Collins *gem*

Collins

BESTSELLING BILINGUAL DICTIONARIES

German
Dictionary

HarperCollins Publishers
Westerhill Road
Bishopbriggs
Glasgow
G64 2QT
Great Britain

Tenth Edition 2009

Reprint 10 9 8 7 6

© William Collins Sons & Co. Ltd
1978, 1988
© HarperCollins Publishers 1993,
1997, 1999, 2000, 2003, 2006, 2007,
2009

ISBN 978-0-00-728448-1

Collins Gem® is a registered
trademark of HarperCollins
Publishers Limited

www.collinslanguage.com

A catalogue record for this book is
available from the British Library

Typeset by RefineCatch Ltd,
Bungay, Suffolk

Supplement typeset by
Davidson Pre-Press, Glasgow

Printed in Italy by
LEGO Spa, Lavis (Trento)

HarperCollins does not warrant
that www.collinsdictionary.com,
www.collinslanguage.com or any
other website mentioned in this
title will be provided
uninterrupted, that any website
will be error free, that defects will
be corrected, or that the website or
the server that makes it available
are free of viruses or bugs. For full
terms and conditions please refer
to the site terms provided on
the website.

Acknowledgements
We would like to thank those
authors and publishers who kindly
gave permission for copyright
material to be used in the Collins
Word Web. We would also like to
thank Times Newspapers Ltd for
providing valuable data.

INHALT

CONTENTS

WARENZEICHEN

NOTE ON TRADEMARKS

PUBLISHING DIRECTOR
Catherine Love

MANAGING EDITOR
Gaëlle Amiot-Cadey

EDITOR
Maggie Seaton

CONTRIBUTORS
Christine Bahr
Susie Beattie
Stuart Fortey
Helen Galloway
Horst Kopleck
Silke Probst
Robin Sawers
Veronika Schnorr

COMPUTING
Thomas Callan

SERIES EDITOR
Rob Scriven

EINFÜHRUNG

Wir freuen uns sehr, dass Sie sich zum Kauf eines Collins Wörterbuchs Deutsch entschlossen haben. Wir wünschen Ihnen viel Spaß beim Gebrauch in der Schule, zu Hause, im Urlaub und im Beruf.

Diese Einführung wird Ihnen einige nützliche Hinweise dazu geben, wie Sie am besten von Ihrem neuen Wörterbuch profitieren. Schließlich bietet Ihnen das Wörterbuch nicht nur Stichwörter und Übersetzungen, sondern auch zahlreiche Zusatzinformationen in jedem einzelnen Eintrag. Mit Hilfe all dieser Informationen können Sie zum einen modernes Deutsch lesen und verstehen, zum anderen auch aktiv auf Deutsch kommunizieren.

Das Collins Wörterbuch Deutsch gibt Ihnen vor dem eigentlichen Wörterbuchtextteil selbst eine Liste aller verwendeten Abkürzungen sowie eine Übersicht zu Aussprache und Gebrauch phonetischer Umschrift. Darüber hinaus finden Sie noch eine Auflistung zu den regelmäßigen deutschen Substantivendungen sowie zu unregelmäßigen englischen und deutschen Verben. Auf den letzten Seiten Ihres Wörterbuchs finden Sie in einem „kleinen Reise-ABC" zahlreiche nützliche Phrasen für verschiedenste Situationen am Urlaubsort.

WIE FINDE ICH WAS?

Die verschiedenen Schriftarten, Schriftgrößen, Symbole, Abkürzungen und Klammern helfen Ihnen dabei, sich innerhalb der Informationen, die das Wörterbuch bietet, zurechtzufinden. Die Konventionen, die diesem Wörterbuch zugrunde liegen, sowie auch der Gebrauch verschiedener Symbole werden im folgenden näher erläutert.

STICHWÖRTER

Die Wörter, die Sie in Ihrem Wörterbuch nachschlagen, die Stichwörter, sind in alphabetischer Reihenfolge angeordnet. Sie sind **fett** gedruckt und in blauer Farbe, sodass Sie sie schnell finden. Die Stichwörter, die rechts und links oben auf jeder Seite erscheinen, sind das jeweils erste Stichwort einer Seite, wenn es sich dabei um eine linke Seite handelt, bzw. das letzte Stichwort einer Seite, wenn es sich um eine rechte Seite handelt. Informationen zu Form und Gebrauch des jeweiligen Stichworts werden im Anschluss an die Lautschrift in Klammern angege ben. Normalerweise sind diese Angaben in abgekürzter Form und *kursiver Schrift* (z.B. *(fam)* für umgangssprachlich oder *(Comm* als Sachgebietsangabe für Wirtschaft).

Wo es sich anbietet, werden zusammengehörige Wörter und Wortgruppen in einem Eintrag zusammengefasst (z.B. gather, gathering; höflich, Höflichkeit). Hierbei sind die Stichwörter in nerhalb des Nests von der Schriftgröße etwas kleiner als das erst Stichwort. Geläufige Ausdrücke, in denen das Stichwort vor kommt, erscheinen ebenfalls **fett**, aber in einer anderen Schriftgröße. Die Tilde (~) steht hierbei für das Hauptstichwor am Anfang eines Eintrags. So steht beispielsweise im Eintrag ,Mitte' der Ausdruck ,~ Juni' für ,**Mitte Juni**'.

PHONETISCHE UMSCHRIFT

Die Aussprache jedes Stichworts findet sich in phonetischer Umschrift in eckigen Klammern jeweils direkt hinter dem Stichwort selbst (z.B. mountain ['maʊntɪn]). Eine Liste der Laut schriftzeichen mit Erklärungen finden Sie auf S. xi.

BEDEUTUNGEN

Die Übersetzung der Stichwörter ist in Normalschrift angegeber Gibt es mehrere Bedeutungen oder Gebrauchsmöglichkeiten, s sind diese durch einen Strichpunkt voneinander zu unter scheiden. Sie finden oft weitere Angaben in Klammern vor der jeweiligen Übersetzungen. Diese zeigen Ihnen typische Kontext auf, in denen das Stichwort verwendet werden kann (z.B. breakup *(of meeting, organisation)*), oder sie liefern Synonyme (z.B fit *(suitable)*).

GRAMMATISCHE HINWEISE

Die Wortartangabe finden Sie als Abkürzung und in *kursiver Schri* direkt hinter der Ausspracheinformation zum jeweiligen Stichwort (z.B. *vt*, *adj*, *n*).

Die Genusangaben zu deutschen Substantiven werden wie folg angegeben: *m* für Maskulinum, *f* für Femininum und *nt* für Neutrum. Darüber hinaus finden Sie neben dem Stichwort in Klammern Genitiv- und Pluralform (Abenteuer *(-s, -)*).

Die Genusangabe zur deutschen Übersetzung findet sich eben falls in *kursiver Schrift* direkt hinter dem Hauptbestandteil der Übersetzung.

INTRODUCTION

We are delighted you have decided to buy the Collins German Dictionary and hope you will enjoy and benefit from using it at school, at home, on holiday or at work.

This introduction gives you a few tips on how to get the most out of your dictionary - not simply from its comprehensive wordlist but also from the information provided in each entry. This will help you to read and understand modern German, as well as to communicate and express yourself in the language.

The Collins German Dictionary begins by listing the abbreviations used in the text and illustrating the sounds shown by the phonetic symbols. Next you will find regular German noun endings and English irregular verbs followed by a section on German irregular verbs. Finally, the new Phrasefinder supplement gives you hundreds of useful phrases which are intended to give you practical help in everyday situations when travelling.

USING YOUR COLLINS DICTIONARY

A wealth of information is presented in the dictionary, using various typefaces, sizes of type, symbols, abbreviations and brackets. The conventions and symbols used are explained in the following sections.

HEADWORDS

The words you look up in the dictionary – 'headwords' – are listed alphabetically. They are printed in **colour** for rapid identification. The headwords appearing at the top of each page indicate the first (if it appears on a left-hand page) and last word (if it appears on a right-hand page) dealt with on the page in question.

Information about the usage or form of certain headwords is given in brackets after the phonetic spelling. This usually appears in abbreviated form and in italics (e.g. (*fam*), (*Comm*)).

Where appropriate, words related to headwords are grouped in the same entry (gather, gathering; höflich, Höflichkeit) in a slightly smaller bold type than the headword. Common expressions in which the headword appears are shown in a different size of bold roman type. The swung dash, ~, represents the main headword at the start of each entry. For example, in the entry for 'Mitte', the phrase '~ Juni' should be read **'Mitte Juni'**.

PHONETIC SPELLINGS

The phonetic spelling of each headword (indicating its pronunciation) is given in square brackets immediately after the headword (e.g. mountain ['maʊntɪn]). A list of these spellings is given on page xi.

MEANINGS

Headword translations are given in ordinary type and, where more than one meaning or usage exists, they are separated by semicolon. You will often find other words in italics in brackets before the translations. These offer suggested contexts in which the headword might appear (e.g. breakup (*of meeting, organisation*)) or provide synonyms (e.g. fit (*suitable*)).

GRAMMATICAL INFORMATION

Parts of speech are given in abbreviated form in italics after the phonetic spellings of headwords (e.g. *vt*, *adj*, *n*).

Genders of German nouns are indicated as follows: *m* for a masculine, *f* for a feminine, and *nt* for a neuter noun. Genitive and plural forms of nouns are also shown next to the headword (Abenteuer (*-s, -*)).

The gender of the German translation appears in *italics* immediately following the key element of the translation.

German	Abbreviation	English
auch	*a.*	also
Abkürzung	*abk, abbr*	abbreviation
Akronym	*acr*	acronym
Adjektiv	*adj*	adjective
Adverb	*adv*	adverb
Landwirtschaft	*Agr*	agriculture
Akkusativ	*akk*	accusative
Akronym	*akr*	acronym
Anatomie	*Anat*	anatomy
Artikel	*art*	article
bildende Künste	*Art*	fine arts
Astronomie, Astrologie	*Astr*	astronomy, astrology
Auto, Verkehr	*Auto*	automobiles, traffic
Luftfahrt	*Aviat*	aviation
Biologie	*Bio*	biology
Botanik	*Bot*	botany
britisch	*BRIT*	British
schweizerisch	*CH*	Swiss
Chemie	*Chem*	chemistry
Film	*Cine*	cinema
Wirtschaft	*Comm*	commerce
Konjunktion	*conj*	conjunction
Dativ	*dat*	dative
Eisenbahn	*Eisenb*	railways
Elektrizität	*Elek, Elec*	electricity
besonders	*esp*	especially
und so weiter	*etc*	et cetera
etwas	*etw*	
Femininum	*f*	feminine
umgangssprachlich	*fam*	familiar, informal
übertragen	*fig*	figurative
Finanzen, Börse	*Fin*	finance
Fotografie	*Foto*	photography
Gastronomie	*Gastr*	cooking, gastronomy
Genitiv	*gen*	genitive
Geographie, Geologie	*Geo*	geography, geology
Geschichte	*Hist*	history
Imperativ	*imper*	imperative
Imperfekt	*imperf*	past tense
Informatik und Computer	*Inform*	computing
Interjektion, Ausruf	*interj*	interjection
unveränderlich	*inv*	invariable
unregelmäßig	*irr*	irregular
jemand, jemandem	*jd, jdm*	
jemanden, jemandes	*jdn, jds*	
Rechtsprechung	*Jur*	law

Konjunktion	konj	conjunction
Bildende Künste	Kunst	fine arts
Sprachwissenschaft, Grammatik	Ling	linguistics, grammar
Maskulinum	m	masculine
Mathematik	Math	mathematics
Medizin	Med	medicine
Meteorologie	Meteo	meteorology
Maskulinum und Femininum	mf	masculine and feminine
Militär	Mil	military
Musik	Mus	music
Substantiv	n	noun
Seefahrt	Naut	nautical, naval
Neutrum	nt	neuter
Zahlwort	num	numeral
oder	o	or
pejorativ, abwertend	pej	pejorative
Physik	Phys	physics
Plural	pl	plural
Politik	Pol	politics
Partizip Perfekt	pp	past participle
Präfix	pref	prefix
Präposition	prep	preposition
Pronomen	pron	pronoun
1. Vergangenheit	pt	past tense
Eisenbahn	Rail	railways
Religion	Rel	religion
siehe	s.	see
	sb	someone, somebody
schottisch	Scot	Scottish
Singular	sing	singular
Skisport	Ski	skiing
	sth	something
Technik	Tech	technology
Nachrichtentechnik	Tel	telecommunications
Theater	Theat	theatre
Fernsehen	TV	television
Typographie, Buchdruck	Typo	printing
unpersönlich	unpers	impersonal
(nord)amerikanisch	US	(North) American
Verb	vb	verb
Hilfsverb	vb aux	auxiliary verb
intransitives Verb	vi	intransitive verb
reflexives Verb	vr	reflexive verb
transitives Verb	vt	transitive verb
vulgär	vulg	vulgar
Zoologie	Zool	zoology
ungefähre Entsprechung	≈	cultural equivalent
abtrennbares Präfix	│	separable prefix

LAUTSCHRIFT   PHONETIC SYMBOLS

[:] Längezeichen, length mark
['] Betonung, stress mark
[*] Bindungs-R, 'r' pronounced before a vowel

alle Vokallaute sind nur ungefähre Entsprechungen
all vowel sounds are approximate only

VOKALE UND DIPHTHONGE

plant, arm, father	[ɑː]	Bahn
fiancé	[ãː]	Ensemble
life	[aɪ]	weit
house	[au]	Haut
man, sad	[æ]	
but, son	[ʌ]	Butler
get, bed	[e]	Metall
name, lame	[eɪ]	
ago, better	[ə]	bitte
bird, her	[ɜː]	
there, care	[ɛə]	mehr
it, wish	[ɪ]	Bischof
bee, me, beat, belief	[iː]	viel
here	[ɪə]	Bier
no, low	[əu]	
not, long	[ɒ]	Post
law, all	[ɔː]	Mond
boy, oil	[ɔɪ]	Heu
push, look	[ʊ]	Pult
you, do	[uː]	Hut
poor, sure	[ʊə]	

KONSONANTEN

been, blind	[b]	Ball
do, had	[d]	dann
jam, object	[dʒ]	
father, wolf	[f]	Fass
go, beg	[g]	Gast
house	[h]	Herr
youth, Indian	[j]	ja
keep, milk	[k]	kalt
lamp, oil, ill	[l]	Last
man, am	[m]	Mast
no, manner	[n]	Nuss
long, sing	[ŋ]	lang

El Niño	[ɲ]	El Niño
paper, happy	[p]	Pakt
red, dry	[r]	rot
stand, sand, yes	[s]	Rasse
ship, station	[ʃ]	Schal
tell, fat	[t]	Tal
thank, death	[θ]	
this, father	[ð]	
church, catch	[tʃ]	Rutsch
voice, live	[v]	was
water, we, which	[w]	
loch	[x]	Bach
zeal, these, gaze	[z]	Hase
pleasure	[ʒ]	Genie

REGULAR GERMAN NOUN ENDINGS

nominative		genitive	plural		nominative		genitive	plural
-ade	f	-ade	-aden		-ist	m	-isten	-isten
-ant	m	-anten	-anten		-ium	nt	-iums	-ien
-anz	f	-anz	-anzen		-ius	m	-ius	-iusse
-ar	m	-ars	-are		-ive	f	-ive	-iven
-är	m	-ärs	-äre		-keit	f	-keit	-keiten
-at	nt	-at(e)s	-ate		-lein	nt	-leins	-lein
-atte	f	-atte	-atten		-ling	m	-lings	-linge
-chen	nt	-chens	-chen		-ment	nt	-ments	-mente
-ei	f	-ei	-eien		-mus	m	-mus	-men
-elle	f	-elle	-ellen		-nis	f	-nis	-nisse
-ent	m	-enten	-enten		-nis	nt	-nisses	-nisse
-enz	f	-enz	-enzen		-nom	m	-nomen	-nomen
-ette	f	-ette	-etten		-rich	m	-richs	-riche
-eur	m	-eurs	-eure		-schaft	f	-schaft	-schaften
-euse	f	-euse	-eusen		-sel	nt	-sels	-sel
-heit	f	-heit	-heiten		-tät	f	-tät	-täten
-ie	f	-ie	-ien		-tiv	nt, m	-tivs	-tive
-ik	f	-ik	-iken		-tor	m	-tors	-toren
-in	f	-in	-innen		-tum	m, nt	-tums	-tümer
-ine	f	-ine	-inen		-ung	f	-ung	-ungen
-ion	f	-ion	-ionen		-ur	f	-ur	-uren

Substantive, die mit einem geklammerten 'r' oder 's' enden (z.B. **Ange-stellte(r)** *mf*, **Beamte(r)** *m*, **Gute(s)** *nt*) werden wie Adjektive dekliniert:

Nouns listed with an 'r' or an 's' in brackets (eg **Angestellte(r)** *mf*, **Beamte(r)** *m*, **Gute(s)** *nt*) take the same endings as adjectives:

der Angestellte *m*	die Angestellte *f*	die Angestellten *pl*
ein Angestellter *m*	eine Angestellte *f*	Angestellte *pl*
der Beamte *m*		die Beamten *pl*
ein Beamter *m*		Beamte *pl*
das Gute *nt*		
ein Gutes *nt*		

UNREGELMÄSSIGE ENGLISCHE VERBEN

present	past tense	past participle	present	past tense	past participle
arise (arising)	arose	arisen	drink	drank	drunk
awake (awaking)	awoke	awaked	drive (driving)	drove	driven
be (am, is, are; being)	was, were	been	eat	ate	eaten
			fall	fell	fallen
bear	bore	born(e)	feed	fed	fed
beat	beat	beaten	feel	felt	felt
become (becoming)	became	become	fight	fought	fought
			find	found	found
begin (beginning)	began	begun	flee	fled	fled
bend	bent	bent	fling	flung	flung
bet (betting)	bet	bet	fly (flies)	flew	flown
bid (bidding)	bid	bid	forbid (forbidding)	forbade	forbidden
bind	bound	bound	foresee	foresaw	foreseen
bite (biting)	bit	bitten	forget (forgetting)	forgot	forgotten
bleed	bled	bled	forgive (forgiving)	forgave	forgiven
blow	blew	blown	freeze (freezing)	froze	frozen
break	broke	broken			
breed	bred	bred	get (getting)	got	got, (US) gotten
bring	brought	brought			
build	built	built	give (giving)	gave	given
burn	burnt (o burned)	burnt (o burned)	go (goes)	went	gone
			grind	ground	ground
burst	burst	burst	grow	grew	grown
buy	bought	bought	hang	hung (o hanged)	hung (o hanged)
can	could	(been able)			
cast	cast	cast			
catch	caught	caught	have (has; having)	had	had
choose (choosing)	chose	chosen	hear	heard	heard
cling	clung	clung	hide (hiding)	hid	hidden
come (coming)	came	come			
cost	cost	cost	hit (hitting)	hit	hit
creep	crept	crept	hold	held	held
cut (cutting)	cut	cut	hurt	hurt	hurt
deal	dealt	dealt	keep	kept	kept
dig (digging)	dug	dug	kneel	knelt (o kneeled)	knelt (o kneeled)
do (does)	did	done			
draw	drew	drawn	know	knew	known
dream	dreamed (o dreamt)	dreamed (o dreamt)	lay	laid	laid
			lead	led	led

xiv

present	past tense	past participle	present	past tense	past participle
lean	leant (o leaned)	leant (o leaned)	shoot	shot	shot
leap	leapt (o leaped)	leapt (o leaped)	show	showed	shown
			shrink	shrank	shrunk
learn	learnt (o learned)	learnt (o learned)	shut (shutting)	shut	shut
			sing	sang	sung
leave (leaving)	left	left	sink	sank	sunk
			sit (sitting)	sat	sat
lend	lent	lent	sleep	slept	slept
let (letting)	let	let	slide (sliding)	slid	slid
lie (lying)	lay	lain			
light	lit (o lighted)	lit (o lighted)	sling	slung	slung
			slit (slitting)	slit	slit
lose (losing)	lost	lost	smell	smelt (o smelled)	smelt (o smelled)
make (making)	made	made			
may	might	–	sow	sowed	sown (o sowed)
mean	meant	meant			
meet	met	met	speak	spoke	spoken
mow	mowed	mown (o mowed)	speed	sped (o speeded)	sped (o speeded)
			spell	spelt (o spelled)	spelt (o spelled)
must	(had to)	(had to)			
pay	paid	paid	spend	spent	spent
put (putting)	put	put	spin (spinning)	spun	spun
quit (quitting)	quit (o quitted)	quit (o quitted)	spit (spitting)	spat	spat
			split (splitting)	split	split
read	read	read	spoil	spoiled (o spoilt)	spoiled (o spoilt)
rid (ridding)	rid	rid			
ride (riding)	rode	ridden	spread	spread	spread
ring	rang	rung	spring	sprang	sprung
rise (rising)	rose	risen	stand	stood	stood
run (running)	ran	run	steal	stole	stolen
saw	sawed	sawn	stick	stuck	stuck
say	said	said	sting	stung	stung
see	saw	seen	stink	stank	stunk
seek	sought	sought	strike (striking)	struck	struck
sell	sold	sold	strive (striving)	strove	striven
send	sent	sent	swear	swore	sworn
set (setting)	set	set	sweep	swept	swept
shake (shaking)	shook	shaken	swell	swelled	swollen (o swelled)
shall	should	–			
shine (shining)	shone	shone			

xv

present	past tense	past participle	present	past tense	past participle
swim (swimming)	swam	swum	wake (waking)	woke (o waked)	woken (o waked)
swing	swung	swung	wear	wore	worn
take (taking)	took	taken	weave (weaving)	wove (o weaved)	woven (o weaved)
teach	taught	taught	weep	wept	wept
tear	tore	torn	win (winning)	won	won
tell	told	told			
think	thought	thought	wind	wound	wound
throw	threw	thrown	write (writing)	wrote	written
thrust	thrust	thrust			
tread	trod	trodden			

IRREGULAR GERMAN VERBS

Infinitiv	Präsens 2., 3. Singular	Imperfekt	Partizip Perfekt
backen	bäckst, bäckt	backte o buk	gebacken
befehlen	befiehlst, befiehlt	befahl	befohlen
beginnen	beginnst, beginnt	begann	begonnen
beißen	beißt, beißt	biss	gebissen
bergen	birgst, birgt	barg	geborgen
betrügen	betrügst, betrügt	betrog	betrogen
biegen	biegst, biegt	bog	gebogen
bieten	bietest, bietet	bot	geboten
binden	bindest, bindet	band	gebunden
bitten	bittest, bittet	bat	gebeten
blasen	bläst, bläst	blies	geblasen
bleiben	bleibst, bleibt	blieb	geblieben
braten	brätst, brät	briet	gebraten
brechen	brichst, bricht	brach	gebrochen
brennen	brennst, brennt	brannte	gebrannt
bringen	bringst, bringt	brachte	gebracht
denken	denkst, denkt	dachte	gedacht
dringen	dringst, dringt	drang	gedrungen
dürfen	darfst, darf	durfte	gedurft
erschrecken	erschrickst, erschrickt	erschrak	erschrocken
essen	isst, isst	aß	gegessen
fahren	fährst, fährt	fuhr	gefahren
fallen	fällst, fällt	fiel	gefallen
fangen	fängst, fängt	fing	gefangen
finden	findest, findet	fand	gefunden
fliegen	fliegst, fliegt	flog	geflogen
fließen	fließt, fließt	floss	geflossen
fressen	frisst, frisst	fraß	gefressen
frieren	frierst, friert	fror	gefroren
geben	gibst, gibt	gab	gegeben
gehen	gehst, geht	ging	gegangen
gelingen	–, gelingt	gelang	gelungen
gelten	giltst, gilt	galt	gegolten
genießen	genießt, genießt	genoss	genossen
geschehen	–, geschieht	geschah	geschehen
gewinnen	gewinnst, gewinnt	gewann	gewonnen
gießen	gießt, gießt	goss	gegossen
gleichen	gleichst, gleicht	glich	geglichen
gleiten	gleitest, gleitet	glitt	geglitten
graben	gräbst, gräbt	grub	gegraben
greifen	greifst, greift	griff	gegriffen
haben	hast, hat	hatte	gehabt
halten	hältst, hält	hielt	gehalten
hängen	hängst, hängt	hing	gehangen

Infinitiv	Präsens 2., 3. Singular	Imperfekt	Partizip Perfekt
heben	hebst, hebt	hob	gehoben
heißen	heißt, heißt	hieß	geheißen
helfen	hilfst, hilft	half	geholfen
kennen	kennst, kennt	kannte	gekannt
klingen	klingst, klingt	klang	geklungen
kommen	kommst, kommt	kam	gekommen
können	kannst, kann	konnte	gekonnt
kriechen	kriechst, kriecht	kroch	gekrochen
laden	lädst, lädt	lud	geladen
lassen	lässt, lässt	ließ	gelassen
laufen	läufst, läuft	lief	gelaufen
leiden	leidest, leidet	litt	gelitten
leihen	leihst, leiht	lieh	geliehen
lesen	liest, liest	las	gelesen
liegen	liegst, liegt	lag	gelegen
lügen	lügst, lügt	log	gelogen
mahlen	mahlst, mahlt	mahlte	gemahlen
meiden	meidest, meidet	mied	gemieden
messen	misst, misst	maß	gemessen
mögen	magst, mag	mochte	gemocht
müssen	musst, muss	musste	gemusst
nehmen	nimmst, nimmt	nahm	genommen
nennen	nennst, nennt	nannte	genannt
pfeifen	pfeifst, pfeift	pfiff	gepfiffen
raten	rätst, rät	riet	geraten
reiben	reibst, reibt	rieb	gerieben
reißen	reißt, reißt	riss	gerissen
reiten	reitest, reitet	ritt	geritten
rennen	rennst, rennt	rannte	gerannt
riechen	riechst, riecht	roch	gerochen
rufen	rufst, ruft	rief	gerufen
saufen	säufst, säuft	soff	gesoffen
saugen	saugst, saugt	sog o saugte	gesogen o gesaugt
schaffen	schaffst, schafft	schuf	geschaffen
scheiden	scheidest, scheidet	schied	geschieden
scheinen	scheinst, scheint	schien	geschienen
schieben	schiebst, schiebt	schob	geschoben
schießen	schießt, schießt	schoss	geschossen
schlafen	schläfst, schläft	schlief	geschlafen
schlagen	schlägst, schlägt	schlug	geschlagen
schleichen	schleichst, schleicht	schlich	geschlichen
schließen	schließt, schließt	schloss	geschlossen
schmeißen	schmeißt, schmeißt	schmiss	geschmissen
schmelzen	schmilzt, schmilzt	schmolz	geschmolzen
schneiden	schneidest, schneidet	schnitt	geschnitten

Infinitiv	Präsens 2., 3. Singular	Imperfekt	Partizip Perfekt
schreiben	schreibst, schreibt	schrieb	geschrieben
schreien	schreist, schreit	schrie	geschrie(e)n
schweigen	schweigst, schweigt	schwieg	geschwiegen
schwellen	schwillst, schwillt	schwoll	geschwollen
schwimmen	schwimmst, schwimmt	schwamm	geschwommen
schwören	schwörst, schwört	schwor	geschworen
sehen	siehst, sieht	sah	gesehen
sein	bist, ist	war	gewesen
senden	sendest, sendet	sandte	gesandt
singen	singst, singt	sang	gesungen
sinken	sinkst, sinkt	sank	gesunken
sitzen	sitzt, sitzt	saß	gesessen
sollen	sollst, soll	sollte	gesollt
sprechen	sprichst, spricht	sprach	gesprochen
springen	springst, springt	sprang	gesprungen
stechen	stichst, sticht	stach	gestochen
stehen	stehst, steht	stand	gestanden
stehlen	stiehlst, stiehlt	stahl	gestohlen
steigen	steigst, steigt	stieg	gestiegen
sterben	stirbst, stirbt	starb	gestorben
stinken	stinkst, stinkt	stank	gestunken
stoßen	stößt, stößt	stieß	gestoßen
streichen	streichst, streicht	strich	gestrichen
streiten	streitest, streitet	stritt	gestritten
tragen	trägst, trägt	trug	getragen
treffen	triffst, trifft	traf	getroffen
treiben	treibst, treibt	trieb	getrieben
treten	trittst, tritt	trat	getreten
trinken	trinkst, trinkt	trank	getrunken
tun	tust, tut	tat	getan
verderben	verdirbst, verdirbt	verdarb	verdorben
vergessen	vergisst, vergisst	vergaß	vergessen
verlieren	verlierst, verliert	verlor	verloren
verschwinden	verschwindest, verschwindet	verschwand	verschwunden
verzeihen	verzeihst, verzeiht	verzieh	verziehen
wachsen	wächst, wächst	wuchs	gewachsen
wenden	wendest, wendet	wandte	gewandt
werben	wirbst, wirbt	warb	geworben
werden	wirst, wird	wurde	geworden
werfen	wirfst, wirft	warf	geworfen
wiegen	wiegst, wiegt	wog	gewogen
wissen	weißt, weiß	wusste	gewusst
wollen	willst, will	wollte	gewollt
ziehen	ziehst, zieht	zog	gezogen
zwingen	zwingst, zwingt	zwang	gezwungen

a

à prep +akk at ... each; **4 Tickets ~ 8 Euro** 4 tickets at 8 euros each

A abk = **Autobahn** ≈ M (Brit), ≈ I (US)

Aal (-(e)s, -e) m eel

 SCHLÜSSELWORT

ab prep +dat from; **Kinder ab 12 Jahren** children from the age of 12; **ab morgen** from tomorrow; **ab sofort** as of now

▷ adv **1** off; **links ab** to the left; **der Knopf ist ab** the button has come off; **ab nach Hause!** off you go home

2 (zeitlich) **von da ab** from then on; **von heute ab** from today, as of today

3 (auf Fahrplänen) **München ab 12.20** leaving Munich 12.20

4 ab und zu o **an** now and then o again

ab|bauen vt (Zelt) to take down; (verringern) to reduce

ab|beißen irr vt to bite off

ab|bestellen vt to cancel

ab|biegen irr vi to turn off; (Straße) to bend; **nach links/rechts ~** to turn left/right

Abbildung f illustration

ab|blasen irr vt (fig) to call off

ab|blenden vt, vi (Auto) (**die Scheinwerfer**) **~** to dip (Brit) (o to dim (US)) one's headlights; **Abblendlicht** nt dipped (Brit) (o dimmed (US)) headlights pl

ab|brechen irr vt to break off; (Gebäude) to pull down; (aufhören) to stop; (Computerprogramm) to abort

ab|bremsen vi to brake, to slow down

ab|bringen irr vt: **jdn von einer Idee ~** to talk sb out of an idea; **jdn vom Thema ~** to get sb away from the subject; **davon lasse ich mich nicht ~** nothing will make me change my mind about it

ab|buchen vt to debit (von to)

ab|danken vi to resign

ab|drehen vt (Gas, Wasser) to turn off; (Licht) to switch off ▷ vi (Schiff, Flugzeug) to change course

Abend (-s, -e) m evening; **am ~** in the evening; **zu ~ essen** to have dinner; **heute/morgen/gestern ~** this/tomorrow/yesterday evening; **guten ~!** good evening; **Abendbrot** nt supper; **Abendessen** nt dinner; **Abendgarderobe** f evening dress (o gown); **Abendkasse** f box office; **Abendkleid** nt evening dress (o gown); **Abendmahl** nt: **das ~** (Holy) Communion; **abends** adv in the evening; **montags ~** on Monday evenings

Abenteuer (-s, -) nt adventure; **Abenteuerurlaub** m adventure holiday

aber conj but; (jedoch) however;
oder ~ alternatively; **~ ja!** (but) of
course; **das ist ~ nett von Ihnen**
that's really nice of you

abergläubisch adj superstitious

abˈfahren irr vi to leave (o to
depart) (nach for); (Ski) to ski
down; **Abfahrt** f departure; (von
Autobahn) exit; (Ski) descent; (Piste)
run; **Abfahrtslauf** m (Ski)
downhill; **Abfahrtszeit** f
departure time

Abfall m waste; (Müll) rubbish
(Brit), garbage (US); **Abfalleimer**
m rubbish bin (Brit), garbage can
(US)

abˈfällig adj disparaging; **~ von
jdm sprechen** to make
disparaging remarks about sb

abˈfärben vi (Wäsche) to run; (fig)
to rub off

abˈfertigen vt (Pakete) to prepare
for dispatch; (an der Grenze) to
clear; **Abfertigungsschalter** m
(am Flughafen) check-in desk

abˈfinden irr vt to pay off ▷ vr:
sich mit etw ~ to come to terms
with sth; **Abfindung** f
(Entschädigung) compensation;
(von Angestellten) redundancy
payment

abˈfliegen irr vi (Flugzeug) to take
off; (Passagier a.) to fly off; **Abflug**
m departure; (Start) takeoff;
Abflughalle f departure lounge;
Abflugzeit f departure time

Abfluss m drain; (am Waschbecken)
plughole (Brit); **Abflussrohr** nt
waste pipe; (außen) drainpipe

abˈfragen vt to test; (Inform) to
call up

abˈführen vi (Med) to have a
laxative effect ▷ vt (Steuern,
Gebühren) to pay; **jdn ~ lassen** to
take sb into custody;
Abführmittel nt laxative

Abgabe f handing in; (von Ball)
pass; (Steuer) tax; (einer Erklärung)
making; **abgabenfrei** adj
tax-free; **abgabenpflichtig** adj
liable to tax

Abgase pl (Auto) exhaust fumes
pl; **Abgas(sonder)untersuchung**
f exhaust emission test

abˈgeben irr vt (Gepäck, Schlüssel)
to leave (bei with); (Schularbeit etc)
to hand in; (Wärme) to give off;
(Erklärung, Urteil) to make ▷ vr:
sich mit jdm ~ to associate with
sb; **sich mit etw ~** to bother with
sth

abgebildet adj: **wie oben ~** as
shown above

abˈgehen irr vi (Post) to go; (Knopf etc)
to come off; (abgezogen
werden) to be taken off; (Straße) to
branch off; **von der Schule ~** to
leave school; **sie geht mir ab** I
really miss her; **was geht denn
hier ab?** (fam) what's going on
here?

abgehetzt adj exhausted,
shattered

abgelaufen adj (Pass) expired;
(Zeit, Frist) up; **die Milch ist ~** the
milk is past its sell-by date

abgelegen adj remote

abgemacht interj OK, it's a deal,
that's settled, then

abgeneigt adj **einer Sache** (dat)
~ sein to be averse to sth; **ich
wäre nicht ~, das zu tun** I
wouldn't mind doing that

Abgeordnete(r) mf Member of
Parliament

abgepackt adj prepacked

abgerissen adj: **der Knopf ist
~** the button has come off

abgesehen adj: **es auf jdn/etw
~ haben** to be after sb/sth; **~ von**
apart from

abgespannt adj (Person)
exhausted, worn out

abgestanden adj stale; (Bier) flat

abgestorben adj (Pflanze) dead; (Finger) numb

abgestumpft adj (Person) insensitive

abgetragen adj (Kleidung) worn

ab|gewöhnen vt: **jdm etw ~** to cure sb of sth; **sich etw ~** to give sth up

ab|haken vt to tick off; **das (Thema) ist schon abgehakt** that's been dealt with

ab|halten irr vt (Versammlung) to hold; **jdn von etw ~** (fernhalten) to keep sb away from sth; (hindern) to keep sb from sth

abhanden adj: **~ kommen** to get lost

Abhang m slope

ab|hängen vt (Bild) to take down; (Anhänger) to uncouple; (Verfolger) to shake off ▷ irr vi: **von jdm/etw ~** to depend on sb/sth; **das hängt davon ab, ob ...** it depends (on) whether ...;

abhängig adj dependent (von on)

ab|hauen irr vt (abschlagen) to cut off ▷ vi (fam: verschwinden) to clear off; **hau ab!** (get lost!, beat it!

ab|heben irr vt (Geld) to withdraw; (Telefonhörer, Spielkarte) to pick up ▷ vi (Flugzeug) to take off; (Rakete) to lift off; (Karten) to cut

ab|holen vt to collect; (am Bahnhof etc) to meet; (mit dem Auto) to pick up; **Abholmarkt** m cash and carry

ab|horchen vt (Med) to listen to

ab|hören vt (Vokabeln) to test; (Telefongespräch) to tap; (Tonband etc) to listen to

Abitur (-s, -e) nt German school-leaving examination, ≈ A-levels (Brit), ≈ High School Diploma (US)

▪ **ABITUR**

- The **Abitur** is the German
- school-leaving examination
- which is taken at the age of 18
- or 19 by pupils at a **Gymnasium**.
- It is taken in four subjects and is
- necessary for entry to
- university.

ab|kaufen vt: **jdm etw ~** to buy sth from sb; **das kauf ich dir nicht ab!** (fam: glauben) I don't believe you

ab|klingen irr vi (Schmerz) to ease; (Wirkung) to wear off

ab|kommen irr vi to get away; **von der Straße ~** to leave the road; **von einem Plan ~** to give up a plan; **vom Thema ~** to stray from the point

Abkommen (-s, -) nt agreement

ab|koppeln vt (Anhänger) to unhitch

ab|kratzen vt to scrape off ▷ vi (fam: sterben) to kick the bucket, to croak

ab|kühlen vi, vt to cool down ▷ vr: **sich ~** to cool down

ab|kürzen vt (Wort) to abbreviate; **den Weg ~** to take a short cut; **Abkürzung** f (Wort) abbreviation; (Weg) short cut

ab|laden irr vt to unload

Ablage f (für Akten) tray; (Aktenordnung) filing system

Ablauf m (Abfluss) drain; (von Ereignissen) course; (einer Frist, Zeit) expiry; **ab|laufen** irr vi (abfließen) to drain away; (Ereignisse) to happen; (Frist, Zeit, Pass) to expire

ab|legen vt to put down; (Kleider) to take off; (Gewohnheit) to get out of; (Prüfung) to take, to sit; (Akten) to file away ▷ vi (Schiff) to cast off

ab|lehnen vt to reject; (Einladung) to decline; (missbilligen) to disapprove of; (*Bewerber*) to turn down ▷ vi to decline

ab|lenken vt to distract; **jdn von der Arbeit ~** to distract sb from their work; **vom Thema ~** to change the subject; **Ablenkung** f distraction

ab|lesen vt (*Text, Rede*) to read; **das Gas/den Strom ~** to read the gas/electricity meter

ab|liefern vt to deliver

ab|machen vt (*entfernen*) to take off; (*vereinbaren*) to agree; **Abmachung** f agreement

ab|melden vt (*Zeitung*) to cancel; (*Auto*) to take off the road ▷ vr: **sich ~** to give notice of one's departure; (*im Hotel*) to check out; (*vom Verein*) to cancel one's membership

ab|messen irr vt to measure

ab|nehmen irr vt to take off, to remove; (*Hörer*) to pick up; (*Führerschein*) to take away; (*Geld*) to get (*jdm out of sb*); (*kaufen, umg: glauben*) to buy (*jdm from sb*) ▷ vi to decrease; (*schlanker werden*) to lose weight; (*Tel*) to pick up the phone; **fünf Kilo ~** to lose five kilos

Abneigung f dislike (*gegen* of); (*stärker*) aversion (*gegen* to)

ab|nutzen vt to wear out ▷ vr: **sich ~** to wear out

Abonnement (-s, -s) nt subscription; **Abonnent(in)** m(f) subscriber; **abonnieren** vt to subscribe to

ab|raten irr vi: **jdm von etw ~** to advise sb against sth

ab|räumen vt: **den Tisch ~** to clear the table; **das Geschirr ~** to clear away the dishes; (*Preis etc*) to walk off with

Abrechnung f settlement; (*Rechnung*) bill

ab|regen vr: **sich ~** (*fam*) to calm

(*o to cool*) down; **reg dich ab!** take it easy

Abreise f departure; **ab|reisen** vi to leave (*nach for*); **Abreisetag** m day of departure

ab|reißen irr vt (*Haus*) to pull down; (*Blatt*) to tear off; **den Kontakt nicht ~ lassen** to stay in touch ▷ vi (*Knopf etc*) to come off

ab|runden vt: **eine Zahl nach oben/unten ~** to round a number up/down

abrupt adj abrupt

ABS nt abk = **Antiblockiersystem** (*Auto*) ABS

Abs. abk = **Absender** from

ab|sagen vt to cancel, to call off; (*Einladung*) to turn down ▷ vi (*ablehnen*) to decline; **ich muss leider ~** I'm afraid I can't come

Absatz m (*Comm*) sales pl; (*neuer Abschnitt*) paragraph; (*Schuh*) heel

ab|schaffen vt to abolish, to do away with

ab|schalten vt, vi (*a. fig*) to switch off

ab|schätzen vt to estimate; (*Lage*) to assess

abscheulich adj disgusting

ab|schicken vt to send off

ab|schieben irr vt (*ausweisen*) to deport

Abschied (-(e)s, -e) m parting; **~ nehmen** to say good-bye (*von jdm to sb*); **Abschiedsfeier** f farewell party

Abschlagszahlung f interim payment

Abschleppdienst m (*Auto*) breakdown service; **ab|schleppen** vt to tow; **Abschleppseil** nt towrope; **Abschleppwagen** m breakdown truck (*Brit*), tow truck (*US*)

ab|schließen irr vt (*Tür*) to lock; (*beenden*) to conclude, to finish; (*Vertrag, Handel*) to conclude;

Abschluss m (Beendigung) close, conclusion; (von Vertrag, Handel) conclusion

ab|schmecken vt (kosten) to taste; (würzen) to season

ab|schminken vr: **sich ~** to take one's make-up off ▷ vt (fam) **sich** (dat) **etw ~** to get sth out of one's mind

ab|schnallen vr: **sich ~** to undo one's seatbelt

ab|schneiden irr vt to cut off ▷ vi: **gut/schlecht ~** to do well/badly

Abschnitt m (von Buch, Text) section; (Kontrollabschnitt) stub

ab|schrauben vt to unscrew

ab|schrecken vt to deter, to put off

ab|schreiben irr vt to copy (bei, von from, off); (verloren geben) to write off; (Comm: absetzen) to deduct

abschüssig adj steep

ab|schwächen vt to lessen; (Behauptung, Kritik) to tone down

ab|schwellen irr vi (Entzündung) to go down; (Lärm) to die down

absehbar adj foreseeable; **in ~er Zeit** in the foreseeable future;

ab|sehen irr vt (Ende, Folgen) to foresee ▷ vi: **von etw ~** to refrain from sth

abseits adv out of the way; (Sport) offside ▷ prep +gen away from; **Abseits** nt (Sport) offside; **Abseitsfalle** f (Sport) offside trap

ab|senden irr vt to send off; (Post) to post; **Absender(in)** (-s, -) m(f) sender

ab|setzen vt (Glas, Brille etc) to put down; (aussteigen lassen) to drop (off); (Comm) to sell; (Fin) to deduct; (streichen) to drop ▷ vr: **sich ~** (sich entfernen) to clear off; (sich ablagern) to be deposited

Absicht f intention; **mit ~** on

purpose; **absichtlich** adj intentional, deliberate

absolut adj absolute

ab|specken vi (fam) to lose weight

ab|speichern vt (Inform) to save

ab|sperren vt to block (o to close) off; (Tür) to lock; **Absperrung** f (Vorgang) blocking (o closing) off; (Sperre) barricade

ab|spielen vt (CD etc) to play ▷ vr: **sich ~** to happen

ab|springen irr vi to jump down/off; (von etw Geplantem) to drop out (von of)

ab|spülen vt to rinse; (Geschirr) to wash (up)

Abstand m distance; (zeitlich) interval; **~ halten** to keep one's distance

ab|stauben vt, vi to dust; (fam: stehlen) to pinch

Abstecher (-s, -) m detour

ab|steigen irr vi (vom Rad etc) to get off, to dismount; (in Gasthof) to stay (in +dat at)

ab|stellen vt (niederstellen) to put down; (Auto) to park; (ausschalten) to turn (o to switch) off; (Missstand, Unsitte) to stop; **Abstellraum** m store room

Abstieg (-(e)s, -e) m (vom Berg) descent; (Sport) relegation

ab|stimmen vi to vote ▷ vt (Termine, Ziele) to fit in (auf +akk with); **Dinge aufeinander ~** to coordinate things ▷ vr: **sich ~** to come to an agreement (o arrangement)

abstoßend adj repulsive

abstrakt adj abstract

ab|streiten irr vt to deny

Abstrich m (Med) smear; **~e machen** to cut back (an +dat on); (weniger erwarten) to lower one's sights

Absturz m fall; (Aviat, Inform)

crash; **ab|stürzen** vi to fall;
(Aviat, Inform) to crash
absurd adj absurd
Abszess (-es, -e) m abscess
ab|tauen vt, vi to thaw;
(Kühlschrank) to defrost
Abtei (-, -en) f abbey
Abteil (-(e)s, -e) nt compartment
Abteilung f (in Firma, Kaufhaus)
department; (in Krankenhaus)
section
ab|treiben irr vt (Kind) to abort
▷ vi to be driven off course; (Med:
Abtreibung vornehmen) to carry out
an abortion; (Abtreibung vornehmen
lassen) to have an abortion;
Abtreibung f abortion
ab|trocknen vt to dry
ab|warten vt to wait for; **das
bleibt abzuwarten** that remains
to be seen ▷ vi to wait
abwärts adv down
Abwasch (-(e)s) m washing-up;
ab|waschen irr vt (Schmutz) to
wash off; (Geschirr) to wash (up)
Abwasser (-s, Abwässer) nt
sewage
ab|wechseln vr: **sich ~ to**
alternate; **sich mit jdm ~ to take
turns with sb; abwechselnd** adv
alternately; **Abwechslung** f
change; **zur ~** for a change
ab|weisen irr vt to turn away;
(Antrag) to turn down; **abweisend**
adj unfriendly
abwesend adj absent;
Abwesenheit f absence
ab|wiegen irr vt to weigh (out)
ab|wimmeln vt (fam) **jdn ~ to**
get rid of sb, to give sb the elbow
ab|wischen vt (Gesicht, Tisch etc)
to wipe; (Schmutz) to wipe off
ab|zählen vt to count; (Geld) to
count out
Abzeichen nt badge
ab|zeichnen vt to draw, to copy;
(Dokument) to initial ▷ vr: **sich**

**~ to stand out; (fig: bevorstehen) to
loom
ab|ziehen irr vt to take off; (Bett)
to strip; (Schlüssel) to take out;
(subtrahieren) to take away, to
subtract ▷ vi to go away
Abzug m (Foto) print; (Öffnung)
vent; (Truppen) withdrawal;
(Betrag) deduction; **nach ~ der
Kosten** charges deducted;
abzüglich prep +gen minus;
~ 20% Rabatt less 20% discount
ab|zweigen vi to branch off ▷ vt
to set aside; **Abzweigung** f
junction
Accessoires pl accessories pl
ach interj oh; **~ so!** oh, I see;
~ was! (Überraschung) really?;
(Ärger) don't talk nonsense
Achse (-, -n) f axis; (Auto) axle
Achsel (-, -n) f shoulder;
(Achselhöhle) f armpit
Achsenbruch m (Auto) broken
axle
acht num eight; **heute in ~ Tagen**
in a week('s time), a week from
today
Acht (-) f: **sich in ~ nehmen** to be
careful (vor +dat of), to watch out
(vor +dat for); **etw außer ~ lassen**
to disregard sth
achte(r, s) adj eighth; siehe auch
dritte; **Achtel** (-s, -) nt (Bruchteil)
eighth; (Wein etc) eighth of a litre;
(Glas Wein) ≈ small glass
achten vt to respect ▷ vi to pay
attention (auf +akk to)
Achterbahn f big dipper, roller
coaster
acht|geben irr vi to take care
(auf +akk of)
achthundert num eight
hundred; **achtmal** adv eight
times
Achtung f attention; (Ehrfurcht)
respect ▷ interj look out
achtzehn num eighteen;

achtzehnte(r, s) adj eighteenth; *siehe auch* **dritte**; **achtzig** *num* eighty; **in den ~er Jahren** in the eighties; **achtzigste(r, s)** adj eightieth

Acker (-s, Äcker) m field

Action (-, -s) f (fam) action; **Actionfilm** m action film

Adapter (-s, -) m adapter

addieren vt to add (up)

Adel (-s) m nobility; **adelig** adj noble

Ader (-, -n) f vein

Adjektiv nt adjective

Adler (-s, -) m eagle

adoptieren vt to adopt; **Adoption** f adoption; **Adoptiveltern** pl adoptive parents pl; **Adoptivkind** nt adopted child

Adrenalin (-s) nt adrenalin

Adressbuch nt directory; (persönliches) address book; **Adresse** (-, -n) f address; **adressieren** vt to address (an +akk to)

ADSL f ADSL

Advent (-s, -) m Advent; **Adventskranz** m Advent wreath

Adverb nt adverb

Aerobic (-s) nt aerobics sing

Affäre (-, -n) f affair

Affe (-n, -n) m monkey

Afghanistan (-s) nt Afghanistan

Afrika (-s) nt Africa; **Afrikaner(in)** (-s, -) m(f) African; **afrikanisch** adj African

After (-s, -) m anus

Aftershave (-(s), -s) nt aftershave

AG (-, -s) f abk = **Aktiengesellschaft** plc (Brit), corp. (US)

Agent(in) m(f) agent; **Agentur** f agency

aggressiv adj aggressive

Ägypten (-s) nt Egypt

ah interj ah, ooh

aha interj I see, aha

ähneln vi +dat to be like, to resemble ▷ vr: **sich ~** to be alike (o similar)

ahnen vt to suspect; **du ahnst es nicht!** would you believe it?

ähnlich adj similar (dat to); **jdm ~ sehen** to look like sb; **Ähnlichkeit** f similarity

Ahnung f idea; (Vermutung) suspicion; **keine ~!** no idea; **ahnungslos** adj unsuspecting

Ahorn (-s, -e) m maple

Aids (-) nt Aids; **aidskrank** adj suffering from Aids; **Aidstest** m Aids test

Airbag (-s, -s) m (Auto) airbag; **Airbus** m airbus

Akademie (-, -n) f academy; **Akademiker(in)** (-s, -) m(f) (university) graduate

akklimatisieren vr: **sich ~** to acclimatize oneself

Akkordeon (-s, -s) nt accordion

Akku (-s, -s) m (storage) battery

Akkusativ m accusative (case)

Akne (-, -) f acne

Akrobat(in) (-s, -en) m(f) acrobat

Akt (-(e)s, -e) m act; (Kunst) nude

Akte (-, -n) f file; **etw zu den ~n legen** (a. fig) to file sth away; **Aktenkoffer** m briefcase

Aktie (-, -n) f share; **Aktiengesellschaft** f public limited company (Brit), corporation (US)

Aktion f (Kampagne) campaign; (Einsatz) operation

Aktionär(in) (-s, -e) m(f) shareholder

aktiv adj active; **aktivieren** vt to activate

aktualisieren vt to update; **aktuell** adj (Thema) topical;

(*modern*) up-to-date; (*Problem*) current; **nicht mehr ~** no longer relevant

Akupunktur f acupuncture

akustisch adj acoustic; **Akustik** f acoustics sing

akut adj acute

AKW (-s, -s) nt abk = **Atomkraftwerk** nuclear power station

Akzent (-(e)s, -e) m accent; (*Betonung*) stress; **mit starkem schottischen ~** with a strong Scottish accent

akzeptieren vt to accept

Alarm (-(e)s, -e) m alarm; **Alarmanlage** f alarm system; **alarmieren** vt to alarm; **die Polizei ~** to call the police

Albanien (-s) nt Albania

Albatros (-ses, -se) m albatross

albern adj silly

Albtraum m nightmare

Album (-s, Alben) nt album

Algen pl algae pl; (*Meeresalgen*) seaweed sing

Algerien (-s) nt Algeria

Alibi (-s, -s) nt alibi

Alimente pl maintenance sing

Alkohol (-s, -e) m alcohol; **alkoholfrei** adj non-alcoholic; **~es Getränk** soft drink; **Alkoholiker(in)** (-s, -) m(f) alcoholic; **alkoholisch** adj alcoholic; **Alkoholtest** m breathalyser® test (*Brit*), alcohol test

All (-s) nt universe

○ SCHLÜSSELWORT

alle(r, s) adj 1 (*sämtliche*) all; **wir alle** all of us; **alle Kinder waren da** all the children were there; **alle Kinder mögen ...** all children like ...; **alle beide** both of us/them; **sie kamen alle** they all came; **alles Gute** all the best; **alles**

in allem all in all
2 (*mit Zeit- oder Maßangaben*) every; **alle vier Jahre** every four years; **alle fünf Meter** every five metres
▷ pron everything; **alles, was er sagt** everything he says, all that he says
▷ adv (*zu Ende, aufgebraucht*) finished; **die Milch ist alle** the milk's all gone, there's no milk left; **etw alle machen** to finish sth up

Allee (-, -n) f avenue

allein adj, adv, alone; (*ohne Hilfe*) on one's own, by oneself; **nicht ~** (*nicht nur*) not only; **allein-erziehend** adj: **~e Mutter** single mother; **Alleinerziehende(r)** mf single mother/father/parent; **alleinstehend** adj single, unmarried

allerbeste(r, s) adj very best

allerdings adv (*zwar*) admittedly; (*gewiss*) certainly, sure (*US*)

allererste(r, s) adj very first; **zu allererst** first of all

Allergie f allergy; **Allergiker(in)** (-s, -) m(f) allergy sufferer; **allergisch** adj allergic (*gegen* to)

allerhand adj inv (*fam*) all sorts of; **das ist doch ~!** (*Vorwurf*) that's the limit

Allerheiligen (-) nt All Saints' Day

allerhöchste(r, s) adj very highest; **allerhöchstens** adv at the very most; **allerlei** adj inv all sorts of; **allerletzte(r, s)** adj very last; **allerwenigste(r, s)** adj very least

alles pron everything; **~ in allem** all in all; *siehe auch* **alle**

Alleskleber (-s, -) m all-purpose glue

allgemein adj general; **im Allgemeinen** in general;

Allgemeinarzt m,

Allgemeinärztin f GP (Brit), family practitioner (US)

Alligator (-s, -en) m alligator

alljährlich adj annual

allmählich adj gradual ▷ adv gradually

Allradantrieb m all-wheel drive

Alltag m everyday life; **alltäglich** adj everyday; (gewöhnlich) ordinary; (tagtäglich) daily

allzu adv all too

Allzweckreiniger (-s, -) m multi-purpose cleaner

Alpen pl: **die ~** the Alps pl

Alphabet (-(e)s, -e) nt alphabet; **alphabetisch** adj alphabetical

Alptraum m siehe Albtraum

⭕ **SCHLÜSSELWORT**

als konj 1 (zeitlich) when; (gleichzeitig) as; **damals, als …** (in the days) when …; **gerade, als …** just as …

2 (in der Eigenschaft) than; **als Antwort** as an answer; **als Kind** as a child

3 (bei Vergleichen) than; **ich kam später als er** I came later than he (did) o later than him; **lieber … als …** rather … than …; **nichts als Ärger** nothing but trouble

4 **als ob/wenn** as if

also conj (folglich) so, therefore ▷ adv, interj so; **~ gut** o (o **schön**)! okay then

alt adj old; **wie ~ sind Sie?** how old are you?; **28 Jahre ~** 28 years old; **vier Jahre älter** four years older

Altar (-(e)s, Altäre) m altar

Alter (-s, -) nt age; (hohes) old age; **im ~ von** at the age of; **er ist in meinem ~** he's my age

alternativ adj alternative; (umweltbewusst) ecologically

minded; (Landwirtschaft) organic; **Alternative** f alternative

Altersheim nt old people's home

Altglas nt used glass; **Altglascontainer** m bottle bank; **altmodisch** adj old-fashioned; **Altpapier** nt waste paper; **Altstadt** f old town

Alt-Taste f Alt key

Alufolie f tin (o kitchen) foil

Aluminium (-s) nt aluminium (Brit), aluminum (US)

Alzheimerkrankheit f Alzheimer's (disease)

am kontr von **an dem**; **~ 2. Januar** on January 2(nd); **~ Morgen** in the morning; **~ Strand** on the beach; **~ Bahnhof** at the station; **was gefällt Ihnen ~ besten?** what do you like best?; **~ besten bleiben wir hier** it would be best if we stayed here

Amateur(in) m(f) amateur

ambulant adj outpatient; **kann ich ~ behandelt werden?** can I have it done as an outpatient?; **Ambulanz** f (Krankenwagen) ambulance; (in der Klinik) outpatients' department

Ameise (-, -n) f ant

amen interj amen

Amerika (-s) nt America; **Amerikaner(in)** m(f) (-s, -) American; **amerikanisch** adj American

Ampel (-, -n) f traffic lights pl

Amphitheater nt amphitheatre

Amsel (-, -n) f blackbird

Amt (-(e)s, Ämter) nt (Dienststelle) office, department; (Posten) post; **amtlich** adj official; **Amtszeichen** nt (Tel) dialling tone (Brit), dial tone (US)

amüsant adj amusing; **amüsieren** vt to amuse ▷ vr: **sich ~** to enjoy oneself, to have a good time

○ SCHLÜSSELWORT

an prep +dat **1** (räumlich) (wo?) at; (auf, bei) on; (nahe bei) near; **an diesem Ort** at this place; **an der Wand** on the wall; **zu nahe an etw** too near to sth; **unten am Fluss** down by the river; **Köln liegt am Rhein** Cologne is on the Rhine
2 (zeitlich: wann?) on; **an diesem Tag** on this day; **an Ostern** at Easter
3 arm an Fett low in fat; **an etw sterben** to die of sth; **an (und für) sich** actually
▷ prep +akk **1** (räumlich: wohin?) to; **er ging ans Fenster** he went (over) to the window; **etw an die Wand hängen/schreiben** to hang/write sth on the wall
2 (woran?) **an etw denken** to think of sth
3 (gerichtet an) to; **ein Gruß/eine Frage an dich** greetings/a question to you
▷ adv **1** (ungefähr) about; **an die hundert** about a hundred
2 (auf Fahrplänen) **Frankfurt an 18.30** arriving Frankfurt 18.30
3 (ab) **von dort/heute an** from there/today onwards
4 (angeschaltet, angezogen) on; **das Licht ist an** the light is on; **ohne etwas an** with nothing on; **siehe auch am**

anal adj anal
analog adj analogous; (Inform) analog
Analyse (-, -n) f analysis; **analysieren** vt to analyse
Ananas (-, -se) f pineapple
an|baggern vt (fam) to chat up (Brit), to come on to (US)
Anbau m (Agr) cultivation;

(Gebäude) extension; **an|bauen** vt (Agr) to cultivate; (Gebäudeteil) to build on
an|behalten irr vt to keep on
anbei adv enclosed; **~ sende ich …** please find enclosed …
an|beten vt to worship
an|bieten irr vt to offer ▷ vr: **sich ~** to volunteer
an|binden irr vt to tie up
Anblick m sight
an|braten irr vt to brown
an|brechen irr vt to start; (Vorräte, Ersparnisse) to break into; (Flasche, Packung) to open ▷ vi to start; (Tag) to break; (Nacht) to fall
an|brennen irr vt, vi to burn; **das Fleisch schmeckt angebrannt** the meat tastes burnt
an|bringen irr vt (herbeibringen) to bring; (befestigen) to fix, to attach
Andacht (-, -en) f devotion; (Gottesdienst) prayers pl
an|dauern vi to continue, to go on; **andauernd** adj continual
Andenken (-s, -) nt memory; (Gegenstand) souvenir
andere(r, s) adj (weitere) other; (verschieden) different; (folgend) next; **am ~n Tag** the next day; **von etw/jmd ~m sprechen** to talk about sth/sb else; **unter ~m** among other things; **andererseits** adv on the other hand
ändern vt to alter, to change ▷ vr: **sich ~** to change
andernfalls adv otherwise
anders adv differently (als from); **jemand/irgendwo ~** someone/somewhere else; **sie ist ~ als ihre Schwester** she's not like her sister; **es geht nicht ~** there's no other way; **anders(he)rum** adv the other way round; **anderswo** adv somewhere else
anderthalb num one and a half

Änderung f change, alteration

an|deuten vt to indicate; (*Wink geben*) to hint at

Andorra (-s) nt Andorra

Andrang m: **es herrschte großer ~** there was a huge crowd

an|drohen vt: **jdm etw ~** to threaten sb with sth

aneinander adv at/on/to one another (o each other); **~ denken** think of each other; **sich ~ gewöhnen** to get used to each other; **aneinander|geraten** irr vi to clash; **aneinander|legen** vt to put together

an|erkennen irr vt (*Staat, Zeugnis etc*) to recognize; (*würdigen*) to appreciate; **Anerkennung** f recognition; (*Würdigung*) appreciation

an|fahren irr vt (*fahren gegen*) to run into; (*Ort, Hafen*) to stop (o call) at; (*liefern*) to deliver; **jdn ~** (*fig: schimpfen*) to jump on sb ▷ vi to start; (*losfahren*) to drive off

Anfall m (*Med*) attack; **anfällig** adj delicate; (*Maschine*) temperamental; **~ für** prone to

Anfang (-(*e*)s, *Anfänge*) m beginning, start; **zu/am ~** to start with; **~ Mai** at the beginning of May; **sie ist ~ 20** she's in her early twenties; **an|fangen** irr vt, vi to begin, to start; **damit kann ich nichts ~** that's no use to me; **Anfänger(in)** (-s, -) m(f) beginner; **anfangs** adv at first; **Anfangsbuchstabe** m first (o initial) letter

an|fassen vt (*berühren*) to touch ▷ vi: **kannst du mal mit ~?** can you give me a hand?

Anflug m (*Aviat*) approach; (*Hauch*) trace

an|fordern vt to demand; **Anforderung** f request (*von* for); (*Anspruch*) demand

Anfrage f inquiry

an|freunden vr: **sich mit jdm ~** to make (o to become) friends with sb

an|fühlen vr: **sich ~** to feel; **es fühlt sich gut an** it feels good

Anführungszeichen pl quotation marks pl

Angabe f (*Tech*) specification; (*fam: Prahlerei*) showing off; (*Tennis*) serve; **~n** pl (*Auskunft*) particulars pl; **die ~n waren falsch** (*Info*) the information was wrong; **an|geben** irr vt (*Name, Grund*) to give; (*zeigen*) to indicate; (*bestimmen*) to set ▷ vi (*fam: prahlen*) to boast; (*Sport*) to serve; **Angeber(in)** (-s, -) m(f) (*fam*) show-off; **angeblich** adj alleged

angeboren adj inborn

Angebot nt offer; (*Comm*) supply (*an +dat* of); **~ und Nachfrage** supply and demand

angebracht adj appropriate

angebunden adj: **kurz ~** curt

angeheitert adj tipsy

an|gehen irr vt to concern; **das geht dich nichts an** that's none of your business; **ein Problem ~** to tackle a problem; **was ihn angeht** as far as he's concerned, as for him ▷ vi (*Feuer*) to catch; (*fam: beginnen*) to begin; **angehend** adj prospective

Angehörige(r) mf relative

Angeklagte(r) mf accused, defendant

Angel (-, -n) f fishing rod; (*an der Tür*) hinge

Angelegenheit f affair, matter

Angelhaken m fish hook; **angeln** vt to catch o ▷ vi to fish; **Angeln** (-s) nt angling, fishing; **Angelrute** (-, -n) f fishing rod

angemessen adj appropriate, suitable

angenehm adj pleasant; **~!** (bei Vorstellung) pleased to meet you

angenommen adj assumed ▷ conj: **~, es regnet, was machen wir dann?** suppose it rains, what do we do then?

angesehen adj respected

angesichts prep +gen in view of, considering

Angestellte(r) mf employee

angetan adj von jdm/etw **~ sein** to be impressed by (a token with) sb/sth

angewiesen adj: **auf jdn/etw ~ sein** to be dependent on sb/sth

an|gewöhnen vt: **sich etw ~** to get used to doing sth; **Angewohnheit** f habit

Angina (-, Anginen) f tonsillitis; **Angina Pectoris** (-) f angina

Angler(in) (-s, -) m(f) angler

Angora (-s) nt angora

an|greifen irr vt to attack; (anfassen) to touch; (beschädigen) to damage; **Angriff** m attack; **etw in ~ nehmen** to get started on sth

Angst (-, Ängste) f fear; **~ haben** to be afraid (vor +dat of); **jdm ~ machen** to scare sb; **ängstigen** vt to frighten ▷ vr: **sich ~** to worry (um, wegen +dat about); **ängstlich** adj nervous; (besorgt) worried

an|haben irr vt (Kleidung) to have on, to wear; (Licht) to have on

an|halten irr vi to stop; (andauern) to continue; **anhaltend** adj continuous; **Anhalter(in)** (-s, -) m(f) hitch-hiker; **per ~ fahren** to hitch-hike

anhand prep +gen with; **~ von** by means of

an|hängen vt to hang up; (Eisenb: Wagen) to couple; (Zusatz) to add (on); **jdm etw ~** (fam: unterschieben) to pin sth on sb;

eine Datei an eine E-Mail **~** (Inform) to attach a file to an email; **Anhänger** (-s, -) m (Auto) trailer; (am Koffer) tag; (Schmuck) pendant; **Anhänger(in)** (-s, -) m(f) supporter; **Anhängerkupplung** f towbar; **anhänglich** adj affectionate; (pej) clinging

Anhieb m: **auf ~** straight away; **das kann ich nicht auf ~ sagen** I can't say offhand

an|himmeln vt to idolize

an|hören vt to listen to ▷ vr: **sich ~** to sound; **das hört sich gut an** that sounds good

Animateur(in) m(f) host/hostess

Anis (-es, -e) m aniseed

Anker (-s, -) m anchor; **ankern** vt, vi to anchor; **Ankerplatz** m anchorage

an|klicken vt (Inform) to click on

an|klopfen vi to knock (an +akk on)

an|kommen irr vi to arrive; **bei jdm gut ~** to go down well with sb; **es kommt darauf an** it depends (ob on whether); **darauf kommt es nicht an** that doesn't matter

an|kotzen vt (vulg) to make sick **mich an** it makes me sick

an|kreuzen vt to mark with a cross

an|kündigen vt to announce

Ankunft (-, Ankünfte) f arrival; **Ankunftszeit** f arrival time

Anlage f (Veranlagung) disposition; (Begabung) talent; (Park) gardens pl; (zu Brief etc) enclosure; (Stereoanlage) stereo; (Tech) plant; (Fin) investment

Anlass (-es, Anlässe) m cause (zu for); (Ereignis) occasion; **aus diesem ~** for this reason; **an|lassen** irr vt (Motor) to start; (Licht, Kleidung) to leave on;

Anlasser (-s, -) m (Auto) starter;
anlässlich prep +gen on the occasion of

Anlauf m run-up; **an|laufen** irr vi to begin; (Film) to open; (Fenster) to mist up; (Metall) to tarnish

an|legen vt to put (an +akk against/on); (Schmuck) to put on; (Garten) to lay out; (Geld) to invest; (Gewehr) to aim (auf +akk at); **es auf etw** (akk) **~** to be out for sth ▷ vi (Schiff) to berth, to dock ▷ vr: **sich mit jdm ~** (fam) to pick a quarrel with sb; **Anlegestelle** f moorings pl

an|lehnen vt to lean (an +akk against); (Tür) to leave ajar ▷ vr: **sich ~** to lean (an +akk against)

an|leiern vt: **etw ~** (fam) to get sth going

Anleitung f instructions pl

Anliegen (-s, -) nt matter; (Wunsch) request

Anlieger(in) (-s, -) m(f) resident; **~ frei** residents only

an|lügen irr vt to lie to

an|machen vt (befestigen) to attach; (einschalten) to switch on; (Salat) to dress; (fam: aufreizen) to turn on; (fam: ansprechen) to chat up (Brit), to come on to (US); (fam: beschimpfen) to have a go at

Anmeldeformular nt application form; (bei Amt) registration form; **an|melden** vt (Besuch etc) to announce ▷ vr: **sich ~** (beim Arzt etc) to make an appointment; (bei Amt, für Kurs etc) to register; **Anmeldeschluss** m deadline for applications, registration deadline; **Anmeldung** f registration; (Antrag) application

an|nähen vt: **einen Knopf (an den Mantel) ~** to sew a button on (one's coat)

annähernd adv roughly; **nicht ~ nowhere near**

Annahme (-, -n) f acceptance; (Vermutung) assumption;
annehmbar adj acceptable;
an|nehmen irr vt to accept; (Namen) to take; (Kind) to adopt; (vermuten) to suppose, to assume

Annonce (-, -n) f advertisement

an|öden vt (fam) to bore stiff (o silly)

annullieren vt to cancel

anonym adj anonymous

Anorak (-s, -s) m anorak

an|packen vt (Problem, Aufgabe) to tackle; **mit ~** to lend a hand

an|passen vt (fig) to adapt (dat to) ▷ vr: **sich ~** to adapt (an +akk to)

an|pfeifen irr vt (Fußballspiel) **das Spiel ~** to start the game; **Anpfiff** m (Sport) (starting) whistle; (Beginn) kick-off; (fam: Tadel) roasting

an|probieren vt to try on

Anrede f form of address;
an|reden vt to address

an|regen vt to stimulate; **Anregung** f stimulation; (Vorschlag) suggestion

Anreise f journey; **an|reisen** vi to arrive; **Anreisetag** m day of arrival

Anreiz m incentive

an|richten vt (Speisen) to prepare; (Schaden) to cause

Anruf m call; **Anrufbeantworter** (-s, -) m answering machine, answerphone; **an|rufen** irr vt (Tel) to call, to phone, to ring (Brit)

ans kontr von **an das**

Ansage f announcement; (auf Anrufbeantworter) recorded message; **an|sagen** vt to announce; **angesagt sein** to be recommended; (modisch sein) to be the in thing

an|schaffen vt to buy

an|schauen vt to look at

Anschein m appearance; **dem** (o allem) **~ nach ...** it looks as if ...; **den ~ erwecken, hart zu arbeiten** to give the impression of working hard; **anscheinend** adj apparent ▷ adv apparently

an|schieben irr vt: **könnten Sie mich mal ~?** (Auto) could you give me a push?

Anschlag m notice; (Attentat) attack; **an|schlagen** irr vt (Plakat) to put up; (beschädigen) to chip ▷ vi (wirken) to take effect; **mit etw an etw** (akk) **~** to bang sth against sth

an|schließen irr vt (Elek, Tech) to connect (an +akk to); (mit Stecker) to plug in ▷ vi, vr (**sich**) **an etw** (akk) **~** (Gebäude etc) to adjoin sth; (zeitlich) to follow sth ▷ vr: **sich ~ to** join (jdm/einer Gruppe sb/a group); **anschließend** adj adjacent; (zeitlich) subsequent ▷ adv afterwards; **~ an** (+akk) following; **Anschluss** m (Elek, Eisenb) connection; (von Wasser, Gas etc) supply; **im ~ an** (+akk) following; **kein ~ unter dieser Nummer** (Tel) the number you have dialled has not been recognized; **Anschlussflug** m connecting flight

an|schnallen vt (Skier) to put on ▷ vr: **sich ~** to fasten one's seat belt

Anschrift f address

an|schwellen irr vi to swell (up)

an|sehen irr vt to look at; (bei etw zuschauen) to watch; **jdn/etw als etw ~** to look on sb/sth as sth; **das sieht man ihm an** he looks it

an sein irr vt siehe **an**

an|setzen vt (Termin) to fix; (zubereiten) to prepare ▷ vi (anfangen) to start, to begin; **zu**

etw ~ to prepare to do sth

Ansicht f (Meinung) view, opinion; (Anblick) sight; **meiner ~ nach** in my opinion; **zur ~** on approval; **Ansichtskarte** f postcard

ansonsten adv otherwise

an|spielen vi **auf etw** (akk) **~** to allude to sth; **Anspielung** f allusion (auf +akk to)

an|sprechen irr vt to speak to; (gefallen) to appeal to ▷ vi **auf etw** (akk) **~** (Patient) to respond to sth; **ansprechend** adj attractive; **Ansprechpartner(in)** m(f) contact

an|springen irr vi (Auto) to start

Anspruch m claim; (Recht) right (auf +akk to); **etw in ~ nehmen** to take advantage of sth; **~ auf etw haben** to be entitled to sth; **anspruchslos** adj undemanding; (bescheiden) modest; **anspruchsvoll** adj demanding

Anstalt (-, -en) f institution

Anstand m decency; **anständig** adj decent; (fig, fam) proper; (groß) considerable

an|starren vt to stare at

anstatt prep +gen instead of

an|stecken vt to pin on; (Med) to infect; **jdn mit einer Erkältung ~** to pass one's cold on to sb ▷ vr: **ich habe mich bei ihm angesteckt** I caught it from him ▷ vi (fig) to be infectious; **ansteckend** adj infectious; **Ansteckungsgefahr** f danger of infection

an|stehen irr vi (in Warteschlange) to queue (Brit), to stand in line (US); (erledigt werden müssen) to be on the agenda

anstelle prep +gen instead of

an|stellen vt (einschalten) to turn on; (Arbeit geben) to employ; (machen) to do; **was hast du**

wieder angestellt? what have you been up to now? ▷ vr: **sich ~** to queue (Brit), to stand in line (US); (fam) **stell dich nicht so an!** stop making such a fuss

Anstoß m impetus; (Sport) kick-off; **an|stoßen** irr vt to push; (mit Fuß) to kick ▷ vi to knock, to bump; (mit Gläsern) to drink (a toast) (auf +akk to); **anstößig** adj offensive; (Kleidung etc) indecent

an|strengen vt to strain ▷ vr: **sich ~** to make an effort; **anstrengend** adj tiring

Antarktis f Antarctic

Anteil m share (an +dat in); **~ nehmen an** (+dat) (mitleidig) to sympathize with; (sich interessieren) to take an interest in

Antenne (-, -n) f aerial

Antibabypille f: **die ~** the pill; **Antibiotikum** (-s, Antibiotika) nt (Med) antibiotic

antik adj antique

Antilope (-, -n) f antelope

Antiquariat nt (für Bücher) second-hand bookshop

Antiquitäten pl antiques pl; **Antiquitätenhändler(in)** m(f) antique dealer

Antiviren- adj (Inform) antivirus; **Antivirensoftware** f antivirus software

an|törnen vt (fam) to turn on

Antrag (-(e)s, Anträge) m proposal; (Pol) motion; (Formular) application form; **einen ~ stellen auf** (+akk) to apply for

an|treffen irr vt to find

an|treiben irr vt (Tech) to drive; (anschwemmen) to wash up; **jdn zur Arbeit ~** to make sb work

an|treten irr vt: **eine Reise ~** to set off on a journey

Antrieb m (Tech) drive; (Motivation) impetus

an|tun irr vt: **jdm etwas ~** to do

sth to sb; **sich** (dat) **etwas ~** (Selbstmord begehen) to kill oneself

Antwort (-, -en) f answer, reply; **um ~ wird gebeten** RSVP (répondez s'il vous plaît); **antworten** vi to answer, to reply; **jdm ~** to answer sb; **auf etw** (akk) **~** to answer sth

an|vertrauen vt: **jdm etw ~** to entrust sb with sth

Anwalt (-s, Anwälte) m, **Anwältin** f lawyer

an|weisen irr vt (anleiten) to instruct; (zuteilen) to allocate (jdm etw sth to sb); **Anweisung** f instruction; (von Geld) money order

an|wenden irr vt to use; (Gesetz, Regel) to apply; **Anwender(in)** (-s, -) m(f) user; **Anwendung** f use; (Inform) application

anwesend adj present; **Anwesenheit** f presence

an|widern vt to disgust

Anwohner(in) (-s, -) m(f) resident

Anzahl f number (an +dat of); **an|zahlen** vt to pay a deposit on; **100 Euro ~** to pay 100 euros as a deposit; **Anzahlung** f deposit

Anzeichen nt sign; (Med) symptom

Anzeige (-, -n) f (Werbung) advertisement; (elektronisch) display; (bei Polizei) report; **an|zeigen** vt (Temperatur, Zeit) to indicate, to show; (elektronisch) to display; (bekannt geben) to announce; **einen Autodiebstahl bei der Polizei ~** to report a stolen car to the police

an|ziehen irr vt to attract; (Kleidung) to put on; (Schraube, Seil) to tighten ▷ vr: **sich ~** to get dressed; **anziehend** adj attractive

Anzug m suit

anzüglich adj suggestive

an|zünden vt to light; (Haus etc)

to set fire to

an|zweifeln vt to doubt

Aperitif (-s, -s (o -e)) m aperitif

Apfel (-s, Äpfel) m apple; **Apfelbaum** m apple tree; **Apfelkuchen** m apple cake; **Apfelmus** nt apple purée; **Apfelsaft** m apple juice; **Apfelsine** f orange; **Apfelwein** m cider

Apostroph (-s, -e) m apostrophe

Apotheke (-, -n) f chemist's (shop) (Brit), pharmacy (US); **apothekenpflichtig** adj only available at the chemist's; **Apotheker(in)** (-s, -) m(f) chemist (Brit), pharmacist (US)

Apparat (-(e)s, -e) m (piece of) apparatus; (Tel) telephone; (Radio, TV) set; **am ~!** (Tel) speaking; **am ~ bleiben** (Tel) to hold the line

Appartement (-s, -s) nt studio flat (Brit) (o apartment (US))

Appetit (-(e)s, -e) m appetite; **guten ~!** bon appétit; **appetitlich** adj appetizing

Applaus (-es, -e) m applause

Aprikose (-, -n) f apricot

April (-(s), -e) m April; siehe auch **juni**; **~, ~!** April fool!; **Aprilscherz** (-es, -e) m April fool's joke

apropos adv by the way; **~ Urlaub ...** while we're on the subject of holidays ...

Aquajogging nt aqua jogging; **Aquaplaning** (-(s)) nt aquaplaning

Aquarell (-s, -e) nt watercolour

Aquarium (-s, Aquarien) nt aquarium

Äquator (-s, -) m equator

Araber(in) (-s, -) m(f) Arab; **arabisch** adj Arab; (Ziffer, Sprache) Arabic; (Meer, Wüste) Arabian

Arbeit (-, -en) f work; (Stelle) job; (Erzeugnis) piece of work; **arbeiten** vi to work; **Arbeiter(in)** (-s, -) m(f) worker; (ungelernt) labourer;

Arbeitgeber(in) (-s, -) m(f) employ; **Arbeitnehmer(in)** (-s, -) m(f) emp **Arbeitsagentur** f job agency (Brit), unemployment agency (US); **Arbeitsamt** nt job centre (Brit), employment office (US); **Arbeitserlaubnis** f work permit; **arbeitslos** adj unemployed; **Arbeitslose(r)** mf unemployed person; **Arbeitslosengeld** nt (income-related) unemployment benefit, job-seeker's allowance (Brit); **Arbeitslosenhilfe** f (non-income related) unemployment benefit; **Arbeitslosigkeit** f unemployment; **Arbeitsplatz** m job; (Ort) workplace; **Arbeitsspeicher** m (Inform) main memory; **Arbeitszeit** f working hours pl; **Arbeitszimmer** nt study

Archäologe (-n, -n) m, **Archäologin** f archaeologist

Architekt(in) (-en, -en) m(f) architect; **Architektur** f architecture

Archiv (-s, -e) nt archives pl

ARD f = **Arbeitsgemeinschaft der öffentlich-rechtlichen Rundfunkanstalten der Bundesrepublik Deutschland** German broadcasting corporation

arg adj bad; (schrecklich) awful ▷ adv (sehr) terribly

Argentinien (-s) nt Argentina

Ärger (-s) m annoyance; (stärker) anger; (Unannehmlichkeiten) trouble; **ärgerlich** adj annoying; (zornig) angry; **ärgern** vt to annoy ▷ vr: **sich ~** to get annoyed

Argument (-s, -e) nt argument

Arktis (-) f Arctic

arm adj poor

Arm (-(e)s, -e) m arm; (Fluss) branch

Armaturenbrett nt instrument panel; (Auto) dashboard

Armband nt bracelet;

Armbanduhr f (wrist)watch
Armee (-, -n) f army
Ärmel (-s, -) m sleeve;
Ärmelkanal m (English) Channel
Armut (-) f poverty
Aroma (-s, Aromen) nt aroma
arrogant adj arrogant
Arsch (-es, Ärsche) m (vulg) arse
(Brit), ass (US); **Arschloch** nt
(vulg: Person) arsehole (Brit),
asshole (US)
Art (-, -en) f (Weise) way; (Sorte)
kind, sort; (bei Tieren) species;
nach ~ des Hauses à la maison;
auf diese ~ (und Weise) in this
way; **das ist nicht seine ~** that's
not like him
Arterie (-, -n) f artery
artig adj good, well-behaved
Artikel (-s, -) m (Ware) article,
item; (Zeitung) article
Artischocke (-, -n) f artichoke
Artist(in) (-en, -en) m(f) (circus)
performer
Arznei f medicine; **Arzt** (-es,
Ärzte) m doctor; **Arzthelfer(in)**
m(f) doctor's assistant; **Ärztin** f
(female) doctor; **ärztlich** adj
medical; **sich ~ behandeln lassen**
to undergo medical treatment
Asche (-, -n) f ashes pl; (von
Zigarette) ash; **Aschenbecher** m
ashtray; **Aschermittwoch** m
Ash Wednesday
Asiat(in) (-en, -en) m(f) Asian;
asiatisch adj Asian; **Asien** (-s) nt
Asia
Aspekt (-(e)s, -e) m aspect
Asphalt (-(e)s, -e) m asphalt
Aspirin® (-s, -e) nt aspirin
aß imperf von **essen**
Ass (-es, -e) nt (Karten, Tennis) ace
Assistent(in) m(f) assistant
Ast (-(e)s, Äste) m branch
Asthma (-s) nt asthma
Astrologie f astrology;
Astronaut(in) (-en, -en) m(f)

astronaut; **Astronomie** f
astronomy
ASU (-, -s) f abk =
Abgassonderuntersuchung
exhaust emission test
Asyl (-s, -e) nt asylum; (Heim)
home; (für Obdachlose) shelter;
Asylant(in) m(f). **Asylbe-
werber(in)** m(f) asylum seeker
Atelier (-s, -s) nt studio
Atem (-s) m breath; **atembe-
raubend** adj breathtaking;
Atembeschwerden pl breathing
difficulties pl; **atemlos** adj breath-
less; **Atempause** f breather
Athen nt Athens
Äthiopien (-s) nt Ethiopia
Athlet(in) (-en, -en) m(f) athlete;
Athletik f athletics sing
Atlantik (-s) m Atlantic (Ocean)
Atlas (- o Atlasses, Atlanten) m
atlas
atmen vt, vi to breathe; **Atmung**
f breathing
Atom (-s, -e) nt atom;
Atombombe f atom bomb;
Atomkraftwerk nt nuclear
power station; **Atommüll** m
nuclear waste; **Atomwaffen** pl
nuclear weapons pl
Attentat (-(e)s, -e) nt
assassination (auf +akk of);
(Versuch) assassination attempt
Attest (-(e)s, -e) nt certificate
attraktiv adj attractive
Attrappe (-, -n) f dummy
ätzend adj (fam) revolting;
(schlecht) lousy
au interj ouch; **~ ja!** yeah
Aubergine (-, -n) f aubergine,
eggplant (US)

O SCHLÜSSELWORT

auch adv **1** (ebenfalls) also, too, as
well; **das ist auch schön** that's
nice too o as well; **er kommt — ich**

auch he's coming — so am I, me too; **auch nicht** not ... either; **ich auch nicht** nor I, me neither; **oder auch** or; **auch das noch!** not that as well!

2 (*selbst, sogar*) even; **auch wenn das Wetter schlecht ist** even if the weather is bad; **ohne auch nur zu fragen** without even asking

3 (*wirklich*) really; **du siehst müde aus—bin ich auch** you look tired— (so) I am; **so sieht es auch aus** it looks like it too

4 (*auch immer*) **wer auch** whoever; **was auch** whatever; **wie dem auch sei** be that as it may; **wie sehr er sich auch bemühte** however much he tried

audiovisuell *adj* audiovisual

SCHLÜSSELWORT

auf *prep* +*dat* (*wo?*) on; **auf dem Tisch** on the table; **auf der Post/dem Fest** at the post office/party; **auf der Straße** on the road; **auf dem Land/der ganzen Welt** in the country/the whole world
▷ *prep* +*akk* **1** (*wohin?*) on(to); **auf den Tisch** on(to) the table; **auf die Post gehen** to go to the post office; **aufs Land** into the country; **etw auf einen Zettel schreiben** to write sth on a piece of paper

2 auf Deutsch in German; **auf Lebenszeit** for my/his lifetime; **bis auf ihn** except for him; **auf einmal** at once; **auf seinen Vorschlag (hin)** at his suggestion
▷ *adv* **1** (*offen*) open; **auf sein** (*fam*) (*Tür, Geschäft*) to be open; **das Fenster ist auf** the window is open

2 (*hinauf*) up; **auf und ab** up and down; **auf und davon** up and away; **auf!** (*los!*) come on!

3 (*aufgestanden*) up; **auf sein** to be up; **ist er schon auf?** is he up yet?
▷ *konj*: **auf dass** (so) that

auf|atmen *vi* to breathe a sigh of relief

auf|bauen *vt* (*errichten*) to put up; (*schaffen*) to build up; (*gestalten*) to construct; (*gründen*) to found, to base (*auf* +*akk* on); **sich eine Existenz ~** to make a life for oneself

auf|bewahren *vt* to keep, to store

auf|bleiben *irr vi* (*Tür, Laden etc*) to stay open; (*Mensch*) to stay up

auf|blenden *vi, vt*: **(die Scheinwerfer) ~** to put one's headlights on full beam

auf|brechen *irr vt* to break open ▷ *vi* to burst open; (*gehen*) to leave; (*abreisen*) to set off

auf|drängen *vt*: **jdm etw ~** to force sth on sb ▷ *vr*: **sich ~** to intrude (*jdm* on sb); **aufdringlich** *adj* pushy

aufeinander *adv* (*übereinander*) on top of each other; **~ achten** to look after each other; **~ vertrauen** to trust each other; **aufeinan-der|folgen** *vi* to follow one another; **aufeinander|prallen** *vi* to crash into one another

Aufenthalt *m* stay; (*Zug*) stop; **Aufenthaltsgenehmigung** *f* residence permit; **Aufenthaltsraum** *m* lounge

auf|essen *irr vt* to eat up

auf|fahren *irr vi* (*Auto*) to run (*o* to crash) (*auf* +*akk* into); (*herankommen*) to drive up; **Auffahrt** *f* (*am Haus*) drive; (*Autobahn*) slip road (Brit), ramp (US); **Auffahrunfall** *m* rear-end collision; (*mehrere Fahrzeuge*) pile-up

auf|fallen *irr vi* to stand out; **jdm ~** to strike sb; **das fällt gar nicht auf** nobody will notice; **auffallend** *adj* striking; **auffällig** *adj* conspicuous; (*Kleidung*) striking

auf|fangen *irr vt* (*Ball*) to catch; (*Stoß*) to cushion

auf|fassen *vt* to understand; **Auffassung** *f* view; (*Meinung*) opinion; (*Auslegung*) concept; (*Auffassungsgabe*) grasp

auf|fordern *vt* (*befehlen*) to call upon; (*bitten*) to ask

auf|frischen *vt* to brush up

auf|führen *vt* (*Theat*) to perform; (*in einem Verzeichnis*) to list; (*Beispiel*) to give ▷ *vr*: **sich ~** (*sich benehmen*) to behave; **Aufführung** *f* (*Theat*) performance

Aufgabe *f* job, task; (*Schule*) exercise; (*Hausaufgabe*) homework

Aufgang *m* (*Treppe*) staircase

auf|geben *irr vt* (*verzichten auf*) to give up; (*Paket*) to post; (*Gepäck*) to check in; (*Bestellung*) to place; (*Inserat*) to insert; (*Rätsel, Problem*) to set ▷ *vi* to give up

auf|gehen *irr vi* (*Sonne, Teig*) to rise; (*sich öffnen*) to open; (*klar werden*) to dawn (*jdm so sb*)

aufgelegt *adj*: **gut/schlecht ~** in a good/bad mood

aufgeregt *adj* excited

aufgeschlossen *adj* open(minded)

aufgeschmissen *adj* (*fam*) in a fix

aufgrund, auf Grund *prep +gen* on the basis of; (*wegen*) because of

auf|haben *irr vt* (*Hut etc*) to have on; **viel ~** (*Schule*) to have a lot of homework to do ▷ *vi* (*Geschäft*) to be open

auf|halten *irr vt* (*jdn*) to detain; (*Entwicklung*) to stop; (*Tür, Hand*) to

hold open; (*Augen*) to keep open ▷ *vr*: **sich ~** (*wohnen*) to live; (*vorübergehend*) to stay

auf|hängen *irr vt* to hang up

auf|heben *irr vt* (*vom Boden etc*) to pick up; (*aufbewahren*) to keep

Aufheiterungen *pl* (*Meteo*) bright periods *pl*

auf|holen *vt* (*Zeit*) to make up ▷ *vi* to catch up

auf|hören *vi* to stop; **~, etw zu tun** to stop doing sth

auf|klären *vt* (*Geheimnis etc*) to clear up; **jdn ~** to enlighten sb; (*sexuell*) to tell sb the facts of life

Aufkleber (*-s, -*) *m* sticker

auf|kommen *irr vi* (*Wind*) to come up; (*Zweifel, Gefühl*) to arise; (*Mode etc*) to appear on the scene; **für den Schaden ~** to pay for the damage

auf|laden *irr vt* to load; (*Handy etc*) to charge; (*Handykarte etc*) to top up; **Aufladegerät** *nt* charger

Auflage *f* edition; (*von Zeitung*) circulation; (*Bedingung*) condition

auf|lassen *irr vt* (*Hut, Brille*) to keep on; (*Tür*) to leave open

Auflauf *m* (*Menschen*) crowd; (*Speise*) bake

auf|legen *vt* (*CD, Schminke etc*) to put on; (*Hörer*) to put down ▷ *vi* (*Tel*) to hang up

auf|leuchten *vi* to light up

auf|lösen *vt* (*in Flüssigkeit*) to dissolve ▷ *vr*: **sich ~** (*in Flüssigkeit*) to dissolve; **der Stau hat sich aufgelöst** traffic is back to normal; **Auflösung** *f* (*von Rätsel*) solution; (*von Bildschirm*) resolution

auf|machen *vt* to open; (*Kleidung*) to undo ▷ *vr*: **sich ~** to set out (*nach for*)

aufmerksam *adj* attentive; **jdn auf etw** (*akk*) **~ machen** to draw sb's attention to sth;

Aufmerksamkeit f attention; (Konzentration) attentiveness; (Geschenk) small token

auf|muntern vt (ermutigen) to encourage; (aufheitern) to cheer up

Aufnahme (-, -n) f (Foto) photo(graph); (einzelne) shot; (in Verein, Krankenhaus etc) admission; (Beginn) beginning; (auf Tonband etc) recording; **Aufnahmeprüfung** f entrance exam; **auf|nehmen** irr vt (in Krankenhaus, Verein etc) to admit; (Musik) to record; (beginnen) to take up; (in Liste) to include; (begreifen) to take in; **mit jdm Kontakt ~** to get in touch with sb

auf|passen vi (aufmerksam sein) to pay attention; (vorsichtig sein) to take care; **auf jdn/etw ~** to keep an eye on sb/sth

Aufprall (-s, -e) m impact; **auf|prallen** vi **auf etw** (akk) **~** to hit sth, to crash into sth

Aufpreis m extra charge

auf|pumpen vt to pump up

Aufputschmittel nt stimulant

auf|räumen vt, vi (Dinge) to clear away; (Zimmer) to tidy up

aufrecht adj upright

auf|regen vt to excite; (ärgern) to annoy ▷ vr: **sich ~** to get worked up; **aufregend** adj exciting; **Aufregung** f excitement

auf|reißen irr vt (Tüte) to tear open; (Tür) to fling open; (fam: Person) to pick up

Aufruf m (Aviat, Inform) call; (öffentlicher) appeal; **auf|rufen** irr vt (auffordern) to call upon (zu for); (Namen) to call out; (Aviat) to call; (Inform) to call up

auf|runden vt (Summe) to round up

aufs kontr von **auf das**

Aufsatz m essay

auf|schieben irr vt (verschieben)

to postpone; (verzögern) to put off; (Tür) to slide open

Aufschlag m (auf Preis) extra charge; (Tennis) service; **auf|schlagen** irr vt (öffnen) to open; (verletzen) to cut open; (Zelt) to pitch, to put up; (Lager) to set up ▷ vi (Tennis) to serve; **auf etw** (+akk) **~** (aufprallen) to hit sth

auf|schließen irr vt to unlock, to open up ▷ vi (aufrücken) to close up

auf|schneiden irr vt to cut open; (in Scheiben) to slice ▷ vi (angeben) to boast, to show off

Aufschnitt m (slices pl of) cold meat; (bei Käse) (assorted) sliced cheeses pl

auf|schreiben irr vt to write down

Aufschrift f inscription; (Etikett) label

Aufschub m (Verzögerung) delay; (Vertagung) postponement

Aufsehen (-s) nt stir; **großes ~ erregen** to cause a sensation; **Aufseher(in)** (-s, -) m(f) guard; (im Betrieb) supervisor; (im Museum) attendant; (im Park) keeper

auf sein irr vi siehe **auf**

auf|setzen vt to put on; (Dokument) to draw up ▷ vi (Flugzeug) to touch down

Aufsicht f supervision; (bei Prüfung) invigilation; **die ~ haben** to be in charge

auf|spannen vt (Schirm) to put up

auf|sperren vt (Mund) to open wide; (aufschließen) to unlock

auf|springen irr vi to jump (auf +akk onto); (hochspringen) to jump up; (sich öffnen) to spring open

auf|stehen irr vi to get up; (Tür) to be open

auf|stellen vt (aufrecht stellen) to

put up; (aufreihen) to line up; (nominieren) to put up; (Liste, Programm) to draw up; (Rekord) to set up

Aufstieg (-(e)s, -e) m (auf Berg) ascent; (Fortschritt) rise; (beruflich, im Sport) promotion

Aufstrich m spread

auf|tanken vt, vi (Auto) to tank up; (Flugzeug) to refuel

auf|tauchen vi to turn up; (aus Wasser etc) to surface; (Frage, Problem) to come up

auf|tauen vt (Speisen) to defrost ▷ vi to thaw; (fig: Person) to unbend

Auftrag (-(e)s, Aufträge) m (Comm) order; (Arbeit) job; (Anweisung) instructions pl; (Aufgabe) task; **im ~ von** on behalf of; **auf|tragen** irr vt (Salbe etc) to apply; (Essen) to serve

auf|treten irr vi to appear; (Problem) to come up; (sich verhalten) to behave; **Auftritt** m (des Schauspielers) entrance; (fig: Szene) scene

auf|wachen vi to wake up

auf|wachsen irr vi to grow up

Aufwand (-(e)s) m expenditure; (Kosten a.) expense; (Anstrengung) effort; **aufwändig** adj costly; **das ist zu ~** that's too much trouble

auf|wärmen vt to warm up ▷ vr: **sich ~** to warm up

aufwärts adv upwards; **mit etw geht es ~** things are looking up for sth

auf|wecken vt to wake up

aufwendig adj siehe **aufwändig**

auf|wischen vt to wipe up; (Fußboden) to wipe

auf|zählen vt to list

auf|zeichnen vt to sketch; (schriftlich) to jot down; (auf Band etc) to record; **Aufzeichnung** f

(schriftlich) note; (Tonband etc) recording; (Film) record

auf|ziehen irr vt (öffnen) to pull open; (Uhr) to wind (up); (fam: necken) to tease; (Kinder) to bring up; (Tiere) to rear ▷ vi (Gewitter) to come up

Aufzug m (Fahrstuhl) lift (Brit), elevator (US); (Kleidung) get-up; (Theat) act

Auge (-s, -n) nt eye; **jdm etw aufs ~ drücken** (fam) to force sth on sb; **ins ~ gehen** (fam) to go wrong; **unter vier ~n** in private; **etw im ~ behalten** to keep sth in mind; **Augenarzt** m, **Augenärztin** f eye specialist, eye doctor (US); **Augenblick** m moment; **im ~** at the moment; **Augenbraue** (-, -n) f eyebrow; **Augenbrauenstift** m eyebrow pencil; **Augenfarbe** f eye colour; **seine ~** the colour of his eyes; **Augenlid** nt eyelid; **Augen-optiker(in)** (-s, -) m(f) optician; **Augentropfen** pl eyedrops pl; **Augenzeuge** m, **Augenzeugin** f eyewitness

August (-(e)s o -, -e) m August; siehe auch **Juni**

Auktion f auction

 SCHLÜSSELWORT

aus prep +dat 1 (räumlich) out of; (von ... her) from; **er ist aus Berlin** he's from Berlin; **aus dem Fenster** out of the window

2 (gemacht/hergestellt aus) made of; **ein Herz aus Stein** a heart of stone

3 (auf Ursache deutend) out of; **aus Mitleid** out of sympathy; **aus Erfahrung** from experience; **aus Spaß** for fun

4 **aus ihr wird nie etwas** she'll never get anywhere

▷ *adv* **1** *(zu Ende)* finished, over; **aus
sein** to be over; **aus und vorbei**
over and done with
2 *(ausgeschaltet, ausgezogen)* out;
(Aufschrift an Geräten) off; **aus sein**
(nicht brennen) to be out;
(abgeschaltet sein: Radio, Herd) to be
off; **Licht aus!** lights out!
3 *(nicht zu Hause)* **aus sein** to be
out
4 *(in Verbindung mit von)* **von Rom
aus** from Rome; **vom Fenster aus**
out of the window; **von sich aus**
(selbstständig) of one's own accord;
von ihm aus as far as he's
concerned

Aus (-) *nt* *(Sport)* touch; *(fig)* end
aus|atmen *vi* to breathe out
aus|bauen *vt* *(Haus, Straße)* to
extend; *(Motor etc)* to remove
aus|bessern *vt* to repair;
(Kleidung) to mend
aus|bilden *vt* to educate;
(Lehrling etc) to train; *(Fähigkeiten)*
to develop; **Ausbildung** *f*
education; *(von Lehrling etc)*
training; *(von Fähigkeiten)*
development
Ausblick *m* view; *(fig)* outlook
aus|brechen *irr vi* to break out;
in Tränen ~ to burst into tears; **in
Gelächter ~** to burst out laughing
aus|breiten *vt* to spread (out);
(Arme) to stretch out ▷ *vr:* **sich
~** to spread
Ausbruch *m* *(Krieg, Seuche etc)*
outbreak; *(Vulkan)* eruption;
(Gefühle) outburst; *(von Gefangenen)*
escape
aus|buhen *vt* to boo
Ausdauer *f* perseverance; *(Sport)*
stamina
aus|dehnen *vt* to stretch; *(fig:
Macht)* to extend
aus|denken *irr vt* **sich** *(dat)* **etw
~** to come up with sth

Ausdruck *m* *(Ausdrücke)*
expression ▷ *m* *(Ausdrucke,
Computerausdruck)* print-out;
aus|drucken *vt* *(Inform)* to print
(out)
aus|drücken *vt* *(formulieren)* to
express; *(Zigarette)* to put out;
(Zitrone etc) to squeeze ▷ *vr:* **sich
~** to express oneself; **ausdrücklich**
adj express ▷ *adv* expressly
auseinander *adv* *(getrennt)*
apart; **~ schreiben** to write as
separate words;
auseinander|gehen *irr vi* *(Men-
schen)* to separate; *(Meinungen)* to
differ; *(Gegenstand)* to fall apart;
auseinander|halten *irr vt* to tell
apart; **auseinander|setzen** *vt*
(erklären) to explain;
auseinander|setzen *vr:* **sich
~** *(sich beschäftigen)* to look *(mit*
at); *(sich streiten)* to argue *(mit*
with); **Auseinandersetzung** *f*
(Streit) argument; *(Diskussion)*
debate
Ausfahrt *f* *(des Zuges etc)*
departure; *(Autobahn, Garage etc)*
exit
aus|fallen *irr vi* *(Haare)* to fall
out; *(nicht stattfinden)* to be
cancelled; *(nicht funktionieren)* to
break down; *(Strom)* to be cut off;
(Resultat haben) to turn out;
groß/klein ~ *(Kleidung, Schuhe)* to
be too big/too small
ausfindig machen *vt* to
discover
aus|flippen *vi* *(fam)* to freak out
Ausflug *m* excursion, outing;
Ausflugsziel *nt* destination
Ausfluss *m* *(Med)* discharge
aus|fragen *vt* to question
Ausfuhr (-, -en) *f* export
aus|führen *vt* *(verwirklichen)* to
carry out; *(Person)* to take out;
(Comm) to export; *(darlegen)* to
explain

ausführlich adj detailed ▷ adv in detail

aus|füllen vt to fill up; (Fragebogen etc) to fill in (o out)

Ausgabe f (Geld) expenditure; (Inform) output; (Buch) edition; (Nummer) issue

Ausgang m way out, exit; (Flugsteig) gate; (Ende) end; (Ergebnis) result; „kein ~" "no exit"

aus|geben irr vt (Geld) to spend; (austeilen) to distribute; **jdm etw ~** (spendieren) to buy sb sth ▷ vr: **sich für etw/jdn ~** to pass oneself off as sth/sb

ausgebucht adj fully booked

ausgefallen adj (ungewöhnlich) unusual

aus|gehen irr vi (abends etc) to go out; (Benzin, Kaffee etc) to run out; (Haare) to fall out; (Feuer, Licht etc) to go out; (Resultat haben) to turn out; **davon ~, dass** to assume that; **ihm ging das Geld aus** he ran out of money

ausgelassen adj exuberant

ausgeleiert adj worn out

ausgenommen conj, prep +gen o dat except

ausgerechnet adv: **~ du** you of all people; **~ heute** today of all days

ausgeschildert adj signposted

ausgeschlafen adj: **bist du ~?** have you had enough sleep?

ausgeschlossen adj (unmöglich) impossible, out of the question

ausgesprochen adj (absolut) out-and-out; (unverkennbar) marked ▷ adv extremely; **~ gut** really good

ausgezeichnet adj excellent

ausgiebig adj (Gebrauch) thorough; (Essen) substantial

aus|gießen irr vt (Getränk) to pour out; (Gefäß) to empty

aus|gleichen irr vt to even out ▷ vi (Sport) to equalize

Ausguss m (Spüle) sink; (Abfluss) outlet

aus|halten irr vt to bear, to stand; **nicht auszuhalten sein** to be unbearable ▷ vi to hold out

aus|händigen vt: **jdm etw ~** to hand sth over to sb

Aushang m notice

Aushilfe f temporary help; (im Büro) temp

aus|kennen irr vr: **sich ~** to know a lot (bei, mit about); (an einem Ort) to know one's way around

aus|kommen irr vi: **gut/schlecht mit jdm ~** to get on well/badly with sb; **mit etw ~** to get by with sth

Auskunft (-, Auskünfte) f information; (nähere) details pl; (Schalter) information desk; (Tel) (directory) enquiries sing (kein Artikel, Brit), information (US)

aus|lachen vt to laugh at

aus|laden irr vt (Gepäck etc) to unload; **jdn ~** (Gast) to tell sb not to come

Auslage f window display; **~n** pl (Kosten) expenses

Ausland nt foreign countries pl; **im/ins ~** abroad; **Ausländer(in)** (-s, -) m(f) foreigner;

ausländerfeindlich adj hostile to foreigners, xenophobic;

ausländisch adj foreign;

Auslandsgespräch nt international call; **Auslands-krankenschein** m health insurance certificate for foreign countries, ≈ E111 (Brit);

Auslandsschutzbrief m international (motor) insurance cover (documents pl)

aus|lassen irr vt to leave out; (Wort etc a.) to omit; (überspringen)

auslaufen | 24

to skip; (Wut, Ärger) to vent (an +dat on) ▷ vr **sich über etw** (akk) ~ to speak one's mind about sth

aus|laufen irr vi (Flüssigkeit) to run out; (Tank etc) to leak; (Schiff) to leave port; (Vertrag) to expire

aus|legen vt (Waren) to display; (Geld) to lend; (Text etc) to interpret; (technisch ausstatten) to design (für, auf +akk for)

aus|leihen irr vt (verleihen) to lend; **sich** (dat) **etw** ~ to borrow sth

aus|loggen vi (Inform) to log out (o off)

aus|lösen vt (Explosion, Alarm) to set off; (hervorrufen) to cause; **Auslöser** (-s, -) m (Foto) shutter release

aus|machen vt (Licht, Radio) to turn off; (Feuer) to put out; (Termin, Preis) to fix; (vereinbaren) to agree; (Anteil darstellen, betragen) to represent; (bedeuten) to matter; **macht es Ihnen etwas aus, wenn ...?** would you mind if ...?; **das macht mir nichts aus** I don't mind

Ausmaß nt extent

Ausnahme (-, -n) f exception; **ausnahmsweise** adv as an exception, just this once

aus|nutzen vt (Zeit, Gelegenheit, Einfluss) to use; (jdn, Gutmütigkeit) to take advantage of

aus|packen vt to unpack

aus|probieren vt to try (out)

Auspuff (-(e)s, -e) m (Tech) exhaust; **Auspuffrohr** nt exhaust (pipe); **Auspufftopf** m (Auto) silencer (Brit), muffler (US)

aus|rauben vt to rob

aus|räumen vt (Dinge) to clear away; (Schrank, Zimmer) to empty; (Bedenken) to put aside

aus|rechnen vt to calculate, to work out

Ausrede f excuse

aus|reden vi to finish speaking ▷ vt: **jdm etw** ~ to talk sb out of sth

ausreichend adj sufficient, satisfactory; (Schulnote) ≈ D

Ausreise f departure; **bei der** ~ on leaving the country; **Ausreiseerlaubnis** f exit visa; **aus|reisen** vi to leave the country

aus|reißen irr vt to tear out ▷ vi to come off; (fam: davonlaufen) to run away

aus|renken vt **sich** (dat) **den Arm** ~ to dislocate one's arm

aus|richten vt (Botschaft) to deliver; (Gruß) to pass on; (erreichen) **ich konnte bei ihr nichts** ~ I couldn't get anywhere with her; **jdm etw** ~ to tell sb sth

aus|rufen irr vt (über Lautsprecher) to announce; **jdn** ~ **lassen** to page sb; **Ausrufezeichen** nt exclamation mark

aus|ruhen vi to rest ▷ vr: **sich** ~ to rest

Ausrüstung f equipment

aus|rutschen vi to slip

aus|schalten vt to switch off; (fig) to eliminate

Ausschau f: ~ **halten** to look out (nach for)

aus|scheiden irr vt (Med) to give off, to secrete ▷ vi to leave (aus etw sth); (Sport) to be eliminated

aus|schlafen irr vi to have a lie-in ▷ vr: **sich** ~ to have a lie-in ▷ vt to sleep off

Ausschlag m (Med) rash; **den** ~ **geben** (fig) to tip the balance; **aus|schlagen** irr vt (Zahn) to knock out; (Einladung) to turn down ▷ vi (Pferd) to kick out; **ausschlaggebend** adj decisive

aus|schließen irr vt to lock out; (fig) to exclude; **ausschließlich**

adv exclusively ▷ *prep* +*gen* excluding

Ausschnitt *m* (*Teil*) section; (*von Kleid*) neckline; (*aus Zeitung*) cutting

Ausschreitungen *pl* riots *pl*

aus|schütten *vt* (*Flüssigkeit*) to pour out; (*Gefäß*) to empty

aus|sehen *irr vi* to look; **krank ~** to look ill; **gut ~** (*Person*) to be good-looking; (*Sache*) to be looking good; **es sieht nach Regen aus** it looks like rain; **es sieht schlecht aus** things look bad

aus sein *irr vi siehe* aus

außen *adv* outside; **nach ~** outwards; **von ~** from (the) outside; **Außenbordmotor** *m* outboard motor; **Außenminister(in)** *m(f)* foreign minister, Foreign Secretary (*Brit*); **Außenseite** *f* outside; **Außenseiter(in)** *m(f)* outsider; **Außenspiegel** *m* wing mirror (*Brit*), side mirror (*US*)

außer *prep* +*dat* (*abgesehen von*) except (for); **nichts ~** nothing but; **~ Betrieb** out of order; **~ sich sein** to be beside oneself (*vor* with); **~ Atem** out of breath ▷ *conj* (*ausgenommen*) except ▷ **~ wenn** unless; **~ dass** except; **außerdem** *conj* besides

äußere(r, s) *adj* outer, external

außergewöhnlich *adj* unusual ▷ *adv* exceptionally; **~ kalt** exceptionally cold; **außerhalb** *prep* +*gen* outside

äußerlich *adj* external

äußern *vt* to express; (*zeigen*) to show ▷ *vr*: **sich ~** to give one's opinion; (*sich zeigen*) to show itself

außerordentlich *adj* extraordinary; **außerplanmäßig** *adj* unscheduled

äußerst *adv* extremely;

äußerste(r, s) *adj* utmost; (*räumlich*) farthest; (*Termin*) last possible

Äußerung *f* remark

aus|setzen *vt* (*Kind, Tier*) to abandon; (*Belohnung*) to offer; **ich habe nichts daran auszusetzen** I have no objection to it ▷ *vi* (*aufhören*) to stop; (*Pause machen*) to drop out; (*beim Spiel*) to miss a turn

Aussicht *f* (*Blick*) view; (*Chance*) prospect; **aussichtslos** *adj* hopeless; **Aussichtsplattform** *f* observation platform; **Aussichtsturm** *m* observation tower

Aussiedler(in) (-s, -) *m(f)* émigré (*person of German descent from Eastern Europe*)

aus|spannen *vi* (*erholen*) to relax ▷ *vt*: **er hat ihm die Freundin ausgespannt** (*fam*) he's nicked his girlfriend

aus|sperren *vt* to lock out ▷ *vr*: **sich ~** to lock oneself out

Aussprache *f* (*von Wörtern*) pronunciation; (*Gespräch*) (*frank*) discussion; **aus|sprechen** *irr vt* to pronounce; (*äußern*) to express ▷ *vr*: **sich ~** to talk (*über* +*akk* about) ▷ *vi* (*zu Ende sprechen*) to finish speaking

aus|spülen *vt* to rinse (out)

Ausstattung *f* (*Ausrüstung*) equipment; (*Einrichtung*) furnishings *pl*; (*von Auto*) fittings *pl*

aus|stehen *irr vt* to endure; **ich kann ihn nicht ~** I can't stand him ▷ *vi* (*noch nicht da sein*) to be outstanding

aus|steigen *irr vi* to get out (*aus* of); **aus dem Bus/Zug ~** to get off the bus/train; **Aussteiger(in)** *m(f)* dropout

aus|stellen *vt* to display; (*auf Messe, in Museum etc*) to exhibit;

(fam: ausschalten) to switch off;
(Scheck etc) to make out; (Pass etc)
to issue; **Ausstellung** f
exhibition

aus|sterben irr vi to die out

aus|strahlen vt to radiate;
(Programm) to broadcast;
Ausstrahlung f (Radio, TV)
broadcast; (fig: von Person)
charisma

aus|strecken vr: **sich ~** to
stretch out ▷ vt (Hand) to reach
out (nach für)

aus|suchen vt to choose

Austausch m exchange;
aus|tauschen vt to exchange
(gegen for)

aus|teilen vt to distribute;
(aushändigen) to hand out

Auster (-, -n) f oyster;
Austernpilz m oyster mushroom

aus|tragen irr vt (Post) to
deliver; (Wettkampf) to hold

Australien (-s) nt Australia;
Australier(in) (-s, -) m(f)
Australian; **australisch** adj
Australian

aus|trinken irr vt (Glas) to drain;
(Getränk) to drink up ▷ vi to finish
one's drink

aus|trocknen vt to dry out;
(Fluss) to dry up

aus|üben vt (Beruf, Sport) to
practise; (Einfluss) to exert

Ausverkauf m sale;
ausverkauft adj (Karten, Artikel)
sold out

Auswahl f selection, choice (an
+dat of); **aus|wählen** vt to
select, to choose

aus|wandern vi to emigrate

auswärtig adj (nicht am/vom Ort)
not local; (ausländisch) foreign;
auswärts adv (außerhalb der Stadt)
out of town; (Sport) **~ spielen** to
play away; **Auswärtsspiel** nt
away match

aus|wechseln vt to replace;
(Sport) to substitute

Ausweg m way out

aus|weichen irr vi to get out of
the way; **jdm/einer Sache ~** to
move aside for sb/sth; (fig) to
avoid sb/sth

Ausweis (-es, -e) m
(Personalausweis) identity card, ID;
(für Bibliothek etc) card; **aus|weisen**
irr vt to expel ▷ vr: **sich ~** to
prove one's identity;
Ausweiskontrolle f ID check;
Ausweispapiere pl identification documents pl

auswendig adv by heart

aus|wuchten vt (Auto: Räder) to
balance

aus|zahlen vt (Summe) to pay
(out); (Person) to pay off ▷ vr: **sich
~** to be worth it

aus|zeichnen vt (ehren) to
honour; (Comm) to price ▷ vr: **sich
~** to distinguish oneself

aus|ziehen irr vt (Kleidung) to
take off ▷ vr: **sich ~** to undress
▷ vi (aus Wohnung) to move out

Auszubildende(r) mf trainee

authentisch adj authentic,
genuine

Auto (-s, -s) nt car; **~ fahren** to
drive; **Autoatlas** m road atlas;
Autobahn f motorway (Brit),
freeway (US); **Autobahnauffahrt**
f motorway access road (Brit),
on-ramp (US); **Autobahnausfahrt**
f motorway exit (Brit), off-ramp
(US); **Autobahngebühr** f toll;
Autobahnkreuz nt motorway
interchange; **Autobahnring** m
motorway ring (Brit), beltway (US);
Autobombe f car bomb;
Autofähre f car ferry;
Autofahrer(in) m(f) driver,
motorist; **Autofahrt** f drive

Autogramm (-s, -e) nt
autograph

Automarke f make of car

Automat (-en, -en) m vending machine

Automatik (-, -en) f (Auto) automatic transmission; **Automatikschaltung** f automatic gear change (Brit) (o shift (US)); **Automatikwagen** m automatic

automatisch adj automatic ▷ adv automatically

Automechaniker(in) m(f) car mechanic; **Autonummer** f registration (Brit) (o license (US)) number

Autor (-s, -en) m author

Autoradio nt car radio; **Autoreifen** m car tyre; **Autoreisezug** m Motorail train® (Brit), auto train (US); **Autorennen** nt motor racing; (einzelnes Rennen) motor race

Autorin f author(ess)

Autoschlüssel m car key; **Autotelefon** nt car phone; **Autounfall** m car accident; **Autoverleih** m, **Autovermietung** f car hire (Brit) (o rental (US)); (Firma) car hire (Brit) (o rental (US)) company; **Autowaschanlage** f car wash; **Autowerkstatt** f car repair shop, garage; **Autozubehör** nt car accessories pl

Avocado (-, -s) f avocado

Axt (-, Äxte) f axe

Azubi (-s, -s) m (-, -s) f akr = **Auszubildende** trainee

b

B abk = **Bundesstraße**

Baby (-s, -s) nt baby; **Babybett** nt cot (Brit), crib (US); **Babyfläschchen** nt baby's bottle; **Babynahrung** f baby food; **Babysitter(in)** m(f) babysitter; **Babysitz** m child seat; **Babywickelraum** m baby-changing room

Bach (-(e)s, Bäche) m stream

Backblech nt baking tray (Brit), cookie sheet (US)

Backbord nt port (side)

Backe (-, -n) f cheek

backen (backte, gebacken) vt, vi to bake

Backenzahn m molar

Bäcker(in) (-s, -) m(f) baker; **Bäckerei** f bakery; (Laden) baker's (shop)

Backofen m oven; **Backpulver** nt baking powder

Backspace-Taste f (Inform)

backspace key
Backstein m brick
Backwaren pl bread, cakes and pastries pl
Bad (-(e)s, Bäder) nt bath; (Schwimmen) swim; (Ort) spa; **ein ~ nehmen** to have (o take) a bath; **Badeanzug** m swimsuit, swimming costume (Brit); **Badehose** f swimming trunks pl; **Badekappe** f swimming cap; **Bademantel** m bathrobe; **Bademeister(in)** m(f) pool attendant; **Bademütze** f swimming cap
baden vi to have a bath; (schwimmen) to swim, to bathe (Brit) ▷ vt to bath (Brit), to bath (US)
Baden-Württemberg (-s) nt Baden-Württemberg
Badeort m spa; **Badesachen** pl swimming things pl; **Badeschaum** m bubble bath, bath foam; **Badetuch** nt bath towel; **Badewanne** f bath (tub); **Badezeug** nt swimming gear; **Badezimmer** nt bathroom
Badminton nt badminton
baff adj: **~ sein** (fam) to be flabbergasted (o gobsmacked)
Bagger (-s, -) m excavator; **Baggersee** m artificial lake in quarry etc, used for bathing
Bahamas pl: **die ~** the Bahamas pl
Bahn (-, -en) f (Eisenbahn) railway (Brit), railroad (US); (Rennbahn) track; (für Läufer) lane; (Astr) orbit; **Deutsche ~** Germany's main railway operator; **bahnbrechend** adj groundbreaking; **BahnCard®** (-, -s) f rail card (allowing 50% o 25% reduction on tickets); **Bahnfahrt** f railway (Brit) o railroad (US) journey; **Bahnhof** m station; **am** (o **auf dem**) **~** at the station;

Bahnlinie f railway (Brit) (o railroad (US)) line; **Bahnpolizei** f railway (Brit) o railroad (US) police; **Bahnsteig** (-(e)s, -e) m platform; **Bahnstrecke** f railway (Brit) (o railroad (US)) line; **Bahnübergang** m level crossing (Brit), grade crossing (US)
Bakterien pl bacteria pl, germs pl
bald adv (zeitlich) soon; (beinahe) almost; **bis ~!** see you soon (o later); **baldig** adj quick, speedy
Balkan (-s) m: **der ~** the Balkans pl
Balken (-s, -) m beam
Balkon (-s, -s o -e) m balcony
Ball (-(e)s, Bälle) m ball; (Tanz) dance, ball
Ballett (-s) nt ballet
Ballon (-s, -s) m balloon
Ballspiel nt ball game
Ballungsgebiet nt conurbation
Baltikum (-s) nt: **das ~** the Baltic States pl
Bambus (-ses, -se) m bamboo; **Bambussprossen** pl bamboo shoots pl
banal adj banal; (Frage, Bemerkung) trite
Banane (-, -n) f banana
band imperf von **binden**
Band (-(e)s, Bände) m (Buch) volume ▷ (-(e)s, Bänder) nt (aus Stoff) ribbon, tape; (Fließband) production line; (Tonband) tape; (Anat) ligament; **etw auf ~ aufnehmen** to tape sth ▷ (-, -s) f (Musikgruppe) band
Bandage (-, -n) f bandage; **bandagieren** vt to bandage
Bande (-, -n) f (Gruppe) gang
Bänderriss m (Med) torn ligament
Bandscheibe f (Anat) disc; **Bandwurm** m tapeworm
Bank (-, Bänke) f (Sitzbank) bench ▷ (-, -en) f (Fin) bank

Bankautomat m cash dispenser; **Bankkarte** f bank card; **Bankkonto** nt bank account; **Bankleitzahl** f bank sort code; **Banknote** f banknote; **Bankverbindung** f banking (o account) details pl

bar adj; **~es Geld** cash; **etw (in) ~ bezahlen** to pay sth (in) cash

Bar (-, -s) f bar

Bär (-en, -en) m bear

barfuß adj barefoot

barg imperf von **bergen**

Bargeld nt cash; **bargeldlos** adj non-cash

Barkeeper (-s, -) m, **Barmann** m barman, bartender (US)

barock adj baroque

Barometer (-s, -) nt barometer

barsch adj brusque

Barsch (-(e)s, -e) m perch

Barscheck m open (o uncrossed) cheque

Bart (-(e)s, Bärte) m beard; **bärtig** adj bearded

Barzahlung f cash payment

Basar (-s, -e) m bazaar

Baseballmütze f baseball cap

Basel (-s) nt Basle

Basilikum (-s) nt basil

Basis (-, Basen) f basis

Baskenland nt Basque region

Basketball m basketball

Bass (-es, Bässe) m bass

basta interj; **und damit ~!** and that's that

basteln vt to make ▷ vi to handicrafts; **Bastler** (-s, -) m do-it-yourselfer

bat imperf von **bitten**

Batterie f battery; **batteriebetrieben** adj battery-powered

Bau (-(e)s) m (Bauen) building, construction; (Aufbau) structure; (Baustelle) building site ▷ m (Baue) (Tier) burrow ▷ m (Bauten)

(Gebäude) building; **Bauarbeiten** pl construction work sing; (Straßenbau) roadworks pl (Brit), roadwork (US); **Bauarbeiter(in)** m(f) construction worker

Bauch (-(e)s, Bäuche) m stomach; **Bauchnabel** m navel; **Bauchredner(in)** m(f) ventriloquist; **Bauchschmerzen** pl stomach-ache sing; **Bauchspeicheldrüse** f pancreas; **Bauchtanz** m belly dance; (das Tanzen) belly dancing; **Bauchweh** (-s) nt stomach-ache

bauen vt, vi to build; (Tech) to construct

Bauer (-n o -s, -n) m farmer; (Schach) pawn; **Bäuerin** f farmer; (Frau des Bauern) farmer's wife; **Bauernhof** m farm

baufällig adj dilapidated; **Baujahr** nt year of construction; **der Wagen ist ~ 2002** the car is a 2002 model, the car was made in 2002

Baum (-(e)s, Bäume) m tree

Baumarkt m DIY centre

Baumwolle f cotton

Bauplatz m building site; **Baustein** m (für Haus) stone; (Spielzeug) brick; (fig) element; **elektronischer ~** chip; **Baustelle** f building site; (bei Straßenbau) roadworks pl (Brit), roadwork (US); **Bauteil** m prefabricated part; **Bauunternehmer(in)** m(f) building contractor; **Bauwerk** nt building

Bayern (-s) nt Bavaria

beabsichtigen vt to intend

beachten vt (Aufmerksamkeit schenken) to pay attention to; (Vorschrift etc) to observe; **nicht ~** to ignore; **beachtlich** adj considerable

Beachvolleyball nt beach volleyball

Beamte(r) (-n, -n) m, **Beamtin** f official; (*Staatsbeamter*) civil servant

beanspruchen vt to claim; (*Zeit, Platz*) to take up; **jdn ~** to keep sb busy

beanstanden vt to complain about; **Beanstandung** f complaint

beantragen vt to apply for

beantworten vt to answer

bearbeiten vt to work; (*Material, Daten*) to process; (*Chem*) to treat; (*Fall etc*) to deal with; (*Buch etc*) to revise; (*fam: beeinflussen wollen*) to work on; **Bearbeitungsgebühr** f handling (o service) charge

beatmen vt: **jdn ~** to give sb artificial respiration

beaufsichtigen vt to supervise; (*bei Prüfung*) to invigilate

beauftragen vt to instruct; **jdn mit etw ~** to give sb the job of doing sth

Becher (-s, -) m mug; (*ohne Henkel*) tumbler; (*für Joghurt*) pot; (*aus Pappe*) tub

Becken (-s, -) nt basin; (*Spüle*) sink; (*zum Schwimmen*) pool; (*Mus*) cymbal; (*Anat*) pelvis

bedanken vr: **sich ~** to say thank you; **sich bei jdm für etw ~** to thank sb for sth

Bedarf (-(e)s) m need (*an +dat* for); (*Comm*) demand (*an +dat* for); **je nach ~** according to demand; **bei ~** if necessary; **Bedarfshaltestelle** f request stop

bedauerlich adj regrettable; **bedauern** vt to regret; (*bemitleiden*) to feel sorry for; **bedauernswert** adj (*Zustände*) regrettable; (*Mensch*) unfortunate

bedeckt adj covered; (*Himmel*) overcast

bedenken irr vt to consider; **Bedenken** (-s, -) nt (*Überlegen*)

consideration; (*Zweifel*) doubt; (*Skrupel*) scruples pl; **bedenklich** adj dubious; (*Zustand*) serious

bedeuten vt to mean; **jdm nichts/viel ~** to mean nothing/a lot to sb; **bedeutend** adj important; (*beträchtlich*) considerable; **Bedeutung** f meaning; (*Wichtigkeit*) importance

bedienen vt to serve; (*Maschine*) to operate ▷ vr: **sich ~** (*beim Essen*) to help oneself; **Bedienung** f service; (*Kellner/Kellnerin*) waiter/waitress; (*Verkäufer(in)*) shop assistant; (*Zuschlag*) service (charge); **Bedienungsanleitung** f operating instructions pl; **Bedienungshandbuch** nt instruction manual

Bedingung f condition; **unter der ~, dass** on condition that; **unter diesen ~en** under these circumstances

bedrohen vt to threaten

Bedürfnis nt need

Beefsteak (-s, -s) nt steak

beeilen vr: **sich ~** to hurry

beeindrucken vt to impress

beeinflussen vt to influence

beeinträchtigen vt to affect

beenden vt to end; (*fertigstellen*) to finish

beerdigen vt to bury; **Beerdigung** f burial; (*Feier*) funeral

Beere (-, -n) f berry; (*Traubenbeere*) grape

Beet (-(e)s, -e) nt bed

befahl imperf von **befehlen**

befahrbar adj passable; (*Naut*) navigable; **befahren** irr vt (*Straße*) to use; (*Pass*) to drive over; (*Fluss etc*) to navigate ▷ adj: **stark/wenig ~** busy/quiet

Befehl (-(e)s, -e) m order; (*Inform*) command; **befehlen** (*befahl, befohlen*) vt to order; **jdm ~, etw zu tun** to order sb to do sth ▷ vi to give orders

befestigen vt to fix; (mit Schnur, Seil) to attach; (mit Klebestoff) to stick

befeuchten vt to moisten

befinden irr vr: **sich ~** to be

befohlen pp von **befehlen**

befolgen vt (Rat etc) to follow

befördern vt (transportieren) to transport; (beruflich) to promote; **Beförderung** f transport; (beruflich) promotion; **Beförderungsbedingungen** pl conditions pl of carriage

Befragung f questioning; (Umfrage) opinion poll

befreundet adj friendly; **~ sein** to be friends (mit jdm with sb)

befriedigen vt to satisfy; **befriedigend** adj satisfactory; (Schulnote) = C; **Befriedigung** f satisfaction

befristet adj limited (auf +akk to)

befruchten vt to fertilize; (fig) to stimulate

Befund (-(e)s, -e) m findings pl; (Med) diagnosis

befürchten vt to fear

befürworten vt to support

begabt adj gifted, talented; **Begabung** f talent, gift

begann imperf von **beginnen**

begegnen vi to meet (jdm sb), to meet with (einer Sache dat sth)

begehen irr vt (Straftat) to commit; (Jubiläum etc) to celebrate

begehrt adj sought-after; (Junggeselle) eligible

begeistern vt to fill with enthusiasm; (inspirieren) to inspire ▷ vr: **sich für etw ~** to be/get enthusiastic about sth; **begeistert** adj enthusiastic

Beginn (-(e)s) m beginning; **zu ~** at the beginning; **beginnen** (begann, begonnen) vt, vi to start, to begin

beglaubigen vt to certify; **Beglaubigung** f certification

begleiten vt to accompany; **Begleiter(in)** m(f) companion; **Begleitung** f company; (Mus) accompaniment

beglückwünschen vt to congratulate (zu on)

begonnen pp von **beginnen**

begraben irr vt to bury; **Begräbnis** nt burial; (Feier) funeral

begreifen irr vt to understand

Begrenzung f boundary; (fig) restriction

Begriff (-(e)s, -e) m concept; (Vorstellung) idea; **im ~ sein, etw zu tun** to be on the point of doing sth; **schwer von ~ sein** to be slow on the uptake

begründen vt (rechtfertigen) to justify; **Begründung** f explanation; (Rechtfertigung) justification

begrüßen vt to greet; (willkommen heißen) to welcome; **Begrüßung** f greeting; (Empfang) welcome

behaart adj hairy

behalten irr vt to keep; (im Gedächtnis) to remember; **etw für sich ~** to keep sth to oneself

Behälter (-s, -) m container

behandeln vt to treat; **Behandlung** f treatment

behaupten vt to claim, to maintain ▷ vr: **sich ~** to assert oneself; **Behauptung** f claim

beheizen vt to heat

behelfen irr vr: **sich mit/ohne etw ~** to make do with/without sth

beherbergen vt to accommodate

beherrschen vt (Situation, Gefühle) to control; (Instrument) to master ▷ vr: **sich ~** to control

oneself; **Beherrschung** f control
(*über +akk* of); **die ~ verlieren** to
lose one's self-control

behilflich adj helpful; **jdm ~ sein**
to help sb (*bei* with)

behindern vt to hinder; (*Verkehr,
Sicht*) to obstruct; **Behinderte(r)**
mf disabled person;
behindertengerecht adj suitable
for disabled people

Behörde (-, -n) f authority; **die
~n** pl the authorities pl

SCHLÜSSELWORT

bei prep +dat **1** (*nahe bei*) near; (*zum
Aufenthalt*) at, with; (*unter,
zwischen*) among; **bei München**
near Munich; **bei uns** at our place;
beim Friseur at the hairdresser's;
bei seinen Eltern wohnen to live
with one's parents; **bei einer
Firma arbeiten** to work for a
firm; **etw bei sich haben** to have
sth on one; **jdn bei sich haben** to
have sb with one; **bei Goethe** in
Goethe; **beim Militär** in the army
2 (*zeitlich*) at, on; (*während*) during;
(*Zustand, Umstand*) in; **bei Nacht** at
night; **bei Nebel** in fog; **bei Regen**
if it rains; **bei solcher Hitze** in
such heat; **bei meiner Ankunft** on
my arrival; **bei der Arbeit** when
I'm *etc* working; **beim Fahren**
while driving

bei|behalten irr vt to keep
Beiboot nt dinghy
bei|bringen irr vt: **jdm etw
~** (*mitteilen*) to break sth to sb;
(*lehren*) to teach sb sth
beide(s) pron both; **meine ~n
Brüder** my two brothers, both my
brothers; **wir ~** both (o the two) of
us; **keiner von ~n** neither of them;
alle ~ both (of them); **~s ist sehr
schön** both are very nice; **30**

~ (*beim Tennis*) 30 all
beieinander adv together
Beifahrer(in) m(f) passenger;
Beifahrerairbag m passenger
airbag; **Beifahrersitz** m
passenger seat
Beifall (-(e)s) m applause
beige adj inv beige
Beigeschmack m aftertaste
Beil (-(e)s, -e) nt axe
Beilage f (*Gastr*) side dish;
(*Gemüse*) vegetables pl; (*zu Buch etc*)
supplement
beiläufig adj casual ▷ adv
casually
Beileid nt condolences pl; (**mein**)
herzliches ~ please accept my
sincere condolences
beiliegend adj enclosed
beim kontr von **bei dem**
Bein (-(e)s, -e) nt leg
beinah(e) adv almost, nearly
beinhalten vt to contain
Beipackzettel m instruction
leaflet
beisammen adv together;
Beisammensein (-s) nt
get-together
beiseite adv aside;
beiseite|legen vt: **etw ~** (*sparen*)
to put sth by
Beispiel (-(e)s, -e) nt example:
sich (*dat*) **an jdm/etw ein
~ nehmen** to take sb/sth as an
example; **zum ~** for example
beißen (*biss, gebissen*) vt to bite
▷ vi to bite; (*stechen: Rauch, Säure*)
to sting ▷ vr: **sich ~** (*Farben*) to
clash
Beitrag (-(e)s, Beiträge) m
contribution; (*für Mitgliedschaft*)
subscription; (*Versicherung*)
premium; **bei|tragen** irr vt, vi to
contribute (*zu* to)
bekannt adj well-known; (*nicht
fremd*) familiar; **mit jdm ~ sein** to
know sb; **~ geben** to announce;

jdn mit jdm ~ machen to introduce sb to sb; **Bekannte(r)** *mf* friend; *(entfernter)* acquaintance; **bekanntlich** *adv* as everyone knows; **Bekanntschaft** *f* acquaintance

bekiffen *vr:* **sich ~** *(fam)* to get stoned

beklagen *vr:* **sich ~** to complain

Bekleidung *f* clothing

bekommen *irr vt* to get; *(erhalten)* to receive; *(Kind)* to have; *(Zug, Grippe)* to catch, to get; **wie viel ~ Sie dafür?** how much is that? ▷ *vi:* **jdm ~** *(Essen)* to agree with sb; **wir ~ schon** *(bedient werden)* we're being served

beladen *irr vt* to load

Belag *(-(e)s, Beläge)* *m* coating; *(auf Zähnen)* plaque; *(auf Zunge)* fur

belasten *vt* to load; *(Körper)* to strain; *(Umwelt)* to pollute; *(fig: mit Sorgen etc)* to burden; *(Comm: Konto)* to debit; *(Jur)* to incriminate

belästigen *vt* to bother; *(stärker)* to pester; *(sexuell)* to harass; **Belästigung** *f* annoyance; **sexuelle ~** sexual harassment

belebt *adj (Straße etc)* busy

Beleg *(-(e)s, -e)* *m* *(Comm)* receipt; *(Beweis)* proof; **belegen** *vt (Brot)* to spread; *(Platz)* to reserve; *(Kurs, Vorlesung)* to register for; *(beweisen)* to prove

belegt *adj (Tel)* engaged *(Brit)*, busy *(US)*; *(Hotel)* full; *(Zunge)* coated; **~es Brötchen** sandwich; **der Platz ist ~** this seat is taken; **Belegzeichen** *nt (Tel)* engaged tone *(Brit)*, busy tone *(US)*

beleidigen *vt* to insult; *(kränken)* to offend; **Beleidigung** *f* insult; *(Jur)* slander; *(schriftliche)* libel

beleuchten *vt* to light; *(bestrahlen)* to illuminate; *(fig)* to examine; **Beleuchtung** *f* lighting; *(Bestrahlung)* illumination

Belgien *(-s)* *nt* Belgium; **Belgier(in)** *(-s, -)* *m(f)* Belgian; **belgisch** *adj* Belgian

belichten *vt* to expose; **Belichtung** *f* exposure; **Belichtungsmesser** *(-s, -)* *m* light meter

Belieben *nt:* **(ganz) nach ~** (just) as you wish

beliebig *adj:* **jedes ~e Muster** any pattern; **jeder ~e** anyone ▷ *adv:* **~ lange** as long as you like; **~ viel** as many (o much) as you like

beliebt *adj* popular; **sich bei jdm ~ machen** to make oneself popular with sb

beliefern *vt* to supply

bellen *vi* to bark

Belohnung *f* reward

Belüftung *f* ventilation

belügen *irr vt* to lie to

bemerkbar *adj* noticeable; **sich ~ machen** *(Mensch)* to attract attention; *(Zustand)* to become noticeable; **bemerken** *vt (wahrnehmen)* to notice; *(sagen)* to remark; **bemerkenswert** *adj* remarkable; **Bemerkung** *f* remark

bemitleiden *vt* to pity

bemühen *vr:* **sich ~** to try (hard), to make an effort; **Bemühung** *f* effort

bemuttern *vt* to mother

benachbart *adj* neighbouring

benachrichtigen *vt* to inform; **Benachrichtigung** *f* notification

benachteiligen *vt* to (put at a) disadvantage; *(wegen Rasse etc)* to discriminate against

benehmen *irr vr:* **sich ~** to behave; **Benehmen** *(-s)* *nt* behaviour

beneiden *vt* to envy; **jdn um etw ~** to envy sb sth

Beneluxländer *pl* Benelux countries *pl*

benommen adj dazed
benötigen vt to need
benutzen vt to use;
Benutzer(in) (-s, -) m(f) user;
benutzerfreundlich adj user-
friendly; Benutzerhandbuch nt
user's guide; Benutzerkennung f
user ID; Benutzeroberfläche f
(Inform) user/system interface;
Benutzung f use;
Benutzungsgebühr f (hire)
charge
Benzin (-s, -e) nt (Auto) petrol
(Brit), gas (US); Benzingutschein
m petrol (Brit) (o gas (US)) coupon;
Benzinkanister m petrol (Brit) (o
gas (US)) can; Benzinpumpe f
petrol (Brit) (o gas (US)) pump;
Benzintank m petrol (Brit) (o gas
(US)) tank; Benzinuhr f fuel
gauge
beobachten vt to observe;
Beobachtung f observation
bequem adj comfortable;
(Ausrede) convenient; (faul) lazy;
machen Sie es sich ~ make
yourself at home; Bequemlichkeit
f comfort; (Faulheit) laziness
beraten irr vt to advise;
(besprechen) to discuss ▷ vr: sich
~ to consult; Beratung f advice;
(bei Arzt etc) consultation
berauben vt to rob
berechnen vt to calculate;
(Comm) to charge; berechnend
adj (Mensch) calculating
berechtigen vt to entitle (zu to);
(fig) to justify; berechtigt adj
justified; zu etw ~ sein to be
entitled to sth
bereden vt (besprechen) to discuss
Bereich (-(e)s, -e) m area;
(Ressort, Gebiet) field
bereisen vt to travel through
bereit adj ready; zu etw ~ sein to
be ready for sth; sich ~ erklären,
etw zu tun to agree to do sth

bereiten vt to prepare; (Kummer)
to cause; (Freude) to give
bereitlegen vt to lay out
bereitmachen vr: sich ~ to get
ready
bereits adv already
Bereitschaft f readiness;
~ haben (Arzt) to be on call
bereitstehen vi to be ready
bereuen vt to regret
Berg (-(e)s, -e) m mountain;
(kleiner) hill; in die ~e fahren to go
to the mountains; bergab adv
downhill; bergauf adv uphill;
Bergbahn f mountain railway
(Brit) (o railroad (US))
bergen (barg, geborgen) vt (retten)
to rescue; (enthalten) to contain
Bergführer(in) m(f) mountain
guide; Berghütte f mountain hut;
bergig adj mountainous;
Bergschuh m climbing boot;
Bergsteigen (-s) nt
mountaineering; Bergsteiger(in)
(-s, -) m(f) mountaineer;
Bergtour f mountain hike
Bergung f (Rettung) rescue; (von
Toten, Fahrzeugen) recovery
Bergwacht (-, -en) f mountain
rescue service; Bergwerk nt
mine
Bericht (-(e)s, -e) m report;
berichten vt, vi to report
berichtigen vt to correct
Bermudadreieck nt Bermuda
triangle; Bermudainseln pl
Bermuda sing; Bermudashorts
pl Bermuda shorts pl
Bernstein m amber
berüchtigt adj notorious,
infamous
berücksichtigen vt to take into
account; (Antrag, Bewerber) to
consider
Beruf (-(e)s, -e) m occupation;
(akademischer) profession;
(Gewerbe) trade; was sind Sie von

~? what do you do (for a living)?;
beruflich *adj* professional
Berufsausbildung *f* vocational
training; **Berufsschule** *f*
vocational college; **berufstätig**
adj employed; **Berufsverkehr** *m*
commuter traffic
beruhigen *vt* to calm ▷ *vr:* **sich**
~ (*Mensch, Situation*) to calm down;
beruhigend *adj* reassuring;
Beruhigungsmittel *nt* sedative
berühmt *adj* famous
berühren *vt* to touch;
(*gefühlsmäßig bewegen*) to move;
(*betreffen*) to affect; (*flüchtig*
erwähnen) to mention, to touch on
▷ *vr:* **sich ~** to touch
besaufen *irr vr:* **sich ~** (*fam*) to
get plastered
beschädigen *vt* to damage
beschäftigen *vt* to occupy;
(*beruflich*) to employ ▷ *vr:* **sich mit**
etw ~ to occupy oneself with sth;
(*sich befassen*) to deal with sth;
beschäftigt *adj* busy, occupied;
Beschäftigung *f* (*Beruf*)
employment; (*Tätigkeit*)
occupation; (*geistige*)
preoccupation (*mit* with)
Bescheid (*-(e)s, -e*) *m*
information; **~ wissen** to be
informed (*o know*) (*über +akk*
about); **ich weiß ~** I know; **jdm**
~ geben (*o sagen*) to let sb know
bescheiden *adj* modest
bescheinigen *vt* to certify;
(*bestätigen*) to acknowledge;
Bescheinigung *f* certificate;
(*Quittung*) receipt
bescheißen *irr vt* (*vulg*) to cheat
(*um* out of)
bescheuert *adj* (*fam, pej*) crazy
beschimpfen *vt* (*mit*
Kraftausdrücken) to swear at
Beschiss (*-es*) *m:* **das ist ~** (*vulg*)
that's a rip-off; **beschissen** *adj*
(*vulg*) shitty

beschlagnahmen *vt* to
confiscate
Beschleunigung *f* acceleration;
Beschleunigungsspur *f*
acceleration lane
beschließen *irr vt* to decide on;
(*beenden*) to end; **Beschluss** *m*
decision
beschränken *vt* to limit, to
restrict (*auf +akk* to) ▷ *vr:* **sich ~** to
restrict oneself (*auf +akk* to);
Beschränkung *f* limitation,
restriction
beschreiben *irr vt* to describe;
(*Papier*) to write on; **Beschreibung**
f description
beschuldigen *vt* to accuse (*gen*
of); **Beschuldigung** *f*
accusation
beschummeln *vt, vi* (*fam*) to
cheat (*um* out of)
beschützen *vt* to protect (*vor*
+dat from)
Beschwerde (*-, -n*) *f* complaint;
~n *pl* (*Leiden*) trouble *sing*;
beschweren *vt* to weight down;
(*fig*) to burden ▷ *vr:* **sich ~** to
complain
beschwipst *adj* tipsy
beseitigen *vt* to remove;
(*Problem*) to get rid of; (*Müll*) to
dispose of; **Beseitigung** *f*
removal; (*von Müll*) disposal
Besen (*-s, -*) *m* broom
besetzen *vt* (*Haus, Land*) to
occupy; (*Platz*) to take; (*Posten*) to
fill; (*Rolle*) to cast; **besetzt** *adj*
full; (*Tel*) engaged (*Brit*), busy (*US*);
(*Platz*) taken; (*WC*) engaged;
Besetztzeichen *nt* engaged tone
(*Brit*), busy tone (*US*)
besichtigen *vt* (*Museum*) to visit;
(*Sehenswürdigkeit*) to have a look at;
(*Stadt*) to tour
besiegen *vt* to defeat
Besitz (*-es*) *m* possession;
(*Eigentum*) property; **besitzen***irr*

vt to own; (*Eigenschaft*) to have; **Besitzer(in)** (*-s, -*) *m(f)* owner
besoffen *adj* (*fam*) plastered
besondere(r, s) *adj* special; (*bestimmt*) particular; (*eigentümlich*) peculiar; **nichts ~s** nothing special; **Besonderheit** *f* special feature; (*besondere Eigenschaft*) peculiarity; **besonders** *adv* especially, particularly; (*getrennt*) separately
besorgen *vt* (*beschaffen*) to get; (*jdm für sb*) (*kaufen a.*) to purchase; (*erledigen: Geschäfte*) to deal with
besprechen *irr vt* to discuss; **Besprechung** *f* discussion; (*Konferenz*) meeting; **Besprechungsraum** *m* consultation room
besser *adj* better; **es geht ihm ~** he feels better; **~ gesagt** or rather; **~ werden** *vt* to improve; **bessern** *vt* to improve ⊳ *vr:* **sich ~** to improve; (*Mensch*) to mend one's ways; **Besserung** *f* improvement; **gute ~I** get well soon
beständig *adj* constant; (*Wetter*) settled
Bestandteil *m* component
bestätigen *vt* to confirm; (*Empfang, Brief*) to acknowledge; **Bestätigung** *f* confirmation; (*von Brief*) acknowledgement
beste(r, s) *adj* best; **das ~ wäre, wir ...** it would be best if we ... ⊳ *adv:* **sie singt am ~n** she sings best; **so ist es am ~n** it's best that way; **am ~n gehst du gleich** you'd better go at once
bestechen *irr vt* to bribe; **Bestechung** *f* bribery
Besteck (*-(e)s, -e*) *nt* cutlery
bestehen *irr vt* to exist; (*andauern*) to last; **~ auf** (+*dat*) to insist on; **~ aus** to consist of ⊳ *vt* (*Probe, Prüfung*) to pass; (*Kampf*) to

win
bestehlen *irr vt* to rob
bestellen *vt* to order; (*reservieren*) to book; (*Grüße, Auftrag*) to pass on (*jdm to sb*); (*kommen lassen*) to send for; **Bestellnummer** *f* order number; **Bestellung** *f* (*Comm*) order; (*das Bestellen*) ordering
bestens *adv* very well
bestimmen *vt* to determine; (*Regeln*) to lay down; (*Tag, Ort*) to fix; (*ernennen*) to appoint; (*vorsehen*) to mean (*für for*); **bestimmt** *adj* definite; (*gewiss*) certain; (*entschlossen*) firm ⊳ *adv* definitely; (*wissen*) for sure; **Bestimmung** *f* (*Verordnung*) regulation; (*Zweck*) purpose
Best.-Nr. *abk* = **Bestellnummer** order number
bestrafen *vt* to punish
bestrahlen *vt* to illuminate; (*Med*) to treat with radiotherapy
bestreiten *irr vt* (*leugnen*) to deny
Bestseller (*-s, -*) *m* bestseller
bestürzt *adj* dismayed
Besuch (*-(e)s, -e*) *m* visit; (*Mensch*) visitor; **~ haben** to have visitors/a visitor; **besuchen** *vt* to visit; (*Schule, Kino etc*) to go to; **Besucher(in)** (*-s, -*) *m(f)* visitor; **Besuchszeit** *f* visiting hours *pl*
betäuben *vt* (*Med*) to anaesthetize; **Betäubung** *f* anaesthetic; **örtliche ~** local anaesthetic; **Betäubungsmittel** *nt* anaesthetic
Bete (*-, -n*) *f*: **Rote ~** beetroot
beteiligen *vr* **sich an etw** (*dat*) **~** to take part in sth, to participate in sth ⊳ *vt* **jdn an etw** (*dat*) **~** to involve sb in sth; **Beteiligung** *f* participation; (*Anteil*) share; (*Besucherzahl*) attendance
beten *vi* to pray
Beton (*-s, -s*) *m* concrete

betonen vt to stress; (hervorheben) to emphasize; **Betonung** f stress; (fig) emphasis

Betr. abk = **Betreff** re

Betracht m: **in ~ ziehen** to take into consideration; **in ~ kommen** to be a possibility; **nicht in ~ kommen** to be out of the question; **betrachten** vt to look at; **~ als** to regard as; **beträchtlich** adj considerable

Betrag (-(e)s, Beträge) m amount, sum; **betragen** irr vt to amount (o come) to ▷ vr: **sich ~** to behave

betreffen irr vt to concern; (Regelung etc) to affect; **was mich betrifft** as for me; **betreffend** adj relevant, in question

betreten irr vt to enter; (Bühne etc) to step onto; „**Betreten verboten**" "keep off/out"

betreuen vt to look after; (Reisegruppe, Abteilung) to be in charge of; **Betreuer(in)** (-s, -) m(f) (Pfleger) carer; (von Kind) child minder; (von Reisegruppe) groupleader

Betrieb (-(e)s, -e) m (Firma) firm; (Anlage) plant; (Tätigkeit) operation; (Treiben) bustle; **außer ~ sein** to be out of order; **in ~ sein** to be in operation; **betriebsbereit** adj operational; **Betriebsrat** m (Gremium) works council; **Betriebssystem** nt (Inform) operating system

betrinken irr vr: **sich ~** to get drunk

betroffen adj (bestürzt) shaken; **von etw ~ werden/sein** to be affected by sth

betrog imperf von **betrügen**; **betrogen** pp von **betrügen**

Betrug (-(e)s) m deception; (Jur) fraud; **betrügen** (betrog, betrogen) vt to deceive; (Jur) to defraud;

(Partner) to cheat on; **Betrüger(in)** (-s, -) m(f) cheat

betrunken adj drunk

Bett (-(e)s, -en) nt bed; **ins** (o zu) **~ gehen** to go to bed; **das ~ machen** to make the bed; **Bettbezug** m duvet cover; **Bettdecke** f blanket

betteln vi to beg

Bettlaken nt sheet

Bettler(in) (-s, -) m(f) beggar

Bettsofa nt sofa bed; **Betttuch** nt sheet; **Bettwäsche** f bed linen; **Bettzeug** nt bedding

beugen vt to bend ▷ vr: **sich ~** to bend; (sich fügen) to submit (dat to)

Beule (-, -n) f (Schwellung) bump; (Delle) dent

beunruhigen vt to worry ▷ vr: **sich ~** to worry

beurteilen vt to judge

Beute (-) f (von Dieb) booty, loot; (von Tier) prey

Beutel (-s, -) m bag

Bevölkerung f population

bevollmächtigt adj authorized (zu etw to do sth)

bevor conj before; **bevor|stehen** irr vi (Schwierigkeiten) to lie ahead; (Gefahr) to be imminent; **jdm ~** (Überraschung etc) to be in store for sb; **bevorstehend** adj forthcoming; **bevorzugen** vt to prefer

bewachen vt to guard; **bewacht** adj: **~er Parkplatz** supervised car park (Brit), guarded parking lot (US)

bewegen vt to move; **jdn dazu ~, etw zu tun** to get sb to do sth ▷ vr: **sich ~** to move; **es bewegt sich etwas** (fig) things are beginning to happen; **Bewegung** f movement; (Phys) motion; (innere) emotion; (körperlich) exercise; **Bewegungsmelder** (-s, -) m sensor (which reacts to *movement*)

Beweis (*-es, -e*) *m* proof; (*Zeugnis*) evidence; **beweisen** *irr vt* to prove; (*zeigen*) to show

bewerben *irr vr:* **sich ~** to apply (*um* for); **Bewerbung** *f* application; **Bewerbungsunterlagen** *pl* application documents *pl*

bewilligen *vt* to allow; (*Geld*) to grant

bewirken *vt* to cause, to bring about

bewohnen *vt* to live in; **Bewohner(in)** (*-s, -*) *m(f)* inhabitant; (*von Haus*) resident

bewölkt *adj* cloudy, overcast; **Bewölkung** *f* clouds *pl*

bewundern *vt* to admire; **bewundernswert** *adj* admirable

bewusst *adj* conscious; (*absichtlich*) deliberate; **sich** (*dat*) **einer Sache** (*gen*) **~ sein** to be aware of sth ▷ *adv* consciously; (*absichtlich*) deliberately; **bewusstlos** *adj* unconscious; **Bewusstlosigkeit** *f* unconsciousness; **Bewusstsein** (*-s*) *nt* consciousness; **bei ~** conscious

bezahlen *vt* to pay; (*Ware, Leistung*) to pay for; **kann ich bar/mit Kreditkarte ~?** can I pay cash/by credit card?; **sich bezahlt machen** to be worth it; **Bezahlung** *f* payment

bezeichnen *vt* (*kennzeichnen*) to mark; (*nennen*) to call; (*beschreiben*) to describe; **Bezeichnung** *f* (*Name*) name; (*Begriff*) term

beziehen *irr vt* (*Bett*) to change; (*Haus, Position*) to move into; (*erhalten*) to receive; (*Zeitung*) to take; **einen Standpunkt ~** (*fig*) to take up a position ▷ *vr:* **sich ~** to refer (*auf +akk* to); **Beziehung** *f* (*Verbindung*) connection; (*Verhältnis*) relationship; **~en**

haben (*vorteilhaft*) to have connections (*o* contacts); **in dieser ~** in this respect; **beziehungsweise** *adv* or; (*genauer gesagt*) or rather

Bezirk (*-(e)s, -e*) *m* district

Bezug (*-(e)s, Bezüge*) *m* (*Überzug*) cover; (*von Kopfkissen*) pillowcase; **in ~ auf** (*+akk*) with regard to; **bezüglich** *prep +gen* concerning

bezweifeln *vt* to doubt

BH (*-s, -s*) *m* bra

Bhf. *abk* = **Bahnhof** station

Biathlon (*-s, -s*) *nt* biathlon

Bibel (*-, -n*) *f* Bible

Biber (*-s, -*) *m* beaver

Bibliothek (*-, -en*) *f* library

biegen (*bog, gebogen*) *vt* to bend ▷ *vr:* **sich ~** to bend ▷ *vi* to turn (*in +akk* into); **Biegung** *f* bend

Biene (*-, -n*) *f* bee

Bier (*-(e)s, -e*) *nt* beer; **helles ~** = lager (*Brit*), beer (*US*); **dunkles ~** = brown ale (*Brit*), dark beer (*US*); **zwei ~, bitte!** two beers, please; **Biergarten** *m* beer garden; **Bierzelt** *nt* beer tent

bieten (*bot, geboten*) *vt* to offer; (*bei Versteigerung*) bid; **sich** (*dat*) **etw ~ lassen** to put up with sth ▷ *vr:* **sich ~** (*Gelegenheit*) to present itself (*dat* to)

Bikini (*-s, -s*) *m* bikini

Bild (*-(e)s, -er*) *nt* picture; (*gedankliches*) image; (*Foto*) photo

bilden *vt* to form; (*geistig*) to educate; (*ausmachen*) to constitute ▷ *vr:* **sich ~** (*entstehen*) to form; (*lernen*) to educate oneself

Bilderbuch *nt* picture book

Bildhauer(in) (*-s, -*) *m(f)* sculptor

Bildschirm *m* screen; **Bildschirmschoner** (*-s, -*) *m* screensaver; **Bildschirmtext** *m* viewdata, videotext

Bildung *f* formation; (*Wissen,*

Benehmen) education;
Bildungsurlaub *m* educational
holiday; *(von Firma)* study leave
Billard *nt* billiards *sing*
billig *adj* cheap; *(gerecht)* fair
Billigflieger *m* budget airline
Billigflug *m* cheap flight
Binde (-, -n) *f* bandage;
(Armbinde) band; *(Damenbinde)*
sanitary towel *(Brit)*, sanitary
napkin *(US)*
Bindehautentzündung *f*
conjunctivitis
binden *(band, gebunden) vt* to tie;
(Buch) to bind; *(Soße)* to thicken
Bindestrich *m* hyphen
Bindfaden *m* string
Bindung *f* bond, tie; *(Skibindung)*
binding
Bio- *in zW* bio-; **Biokost** *f* health
food

- **BIOLADEN**
-
- A **Bioladen** is a shop which
- specializes in selling
- environmentally friendly
- products such as
- phosphate-free washing
- powders, recycled paper and
- organically grown vegetables.

Biologie *f* biology; **biologisch**
adj biological; *(Anbau)* organic
Birke (-, -n) *f* birch
Birne (-, -n) *f (Obst)* pear; *(Elek)*
(light) bulb

🔑 **SCHLÜSSELWORT**

bis *prep +akk, adv* **1** *(zeitlich)* till,
until; *(bis spätestens)* by **Sie haben
bis Dienstag Zeit** you have until o
till Tuesday; **bis Dienstag muss es
fertig sein** it must be ready by
Tuesday; **bis auf Weiteres** until
further notice; **bis in die Nacht**

into the night; **bis bald/gleich** see
you later/soon
2 *(räumlich)* (up) to; **ich fahre bis
Köln** I'm going to o I'm going as far
as Cologne; **bis an unser
Grundstück** (right o up) to our
plot; **bis hierher** this far
3 *(bei Zahlen)* up to; **bis zu** up to
4 bis auf etw akk *(außer)* except
sth; *(einschließlich)* including sth
▷ *konj* **1** *(mit Zahlen)*: **10 bis 20** 10
to 20
2 *(zeitlich)* till, until; **bis es dunkel
wird** till o until it gets dark; **von ...
bis ...** from ,.. to ...

Bischof (-s, *Bischöfe*) *m* bishop
bisher *adv* up to now, so far
Biskuit (-(e)s, -s *o* -e) *nt* sponge
biss *imperf von* **beißen**
Biss (-es, -e) *m* bite
bisschen *adj*: **ein ~** a bit of; **ein
~ Salz/Liebe** a bit of salt/love; **ich
habe kein ~ Hunger** I'm not a bit
hungry ▷ *adv*: **ein ~** a bit; **kein
~** not at all
bissig *adj (Hund)* vicious;
(Bemerkung) cutting
Bit (-s, -s) *nt (Inform)* bit
bitte *interj* please; *(wie)* ~? (I beg
your) pardon?; **~ (schön** *o* **sehr)!**
(als Antwort auf Dank) you're
welcome; **hier, ~** here you are;
Bitte (-, -n) *f* request; **bitten**
(bat, gebeten) vt, vi to ask *(um for)*
bitter *adj* bitter
Blähungen *pl (Med)* wind *sing*
blamieren *vr*: **sich ~** to make a
fool of oneself ▷ *vt*: **jdn ~** to make
sb look a fool
Blankoscheck *m* blank cheque
Blase (-, -n) *f* bubble; *(Med)*
blister; *(Anat)* bladder
blasen *(blies, geblasen) vi* to blow;
jdm einen ~ *(vulg)* to give sb a
blow job
Blasenentzündung *f* cystitis

blass adj pale

Blatt (-(e)s, Blätter) nt leaf; (von Papier) sheet; **blättern** vi (Inform) to scroll; **in etw** (dat) **~ to** leaf through sth; **Blätterteig** m puff pastry; **Blattsalat** m green salad; **Blattspinat** m spinach

blau adj blue; (fam: betrunken) plastered; (Gastr) boiled; **~es Auge** black eye; **~er Fleck** bruise; **Blaubeere** f bilberry, blueberry; **Blaulicht** nt flashing blue light; **blau|machen** vi (fam) to skive work o school; **Blauschimmelkäse** m blue cheese

Blazer (-s, -) m blazer

Blech (-(e)s, -e) nt sheet metal; (Backblech) baking tray (Brit), cookie sheet (US); **Blechschaden** m (Auto) damage to the bodywork

Blei (-(e)s, -e) nt lead

bleiben (blieb, geblieben) vi to stay; **lass das ~!** stop it; **das bleibt unter uns** that's (just) between ourselves; **mir bleibt keine andere Wahl** I have no other choice

bleich adj pale; **bleichen** vt to bleach

bleifrei adj (Benzin) unleaded; **bleihaltig** adj (Benzin) leaded

Bleistift m pencil

Blende (-, -n) f (Foto) aperture

Blick (-(e)s, -e) m look; (kurz) glance; (Aussicht) view; **auf den ersten ~** at first sight; **einen ~ auf etw** (akk) **werfen** to have a look at sth; **blicken** vi to look; **sich ~ lassen** to show up

blieb imperf von **bleiben**

blies imperf von **blasen**

blind adj blind; (Glas etc) dull; **Blinddarm** m appendix; **Blinddarmentzündung** f appendicitis; **Blinde(r)** mf blind person/man/woman; **die ~n** pl the blind pl; **Blindenhund** m guide dog; **Blindenschrift** f

braille

blinken vi (Stern, Lichter) to twinkle; (aufleuchten) to flash; (Auto) to indicate; **Blinker** (-s, -) m (Auto) indicator (Brit), turn signal (US)

blinzeln vi (mit beiden Augen) to blink; (mit einem Auge) to wink

Blitz (-es, -e) m (flash of) lightning; (Foto) flash; **blitzen** vi (Foto) to use a/the flash; **es blitzte und donnerte** there was thunder and lightning; **Blitzlicht** nt flash

Block (-(e)s, Blöcke) m (a. fig) block; (von Papier) pad; **Blockflöte** f recorder; **Blockhaus** nt log cabin; **blockieren** vt to block ▷ vi to jam; (Räder) to lock; **Blockschrift** f block letters pl

blöd adj stupid; **blödeln** vi (fam) to fool around

Blog (-s, -s) nt (Inform) blog; **bloggen** vi to blog

blond adj blond; (Frau) blonde

SCHLÜSSELWORT

bloß adj 1 (unbedeckt) bare; (nackt) naked; **mit der bloßen Hand** with one's bare hand; **mit bloßem Auge** with the naked eye 2 (alleinig, nur) mere; **der bloße Gedanke** the very thought; **bloßer Neid** sheer envy ▷ adv only, merely; **lass das bloß!** just don't do that!; **wie ist das bloß passiert?** how on earth did that happen?

blühen vi to bloom; (fig) to flourish

Blume (-, -n) f flower; (von Wein) bouquet; **Blumenbeet** nt flower bed; **Blumengeschäft** nt florist's (shop); **Blumenkohl** m cauliflower; **Blumenladen** m flower shop; **Blumenstrauß** m bunch of flowers; **Blumentopf** m flowerpot; **Blumenvase** f vase

Bluse (-, -n) f blouse

Blut (-(e)s) nt blood; **Blutbild** nt blood count; **Blutdruck** m blood pressure; **Blutorange** f blood orange

Blüte (-, -n) f (Pflanzenteil) flower, bloom; (Baumblüte) blossom; (fig) prime

bluten vi to bleed

Blütenstaub m pollen

Bluter (-s, -) m (Med) haemophiliac; **Bluterguss** m haematoma; (blauer Fleck) bruise; **Blutgruppe** f blood group; **blutig** adj bloody; **Blutkonserve** f unit of stored blood; **Blutprobe** f blood sample; **Blutspende** f blood donation; **Bluttransfusion** f blood transfusion; **Blutung** f bleeding; **Blutvergiftung** f blood poisoning; **Blutwurst** f black pudding (Brit), blood sausage (US)

BLZ abk = **Bankleitzahl**

Bob (-s, -s) m bob(sleigh)

Bock (-(e)s, Böcke) m (Reh) buck; (Schaf) ram; (Gestell) trestle; (Sport) vaulting horse; **ich hab keinen ~ (drauf)** (fam) I don't feel like it

Boden (-s, Böden) m ground; (Fußboden) floor; (von Meer, Fass) bottom; (Speicher) attic; **Bodennebel** m ground mist; **Bodenpersonal** nt ground staff; **Bodenschätze** pl mineral resources pl

Bodensee m: **der ~** Lake Constance

Body (-s, -s) m body; **Bodybuilding** (-s) nt bodybuilding

bog imperf von **biegen**

Bogen (-s, -) m (Biegung) curve; (in der Architektur) arch; (Waffe, Instrument) bow; (Papier) sheet

Bohne (-, -n) f bean; **grüne ~n** pl green (o French (US)) beans pl; **weiße ~n** pl haricot beans pl; **Bohnenkaffee** m real coffee; **Bohnensprosse** f bean sprout

bohren vt to drill; **Bohrer** (-s, -) m drill

Boiler (-s, -) m water heater

Boje (-, -n) f buoy

Bolivien (-s) nt Bolivia

Bombe (-, -n) f bomb

Bon (-s, -s) m (Kassenzettel) receipt; (Gutschein) voucher, coupon

Bonbon (-s, -s) nt sweet (Brit), candy (US)

Bonus (- o -ses, -se o Boni) m bonus; (Punktvorteil) bonus points pl; (Schadenfreiheitsrabatt) no-claims bonus

Boot (-(e)s, -e) nt boat; **Bootsverleih** m boat hire (Brit) (o rental (US))

Bord (-(e)s, -e) m: **an ~ (eines Schiffes)** on board (a ship); **an ~ gehen** (Schiff) to go on board; (Flugzeug) to board; **von ~ gehen** to disembark; **Bordcomputer** m dashboard computer

Bordell (-s, -e) nt brothel

Bordkarte f boarding card

Bordstein m kerb (Brit), curb (US)

borgen vt to borrow; **jdm etw ~** to lend sb sth; **sich** (dat) **etw ~** to borrow sth

Börse (-, -n) f stock exchange; (Geldbörse) purse

bös adj siehe **böse**; **bösartig** adj malicious; (Med) malignant

Böschung f slope; (Uferböschung) embankment

böse adj bad; (stärker) evil; (Wunde) nasty; (zornig) angry; **bist du mir ~?** are you angry with me?

boshaft adj malicious

Bosnien (-s) nt Bosnia; **Bosnien-Herzegowina** (-s) nt

Bosnia-Herzegovina

böswillig adj malicious

bot imperf von **bieten**

botanisch adj; **~er Garten** botanical gardens pl

Botschaft f message; (Pol) embassy; **Botschafter(in)** m(f) ambassador

Botsuana (-s) nt Botswana

Bouillon (-, -s) f stock

Boutique (-, -n) f boutique

Bowle (-, -n) f punch

Box (-, -en) f (Behälter, Pferdebox) box; (Lautsprecher) speaker; (bei Autorennen) pit

boxen vi to box; **Boxer** (-s, -) m (Hund, Sportler) boxer; **Boxershorts** pl boxer shorts pl; **Boxkampf** m boxing match

Boykott (-s, -e) m boycott

brach imperf von **brechen**

brachte imperf von **bringen**

Brainstorming (-s) nt brainstorming

Branchenverzeichnis nt yellow pages® pl

Brand (-(e)s, Brände) m fire; **einen ~ haben** (fam) to be parched

Brandenburg (-s) nt Brandenburg

Brandsalbe f ointment for burns

Brandung f surf

Brandwunde f burn

brannte imperf von **brennen**

Brasilien (-s) nt Brazil

braten (briet, gebraten) vt to roast; (auf dem Rost) to grill; (in der Pfanne) to fry; **Braten** (-s, -) m roast; (roher) joint; **Bratensoße** f gravy; **Brathähnchen** nt roast chicken; **Bratkartoffeln** pl fried potatoes pl; **Bratpfanne** f frying pan; **Bratspieß** m spit; **Bratwurst** f fried sausage; (gegrillte) grilled sausage

Brauch (-s, Bräuche) m custom

brauchen vt (nötig haben) to need

(für, zu for); (erfordern) to require; (Zeit) to take; (gebrauchen) to use; **wie lange wird er ~?** how long will it take him?; **du brauchst es nur zu sagen** you only need to say; **das braucht (seine) Zeit** it takes time; **ihr braucht es nicht zu tun** you don't have (o need) to do it; **sie hätte nicht zu kommen ~** she needn't have come

brauen vt to brew; **Brauerei** f brewery

braun adj brown; (von Sonne) tanned; **Bräune** (-, -n) f brownness; (von Sonne) tan; **Bräunungsstudio** nt tanning studio

Brause (-, -n) f (Dusche) shower; (Getränk) fizzy drink (Brit), soda (US)

Braut (-, Bräute) f bride; **Bräutigam** (-s, -e) m bridegroom

brav adj (artig) good, well-behaved

bravo interj well done

BRD (-) f abk = **Bundesrepublik Deutschland** FRG

● **BRD**
●
● The **BRD** is the official name for
● the Federal Republic of
● Germany. It comprises 16
● **Länder** (see **Land**). It was the
● name given to the former West
● Germany as opposed to East
● Germany (the **DDR**). The two
● Germanies were reunited on 3rd
● October 1990.

brechen (brach, gebrochen) vt to break; (erbrechen) to bring up; **sich** (dat) **den Arm ~** to break one's arm ▷ vi to break; (erbrechen) to vomit, to be sick; **Brechreiz** m nausea

Brei (-(e)s, -e) m (Breimasse) mush, pulp; (Haferbrei) porridge; (für

Kinder) pap
breit *adj* wide; *(Schultern)* broad;
zwei Meter ~ two metres wide;
Breite (-, -n) *f* breadth; *(bei
Maßangaben)* width; *(Geo)* latitude;
der ~ nach widthways;
Breitengrad *m* (degree of)
latitude
Bremen (-s) *nt* Bremen
Bremsbelag *m* brake lining;
Bremse (-, -n) *f* brake; *(Zool)*
horsefly; **bremsen** *vi* to brake
▷ *vt (Auto)* to brake; *(fig)* to slow
down; **Bremsflüssigkeit** *f* brake
fluid; **Bremslicht** *nt* brake light;
Bremspedal *nt* brake pedal;
Bremsspur *f* tyre marks *pl*;
Bremsweg *m* braking distance
brennen *(brannte, gebrannt) vi* to
burn; *(in Flammen stehen)* to be on
fire; **es brennt!** fire!; **mir ~ die
Augen** my eyes are smarting; **das
Licht ~ lassen** to leave the light
on; **Brennholz** *nt* firewood;
Brennnessel *f* stinging nettle;
Brennspiritus *m* methylated
spirits *pl*; **Brennstab** *m* fuel rod;
Brennstoff *m* fuel
Brett (-(e)s, -er) *nt* board; *(länger)*
plank; *(Regal)* shelf; *(Spielbrett)*
board; **Schwarzes ~** notice board,
bulletin board (US); **~er** *pl* (ski) skis
pl; **Brettspiel** *nt* board game
Brezel (-, -n) *f* pretzel
Brief (-(e)s, -e) *m* letter;
Briefbombe *f* letter bomb;
Brieffreund(in) *m(f)* penfriend,
pen pal; **Briefkasten** *m* letterbox
(Brit), mailbox (US);
elektronischer ~ electronic
mailbox; **Briefmarke** *f* stamp;
Briefpapier *nt* writing paper;
Brieftasche *f* wallet;
Briefträger(in) *m(f)* post-
man/-woman; **Briefumschlag** *m*
envelope; **Briefwaage** *f* letter
scales *pl*

brief *imperf von* **braten**
Brille (-, -n) *f* glasses *pl*;
(Schutzbrille) goggles *pl*; **Brillenetui**
nt glasses case
bringen *(brachte, gebracht) vt*
(herbringen) to bring; *(mitnehmen,
vom Sprecher weg)* to take; *(holen,
herbringen)* to get, to fetch; *(Theat,
Cine)* to show; *(Radio, TV)* to
broadcast; **~ Sie mir bitte noch
ein Bier** could you bring me
another beer, please?; **jdn nach
Hause ~** to take sb home; **jdn
dazu ~, etw zu tun** to make sb do
sth; **jdn auf eine Idee ~** to give sb
an idea
Brise (-, -n) *f* breeze
Brite (-n, -n) *m*, **Britin** *f* British
person, Briton; **er ist ~** he is
British; **die ~n** the British; **britisch**
adj British
Brocken (-s, -) *m* bit; *(größer)*
lump, chunk
Brokkoli *m* broccoli
Brombeere *f* blackberry
Bronchitis (-) *f* bronchitis
Bronze (-, -n) *f* bronze
Brosche (-, -n) *f* brooch
Brot (-(e)s, -e) *nt* bread; *(Laib)* loaf;
Brotaufstrich *m* spread;
Brötchen *nt* roll; **Brotzeit** *f*
(Pause) break; *(Essen)* snack;
~ machen to have a snack
Browser (-s, -) *m (Inform)*
browser
Bruch (-(e)s, Brüche) *m (Brechen)*
breaking; *(Bruchstelle; mit Partei,
Tradition etc)* break; *(Med:
Eingeweidebruch)* rupture, hernia;
(Knochenbruch) fracture; *(Math)*
fraction; **brüchig** *adj* brittle
Brücke (-, -n) *f* bridge
Bruder (-s, Brüder) *m* brother
Brühe (-, -n) *f (Suppe)* (clear)
soup; *(Grundlage)* stock; *(pej:
Getränk)* muck; **Brühwürfel** *m*
stock cube

brüllen vi to roar; (Stier) to bellow; (vor Schmerzen) to scream (with pain)

brummen vi (Bär, Mensch) to growl; (brummeln) to mutter; (Insekt) to buzz; (Motor, Radio) to drone ▶ vt to growl

brünett adj brunette

Brunnen (-s, -) m fountain; (tief) well; (natürlich) spring

Brust (-, Brüste) f breast; (beim Mann) chest; **Brustschwimmen** (-s) nt breaststroke; **Brustwarze** f nipple

brutal adj brutal

brutto adv gross

BSE (-) nt abk = **bovine spongiforme Enzephalopathie** BSE

Bube (-n, -n) m boy, lad; (Karten) jack

Buch (-(e)s, Bücher) nt book

Buche (-, -n) f beech (tree)

buchen vt to book; (Betrag) to enter

Bücherei f library

Buchfink m chaffinch

Buchhalter(in) m(f) accountant

Buchhandlung f bookshop

Büchse (-, -n) f tin (Brit), can

Buchstabe (-ns, -n) m letter; **buchstabieren** vt to spell

Bucht (-, -en) f bay

Buchung f booking; (Comm) entry

Buckel (-s, -) m hump

bücken vr: **sich ~** to bend down

Buddhismus (-) m Buddhism

Bude (-, -en) f (auf Markt) stall; (fam: Wohnung) pad, place

Büfett (-s, -s) nt sideboard; **kaltes ~** cold buffet

Büffel (-s, -) m buffalo

Bügel (-s, -) m (Kleidung) hanger; (Steigbügel) stirrup; (Brille) sidepiece; (von Skilift) T-bar; **Bügelbrett** nt ironing board;

Bügeleisen nt iron; **Bügelfalte** f crease; **bügelfrei** adj non-iron; **bügeln** vt, vi to iron

buh interj boo

Bühne (-, -n) f stage; **Bühnenbild** nt set

Bulgare (-n, -n) m, **Bulgarin** f Bulgarian; **Bulgarien** (-s) nt Bulgaria; **bulgarisch** adj Bulgarian; **Bulgarisch** nt Bulgarian

Bulimie f bulimia

Bulle (-n, -n) m bull; (fam: Polizist) cop

Bummel (-s, -) m stroll; **bummeln** vi to stroll; (trödeln) to dawdle; (faulenzen) to loaf around; **Bummelzug** m slow train

bums interj bang

bumsen vi (vulg) to screw

Bund (-(e)s, Bünde) m (von Hose, Rock) waistband; (Freundschaftsbund) bond; (Organisation) association; (Pol) confederation; **der ~** (fam: Bundeswehr) the army ▶ (-(e)s, -e) nt bunch; (von Stroh etc) bundle

Bundes- in zW Federal; (auf Deutschland bezogen a.) German; **Bundeskanzler(in)** m(f) Chancellor; **Bundesland** nt state, Land; **Bundesliga** f: **erste/zweite ~** First/Second Division; **Bundespräsident(in)** m(f) President; **Bundesrat** m (in Deutschland) Upper House of the German Parliament; (in der Schweiz) Council of Ministers; **Bundesregierung** f Federal Government; **Bundesrepublik** f Federal Republic; **~ Deutschland** Federal Republic of Germany; **Bundesstraße** f ≈ A road (Brit), ≈ state highway (US); **Bundestag** m Lower House of the German Parliament; **Bundeswehr** f (German) armed forces pl

BUNDESWEHR

The **Bundeswehr** is the name for the German armed forces. It was established in 1955, first of all for volunteers, but since 1956 there has been compulsory military service for all able-bodied young men of 18. In peacetime the Defence Minister is the head of the 'Bundeswehr', but in wartime the **Bundeskanzler** takes over. The 'Bundeswehr' comes under the jurisdiction of NATO.

Bündnis nt alliance
Bungalow (-s, -s) m bungalow
Bungeejumping (-s) nt bungee jumping
bunt adj colourful; (von Programm etc) varied; **-e Farben** bright colours ▷ adv (anstreichen) in bright colours; **Buntstift** m crayon, coloured pencil
Burg (-, -en) f castle
Bürger(in) (-s, -) m(f) citizen; **bürgerlich** adj (Rechte, Ehe etc) civil; (vom Mittelstand) middle-class; (pej) bourgeois; **Bürgermeister(in)** m(f) mayor; **Bürgersteig** (-(e)s, -e) m pavement (Brit), sidewalk (US)
Büro (-s, -s) nt office; **Büroklammer** f paper clip
Bürokratie f bureaucracy
Bursche (-n, -n) m lad; (Typ) guy
Bürste (-, -n) f brush; **bürsten** vt to brush
Bus (-ses, -se) m bus; (Reisebus) coach (Brit), bus; **Busbahnhof** m bus station
Busch (-(e)s, Büsche) m bush; (Strauch) shrub
Busen (-s, -) m breasts pl, bosom
Busfahrer(in) m(f) bus driver; **Bushaltestelle** f bus stop

Businessclass (-) f business class
Buslinie f bus route; **Busreise** f coach tour (Brit), bus tour
Bußgeld nt fine
Büstenhalter (-s, -) m bra
Busverbindung f bus connection
Butter (-) f butter; **Butterbrot** nt slice of bread and butter; **Butterkäse** m type of mild, full-fat cheese; **Buttermilch** f buttermilk; **Butterschmalz** nt clarified butter
Button (-s, -s) m badge (Brit), button (US)
b. w. abk = **bitte wenden** pto
Byte (-s, -s) nt byte
bzw. adv abk = **beziehungsweise**

C

ca. adv abk = **circa** approx

Cabrio (-s, -s) nt convertible

Café (-s, -s) nt café

Cafeteria (-, -s) f cafeteria

Call-Center (-s, -) nt call centre

campen vi to camp; **Camping** (-s) nt camping; **Campingbus** m camper; **Campingplatz** m campsite, camping ground (US)

Cappuccino (-s, -) m cappuccino

Carving (-s) nt (Ski) carving; **Carvingski** m carving ski

CD (-, -s) f abk = **Compact Disc** CD; **CD-Brenner** (-s, -) m CD burner, CD writer; **CD-Player** (-s, -) m CD player; **CD-ROM** (-, -s) f abk = **Compact Disc Read Only Memory** CD-ROM; **CD-ROM-Laufwerk** nt CD-ROM drive; **CD-Spieler** m CD player

Cello (-s, -s o Celli) nt cello

Celsius nt celsius; **20 Grad ~** 20 degrees Celsius, 68 degrees Fahrenheit

Cent (-, -s) m (von Dollar und Euro) cent

Chamäleon (-s, -s) nt chameleon

Champagner (-s, -) m champagne

Champignon (-s, -s) m mushroom

Champions League (-, -s) f Champions League

Chance (-, -n) f chance; **die -n stehen gut** the prospects are good

Chaos (-) nt chaos; **Chaot(in)** (-en, -en) m(f) (fam) disorganized person, scatterbrain; **chaotisch** adj chaotic

Charakter (-s, -e) m character; **charakteristisch** adj characteristic (für of)

Charisma (-s, Charismen o Charismata) nt charisma

charmant adj charming

Charterflug m charter flight; **chartern** vt to charter

Chat (-s, -s) m (Inform) chat; **chatten** vi (Inform) to chat

checken vt (überprüfen) to check; (fam: verstehen) to get

Check-in (-s, -s) m check-in; **Check-in-Schalter** m check-in desk

Chef(in) (-s, -s) m(f) boss; **Chefarzt** m, **Chefärztin** f senior consultant (Brit), medical director (US)

Chemie (-) f chemistry; **chemisch** adj chemical; **~e Reinigung** dry cleaning

Chemotherapie f chemotherapy

Chicoree (-s) m chicory

Chiffre (-, -n) f (Geheimzeichen) cipher; (in Zeitung) box number

Chile (-s) nt Chile

Chili (-s, -s) m chilli

China (-s) nt China; **Chinakohl** m Chinese leaves pl (Brit), bok choy (US); **Chinarestaurant** nt Chinese restaurant; **Chinese** (-n, -n) m Chinese; **Chinesin** (-, -nen) f Chinese (woman); **sie ist ~** she's Chinese; **chinesisch** adj Chinese; **Chinesisch** nt Chinese

Chip (-s, -s) m (Inform) chip; **Chipkarte** f smart card

Chips pl (Kartoffelchips) crisps pl (Brit), chips pl (US)

Chirurg(in) (-en, -en) m(f) surgeon

Chlor (-s) nt chlorine

Choke (-s, -s) m choke

Cholera (-) f cholera

Cholesterin (-s) nt cholesterol

Chor (-(e), Chöre) m choir; (Theat) chorus

Choreografie f choreography

Christ(in) (-en, -en) m(f) Christian; **Christbaum** m Christmas tree; **Christi Himmelfahrt** f the Ascension (of Christ); **Christkind** nt baby Jesus; (das Geschenke bringt) ≈ Father Christmas, Santa Claus; **christlich** adj Christian

Chrom (-s) nt chrome; (Chem) chromium

chronisch adj chronic

chronologisch adj chronological ▷ adv in chronological order

Chrysantheme (-, -n) f chrysanthemum

circa adv about, approximately

City (-) f city centre, downtown (US)

Clementine (-, -n) f clementine

clever adj clever, smart

Clique (-, -n) f group; (pej) clique; **David und seine ~** David and his lot o crowd

Clown (-s, -s) m clown

Club (-s, -s) m club; **Cluburlaub** m club holiday (Brit), club vacation (US)

Cocktail (-s, -s) m cocktail; **Cocktailtomate** f cherry tomato

Cognac (-s) m cognac

Cola (-, -s) f Coke®, cola

Comic (-s, -s) m comic strip; (Heft) comic

Compact Disc (-, -s) f compact disc

Computer (-s, -) m computer; **Computerfreak** m computer nerd; **computergesteuert** adj computer-controlled; **Computergrafik** f computer graphics pl; **computerlesbar** adj machine-readable; **Computerspiel** nt computer game; **Computertomografie** f computer tomography, scan; **Computervirus** m computer virus

Container (-s, -) m (zum Transport) container; (für Bauschutt etc) skip

Control-Taste f control key

Cookie (-s, -s) nt (Inform) cookie

cool adj (fam) cool

Cornflakes pl cornflakes pl

Couch (-, -en) f couch; **Couchtisch** m coffee table

Coupé (-s, -s) nt coupé

Coupon (-s, -s) m coupon

Cousin (-s, -s) m cousin; **Cousine** f cousin

Crack (-s) nt (Droge) crack

Creme (-, -s) f cream; (Gastr) mousse

Creutzfeld-Jakob-Krankheit f Creutzfeld-Jakob disease, CJD

Croissant (-s, -s) nt croissant

Curry (-s) m curry powder ▷ (-s) nt (indisches Gericht) curry; **Currywurst** f fried sausage with ketchup and curry powder

Cursor (-s, -) m (Inform) cursor

Cybercafé nt cybercafé; **Cyberspace** (-) m cyberspace

d

even though he has no idea; **ich finde nichts ~** I don't see anything wrong with it; **es bleibt ~** that's settled; **~ sein** (anwesend) to be present; (beteiligt) to be involved; **ich bin ~** I count me in; **er war gerade ~ zu gehen** he was just (o on the point of) leaving

dabei|bleiben irr vi to stick with it; **ich bleibe dabei** i'm not changing my mind

dabei|haben irr vt: **er hat seine Schwester dabei** he's brought his sister; **ich habe kein Geld dabei** I haven't got any money on me

Dach (-(e)s, Dächer) nt roof; **Dachboden** m attic, loft; **Dachgepäckträger** m roofrack; **Dachrinne** f gutter

Dachs (-es, -e) m badger

dachte imperf von **denken**

Dackel (-s, -) m dachshund

dadurch adv (räumlich) through it; (durch diesen Umstand) in that way; (deshalb) because of that, for that reason ▷ conj: **~, dass** because; **~, dass er hart arbeitete** (indem) by working hard

dafür adv for it; (anstatt) instead; **~ habe ich 50 Euro bezahlt** I paid 50 euros for it; **ich bin ~ zu bleiben** i'm for (o in favour of) staying; **~ ist er ja da** that's what he's there for; **er kann nichts ~** he can't help it

dagegen adv against it; (im Vergleich damit) in comparison; (bei Tausch) for it; **ich habe nichts ~** I don't mind

daheim adv at home

daher adv (räumlich) from there; (Ursache) that's why ▷ conj (deshalb) that's why

dahin adv (räumlich) there; (zeitlich) then; (vergangen) gone; **bis ~** (zeitlich) till then; (örtlich) up to there; **bis ~ muss die Arbeit fertig**

○ SCHLÜSSELWORT

da adv 1 (örtlich) there; (hier) here; **da draußen** out there; **da sein** to be there; **da bin ich** here I am; **da, wo** where; **ist noch Milch da?** is there any milk left?
2 (zeitlich) then; (folglich) so
3 **da haben wir Glück gehabt** we were lucky there; **da kann man nichts machen** nothing can be done about it
▷ konj (weil) as, since

dabei adv (räumlich) close to it; (zeitlich) at the same time; (obwohl, doch) though; **sie hörte Radio und rauchte** she was listening to the radio and smoking (at the same time); **~ fällt mir ein ...** that reminds me ...; **~ kam es zu einem Unfall** this led to an accident; **... und ~ hat er gar keine Ahnung ...**

sein the work must be finished by then

dahinter adv behind it; **~ kommen** to find out

Dahlie f dahlia

Dalmatiner (-s, -) m dalmatian

damals adv at that time, then

Dame (-, -n) f lady; (Karten) queen; (Spiel) draughts sing (Brit), checkers sing (US); **Damenbinde** f sanitary towel (Brit), sanitary napkin (US); **Damenkleidung** f ladies' wear; **Damentoilette** f ladies' toilet (o restroom (US))

damit adv with it; (begründend) by that; **was meint er ~?** what does he mean by that?; **genug ~!** that's enough ▷ conj so that

Damm (-(e)s, Dämme) m dyke; (Staudamm) dam; (am Hafen) mole; (Bahn-, Straßendamm) embankment

Dämmerung f twilight; (am Morgen) dawn; (am Abend) dusk

Dampf (-(e)s, Dämpfe) m steam; (Dunst) vapour; **Dampfbad** nt Turkish bath; **Dampfbügeleisen** nt steam iron; **dampfen** vi to steam

dämpfen vt (Gastr) to steam; (Geräusch) to deaden; (Begeisterung) to dampen

Dampfer (-s, -) m steamer

Dampfkochtopf m pressure cooker

danach adv after that; (zeitlich a.) afterwards; (demgemäß) accordingly; **mir ist nicht ~** I don't feel like it; **~ sieht es aus** that's what it looks like

Däne (-n, -n) m Dane

daneben adv beside it; (im Vergleich) in comparison

Dänemark (-s) nt Denmark; **Dänin** f Dane, Danish woman/girl; **dänisch** adj Danish; **Dänisch** nt Danish

dank prep +dat o gen thanks to; **Dank** (-(e)s) m thanks pl; **vielen ~!** thank you very much; **jdm ~ sagen** to thank sb; **dankbar** adj grateful; (Aufgabe) rewarding; **danke** interj thank you, thanks; **~ schön** (o sehr) thank you very much; **nein ~!** no, thank you; **~, gerne!** yes, please; **~, gleichfalls!** thanks, and the same to you; **danken** vi: **jdm für etw ~** to thank sb for sth; **nichts zu ~!** you're welcome

dann adv then; **bis ~!** see you (later); **~ eben nicht** okay, forget it, suit yourself

daran adv (räumlich) on it; (befestigen) to it; (stoßen) against it; **es liegt ~, dass ...** it's because ...

darauf adv (räumlich) on it; (zielgerichtet) towards it; (danach) afterwards; **es kommt ganz ~ an, ob ...** it all depends whether ...; **ich freue mich ~** I'm looking forward to it; **am Tag ~** the next day; **~ folgend** (Tag, Jahr) next, following

darauffolgend adj (Tag, Jahr) next, following

daraus adv from it; **was ist ~ geworden?** what became of it?

darin adv in it; **das Problem liegt ~, dass ...** the basic problem is that ...

Darlehen (-s, -) nt loan

Darm (-(e)s, Därme) m intestine; (Wurstdarm) skin; **Darmgrippe** f gastroenteritis

darstellen vt to represent; (Theat) to play; (beschreiben) to describe; **Darsteller(in)** m(f) actor/actress; **Darstellung** f representation; (Beschreibung) description

darüber adv (räumlich) above it, over it; (fahren) over it; (mehr) more; (*währenddessen*) meanwhile; (*sprechen, streiten, sich freuen*) about it

darum adv (*deshalb*) that's why; **es geht ~, dass ...** the point (o thing) is that ...

darunter adv (*räumlich*) under it; (*dazwischen*) among them; (*weniger*) less; **was verstehen Sie ~?** what do you understand by that?; **~ fallen** to be included

darunterfallen vi to be included

das art the; **~ Auto da** that car; **er hat sich ~ Bein gebrochen** he's broken his leg; **vier Euro ~ Kilo** four euros a kilo ▷ pron that (one), this (one); (*relativ, Sache*) that, which; (*relativ, Person*) who, that; (*demonstrativ*) this/that one; **~ Auto da** that car; **ich nehme ~ da** I'll take that one; **~ Auto, ~ er kaufte** the car (that (o which)) he bought; **~ Mädchen, ~ nebenan wohnt** the girl who (o that) lives next door; **~ heißt** that is; **~ sind Amerikaner** they're American

da sein irr vi siehe **da**

dass conj that; **so ~** so that; **es sei denn, ~** unless; **ohne ~ er grüßte** without saying hello

dasselbe pron the same

Datei f (*Inform*) file;

Dateimanager m file manager

Daten pl data pl; **Datenbank** f database; **Datenmissbrauch** m misuse of data; **Datenschutz** m data protection; **Datenträger** m data carrier; **Datenverarbeitung** f data processing

datieren vt to date

Dativ m dative (case)

Dattel (-, -n) f date

Datum (-s, Daten) nt date

Dauer (-, -n) f duration; (*Länge*) length; **auf die ~** in the long run; **für die ~ von zwei Jahren** for a

period of) two years;

Dauerauftrag m (Fin) standing order; **dauerhaft** adj lasting; (*Material*) durable; **Dauerkarte** f season ticket; **dauern** vi to last; (*Zeit benötigen*) to take; **es hat sehr lange gedauert, bis er ...** it took him a long time to ...; **wie lange dauert es denn noch?** how much longer will it be?; **das dauert mir zu lange** I can't wait that long; **dauernd** adj lasting; (*ständig*) constant ▷ adv always, constantly; **er lachte ~** he kept laughing; **unterbrich mich nicht ~** stop interrupting me; **Dauerwelle** f perm (Brit), permanent (US)

Daumen (-s, -) m thumb

Daunendecke f eiderdown

davon adv of it; (*räumlich*) away; (*weg von*) from it; (*Grund*) because of it; **ich hätte gerne ein Kilo ~** I'd like one kilo of that; **~ habe ich gehört** I've heard of it; (*Geschehen*) I've heard about it; **das kommt ~, wenn ...** that's what happens when ...; **was habe ich ~?** what's the point?; **auf und ~** up and away; **davon|laufen** irr vi to run away

davor adv (*räumlich*) in front of it; (*zeitlich*) before; **ich habe Angst ~** I'm afraid of it

dazu adv (*zusätzlich*) on top of that, as well; (*zu diesem Zweck*) for it, for that purpose; **ich möchte Reis ~** I'd like rice with it; **und ~ noch** and in addition; **~ fähig sein, etw zu tun** to be capable of doing sth; **wie kam es ~** how did it happen?; **dazu|gehören** vi to belong to it; **dazu|kommen** irr vi (zu jdm ~) to join sb; **kommt noch etwas dazu?** anything else?

dazwischen adv in between; (*Unterschied etc*) between them; (*in einer Gruppe*) among them

dazwischen|kommen irr vi:
wenn nichts dazwischenkommt
if all goes well; **mir ist etwas
dazwischengekommen**
something has cropped up
DDR (-) f abk = **Deutsche
Demokratische Republik** (Hist)
GDR
dealen vi (fam: mit Drogen) to deal
in drugs; **Dealer(in)** (-s, -) m(f)
(fam) dealer, pusher
Deck (-(e)s, -s o -e) nt deck
Decke (-, -n) f cover; (für Bett)
blanket; (für Tisch) tablecloth; (von
Zimmer) ceiling
Deckel (-s, -) m lid
decken vt to cover; (Tisch) to lay,
to set ▷ vr: **sich ~** (Interessen) to
coincide; (Aussagen) to correspond
▷ vi (den Tisch decken) to lay (o set)
the table
Decoder (-s, -) m decoder
defekt adj faulty; **Defekt** (-(e)s,
-e) m fault, defect
definieren vt to define;
Definition (-, -en) f definition
deftig adj (Preise) steep; **ein ~es
Essen** a good solid meal
dehnbar adj flexible, elastic;
dehnen vt to stretch ▷ vr: **sich
~** to stretch
Deich (-(e)s, -e) m dyke
dein pron (adjektivisch) your;
deine(r, s) pron (substantivisch)
yours; **deiner** pron gen von **du**; of you; **deinetwegen** adv
(wegen dir) because of you; (dir
zuliebe) for your sake; (um dich)
about you
deinstallieren vt (Programm) to
uninstall
Dekolleté (-s, -s) nt low neckline
Dekoration f decoration; (in
Laden) window dressing;
dekorativ adj decorative;
dekorieren vt to decorate; (Schaufenster) to dress

Delfin (-s, -e) m dolphin
delikat adj (lecker) delicious;
(heikel) delicate
Delikatesse (-, -n) f delicacy
Delle (-, -en) f (fam) dent
Delphin (-s, -e) m dolphin
dem dat sing von **der/das**; **wie
~ auch sein mag** be that as it may
demnächst adv shortly, soon
Demo (-, -s) f (fam) demo
Demokratie (-, -n) f democracy;
demokratisch adj democratic
demolieren vt to demolish
Demonstration f demonstration; **demonstrieren** vt, vi to
demonstrate
den art akk sing, dat pl von **der**; **sie
hat sich ~ Arm gebrochen** she's
broken her arm ▷ pron him;
(Sache) that one; (relativ: Person)
who, that, whom; (relativ: Sache)
which, that; **~ hab ich schon ewig
nicht mehr gesehen** I haven't
seen him in ages ▷ pron (Person)
who, that, whom; (Sache) which,
that; **der Typ, auf ~ sie steht** the
guy (who) she fancies; **der Berg,
auf ~ wir geklettert sind** the
mountain (that) we climbed
denkbar adj: **das ist ~** that's
possible ▷ adv: **~ einfach**
extremely simple; **denken** (dachte,
gedacht) vt, vi to think (über +akk
about); **an jdn/etw ~** to think of
sb/sth; (sich erinnern,
berücksichtigen) to remember
sb/sth; **woran denkst Du?** what
are you thinking about?; **denk an
den Kaffee!** don't forget the coffee
▷ vr: **sich ~** (sich vorstellen) to
imagine; **das kann ich mir ~** I can
(well) imagine
Denkmal (-s, Denkmäler) nt
monument; **Denkmalschutz** m
monument preservation; **unter
~ stehen** to be listed
denn conj for, because ▷ adv

then; (*nach Komparativ*) than; **was ist ~?** what's wrong?; **ist das ~ so schwierig?** is it really that difficult?

dennoch *conj* still, nevertheless

Deo (*-s, -s*) *nt*, **Deodorant** (*-s, -s*) *nt* deodorant; **Deoroller** *m* roll-on deodorant; **Deospray** *m* o *nt* deodorant spray

Deponie (*-, -n*) *f* waste disposal site, tip

Depressionen *pl*: **an ~ leiden** to suffer from depression *sing*; **deprimieren** *vt* to depress

🔵 SCHLÜSSELWORT

der (*f* **die**, *nt* **das**, *gen* **des, der, des**, *dat* **dem, der, dem**, *akk* **den, die, das**, *pl* **die**) *def art* the; **der Rhein** the Rhine; **der Klaus** (*fam*) Klaus; **die Frau** (*im Allgemeinen*) women; **der Tod/das Leben** death/life; **der Fuß des Berges** the foot of the hill; **gib es der Frau** give it to the woman; **er hat sich die Hand verletzt** he has hurt his hand

▷ *relativ pron* (*bei Menschen*) who, that; (*bei Tieren, Sachen*) which, that; **der Mann, den ich gesehen habe** the man who o whom o that I saw

▷ *demonstrativ pron* he/she/it (*jener, dieser*) that; (*pl*) those; **der/die war es** it was him/her; **der mit der Brille** the one with glasses; **ich will den (da)** I want that one

derart *adv* so; (*solcher Art*) such; **derartig** *adj*: **ein ~er Fehler** such a mistake, a mistake like that

deren *gen von* **die** o *pron* (*Person*) her; (*Sache*) its; (*Plural*) their o *pron* (*Person*) whose; (*Sache*) of which; **meine Freundin und ~ Mutter** my

friend and her mother; **das sind ~ Sachen** that's their stuff; **die Frau, ~ Tochter ...** the woman whose daughter ...; **ich bin mir ~ bewusst** I'm aware of that

dergleichen *pron*: **und ~ mehr** and the like, and so on; **nichts ~** no such thing

derjenige *pron* the one; **~, der** (*relativ*) the one who (o that)

dermaßen *adv* so much; (*mit Adj*) so

derselbe *pron* the same (person/thing)

deshalb *adv* therefore; **~ frage ich ja** that's why I'm asking

Design (*-s, -s*) *nt* design; **Designer(in)** (*-s, -*) *m(f)* designer

Desinfektionsmittel *nt* disinfectant; **desinfizieren** *vt* to disinfect

dessen *gen von* **der, das** ▷ *pron* (*Person*) his; (*Sache*) its; **ich bin mir ~ bewusst** I'm aware of that ▷ *pron* (*Person*) whose; (*Sache*) of which; **mein Freund und ~ Mutter** my friend and his mother; **der Mann, ~ Tochter ...** the man whose daughter ...; **ich bin mir ~ bewusst** I'm aware of that

Dessert (*-s, -s*) *nt* dessert; **zum** (*o* **als**) **~** for dessert

destilliert *adj* distilled

desto *adv*: **je eher, ~ besser** the sooner, the better

deswegen *conj* therefore

Detail (*-s, -s*) *nt* detail; **ins ~ gehen** to go into detail

Detektiv(in) (*-s, -e*) *m(f)* detective

deutlich *adj* clear; (*Unterschied*) distinct

deutsch *adj* German; **Deutsch** *nt* German; **auf ~** in German; **ins ~e übersetzen** to translate into German; **Deutsche(r)** *mf*

German; **Deutschland** nt Germany

Devise (-, -n) f motto; **~n** pl (Fin) foreign currency sing; **Devisenkurs** m exchange rate

Dezember (-(s), -) m December; *siehe auch* **Juni**

dezent adj discreet

d.h. abk von **das heißt** i.e. (gesprochen: i.e. oder that is)

Dia (-s, -s) nt slide

Diabetes (-, -) m (Med) diabetes; **Diabetiker(in)** (-s, -) m(f) diabetic

Diagnose (-, -n) f diagnosis

diagonal adj diagonal

Dialekt (-(e)s, -e) m dialect

Dialog (-(e)s, -e) m dialogue; (Inform) dialog

Dialyse (-, -n) f (Med) dialysis

Diamant m diamond

Diaprojektor m slide projector

Diät (-, -en) f diet; **eine ~ machen** to be on a diet; (anfangen) to go on a diet

dich pron akk von **du** you; **~ (selbst)** (reflexiv) yourself; **pass auf ~ auf** look after yourself; **reg ~ nicht auf** don't get upset

dicht adj dense; (Nebel) thick; (Gewebe) close; (wasserdicht) watertight; (Verkehr) heavy ▷ adv: **~ an/bei** close to; **~ bevölkert** densely populated

Dichter(in) (-s, -) m(f) poet; (Autor) writer

Dichtung f (Auto) gasket; (Dichtungsring) washer; (Gedichte) poetry

Dichtungsring m (Tech) washer

dick adj thick; (Person) fat; **jdn ~ haben** to be sick of sb; **Dickdarm** m colon; **Dickkopf** m stubborn (o pig-headed) person; **Dickmilch** f sour milk

die art the; **~ arme Sarah** poor Sarah ▷ pron (sing, Person, als Subjekt, als) she; (Person, als Subjekt, Plural) they; (Person, als Objekt) her; (Person, als Objekt, Plural) them; (Sache) that (one), this (one); (Plural) those (ones) (Sache, Plural) those (ones); (relativ, auf Person) who, that; (relativ, auf Sache) which, that; **~ mit den langen Haaren** the one (o her) with the long hair; **sie war ~ erste, ~ es erfuhr** she was the first to know; **ich nehme ~ da** I'll take that one/those ▷ pl von **der, die, das**

Dieb(in) (-(e)s, -e) m(f) thief; **Diebstahl** (-(e)s, Diebstähle) m theft; **Diebstahlsicherung** f burglar alarm

diejenige pron the one; **~, die** (relativ) the one who (o that); **~n** pl those pl, the ones

Diele (-, -n) f hall

Dienst (-(e)s, -e) m service; **außer ~** retired; **~ haben** to be on duty

Dienstag m Tuesday; *siehe auch* **Mittwoch**; **dienstags** adv on Tuesdays; *siehe auch* **mittwochs**

Dienstbereitschaft f: **~ haben** (Arzt) to be on call; **diensthabend** adj: **der ~e Arzt** the doctor on duty; **Dienstleistung** f service; **dienstlich** adj official; **er ist ~ unterwegs** he's away on business; **Dienstreise** f business trip; **Dienststelle** f department; **Dienstwagen** m company car; **Dienstzeit** f office hours pl; (Mil) period of service

diesbezüglich adj (formell) on this matter

diese(r, s) pron this (one); pl these; **~ Frau** this woman; **~r Mann** this man; **~s Mädchen** this girl; **~ Leute** these people; **ich nehme ~/~n/~s** (hier) I'll take this one; (dort) I'll take that one; **ich nehme ~** pl (hier) I'll take these (ones); (dort) I'll take those (ones)

Diesel (-s, -) m (Auto) diesel

dieselbe pron the same; **es sind immer ~n** it's always the same people

Dieselmotor m diesel engine; **Dieselöl** nt diesel (oil)

diesig adj hazy, misty

diesmal adv this time

Dietrich (-s, -e) m skeleton key

Differenz (-, -en) f difference

digital adj digital; **Digital-** in zW (Anzeige etc) digital; **Digitalfernsehen** nt digital television, digital TV; **Digitalkamera** f digital camera

Diktat (-(e)s, -e) nt dictation

Diktatur f dictatorship

Dill (-s) m dill

DIN abk = **Deutsche Industrienorm** DIN; **~ A4** A4

Ding (-(e)s, -e) nt thing; **vor allen ~en** above all; **der Stand der ~e** the state of affairs; **das ist nicht mein ~** (fam) it's not my sort of thing (o cup of tea); **Dingsbums** (-) nt (fam) thingy, thingummybob

Dinkel (-s, -) m (Bot) spelt

Dinosaurier (-s, -) m dinosaur

Diphtherie (-, -n) f diphtheria

Diplom (-(e)s, -e) nt diploma

Diplomat(in) (-en, -en) m(f) diplomat

dir pron dat von **du** (to) you; **hat er ~ geholfen?** did he help you?; **ich werde es ~ erklären** I'll explain it to you; (reflexiv) **wasch ~ die Hände** go and wash your hands; **ein Freund von ~** a friend of yours

direkt adj direct; (Frage) straight; **~e Verbindung** through service ▷ adv directly; (sofort) immediately; **~ am Bahnhof** right next to the station; **Direktflug** m direct flight

Direktor(in) m(f) director; (Schule) headmaster/-mistress

(Brit), principal (US)

Direktübertragung f live broadcast

Dirigent(in) m(f) conductor; **dirigieren** vt to direct; (Mus) to conduct

Discman® (-s, -s) m Discman®

Diskette f disk, diskette; **Diskettenlaufwerk** nt disk drive

Diskjockey (-s, -s) m disc jockey; **Disko** (-, -s) f (fam) disco, club; **Diskothek** (-, -en) f discotheque, club

diskret adj discreet

diskriminieren vt to discriminate against

Diskussion f discussion; **diskutieren** vt, vi to discuss ·

Display (-s, -s) nt display

disqualifizieren vt to disqualify

Distanz f distance

Distel (-, -n) f thistle

Disziplin (-, -en) f discipline

divers adj various

dividieren vt to divide (durch by); **8 dividiert durch 2 ist 4** 8 divided by 2 is 4

DJ (-s, -s) m abk = **Diskjockey** DJ

SCHLÜSSELWORT

doch adv 1 (dennoch) after all; (sowieso) anyway; **er kam doch noch** he came after all; **du weißt es ja doch besser** you know better than I do anyway; **und doch ...** and yet ...

2 (als bejahende Antwort) yes I do/it does etc; **das ist nicht wahr — doch!** that's not true — yes it is!

3 (auffordernd) **komm doch** do come; **lass ihn doch** just leave him; **nicht doch!** oh no!

4 **sie ist doch noch so jung** but she's still so young; **Sie wissen doch, wie das ist** you know how

it is(, don't you?); **wenn doch** if
only
▷ *konj (aber)* but; *(trotzdem)* all the
same; **und doch hat er es getan**
but still he did it

Doktor(in) *m(f)* doctor
Dokument *nt* document;
 Dokumentarfilm *m* docu-
 mentary (film); **dokumentieren**
 vt to document;
 Dokumentvorlage *f (Inform)*
 document template
Dolch (-(e)s, -e) *m* dagger
Dollar (-(s), -s) *m* dollar
dolmetschen *vt, vi* to interpret;
 Dolmetscher(in) (-s, -) *m(f)*
 interpreter
Dolomiten *pl* Dolomites *pl*
Dom (-(e)s, -e) *m* cathedral
Domäne (-, -n) *f* domain,
 province; *(Inform: Domain)* domain
Dominikanische Republik *f*
 Dominican Republic
Domino (-s, -s) *nt* dominoes *sing*
Donau (-) *f* Danube
Döner (-s, -) *m*, **Döner Kebab**
 (-(s), -s) *m* doner kebab
Donner (-s, -) *m* thunder;
 donnern *vi*: **es donnert** it's
 thundering
Donnerstag *m* Thursday; *siehe*
 auch **Mittwoch**; **donnerstags**
 adv on Thursdays; *siehe auch*
 mittwochs
doof *adj (fam)* stupid
dopen *vt* to dope; **Doping** (-s) *nt*
 doping; **Dopingkontrolle** *f*
 drugs test
Doppel (-s, -) *nt* duplicate; *(Sport)*
 doubles *sing*; **Doppelbett** *nt*
 double bed; **Doppeldecker** *m*
 double-decker; **Doppelhaus-**
 hälfte *f* semi-detached house
 (Brit), duplex (US); **doppelklicken**
 vi to double-click; **Doppelname**
 m double-barrelled name;

Doppelpunkt *m* colon;
 Doppelstecker *m* two-way
 adaptor; **doppelt** *adj* double; **in**
 ~er Ausführung in duplicate;
 Doppelzimmer *nt* double room
Dorf (-(e)s, Dörfer) *nt* village
Dorn (-(e)s, -en) *m (Bot)* thorn
Dörrobst *nt* dried fruit
Dorsch (-(e)s, -e) *m* cod
dort *adv* there; **~ drüben** over
 there; **dorther** *adv* from there
Dose (-, -n) *f* box; *(Blechdose)* tin
 (Brit), can; *(Bierdose)* can
dösen *vi* to doze
Dosenbier *nt* canned beer;
 Dosenmilch *f* canned milk,
 tinned milk (Brit); **Dosenöffner**
 m tin opener (Brit), can opener
Dotter (-s, -) *m (egg)* yolk
downloaden *vt* to download
Downsyndrom (-(e)s, -e) *nt*
 (Med) Down's syndrome
Dr. *abk* = **Doktor**
Drache (-n, -n) *m* dragon;
 Drachen (-s, -) *m (Spielzeug)* kite;
 (Sport) hang-glider;
 Drachenfliegen (-s) *nt*
 hang-gliding; **Drachenflieger(in)**
 (-s, -) *m(f)* hang-glider
Draht (-(e)s, Drähte) *m* wire;
 Drahtseilbahn *f* cable railway
Drama (-s, Dramen) *nt* drama;
 dramatisch *adj* dramatic
dran *adv (fam) kontr von* **daran**;
 gut ~ sein *(reich)* to be well-off;
 (glücklich) to be fortunate;
 (gesundheitlich) to be well;
 schlecht ~ sein to be in a bad way;
 wer ist ~? whose turn is it?; **ich**
 bin ~ it's my turn; **bleib ~!** *(Tel)*
 hang on
drang *imperf von* **dringen**
Drang (-(e)s, Dränge) *m (Trieb)*
 urge *(nach* for); *(Druck)* pressure
drängeln *vt, vi* to push
drängen *vt (schieben)* to push;

(*antreiben*) to urge ▷ *vi* (*eilig sein*) to be urgent; (*Zeit*) to press; **auf etw** (*akk*) **~** to press for sth

dran|kommen *irr vi*: **wer kommt dran?** who's turn is it?, who's next?

drauf (*fam*) *kontr von* **darauf**; **gut/schlecht ~ sein** to be in a good/bad mood

Draufgänger(in) (*-s, -*) *m(f)* daredevil

drauf|kommen *irr vi* to remember; **ich komme nicht drauf** I can't think of it

drauf|machen *vi* (*fam*) **einen ~** to go on a binge

draußen *adv* outside

Dreck (*-(e)s, -*) *m* dirt, filth; **dreckig** *adj* dirty, filthy

drehen *vi, vt* to turn; (*Zigaretten*) to roll; (*Film*) to shoot ▷ *vr*: **sich ~** to turn; (*um Achse*) to rotate; **sich ~ um** (*handeln von*) to be about

Drehstrom *m* three-phase current; **Drehtür** *f* revolving door; **Drehzahlmesser** *m* rev counter

drei *num* three; **~ viertel voll** three-quarters full; **es ist ~ viertel neun** it's a quarter to nine; **Drei** (*-, -en*) *f* three; (*Schulnote*) ≈ C; **Dreieck** *nt* triangle; **dreieckig** *adj* triangular; **dreifach** *adj* triple ▷ *adv* three times; **dreihundert** *num* three hundred; **Dreikönigstag** *m* Epiphany; **dreimal** *adv* three times; **Dreirad** *nt* tricycle; **dreispurig** *adj* three-lane

dreißig *num* thirty; **dreißigste(r, s)** *adj* thirtieth; *siehe auch* **dritte**

Dreiviertelstunde *f*: **eine ~** three quarters of an hour

dreizehn *num* thirteen; **dreizehnte(r, s)** *adj* thirteenth; *siehe auch* **dritte**

dressieren *vt* to train

Dressing (*-s, -s*) *nt* (salad) dressing

Dressman (*-s, Dressmen*) *m* (male) model

Dressur (*-, -en*) *f* training

drin (*fam*) *kontr von* **darin** in it; **mehr war nicht ~** that was the best I could do

dringen (*drang, gedrungen*) *vi* (*Wasser, Licht, Kälte*) to penetrate (*durch* through, *in +akk* into); **auf etw** (*akk*) **~** to insist on sth; **dringend, dringlich** *adj* urgent

drinnen *adv* inside

dritt *adv*: **wir sind zu ~** there are three of us; **dritte(r, s)** *adj* third; **die Dritte Welt** the Third World; **7. Juni** 7(th) June (*gesprochen*: the seventh of June); **am 7. Juni** on 7(th) June, on June 7(th) (*gesprochen*: on the seventh of June); **München, den 7. Juni** Munich, June 7(th); **Drittel** (*-s, -*) *nt* (*Bruchteil*) third; **drittens** *adv* thirdly

Droge (*-, -n*) *f* drug; **drogenabhängig, drogensüchtig** *adj* addicted to drugs

Drogerie *f* chemist's (Brit), drugstore (US); **Drogeriemarkt** *m* discount chemist's (Brit) (*o* drugstore (US))

> **DROGERIE**
>
> The **Drogerie** as opposed to the **Apotheke** sells medicines not requiring a prescription. It tends to be cheaper and also sells cosmetics, perfume and toiletries.

drohen *vi* to threaten (*jdm* sb); **mit etw ~** to threaten to do sth

dröhnen *vi* (*Motor*) to roar; (*Stimme, Musik*) to boom; (*Raum*) to resound

Drohung *f* threat

Drossel (-, -n) f thrush

drüben adv over there; (auf der anderen Seite) on the other side

drüber (fam) kontr von **darüber**

Druck (-(e)s, Drücke) m (Phys) pressure; (fig: Belastung) stress; **jdn unter ~ setzen** to put sb under pressure ▷ (-(e)s, -e) m (Typo: Vorgang) printing; (Produkt, Schriftart) print; **Druckbuchstabe** m block letter; **in ~n schreiben** to print; **drucken** vt, vi to print

drücken vt, vi (Knopf, Hand) to press; (zu eng sein) to pinch; (fig: Preise) to keep down; **jdm etw in die Hand ~** to press sth into sb's hand ▷ vr **sich vor etw** (dat) ~ to get out of sth; **drückend** adj oppressive

Drucker (-s, -) m (Inform) printer; **Druckertreiber** m printer driver

Druckknopf m press stud (Brit), snap fastener (US); **Drucksache** f printed matter; **Druckschrift** f block letters pl

drunten adv down there

drunter (fam) kontr von **darunter**

Drüse (-, -n) f gland

Dschungel (-s, -) m jungle

du pron you; **bist ~ es?** is it you?; **wir sind per ~** we're on first-name terms

Dübel (-s, -) m Rawlplug®

ducken vt to duck ▷ vr: **sich ~** to duck

Dudelsack m bagpipes pl

Duett (-s, -e) nt duet

Duft (-(e)s, Düfte) m scent; **duften** vi to smell nice; **es duftet nach ...** it smells of ...

dulden vt to tolerate

dumm adj stupid; **Dummheit** f stupidity; (Tat) stupid thing; **Dummkopf** m idiot

dumpf adj (Ton) muffled; (Erinnerung) vague; (Schmerz) dull

Düne (-, -n) f dune

Dünger (-s, -) m fertilizer

dunkel adj dark; (Stimme) deep; (Ahnung) vague; (rätselhaft) obscure; (verdächtig) dubious; **im Dunkeln tappen** (fig) to be in the dark; **dunkelblau** adj dark blue; **dunkelblond** adj light brown; **dunkelhaarig** adj dark-haired; **Dunkelheit** f darkness

dünn adj thin; (Kaffee) weak

Dunst (-es, Dünste) m haze; (leichter Nebel) mist; (Chem) vapour

dünsten vt (Gastr) to steam

Duo (-s, -s) nt duo

Dur (-) nt (Mus) major (key); **in G-~** in G major

SCHLÜSSELWORT

durch prep +akk 1 (hindurch) through; **durch den Urwald** through the jungle; **durch die ganze Welt reisen** to travel all over the world
2 (mittels) through, by (means of); (aufgrund) due to, owing to; **Tod durch Herzschlag/den Strang** death from a heart attack/by hanging; **durch die Post** by post; **durch seine Bemühungen** through his efforts
▷ adv 1 (hindurch) through; **die ganze Nacht durch** all through the night; **den Sommer durch** during the summer; **8 Uhr durch** past 8 o'clock; **durch und durch** completely
2 (durchgebraten etc) (gut) durch well-done

durchaus adv absolutely; **~ nicht** not at all

Durchblick m view; **den ~ haben** (fig) to know what's going on; **durch|blicken** vi to look through; (fam: verstehen) to understand (bei etw sth); **etw**

~ lassen (fig) to hint at sth
Durchblutung f circulation
durch|brennen irr vi (Sicherung) to blow; (Draht) to burn through; (fam: davonlaufen) to run away

durchdacht adv: **gut ~** well thought-out

durch|drehen vt (Fleisch) to mince ▷ vi (Räder) to spin; (fam: nervlich) to crack up

durcheinander adv in a mess; (fam: verwirrt) confused; **Durcheinander** (-s) nt (Verwirrung) confusion; (Unordnung) mess; **durcheinander|bringen** irr vt to mess up; (verwirren) to confuse; **durcheinander|reden** irr vi to talk all at the same time; **durcheinander|trinken** irr vi to mix one's drinks

Durchfahrt f way through; **„~ verboten!"** "no thoroughfare"

Durchfall m (Med) diarrhoea
durch|fallen irr vi to fall through; (in Prüfung) to fail

durch|fragen vr: **sich ~** to ask one's way

durch|führen vt to carry out
Durchgang m passage; (Sport) round; (bei Wahl) ballot; **Durchgangsverkehr** m through traffic

durchgebraten adj well done
durchgefroren adj frozen to the bone

durch|gehen irr vi to go through (durch etw sth); (ausreißen: Pferd) to break loose; (Mensch) to run away; **durchgehend** adj (Zug) through; **~ geöffnet** open all day

durch|halten irr vi to hold out ▷ vt (Tempo) to keep up; **etw ~** (bis zum Schluss) to see sth through

durch|kommen irr vi to get through; (Patient) to pull through

durch|lassen irr vt (jdn) to let through; (Wasser) to let in

durch|lesen irr vt to read through

durchleuchten vt to X-ray
durch|machen vt to go through; (Entwicklung) to undergo; **die Nacht ~** to make a night of it, to have an all-nighter

Durchmesser (-s, -) m diameter
Durchreise f journey through; **auf der ~** passing through; (Güter) in transit; **Durchreisevisum** nt transit visa

durch|reißen irr vt, vi to tear (in two)

durchs kontr von **durch das**
Durchsage (-, -n) f announcement

durchschauen vt (jdn, Lüge) to see through

durch|schlagen irr vr: **sich ~** to struggle through

durch|schneiden irr vt to cut (in two)

Durchschnitt m (Mittelwert) average; **im ~** on average; **durchschnittlich** adj average ▷ adv (im Durchschnitt) on average; **Durchschnittsgeschwindigkeit** f average speed

durch|setzen vt to get through ▷ vr: **sich ~** (Erfolg haben) to succeed; (sich behaupten) to get one's way

durchsichtig adj transparent, see-through

durch|stellen vt (Tel) to put through

durch|streichen irr vt to cross out

durchsuchen vt to search (nach for); **Durchsuchung** f search
durchwachsen adj (Speck) streaky; (fig: mittelmäßig) so-so
Durchwahl f direct dialling; (Nummer) extension

durch|ziehen *irr vt* (*Plan*) to carry through
Durchzug *m* draught

○ SCHLÜSSELWORT

dürfen *unreg vi* 1 (*Erlaubnis haben*) to be allowed to; **ich darf das** I'm allowed to (do that); **darf ich?** may I?; **darf ich ins Kino?** can o may I go to the cinema?; **es darf geraucht werden** you may smoke 2 (*in Verneinungen*) **er darf das nicht** he's not allowed to (do that); **das darf nicht geschehen** that must not happen; **da darf sie sich nicht wundern** that shouldn't surprise her
3 (*in Höflichkeitsformeln*) **darf ich Sie bitten, das zu tun?** may o could I ask you to do that?; **was darf es sein?** what can I do for you?
4 (*können*) **das dürfen Sie mir glauben** you can believe me
5 (*Möglichkeit*) **das dürfte genug sein** that should be enough; **es dürfte Ihnen bekannt sein, dass ...** as you will probably know ...

dürftig *adj* (*ärmlich*) poor; (*unzulänglich*) inadequate
dürr *adj* dried-up; (*Land*) arid; (*mager*) skinny
Durst (-(e)s) *m* thirst; **~ haben** to be thirsty; **durstig** *adj* thirsty
Dusche (-, -n) *f* shower; **duschen** *vi* to have a shower ▷ *vr*: **sich ~** to have a shower; **Duschgel** *nt* shower gel; **Duschvorhang** *m* shower curtain
Düse (-, -n) *f* nozzle; (*Tech*) jet; **Düsenflugzeug** *nt* jet (aircraft)
Dussel (-s, -) *m* (*fam*) dope; **duss(e)lig** *adj* (*fam*) stupid

düster *adj* dark; (*Gedanken, Zukunft*) gloomy
Dutyfreeshop (-s, -s) *m* duty-free shop
Dutzend (-s, -e) *nt* dozen
duzen *vt* to address as "du" ▷ *vr*: **sich ~ (mit jdm)** to address each other as "du", to be on first-name terms
DVD (-, -s) *f abk =* **Digital Versatile Disk** DVD; **DVD-Player** (-s, -) *m* DVD player; **DVD-Rekorder** (-s, -) *m* DVD recorder
dynamisch *adj* dynamic
Dynamo (-s, -s) *m* dynamo
D-Zug *m* fast train

e

Ebbe (-, -n) f low tide
eben adj level; (glatt) smooth
▷ adv just; (bestätigend) exactly
Ebene (-, -n) f plain; (fig) level
ebenfalls adv also, as well;
(Antwort: gleichfalls!) you too;
ebenso adv just as; **~ gut** just as
well; **~ viel** just as much
Eber (-s, -) m boar
EC (-, -s) m abk = **Eurocityzug**
Echo (-s, -s) nt echo
echt adj (Leder, Gold) real, genuine;
ein ~er Verlust a real loss
EC-Karte f = debit card
Ecke (-, -n) f corner; (Math) angle;
an der ~ at the corner; **gleich um
die ~** just round the corner; **eckig**
adj rectangular; **Eckzahn** m
canine
Economyclass (-) f coach
(class), economy class
Ecstasy (-) f (Droge) ecstasy
edel adj noble; **Edelstein** m
precious stone
EDV (-) f abk = **elektronische
Datenverarbeitung** EDP
Efeu (-s) m ivy
Effekt (-s, -e) m effect
egal adj: **das ist ~** it doesn't
matter; **das ist mir ~** I don't care,
it's all the same to me; **~ wie teuer**
no matter how expensive
egoistisch adj selfish
ehe conj before
Ehe (-, -n) f marriage; **Ehefrau** f
wife; (verheiratete Frau) married
woman; **Eheleute** pl married
couple sing
ehemalig adj former; **ehemals**
adv formerly
Ehemann m husband;
(verheirateter Mann) married man;
Ehepaar nt married couple
eher adv (früher) sooner; (lieber)
rather, sooner; (mehr) more; **je ~,
desto besser** the sooner the
better
Ehering m wedding ring
eheste(r, s) adj (früheste) first
▷ adv: **am ~n** (am
wahrscheinlichsten) most likely
Ehre (-, -n) f honour; **ehren** vt
to honour; **ehrenamtlich** adj
voluntary; **Ehrengast** m guest
of honour; **Ehrenwort** nt word
of honour; **~! I** promise; **ich gebe
dir mein ~** I give you my word
ehrgeizig adj ambitious
ehrlich adj honest
Ei (-(e)s, -er) nt egg; **hart
gekochtes/weiches
~** hard-boiled/soft-boiled egg
Eiche (-, -n) f oak (tree); **Eichel**
(-, -n) f acorn
Eichhörnchen nt squirrel
Eid (-(e)s, -e) m oath
Eidechse (-, -n) f lizard
Eierbecher m eggcup; **Eierstock**
m ovary; **Eieruhr** f egg timer
Eifersucht f jealousy;

eifersüchtig adj jealous (auf +akk of)

Eigelb (-(e)s, -) nt egg yolk

eigen adj own; (typisch) characteristic (jdm of sb); (eigenartig) peculiar; **eigenartig** adj peculiar; **Eigenschaft** f quality; (Chem, Phys) property; (Merkmal) characteristic

eigentlich adj actual, real ▷ adv actually, really; **was denken Sie sich ~ dabei?** what on earth do you think you're doing?

Eigentum nt property; **Eigentümer(in)** m(f) owner; **Eigentumswohnung** f owner-occupied flat (Brit), condominium (US)

eignen vr: **sich ~ für** to be suited for; **er würde sich als Lehrer ~** he'd make a good teacher

Eilbrief m express letter, special-delivery letter; **Eile** (-) f hurry; **eilen** vi (dringend sein) to be urgent; **es eilt nicht** there's no hurry; **eilig** adj hurried; (dringlich) urgent; **es ~ haben** to be in a hurry

Eimer (-s, -) m bucket

ein adv: **nicht ~ noch aus wissen** not to know what to do; **~ ~ aus** (Schalter) on - off

ein(e) art a; (vor gesprochenem Vokal) an; **~ Mann** a man; **~ Apfel** an apple; **~e Stunde** an hour; **~ Haus** a house; **(gewisser) Herr Miller** a (certain) Mr Miller; **~es Tages** one day

einander pron one another, each other

ein|arbeiten vt to train ▷ vr: **sich ~** to get used to the work

ein|atmen vt, vi to breathe in

Einbahnstraße f one-way street

ein|bauen vt to build in; (Motor etc) to install, to fit; **Einbauküche** f fitted kitchen

ein|biegen irr vi to turn (in +akk into)

ein|bilden vt: **sich** (dat) **etw ~** to imagine sth

ein|brechen irr vi (in Haus) to break in; (Dach etc) to fall in, to collapse; **Einbrecher(in)** (-s, -) m(f) burglar

ein|bringen irr vt (Ernte) to bring in; (Gewinn) to yield; **jdm etw ~** to bring (o earn) sb sth ▷ vr: **sich in** (akk) **etw ~** to make a contribution to sth

Einbruch m (Haus) break-in, burglary; **bei ~ der Nacht** at nightfall

Einbürgerung f naturalization

ein|checken vt to check in

ein|cremen vt to put some cream on ▷ vr: **sich ~** to put some cream on

eindeutig adj clear, obvious ▷ adv clearly; **~ falsch** clearly wrong

ein|dringen irr vi (gewaltsam) to force one's way in (in +akk -to); (in Haus) to break in (in +akk -to); (Gas, Wasser) to get in (in +akk -to)

Eindruck m impression; **großen ~ auf jdn machen** to make a big impression on sb

eine(r, s) pron one; (jemand) someone; **~r meiner Freunde** one of my friends; **~r nach dem andern** one after the other

eineiig adj (Zwillinge) identical

eineinhalb num one and a half

einerseits adv on the one hand

einfach adj (nicht kompliziert) simple; (Mensch) ordinary; (Essen) plain; (nicht mehrfach) single; **~e Fahrkarte** single ticket (Brit), one-way ticket (US) ▷ adv simply; (nicht mehrfach) once

Einfahrt f (Vorgang) driving in; (eines Zuges) arrival; (Ort) entrance

Einfall m (Idee) idea; **ein|fallen** irr vi (Licht etc) to fall in; (einstürzen) to collapse; **ihm fiel ein, dass ...** it occurred to him that ...; **ich werde mir etwas ~ lassen** I'll think of something; **was fällt Ihnen ein!** what do you think you're doing?

Einfamilienhaus nt detached house

einfarbig adj all one colour; (Stoff etc) self-coloured

Einfluss m influence

ein|frieren irr vt, vi to freeze

ein|fügen vt to fit in; (zusätzlich) to add; (Inform) to insert; **Einfügetaste** f (Inform) insert key

Einfuhr (-, -en) f import; **Einfuhrbestimmungen** pl import regulations pl

ein|führen vt to introduce; (Ware) to import; **Einführung** f introduction

Eingabe f (Dateneingabe) input; **Eingabetaste** f (Inform) return (o enter) key

Eingang m entrance; **Eingangshalle** f entrance hall, lobby (US)

ein|geben irr vt (Daten etc) to enter, to key in

eingebildet adj imaginary; (eitel) arrogant

Eingeborene(r) mf native

ein|gehen irr vi (Sendung, Geld) to come in, to arrive; (Tier, Pflanze) to die; (Stoff) to shrink; **auf etw** (akk) **~ to** agree to sth; **auf jdn ~** to respond to sb ▷ vt (Vertrag) to enter into; (Wette) to make; (Risiko) to take

eingelegt adj (in Essig) pickled

eingeschaltet adj (switched) on

eingeschlossen adj locked in; (inklusive) included

ein|gewöhnen vr: **sich ~** to settle in

ein|gießen irr vt to pour

ein|greifen irr vi to intervene; **Eingriff** m intervention; (Operation) operation

ein|halten irr vt (Versprechen etc) to keep

einheimisch adj (Produkt, Mannschaft) local; **Einheimische(r)** mf local

Einheit f (Geschlossenheit) unity; (Maß) unit; **einheitlich** adj uniform

ein|holen vt (Vorsprung aufholen) to catch up with; (Verspätung) to make up for; (Rat, Erlaubnis) to ask for

Einhorn nt unicorn

einhundert num one (o a) hundred

einig adj (vereint) united; **sich** (dat) **~ sein** to agree

einige pron pl some; (mehrere) several ▷ adj some; **nach ~er Zeit** after some time; **~e hundert Euro** some hundred euros

einigen vr: **sich ~** to agree (auf +akk on)

einigermaßen adv fairly, quite; (leidlich) reasonably

einiges pron something; (ziemlich viel) quite a bit; (mehreres) a few things; **es gibt noch ~ zu tun** there's still a fair bit to do

Einkauf m purchase; **Einkäufe** (machen) (to do one's) shopping; **ein|kaufen** vt to buy ▷ vi to go shopping; **Einkaufsbummel** m shopping trip; **Einkaufstasche** f, **Einkaufstüte** f shopping bag; **Einkaufswagen** m shopping trolley (Brit) (o cart (US)); **Einkaufszentrum** nt shopping centre (Brit) (o mall (US))

ein|klemmen vt to jam; **er hat sich** (dat) **den Finger eingeklemmt** he got his finger caught

Einkommen (-s, -) nt income

ein|laden *irr vt* (*jdn*) to invite; (*Gegenstände*) to load; **jdn zum Essen ~** to take sb out for a meal; **ich lade dich ein** (*bezahle*) it's my treat; **Einladung** *f* invitation

Einlass (*-es, Einlässe*) *m* admittance; **~ ab 18 Uhr** doors open at 6 pm; **ein|lassen** *irr vr* **sich mit jdm/auf etw ~** to get involved with sb/sth

ein|leben *vr*: **sich ~** to settle down

ein|legen *vt* (*Film etc*) to put in; (*marinieren*) to marinate; **eine Pause ~** to take a break

ein|leiten *vt* to start; (*Maßnahmen*) to introduce; (*Geburt*) to induce; **Einleitung** *f* introduction; (*von Geburt*) induction

ein|leuchten *vi*: **jdm ~** to be (*o* become) clear to sb; **einleuchtend** *adj* clear

ein|loggen *vi* (*Inform*) to log on (*o* in)

ein|lösen *vt* (*Scheck*) to cash; (*Gutschein*) to redeem; (*Versprechen*) to keep

einmal *adv* once; (*früher*) before; (*in Zukunft*) some day; (*erstens*) first; **~ im Jahr** once a year; **noch ~** once more, again; **ich war schon ~ hier** I've been here before; **warst du schon ~ in London?** have you ever been to London?; **nicht ~** not even; **auf ~** suddenly; (*gleichzeitig*) at once; **einmalig** *adj* unique; (*einmal geschehend*) single; (*prima*) fantastic

ein|mischen *vr*: **sich ~** to interfere (*in +akk* with)

Einnahme (*-, -n*) *f* (*Geld*) takings *pl*; (*von Medizin*) taking; **ein|nehmen** *irr vt* (*Medizin*) to take; (*Geld*) to take in; (*Standpunkt, Raum*) to take up; **jdn für sich ~** to win sb over

ein|ordnen *vt* to put in order; (*klassifizieren*) to classify; (*Akten*) to file ▷ *vr*: **sich ~** (*Auto*) to get in lane; **sich rechts/links ~** to get into the right/left lane

ein|packen *vt* to pack (up)

ein|parken *vt, vi* to park

ein|planen *vt* to allow for

ein|prägen *vt* **sich** (*dat*) **etw ~** to remember (*o* memorize) sth

ein|räumen *vt* (*Bücher, Geschirr*) to put away; (*Schrank*) to put things in

ein|reden *vt*: **jdm/sich etw ~** to talk sb/oneself into (believing) sth

ein|reiben *irr vt*: **sich mit etw ~** to rub sth into one's skin

ein|reichen *vt* to hand in; (*Antrag*) to submit

Einreise *f* entry; **Einreisebestimmungen** *pl* entry regulations *pl*; **Einreiseerlaubnis** *f*, **Einreisegenehmigung** *f* entry permit; **ein|reisen** *vi* to enter (*in ein Land* a country); **Einreisevisum** *nt* entry visa

ein|renken *vt* (*Arm, Bein*) to set

ein|richten *vt* (*Wohnung*) to furnish; (*gründen*) to establish, to set up; (*arrangieren*) to arrange ▷ *vr*: **sich ~** (*in Haus*) to furnish one's home; (*sich vorbereiten*) to prepare oneself (*auf +akk* for); (*sich anpassen*) to adapt (*auf +akk* to); **Einrichtung** *f* (*Wohnung*) furnishings *pl*; (*öffentliche Anstalt*) institution; (*Schwimmbad etc*) facility

eins *num* one; **Eins** (*-, -en*) *f* one; (*Schulnote*) ~ A

einsam *adj* lonely

ein|sammeln *vt* to collect

Einsatz *m* (*Teil*) insert; (*Verwendung*) use; (*Spieleinsatz*) stake; (*Risiko*) risk; (*Mus*) entry

ein|schalten *vt* (*Elek*) to switch on

ein|schätzen vt to estimate, to assess

ein|schenken vt to pour

ein|schiffen vr: **sich ~** to embark (nach for)

ein|schlafen irr vi to fall asleep, to drop off; **mir ist der Arm eingeschlafen** my arm's gone to sleep

ein|schlagen irr vt (Fenster) to smash; (Zähne, Schädel) to smash in; (Weg, Richtung) to take ▷ vi to hit (in etw akk sth, auf jdn sb); (Blitz) to strike; (Anklang finden) to be a success

ein|schließen irr vt (jdn) to lock in; (Gegenstand) to lock away; (umgeben) to surround; (fig: beinhalten) to include; **einschließlich** adv inclusive ▷ prep +gen including; **von Montag bis ~ Freitag** from Monday up to and including Friday, Monday through Friday (US)

ein|schränken vt to limit, to restrict; (verringern) to cut down on ▷ vr: **sich ~** to cut down (on expenditure)

ein|schreiben irr vr: **sich ~** to register; (Schule) to enrol; **Einschreiben** (-s, -) nt registered letter; **etw per ~ schicken** to send sth by special delivery

ein|schüchtern vt to intimidate

ein|sehen irr vt (verstehen) to see; (Fehler) to recognize; (Akten) to have a look at

einseitig adj one-sided

ein|senden irr vt to send in

ein|setzen vt to put in; (in Amt) to appoint; (Geld) to stake; (verwenden) to use ▷ vi (beginnen) to set in; (Mus) to enter, to come in ▷ vr: **sich ~** to work hard; **sich für jdn/etw ~** to support sb/sth

Einsicht f insight; **zu der**

~ kommen, dass ... to come to realize that ...

ein|sperren vt to lock up

ein|spielen vt (Geld) to bring in

ein|springen irr vi (aushelfen) to step in (für for)

Einspruch m objection (gegen to)

einspurig adj single-lane

Einstand m (Tennis) deuce

ein|stecken vt to pocket; (Elek: Stecker) to plug in; (Brief) to post, to mail (US); (mitnehmen) to take; (hinnehmen) to swallow

ein|steigen irr vi (in Auto) to get in; (in Bus, Zug, Flugzeug) to get on; (sich beteiligen) to get involved

ein|stellen vt (beenden) to stop; (Geräte) to adjust; (Kamera) to focus; (Sender, Radio) to tune in; (unterstellen) to put; (in Firma) to employ, to take on ▷ vr: **sich auf jdn/etw ~** to adapt to sb/prepare oneself for sth; **Einstellung** f (von Gerät) adjustment; (von Kamera) focusing; (von Arbeiter) taking on; (Meinung) attitude

ein|stürzen vi to collapse

eintägig adj one-day

ein|tauschen vt to exchange (gegen for)

eintausend num one (o a) thousand

ein|teilen vt (in Teile) to divide (up) (in +akk into); (Zeit) to organize

eintönig adj monotonous

Eintopf m stew

ein|tragen irr vt (in eine Liste) to put down, to enter ▷ vr: **sich ~** to put one's name down, to register

ein|treffen irr vi to happen; (ankommen) to arrive

ein|treten irr vi (hineingehen) to enter (in etw akk sth); (in Klub, Partei) to join (in etw akk sth); (sich ereignen) to occur; **~ für** to support; **Eintritt** m admission; **„~ frei"**

"admission free"; **Eintrittskarte** f (entrance) ticket; **Eintrittspreis** m admission charge

einverstanden interj okay, all right ▷ adj: **mit etwas ~ sein** to agree to sth, to accept sth

Einwanderer m, **Einwanderin** f immigrant; **ein|wandern** vi to immigrate

einwandfrei adj perfect, flawless

Einwegflasche f non-returnable bottle

ein|weichen vt to soak

ein|weihen vt (Gebäude) to inaugurate, to open; **jdn in etw** (akk) **~ to let sb in on sth;** **Einweihungsparty** f house-warming party

ein|werfen irr vt (Ball, Bemerkung etc) to throw in; (Brief) to post, to mail (US); (Geld) to put in, to insert; (Fenster) to smash

ein|wickeln vt to wrap up; (fig) **jdn ~** to take sb in

Einwohner(in) (-s, -) m(f) inhabitant; **Einwohnermeldeamt** nt registration office for residents

Einwurf m (Öffnung) slot; (Sport) throw-in

Einzahl f singular

ein|zahlen vt to pay in (auf ein Konto -to an account)

Einzel (-s, -) nt (Tennis) singles sing; **Einzelbett** nt single bed; **Einzelfahrschein** m single ticket (Brit), one-way ticket (US); **Einzelgänger(in)** m(f) loner; **Einzelhandel** m retail trade; **Einzelkind** nt only child

einzeln adj individual; (getrennt) separate; (einzig) single; **~e ...** several ...; some ...; **der/die Einzelne** the individual; **im Einzelnen** in detail ▷ adv separately; (verpacken, aufführen) individually; **~ angeben** to specify; **~ eintreten** to enter one

by one

Einzelzimmer nt single room; **Einzelzimmerzuschlag** m single-room supplement

ein|ziehen irr vt: **den Kopf ~** to duck ▷ vi (in ein Haus) to move in

einzig adj only; (einzeln) single; (einzigartig) unique; **kein ~er Fehler** not a single mistake; **das Einzige** the only thing; **der/die Einzige** the only person ▷ adv only; **die ~ richtige Lösung** the only correct solution; **einzigartig** adj unique

Eis (-es, -) nt ice; (Speiseeis) ice-cream; **Eisbahn** f ice(skating) rink; **Eisbär** m polar bear; **Eisbecher** m (ice-cream) sundae; **Eisberg** m iceberg; **Eisbergsalat** m iceberg lettuce; **Eiscafé** nt, **Eisdiele** f ice-cream parlour

Eisen (-s, -) nt iron; **Eisenbahn** f railway (Brit), railroad (US); **eisern** adj iron

eisgekühlt adj chilled; **Eishockey** nt ice hockey; **Eiskaffee** m iced coffee; **eiskalt** adj ice-cold; (Temperatur) freezing; **Eiskunstlauf** m figure skating; **eis|laufen** irr vi to skate; **Eisschokolade** f iced chocolate; **Eisschrank** m fridge, ice-box (US); **Eistee** m iced tea; **Eiswürfel** m ice cube; **Eiszapfen** m icicle

eitel adj vain

Eiter (-s) m pus

Eiweiß (-es, -e) nt egg white; (Chem, Bio) protein

ekelhaft, ek(e)lig adj disgusting, revolting; **ekeln** vr: **sich ~** to be disgusted (vor +dat at)

EKG (-s, -s) nt abk = **Elektrokardiogramm** ECG

Ekzem (-s, -e) nt (Med) eczema

elastisch adj elastic

Elch (-(e)s, -e) m elk; (nordamerikanischer) moose

Elefant m elephant

elegant adj elegant

Elektriker(in) (-s, -) m(f) electrician; **elektrisch** adj electric; **Elektrizität** f electricity; **Elektroauto** nt electric car; **Elektrogerät** nt electrical appliance; **Elektrogeschäft** nt electrical shop; **Elektroherd** m electric cooker; **Elektromotor** m electric motor; **Elektronik** f electronics sing; **elektronisch** adj electronic; **Elektrorasierer** (-s, -) m electric razor

Element (-s, -e) nt element

elend adj miserable; **Elend** (-(e)s) nt misery

elf num eleven; **Elf** (-, -en) f (Sport) eleven

Elfenbein nt ivory

Elfmeter m (Sport) penalty (kick)

elfte(r, s) adj eleventh; siehe auch **dritte**

Ell(en)bogen m elbow

Elster (-, -n) f magpie

Eltern pl parents pl; **Elternteil** m parent

EM f abk = **Europameisterschaft** European Championship(s)

E-Mail (-, -s) f (Inform) e-mail; **jdm eine ~ schicken** to e-mail sb, to send sb an e-mail; **jdm etwas per ~ schicken** to e-mail sth to sb; **E-Mail-Adresse** f e-mail address; **e-mailen** vt to e-mail

Emoticon (-s, -s) nt emoticon

emotional adj emotional

empfahl imperf von **empfehlen**

empfand imperf von **empfinden**

Empfang (-(e)s, Empfänge) m reception; (Erhalten) receipt; **in ~ nehmen** to receive; **empfangen** (empfing, empfangen) vt to receive; **Empfänger(in)** (-s, -) m(f) recipient; (Adressat) addressee ▷ m (Tech) receiver; **Empfängnisverhütung** f contraception; **Empfangshalle** f reception area

empfehlen (empfahl, empfohlen) vt to recommend; **Empfehlung** f recommendation

empfinden (empfand, empfunden) vt to feel; **empfindlich** adj (Mensch) sensitive; (Stelle) sore; (reizbar) touchy; (Material) delicate

empfing imperf von **empfangen**

empfohlen pp von **empfehlen**

empfunden pp von **empfinden**

empört adj indignant (über +akk at)

Ende (-s, -n) nt end; (Film, Roman) ending; **am ~** at the end; (schließlich) in the end; **~ Mai** at the end of May; **~ der Achtzigerjahre** in the late eighties; **sie ist ~ zwanzig** she's in her late twenties; **zu ~** over, finished; **enden** vi to end; **der Zug endet hier** this service (o train) terminates here; **endgültig** adj final; (Beweis) conclusive

Endivie f endive

endlich adv at last, finally; (am Ende) eventually; **Endspiel** nt final; (Endrunde) finals pl; **Endstation** f terminus; **Endung** f ending

Energie f energy; **~ sparend** energy-saving; **Energiebedarf** m energy requirement; **Energieverbrauch** m energy consumption

energisch adj (entschlossen) forceful

eng adj narrow; (Kleidung) tight; (fig: Freundschaft, Verhältnis) close; **das wird ~** (fam: zeitlich) we're running out of time, it's getting tight ▷ adv: **~ befreundet sein** to be close friends

engagieren vt to engage ▷ vr: **sich ~** to commit oneself, to be committed (für to)

Engel (-s, -) m angel

England nt England;
Engländer(in) (-s, -) m(f)
Englishman/ -woman; **die ~** pl
the English pl; **englisch** adj English;
(Gastr) rare; **Englisch** nt English;
ins ~e übersetzen to translate
into English

Enkel (-s, -) m grandson; **Enkelin**
f granddaughter

enorm adj enormous; (fig)
tremendous

Entbindung f (Med) delivery

entdecken vt to discover;
Entdeckung f discovery

Ente (-, -n) f duck

Enter-Taste f (Inform) enter (o
return) key

entfernen vt to remove; (Inform)
to delete ▷ vr: **sich ~** to go away;
entfernt adj distant; **15 km von X
~** 15 km away from X; **20 km
voneinander ~** 20 km apart;
Entfernung f distance; **aus der
~** from a distance

entführen vt to kidnap;
Entführer(in) m(f) kidnapper;
Entführung f kidnapping

entgegen prep +dat contrary to
▷ adv towards; **dem Wind
~** against the wind;
entgegengesetzt adj (Richtung)
opposite; (Meinung) opposing;
entgegen|kommen irr vi: **jdm
~** to come to meet sb; (fig) to
accommodate sb;
entgegenkommend adj (Verkehr)
oncoming; (fig) obliging

entgegnen vt to reply (auf +akk
to)

entgehen irr vi: **jdm ~** to escape
sb's notice; **sich** (dat) **etw ~ lassen**
to miss sth

entgleisen vi (Eisenb) to be
derailed; (fig: Mensch) to
misbehave

Enthaarungscreme f hair
remover

enthalten irr vt (Behälter) to
contain; (Preis) to include ▷ vr:
sich ~ to abstain (gen from)

entkoffeiniert adj
decaffeinated

entkommen irr vi to escape

entkorken vt to uncork

entlang prep +akk o dat – **dem
Fluss, den Fluss ~** along the river;
entlang|gehen irr vi to walk
along

entlassen irr vt (Patient) to
discharge; (Arbeiter) to dismiss

entlasten vt: **jdn ~** (Arbeit
abnehmen) to relieve sb of some of
his/her work

entmutigen vt to discourage

entnehmen irr vt to take (dat from)

entrahmt adj (Milch) skimmed

entschädigen vt to
compensate; **Entschädigung** f
compensation

entscheiden irr vt, vi to decide
▷ vr: **sich ~** to decide; **sich
für/gegen etw ~** to decide
on/against sth; **wir haben uns
entschieden, nicht zu gehen** we
decided not to go; **das
entscheidet sich morgen** that'll
be decided tomorrow;
entscheidend adj (Stimme)
casting; (Frage, Problem) crucial;
Entscheidung f decision

entschließen irr vr: **sich ~** to
decide (zu, für on), to make up
one's mind; **Entschluss** m
decision

entschuldigen vt to excuse
▷ vr: **sich ~** to apologize; **sich bei
jdm für etw ~** to apologize to sb
for sth ▷ vi: **entschuldige!, ~ Sie!**
(vor einer Frage) excuse me;
(Verzeihung!) (I'm) sorry, excuse me
(US); **Entschuldigung** f apology;

entsetzlich | 68

(*Grund*) excuse; **jdn um ~ bitten** to apologize to sb; **~!** (*bei Zusammenstoß*) (I'm) sorry, excuse me (*US*); (*vor einer Frage*) excuse me; (*wenn man etw nicht verstanden hat*) (I beg your) pardon?

entsetzlich *adj* dreadful, appalling

entsorgen *vt* to dispose of

entspannen *vt* (*Körper*) to relax; (*Pol: Lage*) to ease ▷ *vr:* **sich ~** to relax; (*fam*) to chill out; **Entspannung** *f* relaxation

entsprechen *irr vi* +*dat* to correspond to; (*Anforderungen, Wünschen etc*) to comply with; **entsprechend** *adj* appropriate ▷ *adv* accordingly ▷ *prep* +*dat* according to, in accordance with

entstehen *irr vi* (*Schwierigkeiten*) to arise; (*gebaut werden*) to be built; (*hergestellt werden*) to be created

enttäuschen *vt* to disappoint; **Enttäuschung** *f* disappointment

entweder *conj:* **~ ... oder ...** either ... or ...; **~ oder!** take it or leave it

entwerfen *irr vt* (*Möbel, Kleider*) to design; (*Plan, Vertrag*) to draft

entwerten *vt* to devalue; (*Fahrschein*) to cancel; **Entwerter** (*-s, -*) *m* ticket-cancelling machine

entwickeln *vt* (*a. Foto*) to develop; (*Mut, Energie*) to show, to display ▷ *vr:* **sich ~** to develop; **Entwicklung** *f* development; (*Foto*) developing; **Entwicklungshelfer(in)** (*-s, -*) *m(f)* development worker; **Entwicklungsland** *nt* developing country

Entwurf *m* outline; (*Design*) design; (*Vertragsentwurf*) draft

entzückend *adj* delightful, charming

Entzug *m* withdrawal; (*Behandlung*) detox;

Entzugserscheinung *f* withdrawal symptom

entzünden *vr:* **sich ~** to catch fire; (*Med*) to become inflamed; **Entzündung** *f* (*Med*) inflammation

Epidemie (*-, -n*) *f* epidemic

Epilepsie (*-, -n*) *f* epilepsy

epilieren *vt* to remove body hair, to depilate; **Epiliergerät** *nt* Ladyshave®

er *pron* (*Person*) he; (*Sache*) it; **er ist's** it's him; **wo ist mein Mantel? — ~ ist ...** where's my coat? — it's ...

Erbe (*-n, -n*) *m* heir ▷ (*-s*) *nt* inheritance; (*fig*) heritage; **erben** *vt* to inherit; **Erbin** *f* heiress; **erblich** *adj* hereditary

erblicken *vt* to catch sight of

erbrechen *irr vt* to vomit ▷ *vr:* **sich ~** to vomit; **Erbrechen** *nt* vomiting

Erbschaft *f* inheritance

Erbse (*-, -n*) *f* pea

Erdapfel *m* potato; **Erdbeben** *nt* earthquake; **Erdbeere** *f* strawberry; **Erde** (*-, -n*) *f* (*Planet*) earth; (*Boden*) ground; **Erdgas** *nt* natural gas; **Erdgeschoss** *nt* ground floor (*Brit*), first floor (*US*); **Erdkunde** *f* geography; **Erdnuss** *f* peanut; **Erdöl** *nt* (mineral) oil; **Erdrutsch** *m* landslide; **Erdteil** *m* continent

ereignen *vr:* **sich ~** to happen, to take place; **Ereignis** *nt* event

erfahren *irr vt* to learn, to find out; (*erleben*) to experience ▷ *adj* experienced; **Erfahrung** *f* experience

erfinden *irr vt* to invent; **erfinderisch** *adj* inventive, creative; **Erfindung** *f* invention

Erfolg (*-(e)s, -e*) *m* success; (*Folge*) result; **~ versprechend** promising; **viel ~!** good luck;

erfolglos adj unsuccessful;
erfolgreich adj successful
erforderlich adj necessary
erforschen vt to explore; (untersuchen) investigate
erfreulich adj pleasing, pleasant; (Nachricht) good;
erfreulicherweise adv fortunately
erfrieren irr vi to freeze to death; (Pflanzen) to be killed by frost
Erfrischung f refreshment
erfüllen vt (Raum) to fill; (Bitte, Wunsch etc) to fulfil ▷ vr: sich ~ to come true
ergänzen vt (hinzufügen) to add; (vervollständigen) to complete ▷ vr: sich ~ to complement one another; **Ergänzung** f completion; (Zusatz) supplement
ergeben irr vt (Betrag) to come to; (zum Ergebnis haben) to result in ▷ irr vr: sich ~ to surrender; (folgen) to result (aus from) ▷ adj devoted; (demütig) humble
Ergebnis nt result
ergreifen irr vt to seize; (Beruf) to take up; (Maßnahme, Gelegenheit) to take; (rühren) to move
erhalten irr vt (bekommen) to receive; (bewahren) to preserve; **gut ~ sein** to be in good condition; **erhältlich** adj available
erheblich adj considerable
erhitzen vt to heat (up)
erhöhen vt to raise; (verstärken) to increase ▷ vr: sich ~ to increase
erholen vr: sich ~ to recover; (sich ausruhen) to have a rest; **erholsam** adj restful; **Erholung** f recovery; (Entspannung) relaxation
erinnern vt to remind (an +akk of) ▷ vr: sich ~ to remember (an etw akk sth); **Erinnerung** f memory; (Andenken) souvenir;

(Mahnung) reminder
erkälten vr: sich ~ to catch a cold; **erkältet** adj: (stark) ~ sein to have a (bad) cold; **Erkältung** f cold
erkennen irr vt to recognize; (sehen, verstehen) to see; ~, dass ... to realize that ...; **erkenntlich** adj: sich ~ zeigen to show one's appreciation
Erker (-s, -) m bay
erklären vt to explain; (kundtun) to declare; **Erklärung** f explanation; (Aussage) declaration
erkundigen vr: sich ~ to enquire (nach about)
erlauben vt to allow, to permit; **jdm ~, etw zu tun** to allow (o permit) sb to do sth; **sich (dat) etw ~** to permit oneself sth; ~ **Sie(, dass ich rauche)?** do you mind (if I smoke)?; **was ~ Sie sich?** what do you think you're doing?; **Erlaubnis** f permission
Erläuterung f explanation; (zu Text) comment
erleben vt to experience; (schöne Tage etc) to have; (Schlimmes) to go through; (miterleben) to witness; (noch miterleben) to live to see; **Erlebnis** nt experience
erledigen vt (Angelegenheit, Aufgabe) to deal with; (fam: ruinieren) to finish; **erledigt** adj (beendet) finished; (gelöst) dealt with; (fam: erschöpft) whacked, knackered (Brit)
erleichtert adj relieved
Erlös (-es, -e) m proceeds pl
ermahnen vt (warnend) to warn
ermäßigt adj reduced; **Ermäßigung** f reduction
ermitteln vt to find out; (Täter) to trace ▷ vi (Jur) to investigate
ermöglichen vt to make possible (dat for)
ermorden vt to murder

ermüdend adj tiring
ermutigen vt to encourage
ernähren vt to feed; (Familie)
to support ▷ vr: **sich ~** to
support oneself; **sich ~ von** to
live on; **Ernährung** f (Essen)
food; **Ernährungsberater(in)**
m(f) nutritional (o dietary)
adviser
erneuern vt to renew;
(restaurieren) to restore; (renovieren)
to renovate; (auswechseln) to
replace
ernst adj serious ▷ adv: **jdn/etw
~ nehmen** take sb/sth seriously;
Ernst (-es) m seriousness; **das ist
mein ~** I'm quite serious; **im ~?**
seriously?; **ernsthaft** adj serious
▷ adv seriously
Ernte (-, -n) f harvest;
Erntedankfest nt harvest festival
(Brit), Thanksgiving (Day) (US: 4.
Donnerstag im November); **ernten**
vt to harvest; (Lob etc) to earn
erobern vt to conquer
eröffnen vt to open; **Eröffnung**
f opening
erogen adj erogenous
erotisch adj erotic
erpressen vt (jdn) to blackmail;
(Geld etc) to extort; **Erpressung** f
blackmail; (von Geld) extortion
erraten irr vt to guess
erregen vt to excite; (sexuell) to
arouse; (ärgern) to annoy;
(hervorrufen) to arouse ▷ vr: **sich
~ to get worked up; **Erreger** (-s, -)
m (Med) germ; (Virus) virus
erreichbar adj: **~ sein** to be
within reach; (Person) to be
available; **das Stadtzentrum ist
zu Fuß/mit dem Wagen leicht
~** the city centre is within easy
walking/driving distance;
erreichen vt to reach; (Zug etc) to
catch
Ersatz (-es) m replacement; (auf

Zeit) substitute; (Ausgleich)
compensation; **Ersatzreifen** m
(Auto) spare tyre; **Ersatzteil** nt
spare (part)
erscheinen irr vi to appear;
(wirken) to seem
erschöpft adj exhausted;
Erschöpfung f exhaustion
erschrecken vt to frighten
▷ (erschrak, erschrocken) vi to get a
fright; **erschreckend** adj
alarming; **erschrocken** adj
frightened
erschwinglich adj affordable
ersetzen vt to replace; (Auslagen)
to reimburse

SCHLÜSSELWORT

erst adv 1 first; **mach erst mal die
Arbeit fertig** finish your work
first; **wenn du das erst mal
hinter dir hast** once you've got
that behind you
2 (nicht früher als, nur) only; (nicht
bis) not till; **erst gestern** only
yesterday; **erst morgen** not until
tomorrow; **erst als** only when, not
until; **wir fahren erst später**
we're not going until later; **er ist
(gerade) erst angekommen** he's
only just arrived
3 **wäre er doch erst zurück!** if
only he were back!

erstatten vt (Kosten) to refund;
Bericht ~ to report (über +akk on);
Anzeige gegen jdn ~ to report sb
to the police
erstaunlich adj astonishing;
erstaunt adj surprised
erstbeste(r, s) adj: **das ~ Hotel**
any old hotel; **der Erstbeste** just
anyone
erste(r, s) adj first; siehe auch
dritte; **zum ~n Mal** for the first
time; **er wurde Erster** he came

first; **auf den ~n Blick** at first sight

erstens adv first(ly), in the first place

ersticken vi (Mensch) to suffocate; **in Arbeit ~** to be snowed under with work

erstklassig adj first-class;

erstmals adv for the first time

erstrecken vr: **sich ~** to extend, to stretch (auf +akk to; über +akk over)

ertappen vt to catch

erteilen vt (Rat, Erlaubnis) to give

Ertrag (-(e)s, Erträge) m yield; (Gewinn) proceeds pl; **ertragen** vt (Schmerzen) to bear, to stand; (dulden) to put up with; **erträglich** adj bearable; (nicht zu schlecht) tolerable

ertrinken irr vi to drown

erwachsen adj grown-up; **~ werden** to grow up; **Erwachsene(r)** mf adult, grown-up

erwähnen vt to mention

erwarten vt to expect; (warten auf) to wait for; **ich kann den Sommer kaum ~** I can hardly wait for the summer

erwerbstätig adj employed

erwidern vt to reply; (Gruß, Besuch) to return

erwischen vt (fam) to catch (bei etw doing sth)

erwünscht adj desired; (willkommen) welcome

Erz (-es, -e) nt ore

erzählen vt to tell (jdm etw sb sth); **Erzählung** f story, tale

erzeugen vt to produce; (Strom) to generate; **Erzeugnis** nt product

erziehen irr vt to bring up; (geistig) to educate; (Tier) to train; **Erzieher(in)** (-s, -) m(f) educator; (Kindergarten) (nursery school)

teacher; **Erziehung** f upbringing; (Bildung) education

es pron (Sache, im Nom und Akk) it; (Baby, Tier) he/she; **ich bin ~** it's me; **~ ist kalt** it's cold; **~ gibt ...** there is .../there are ...; **ich hoffe ~** I hope so; **ich kann ~** I can do it

Escape-Taste f (Inform) escape key

Esel (-s, -) m donkey

Espresso (-s, -) m espresso

essbar adj edible; **essen** (aß, gegessen) vt, vi to eat; **zu Mittag/Abend ~** to have lunch/dinner; **was gibt's zu ~?** what's for lunch/dinner?; **~ gehen** to eat out; **gegessen sein** (fig, fam) to be history; **Essen** (-s, -) nt (Mahlzeit) meal; (Nahrung) food

Essig (-s, -e) m vinegar

Esslöffel m dessert spoon; **Esszimmer** nt dining room

Estland nt Estonia

Etage (-, -n) f floor, storey; **in** (o **auf**) **der ersten ~** on the first (Brit) (o second US)) floor; **Etagenbett** nt bunk bed

Etappe (-, -n) f stage

ethnisch adj ethnic

Etikett (-(e)s, -e) nt label

etliche pron pl several, quite a few; **etliches** pron quite a lot

etwa adv (ungefähr) about; (vielleicht) perhaps; (beispielsweise) for instance

etwas pron something; (verneinend, fragend) anything; (ein wenig) a little; **~ Neues** something/anything new; **~ zu essen** something to eat; **~ Salz** some salt; **wenn ich noch ~ tun kann ...** if I can do anything else ...; ▷ adv a bit, a little; **~ mehr** a little more

EU (-) f abk = **Europäische Union** EU

euch pron akk, dat von **ihr**; you, (to)

you; **~ (selbst)** *(reflexiv)* yourselves; **wo kann ich ~ treffen?** where can I meet you?; **sie schickt es ~** she'll send it to you; **ein Freund von ~** a friend of yours; **setzt ~ bitte** please sit down; **habt ihr ~ amüsiert?** did you enjoy yourselves?

euer *pron (adjektivisch)* your; **~ David** *(am Briefende)* Yours, David ▷ *pron gen von* **ihr**; of you; **euere(r, s)** *pron siehe* **eure**

Eule *(-, -n) f* owl

eure(r, s) *pron (substantivisch)* yours; **das ist ~** that's yours; **euretwegen** *adv (wegen euch)* because of you; *(euch zuliebe)* for your sake; *(um euch)* about you

Euro *(-, -) m (Währung)* euro; **Eurocent** *m* eurocent; **Eurocity** *(-(s), -s) m*, **Eurocityzug** *m* European Intercity train; **Europa** *(-s) nt* Europe; **Europäer(in)** *(-s, -) m(f)* European; **europäisch** *adj* European; **Europäische Union** European Union; **Europameister(in)** *m(f)* European champion; *(Mannschaft)* European champions *pl*; **Europaparlament** *nt* European Parliament

Euter *(-s, -) nt* udder

evangelisch *adj* Protestant

eventuell *adj* possible ▷ *adv* possibly, perhaps

ewig *adj* eternal; **er hat ~ gebraucht** it took him ages; **Ewigkeit** *f* eternity

Ex *mf* ex

Ex- *in zW* ex-, former; **~frau** ex-wife; **~freund** *m* ex-boyfriend; **~minister** former minister

exakt *adj* precise

Examen *(-s, -) nt* exam

Exemplar *(-s, -e) nt* specimen; *(Buch)* copy

Exil *(-s, -e) nt* exile

Existenz *f* existence; *(Unterhalt)* livelihood, living; **existieren** *vi* to exist

exklusiv *adj* exclusive; **exklusive** *adv, prep +gen* excluding

exotisch *adj* exotic

Experte *(-n, -n) m*, **Expertin** *f* expert

explodieren *vi* to explode; **Explosion** *f* explosion

Export *(-(e)s, -e) m* export; **exportieren** *vt* to export

Express *(-es) m*, **Expresszug** *m* express (train)

extra *adj inv (fam: gesondert)* separate; *(zusätzlich)* extra ▷ *adv (gesondert)* separately; *(speziell)* specially; *(absichtlich)* on purpose; **Extra** *(-s, -s) nt* extra

extrem *adj* extreme ▷ *adv* extreme; **~ kalt** extremely cold

exzellent *adj* excellent

Eyeliner *(-s, -) m* eyeliner

f

fabelhaft adj fabulous, marvellous

Fabrik f factory

Fach (-(e)s, Fächer) nt compartment; (Schulfach, Sachgebiet) subject; **Facharzt** m, **Fachärztin** f specialist; **Fachausdruck** (-s, Fachausdrücke) m technical term

Fächer (-s, -) m fan

Fachfrau f specialist, expert; **Fachmann** (-leute) m specialist, expert; **Fachwerkhaus** nt half-timbered house

Fackel (-, -n) f torch

fad(e) adj (Essen) bland; (langweilig) dull

Faden (-s, Fäden) m thread

fähig adj capable (zu, gen of); **Fähigkeit** f ability

Fahndung f search

Fahne (-, -n) f flag

Fahrausweis m ticket

Fahrbahn f road; (Spur) lane

Fähre (-, -n) f ferry

fahren (fuhr, gefahren) vt to drive; (Rad) to ride; (befördern) to drive, to take; **50 km/h ~** to drive at (o do) 50 kph ▷ vi (sich bewegen) to go; (Autofahrer) to drive; (Schiff) to sail; (abfahren) to leave; **mit dem Auto/Zug ~** to go by car/train; **rechts ~!** keep to the right; **Fahrer(in)** (-s, -) m(f) driver; **Fahrerairbag** m driver airbag; **Fahrerflucht** f: **~ begehen** to fail to stop after an accident; **Fahrersitz** m driver's seat

Fahrgast m passenger; **Fahrgeld** nt fare; **Fahrgemeinschaft** f car pool; **Fahrkarte** f ticket; **Fahrkartenautomat** m ticket machine; **Fahrkartenschalter** m ticket office

fahrlässig adj negligent

Fahrlehrer(in) m(f) driving instructor; **Fahrplan** m timetable; **Fahrplanauszug** m individual timetable; **fahrplanmäßig** adj (Eisenb) scheduled; **Fahrpreis** m fare; **Fahrpreisermäßigung** f fare reduction; **Fahrrad** nt bicycle; **Fahrradschlauch** m bicycle tube; **Fahrradschloss** nt bicycle lock; **Fahrradverleih** m cycle hire (Brit) (o rental) (US); **Fahrradweg** m cycle path; **Fahrschein** m ticket; **Fahrscheinautomat** m ticket machine; **Fahrscheinentwerter** m ticket-cancelling machine; **Fahrschule** f driving school; **Fahrschüler(in)** m(f) learner (driver) (Brit), student driver (US); **Fahrspur** f lane; **Fahrstreifen** m lane; **Fahrstuhl** m lift (Brit), elevator (US)

Fahrt (-, -en) f journey; (kurz) trip; (Auto) drive; **auf der ~ nach London** on the way to London; **nach drei Stunden ~** after travelling for three hours; **gute ~!** have a good time; **Fahrtkosten** pl travelling expenses pl; **Fahrtrichtung** f direction of travel

fahrtüchtig f (Person) fit to drive; (Fahrzeug) roadworthy

Fahrtunterbrechung f break in the journey, stop

Fahrverbot nt: **~ erhalten/ haben** to be banned from driving; **Fahrzeug** nt vehicle; **Fahrzeugbrief** m (vehicle) registration document; **Fahrzeughalter(in)** m(f) registered owner; **Fahrzeugpapiere** pl vehicle documents pl

fair adj fair

Fakultät f faculty

Falke (-n, -n) m falcon

Fall (-(e)s, Fälle) m (Sturz) fall; (Sachverhalt, juristisch) case; **auf jeden ~, auf alle Fälle** in any case; (bestimmt) definitely; **auf keinen ~** on no account; **für den ~, dass ...** in case ...

Falle (-, -n) f trap

fallen (fiel, gefallen) vi to fall; **etw ~ lassen** to drop sth

fällig adj due

falls adv if; (für den Fall, dass) in case

Fallschirm m parachute; **Fallschirmspringen** nt parachuting, parachute jumping; **Fallschirmspringer(in)** m(f) parachutist

falsch adj (unrichtig) wrong; (unehrlich, unecht) false; (Schmuck) fake; **~ verbunden** sorry, wrong number; **fälschen** vt to forge; **Falschfahrer(in)** m(f) person driving the wrong way on the motorway; **Falschgeld** nt counterfeit money; **Fälschung** f forgery, fake

Faltblatt nt leaflet

Falte (-, -n) f (Knick) fold; (Haut) wrinkle; (Rock) pleat; (Bügel) crease; **falten** vt to fold; **faltig** adj (zerknittert) creased; (Haut, Gesicht) wrinkled

Familie f family; **Familienangehörige(r)** mf family member; **Familienname** m surname; **Familienstand** m marital status

Fan (-s, -s) m fan

fand imperf von **finden**

fangen (fing, gefangen) vt to catch ▷ vr: **sich ~** (nicht fallen) to steady oneself; (fig) to compose oneself

Fantasie f imagination

fantastisch adj fantastic

Farbdrucker m colour printer; **Farbe** (-, -n) f colour; (zum Malen etc) paint; (für Stoff) dye; **färben** vt to colour; (Stoff, Haar) to dye; **Farbfernsehen** nt colour television; **Farbfilm** m colour film; **farbig** adj coloured; **Farbkopierer** m colour copier; **farblos** adj colourless; **Farbstoff** m dye; (für Lebensmittel) colouring

Farn (-(e)s, -e) m fern

Fasan (-(e)s, -e(n)) m pheasant

Fasching (-s, -e) m carnival, Mardi Gras (US); **Faschingsdienstag** (-s, -e) m Shrove Tuesday, Mardi Gras (US)

Faschismus m fascism

Faser (-, -n) f fibre

Fass (-es, Fässer) nt barrel; (Öl) drum

fassen vt (ergreifen) to grasp; (enthalten) to hold; (Entschluss) to take; (verstehen) to understand; **nicht zu ~!** unbelievable ▷ vr: **sich ~** to compose oneself; **Fassung** f (Umrahmung) mount; (Brille) frame; (Lampe) socket; (Wortlaut) version; (Beherrschung) composure; **jdn aus der ~ bringen**

to throw sb; **die ~ verlieren** to lose one's cool

fast adv almost, nearly

fasten vi to fast; **Fastenzeit** f: **die ~** (christlich) Lent; (muslimisch) Ramadan

Fast Food (-s) nt fast food

Fastnacht f (Fasching) carnival

fatal adj (verhängnisvoll) disastrous; (peinlich) embarrassing

faul adj (Obst, Gemüse) rotten; (Mensch) lazy; (Ausreden) lame; **faulen** vi to rot

faulenzen vi to do nothing, to hang around; **Faulheit** f laziness

faulig adj rotten; (Geruch, Geschmack) foul

Faust (-, Fäuste) f fist; **Fausthandschuh** m mitten

Fax (-, -(e)) nt fax; **faxen** vi, vt to fax; **Faxgerät** nt fax machine; **Faxnummer** f fax number

FCKW (-, -s) nt abk = **Fluorchlorkohlenwasserstoff** CFC

Februar (-(s), -e) m February; siehe auch **Juni**

Fechten vt fencing

Feder (-, -n) f feather; (Schreibfeder) (pen-)nib; (Tech) spring; **Federball** m (Ball) shuttlecock; (Spiel) badminton; **Federung** f suspension

Fee (-, -n) f fairy

fegen vi, vt to sweep

fehl adj: **~ am Platz** (o Ort) out of place

fehlen vi (abwesend sein) to be absent; **etw fehlt jdm** sb lacks sth; **was fehlt ihm?** what's wrong with him?; **du fehlst mir** I miss you; **es fehlt an ...** there's no...

Fehler (-s, -) m mistake, error; (Mangel, Schwäche) fault; **Fehlerbeseitigung** f (Inform) debugging; **Fehlermeldung** f (Inform) error message

Fehlzündung f (Auto) misfire

Feier (-, -n) f celebration; (Party) party; **Feierabend** m end of the working day; **~ haben** to finish work; **nach ~** after work; **feierlich** adj solemn; **feiern** vt, vi to celebrate, to have a party; **Feiertag** m holiday; **gesetzlicher ~** public holiday

feig(e) adj cowardly

Feige (-, -n) f fig

Feigling m coward

Feile (-, -n) f file

fein adj fine; (vornehm) refined; **~!** great!; **das schmeckt ~** that tastes delicious

Feind(in) (-(e)s, -e) m(f) enemy; **feindlich** adj hostile

Feinkost (-) f delicacies pl; **Feinkostladen** m delicatessen; **Feinschmecker(in)** (-s, -) m(f) gourmet; **Feinstaub** m particulate matter; **Feinwaschmittel** nt washing powder for delicate fabrics

Feld (-(e)s, -er) nt field; (Schach) square; (Sport) pitch; **Feldsalat** m lamb's lettuce; **Feldweg** m path across the fields

Felge (-, -n) f (wheel) rim

Fell (-(e)s, -e) nt fur; (von Schaf) fleece

Fels (-en, -en) m, **Felsen** (-s, -) m rock; (Klippe) cliff; **felsig** adj rocky

feminin adj feminine; **Femininum** (-s, Feminina) nt (Ling) feminine noun

feministisch adj feminist

Fenchel (-s, -) m fennel

Fenster (-s, -) nt window; **Fensterbrett** nt windowsill; **Fensterladen** m shutter; **Fensterplatz** m windowseat; **Fensterscheibe** f windowpane

Ferien pl holidays pl (Brit), vacation sing (US); **~ haben/machen** to be/go on holiday (Brit)

(o vacation (US)); **Ferienhaus** nt
holiday (Brit) (o vacation (US))
home; **Ferienkurs** m holiday
(Brit) (o vacation (US)) course;
Ferienlager nt holiday camp
(Brit), vacation camp (US); (für
Kinder im Sommer) summer camp;
Ferienort m holiday (Brit) (o
vacation (US)) resort;
Ferienwohnung f holiday flat
(Brit), vacation apartment (US)
Ferkel (-s, -) nt piglet
fern adj distant, far-off; **von
~** from a distance; **Fernabfrage** f
remote-control access;
Fernbedienung f remote control; **Ferne** f distance; **aus der ~** from
a distance
ferner adj, adv further; (außerdem)
besides
Fernflug m long-distance flight;
Ferngespräch nt long-distance
call; **ferngesteuert** adj
remote-controlled; **Fernglas** nt
binoculars pl; **Fernlicht** nt full
beam (Brit), high beam (US)
Fernsehapparat m TV (set);
fern|sehen irr vi to watch
television; **Fernsehen** nt
television; **im ~** on television;
Fernseher m TV (set);
Fernsehkanal m TV channel;
Fernsehprogramm nt (Sendung)
TV programme; (Zeitschrift) TV
guide; **Fernsehserie** f TV series
sing; **Fernsehturm** m TV tower;
Fernsehzeitschrift f TV guide
Fernstraße f major road;
Ferntourismus m long-haul
tourism; **Fernverkehr** m
long-distance traffic
Ferse (-, -n) f heel
fertig adj (bereit) ready; (beendet)
finished; (gebrauchsfertig)
ready-made; **~ machen** (beenden)
to finish; **sich ~ machen** to get
ready; **mit etw ~ werden** to be

able to cope with sth; **auf die
Plätze, ~, los!** on your marks, get
set, go!; **Fertiggericht** nt ready
meal; **fertig|machen** vt (jdn
kritisieren) to give sb hell; (jdn zur
Verzweiflung bringen) to drive sb
mad; (jdn deprimieren) to get sb
down
fest adj firm; (Nahrung) solid;
(Gehalt) regular; (Schuhe) sturdy;
(Schlaf) sound
Fest (-(e)s, -e) nt party; (Rel)
festival
Festbetrag m fixed amount
fest|binden irr vt to tie (an +dat
to); **fest|halten** irr vt to hold
onto ▷ vr: **sich ~** to hold on (an
+dat to)
Festiger (-s, -) m setting lotion
Festival (-s, -s) nt festival
Festland nt mainland; **das
europäische ~** the (European)
continent
fest|legen vt to fix ▷ vr: **sich
~** to commit oneself
festlich adj festive
fest|machen vt to fasten;
(Termin etc) to fix; **fest|nehmen** irr
vt to arrest; **Festnetz** nt (Tel)
fixed-line network; **Festplatte** f
(Inform) hard disk
fest|setzen vt to fix
Festspiele pl festival sing
fest|stehen irr vi to be fixed
fest|stellen vt to establish;
(sagen) to remark
Feststelltaste f shift lock
Festung f fortress
Festzelt nt marquee
Fete (-, -n) f party
fett adj (dick) fat; (Essen etc)
greasy; (Schrift) bold; **Fett** (-(e)s,
-e) nt fat; (Tech) grease; **fettarm**
adj low-fat; **fettig** adj fatty;
(schmierig) greasy
feucht adj damp; (Luft) humid;
Feuchtigkeit f dampness;

(*Luftfeuchtigkeit*) humidity; **Feuchtigkeitscreme** f moisturizing cream

Feuer (-s, -) nt fire; **haben Sie ~?** have you got a light?; **Feueralarm** m fire alarm; **feuerfest** adj fireproof; **Feuerlöscher** (-s, -) m fire extinguisher; **Feuermelder** (-s, -) m fire alarm; **Feuertreppe** f fire escape; **Feuerwehr** (-, -en) f fire brigade; **Feuerwehrfrau** f firewoman, fire fighter; **Feuerwehrmann** m fireman, fire fighter; **Feuerwerk** nt fireworks pl; **Feuerzeug** nt (cigarette) lighter

Fichte (-, -n) f spruce

ficken vt, vi (vulg) to fuck

Fieber (-s, -) nt temperature, fever; **~ haben** to have a high temperature; **Fieberthermometer** nt thermometer

fiel imperf von **fallen**

fies adj (fam) nasty

Figur (-, -en) f figure; (im Schach) piece

Filet (-s, -s) nt fillet; **filetieren** vt to fillet; **Filetsteak** nt fillet steak

Filiale (-, -n) f (Comm) branch

Film (-(e)s, -e) m film, movie; **filmen** vt, vi to film

Filter (-s, -) m filter; **Filterkaffee** m filter coffee; **filtern** vt to filter; **Filterpapier** nt filter paper

Filz (-es, -e) m felt; **Filzschreiber** m, **Filzstift** m felt(-tip) pen, felt-tip

Finale (-s, -) nt (Sport) final

Finanzamt nt tax office; **finanziell** adj financial; **finanzieren** vt to finance

finden (fand, gefunden) vt to find; (meinen) to think; **ich finde nichts dabei, wenn ...** I don't see what's

wrong if ...; **ich finde es gut/schlecht** I like/don't like it ▷ vr: **es fanden sich nur wenige Helfer** there were only a few helpers

fing imperf von **fangen**

Finger (-s, -) m finger; **Fingerabdruck** m fingerprint; **Fingerhandschuh** m glove; **Fingernagel** m fingernail

Fink (-en, -en) m finch

Finne (-n, -n) m, **Finnin** f Finn, Finnish man/woman; **finnisch** adj Finnish; **Finnisch** nt Finnish; **Finnland** nt Finland

finster adj dark; (verdächtig) dubious; (verdrossen) grim; (Gedanke) dark; **Finsternis** f darkness

Firewall (-, -s) f (Inform) firewall

Firma (-, Firmen) f firm

Fisch (-(e)s, -e) m fish; **~e pl** (Astr) Pisces sing; **fischen** vt, vi to fish; **Fischer(in)** (-s, -) m(f) fisherman/-woman; **Fischerboot** nt fishing boat; **Fischgericht** nt fish dish; **Fischhändler(in)** m(f) fishmonger; **Fischstäbchen** nt fish finger (Brit) (o stick (US))

Fisole (-, -n) f French bean

fit adj fit; **Fitness** (-) f fitness; **Fitnesscenter** (-s, -) nt fitness centre; **Fitnesstrainer(in)** m(f) fitness trainer, personal trainer

fix adj (schnell) quick; **~ und fertig** exhausted

fixen vi (fam) to shoot up; **Fixer(in)** (-s, -) m(f) (fam) junkie

FKK f abk = **Freikörperkultur** nudism; **FKK-Strand** m nudist beach

flach adj flat; (Gewässer; Teller) shallow; **~er Absatz** low heel; **Flachbildschirm** m flat screen

Fläche (-, -n) f area; (Oberfläche) surface

Flagge (-, -n) f flag

flambiert adj flambé(ed)

Flamme (-, -n) f flame

Flanell (-s) m flannel

Flasche (-, -n) f bottle; **eine ~ sein** (fam) to be useless; **Flaschenbier** nt bottled beer; **Flaschenöffner** m bottle opener; **Flaschenpfand** nt deposit; **Flaschentomate** f plum tomato

flatterhaft adj fickle; **flattern** vi to flutter

flauschig adj fluffy

Flausen pl (fam) daft ideas pl

Flaute (-, -n) f calm; (Comm) recession

Flechte (-, -n) f plait; (Med) scab; (Bot) lichen; **flechten** (flocht, geflochten) vt to plait; (Kranz) to bind

Fleck (-(e)s, -e) m, **Flecken** (-s, -) m spot; (Schmutz) stain; (Stoff~) patch; (Makel) blemish; **Fleckentferner** (-s, -) m stain remover; **fleckig** adj spotted; (mit Schmutzflecken) stained

Fledermaus f bat

Fleisch (-(e)s) nt flesh; (Essen) meat; **Fleischbrühe** f meat stock; **Fleischer(in)** (-s, -) m(f) butcher; **Fleischerei** f butcher's (shop); **Fleischtomate** f beef tomato

fleißig adj diligent, hard-working

flennen vi (fam) to cry, to howl

flexibel adj flexible

flicken vt to mend; **Flickzeug** nt repair kit

Flieder (-s, -) m lilac

Fliege (-, -n) f fly; (Krawatte) bow tie

fliegen (flog, geflogen) vt, vi to fly

Fliese (-, -n) f tile

Fließband nt conveyor belt; (als Einrichtung) production (o assembly) line; **fließen** (floss, geflossen) vi to flow; **fließend** adj fluent; (Übergänge) smooth; **~(es) Wasser** running water

Flipper (-s, -) m pinball machine; **flippern** vi to play pinball

flippig adj (fam) eccentric

flirten vi to flirt

Flitterwochen pl honeymoon sing

flocht imperf von **flechten**

Flocke (-, -n) f flake

flog imperf von **fliegen**

Floh (-(e)s, Flöhe) m flea; **Flohmarkt** m flea market

Flop (-s, -s) m flop

Floskel (-, -n) f empty phrase

floss imperf von **fließen**

Floß (-es, Flöße) nt raft

Flosse (-, -n) f fin; (Schwimmflosse) flipper

Flöte (-, -n) f flute; (Blockflöte) recorder

flott adj lively; (elegant) smart; (Naut) afloat

Fluch (-(e)s, Flüche) m curse; **fluchen** vi to swear, to curse

Flucht (-, -en) f flight; **flüchten** vi to flee (vor +dat from); **flüchtig** adj: **ich kenne ihn nur ~** I don't know him very well at all; **Flüchtling** m refugee

Flug (-(e)s, Flüge) m flight; **Flugbegleiter(in)** (-s, -) m(f) flight attendant; **Flugblatt** nt leaflet

Flügel (-s, -) m wing; (Mus) grand piano

Fluggast m passenger (on a plane); **Fluggesellschaft** f airline; **Flughafen** m airport; **Flugkarte** f airline ticket; **Fluglotse** m air-traffic controller; **Flugnummer** f flight number; **Flugplan** m flight schedule; **Flugplatz** m airport; (klein) airfield; **Flugschein** m plane ticket; **Flugschreiber** m flight recorder, black box; **Flugsteig** (-s, -e) m gate; **Flugstrecke** f air route; **Flugticket** nt plane ticket; **Flugverbindung** f flight connection; **Flugverkehr** m air traffic; **Flugzeit** f flying time; **Flugzeug** nt plane; **Flugzeugentführung** f hijacking

Flunder (-, -n) f flounder

Fluor (-s) nt fluorine

Flur (-(e)s, -e) m hall

Fluss (-es, Flüsse) m river; (Fließen) flow

flüssig adj liquid; **Flüssigkeit** (-, -en) f liquid; **Flüssigseife** f liquid soap

flüstern vt, vi to whisper

Flut (-, -en) f (a. fig) flood; (Gezeiten) high tide; **Flutlicht** nt floodlight

Fohlen (-s, -) nt foal

Föhn (-(e)s, -e) m hairdryer; (Wind) foehn; **föhnen** vt to dry; (beim Friseur) to blow-dry

Folge (-, -n) f (Reihe, Serie) series sing; (Aufeinanderfolge) sequence; (Fortsetzung eines Romans) instalment; (Fortsetzung einer Fernsehserie) episode; (Auswirkung) result; **etw zur ~ haben** to result in sth; **~n haben** to have consequences; **folgen** vi to follow (jdm sb); (gehorchen) to obey (jdm sb); **jdm ~ können** (fig) to be able to follow sb; **folgend** adj following; **folgendermaßen** adv as follows; **folglich** adv consequently

Folie f foil; (für Projektor) transparency

Fön® m siehe **Föhn**

Fondue (-s, -s) nt fondue

fönen vt siehe **föhnen**

fordern vt to demand

fördern vt to promote; (unterstützen) to help

Forderung f demand

Forelle f trout

Form (-, -en) f form; (Gestalt) shape; (Gussform) mould; (Backform) baking tin (Brit) (o pan

(US)); **in ~ sein** to be in good form; **Formalität** f formality; **Format** nt format; **von internationalem ~** of international standing; **formatieren** vt (Diskette) to format; (Text) to edit

Formblatt nt form; **formen** vt to form, to shape; **förmlich** adj formal; (buchstäblich) real; **formlos** adj informal; **Formular** (-s, -e) nt form; **formulieren** vt to formulate

forschen vi to search (nach for); (wissenschaftlich) to (do) research; **Forscher(in)** m(f) researcher; **Forschung** f research

Förster(in) (-s, -) m(f) forester; (für Wild) gamekeeper

fort adv away; (verschwunden) gone; **fort|bewegen** vt to move away ▷ vr: **sich ~** to move; **Fortbildung** f further education; (im Beruf) further training; **fort|fahren** irr vi to go away; (weitermachen) to continue; **fort|gehen** irr vi to go away; **fortgeschritten** adj advanced; **Fortpflanzung** f reproduction

Fortschritt m progress; **~e machen** to make progress; **fortschrittlich** adj progressive; **fort|setzen** vt to continue; **Fortsetzung** f continuation; (folgender Teil) instalment; **~ folgt** to be continued

Foto (-s, -s) nt photo ▷ (-s, -s) m (Fotoapparat) camera; **Fotograf(in)** (-en, -en) m(f) photographer; **Fotografie** f photography; (Bild) photograph; **fotografieren** vt to photograph ▷ vi to take photographs; **Fotohandy** nt camera phone; **Fotokopie** f photocopy; **fotokopieren** vt to photocopy

Foul (-s, -s) nt foul

Foyer (-s, -s) nt foyer

Fr. f abk = **Frau** Mrs; (unverheiratet, neutral) Ms

Fracht (-, -en) f freight; (Naut) cargo; (Preis) carriage; **Frachter** (-s, -) m freighter

Frack (-(e)s, Fräcke) m tails pl

Frage (-, -n) f question; **das ist eine - der Zeit** that's a matter (o question) of time; **das kommt nicht in ~** that's out of the question; **Fragebogen** m questionnaire; **fragen** vt, vi to ask; **Fragezeichen** nt question mark; **fragwürdig** adj dubious

Franken (-s, -) m (Schweizer Währung) Swiss franc ▷ (-s) nt (Land) Franconia

frankieren vt to stamp; (maschinell) to frank

Frankreich (-s) nt France; **Franzose** (-n, -n) m, **Französin** f Frenchman/-woman; **die ~ n** pl the French pl; **französisch** adj French; **Französisch** nt French

fraß imperf von **fressen**

Frau (-, -en) f woman; (Ehefrau) wife; (Anrede) Mrs; (unverheiratet, neutral) Ms; **Frauenarzt** m, **Frauenärztin** f gynaecologist; **Frauenbewegung** f women's movement; **frauenfeindlich** adj misogynous; **Frauenhaus** nt refuge (for battered women)

Fräulein nt (junge Dame) young lady; (veraltet als Anrede) Miss

Freak (-s, -s) m (fam) freak

frech adj cheeky; **Frechheit** f cheek; **so eine ~!** what a cheek

Freeclimbing (-s) nt free climbing

frei adj free; (Straße) clear; (Mitarbeiter) freelance; **ein ~er Tag** a day off; **~e Arbeitsstelle** vacancy; **Zimmer ~** room(s) to let (Brit), room(s) for rent (US); **im Freien** in the open air; **Freibad** nt open-air (swimming) pool;

freiberuflich adj freelance; **freig(i)ebig** adj generous; **Freiheit** f freedom; **Freikarte** f free ticket; **frei|lassen** irr vt to (set) free

freilich adv of course

Freilichtbühne f open-air theatre; **frei|machen** vr: **sich ~** to undress; **frei|nehmen** irr vt **sich** (dat) **einen Tag ~** to take a day off; **Freisprechanlage** f hands-free phone; **Freistoß** m free kick

Freitag m Friday; siehe auch **Mittwoch**; **freitags** adv on Fridays; siehe auch **mittwochs**

freiwillig adj voluntary

Freizeichen nt (Tel) ringing tone

Freizeit f spare (o free) time; **Freizeithemd** nt sports shirt; **Freizeitkleidung** f leisure wear; **Freizeitpark** m leisure park

fremd adj (nicht vertraut) strange; (ausländisch) foreign; (nicht eigen) someone else's; **Fremde(r)** mf (Unbekannter) stranger; (Ausländer) foreigner; **fremdenfeindlich** adj anti-foreigner, xenophobic; **Fremdenführer(in)** m(f) (tourist) guide; **Fremdenverkehr** m tourism; **Fremdenverkehrsamt** nt tourist information office; **Fremdenzimmer** nt (guest) room; **Fremdsprache** f foreign language; **Fremdsprachenkenntnisse** pl knowledge sing of foreign languages; **Fremdwort** nt foreign word

Frequenz f (Radio) frequency

fressen (fraß, gefressen) vt, vi (Tier) to eat; (Mensch) to guzzle

Freude (-, -n) f joy, delight; **freuen** vt to please; **es freut mich, dass ...** I'm pleased that ... ▷ vr: **sich ~** to be pleased (über +akk about); **sich auf etw** (akk) **~** to look forward to sth

Freund (-(e)s, -e) m friend; (in Beziehung) boyfriend; **Freundin** f friend; (in Beziehung) girlfriend; **freundlich** adj friendly; (liebenswürdig) kind; **freundlicherweise** adv kindly; **Freundlichkeit** f friendliness; (Liebenswürdigkeit) kindness; **Freundschaft** f friendship

Frieden (-s, -) m peace; **Friedhof** m cemetery; **friedlich** adj peaceful

frieren (fror, gefroren) vt, vi to freeze; **ich friere, es friert mich** I'm freezing

Frikadelle f rissole

Frisbee® nt, **Frisbeescheibe** f frisbee®

frisch adj fresh; (lebhaft) lively; **„~ gestrichen"** "wet paint"; **sich ~ machen** to freshen up; **Frischhaltefolie** f clingfilm® (Brit), plastic wrap (US); **Frischkäse** m cream cheese

Friseur(in) (-s, -e) m(f) hairdresser; **frisieren** vt: **jdn ~** to do sb's hair ▷ vr: **sich ~** to do one's hair

Frist (-, -en) f period; (Zeitpunkt) deadline; **innerhalb einer ~ von zehn Tagen** within a ten-day period; **eine ~ einhalten** to meet a deadline; **die ~ ist abgelaufen** the deadline has expired; **fristgerecht** adj, adv within the specified time; **fristlos** adj: **~e Entlassung** dismissal without notice

Frisur f hairdo, hairstyle

frittieren vt to deep-fry

Frl. f abk = **Fräulein** Miss

froh adj happy; **~e Weihnachten!** Merry Christmas

fröhlich adj happy, cheerful

Fronleichnam (-(e)s) m Corpus Christi

frontal adj frontal

fror imperf von **frieren**

Frosch (-(e)s, Frösche) m frog

Frost (-(e)s, Fröste) m frost; **bei ~** in frosty weather; **Frostschutzmittel** nt anti-freeze

Frottee nt terry(cloth); **Frottier(hand)tuch** nt towel

Frucht (-, Früchte) f (a. fig) fruit; (Getreide) corn; **Fruchteis** nt fruit-flavoured ice-cream; **Früchtetee** m fruit tea; **fruchtig** adj fruity; **Fruchtpresse** f juicer; **Fruchtsaft** m fruit juice; **Fruchtsalat** m fruit salad

früh adj, adv early; **heute ~** this morning; **um fünf Uhr ~** at five (o'clock) in the morning; **~ genug** soon enough; **früher** adj earlier; (ehemalig) former ▷ adv formerly, in the past; **frühestens** adv at the earliest

Frühjahr nt, **Frühling** m spring; **Frühlingsrolle** f spring roll; **Frühlingszwiebel** f spring onion (Brit), scallion (US)

frühmorgens adv early in the morning

Frühstück nt breakfast; **frühstücken** vi to have breakfast; **Frühstücksbüfett** nt breakfast buffet; **Frühstücksfernsehen** nt breakfast television; **Frühstücksspeck** m bacon

frühzeitig adj early

Frust (-s) m (fam) frustration; **frustrieren** vt to frustrate

Fuchs (-es, Füchse) m fox

fühlen vt, vi to feel ▷ vr: **sich ~** to feel

fuhr imperf von **fahren**

führen vt to lead; (Geschäft) to run; (Name) to bear; (Buch) to keep ▷ vi to lead, to be in the lead ▷ vr: **sich ~** to behave; **Führerschein** m driving licence (Brit), driver's license (US); **Führung** f leadership; (eines Unternehmens) management; (*Mil*) command; (*in Museum, Stadt*) guided tour; **in ~ liegen** to be in the lead

füllen *vt* to fill; (*Gastr*) to stuff ▷ *vr:* **sich ~** to fill

Füller (-s, -) *m*, **Füllfederhalter** (-s, -) *m* fountain pen

Füllung *f* filling

Fund (-(e)s, -e) *m* find; **Fundbüro** *nt* lost property office (*Brit*), lost and found (*US*); **Fundsachen** *pl* lost property *sing*

fünf *num* five; **Fünf** (-, -en) *f* five; (*Schulnote*) ≈ E; **fünfhundert** *num* five hundred; **fünfmal** *adv* five times; **fünfte(r, s)** *adj* fifth; *siehe auch* **dritte**; **Fünftel** (-s, -) *nt* (*Bruchteil*) fifth; **fünfzehn** *num* fifteen; **fünfzehnte(r, s)** *adj* fifteenth; *siehe auch* **dritte**; **fünfzig** *num* fifty; **fünfzigste(r, s)** *adj* fiftieth

Funk (-s) *m* radio; **über ~** by radio

Funke (-ns, -n) *m* spark; **funkeln** *vi* to sparkle

Funkgerät *nt* radio set; **Funktaxi** *nt* radio taxi, radio cab

Funktion *f* function; **funktionieren** *vi* to work, to function; **Funktionstaste** *f* (*Inform*) function key

für *prep* +*akk* for; **was ~ (ein) ...?** what kind (*o* sort) of ...?; **Tag ~ Tag** day after day

Furcht (-) *f* fear; **furchtbar** *adj* terrible; **fürchten** *vt* to be afraid of, to fear ▷ *vr:* **sich ~** to be afraid (*vor* +*dat* of); **fürchterlich** *adj* awful

füreinander *adv* for each other

fürs *kontr von* **für das**

Fürst(in) (-en, -en) *m(f)* prince/princess; **Fürstentum** *nt* principality; **fürstlich** *adj* (*fig*) splendid

Furunkel (-s, -) *nt* boil

Furz (-es, -e) *m* (*vulg*) fart; **furzen** *vi* (*vulg*) to fart

Fuß (-es, Füße) *m* foot; (*von Glas, Säule etc*) base; (*von Möbel*) leg; **zu ~** on foot; **zu ~ gehen** to walk; **Fußball** *m* football (*Brit*), soccer; **Fußballmannschaft** *f* football (*Brit*) (*o* soccer) team; **Fußballplatz** *m* football pitch (*Brit*), soccer field (*US*); **Fußballspiel** *nt* football (*Brit*) (*o* soccer) match; **Fußballspieler(in)** *m(f)* footballer (*Brit*), soccer player; **Fußboden** *m* floor; **Fußgänger(in)** (-s, -) *m(f)* pedestrian; **Fußgängerüberweg** *m* pedestrian crossing (*Brit*), crosswalk (*US*); **Fußgängerzone** *f* pedestrian precinct (*Brit*) (*o* zone (*US*)); **Fußgelenk** *nt* ankle; **Fußpilz** *m* athlete's foot; **Fußtritt** *m* kick; **jdm einen ~ geben** to give sb a kick, to kick sb; **Fußweg** *m* footpath

Futon (-s, -s) *m* futon

Futter (-s, -) *nt* feed; (*Heu etc*) fodder; (*Stoff*) lining; **füttern** *vt* to feed; (*Kleidung*) to line

Futur (-s, -e) *nt* (*Ling*) future (tense)

Fuzzi (-s, -s) *m* (*fam*) guy

g

gab *imperf von* **geben**

Gabe (-, -n) *f* gift

Gabel (-, -n) *f* fork; **Gabelung** *f* fork

gaffen *vi* to gape

Gage (-, -n) *f* fee

gähnen *vi* to yawn

Galerie *f* gallery

Galle (-, -n) *f* gall; (*Organ*) gall bladder; **Gallenstein** *m* gallstone

Galopp (-s) *m* gallop; **galoppieren** *vi* to gallop

galt *imperf von* **gelten**

Gameboy® (-s, -s) *m* Gameboy®

Gameshow *f* game show

gammeln *vi* to loaf around; **Gammler(in)** (-s, -) *m(f)* layabout

gang *adj*: **~ und gäbe sein** to be quite normal

Gang (-(e)s, Gänge) *m* walk; (*im Flugzeug*) aisle; (*Essen, Ablauf*) course; (*Flur etc*) corridor; (*Durchgang*) passage; (*Auto*) gear; **den zweiten ~ einlegen** to change into second (gear); **etw in ~ bringen** to get sth going; **Gangschaltung** *f* gears *pl*; **Gangway** (-, -s) *f* (*Aviat*) steps *pl*; (*Naut*) gangway

Gans (-, Gänse) *f* goose; **Gänseblümchen** *nt* daisy; **Gänsehaut** *f* goose pimples *pl* (*Brit*), goose bumps *pl* (*US*)

ganz *adj* whole; (*vollständig*) complete; **~ Europa** all of Europe; **sein ~es Geld** all his money; **den ~en Tag** all day; ▷ *adv* quite; (*völlig*) completely; **es hat mir ~ gut gefallen** I quite liked it; **~ schön viel** quite a lot; **~ und gar nicht** not at all; **das ist etwas ~ anderes** that's a completely different matter; **ganztägig** *adj* all-day; (*Arbeit, Stelle*) full-time; **ganztags** *adv* (*arbeiten*) full-time; **Ganztagsschule** *f* all-day school; **Ganztagsstelle** *f* full-time job

gar *adj* done, cooked ▷ *adv* at all; **~ nicht/nichts** not/nothing at all; **~ nicht schlecht** not bad at all

Garage (-, -n) *f* garage

Garantie *f* guarantee; **garantieren** *vt* to guarantee

Garderobe (-, -n) *f* (*Kleidung*) wardrobe; (*Abgabe*) cloakroom

Gardine *f* curtain

Garn (-(e)s, -e) *nt* thread

Garnele (-, -n) *f* shrimp

garnieren *vt* to decorate; (*Speisen*) to garnish

Garten (-s, Gärten) *m* garden; **Gärtner(in)** (-s, -) *m(f)* gardener; **Gärtnerei** *f* nursery; (*Gemüsegärtnerei*) market garden (*Brit*), truck farm (*US*)

Gas (-es, -e) *nt* gas; **~ geben** (*Auto*) to accelerate; (*fig*) to get a move on; **Gasanzünder** *m* gas lighter; **Gasbrenner** *m* gas burner;

Gasflasche f gas bottle;
Gasheizung f gas heating;
Gasherd m gas stove, gas cooker
(Brit); **Gaskocher** (-s, -) m
camping stove; **Gaspedal** nt
accelerator, gas pedal (US)

Gasse (-, -n) f alley

Gast (-es, Gäste) m guest; **Gäste
haben** to have guests;
Gastarbeiter(in) m(f) foreign
worker; **Gästebett** nt spare bed;
Gästebuch nt visitors' book;
Gästehaus nt guest house;
Gästezimmer nt guest room;
gastfreundlich adj hospitable;
Gastfreundschaft f hospitality;
Gastgeber(in) (-s, -) m(f) host/
hostess; **Gasthaus** nt, **Gasthof** m
inn; **Gastland** nt host country

Gastritis (-) f gastritis

Gastronomie f catering trade

Gastspiel nt (Sport) away game;
Gaststätte f restaurant;
(Trinklokal) pub (Brit), bar;
Gastwirt(in) m(f) landlord/-lady

GAU (-s, -s) m akr = **größter
anzunehmender Unfall** MCA

Gaumen (-s, -) m palate

Gaze (-, -n) f gauze

geb. adj abk = **geboren** b. ▷ adj
abk = **geborene** née; siehe **geboren**

Gebäck (-(e)s, -e) nt pastries pl;
(Kekse) biscuits pl (Brit), cookies pl
(US)

gebacken pp von **backen**

Gebärdensprache f sign
language

Gebärmutter f womb

Gebäude (-s, -) nt building

geben (gab, gegeben) vt, vi to give
(jdm etw sb sth, sth to sb); (Karten)
to deal; **lass dir eine Quittung
~** ask for a receipt ▷ vt impers: **es
gibt** there is/are; (in Zukunft) there
will be; **das gibt's nicht** I don't
believe it ▷ vr: **sich ~** (sich
verhalten) to behave, to act; **das**

gibt sich wieder it'll sort itself out

Gebet (-(e)s, -e) nt prayer

gebeten pp von **bitten**

Gebiet (-(e)s, -e) nt area;
(Hoheitsgebiet) territory; (fig) field

gebildet adj educated; (belesen)
well-read

Gebirge (-s, -) nt mountains pl;
gebirgig adj mountainous

Gebiss (-es, -e) nt teeth pl;
(künstlich) dentures pl; **gebissen**
pp von **beißen**; **Gebissreiniger** m
denture tablets pl

Gebläse (-s, -) nt fan, blower

geblasen pp von **blasen**

geblieben pp von **bleiben**

gebogen pp von **biegen**

geboren pp von **gebären** ▷ adj
born; **Andrea Jordan, geborene
Christian** Andrea Jordan, née
Christian

geborgen pp von **bergen** ▷ adj
secure, safe

geboten pp von **bieten**

gebracht pp von **bringen**

gebrannt pp von **brennen**

gebraten pp von **braten**

gebrauchen vt to use;
Gebrauchsanweisung f direc-
tions pl for use; **gebrauchsfertig**
adj ready to use; **gebraucht** adj
used; **etw ~ kaufen** to buy sth
secondhand; **Gebrauchtwagen**
m secondhand (o used) car

gebräunt adj tanned

gebrochen pp von **brechen**

Gebühr (-, -en) f charge; (Maut)
toll; (Honorar) fee; **Gebühren-
einheit** f (Tel) unit;
gebührenfrei adj free of charge;
(Telefonnummer) freefone® (Brit),
toll-free (US); **gebührenpflichtig**
adj subject to charges; **~e Straße**
toll road

gebunden pp von **binden**

Geburt (-, -en) f birth; **gebürtig**
adj: **er ist ~er Schweizer** he is

Swiss by birth; **Geburtsdatum** nt date of birth; **Geburtsjahr** nt year of birth; **Geburtsname** m birth name; (einer Frau) maiden name; **Geburtsort** m birthplace; **Geburtstag** m birthday; **herzlichen Glückwunsch zum ~!** Happy Birthday; **Geburtsurkunde** f birth certificate

Gebüsch (-(e)s, -e) nt bushes pl

gedacht pp von **denken**

Gedächtnis nt memory; **im ~ behalten** to remember

Gedanke (-ns, -n) m thought; **sich** (dat) **über etw** (akk) **~n machen** to think about sth; (besorgt) to be worried about sth; **Gedankenstrich** m dash

Gedeck (-(e)s, -e) nt place setting; (Speisenfolge) set meal

Gedenkstätte f memorial; **Gedenktafel** f commemorative plaque

Gedicht (-(e)s, -e) nt poem

Gedränge (-s) nt crush, crowd

gedrungen pp von **dringen**

Geduld (-) f patience; **geduldig** adj patient

gedurft pp von **dürfen**

geehrt adj: **Sehr ~er Herr Young** Dear Mr Young

geeignet adj suitable

Gefahr (-, -en) f danger; **auf eigene ~** at one's own risk; **außer ~** out of danger; **gefährden** vt to endanger

gefahren pp von **fahren**

gefährlich adj dangerous

Gefälle (-s, -) nt gradient, slope

gefallen pp von **fallen** ♦ irr vi: **jdm ~** to please sb; **er/es gefällt mir** I like him/it; **sich** (dat) **etw ~ lassen** to put up with sth

Gefallen (-s, -) m favour; **jdm einen ~ tun** to do sb a favour

gefälligst adv ..., will you!; **sei ~ still!** be quiet, will you!

gefangen pp von **fangen**

Gefängnis nt prison

Gefäß (-es, -e) nt (Behälter) container, receptacle; (Anat, Bot) vessel

gefasst adj composed, calm; **auf etw** (akk) **~ sein** to be prepared (o ready) for sth

geflochten pp von **flechten**

geflogen pp von **fliegen**

geflossen pp von **fließen**

Geflügel (-s) nt poultry

gefragt adj in demand

gefressen pp von **fressen**

Gefrierbeutel m freezer bag; **gefrieren** irr vi to freeze; **Gefrierfach** nt freezer compartment; **Gefrierschrank** m (upright) freezer; **Gefriertruhe** f (chest) freezer

gefroren pp von **frieren**

Gefühl (-(e)s, -e) nt feeling

gefunden pp von **finden**

gegangen pp von **gehen**

gegeben pp von **geben**; **gegebenenfalls** adv if need be

⭕ SCHLÜSSELWORT

gegen prep +akk **1** against; **nichts gegen jdn haben** to have nothing against sb; **X gegen Y** (Sport, Jur) X versus Y; **ein Mittel gegen Schnupfen** something for colds

2 (in Richtung auf) towards; **gegen Osten** to(wards) the east; **gegen Abend** towards evening; **gegen einen Baum fahren** to drive into a tree

3 (ungefähr) round about; **gegen 3 Uhr** around 3 o'clock

4 (gegenüber) towards; (ungefähr) around; **gerecht gegen alle** fair to all

5 (im Austausch für) for; **gegen bar** for cash; **gegen Quittung** against

a receipt
6 (*verglichen mit*) compared with

Gegend (-, -en) *f* area; **hier in der
~** around here
gegeneinander *adv* against one
another
Gegenfahrbahn *f* opposite
lane; **Gegenmittel** *nt* remedy
(*gegen* for); **Gegenrichtung** *f*
opposite direction; **Gegensatz**
m contrast; **im ~ zu** in contrast to;
gegensätzlich *adj* conflicting;
gegenseitig *adj* mutual; **sich
~ helfen** to help each other
Gegenstand *m* object; (*Thema*)
subject
Gegenteil *nt* opposite; **im ~ on**
the contrary; **gegenteilig** *adj*
opposite, contrary
gegenüber *prep* +*dat* opposite;
(*zu jdm*) to(wards); (*angesichts*) in
the face of ▷ *adv* opposite;
gegenüber|stehen *vt* to face;
(*Problemen*) to be faced with;
gegenüber|stellen *vt* to confront
(*dat* with); (*fig*) compare (*dat*
with)
Gegenverkehr *m* oncoming
traffic; **Gegenwart** (-) *f* present
(tense)
Gegenwind *m* headwind
gegessen *pp von* **essen**
geglichen *pp von* **gleichen**
geglitten *pp von* **gleiten**
Gegner(in) (-s, -) *m(f)* opponent
gegolten *pp von* **gelten**
gegossen *pp von* **gießen**
gegraben *pp von* **graben**
gegriffen *pp von* **greifen**
gehabt *pp von* **haben**
Gehackte(s) *nt* mince(d meat)
(*Brit*), ground meat (*US*)
Gehalt (-(*e*)s, -e) *m* content
▷ (-(*e*)s, *Gehälter*) *nt* salary
gehalten *pp von* **halten**
gehangen *pp von* **hängen**

gehässig *adj* spiteful, nasty
gehauen *pp von* **hauen**
gehbehindert *adj*: **sie ist ~** she
can't walk properly
geheim *adj* secret; **etw ~ halten**
to keep sth secret; **Geheimnis** *nt*
secret; (*rätselhaft*) mystery;
geheimnisvoll *adj* mysterious;
Geheimnummer *f*, **Geheimzahl**
f (*von Kreditkarte*) PIN number
geheißen *pp von* **heißen**
gehen (ging, gegangen) *vt*, *vi* to
go; (*zu Fuß*) to walk; (*funktionieren*)
to work; **über die Straße ~** to
cross the street; **~ nach** (*Fenster*) to
face ▷ *vi impers*: **wie geht es** (o *things*)?;
**mir/ihm
geht es gut** I'm/he's (doing) fine;
geht das? is that possible?; **geht's
noch?** can you still manage?; **es
geht** not too bad, OK; **das geht
nicht** that's not on; **es geht um ...**
it's about ...
Gehirn (-(*e*)s, -e) *nt* brain;
Gehirnerschütterung *f*
concussion
gehoben *pp von* **heben**
geholfen *pp von* **helfen**
Gehör (-(*e*)s) *nt* hearing
gehorchen *vi* to obey (*jdm* sb)
gehören *vi* to belong (*jdm* to sb);
wem gehört das Buch? whose
book is this?; **gehört dir?** is it
yours? ▷ *vi impers*: **das gehört
sich nicht** it's not done
gehörlos *adj* deaf
gehorsam *adj* obedient
Gehsteig *m*, **Gehweg** (-s, -e) *m*
pavement (*Brit*), sidewalk (*US*)
Geier (-s, -) *m* vulture
Geige (-, -n) *f* violin
geil *adj* randy (*Brit*), horny (*US*);
(*fam*: *toll*) fantastic
Geisel (-, -n) *f* hostage
Geist (-(*e*)s, -er) *m* spirit;
(*Gespenst*) ghost; (*Verstand*) mind;
Geisterbahn *f* ghost train, tunnel

of horror (US); **Geisterfahrer(in)**
m(f) person driving the wrong way on
the motorway
geizig adj stingy
gekannt pp von **kennen**
geklungen pp von **klingen**
geknickt adj (fig) dejected
gekniffen pp von **kneifen**
gekommen pp von **kommen**
gekonnt pp von **können** ▷ adj
skilful
gekrochen pp von **kriechen**
Gel (-s, -s) nt gel
Gelächter (-s, -) nt laughter
geladen pp von **laden** ▷ adj
loaded; (Elek) live; (fig) furious
gelähmt adj paralysed
Gelände (-s, -) nt land, terrain;
(Fabrik, Sportgelände) grounds pl;
(Baugelände) site
Geländer (-s, -) nt railing;
(Treppengeländer) banister
Geländewagen m off-road
vehicle
gelang imperf von **gelingen**
gelassen pp von **lassen** ▷ adj
calm, composed
Gelatine f gelatine
gelaufen pp von **laufen**
gelaunt adj: **gut/schlecht ~** in a
good/bad mood
gelb adj yellow; (Ampel) amber,
yellow (US); **gelblich** adj
yellowish; **Gelbsucht** f jaundice
Geld (-(e)s, -er) nt money;
Geldautomat m cash machine (o
dispenser (Brit)); ATM (US);
Geldbeutel m, **Geldbörse** f
purse; **Geldbuße** f fine;
Geldschein m (bank)note (Brit),
bill (US); **Geldstrafe** f fine;
Geldstück nt coin; **Geldwechsel**
m exchange of money; (Ort)
bureau de change;
Geldwechselautomat m,
Geldwechsler (-s, -) m change
machine

Gelee (-s, -s) nt jelly
gelegen pp von **liegen** ▷ adj
situated; (passend) convenient;
etw kommt jdm ~ sth is
convenient for sb
Gelegenheit f opportunity;
(Anlass) occasion
gelegentlich adj occasional
▷ adv occasionally; (bei
Gelegenheit) some time (or other)
Gelenk (-(e)s, -e) nt joint
gelernt adj skilled
gelesen pp von **lesen**
geliehen pp von **leihen**
gelingen (gelang, gelungen) vi to
succeed; **es ist mir gelungen, ihn
zu erreichen** I managed to get
hold of him
gelitten pp von **leiden**
gelockt adj curly
gelogen pp von **lügen**
gelten (galt, gegolten) vt (wert
sein) to be worth; **jdm viel/wenig
~** to mean a lot/not to mean much
to sb ▷ vi (gültig sein) to be valid;
(erlaubt sein) to be allowed; **jdm
~** (gemünzt sein auf) to be meant for
(o aimed at) sb; **etw ~ lassen** to
accept sth; **als etw ~** to be
considered to be sth;
Geltungsdauer f: **eine ~ von
fünf Tagen haben** to be valid for
five days
gelungen pp von **gelingen**
gemahlen pp von **mahlen**
Gemälde (-s, -) nt painting,
picture
gemäß prep +dat in accordance
with ▷ adj appropriate (dat to)
gemein adj (niederträchtig) mean,
nasty; (gewöhnlich) common
Gemeinde (-, -n) f district,
community; (Pfarrgemeinde)
parish; (Kirchengemeinde)
congregation
gemeinsam adj joint, common
▷ adv together, jointly; **das Haus**

gehört uns beiden ~ the house belongs to both of us

Gemeinschaft f community; **~ Unabhängiger Staaten** Commonwealth of Independent States

gemeint pp von **meinen; das war nicht so ~** I didn't mean it like that

gemessen pp von **messen**

gemieden pp von **meiden**

gemischt adj mixed

gemocht pp von **mögen**

Gemüse (-s, -) nt vegetables pl; **Gemüsehändler(in)** m(f) greengrocer

gemusst pp von **müssen**

gemustert adj patterned

gemütlich adj comfortable, cosy; (Mensch) good-natured, easy-going; **mach es dir ~** make yourself at home

genannt pp von **nennen**

genau adj exact, precise ▷ adv exactly, precisely; **~ in der Mitte** right in the middle; **es mit etw ~ nehmen** to be particular about sth; **~ genommen** strictly speaking; **ich weiß es ~** I know for certain (o for sure); **genauso** adv exactly the same (way); **~ gut/viel/viele Leute** just as well/much/many people (wie as)

genehmigen vt to approve; **sich** (dat) **etw ~** to indulge in sth; **Genehmigung** f approval

Generalkonsulat nt consulate general

Generation (-s) f generation

Genf (-s) nt Geneva; **~er See** Lake Geneva

Genforschung f genetic research

genial adj brilliant

Genick (-(e)s, -e) nt (back of the) neck

Genie (-s, -s) nt genius

genieren vr: **sich ~** to feel awkward; **ich geniere mich vor ihm** he makes me feel embarrassed

genießen (genoss, genossen) vt to enjoy

Genitiv m genitive (case)

genmanipuliert adj genetically modified, GM

genommen pp von **nehmen**

genoss imperf von **genießen**

genossen pp von **genießen**

Gentechnik f genetic technology; **gentechnisch** adv: **~ verändert** genetically modified, GM

genug adv enough

genügen vi to be enough (jdm for sb); **danke, das genügt** thanks, that's enough (o that will do)

Genuss (-es, Genüsse) m pleasure; (Zusichnehmen) consumption

geöffnet adj (Geschäft etc) open

Geografie f geography

Geologie f geology

Georgien (-s) nt Georgia

Gepäck (-(e)s) nt luggage (Brit), baggage; **Gepäckabfertigung** f luggage (Brit) (o baggage) check-in; **Gepäckablage** f luggage (Brit) (o baggage) rack; **Gepäckannahme** f (zur Beförderung) luggage (Brit) (o baggage) office; (zur Aufbewahrung) left-luggage office (Brit), baggage checkroom (US); **Gepäckaufbewahrung** f left-luggage office (Brit), baggage checkroom (US); **Gepäckausgabe** f luggage (Brit) (o baggage) office; (am Flughafen) baggage reclaim; **Gepäckband** nt luggage (Brit) (o baggage) conveyor; **Gepäckkontrolle** f luggage (Brit) (o baggage) check; **Gepäckstück** nt item of luggage (Brit) (o baggage (US)); **Gepäckträger** m porter; (an Fahrrad) carrier;

Gepäckversicherung f luggage (Brit) (o baggage) insurance;
Gepäckwagen m luggage van (Brit), baggage car (US)
gepfiffen pp von **pfeifen**
gepflegt adj well-groomed; (Park) well looked after
gequollen pp von **quellen**

○ SCHLÜSSELWORT

gerade adj straight; (aufrecht) upright; **eine gerade Zahl** an even number
▷ adv **1** (genau) just, exactly; (speziell) especially; **gerade deshalb** that's just o exactly why; **das ist es ja gerade!** that's just it!; **gerade du** you especially; **warum gerade ich?** why me (of all people)?; **jetzt gerade nicht!** not now!; **gerade neben** right next to **2** (eben, soeben) just; **er wollte gerade aufstehen** he was just about to get up; **gerade erst** only just; **gerade noch** (only) just

geradeaus adv straight ahead
gerannt pp von **rennen**
geraspelt adj grated
Gerät (-(e)s, -e) nt device, gadget; (Werkzeug) tool; (Radio, Fernseher) set; (Zubehör) equipment
geraten pp von **raten** ▷ irr vi to turn out; **gut/schlecht ~** to turn out well/badly; **an jdn ~** to come across sb; **in etw** (akk) **~** to get into sth
geräuchert adj smoked
geräumig adj roomy
Geräusch (-(e)s, -e) nt sound; (unangenehm) noise
gerecht adj fair; (Strafe, Belohnung) just; **jdm/einer Sache ~ werden** to do justice to sb/sth
gereizt adj irritable

Gericht (-(e)s, -e) nt (Jur) court; (Essen) dish
gerieben pp von **reiben**
gering adj small; (unbedeutend) slight; (niedrig) low; (Zeit) short; **geringfügig** adj slight, minor ▷ adv slightly
gerissen pp von **reißen**
geritten pp von **reiten**
gern(e) adv willingly, gladly; **etw ~ tun** to like doing sth; **~ geschehen** you're welcome; **gern haben, gern mögen** irr vt to like
gerochen pp von **riechen**
Gerste (-, -n) f barley; **Gerstenkorn** nt (im Auge) stye
Geruch (-(e)s, Gerüche) m smell
Gerücht (-(e)s, -e) nt rumour
gerufen pp von **rufen**
Gerümpel (-s) nt junk
gerungen pp von **ringen**
Gerüst (-(e)s, -e) nt (auf Bau) scaffolding; (Gestell) trestle; (fig) framework (zu of)

gesalzen pp von **salzen**
gesamt adj whole, entire; (Kosten) total; (Werke) complete; **Gesamtschule** f ≈ comprehensive school
gesandt pp von **senden**
Gesäß (-es, -e) nt bottom
geschaffen pp von **schaffen**
Geschäft (-(e)s, -e) nt business; (Laden) shop; (Geschäftsabschluss) deal; **geschäftlich** adj commercial ▷ adv on business; **Geschäftsfrau** f businesswoman; **Geschäftsführer(in)** m(f) managing director; (von Laden) manager; **Geschäftsleitung** f executive board; **Geschäftsmann** m businessman; **Geschäftsreise** f business trip; **Geschäftsstraße** f shopping street; **Geschäftszeiten** pl business (o opening) hours pl

geschehen (geschah, geschehen) vi to happen

Geschenk (-(e)s, -e) nt present, gift; **Geschenkgutschein** m gift voucher; **Geschenkpapier** nt gift-wrapping paper, giftwrap

Geschichte (-, -n) f story; (Sache) affair; (Hist) history

geschickt adj skilful

geschieden pp von **scheiden**
▷ adj divorced

geschienen pp von **scheinen**

Geschirr (-(e)s, -e) nt crockery; (zum Kochen) pots and pans pl; (von Pferd) harness; **~ spülen** to do (o wash) the dishes, to do the washing-up (Brit);
Geschirrspülmaschine f dishwasher; **Geschirrspülmittel** nt washing-up liquid (Brit), dishwashing liquid (US);
Geschirrtuch nt tea towel (Brit), dish towel (US)

geschissen pp von **scheißen**

geschlafen pp von **schlafen**

geschlagen pp von **schlagen**

Geschlecht (-(e)s, -er) nt sex; (Ling) gender; **Geschlechtskrankheit** f sexually transmitted disease, STD; **Geschlechtsorgan** nt sexual organ;
Geschlechtsverkehr m sexual intercourse

geschlichen pp von **schleichen**

geschliffen pp von **schleifen**

geschlossen adj closed

Geschmack (-(e)s, Geschmäcke) m taste; **geschmacklos** adj tasteless; **Geschmack(s)sache** f: **das ist ~** that's a matter of taste; **geschmackvoll** adj tasteful

geschmissen pp von **schmeißen**

geschmolzen pp von **schmelzen**

geschnitten pp von **schneiden**

geschoben pp von **schieben**

Geschoss (-es, -e) nt (Stockwerk) floor

geschossen pp von **schießen**

Geschrei (-s) nt cries pl; (fig) fuss

geschrieben pp von **schreiben**

geschrie(e)n pp von **schreien**

geschützt adj protected

Geschwätz (-es) nt chatter; (Klatsch) gossip; **geschwätzig** adj talkative, gossipy

geschweige adv: **~ (denn)** let alone

geschwiegen pp von **schweigen**

Geschwindigkeit f speed; (Phys) velocity; **Geschwindigkeitsbegrenzung** f speed limit

Geschwister pl brothers and sisters pl

geschwollen adj (angeschwollen) swollen; (Rede) pompous

geschwommen pp von **schwimmen**

geschworen pp von **schwören**

Geschwulst (-, Geschwülste) f growth

Geschwür (-(e)s, -e) nt ulcer

gesehen pp von **sehen**

gesellig adj sociable;
Gesellschaft f society; (Begleitung) company; (Abend~) party; **~ mit beschränkter Haftung** limited company (Brit), limited corporation (US)

gesessen pp von **sitzen**

Gesetz (-es, -e) nt law; **gesetzlich** adj legal; **~er Feiertag** public (o bank (Brit) o legal (US)) holiday; **gesetzwidrig** adj illegal

Gesicht (-(e)s, -er) nt face; (Miene) expression; **mach doch nicht so ein ~!** stop pulling such a face!; **Gesichtscreme** f face cream; **Gesichtswasser** nt toner

gesoffen pp von **saufen**

gesogen pp von **saugen**

gespannt adj tense; (begierig) eager; **ich bin ~, ob ...** I wonder if ...; **auf etw/jdn ~ sein** to look

forward to sth/to seeing sb
Gespenst (-(e)s, -er) nt ghost
gesperrt adj closed
gesponnen pp von **spinnen**
Gespräch (-(e)s, -e) nt talk,
conversation; (Diskussion)
discussion; (Anruf) call
gesprochen pp von **sprechen**
gesprungen pp von **springen**
Gestalt (-, -en) f form, shape;
(Mensch) figure
gestanden pp von **stehen,
gestehen**
Gestank (-(e)s) m stench
gestatten vt to permit, to allow;
~ **Sie?** may I?
Geste (-, -n) f gesture
gestehen irr vt to confess
gestern adv yesterday;
~ **Abend/Morgen** yesterday
evening/morning
gestiegen pp von **steigen**
gestochen pp von **stechen**
gestohlen pp von **stehlen**
gestorben pp von **sterben**
gestört adj disturbed; (Empfang)
poor
gestoßen pp von **stoßen**
gestreift adj striped
gestrichen pp von **streichen**
gestritten pp von **streiten**
gestunken pp von **stinken**
gesund adj healthy; **wieder
~ werden** to get better;
Gesundheit f health; ~! bless
you!; **gesundheitsschädlich** adj
unhealthy
gesungen pp von **singen**
gesunken pp von **sinken**
getan pp von **tun**
getragen pp von **tragen**
Getränk (-(e)s, -e) nt drink;
Getränkeautomat m drinks
machine; **Getränkekarte** f list
of drinks
Getreide (-s, -) nt cereals pl,
grain

getrennt adj separate; ~ **leben**
to live apart; ~ **zahlen** to pay
separately
getreten pp von **treten**
Getriebe (-s, -) nt (Auto) gearbox
getrieben pp von **treiben**
Getriebeschaden m gearbox
damage
getroffen pp von **treffen**
getrunken pp von **trinken**
Getue nt fuss
geübt adj experienced
gewachsen pp von **wachsen**
▷ adj: **jdm/einer Sache ~ sein** to
be a match for sb/up to sth
Gewähr (-) f guarantee; **keine
~ übernehmen für** to accept no
responsibility for
Gewalt (-, -en) f (Macht) power;
(Kontrolle) control; (große Kraft)
force; (-taten) violence; **mit aller
~** with all one's might; **gewaltig**
adj tremendous; (Irrtum) huge
gewandt pp von **wenden** ▷ adj
(flink) nimble; (geschickt) skilful
gewann imperf von **gewinnen**
gewaschen pp von **waschen**
Gewebe (-s, -) nt (Stoff) fabric;
(Bio) tissue
Gewehr (-(e)s, -e) nt rifle, gun
Geweih (-(e)s, -e) nt antlers pl
gewellt adj (Haare) wavy
gewendet pp von **wenden**
Gewerbe (-s, -) nt trade;
Gewerbegebiet nt industrial
estate (Brit) (o park (US));
gewerblich adj commercial
Gewerkschaft f trade union
gewesen pp von **sein**
Gewicht (-(e)s, -e) nt weight;
(fig) importance
gewiesen pp von **weisen**
Gewinn (-(e)s, -e) m profit; (bei
Spiel) winnings pl; **gewinnen**
(gewann, gewonnen) vt to win;
(erwerben) to gain; (Kohle, Öl) to
extract ▷ vi to win; (profitieren) to

gewiss | 92

gain; **Gewinner(in)** (-s, -) m(f) winner

gewiss adj certain ▷ adv certainly

Gewissen (-s, -) nt conscience; **ein gutes/schlechtes ~ haben** to have a clear/bad conscience

Gewitter (-s, -) nt thunderstorm; **gewittern** vi impers: **es gewittert** it's thundering

gewogen pp von **wiegen**

gewöhnen vt **jdn an etw** (akk) **~** to accustom sb to sth ▷ vr: **sich an jdn/etw ~** to get used (o accustomed) to sb/sth; **Gewohnheit** f habit; (Brauch) custom; **gewöhnlich** adj usual; (durchschnittlich) ordinary; (pej) common; **wie ~** as usual; **gewohnt** adj usual; **etw ~ sein** to be used to sth

Gewölbe (-s, -) nt (Deckengewölbe) vault

gewonnen pp von **gewinnen**

geworben pp von **werben**

geworden pp von **werden**

geworfen pp von **werfen**

Gewürz (-es, -e) nt spice; **Gewürznelke** f clove; **gewürzt** adj seasoned

gewusst pp von **wissen**

Gezeiten pl tides pl

gezogen pp von **ziehen**

gezwungen pp von **zwingen**

Gibraltar (-s) nt Gibraltar

Gicht (-) f gout

Giebel (-s, -) m gable

gierig adj greedy

gießen (goss, gegossen) vt to pour; (Blumen) to water; (Metall) to cast; **Gießkanne** f watering can

Gift (-(e)s, -e) nt poison; **giftig** adj poisonous

Gigabyte nt gigabyte

Gin (-s, -s) m gin

ging imperf von **gehen**

Gin Tonic (-(s), -s) m gin and tonic

Gipfel (-s, -) m summit, peak; (Pol) summit; (fig: Höhepunkt) height

Gips (-es, -e) m (a. Med) plaster; **Gipsbein** nt: **sie hat ein ~** she's got her leg in plaster; **Gipsverband** m plaster cast

Giraffe (-, -n) f giraffe

Girokonto nt current account (Brit), checking account (US)

Gitarre (-, -n) f guitar

Gitter (-s, -) nt bars pl

glänzen vi (a. fig) to shine; **glänzend** adj shining; (fig) brilliant

Glas (-es, Gläser) nt glass; (Marmelade) jar; **zwei ~ Wein** two glasses of wine; **Glascontainer** m bottle bank; **Glaser(in)** m(f) glazier; **Glasscheibe** f pane (of glass); **Glassplitter** m splinter of glass

Glasur f glaze; (Gastr) icing

glatt adj smooth; (rutschig) slippery; (Lüge) downright; **Glatteis** nt (black) ice

Glatze (-, -n) f bald head; (fam: Skinhead) skinhead

glauben vt, vi to believe (an +akk in); (meinen) to think; **jdm ~** to believe sb

gleich adj equal; (identisch) same, identical; **alle Menschen sind ~** all people are the same; **es ist mir ~** it's all the same to me ▷ adv equally; (sofort) straight away; (bald) in a minute; **~ groß/alt** the same size/age; **~ nach/an** right after/at; **Gleichberechtigung** f equal rights pl; **gleichen** (glich, geglichen) vi: **jdm/einer Sache ~** to be like sb/sth ▷ vr: **sich ~** to be alike; **gleichfalls** adv likewise; **danke ~!** thanks, and the same to you; **gleichgültig** adj indifferent; **gleichmäßig** adj regular; (Verteilung) even, equal;

gleichzeitig adj simultaneous ▷ adv at the same time

Gleis (-es, -e) nt track, rails pl; (Bahnsteig) platform

gleiten (glitt, geglitten) vi to glide; (rutschen) to slide; **Gleitschirmfliegen** (-s) nt paragliding

Gletscher (-s, -) m glacier; **Gletscherskifahren** nt glacier skiing; **Gletscherspalte** f crevasse

glich imperf von **gleichen**

Glied (-(e)s, -er) nt (Arm, Bein) limb; (von Kette) link; (Penis) penis; **Gliedmaßen** pl limbs pl

glitschig adj slippery

glitt imperf von **gleiten**

glitzern vi to glitter; (Sterne) to twinkle

Glocke (-, -n) f bell; **Glockenspiel** nt chimes pl

Glotze (-, -n) f (fam: TV) box; **glotzen** vi (fam) to stare

Glück (-(e)s) nt luck; (Freude) happiness; **~ haben** to be lucky; **viel ~!** good luck; **zum ~** fortunately; **glücklich** adj lucky; (froh) happy; **glücklicherweise** adv fortunately; **Glückwunsch** m congratulations pl; **herzlichen ~ zur bestandenen Prüfung** congratulations on passing your exam; **herzlichen ~ zum Geburtstag!** Happy Birthday

Glühbirne f light bulb; **glühen** vi to glow; **Glühwein** m mulled wine

GmbH (-, -s) f abk = **Gesellschaft mit beschränkter Haftung** ≈ Ltd (Brit), ≈ Inc (US)

Gokart (-(s), -s) m go-kart

Gold (-(e)s) nt gold; **golden** adj gold; (fig) golden; **Goldfisch** m goldfish; **Goldmedaille** f gold medal; **Goldschmied(in)** m(f)

goldsmith

Golf (-(e)s, -e) m gulf; **der ~ von Biskaya** the Bay of Biscay ▷ (-s) nt golf; **Golfplatz** m golf course; **Golfschläger** m golf club

Gondel (-, -n) f gondola; (Seilbahn) cable-car

gönnen vt: **ich gönne es ihm** I'm really pleased for him; **sich** (dat) **etw ~** to allow oneself sth

goss imperf von **gießen**

gotisch adj Gothic

Gott (-es, Götter) m God; (Gottheit) god; **Gottesdienst** m service; **Göttin** f goddess

Grab (-(e)s, Gräber) nt grave

graben (grub, gegraben) vt to dig; **Graben** (-s, Gräben) m ditch

Grabstein m gravestone

Grad (-(e)s, -e) m degree; **wir haben 30 ~ Celsius** it's 30 degrees Celsius, it's 86 degrees Fahrenheit; **bis zu einem gewissen ~** up to a certain extent

Graf (-en, -en) m count; (in Großbritannien) earl

Graffiti pl graffiti sing

Grafik (-, -en) f graph; (Kunstwerk) graphic; (Illustration) diagram; **Grafikkarte** f (Inform) graphics card; **Grafikprogramm** nt (Inform) graphics software

Gräfin (-, -nen) f countess

Gramm (-s) nt gram(me)

Grammatik f grammar

Grapefruit (-, -s) f grapefruit

Graphik f siehe **Grafik**

Gras (-es, Gräser) nt grass

grässlich adj horrible

Gräte (-, -n) f (fish)bone

gratis adj, adv free (of charge)

gratulieren vi: **jdm (zu etw) ~** to congratulate sb (on sth); **(ich) gratuliere!** congratulations!

grau adj grey, gray (US); **grauhaarig** adj grey-haired

grausam adj cruel

gravierend adj (Fehler) serious
greifen (griff, gegriffen) vt to seize; **zu etw ~** (fig) to resort to sth ▷ vi (Regel etc) to have an effect (bei on)
grell adj harsh
Grenze (-, -n) f boundary; (Staat) border; (Schranke) limit; **grenzen** vi to border (an +akk on); **Grenzkontrolle** f border control; **Grenzübergang** m border crossing point; **Grenzverkehr** m border traffic
Grieche (-n, -n) m Greek; **Griechenland** nt Greece; **Griechin** f Greek; **griechisch** adj Greek; **Griechisch** nt Greek
griesgrämig adj grumpy
Grieß (-es, -e) m (Gastr) semolina
griff imperf von **greifen**
Griff (-(e)s, -e) m grip; (Tür etc) handle; **griffbereit** adj handy
Grill (-s, -s) m grill; (im Freien) barbecue
Grille (-, -n) f cricket
grillen vt to grill ▷ vi to have a barbecue; **Grillfest** nt, **Grillfete** f barbecue; **Grillkohle** f charcoal
grinsen vi to grin; (höhnisch) to sneer
Grippe (-, -n) f flu; **Grippeschutzimpfung** f flu vaccination
grob adj coarse; (Fehler, Verstoß) gross; (Einschätzung) rough
Grönland (-s) nt Greenland
groß adj big, large; (hoch) tall; (fig) great; (Buchstabe) capital; (erwachsen) grown-up; **im Großen und Ganzen** on the whole ▷ adv greatly; **großartig** adj wonderful
Großbritannien (-s) nt (Great) Britain
Großbuchstabe m capital letter
Größe (-, -n) f size; (Länge) height; (fig) greatness; **welche**

~ haben Sie? what size do you take?
Großeltern pl grandparents pl; **Großhandel** m wholesale trade; **Großmarkt** m hypermarket; **Großmutter** f grandmother; **Großraum** m: **der ~ Manchester** Greater Manchester; **groß|schreiben** irr vt to write with a capital letter; **Großstadt** f city; **Großvater** m grandfather; **großzügig** adj generous; (Planung) on a large scale
Grotte (-, -n) f grotto
grub imperf von **graben**
Grübchen nt dimple
Grube (-, -n) f pit
grüezi (interj) f (schweizerisch) hello
Gruft (-, -en) f vault
grün adj green; **~er Salat** lettuce; **~e Bohnen** French beans; **der ~e Punkt** symbol for recyclable packaging; **im ~en Bereich** hunky-dory

● **GRÜNER PUNKT**
●
● The **grüner Punkt** is the green
● spot symbol which appears on
● packaging, indicating that the
● packaging should not be
● thrown into the normal
● household refuse but kept
● separate to be recycled through
● the **DSD** (Duales System
● Deutschland) system. The
● recycling is financed by licences
● bought by the manufacturer
● from the 'DSD' and the cost of
● this is often passed on to the
● consumer.

Grünanlage f park
Grund (-(e)s, Gründe) m (Ursache) reason; (Erdboden) ground; (See, Gefäß) bottom; (Grundbesitz) land, property; **aus gesundheitlichen**

Gründen for health reasons; **im ~e** basically; **aus diesem ~** for this reason

gründen vt to found; **Gründer(in)** m(f) founder

Grundgebühr f basic charge; **Grundgesetz** nt (German) Constitution

gründlich adj thorough

Gründonnerstag m Maundy Thursday

grundsätzlich adj fundamental, basic; **sie kommt ~ zu spät** she's always late; **Grundschule** f primary school; **Grundstück** nt plot; (Anwesen) estate; (Baugrundstück) site; **Grundwasser** nt ground water

Grüne(r) mf (Pol) Green; **die ~n** the Green Party

Gruppe (-, -n) f group; **Gruppenermäßigung** f group discount; **Gruppenreise** f group tour

Gruselfilm m horror film

Gruß (-es, Grüße) m greeting; **viele Grüße** best wishes; **Grüße an** (+akk) regards to; **mit freundlichen Grüßen** Yours sincerely (Brit), Sincerely yours (US); **sag ihm einen schönen ~ von mir** give him my regards; **grüßen** vt to greet; **grüß deine Mutter von mir** give your mother my regards; **Julia lässt (euch) ~ Julia** sends (you) her regards

gucken vi to look

Gulasch (-(e)s, -e) nt goulash

gültig adj valid

Gummi (-s, -s) m o nt rubber; **Gummiband** nt rubber (o elastic (Brit)) band; **Gummibärchen** nt gums pl (in the shape of a bear) (Brit), gumdrops pl (in the shape of a bear) (US); **Gummihandschuhe** pl rubber gloves pl; **Gummistiefel** m wellington (boot) (Brit), rubber

boot (US)

günstig adj favourable; (Preis) good

gurgeln vi to gurgle; (im Mund) to gargle

Gurke (-, -n) f cucumber; **saure ~** gherkin

Gurt (-(e)s, -e) m belt

Gürtel (-s, -) m belt; (Geo) zone; **Gürtelrose** f shingles sing

GUS (-) f akr = **Gemeinschaft Unabhängiger Staaten** CIS

⊙ SCHLÜSSELWORT

gut adj good; **alles Gute** all the best; **also gut** all right then
▷ adv well; **gut gehen** to work, to come off; **es geht jdm gut** sb's doing fine; **gut gemeint** well meant; **gut schmecken** to taste good; **jdm guttun** to do sb good; **gut, aber ...** OK, but ...; **(na) gut, ich komme** all right, I'll come; **gut drei Stunden** a good three hours; **das kann gut sein** that may well be; **lass es gut sein** that'll do

Gutachten (-s, -) nt report; **Gutachter(in)** (-s, -) m(f) expert

gutartig adj (Med) benign

Güter pl goods pl; **Güterbahnhof** m goods station; **Güterzug** m goods train

gutgläubig adj trusting; **Guthaben** (-s) nt (Fin) credit balance

gutmütig adj good-natured

Gutschein (-s, -e) m voucher; **Gutschrift** f credit

Gymnasium nt ≈ grammar school (Brit), ≈ high school (US)

Gymnastik f exercises pl, keep-fit

Gynäkologe m, **Gynäkologin** f gynaecologist

Gyros (-, -) nt doner kebab

h

you mind if ...?; **was hast du denn?** what's the matter (with you)?

Haben nt (Comm) credit

Habicht (-(e)s, -e) m hawk

Hacke (-, -n) f (im Garten) hoe; (Ferse) heel; **hacken** vt to chop; (Loch) to hack; (Erde) to hoe; **Hacker(in)** (-s, -) m(f) (Inform) hacker; **Hackfleisch** nt mince(d meat) (Brit), ground meat (US)

Hafen (-s, Häfen) m harbour; (großer) port; **Hafenstadt** f port

Hafer (-s, -) m oats pl; **Haferflocken** pl rolled oats pl

Haft (-) f custody; **haftbar** adj liable, responsible; **haften** vi to stick; **~ für** to be liable (o responsible) for; **Haftnotiz** f Post-it®; **Haftpflichtversicherung** f third party insurance; **Haftung** f liability

Hagebutte (-, -n) f rose hip

Hagel (-s) m hail; **hageln** vi impers to hail

Hahn (-(e)s, Hähne) m cock; (Wasserhahn) tap (Brit), faucet (US); **Hähnchen** nt cockerel; (Gastr) chicken

Hai(fisch) (-(e)s, -e) m shark

häkeln vi, vt to crochet; **Häkelnadel** f crochet hook

Haken (-s, -) m hook; (Zeichen) tick

halb adj half; **~ eins** half past twelve; (fam) half twelve; **eine ~e Stunde** half an hour; **~ offen** half-open; **Halbfinale** nt semifinal; **halbieren** vt to halve; **Halbinsel** f peninsula; **Halbjahr** nt half-year; **halbjährlich** adj half-yearly; **Halbmond** m (Astr) half-moon; (Symbol) crescent; **Halbpension** f half board; **halbseitig** adj: **~ gelähmt** paralyzed on one side; **halbtags**

Haar (-(e)s, -e) nt hair; **um ein ~** nearly; **sich** (dat) **die ~e schneiden lassen** to have one's hair cut; **Haarbürste** f hairbrush; **Haarfestiger** m setting lotion; **Haargel** nt hair gel; **haarig** adj hairy; (fig) nasty; **Haarschnitt** m haircut; **Haarspange** f hair slide (Brit), barrette (US); **Haarspliss** m split ends pl; **Haarspray** nt hair spray; **Haartrockner** (-s, -) m hairdryer; **Haarwaschmittel** nt shampoo; **Haarwasser** nt hair tonic

haben (hatte, gehabt) vt, vaux to have; **Hunger/Angst ~** to be hungry/afraid; **Ferien ~** to be on holiday (Brit) (o vacation (US)); **welches Datum ~ wir heute?** what's the date today?; **ich hätte gerne ...** I'd like ...; **hätten Sie etwas dagegen, wenn ...?** would

adv (arbeiten) part-time; **halbwegs**
adv (leidlich) reasonably; **Halbzeit**
f half; (Pause) half-time

half *imperf von* **helfen**; **Hälfte**
(-, -n) f half

Halle (-, -n) f hall; **Hallenbad** nt
indoor (swimming) pool

hallo *interj* hello, hi

Halogenlampe f halogen lamp;
Halogenscheinwerfer m halogen headlight

Hals (-es, Hälse) m neck; (Kehle)
throat; **Halsband** nt (für Tiere)
collar; **Halsentzündung** f sore
throat; **Halskette** f necklace;
Hals-Nasen-Ohren-Arzt m,
Hals-Nasen-Ohren-Ärztin f ear,
nose and throat specialist;
Halsschmerzen pl sore throat
sing; **Halstuch** nt scarf

halt *interj* stop ▷ *adv*: **das ist ~ so**
that's just the way it is; **Halt** (-(e)s,
-e) m stop; (fester) hold; (innerer)
stability

haltbar *adj* durable; (Lebensmittel)
non-perishable; **Haltbarkeitsdatum** nt best-before
date

halten (hielt, gehalten) vt to keep;
(festhalten) to hold; **~ für** to regard
as; **~ von** to think of; **den
Elfmeter ~** to save the penalty;
eine Rede ~ to give (o make) a
speech ▷ vi to hold; (frisch bleiben)
to keep; (stoppen) to stop; **zu jdm
~** to stand by sb ▷ vr: **sich ~** (frisch
bleiben) to keep; (sich behaupten) to
hold out

Haltestelle f stop; **Halteverbot**
nt: **hier ist ~** you can't stop here

Haltung f (Körper) posture; (fig)
attitude; (Selbstbeherrschung)
composure; **~ bewahren** to keep
one's composure

Hamburg (-s) nt Hamburg;
Hamburger (-s, -) m (Gastr)
hamburger

Hammelfleisch nt mutton
Hammer (-s, Hämmer) m hammer; (fig, fam: Fehler) howler; **das
ist der ~** (unerhört) that's a bit
much

Hämorr(ho)iden pl haemorrhoids pl, piles pl

Hamster (-s, -) m hamster

Hand (-, Hände) f hand; **jdm die
~ geben** to shake hands with sb;
jdn bei der ~ nehmen to take sb
by the hand; **eine ~ voll
Reis/Leute** a handful of
rice/people; **zu Händen von**
attention; **Handarbeit** f
(Schulfach) handicraft; **~ sein** to be
handmade; **Handball** m
handball; **Handbremse** f
handbrake; **Handbuch** nt
handbook, manual; **Handcreme** f
hand cream; **Händedruck** m
handshake

Handel (-s) m trade; (Geschäft)
transaction; **handeln** vi to act;
(Comm) to trade; **~ von** to be
about ▷ vr impers: **sich ~ um** to
be about; **es handelt sich um ...**
it's about ...; **Handelskammer** f
chamber of commerce;
Handelsschule f business school

Handfeger (-s, -) m brush;
Handfläche f palm; **Handgelenk**
nt wrist; **handgemacht** adj
handmade; **Handgepäck** nt
hand luggage (Brit) (o baggage)

Händler(in) (-s, -) m(f) dealer

handlich adj handy

Handlung f act, action; (von
Roman, Film) plot

Handschellen pl handcuffs pl;
Handschrift f handwriting;
Handschuh m glove;
Handschuhfach nt glove
compartment; **Handtasche** f
handbag, purse (US); **Handtuch**
nt towel; **Handwerk** nt trade;
(Kunst~) craft; **Handwerker** (-s, -)

m workman

Handy (-s, -s) *nt* mobile (phone) (Brit), cell phone (US);
Handynummer *f* mobile number (Brit), cell phone number (US)

Hanf (-(e)s) *m* hemp

Hang (-(e)s, **Hänge**) *m* (Abhang) slope; (fig) tendency

Hängebrücke *f* suspension bridge; **Hängematte** *f* hammock

hängen (hing, gehangen) *vi* to hang; **an der Wand/an der Decke ~** to hang on the wall/from the ceiling; **an jdm ~** (fig) to be attached to sb; **~ bleiben** to get caught (an +dat on); (fig) to get stuck ▷ *vt* to hang (an +akk on)

Hantel (-, -n) *f* dumbbell

Hardware (-, -s) *f* (Inform) hardware

Harfe (-, -n) *f* harp

harmlos *adj* harmless

harmonisch *adj* harmonious

Harn (-(e)s, -e) *m* urine; **Harnblase** *f* bladder

Harpune (-, -n) *f* harpoon

hart *adj* hard; (fig) harsh; **zu jdm ~ sein** to be hard on sb; **~ gekocht** (Ei) hard-boiled; **hartnäckig** *adj* stubborn

Haschee (-s, -s) *nt* hash

Haschisch (-) *nt* hashish

Hase (-n, -n) *m* hare

Haselnuss *f* hazelnut

Hasenscharte *f* (Med) harelip

Hass (-es) *m* hatred (auf, gegen +akk of), hate; **einen ~ kriegen** (fam) to see red; **hassen** *vt* to hate

hässlich *adj* ugly; (gemein) nasty

Hast (-) *f* haste, hurry; **hastig** *adj* hasty

hatte *imperf von* **haben**

Haube (-, -n) *f* hood; (Mütze) cap; (Auto) bonnet (Brit), hood (US)

Hauch (-(e)s, -e) *m* breath; (Luft~)

breeze; (fig) trace; **hauchdünn** *adj* (Schicht, Scheibe) wafer-thin

hauen (haute, gehauen) *vt* to hit

Haufen (-s) *m* pile; **ein ~ Geld** (viel Geld) a lot of money

häufig *adj* frequent ▷ *adv* frequently, often

Haupt- *in zW* main: **Hauptbahnhof** *m* central (o main) station; **Hauptdarsteller(in)** *m(f)* leading actor/lady; **Haupteingang** *m* main entrance; **Hauptgericht** *nt* main course; **Hauptgeschäftszeiten** *pl* peak shopping hours *pl*; **Hauptgewinn** *m* first prize

Häuptling *m* chief

Hauptquartier *nt* headquarters *pl*; **Hauptreisezeit** *f* peak tourist season; **Hauptrolle** *f* leading role; **Hauptsache** *f* main thing; **hauptsächlich** *adv* mainly, chiefly; **Hauptsaison** *f* high (o peak) season; **Hauptsatz** *m* main clause; **Hauptschule** *f* ≈ secondary school (Brit), ≈ junior high school (US); **Hauptspeicher** *m* (Inform) main storage (o memory); **Hauptstadt** *f* capital; **Hauptstraße** *f* main road; (im Stadtzentrum) main street; **Hauptverkehrszeit** *f* rush hour

Haus (-es, **Häuser**) *nt* house; **nach ~e** home; **zu ~e** at home; **jdn nach ~e bringen** to take sb home; **bei uns zu ~e** (Heimat) where we come from; (Familie) in my family; (Haus) at our place; **Hausarbeit** *f* housework; **Hausaufgabe** *f* (Schule) homework; **~n** *pl* homework sing; **Hausbesitzer(in)** (-s, -) *m(f)* house owner; (Vermieter) landlord/-lady; **Hausbesuch** *m* home visit; **Hausbewohner(in)** (-s, -) *m(f)* occu[...]; **Hausflur** *m* hall; **Hausfrau** *f* housewife; **hausgemacht** adj homemade; **Haushalt** m household; (Pol) budget; **Hausherr(in)** m(f) host/hostess; (Vermieter) landlord/-lady

häuslich adj domestic

Hausmann m house-husband; **Hausmannskost** f good plain cooking; **Hausmeister(in)** m(f) caretaker (Brit), janitor (US); **Hausnummer** f house number; **Hausordnung** f (house) rules pl; **Hausschlüssel** m front-door key; **Hausschuh** m slipper; **Haustier** nt pet; **Haustür** f front door

Haut (-, Häute) f skin; (Tier) hide; **Hautarzt** m, **Hautärztin** f dermatologist; **Hautausschlag** m skin rash; **Hautcreme** f skin cream; **Hautfarbe** f skin colour; **Hautkrankheit** f skin disease

Hawaii (-s) nt Hawaii

Hbf. abk = **Hauptbahnhof** central station

Hebamme (-, -n) f midwife

Hebel (-s, -) m lever

heben (hob, gehoben) vt to raise, to lift

Hebräisch (-) nt Hebrew

Hecht (-(e)s, -e) m pike

Heck (-(e)s, -e) nt (von Boot) stern; (von Auto) rear; **Heckantrieb** m rear-wheel drive

Hecke (-, -n) f hedge

Heckklappe f tailgate; **Hecklicht** nt tail-light; **Heckscheibe** f rear window

Hefe (-, -n) f yeast

Heft (-(e)s, -e) nt notebook, exercise book; (Ausgabe) issue **heftig** adj violent; (Kritik, Streit) fierce

Heftklammer f paper clip; **Heftpflaster** nt plaster (Brit), Band-Aid® (US)

Heide (-, -n) f heath, moor; **Heidekraut** nt heather

Heidelbeere f bilberry, blueberry

heidnisch adj (Brauch) pagan

heikel adj (Angelegenheit) awkward; (wählerisch) fussy

heil adj (Sache) in one piece, intact; (Person) unhurt; **heilbar** adj curable

Heilbutt f -(e)s, -e) m halibut

heilen vt to cure ▷ vi to heal

heilig adj holy; **Heiligabend** m Christmas Eve; **Heilige(r)** mf saint

Heilmittel n remedy, cure (gegen for); **Heilpraktiker(in)** (-s, -) m(f) non-medical practitioner

heim adv home; **Heim** (-(e)s, -e) nt home

Heimat (-, -en) f home (town/country); **Heimatland** nt home country

heim|fahren irr vi to drive home; **Heimfahrt** f journey home; **heimisch** adj (Bevölkerung, Brauchtum) local; (Tiere, Pflanzen) native; **heim|kommen** irr vi to come (o return) home

heimlich adj secret

Heimreise f journey home; **Heimspiel** nt (Sport) home game; **Heimvorteil** m (Sport) home advantage; **Heimweg** m way home; **Heimweh** (-s) nt homesickness; **~ haben** to be homesick; **Heimwerker(in)** m(f) DIY enthusiast

Heirat (-, -en) f marriage; **heiraten** vi to get married ▷ vt to marry; **Heiratsantrag** m proposal; **er hat ihr einen ~ gemacht** he proposed to her

heiser adj hoarse

heiß adj hot; (Diskussion) heated; **mir ist ~** I'm hot

heißen (hieß, geheißen) vi to be called; (bedeuten) to mean; **ich heiße Tom** my name is Tom; **wie**

~ Sie? what's your name?; **wie heißt sie mit Nachnamen?** what's her surname?; **wie heißt das auf Englisch?** what's that in English? ▷ *vi impers:* **es heißt** (*man sagt*) it is said; **es heißt in dem Brief ...** it says in the letter ...; **das heißt** that is

Heißluftherd *m* fan-assisted oven

heiter *adj* cheerful; (*Wetter*) bright

heizen *vt* to heat; **Heizkissen** *nt* (*Med*) heated pad; **Heizkörper** *m* radiator; **Heizöl** *nt* fuel oil; **Heizung** *f* heating

Hektar (*-s, -*) *nt* hectare

Hektik (*-, -en*) *f:* **nur keine ~!** take it easy; **hektisch** *adj* hectic

Held (*-en, -en*) *m* hero; **Heldin** *f* heroine

helfen (*half, geholfen*) *vi* to help (*jdm bei etw* sb with sth); (*nützen*) to be of use; **sie weiß sich** (*dat*) **zu ~ she** can manage ▷ *vi impers:* **es hilft nichts, du musst ...** it's no use, you have to ...; **Helfer(in)** *m(f)* helper; (*Mitarbeiter*) assistant

Helikopter-Skiing (*-s*) *nt* heliskiing, helicopter skiing

hell *adj* bright; (*Farbe*) light; (*Hautfarbe*) fair; **hellblau** *adj* light blue; **hellblond** *adj* ash-blond; **hellgelb** *adj* pale yellow; **hellgrün** *adj* light green; **Hellseher(in)** *m(f)* clairvoyant

Helm (*-(e)s, -e*) *m* helmet; **Helmpflicht** *f* compulsory wearing of helmets

Hemd (*-(e)s, -en*) *nt* shirt; (*Unter-*) vest

hemmen *vt* to check; (*behindern*) to hamper; **gehemmt sein** to be inhibited; **Hemmung** *f* (*psychisch*) inhibition; **sie hatte keine ~, ihn zu betrügen** she had no scruples about deceiving him; (*moralisch*) scruple

Henkel (*-s, -*) *m* handle

Henna (*-s*) *nt* henna

Henne (*-, -n*) *f* hen

Hepatitis (*-, Hepatitiden*) *f* hepatitis

⭕ **SCHLÜSSELWORT**

her *adv* **1** (*Richtung*) **komm her zu mir** come here (to me); **von England her** from England; **von weit her** from a long way away; **her damit!** hand it over!; **wo hat er das her?** where did he get that from?; **wo bist du her?** where do you come from?
2 (*Blickpunkt*) **von der Form her** as far as the form is concerned
3 (*zeitlich*) **das ist 5 Jahre her** that was 5 years ago; **ich kenne ihn von früher her** I know him from before

herab *adv* down; **herablassend** *adj* (*Bemerkung*) condescending; **herab|sehen** *irr vi:* **auf jdn ~** to look down on sb; **herab|setzen** *vt* to reduce; (*fig*) to disparage

heran *adv* **näher ~!** come closer; **heran|kommen** *irr vi* to approach; **~ an** (*+akk*) to be able to get at; (*fig*) to be able to get hold of; **heran|wachsen** *irr vi* to grow up

herauf *adv* up; **herauf|beschwören** *irr vt* to evoke; (*verursachen*) to cause; **herauf|ziehen** *irr vt* to pull up ▷ *vi* to approach; (*Sturm*) to gather

heraus *adv* out; **heraus|bekommen** *irr vt* (*Geheimnis*) to find out; (*Rätsel*) to solve; **ich bekomme noch zwei Euro heraus** I've got two euros change to come; **heraus|bringen** *irr vt* to bring out; **heraus|finden**

irr vt to find out; **heraus|fordern**
vt to challenge; **Herausforderung**
f challenge; **heraus|geben** *irr vt*
(*Buch*) to edit; (*veröffentlichen*) to
publish; **jdm zwei Euro ~** to give
sb two euros change; **geben Sie
mir bitte auf 20 Euro heraus**
could you give me change for 20
euros, please?; **heraus|holen** *vt*
to get out (*aus of*); **heraus|-
kommen** *irr vi* to come
out; **dabei kommt nichts heraus**
nothing will come of it;
heraus|stellen *vr*: **sich ~** to turn
out (*als* to be); **heraus|ziehen** *irr*
vt to pull out

Herbergseltern *pl* (youth hostel)
wardens *pl*

Herbst (*-(e)s, -e*) *m* autumn, fall
(*US*)

Herd (*-(e)s, -e*) *m* cooker, stove

Herde (*-, -n*) *f* herd; (*Schafe*) flock

herein *adv* in; **~!** come in;
herein|fallen *irr vi*: **wir sind auf
einen Betrüger hereingefallen**
we were taken in by a swindler;
herein|legen *vt*: **jdn ~** (*fig*) to
take sb for a ride

Herfahrt *f* journey here; **auf der
~** on the way here

Hergang *m* course (of events);
schildern Sie mir den ~ tell me
what happened

Hering (*-s, -e*) *m* herring

her|kommen *irr vi* to come; **wo
kommt sie her?** where does she
come from?

Heroin (*-s*) *nt* heroin

Herpes (*-*) *m* (*Med*) herpes

Herr (*-(e)n, -en*) *m* (*vor Namen*) Mr;
(*Mann*) gentleman; (*Adliger, Gott*)
Lord; **mein ~!** sir; **meine ~en!**
gentlemen; **Sehr geehrte Damen
und ~en** Dear Sir or Madam;
herrenlos *adj* (*Gepäck*) abandoned;
(*Tier*) stray; **Herrentoilette** *f*
men's toilet, gents

her|richten *vt* to prepare

herrlich *adj* marvellous, splendid

Herrschaft *f* rule; (*Macht*) power;
meine ~en! ladies and gentlemen!

herrschen *vi* to rule; (*bestehen*) to
be

her|stellen *vt* to make;
(*industriell*) to manufacture; **Her-
steller(in)** *m(f)* manufacturer;
Herstellung *f* production

herüber *adv* over

herum *adv* around; (*im Kreis*)
round; **anders ~** around sth; **du
hast den Pulli falsch ~ an** your
sweater's inside out; **anders ~** the
other way round; **herum|fahren**
irr vi to drive around; **herum|
führen** *vt*: **jdn in der Stadt ~** to
show sb around the town ▷ *vi*:
**die Straße führt um das Zentrum
herum** the road goes around the
city centre; **herum|kommen** *irr*
vi: **sie ist viel in der Welt
herumgekommen** she's been
around the world; **um etw
~** (*vermeiden*) to get out of sth;
herum|kriegen *vt* to talk round;
herum|treiben *irr vr*: **sich ~** to
hang around

herunter *adv* down;
heruntergekommen *adj* (*Gebäude,
Gegend*) run-down; (*Person*)
down-at-heel; **herunter|handeln**
vt to get-at-heel; **herunter|holen**
vt to bring down;
herunter|kommen *irr vi* to come
down; **herunterladbar** *adj*
(*Inform*) downloadable;
herunter|laden *irr vt* (*Inform*) to
download

hervor *adv* out; **hervor|bringen**
irr vt to produce; (*Wort*) to utter;
hervor|heben *irr vt* to
emphasize; **hervorragend** *adj*
excellent; **hervor|rufen** *irr vt* to
cause, to give rise to

Herz (*-ens, -en*) *nt* heart; (*Karten*)

hearts pl; **von ganzem ~en**
wholeheartedly; **sich** (dat) **etw zu
~en nehmen** to take sth to heart;
Herzanfall m heart attack;
Herzbeschwerden pl heart
trouble sing; **Herzfehler** m heart
defect; **herzhaft** adj (Essen)
substantial; **~ lachen** to have a
good laugh; **Herzinfarkt** m
heart attack; **Herzklopfen** (-s) nt
(Med) palpitations pl; **ich hatte
~ (vor Aufregung)** my heart was
pounding (with excitement);
herzkrank adj: **sie ist ~** she's got
a heart condition; **herzlich** adj
(Empfang, Mensch) warm; **~en
Glückwunsch** congratulations
Herzog(in) (-s, Herzöge) m(f)
duke/duchess
Herzschlag m heartbeat;
(Herzversagen) heart failure;
Herzschrittmacher m pacemaker; **Herzstillstand** m
cardiac arrest
Hessen (-s) nt Hessen
heterosexuell adj heterosexual;
Heterosexuelle(r) mf
heterosexual
Hetze (-, -n) f (Eile) rush; **hetzen**
vt to rush ▶ vr: **sich ~** to rush
Heu (-(e)s) nt hay
heuer adv this year
heulen vi to howl; (weinen) to cry
Heuschnupfen m hay fever;
Heuschrecke (-, -n) f grasshopper; (größer) locust
heute adv today; **~ Abend/früh**
this evening/morning; **~ Morgen**
this morning; **~ Nacht** tonight;
(letzte Nacht) last night; **~ in acht
Tagen** a week (from) today; **sie
hat bis ~ nicht bezahlt** she hasn't
paid to this day; **heutig** adj: **die
~e Zeitung/Generation** today's
paper/generation; **heutzutage**
adv nowadays
Hexe (-, -n) f witch;

Hexenschuss m lumbago
hielt imperf von **halten**
hier adv here; **~ entlang** this way;
ich bin auch nicht von ~ I'm a
stranger here myself; **hier|bleiben**
irr vi to stay here; **hier|lassen** irr
vt to leave here; **hierher** adv
here; **das gehört nicht ~** that
doesn't belong here; **hiermit** adv
with this; **hierzulande** adv in
this country
hiesig adj local
hieß imperf von **heißen**
Hi-Fi-Anlage f hi-fi (system)
high adj (fam) high; **Highlife** (-s)
nt high life; **~ machen** to live it
up; **Hightech** (-s) nt high tech
Hilfe (-, -n) f help; (für Notleidende,
finanziell) aid; **~!** help!; **Erste
~ leisten** to give first aid; **um
~ bitten** to ask for help; **hilflos**
adj helpless; **hilfsbereit** adj
helpful; **Hilfsmittel** nt aid
Himbeere f raspberry
Himmel (-s, -) m sky; (Rel)
heaven; **Himmelfahrt** f
Ascension; **Himmelsrichtung** f
direction; **himmlisch** adj
heavenly

○ **SCHLÜSSELWORT**

hin adv **1** (Richtung) **hin und zurück**
there and back; **hin und her** to
and fro; **bis zur Mauer hin** up to
the wall; **wo ist er hin?** where has
he gone?; **Geld hin, Geld her**
money or no money
2 (auf ... hin) **auf meine Bitte hin**
at my request; **auf seinen Rat hin**
on the basis of his advice
3 **mein Glück ist hin** my happiness
has gone

hinab adv down; **hinab|gehen** irr
vi to go down
hinauf adv up; **hinauf|gehen** irr

vi, vt to go up; **hinauf|steigen** irr vi to climb (up)

hinaus adv out; **hinaus|gehen** irr vi to go out; **das Zimmer geht auf den See hinaus** the room looks out onto the lake; **~ über** (+akk) to exceed; **hinaus|laufen** irr vi to run out; **~ auf** (+akk) to come to, to amount to; **hinaus|schieben** irr vi to put off, to postpone; **hinaus|werfen** irr vt to throw out; (aus Firma) to fire, to sack (Brit); **hinaus|zögern** vr: **sich ~** to take longer than expected

Hinblick m in (o **im**) **~ auf** (+akk) with regard to; (wegen) in view of

hin|bringen irr vt: **ich bringe Sie hin** I'll take you there

hindern vt to prevent; **jdn daran ~, etw zu tun** to stop (o prevent) sb from doing sth; **Hindernis** nt obstacle

Hinduismus m Hinduism

hindurch adv through; **das ganze Jahr ~** throughout the year, all year round; **die ganze Nacht ~** all night (long)

hinein adv in; **hinein|gehen** vi to go in; **~ in** (+akk) to go into, to enter; **hinein|passen** vi to fit in; **~ in** (+akk) to fit into

hin|fahren irr vi to go there ▷ vt to take there; **Hinfahrt** f outward journey

hin|fallen irr vi to fall (down)

Hinflug m outward flight

hing imperf von **hängen**

hin|gehen irr vi to go there; (Zeit) to pass; **hin|halten** irr vt to hold out; (warten lassen) to put off

hinken vi to limp; **der Vergleich hinkt** the comparison doesn't work

hin|knien vr: **sich ~** to kneel down; **hin|legen** vt to put down ▷ vr: **sich ~** to lie down; **hin|nehmen** irr vt (fig) to put up

with, to take; **Hinreise** f outward journey; **hin|setzen** vr: **sich ~** to sit down; **hinsichtlich** prep +gen with regard to; **hin|stellen** vt to put (down) ▷ vr: **sich ~** to stand

hinten adv at the back; (im Auto) in the back; (dahinter) behind

hinter prep +dat o akk behind; (nach) after; **~ jdm her sein** to be after sb; **etw ~ sich (dat) bringen** to get sth over (and done) with; **Hinterachse** f rear axle; **Hinterausgang** m rear exit; **Hinterbein** nt hind leg; **Hinterbliebene(r)** mf dependant; **hintere(r, s)** adj rear, back; **hintereinander** adv (in einer Reihe) one behind the other; (hintereinander her) one after the other; **drei Tage ~** three days running (o in a row); **Hintereingang** m rear entrance; **Hintergedanke** m ulterior motive; **hintergehen** irr vt to deceive; **Hintergrund** m background; **hinterher** adv (zeitlich) afterwards; **los, ~!** come on, after him/her/them; **Hinterkopf** m back of the head; **hinterlassen** irr vt to leave; **jdm eine Nachricht ~** to leave a message for sb; **hinterlegen** vt to leave (bei with)

Hintern (-, -) m (fam) backside, bum

Hinterradantrieb m (Auto) rear-wheel drive; **Hinterteil** nt back (part); (Hintern) behind; **Hintertür** f back door

hinüber adv over; **~ sein** (fam: kaputt) to be ruined; (verdorben) to have gone bad; **hinüber|gehen** irr vi to go over

hinunter adv down; **hinunter|gehen** irr vi, vt to go down; **hinunter|schlucken** vt to

(a. fig) to swallow

Hinweg m outward journey

hinweg|setzen vr **sich über etw** (akk) ~ to ignore sth

Hinweis (-es, -e) m (Andeutung) hint; (Anweisung) instruction; (Verweis) reference; **hin|weisen** irr vi **jdn auf etw** (acc) ~ to point sth out to sb; **jdn nochmal auf etw** ~ to remind sb of sth

hinzu adv in addition; **hinzu|fügen** vt to add; **hinzu|kommen** irr vi: **zu jdm** ~ to join sb; **es war kalt, hinzu kam, dass es auch noch regnete** it was cold, and on top of that it was raining

Hirn (-(e)s, -e) nt brain; (Verstand) brains pl; **Hirnhautentzündung** f meningitis

Hirsch (-(e)s, -e) m deer; (als Speise) venison

Hirte (-n, -n) m shepherd

historisch adj historical

Hit (-s, -s) m (fig, Mus, Inform) hit; **Hitliste** f, **Hitparade** f charts pl

Hitze (-) f heat; **hitzebeständig** adj heat-resistant; **Hitzewelle** f heatwave; **hitzig** adj hot-tempered; (Debatte) heated; **Hitzschlag** m heatstroke

HIV (-(s), -(s)) nt abk = **Human Immunodeficiency Virus** HIV; **HIV-negativ** adj HIV-negative; **HIV-positiv** adj HIV-positive

H-Milch f long-life milk

hob imperf von **heben**

Hobby (-s, -s) nt hobby

Hobel (-s, -) m plane

hoch adj high; (Baum) tall; (Schnee) deep; **der Zaun ist drei Meter** ~ the fence is three metres high; ~ **auflösend** high-resolution; ~ **begabt** extremely gifted; **das ist mir zu** ~ that's above my head; ~ **soll sie leben!, sie lebe** ~! three cheers for her; **4 ÷ 2 ist 16** 4 squared

is 16; **4 ÷ 5** 4 to the power of 5

Hoch (-s, -s) nt (Ruf) cheer; (Meteo) high; **hochachtungsvoll** adv (in Briefen) Yours faithfully; **Hochbetrieb** m: **es herrscht** ~ they/we are extremely busy; **Hochdeutsch** nt High German; **Hochgebirge** nt high mountains pl; **Hochgeschwindigkeitszug** m high-speed train; **Hochhaus** nt high rise; **hoch|heben** irr vt to lift (up); **hochprozentig** adj (Alkohol) high-proof; **Hochsaison** f high season; **Hochschule** f college; (Universität) university; **Hochschulreife** f **er hat (die)** ~ he's got his A-levels (Brit), he's graduated from high school (US); **Hochsommer** m midsummer; **Hochspannung** f great tension; (Elek) high voltage; **Hochsprung** m high jump

höchst adv highly, extremely; **höchste(r, s)** adj highest; (äußerste) extreme; **höchstens** adv at the most; **Höchstform** f (Sport) top form; **Höchstgeschwindigkeit** f maximum speed; **Höchstparkdauer** f maximum stay

Hochstuhl m high chair

höchstwahrscheinlich adv very probably

Hochwasser nt high water; (Überschwemmung) floods pl; **hochwertig** adj high-quality

Hochzeit (-, -en) f wedding; **Hochzeitsnacht** f wedding night; **Hochzeitsreise** f honeymoon; **Hochzeitstag** m wedding day; (Jahrestag) wedding anniversary

hocken vi to squat, to crouch

Hocker (-s, -) m stool

Hockey (-s) nt hockey

Hoden (-s, -) m testicle

Hof (-(e)s, Höfe) m (Hinterhof) yard;

(Innenhof) courtyard; (Bauernhof) farm; (Königshof) court

hoffen vi to hope (auf +akk for); **ich hoffe es** I hope so; **hoffentlich** adv hopefully; **~ nicht** I hope not; **Hoffnung** f hope; **hoffnungslos** adj hopeless

höflich adj polite; **Höflichkeit** f politeness

hohe(r, s) adj siehe hoch

Höhe (-, -n) f height; (Anhöhe) hill; (einer Summe) amount; **in einer ~ von 5000 Metern** at an altitude of 5,000 metres; (Flughöhe) altitude; **Höhenangst** f vertigo

Höhepunkt m (einer Reise) high point; (einer Veranstaltung) highlight; (eines Films; sexuell) climax

höher adj, adv higher

hohl adj hollow

Höhle (-, -n) f cave

holen vt to get, to fetch; (abholen) to pick up; (Atem) to catch; **die Polizei ~** to call the police; **jdn/etw ~ lassen** to send for sb/sth

Holland nt Holland; **Holländer(in)** (-s, -) m(f) Dutchman/ -woman; **holländisch** adj Dutch

Hölle (-, -n) f hell

Hologramm nt hologram

holperig adj bumpy

Holunder (-s, -) m elder

Holz (-es, Hölzer) nt wood; **Holzboden** m wooden floor; **hölzern** adj wooden; **holzig** adj (Stängel) woody; **Holzkohle** f charcoal

Homebanking (-s) nt home banking, online banking; **Homepage** f home page; **Hometrainer** m exercise machine

Homoehe f (fam) gay marriage

homöopathisch adj homeopathic

homosexuell adj homosexual; **Homosexuelle(r)** mf homosexual

Honig (-s, -e) m honey; **Honigmelone** f honeydew melon

Honorar (-s, -e) nt fee

Hopfen (-s, -) m (Bot) hop; (beim Brauen) hops pl

hoppla interj whoops, oops

horchen vi to listen (auf +akk to); (an der Tür) to eavesdrop

hören vt, vi (passiv, mitbekommen) to hear; (zufällig) to overhear; (aufmerksam zuhören; Radio, Musik) to listen to; **ich habe schon viel von Ihnen gehört** I've heard a lot about you; **Hörer** m (Tel) receiver; **Hörer(in)** m(f) listener; **Hörgerät** nt hearing aid

Horizont (-(e)s, -e) m horizon; **das geht über meinen ~** that's beyond me

Hormon (-s, -e) nt hormone

Hornhaut f hard skin; (des Auges) cornea

Hornisse (-, -n) f hornet

Horoskop (-s, -e) nt horoscope

Hörsaal m lecture hall; **Hörsturz** m acute hearing loss; **Hörweite** f: **in/außer ~** within/out of earshot

Höschenwindel (-, -n) f nappy (Brit), diaper (US)

Hose (-, -n) f trousers pl (Brit), pants pl (US); (Unterhose) (under)pants pl; **eine ~** a pair of trousers/pants; **kurze ~** (pair of) shorts pl; **Hosenanzug** m trouser suit (Brit), pantsuit (US); **Hosenschlitz** m fly, flies (Brit); **Hosentasche** f trouser pocket (Brit), pant pocket (US); **Hosenträger** m braces pl (Brit), suspenders pl (US)

Hospital (-s, Hospitäler) nt hospital

Hotdog (-s, -s) nt o m hot dog

Hotel (-s, -s) nt hotel; **in welchem ~ seid ihr?** which hotel are you staying at?; **Hoteldirektor(in)** m(f) hotel manager; **Hotelkette** f hotel chain; **Hotelzimmer** nt hotel room

Hotline (-, -s) f hot line; **Hotspot** m (wireless) hotspot

Hubraum m cubic capacity

hübsch adj (Mädchen, Kind, Kleid) pretty; (gutaussehend; Mann, Frau) good-looking, cute

Hubschrauber (-s, -) m helicopter

Huf (-(e)s, -e) m hoof; **Hufeisen** nt horseshoe

Hüfte (-, -n) f hip

Hügel (-s, -) m hill; **hügelig** adj hilly

Huhn (-(e)s, Hühner) nt hen; (Gastr) chicken; **Hühnchen** nt chicken; **Hühnerauge** nt corn; **Hühnerbrühe** f chicken broth

Hülle (-, -n) f cover; (für Ausweis) case; (Zellophan) wrapping

Hummel (-, -n) f bumblebee

Hummer (-s, -) m lobster; **Hummerkrabbe** f king prawn

Humor (-s) m humour; **~ haben** to have a sense of humour; **humorlos** adj humourless; **humorvoll** adj humorous

humpeln vi to hobble

Hund (-(e)s, -e) m dog; **Hundeleine** f dog lead (Brit), dog leash (US)

hundert num hundred; **Hundertjahrfeier** f centenary; **hundertprozentig** adj, adv one hundred per cent; **hundertste(r, s)** adj hundredth

Hündin f bitch

Hunger (-s) m hunger; **~ haben/bekommen** to be/get hungry; **hungern** vi to go

hungry; (ernsthaft, dauernd) to starve

Hupe (-, -n) f horn; **hupen** vi to sound one's horn

Hüpfburg f bouncy castle®; **hüpfen** vi to hop; (springen) to jump

Hürde (-, -n) f hurdle

Hure (-, -n) f whore

hurra interj hooray

husten vi to cough; **Husten** (-s) m cough; **Hustenbonbon** nt cough sweet; **Hustensaft** m cough mixture

Hut (-(e)s, Hüte) m hat

hüten vt to look after ▷ vr: **sich ~** to watch out; **sich ~, etw zu tun** to take care not to do sth; **sich ~ vor** (+dat) to beware of

Hütte (-, -n) f hut, cottage; **Hüttenkäse** m cottage cheese

Hyäne (-, -n) f hyena

Hydrant m hydrant

hygienisch adj hygienic

Hyperlink (-s, -s) m hyperlink

Hypnose (-, -n) f hypnosis; **Hypnotiseur(in)** m(f) hypnotist; **hypnotisieren** vt to hypnotize

Hypothek (-, -en) f mortgage

hysterisch adj hysterical

i

Igel (-s, -) m hedgehog
ignorieren vt to ignore
ihm pron dat sing von **er/es**; (to) him, (to) it; **wie geht es ~?** how is he?; **ein Freund von ~** a friend of his ▷ pron dat von **es**; (to) it
ihn pron akk sing von **er**; (Person) him; (Sache) it
ihnen pron dat pl von **sie**; (to) them; **wie geht es ~?** how are they?; **ein Freund von ~** a friend of theirs
Ihnen pron dat sing u pl von **Sie**; (to) you; **wie geht es ~?** how are you?; **ein Freund von ~** a friend of yours

ihr pron 1 (nom pl) you; **ihr seid es** it's you
2 (dat von sie) to her; **gib es ihr** give it to her; **er steht neben ihr** he is standing beside her
▷ possessiv pron 1 (sg) her; (bei Tieren, Dingen) its; **ihr Mann** her husband
2 (pl) their; **die Bäume und ihre Blätter** the trees and their leaves

i. A. abk = **im Auftrag** pp
IC (-, -s) m abk = **Intercityzug** Intercity (train)
ICE (-, -s) m abk = **Intercityexpresszug** German high-speed train
ich pron I; **~ bin's** it's me; **~ nicht** not me; **du und ~** you and me; **hier bin ~!** here I am; **~ Idiot!** stupid me
Icon (-s, -s) nt (Inform) icon
IC-Zuschlag m Intercity supplement
ideal adj ideal; **Ideal** (-s, -e) nt ideal
Idee (-, -n) f idea
identifizieren vt to identify ▷ vr: **sich mit jdm/etw ~** to identify with sb/sth
identisch adj identical
Idiot(in) (-en, -en) m(f) idiot; **idiotisch** adj idiotic
Idol (-s, -e) nt idol
Idylle f idyll; **idyllisch** adj idyllic

Ihr pron von **Sie**; (adjektivisch) your; **~ XY** (am Briefende) Yours, XY
ihre(r, s) pron (substantivisch, sing) hers; (pl) theirs; **das ist ~/~r/ihr(e)s** that's hers; (pl) that's theirs
Ihre(r, s) pron (substantivisch) yours; **das ist ~/~r/Ihr(e)s** that's yours
ihretwegen adv (wegen ihr) because of her; (ihr zuliebe) for her sake; (um sie) about her; (von ihr aus) as far as she is concerned ▷ adv (wegen ihnen) because of them; (ihnen zuliebe) for their sake; (um sie) about them; (von ihnen aus)

as far as they are concerned; **Ihretwegen** *adv* (*wegen Ihnen*) because of you; (*Ihnen zuliebe*) for your sake; (*um Sie*) about you; (*von Ihnen aus*) as far as you are concerned

Ikone (-, -n) *f* icon

illegal *adj* illegal

Illusion *f* illusion; **sich** (*dat*) **~en machen** to delude oneself; **illusorisch** *adj* illusory

Illustration *f* illustration

Illustrierte (-n, -n) *f* (glossy) magazine

im *kontr von* **in dem**; **~ Bett** in bed; **~ Fernsehen** on TV; **~ Radio** on the radio; **~ Bus/Zug** on the bus/train; **~ Januar** in January; **~ Stehen** (while) standing up

Imbiss (-es, -e) *m* snack; **Imbissbude** *f*, **Imbissstube** *f* snack bar

Imbussschlüssel *m* hex key

immer *adv* always; **~ mehr** more and more; **~ wieder** again and again; **~ noch** still; **~ noch nicht** still not; **für ~** forever; **~ wenn ich ...** every time I ...; **~ schöner/ trauriger** more and more beautiful/sadder and sadder; **was/wer/wo/wann (auch)** whatever/whoever/ wherever/whenever; **immerhin** *adv* after all; **immerzu** *adv* all the time

Immigrant(in) *m(f)* immigrant

Immobilien *pl* property *sing*, real estate *sing*; **Immobilien- makler(in)** *m(f)* estate agent (*Brit*), realtor (*US*)

immun *adj* immune (**gegen** to); **Immunschwäche** *f* immuno- deficiency; **Immun- schwächekrankheit** *f* immune deficiency syndrome; **Immunsystem** *nt* immune system

impfen *vt* to vaccinate; **ich muss mich gegen Pocken ~ lassen** I've got to get myself vaccinated against smallpox; **Impfpass** *m* vaccination card; **Impfstoff** *m* vaccine; **Impfung** *f* vaccination

imponieren *vi* to impress (*jdm* sb)

Import (-(e)s, -e) *m* import; **importieren** *vt* to import

impotent *adj* impotent

imstande *adj*: **~ sein** to be in a position; (*fähig*) to be able

○ **SCHLÜSSELWORT**

in *prep* +*akk* **1** (*räumlich: wohin?*) in, into; **in die Stadt** into town; **in die Schule gehen** to go to school
2 (*zeitlich*) **bis ins 20. Jahrhundert** into o up to the 20th century
▷ *prep* +*dat* **1** (*räumlich: wo?*) in; **in der Stadt** in town; **in der Schule sein** to be at school
2 (*zeitlich: wann?*) **in diesem Jahr** this year; (*in jenem Jahr*) in that year; **heute in zwei Wochen** two weeks today

inbegriffen *adj* included

indem *conj*: **sie gewann, ~ sie mogelte** she won by cheating

Inder(in) (-s, -) *m(f)* Indian

Indianer(in) (-s, -) *m(f)* American Indian, Native American; **indianisch** *adj* American Indian, Native American

Indien (-s) *nt* India

indirekt *adj* indirect

indisch *adj* Indian

indiskret *adj* indiscreet

individuell *adj* individual

Indonesien (-s) *nt* Indonesia

Industrie *f* industry; **Industrie- in** *zW* industrial; **Industriegebiet** *nt* industrial area; **industriell** *adj* industrial

ineinander adv in(to) one another (o each other)

Infarkt (-(e)s, -e) m (Herzinfarkt) heart attack

Infektion f infection; **Infektionskrankheit** f infectious disease; **infizieren** vt to infect ▷ vr: **sich ~** to be infected

Info (-, -s) f (fam) info

infolge prep +gen as a result of, owing to; **infolgedessen** adv consequently

Infomaterial nt (fam) bumf, info

Informatik f computer science; **Informatiker(in)** (-s, -) m(f) computer scientist

Information f information; **Informationsschalter** m information desk; **informieren** vt to inform; **falsch ~** to misinform ▷ vr: **sich ~** to find out (über +akk about)

infrage adv: **das kommt nicht ~** that's out of the question; **etw ~ stellen** to question sth

Infrastruktur f infrastructure

Infusion f infusion

Ingenieur(in) m(f) engineer

Ingwer (-s) m ginger

Inhaber(in) (-s, -) m(f) owner; (Haus~) occupier; (von Lizenz) holder; (Fin) bearer

Inhalt (-(e)s, -e) m contents pl; (eines Buchs etc) content; (Math) volume; (Flächeninhalt) area; **Inhaltsangabe** f summary; **Inhaltsverzeichnis** nt table of contents

Initiative f initiative; **die ~ ergreifen** to take the initiative

Injektion f injection

inklusive adv, prep inclusive (gen of)

inkonsequent adj inconsistent

Inland nt (Pol, Comm) home; **im ~** at home; (Geo) inland;

inländisch adj domestic; **Inlandsflug** m domestic flight; **Inlandsgespräch** nt national call

Inliner pl, **Inlineskates** pl (Sport) Rollerblades® pl, in-line skates pl

innen adv inside; **Innenarchitekt(in)** m(f) interior designer; **Innenhof** m (inner) courtyard; **Innenminister(in)** m(f) minister of the interior, Home Secretary (Brit); **Innenseite** f inside; **Innenspiegel** m rearview mirror; **Innenstadt** f town centre; (von Großstadt) city centre

innere(r, s) adj inner; (im Körper, inländisch) internal; **Innere(s)** nt inside; (Mitte) centre; (fig) heart

Innereien pl innards pl

innerhalb adv, prep +gen within; (räumlich) inside

innerlich adj internal; (geistig) inner

innerste(r, s) adj innermost

Innovation f innovation; **innovativ** adj innovative

inoffiziell adj unofficial; (zwanglos) informal

ins kontr von in das

Insasse (-n, -n) m, **Insassin** f (Auto) passenger; (Anstalt) inmate

insbesondere adv particularly, in particular

Inschrift f inscription

Insekt (-(e)s, -en) nt insect, bug (US); **Insektenschutzmittel** nt insect repellent; **Insektenstich** m insect bite

Insel (-, -n) f island

Inserat nt advertisement

insgesamt adv altogether, all in all

Insider(in) (-s, -) m(f) insider

insofern adv in that respect; (deshalb) (and) so ▷ conj if; **~ als** in so far as

Installateur | 110

Installateur(in) *m(f)* (Klempner) plumber; (Elektroinstallateur) electrician; **installieren** *vt* (Inform) to install

Instinkt (-(e)s, -e) *m* instinct

Institut (-(e)s, -e) *nt* institute

Institution *f* institution

Instrument *nt* instrument

Insulin (-s) *nt* insulin

Inszenierung *f* production

intakt *adj* intact

intellektuell *adj* intellectual

intelligent *adj* intelligent; **Intelligenz** *f* intelligence

intensiv *adj* (gründlich) intensive; (Gefühl, Schmerz) intense; **Intensivkurs** *m* crash course; **Intensivstation** *f* intensive care unit

interaktiv *adj* interactive

Intercityexpress(zug) *m* German high-speed train; **Intercityzug** *m* Intercity (train); **Intercityzuschlag** *m* Intercity supplement

interessant *adj* interesting; **Interesse** (-s, -n) *nt* interest; **~ haben an** (+dat) to be interested in; **interessieren** *vt* to interest ▷ *vr*: **sich ~** to be interested (für in)

Interface (-, -s) *nt* (Inform) interface

Internat *nt* boarding school

international *adj* international

Internet (-s) *nt* internet, net; **im ~ on** the internet; **im ~ surfen** to surf the net; **Internetanschluss** *m* internet connection; **Internetauktion** *f* internet auction; **Internetcafé** *nt* internet café, cybercafé; **Internetfirma** *f* dotcom company; **Internethandel** *m* e-commerce; **Internetseite** *f* web page; **Internetzugang** *m* internet access

interpretieren *vt* to interpret (als as)

Interpunktion *f* punctuation

Interview (-s, -s) *nt* interview; **interviewen** *vt* to interview

intim *adj* intimate

intolerant *adj* intolerant

investieren *vt* to invest

inwiefern *adv* in what way; (in welchem Ausmaß) to what extent; **inwieweit** *adv* to what extent

inzwischen *adv* meanwhile

iPod® *m* iPod®

Irak (-(s)) *m*: **(der) ~** Iraq

Iran (-(s)) *m*: **(der) ~** Iran

Ire (-n, -n) *m* Irishman

irgend *adv*: **~ so ein Idiot** some idiot; **wenn ~ möglich** if at all possible; **irgendein** *pron*, **irgendeine(r, s)** *adj* some; (fragend, im Bedingungssatz; beliebig) any; **irgendetwas** *pron* something; (fragend, im Bedingungssatz) anything; **irgendjemand** *pron* somebody; (fragend, im Bedingungssatz) anybody; **irgendwann** *adv* sometime; (zu beliebiger Zeit) any time; **irgendwie** *adv* somehow; **irgendwo** *adv* somewhere; (fragend, im Bedingungssatz) anywhere

Irin *f* Irishwoman; **irisch** *adj* Irish; **Irland** *nt* Ireland

ironisch *adj* ironic

irre *adj* crazy, mad; (toll) terrific; **Irre(r)** *mf* lunatic; **irreführen** *irr vt* to mislead; **irremachen** *vt* to confuse; **irren** *vi* to be mistaken; (umherirren) to wander ▷ *vr*: **sich ~** to be mistaken; **wenn ich mich nicht irre** if I'm not mistaken; **sich in der Nummer ~** (Telefon) to get the wrong number; **irrsinnig** *adj* mad, crazy; **Irrtum** (-s, -tümer) *m* mistake, error; **irrtümlich** *adj* mistaken ▷ *adv* by mistake

ISBN (-) *nt abk* = **industrial standard business network** ISBN

▷ (-) *f abk* = **Internationale Standard Buchnummer** ISBN
Ischias (-) *m* sciatica
ISDN (-) *nt abk* = **integrated services digital network** ISDN
Islam (-s) *m* Islam; **islamisch** *adj* Islamic
Island *nt* Iceland; **Isländer(in)** (-s, -) *m(f)* Icelander; **isländisch** *adj* Icelandic; **Isländisch** *nt* Icelandic
Isolierband *nt* insulating tape; **isolieren** *vt* to isolate; (*Elek*) to insulate
Isomatte *f* thermomat, karrymat®
Israel (-s) *nt* Israel; **Israeli** (-(s), -(s)) *m* (-, -(s)) *f* Israeli; **israelisch** *adj* Israeli
IT (-) *f abk* = **Informationstechnologie** IT
Italien (-s) *nt* Italy; **Italiener(in)** (-s, -) *m(f)* Italian; **italienisch** *adj* Italian; **Italienisch** *nt* Italian

SCHLÜSSELWORT

ja *adv* **1** yes; **haben Sie das gesehen? — ja** did you see it? — yes;(I did); **ich glaube ja** (yes,) I think so
2 (*fragend*) really?; **ich habe gekündigt — ja?** I've quit — have you?; **du kommst, ja?** you're coming, aren't you?
3 sei ja vorsichtig do be careful; **Sie wissen ja, dass ...** as you know, ...; **tu das ja nicht!** don't do that!; **ich habe es ja gewusst** I just knew it; **ja, also ...** well you see ...

Jacht (-, -en) *f* yacht; **Jachthafen** *m* marina
Jacke (-, -n) *f* jacket; (*Wolljacke*) cardigan
Jackett (-s, -s *o* -e) *nt* jacket
Jagd (-, -en) *f* hunt; (*Jagen*) hunting; **jagen** *vi* to hunt ▷ *vt* to

hunt; (*verfolgen*) to chase; **Jäger(in)** *m(f)* hunter

Jaguar (-s, -e) *m* jaguar

Jahr (-(e)s, -e) *nt* year; **ein halbes ~** six months *pl*; **Anfang der neunziger ~e** in the early nineties; **mit sechzehn ~en** at (the age of) sixteen; **Jahrestag** *m* anniversary; **Jahreszahl** *f* date, year; **Jahreszeit** *f* season; **Jahrgang** *m* (*Wein*) year, vintage; **der ~ 1989** (*Personen*) those born in 1989; **Jahrhundert** (-s, -e) *nt* century; **jährlich** *adj* yearly, annual; **Jahrmarkt** *m* fair; **Jahrtausend** *nt* millennium; **Jahrzehnt** *nt* decade

jähzornig *adj* hot-tempered

Jakobsmuschel *f* scallop

Jalousie *f* (venetian) blind

Jamaika (-s) *nt* Jamaica

jämmerlich *adj* pathetic

jammern *vi* to moan

Januar (-(s), -e) *m* January; *siehe auch* **Juni**

Japan (-s) *nt* Japan; **Japaner(in)** (-s, -) *m(f)* Japanese; **japanisch** *adj* Japanese; **Japanisch** *nt* Japanese

jaulen *vi* to howl

jawohl *adv* yes (of course)

Jazz (-) *m* jazz

○ **SCHLÜSSELWORT**

je *adv* 1 (*jemals*) ever; **hast du so was je gesehen?** did you ever see anything like it?
2 (*jeweils*) every, each; **sie zahlten je 3 Euro** they paid 3 euros each ▷ *konj* 1 **je nach** depending on; **je nachdem** it depends; **je nachdem, ob ...** depending on whether ...
2 **je eher, desto** *o* **umso besser** the sooner the better

Jeans (-, -) *f* jeans *pl*

jede(r, s) *unbest Zahlwort* (*insgesamt gesehen*) every; (*einzeln gesehen*) each; (*jede(r, s) beliebige*) any; **~s Mal** every time, each time; **~n zweiten Tag** every other day; **sie hat an ~m Finger einen Ring** she's got a ring on each finger; **~r Computer reicht aus** any computer will do; **bei ~m Wetter** in any weather ▷ *pron* everybody; (*jeder Einzelne*) each; **~r von euch/uns** each of you/us; **jedenfalls** *adv* in any case; **jederzeit** *adv* at any time; **jedesmal** *adv* every time

jedoch *adv* however

jemals *adv* ever

jemand *pron* somebody; (*in Frage und Verneinung*) anybody

Jemen (-(s)) *m* Yemen

jene(r, s) *adj* that, those *pl* ▷ *pron* that (one), those *pl*

jenseits *adv* on the other side ▷ *prep* +*gen* on the other side of; (*fig*) beyond

Jetlag (-s) *m* jet lag

jetzig *adj* present

jetzt *adv* now; **erst ~** only now; **~ gleich** right now; **bis ~** so far, up to now; **von ~ an** from now on

jeweils *adv* **~ zwei zusammen** two at a time; **zu ~ 5 Euro** at 5 euros each

Job (-s, -s) *m* job; **jobben** *vi* (*fam*) to work, to have a job

Jod (-(e)s) *nt* iodine

joggen *vi* to jog; **Jogging** (-s) *nt* jogging; **Jogginganzug** *m* jogging suit, tracksuit; **Jogginghose** *f* jogging pants *pl*

Jog(h)urt (-s, -s) *m* o *nt* yoghurt

Johannisbeere *f*: **Schwarze ~** blackcurrant; **Rote ~** redcurrant

Joint (-s, -s) *m* (*fam*) joint

jonglieren *vi* to juggle

Jordanien (-s) *nt* Jordan

Journalist(in) *m(f)* journalist

Joystick (-s, -s) m (Inform) joystick

jubeln vi to cheer

Jubiläum (-s, Jubiläen) nt jubilee; (Jahrestag) anniversary

jucken vi to itch ▷ vt: **es juckt mich am Arm** my arm is itching; **das juckt mich nicht** (fam) I couldn't care less; **Juckreiz** m itch

Jude (-n, -n) m, **Jüdin** f Jew; **sie ist Jüdin** she's Jewish; **jüdisch** adj Jewish

Judo (-(s)) nt judo

Jugend (-) f youth; **jugendfrei** adj: **ein ~er Film** a U-rated film (Brit), a G-rated film (US); **ein nicht ~er Film** an X-rated film; **Jugendgruppe** f youth group; **Jugendherberge** (-, -n) f youth hostel; **Jugendherbergsausweis** m youth hostel card; **jugendlich** adj youthful; **Jugendliche(r)** mf young person; **Jugendstil** m art nouveau; **Jugendzentrum** nt youth centre

Jugoslawien (-s) nt (Hist) Yugoslavia; **das ehemalige ~** the former Yugoslavia

Juli (-(s), -s) m July; siehe auch **Juni**

jung adj young

Junge (-n, -n) m boy

Junge(s) (-n, -n) nt young animal; **die ~n** pl the young pl

Jungfrau f virgin; (Astr) Virgo

Junggeselle (-n, -n) m bachelor; **Junggesellin** f single woman

Juni (-(s), -s) m June; **im ~** in June; **am 4. ~** on 4(th) June, on June 4(th) (gesprochen: on the fourth of June); **Anfang/Mitte/Ende ~** at the beginning/in the middle/at the end of June; **letzten/nächsten ~** last/next June

Jupiter (-s) m Jupiter

Jura ohne Artikel (Studienfach) law; **~ studieren** to study law; **Jurist(in)** m(f) lawyer; **juristisch** adj legal

Justiz (-) f justice; **Justizminister(in)** m(f) minister of justice

Juwel (-s, -en) nt jewel; **Juwelier(in)** (-s, -e) m(f) jeweller

k

Kabel (-s, -) nt (Elek) wire; (stark) cable; **Kabelfernsehen** nt cable television

Kabeljau (-s, -e o -s) m cod

Kabine f cabin; (im Schwimmbad) cubicle

Kabrio (-s, -s) nt convertible

Kachel (-, -n) f tile; **Kachelofen** m tiled stove

Käfer (-s, -) m beetle, bug (US)

Kaff (-s, -s) nt dump, hole

Kaffee (-s, -s) m coffee; ~ **kochen** to make some coffee; **Kaffeefilter** m coffee filter; **Kaffeekanne** f coffeepot; **Kaffeeklatsch** (-(e)s, -e) m chat over coffee and cakes, coffee klatch (US); **Kaffeelöffel** m coffee spoon; **Kaffeemaschine** f coffee maker (o machine); **Kaffeetasse** f coffee cup

Käfig (-s, -e) m cage

kahl adj bald; (Baum, Wand) bare

Kahn (-(e)s, Kähne) m boat; (Lastkahn) barge

Kai (-s, -e o -s) m quay

Kaiser (-s, -) m emperor; **Kaiserin** f empress; **Kaiserschnitt** m (Med) caesarean (section)

Kajak (-s, -s) nt kayak; **Kajakfahren** nt kayaking

Kajal (-s) m kohl

Kajüte (-, -n) f cabin

Kakao (-s, -s) m cocoa; (Getränk) (hot) chocolate

Kakerlake (-, -n) f cockroach

Kaki (-, -s) f kaki

Kaktee (-, -n) f, **Kaktus** (-, -se) m cactus

Kalb (-(e)s, Kälber) nt calf; **Kalbfleisch** nt veal; **Kalbsbraten** m roast veal; **Kalbsschnitzel** nt veal cutlet; (paniert) escalope of veal

Kalender (-s, -) m calendar; (Taschenkalender) diary

Kalk (-(e)s, -e) m lime; (in Knochen) calcium

Kalorie f calorie; **kalorienarm** adj low-calorie

kalt adj cold; **mir ist (es)** ~ I'm cold; **kaltblütig** adj cold-blooded; **Kälte** (-) f cold; (fig) coldness

kam imperf von **kommen**

Kambodscha (-s) nt Cambodia

Kamel (-(e)s, -e) nt camel

Kamera (-, -s) f camera

Kamerad(in) (-en, -en) m(f) friend; (als Begleiter) companion

Kamerafrau f camerawoman; **Kamerahandy** nt cameraphone; **Kameramann** m cameraman

Kamille (-, -n) f camomile; **Kamillentee** m camomile tea

Kamin (-s, -e) m (außen) chimney; (innen) fireplace

Kamm (-(e)s, Kämme) m comb; (Berg) ridge; (Hahn) crest; **kämmen** vr **sich** ~, **sich** (dat) **die Haare** ~ to comb one's hair; **Kammermusik** f chamber music

Kampf (-(e)s, Kämpfe) m fight; (Schlacht) battle; (Wettbewerb) contest; (fig: Anstrengung) struggle; **kämpfen** vi to fight (für, um for); **Kampfsport** m martial art

Kanada (-s) nt Canada; **Kanadier(in)** (-s, -) m(f) Canadian; **kanadisch** adj Canadian

Kanal (-s, Kanäle) m (Fluss) canal; (Rinne, TV) channel; (für Abfluss) drain; **der ~** (Ärmelkanal) the (English) Channel; **Kanalinseln** pl Channel Islands pl; **Kanalisation** f sewerage system; **Kanaltunnel** m Channel Tunnel

Kanarienvogel m canary

Kandidat(in) (-en, -en) m(f) candidate

Kandis(zucker) (-) m rock candy

Känguru (-s) nt kangaroo

Kaninchen nt rabbit

Kanister (-s, -) m can

Kännchen nt pot; **ein ~ Kaffee/Tee** a pot of coffee/tea; **Kanne** (-, -n) f (Krug) jug; (Kaffeekanne) pot; (Milchkanne) churn; (Gießkanne) can

kannte imperf von **kennen**

Kante (-, -n) f edge

Kantine f canteen

Kanton (-s, -e) m canton

Kanu (-s, -s) nt canoe

Kanzler(in) (-s, -) m(f) chancellor

Kap (-s, -s) nt cape

Kapazität f capacity; (Fachmann) authority

Kapelle f (Gebäude) chapel; (Mus) band

Kaper (-, -n) f caper

kapieren vt, vi (fam) to understand; **kapiert?** got it?

Kapital (-s, -e o -ien) nt capital

Kapitän (-s, -e) m captain

Kapitel (-s, -) nt chapter

Kappe (-, -n) f cap

Kapsel (-, -n) f capsule

kaputt adj (fam) broken; (Mensch) exhausted; **kaputt|gehen** irr vi to break; (Schuhe) to fall apart; (Firma) to go bust; (Stoff) to wear out; **kaputt|machen** vt to break; (jdn) to wear out

Kapuze (-, -n) f hood

Kap Verde (-s) nt Cape Verde

Karaffe (-, -n) f carafe; (mit Stöpsel) decanter

Karamell (-s) m caramel, toffee

Karaoke (-(s)) nt karaoke

Karat (-s, -e) nt carat

Karate (-s) nt karate

Kardinal (-s, Kardinäle) m cardinal

Karfreitag m Good Friday

kariert adj checked; (Papier) squared

Karies (-) f (tooth) decay

Karikatur f caricature

Karneval (-s, -e o -s) m carnival

○ **KARNEVAL**
○
○ **Karneval** is the name given to
○ the days immediately before
○ Lent when people gather to
○ sing, dance, eat, drink and
○ generally make merry before the
○ fasting begins. **Rosenmontag**,
○ the day before Shrove Tuesday,
○ is the most important day of
○ 'Karneval' on the Rhine. Most
○ firms take a day's holiday on
○ that day to enjoy the parades
○ and revelry. In South Germany
○ 'Karneval' is called **Fasching**.

Kärnten (-s) nt Carinthia

Karo (-s, -s) nt square; (Karten) diamonds pl

Karosserie f (Auto) body(work)

Karotte (-, -n) f carrot

Karpfen (-s, -) m carp

Karriere (-, -n) f career

Karte (-, -n) f card; (Landkarte) map; (Speisekarte) menu; (Eintrittskarte, Fahrkarte) ticket; **mit ~ bezahlen** to pay by credit card; **~n spielen** to play cards; **die ~n mischen/geben** to shuffle/deal the cards

Kartei f card index; **Karteikarte** f index card

Kartenspiel nt card game; **Kartentelefon** nt cardphone; **Kartenvorverkauf** m advance booking

Kartoffel (-, -n) f potato; **Kartoffelbrei** m mashed potatoes pl; **Kartoffelchips** pl crisps pl (Brit), chips pl (US); **Kartoffelpuffer** m potato cake (made from grated potatoes); **Kartoffelpüree** nt mashed potatoes pl; **Kartoffelsalat** m potato salad

Karton (-s, -s) m cardboard; (Schachtel) (cardboard) box

Kartusche (-, -n) f cartridge

Karussell (-s, -s) nt roundabout (Brit), merry-go-round

Kaschmir (-s, e) m (Stoff) cashmere

Käse (-s, -) m cheese; **Käsekuchen** m cheesecake; **Käseplatte** f cheeseboard

Kasino (-s, -s) nt (Spielkasino) casino

Kaskoversicherung f comprehensive insurance

Kasper(l) (-s, -) m Punch; (fig) clown; **Kasperl(e)theater** nt (Vorstellung) Punch and Judy show; (Gebäude) Punch and Judy theatre

Kasse (-, -n) f (in Geschäft) till, cash register; (im Supermarkt) checkout; (Geldkasten) cashbox;

(Theater) box office; (Kino) ticket office; (Krankenkasse) health insurance; (Spar~) savings bank; **Kassenbon** (-s, -s) m, **Kassenzettel** m receipt

Kassette f (small) box; (Tonband) cassette; **Kassettenrekorder** m cassette recorder

kassieren vt to take ▷ vi: **darf ich ~?** would you like to pay now?; **Kassierer(in)** m(f) cashier

Kastanie f chestnut

Kasten (-s, Kästen) m (Behälter) box; (Getränkekasten) crate

Kat m abk = **Katalysator**

Katalog (-(e)s, -e) m catalogue

Katalysator m (Auto) catalytic converter; (Phys) catalyst

Katar (-s) nt Qatar

Katarr(h) (-s, -e) m catarrh

Katastrophe (-, -n) f catastrophe, disaster

Kategorie (-, -n) f category

Kater (-s, -) m tomcat; (fam: nach zu viel Alkohol) hangover

Kathedrale (-, -n) f cathedral

Katholik(in) m(f) Catholic; **katholisch** adj Catholic

Katze (-, -n) f cat

Kauderwelsch (-(s)) nt (unverständlich) gibberish; (Fachjargon) jargon

kauen vt, vi to chew

Kauf (-(e)s, Käufe) m purchase; (Kaufen) buying; **ein guter ~** a bargain; **etw in ~ nehmen** to put up with sth; **kaufen** vt to buy; **Käufer(in)** m(f) buyer; **Kauffrau** f businesswoman; **Kaufhaus** nt department store; **Kaufmann** m businessman; (im Einzelhandel) shopkeeper (Brit), storekeeper (US); **Kaufpreis** m purchase price; **Kaufvertrag** m purchase agreement

Kaugummi m chewing gum

Kaulquappe (-, -n) f tadpole

kaum adv hardly, scarcely

Kaution f deposit; (Jur) bail

Kaviar m caviar

KB (-, -) nt, **Kbyte** (-, -) nt abk = **Kilobyte** KB

Kebab (-(s), -s) m kebab

Kegel (-s, -) m skittle; (beim Bowling) pin; (Math) cone; **Kegelbahn** f bowling alley; **kegeln** vi to play skittles; (bowlen) to bowl

Kehle (-, -n) f throat; **Kehlkopf** m larynx

Kehre (-, -n) f sharp bend

kehren vt (fegen) to sweep

Keilriemen m (Auto) fan belt

kein pron no, not ... any; **ich habe ~ Geld** I have no money, I don't have any money; **~ Mensch** no one; **du bist ~ Kind mehr** you're not a child any more; **keine(r, s)** pron (Person) no one, nobody; (Sache) not ... any, none; **~r von ihnen** none of them; (bei zwei Personen/Sachen) neither of them; **ich will keins von beiden** I don't want either (of them); **keinesfalls** adv on no account, under no circumstances

Keks (-es, -e) m biscuit (Brit), cookie (US); **jdm auf den ~ gehen** (fam) to get on sb's nerves

Keller (-s, -) m cellar; (Geschoss) basement

Kellner (-s, -) m waiter; **Kellnerin** f waitress

Kenia (-s) nt Kenya

kennen (kannte, gekannt) vt to know; **wir ~ uns seit 1990** we've known each other since 1990; **wir ~ uns schon** we've already met; **kennst du mich noch?** do you remember me?; **kennenlernen** vt to get to know; **sich ~** to get to know each other; (zum ersten Mal) to meet

Kenntnis f knowledge; **seine ~se**

his knowledge

Kennwort nt (a. Inform) password; **Kennzeichen** nt mark, sign; (Auto) number plate (Brit), license plate (US); **besondere ~** distinguishing marks

Kerl (-s, -e) m guy, bloke (Brit)

Kern (-(e)s, -e) m (Obst) pip; (Pfirsich, Kirsche etc) stone; (Nuss) kernel; (Atomkern) nucleus; (fig) heart, core

Kernenergie f nuclear energy; **Kernkraft** f nuclear power; **Kernkraftwerk** nt nuclear power station

Kerze (-, -n) f candle; (Zündkerze) plug

Ket(s)chup (-(s), -s) m o nt ketchup

Kette (-, -n) f chain; (Halskette) necklace

keuchen vi to pant; **Keuchhusten** m whooping cough

Keule (-, -n) f club; (Gastr) leg; (von Hähnchen a.) drumstick

Keyboard (-s, -s) nt (Mus) keyboard

Kfz nt abk = **Kraftfahrzeug**
Kfz-Brief m = logbook
Kfz-Steuer f = road tax (Brit), vehicle tax (US)

KG (-, -s) f abk = **Kommanditgesellschaft** limited partnership

Kichererbse f chick pea

kichern vi to giggle

Kickboard® (-s, -s) nt micro scooter

Kicker (-s, -) m (Spiel) table football (Brit), foosball (US)

kidnappen vt to kidnap

Kidney-Bohne f kidney bean

Kiefer (-s, -) m jaw ▷ (-, -n) f pine; **Kieferchirurg(in)** m(f) oral surgeon

Kieme (-, -n) f gill

Kies (-es, -e) m gravel; **Kiesel** (-s, -) m, **Kieselstein** m pebble

Kilo (-s, -(s)) nt kilo; **Kilobyte** nt kilobyte; **Kilogramm** nt kilogram; **Kilometer** m kilometre; **Kilometerstand** m ≈ mileage; **Kilometerzähler** m ≈ mileometer; **Kilowatt** nt kilowatt

Kind (-(e)s, -er) nt child; **sie bekommt ein ~** she's having a baby; **Kinderarzt** m, **Kinderärztin** f paediatrician; **Kinderbetreuung** f childcare; **Kinderbett** nt cot (Brit), crib (US); **Kinderfahrkarte** f child's ticket; **Kindergarten** m nursery school, kindergarten; **Kindergärtner(in)** m(f) nursery-school teacher; **Kindergeld** nt child benefit; **Kinderkrippe** f crèche (Brit), daycare center (US); **Kinderlähmung** f polio; **Kindermädchen** nt nanny (Brit), nurse(maid); **kindersicher** adj childproof; **Kindersicherung** f childproof safety catch; (an Flasche) childproof cap; **Kindersitz** m child seat; **Kindertagesstätte** f day nursery; **Kinderteller** m (im Restaurant) children's portion; **Kinderwagen** m pram (Brit), baby carriage (US); **Kinderzimmer** nt children's (bed)room; **Kindheit** f childhood; **kindisch** adj childish; **kindlich** adj childlike

Kinn (-(e)s, -e) nt chin

Kino (-s, -s) nt cinema (Brit), movie theater (US); **ins ~ gehen** to go to the cinema (Brit) (o to the movies (US))

Kiosk (-(e)s, -e) m kiosk

Kippe f (fam: Zigarettenstummel) cigarette end, fag end (Brit)

kippen vi to tip over ▷ vt to tilt; (Regierung, Minister) to topple

Kirche (-, -n) f church; **Kirchturm** m church tower; (mit Spitze) steeple; **Kirchweih** f fair

Kirmes (-, -sen) f fair

Kirsche (-, -n) f cherry; **Kirschtomate** f cherry tomato

Kissen (-s, -) nt cushion; (Kopfkissen) pillow; **Kissenbezug** m cushion cover; (für Kopfkissen) pillowcase

Kiste (-, -n) f box; (Truhe) chest

KITA (-, -s) f abk =
Kindertagesstätte day-care centre (Brit), day-care center (US)

kitschig adj kitschy, cheesy

kitzelig adj (a. fig) ticklish; **kitzeln** vt, vi to tickle

Kiwi (-, -s) f (Frucht) kiwi (fruit)

Klage (-, -n) f complaint; (Jur) lawsuit; **klagen** vi to complain (über +akk about, bei to); **kläglich** adj wretched

Klammer (-, -n) f (in Text) bracket; (Büroklammer) clip; (Wäscheklammer) peg (Brit), clothespin (US); (Zahnklammer) brace; **Klammeraffe** m (fam) at-sign, @; **klammern** vr: **sich ~ to cling** (an +akk to)

Klamotten pl (fam: Kleider) clothes pl

klang imperf von **klingen**

Klang (-(e)s, Klänge) m sound

Klappbett nt folding bed

klappen vi impers (gelingen) to work; **es hat gut geklappt** it went well

klappern vi to rattle; (Geschirr) to clatter; **Klapperschlange** f rattlesnake

Klappfahrad nt folding bicycle; **Klappstuhl** m folding chair

klar adj clear; **sich** (dat) **im Klaren sein** to be clear (über +akk about); **alles ~?** everything okay?

klären vt (Flüssigkeit) to purify; (Probleme, Frage) to clarify ▷ vr:

sich ~ to clear itself up
Klarinette (-, -n) f clarinet
klar|kommen irr vi: **mit etw ~** to cope with something; **kommst du klar?** are you managing all right?; **mit jdm ~** to get along with sb; **klar|machen** vt: **jdm etw ~** to make sth clear to sb; **klar|stellen** vt to clarify
Klärung f (von Frage, Problem) clarification
klasse adj inv (fam) great, brilliant
Klasse (-, -n) f class (Schuljahr) form (Brit), grade (US); **erster ~ reisen** to travel first class; **in welche ~ gehst du?** which form (Brit) (o grade (US)) are you in?; **Klassenarbeit** f test; **Klassenlehrer(in)** m(f) class teacher; **Klassenzimmer** nt classroom
Klassik f (Zeit) classical period; (Musik) classical music
Klatsch (-(e)s, -e) m (Gerede) gossip; **klatschen** vi (schlagen) to smack; (Beifall) to applaud, to clap; (reden) to gossip; **Klatschmohn** m (corn) poppy; **klatschnass** adj soaking (wet)
Klaue (-, -n) f claw; (fam: Schrift) scrawl; **klauen** vt (fam) to pinch
Klavier (-s, -e) nt piano
Klebeband nt adhesive tape; **kleben** vt to stick (an +akk to) ▸ vi (klebrig sein) to be sticky; **klebrig** adj sticky; **Klebstoff** m glue; **Klebstreifen** m adhesive tape
Klecks (-es, -e) m blob; (Tinte) blot
Klee (-s) m clover
Kleid (-(e)s, -er) nt (Frauen~) dress; **~er** pl (Kleidung) clothes pl; **Kleiderbügel** m coat hanger; **Kleiderschrank** m wardrobe (Brit), closet (US); **Kleidung** f clothing
klein adj small, little; (Finger) little; **mein ~er Bruder** my little (o

younger) brother; **als ich noch ~ war** when I was a little boy/girl; **etw ~ schneiden** to chop sth up; **Kleinanzeige** f classified ad; **Kleinbuchstabe** m small letter; **Kleinbus** m minibus; **Kleingeld** nt change; **Kleinigkeit** f trifle; (Zwischenmahlzeit) snack; **Kleinkind** nt toddler; **klein|schreiben** vt (mit kleinem Anfangsbuchstaben) to write with a small letter; **Kleinstadt** f small town
Kleister (-s, -) m paste
Klempner(in) m(f) plumber
klettern vi to climb
Klettverschluss m Velcro® fastening
klicken vi (a. Inform) to click
Klient(in) (-en, -en) m(f) client
Klima (-s, -s) nt climate; **Klimaanlage** f air conditioning; **klimatisiert** adj air-conditioned
Klinge (-, -n) f blade
Klingel (-, -n) f bell; **klingeln** vi to ring
klingen (klang, geklungen) vi to sound
Klinik f clinic; (Krankenhaus) hospital
Klinke (-, -n) f handle
Klippe (-, -n) f cliff; (im Meer) reef; (fig) hurdle
Klischee (-s, -s) nt (fig) cliché
Klo (-s, -s) nt (fam) loo (Brit), john (US); **Klobrille** f toilet seat; **Klopapier** nt toilet paper
klopfen vt, vi to knock; (Herz) to thump
Kloß (-es, Klöße) m (im Hals) lump; (Gastr) dumpling
Kloster (-s, Klöster) nt (für Männer) monastery; (für Frauen) convent
Klub (-s, -s) m club
klug adj clever
knabbern vt, vi to nibble

Knäckebrot nt crispbread

knacken vt, vi to crack

Knall (-(e)s, -e) m bang; **knallen** vi to bang

knapp adj (kaum ausreichend) scarce; (Sieg) narrow; **~ bei Kasse sein** to be short of money; **~ zwei Stunden** just under two hours

Knauf (-s, Knäufe) m knob

kneifen (kniff, gekniffen) vt, vi to pinch; (sich drücken) to back out (vor +dat of); **Kneifzange** f pincers pl

Kneipe (-, -n) f (fam) pub (Brit), bar

Knete (-) f (fam: Geld) dough; **kneten** vt to knead; (formen) to mould

knicken vt, vi (brechen) to break; (Papier) to fold; **geknickt sein** (fig) to be downcast

Knie (-s, -) nt knee; **in die ~ gehen** to bend one's knees; **Kniebeuge** f knee bend; **Kniegelenk** nt knee joint; **Kniekehle** f back of the knee; **knien** vi to kneel; **Kniescheibe** f kneecap; **Knieschoner** (-s, -) m, **Knieschützer** (-s, -) m knee pad; **Kniestrumpf** m knee-length sock

kniff imperf von **kneifen**

knipsen vt to punch; (Foto) to snap ▷ vi (Foto) to take snaps

knirschen vi to crunch; **mit den Zähnen ~** to grind one's teeth

knitterfrei adj non-crease; **knittern** vi to crease

Knoblauch m garlic; **Knoblauchbrot** nt garlic bread; **Knoblauchzehe** f clove of garlic

Knöchel (-s, -) m (Finger) knuckle; (Fuß) ankle

Knochen (-s, -) m bone; **Knochenbruch** m fracture; **Knochenmark** nt marrow

Knödel (-s, -) m dumpling

Knollensellerie m celeriac

Knopf (-(e)s, Knöpfe) m button; **Knopfdruck** m: **auf ~** at the touch of a button; **Knopfloch** nt buttonhole

Knospe (-, -n) f bud

knoten vt to knot; **Knoten** (-s, -) m knot; (Med) lump

Know-how (-(s)) nt know-how, expertise

knurren vi (Hund) to growl; (Magen) to rumble; (Mensch) to grumble

knusprig adj crisp; (Keks) crunchy

knutschen vi (fam) to smooch

k. o. adj inv (Sport) knocked out; (fig) knackered

Koalition f coalition

Koch (-(e)s, Köche) m cook; **Kochbuch** nt cookery book, cookbook; **kochen** vt, vi to cook; (Wasser) to boil; (Kaffee, Tee) to make; **Köchin** f cook; **Kochlöffel** m wooden spoon; **Kochnische** f kitchenette; **Kochplatte** f hotplate; **Kochrezept** nt recipe; **Kochtopf** m saucepan

Kode (-s) m code

Köder (-s, -) m bait

Koffein (-s) nt caffeine; **koffeinfrei** adj decaffeinated

Koffer (-s, -) m (suit)case; **Kofferraum** m (Auto) boot (Brit), trunk (US)

Kognak (-s, -s) m brandy

Kohl (-(e)s, -e) m cabbage

Kohle (-, -n) f coal; (Holzkohle) charcoal; (Chem) carbon; (fam: Geld) cash, dough; **Kohlehydrat** nt carbohydrate; **Kohlendioxid** nt carbon dioxide; **Kohlensäure** f (in Getränken) fizz; **ohne ~** still, non-carbonated (US); **mit ~** sparkling, carbonated (US); **Kohletablette** f charcoal tablet

Kohlrabi (-(s), -(s)) m kohlrabi

Koje (-, -n) f cabin; (Bett) bunk

Kokain (-s) nt cocaine

Kokosnuss f coconut

Kolben (-s, -) m (Tech) piston; (Mais~) cob

Kolik (-, -en) f colic

Kollaps (-es, -e) m collapse

Kollege (-n, -n) m, **Kollegin** f colleague

Köln (-s) nt Cologne; **Kölnischwasser** nt eau du cologne

Kolonne (-, -n) f convoy

Kolumbien (-s) nt Columbia

Koma (-s, -s) nt coma

Kombi (-(s), -s) m estate (car) (Brit), station wagon (US); **Kombination** f combination; (Folgerung) deduction; (Hemdhose) combinations pl; (Aviat) flying suit; **kombinieren** vt to combine ▷ vi to reason; (vermuten) to guess; **Kombizange** f (pair of) pliers pl

Komfort (-s) m conveniences pl; (Bequemlichkeit) comfort

Komiker(in) m(f) comedian, comic; **komisch** adj funny

Komma (-s, -s) nt comma

Kommanditgesellschaft f limited partnership

kommen (kam, gekommen) vi to come; (näher kommen) to approach; (passieren) to happen; (gelangen, geraten) to get; (erscheinen) to appear; (in die Schule, das Gefängnis etc) to go; ~ **lassen** to send for; **zu sich ~** to come round (o to); **zu etw ~** (bekommen) to acquire sth; (Zeit dazu finden) to get round to sth; **wer kommt zuerst?** who's first?; **kommend** adj coming; **~e Woche** next week; **in den ~en Jahren** in the years to come

Kommentar m commentary; **kein ~** no comment

Kommilitone (-n, -n) m,

Kommilitonin f fellow student

Kommissar(in) m(f) inspector

Kommode (-, -n) f chest of drawers

Kommunikation f communication

Kommunion f (Rel) communion

Kommunismus m communism

Komödie f comedy

kompakt adj compact

Kompass (-es, -e) m compass

kompatibel adj compatible

kompetent adj competent

komplett adj complete

Kompliment nt compliment; **jdm ein ~ machen** to pay sb a compliment; **~!** congratulations

Komplize (-n, -n) m accomplice

kompliziert adj complicated

Komponist(in) m(f) composer

Kompost (-(e)s, -e) m compost; **Komposthaufen** m compost heap; **kompostierbar** adj biodegradable

Kompott (-(e)s, -e) nt stewed fruit

Kompresse (-, -n) f compress

Kompromiss (-es, -e) m compromise

Kondensmilch f condensed milk, evaporated milk

Kondition f (Leistungsfähigkeit) condition; **sie hat eine gute ~** she's in good shape

Konditorei f cake shop; (mit Café) café

Kondom (-s, -e) nt condom

Konfektionsgröße f size

Konferenz f conference

Konfession f religion; (christlich) denomination

Konfetti (-(s)) nt confetti

Konfirmation f (Rel) confirmation

Konfitüre (-, -n) f jam

Konflikt (-(e)s, -e) m conflict

konfrontieren vt to confront

Kongress (-es, -e) m conference; **der ~** (Parlament der USA) Congress

König (-(e)s, -e) m king; **Königin** f queen; **königlich** adj royal; **Königreich** nt kingdom

Konkurrenz f competition

🔵 SCHLÜSSELWORT

können (pt **konnte**, pp **gekonnt** o (als Hilfsverb) **können**) vt, vi 1 to be able to; **ich kann es machen** I can do it, I am able to do it; **ich kann es nicht machen** I can't do it, I'm not able to do it; **ich kann nicht ...** I can't ..., I cannot ...; **ich kann nicht mehr** I can't go on

2 (wissen, beherrschen) to know; **können Sie Deutsch?** can you speak German?; **er kann gut Englisch** he speaks English well; **sie kann keine Mathematik** she can't do mathematics

3 (dürfen) to be allowed to; **kann ich gehen?** can I go?; **könnte ich ...?** could I ...?; **kann ich mit?** (fam) can I come with you?

4 (möglich sein) **Sie könnten recht haben** you may be right; **das kann sein** that's possible; **kann sein** maybe

konsequent adj consistent; **Konsequenz** f consequence

konservativ adj conservative

Konserven pl tinned food sing (Brit), canned food sing; **Konservendose** f tin (Brit), can

konservieren vt to preserve; **Konservierungsmittel** nt preservative

Konsonant m consonant

Konsul(in) (-s, -n) m(f) consul; **Konsulat** nt consulate

Kontakt (-(e)s, -e) m contact; **kontaktarm** adj: **er ist ~** he lacks

contact with other people; **kontaktfreudig** adj sociable; **Kontaktlinsen** pl contact lenses pl

Kontinent m continent

Konto (-s, **Konten**) nt account; **Kontoauszug** m (bank) statement; **Kontoauszugsdrucker** m bank-statement machine; **Kontoinhaber(in)** m(f) account holder; **Kontonummer** f account number; **Kontostand** m balance

Kontrabass m double bass

Kontrast (-(e)s, -e) m contrast

Kontrolle (-, -n) f control; (Aufsicht) supervision; (Passkontrolle) passport control; **kontrollieren** vt to control; (nachprüfen) to check

Konzentration f concentration; **Konzentrationslager** nt (Hist) concentration camp; **konzentrieren** vt to concentrate ▷ vr: **sich ~** to concentrate

Konzept (-(e)s, -e) nt rough draft; **jdn aus dem ~ bringen** to put sb off

Konzern (-(e)s, -e) m firm

Konzert (-(e)s, -e) nt concert; (Stück) concerto; **Konzertsaal** m concert hall

koordinieren vt to coordinate

Kopf (-(e)s, **Köpfe**) m head; **pro ~** per person; **sich den ~ zerbrechen** to rack one's brains; **Kopfhörer** m headphones pl; **Kopfkissen** nt pillow; **Kopfsalat** m lettuce; **Kopfschmerzen** pl headache sing; **Kopfstütze** f headrest; **Kopftuch** nt headscarf; **kopfüber** adv headfirst

Kopie f copy; **kopieren** vt (a. Inform) to copy; **Kopierer** (-s, -) m, **Kopiergerät** nt copier

Kopilot(in) m(f) co-pilot

Koralle (-, -n) f coral

Koran (-s) m (Rel) Koran

Korb (-(e)s, Körbe) m basket; **jdm einen ~ geben** (fig) to turn sb down

Kord (-(e)s, -e) m corduroy

Kordel (-, -n) f cord

Kork (-(e)s, -e) m cork; **Korken** (-s, -) m cork; **Korkenzieher** (-s, -) m corkscrew

Korn (-(e)s, Körner) nt grain; **Kornblume** f cornflower

Körper (-s, -) m body; **Körperbau** m build; **Körpergeruch** m body odour; **Körpergröße** f height; **körperlich** adj physical; **Körperteil** m part of the body; **Körperverletzung** f physical injury

korrekt adj correct

Korrespondent(in) m(f) correspondent; **Korrespondenz** f correspondence

korrigieren vt to correct

Kosmetik f cosmetics pl; **Kosmetikkoffer** m vanity case; **Kosmetiksalon** m beauty parlour; **Kosmetiktuch** nt paper tissue

Kost (-) f (Nahrung) food; (Verpflegung) board

kostbar adj precious; (teuer) costly, expensive

kosten vt to cost ▷ vt, vi (versuchen) to taste; **Kosten** pl costs pl, cost; (Ausgaben) expenses pl; **auf ~ von** at the expense of; **kostenlos** adj free (of charge); **Kostenvoranschlag** m estimate

köstlich adj (Essen) delicious; (Einfall) delightful; **sich ~ amüsieren** to have a marvellous time

Kostprobe f taster; (fig) sample; **kostspielig** adj expensive

Kostüm (-s, -e) nt costume;

(Damenkostüm) suit

Kot (-(e)s) m excrement

Kotelett (-(e)s, -e o -s) nt chop, cutlet

Koteletten pl sideboards pl (Brit), sideburns pl (US)

Kotflügel m (Auto) wing

kotzen vi (vulg) to puke, to throw up

Krabbe (-, -n) f shrimp; (größer) prawn; (Krebs) crab

krabbeln vi to crawl

Krach (-(e)s, -s o -e) m crash; (andauernd) noise; (fam: Streit) row

Kraft (-, Kräfte) f strength; (Pol, Phys) force; (Fähigkeit) power; (Arbeits~) worker; **in ~ treten** to come into effect; **Kraftausdruck** m swearword; **Kraftfahrzeug** nt motor vehicle; **Kraftfahrzeugbrief** m = logbook; **Kraftfahrzeugschein** m vehicle registration document; **Kraftfahrzeugsteuer** f = road tax (Brit), vehicle tax (US); **Kraftfahrzeugversicherung** f car insurance; **kräftig** adj strong; (gesund) healthy; (Farben) intense, strong; **Kraftstoff** m fuel; **Kraftwerk** nt power station

Kragen (-s, -) m collar

Krähe (-, -n) f crow

Kralle (-, -n) f claw; (Parkkralle) wheel clamp

Kram (-(e)s) m stuff

Krampf (-(e)s, Krämpfe) m cramp; (zuckend) spasm; **Krampfader** f varicose vein

Kran (-(e)s, Kräne) m crane

Kranich (-s, -e) m (Zool) crane

krank adj ill, sick

kränken vt to hurt

Krankengymnastik f physiotherapy; **Krankenhaus** nt hospital; **Krankenkasse** f health insurance; **Krankenpfleger** (-s, -) m (male) nurse;

Krankenschein m health insurance certificate; **Krankenschwester** f nurse; **Krankenversicherung** f health insurance; **Krankenwagen** m ambulance; **Krankheit** f illness; (durch Infektion hervorgerufen) disease

Kränkung f insult

Kranz (-es, Kränze) m wreath

krass adj crass; (fam: toll) wicked

kratzen vt, vi to scratch; **Kratzer** (-s, -) m scratch

kraulen vi (schwimmen) to do the crawl ▷ vt (streicheln) to pet

Kraut (-(e)s, Kräuter) nt plant; (Gewürz) herb; (Gemüse) cabbage; **Kräuter** pl herbs pl; **Kräuterbutter** f herb butter; **Kräutertee** m herbal tea; **Krautsalat** m coleslaw

Krawatte f tie

kreativ adj creative

Krebs (-es, -e) m (Zool) crab; (Med) cancer; (Astr) Cancer

Kredit (-(e)s, -e) m credit; **auf ~** on credit; **einen ~ aufnehmen** to take out a loan; **Kreditkarte** f credit card

Kreide (-, -n) f chalk

Kreis (-es, -e) m circle; (Bezirk) district

kreischen vi to shriek; (Bremsen, Säge) to screech

Kreisel (-s, -) m (Spielzeug) top; (Verkehrskreisel) roundabout (Brit), traffic circle (US)

Kreislauf m (Med) circulation; (fig: der Natur etc) cycle; **Kreislaufstörungen** pl (Med) **ich habe ~** I've got problems with my circulation; **Kreisverkehr** m roundabout (Brit), traffic circle (US)

Kren (-s) m horseradish

Kresse (-, -n) f cress

Kreuz (-es, -e) nt cross; (Anat) small of the back; (Karten) clubs pl;

mir tut das ~ weh I've got backache; **Kreuzband** nt cruciate ligament; **kreuzen** vt to cross ▷ vr: **sich ~** to cross ▷ vi (Naut) to cruise; **Kreuzfahrt** f cruise; **Kreuzgang** m cloisters pl; **Kreuzotter** (-, -n) f adder; **Kreuzschlitzschraubenzieher** m Phillips® screwdriver; **Kreuzschlüssel** m (Auto) wheel brace; **Kreuzschmerzen** pl backache sing; **Kreuzung** f (Verkehrskreuzung) crossroads sing, intersection; (Züchtung) cross; **Kreuzworträtsel** nt crossword (puzzle)

kriechen (kroch, gekrochen) vi to crawl; (unauffällig) to creep; (fig, pej) (vor jdm) ~ to crawl (to sb); **Kriechspur** f crawler lane

Krieg (-(e)s, -e) m war

kriegen vt (fam) to get; (erwischen) to catch; **sie kriegt ein Kind** she's having a baby; **ich kriege noch Geld von dir** you still owe me some money

Krimi (-s, -s) m (fam) thriller; **Kriminalität** f criminality; **Kriminalpolizei** f detective force, ≈ CID (Brit), = FBI (US); **Kriminalroman** m detective novel; **kriminell** adj criminal

Krippe (-, -n) f (Futterkrippe) manger; (Weihnachtskrippe) crib (Brit), crèche (US); (Kinderkrippe) crèche (Brit), daycare center (US)

Krise (-, -n) f crisis

Kristall (-s, -e) m crystal ▷ (-s) nt (Glas) crystal

Kritik f criticism; (Rezension) review; **Kritiker(in)** m(f) critic; **kritisch** adj critical

kritzeln vt, vi to scribble, to scrawl

Kroate (-n, -n) m Croat; **Kroatien** (-s) nt Croatia; **Kroatin** f Croat; **kroatisch** adj Croatian;

Kroatisch nt Croatian

kroch imperf von **kriechen**

Krokodil (-s, -e) nt crocodile

Krokus (-, -o -se) m crocus

Krone (-, -n) f crown;
Kronleuchter m chandelier

Kropf (-(e)s, Kröpfe) m (Med)
goitre; (von Vogel) crop

Kröte (-, -n) f toad

Krücke (-, -n) f crutch

Krug (-(e)s, Krüge) m jug;
(Bierkrug) mug

Krümel (-s, -) m crumb

krumm adj crooked

Krüppel (-s, -) m cripple

Kruste (-, -n) f crust

Kruzifix (-es, -e) nt crucifix

Kuba (-s) nt Cuba

Kübel (-s, -) m tub; (Eimer) bucket

Kubikmeter m cubic metre

Küche (-, -n) f kitchen; (Kochen)
cooking

Kuchen (-s, -) m cake; (mit
Teigdeckel) pie; Kuchengabel f
cake fork

Küchenmaschine f food
processor; Küchenpapier nt
kitchen roll; Küchenschrank m
(kitchen) cupboard

Kuckuck (-, -e) m cuckoo

Kugel (-, -n) f ball; (Math) sphere;
(Mil) bullet; (Weihnachtskugel)
bauble; Kugellager nt ball
bearing; Kugelschreiber m
(ball-point) pen, biro® (Brit);
Kugelstoßen (-s) nt shot put

Kuh (-, Kühe) f cow

kühl adj cool; Kühlakku (-s, -s) m
ice pack; Kühlbox f cool box;
kühlen vt to cool; Kühler (-s, -)
m (Auto) radiator; Kühlerhaube
f (Auto) bonnet (Brit), hood (US);
Kühlschrank m fridge,
refrigerator; Kühltasche f cool
bag; Kühltruhe f freezer;
Kühlwasser nt (Auto) radiator
water

Kuhstall m cowshed

Küken (-s, -) nt chick

Kuli (-s, -s) m (fam: Kugelschreiber)
pen, biro® (Brit)

Kulisse (-, -n) f scenery

Kult (-s, -e) m cult; Kultfigur f
cult figure

Kultur f culture; (Lebensform)
civilization; Kulturbeutel m
toilet bag (Brit), washbag;
kulturell adj cultural

Kümmel (-s, -) m caraway
seeds pl

Kummer (-s) m grief, sorrow

kümmern vr: **sich um jdn** ~ to
look after sb; **sich um etw** ~ to see
to sth ▷ vt to concern; **das
kümmert mich nicht** that doesn't
worry me

Kumpel (-s, -) m (fam) mate, pal

Kunde (-n, -n) m customer;
Kundendienst m after-sales (o
customer) service;
Kunden(kredit)karte f storecard, chargecard; Kunden-
nummer f customer number

kündigen vi to hand in one's
notice; (Mieter) to give notice that
one is moving out; **jdm** ~ to give
sb his/her notice; (Vermieter) to
give sb notice to quit ▷ vt to
cancel; (Vertrag) to terminate; **jdm
die Stellung** ~ to give sb his/her
notice; **jdm die Wohnung** ~ to
give sb notice to quit; **Kündigung**
f (Arbeitsverhältnis) dismissal;
(Vertrag) termination;
(Abonnement) cancellation; (Frist)
notice; Kündigungsfrist f
period of notice

Kundin f customer; Kundschaft
f customers pl

künftig adj future

Kunst (-, Künste) f art; (Können)
skill; Kunstausstellung f art
exhibition; Kunstgewerbe nt arts
and crafts pl; Künstler(in) (-s, -)

künstlich | 126

m(f) artist; **künstlerisch** *adj* artistic

künstlich *adj* artificial
Kunststoff *m* synthetic material; **Kunststück** *nt* trick; **Kunstwerk** *nt* work of art
Kupfer *(-s, -)* *nt* copper
Kuppel *(-, -n)* *f* dome
kuppeln *vi (Auto)* to operate the clutch; **Kupplung** *f* coupling; *(Auto)* clutch
Kur *(-, -en)* *f* course of treatment; *(am Kurort)* cure
Kür *(-, -en)* *f (Sport)* free programme
Kurbel *(-, -n)* *f* crank; *(von Rollo, Fenster)* winder
Kürbis *(-ses, -se)* *m* pumpkin
Kurierdienst *m* courier service
kurieren *vt* to cure
Kurort *m* health resort
Kurs *(-es, -e)* *m* course; *(Fin)* rate; *(Wechselkurs)* exchange rate
kursiv *adj* italic ⊳ *adv* in italics
Kursleiter(in) *m(f)* course tutor; **Kursteilnehmer(in)** *m(f)* (course) participant; **Kurswagen** *m* (Eisenb) through carriage
Kurve *(-, -n)* *f* curve; *(Straßenkurve)* bend; **kurvenreich** *adj* (Straße) winding
kurz *adj* short; *(zeitlich a.)* brief; **~ vorher/darauf** shortly before/after; **kannst du ~ kommen?** could you come here for a minute?; **~ gesagt** in short; **kurzärmelig** *adj* short-sleeved; **kürzen** *vt* to cut short; *(in der Länge)* to shorten; *(Gehalt)* to reduce; **kurzerhand** *adv* on the spot; **kurzfristig** *adj* short-term; **das Konzert wurde ~ abgesagt** the concert was called off at short notice; **Kurzgeschichte** *f* short story; **kurzhaarig** *adj* short-haired; **kürzlich** *adv* recently; **Kurzparkzone** *f*

short-stay (Brit) (o short-term (US)) parking zone; **Kurzschluss** *m* (Elek) short circuit; **kurzsichtig** *adj* short-sighted; **Kurztrip** *m* trip, break; **Kurzurlaub** *m* short holiday (Brit), short vacation (US); **Kurzwelle** *f* short wave
Kusine *f* cousin
Kuss *(-es, Küsse)* *m* kiss; **küssen** *vt* to kiss ⊳ *vr*: **sich ~** to kiss
Küste *(-, -n)* *f* coast; *(Ufer)* shore; **Küstenwache** *f* coastguard
Kutsche *(-, -n)* *f* carriage; *(geschlossene)* coach
Kuvert *(-s, -s)* *nt* envelope
Kuvertüre *(-, -n)* *f* coating
Kuwait *(-s)* *nt* Kuwait
KZ *(-s, -s)* *nt* abk = **Konzentrationslager** (Hist) concentration camp

I

Labor (-s, -e o -s) nt lab
Labyrinth (-s, -e) nt maze
Lache (-, -n) f (Pfütze) puddle;
(Blut~, Öl~) pool
lächeln vi to smile; **Lächeln** (-s)
nt smile; **lachen** vi to laugh;
lächerlich adj ridiculous
Lachs (-es, -e) m salmon
Lack (-(e)s, -e) m varnish;
(Farblack) lacquer; (an Auto) paint;
lackieren vt to varnish; (Auto) to
spray; **Lackschaden** m scratch
(on the paintwork)
Ladegerät nt (battery) charger;
laden (lud, geladen) vt (a. Inform)
to load; (einladen) to invite; (Handy
etc) to charge
Laden (-s, Läden) m shop;
(Fensterladen) shutter;
Ladendieb(in) m(f) shoplifter;
Ladendiebstahl m shoplifting;
Ladenschluss m closing time
Ladung f load; (Naut, Aviat)

cargo; (Jur) summons sing
lag imperf von **liegen**
Lage (-, -n) f position, situation;
(Schicht) layer; **in der ~ sein zu** to
be in a position to
Lager (-s, -) nt camp; (Comm)
warehouse; (Tech) bearing;
Lagerfeuer nt campfire; **lagern**
vi (Dinge) to be stored; (Menschen)
to camp ▷ vt to store
Lagune f lagoon
lahm adj lame; (langweilig) dull;
lähmen vt to paralyse; **Lähmung**
f paralysis
Laib (-s, -e) m loaf
Laie (-n, -n) m layman
Laken (-s, -) nt sheet
Lakritze (-, -n) f liquorice
Lamm (-(e)s, Lämmer) nt lamb
Lampe (-, -n) f lamp; (Glühbirne)
bulb; **Lampenfieber** nt stage
fright; **Lampenschirm** m
lampshade
Lampion (-s, -s) m Chinese
lantern
Land (-(e)s, Länder) nt (Gelände)
land; (Nation) country; (Bundesland)
state, Land; **auf dem ~(e)** in the
country

○ **LAND**

○ A **Land** (plural **Länder**) is a
○ member state of the **BRD**. There
○ are 16 **Länder**, namely
○ Baden-Württemberg, Bayern,
○ Berlin, Brandenburg, Bremen,
○ Hamburg, Hessen,
○ Mecklenburg-Vorpommern,
○ Niedersachsen,
○ Nordrhein-Westfalen,
○ Rheinland-Pfalz, Saarland,
○ Sachsen, Sachsen-Anhalt,
○ Schleswig-Holstein and
○ Thüringen. Each "Land" has its
○ own parliament and
○ constitution.

Landebahn f runway; **landen**
vt, vi to land; (Schiff) to dock
Länderspiel nt international
(match)
Landesgrenze f national
border, frontier; **Landesinnere**
nt interior; **landesüblich** adj
customary; **Landeswährung** f
national currency; **landesweit**
adj nationwide
Landhaus nt country house;
Landkarte f map; **Landkreis** m
administrative region, ≈ district
ländlich adj rural
Landschaft f countryside;
(schöne) scenery; (Kunst)
landscape; **Landstraße** f
country road, B road (Brit)
Landung f landing,
Landungsbrücke f,
Landungssteg m gangway
Landwirt(in) m(f) farmer;
Landwirtschaft f agriculture,
farming; **landwirtschaftlich** adj
agricultural
lang adj long; (Mensch) tall; **ein
zwei Meter ~er Tisch** a table two
metres long; **den ganzen Tag ~** all
day long; **die Straße ~** along the
street; **langärmelig** adj
long-sleeved; **lange ~** (for) a
long time; **ich musste ~ warten** I
had to wait (for) a long time; **ich
bleibe nicht ~** I won't stay long; **es
ist ~ her, dass wir uns gesehen
haben** it's a long time since we
saw each other; **Länge** (-, -n) f
length; (Geo) longitude
langen vi (fam: ausreichen) to be
enough; (fam: fassen) to reach (nach
for); **mir langt's** I've had enough
Langeweile f boredom
langfristig adj long-term ▷ adv in
the long term
Langlauf m cross-country skiing
längs prep +gen **die Bäume ~ der
Straße** the trees along(side) the

road ▷ adv: **die Streifen laufen
~ über das Hemd** the stripes run
lengthways down the shirt
langsam adj slow ▷ adv slowly
Langschläfer(in) (-s, -) m(f) late
riser
längst adv: **das ist ~ fertig** that
was finished a long time ago;
sie sollte ~ da sein she should
have been here long ago; **als
sie kam, waren wir ~ weg** when
she arrived we had long since
left
Langstreckenflug m long-haul
flight
Languste (-, -n) f crayfish,
crawfish (US)
langweilen vt to bore; **ich
langweile mich** I'm bored;
langweilig adj boring; **Langwelle**
f long wave
Laos (-) nt Laos
Lappen (-s, -) m cloth, rag;
(Staublappen) duster
läppisch adj silly; (Summe)
ridiculous
Laptop (-s, -s) m laptop
Lärche (-, -n) f larch
Lärm (-(e)s) m noise
las imperf von **lesen**
Lasche (-, -n) f flap
Laser (-s, -) m laser;
Laserdrucker m laser printer

O SCHLÜSSELWORT

lassen (pt **ließ**, pp **gelassen** o (als
Hilfsverb) **lassen**) vt **1** (unterlassen)
to stop; (momentan) to leave; **lass
das (sein)!** don't (do it)!; (hör auf!)
stop it!; **lass mich!** leave me alone;
lassen wir das! let's leave it; **er
kann das Trinken nicht lassen** he
can't stop drinking
2 (zurücklassen) to leave; **etw
lassen, wie es ist** to leave sth
(just) as it is

3 (*überlassen*) **jdn ins Haus lassen** to let sb into the house
▷ *vi* ; **lass mal, ich mache das schon** leave it, I'll do it
▷ **Hilfsverb 1** (*veranlassen*) **etw machen lassen** to have o get sth done; **sich** *dat* **etw schicken lassen** to have sth sent (to one)
2 (*zulassen*) **jdn etw wissen lassen** to let sb know sth; **das Licht brennen lassen** to leave the light on; **jdn warten lassen** to keep sb waiting; **das lässt sich machen** that can be done
3 **lass uns gehen** let's go

lässig *adj* casual
Last (-, -en) *f* load; (*Bürde*) burden; (*Naut, Aviat*) cargo
Laster (-s, -) *nt* vice; (*fam*) truck, lorry (*Brit*)
lästern *vi*: **über jdn/etw ~ to** make nasty remarks about sb/sth
lästig *adj* annoying; (*Person*) tiresome
Last-Minute-Angebot *nt* last-minute offer; **Last-Minute-Flug** *m* last-minute flight; **Last-Minute-Ticket** *nt* last-minute ticket
Lastwagen *m* truck, lorry (*Brit*)
Latein (-s) *nt* Latin
Laterne (-, -n) *f* lantern; (*Straßenlaterne*) streetlight
Latte (-, -n) *f* slat; (*Sport*) bar
Latz (-es, *Lätze*) *m* bib; **Lätzchen** *nt* bib; **Latzhose** *f* dungarees *pl*
lau *adj* (*Wind, Luft*) mild
Laub (-(e)s) *nt* foliage; **Laubfrosch** *m* tree frog; **Laubsäge** *f* fretsaw
Lauch (-(e)s, -e) *m* leeks *pl*; **eine Stange ~** a leek; **Lauchzwiebel** *f* spring onions *pl* (*Brit*), scallions *pl* (*US*)
Lauf (-(e)s, *Läufe*) *m* run; (*Wettlauf*) race; (*Entwicklung*) course; (*von*

Gewehr) barrel; **Laufbahn** *f* career;
laufen (*lief, gelaufen*) *vi, vt* to run; (*gehen*) to walk; (*funktionieren*) to work; **mir läuft die Nase** my nose is running; **was läuft im Kino?** what's on at the cinema?; **wie läuft's so?** how are things?;
laufend *adj* running; (*Monat, Ausgaben*) current; **auf dem Laufenden sein/halten** to be/to keep up-to-date; **Läufer** (-s, -) *m* (*Teppich*) rug; (*Schach*) bishop;
Läufer(in) *m(f)* (*Sport*) runner;
Laufmasche *f* ladder (*Brit*), run (*US*); **Laufwerk** *nt* (*Inform*) drive
Laune (-, -n) *f* mood;
gute/schlechte ~ haben to be in a good/bad mood; **launisch** *adj* moody
Laus (-, *Läuse*) *f* louse
lauschen *vi* to listen; (*heimlich*) to eavesdrop
laut *adj* loud ▷ *adv* loudly; (*lesen*) aloud ▷ *prep +gen o dat* according to
läuten *vt, vi* to ring
lauter *adv* (*fam: nichts als*) nothing but
Lautsprecher *m* loudspeaker;
Lautstärke *f* loudness; (*Radio, TV*) volume
lauwarm *adj* lukewarm
Lava (-, *Laven*) *f* lava
Lavendel (-s, -) *m* lavender
Lawine *f* avalanche
LCD-Anzeige *f* LCD-display
leasen *vt* to lease; **Leasing** (-s) *nt* leasing
leben *vt, vi* to live; (*am Leben sein*) to be alive; **wie lange ~ Sie schon hier?** how long have you been living here?; **von ... ~** (*Nahrungsmittel etc*) to live on ...; (*Beruf, Beschäftigung*) to make one's living from ...; **Leben** (-s, -) *nt* life;
lebend *adj* living; **lebendig** *adj* alive; (*lebhaft*) lively;

lebensgefährlich adj very dangerous; (Verletzung) critical; **Lebensgefährte** m, **Lebensgefährtin** f partner; **Lebenshaltungskosten** pl cost sing of living; **lebenslänglich** adj for life; **~ bekommen** to get life; **Lebenslauf** m curriculum vitae (Brit), CV (Brit), resumé (US); **Lebensmittel** pl food sing; **Lebensmittelgeschäft** nt grocer's (shop); **Lebensmittelvergiftung** f food poisoning; **lebensnotwendig** adj vital; **Lebensretter(in)** m(f) rescuer; **Lebensstandard** m standard of living; **Lebensunterhalt** m livelihood; **Lebensversicherung** f life insurance (o assurance (Brit)); **Lebenszeichen** nt sign of life

Leber (-, -n) f liver; **Leberfleck** m mole; **Leberpastete** f liver pâté

Lebewesen nt living being **lebhaft** adj lively; (Erinnerung, Eindruck) vivid; **Lebkuchen** m gingerbread; **ein ~** a piece of gingerbread; **leblos** adj lifeless

Leck nt leak

lecken vi (Loch haben) to leak ▷ vt, vi (schlecken) to lick

lecker adj delicious, tasty

Leder (-s, -) nt leather

ledig adj single

leer adj empty; (Seite) blank; (Batterie) dead; **leeren** vt to empty ▷ vr: **sich ~** to empty; **Leerlauf** m (Gang) neutral; **Leertaste** f space bar; **Leerung** f emptying; (Briefkasten) collection; **Leerzeichen** nt blank, space

legal adj legal, lawful

legen vt to put, to place; (Eier) to lay ▷ vr: **sich ~** to lie down; (Sturm, Begeisterung) to die down; (Schmerz, Gefühl) to wear off

Legende (-, -n) f legend

leger adj casual

Lehm (-(e)s, -e) m loam; (Ton) clay

Lehne (-, -n) f arm(rest); (Rückenlehne) back(rest); **lehnen** vt to lean ▷ vr: **sich ~** to lean (an/gegen +akk against); **Lehnstuhl** m armchair

Lehrbuch nt textbook; **Lehre** (-, -n) f teaching; (beruflich) apprenticeship; (moralisch) lesson; **lehren** vt to teach; **Lehrer(in)** (-s, -) m(f) teacher; **Lehrgang** m course; **Lehrling** m apprentice; **lehrreich** adj instructive

Leib (-(e)s, -er) m body; **Leibgericht** nt, **Leibspeise** f favourite dish; **Leibwächter(in)** m(f) bodyguard

Leiche (-, -n) f corpse; **Leichenhalle** f mortuary; **Leichenwagen** m hearse

leicht adj light; (einfach) easy, simple; (Erkrankung) slight; **es sich** (dat) **~ machen** to take the easy way out ▷ adv (mühelos, schnell) easily; (geringfügig) slightly; **Leichtathletik** f athletics sing; **leicht|fallen** irr vi: **jdm ~** to be easy for sb; **leichtsinnig** adj careless; (stärker) reckless

leid adj: **jdn/etw ~ sein** to be tired of sb/sth; **Leid** (-(e)s) nt grief, sorrow; **leiden** (litt, gelitten) vi, vt to suffer (an, unter +dat from); **ich kann ihn/es nicht ~** I can't stand him/it; **Leiden** (-s, -) nt suffering; (Krankheit) illness

Leidenschaft f passion; **leidenschaftlich** adj passionate

leider adv unfortunately; **wir müssen jetzt ~ gehen** I'm afraid we have to go now; **~ ja/nein** I'm afraid so/not

leid|tun irr vi: **es tut mir/ihm leid** I'm/he's sorry; **er tut mir leid** I'm sorry for him

Leihbücherei f lending library
leihen (*lieh, geliehen*) vt: **jdm etw ~** to lend sb sth; **sich** (*dat*) **etw von jdm ~** to borrow sth from sb;
Leihfrist f lending period;
Leihgebühr f hire charge; (*für Buch*) lending charge; **Leihwagen** m hire car (*Brit*), rental car (*US*)

Leim (-(e)s, -e) m glue
Leine (-, -n) f cord; (*für Wäsche*) line; (*Hundeleine*) lead (*Brit*), leash (*US*)

Leinen (-s, -) nt linen; **Leintuch** nt (*für Bett*) sheet; **Leinwand** f (*Kunst*) canvas; (*Cine*) screen
leise adj quiet; (*sanft*) soft ▷ adv quietly

Leiste (-, -n) f ledge; (*Zierleiste*) strip; (*Anat*) groin
leisten vt (*Arbeit*) to do; (*vollbringen*) to achieve; **jdm Gesellschaft ~** to keep sb company; **sich** (*dat*) **etw ~** (*gönnen*) to treat oneself to sth; **ich kann es mir nicht ~** I can't afford it
Leistenbruch m hernia
Leistung f performance; (*gute*) achievement
Leitartikel m leading article (*Brit*), editorial (*US*)
leiten vt to lead; (*Firma*) to run; (*in eine Richtung*) to direct; (*Elek*) to conduct
Leiter (-, -n) f ladder
Leiter(in) (-s, -) m(f) (*von Geschäft*) manager
Leitplanke (-, -n) f crash barrier
Leitung f (*Führung*) direction; (*Tel*) line; (*von Firma*) management; (*Wasserleitung*) pipe; (*Kabel*) cable; **eine lange ~ haben** to be slow on the uptake; **Leitungswasser** nt tap water
Lektion f lesson
Lektüre (-, -n) f (*Lesen*) reading; (*Lesestoff*) reading matter

Lende (-, -n) f (*Speise*) loin; (*vom Rind*) sirloin; **die ~n** pl (*Med*) the lumbar region *sing*
lenken vt to steer; (*Blick*) to direct (*auf+akk* towards); **jds Aufmerksamkeit auf etw** (*akk*) **~** to draw sb's attention to sth; **Lenker** m (*von Fahrrad, Motorrad*) handlebars pl; **Lenkrad** nt steering wheel; **Lenkradschloss** nt steering lock; **Lenkstange** f handlebars pl
Leopard (-en, -en) m leopard
Lepra (-) f leprosy
Lerche (-, -n) f lark
lernen vt, vi to learn; (*für eine Prüfung*) to study, to revise
lesbisch adj lesbian
Lesebuch nt reader; **lesen** (*las, gelesen*) vi, vt to read; (*ernten*) to pick; **Leser(in)** m(f) reader;
Leserbrief m letter to the editor;
leserlich adj legible; **Lesezeichen** nt bookmark
Lettland nt Latvia
letzte(r, s) adj last; (*neueste*) latest; (*endgültig*) final; **zum ~n Mal** for the last time; **am ~n Montag** last Monday; **in ~r Zeit** lately, recently; **letztens** also recently; **letztere(r, s)** adj the latter
Leuchtanzeige f illuminated display; **Leuchte** (-, -n) f lamp, light; **leuchten** vi to shine; (*Feuer, Zifferblatt*) to glow;
Leuchter (-s, -) m candlestick;
Leuchtfarbe f fluorescent colour; (*Anstrichfarbe*) luminous paint;
Leuchtreklame f neon sign;
Leuchtstoffröhre f strip light;
Leuchtturm m lighthouse
leugnen vt to deny ▷ vi to deny everything
Leukämie f leukaemia (*Brit*), leukemia (*US*)

Leukoplast® (-(e)s, -e) nt
Elastoplast® (Brit), Band-Aid®
(US)

Leute pl people pl

Lexikon (-s, Lexika) nt encyclopaedia (Brit), encyclopedia (US);
(Wörterbuch) dictionary

Libanon (-s) m: **der ~** Lebanon

Libelle f dragonfly

liberal adj liberal

Libyen (-s) nt Libya

Licht (-(e)s, -er) nt light;
Lichtblick m ray of hope;
lichtempfindlich adj sensitive to
light; **Lichtempfindlichkeit** f
(Foto) speed; **Lichthupe** f: **die
~ betätigen** to flash one's lights;
Lichtjahr nt light year;
Lichtmaschine f dynamo;
Lichtschalter m light switch;
Lichtschranke f light barrier;
Lichtschutzfaktor m sun
protection factor, SPF

Lichtung f clearing

Lid (-(e)s, -er) nt eyelid;
Lidschatten m eyeshadow

lieb adj (nett) nice; (teuer, geliebt)
dear; (liebenswert) sweet; **das ist
~ von dir** that's nice of you; **Lieber
Herr X** Dear Mr X; **Liebe** (-, -n) f
love; **lieben** vt to love; (sexuell) to
make love to; **liebenswürdig** adj
kind; **lieber** adv rather; **ich
möchte ~ nicht** I'd rather not;
welches ist dir ~? which one do
you prefer?; **siehe auch gern, lieb**;
Liebesbrief m love letter;
Liebeskummer m: **~ haben** to be
lovesick; **Liebespaar** nt lovers pl;
liebevoll adj loving;
Liebhaber(in) (-s, -) m(f) lover;
lieblich adj loving; (Wein) sweet;
Liebling m darling; (Günstling)
favourite; **Lieblings-** in zW
favourite; **liebste(r, s)** adj
favourite; **liebsten** adv: **am
~ esse ich ...** my favourite food

is ...; **am ~ würde ich bleiben** I'd
really like to stay

Liechtenstein (-s) nt
Liechtenstein

Lied (-(e)s, -er) nt song; (Rel) hymn

lief imperf von **laufen**

Lieferant(in) m(f) supplier

lieferbar adj available

liefern vt to deliver; (beschaffen)
to supply

Lieferschein m delivery note;
Lieferung f delivery;
Lieferwagen m delivery van

Liege (-, -n) f (beim Arzt) couch;
(Notbett) campbed; (Gartenliege)
lounger; **liegen** (lag, gelegen) vi to
lie; (sich befinden) to be; **mir liegt
nichts/viel daran** it doesn't
matter to me/it matters a lot to
me; **woran liegt es nur, dass ...?**
why is it that ...?; **~ bleiben**
(Mensch) to stay lying down; (im
Bett) to stay in bed; (Ding) to be left
(behind); **~ lassen** (vergessen) to
leave behind; **Liegestuhl** m deck
chair; **Liegestütz** m press-up
(Brit), push-up (US); **Liegewagen**
m (Eisenb) couchette car

lieh imperf von **leihen**

ließ imperf von **lassen**

Lift (-(e)s, -e o -s) m lift, elevator
(US)

Liga (-, Ligen) f league, division

light adj (Cola) diet; (fettarm)
low-fat; (kalorienarm) low-calorie;
(Zigaretten) mild

Likör (-s, -e) m liqueur

lila adj inv purple

Lilie f lily

Limette (-, -n) f lime

Limo (-, -s) f (fam) fizzy drink
(Brit), soda (US); **Limonade** f
fizzy drink (Brit), soda (US); (mit
Zitronengeschmack) lemonade

Limone (-, -n) f lime

Limousine (-, -n) f saloon (car)
(Brit), sedan (US); (fam) limo

Linde (-, -n) f lime tree

lindern vt to relieve, to soothe

Lineal (-s, -e) nt ruler

Linie f line; **Linienflug** m scheduled flight; **liniert** adj ruled, lined

Link (-s, -s) m (Inform) link

Linke (-n, -n) f left-hand side; (Hand) left hand; (Pol) left (wing); **linke(r, s)** adj left; **auf der ~n Seite** on the left, on the left-hand side; **links** adv on the left; **~ abbiegen** to turn left; **~ von** to the left of; **~ oben** at the top left; **Linkshänder(in)** (-s, -) m(f) left-hander; **linksherum** adv to the left, anticlockwise; **Linksverkehr** m driving on the left

Linse (-, -n) f lentil; (optisch) lens

Lippe (-, -n) f lip; **Lipgloss** nt lip gloss; **Lippenstift** m lipstick

lispeln vi to lisp

List (-, -en) f cunning; (Trick) trick

Liste (-, -n) f list

Litauen (-s) nt Lithuania

Liter (-s, -) m or nt litre

literarisch adj literary; **Literatur** f literature

Litschi (-, -s) f lychee, litchi

litt imperf von **leiden**

live adv (Radio, TV) live

Lizenz f licence

Lkw (-(s), -(s)) m abk = **Lastkraftwagen** truck, lorry (Brit); **Lkw-Maut** f heavy goods vehicle toll

Lob (-(e)s) nt praise; **loben** vt to praise

Loch (-(e)s, Löcher) nt hole; **lochen** vt to punch; **Locher** (-s, -) m (hole) punch

Locke (-, -n) f curl; **locken** vt (anlocken) to lure; (Haare) to curl; **Lockenstab** m curling tongs pl (Brit), curling irons pl (US); **Lockenwickler** (-s, -) m curler

locker adj (Schraube, Zahn) loose; (Haltung) relaxed; (Person) easy-going; **das schaffe ich ~** (fam) I'll manage it, no problem; **lockern** vt to loosen ▷ vr: **sich ~** to loosen

lockig adj curly

Löffel (-s, -) m spoon; **einen ~ Mehl zugeben** add a spoonful of flour; **Löffelbiskuit** (-s, -s) m sponge finger

log imperf von **lügen**

Loge (-, -n) f (Theat) box

logisch adj logical

Logo (-s, -s) nt logo

Lohn (-(e)s, Löhne) m reward; (Arbeitslohn) pay, wages pl

lohnen vr: **sich ~** to be worth it; **es lohnt sich nicht zu warten** it's no use waiting

Lohnerhöhung f pay rise (Brit), pay raise (US); **Lohnsteuer** f income tax

Lokal (-(e)s, -e) nt (Gaststätte) restaurant; (Kneipe) pub (Brit), bar

Lokomotive f locomotive

London (-s) nt London

Lorbeer (-s, -en) m laurel; **Lorbeerblatt** nt (Gastr) bay leaf

los adj loose; **~!** go on!; **jdn/etw ~ sein** to be rid of sb/sth; **was ist ~?** what's the matter?, what's up?; **dort ist nichts/viel ~** there's nothing/a lot going on there

Los (-es, -e) nt (Schicksal) lot, fate; (Lotterie etc) ticket

losbinden irr vt to untie

löschen vt (Feuer, Licht) to put out, to extinguish; (Durst) to quench; (Tonband) to erase; (Daten, Zeile) to delete; **Löschtaste** f delete key

lose adj loose

Lösegeld nt ransom

losen vi to draw lots

lösen vt (lockern) to loosen; (Rätsel) to solve; (Chem) to

dissolve; (Fahrkarte) to buy ▷ vr:
sich ~ (abgehen) to come off;
(Zucker etc) to dissolve; (Problem,
Schwierigkeit) to (re)solve itself
los|fahren irr vi to leave;
los|gehen irr vi to set out;
(anfangen) to start; **los|lassen** irr
vt to let go
löslich adj soluble
Lösung f (eines Rätsels, Problems,
Flüssigkeit) solution
los|werden irr vt to get rid of
Lotterie f lottery; **Lotto** (-s) nt
National Lottery; **~ spielen** to play
the lottery
Löwe (-n, -n) m (Zool) lion; (Astr)
Leo; **Löwenzahn** m dandelion
Luchs (-es, -e) m lynx
Lücke (-, -n) f gap;
Lückenbüßer(in) (-s, -) m(f)
stopgap
lud imperf von **laden**
Luft (-, Lüfte) f air; (Atem) breath;
Luftballon m balloon; **Luftblase**
f (air) bubble; **luftdicht** adj
airtight; **Luftdruck** m (Meteo)
atmospheric pressure; (in Reifen)
air pressure
lüften vt to air; (Geheimnis) to
reveal
Luftfahrt f aviation;
Luftfeuchtigkeit f humidity;
Luftfilter m air filter; **Luftfracht**
f air freight; **Luftkissenboot** nt,
Luftkissenfahrzeug nt hovercraft;
Luftlinie f: **10 km** ~ 10 km as the
crow flies; **Luftmatratze** f airbed;
Luftpirat(in) m(f) hijacker;
Luftpost f airmail; **Luftpumpe** f
(bicycle) pump; **Luftröhre** f
windpipe
Lüftung f ventilation
Luftveränderung f change of
air; **Luftverschmutzung** f air
pollution; **Luftwaffe** f air force;
Luftzug m draught (Brit), draft
(US)

Lüge (-, -n) f lie; **lügen** (log,
gelogen) vi to lie; **Lügner(in)** (-s, -)
m(f) liar
Luke (-, -n) f hatch
Lumpen (-s, -) m rag
Lunchpaket nt packed lunch
Lunge (-, -n) f lungs pl;
Lungenentzündung f
pneumonia
Lupe (-, -n) f magnifying glass;
etw unter die ~ nehmen (fig) to
have a close look at sth
Lust (-, Lüste) f joy, delight;
(Neigung) desire; **~ auf etw** (akk)
haben to feel like sth; **~ haben,
etw zu tun** to feel like doing sth
lustig adj (komisch) amusing,
funny; (fröhlich) cheerful
lutschen vt to suck ▷ vi **~ an**
(+dat) to suck; **Lutscher** (-s, -) m
lollipop
Luxemburg (-s) nt Luxembourg
luxuriös adj luxurious
Luxus (-) m luxury
Lymphdrüse f lymph gland;
Lymphknoten m lymph node
Lyrik (-) f poetry

m

machbar adj feasible

○ SCHLÜSSELWORT

machen vt 1 to do; (herstellen, zubereiten) to make; **was machst du da?** what are you doing (there)?; **das ist nicht zu machen** that can't be done; **das Radio leiser machen** to turn the radio down; **aus Holz gemacht** made of wood

2 (verursachen, bewirken) to make; **jdm Angst machen** to make sb afraid; **das macht die Kälte** it's the cold that does this

3 (ausmachen) to matter; **das macht nichts** that doesn't matter; **die Kälte macht mir nichts** I don't mind the cold

4 (kosten, ergeben) to be; **3 und 5 macht 8** 3 and 5 is o are 8; **was o wie viel macht das?** how much

does that make?

5 was macht die Arbeit? how's the work going?; **was macht dein Bruder?** how is your brother doing?; **das Auto machen lassen** to have the car done; **mach's gut!** take care!; **(viel Glück)** good luck!
▷ vi: **mach schnell!** hurry up!; **Schluss machen** to finish (off); **mach schon!** come on!; **das macht müde** it makes you tired; **in etw** dat **machen** to be o deal in sth
▷ vr to come along (nicely); **sich an etw** akk **machen** to set about sth; **sich verständlich machen** to make o.s. understood; **sich** dat **viel aus jdm/etw machen** to like sb/sth

Macho (-s, -s) m (fam) macho (type)

Macht (-, *Mächte*) f power; **mächtig** adj powerful; (fam: ungeheuer) enormous; **machtlos** adj powerless; **da ist man ~** there's nothing you can do (about it)

Mädchen nt girl; **Mädchenname** m maiden name

Made (-, -n) f maggot

Magazin (-s, -e) nt magazine

Magen (-s, - o *Mägen*) m stomach; **Magenbeschwerden** pl stomach trouble sing; **Magen-Darm-Infektion** f gastroenteritis; **Magengeschwür** nt stomach ulcer; **Magenschmerzen** pl stomachache sing

mager adj (Fleisch, Wurst) lean; (Person) thin; (Käse, Joghurt) low-fat; **Magermilch** f skimmed milk; **Magersucht** f anorexia; **magersüchtig** adj anorexic

magisch adj magical

Magnet (-s o -en, -en) m magnet

mähen vt, vi to mow

mahlen (mahlte, gemahlen) vt to grind

Mahlzeit f meal; (für Baby) feed ▷ interj (guten Appetit) enjoy your meal

Mähne (-, -n) f mane

mahnen vt to urge; **jdn schriftlich ~** to send sb a reminder; **Mahngebühr** f fine; **Mahnung** f warning; (schriftlich) reminder

Mai (-(s), -e) m May; siehe auch **Juni**; **Maifeiertag** m May Day; **Maiglöckchen** nt lily of the valley; **Maikäfer** m cockchafer

Mail (-, -s) f e-mail; **jdm eine~ schicken** to mail sb, to e-mail sb; **Mailbox** f (Inform) mailbox; **mailen** vi, vt to e-mail

Mais (-es, -e) m maize, corn (US); **Maiskolben** m corn cob; (Gastr) corn on the cob

Majestät (-, -en) f Majesty

Majonäse (-, -n) f mayonnaise

Majoran (-s, -e) m marjoram

makaber adj macabre

Make-up (-s, -s) nt make-up

Makler(in) (-s, -) m(f) broker; (Immobilienmakler) estate agent (Brit), Realtor® (US)

Makrele (-, -n) f mackerel

Makro (-s, -s) nt (Inform) macro

Makrone (-, -n) f macaroon

mal adv (beim Rechnen) times, multiplied by; (beim Messen) by; (fam: einmal = früher) once; (einmal = zukünftig) some day; **4 ~ 3 ist 12** 4 times 3 is (o equals) twelve; **da habe ich ~ gewohnt** I used to live there; **irgendwann ~ werde ich dort hinfahren** I'll go there one day; **das ist nun ~ so** well, that's just the way it is (o goes); **Mal** (-(e)s, -e) nt (Zeitpunkt) time; (Markierung) mark; **jedes ~** every time; **ein paar ~** a few times; **ein einziges ~** just once

Malaria (-) f malaria

Malaysia (-s) nt Malaysia

Malbuch nt colouring book

Malediven pl Maldives pl

malen vt, vi to paint; **Maler(in)** (-s, -) m(f) painter; **Malerei** f painting; **malerisch** adj picturesque

Mallorca (-s) nt Majorca, Mallorca

mal|nehmen irr vt to multiply (mit by)

Malta (-s) nt Malta

Malventee m mallow tea

Malz (-es) nt malt; **Malzbier** nt malt beer

Mama (-, -s) f mum(my) (Brit), mom(my) (US)

man pron you; (förmlich) one; (jemand) someone, somebody; (die Leute) they, people pl; **wie schreibt ~ das?** how do you spell that?; **~ hat ihr das Fahrrad gestohlen** someone stole her bike; **~ sagt, dass ...** they (o people) say that ...

managen vt (fam) to manage; **Manager(in)** (-s, -) m(f) manager

manche(r, s) adj many a; (mit pl) a number of, quite a ▷ pron (einige) some; (viele) many; **~ Politiker** many politicians pl, many a politician; **manchmal** adv sometimes

Mandant(in) m(f) client

Mandarine f mandarin, tangerine

Mandel (-, -n) f almond; **~n** (Anat) tonsils pl; **Mandelentzündung** f tonsillitis

Manege (-, -n) f ring

Mangel (-s, Mängel) m (Fehlen) lack; (Knappheit) shortage (an +dat of); (Fehler) defect, fault; **mangelhaft** adj (Ware) faulty; (Schulnote) = E

Mango (-, -s) f mango

Mangold (-s) m mangel(wurzel)

Manieren pl manners pl

Maniküre (-, -n) f manicure

manipulieren vt to manipulate

Manko (-s, -s) nt deficiency

Mann (-(e)s, Männer) m man; (Ehemann) husband; **Männchen** nt: **es ist ein ~** (Tier) it's a he; **männlich** adj masculine; (Bio) male

Mannschaft f (Sport, fig) team; (Naut, Aviat) crew

Mansarde (-, -n) f attic

Manschettenknopf m cufflink

Mantel (-s, Mäntel) m coat; (Tech) casing, jacket

Mappe (-, -n) f briefcase; (Aktenmappe) folder

Maracuja (-, -s) f passion fruit

Marathon (-s, -s) m marathon

Märchen nt fairy tale

Marder (-s, -) m marten

Margarine f margarine

Marienkäfer m ladybird (Brit), ladybug (US)

Marihuana (-s) nt marijuana

Marille (-, -n) f apricot

Marinade f marinade

Marine f navy

marinieren vt to marinate

Marionette f puppet

Mark (-(e)s) nt (Knochenmark) marrow; (Fruchtmark) pulp

Marke (-, -n) f (Warensorte) brand; (Fabrikat) make; (Briefmarke) stamp; (Essenmarke) voucher, ticket; (aus Metall etc) disc; (Messpunkt) mark; **Markenartikel** m branded item, brand name product; **Markenzeichen** nt trademark

markieren vt to mark; **Markierung** f marking; (Zeichen) mark

Markise (-, -n) f awning

Markt (-(e)s, Märkte) m market; **auf den ~ bringen** to launch; **Markthalle** f covered market;

Marktlücke f gap in the market; **Marktplatz** m market place; **Marktwirtschaft** f market economy

Marmelade f jam; (Orangenmarmelade) marmalade

Marmor (-s, -e) m marble; **Marmorkuchen** m marble cake

Marokko (-s) nt Morocco

Marone (-, -n) f chestnut

Mars (-) m Mars

Marsch (-(e)s, Märsche) m march

Märtyrer(in) (-s, -) m(f) martyr

März (-(es), -e) m March; siehe auch **Juni**

Marzipan (-s, -e) nt marzipan

Maschine f machine; (Motor) engine; **maschinell** adj mechanical, machine-; **Maschinenbau** m mechanical engineering

Masern pl (Med) measles sing

Maske (-, -n) f mask; **Maskenball** m fancy-dress ball; **maskieren** vr: **sich ~** (Maske aufsetzen) to put on a mask; (verkleiden) to dress up

Maskottchen nt mascot

maß imperf von **messen**

Maß (-es, -e) nt measure; (Mäßigung) moderation; (Grad) degree, extent; **~e** (Person) measurements; (Raum) dimensions; **in gewissem/hohem ~e** to a certain/high degree; **in zunehmendem ~e** increasingly

Mass (-, -(en)) f (Bier) litre of beer

Massage (-, -n) f massage

Masse (-, -n) f mass; (von Menschen) crowd; (Großteil) majority; **massenhaft** adv masses (o loads) of; **am See sind ~ Mücken** there are masses of mosquitoes at the lake; **Massenkarambolage** f pile-up; **Massenmedien** pl mass media pl; **Massenproduktion** f mass

production; **Massentourismus** m mass tourism
Masseur(in) m(f) masseur/masseuse
maßgeschneidert adj (Kleidung) made-to-measure
massieren vt to massage
mäßig adj moderate
massiv adj solid; (fig) massive
maßlos adj extreme
Maßnahme (-, -n) f measure, step
Maßstab m rule, measure; (fig) standard; **im ~ von 1:5** on a scale of 1:5
Mast (-(e)s, -e(n)) m mast; (Elek) pylon
Material (-s, -ien) nt material; (Arbeitsmaterial) materials pl; **materialistisch** adj materialistic
Materie f matter; **materiell** adj material
Mathe (-) f (fam) maths (Brit), math (US); **Mathematik** f mathematics sing; **Mathematiker(in)** m(f) mathematician
Matinee (-, -n) f ≈ matinee
Matratze (-, -n) f mattress
Matrose (-n, -n) m sailor
Matsch (-(e)s) m mud; (Schnee) slush; **matschig** adj muddy; (Schnee) slushy; (Obst) mushy
matt adj weak; (glanzlos) dull; (Foto) matt; (Schach) mate
Matte (-, -n) f mat
Matura (-) f Austrian school-leaving examination; ≈ A-levels (Brit), ≈ High School Diploma (US)
Mauer (-, -n) f wall
Maul (-(e)s, Mäuler) nt mouth; (fam) gob; **halt's ~!** shut your face (o gob); **Maulbeere** f mulberry; **Maulesel** m mule; **Maulkorb** m muzzle; **Maul- und Klauenseuche** f foot-and-mouth disease; **Maulwurf** m mole

Maurer(in) (-s, -) m(f) bricklayer
Mauritius (-) nt Mauritius
Maus (-, Mäuse) f mouse; **Mausefalle** f mousetrap; **Mausklick** (-s, -s) m mouse click; **Mauspad** (-s, -s) nt mouse mat (o pad); **Maustaste** f mouse key (o button)
Maut (-, -en) f toll; **Mautgebühr** f toll; **mautpflichtig** adj: **-e Straße** toll road, turnpike (US); **Mautstelle** f tollbooth, tollgate; **Mautstraße** f toll road, turnpike (US)
maximal adv: **ihr habt ~ zwei Stunden Zeit** you've got two hours at (the) most; **~ vier Leute** a maximum of four people
Mayonnaise f siehe **Majonäse**
Mazedonien (-s) nt Macedonia
MB (-, -) nt, **Mbyte** (-, -) nt abk = **Megabyte** MB
Mechanik f mechanics sing; (Getriebe) mechanics pl; **Mechaniker(in)** (-s, -) m(f) mechanic; **mechanisch** adj mechanical; **Mechanismus** m mechanism
meckern vi (Ziege) to bleat; (fam: schimpfen) to moan
Mecklenburg-Vorpommern (-s) nt Mecklenburg-Western Pomerania
Medaille (-, -n) f medal
Medien pl media pl
Medikament nt medicine
Meditation f meditation; **meditieren** vi to meditate
medium adj (Steak) medium
Medizin (-, -en) f medicine (gegen for); **medizinisch** adj medical
Meer (-(e)s, -e) nt sea; **am ~** by the sea; **Meerenge** f straits pl; **Meeresfrüchte** pl seafood sing; **Meeresspiegel** m sea level; **Meerrettich** m horseradish; **Meerschweinchen** nt guinea pig; **Meerwasser** nt seawater

Megabyte nt megabyte;
Megahertz nt megahertz

Mehl (-(e)s, -e) nt flour;
Mehlspeise f sweet dish made from
flour, eggs and milk

mehr pron, adv more; **~ will ich
nicht ausgeben** I don't want to
spend any more, that's as much as
I want to spend; **was willst du ~?**
what more do you want? ▷ adv:
immer ~ (Leute) more and more
(people); **~ als fünf Minuten** more
than five minutes; **je ~ ..., desto
besser** the more ..., the better; **ich
kann nicht ~ stehen** I can't stand
any more (o longer); **es ist kein
Brot ~ da** there's no bread left; **nie
~** never again; **mehrdeutig** adj
ambiguous; **mehrere** pron
several; **mehreres** pron several
things; **mehrfach** adj multiple;
(wiederholt) repeated;
Mehrfachstecker m multiple
plug; **Mehrheit** f majority;
mehrmals adv repeatedly;
mehrsprachig adj multilingual;
Mehrwegflasche f returnable
bottle, deposit bottle;
Mehrwertsteuer f value added
tax, VAT; **Mehrzahl** f majority;
(Plural) plural

meiden (mied, gemieden) vt to
avoid

Meile (-, -n) f mile

mein pron (adjektivisch) my;
meine(r, s) pron (substantivisch)
mine

meinen vt, vi (glauben, der Ansicht
sein) to think; (sagen) to say;
(sagen wollen, beabsichtigen) to mean; **das
war nicht so gemeint** I didn't
mean it like that

meinetwegen adv (wegen mir)
because of me; (mir zuliebe) for my
sake; (von mir aus) as far as I'm
concerned

Meinung f opinion; **meiner**

~ nach in my opinion;
Meinungsumfrage f opinion
poll; **Meinungsverschiedenheit**
f disagreement (über +akk about)

Meise (-, -n) f tit; **eine ~ haben**
(fam) to be crazy

Meißel (-s, -) m chisel

meist adv mostly; **meiste(r, s)**
pron (adjektivisch) most; **die ~n**
(Leute) most people; **die ~ Zeit**
most of the time; **das ~** (davon)
most of it; **die ~n von ihnen** most
of them; (substantivisch) most of
them; **am ~n** (the) most;
meistens adv mostly; (zum
größten Teil) for the most part

Meister(in) (-s, -) m(f) master;
(Sport) champion; **Meisterschaft**
f championship; **Meisterwerk**
nt masterpiece

melden vt to report ▷ vr: **sich
~** to report (bei to); (Schule) to put
one's hand up; (freiwillig) to
volunteer; (auf etw, am Telefon) to
answer; **Meldung** f
announcement; (Bericht) report;
(Inform) message

Melodie f tune, melody

Melone (-, -n) f melon

Memoiren pl memoirs pl

Menge (-, -n) f quantity;
(Menschen) crowd; **eine ~** (große
Anzahl) a lot (gen of);
Mengenrabatt m bulk discount

Meniskus (-, Menisken) m
meniscus

Mensa (-, Mensen) f canteen,
cafeteria (US)

Mensch (-en, -en) m human
being, man; (Person) person; **kein
~** nobody; **~!** (bewundernd) wow!;
(verärgert) bloody hell!;
Menschenmenge f crowd;
Menschenrechte pl human
rights pl; **Menschenverstand** m:
gesunder ~ common sense;
Menschheit f humanity,

mankind; **menschlich** adj
human; *(human)* humane
Menstruation f menstruation
Mentalität f mentality, mindset
Menthol (-s) nt menthol
Menü (-s, -s) nt set meal; *(Inform)*
menu; **Menüleiste** f *(Inform)*
menu bar
Merkblatt nt leaflet; **merken** vt
(bemerken) to notice; **sich** *(dat)* **etw**
~ to remember sth; **Merkmal** nt
feature
Merkur (-s) m Mercury
merkwürdig adj odd
Messbecher m measuring jug
Messe (-, -n) f fair; *(Rel)* mass;
Messebesucher(in) m(f) visitor
to a/the fair; **Messegelände** nt
exhibition site
messen *(maß, gemessen)* vt to
measure; *(Temperatur, Puls)* to take
▷ vr: **sich** ~ *(Comm)* to compete; **sie kann
sich mit ihm nicht** ~ she's no
match for him
Messer (-s, -) nt knife
Messgerät nt measuring device,
gauge
Messing (-s) nt brass
Metall (-s, -e) nt metal
Meteorologe m, **Meteorologin**
f meteorologist
Meter (-s, -) m o nt metre;
Metermaß nt tape measure
Methode (-, -n) f method
Metzger(in) (-s, -) m(f) butcher;
Metzgerei f butcher's (shop)
Mexiko (-s) nt Mexico
MEZ f abk = **mitteleuropäische
Zeit** CET
miau interj miaow
mich pron akk von **ich** me;
~ *(selbst)* *(reflexiv)* myself; **stell
dich hinter** ~ stand behind me;
ich fühle ~ **wohl** I feel fine
mied imperf von **meiden**
Miene (-, -n) f look, expression
mies adj *(fam)* lousy

Miesmuschel f mussel
Mietauto nt siehe **Mietwagen**;
Miete (-, -n) f rent; **mieten** vt to
rent; *(Auto)* to hire (Brit), to rent
(US); **Mieter(in)** (-s, -) m(f)
tenant; **Mietshaus** nt block of
flats (Brit), apartment house (US);
Mietvertrag m rental
agreement; **Mietwagen** m hire
car (Brit), rental car (US); **sich** *(dat)*
einen ~ **nehmen** to hire (Brit) (o
rent (US)) a car
Migräne (-, -n) f migraine
Migrant(in) (-en, -en) m(f)
migrant (worker)
Mikrofon (-s, -e) nt microphone
Mikrowelle (-, -n) f,
Mikrowellenherd m microwave
(oven)
Milch (-) f milk; **Milcheis** nt
ice-cream *(made with milk)*;
Milchglas nt *(dickes, trübes Glas)*
frosted glass; **Milchkaffee** m
milky coffee; **Milchprodukte** pl
dairy products pl; **Milchpulver** nt
powdered milk; **Milchreis** m rice
pudding; **Milchshake** m milk
shake; **Milchstraße** f Milky Way
mild adj mild; *(Richter)* lenient;
(freundlich) kind
Militär (-s) nt military, army
Milliarde (-, -n) f billion;
Milligramm nt milligram;
Milliliter m millilitre; **Millimeter**
m millimetre; **Million** f million;
Millionär(in) m(f) millionaire
Milz (-, -en) f spleen
Mimik f facial expression(s)
Minderheit f minority
minderjährig adj underage
minderwertig adj inferior;
Minderwertigkeitskomplex m
inferiority complex
Mindest- in zW minimum;
mindeste(r, s) adj least;
mindestens adv at least;
Mindesthaltbarkeitsdatum nt

best-before date, sell-by date
(Brit)

Mine (-, -n) f mine; (Bleistift) lead;
(Kugelschreiber) refill

Mineralwasser nt mineral
water

Minibar f minibar; **Minigolf** nt
miniature golf, crazy golf (Brit)

minimal adj minimal

Minimum (-s, Minima) nt
minimum

Minirock m miniskirt

Minister(in) (-s, -) m(f) minister;
Ministerium nt ministry;
Ministerpräsident(in) m(f) (von
Bundesland) Minister President
(Prime Minister of a Bundesland)

minus adv minus; **Minus** (-, -) nt
deficit; **im ~ sein** to be in the red;
(Konto) to be overdrawn

Minute (-, -n) f minute

Minze (-, -n) f mint

Mio. nt abk von **Million(en)** m

mir pron dat von **ich** (to) me;
kannst du ~ helfen? can you help
me?; **kannst du es ~ erklären?** can
you explain it to me?; **ich habe
~ einen neuen Rechner gekauft** I
bought (myself) a new computer;
ein Freund von ~ a friend of mine

Mirabelle (-, -n) f mirabelle
(small yellow plum)

mischen vt to mix; (Karten) to
shuffle; **Mischmasch** m (fam)
hotchpotch; **Mischung** f
mixture (aus of)

missachten vt to ignore;
Missbrauch m abuse; (falscher
Gebrauch) misuse; **missbrauchen**
vt to misuse (zu for); (sexuell) to
abuse; **Misserfolg** m failure;
Missgeschick nt (Panne) mishap;
misshandeln vt to ill-treat

Mission f mission

misslingen (misslang, misslungen)
vi to fail; **der Versuch ist mir
misslungen** my attempt failed;

misstrauen vt +dat to distrust;
Misstrauen (-s) nt mistrust,
suspicion (gegenüber of);
misstrauisch adj distrustful;
(argwöhnisch) suspicious;

Missverständnis nt misunderstanding; **missverstehen** irr vt
to misunderstand

Mist (-(e)s) m (fam) rubbish; (von
Kühen) dung; (als Dünger) manure

Mistel (-, -n) f mistletoe

mit prep +dat with; (mittels) by;
~ der Bahn by train; **~ der
Kreditkarte bezahlen** to pay
by credit card; **~ 10 Jahren** at the
age of 10; **wie wärs ~ ...?** how
about ...? ▷ adv along, too; **wollen
Sie ~?** do you want to come along?

Mitarbeiter(in) m(f) (Angestellter) employee; (an Projekt)
collaborator; (freier) freelancer

mit|bekommen irr vt (fam:
aufschnappen) to catch; (hören) to
hear; (verstehen) to get

mit|benutzen vt to share

Mitbewohner(in) m(f) (in
Wohnung) flatmate (Brit),
roommate (US)

mit|bringen irr vt to bring
along; **Mitbringsel** (-s, -) nt small
present

miteinander adv with one
another; (gemeinsam) together

mit|erleben vt to see (with one's
own eyes)

Mitesser (-s, -) m blackhead

Mitfahrgelegenheit f ~ lift,
ride (US); **Mitfahrzentrale** f
agency for arranging lifts

mit|geben irr vt: **jdm etw ~** to
give sb sth (to take along)

Mitgefühl nt sympathy

mit|gehen irr vi to go/come
along

mitgenommen adj worn out,
exhausted

Mitglied nt member

mithilfe prep +gen ~ **von** with the help of

mit|kommen irr vi to come along; (verstehen) to follow

Mitleid nt pity; ~ **haben mit** to feel sorry for

mit|machen vt to take part in ▷ vi to take part

mit|nehmen irr vt to take along; (anstrengen) to wear out, to exhaust

mit|schreiben irr vi to take notes ▷ vt to take down

Mitschüler(in) m(f) schoolmate

mit|spielen vi (in Mannschaft) to play; (bei Spiel) to join in; **in einem Film/Stück ~** to act in a film/play

Mittag m midday; **gestern ~** at midday yesterday, yesterday lunchtime; **über ~ geschlossen** closed at lunchtime; **zu ~ essen** to have lunch; **Mittagessen** nt lunch; **mittags** adv at lunchtime, at midday; **Mittagspause** f lunch break

Mitte (-, -n) f middle; ~ **Juni** in the middle of June; **sie ist ~ zwanzig** she's in her mid-twenties

mit|teilen vt: **jdm etw ~** to inform sb of sth; **Mitteilung** f notification

Mittel (-s -) nt means sing; (Maßnahme, Methode) method; (Med) remedy (gegen for); **das ist ein gutes ~, (um) junge Leute zu erreichen** that's a good way of engaging with young people

Mittelalter nt Middle Ages pl; **mittelalterlich** adj medieval; **Mittelamerika** nt Central America; **Mitteleuropa** nt Central Europe; **Mittelfeld** nt midfield; **Mittelfinger** m middle finger; **mittelmäßig** adj mediocre; **Mittelmeer** nt Mediterranean (Sea);

Mittelohrentzündung f inflammation of the middle ear; **Mittelpunkt** m centre; **im ~ stehen** to be the centre of attention

mittels prep +gen by means of

Mittelstreifen m central reservation (Brit), median (US); **Mittelstürmer(in)** m(f) striker, centre-forward; **Mittelwelle** f medium wave

mitten adv in the middle; ~ **auf der Straße/in der Nacht** in the middle of the street/night

Mitternacht f midnight

mittlere(r, s) adj middle; (durchschnittlich) average

mittlerweile adv meanwhile

Mittwoch (-s, -e) m Wednesday; **(am)** ~ on Wednesday; **(am) ~ Morgen/Nachmittag/Abend** (on) Wednesday morning/afternoon/evening; **diesen/letzten/nächsten ~** this/last/next Wednesday; **jeden ~** every Wednesday; **~ in einer Woche** a week on Wednesday, Wednesday week; **mittwochs** adv on Wednesdays; **~ abends** (jeden Mittwochabend) on Wednesday evenings

mixen vt to mix; **Mixer** (-s, -) m (Küchengerät) blender

MKS f abk = **Maul- und Klauenseuche** FMD

mobben vt to harass (o to bully) (at work)

Mobbing (-s) nt workplace bullying (o harassment)

Möbel (-s, -) nt piece of furniture; **die ~** pl the furniture sing; **Möbelwagen** m removal van

mobil adj mobile

Mobilfunknetz nt cellular network; **Mobiltelefon** nt mobile phone

möblieren vt to furnish

mochte imperf von **mögen**

Mode (-, -n) f fashion

Model (-s, -s) nt model

Modell (-s, -e) nt model

Modem (-s, -s) nt (Inform) modem

Mode(n)schau f fashion show

Moderator(in) m(f) presenter

modern adj modern; (modisch) fashionable

Modeschmuck m costume jewellery; **modisch** adj fashionable

Modus (-, Modi) m (Inform) mode; (fig) way

Mofa (-s, -s) nt moped

mogeln vi to cheat

○ SCHLÜSSELWORT

mögen (pt **mochte**, pp **gemocht** o (als Hilfsverb) **mögen**) vt, vi to like; **magst du/mögen Sie ihn?** do you like him?; **ich möchte ...** I would like ..., I'd like ...; **er möchte in die Stadt** he'd like to go into town; **ich möchte nicht, dass du ...** I wouldn't like you to ...; **ich mag nicht mehr** I've had enough
▷ Hilfsverb to like to; (wollen) to want; **möchtest du etwas essen?** would you like something to eat?; **sie mag nicht bleiben** she doesn't want to stay; **das mag wohl sein** that may well be; **was mag das heißen?** what might that mean?; **Sie möchten zu Hause anrufen** could you please call home?

möglich adj possible; **so bald wie ~** as soon as possible; **möglicherweise** adv possibly; **Möglichkeit** f possibility; **möglichst** adv as ... as possible

Mohn (-(e)s, -e) m (Blume) poppy; (Samen) poppy seed

Möhre (-, -n) f, **Mohrrübe** f carrot

Mokka (-s, -s) m mocha

Moldawien (-s) nt Moldova

Molkerei (-, -en) f dairy

Moll (-) nt minor (key); **a-~** A minor

mollig adj cosy; (dicklich) plump

Moment (-(e)s, -e) m moment; **im ~** at the moment; **einen ~ bitte!** just a minute; **momentan** adj momentary ▷ adv at the moment

Monaco (-s) nt Monaco

Monarchie f monarchy

Monat (-(e)s, -e) m month; **sie ist im dritten ~** (schwanger) she's three months pregnant; **monatlich** adj, adv monthly; **~ 100 Euro zahlen** to pay 100 euros a month (o every month); **Monatskarte** f monthly season ticket

Mönch (-s, -e) m monk

Mond (-(e)s, -e) m moon; **Mondfinsternis** f lunar eclipse

Mongolei (-) f: **die ~** Mongolia

Monitor m (Inform) monitor

monoton adj monotonous

Monsun (-s, -e) m monsoon

Montag m Monday; siehe auch **Mittwoch**; **montags** adv on Mondays; siehe auch **mittwochs**

Montenegro (-s) nt Montenegro

Monteur(in) (-s, -e) m(f) fitter; **montieren** vt to assemble, to set up

Monument nt monument

Moor (-(e)s, -e) nt moor

Moos (-es, -e) nt moss

Moped (-s, -s) nt moped

Moral (-) f (Werte) morals pl; (einer Geschichte) moral; **moralisch** adj moral

Mord (-(e)s, -e) m murder;

Mörder(in) (-s, -) m(f) murderer/murderess

morgen adv tomorrow; **~ früh** tomorrow morning

Morgen (-s, -) m morning; **am ~** in the morning; **Morgenmantel** m, **Morgenrock** m dressing gown; **Morgenmuffel** m: **er ist ein ~** he's not a morning person; **morgens** adv in the morning; **um 3 Uhr ~** at 3 (o'clock) in the morning, at 3 am

Morphium (-s) nt morphine

morsch adj rotten

Mosaik (-s, -e(n)) nt mosaic

Mosambik (-s) nt Mozambique

Moschee (-, -n) f mosque

Moskau (-s) nt Moscow

Moskito (-s, -s) m mosquito; **Moskitonetz** nt mosquito net

Moslem (-s, -s) m, **Moslime** (-, -n) f Muslim

Most (-(e)s, -e) m (unfermented) fruit juice; (Apfelwein) cider

Motel (-s, -s) nt motel

motivieren vt to motivate

Motor m engine; (Elek) motor; **Motorboot** nt motorboat; **Motoröl** nt engine oil; **Motorhaube** f bonnet (Brit), hood (US); **Motorrad** nt motorbike, motorcycle; **Motorradfahrer(in)** m(f) motorcyclist; **Motorroller** m (motor) scooter; **Motorschaden** m engine trouble

Motte (-, -n) f moth

Motto (-s, -s) nt motto

Mountainbike (-s, -s) nt mountain bike

Möwe (-, -n) f (sea)gull

MP3-Player (-s, -) m MP3 player

Mrd. f abk = **Milliarde(n)**

MS (-) f abk = **multiple Sklerose** MS

Mücke (-, -n) f midge; (tropische) mosquito; **Mückenstich** m mosquito bite

müde adj tired

muffig adj (Geruch) musty; (Gesicht, Mensch) grumpy

Mühe (-, -n) f trouble, pains pl; **sich** (dat) **große ~ geben** to go to a lot of trouble

muhen vi to moo

Mühle (-, -n) f mill; (Kaffeemühle) grinder

Müll (-(e)s) m rubbish (Brit), garbage (US); **Müllabfuhr** f rubbish (Brit) or garbage (US) disposal

Mullbinde f gauze bandage

Müllcontainer m waste container; **Mülldeponie** f rubbish (Brit) or garbage (US) dump; **Mülleimer** m rubbish bin (Brit), garbage can (US); **Mülltonne** f dustbin (Brit), garbage can (US); **Mülltrennung** f sorting and collecting household waste according to type of material; **Müllverbrennungsanlage** f incineration plant; **Müllwagen** m dustcart (Brit), garbage truck (US)

multikulturell adj multicultural

Multimedia- in zW multimedia

Multiple-Choice-Verfahren nt multiple choice

multiple Sklerose (-n, -n) f multiple sclerosis

Multiplexkino nt multiplex (cinema)

multiplizieren vt to multiply (mit by)

Mumie f mummy

Mumps (-) m mumps sing

München (-s) nt Munich

Mund (-(e)s, Münder) m mouth; **halt den ~!** shut up; **Mundart** f dialect; **Munddusche** f dental water jet

münden vi to flow (in +akk into)

Mundgeruch m bad breath; **Mundharmonika** (-, -s) f mouth organ

mündlich *adj* oral
Mundschutz *m* mask;
Mundwasser *nt* mouthwash
Munition *f* ammunition
Münster *(-s, -)* *nt* minster,
cathedral
munter *adj* lively
Münzautomat *m* vending
machine; **Münze** *(-, -n)* *f* coin;
Münzeinwurf *m* slot;
Münzrückgabe *f* coin return;
Münztelefon *nt* pay phone;
Münzwechsler *m* change
machine
murmeln *vt, vi* to murmur, to
mutter
Murmeltier *nt* marmot
mürrisch *adj* sullen, grumpy
Mus *(-es, -e)* *nt* puree
Muschel *(-, -n)* *f* mussel; *(~schale)*
shell
Museum *(-s, Museen)* *nt*
museum
Musical *(-s, -s)* *nt* musical
Musik *f* music; **musikalisch** *adj*
musical; **Musiker(in)** *(-s, -)* *m(f)*
musician; **Musikinstrument** *nt*
musical instrument; **musizieren**
vi to play music
Muskat *(-(e)s)* *m* nutmeg
Muskel *(-s, -n)* *m* muscle;
Muskelkater *m*: **~ haben** to be
stiff; **Muskelriss** *m* torn muscle;
Muskelzerrung *f* pulled muscle;
muskulös *adj* muscular
Müsli *(-s, -)* *nt* muesli
Muslim(in) *(-s, -s)* *m(f)* Muslim
Muss *(-)* *nt* must

○ **SCHLÜSSELWORT**

müssen *(pt* **musste,** *pp* **gemusst**
o (als Hilfsverb) **müssen)** *vi*
1 *(Zwang)* must; *(nur im Präsens)* to
have to; **ich muss es tun** I must do
it, I have to do it; **ich musste es
tun** I had to do it; **er muss es**

nicht tun he doesn't have to do it;
muss ich? must I?, do I have to?;
wann müsst ihr zur Schule?
when do you have to go to
school?; **er hat gehen müssen** he
(has) had to go; **muss das sein?** is
that really necessary?; **ich muss
mal** *(fam)* I need the toilet
2 *(sollen)* **das musst du nicht tun!**
you oughtn't to *o* shouldn't do
that; **Sie hätten ihn fragen
müssen** you should have asked
him
3 es muss geregnet haben it
must have rained; **es muss nicht
wahr sein** it needn't be true

Muster *(-s, -)* *nt (Dessin)* pattern,
design; *(Probe)* sample; *(Vorbild)*
model; **mustern** *vt* to have a
close look at; **jdn ~** to look sb up
and down
Mut *(-(e)s)* *m* courage; **jdm
~ machen** to encourage sb; **mutig**
adj brave, courageous
Mutter *(-, Mütter)* *f* mother
▷ *(-, -n)* *f (Schraubenmutter)* nut;
Muttersprache *f* mother
tongue; **Muttertag** *m* Mother's
Day; **Mutti** *f* mum(my) (Brit),
mom(my) (US)
mutwillig *adj* deliberate
Mütze *(-, -n)* *f* cap
MwSt. *abk* = **Mehrwertsteuer**
VAT
Myanmar *(-s)* *nt* Myanmar

n

N abk = **Nord** N

na interj: ~ **also!**, ~ **bitte!** see?, what did I tell you?; ~ **ja** well; ~ **und?** so what?

Nabel (-s, -) m navel

SCHLÜSSELWORT

nach prep +dat 1 (örtlich) to; **nach Berlin** to Berlin; **nach links/rechts** (to the) left/right; **nach oben/hinten** up/back
2 (zeitlich) after; **einer nach dem anderen** one after the other; **nach Ihnen!** after you!; **zehn (Minuten) nach drei** ten (minutes) past three
3 (gemäß) according to; **nach dem Gesetz** according to the law; **dem Namen nach** judging by his/her name; **nach allem, was ich weiß** as far as I know
▷ adv: **ihm nach!** after him! **nach und nach** gradually, little by little; **nach wie vor** still

nach|ahmen vt to imitate

Nachbar(in) (-n, -n) m(f) neighbour; **Nachbarschaft** f neighbourhood

nach|bestellen vt to order some more

nachdem conj after; (weil) since; **je ~ (ob/wie)** depending on (whether/how)

nach|denken irr vi to think (über +akk about); **nachdenklich** adj thoughtful

nacheinander adv one after another (o the other)

Nachfolger(in) (-s, -) m(f) successor

nach|forschen vt to investigate

Nachfrage f inquiry; (Comm) demand; **nach|fragen** vi to inquire

nach|geben irr vi to give in (jdm to sb)

Nachgebühr f surcharge; (für Briefe etc) excess postage

nach|gehen irr vi to follow (jdm sb); (erforschen) to inquire (einer Sache dat into sth); **die Uhr geht (zehn Minuten) nach** this watch is (ten minutes) slow

nachher adv afterwards; **bis ~!** see you later

Nachhilfe f extra tuition

nach|holen vt to catch up with; (Versäumtes) to make up for

nach|kommen irr vi to follow; **einer Verpflichtung** (dat) ~ to fulfil an obligation

nach|lassen irr vt (Summe) to take off ▷ vi to decrease, to ease off; (schlechter werden) to deteriorate; **nachlässig** adj negligent, careless

nach|laufen irr vi to run after, to chase (jdm sb)

nach|lösen vt: **eine Fahrkarte ~** to buy a ticket on the bus/train
nach|machen vt to imitate, to copy (jdm etw sth from sb); (fälschen) to counterfeit
Nachmittag m afternoon; **heute ~** this afternoon; **am ~** in the afternoon; **nachmittags** adv in the afternoon; **um 3 Uhr ~** at 3 (o'clock) in the afternoon, at 3 pm
Nachnahme (-, -n) f cash on delivery; **per ~** COD
Nachname m surname
nach|prüfen vt to check
nach|rechnen vt to check
Nachricht (-, -en) f (piece of) news sing; (Mitteilung) message; **Nachrichten** pl news sing
Nachsaison f off-season
nach|schauen vi: **jdm ~** to gaze after sb ▷ vt (prüfen) to check
nach|schicken vt to forward
nach|schlagen irr vt to look up
nach|sehen irr vt (prüfen) to check
Nachspeise f dessert
nächstbeste(r, s) adj: **der ~ Zug/Job** the first train/job that comes along; **nächste(r, s)** adj next; (nächstgelegen) nearest
Nacht (-, Nächte) f night; **in der ~** during the night; (bei Nacht) at night; **Nachtclub** m nightclub; **Nachtdienst** m night duty; **~ haben** (Apotheke) to be open all night
Nachteil m disadvantage
Nachtflug m night flight; **Nachtfrost** m overnight frost; **Nachthemd** nt (für Damen) nightdress; (für Herren) nightshirt
Nachtigall (-, -en) f nightingale
Nachtisch m dessert, sweet (Brit), pudding (Brit); **Nachtleben** nt nightlife

nach|tragen irr vt: **jdm etw ~** (übel nehmen) to hold sth against sb
nachträglich adv: **~ alles Gute zum Geburtstag!** Happy belated birthday
nachts adv at night; **um 11 Uhr ~** at 11 (o'clock) at night, at 11 pm; **um 2 Uhr ~** at 2 (o'clock) in the morning, at 2 am; **Nachtschicht** f night shift; **Nachttarif** m off-peak rate; **Nachttisch** m bedside table; **Nachtzug** m night train
Nachweis (-es, -e) m proof
Nachwirkung f after-effect
nach|zahlen vi to pay extra ▷ vt: **20 Euro ~** to pay 20 euros extra
nach|zählen vt to check
Nacken (-s, -) m (nape of the) neck
nackt adj naked; (Tatsachen) plain, bare; **Nacktbadestrand** m nudist beach
Nadel (-, -n) f needle; (Stecknadel) pin; **Nadelstreifen** pl pinstripes pl
Nagel (-s, Nägel) m nail; **Nagelbürste** f nail brush; **Nagelfeile** f nail-file; **Nagellack** m nail varnish (or polish); **Nagellackentferner** (-s, -) m nail-varnish (o nail-polish) remover; **Nagelschere** f nail scissors pl
nah(e) adj (räumlich) near(by); (zeitlich) near; (Verwandte, Freunde) close; **Nähe** (-) f (Umgebung) vicinity; **in der ~** nearby; **in der ~ von** near to; **nahe|gehen** irr vi: **jdm ~** to upset sb; **nahe|legen** vt: **jdm etw ~** to suggest sth to sb; **nahe|liegen** irr vi to be obvious ▷ prep +dat near (to), close to
nähen vt, vi to sew
nähere(r, s) adj (Erklärung, Erkundigung) more detailed; **die ~ Umgebung** the immediate area;

Nähere(s) nt details pl; **nähern**
vr: **sich ~** to approach

nahezu adv virtually, almost

nahm imperf von **nehmen**

Nähmaschine f sewing
machine

nahrhaft adj nourishing,
nutritious; **Nahrung** f food;
Nahrungsmittel nt food

Naht (-, **Nähte**) f seam; (Med)
stitches pl, suture; (Tech) join

Nahverkehr m local traffic;
Nahverkehrszug m local train

Nähzeug nt sewing kit

naiv adj naive

Name (-ns, -n) m name

nämlich adv that is to say,
namely; (denn) since

nannte imperf von **nennen**

Napf (-(e)s, **Näpfe**) m bowl, dish

Narbe (-, -n) f scar

Narkose (-, -n) f anaesthetic

Narzisse (-, -n) f narcissus

naschen vt, vi to nibble;
Naschkatze f (fam) nibbler; **eine
~ sein** to have a sweet tooth

Nase (-, -n) f nose; **Nasenbluten**
(-s) nt nosebleed; **~ haben** to
have a nosebleed; **Nasenloch** nt
nostril; **Nasentropfen** pl nose
drops pl

Nashorn nt rhinoceros

nass adj wet; **Nässe** (-) f
wetness; **nässen** vi (Wunde) to
weep

Nation (-, -en) f nation; **national**
adj national; **Nationalfeiertag** m
national holiday; **Nationalhymne**
(-, -n) f national anthem;
Nationalität f nationality;
Nationalmannschaft f national
team; **Nationalpark** m National
Park; **Nationalspieler(in)** m(f)
international player

NATO (-) f abk = **North Atlantic
Treaty Organization** NATO, Nato

Natur f nature; **Naturkost** f
health food; **natürlich** adj natural
▶ adv naturally; (selbstverständlich)
of course; **Naturpark** m nature
reserve; **naturrein** adj natural,
pure; **Naturschutz** m
conservation; **Naturschutzgebiet**
nt nature reserve; **Naturwissenschaft** f (natural) science;
Naturwissenschaftler(in) m(f)
scientist

Navigationssystem nt (Auto)
navigation system

n. Chr. abk = **nach Christus** AD

Nebel (-s, -) m fog, mist; **nebelig**
adj foggy, misty; **Nebelschein-
werfer** m foglamp; **Nebelschlussleuchte** f (Auto) rear foglight

neben prep +akk o dat next to;
(außer) apart from, besides;
nebenan adv next door;
Nebenausgang m side exit;
nebenbei adv at the same time;
(außerdem) additionally; (beiläufig)
incidentally; **nebeneinander** adv
side by side; **Nebeneingang** m
side entrance; **Nebenfach** nt
subsidiary subject

nebenher adv (zusätzlich)
besides; (gleichzeitig) at the same
time; (daneben) alongside

Nebenkosten pl extra charges
pl, extras pl; **Nebensache** f
minor matter; **nebensächlich**
adj minor; **Nebensaison** f low
season; **Nebenstraße** f side
street; **Nebenwirkung** f side
effect

neblig adj foggy, misty

necken vt to tease

Neffe (-n, -n) m nephew

negativ adj negative; **Negativ**
nt (Foto) negative

nehmen (nahm, genommen) vt to
take; **wie man's nimmt** it
depends on how you look at it;
den Bus/Zug ~ to take the
bus/train; **jdn/etw ernst ~** to

take sb/sth seriously; **etw zu sich ~** to eat sth; **jdn zu sich ~** to have sb come and live with one; **jdn an die Hand ~** to take sb by the hand

neidisch adj envious

neigen vi: **zu etw ~** to tend towards sth; **Neigung** f (des Geländes) slope; (Tendenz) inclination; (Vorliebe) liking

nein adv no

Nektarine f nectarine

Nelke (-, -n) f carnation; (Gewürz) clove

nennen (nannte, genannt) vt to name; (mit Namen) to call

Neonazi (-s, -s) m neo-Nazi

Nepal (-s) nt Nepal

Neptun (-s) m Neptune

Nerv (-s, -en) m nerve; **jdm auf die ~en gehen** to get on sb's nerves; **nerven** vt: **jdn ~** (fam) to get on sb's nerves; **Nervenzusammenbruch** m nervous breakdown; **nervös** adj nervous

Nest (-(e)s, -er) nt nest; (pej: Ort) dump

nett adj nice; (freundlich) kind; **sei so ~ und ...** do me a favour and ...

netto adv net

Netz (-es, -e) nt net; (für Einkauf) string bag; (System) network; (Stromnetz) mains, power (US); **Netzanschluss** m mains connection; **Netzbetreiber(in)** m(f) network operator; (Inform) Internet operator; **Netzgerät** nt power pack; **Netzkarte** f season ticket; **Netzwerk** nt (Inform) network; **Netzwerken** nt (social) networking; **Netzwerkkarte** f network card

neu adj new; (Sprache, Geschichte) modern; **die ~esten Nachrichten** the latest news; **Neubau** m new building; **neuerdings** adv recently; **Neueröffnung** f

new business; **Neuerung** f innovation; (Reform) reform

Neugier f curiosity; **neugierig** adj curious (auf +akk about); **ich bin ~, ob ...** I wonder whether (o if) ...; **ich bin ~, was du dazu sagst** I'll be interested to hear what you have to say about it

Neuheit f novelty; **Neuigkeit** f news sing; **eine ~** a piece of news; **Neujahr** nt New Year; **prosit ~!** Happy New Year!; **neulich** adv recently, the other day; **Neumond** m new moon

neun num nine; **neunhundert** num nine hundred; **neunmal** adv nine times; **neunte(r, s)** adj ninth; siehe auch **dritte**; **Neuntel** (-s, -) nt ninth; **neunzehn** num nineteen; **neunzehnte(r, s)** adj nineteenth; siehe auch **dritte**; **neunzig** num ninety; **in den -er Jahren** in the nineties; **Neunzigerjahre** pl nineties pl; **neunzigste(r, s)** adj ninetieth

neureich adj nouveau riche

Neurologe m, **Neurologin** f neurologist; **Neurose** (-, -n) f neurosis; **neurotisch** adj neurotic

Neuseeland nt New Zealand

Neustart m (Inform) restart, reboot

neutral adj neutral

neuwertig adj nearly new

Nicaragua (-s) nt Nicaragua

 SCHLÜSSELWORT

nicht adv **1** (Verneinung) not; **er ist es nicht** it's not him, it isn't him; **er raucht nicht** (gerade) he isn't smoking; (gewöhnlich) he doesn't smoke; **ich kann das nicht — ich auch nicht** I can't do it — neither o nor can I; **es regnet nicht mehr** it's not raining any more; **nicht rostend** stainless

2 (Bitte, Verbot) **nicht!** don't!, no!; **nicht berühren!** do not touch!; **nicht doch!** don't!

3 (rhetorisch) **du bist müde, nicht (wahr)?** you're tired, aren't you?; **das ist schön, nicht (wahr)?** it's nice, isn't it?

4 was du nicht sagst! the things you say!

Nichte (-, -n) f niece
Nichtraucher(in) m(f) non-smoker; **Nichtraucherabteil** nt non-smoking compartment; **Nichtraucherzone** f non-smoking area

nichts pron nothing; **für ~ und wieder ~** for nothing at all; **ich habe ~ gesagt** I didn't say anything; **macht ~** never mind

Nichtschwimmer(in) m(f) non-swimmer

nichtssagend adj meaningless
nicken vi to nod
Nickerchen nt nap
nie adv never; **~ wieder** (o **mehr**) never again; **fast ~** hardly ever

nieder adj (niedrig) low; (gering) inferior ▷ adv down; **niedergeschlagen** adj depressed; **Niederlage** f defeat

Niederlande pl Netherlands pl; **Niederländer(in)** m(f) Dutchman/Dutchwoman; **niederländisch** adj Dutch; **Niederländisch** nt Dutch

Niederlassung f branch
Niederösterreich nt Lower Austria; **Niedersachsen** nt Lower Saxony

Niederschlag m (Meteo) precipitation; (Regen) rainfall

niedlich adj sweet, cute
niedrig adj low; (Qualität) inferior

niemals adv never
niemand pron nobody, no one;

ich habe ~en gesehen I haven't seen anyone; **~ von ihnen** none of them

Niere (-, -n) f kidney; **Nierenentzündung** f kidney infection; **Nierensteine** pl kidney stones pl

nieseln vi impers to drizzle; **Nieselregen** m drizzle

niesen vi to sneeze
Niete (-, -n) f (Los) blank; (Reinfall) flop; (pej: Mensch) failure; (Tech) rivet

Nigeria (-s) nt Nigeria
Nikotin (-s) nt nicotine
Nilpferd nt hippopotamus
nippen vi to sip; **an etw** (dat) **~** to sip sth

nirgends adv nowhere
Nische (-, -n) f niche
Niveau (-s, -s) nt level; **sie hat ~** she's got class

nobel adj (großzügig) generous; (fam: luxuriös) classy, posh; **Nobelpreis** m Nobel Prize

O SCHLÜSSELWORT

noch adv **1** (weiterhin) still; **noch nicht** not yet; **noch nie** never (yet); **noch immer** o **immer noch** still; **bleiben Sie doch noch** stay a bit longer

2 (in Zukunft) still, yet; **das kann noch passieren** that might still happen; **er wird noch kommen** he'll come (yet)

3 (nicht später als) **noch vor einer Woche** only a week ago; **noch am selben Tag** the very same day; **noch im 19. Jahrhundert** as late as the 19th century; **noch heute** today

4 (zusätzlich) **wer war noch da?** who else was there?; **noch einmal** once more, again; **noch dreimal** three more times; **noch einer** another one

5 (bei Vergleichen) **noch größer** even bigger; **das ist noch besser** that's better still; **und wenn es noch so schwer ist** however hard it is
6 Geld noch und noch heaps (and heaps) of money; **sie hat noch und noch versucht, ...** she tried again and again to ...
▷ konj: **weder A noch B** neither A nor B

nochmal(s) adv again, once more
Nominativ m nominative (case)
Nonne (-, -n) f nun
Nonstop-Flug m nonstop flight
Nord north; **Nordamerika** nt North America; **Norddeutschland** nt Northern Germany; **Norden** (-s) m north; **im ~ Deutschlands** in the north of Germany; **Nordeuropa** nt Northern Europe
Nordic Walking nt (Sport) Nordic Walking
Nordirland nt Northern Ireland; **nordisch** adj (Völker, Sprache) Nordic; **Nordkorea** (-s) nt North Korea; **nördlich** adj northern; (Kurs, Richtung) northerly; **Nordost(en)** m northeast; **Nordpol** m North Pole; **Nordrhein-Westfalen** (-s) nt North Rhine-Westphalia; **Nordsee** f North Sea; **nordwärts** adv north, northwards; **Nordwest(en)** m northwest; **Nordwind** m north wind
nörgeln vi to grumble
Norm (-, -en) f norm; (Größenvorschrift) standard
normal adj normal; **Normalbenzin** nt regular (petrol (Brit) o gas (US)); **normalerweise** adv normally
normen vt to standardize
Norwegen (-s) nt Norway;

Norweger(in) m(f) Norwegian; **norwegisch** adj Norwegian; **Norwegisch** nt Norwegian
Not (-, Nöte) f need; (Armut) poverty; (Elend) hardship; (Bedrängnis) trouble; (Mangel) want; (Mühe) trouble; (Zwang) necessity; **zur ~** if necessary; (gerade noch) just about
Notar(in) m(f) public notary; **notariell** adj: **~ beglaubigt** attested by a notary
Notarzt m, **Notärztin** f emergency doctor; **Notarztwagen** m emergency ambulance; **Notaufnahme** f A&E, casualty (Brit), emergency room (US); **Notausgang** m emergency exit; **Notbremse** f emergency brake; **Notdienst** m emergency service, after-hours service; **notdürftig** adj scanty; (behelfsmäßig) makeshift
Note (-, -n) f note; (in Schule) mark, grade (US); (Mus) note
Notebook (-(s), -s) nt (Inform) notebook
Notfall m emergency; **notfalls** adv if necessary
notieren vt to note down
nötig adj necessary; **etw ~ haben** to need sth
Notiz (-, -en) f note; (Zeitungs~) item; **Notizblock** m notepad; **Notizbuch** nt notebook
Notlage f crisis; (Elend) plight; **notlanden** vi to make a forced (o emergency) landing; **Notlandung** f emergency landing; **Notruf** m emergency call; **Notrufnummer** f emergency number; **Notrufsäule** f emergency telephone
notwendig adj necessary
Nougat (-s, -s) m od nt nougat
November (-(s), -) m November; siehe auch **Juni**

n

Nr. *abk* = **Nummer** No., no.

Nu *m*: **im ~** in no time

nüchtern *adj* sober; (*Magen*) empty

Nudel (-, -n) *f* noodle; **~n** *pl* (*italienische*) pasta *sing*

null *num* zero; (*Tel*) O (*Brit*), zero (*US*); **~ Fehler** no mistakes; **~ Uhr** midnight; **Null** (-, -en) *f* nought, zero; (*pej: Mensch*) dead loss; **Nulltarif** *m*: **zum ~** free of charge

Numerus clausus (-) *m* restriction on the number of students allowed to study a particular subject

Nummer (-, -n) *f* number; **nummerieren** *vt* to number; **Nummernschild** *nt* (*Auto*) number plate (*Brit*), license plate (*US*)

nun *adv* now; **von ~ an** from now on ▷ *interj* well; **~ gut!** all right, then; **es ist ~ mal so** that's the way it is

nur *adv* only; **nicht ~ ..., sondern auch ...** not only ..., but also ...; **~ Anna nicht** except Anna

Nürnberg (-s) *nt* Nuremberg

Nuss (-, *Nüsse*) *f* nut; **Nussknacker** (-s, -) *m* nutcracker; **Nuss-Nougat-Creme** *f* chocolate nut cream

Nutte (-, -n) *f* (*fam*) tart

nutz, nütze *adj*: **zu nichts ~ sein** to be useless; **nutzen, nützen** *vt* to use (*zu etw* for sth); **was nützt es?** what use is it? ▷ *vi* to be of use; **das nützt nicht viel** that doesn't help much; **es nützt nichts(, es zu tun)** it's no use (doing it); **Nutzen** (-s, -) *m* usefulness; (*Gewinn*) profit; **nützlich** *adj* useful

Nylon (-s) *nt* nylon

O

o *interj* oh

O *abk* = **Ost** E

Oase (-, -n) *f* oasis

ob *conj* if, whether; **so als ~** as if; **er tut so, als ~ er krank wäre** he's pretending to be sick; **und ~!** you bet

obdachlos *adj* homeless

oben *adv* (*am oberen Ende*) at the top; (*obenauf*) on (the) top; (*im Haus*) upstairs; (*in einem Text*) above; **~ erwähnt** (*o genannt*) above-mentioned; **mit dem Gesicht nach ~** face up; **da ~** up there; **von ~ bis unten** from top to bottom; **siehe ~** see above

Ober (-s, -) *m* waiter

obere(r, s) *adj* upper, top

Oberfläche *f* surface; **oberflächlich** *adj* superficial; **Obergeschoss** *nt* upper floor

oberhalb *adv, prep* +gen above

Oberhemd *nt* shirt; **Oberkörper**

m upper body; **Oberlippe** *f* upper lip; **Oberösterreich** *nt* Upper Austria; **Oberschenkel** *m* thigh

oberste(r, s) *adj* very top, topmost

Oberteil *nt* top; **Oberweite** *f* bust/chest measurement

obig *adj* above(-mentioned)

Objekt (-(e)s, -e) *nt* object

objektiv *adj* objective; **Objektiv** *nt* lens

obligatorisch *adj* compulsory, obligatory

Oboe (-, -n) *f* oboe

Observatorium *nt* observatory

Obst (-(e)s) *nt* fruit; **Obstkuchen** *m* fruit tart; **Obstsalat** *m* fruit salad

obszön *adj* obscene

obwohl *conj* although

Ochse (-n, -n) *m* ox; **Ochsenschwanzsuppe** *f* oxtail soup

ocker *adj* ochre

öd(e) *adj* waste; (*unbebaut*) barren; (*fig*) dull

oder *conj* or; **~ aber** or else; **er kommt doch, ~?** he's coming, isn't he?

Ofen (-s, Öfen) *m* oven; (*Heizofen*) heater; (*Kohleofen*) stove; (*Herd*) cooker, stove; **Ofenkartoffel** *f* baked (*o* jacket) potato

offen *adj* open; (*aufrichtig*) frank; (*Stelle*) vacant ▷ *adv* frankly; **~ gesagt** to be honest

offenbar *adj* obvious; **offensichtlich** *adj* evident, obvious

öffentlich *adj* public; **Öffentlichkeit** *f* (*Leute*) public; (*einer Versammlung etc*) public nature

offiziell *adj* official

offline *adv* (*Inform*) offline

öffnen *vt* to open ▷ *vr*: **sich ~** to open; **Öffner** (-s, -) *m* opener;

Öffnung *f* opening; **Öffnungszeiten** *pl* opening times *pl*

oft *adv* often; **schon ~** many times; **öfter** *adv* more often (*o* frequently); **öfters** *adv* often, frequently

ohne *conj, prep* +*akk* without; **~ weiteres** without a second thought; (*sofort*) immediately; **~ ein Wort zu sagen** without saying a word; **~ mich** count me out

Ohnmacht (-machten) *f* unconsciousness; (*Hilflosigkeit*) helplessness; **in ~ fallen** to faint; **ohnmächtig** *adj* unconscious; **sie ist ~** she has fainted

Ohr (-(e)s, -en) *nt* ear; (*Gehör*) hearing

Öhr (-(e)s, -e) *nt* eye

Ohrenarzt *m*, **Ohrenärztin** *f* ear specialist; **Ohrenschmerzen** *pl* earache; **Ohrentropfen** *pl* ear drops *pl*; **Ohrfeige** *f* slap (in the face); **Ohrläppchen** *nt* earlobe; **Ohrringe** *pl* earrings *pl*

oje *interj* oh dear

okay *interj* OK, okay

Ökoladen *m* health food store; **ökologisch** *adj* ecological; **~e Landwirtschaft** organic farming

ökonomisch *adj* economic; (*sparsam*) economical

Ökosystem *nt* ecosystem

Oktanzahl *f* (*bei Benzin*) octane rating

Oktober (-(s), -) *m* October; *siehe auch* **Juni**

● **OKTOBERFEST**
●
● The annual October beer
● festival, the **Oktoberfest**,
● takes place in Munich on a
● huge field where beer tents,
● roller coasters and many other

amusements are set up. People sit at long wooden tables, drink beer from enormous litre beer mugs, eat pretzels and listen to brass bands. It is a great attraction for tourists and locals alike.

Öl (-(e)s, -e) nt oil; **Ölbaum** m olive tree; **ölen** vt to oil; (Tech) to lubricate; **Ölfarbe** f oil paint; **Ölfilter** m oil filter; **Ölgemälde** nt oil painting; **Ölheizung** f oil-fired central heating; **ölig** adj oily

oliv adj inv olive-green; **Olive** (-, -n) f olive; **Olivenöl** nt olive oil

Ölmessstab m dipstick; **Ölofen** m oil stove; **Ölpest** f oil pollution; **Ölsardine** f sardine in oil; **Ölstandanzeiger** m (Auto) oil gauge; **Ölteppich** m oil slick; **Ölwechsel** m oil change

Olympiade f Olympic Games pl; **olympisch** adj Olympic

Oma f, **Omi** (-s, -s) f grandma, gran(ny)

Omelett (-(e)s, -s) nt, **Omelette** f omelette

Omnibus m bus

onanieren vi to masturbate

Onkel (-s, -) m uncle

online adv (Inform) online; **Onlinedienst** m (Inform) online service

OP (-s, -s) m abk =
Operationssaal operating theatre (Brit) (o room (US))

Opa m, **Opi** (-s, -s) m grandpa, grandad

Open-Air-Konzert nt open-air concert

Oper (-, -n) f opera; (Gebäude) opera house

Operation f operation

Operette f operetta

operieren vi to operate ▷ vt to operate on

Opernhaus nt opera house, opera; **Opernsänger(in)** m(f) opera singer

Opfer (-s, -) nt sacrifice; (Mensch) victim; **ein ~ bringen** to make a sacrifice

Opium (-s) nt opium

Opposition f opposition

Optiker(in) (-s, -) m(f) optician

optimal adj optimal, optimum

optimistisch adj optimistic

oral adj oral; **Oralverkehr** m oral sex

orange adj inv orange; **Orange** (-, -n) f orange; **Orangenmarmelade** f marmalade; **Orangensaft** m orange juice

Orchester (-s, -) nt orchestra

Orchidee (-, -n) f orchid

Orden (-s, -) m (Rel) order; (Mil) decoration

ordentlich adj (anständig) respectable; (geordnet) tidy, neat; (fam: annehmbar) not bad; (fam: tüchtig) proper ▷ adv properly

ordinär adj common, vulgar; (Witz) dirty

ordnen vt to sort out; **Ordner** (-s, -) m (bei Veranstaltung) steward; (Aktenordner) file; **Ordnung** f order; (Geordnetsein) tidiness; **(geht) in ~!** (that's) all right; **mit dem Drucker ist etwas nicht in ~** there's something wrong with the printer

Oregano (-s) m oregano

Organ (-s, -e) nt organ; (Stimme) voice

Organisation f organization; **organisieren** vt to organize; (fam: beschaffen) to get hold of ▷ vr: **sich ~** to organize

Organismus m organism

Orgasmus m orgasm

Orgel (-, -n) f organ

Orgie f orgy
orientalisch adj oriental
orientieren vr: **sich ~** to get
one's bearings; **Orientierung** f
orientation; **Orientierungssinn**
m sense of direction
original adj original; (echt)
genuine; **Original** (-s, -e) nt
original
originell adj original; (komisch)
witty
Orkan (-(e)s, -e) m hurricane
Ort (-(e)s, -e) m place; (Dorf)
village; **an ~ und Stelle, vor ~** on
the spot
Orthopäde (-n, -n) m,
Orthopädin f orthopaedist
örtlich adj local; **Ortschaft** f
village, small town; **Ortsgespräch**
nt local call; **Ortstarif** m local
rate; **Ortszeit** f local time

- **OSSI**
-
- **Ossi** is a colloquial and rather
- derogatory word used to
- describe a German from the
- former **DDR**.

Ost east; **Ostdeutschland** nt
(als Landesteil) Eastern Germany;
(Hist) East Germany; **Osten** (-s) m
east
Osterei nt Easter egg;
Osterglocke f daffodil;
Osterhase m Easter bunny;
Ostermontag m Easter Monday;
Ostern (-, -) nt Easter; **an** (o zu)
~ at Easter; **frohe ~** Happy Easter
Österreich (-s) nt Austria;
Österreicher(in) (-s, -) m(f) Austrian;
österreichisch adj Austrian
Ostersonntag m Easter Sunday
Osteuropa nt Eastern Europe;
Ostküste f east coast; **östlich**
adj eastern; (Kurs, Richtung)
easterly; **Ostsee** f: **die ~** the

Baltic (Sea); **Ostwind** m
east(erly) wind
OSZE (-) f abk = **Organisation für
Sicherheit und Zusammenarbeit
in Europa** OSCE
Otter (-s, -) m otter
out adj (fam) out; **outen** vt to
out
oval adj oval
Overheadprojektor m overhead projector
Ozean (-s, -e) m ocean; **der Stille
~** the Pacific (Ocean)
Ozon (-s) nt ozone;
Ozonbelastung f ozone level;
Ozonloch nt hole in the ozone
layer; **Ozonschicht** f ozone
layer; **Ozonwerte** pl ozone
levels pl

o

p

paar adj inv **ein ~** a few; **ein ~ Mal** a few times; **ein ~ Äpfel** some apples

Paar (-(e)s, -e) nt pair; (Ehepaar) couple; **ein ~ Socken** a pair of socks

pachten vt to lease

Päckchen nt package; (Zigaretten) packet; (zum Verschicken) small parcel; **packen** vt to pack; (fassen) to grasp, to seize; (fam: schaffen) to manage; (fig: fesseln) to grip; **Packpapier** nt brown paper; **Packung** f packet, pack (US); **Packungsbeilage** f package insert, patient information leaflet

Pädagoge (-n, -n) m, **Pädagogin** f teacher; **pädagogisch** adj educational; **~e Hochschule** college of education

Paddel (-s, -) nt paddle; **Paddelboot** nt canoe; **paddeln**

vi to paddle

Paket (-(e)s, -e) nt packet; (Postpaket) parcel; (Inform) package; **Paketbombe** f parcel bomb; **Paketkarte** f dispatch form (to be filled in with details of the sender and the addressee when handing in a parcel at the post office)

Pakistan (-s) nt Pakistan

Palast (-es, Paläste) m palace

Palästina (-s) nt Palestine; **Palästinenser(in)** (-s, -) m(f) Palestinian

Palatschinken pl filled pancakes pl

Palette f (von Maler) palette; (Ladepalette) pallet; (Vielfalt) range

Palme (-, -n) f palm (tree); **Palmsonntag** m Palm Sunday

Pampelmuse (-, -n) f grapefruit

pampig adj (fam: frech) cheeky; (breiig) gooey

Panda(bär) (-s, -s) m panda

Pandemie (-, -n) f pandemic

panieren vt (Gastr) to coat with breadcrumbs; **paniert** adj breaded

Panik f panic

Panne (-, -n) f (Auto) breakdown; (Missgeschick) slip; **Pannendienst** m, **Pannenhilfe** f breakdown (o rescue) service

Pant(h)er (-s, -) m panther

Pantomime (-, -n) f mime

Panzer (-s, -) m (Panzerung) armour (plating); (Mil) tank

Papa (-s, -s) m dad(dy), pa (US)

Papagei (-s, -en) m parrot

Papaya (-, -s) f papaya

Papier (-s, -e) nt paper; **~e** pl (Ausweispapiere) papers pl; (Dokumente, Urkunden) papers pl, documents pl; **Papiercontainer** m paper bank; **Papierformat** nt paper size; **Papiergeld** nt paper money; **Papierkorb** m wastepaper basket; (Inform)

recycle bin; **Papiertaschentuch**
nt (paper) tissue; **Papiertonne** f
paper bank
Pappbecher m paper cup;
Pappe (-, -n) f cardboard;
Pappkarton m cardboard box;
Pappteller m paper plate
Paprika (-s, -s) m (Gewürz)
paprika; (Schote) pepper
Papst (-(e)s, Päpste) m pope
Paradeiser (-s, -) m tomato
Paradies (-es, -e) nt paradise
Paragliding (-s) nt paragliding
Paragraph (-en, -en) m
paragraph; (Jur) section
parallel adj parallel
Paranuss f Brazil nut
Parasit (-en, -en) m parasite
parat adj ready; **etw ~ haben** to
have sth ready
Pärchen nt couple
Parfüm (-s, -s o -e) nt perfume;
Parfümerie f perfumery;
parfümieren vt to scent, to
perfume
Pariser (-s, -) m (fam: Kondom)
rubber
Park (-s, -s) m park
Park-and-ride-System nt
park-and-ride system; **Parkbank** f
park bench; **Parkdeck** nt parking
level; **parken** vt, vi to park
Parkett (-s, -e) nt parquet
flooring; (Theat) stalls pl (Brit),
parquet (US)
Parkhaus nt multi-storey car
park (Brit), parking garage (US)
parkinsonsche Krankheit f
Parkinson's disease
Parkkralle f (Auto) wheel clamp;
Parklicht nt parking light;
Parklücke f parking space;
Parkplatz m (für ein Auto) parking
space; (für mehrere Autos) car park
(Brit), parking lot (US);
Parkscheibe f parking disc;
Parkscheinautomat m pay

point; (Parkscheinausgabegerät)
ticket machine; **Parkuhr** f
parking meter; **Parkverbot** nt
(Stelle) no-parking zone; **hier ist
~** you can't park here
Parlament nt parliament
Parmesan (-s) m Parmesan
(cheese)
Partei f party
Parterre (-s, -s) nt ground floor
(Brit), first floor (US)
Partie f part; (Spiel) game; (Mann,
Frau) catch; **mit von der ~ sein** to
be in on it
Partitur f (Mus) score
Partizip (-s, -ien) nt participle
Partner(in) (-s, -) m(f) partner;
Partnerschaft f partnership;
eingetragene ~ civil partnership;
Partnerstadt f twin town
Party (-, -s) f party; **Partymuffel**
(-s, -) m party pooper;
Partyservice m catering service
Pass (-es, Pässe) m pass; (Ausweis)
passport
passabel adj reasonable
Passagier (-s, -e) m passenger
Passamt nt passport office
Passant(in) m(f) passer-by;
Passbild nt passport photo
passen vi (Größe) to fit; (Farbe,
Stil) to go with; (auf Frage) to
pass; **passt (es) dir morgen?** does
tomorrow suit you?; **das passt
mir gut** that suits me fine;
passend adj suitable;
(zusammenpassend) matching;
(angebracht) fitting; (Zeit)
convenient; **haben Sie es nicht ~?**
(Kleingeld) have you got the right
change?
passieren vi to happen
passiv adj passive
Passkontrolle f passport
control
Passwort nt password
Paste (-, -n) f paste

Pastellfarbe f pastel colour

Pastete (-, -n) f (warmes Gericht)
pie; (Pastetchen) vol-au-vent; (ohne
Teig) pâté

Pastor, in (-s, -en) m(f) minister,
vicar

Pate (-n, -n) m godfather;
Patenkind nt godchild

Patient(in) m(f) patient

Patin f godmother

Patrone (-, -n) f cartridge

patsch interj splat; **patschnass**
adj soaking wet

pauschal adj (Kosten) inclusive;
(Urteil) sweeping; **Pauschale**
(-, -n) f, **Pauschalgebühr** f flat
rate (charge); **Pauschalpreis** m
flat rate; (für Hotel, Reise)
all-inclusive price; **Pauschalreise**
f package tour

Pause (-, -n) f break; (Theat)
interval; (Kino etc) intermission;
(Innehalten) pause

Pavian (-s, -e) m baboon

Pavillon (-s, -s) m pavilion

Pay-TV (-s) nt pay-per-view
television, pay TV

Pazifik (-s) m Pacific (Ocean)

PC (-s, -s) m abk = **Personal
Computer** PC

Pech (-s) nt (fig) bad luck;
~ **haben** to be unlucky; ~ **gehabt!**
tough (luck)

Pedal (-s, -s) nt pedal

Pediküre (-, -en) f pedicure

Peeling (-s, -s) nt (facial/body)
scrub

peinlich adj (unangenehm)
embarrassing, awkward; (genau)
painstaking; **es war mir sehr ~** I
was totally embarrassed

Peitsche (-, -n) f whip

Pelikan (-s, -e) m pelican

Pellkartoffeln pl potatoes pl
boiled in their skins

Pelz (-es, -e) m fur; **pelzig** adj
(Zunge) furred

pendeln vi (Zug, Bus) to shuttle;
(Mensch) to commute;
Pendelverkehr m shuttle traffic;
(für Pendler) commuter traffic;
Pendler(in) (-s, -) m(f)
commuter

penetrant adj sharp; (Mensch)
pushy

Penis (-, -se) m penis

Pension f (Geld) pension;
(Ruhestand) retirement; (für Gäste)
guesthouse, B&B; **pensioniert**
adj retired; **Pensionsgast** m
guest (in a guesthouse)

Peperoni (-, -) f chilli

per prep +akk by, per; (pro) per; (bis)
by

perfekt adj perfect

Pergamentpapier nt grease-
proof paper

Periode (-, -n) f period

Perle (-, -n) f (a. fig) pearl

perplex adj dumbfounded

Person (-, -en) f person; **ein Tisch
für drei ~en** a table for three;
Personal (-s) nt staff, personnel;
(Bedienung) servants pl;
Personalausweis m identity
card; **Personalien** pl particulars
pl; **Personenschaden** m injury
to persons; **Personenwaage** f
(bathroom) scales pl;
Personenzug m passenger train;
persönlich adj personal; (auf
Briefen) private ▷ adv personally;
(selbst) in person; **Persönlichkeit**
f personality

Peru (-s) nt Peru

Perücke (-, -n) f wig

pervers adj perverted

pessimistisch adj pessimistic

Pest (-) f plague

Petersilie (-, -n) f parsley

Petroleum (-s) nt paraffin (Brit),
kerosene (US)

Pfad (-(e)s, -e) m path;
Pfadfinder (-s, -) m boy scout;

Pfadfinderin f girl guide
Pfahl (-(e)s, Pfähle) m post, stake
Pfand (-(e)s, Pfänder) nt security;
(Flaschenpfand) deposit; (im Spiel)
forfeit; **Pfandflasche** f
returnable bottle
Pfanne (-, -n) f (frying) pan
Pfannkuchen m pancake
Pfarrei f parish; **Pfarrer(in)**
(-s, -) m(f) priest
Pfau (-(e)s, -en) m peacock
Pfeffer (-s, -) m pepper;
Pfefferkuchen m gingerbread;
Pfefferminze (-e) f peppermint;
Pfefferminztee m peppermint
tea; **Pfeffermühle** f pepper mill;
pfeffern vt to put pepper on/in;
Pfefferstreuer (-s, -) m pepper
pot
Pfeife (-, -n) f whistle; (für Tabak,
von Orgel) pipe; **pfeifen** (pfiff,
gepfiffen) vt, vi to whistle
Pfeil (-(e)s, -e) m arrow
Pfeiltaste f (Inform) arrow key
Pferd (-(e)s, -e) nt horse;
Pferdeschwanz m (Frisur)
ponytail; **Pferdestall** m stable;
Pferdestärke f horsepower
pfiff imperf von **pfeifen**
Pfifferling m chanterelle
Pfingsten (-, -) nt Whitsun,
Pentecost (US); **Pfingstmontag**
m Whit Monday; **Pfingstsonntag**
m Whit Sunday, Pentecost (US)
Pfirsich (-s, -e) m peach
Pflanze (-, -n) f plant; **pflanzen**
vt to plant; **Pflanzenfett** nt
vegetable fat
Pflaster (-s, -) nt (für Wunde)
plaster, Band Aid® (US);
(Straßenpflaster) road surface,
pavement (US)
Pflaume (-, -n) f plum
Pflege (-, -n) f care;
(Krankenpflege) nursing; (von Autos,
Maschinen) maintenance;
pflegebedürftig adj in need of

care; **pflegeleicht** adj easy-care;
(fig) easy to handle; **pflegen** vt
to look after; (Kranke) to nurse;
(Beziehungen) to foster; (Fingernägel,
Gesicht) to take care of; (Daten) to
maintain; **Pflegepersonal** nt
nursing staff; **Pflegeversicherung**
f long-term care insurance
Pflicht (-, -en) f duty; (Sport)
compulsory section; **pflicht-
bewusst** adj conscientious;
Pflichtfach nt (Schule)
compulsory subject; **Pflicht-
versicherung** f compulsory
insurance
pflücken vt to pick
Pforte (-, -n) f gate; **Pförtner(in)**
(-s, -) m(f) porter
Pfosten (-s, -) m post
Pfote (-, -n) f paw
pfui interj ugh
Pfund (-(e)s, -e) nt pound
pfuschen vi (fam) to be sloppy
Pfütze (-, -n) f puddle
Phantasie f siehe **Fantasie**;
phantastisch adj siehe
fantastisch
Phase (-, -n) f phase
Philippinen pl Philippines pl
Philosophie f philosophy
Photo nt siehe **Foto**
pH-neutral adj pH-balanced;
pH-Wert m pH-value
Physalis (-, Physalen) f physalis
Physik f physics sing
physisch adj physical
Pianist(in) (-en, -en) m(f) pianist
Pickel (-s, -) m pimple; (Werkzeug)
pickaxe; (Berg-) ice-axe
Picknick (-s, -e o -s) nt picnic; **ein
~ machen** to have a picnic
piepsen vi to chirp
piercen vt: **sich die Nase
~ lassen** to have one's nose
pierced; **Piercing** (-s) nt (body)
piercing
pieseln vi (fam) to pee

Pik (-, -) nt (Karten) spades pl
pikant adj spicy
Pilates nt (Sport) Pilates
Pilger(in) m(f) pilgrim;
Pilgerfahrt f pilgrimage
Pille (-, -n) f pill; **sie nimmt die
~** she's on the pill
Pilot(in) (-en, -en) m(f) pilot
Pils (-, -) nt (Pilsner) lager
Pilz (-es, -e) m (essbar) mushroom;
(giftig) toadstool; (Med) fungus
PIN (-, -s) f PIN (number)
pingelig adj (fam) fussy
Pinguin (-s, -e) m penguin
Pinie f pine; **Pinienkern** m pine
nut
pink adj shocking pink
pinkeln vi (fam) to pee
Pinsel (-s, -) m (paint)brush
Pinzette f tweezers pl
Pistazie f pistachio
Piste (-, -n) f (Ski) piste; (Aviat)
runway
Pistole (-, -n) f pistol
Pixel (-s) nt (Inform) pixel
Pizza (-, -s) f pizza; **Pizzaservice**
m pizza delivery service; **Pizzeria**
(-, Pizzerien) f pizzeria
Pkw (-(s), -(s)) m abk =
Personenkraftwagen car
Plakat nt poster
Plakette f (Schildchen) badge;
(Aufkleber) sticker
Plan (-(e)s, Pläne) m plan; (Karte)
map; **planen** vt to plan
Planet (-en, -en) m planet;
Planetarium nt planetarium
planmäßig adj scheduled
Plan(t)schbecken nt paddling
pool; **plan(t)schen** vi to splash
around
Planung f planning
Plastik f sculpture ▷ (-s) nt
plastic; **Plastikfolie** f plastic film;
Plastiktüte f plastic bag
Platin (-s) nt platinum
platsch interj splash

platt adj flat; (fam: überrascht)
flabbergasted; (fig: geistlos) flat,
boring
Platte (-, -n) f (Foto, Tech, Gastr)
plate; (Steinplatte) flag;
(Schallplatte) record;
Plattenspieler m record player
Plattform f platform; **Plattfuß**
m flat foot; (Reifen) flat (tyre)
Platz (-es, Plätze) m place;
(Sitzplatz) seat; (freier Raum) space,
room; (in Stadt) square; (Sportplatz)
playing field; **nehmen Sie ~** please
sit down, take a seat; **ist dieser
~ frei?** is this seat taken?;
Platzanweiser(in) m(f)
usher/usherette
Plätzchen nt spot; (Gebäck)
biscuit
platzen vi to burst; (Bombe) to
explode
Platzkarte f seat reservation;
Platzreservierung f seat
reservation; **Platzverweis** m: **er
erhielt einen ~** he was sent off;
Platzwunde f laceration, cut
plaudern vi to chat, to talk
pleite adj (fam) broke; **Pleite**
(-, -n) f (Bankrott) bankruptcy;
(fam: Reinfall) flop
Plombe (-, -n) f lead seal;
(Zahnplombe) filling; **plombieren**
vt (Zahn) to fill
plötzlich adj sudden ▷ adv suddenly,
all at once
plump adj clumsy; (Hände)
ungainly; (Körper) shapeless
plumps interj thud; (in Flüssigkeit)
plop
Plural (-s, -e) m plural
plus adv plus; **fünf ~ sieben ist
zwölf** five plus seven is (o are)
twelve; **zehn Grad ~** ten degrees
above zero; **Plus** (-, -) nt plus;
(Fin) profit; (Vorteil) advantage
Plüsch (-(e)s, -e) m plush
Pluto (-) m Pluto

PLZ *abk* = **Postleitzahl** postcode (Brit), zip code (US)

Po (-s, -s) *m* (*fam*) bottom, bum

Pocken *pl* smallpox *sing*

Podcast (-s, -s) *m* podcast

poetisch *adj* poetic

Pointe (-, -n) *f* punch line

Pokal (-s, -e) *m* goblet; (*Sport*) cup

pökeln *vt* to pickle

Pol (-s, -e) *m* pole

Pole (-n, -n) *m* Pole; **Polen** (-s) *nt* Poland

Police (-, -n) *f* (insurance) policy

polieren *vt* to polish

Polin *f* Pole, Polish woman

Politik *f* politics *sing*; (*eine bestimmte*) policy; **Politiker(in)** *m(f)* politician; **politisch** *adj* political

Politur *f* polish

Polizei *f* police *pl*; **Polizeibeamte(r)** *m*, **Polizeibeamtin** *f* police officer; **polizeilich** *adj* police; **sie wird ~ gesucht** the police are looking for her; **Polizeirevier** *nt*, **Polizeiwache** *f* police station; **Polizeistunde** *f* closing time; **Polizeiwache** *f* police station; **Polizist(in)** *m(f)* policeman/-woman

Pollen (-s, -s) *m* pollen; **Pollenflug** (-s) *m* pollen count

polnisch *adj* Polish; **Polnisch** *nt* Polish

Polo (-s) *nt* polo; **Polohemd** *nt* polo shirt

Polster (-s, -) *nt* cushion; (*Polsterung*) upholstery; (*in Kleidung*) padding; (*fig: Geld*) reserves *pl*; **Polstergarnitur** *f* living-room suite; **Polstermöbel** *pl* upholstered furniture *sing*; **polstern** *vt* to upholster; (*Kleidung*) to pad

Polterabend *m* party prior to a wedding, at which old crockery is

smashed to bring good luck

poltern *vi* (Krach machen) to crash; (schimpfen) to rant

Polyester (-s, -) *m* polyester

Polypen *pl* (Med) adenoids *pl*

Pommes frites *pl* chips *pl* (Brit), French fries *pl* (US)

Pony (-s, -s) *m* (Frisur) fringe (Brit), bangs *pl* (US) ▷ (-s, -s) *nt* (Pferd) pony

Popcorn (-s) *nt* popcorn

Popmusik *f* pop (music)

populär *adj* popular

Pore (-, -n) *f* pore

Pornografie *f* pornography

Porree (-s, -s) *m* leeks *pl*; **eine Stange ~** a leek

Portemonnaie, Portmonee (-s, -s) *nt* purse

Portier (-s, -s) *m* porter

Portion *f* portion, helping

Porto (-s, -s) *nt* postage

Portrait, Porträt (-s, -s) *nt* portrait

Portugal (-s) *nt* Portugal; **Portugiese** (-n, -n) *m* Portuguese; **Portugiesin** (-, -nen) *f* Portuguese; **portugiesisch** *adj* Portuguese; **Portugiesisch** *nt* Portuguese

Portwein (-s, -e) *m* port

Porzellan (-s, -e) *nt* china

Posaune (-, -n) *f* trombone

Position *f* position

positiv *adj* positive

Post® (-, -en) *f* post office; (Briefe) post (Brit), mail; **Postamt** *nt* post office; **Postanweisung** *f* postal order (Brit), money order (US); **Postbank** *f* German post office bank; **Postbote** *m*, **-botin** *f* postman/-woman

Posten (-s, -e) *m* post, position; (Comm) item; (auf Liste) entry

Poster (-s, -) *nt* poster

Postfach *nt* post-office box, PO box; **Postkarte** *f* postcard;

postlagernd adv poste restante;
Postleitzahl f postcode (Brit), zip
code (US)

postmodern adj postmodern

Postsparkasse f post office
savings bank; **Poststempel** m
postmark; **Postweg** m: **auf dem
~** by mail

Potenz f (Math) power; (eines
Mannes) potency

PR (-, -s) f abk = **Public Relations**
PR

prächtig adj splendid

prahlen vi to boast, to brag

Praktikant(in) m(f) trainee;
Praktikum (-s, Praktika) nt practical training; **praktisch** adj
practical; **-er Arzt** general
practitioner

Praline f chocolate

Prämie f (bei Versicherung)
premium; (Belohnung) reward; (von
Arbeitgeber) bonus

Präparat nt (Med) medicine; (Bio)
preparation

Präservativ nt condom

Präsident(in) m(f) president

Praxis (-, Praxen) f practice;
(Behandlungsraum) surgery; (von
Anwalt) office; **Praxisgebühr** f
surgery surcharge

präzise adj precise, exact

predigen vt, vi to preach; **Predigt**
(-, -en) f sermon

Preis (-es, -e) m (zu zahlen) price;
(bei Sieg) prize; **den ersten
~ gewinnen** to win first prize;
Preisausschreiben nt
competition

Preiselbeere f cranberry

preisgünstig adj inexpensive;
Preislage f price range; **Preisliste**
f price list; **Preisschild** nt price
tag; **Preisträger(in)** m(f)
prizewinner; **preiswert** adj
inexpensive

Prellung f bruise

Premiere (-, -n) f premiere, first
night

Premierminister(in) m(f) prime
minister, premier

Prepaidhandy nt prepaid
mobile (Brit), prepaid cell phone
(US); **Prepaidkarte** f prepaid
card

Presse f press

pressen vt to press

prickeln vi to tingle

Priester(in) (-s, -) m(f) priest/(woma
priest

Primel (-, -n) f primrose

primitiv adj primitive

Prinz (-en, -en) m prince;
Prinzessin f princess

Prinzip (-s, -ien) nt principle; **im
~** basically; **aus ~** on principle

Priorität f priority

privat adj private;
Privatfernsehen nt commercial
television; **Privatgrundstück** nt
private property; **privatisieren**
vt to privatize

pro prep +akk per; **5 Euro
~ Stück/Person** 5 euros each/per
person; **Pro** (-s) nt pro

Probe (-, -n) f test; (Teststück)
sample; (Theat) rehearsal;
Probefahrt f test drive; **eine
~ machen** to go for a test drive;
Probezeit f trial period;
probieren vt, vi to try; (Wein,
Speise) to taste, to sample

Problem (-s, -e) nt problem

Produkt (-(e)s, -e) nt product;
Produktion f production;
(produzierte Menge) output;
produzieren vt to produce

Professor(in) (-s, -en) m(f)
professor

Profi (-s, -s) m pro

Profil (-s, -e) nt profile; (von
Reifen, Schuhsohle) tread

Profit (-(e)s, -e) m profit;
profitieren vi to profit (von from)

Prognose (-, -n) f prediction; (Wetter) forecast

Programm (-s, -e) nt programme; (Inform) program; (TV) channel; **Programmheft** nt programme; **programmieren** vt to program; **Programmierer(in)** (-s, -) m(f) programmer; **Programmkino** nt arts (o repertory (US)) cinema

Projekt (-(e)s, -e) nt project

Projektor m projector

Promenade (-, -n) f promenade

Promille (-(s), -) nt (blood) alcohol level; **0,8 ~** 0,08 per cent; **Promillegrenze** f legal alcohol limit

prominent adj prominent; **Prominenz** f VIPs pl, prominent figures pl; (fam: Stars) the glitterati pl

Propeller (-s, -) m propeller

prosit interj cheers

Prospekt (-(e)s, -e) m leaflet, brochure

prost interj cheers

Prostituierte(r) mf prostitute

Protest (-(e)s, -e) m protest

Protestant(in) m(f) Protestant; **protestantisch** adj Protestant

protestieren vi to protest (gegen against)

Prothese (-, -n) f artificial arm/leg; (Gebiss) dentures pl

Protokoll (-s, -e) nt (bei Sitzung) minutes pl; (diplomatisch, Inform) protocol; (bei Polizei) statement

protzen vi to show off; **protzig** adj flashy

Proviant (-s, -e) m provisions pl

Provider (-s, -) m (Inform) (service) provider

Provinz (-, -en) f province

Provision f (Comm) commission

provisorisch adj provisional; **Provisorium** (-s, Provisorien) nt stopgap; (Zahn) temporary filling

provozieren vt to provoke

Prozent (-(e)s, -e) nt per cent

Prozess (-es, -e) m (Vorgang) process; (Jur) trial; (Rechtsfall) (court) case; **prozessieren** vi to go to law (mit against)

Prozession f procession

Prozessor (-s, -en) m (Inform) processor

prüde adj prudish

prüfen vt to test; (nachprüfen) to check; **Prüfung** f (Schule) exam; (Überprüfung) check; **eine ~ machen** (Schule) to take an exam

Prügelei f fight; **prügeln** vt to beat ▷ vr: **sich ~** to fight

PS abk = **Pferdestärke** hp; = **Postskript(um)** PS

pseudo- präf pseudo; **Pseudokrupp** (-s) m (Med) pseudocroup; **Pseudonym** (-s, -e) nt pseudonym

pst interj ssh

Psychiater(in) (-s, -) m(f) psychiatrist; **psychisch** adj psychological; (Krankheit) mental;

Psychoanalyse f psychoanalysis;

Psychologe (-n, -n) m, **Psychologin** f psychologist; **Psychologie** f psychology

Psychopharmaka pl mind-affecting drugs pl, psychotropic drugs pl; **psychosomatisch** adj psychosomatic; **Psychoterror** m psychological intimidation; **Psychotherapie** f psychotherapy

Pubertät f puberty

Publikum (-s) nt audience; (Sport) crowd

Pudding (-s, -e o -s) m blancmange

Pudel (-s, -) m poodle

Puder (-s, -) m powder; **Puderzucker** m icing sugar

Puerto Rico (-s) nt Puerto Rico

Pulli (-s, -s) m, **Pullover** (-s, -) m sweater, pullover, jumper (Brit)

Puls (-es, -e) m pulse

Pulver (-s, -) nt powder;
Pulverkaffee m instant coffee;
Pulverschnee m powder snow

pummelig adj chubby

Pumpe (-, -n) f pump; **pumpen**
vt to pump; (fam: verleihen) to lend;
(fam: sich ausleihen) to borrow

Pumps pl court shoes pl (Brit),
pumps pl (US)

Punk (-s, -s) m (Musik, Mensch)
punk

Punkt (-(e)s, -e) m point; (bei
Muster) dot; (Satzzeichen) full stop
(Brit), period (US); **~ zwei Uhr** at
two o'clock sharp

pünktlich adj punctual, on time;
Pünktlichkeit f punctuality

Punsch (-(e)s, -e) m punch

Pupille (-, -n) f pupil

Puppe (-, -n) f doll

pur adj pure; (völlig) sheer;
(Whisky) neat

Püree (-s, -s) nt puree;
(Kartoffelpüree) mashed potatoes pl

Puste (-) f (fam) puff; **außer**
~ sein to be puffed

Pustel (-, -n) f pustule; (Pickel)
pimple; **pusten** vi to blow;
(keuchen) to puff

Pute (-, -n) f turkey;
Putenschnitzel nt turkey
escalope

Putsch (-es, -e) m putsch

Putz (-es) m (Mörtel) plaster

putzen vt to clean; **sich** (dat) **die**
Nase ~ to blow one's nose; **sich**
(dat) **die Zähne ~** to brush one's
teeth; **Putzfrau** f cleaner;
Putzlappen m cloth, **Putzmann**
m cleaner; **Putzmittel** nt
cleaning agent, cleaner

Puzzle (-s, -s) nt jigsaw (puzzle)

Pyjama (-s, -s) m pyjamas pl

Pyramide (-, -n) f pyramid

Python (-s, -s) m python

q

Quadrat nt square; **quadratisch**
adj square; **Quadratmeter** m
square metre

quaken vi (Frosch) to croak; (Ente)
to quack

Qual (-, -en) f pain, agony;
(seelisch) anguish; **quälen** vt to
torment ▷ vr: **sich ~** to struggle;
(geistig) to torment oneself;
Quälerei f torture, torment

qualifizieren vt to qualify;
(einstufen) to label ▷ vr: **sich ~** to
qualify

Qualität f quality

Qualle (-, -n) f jellyfish

Qualm (-(e)s) m thick smoke;
qualmen vt, vi to smoke

Quantität f quantity

Quarantäne (-, -n) f quarantine

Quark (-s) m quark; (fam: Unsinn)
rubbish

Quartett (-s, -e) nt quartet;
(Kartenspiel) happy families sing

Quartier (-s, -e) nt
accommodation

quasi adv more or less

Quatsch (-es) m (fam) rubbish;
quatschen vi (fam) to chat

Quecksilber nt mercury

Quelle (-, -n) f spring; (eines
Flusses) source

quellen vi to pour

quer adv crossways, diagonally;
(rechtwinklig) at right angles;
~ über die Straße straight across
the street; **querfeldein** adv
across country; **Querflöte** f
flute; **Querschnitt** m cross
section; **querschnittsgelähmt**
adj paraplegic; **Querstraße** f
side street

quetschen vt to squash, to
crush; (Med) to bruise;
Quetschung f bruise

Queue (-s, -s) m (billiard) cue

quietschen vi to squeal; (Tür,
Bett) to squeak; (Bremsen) to
screech

quitt adj quits, even

Quitte (-, -n) f quince

Quittung f receipt

Quiz (-, -) nt quiz

Quote (-, -n) f rate; (Comm) quota

r

Rabatt (-(e)s, -e) m discount

Rabbi (-(s), -s) m rabbi; **Rabbiner**
(-s, -) m rabbi

Rabe (-n, -n) m raven

Rache (-) f revenge, vengeance

Rachen (-s, -) m throat

rächen vt to avenge ▷ vr: **sich
~** to take (one's) revenge (an +dat
on)

Rad (-(e)s, Räder) nt wheel;
(Fahrrad) bike; **~ fahren** to
cycle; **mit dem ~ fahren** to go
by bike

Radar (-s) m o nt radar;
Radarfalle f speed trap;
Radarkontrolle f radar speed
check

radeln vi (fam) to cycle;
Radfahrer(in) m(f) cyclist;
Radfahrweg m cycle track (o
path)

Radicchio (-s) m (Salatsorte)
radicchio

radieren vt to rub out, to erase; **Radiergummi** m rubber (Brit), eraser; **Radierung** f (Kunst) etching

Radieschen nt radish

radikal adj radical

Radio (-s, -s) nt radio; **im ~** on the radio

radioaktiv adj radioactive

Radiologe (-n, -n) m, **Radiologin** f radiologist

Radiorekorder m radio cassette recorder; **Radiosender** m radio station; **Radiowecker** m radio alarm (clock)

Radkappe f (Auto) hub cap

Radler(in) (-s, -) m(f) cyclist

Radler (-s, -) m ≈ shandy

Radlerhose f cycling shorts pl;
Radrennen nt cycle racing;
(einzelnes Rennen) cycle race;
Radtour f cycling tour; **Radweg** m cycle track (o path)

raffiniert adj crafty, cunning;
(Zucker) refined

Rafting (-s) nt white water rafting

Ragout (-s, -s) nt ragout

Rahm (-s) m cream

rahmen vt to frame; **Rahmen** (-s, -) m frame

Rakete (-, -n) f rocket

rammen vt to ram

Rampe (-, -n) f ramp

ramponieren vt (fam) to damage, to batter

Ramsch (-(e)s, -e) m junk

ran (fam) kontr von **heran**

Rand (-(e)s, Ränder) m edge; (von Brille, Tasse etc) rim; (auf Papier) margin; (Schmutzrand, unter Augen) ring; (fig) verge, brink

randalieren vi to (go on the) rampage; **Randalierer(in)** (-s, -) m(f) hooligan

Randstein m kerb (Brit), curb (US); **Randstreifen** m shoulder

rang imperf von **ringen**

Rang (-(e)s, Ränge) m rank; (in Wettbewerb) place; (Theat) circle

rannte imperf von **rennen**

ranzig adj rancid

Rap (-(s), -s) m (Mus) rap; **rappen** vi (Mus) to rap; **Rapper(in)** (-s, -) m(f) (Mus) rapper

rar adj rare, scarce

rasant adj quick, rapid

rasch adj quick

rascheln vi to rustle

rasen vi (sich schnell bewegen) to race; (toben) to rave; **gegen einen Baum ~** to crash into a tree

Rasen (-s, -) m lawn

rasend adj (vor Wut) furious

Rasenmäher (-s, -) m lawnmower

Rasierapparat m razor; (elektrischer) shaver; **Rasiercreme** f shaving cream; **rasieren** vt to shave ▷ vr: **sich ~** to shave; **Rasierer** m shaver; **Rasiergel** nt shaving gel; **Rasierklinge** f razor blade; **Rasiermesser** nt (cutthroat) razor; **Rasierpinsel** m shaving brush; **Rasierschaum** m shaving foam; **Rasierzeug** nt shaving tackle, shaving equipment

Rasse (-, -n) f race; (Tiere) breed

Rassismus m racism;
Rassist(in) m(f) racist;
rassistisch adj racist

Rast (-, -en) f rest, break; **~ machen** to have a rest (o break); **rasten** vi to rest; **Rastplatz** m (Auto) rest area; **Raststätte** f (Auto) service area; (Gaststätte) motorway (Brit) (o highway (US)) restaurant

Rasur f shave

Rat (-(e)s, Ratschläge) m (piece of) advice; **sie hat mir einen ~ gegeben** she gave me some advice; **um ~ fragen** to ask for advice

Rate (-, -n) f instalment; **etw auf ~n kaufen** to buy sth in instalments (Brit), to buy sth on the instalment plan (US)

raten (riet, geraten) vt, vi to guess; (empfehlen) to advise (jdm sb)

Rathaus nt town hall

Ration f ration

ratlos adj at a loss, helpless; **ratsam** adj advisable

Rätsel (-s, -) nt puzzle; (Worträtsel) riddle; **das ist mir ein ~** it's a mystery to me; **rätselhaft** adj mysterious

Ratte (-, -n) f rat

rau adj rough, coarse; (Wetter) harsh

Raub (-(e)s) m robbery; (Beute) loot, booty; **rauben** vt to steal; **jdm etw ~** to rob sb of sth; **Räuber(in)** (-s, -) m(f) robber; **Raubfisch** m predatory fish; **Raubkopie** f pirate copy; **Raubmord** m robbery with murder; **Raubtier** nt predator; **Raubüberfall** m mugging; **Raubvogel** m bird of prey

Rauch (-(e)s) m smoke; (Abgase) fumes pl; **rauchen** vt, vi to smoke; **Raucher(in)** (-s, -) m(f) smoker; **Raucherabteil** nt smoking compartment

Räucherlachs m smoked salmon; **räuchern** vt to smoke

rauchig adj smoky; **Rauchmelder** m smoke detector; **Rauchverbot** nt smoking ban; **hier ist ~** there's no smoking here

rauf (fam) kontr von **herauf**

rauh adj siehe **rau**; **Rauhreif** m siehe **Raureif**

Raum (-(e)s, Räume) m space; (Zimmer, Platz) room; (Gebiet) area

räumen vt to clear; (Wohnung, Platz) to vacate; (wegbringen) to

shift, to move; (in Schrank etc) to put away

Raumfähre f space shuttle; **Raumfahrt** f space travel; **Raumschiff** nt spacecraft, spaceship; **Raumsonde** f space probe; **Raumstation** f space station

Raumtemperatur f room temperature

Räumungsverkauf m clearance sale, closing-down sale

Raupe (-, -n) f caterpillar

Raureif m hoarfrost

raus (fam) kontr von **heraus**, **hinaus**, **~!** (get) out!

Rausch (-(e)s, Räusche) m intoxication; **einen ~ haben/kriegen** to be/get drunk

rauschen vi (Wasser) to rush; (Baum) to rustle; (Radio etc) to hiss; **Rauschgift** nt drug; **Rauschgiftsüchtige(r)** mf drug addict

rausfliegen irr vi (fam) to be kicked out

raushalten irr vr (fam) **halt du dich da raus!** you (just) keep out of it

räuspern vr: **sich ~** to clear one's throat

rausschmeißen irr vt (fam) to throw out

Razzia (-, Razzien) f raid

reagieren vi to react (auf +akk to); **Reaktion** f reaction

real adj real; **realisieren** vt (merken) to realize; (verwirklichen) to implement; **realistisch** adj realistic; **Realität** (-, -en) f reality; **Reality-TV** (-s) nt reality TV

Realschule f ≈ secondary school, junior high (school) (US)

Rebe (-, -n) f vine

rebellieren vi to rebel

Rebhuhn nt partridge

rechnen vt, vi to calculate; ~ **mit** to expect; (bauen auf) to count on ▷ vr: **sich** ~ to pay off, to turn out to be profitable; **Rechner** (-s, -) m calculator; (Computer) computer; **Rechnung** f calculation(s); (Comm) bill (Brit), check (US); **die** ~, **bitte!** can I have the bill, please?; **das geht auf meine** ~ this is on me

recht adj (richtig, passend) right; ~ **haben** to be right; **jdm** ~ **geben** to agree with sb; **mir soll's** ~ **sein** it's alright by me; **mir ist es** ~ I don't mind ▷ adv really, quite; (richtig) right(ly); **ich weiß nicht** ~ I don't really know; **es geschieht ihm** ~ it serves him right

Recht (-(e)s, -e) nt right; (Jur) law

Rechte (-n, -n) f right-hand side; (Hand) right hand; (Pol) right (wing); **rechte(r, s)** adj right; **auf der ~n Seite** on the right, on the right-hand side; **Rechte(s)** nt right thing; **etwas/nichts ~s** something/nothing proper

Rechteck (-s, -e) nt rectangle; **rechteckig** adj rectangular

rechtfertigen vt to justify ▷ vr: **sich** ~ to justify oneself

rechtlich adj legal; **rechtmäßig** adj legal, lawful

rechts adv on the right; ~ **abbiegen** to turn right; ~ **von** to the right of; ~ **oben** at the top right

Rechtsanwalt m, **-anwältin** f lawyer

Rechtschreibung f spelling **Rechtshänder(in)** (-s, -) m(f) right-hander; **rechtsherum** adv to the right, clockwise; **rechtsradikal** adj (Pol) extreme right-wing

Rechtsschutzversicherung f legal costs insurance

Rechtsverkehr m driving on the right

rechtswidrig adj illegal **rechtwinklig** adj right-angled; **rechtzeitig** adj timely ▷ adv in time

recycelbar adj recyclable; **recyceln** vt to recycle; **Recycling** (-s) nt recycling; **Recyclingpapier** nt recycled paper

Redakteur(in) m(f) editor; **Redaktion** f editing; (Leute) editorial staff; (Büro) editorial office(s)

Rede (-, -n) f speech; (Gespräch) talk; **eine** ~ **halten** to make a speech; **reden** vi to talk, to speak ▷ vt to say; (Unsinn etc) to talk; **Redewendung** f idiom; **Redner(in)** m(f) speaker

reduzieren vt to reduce

Referat (-s, -e) nt paper; **ein** ~ **halten** to give a paper (über +akk on)

reflektieren vt to reflect

Reform (-, -en) f reform; **Reformhaus** nt health food shop; **reformieren** vt to reform

Regal (-s, -e) nt shelf; (Möbelstück) shelves pl

Regel (-, -n) f rule; (Med) period; **regelmäßig** adj regular; **regeln** vt to regulate, to control; (Angelegenheit) to settle ▷ vr: **sich von selbst** ~ to sort itself out; **Regelung** f regulation

Regen (-s, -) m rain; **Regenbogen** m rainbow; **Regenmantel** m raincoat; **Regenrinne** f gutter; **Regenschauer** m shower; **Regenschirm** m umbrella; **Regenwald** m rainforest; **Regenwurm** m earthworm

Regie f direction

regieren vt, vi to govern, to rule;

Regierung f government; (von Monarch) reign

Region f region; **regional** adj regional

Regisseur(in) m(f) director

registrieren vt to register; (bemerken) to notice

regnen vi impers to rain; **regnerisch** adj rainy

regulär adj regular; **regulieren** vt to regulate, to adjust

Reh (-(e)s, -e) nt deer; (Fleisch) venison

Rehabilitationszentrum nt (Med) rehabilitation centre

Reibe (-, -n) f, **Reibeisen** nt grater; **reiben** (rieb, gerieben) vt to rub; (Gastr) to grate; **reibungslos** adj smooth

reich adj rich

Reich (-(e)s, -e) nt empire; (eines Königs) kingdom

reichen vi to reach; (genügen) to be enough, to be sufficient (jdm for sb) ▷ vt to hold out; (geben) to pass, to hand; (anbieten) to offer

reichhaltig adj ample, rich; **reichlich** adj (Trinkgeld) generous; (Essen) ample; **~ Zeit** plenty of time; **Reichtum** (-s, -tümer) m wealth

reif adj ripe; (Mensch, Urteil) mature

Reif (-(e)s) m (Raureif) hoarfrost ▷ (-(e)s, -e) m (Ring) ring, hoop

reifen vi to mature; (Obst) to ripen

Reifen (-s, -) m ring, hoop; (von Auto) tyre; **Reifendruck** m tyre pressure; **Reifenpanne** f puncture; **Reifenwechsel** m tyre change

Reihe (-, -n) f row; (von Tagen etc, fam: Anzahl) series sing; **der ~ nach** one after the other; **er ist an der ~** it's his turn; **Reihenfolge** f order, sequence; **Reihenhaus** nt terraced house (Brit), row house (US)

Reiher (-s, -) m heron

rein (fam) kontr von **herein, hinein** ▷ adj pure; (sauber) clean

Reinfall m (fam) letdown; **rein|fallen** irr vi (fam) **auf etw** (akk) ~ to fall for sth

reinigen vt to clean; **Reinigung** f cleaning; (Geschäft) (dry) cleaner's; **Reinigungsmittel** nt cleaning agent, cleaner

rein|legen vt: **jdn ~** to take sb for a ride

Reis (-es, -e) m rice

Reise (-, -n) f journey; (auf Schiff) voyage; **Reiseapotheke** f first-aid kit; **Reisebüro** nt travel agent's; **Reisebus** m coach; **Reiseführer(in)** m(f) (Mensch) courier; (Buch) guide(book); **Reisegepäck** nt luggage (Brit), baggage; **Reisegesellschaft** f (Veranstalter) tour operator; **Reisegruppe** f tourist party; (mit Reisebus) coach party; **Reiseleiter(in)** m(f) courier; **reisen** vi to travel; **~ nach** to go to; **Reisende(r)** mf traveller; **Reisepass** m passport; **Reiseroute** f route, itinerary; **Reiserücktrittversicherung** f holiday cancellation insurance; **Reisescheck** m traveller's cheque; **Reisetasche** f holdall (Brit), carryall (US); **Reiseveranstalter** m tour operator; **Reiseverkehr** m holiday traffic; **Reiseversicherung** f travel insurance; **Reiseziel** nt destination

Reiskocher (-s, -) m rice steamer

reißen (riss, gerissen) vt, vi to tear; (ziehen) to pull, to drag; (Witz) to crack

Reißnagel m drawing pin (Brit), thumbtack (US); **Reißverschluss** m zip (Brit), zipper (US); **Reißzwecke** f drawing pin (Brit), thumbtack (US)

reiten (ritt, geritten) vt, vi to ride; **Reiter(in)** m(f) rider; **Reithose** f riding breeches pl; **Reitsport** m riding; **Reitstiefel** m riding boot

Reiz (-es, -e) m stimulus; (angenehm) charm; (Verlockung) attraction; **reizen** vt to stimulate; (unangenehm) to annoy; (verlocken) to appeal to, to attract; **reizend** adj charming; **Reizgas** nt irritant gas; **Reizung** f irritation

Reklamation f complaint

Reklame (-, -n) f advertising; (Einzelwerbung) advertisement; (im Fernsehen) commercial

reklamieren vi to complain (wegen about)

Rekord (-(e)s, -e) m record

relativ adj relative ▷ adv relatively

relaxen vi to relax, to chill out

Religion f religion; **religiös** adj religious

Remoulade (-, -n) f tartar sauce

Renaissance f renaissance, revival; (Hist) Renaissance

Rennbahn f racecourse; (Auto) racetrack; **rennen** (rannte, gerannt) vt, vi to run; **Rennen** (-s, -) nt running; (Wettbewerb) race; **Rennfahrer(in)** m(f) racing driver; **Rennrad** nt racing bike; **Rennwagen** m racing car

renommiert adj famous, noted (wegen, für for)

renovieren vt to renovate; **Renovierung** f renovation

rentabel adj profitable

Rente (-, -n) f pension; **Rentenversicherung** f pension scheme

Rentier nt reindeer

rentieren vr: **sich ~** to pay, to be profitable

Rentner(in) (-s, -) m(f) pensioner, senior citizen

Reparatur f repair; **Reparaturwerkstatt** f repair shop; (Auto) garage; **reparieren** vt to repair

Reportage f report; **Reporter(in)** (-s, -) m(f) reporter

Reptil (-s, -ien) nt reptile

Republik f republic

Reservat (-s, -e) nt nature reserve; (für Ureinwohner) reservation; **Reserve** (-, -n) f reserve; **Reservekanister** m spare can; **Reserverad** nt (Auto) spare wheel; **reservieren** vt to reserve; **Reservierung** f reservation

resignieren vi to give up; **resigniert** adj resigned

Respekt (-(e)s) m respect; **respektieren** vt to respect

Rest (-(e)s, -e) m rest, remainder; (Überreste) remains pl; **der ~ ist für Sie** keep the change

Restaurant (-s, -s) nt restaurant

restaurieren vt to restore

Restbetrag m balance; **restlich** adj remaining; **restlos** adj complete; **Restmüll** m non-recyclable waste

Resultat nt result

retten vt to save, to rescue

Rettich (-s, -e) m radish (large white or red variety)

Rettung f rescue; (Hilfe) help; (Rettungsdienst) ambulance service; **Rettungsboot** nt lifeboat; **Rettungshubschrauber** m rescue helicopter; **Rettungsring** m lifebelt, life preserver (US); **Rettungswagen** m ambulance

Reue (-) f remorse; (Bedauern)

regret; **reuen** vt: **es reut ihn** he regrets it

revanchieren vr: **sich ~** (sich rächen) to get one's own back, to get one's revenge; (für Hilfe etc) to return the favour

Revolution f revolution

Rezept (-(e)s, -e) nt (Gastr) recipe; (Med) prescription; **rezeptfrei** adj over-the-counter, non-prescription

Rezeption f (in Hotel) reception

rezeptflichtig adj available only on prescription

R-Gespräch nt reverse-charge (Brit) (o collect (US)) call

Rhabarber (-s) m rhubarb

Rhein (-s) m Rhine; **Rheinland-Pfalz** (-) nt Rhineland-Palatinate

Rheuma (-s) nt rheumatism

Rhythmus m rhythm

richten vt (lenken) to direct (auf +akk to); (Waffe, Kamera) to point (auf +akk at); (Brief, Anfrage) to address (an +akk to); (einstellen) to adjust; (instand setzen) to repair; (zurechtmachen) to prepare ▷ vr: **sich ~ nach** (Regel etc) to keep to; (Mode, Beispiel) to follow; (abhängen von) to depend on

Richter(in) (-s, -) m(f) judge

Richtgeschwindigkeit f recommended speed

richtig adj right, correct; (echt) proper ▷ adv (fam: sehr) really; **richtig|stellen** vt: **etw ~** (berichtigen) to correct sth

Richtlinie f guideline

Richtung f direction; (Tendenz) tendency; **Richtungstaste** f arrow key

rieb imperf von **reiben**

riechen (roch, gerochen) vt, vi to smell; **nach etw ~** to smell of sth; **an etw** (dat) **~** to smell sth

rief imperf von **rufen**

Riegel (-s, -) m bolt; (Gastr) bar

Riemen (-s, -) m strap; (Gürtel) belt

Riese (-n, -n) m giant; **Riesengarnele** f king prawn; **riesengroß** adj gigantic, huge; **Riesenrad** nt big wheel; **riesig** adj enormous, huge

riet imperf von **raten**

Riff (-(e)s, -e) nt reef

Rind (-(e)s, -er) nt cow; (Bulle) bull; (Gastr) beef; **-er** pl cattle pl

Rinde (-, -n) f (Baum) bark; (Käse) rind; (Brot) crust

Rinderbraten m roast beef; **Rinderwahn(sinn)** m mad cow disease; **Rindfleisch** nt beef

Ring (-(e)s, -e) m ring; (Straße) ring road; **Ringbuch** nt ring binder

ringen (rang, gerungen) vi to wrestle; **Ringer(in)** m(f) wrestler; **Ringfinger** m ring finger; **Ringkampf** m wrestling match; **ringsherum** adv round about

Rippe (-, -n) f rib; **Rippenfellentzündung** f pleurisy

Risiko (-s, -s o Risiken) nt risk; **auf eigenes ~** at one's own risk; **riskant** adj risky; **riskieren** vt to risk

riss imperf von **reißen**

Riss (-es, -e) m tear; (in Mauer, Tasse etc) crack; **rissig** adj cracked; (Haut) chapped

ritt imperf von **reiten**

Ritter (-s, -) m knight

Rivale (-n, -n) m, **Rivalin** f rival

Rizinusöl nt castor oil

Robbe (-, -n) f seal

Roboter (-s, -) m robot

robust adj robust

roch imperf von **riechen**

Rock (-(e)s, Röcke) m skirt

Rockband f (Musikgruppe) rock band; **Rockmusik** f rock (music)

Rodelbahn f toboggan run; **rodeln** vi to toboggan

Roggen (-s, -) m rye; **Roggenbrot** nt rye bread

roh adj raw; (Mensch) coarse, crude; **Rohkost** f raw vegetables and fruit pl

Rohr (-(e)s, -e) nt pipe; (Bot) cane; (Schilf) reed; **Röhre** (-, -n) f tube; (Leitung) pipe; (Elek) valve; (Backröhre) oven; **Rohrzucker** m cane sugar

Rohstoff m raw material

Rokoko (-s) nt rococo

Rollbrett nt skateboard

Rolle (-, -n) f (etw Zusammengerolltes) roll; (Theat) role

rollen vt, vi to roll

Roller (-s, -) m scooter

Rollerblades® pl Rollerblades® pl; **Rollerskates** pl roller skates pl

Rollkragenpullover m polo-neck (Brit) (o turtleneck (US)) sweater; **Rollladen** m, **Rollo** (-s, -s) m (roller) shutters pl; **Rollschuh** m roller skate; **Rollstuhl** m wheelchair; **rollstuhlgerecht** adj suitable for wheelchairs; **Rolltreppe** f escalator

Roman (-s, -e) m novel

Romantik f romance; **romantisch** adj romantic

römisch-katholisch adj Roman Catholic

röntgen vt to X-ray; **Röntgenaufnahme** f, **Röntgenbild** nt X-ray; **Röntgenstrahlen** pl X-rays pl

rosa adj inv pink

Rose (-, -n) f rose

Rosenkohl m (Brussels) sprouts pl

Rosé(wein) m rosé (wine)

rosig adj rosy

Rosine f raisin

Rosmarin (-s) m rosemary

Rosskastanie f horse chestnut

Rost (-(e)s, -e) m rust; (zum Braten) grill, gridiron; **Rostbratwurst** f grilled sausage; **rosten** vi to rust; **rösten** vt to roast, to grill; (Brot) to toast; **rostfrei** adj rustproof; (Stahl) stainless; **rostig** adj rusty; **Rostschutz** m rustproofing

rot adj red; **~ werden** to blush; **Rote Karte** red card; **Rote Bete** beetroot; **bei Rot über die Ampel fahren** to jump the lights; **das Rote Kreuz** the Red Cross

Röteln pl German measles sing

röten vt to redden ▷ vr: **sich ~** to redden

rothaarig adj red-haired

rotieren vi to rotate; **am Rotieren sein** (fam) to be rushing around like a mad thing

Rotkehlchen nt robin; **Rotkohl** m, **Rotkraut** nt red cabbage; **Rotlichtviertel** nt red-light district; **Rotwein** m red wine

Rouge (-s, -s) nt rouge

Route (-, -n) f route

Routine f experience; (Trott) routine

Rubbellos nt scratchcard; **rubbeln** vt to rub

Rübe (-, -n) f turnip; **Gelbe ~** carrot; **Rote ~** beetroot

rüber (fam) kontr von **herüber**, **hinüber**

rückbestätigen vt (Flug etc) to reconfirm

rücken vt, vi to move; **könntest du ein bisschen ~?** could you move over a bit?

Rücken (-s, -) m back; **Rückenlehne** f back(rest); **Rückenmark** nt spinal cord; **Rückenschmerzen** pl backache sing; **Rückenschwimmen** nt backstroke; **Rückenwind** m tailwind

Rückerstattung f refund;
Rückfahrkarte f return ticket
(Brit), round-trip ticket (US);
Rückfahrt f return journey;
Rückfall m relapse; **Rückflug** m
return flight; **Rückgabe** f return;
rückgängig adj: **etw ~ machen**
to cancel sth; **Rückgrat** (-(e)s, -e)
nt spine, backbone; **Rückkehr**
(-, -en) f return; **Rücklicht** nt
rear light; **Rückreise** f return
journey; **auf der ~** on the way
back
Rucksack m rucksack, backpack;
Rucksacktourist(in) m(f)
backpacker
Rückschritt m step back;
Rückseite f back; (hinterer Teil)
rear; **siehe ~** see overleaf;
Rücksicht f consideration;
~ nehmen auf (+akk) to show
consideration for; **rücksichtslos**
adj inconsiderate; (Fahren)
reckless; (unbarmherzig) ruthless;
rücksichtsvoll adj considerate;
Rücksitz m back seat;
Rückspiegel m (Auto) rear-view
mirror; **Rückstand** m: **sie sind
zwei Tore im ~** they're two goals
down; **im ~ sein mit** (Arbeit, Miete)
to be behind with; **Rücktaste** f
backspace key; **Rückvergütung**
f refund; **rückwärts** adv
backwards, back; **Rückwärtsgang** m (Auto) reverse (gear);
Rückweg m return journey, way
back; **Rückzahlung** f repayment
Ruder (-s, -) nt oar; (Steuer)
rudder; **Ruderboot** nt rowing
boat (Brit), rowboat (US); **rudern**
vt, vi to row
Ruf (-(e)s, -e) m call, cry; (Ansehen)
reputation; **rufen** (rief, gerufen) vt,
vi to call; (schreien) to cry;
Rufnummer f telephone number
Ruhe (-) f rest; (Ungestörtheit)
peace, quiet; (Gelassenheit, Stille)

calm; (Schweigen) silence; **lass
mich in ~!** leave me alone; **ruhen**
vi to rest; **Ruhestand** m
retirement; **im ~ sein** to be retired;
Ruhestörung f disturbance of
the peace; **Ruhetag** m closing
day; **montags ~ haben** to be
closed on Mondays
ruhig adj quiet; (bewegungslos)
still; (Hand) steady; (gelassen) calm
Ruhm (-(e)s) m fame, glory
Rührei nt scrambled egg(s);
rühren vt to move; (umrühren) to
stir ⊳ vr: **sich ~** to move; (sich
bemerkbar machen) to say
something; **rührend** adj
touching, moving; **Rührung** f
emotion
Ruine (-, -n) f ruin; **ruinieren** vt
to ruin
rülpsen vi to burp, to belch
rum (fam) kontr von **herum**
Rumänien (-s) nt Romania
Rummel (-s) m (Trubel) hustle
and bustle; (Jahrmarkt) fair;
(Medienrummel) hype;
Rummelplatz m fairground
rumoren vi: **es rumort in
meinem Bauch/Kopf** my
stomach is rumbling/my head is
spinning
Rumpf (-(e)s, Rümpfe) m (Anat)
trunk; (Aviat) fuselage; (Naut)
hull
rümpfen vt: **die Nase ~** to turn
one's nose up (über at)
Rumpsteak nt rump steak
rund adj round ⊳ adv (etwa)
around; **~ um etw** a)round sth;
Runde (-, -n) f round; (in Rennen)
lap; **Rundfahrt** f tour (durch of);
Rundfunk m broadcasting;
(Rundfunkanstalt) broadcasting
service; **im ~ on** the radio;
Rundgang m tour (durch of); (von
Wächter) round

rundlich adj plump; **Rundreise** f tour (durch of)
runter (fam) kontr von **herunter, hinunter**; **runterscrollen** vt (Inform) to scroll down
runzeln vt: **die Stirn ~** to frown; **runzelig** adj wrinkled
ruppig adj gruff
Rüsche (-, -n) f frill
Ruß (-es) m soot
Russe (-n, -n) m Russian
Rüssel (-s, -) m (Elefant) trunk; (Schwein) snout
Russin f Russian; **russisch** adj Russian; **Russisch** nt Russian; **Russland** nt Russia
Rüstung f (mit Waffen) arming; (Ritterrüstung) armour; (Waffen) armaments pl
Rutsch (-(e)s, -e) m: **guten ~ (ins neue Jahr)!** Happy New Year; **Rutschbahn** f, **Rutsche** f slide; **rutschen** vi to slide; (ausrutschen) to slip; **rutschig** adj slippery
rütteln vt, vi to shake

S

S abk = **Süd** S
s. abk = **siehe** see; = **Seite** p.
Saal (-(e)s, Säle) m hall; (für Sitzungen) room
Saarland nt Saarland
sabotieren vt to sabotage
Sache (-, -n) f thing; (Angelegenheit) affair, business; (Frage) matter; **bei der ~ bleiben** to keep to the point; **sachkundig** adj competent; **Sachlage** f situation; **sachlich** adj (objektiv) objective; (nüchtern) matter-of-fact; (inhaltlich) factual; **sächlich** adj (Ling) neuter; **Sachschaden** m material damage
Sachsen (-s) nt Saxony; **Sachsen-Anhalt** (-s) nt Saxony-Anhalt
sacht(e) adv softly, gently
Sachverständige(r) mf expert
Sack (-(e)s, Säcke) m sack; (pej:

Mensch) bastard, bugger;
Sackgasse f dead end, cul-de-sac
Safe (-s, -s) m safe
Safer Sex m safe sex
Safran (-s, -e) m saffron
Saft (-(e)s, Säfte) m juice; **saftig**
adj juicy
Sage (-, -n) f legend
Säge (-, -n) f saw; **Sägemehl** nt
sawdust
sagen vt, vi to say (jdm to sb),
to tell (jdm sb); **wie sagt man ...
auf Englisch?** what's ... in
English?
sägen vt, vi to saw
sagenhaft adj legendary; (fam:
großartig) fantastic
sah imperf von **sehen**
Sahne (-) f cream
Saison (-, -s) f season;
außerhalb der ~ out of season
Saite (-, -n) f string
Sakko (-s, -s) nt jacket
Salami (-, -s) f salami
Salat (-(e)s, -e) m salad;
(Kopfsalat) lettuce; **Salatbar** f
salad bar; **Salatschüssel** f salad
bowl; **Salatsoße** f salad
dressing
Salbe (-, -n) f ointment
Salbei (-s) m sage
Salmonellenvergiftung f
salmonella (poisoning)
salopp adj (Kleidung) casual;
(Sprache) slangy
Salsamusik f salsa (music)
Salto (-s, -s) m somersault
Salz (-es, -e) nt salt; **salzarm** adj
low-salt; **salzen** (salzte, gesalzen)
vt to salt; **Salzgurke** f pickled
gherkin; **Salzhering** m pickled
herring; **salzig** adj salty;
Salzkartoffeln pl boiled potatoes
pl; **Salzstange** f pretzel stick;
Salzstreuer m salt cellar (Brit) (o
shaker (US)); **Salzwasser** nt salt
water

Samba (-, -s) f samba
Samen (-s, -) m seed; (Sperma)
sperm
sammeln vt to collect;
Sammler(in) m(f) collector;
Sammlung f collection;
(Ansammlung, Konzentration)
concentration
Samstag m Saturday; siehe auch
Mittwoch; samstags adv on
Saturdays; siehe auch **mittwochs**
samt prep +dat (along) with,
together with
Samt (-(e)s, -e) m velvet
sämtliche(r, s) adj all (the)
Sanatorium (-s, Sanatorien) nt
sanatorium (Brit), sanitarium (US)
Sand (-(e)s, -e) m sand
Sandale (-, -n) f sandal
sandig adj sandy; **Sandkasten**
m sandpit (Brit), sandbox (US);
Sandpapier nt sandpaper;
Sandstrand m sandy beach
sandte imperf von **senden**
sanft adj soft, gentle
sang imperf von **singen**;
Sänger(in) (-s, -) m(f) singer
Sangria (-, -s) f sangria
sanieren vt to redevelop;
(Gebäude) to renovate; (Betrieb) to
restore to profitability
sanitär adj sanitary; **~e Anlagen**
pl sanitation
Sanitäter(in) (-s, -) m(f) ambu-
lance man/woman, paramedic
sank imperf von **sinken**
Sankt Gallen (-s) nt St Gallen
Saphir (-s, -e) m sapphire
Sardelle f anchovy
Sardine f sardine
Sarg (-(e)s, Särge) m coffin
saß imperf von **sitzen**
Satellit (-en, -en) m satellite;
Satellitenfernsehen nt satellite
TV; **Satellitenschüssel** f (fam)
satellite dish
Satire (-, -n) f satire (auf +akk on)

satt adj full; (Farbe) rich, deep;
~ **sein** (gesättigt) to be full;
~ **machen** to be filling; **jdn/etw**
~ **sein** to be fed up with sb/sth
Sattel (-s, Sättel) m saddle
satt|haben irr vt: **jdn/etw**
~ (nicht mehr mögen) to be fed up
with sb/sth
Saturn (-s) m Saturn
Satz (-es, Sätze) m (Ling) sentence;
(Mus) movement; (Tennis) set;
(Kaffee) grounds pl; (Comm) rate;
(Sprung) jump; (Comm) rate
Satzzeichen nt punctuation
mark
Sau (-, Säue) f sow; (pej: Mensch)
dirty bugger
sauber adj clean; (ironisch) fine;
~ **machen** to clean; **Sauberkeit** f
cleanness; (von Person) cleanliness;
säubern vt to clean
saublöd adj (fam) really stupid,
dumb
Sauce (-, -n) f sauce; (zu Braten)
gravy
Saudi-Arabien (-s) nt Saudi
Arabia
sauer adj sour; (Chem) acid; (fam:
verärgert) cross; **saurer Regen** acid
rain; **Sauerkirsche** f sour
cherry; **Sauerkraut** nt
sauerkraut; **säuerlich** adj
slightly sour; **Sauermilch** f
sour milk; **Sauerrahm** m sour
cream; **Sauerstoff** m oxygen
saufen (soff, gesoffen) vt to drink;
(fam: Mensch) to knock back ▷ vi
to drink; (fam: Mensch) to booze
saugen (sog o saugte, gesogen o
gesaugt) vt, vi to suck; (mit
Staubsauger) to vacuum, to hoover
(Brit); **Sauger** (-s, -) m (auf Flasche)
teat; **Säugetier** nt mammal;
Säugling m infant, baby
Säule (-, -n) f column, pillar
Saum (-s, Säume) m hem; (Naht)
seam

Sauna (-, -s) f sauna
Säure (-, -n) f acid
sausen vi (Ohren) to buzz; (Wind)
to howl; (Mensch) to rush
Saustall m pigsty; **Sauwetter**
nt: **was für ein** ~ (fam) what lousy
weather
Saxophon (-s, -e) nt saxophone
S-Bahn f suburban railway;
S-Bahn-Haltestelle f, **S-Bahnhof**
m suburban (train) station
scannen vt to scan; **Scanner**
(-s, -) m scanner
schäbig adj shabby
Schach (-s, -s) nt chess; (Stellung)
check; **Schachbrett** nt
chessboard; **Schachfigur** f
chess piece; **schachmatt** adj
checkmate
Schacht (-(e)s, Schächte) m shaft
Schachtel (-, -n) f box
schade interj what a pity
Schädel (-s, -) m skull;
Schädelbruch m fractured skull
schaden vi to damage, to harm
(jdm sb); **das schadet nichts** it
won't do any harm; **Schaden**
(-s, Schäden) m damage;
(Verletzung) injury; (Nachteil)
disadvantage; **einen**
~ **verursachen** to cause damage;
Schadenersatz m compensation, damages pl; **schadhaft** adj
faulty; (beschädigt) damaged;
schädigen vt to damage; (jdn) to
do harm to, to harm; **schädlich**
adj harmful (für to); **Schadstoff**
m harmful substance;
schadstoffarm adj low-emission
Schaf (-(e)s, -e) nt sheep;
Schafbock m ram; **Schäfer** (-s, -)
m shepherd; **Schäferhund** m
Alsatian (Brit), German shepherd;
Schäferin f shepherdess
schaffen (schuf, geschaffen) vt to
create; (Platz) to make ▷ vt
(erreichen) to manage, to do;

(erledigen) to finish; *(Prüfung)* to pass; *(transportieren)* to pass; **jdm zu ~ machen** to cause sb trouble

Schaffner(in) *(-s, -) m(f)* (in Bus) conductor/conductress; *(Eisenb)* guard

Schafskäse *m* sheep's (milk) cheese

schal *adj (Getränk)* flat

Schal *(-s, -e o -s) m* scarf

Schälchen *nt* (small) bowl

Schale *(-, -n) f* skin; *(abgeschält)* peel; *(Nuss, Muschel, Ei)* shell; *(Geschirr)* bowl, dish

schälen *vt* to peel; *(Tomate, Mandel)* to skin; *(Erbsen, Eier, Nüsse)* to shell; *(Getreide)* to husk ▷ *vr:* **sich ~** to peel

Schall *(-(e)s, -e) m* sound; **Schalldämpfer** *(-s, -) m (Auto)* silencer *(Brit)*, muffler *(US)*; **Schallplatte** *f* record

Schalotte *(-, -n) f* shallot

schalten *vt* to switch ▷ *vi (Auto)* to change gear; *(fam: begreifen)* to catch on; **Schalter** *(-s, -) m* (auf Post, Bank) counter; *(an Gerät)* switch; **Schalterhalle** *f* main hall; **Schalteröffnungszeiten** *pl* business hours *pl*

Schaltfläche *f (Inform)* button; **Schalthebel** *m* gear lever *(Brit)* (o shift *(US)*); **Schaltjahr** *nt* leap year; **Schaltknüppel** *m* gear lever *(Brit)* (o shift *(US)*); **Schaltung** *f* gear change *(Brit)*, gearshift *(US)*

Scham *(-) f* shame; *(Schamgefühl)* modesty; **schämen** *vr:* **sich ~** to be ashamed

Schande *(-) f* disgrace

Schanze *(-, -n) f* ski jump

Schar *(-, -en) f (von Vögeln)* flock; *(Menge)* crowd; **in ~en** in droves

scharf *adj (Messer, Kritik)* sharp; *(Essen)* hot; **auf etw (akk) ~ sein** *(fam)* to be keen on sth

Schärfe *(-, -n) f* sharpness; *(Strenge)* rigour; *(Foto)* focus

Scharlach *(-s) m (Med)* scarlet fever

Scharnier *(-s, -e) nt* hinge

Schaschlik *(-s, -s) m o nt* (shish) kebab

Schatten *(-s, -) m* shadow; **30 Grad im ~** 30 degrees in the shade; **schattig** *adj* shady

Schatz *(-es, Schätze) m* treasure; *(Mensch)* love

schätzen *vt (abschätzen)* to estimate; *(Gegenstand)* to value; *(würdigen)* to value, to esteem; *(vermuten)* to reckon; **Schätzung** *f* estimate; *(das Schätzen)* estimation; *(von Wertgegenstand)* valuation; **schätzungsweise** *adv* roughly, approximately

Schau *(-, -en) f* show; *(Ausstellung)* exhibition

schauen *vi* to look; **ich schau mal, ob ...** I'll go and have a look whether ...; **schau, dass ...** see (to it) that ...

Schauer *(-s, -) m (Regen)* shower; *(Schreck)* shudder

Schaufel *(-, -n) f* shovel; **~ und Besen** dustpan and brush; **schaufeln** *vt* to shovel; **Schnee ~** to clear the snow away

Schaufenster *nt* shop window; **Schaufensterbummel** *m* window-shopping expedition

Schaukel *(-, -n) f* swing; **schaukeln** *vi* to rock; *(mit Schaukel)* to swing

Schaulustige(r) *mf* gawper *(Brit)*, rubbernecker *(US)*

Schaum *(-(e)s, Schäume) m* foam; *(Seifenschaum)* lather; *(Bierschaum)* froth; **Schaumbad** *nt* bubble bath; **schäumen** *vi* to foam; **Schaumfestiger** *(-s, -) m* styling mousse; **Schaumgummi** *m*

foam (rubber); **Schaumwein** m sparkling wine

Schauplatz m scene;
Schauspiel nt spectacle; (*Theat*)
play; **Schauspieler(in)** m(f)
actor/actress

Scheck (-s, -s) m cheque;
Scheckheft nt chequebook;
Scheckkarte f cheque card

Scheibe (-, -n) f disc; (*von Brot,
Käse etc*) slice; (*Glasscheibe*) pane;
Scheibenbremse f (*Auto*) disc
brake; **Scheibenwaschanlage** f
(*Auto*) windscreen (*Brit*) (*o
windshield* (*US*)) washer unit;
Scheibenwischer (-s, -) m (*Auto*)
windscreen (*Brit*) (*o windshield*
(*US*)) wiper

Scheich (-s, -s) m sheik(h)

Scheide (-, -n) f (*Anat*) vagina

scheiden (*schied, geschieden*) vt
(*trennen*) to separate; (*Ehe*) to
dissolve; **sich ~ lassen** to get a
divorce; **sie hat sich von ihm
~ lassen** she divorced him;
Scheidung f divorce

Schein (-(e)s, -e) m light;
(*Anschein*) appearance; (*Geld*)
(bank)note; **scheinbar** adj
apparent; **scheinen** (*schien,
geschienen*) vi (*Sonne*) to shine;
(*den Anschein haben*) to seem;
Scheinwerfer (-s, -) m floodlight; (*Theat*) spotlight; (*Auto*)
headlight

Scheiß- in zW (*vulg*) damned,
bloody (*Brit*); **Scheiße** (-) f (*vulg*)
shit, crap; **scheißegal** adj (*vulg*)
das ist mir ~ I don't give a damn (*o
toss*); **scheißen** (*schiss, geschissen*)
vi (*vulg*) to shit

Scheitel (-s, -) m parting (*Brit*),
part (*US*)

scheitern vi to fail (*an +dat*)
because of)

Schellfisch m haddock

Schema (-s, -s *o* Schemata) nt

scheme, plan; (*Darstellung*)
diagram

Schenkel (-s, -) m thigh

schenken vt to give; **er hat es
mir geschenkt** he gave it to me
(as a present); **sich** (*dat*) **etw
~ können** (*fam: weglassen*) to skip sth

Scherbe (-, -n) f broken piece,
fragment

Schere (-, -n) f scissors pl; (*groß*)
shears pl; **eine ~** a pair of
scissors/shears

Scherz (-es, -e) m joke

scheu adj shy

scheuen vr **sich ~ vor** (+dat) to be
afraid of, to shrink from ▷ vt to
shun ▷ vi (*Pferd*) to shy

scheuern vt to scrub; **jdm eine
~** (*fam*) to slap sb in the face

Scheune (-, -n) f barn

scheußlich adj dreadful

Schi (-s, -er) m siehe **Ski**

Schicht (-, -en) f layer; (*in
Gesellschaft*) class; (*in Fabrik etc*)
shift

schick adj stylish, chic

schicken vt to send ▷ vr: **sich
~ (sich beeilen)** to hurry up

Schickimicki (-(s), -s) m (*fam*)
trendy

Schicksal (-s, -e) nt fate

Schiebedach nt (*Auto*) sunroof;
schieben (*schob, geschoben*) vt, vi
to push; **die Schuld auf jdn ~** to
put the blame on sb; **Schiebetür**
f sliding door

schied imperf von **scheiden**

Schiedsrichter(in) m(f) referee;
(*Tennis*) umpire; (*Schlichter*)
arbitrator

schief adj crooked; (*Blick*) funny
▷ adv crooked(ly); **schiefgehen**
irr vi (*fam: misslingen*) to go wrong

schielen vi to squint

schien imperf von **scheinen**

Schienbein nt shin

Schiene (-, -n) f rail; (*Med*) splint

schlau adj clever, smart; (raffiniert) crafty, cunning

Schlauch (-(e)s, Schläuche) m hose; (in Reifen) inner tube; **Schlauchboot** nt rubber dinghy

schlecht adj bad; **mir ist ~** I feel sick; **die Milch ist ~** the milk has gone off ▷ adv badly; **es geht ihm ~** he's having a hard time; (gesundheitlich) he's not feeling well; (finanziell) he's pretty hard up; **schlecht machen** vt: **jdn ~** (herabsetzen) to run sb down

schleichen (schlich, geschlichen) vi to creep

Schleier (-s, -) m veil

Schleife (-, -n) f (Inform, Aviat, Elek) loop; (Band) bow

schleifen vt (ziehen, schleppen) to drag ▷ (schliff, geschliffen) vt (schärfen) to grind; (Edelstein) to cut

Schleim (-(e)s, -e) m slime; (Med) mucus; **Schleimer** (-s, -) m (fam) creep; **Schleimhaut** f mucous membrane

schlendern vi to stroll

schleppen vt to drag; (Auto, Schiff) to tow; (tragen) to lug; **Schlepplift** m ski tow

Schleswig-Holstein (-s) nt Schleswig-Holstein

Schleuder (-, -n) f catapult; (für Wäsche) spin-dryer; **schleudern** vt to hurl; (Wäsche) to spin-dry ▷ vi (Auto) to skid; **Schleudersitz** m ejector seat

schlich imperf von **schleichen**

schlicht adj simple, plain

schlichten vt (Streit) to settle

schlief imperf von **schlafen**

schließen (schloss, geschlossen) vt, vi to close, to shut; (beenden) to close; (Freundschaft, Ehe) to enter into; (folgern) to infer (aus from) ▷ vr: **sich ~** to close, to shut; **Schließfach** nt locker

schließlich adv finally; (schließlich doch) after all

schliff imperf von **schleifen**

schlimm adj bad; **schlimmer** adj worse; **schlimmste(r, s)** adj worst; **schlimmstenfalls** adv at (the) worst

Schlinge (-, -n) f loop; (Med) sling

Schlips (-es, -e) m tie

Schlitten (-s, -) m sledge, toboggan; (mit Pferden) sleigh; **Schlittenfahren** (-s) nt tobogganing

Schlittschuh m ice skate; **~ laufen** to ice-skate

Schlitz (-es, -e) m slit; (für Münze) slot; (an Hose) flies pl

schloss imperf von **schließen**

Schloss (-es, Schlösser) nt lock; (Burg) castle

Schlosser(in) m(f) mechanic

Schlucht (-, -en) f gorge, ravine

schluchzen vi to sob

Schluck (-(e)s, -e) m swallow; **Schluckauf** (-s) m hiccups pl; **schlucken** vt, vi to swallow

schludern vi (fam) to do sloppy work

schlug imperf von **schlagen**

Schlüpfer (-s, -) m panties pl

schlürfen vt, vi to slurp

Schluss (-es, Schlüsse) m end; (Schlussfolgerung) conclusion; **am ~** at the end; **mit jdm ~ machen** to finish (o split up) with sb

Schlüssel (-s, -) m (a. fig) key; **Schlüsselbein** nt collarbone; **Schlüsselbund** m bunch of keys; **Schlüsseldienst** m key-cutting service; **Schlüsselloch** nt keyhole

Schlussfolgerung f conclusion; **Schlusslicht** nt tail-light; (fig) tail-ender; **Schlussverkauf** m clearance sale

schmächtig adj frail

schmal adj narrow; (Mensch, Buch etc) slim; (karg) meagre

Schmalz (-es, -e) nt dripping, lard; (fig: Sentimentalitäten) schmaltz

schmatzen vi to eat noisily

schmecken vt, vi to taste (nach of); **es schmeckt ihm** he likes it; **lass es dir ~!** bon appétit

Schmeichelei f flattery; **schmeichelhaft** adj flattering; **schmeicheln** vi: **jdm ~** to flatter sb

schmeißen (schmiss, geschmissen) vt (fam) to chuck, to throw

schmelzen (schmolz, geschmolzen) vt, vi to melt; (Metall, Erz) to smelt; **Schmelzkäse** m cheese spread

Schmerz (-es, -en) m pain; (Trauer) grief; **~en haben** to be in pain; **~en im Rücken haben** to have a pain in one's back; **schmerzen** vt, vi to hurt; **Schmerzensgeld** nt compensation; **schmerzhaft**, **schmerzlich** adj painful; **schmerzlos** adj painless; **Schmerzmittel** nt painkiller; **schmerzstillend** adj painkilling; **Schmerztablette** f painkiller

Schmetterling m butterfly

Schmied(in) (-(e)s, -e) m(f) blacksmith; **schmieden** vt to forge; (Pläne) to make

schmieren vt to smear; (ölen) to lubricate, to grease; (bestechen) to bribe ▷ vt, vi (unsauber schreiben) to scrawl; **Schmiergeld** nt (fam) bribe; **schmierig** adj greasy; **Schmierseife** f soft soap

Schminke (-, -n) f make-up; **schminken** vr: **sich ~** to put one's make-up on

schmiss imperf von **schmeißen**

schmollen vi to sulk; **schmollend** adj sulky

schmolz imperf von **schmelzen**

Schmuck (-(e)s, -e) m jewellery (Brit), jewelry (US); (Verzierung) decoration; **schmücken** vt to decorate

schmuggeln vt, vi to smuggle

schmunzeln vi to smile

schmusen vi to (kiss and) cuddle

Schmutz (-es) m dirt, filth; **schmutzig** adj dirty

Schnabel (-s, Schnäbel) m beak, bill; (Ausguss) spout

Schnake (-, -n) f mosquito

Schnalle (-, -n) f buckle

Schnäppchen nt (fam) bargain; **schnappen** vt (fangen) to catch ▷ vi: **nach Luft ~** to gasp for breath; **Schnappschuss** m (Foto) snap(shot)

Schnaps (-es, Schnäpse) m schnapps

schnarchen vi to snore

schnaufen vi to puff, to pant

Schnauzbart m moustache; **Schnauze** (-, -n) f snout, muzzle; (Ausguss) spout; (fam: Mund) trap; **die ~ voll haben** to have had enough

schnäuzen vr: **sich ~** to blow one's nose

Schnecke (-, -n) f snail; **Schneckenhaus** nt snail's shell

Schnee (-s) m snow; **Schneeball** m snowball; **Schneebob** m snowmobile; **Schneebrille** f snow goggles pl; **Schneeflocke** f snowflake; **Schneegestöber** (-s, -) nt snow flurry; **Schneeglöckchen** nt snowdrop; **Schneegrenze** f snowline; **Schneekanone** f snow thrower; **Schneekette** f (Auto) snow chain; **Schneemann** m snowman; **Schneepflug** m snowplough; **Schneeregen** m sleet; **Schneeschmelze** f thaw; **Schneesturm** m snowstorm, blizzard; **Schneetreiben** nt light blizzards pl; **Schneewehe** f snowdrift

Schneide (-, -n) f edge; (Klinge)
blade; **schneiden** (schnitt,
geschnitten) vt to cut; **sich** (dat) **die
Haare ~ lassen** to have one's hair
cut ▷ vr: **sich ~** to cut oneself;
Schneider(in) (-s, -) m(f) tailor;
(für Damenmode) dressmaker;
Schneiderin f dressmaker;
Schneidezahn m incisor
schneien vi impers to snow
schnell adj quick, fast ▷ adv
quickly, fast; **mach ~!** hurry up;
Schnelldienst m express service;
Schnellhefter m loose-leaf
binder; **Schnellimbiss** m snack
bar; **Schnellkochtopf** m
pressure cooker;
Schnellreinigung f express dry
cleaning; (Geschäft) express (dry)
cleaner's; **Schnellstraße** f
expressway; **Schnellzug** m fast
train
schneuzen vr siehe **schnäuzen**
schnitt imperf von **schneiden**
Schnitt (-(e)s, -e) m cut;
(Schnittpunkt) intersection;
(Querschnitt) (cross) section;
(Durchschnitt) average; (eines
Kleides) style; **Schnitte** (-, -n) f
slice; (belegt) sandwich;
Schnittkäse m cheese slices pl;
Schnittlauch m chives pl;
Schnittmuster m pattern;
Schnittstelle f (Inform, fig)
interface; **Schnittwunde** f cut,
gash
Schnitzel (-s, -) nt (Papier) scrap;
(Gastr) escalope
schnitzen vt to carve
Schnorchel (-s, -) m snorkel;
schnorcheln vi to go snorkelling,
to snorkel
schnüffeln vi to sniff
Schnuller (-s, -) m dummy (Brit),
pacifier (US)
Schnulze (-, -n) f (Film, Roman)
weepie

Schnupfen (-s, -) m cold
schnuppern vi to sniff
Schnur (-, Schnüre) f string, cord;
(Elek) lead; **schnurlos** adj
(Telefon) cordless
Schnurrbart m moustache
schnurren vi to purr
Schnürsenkel (-s, -) m shoelace
schob imperf von **schieben**
Schock (-(e)s, -e) m shock; **unter
~ stehen** to be in a state of shock;
schockieren vt to shock
Schokolade f chocolate;
Schokoriegel m chocolate bar
Scholle (-, -n) f (Fisch) plaice; (Eis)
ice floe

 SCHLÜSSELWORT

schon adv 1 (bereits) already; **er ist
schon da** he's there already, he's
already there; **ist er schon da?** is
he there yet?; **warst du schon
einmal da?** have you ever been
there?; **ich war schon einmal da**
I've been there before; **das war
schon immer so** that has always
been the case; **schon oft** often;
hast du schon gehört? have you
heard?
2 (bestimmt) all right; **du wirst
schon sehen** you'll see (all right);
das wird schon noch gut that'll
be OK
3 (bloß) just; **allein schon das
Gefühl ...** just the very feeling ...;
schon der Gedanke the very
thought; **wenn ich das schon
höre** I only have to hear that
4 (einschränkend) **ja schon, aber ...**
yes (well), but ...
5 **schon möglich** possible; **schon
gut!** OK!; **du weißt schon** you
know; **komm schon!** come on!

schön adj beautiful; (nett) nice;
(Frau) beautiful, pretty; (Mann)

beautiful, handsome; (*Wetter*) fine; **~e Grüße** best wishes; **~es Wochenende** have a nice weekend

schonen vt (*pfleglich behandeln*) to look after ▷ vr: **sich ~** to take it easy

Schönheit f beauty

Schonkost f light diet

schöpfen vt to scoop; (*mit Kelle*) to ladle; **Schöpfkelle** f, **Schöpflöffel** m ladle

Schöpfung f creation

Schoppen (-s, -) m glass (of wine)

Schorf (-(e)s, -e) m scab

Schorle (-, -n) f spritzer

Schornstein m chimney; **Schornsteinfeger(in)** (-s, -) m(f) chimney sweep

schoss *imperf von* **schießen**

Schoß (-es, Schöße) m lap

Schotte (-n, -n) m Scot, Scotsman; **Schottin** f Scot, Scotswoman; **schottisch** adj Scottish, Scots; **Schottland** nt Scotland

schräg adj slanting; (*Dach*) sloping; (*Linie*) diagonal; (*fam: unkonventionell*) wacky

Schrank (-(e)s, Schränke) m cupboard; (*Kleiderschrank*) wardrobe (Brit), closet (US)

Schranke (-, -n) f barrier

Schrankwand f wall unit

Schraube (-, -n) f screw; **schrauben** vt to screw; **Schraubendreher** (-s, -) m screwdriver; **Schraubenschlüssel** m spanner; **Schraubenzieher** (-s, -) m screwdriver; **Schraubverschluss** m screw top, screw cap

Schreck (-(e)s, -e) m, **Schrecken** (-s, -) m terror; (*Angst*) fright; **jdm einen ~ einjagen** to give sb a fright; **schreckhaft** adj jumpy; **schrecklich** adj terrible, dreadful

Schrei (-(e)s, -e) m scream; (*Ruf*) shout

Schreibblock m writing pad; **schreiben** (schrieb, geschrieben) vt, vi to write; (*buchstabieren*) to spell; **wie schreibt man ...?** how do you spell ...?; **Schreiben** (-s, -) nt writing; (*Brief*) letter; **Schreibfehler** m spelling mistake; **schreibgeschützt** adj (*Diskette*) write-protected; **Schreibtisch** m desk; **Schreibwaren** pl stationery sing; **Schreibwarenladen** m stationer's

schreien (schrie, geschrie(e)n) vt, vi to scream; (*rufen*) to shout

Schreiner(in) m(f) joiner; **Schreinerei** f joiner's workshop

schrie *imperf von* **schreien**

schrieb *imperf von* **schreiben**

Schrift (-, -en) f writing; (*Handschrift*) handwriting; (*Schriftart*) typeface; (*Schrifttyp*) font; **schriftlich** adj written ▷ adv in writing; **würden Sie uns das bitte ~ geben?** could we have that in writing, please?; **Schriftsteller(in)** (-s, -) m(f) writer

Schritt (-(e)s, -e) m step; **~ für ~** step by step; **~e gegen etw unternehmen** to take steps against sth; **Schrittgeschwindigkeit** f walking speed; **Schrittmacher** m (*Med*) pacemaker

Schrott (-(e)s, -e) m scrap metal; (*fig*) rubbish

schrubben vi, vt to scrub; **Schrubber** (-s, -) m scrubbing brush

schrumpfen vi to shrink

Schubkarren (-s, -) m wheelbarrow; **Schublade** f drawer

schubsen vt to shove, to push

schüchtern adj shy

schuf *imperf von* **schaffen**

Schuh (-(e)s, -e) m shoe;
Schuhcreme f shoe polish;
Schuhgeschäft nt shoe shop;
Schuhgröße f shoe size;
Schuhlöffel m shoehorn
Schulabschluss m school-
leaving qualification
schuld adj: **wer ist ~ daran?**
whose fault is it?; **er ist ~** it's his
fault, he's to blame; **Schuld** (-) f
guilt; (Verschulden) fault; **~ haben**
to be to blame (an +dat for); **er hat
~** it's his fault; **sie gibt mir die
~ an dem Unfall** she blames me
for the accident; **schulden** vt to
owe (jdm etw sb sth); **Schulden** pl
debts pl; **~ haben** to be in debt;
~ machen to run up debts; **seine
~ bezahlen** to pay off one's debts;
schuldig adj guilty (an +dat of);
(gebührend) due; **jdm etw ~ sein** to
owe sb sth
Schule (-, -n) f school; **in der ~** at
school; **in die ~ gehen** to go to
school; **Schüler(in)** (-s, -) m(f)
(jüngerer) pupil; (älterer) student;
Schüleraustausch m school
exchange; **Schulfach** nt subject;
Schulferien pl school holidays pl
(Brit) (o vacation (US)); **schulfrei**
adj: **morgen ist ~** there's no school
tomorrow; **Schulfreund(in)** m(f)
schoolmate; **Schuljahr** nt school
year; **Schulkenntnisse** pl: **~ in
Französisch** school(-level) French;
Schulklasse f class; **Schul-
leiter(in)** m(f) headmaster/
headmistress (Brit), principal (US)
Schulter (-, -n) f shoulder;
Schulterblatt nt shoulder blade
Schulung f training;
(Veranstaltung) training course
schummeln vi (fam) to cheat
Schuppe (-, -n) f (von Fisch) scale;
schuppen vt to scale ▷ vr: **sich
~** to peel; **Schuppen** pl (im Haar)
dandruff sing

Schürfwunde f graze
Schürze (-, -n) f apron
Schuss (-es, Schüsse) m shot; **mit
einem ~ Wodka** with a dash of
vodka
Schüssel (-, -n) f bowl
Schuster(in) (-s, -) m(f)
shoemaker
Schutt (-(e)s) m rubble
Schüttelfrost m shivering fit;
schütteln vt to shake ▷ vr: **sich
~** to shake
schütten vt to pour; (Zucker, Kies
etc) to tip ▷ vi impers to pour
(down)
Schutz (-es) m protection (gegen,
vor against, from); (Unterschlupf)
shelter; **jdn in ~ nehmen** to stand
up for sb; **Schutzblech** nt
mudguard; **Schutzbrief** m travel
insurance document for drivers;
Schutzbrille f (safety) goggles pl
Schütze (-n, -n) m (beim Fußball)
scorer; (Astr) Sagittarius
schützen vt: **jdn gegen/vor etw
~** to protect sb against/from sth;
Schutzimpfung f inoculation,
vaccination
schwach adj weak; **~e Augen**
poor eyesight sing; **Schwäche**
(-, -n) f weakness; **Schwachstelle**
f weak point; **Schwachstrom** m
low-voltage current
Schwager (-s, Schwäger) m
brother-in-law; **Schwägerin** f
sister-in-law
Schwalbe (-, -n) f swallow; (beim
Fußball) dive
schwamm imperf von
schwimmen
Schwamm (-(e)s, Schwämme) m
sponge; **~ drüber!** (fam) let's forget
it!
Schwan (-(e)s,
Schwäne) m swan
schwanger adj pregnant; **im
vierten Monat ~ sein** to be four

months pregnant; **Schwangerschaft** f pregnancy; **Schwangerschaftsabbruch** m abortion; **Schwangerschaftstest** m pregnancy test

schwanken vi to sway; (*Preise, Zahlen*) to fluctuate; (*zögern*) to hesitate; (*taumeln*) to stagger; **ich schwanke zwischen A und B** I can't decide between A and B

Schwanz (-es, Schwänze) m tail; (*vulg: Penis*) cock

Schwarm (-(e)s, Schwärme) m swarm; (*fam: angehimmelte Person*) heartthrob; **schwärmen** vi to swarm; ~ **für** to be mad about

schwarz adj black; **mir wurde ~ vor Augen** everything went black; **Schwarzarbeit** f illicit work; **Schwarzbrot** nt black bread; **schwarz|fahren** irr vi to travel without a ticket; (*ohne Führerschein*) to drive without a licence; **Schwarzfahrer(in)** m(f) fare-dodger; **Schwarzmarkt** m black market; **schwarz|sehen** irr vi (*fam: pessimistisch sein*) to be pessimistic (*für* about); **Schwarzwald** m Black Forest; **schwarzweiß** adj black and white; **Schwarzwurzel** f salsify

schwatzen vi to chatter; **Schwätzer(in)** (-s, -) m(f) chatterbox; (*Schwafler*) gasbag; (*Klatschmaul*) gossip

Schwebebahn f suspension railway; **schweben** vi to float; (*hoch*) to soar

Schwede (-n, -n) m Swede; **Schweden** (-s) nt Sweden; **Schwedin** f Swede; **schwedisch** adj Swedish; **Schwedisch** nt Swedish

Schwefel (-s) m sulphur

schweigen (schwieg, geschwiegen) vi to be silent; (*nicht mehr reden*) to

stop talking; **Schweigen** (-s) nt silence; **Schweigepflicht** f duty of confidentiality; **die ärztliche ~** medical confidentiality

Schwein (-(e)s, -e) nt pig; (*fam: Glück*) luck; (*fam: gemeiner Mensch*) swine; **Schweinebraten** m roast pork; **Schweinefleisch** nt pork; **Schweinerei** f mess; (*Gemeinheit*) dirty trick

Schweiß (-es) m sweat

schweißen vt, vi to weld

Schweiz (-) f: **die ~** Switzerland; **Schweizer(in)** (-s, -) m(f) Swiss; **Schweizerdeutsch** nt Swiss German; **schweizerisch** adj Swiss

Schwelle (-, -n) f doorstep; (*a. fig*) threshold

schwellen vi to swell (up); **Schwellung** f swelling

schwer adj heavy; (*schwierig*) difficult, hard; (*schlimm*) serious, bad; **er ist ~ zu verstehen** it's difficult to understand what he's saying ▷ adv (*sehr*) really; (*verletzt etc*) seriously, badly; **etw ~ nehmen** to take sth hard; **Schwerbehinderte(r)** mf severely disabled person; **schwer|fallen** irr vi (*Schwierigkeiten bereiten*) **jdm ~** to be difficult for sb; **schwerhörig** adj hard of hearing

Schwert (-(e)s, -er) nt sword; **Schwertlilie** f iris

Schwester (-, -n) f sister; (*Med*) nurse

schwieg imperf von **schweigen**

Schwiegereltern pl parents-in-law pl; **Schwiegermutter** f mother-in-law; **Schwiegersohn** m son-in-law; **Schwiegertochter** f daughter-in-law; **Schwiegervater** m father-in-law

schwierig adj difficult, hard; **Schwierigkeit** f difficulty; **in ~en kommen** to get into trouble; **jdm**

~en machen to make things difficult for sb
Schwimmbad nt swimming pool; **Schwimmbecken** nt swimming pool; **schwimmen** (schwamm, geschwommen) vi to swim; (treiben) to float; (fig: unsicher sein) to be all at sea; **Schwimmer(in)** m(f) swimmer; **Schwimmflosse** f flipper; **Schwimmflügel** m water wing; **Schwimmreifen** m rubber ring; **Schwimmweste** f life jacket
Schwindel (-s) m dizziness; (Anfall) dizzy spell; (Betrug) swindle; **schwindelfrei** adj: **nicht ~ sein** to suffer from vertigo; **~ sein** to have a head for heights; **schwindlig** adj dizzy; **mir ist ~ I** feel dizzy
Schwips m: **einen ~ haben** to be tipsy
schwitzen vi to sweat
schwoll imperf von **schwellen**
schwor imperf von **schwören**
schwören (schwor, geschworen) vt, vi to swear; **einen Eid ~** to take an oath
schwul adj gay
schwül adj close
Schwung (-(e)s, Schwünge) m swing; (Triebkraft) momentum; (fig: Energie) energy; (fam: Menge) batch; **in ~ kommen** to get going
Schwur (-s, Schwüre) m oath
scrollen vi (Inform) to scroll
sechs num six; **Sechs** (-, -en) f six; (Schulnote) = F; **Sechserpack** m sixpack; **sechshundert** num six hundred; **sechsmal** adv six times; **sechste(r, s)** adj sixth; siehe auch **dritte**; **Sechstel** (-s, -) nt sixth; **sechzehn** num sixteen; **sechzehnte(r, s)** adj sixteenth; siehe auch **dritte**; **sechzig** num sixty; **in den ~er Jahren** in the

sixties; **sechzigste(r, s)** adj sixtieth
Secondhandladen m secondhand shop
See (-, -n) f sea: **an der ~** by the sea ▷ (-s, -n) m lake; **am ~** by the lake; **Seegang** m waves; **hoher/schwerer/leichter ~** rough/heavy/calm seas pl; **Seehund** m seal; **Seeigel** m sea urchin; **seekrank** adj seasick
Seele (-, -n) f soul
Seeleute pl seamen pl, sailors pl
seelisch adj mental, psychological
Seelöwe m sea lion; **Seemann** m sailor, seaman; **Seemeile** f nautical mile; **Seemöwe** f seagull; **Seenot** f distress (at sea); **Seepferdchen** nt sea horse; **Seerose** f water lily; **Seestern** m starfish; **Seezunge** f sole
Segel (-s, -) nt sail; **Segelboot** nt yacht; **Segelfliegen** (-s) nt gliding; **Segelflugzeug** nt glider; **segeln** vt, vi to sail; **Segelschiff** nt sailing ship
sehbehindert adj partially sighted
sehen (sah, gesehen) vt, vi to see; (in bestimmte Richtung) to look; **gut/schlecht ~** to have good/bad eyesight; **auf die Uhr ~** to look at one's watch; **kann ich das mal ~?** can I have a look at it?; **wir ~ uns morgen!** see you tomorrow; **ich kenne sie nur vom Sehen** I only know her by sight; **Sehenswürdigkeiten** pl sights pl
Sehne (-, -n) f tendon; (an Bogen) string
sehnen vr: **sich ~** to long (nach for)
Sehnenscheidenentzündung f (Med) tendovaginitis;

Sehnenzerrung f (Med) pulled tendon
Sehnsucht f longing; **sehnsüchtig** adj longing
sehr adv (vor Adjektiv, Adverb) very; (mit Verben) a lot, very much; **zu ~** too much
seicht adj shallow
Seide (-, -n) f silk
Seife (-, -n) f soap; **Seifenoper** f soap (opera); **Seifenschale** f soap dish
Seil (-(e)s, -e) nt rope; (Kabel) cable; **Seilbahn** f cable railway

○ SCHLÜSSELWORT

sein¹ (pt war, pp gewesen) vi 1to be; **ich bin** I am; **du bist** you are; **er/sie/es ist** he/she/it is; **wir sind/ihr seid/sie sind** we/you/they are; **wir waren** we were; **wir sind gewesen** we have been
2**seien Sie nicht böse** don't be angry; **sei so gut und ...** be so kind as to ...; **das wäre gut** that would o that'd be a good thing; **wenn ich Sie wäre** if I were o was you; **das wär's** that's all, that's it; **morgen bin ich in Rom** tomorrow I'll o I will o I shall be in Rome; **waren Sie mal in Rom?** have you ever been to Rome?
3**wie ist das zu verstehen?** how is that to be understood?; **er ist nicht zu ersetzen** he cannot be replaced; **mit ihr ist nicht zu reden** you can't talk to her
4**mir ist kalt** I'm cold; **was ist?** what's the matter?, what is it?; **ist was?** is something the matter?; **es sei denn, dass ...** unless ...; **wie dem auch sei** be that as it may; **wie wäre es mit ...?** how o what about ...?; **lass das sein!** stop that!

sein² pron possessive von **er**; (adjektivisch) his ▷ pron possessive von **es**; (adjektivisch) its; (adjektivisch, männlich) his; (weiblich) her; (sächlich) its; **das ist ~e Tasche** that's his bag; **jeder hat ~e Sorgen** everyone has their problems; **seine(r, s)** pron possessiv von **er**; (substantivisch) his ▷ pron possessiv von **es**; (substantivisch) its; (substantivisch, männlich) his; (weiblich) hers; **das ist ~r/~/~s** that's his/hers; **seiner** gen von **er**; of him ▷ pron adv von **es**; of it; **seinetwegen** adv (wegen ihm) because of him; (ihm zuliebe) for his sake; (um ihn) about him; (von ihm aus) as far as he is concerned
seit conj (bei Zeitpunkt) since; (bei Zeitraum) for; **er ist ~ Montag hier** he's been here since Monday; **er ist ~ einer Woche hier** he's been here for a week; **~ langem** for a long time; **seitdem** adv, conj since
Seite (-, -n) f side; (in Buch) page; **zur ~ gehen** to step aside; **Seitenairbag** m side-impact airbag; **Seitenaufprallschutz** m (Auto) side-impact protection; **Seitensprung** m affair; **Seitenstechen** (-s) nt: **~ haben/bekommen** to have/get a stitch; **Seitenstraße** f side street; **Seitenstreifen** m hard shoulder (Brit), shoulder (US); **Seitenwind** m crosswind
seither adv since (then)
seitlich adj side
Sekretär(in) m(f) secretary; **Sekretariat** (-s, -e) nt secretary's office
Sekt (-(e)s, -e) m sparkling wine (similar to champagne)
Sekte (-, -n) f sect

Sekunde | 188

Sekunde (-, -n) f second; **Sekundenkleber** (-s, -) m superglue; **Sekundenschnelle** f: **es geschah alles in ~** it was all over in a matter of seconds

⊙ SCHLÜSSELWORT

selbst pron 1 ich/er/wir **selbst** I myself/he himself/we ourselves; **sie ist die Tugend selbst** she's virtue itself; **er braut sein Bier selbst** he brews his own beer; **wie geht's? — gut, und selbst?** how are things? — fine, and yourself? 2 (ohne Hilfe) alone, on my/his/one's etc own; **von selbst** by itself; **er kam von selbst** he came of his own accord; **selbst gemacht** home-made
▷ adv even; **selbst wenn** even if; **selbst Gott** even God (himself)

selbständig adj siehe **selbstständig**
Selbstauslöser (-s, -) m (Foto) self-timer; **Selbstbedienung** f self-service; **Selbstbefriedigung** f masturbation; **Selbstbeherrschung** f self-control; **Selbstbeteiligung** f (einer Versicherung) excess; **selbstbewusst** adj (self-)confident; **Selbstbräuner** (-s, -) m self-tanning lotion; **selbstgemacht** adj self-made; **selbstklebend** adj self-adhesive; **Selbstlaut** m vowel; **Selbstmord** m suicide; **Selbstmordattentat** nt suicide bombing; **Selbstmordattentäter(in)** m(f) suicide bomber; **selbstsicher** adj self-assured; **selbstständig** adj independent; (arbeitend) self-employed; **Selbstverpflegung** f self-catering; **selbstverständlich** adj obvious;

ich halte das für ~ I take that for granted ▷ adv naturally; **Selbstvertrauen** nt self-confidence

Sellerie (-s, -(s)) m (-, -n) f (Knollensellerie) celeriac; (Stangensellerie) celery

selten adj rare ▷ adv seldom, rarely
seltsam adj strange; **~ schmecken/riechen** to taste/smell strange
Semester (-s, -) nt semester; **Semesterferien** pl vacation sing
Semikolon (-s, Semikola) nt semicolon
Seminar (-s, -e) nt seminar
Semmel (-, -n) f roll; **Semmelbrösel** pl breadcrumbs
Senat (-(e)s, -e) m senate
senden (sandte, gesandt) vt to send ▷ vt, vi (Radio, TV) to broadcast; **Sender** (-s, -) m (TV) channel; (Radio) station; (Anlage) transmitter; **Sendung** f (Radio, TV) broadcasting; (Programm) programme
Senf (-(e)s, -e) m mustard
Senior(in) m(f) senior citizen; **Seniorenpass** m senior citizen's travel pass
senken vt to lower ▷ vr: **sich ~** to sink
senkrecht adj vertical
Sensation (-, -en) f sensation
sensibel adj sensitive
sentimental adj sentimental
separat adj separate
September (-(s), -) m September; siehe auch **Juni**
Serbien (-s) nt Serbia
Serie f series sing
seriös adj (ernsthaft) serious; (anständig) respectable
Serpentine f hairpin (bend)
Serum (-s, Seren) nt serum
Server (-s, -) m (Inform) server

Service (-(s), -s) nt (Geschirr)
service ▷ (-s) m service
servieren vt, vi to serve
Serviette f napkin, serviette
Servolenkung f (Auto) power
steering
Sesam (-s, -s) m sesame seeds pl
Sessel (-s, -) m armchair;
Sessellift m chairlift
Set (-s, -s) m o nt set; (Tischset)
tablemat
setzen vt to put; (Baum etc) to
plant; (Segel) to set ▷ vr: **sich ~** to
settle; (hinsetzen) to sit down; **~ Sie
sich doch** please sit down
Seuche (-, -n) f epidemic
seufzen vt, vi to sigh
Sex (-(es)) m sex; **Sexismus** m
sexism; **sexistisch** adj sexist;
Sextourismus m sex tourism;
Sexualität f sexuality; **sexuell**
adj sexual
Seychellen pl Seychelles pl
sfr abk = **Schweizer Franken** Swiss
franc(s)
Shampoo (-s, -s) nt shampoo
Shareware (-, -s) f (Inform)
shareware
Shorts f shorts pl
Shuttlebus m shuttle bus

⭕ SCHLÜSSELWORT

sich pron 1 (akk) **er/sie/es … sich**
he/she/it … himself/herself/itself;
sie pl/**man … sich** they/one …
themselves/oneself; **Sie … sich**
you … yourself/yourselves pl; **sich
wiederholen** to repeat
oneself/itself
2 (dat) **er/sie/es … sich** he/she/it
… to himself/herself/itself; **sie**
pl/**man … sich** they/one … to
themselves/oneself; **Sie … sich**
you … to yourself/yourselves pl;
**sie hat sich einen Pullover
gekauft** she bought herself a

jumper; **sich die Haare waschen**
to wash one's hair
3 (mit Präposition) **haben Sie Ihren
Ausweis bei sich?** do you have
your pass on you?; **er hat nichts
bei sich** he's got nothing on him;
sie bleiben gern unter sich they
keep themselves to themselves
4 (einander) each other, one
another; **sie bekämpfen sich** they
fight each other o one another
5 **dieses Auto fährt sich gut** this
car drives well; **hier sitzt es sich
gut** it's good to sit here

sicher adj safe (vor +dat from);
(gewiss) certain (gen of);
(zuverlässig) reliable; (selbstsicher)
confident; **aber ~!** of course, sure;
Sicherheit f safety; (Aufgabe von
Sicherheitsbeamten) (Fin) security;
(Gewissheit) certainty;
(Selbstsicherheit) confidence; **mit
~** definitely; **Sicherheitsabstand**
m safe distance; **Sicherheitsgurt**
m seat belt; **sicherheitshalber**
adv just to be on the safe side;
Sicherheitsnadel f safety pin;
Sicherheitsvorkehrung f safety
precaution; **sicherlich** adv
certainly; (wahrscheinlich) probably
sichern vt to secure (gegen
against); (schützen) to protect;
(Daten) to back up; **Sicherung** f
(Sichern) securing; (Vorrichtung)
safety device; (an Waffen) safety
catch; (Elek) fuse; (Inform) backup;
die ~ ist durchgebrannt the fuse
has blown
Sicht (-) f sight; (Aussicht) view;
sichtbar adj visible; **sichtlich**
adj evident, obvious;
Sichtverhältnisse pl visibility
sing; **Sichtweite** f: **in/außer
~** within/out of sight
sie pron (3. Person sing) she; (3.
Person pl) they; (akk von sing) her;

(akk von pl) them; (für eine Sache) it; **da ist ~ ja** there she is; **da sind ~ ja** there they are; **ich kenne ~ (Frau)** I know her; (mehrere Personen) I know them; **~ lag gerade noch hier** (meine Jacke, Uhr) it was here just a minute ago; **ich hab ~ gefunden** (meine Jacke, Uhr) I've found it; **hast du meine Brille/Hose gesehen? — ich kann ~ nirgends finden** have you seen my glasses/trousers? — I can't find them anywhere

Sie pron (Höflichkeitsform, Nom und Akk) you

Sieb (-(e)s, -e) nt sieve; (Teesieb) strainer

sieben num seven; **siebenhundert** num seven hundred; **siebenmal** adv seven times; **siebte(r, s)** adj seventh; siehe auch **dritte**; **Siebtel** (-s, -) nt seventh; **siebzehn** num seventeen; **siebzehnte(r, s)** adj seventeenth; siehe auch **dritte**; **siebzig** num seventy; **in den ~er Jahren** in the seventies; **siebzigste(r, s)** adj seventieth

Siedlung (-, -en) f (Wohngebiet) housing estate (Brit) (o development (US))

Sieg (-(e)s, -e) m victory; **siegen** vi to win; **Sieger(in)** (-s, -) m(f) winner; **Siegerehrung** f presentation ceremony

siehe imper see

siezen vt to address as "Sie"

Signal (-s, -e) nt signal

Silbe (-, -n) f syllable

Silber (-s) nt silver; **Silberhochzeit** f silver wedding; **Silbermedaille** f silver medal

Silikon (-s, -e) nt silicone

Silvester (-s, -) nt, **Silvesterabend** m New Year's Eve, Hogmanay (Scot)

Simbabwe (-s) nt Zimbabwe

SIM-Karte f SIM card

simpel adj simple

simultan adj simultaneous

simsen vt, vi (fam) to text

Sinfonie (-, -n) f symphony; **Sinfonieorchester** nt symphony orchestra

Singapur (-s) nt Singapore

singen (sang, gesungen) vt, vi to sing; **richtig/falsch ~** to sing in tune/out of tune

Single (-, -s) f (CD) single ▷ (-s, -s) m (Mensch) single

Singular m singular

sinken (sank, gesunken) vi to sink; (Preise etc) to fall, to go down

Sinn (-(e)s, -e) m (Denken) mind; (Wahrnehmung) sense; (Bedeutung) sense, meaning; **~ machen** to make sense; **das hat keinen ~** it's no use; **sinnlich** adj sensuous; (erotisch) sensual; (Wahrnehmung) sensory; **sinnlos** adj (unsinnig) stupid; (Verhalten) senseless; (zwecklos) pointless; (bedeutungslos) meaningless; **sinnvoll** adj meaningful; (vernünftig) sensible

Sirup (-s, -e) m syrup

Sitte (-, -n) f custom

Situation f situation

Sitz (-es, -e) m seat; **sitzen** (saß, gesessen) vi to sit; (Bemerkung, Schlag) to strike home; (Gelerntes) to have sunk in; **der Rock sitzt**

gut the skirt is a good fit;
~ bleiben (*Schule*) to have to repeat
a year; **Sitzgelegenheit** f place to
sit down; **Sitzplatz** m seat;
Sitzung f meeting

Sizilien (-s) nt Sicily

Skandal (-s, -e) m scandal

Skandinavien (-s) nt
Scandinavia

Skateboard (-s, -s) nt
skateboard; **skateboarden** vi to
skateboard

Skelett (-s, -e) nt skeleton

skeptisch adj sceptical

Ski (-s, -er) m ski; **~ laufen** (o
fahren) to ski; **Skianzug** m ski
suit; **Skibrille** f ski goggles pl;
Skifahren (-s) nt skiing; **Skigebiet**
(-s, -e) nt skiing area; **Skihose** f
skiing trousers pl; **Skikurs** m
skiing course; **Skilanglauf** m
cross-country skiing; **Skiläufer(in)**
m(f) skier; **Skilehrer(in)** m(f) ski
instructor; **Skilift** m ski-lift

Skinhead (-s, -s) m skinhead

Skipiste f ski run; **Skischanze**
(-, -n) f ski jump; **Skischuh** m
ski boot; **Skischule** f ski school;
Skispringen (-s, -n) nt ski jumping;
Skistiefel (-s, -) m ski boot;
Skistock m ski pole; **Skiträger** m
ski rack; **Skiurlaub** m skiing
holiday (Brit) o vacation (US)

Skizze (-, -n) f sketch

Skonto (-s, -s) m o nt discount

Skorpion (-s, -e) m (Zool)
scorpion; (Astr) Scorpio

Skulptur (-, -en) f sculpture

S-Kurve f double bend

Slalom (-s, -s) m slalom

Slip (-s, -s) m (pair of) briefs pl;
Slipeinlage f panty liner

Slowakei (-) f Slovakia;
slowakisch adj Slovakian;
S~ Republik f Slovak Republic;
Slowakisch nt Slovakian

Slowenien (-s) nt Slovenia;

slowenisch adj Slovenian;
Slowenisch nt Slovenian

Smiley (-s, -s) m smiley

Smog (-s) m smog; **Smogalarm**
m smog alert

Smoking (-s, -s) m dinner jacket
(Brit), tuxedo (US)

SMS nt abk = **Short Message
Service** ▷ f (Nachricht) text
message; **ich schicke dir eine ~** I'll
text you, I'll send you a text

Snowboard (-s, -s) nt snowboard; **snowboarden** vi to
snowboard; **Snowboardfahren**
(-s) nt snowboarding;
Snowboardfahrer(in) m(f)
snowboarder

SCHLÜSSELWORT

so adv 1 (so sehr) so; **so groß/schön**
etc so big/nice etc; **so groß/schön
wie ...** as big/nice as ...; **so viel
(wie)** as much as; **rede nicht so
viel** don't talk so much; **so weit
sein** to be ready; **so weit wie** o **als
möglich** as far as possible; **ich bin
so weit zufrieden** by and large I'm
quite satisfied; **so wenig (wie)** as
little (as); **das hat ihn so
geärgert, dass ...** that annoyed
him so much that ...; **so einer wie
ich** somebody like me; **na so was!**
well, well!

2 (auf diese Weise) like this; **mach
es nicht so** don't do it like that; **so
oder so** in one way or the other;
und so weiter and so on; **... oder
so was** ... or something like that;
das ist gut so that's fine

3 (fam) (umsonst) **ich habe es so
bekommen** I got it for nothing
▷ konj: **sodass** so that; **so wie es
jetzt ist** as things are at the
moment
▷ excl: **so?** really?; **so, das wär's**
so, that's it then

s. o. *abk* = **siehe oben** see above

sobald *conj* as soon as

Socke (-, -n) *f* sock

Sodbrennen (-s) *nt* heartburn

Sofa (-s, -s) *nt* sofa

sofern *conj* if, provided (that)

soff *imperf von* **saufen**

sofort *adv* immediately, at once; **Sofortbildkamera** *f* instant camera

Softeis *nt* soft ice-cream

Software (-, -s) *f* software

sog *imperf von* **saugen**

sogar *adv* even; **kalt, ~ sehr kalt** cold, in fact very cold

sogenannt *adj* so-called

Sohle (-, -n) *f* sole

Sohn (-(e)s, Söhne) *m* son

Soja (-, Sojen) *f* soya; **Sojasprossen** *pl* bean sprouts *pl*

solang(e) *conj* as long as

Solarium *nt* solarium

Solarzelle *f* solar cell

solche(r, s) *pron* such; **eine ~ Frau, solch eine Frau** such a woman, a woman like that; **~ Sachen** things like that, such things; **ich habe ~ Kopfschmerzen** I've got such a headache; **ich habe ~n Hunger** I'm so hungry

Soldat(in) (-en, -en) *m(f)* soldier

solidarisch *adj* showing solidarity; **sich ~ erklären mit** to declare one's solidarity with

solid(e) *adj* solid; (Leben, Mensch) respectable

Soll (-(s), -(s)) *nt* (Fin) debit; (Arbeitsmenge) quota, target

⭕ **SCHLÜSSELWORT**

sollen (pt **sollte**, pp **gesollt** o (als Hilfsverb) **sollen**) Hilfsverb **1** (Pflicht, Befehl) to be supposed to; **du hättest nicht gehen sollen** you shouldn't have gone, you oughtn't to have gone; **soll ich?** shall I?; **soll**

ich dir helfen? shall I help you?; **sag ihm, er soll warten** tell him he's to wait; **was soll ich machen?** what should I do?

2 (Vermutung) **sie soll verheiratet sein** she's said to be married; **was soll das heißen?** what's that supposed to mean?; **man sollte glauben, dass ...** you would think that ...; **sollte das passieren, ...** if that should happen ...

▷ *vt, vi*: **was soll das?** what's all this?; **das sollst du nicht** you shouldn't do that; **was soll's?** what the hell!

Solo (-s, -) *nt* solo

Sommer (-s, -) *m* summer; **Sommerfahrplan** *m* summer timetable; **Sommerferien** *pl* summer holidays *pl* (Brit) (o vacation sing (US)); **sommerlich** *adj* summery; (Sommer-) summer; **Sommerreifen** *m* normal tyre; **Sommersprossen** *f* freckles *pl*; **Sommerzeit** *f* summertime; (Uhrzeit) daylight saving time

Sonderangebot *nt* special offer; **sonderbar** *adj* strange, odd; **Sondermarke** *f* special stamp; **Sondermaschine** *f* special plane; **Sondermüll** *m* hazardous waste

sondern *conj* but; **nicht nur ..., ~ auch** not only ..., but also

Sonderpreis *m* special price; **Sonderschule** *f* special school; **Sonderzeichen** *nt* (Inform) special character; **Sonderzug** *m* special train

Song (-s, -s) *m* song

Sonnabend *m* Saturday; siehe auch **Mittwoch**; **sonnabends** *adv* on Saturdays; **~ morgens** on Saturday mornings; siehe auch **mittwochs**

Sonne (-, -n) f sun; **sonnen** vr: **sich ~** to sunbathe; **Sonnenallergie** f sun allergy; **Sonnenaufgang** m sunrise; **Sonnenblume** f sunflower; **Sonnenblumenkern** m sunflower seed; **Sonnenbrand** m sunburn; **Sonnenbrille** f sunglasses pl, shades pl; **Sonnencreme** f sun cream; **Sonnendach** nt (an Haus) awning; (Auto) sunroof; **Sonnendeck** nt sun deck; **Sonnenmilch** f suntan lotion; **Sonnenöl** nt suntan oil; **Sonnenschein** m sunshine; **Sonnenschirm** m parasol, sunshade; **Sonnenschutzcreme** f sunscreen; **Sonnenstich** m sunstroke; **Sonnenstudio** nt solarium; **Sonnenuhr** f sundial; **Sonnenuntergang** m sunset; **sonnig** adj sunny

Sonntag m Sunday; siehe auch **Mittwoch**; **sonntags** adv on Sundays; siehe auch **mittwochs**

sonst adv, conj (außerdem) else; (andernfalls) otherwise; (or) else; (mit Pron, in Fragen) else; (normalerweise) normally, usually; **~ noch etwas?** anything else?; **~ nichts** nothing else

sooft conj whenever

Sopran (-s, -e) m soprano

Sorge (-, -n) f worry; (Fürsorge) care; **sich** (dat) **~n machen** to be worried about sb; **sorgen** vi: **für jdn ~** to look after sb; **für etw ~** to take care of sth, to see to sth ▷ vr: **sich ~** to worry (um about); **sorgfältig** adj careful

sortieren vt to sort (out)

Sortiment nt assortment

sosehr conj however much

Soße (-, -n) f sauce; (zu Braten) gravy

Soundkarte f (Inform) sound card

Souvenir (-s, -s) nt souvenir

soviel conj as far as

soweit conj as far as

sowie conj (wie auch) as well as; (sobald) as soon as

sowohl conj: **~ ... als** (o wie) **auch** both ... and

sozial adj social; **~er Wohnungsbau** public-sector housing (programme); **Sozialhilfe** f income support (Brit), welfare (aid) (US); **Sozialismus** m socialism; **Sozialkunde** f social studies pl; **Sozialversicherung** f social security; **Sozialwohnung** f council flat (Brit), state-subsidized apartment (US)

Soziologie f sociology

sozusagen adv so to speak

Spachtel (-s, -) m spatula

Spag(h)etti pl spaghetti sing

Spalte (-, -n) f crack; (Gletscher) crevasse; (in Text) column

spalten vt to split

Spam (-s, -s) m (Inform) spam

Spange (-, -n) f clasp; (Haarspange) slide (Brit), barrette (US)

Spanien (-s) nt Spain; **Spanier(in)** (-s, -) m(f) Spaniard; **spanisch** adj Spanish; **Spanisch** nt Spanish

spann imperf von **spinnen**

spannen vt (straffen) to tighten; (befestigen) to brace ▷ vi to be tight

spannend adj exciting, gripping; **Spannung** f tension; (Elek) voltage; (fig) suspense

Sparbuch nt savings book; (Konto) savings account; **sparen** vt, vi to save

Spargel (-s, -) m asparagus

Sparkasse f savings bank; **Sparkonto** nt savings account

spärlich adj meagre; (Bekleidung) scanty

sparsam adj economical; **Sparschwein** nt piggy bank

Spaß (-es, Späße) m joke; (Freude) fun; **es macht mir ~** I enjoy it, it's (great) fun; **viel ~!** have fun

spät adj, adv late; **zu ~ kommen** to be late

Spaten (-s, -) m spade

später adj, adv later; **spätestens** adv at the latest; **Spätlese** f late vintage (wine); **Spätvorstellung** f late-night performance

Spatz (-en, -en) m sparrow

spazieren vi to stroll, to walk; **~ gehen** to go for a walk; **Spaziergang** m walk

Specht (-(e)s, -e) m woodpecker

Speck (-(e)s, -e) m bacon fat; (durchwachsen) bacon

Spedition f (für Umzug) removal firm

Speiche f (-, -n) f spoke

Speichel (-s) m saliva

Speicher (-s, -) m storehouse; (Dachboden) attic; (Inform) memory; **speichern** vt (Inform) to store; (sichern) to save

Speise (-, -n) f food; (Gericht) dish; **Speisekarte** f menu; **Speiseröhre** f gullet, oesophagus; **Speisesaal** m dining hall; **Speisewagen** m dining car

Spende (-, -n) f donation; **spenden** vt to donate, to give

spendieren vt: **jdm etw ~** to treat sb to sth

Sperre (-, -n) f barrier; (Verbot) ban; **sperren** vt to block; (Sport) to suspend; (verbieten) to ban

Sperrgepäck nt bulky luggage; **Sperrmüll** m bulky refuse; **Sperrstunde** f closing time; **Sperrung** f closing

Spesen pl expenses pl

spezialisieren vr: **sich ~** to specialize (auf +akk in); **Spezialist(in)** m(f) specialist; **Spezialität** f speciality (Brit),

specialty (US); **speziell** adj special ▷ adv especially

Spiegel (-s, -) m mirror; **Spiegelei** nt fried egg (sunny-side up (US)); **spiegelglatt** adj very slippery; **Spiegelreflexkamera** f reflex camera

Spiel (-(e)s, -e) nt game; (Tätigkeit) play(ing); (Karten) pack, deck; (Tech) (free) play; **Spielautomat** m (ohne Geldgewinn) gaming machine; (mit Geldgewinn) slot machine; **spielen** vt, vi to play; (um Geld) to gamble; (Theat) to perform, to act; **Klavier ~** to play the piano; **spielend** adv easily; **Spieler(in)** (-s, -) m(f) player; (um Geld) gambler; **Spielfeld** nt (für Fußball, Hockey) field; (für Basketball) court; **Spielfilm** m feature film; **Spielkasino** nt casino; **Spielplatz** m playground; **Spielraum** m room to manoeuvre; **Spielregel** f rule; **sich an die ~n halten** to stick to the rules; **Spielsachen** pl toys pl; **Spielzeug** nt toys pl; (einzelnes) toy

Spieß (-es, -e) m spear; (Bratspieß) spit; **Spießer(in)** (-s, -) m(f) square, stuffy type; **spießig** adj square, uncool

Spikes pl (Sport) spikes pl; (Aut) studs pl

Spinat (-(e)s, -e) m spinach

Spinne (-, -n) f spider; **spinnen** (spann, gesponnen) vt, vi to spin; (fam: Unsinn reden) to talk rubbish; (verrückt sein) to be crazy; **du spinnst!** you must be mad; **Spinnwebe** (-, -n) f cobweb

Spion(in) (-s, -e) m(f) spy; **spionieren** vi to spy; (fig) to snoop around

Spirale (-, -n) f spiral; (Med) coil

Spirituosen pl spirits pl, liquor sing (US)

Spiritus (-, -se) m spirit

spitz adj (Nase, Kinn) pointed; (Bleistift, Messer) sharp; (Winkel) acute; **Spitze** (-, -n) f point; (von Finger, Nase) tip; (Bemerkung) taunt, dig; (erster Platz) lead; (Gewebe) lace; **Spitzer** (-s, -) m pencil sharpener; **Spitzname** m nickname

Spliss (-) m split ends pl

sponsern vt to sponsor; **Sponsor(in)** (-s, -en) m(f) sponsor

spontan adj spontaneous

Sport (-(e)s, -e) m sport; **~ treiben** to do sport; **Sportanlage** f sports grounds pl; **Sportart** f sport; **Sportbekleidung** f sportswear; **Sportgeschäft** nt sports shop; **Sporthalle** f gymnasium, gym; **Sportlehrer(in)** (-s, -) m(f) sports instructor; (Schule) PE teacher; **Sportler(in)** (-s, -) m(f) sportsman/-woman; **sportlich** adj sporting; (Mensch) sporty; **Sportplatz** m playing field; **Sporttauchen** nt (skin-)diving; (mit Gerät) scuba-diving; **Sportverein** m sports club; **Sportwagen** m sports car

sprach imperf von **sprechen**

Sprache (-, -n) f language; (Sprechen) speech; **Sprachenschule** f language school; **Sprachführer** m phrasebook; **Sprachkenntnisse** pl knowledge sing of languages; **gute englische ~ haben** to have a good knowledge of English; **Sprachkurs** m language course; **Sprachunterricht** m language teaching

sprang imperf von **springen**

Spray (-s, -s) m ont o f spray

Sprechanlage f intercom; **sprechen** (sprach, gesprochen) vt, vi

to speak (jdn, mit jdm to sb); (sich unterhalten) to talk (mit to, über, von about); **~ Sie Deutsch?** do you speak German?; **kann ich bitte mit David ~?** (am Telefon) can I speak to David, please?; **Sprecher(in)** m(f) speaker; (Ansager) announcer; **Sprechstunde** f consultation; (Arzt) surgery hours pl; (Anwalt etc) office hours pl; **Sprechzimmer** nt consulting room

Sprengstoff m explosive

Sprichwort nt proverb

Springbrunnen m fountain

springen (sprang, gesprungen) vi to jump; (Glas) to crack; (mit Kopfsprung) to dive

Sprit (-(e)s, -e) m (fam: Benzin) petrol (Brit), gas (US)

Spritze (-, -n) f (Gegenstand) syringe; (Injektion) injection; (an Schlauch) nozzle; **spritzen** vt to spray; (Med) to inject ▷ vi to splash; (Med) to give injections

Spruch (-(e)s, Sprüche) m saying

Sprudel (-s, -) m sparkling mineral water; (süßer) fizzy drink (Brit), soda (US); **sprudeln** vi to bubble

Sprühdose f aerosol (can); **sprühen** vt, vi to spray; (fig) to sparkle; **Sprühregen** m drizzle

Sprung (-(e)s, Sprünge) m jump; (Riss) crack; **Sprungbrett** nt springboard; **Sprungschanze** f ski jump; **Sprungturm** m diving platforms pl

Spucke (-) f spit; **spucken** vt, vi to spit; (fam: sich erbrechen) to vomit; **Spucktüte** f sick bag

spuken vi (Geist) to walk; **hier spukt es** this place is haunted

Spülbecken nt sink

Spule (-, -n) f spool; (Elek) coil

Spüle (-, -n) f sink; **spülen** vt, vi to rinse; (Geschirr) to wash up;

(Toilette) to flush; **Spülmaschine**
f dishwasher; **Spülmittel** nt
washing-up liquid (Brit),
dishwashing liquid (US); **Spültuch**
nt dishcloth; **Spülung** f (von WC)
flush

Spur (-, -en) f trace; (Fußspur,
Radspur) track; (Fährte) trail;
(Fahrspur) lane; **die ~ wechseln** to
change lanes pl

spüren vt to feel; (merken) to
notice; **Spürhund** m sniffer dog

Squash (-) nt squash;
Squashschläger m squash racket

Sri Lanka (-s) nt Sri Lanka

Staat (-(e)s, -en) m state;
staatlich adj state(-); (vom Staat
betrieben) state-run;
Staatsangehörigkeit f
nationality; **Staatsanwalt** m,
-**anwältin** f prosecuting counsel
(Brit), district attorney (US);
Staatsbürger(in) m(f) citizen;
Staatsbürgerschaft f nationality; **doppelte ~** dual nationality;
Staatsexamen nt final exam
taken by trainee teachers, medical and
law students

Stab (-(e)s, Stäbe) m rod; (Gitter)
bar; **Stäbchen** nt (Essstäbchen)
chopstick; **Stabhochsprung** m
pole vault

stabil adj stable; (Möbel) sturdy

stach imperf von **stechen**

Stachel (-s, -n) m spike; (von Tier)
spine; (von Insekten) sting;
Stachelbeere f gooseberry;
Stacheldraht m barbed wire;
stachelig adj prickly

Stadion (-s, Stadien) nt stadium

Stadt (-, Städte) f town; (groß)
city; **in der ~** in town;
Stadtautobahn f urban
motorway (Brit) (o expressway
(US)); **Stadtbummel** (-s, -) m:
einen ~ machen to go round
town; **Stadtführer** m (Heft) city

guide; **Stadtführung** f city
sightseeing tour; **Stadthalle** f
municipal hall; **städtisch** adj
municipal; **Stadtmauer** f city
wall(s); **Stadtmitte** f town/city
centre, downtown (US);
Stadtplan m (street) map;
Stadtrand m outskirts pl;
Stadtrundfahrt f city tour;
Stadtteil m, **Stadtviertel** nt
district, part of town;
Stadtzentrum nt town/city
centre, downtown (US)

stahl imperf von **stehlen**

Stahl (-(e)s, Stähle) m steel

Stall (-(e)s, Ställe) m stable;
(Kaninchen) hutch; (Schweine)
pigsty; (Hühner) henhouse

Stamm (-(e)s, Stämme) m (Baum)
trunk; (von Menschen) tribe;
stammen vi: **~ aus** to come from;
Stammgast m regular (guest);
Stammkunde m, **Stammkundin**
f regular (customer); **Stammtisch**
m table reserved for regulars

stampfen vt, vi to stamp; (mit
Werkzeug) to pound; (stapfen) to
tramp

stand imperf von **stehen**

Stand (-(e)s, Stände) m (Wasser,
Benzin) level; (Stehen) standing
position; (Zustand) state;
(Spielstand) score; (auf Messe etc)
stand; (Klasse) class; **im ~e sein** to
be in a position; (fähig) to be able

Stand-by-Betrieb m stand-by;
Stand-by-Ticket nt stand-by
ticket

Ständer (-s, -) m (Gestell) stand;
(fam: Erektion) hard-on

Standesamt nt registry office

ständig adj permanent;
(ununterbrochen) constant,
continual

Standlicht nt sidelights pl (Brit),
parking lights pl (US); **Standort**
m position; **Standpunkt** m

standpoint; **Standspur** f (Auto) hard shoulder (Brit), shoulder (US)

Stange (-, -n) f stick; (Stab) pole; (Metall) bar; (Zigaretten) carton; **Stangenbohne** f runner (Brit) (o string (US)) bean; **Stangenbrot** nt French stick; **Stangensellerie** m celery

stank imperf von **stinken**

Stapel (-s, -) m pile

Star (-(e)s, -e) m (Vogel) starling; (Med) cataract ▷ (-s, -s) m (in Film etc) star

starb imperf von **sterben**

stark adj strong; (heftig, groß) heavy; (Maßangabe) thick; **Stärke** (-, -n) f strength; (Dicke) thickness; (Wäschestärke, Speisestärke) starch; **stärken** vt to strengthen; (Wäsche) to starch; **Starkstrom** m high-voltage current; **Stärkung** f strengthening; (Essen) refreshment

starr adj stiff; (unnachgiebig) rigid; (Blick) staring

starren vi to stare

Start (-(e)s, -e) m start; (Aviat) takeoff; **Startautomatik** f automatic choke; **Startbahn** f runway; **starten** vt, vi to start; (Aviat) to take off; **Starthilfekabel** nt jump leads pl (Brit), jumper cables pl (US); **Startmenü** nt (Inform) start menu

Station f (Haltestelle) stop; (Bahnhof) station; (im Krankenhaus) ward; **stationär** adj stationary; **~e Behandlung** in-patient treatment; **jdn ~ behandeln** to treat sb as an in-patient

Statistik f statistics pl

Stativ nt tripod

statt conj, prep +gen o dat instead of; **~ zu arbeiten** instead of working

statt|finden irr vi to take place

Statue (-, -n) f statue

Statusleiste f, **Statuszeile** f (Inform) status bar

Stau (-(e)s, -e) m (im Verkehr) (traffic) jam; **im ~ stehen** to be stuck in a traffic jam

Staub (-(e)s) m dust; **~ wischen** to dust; **staubig** adj dusty; **staubsaugen** vt, vi to vacuum, to hoover (Brit); **Staubsauger** m vacuum cleaner, Hoover® (Brit); **Staubtuch** nt duster

Staudamm m dam

staunen vi to be astonished (über +akk at)

Stausee m reservoir; **Stauung** f (von Wasser) damming-up; (von Blut, Verkehr) congestion; **Stauwarnung** f traffic report

Std. abk = **Stunde** h

Steak (-s, -s) nt steak

stechen (stach, gestochen) vt, vi (mit Nadel etc) to prick; (mit Messer) to stab; (mit Finger) to poke; (Biene) to sting; (Mücke) to bite; (Sonne) to burn; (Kartenspiel) to trump; **Stechen** (-s, -) nt sharp pain, stabbing pain; **Stechmücke** f mosquito

Steckdose f socket; **stecken** vt to put; (Nadel) to stick; (beim Nähen) to pin ▷ vi (festsitzen) to be stuck; (Nadeln) to be (sticking); **der Schlüssel steckt** the key is in the door; **Stecker** (-s, -) m plug; **Steckrübe** f swede (Brit), rutabaga (US)

Steg (-s, -e) m bridge

stehen (stand, gestanden) vi to stand (zu by); (sich befinden) to be; (stillstehen) to have stopped; **was steht im Brief?** what does it say in the letter?; **jdm (gut) ~** to suit sb; **~ bleiben** (Uhr) to stop; **~ lassen** to leave ▷ vi impers: **wie steht's?** (Sport) what's the score?

stehlen (stahl, gestohlen) vt to steal

Stehplatz m (im Konzert etc) standing ticket

Steiermark (-) f Styria

steif adj stiff

steigen (stieg, gestiegen) vi (Preise, Temperatur) to rise; (klettern) to climb; **~ in/auf** (+akk) to get in/on

steigern vt to increase ▷ vr: **sich ~** to increase

Steigung f incline, gradient

steil adj steep; **Steilhang** m steep slope; **Steilküste** f steep coast

Stein (-(e)s, -e) m stone; **Steinbock** m (Zool) ibex; (Astr) Capricorn; **steinig** adj stony; **Steinschlag** m falling rocks pl

Stelle (-, -n) f place, spot; (Arbeit) post, job; (Amt) office; **ich an deiner ~** if I were you; **auf der ~** straightaway; **stellen** vt to put; (Uhr etc) to set (auf +akk to); (zur Verfügung stellen) to provide ▷ vr: **sich ~** (bei Polizei) to give oneself up; **sich schlafend ~** to pretend to be asleep; **Stellenangebot** nt job offer, vacancy; **stellenweise** adv in places; **Stellenwert** m (fig) status; **einen hohen ~ haben** to play an important role; **Stellplatz** m parking space; **Stellung** f position; **zu etw ~ nehmen** to comment on sth; **Stellvertreter(in)** m(f) representative; (amtlich) deputy; (von Arzt) locum (Brit), locum tenens (US)

Stempel (-s, -) m stamp; **stempeln** vt to stamp; (Briefmarke) to cancel

sterben (starb, gestorben) vi to die

Stereoanlage f stereo (system)

steril adj sterile; **sterilisieren** vt to sterilize

Stern (-(e)s, -e) m star; **ein Hotel mit vier ~en** a four-star hotel; **Sternbild** nt constellation; (Sternzeichen) star sign, sign of the zodiac; **Sternfrucht** f star fruit; **Sternschnuppe** (-, -n) f shooting star; **Sternwarte** (-e, -n) f observatory; **Sternzeichen** nt star sign, sign of the zodiac; **welches ~ bist du?** what's your star sign?

stets adv always

Steuer (-s, -) nt (Auto) steering wheel ▷ (-, -n) f tax; **Steuerberater(in)** m(f) tax adviser; **Steuerbord** nt starboard; **Steuererklärung** f tax declaration; **steuerfrei** adj tax-free; (Waren) duty-free; **Steuerknüppel** m control column; (Aviat, Inform) joystick; **steuern** vt, vi to steer; (Flugzeug) to pilot; (Entwicklung, Tonstärke) (Inform) to control; **steuerpflichtig** adj taxable; **Steuerung** f (Auto) steering; (Vorrichtung) controls pl; (Aviat) piloting; (fig) control; **Steuerungstaste** f (Inform) control key

Stich (-(e)s, -e) m (von Insekt) sting; (von Mücke) bite; (durch Messer) stab; (beim Nähen) stitch; (Färbung) tinge; (Kartenspiel) trick; (Kunst) engraving

sticken vt, vi to embroider

Sticker (-s, -) m sticker

Stickerei f embroidery

stickig adj stuffy, close

Stiefbruder m stepbrother

Stiefel (-s, -) m boot

Stiefmutter f stepmother

Stiefmütterchen nt pansy

Stiefschwester f stepsister;

Stiefsohn m stepson; **Stieftochter** f stepdaughter; **Stiefvater** m stepfather

stieg imperf von **steigen**

Stiege (-, -n) f steps pl

Stiel (-(e)s, -e) m (Bot) stalk; **ein Eis am ~** an ice lolly (Brit), a Popsicle® (US)

Stier (-(e)s, -e) m (Zool) bull; (Astr) Taurus; **Stierkampf** m bullfight

stieß imperf von **stoßen**

Stift (-(e)s, -e) m (aus Holz) peg; (Nagel) tack; (zum Schreiben) pen; (Farbstift) crayon; (Bleistift) pencil

Stil (-s, -e) m style

still adj quiet; (unbewegt) still

stillen vt (Säugling) to breast-feed

stillhalten irr vi to keep still; **stillstehen** irr vi to stand still

Stimme (-, -n) f voice; (bei Wahl) vote

stimmen vi to be right; **stimmt!** that's right; **hier stimmt was nicht** there's something wrong here; **stimmt so!** (beim Bezahlen) keep the change

Stimmung f mood; (Atmosphäre) atmosphere

Stinkefinger m (fam) **jdm den ~ zeigen** to give sb the finger (o bird (US))

stinken (stank, gestunken) vi to stink (nach of)

Stipendium nt scholarship; (als Unterstützung) grant

Stirn (-, -en) f forehead; **Stirnhöhle** f sinus

Stock (-(e)s, Stöcke) m stick; (Bot) stock ▷ m (Stockwerke) floor, storey; **Stockbett** nt bunk bed; **Stöckelschuhe** pl high-heels; **Stockwerk** nt floor; **im ersten ~** on the first floor (Brit), on the second floor (US)

Stoff (-(e)s, -e) m (Gewebe) material; (Materie) matter; (von Buch etc) subject (matter); (fam: Rauschgift) stuff

stöhnen vi to groan (vor with)

stolpern vi to stumble, to trip

stolz adj proud

stopp interj hold it; (Moment mal!) hang on a minute; **stoppen** vt, vi to stop; (mit Uhr) to time; **Stoppschild** nt stop sign; **Stoppuhr** f stopwatch

Stöpsel (-s, -) m plug; (für Flaschen) stopper

Storch (-(e)s, Störche) m stork

stören vt to disturb; (behindern) to interfere with; **darf ich dich kurz ~?** can I trouble you for a minute?; **stört es dich, wenn ...?** do you mind if ...?

stornieren vt to cancel; **Stornogebühr** f cancellation fee

Störung f disturbance; (in der Leitung) fault

Stoß (-es, Stöße) m (Schub) push; (Schlag) blow; (mit Fuß) kick; (Haufen) pile; **Stoßdämpfer** (-s, -) m shock absorber

stoßen (stieß, gestoßen) vt (mit Druck) to shove, to push; (mit Schlag) to knock; (mit Fuß) to kick; (anstoßen) to bump; (zerkleinern) to pulverize ▷ vr: **sich ~** to bang oneself; **sich ~ an** (+dat) (fig) to take exception to

Stoßstange f (Auto) bumper

stottern vt, vi to stutter

Str. abk von **Straße** St, Rd

Strafe (-, -n) f punishment; (Sport) penalty; (Gefängnisstrafe) sentence; (Geldstrafe) fine; **strafen** vt to punish; **Straftat** f (criminal) offence; **Strafzettel** m ticket

Strahl (-s, -en) m ray, beam; (Wasser) jet; **strahlen** vi to radiate; (fig) to beam

Strähne (-, -n) f strand; (weiß, gefärbt) streak

Strand (-(e)s, Strände) m beach; **am ~** on the beach; **Strandcafé** nt beach café; **Strandkorb** m wicker beach chair with a hood; **Strandpromenade** f promenade

strapazieren vt (Material) to be hard on; (Mensch, Kräfte) to be a strain on

Straße (-, -n) f road; (in der Stadt) street; **Straßenarbeiten** pl roadworks pl (Brit), road repairs pl (US); **Straßenbahn** f tram (Brit), streetcar (US); **Straßencafé** nt pavement café (Brit), sidewalk café (US); **Straßenfest** nt street party; **Straßenglätte** f slippery roads pl; **Straßenkarte** f road map; **Straßenrand** m: **am ~** at the roadside; **Straßenschild** nt street sign; **Straßensperre** f roadblock; **Straßenverhältnisse** pl road conditions pl

Strategie (-, -n) f strategy

Strauch (-(e)s, Sträucher) m bush, shrub; **Strauchtomate** f vine-ripened tomato

Strauß (-es, Sträuße) m bunch; (als Geschenk) bouquet ▷ m (Strauße) (Vogel) ostrich

Strecke (-, -n) f route; (Entfernung) distance; (Eisenb) line

strecken vt to stretch ▷ vr: **sich ~** to stretch

streckenweise adv (teilweise) in parts; (zeitweise) at times

Streich (-(e)s, -e) m trick, prank

streicheln vt to stroke

streichen (strich, gestrichen) vt (anmalen) to paint; (berühren) to stroke; (auftragen) to spread; (durchstreichen) to delete; (nicht genehmigen) to cancel

Streichholz nt match; **Streichholzschachtel** f matchbox; **Streichkäse** m cheese spread

Streifen (-s, -) m (Linie) stripe; (Stück) strip; (Film) film

Streifenwagen m patrol car

Streik (-(e)s, -s) m strike; **streiken** vi to be on strike

Streit (-(e)s, -e) m argument (um, wegen about, over); **streiten** (stritt, gestritten) vi to argue (um, wegen about, over) ▷ vr: **sich ~** to argue (um, wegen about, over)

streng adj (Blick) severe; (Lehrer) strict; (Geruch) sharp

Stress (-es) m stress; **stressen** vt to stress (out); **stressig** adj (fam) stressful

Stretching (-s) nt (Sport) stretching exercises pl

streuen vt to scatter; **die Straßen ~** to grit the roads; (mit Salz) to put salt down on the roads; **Streufahrzeug** nt gritter lorry (Brit), salt truck (US)

strich imperf von **streichen**

Strich (-(e)s, -e) m (Linie) line; **Stricher** m (fam: Strichjunge) rent boy (Brit), boy prostitute; **Strichkode** (-s, -s) m bar code; **Stricherin** f (fam: Strichmädchen) hooker; **Strichpunkt** m semicolon

Strick (-(e)s, -e) m rope

stricken vt, vi to knit; **Strickjacke** f cardigan; **Stricknadel** f knitting needle

String (-s, -s) m, **Stringtanga** m G-string

Stripper(in) m(f) stripper; **Striptease** (-) m striptease

stritt imperf von **streiten**

Stroh (-(e)s) nt straw; **Strohdach** nt thatched roof; **Strohhalm** m (drinking) straw

Strom (-(e)s, Ströme) m river; (fig) stream; (Elek) current; **Stromanschluss** m connection; **Stromausfall** m power failure

strömen vi to stream, to pour; **Strömung** f current

Stromverbrauch m power consumption; **Stromzähler** m electricity meter

Strophe (-, -n) f verse

Strudel (-s, -) m (in Fluss) whirlpool; (Gebäck) strudel

Struktur f structure; (von Material) texture

Strumpf (-(e)s, Strümpfe) m (Damenstrumpf) stocking; (Socke) sock; **Strumpfhose** f (pair of) tights pl (Brit), pantyhose (US)

Stück (-(e)s, -e) nt piece; (von Zucker) lump; (etwas) bit; (Zucker) lump; (Theat) play; **ein ~ Käse** a piece of cheese

Student(in) m(f) student; **Studentenausweis** m student card; **Studentenwohnheim** nt hall of residence (Brit), dormitory (US); **Studienabschluss** m qualification (at the end of a course of higher education); **Studienfahrt** f study trip; **Studienplatz** m university/college place; **studieren** vt, vi to study; **Studium** nt studies pl; **während seines ~s** while he is/was studying

Stufe (-, -n) f step; (Entwicklungsstufe) stage

Stuhl (-(e)s, Stühle) m chair

stumm adj silent; (Med) dumb

stumpf adj blunt; (teilnahmslos, glanzlos) dull; **stumpfsinnig** adj dull

Stunde (-, -n) f hour; (Unterricht) lesson; **eine halbe ~** half an hour; **Stundenkilometer** m: **80 ~** 80 kilometres an hour; **stundenlang** adv for hours; **Stundenlohn** m hourly wage; **Stundenplan** m timetable; **stündlich** adj hourly

Stuntman (-s, Stuntmen) m stuntman; **Stuntwoman** (-, Stuntwomen) f stuntwoman

stur adj stubborn; (stärker) pigheaded

Sturm (-(e)s, Stürme) m storm; **stürmen** vi (Wind) to blow hard; (rennen) to storm; **Stürmer(in)** m(f) striker, forward; **Sturmflut** f storm tide; **stürmisch** adj stormy; (fig) tempestuous; (Zeit) turbulent; (Liebhaber) passionate; (Beifall, Begrüßung) tumultuous; **Sturmwarnung** f gale warning

Sturz (-es, Stürze) m fall; (Pol) overthrow; **stürzen** vt (werfen) to hurl; (Pol) to overthrow; (umkehren) to overturn ▷ vi to fall; (rennen) to dash; **Sturzhelm** m crash helmet

Stute (-, -n) f mare

Stütze (-, -n) f support; (Hilfe) help; (fam: Arbeitslosenunterstützung) dole (Brit), welfare (US)

stützen vt to support; (Ellbogen) to prop

stutzig adj perplexed, puzzled; (misstrauisch) suspicious

Styropor® (-s) nt polystyrene (Brit), styrofoam (US)

subjektiv adj subjective

Substanz (-, -en) f substance

subtrahieren vt to subtract

Subvention f subsidy; **subventionieren** vt to subsidize

Suche (-, -n) f search (nach for); **auf der ~ nach etw sein** to be looking for sth; **suchen** vt to look for; (Inform) to search ▷ vi to look, to search (nach for); **Suchmaschine** f (Inform) search engine

Sucht (-, Süchte) f mania; (Med) addiction; **süchtig** adj addicted; **Süchtige(r)** mf addict

Süd south; **Südafrika** nt South Africa; **Südamerika** nt South America; **Süddeutschland** nt Southern Germany; **Süden** (-s) m south; **im ~ Deutschlands** in the south of Germany; **Südeuropa** nt Southern Europe; **Südkorea** (-s) nt South Korea; **südlich** adj southern; (Kurs, Richtung) southerly; **Verkehr in ~er**

Richtung southbound traffic; **Südost(en)** m southeast; **Südpol** m South Pole; **Südstaaten** pl (der USA) the Southern States pl, the South sing; **südwärts** adv south, southwards; **Südwest(en)** m southwest; **Südwind** m south wind

Sülze (-, -n) f jellied meat

Summe (-, -n) f sum; (Gesamtsumme) total

summen vi, vt to hum; (Insekt) to buzz

Sumpf (-(e)s, Sümpfe) m marsh; (subtropischer) swamp; **sumpfig** adj marshy

Sünde (-, -n) f sin

super adj (fam) super, great; **Super** (-s) nt (Benzin) four star (petrol) (Brit), premium (US); **Supermarkt** m supermarket

Suppe (-, -n) f soup; **Suppengrün** nt bunch of herbs and vegetables for flavouring soup; **Suppenlöffel** m soup spoon; **Suppenschüssel** f soup tureen; **Suppentasse** f soup cup; **Suppenteller** m soup plate; **Suppenwürfel** m stock cube

Surfbrett nt surfboard; **surfen** vi to surf; **im Internet ~** to surf the Internet; **Surfer(in)** (-s, -) m(f) surfer

Surrealismus m surrealism

Sushi (-s, -s) nt sushi

süß adj sweet; **süßen** vt to sweeten; **Süßigkeit** f (Bonbon etc) sweet (Brit), candy (US); **Süßkartoffel** f sweet potato (Brit), yam (US); **süßsauer** adj sweet-and-sour; **Süßspeise** f dessert; **Süßstoff** m sweetener; **Süßwasser** nt fresh water

Sweatshirt (-s, -s) nt sweatshirt

Swimmingpool (-s, -s) m (swimming) pool

Sylvester nt siehe **Silvester**

Symbol (-s, -e) nt symbol; **Symbolleiste** f (Inform) toolbar

Symmetrie (-, -n) f symmetry; **symmetrisch** adj symmetrical

sympathisch adj nice; **jdn ~ finden** to like sb

Symphonie (-, -n) f symphony

Symptom (-s, -e) nt symptom (für of)

Synagoge (-, -n) f synagogue

synchronisiert adj (Film) dubbed; **Synchronstimme** f dubbing voice

Synthetik (-, -en) f synthetic (fibre); **synthetisch** adj synthetic

Syrien (-s) nt Syria

System (-s, -e) nt system; **systematisch** adj systematic; **Systemsteuerung** f (Inform) control panel

Szene (-, -n) f scene

t

Tabak (-s, -e) m tobacco;
Tabakladen m tobacconist's
Tabelle f table
Tablett (-s, -s) nt tray
Tablette f tablet, pill
Tabulator m tabulator, tab
Tacho(meter) (-s, -s) m (Auto)
speedometer
Tafel (-, -n) f (a. Math) table;
(Anschlagtafel) board; (Wandtafel)
blackboard; (Schiefer~) slate;
(Gedenktafel) plaque; **eine
~ Schokolade** a bar of chocolate;
Tafelwasser nt table water;
Tafelwein m table wine
Tag (-(e)s, -e) m day; (Tageslicht)
daylight; **guten ~!** good
morning/afternoon; **am ~** during
the day; **sie hat ihre ~e** she's got
her period; **eines ~es** one day;
~ der Arbeit Labour Day;
Tagebuch nt diary; **tagelang**
adj for days (on end);

Tagesanbruch m daybreak;
Tagesausflug m day trip;
Tagescreme f day cream;
Tagesdecke f bedspread;
Tagesgericht nt dish of the day;
Tageskarte f (Fahrkarte) day
ticket; **die ~** (Speisekarte) today's
menu; **Tageslicht** nt daylight;
Tagesmutter f child minder;
Tagesordnung f agenda;
Tagestour f day trip;
Tageszeitung f daily newspaper;
täglich adj, adv daily; **tags(über)**
adv during the day; **Tagung** f
conference
Tai Chi (-) nt tai chi
Taille (-, -n) f waist
Taiwan (-s) nt Taiwan
Takt (-(e)s, -e) m (Taktgefühl) tact;
(Mus) time
Taktik (-, -en) f tactics pl
taktlos adj tactless; **taktvoll** adj
tactful
Tal (-(e)s, Täler) nt valley
Talent (-(e)s, -e) nt talent;
talentiert adj talented
Talkmaster(in) (-s, -) m(f) talk-show
host; **Talkshow** (-, -s) f talkshow
Tampon (-s, -s) m tampon
Tandem (-s, -s) nt tandem
Tang (-s, -e) m seaweed
Tanga (-s, -s) m thong
Tank (-s, -s) m tank;
Tankanzeige f fuel gauge;
Tankdeckel m fuel cap; **tanken** vi
to get some petrol (Brit) (o gas
(US)); (Aviat) to refuel; **Tanker**
(-s, -) m (oil) tanker; **Tankstelle** f
petrol station (Brit), gas station
(US); **Tankwart(in)** (-s, -e) m(f)
petrol pump attendant (Brit), gas
station attendant (US)
Tanne (-, -n) f fir; **Tannenzapfen**
m fir cone
Tansania (-s) nt Tanzania
Tante (-, -n) f aunt;
Tante-Emma-Laden m corner

shop (Brit), grocery store (US)

Tanz (-es, Tänze) m dance; **tanzen** vt, vi to dance; **Tänzer(in)** m(f) dancer; **Tanzfläche** f dance floor; **Tanzkurs** m dancing course; **Tanzlehrer(in)** m(f) dancing instructor; **Tanzstunde** f dancing lesson

Tapete (-, -n) f wallpaper; **tapezieren** vt, vi to wallpaper

Tarantel (-, -n) f tarantula

Tarif (-s, -e) m tariff, (scale of) fares; charges pl

Tasche (-, -n) f bag; (Hosentasche) pocket; (Handtasche) bag (Brit), purse (US)

Taschen- in zW pocket; **Taschenbuch** nt paperback; **Taschendieb(in)** m(f) pickpocket; **Taschengeld** nt pocket money; **Taschenlampe** f torch (Brit), flashlight (US); **Taschenmesser** nt penknife; **Taschenrechner** m pocket calculator; **Taschentuch** nt handkerchief

Tasse (-, -n) f cup; **eine ~ Kaffee** a cup of coffee

Tastatur f keyboard; **Taste** (-, -n) f button; (von Klavier, Computer) key; **Tastenkombination** f (Inform) shortcut

tat imperf von **tun**

Tat (-, -en) f action

Tatar (-s, -s) nt raw minced beef

Täter(in) (-s, -) m(f) culprit

tätig adj active; **in einer Firma ~ sein** to work for a firm; **Tätigkeit** f activity; (Beruf) occupation

tätowieren vt to tattoo; **Tätowierung** f tattoo (an +dat on)

Tatsache f fact; **tatsächlich** adj actual ▷ adv really

Tau (-(e)s, -e) nt (Seil) rope ▷ (-(e)s) m dew

taub adj deaf; (Füße etc) numb (vor Kälte with cold)

Taube (-, -n) f pigeon; (Turtel-, fig: Friedenssymbol) dove

taubstumm adj deaf-and-dumb; **Taubstumme(r)** mf deaf-mute

tauchen vt to dip ▷ vi to dive; (Naut) to submerge; **Tauchen** (-s) nt diving; **Taucher(in)** (-s, -) m(f) diver; **Taucheranzug** m diving (o wet) suit; **Taucherbrille** f diving goggles pl; **Tauchermaske** f diving mask; **Tauchkurs** m diving course; **Tauchsieder** (-s, -) m portable immersion coil for heating water

tauen vi impers to thaw

Taufe (-, -n) f baptism; **taufen** vt to baptize; (nennen) to christen

taugen vi to be suitable (für for); **nichts ~** to be no good

Tausch (-(e)s, -e) m exchange; **tauschen** vt to exchange, to swap

täuschen vt to deceive ▷ vi to be deceptive ▷ vr: **sich ~** to be wrong; **täuschend** adj deceptive; **Täuschung** f deception; (optisch) illusion

tausend num a thousand; **vier~** four thousand; **~ Dank!** thanks a lot; **tausendmal** adv a thousand times; **tausendste(r, s)** adj thousandth; **Tausendstel** (-s, -) nt (Bruchteil) thousandth

Taxi (-s, -s) nt taxi; **Taxifahrer(in)** m(f) taxi driver; **Taxistand** m taxi rank (Brit), taxi stand (US)

Team (-s, -s) nt team; **Teamarbeit** f team work; **teamfähig** adj able to work in a team

Technik f technology; (angewandte) engineering; (Methode) technique; **Techniker(in)** (-s, -) m(f) engineer; (Sport, Mus) technician;

technisch adj technical
Techno (-s) m (Mus) techno
Teddybär m teddy bear
TEE abk = **Trans-Europ-Express**
Trans-Europe-Express
Tee (-s, -s) m tea; **Teebeutel** m
teabag; **Teekanne** f teapot;
Teelöffel m teaspoon
Teer (-(e)s, -e) m tar
Teesieb nt tea strainer; **Teetasse**
f teacup
Teich (-(e)s, -e) m pond
Teig (-(e)s, -e) m dough;
Teigwaren pl pasta sing
Teil (-(e)s, -e) m or nt (Anteil)
share; **zum ~** partly ▷ (-(e)s, -e) nt
part; (Bestandteil) component;
teilen vt to divide; (mit jdm) to
share (mit with); **20 durch 4 ~** to
divide 20 by 4 ▷ vr: **sich ~** to
divide
Teilkaskoversicherung f third
party, fire and theft insurance
teilmöbliert adj partly furnished
Teilnahme (-, -n) f participation
(an +dat in); **teilnehmen** irr vi to
take part (an +dat in); **Teilneh-
mer(in)** (-s, -) m(f) participant
teils adv partly; **teilweise** adv
partially, in part; **Teilzeit** f:
~ arbeiten to work part-time
Teint (-s, -s) m complexion
Tel. abk von **Telefon** tel.
Telefon (-s, -e) nt telephone;
Telefonanruf m, **Telefonat** nt
(tele)phone call;
Telefonanschluss m telephone
connection; **Telefonauskunft** f
directory enquiries pl (Brit),
directory assistance (US);
Telefonbuch nt telephone
directory; **Telefongebühren** pl
telephone charges pl;
Telefongespräch nt telephone
conversation; **telefonieren** vi:
ich telefoniere gerade (mit ...)
I'm on the phone (to ...);

telefonisch adj telephone;
(Benachrichtigung) by telephone;
Telefonkarte f phonecard;
Telefonnummer f (tele)phone
number; **Telefonrechnung** f
phone bill; **Telefonverbindung** f
telephone connection;
Telefonzelle f phone box (Brit),
phone booth; **Telefonzentrale** f
switchboard; **über die ~** through
the switchboard
Telegramm nt telegram;
Teleobjektiv nt telephoto lens;
Teleshopping (-s) nt teleshopping; **Teleskop** (-s, -e) nt
telescope
Teller (-s, -) m plate
Tempel (-s, -) m temple
Temperament nt temperament; (Schwung) liveliness;
temperamentvoll adj lively
Temperatur f temperature; **bei
-en von 30 Grad** at temperatures
of 30 degrees; **~ haben** to have a
temperature; **~ bei jdm messen** to
take sb's temperature
Tempo (-s, -s) nt (Geschwindigkeit)
speed; **Tempolimit** (-s, -s) nt
speed limit
Tempotaschentuch® nt
(Papiertaschentuch) (paper) tissue
Tendenz f tendency; (Absicht)
intention
Tennis (-) nt tennis; **Tennisball**
m tennis ball; **Tennisplatz** m
tennis court; **Tennisschläger** m
tennis racket; **Tennisspieler(in)**
m(f) tennis player
Tenor (-s, Tenöre) m tenor
Teppich (-s, -e) m carpet;
Teppichboden m (fitted) carpet
Termin (-s, -e) m (Zeitpunkt) date;
(Frist) deadline; (Arzttermin etc)
appointment
Terminal (-s, -s) nt (Inform, Aviat)
terminal
Terminkalender m diary;

Terminplaner m (in Buchform) personal organizer, Filofax®; (Taschencomputer) personal digital assistant, PDA

Terpentin (-s, -e) nt turpentine, turps sing

Terrasse (-, -n) f terrace; (hinter einem Haus) patio

Terror (-s) m terror; **Terroranschlag** m terrorist attack; **terrorisieren** vt to terrorize; **Terrorismus** m terrorism; **Terrorist(in)** m(f) terrorist

Tesafilm® m = sellotape® (Brit), = Scotch tape® (US)

Test (-s, -s) m test

Testament nt will; **das Alte/Neue ~** the Old/New Testament

testen vt to test; **Testergebnis** nt test results pl

Tetanus (-) m tetanus; **Tetanusimpfung** f (anti-)tetanus injection

teuer adj expensive, dear (Brit)

Teufel (-s, -) m devil; **was/wo zum ~** what/where the devil; **Teufelskreis** m vicious circle

Text (-(e)s, -e) m text; (Liedertext) words pl, lyrics pl; **Textmarker** (-s, -) m highlighter; **Textverarbeitung** f word processing; **Textverarbeitungsprogramm** nt word processing program

Thailand nt Thailand

Theater (-s, -) nt theatre; (fam) fuss; **ins ~ gehen** to go to the theatre; **Theaterkasse** f box office; **Theaterstück** nt (stage) play; **Theatervorstellung** f (stage) performance

Theke (-, -n) f (Schanktisch) bar; (Ladentisch) counter

Thema (-s, Themen) nt subject, topic; **kein ~!** no problem

Themse (-) f Thames

Theologie f theology

theoretisch adj theoretical; **~ stimmt das** that's right in theory; **Theorie** f theory

Therapeut(in) m(f) therapist; **Therapie** f therapy; **eine ~ machen** to undergo therapy

Thermalbad nt thermal bath; (Ort) thermal spa; **Thermometer** (-s, -) nt thermometer

Thermosflasche® f, **Thermoskanne®** f Thermos® (flask); **Thermostat** (-(e)s, -e) m thermostat

These (-, -n) f theory

Thron (-(e)s, -e) m throne

Thunfisch (-(e)s, -e) m tuna

Thüringen (-s) nt Thuringia

Thymian (-s, -e) m thyme

Tick (-(e)s, -s) m tic; (Eigenart) quirk; (Fimmel) craze; **ticken** vi to tick; **er tickt nicht ganz richtig** he's off his rocker

Ticket (-s, -s) nt (plane) ticket

tief adj deep; (Ausschnitt, Ton, Sonne) low; **2 Meter ~** 2 metres deep; **Tief** (-s, -s) nt (Meteo) low; (seelisch) depression; **Tiefdruck** m (Meteo) low pressure; **Tiefe** (-, -n) f depth; **Tiefgarage** f underground car park (Brit) (o garage (US)); **tiefgekühlt** adj frozen; **Tiefkühlfach** nt freezer compartment; **Tiefkühlkost** f frozen food; **Tiefkühltruhe** f freezer; **Tiefpunkt** m low

Tier (-(e)s, -e) nt animal; **Tierarzt** m, **Tierärztin** f vet; **Tiergarten** m zoo; **Tierhandlung** f pet shop; **Tierheim** nt animal shelter; **tierisch** adj animal ▷ adv (fam) really; **~ ernst** deadly serious; **ich hatte ~ Angst** I was dead scared; **Tierkreiszeichen** nt sign of the zodiac; **Tierpark** m zoo; **Tierquälerei** f cruelty to animals;

Tierschützer(in) (-s, -) m(f) animal rights campaigner; **Tierversuch** m animal experiment

Tiger (-s, -) m tiger

timen vt to time; **Timing** (-s) nt timing

Tinte (-, -n) f ink; **Tintenfisch** m cuttlefish; (klein) squid; (achtarmig) octopus; **Tintenfischringe** pl calamari pl; **Tintenstrahldrucker** m ink-jet printer

Tipp (-s, -s) m tip; **tippen** vi, vi to tap; (fam: schreiben) to type; (fam: raten) to guess

Tirol (-s) nt Tyrol

Tisch (-(e)s, -e) m table; **Tischdecke** f tablecloth; **Tischlerei** f joiner's workshop; (Arbeit) joinery; **Tischtennis** nt table tennis; **Tischtennisschläger** m table-tennis bat

Titel (-s, -) m title; **Titelbild** nt cover picture

Toast (-(e)s, -s) m toast; **toasten** vt to toast; **Toaster** (-s, -) m toaster

Tochter (-, Töchter) f daughter

Tod (-(e)s, -e) m death; **Todesopfer** nt casualty; **Todesstrafe** f death penalty; **todkrank** adj terminally ill; (sehr krank) seriously ill; **tödlich** adj deadly, fatal; **er ist ~ verunglückt** he was killed in an accident; **todmüde** adj (fam) dead tired; **todsicher** adj (fam) dead certain

Tofu (-(s)) m tofu, bean curd

Toilette f toilet, restroom (US); **Toilettenpapier** nt toilet paper

toi, toi, toi (interj) good luck

tolerant adj tolerant (gegen of)

toll adj mad; (Treiben) wild; (fam: großartig) great; **Tollkirsche** f deadly nightshade; **Tollwut** f rabies sing

Tomate (-, -n) f tomato; **Tomatenmark** nt tomato purée (Brit) (o paste (US)); **Tomatensaft** m tomato juice

Tombola (-, -s) f raffle, tombola (Brit)

Ton (-(e)s, -e) m (Erde) clay ▷ m (Töne; Laut) sound; (Mus) note; (Redeweise) tone; (Farbton, Nuance) shade; **Tonband** nt tape; **Tonbandgerät** nt tape recorder

tönen vi to sound ▷ vt to shade; (Haare) to tint

Toner (-s, -) m toner; **Tonerkassette** f toner cartridge

Tonne (-, -n) f (Fass) barrel; (Gewicht) tonne, metric ton

Tontechniker(in) m(f) sound engineer

Tönung f hue; (für Haar) rinse

Top (-s, -s) nt top

Topf (-(e)s, Töpfe) m pot

Töpfer(in) (-s, -) m(f) potter; **Töpferei** f pottery; (Gegenstand) piece of pottery

Tor (-(e)s, -e) nt gate; (Sport) goal; **ein ~ schießen** to score a goal; **Torhüter(in)** m(f) goalkeeper

torkeln vi to stagger

Tornado (-s, -s) m tornado

Torschütze m, **Torschützin** f (goal)scorer

Torte (-, -n) f cake; (Obsttorte) flan; (Sahnetorte) gateau

Torwart(in) (-s, -e) m(f) goalkeeper

tot adj dead; **~er Winkel** blind spot

total adj total, complete; **Totalschaden** m complete write-off

Tote(r) mf dead man/woman; (Leiche) corpse; **töten** vt, vi to kill; **Totenkopf** m skull

tot|**lachen** vr: **sich ~** to kill oneself laughing

Toto (-s, -s) m o nt pools pl

tot|schlagen irr vt to beat to death; **die Zeit ~** to kill time

Touchscreen (-s, -s) m touch screen

Tour (-, -en) f trip; (Rundfahrt) tour; **eine ~ nach York machen** to go on a trip to York; **Tourenski** m touring skis

Tourismus m tourism; **Tourist(in)** m(f) tourist; **Touristenklasse** f tourist class; **touristisch** adj tourist; (pej) touristy

traben vi to trot

Tournee (-, -n) f tour

Tracht (-, -en) f (Kleidung) traditional costume

Trackball (-s, -s) m (Inform) trackball

Tradition f tradition; **traditionell** adj traditional

traf imperf von **treffen**

Trafik (-, -en) f tobacconist's

Tragbahre (-, -n) f stretcher

tragbar adj portable

träge adj sluggish, slow

tragen (trug, getragen) vt to carry; (Kleidung, Brille, Haare) to wear; (Namen, Früchte) to bear; **Träger** (-s, -) m (an Kleidung) strap; (Hosen~) braces pl (Brit), suspenders pl (US); (in der Architektur) beam; (Stahl~, Eisen~) girder

Tragfläche f wing; **Tragflügelboot** nt hydrofoil

tragisch adj tragic; **Tragödie** f tragedy

Trainer(in) (-s, -) m(f) trainer, coach; **trainieren** vt, vi to train; (jdn a.) to coach; (Übung) to practise; **Training** (-s, -s) nt training; **Trainingsanzug** m tracksuit

Traktor m tractor

Trambahn f tram (Brit), streetcar (US)

trampen vi to hitchhike; **Tramper(in)** m(f) hitchhiker

Träne (-, -n) f tear; **tränen** vi to water; **Tränengas** nt teargas

trank imperf von **trinken**

Transfusion f transfusion

Transitverkehr m transit traffic; **Transitvisum** nt transit visa

Transplantation f transplant; (Hauttransplantation) graft

Transport (-(e)s, -e) m transport; **transportieren** vt to transport; **Transportmittel** nt means sing of transport; **Transportunternehmen** nt haulage firm

Transvestit (-en, -en) m transvestite

trat imperf von **treten**

Traube (-, -n) f (einzelne Beere) grape; (ganze Frucht) bunch of grapes; **Traubensaft** m grape juice; **Traubenzucker** m glucose

trauen jdm/einer Sache **~** to trust sb/sth; **ich traute meinen Ohren nicht** I couldn't believe my ears ▷ vr: **sich ~** to dare ▷ vt to marry; **sich ~ lassen** to get married

Trauer (-) f sorrow; (für Verstorbenen) mourning

Traum (-(e)s, Träume) m dream; **träumen** vt, vi to dream (von of, about); **traumhaft** adj dreamlike; (fig) wonderful

traurig adj sad (über +akk about)

Trauschein m marriage certificate; **Trauung** f wedding ceremony; **Trauzeuge** m, **Trauzeugin** f witness (at wedding ceremony), = best man/maid of honour

Travellerscheck m traveller's cheque

treffen (traf, getroffen) vr: **sich ~** to meet ▷ vt, vi to hit; (Bemerkung) to hurt; (begegnen) to meet; (*Entscheidung*) to make; (*Maßnahmen*) to take; **Treffen** (-s, -) nt meeting; **Treffer** (-s, -) m (*Tor*) goal; **Treffpunkt** m meeting place

treiben (trieb, getrieben) vt to drive; (*Sport*) to do ▷ vi (*im Wasser*) to drift; (*Pflanzen*) to sprout; (*Tee, Kaffee*) to be diuretic; **Treiber** (-s, -) m (*Inform*) driver

Treibgas nt propellant; **Treibhaus** nt greenhouse; **Treibstoff** m fuel

trennen vt to separate; (*teilen*) to divide ▷ vr: **sich ~** to separate; **sich von jdm ~** to leave sb; **sich von etw ~** to part with sth; **Trennung** f separation

Treppe (-, -n) f stairs pl; (*im Freien*) steps pl; **Treppengeländer** nt banister; **Treppenhaus** nt staircase

Tresen (-s, -) m (*in Kneipe*) bar; (*in Laden*) counter

Tresor (-s, -e) m safe

Tretboot nt pedal boat; **treten** (trat, getreten) vi to step; **mit jdm in Verbindung ~** to get in contact with sb ▷ vt to kick; (*nieder~*) to tread

treu adj (*gegenüber Partner*) faithful; (*Kunde, Fan*) loyal; **Treue** (-) f (*eheliche*) faithfulness; (*von Kunde, Fan*) loyalty

Triathlon (-s, -s) m triathlon

Tribüne (-, -n) f stand; (*Rednertribüne*) platform

Trick (-s e o -s) m trick; **Trickfilm** m cartoon

trieb imperf von **treiben**

Trieb (-(e)s, -e) m urge; (*Instinkt*) drive; (*Neigung*) inclination; (*an Baum etc*) shoot; **Triebwerk** nt engine

Trikot (-s, -s) nt shirt, jersey

Trimm-Dich-Pfad m fitness trail

trinkbar adj drinkable; **trinken** (trank, getrunken) vt, vi to drink; **einen ~ gehen** to go out for a drink; **Trinkgeld** nt tip; **Trinkhalm** m (drinking) straw; **Trinkwasser** nt drinking water

Trio (-s, -s) nt trio

Tripper (-s, -) m gonorrhoea

Tritt (-(e)s, -e) m (*Schritt*) step; (*Fußtritt*) kick; **Trittbrett** nt running board

Triumph (-(e)s, -e) m triumph; **triumphieren** vi to triumph (*über +akk* over)

trivial adj trivial

trocken adj dry; **Trockenhaube** f hair-dryer; **Trockenheit** f dryness; **trocken|legen** vt (*Baby*) to change; **trocknen** vt, vi to dry; **Trockner** (-s, -) m dryer

Trödel (-s) m (*fam*) junk; **Trödelmarkt** m flea market

trödeln vi (*fam*) to dawdle

Trommel (-, -n) f drum; **Trommelfell** nt eardrum; **trommeln** vt, vi to drum

Trompete (-, -n) f trumpet

Tropen pl tropics pl

Tropf (-(e)s, -e) m (*Med*) drip; **am ~ hängen** to be on a drip; **tröpfeln** vi to drip; **es tröpfelt** it's drizzling; **tropfen** vt, vi to drip; **Tropfen** (-s, -) m drop; **tropfenweise** adv drop by drop; **tropfnass** adj dripping wet; **Tropfsteinhöhle** f stalactite cave

tropisch adj tropical

Trost (-es) m consolation, comfort; **trösten** vt to console, to comfort; **trostlos** adj bleak; (*Verhältnisse*) wretched; **Trostpreis** m consolation prize

Trottoir (-s, -s) nt pavement (*Brit*), sidewalk (*US*)

trotz prep +gen o dat in spite of; **Trotz** (-es) m defiance; **trotzdem** adv nevertheless ▷ conj although;

trotzig adj defiant

trüb adj dull; (Flüssigkeit, Glas) cloudy; (fig) gloomy

Trüffel (-, -n) f truffle

trug imperf von **tragen**

trügerisch adj deceptive

Truhe (-, -n) f chest

Trümmer pl wreckage sing; (Bau~) ruins pl

Trumpf (-(e)s, Trümpfe) m trump

Trunkenheit f intoxication; **~ am Steuer** drink driving (Brit), drunk driving (US)

Truthahn m turkey

Tscheche (-n, -n) m, **Tschechin** f Czech; **Tschechien** (-s) nt Czech Republic; **tschechisch** adj Czech; **Tschechische Republik** Czech Republic; **Tschechisch** nt Czech

Tschetschenien (-s) nt Chechnya

tschüs(s) interj bye

T-Shirt (-s, -s) nt T-shirt

Tube (-, -n) f tube

Tuberkulose (-, -n) f tuberculosis, TB

Tuch (-(e)s, Tücher) nt cloth; (Halstuch) scarf; (Kopftuch) headscarf

tüchtig adj competent; (fleißig) efficient; (fam: kräftig) good

Tugend (-, -en) f virtue; **tugendhaft** adj virtuous

Tulpe (-, -n) f tulip

Tumor (-s, -en) m tumour

tun (tat, getan) vt (machen) to do; (legen) to put; **was tust du da?** what are you doing?; **das tut man nicht** you shouldn't do that; **jdm etw ~** (antun) to do sth to sb; **das tut es auch** that'll do ▸ vi to act; **so ~, als ob** to act as if ▸ vr impers: **es tut sich etwas/viel** something/a lot is happening

Tuner (-s, -) m tuner

Tunesien (-s) nt Tunisia

Tunfisch m siehe **Thunfisch** tuna

Tunnel (-s, -s o -) m tunnel

Tunte (-, -n) f (pej, fam) fairy

tupfen vt, vi to dab; (mit Farbe) to dot; **Tupfen** (-s, -) m dot

Tür (-, -en) f door; **vor/an der ~** at the door; **an die ~ gehen** to answer the door

Türke (-n, -n) m Turk; **Türkei** (-) f: **die ~** Turkey; **Türk** f Turk

Türkis (-es, -e) m turquoise; **türkisch** adj Turkish; **Türkisch** nt Turkish

Turm (-(e)s, Türme) m tower; (spitzer Kirchturm) steeple; (Sprung~) diving platform; (Schach) rook, castle

turnen vi to do gymnastics; **Turnen** (-s) nt gymnastics sing; (Schule) physical education, PE; **Turner(in)** m(f) gymnast; **Turnhalle** f gym(nasium); **Turnhose** f gym shorts pl

Turnier (-s, -e) nt tournament

Turnschuh m gym shoe, sneaker (US)

Türschild nt doorplate; **Türschloss** nt lock

tuscheln vt, vi to whisper

Tussi (-, -s) f (pej, fam) chick

Tüte (-, -n) f bag

TÜV (-s, -s) m akr = **Technischer Überwachungsverein** ≈ MOT (Brit), vehicle inspection (US)

○ **TÜV**

● The **TÜV** is the organization
● responsible for checking the
● safety of machinery, particularly
● vehicles. Cars over three years
● old have to be examined every
● two years for their safety and
● for their exhaust emissions.
● **TÜV** is also the name given to
● the test itself.

TÜV-Plakette *f* badge attached to a vehicle's numberplate, indicating that it has passed the "TÜV"

Tweed (-s, -s) *m* tweed

Typ (-s, -en) *m* type; (*Auto*) model; (*Mann*) guy, bloke

Typhus (-) *m* typhoid

typisch *adj* typical (*für* of); **ein ~er Fehler** a common mistake; **~ Marcus!** that's just like Marcus; **~ amerikanisch!** that's so American

u

u. *abk* = **und**

u. a. *abk* = **und andere(s)** and others; = **unter anderem, unter anderen** among other things

u. A. w. g. *abk* = **um Antwort wird gebeten** RSVP

U-Bahn *f* underground (*Brit*), subway (US)

übel *adj* bad; (*moralisch*) wicked; **mir ist ~** I feel sick; **diese Bemerkung hat er mir ~ genommen** he took offence at my remark; **Übelkeit** *f* nausea

üben *vt, vi* to practise

 SCHLÜSSELWORT

über *prep* +*dat* **1** (*räumlich*) over, above; **zwei Grad über null** two degrees above zero
2 (*zeitlich*) over; **über der Arbeit einschlafen** to fall asleep over one's work

▷ prep +akk **1** (räumlich) over; (hoch über auch) above; (quer über auch) across

2 (zeitlich) over; **über Weihnachten** over Christmas; **über kurz oder lang** sooner or later

3 (mit Zahlen) **Kinder über 12 Jahren** children over o above 12 years of age; **ein Scheck über 200 Euro** a cheque for 200 euros

4 (auf dem Wege) via; **nach Köln über Aachen** to Cologne via Aachen; **ich habe es über die Auskunft erfahren** I found out from information

5 (betreffend) about; **ein Buch über ...** a book about o on ...; **über jdn/etw lachen** to laugh about o at sb/sth

6 Macht über jdn haben to have power over sb; **sie liebt ihn über alles** she loves him more than everything

▷ adv over; **über und über** over and over; **den ganzen Tag über** all day long; **jdm in etw** dat **über sein** to be superior to sb in sth

überall adv everywhere
überanstrengen vr: **sich ~ to** overexert oneself
überbacken adj: (mit Käse) **~ au** gratin; **überbelichten** vt (Foto) to overexpose; **überbieten** irr vt to outbid; (übertreffen) to surpass; (Rekord) to break
Überbleibsel (-s, -) nt remnant
Überblick m overview; (fig: in Darstellung) survey; (Fähigkeit zu verstehen) grasp (über +akk of)
überbuchen vt to overbook; **Überbuchung** f overbooking
überdurchschnittlich adj above average
übereinander adv on top of each other; (sprechen etc) about

each other
übereinstimmen vi to agree (mit with)
überempfindlich adj hypersensitive
überfahren irr vt (Auto) to run over; **Überfahrt** f crossing
Überfall m (Banküberfall) robbery; (Mil) raid; (auf jdn) assault; **überfallen** irr vt to attack; (Bank) to raid
überfällig adj overdue
überfliegen irr vt to fly over; (Buch) to skim through
Überfluss m overabundance, excess (an +dat of); **überflüssig** adj superfluous
überfordern vt to demand too much of; (Kräfte) to overtax; **da bin ich überfordert** (bei Antwort) you've got me there
Überführung f (Brücke) flyover (Brit), overpass (US)
überfüllt adj overcrowded
Übergabe f handover
Übergang m crossing; (Wandel, Überleitung) transition; **Übergangslösung** f temporary solution, stopgap
übergeben irr vt to hand over
▷ vr: **sich ~ to** be sick, to vomit
Übergepäck nt excess baggage
Übergewicht nt excess weight; **(10 Kilo) ~ haben** to be (10 kilos) overweight
überglücklich adj overjoyed; (fam) over the moon
Übergröße f outsize
überhaupt adv at all; (im Allgemeinen) in general; (besonders) especially; **was willst du ~?** what is it you want?
überheblich adj arrogant
überholen vt to overtake; (Tech) to overhaul; **Überholspur** f overtaking (Brit) (o passing (US)) lane; **überholt** adj outdated

Überholverbot nt: **hier herrscht ~** you can't overtake here
überhören ~ vt to miss, not to catch; (absichtlich) to ignore;
überladen irr vt to overload ▷ adj (fig) cluttered; **überlassen** irr vt: **jdm etw ~** to leave sth to sb; **überlaufen** irr vi (Flüssigkeit) to overflow
überleben vt, vi to survive; **Überlebende(r)** mf survivor
überlegen vt to consider; **sich** (dat) **etw ~** to think about sth; **er hat es sich** (dat) **anders überlegt** he's changed his mind ▷ adj superior (dat to); **Überlegung** f consideration
überm kontr von **über dem**
übermäßig adj excessive
übermorgen adv the day after tomorrow
übernächste(r, s) adj: **~ Woche** the week after next
übernachten vt to spend the night (bei jdm at sb's place);
übernächtigt adj bleary-eyed, very tired; **Übernachtung** f overnight stay; **~ mit Frühstück** bed and breakfast
übernehmen irr vt to take on; (Amt, Geschäft) to take over ▷ vr: **sich ~** to take on too much
überprüfen vt to check; **Überprüfung** f check; (Überprüfen) checking
überqueren vt to cross
überraschen vt to surprise; **Überraschung** f surprise
überreden vt to persuade; **er hat mich überredet** he talked me into it
überreichen vt to hand over
übers kontr von **über das**
überschätzen vt to overestimate; **überschlagen** irr vt (berechnen) to estimate; (auslassen: Seite) to skip ▷ vr: **sich**

~ to somersault; (Auto) to overturn; (Stimme) to crack;
überschneiden irr vr: **sich ~** (Linien etc) to intersect; (Termine) to clash
Überschrift f heading
Überschwemmung f flood
Übersee f: **nach/in ~** overseas
übersehen irr vt (Gelände) to look (out) over; (nicht beachten) to overlook
übersetzen vt to translate (aus from, in +akk into); **Übersetzer(in)** (-s, -) m(f) translator; **Übersetzung** f translation
Übersicht f overall view; (Darstellung) survey; **übersichtlich** adj clear
überstehen irr vt (durchstehen) to get over; (Winter etc) to get through
Überstunden pl overtime sing
überstürzt adj hasty
überteuert adj overpriced
übertragbar adj transferable; (Med) infectious; **übertragen** irr vt to transfer (auf +akk to); (Radio) to broadcast; (Krankheit) to transmit ▷ vr to spread (auf +akk to) ▷ adj figurative;
Übertragung f (Radio) broadcast; (von Daten) transmission
übertreffen irr vt to surpass
übertreiben irr vt, vi to exaggerate, to overdo;
Übertreibung f exaggeration; **übertrieben** adj exaggerated, overdone
überwachen vt to supervise; (Verdächtigen) to keep under surveillance
überwand imperf von **überwinden**
überweisen irr vt to transfer; (Patienten) to refer (an +akk to);
Überweisung f transfer; (von Patienten) referral

überwiegend adv mainly
überwinden (überwand, überwunden) vt to overcome ▷ vr: **sich ~** to make an effort, to force oneself; **überwunden** pp von **überwinden**
Überzelt nt flysheet
überzeugen vt to convince; **Überzeugung** f conviction
überziehen irr vt (bedecken) to cover; (Jacke etc) to put on; (Konto) to overdraw; **die Betten frisch ~** to change the sheets
üblich adj usual
übrig adj remaining; **ist noch Saft ~?** is there any juice left?; **die Übrigen** pl the rest pl; **im Übrigen** besides; **~ bleiben** to be left (over); **mir blieb nichts anderes ~(, als zu gehen)** I had no other choice (but to go); **übrigens** adv besides; (nebenbei bemerkt) by the way; **übrig haben** irr vt: **für jdn etwas ~** (fam: jdn mögen) to have a soft spot for sb
Übung f practice; (im Sport, Aufgabe etc) exercise
Ufer (-s, -) nt (Fluss) bank; (Meer, See) shore; **am ~** on the bank/shore
Ufo (-(s), -s) nt akr = **unbekanntes Flugobjekt** UFO
Uhr (-, -en) f clock; (am Arm) watch; **wie viel ~ ist es?** what time is it?; **1 ~** 1 o'clock; **20 ~** 8 o'clock, 8 pm; **Uhrzeigersinn** m: **im ~** clockwise; **gegen den ~** anticlockwise (Brit), counterclockwise (US); **Uhrzeit** f time (of day)
Ukraine (-) f: **die ~** the Ukraine
UKW abk = **Ultrakurzwelle** VHF
Ulme (-, -n) f elm
Ultrakurzwelle f very high frequency; **Ultraschallaufnahme** f (Med) scan

um prep +akk **1** (um herum) (a)round; **um Weihnachten** around Christmas; **er schlug um sich** he hit about him
2 (mit Zeitangabe) at; **um acht (Uhr)** at eight (o'clock)
3 (mit Größenangabe) by; **etw um 4 cm kürzen** to shorten sth by 4 cm; **um 10% teurer** 10% more expensive; **um vieles besser** better by far; **um so besser** so much the better
4 **der Kampf um den Titel** the battle for the title; **um Geld spielen** to play for money; **Stunde um Stunde** hour after hour; **Auge um Auge** an eye for an eye
▷ prep +gen: **um ... willen** for the sake of ...; **um Gottes willen** for goodness' o (stärker) God's sake
▷ konj: **um ... zu** (in order) to ...; **zu klug, um zu ...** too clever to ...; siehe umso
▷ adv **1** (ungefähr) about; **um (die) 30 Leute** about o around 30 people
2 (vorbei) **die 2 Stunden sind um** the two hours are up

umarmen vt to embrace
Umbau m rebuilding; (zu etwas) conversion (zu into); **umbauen** vt to rebuild; (zu etwas) to convert (zu into)
um|blättern vt, vi to turn over
um|bringen irr vt to kill
um|buchen vi to change one's reservation/flight
um|drehen vt to turn (round); (obere Seite nach unten) to turn over ▷ vr: **sich ~** to turn (round); **Umdrehung** f turn; (Phys, Auto) revolution
um|fahren irr vt to knock down

um|fallen irr vi to fall over

Umfang m (Ausmaß) extent; (von Buch) size; (Reichweite) range; (Math) circumference;
umfangreich adj extensive

Umfeld nt environment

Umfrage f survey

Umgang m company; (mit jdm) dealings pl; **umgänglich** adj sociable; **Umgangssprache** f colloquial language, slang

Umgebung f surroundings pl; (Milieu) environment; (Personen) people around one

umgehen irr vi (Gerücht) to go round; **~ (können) mit** (know how to) handle ▷ irr vt to avoid; (Schwierigkeit, Verbot) to get round

um|gehen irr vi: **mit etw ~** to handle sth; **Umgehungsstraße** f bypass

umgekehrt adj reverse; (gegenteilig) opposite ▷ adv the other way round; **und ~** and vice versa

um|hören vr: **sich ~** to ask around; **um|kehren** vi to turn back ▷ vt to reverse; (Kleidungsstück) to turn inside out; **um|kippen** vt to tip over ▷ vi to overturn; (fig) to change one's mind; (fam: ohnmächtig werden) to pass out

Umkleidekabine f changing cubicle (Brit), dressing room (US); **Umkleideraum** m changing room

Umkreis m neighbourhood; **im ~ von** within a radius of

um|leiten vt to divert; **Umleitung** f diversion

um|rechnen vt to convert (in +akk into); **Umrechnung** f conversion; **Umrechnungskurs** m rate of exchange

Umriss m outline

um|rühren vi, vt to stir

ums kontr von **um das**

Umsatz m turnover

um|schalten vi to turn over

Umschlag m (von Buch) jacket; (Med) compress; (Brief) envelope

Umschulung f retraining

um|sehen irr vr: **sich ~** to look around; (suchen) to look out (nach for)

umso adv all the; **~ mehr** all the more; **~ besser** so much the better

umsonst adv (vergeblich) in vain; (gratis) for nothing

Umstand m circumstance; **Umstände** (pl) (fig) fuss; **in anderen Umständen sein** to be pregnant; **jdm Umstände machen** to cause sb a lot of trouble; **machen Sie bitte keine Umstände** please, don't put yourself out; **unter diesen/keinen Umständen** under these/no circumstances; **unter Umständen** possibly; **umständlich** adj (Methode) complicated; (Ausdrucksweise) long-winded; (Mensch) ponderous; **Umstandsmode** f maternity wear

um|steigen irr vi to change (trains/buses)

um|stellen vt (an anderen Ort) to change round; (Tech) to convert ▷ vr: **sich ~** to adapt (auf +akk to); **Umstellung** f change; (Umgewöhnung) adjustment; (Tech) conversion

Umtausch m exchange; **um|tauschen** vt to exchange; (Währung) to change

Umweg m detour

Umwelt f environment; **Umweltbelastung** f ecological damage; **umweltbewusst** adj environmentally aware

umweltfreundlich adj
environment-friendly;
Umweltpapier nt recycled paper;
umweltschädlich adj harmful to
the environment; **Umweltschutz**
m environmental protection;
Umweltschützer(in) (-s, -) m(f)
environmentalist;
Umweltverschmutzung f
pollution; **umweltverträglich** adj
environment-friendly

um|werfen irr vt to knock over;
(fig: ändern) to upset; (fig, fam: jdn)
to flabbergast

um|ziehen irr vt to change ▷ vr:
sich ~ to change ▷ vi to move
(house); **Umzug** m
(Straßenumzug) procession;
(Wohnungsumzug) move

unabhängig adj independent;
Unabhängigkeitstag m
Independence Day, Fourth of July
(US)

unabsichtlich adv
unintentionally

unangenehm adj unpleasant;
Unannehmlichkeit f inconvenience;
~en pl trouble sing

unanständig adj indecent;
unappetitlich adj (Essen)
unappetizing; (abstoßend)
off-putting; **unbeabsichtigt** adj
unintentional; **unbedeutend** adj
insignificant, unimportant;
(Fehler) slight

unbedingt adj unconditional
▷ adv absolutely

unbefriedigend adj unsatisfactory; **unbegrenzt** adj
unlimited; **unbekannt** adj
unknown; **unbeliebt** adj
unpopular; **unbemerkt** adj
unnoticed; **unbequem** adj
(Stuhl, Mensch) uncomfortable;
(Regelung) inconvenient;
unbeständig adj (Wetter)
unsettled; (Lage) unstable;

(Mensch) unreliable; **unbestimmt**
adj indefinite; **unbeteiligt** adj
(nicht dazugehörig) uninvolved;
(innerlich nicht berührt) indifferent,
unconcerned; **unbewacht** adj
unguarded; **unbewusst** adj
unconscious; **unbezahlt** adj
unpaid; **unbrauchbar** adj
useless

und conj and; **~ so weiter** and so
on; **na ~?** so what?

undankbar adj (Person)
ungrateful; (Aufgabe) thankless;
undenkbar adj inconceivable;
undeutlich adj indistinct;
undicht adj leaky; **uneben** adj
uneven; **unecht** adj (Schmuck etc)
fake; **unehelich** adj (Kind)
illegitimate; **unendlich** adj
endless; (Math) infinite;
unentbehrlich adj indispensable;
unentgeltlich adj free (of charge)

unentschieden adj undecided;
~ enden (Sport) to end in a draw

unerfreulich adj unpleasant

unerhört adj unheard-of; (Bitte)
outrageous; **unerlässlich** adj
indispensable; **unerträglich** adj
unbearable; **unerwartet** adj
unexpected

unerwünscht adj unwelcome;
(Eigenschaften) undesirable;
unfähig adj incompetent; **~ sein,
etw zu tun** to be incapable of
doing sth; **unfair** adj unfair

Unfall m accident; **Unfallbericht**
m accident report; **Unfallflucht** f
failure to stop after an accident;
Unfallhergang m: **den
~ schildern** to give details of the
accident; **Unfallstation** f
casualty ward; **Unfallstelle** f
scene of the accident;
Unfallversicherung f accident
insurance

unfreundlich adj unfriendly
Ungarn (-s) nt Hungary

Ungeduld f impatience; **ungeduldig** adj impatient
ungeeignet adj unsuitable
ungefähr adj approximate ▷ adv approximately; **~ 10 Kilometer** about 10 kilometres; **wann ~?** about what time?; **wo ~?** whereabouts?
ungefährlich adj harmless; (sicher) safe
ungeheuer adj huge ▷ adv (fam) enormously; **Ungeheuer** (-s, -) nt monster
ungehorsam adj disobedient (gegenüber to)
ungelegen adj inconvenient; **ungemütlich** adj unpleasant; (Mensch) disagreeable; **ungenießbar** adj inedible; (Getränk) undrinkable; **ungenügend** adj unsatisfactory; (Schulnote) ≈ F; **ungepflegt** adj (Garten) untended; (Aussehen) unkempt; (Hände) neglected; **ungerade** adj odd
ungerecht adj unjust; **ungerechtfertigt** adj unjustified; **Ungerechtigkeit** f injustice, unfairness
ungern adv reluctantly; **ungeschickt** adj clumsy; **ungeschminkt** adj without make-up; **ungesund** adj unhealthy; **ungewiss** adj uncertain; **ungewöhnlich** adj unusual
Ungeziefer (-s) nt vermin pl
ungezogen adj ill-mannered
ungezwungen adj relaxed
ungiftig adj non-toxic
unglaublich adj incredible
Unglück (-(e)s, -e) nt (Unheil) misfortune; (Pech) bad luck; (Unglücksfall) disaster; (Verkehrs~) accident; **das bringt ~** that's unlucky; **unglücklich** adj unhappy; (erfolglos) unlucky;

(unerfreulich) unfortunate; **unglücklicherweise** adv unfortunately
ungültig adj invalid
ungünstig adj inconvenient
unheilbar adj incurable; **~ krank sein** to be terminally ill
unheimlich adj eerie ▷ adv (fam) incredibly
unhöflich adj impolite
uni adj plain
Uni (-, -s) f uni
Uniform (-, -en) f uniform
Universität f university
Unkenntnis f ignorance
unklar adj unclear
Unkosten pl expenses pl; **Unkostenbeitrag** m contribution (towards expenses)
Unkraut nt weeds pl, ~art, weed
unlogisch adj illogical
unmissverständlich adj unambiguous
unmittelbar adj immediate; **~ darauf** immediately afterwards
unmöbliert adj unfurnished
unmöglich adj impossible
unnahbar adj unapproachable
unnötig adj unnecessary
UNO (-) f akr = **United Nations Organization** UN
unordentlich adj untidy; **Unordnung** f disorder
unpassend adj inappropriate; (Zeit) inconvenient; **unpersönlich** adj impersonal; **unpraktisch** adj impractical
Unrecht nt wrong; **zu ~** wrongly; **im ~ sein** to be wrong; **unrecht** adj wrong; **~ haben** to be wrong
unregelmäßig adj irregular; **unreif** adj unripe; **unruhig** adj restless; **~ schlafen** to have a bad night
uns pron akk, dat von **wir**; us, (to) us; **~ (selbst)** (reflexiv) ourselves;

sehen Sie ~? can you see us?; **er schickte es ~** he sent it to us; **lasst ~ in Ruhe** leave us alone; **ein Freund von ~** a friend of ours; **wir haben ~ hingesetzt** we sat down; **wir haben ~ amüsiert** we enjoyed ourselves; **wir mögen ~** we like each other

unscharf adj (Foto) blurred, out of focus

unscheinbar adj insignificant; (Aussehen) unprepossessing

unschlüssig adj undecided

unschuldig adj innocent

unser pron (adjektivisch) our
▷ pron gen von **wir**; of us; **unsere(r, s)** pron (substantivisch) ours; **unseretwegen** adv (wegen uns) because of us; (uns zuliebe) for our sake; (um uns) about us; (von uns aus) as far as we are concerned

unseriös adj dubious; **unsicher** adj (ungewiss) uncertain; (Person, Job) insecure

Unsinn m nonsense

unsterblich adj immortal; **~ verliebt** madly in love

unsympathisch adj unpleasant; **er ist mir ~** I don't like him

unten adv below; (im Haus) downstairs; (an der Treppe etc) at the bottom; **nach ~ down**

⊙ SCHLÜSSELWORT

unter prep +dat 1 (räumlich, mit Zahlen) under; (drunter) underneath, below; **unter 18 Jahren** under 18 years
2 (zwischen) among(st); **sie waren unter sich** they were by themselves; **einer unter ihnen** one of them; **unter anderem** among other things
▷ prep +akk under, below

Unterarm m forearm

unterbelichtet adj (Foto) underexposed

Unterbewusstsein nt subconscious

unterbrechen irr vt to interrupt; **Unterbrechung** f interruption; **ohne ~** nonstop

unterdrücken vt to suppress; (Leute) to oppress

unterdurchschnittlich adj below average

untere(r, s) adj lower

untereinander adv (räumlich) one below the other; (gegenseitig) each other; (miteinander) among themselves/yourselves/ourselves

Unterführung f underpass

untergehen irr vi to go down; (Sonne) to set; (Volk) to perish; (Welt) to come to an end; (im Lärm) to be drowned out

Untergeschoss nt basement; **Untergewicht** nt: (**3 Kilo**) **~ haben** to be (3 kilos) underweight; **Untergrund** m foundation; (Pol) underground; **Untergrundbahn** f underground (Brit), subway (US)

unterhalb adv, prep +gen below; **~ von** below

Unterhalt m maintenance; **unterhalten** irr vt to maintain; (belustigen) to entertain ▷ vr: **sich ~** to talk; (sich belustigen) to enjoy oneself; **Unterhaltung** f (Belustigung) entertainment; (Gespräch) talk, conversation

Unterhemd nt vest (Brit), undershirt (US); **Unterhose** f underpants pl; (für Damen) briefs pl

unterirdisch adj underground

Unterkiefer m lower jaw

Unterkunft (-, -künfte) f accommodation

Unterlage f (Beleg) document; (Schreibunterlage) pad

unterlassen irr vt: **es ~, etw zu tun** (versäumen) to fail to do sth; (bleiben lassen) to refrain from doing sth
unterlegen adj inferior (dat to); (besiegt) defeated
Unterleib m abdomen
Unterlippe f lower lip
Untermiete f: **zur ~ wohnen** to be a subtenant; **Untermieter(in)** m(f) subtenant
unternehmen irr vt (Reise) to go on; (Versuch) to make; **etwas ~ to do something** (gegen about); **Unternehmen** (-s, -) nt undertaking; (Comm) company; **Unternehmensberater(in)** (-s, -) m(f) management consultant; **Unternehmer(in)** (-s, -) m(f) entrepreneur
Unterricht (-(e)s, -e) m lessons pl; **unterrichten** vt to teach
unterschätzen vt to underestimate
unterscheiden irr vt to distinguish (von from, zwischen +dat between) ▷ vr: **sich ~ to differ** (von from)
Unterschenkel m lower leg
Unterschied (-(e)s, -e) m difference; **im ~ zu dir** unlike you; **unterschiedlich** adj different
unterschreiben irr vt to sign; **Unterschrift** f signature
Untersetzer (-s, -) m tablemat; (für Gläser) coaster
unterste(r, s) adj lowest, bottom
unter|stellen vr: **sich ~ to take** shelter
unterstellen vt (rangmäßig) to subordinate (dat to); (fig) to impute (jdm etw sth to sb)
unterstreichen irr vt (a. fig) to underline
Unterstrich m (Inform) underscore

unterstützen vt to support; **Unterstützung** f support
untersuchen vt (Med) to examine; (Polizei) to investigate; **Untersuchung** f examination; (polizeiliche) investigation
untertags adv during the day
Untertasse f saucer
Unterteil nt lower part, bottom
Untertitel m subtitle
untervermieten vt to sublet
Unterwäsche f underwear
unterwegs adv on the way
unterzeichnen vt to sign
untreu adj unfaithful
untröstlich adj inconsolable; **unüberlegt** adj ill-considered ▷ adv without thinking; **unüblich** adj unusual; **unverantwortlich** adj irresponsible; (unentschuldbar) inexcusable
unverbindlich adj not binding; (Antwort) noncommittal ▷ adv (Comm) without obligation
unverbleit adj unleaded; **unverheiratet** adj unmarried, single; **unvermeidlich** adj unavoidable; **unvernünftig** adj silly; **unverschämt** adj impudent; **unverständlich** adj incomprehensible; **unverträglich** adj (Person) quarrelsome; (Essen) indigestible
unverwüstlich adj indestructible; (Mensch) irrepressible
unverzeihlich adj unpardonable; **unverzüglich** adj immediate; **unvollständig** adj incomplete; **unvorsichtig** adj careless
unwahrscheinlich adj improbable, unlikely ▷ adv (fam) incredibly
Unwetter nt thunderstorm
unwichtig adj unimportant
unwiderstehlich adj irresistible

unwillkürlich adj involuntary
▷ adv instinctively; **ich musste
~ lachen** I couldn't help laughing
unwohl adj unwell, ill
unzählig adj innumerable,
countless
unzerbrechlich adj unbreak-
able; **unzertrennlich** adj
inseparable; **unzufrieden** adj
dissatisfied; **unzugänglich** adj
inaccessible; **unzumutbar** adj
unacceptable
unzusammenhängend adj
disconnected; (Äußerung)
incoherent; **unzutreffend** adj
inapplicable; (unwahr) incorrect;
unzuverlässig adj unreliable
Update (-s, -s) nt (Inform) update
üppig adj (Essen) lavish;
(Vegetation) lush
uralt adj ancient, very old
Uran (-s) nt uranium
Uranus (-) m Uranus
Uraufführung f premiere
Urenkel m great-grandson;
Urenkelin f great-grand-
daughter; **Urgroßeltern** pl
great-grandparents pl;
Urgroßmutter f great-grandmother; **Urgroßvater** m
great-grandfather
Urheber(in) (-s, -) m(f) origin-
ator; (Autor) author
Urin (-s, -e) m urine; **Urinprobe**
f urine specimen
Urkunde (-, -n) f document
Urlaub (-(e)s, -e) m holiday (Brit),
vacation (US); **im ~** on holiday
(Brit), on vacation (US); **in ~ fahren**
to go on holiday (Brit) (o vacation
(US)); **Urlauber(in)** (-s, -) m(f)
holiday-maker (Brit), vacationer
(US); **Urlaubsort** m holiday
resort; **urlaubsreif** adj ready for
a holiday (Brit) (o vacation (US));
Urlaubszeit f holiday season
(Brit), vacation period (US)

Urne (-, -n) f urn
Urologe m, **Urologin** f
urologist
Ursache f cause (für of); **keine ~!**
not at all; (bei Entschuldigung) that's
all right
Ursprung m origin; (von Fluss)
source; **ursprünglich** adj
original ▷ adv originally;
Ursprungsland adj country of
origin
Urteil (-s, -e) nt (Meinung)
opinion; (Jur) verdict; (Strafmaß)
sentence; **urteilen** vi to judge
Uruguay (-s) nt Uruguay
Urwald m jungle
USA pl USA sing
User(in) (-s, -) m(f) (Inform) user
usw. abk = **und so weiter** etc
Utensilien pl utensils pl

V

vage *adj* vague

Vagina (-, *Vaginen*) *f* vagina

Valentinstag *m* St Valentine's Day

Vandalismus *m* vandalism

Vanille (-) *f* vanilla

variieren *vt, vi* to vary

Vase (-, -n) *f* vase

Vaseline (-) *f* Vaseline®

Vater (-s, *Väter*) *m* father; **väterlich** *adj* paternal; **Vaterschaft** *f* fatherhood; *(Jur)* paternity; **Vatertag** *m* Father's Day; **Vaterunser** *nt*: **das ~ (beten)** (to say) the Lord's Prayer

V-Ausschnitt *m* V-neck

v. Chr. *abk* = **vor Christus** BC

Veganer(in) (-s, -) *m(f)* vegan; **Vegetarier(in)** (-s, -) *m(f)* vegetarian; **vegetarisch** *adj* vegetarian

Veilchen *nt* violet

Velo (-s, -s) *nt* (*schweizerisch*)

bicycle

Vene (-, -n) *f* vein

Venedig (-s) *nt* Venice

Venezuela (-s) *nt* Venezuela

Ventil (-s, -e) *nt* valve

Ventilator *m* ventilator

Venus (-) *f* Venus

Venusmuschel *f* clam

verabreden *vt* to arrange ▷ *vr*: **sich ~** to arrange to meet (*mit jdm* sb); **ich bin schon verabredet** I'm already meeting someone; **Verabredung** *f* arrangement; (*Termin*) appointment; (*zum Ausgehen*) date

verabschieden *vt* (*Gäste*) to say goodbye to; (*Gesetz*) to pass ▷ *vr*: **sich ~** to say goodbye

verachten *vt* to despise; **verächtlich** *adj* contemptuous; (*verachtenswert*) contemptible; **Verachtung** *f* contempt

verallgemeinern *vt* to generalize

Veranda (-, *Veranden*) *f* veranda, porch (US)

veränderlich *adj* changeable; **verändern** *vt* to change ▷ *vr*: **sich ~** to change; **Veränderung** *f* change

veranlassen *vt* to cause

veranstalten *vt* to organize; **Veranstalter(in)** (-s, -) *m(f)* organizer; **Veranstaltung** *f* event; **Veranstaltungsort** *m* venue

verantworten *vt* to take responsibility for ▷ *vr*: **sich für etw ~** to answer for sth; **verantwortlich** *adj* responsible (*für* for); **Verantwortung** *f* responsibility (*für* for)

verärgern *vt* to annoy

verarschen *vt* (*fam*) to take the piss out of (*Brit*), to make a sucker out of (*US*)

Verb (-s, -en) *nt* verb

Verband m (Med) bandage; (Bund) association; **Verband(s)kasten** m first-aid box; **Verband(s)zeug** nt dressing material

verbessern vt to improve; (berichtigen) to correct ▷ vr: **sich ~** to improve; (berichtigen) to correct oneself; **Verbesserung** f improvement; (Berichtigung) correction

verbiegen irr vi to bend ▷ vr: **sich ~** to bend

verbieten irr vt to forbid; **jdm ~, etw zu tun** to forbid sb to do sth

verbinden irr vt to connect; (kombinieren) to combine; (Med) to bandage; **können Sie mich mit ... ~?** (Tel) can you put me through to ...?; **ich verbinde** (Tel) I'm putting you through ▷ vr (Chem) **sich ~** to combine

verbindlich adj binding; (freundlich) friendly; **Verbindung** f connection

verbleit adj leaded

verblüffen vt to amaze

verblühen vi to fade

verborgen adj hidden

Verbot (-(e)s, -e) nt ban (für, von on); **verboten** adj forbidden; **es ist ~** it's not allowed; **es ist ~, hier zu parken** no parking here; **Rauchen ~** no smoking

verbrannt adj burnt

Verbrauch (-(e)s) m consumption; **verbrauchen** vt to use up; **Verbraucher(in)** (-s, -) m(f) consumer

Verbrechen (-s, -) nt crime; **Verbrecher(in)** (-s, -) m(f) criminal

verbreiten vt to spread ▷ vr: **sich ~** to spread

verbrennen irr vt to burn; **Verbrennung** f burning; (in Motor) combustion

verbringen irr vt to spend

verbunden adj: **falsch ~** sorry, wrong number

Verdacht (-(e)s) m suspicion; **verdächtig** adj suspicious; **verdächtigen** vt to suspect

verdammt interj (fam) damn

verdanken vt: **jdm etw ~** to owe sth to sb

verdarb imperf von **verderben**

verdauen vt (a. fig) to digest; **verdaulich** adj digestible; **das ist schwer ~** that is hard to digest; **Verdauung** f digestion

Verdeck (-(e)s, -e) nt top

verderben (verdarb, verdorben) vt to spoil; (schädigen) to ruin; (moralisch) to corrupt; **es soll** mit jdm ~ to get into sb's bad books; **ich habe mir den Magen verdorben** I've got an upset stomach ▷ vi (Lebensmittel) to go off

verdienen vt to earn; (moralisch) to deserve; **Verdienst** (-(e)s, -e) m earnings pl ▷ (-(e)s, -e) nt merit; (Leistung) service (um to)

verdoppeln vt to double

verdorben pp von **verderben** ▷ adj spoilt; (geschädigt) ruined; (moralisch) corrupt

verdrehen vt to twist; (Augen) to roll; **jdm den Kopf ~** (fig) to turn sb's head

verdünnen vt to dilute

verdunsten vi to evaporate

verdursten vi to die of thirst

verehren vt to admire; (Rel) to worship; **Verehrer(in)** (-s, -) m(f) admirer

Verein (-(e)s, -e) m association; (Klub) club

vereinbar adj compatible

vereinbaren vt to arrange; **Vereinbarung** f agreement, arrangement

vereinigen vt to unite ▷ vr: **sich ~** to unite; **Vereinigtes Königreich** nt United Kingdom; **Vereinigte Staaten (von Amerika)** pl United States sing (of America); **Vereinigung** f union; (Verein) association; **Vereinte Nationen** pl United Nations pl

vereisen vi (Straße) to freeze over; (Fenster) to ice up ▷ vt (Med) to freeze

vererben vt: **jdm etw ~** to leave sth to sb; (Bio) to pass sth on to sb ▷ vr: **sich ~** to be hereditary; **vererblich** adj hereditary

verfahren irr vi to proceed ▷ vr: **sich ~** to get lost; **Verfahren** (-s, -) nt procedure; (Tech) method; (Jur) proceedings pl

verfallen irr vi to decline; (Haus) to be falling apart; (Fahrkarte etc) to expire; **~ in** (+akk) to lapse into; **Verfallsdatum** nt expiry (Brit) (o expiration (US)) date; (von Lebensmitteln) best-before date

verfärben vr: **sich ~** to change colour; (Wäsche) to discolour

Verfasser(in) (-s, -) m(f) author, writer; **Verfassung** f (gesundheitlich) condition; (Pol) constitution

verfaulen vi to rot

verfehlen vt to miss

verfeinern vt to refine

Verfilmung f film (o screen) version

verfluchen vt to curse

verfolgen vt to pursue; (Pol) to persecute

verfügbar adj available; **verfügen** vi **über etw** (akk) **~** to have sth at one's disposal;

Verfügung f order; **jdm zur ~ stehen** to be at sb's disposal; **jdm etw zur ~ stellen** to put sth at sb's disposal

verführen vt to tempt; (sexuell) to seduce; **verführerisch** adj seductive

vergangen adj past; **~e Woche** last week; **Vergangenheit** f past

Vergaser (-s, -) m (Auto) carburettor

vergaß imperf von **vergessen**

vergeben irr vt to forgive (jdm etw sb for sth); (weggeben) to award, to allocate; **vergebens** adv in vain; **vergeblich** adv in vain ▷ adj vain, futile

vergehen irr vi to pass ▷ vr: **sich an jdm ~** to indecently assault sb; **Vergehen** (-s, -) nt offence

Vergeltung f retaliation

vergessen (vergaß, vergessen) vt to forget; **vergesslich** adj forgetful

vergeuden vt to squander, to waste

vergewaltigen vt to rape; **Vergewaltigung** f rape

vergewissern vr: **sich ~** to make sure

vergiften vt to poison; **Vergiftung** f poisoning

Vergissmeinnicht (-(e)s, -e) nt forget-me-not

Vergleich (-(e)s, -e) m comparison; (Jur) settlement; **im ~ zu** compared to (o with); **vergleichen** irr vt to compare (mit to, with)

Vergnügen (-s, -) nt pleasure; **viel ~!** enjoy yourself; **vergnügt** adj cheerful; **Vergnügungspark** m amusement park

vergoldet adj gold-plated

vergriffen adj (Buch) out of print; (Ware) out of stock

vergrößern vt to enlarge;
(Menge) to increase; (mit Lupe) to
magnify; **Vergrößerung** f
enlargement; (Menge) increase;
(mit Lupe) magnification;
Vergrößerungsglas nt magnifying glass
verh. adj abk = **verheiratet**
married
verhaften vt to arrest
verhalten irr vr: **sich ~** (sich
benehmen) to behave; (Sache) to be;
Verhalten (-s) nt behaviour
Verhältnis nt relationship (zu
with); (Math) ratio; **~se** pl
circumstances pl, conditions pl; **im
~ von 1 zu 2** in a ratio of 1 to 2;
verhältnismäßig adj relative
▷ adv relatively
verhandeln vi to negotiate (über
etw akk sth); **Verhandlung** f
negotiation
verheimlichen vt to keep secret
(jdm from sb)
verheiratet adj married
verhindern vt to prevent; **sie
ist verhindert** she can't make
it
Verhör (-(e)s, -e) nt
interrogation; (gerichtlich)
examination; **verhören** vt to
interrogate; (bei Gericht) to
examine ▷ vr: **sich ~** to mishear
verhungern vi to starve to
death
verhüten vt to prevent;
Verhütung f prevention; (mit
Pille, Kondom etc) contraception;
Verhütungsmittel nt
contraceptive
verirren vr: **sich ~** to get lost
Verkauf m sale; **verkaufen** vt to
sell; **zu ~** for sale; **Verkäufer(in)**
m(f) seller; (beruflich) salesperson;
(in Laden) shop assistant (Brit),
salesperson (US); **verkäuflich** adj
for sale

Verkehr (-s, -e) m traffic; (Sex)
intercourse; (Umlauf) circulation;
verkehren vi (Bus etc) to run; **~ in**
to frequent; **~ mit** to associate (o
mix) with; **Verkehrsampel** f
traffic lights pl; **Verkehrsamt** nt
tourist information office;
verkehrsfrei adj traffic-free;
Verkehrsfunk m travel news sing;
Verkehrsinsel f traffic island;
Verkehrsmeldung f traffic
report; **Verkehrsmittel** nt means
sing of transport; **öffentliche ~** pl
public transport sing;
Verkehrsschild nt traffic sign;
Verkehrstote(r) mf road
casualty; **die Zahl der ~n** the
number of deaths on the road;
Verkehrsunfall m road accident;
Verkehrszeichen nt traffic sign
verkehrt adj wrong; (verkehrt
herum) the wrong way round;
(Pullover etc) inside out; **du machst
es ~** you're doing it wrong
verklagen vt to take to court
verkleiden vt to dress up (als as)
▷ vr: **sich ~** to dress up (als as); (um
unerkannt zu bleiben) to disguise
oneself; **Verkleidung** f (Karneval)
fancy dress; (um nicht erkannt zu
werden) disguise
verkleinern vt to reduce;
(Zimmer, Gebiet etc) to make smaller
verkneifen irr vt sich (dat) etw
~ (Lachen) to stifle sth; (Schmerz) to
hide sth; (sich versagen) to do
without sth; **verkommen** irr vi
(Mensch) to go
downhill ▷ adj (Haus) dilapidated;
(moralisch) depraved; **verkraften**
vt to cope with
verkratzt adj scratched
verkühlen vr: **sich ~** to get a chill
verkürzen vt to shorten
Verlag (-(e)s, -e) m publishing
company
verlangen vt (fordern) to

demand; (wollen) to want; (Preis) to
ask; (Qualifikation) to require;
(erwarten) to ask (von of); (fragen
nach) to ask for; (Pass etc) to ask to
see; **~ Sie Herrn X** ask for Mr X
▷ vi: **~ nach** to ask for
verlängern vt to extend; (Pass,
Erlaubnis) renew; **Verlängerung** f
extension; (Sport) extra time; (von
Pass, Erlaubnis) renewal;
Verlängerungsschnur f extension cable; **Verlängerungswoche**
f extra week
verlassen irr vt to leave ▷ irr vr:
sich ~ to rely (auf +akk on) ▷ adj
desolate; (Mensch) abandoned;
verlässlich adj reliable
Verlauf m course; **verlaufen** irr
vi (Weg, Grenze) to run (entlang
along); (zeitlich) to pass; (Farben) to
run ▷ vr: **sich ~** to get lost;
(Menschenmenge) to disperse
verlegen vt to move; (verlieren) to
mislay; (Buch) to publish ▷ adj
embarrassed; **Verlegenheit** f
embarrassment; (Situation)
difficulty
Verleih (-(e)s, -e) m (Firma) hire
company (Brit), rental company
(US); **verleihen** irr vt to lend;
(vermieten) to hire (out) (Brit), to
rent (out) (US); (Preis, Medaille) to
award
verleiten vt: **jdn dazu ~, etw zu
tun** to induce sb to do sth
verlernen vt to forget
verletzen vt to injure; (fig) to
hurt; **Verletzte(r)** mf injured
person; **Verletzung** f injury;
(Verstoß) violation
verlieben vr: **sich ~** to fall in love
(in jdn with sb); **verliebt** adj in
love
verlieren (verlor, verloren) vt, vi to
lose
verloben vr: **sich ~** to get
engaged (mit to); **Verlobte(r)** mf

fiancé/fiancée; **Verlobung** f
engagement
verlor imperf von **verlieren**
verloren pp von **verlieren** ▷ adj
lost; (Eier) poached; **~ gehen** to go
missing
verlosen vt to raffle; **Verlosung** f
raffle
Verlust (-(e)s, -e) m loss
vermehren vt to multiply;
(Menge) to increase ▷ vr: **sich ~** to
multiply; (Menge) to increase
vermeiden irr vt to avoid
vermeintlich adj supposed
vermieten vt to rent (out), to let
(out) (Brit); (Auto) to hire (out)
(Brit), to rent (out) (US);
Vermieter(in) m(f)
landlord/-lady
vermischen vt to mix ▷ vr: **sich ~** to mix
vermissen vt to miss; **vermisst**
adj missing; **jdn als ~ melden** to
report sb missing
Vermittlung f (bei Streit)
mediation; (Herbeiführung)
arranging; (Stelle) agency
Vermögen (-s, -) nt fortune
vermuten vt to suppose;
(argwöhnen) to suspect;
vermutlich adj probable ▷ adv
probably; **Vermutung** f
supposition; (Verdacht) suspicion
vernachlässigen vt to neglect
vernichten vt to destroy;
vernichtend adj (fig) crushing;
(Blick) withering; (Kritik) scathing
Vernunft (-) f reason; **ich kann
ihn nicht zur ~ bringen** I can't
make him see reason; **vernünftig**
adj sensible; (Preis) reasonable
veröffentlichen vt to publish
verordnen vt (Med) to prescribe;
Verordnung f order; (Med)
prescription
verpachten vt to lease (out) (an
+akk to)

verpacken vt to pack; (*einwickeln*) to wrap up

Verpackung f packaging; **Verpackungskosten** pl packing charges pl

verpassen vt to miss

verpflegen vt to feed; **Verpflegung** f feeding; (*Kost*) food; (*in Hotel*) board

verpflichten vt to oblige; (*anstellen*) to engage ▷ vr: **sich ~** to commit oneself (*etw zu tun* to doing sth)

verprügeln vt to beat up

verraten irr vt to betray; (*Geheimnis*) to divulge; **aber nicht ~!** but don't tell anyone ▷ vr: **sich ~** to give oneself away

verrechnen vt: **~ mit** to set off against ▷ vr: **sich ~** to miscalculate; **Verrechnungsscheck** m crossed cheque (*Brit*), check for deposit only (*US*)

verregnet adj rainy

verreisen vi to go away (*nach* to); **sie ist (geschäftlich) verreist** she's away (on business)

verrenken vt to contort; (*Med*) to dislocate; **sich** (*dat*) **den Knöchel ~** to sprain (o twist) one's ankle;

verringern vt to reduce

verrostet adj rusty

verrückt adj mad, crazy; **es macht mich ~** it's driving me mad

versagen vi to fail; **Versagen** (*-s*) nt failure; **Versager(in)** (*-s, -*) m(f) failure

versalzen irr vt to put too much salt in/on

versammeln vt to assemble, to gather ▷ vr: **sich ~** to assemble, to gather; **Versammlung** f meeting

Versand (*-(e)s*) m dispatch; (*Abteilung*) dispatch department; **Versandhaus** nt mail-order company

versäumen vt to miss; (*unterlassen*) to neglect; **~, etw zu tun** to fail to do sth

verschätzen vr: **sich ~** to miscalculate

verschenken vt to give away; (*Chance*) to waste

verschicken vt to send off

verschieben vt irr (*auf später*) to postpone, to put off; (*an anderen Ort*) to move

verschieden adj (*unterschiedlich*) different; (*mehrere*) various; **sie sind ~ groß** they are of different sizes; **Verschiedene** pl various people/things pl; **Verschiedenes** various things pl

verschimmelt adj mouldy

verschlafen irr vt to sleep through; (*fig*) to miss ▷ vi to oversleep

verschlechtern vr: **sich ~** to deteriorate, to get worse; **Verschlechterung** f deterioration

Verschleiß (*-es*) m wear and tear

verschließbar adj lockable; **verschließen** irr vt to close; (*mit Schlüssel*) to lock

verschlimmern vt to make worse ▷ vr: **sich ~** to get worse

verschlossen adj locked; (*fig*) reserved

verschlucken vt to swallow ▷ vr: **sich ~** to choke (*an +dat* on)

Verschluss m lock; (*von Kleid*) fastener; (*Foto*) shutter; (*Stöpsel*) stopper

verschmutzen vt to get dirty; (*Umwelt*) to pollute

verschnaufen vi: **ich muss mal ~** I need to get my breath back

verschneit adj snow-covered

verschnupft adj: **~ sein** to have a cold; (*fam: beleidigt*) to be peeved

verschonen vt to spare (*jdn mit etw* sb sth)

verschreiben *irr vt (Med)* to prescribe; **verschreibungspflichtig** *adj* available only on prescription

verschwand *imperf von* **verschwinden**

verschweigen *irr vt* to keep secret; **jdm etw ~** to keep sth from sb

verschwenden *vt* to waste; **Verschwendung** *f* waste

verschwiegen *adj* discreet; *(Ort)* secluded

verschwinden *(verschwand, verschwunden) vi* to disappear, to vanish; **verschwinde!** get lost!; **verschwunden** *pp von* **verschwinden**

Versehen *(-s, -) nt:* **aus ~** by mistake; **versehentlich** *adv* by mistake

versenden *irr vt* to send off

versessen *adj:* **~ auf** *(+akk)* mad about

versetzen *vt* to transfer; *(verpfänden)* to pawn; *(fam: bei Verabredung)* to stand up ▷ *vr:* **sich in jdn** *o* **jds Lage ~** to put oneself in sb's place

verseuchen *vt* to contaminate

versichern *vt* to insure; *(bestätigen)* to assure; **versichert sein** to be insured; **Versichertenkarte** *f* health-insurance card; **Versicherung** *f* insurance; **Versicherungskarte** *f:* **grüne ~** green card *(Brit)*, insurance document for driving abroad; **Versicherungspolice** *f* insurance policy

versilbert *adj* silver-plated

versinken *irr vi* to sink

Version *f* version

versöhnen *vt* to reconcile ▷ *vr:* **sich ~** to become reconciled

versorgen *vt* to provide, to supply *(mit* with); *(Familie)* to look

after ▷ *vr:* **sich ~** to look after oneself; **Versorgung** *f* provision; *(Unterhalt)* maintenance; *(für Alter etc)* benefit

verspäten *vr:* **sich ~** to be late; **verspätet** *adj* late; **Verspätung** *f* delay; **(eine Stunde) ~ haben** to be (an hour) late

versprechen *irr vt* to promise ▷ *vr:* **ich habe mich versprochen** I didn't mean to say that

Verstand *m* mind; *(Vernunft)* (common) sense; **den ~ verlieren** to lose one's mind; **verständigen** *vt* to inform ▷ *vr:* **sich ~** to communicate; *(sich einigen)* to come to an understanding; **Verständigung** *f* communication; **verständlich** *adj* understandable; **Verständnis** *nt* understanding *(für* of); *(Mitgefühl)* sympathy; **verständnisvoll** *adj* understanding

verstauchen *vt* to sprain; **verstaucht** *pp von* **verstauchen** sprained

Versteck *(-(e)s, -e) nt* hiding place; **~ spielen** to play hide-and-seek; **verstecken** *vt* to hide *(vor+dat* from) ▷ *vr:* **sich ~** to hide *(vor+dat* from)

verstehen *irr vt* to understand; **falsch ~** to misunderstand ▷ *vr:* **sich ~** to get on *(mit* with)

Versteigerung *f* auction

verstellbar *adj* adjustable; **verstellen** *vt* to move; *(Uhr)* to adjust; *(versperren)* to block; *(Stimme, Handschrift)* to disguise ▷ *vr:* **sich ~** to pretend, to put on an act

verstopfen *vt* to block up; *(Med)* to constipate; **Verstopfung** *f* obstruction; *(Med)* constipation

Verstoß *m* infringement, violation *(gegen* of)

Versuch (-(e)s, -e) m attempt; (wissenschaftlich) experiment; **versuchen** vt to try

vertauschen vt to exchange; (versehentlich) to mix up

verteidigen vt to defend; **Verteidiger(in)** (-s, -) m(f) (Sport) defender; (Jur) defence counsel; **Verteidigung** f defence

verteilen vt to distribute

Vertrag (-(e)s, Verträge) m contract; (Pol) treaty

vertragen irr vt to stand, to bear ▷ vr: **sich ~** to get along (with each other); (sich aussöhnen) to make it up

verträglich adj (Mensch) good-natured; (Speisen) digestible

vertrauen vi: **jdm/einer Sache ~** to trust sb/sth; **Vertrauen** (-s) nt trust (in +akk in, zu in); **ich habe kein ~ zu ihm** I don't trust him; **ich hab's ihm im ~ gesagt** I told him in confidence; **vertraulich** adj (geheim) confidential; **vertraut** adj: **sich mit etw ~ machen** to familiarize oneself with sth

vertreten irr vt to represent; (Ansicht) to hold; **Vertreter(in)** (-s, -) m(f) representative

Vertrieb (-(e)s, -e) m (Abteilung) sales department

vertrocknen vi to dry up

vertun irr vr: **sich ~** to make a mistake

vertuschen vt to cover up

verunglücken vi to have an accident; **tödlich ~** to be killed in an accident

verunsichern vt to make uneasy

verursachen vt to cause

verurteilen vt to condemn

vervielfältigen vt to make copies of

verwählen vr: **sich ~** to dial the wrong number

verwalten vt to manage; (behördlich) to administer; **Verwalter(in)** (-s, -) m(f) manager; (Vermögens~) trustee; **Verwaltung** f management; (amtlich) administration

verwandt adj related (mit to); **Verwandte(r)** mf relative, relation; **Verwandtschaft** f relationship; (Menschen) relations pl

verwarnen vt to warn; (Sport) to caution

verwechseln vt to confuse (mit with); (halten für) to mistake (mit for)

verweigern vt to refuse

verwenden vt to use; (Zeit) to spend; **Mühe auf etw (akk) ~** to take trouble over sth; **Verwendung** f use

verwirklichen vt to realize; **sich selbst ~** to fulfil oneself

verwirren vt to confuse; **Verwirrung** f confusion

verwitwet adj widowed

verwöhnen vt to spoil

verwunderlich adj surprising; **Verwunderung** f astonishment

verwüsten vt to devastate

verzählen vr: **sich ~** to miscount

verzehren vt to consume

Verzeichnis nt (Liste) list; (Katalog) catalogue; (in Buch) index; (Inform) directory

verzeihen (verzieh, verziehen) vt, vi to forgive (jdm etw sb for sth); **~ Sie bitte, ...** (vor Frage etc) excuse me, ...; **~ Sie die Störung** sorry to disturb you; **Verzeihung** f: **~!** sorry; **~, ...** (vor Frage etc) excuse me, ...; **(jdn) um ~ bitten** to apologize (to sb)

verzichten vi: **auf etw (akk) ~** to do without sth; (aufgeben) to give sth up

verzieh _imperf von_ **verzeihen**

verziehen _pp von_ **verziehen**

verziehen _irr vt_ (_Kind_) to spoil; **das Gesicht ~** to pull a face ▷ _vr:_ **sich ~** to go out of shape; (_Gesicht_) to contort; (_verschwinden_) to disappear

verzieren _vt_ to decorate

verzögern _vt_ to delay ▷ _vr:_ **sich ~** to be delayed; **Verzögerung** _f_ delay

verzweifeln _vi_ to despair (_an +dat of_); **verzweifelt** _adj_ desperate; **Verzweiflung** _f_ despair

Veterinär(in) (_-s, -e_) _m(f)_ veterinary surgeon (Brit), veterinarian (US)

Vetter (_-s, -n_) _m_ cousin

vgl. _abk_ = **vergleiche**

Viagra® (_-s_) _nt_ Viagra®

Vibrator (_-s, -en_) _m_ vibrator; **vibrieren** _vi_ to vibrate

Video (_-s, -s_) _nt_ video; **auf ~ aufnehmen** to video; **Videoclip** (_-s, -s_) _m_ video clip; **Videofilm** _m_ video; **Videogerät** _nt_ video (recorder); **Videokamera** _f_ video camera; **Videokassette** _f_ video (cassette); **Videorekorder** _m_ video recorder; **Videospiel** _nt_ video game; **Videothek** (_-, -en_) _f_ video library

Vieh (_-(e)s_) _nt_ cattle

viel _pron_ a lot (of), lots of; **~ Arbeit** a lot of work, lots of work; **~e Leute** a lot of people, lots of people, many people; **zu ~** too much; **zu ~e** too many; **sehr ~** a great deal of; **sehr ~e** a great many; **ziemlich ~/~e** quite a lot of; **nicht ~** not much, not a lot of; **nicht ~e** not many, not a lot of ▷ _pron_ a lot; **sie sagt nicht ~** she doesn't say a lot; **nicht ~** not much, not a lot of; **nicht ~e** not many, not a lot of; **gibt es ~?** is

there much?, is there a lot?; **gibt es ~e?** are there many?, are there a lot? ▷ _adv_ a lot; **er geht ~ ins Kino** he goes a lot to the cinema; **sehr ~** a great deal; **ziemlich ~** quite a lot, **~ besser** much better; **~ teurer** much more expensive; **~ zu ~** far too much

vielleicht _adv_ perhaps; **~ ist sie krank** perhaps she's ill, she might be ill; **weißt du ~, wo er ist?** do you know where he is (by any chance)?

vielmal(s) _adv_ many times; **danke ~s** many thanks; **vielmehr** _adv_ rather; **vielseitig** _adj_ very varied; (_Mensch, Gerät_) versatile

vier _num_ four; **auf allen ~en** on all fours; **unter ~ Augen** in private, privately; **Vier** (_-, -en_) _f_ four; (_Schulnote_) = D; **Vierbettzimmer** _nt_ four-bed room; **Viereck** (_-(e)s, -e_) _nt_ four-sided figure; (_Quadrat_) square; **viereckig** _adj_ four-sided; (_quadratisch_) square; **vierfach** _adj_: **die ~e Menge** four times the amount; **vierhundert** _num_ four hundred; **viermal** _adv_ four times; **vierspurig** _adj_ four-lane

viert _adv_: **wir sind zu ~** there are four of us; **vierte(r, s)** _adj_ fourth; _siehe auch_ **dritte**

Viertel (_-s, -_) _nt_ (_Stadtviertel_) quarter, district; (_Bruchteil_) quarter; (_Viertelliter_) quarter-litre; (_Uhrzeit_) quarter; **~ vor/nach drei** a quarter to/past three; **viertel drei** a quarter past two; **drei viertel drei** a quarter to three; **Viertelfinale** _nt_ quarter-final; **vierteljährlich** _adj_ quarterly; **Viertelstunde** _f_ quarter of an hour

vierzehn _num_ fourteen; **in ~ Tagen** in two weeks, in a fortnight (Brit); **vierzehntägig** _adj_ two-week, fortnightly (Brit);

vierzehnte(r, s) adj fourteenth; siehe auch **dritte**; **vierzig** num forty; **vierzigste(r, s)** adj fortieth

Vietnam (-s) nt Vietnam

Vignette f (Autobahn~) motorway (Brit) (o freeway (US)) permit

Villa (-, Villen) f villa

violett adj purple

Violine f violin

Virus (-, Viren) m o nt virus

Visitenkarte f card

Visum (-s, Visa o Visen) nt visa

Vitamin (-s, -e) nt vitamin

Vitrine (-, -n) f (glass) cabinet; (Schaukasten) display case

Vogel (-s, Vögel) m bird; **Vogelgrippe** f bird flu, avian flu; **vögeln** vi, vt (vulg) to screw

Voicemail (-, -s) f voice mail

Vokal (-s, -e) m vowel

Volk (-(e)s, Völker) nt people pl; (Nation) nation; **Volksfest** nt festival; (Jahrmarkt) funfair; **Volkshochschule** f adult education centre; **Volkslied** nt folksong; **Volksmusik** f folk music; **volkstümlich** adj (einfach und beliebt) popular; (herkömmlich) traditional; (Kunst) folk

voll adj full (von of); **voll|machen** vt to fill (up); **voll|tanken** vi to fill up

Vollbart m beard; **Vollbremsung** f: **eine ~ machen** to slam on the brakes; **vollends** adv completely

Volleyball m volleyball

Vollgas nt: **mit ~** at full throttle; **~ geben** to step on it

völlig adj complete ▷ adv completely

volljährig adj of age; **Vollkaskoversicherung** f fully comprehensive insurance; **vollklimatisiert** adj fully

air-conditioned; **vollkommen** adj perfect; **~er Unsinn** complete rubbish ▷ adv completely

Vollkornbrot nt wholemeal (Brit) (o whole wheat (US)) bread

Vollmacht (-, -en) f authority; (Urkunde) power of attorney

Vollmilch f full-fat milk (Brit), whole milk (US); **Vollmilchschokolade** f milk chocolate; **Vollmond** m full moon; **Vollnarkose** f general anaesthetic; **Vollpension** f full board

vollständig adj complete

Volltreffer m direct hit; **Vollwertkost** f wholefood; **vollzählig** adj complete

Volt (-, -) nt volt

Volumen (-s, -) nt volume

vom kontr von **von dem** (räumlich, zeitlich, Ursache) from; **ich kenne sie nur ~ Sehen** I only know her by sight

⭕ SCHLÜSSELWORT

von prep +dat 1 (Ausgangspunkt) from; **von ... bis from ... to**; **von morgens bis abends** from morning till night; **von ... nach ...** from ... to ...; **von ... an** from ...; **von ... aus** from ...; **von dort aus** from there; **etw von sich aus tun** to do sth of one's own accord; **von mir aus** (fam) if you like, I don't mind; **von wo/wann ...?** where/when ... from?

2 (Ursache, im Passiv) by; **ein Gedicht von Schiller** a poem by Schiller; **von etw müde** tired from sth

3 (als Genitiv) of; **ein Freund von mir** a friend of mine; **nett von dir** nice of you; **jeweils zwei von zehn** two out of every ten

4 (über) about; **er erzählte vom**

Urlaub he talked about his holiday
5 von wegen! (fam) no way!

voneinander adv from each
other

⊙ SCHLÜSSELWORT

vor prep +dat **1** (räumlich) in front
of; **vor der Kirche links abbiegen**
turn left before the church
2 (zeitlich) before; **ich war vor ihm
da** I was there before him; **vor 2
Tagen** 2 days ago; **5 (Minuten) vor
4** 5 (minutes) to 4; **vor Kurzem** a
little while ago
3 (Ursache) with; **vor Wut/Liebe**
with rage/love; **vor Hunger
sterben** to die of hunger; **vor
lauter Arbeit** because of work
4 vor allem, vor allen Dingen
most of all
▷ prep +akk (räumlich) in front of
▷ adv: **vor und zurück** backwards
and forwards

vorangehen irr vi to go ahead;
einer Sache (dat) **~** to precede sth;
vorankommen irr vi to make
progress

Vorarlberg (-s) nt Vorarlberg
voraus adv ahead; **im Voraus** in
advance; **vorausfahren** irr vi to
drive on ahead; **vorausgesetzt**
conj provided (that); **Voraussage** f
prediction; (Wetter) forecast;
voraussagen vt to predict;
voraussehen irr vt to foresee;
vorausseín irr vi: **jdm ~** to be
ahead of sb; **voraussetzen** vt to
assume; **Voraussetzung** f
requirement, prerequisite;
voraussichtlich adj expected
▷ adv probably; **vorauszahlen**
vt to pay in advance
Vorbehalt (-(e)s, -e) m
reservation; **vorbehalten** irr vt:

sich/jdm etw ~ to reserve sth (for
oneself)/for sb
vorbei adv past, over, finished;
vorbeibringen irr vt to drop by
(o in); **vorbeifahren** irr vi to
drive past; **vorbeigehen** irr vi to
pass by, to go past; (verstreichen,
aufhören) to pass; **vorbeikommen**
irr vi to drop by; **vorbeilassen** irr
vt: **kannst du die Leute ~?** would
you let these people pass?; **lässt
du mich bitte mal vorbei?** can I
get past, please?; **vorbeireden**
vi: **aneinander ~** to talk at
cross-purposes
vorbereiten vt to prepare ▷ vr:
sich ~ to get ready (auf +akk, für
for); **Vorbereitung** f preparation
vorbestellen vt to book in
advance; (Essen) to order in
advance; **Vorbestellung** f
booking, reservation
vorbeugen vi to prevent (dat
sth); **vorbeugend** adj preven-
tive; **Vorbeugung** f prevention
Vorbild nt (role) model;
vorbildlich adj model, ideal
Vorderachse f front axle;
vordere(r, s) adj front;
Vordergrund m foreground;
Vorderradantrieb m (Auto)
front-wheel drive; **Vorderseite** f
front; **Vordersitz** m front seat;
Vorderteil m o nt front (part)
Vordruck m form
voreilig adj hasty, rash; **~e
Schlüsse ziehen** to jump to
conclusions; **voreingenommen**
adj biased
vorenthalten irr vt: **jdm etw
~** to withhold sth from sb
vorerst adv for the moment
vorfahren irr vi (vorausfahren) to
drive on ahead; **vor das Haus ~** to
drive up to the house; **fahren Sie
bis zur Ampel vor** drive as far as
the traffic lights

Vorfahrt f (Auto) right of way; **~ achten** give way (Brit), yield (US); **Vorfahrtsschild** nt give way (Brit) (o yield (US)) sign; **Vorfahrtsstraße** f major road

Vorfall m incident

vor|führen vt to demonstrate; (Film) to show; (Theaterstück, Trick) to perform

Vorgänger(in) m(f) predecessor

vor|gehen irr vi (vorausgehen) to go on ahead; (nach vorn) to go forward; (handeln) to act, to proceed; (Uhr) to be fast; (Vorrang haben) to take precedence; (passieren) to go on; **Vorgehen** (-s) nt procedure

Vorgesetzte(r) mf superior

vorgestern adv the day before yesterday

vor|haben irr vt to plan; **hast du schon was vor?** have you got anything on?; **ich habe vor, nach Rom zu fahren** I'm planning to go to Rome

vor|halten irr vt: **jdm etw ~** to accuse sb of sth

Vorhand f forehand

vorhanden adj existing; (erhältlich) available

Vorhang m curtain

Vorhaut f foreskin

vorher adv before; **zwei Tage ~** two days before; **~ essen wir** we'll eat first; **Vorhersage** f forecast; **vorher|sehen** irr vt to foresee

vorhin adv just now, a moment ago

Vorkenntnisse pl previous knowledge sing

vor|kommen irr vi (nach vorne kommen) to come forward; (geschehen) to happen; (sich finden) to occur; (scheinen) to seem (to be); **sich** (dat) **dumm ~** to feel stupid

Vorlage f model

vor|lassen irr vt: **jdn ~** to let sb go first

vorläufig adj temporary

vor|lesen irr vt to read out

Vorlesung f lecture

vorletzte(r, s) adj last but one; **am ~n Samstag** (on) the Saturday before last

Vorliebe f preference

vor|machen vt: **kannst du es mir ~?** can you show me how to do it?; **jdm etwas ~** (fig: täuschen) to fool sb

vor|merken vt to note down; (Plätze) to book

Vormittag m morning; **am ~** in the morning; **heute ~** this morning; **vormittags** adv in the morning; **um 9 Uhr ~** at 9 (o'clock) in the morning, at 9 am

vorn(e) adv in front; **von ~ anfangen** to start at the beginning; **nach ~** to the front; **weiter ~** further up; **von ~ bis hinten** from beginning to end

Vorname m first name; **wie heißt du mit ~** what's your first name?

vornehm adj (von Rang) distinguished; (Benehmen) refined; (fein, elegant) elegant

vor|nehmen irr vt sich (dat) etw **~** to start on sth; sich (dat) **~, etw zu tun** (beschließen) to decide to do sth

vornherein adv: **von ~** from the start

Vorort m suburb

vorrangig adj priority

Vorrat m stock, supply; **vorrätig** adj in stock

Vorrecht nt privilege

Vorruhestand m early retirement

Vorsaison f early season

Vorsatz m intention; (Jur) intent;

vorsätzlich adj intentional; (Jur) premeditated

Vorschau f preview; (Film) trailer

Vorschlag m suggestion, proposal; **vorschlagen** irr vt to suggest, to propose; **ich schlage vor, dass wir gehen** I suggest we go

vor|schreiben irr vt (befehlen) to stipulate; **jdm etw ~** to dictate sth to sb

Vorschrift f regulation, rule; (Anweisung) instruction; **vorschriftsmäßig** adj correct

Vorschule f nursery school, pre-school (US)

Vorsicht f care; **~!** look out; (Schild) caution; **~ Stufe!** mind the step; **vorsichtig** adj careful; **vorsichtshalber** adv just in case

Vorsorge f precaution; (Vorbeugung) prevention; **Vorsorgeuntersuchung** f checkup; **vorsorglich** adv as a precaution

Vorspann (-(e)s, -e) m credits pl

Vorspeise f starter

Vorsprung m projection; (Abstand) lead

vor|stellen vt (bekannt machen) to introduce; (Uhr) to put forward; (vor etw) to put in front; **sich** (dat) **etw ~** to imagine sth; **Vorstellung** f (Bekanntmachen) introduction; (Theat) performance; (Gedanke) idea; **Vorstellungsgespräch** nt interview

vor|täuschen vt to feign

Vorteil m advantage (gegenüber over); **die Vor- und Nachteile** the pros and cons; **vorteilhaft** adj advantageous

Vortrag (-(e)s, Vorträge) m talk (über +akk on); (akademisch) lecture; **einen ~ halten** to give a talk

vorüber adv over; **vorüber|gehen** irr vi to pass; **vorübergehend** adj temporary

▷ adv temporarily, for the time being

Vorurteil nt prejudice

Vorverkauf m advance booking

vor|verlegen vt to bring forward

Vorwahl f (Tel) dialling code (Brit), area code (US)

Vorwand (-(e)s, Vorwände) m pretext, excuse; **unter dem ~, dass** with the excuse that

vorwärts adv forward; **vorwärts|gehen** irr vi (fig) to progress

vorweg adv in advance; **vorweg|nehmen** irr vt to anticipate

Vorweihnachtszeit f pre-Christmas period, run-up to Christmas (Brit)

vor|werfen irr vt: **jdm etw ~** to accuse sb of sth

vorwiegend adv mainly

Vorwort nt preface

Vorwurf m reproach; **sich** (dat) **Vorwürfe machen** to reproach oneself; **jdm Vorwürfe machen** to accuse sb; **vorwurfsvoll** adj reproachful

vor|zeigen vt to show

vorzeitig adj premature, early

vor|ziehen irr vt (lieber haben) to prefer

Vorzug m preference; (gute Eigenschaft) merit; (Vorteil) advantage

vorzüglich adj excellent

vulgär adj vulgar

Vulkan (-s, -e) m volcano; **Vulkanausbruch** m volcanic eruption

W *abk* = **West** W

Waage (-, -n) *f* scales *pl*; (*Astr*) Libra; **waagerecht** *adj* horizontal

wach *adj* awake; **~ werden** to wake up; **Wache** (-, -n) *f* guard

Wachs (-es, -e) *nt* wax

wachsen (wuchs, gewachsen) *vi* to grow

wachsen *vt* (Skier) to wax

Wachstum *nt* growth

Wachtel (-, -n) *f* quail

Wächter(in) (-s, -) *m(f)* guard; (*auf Parkplatz*) attendant

wackelig *adj* wobbly; (*fig*) shaky; **Wackelkontakt** *m* loose connection; **wackeln** *vi* (Stuhl) to be wobbly; (Zahn, Schraube) to be loose; **mit dem Kopf ~** to waggle one's head

Wade (-, -n) *f* (Anat) calf

Waffe (-, -n) *f* weapon

Waffel (-, -n) *f* waffle; (Keks, Eiswaffel) wafer

wagen *vt* to risk; **es ~, etw zu tun** to dare to do sth

Wagen (-s, -) *m* (Auto) car; (Eisenb) carriage; **Wagenheber** (-s, -) *m* jack; **Wagentyp** *m* model, make

Wahl (-, -en) *f* choice; (Pol) election

wählen *vt* to choose; (Tel) to dial; (Pol) to vote for; (durch Wahl ermitteln) to elect ▷ *vi* to choose; (Tel) to dial; (Pol) to vote; **Wähler(in)** (-s, -) *m(f)* voter; **wählerisch** *adj* choosy

Wahlkampf *m* election campaign; **wahllos** *adv* at random; **Wahlwiederholung** *f* redial

Wahnsinn *m* madness; **~!** amazing!; **wahnsinnig** *adj* insane, mad ▷ *adv* (fam) incredibly

wahr *adj* true; **das darf doch nicht ~ sein!** I don't believe it!; **nicht ~?** that's right, isn't it?

während *prep* +gen during ▷ *conj* while; **währenddessen** *adv* meanwhile, in the meantime

Wahrheit *f* truth

wahrnehmbar *adj* noticeable, perceptible; **wahr|nehmen** *irr vt* to perceive

Wahrsager(in) (-s, -) *m(f)* fortune-teller

wahrscheinlich *adj* probable, likely ▷ *adv* probably; **ich komme ~ zu spät** I'll probably be late; **Wahrscheinlichkeit** *f* probability

Währung *f* currency

Wahrzeichen *nt* symbol

Waise (-, -n) *f* orphan

Wal (-(e)s, -e) *m* whale

Wald (-(e)s, Wälder) *m* wood; (groß) forest; **Waldbrand** *m* forest fire; **Waldsterben** (-s) *nt* forest dieback

Wales (-) nt Wales; **Waliser(in)** m(f) Welshman/Welshwoman; **walisisch** adj Welsh; **Walisisch** nt Welsh

Walkie-Talkie (-(s), -s) nt walkie-talkie

Walkman® (-s, -s) m walkman®, personal stereo

Wall (-(e)s, Wälle) m embankment

Wallfahrt f pilgrimage; **Wallfahrtsort** m place of pilgrimage

Walnuss f walnut

Walross (-es, -e) nt walrus

wälzen vt to roll; (Bücher) to pore over; (Probleme) to deliberate on ▷ vr: **sich ~** to wallow; (vor Schmerzen) to roll about; (im Bett) to toss and turn

Walzer (-s, -) m waltz

Wand (-, Wände) f wall; (Trenn~) partition; (Berg~) (rock) face

Wandel (-s) m change; **wandeln** vt to change ▷ vr: **sich ~** to change

Wanderer (-s, -) m, **Wanderin** f hiker; **Wanderkarte** f hiking map; **wandern** vi to hike; (Blick) to wander; (Gedanken) to stray; **Wanderschuh** m walking shoe; **Wanderstiefel** m hiking boot; **Wanderung** f hike; **eine ~ machen** to go on a hike; **Wanderweg** m walking (o hiking) trail

Wandleuchte f wall lamp; **Wandmalerei** f mural; **Wandschrank** m built-in cupboard (Brit), closet (US)

wandte imperf von **wenden**

Wange (-, -n) f cheek

wann adv when; **seit ~ ist sie da?** how long has she been here?; **bis ~ bleibt ihr?** how long are you staying?

Wanne (-, -n) f (bath) tub

Wappen (-s, -) nt coat of arms

war imperf von **sein**

warb imperf von **werben**

Ware (-, -n) f product; **~n** goods pl; **Warenhaus** nt department store; **Warenprobe** f sample; **Warenzeichen** nt trademark

warf imperf von **werfen**

warm adj warm; (Essen) hot; **~ laufen** to warm up; **mir ist es zu ~** I'm too warm; **Wärme** (-, -f) f warmth; **wärmen** vt to warm; (Essen) to warm (o to heat) up ▷ vi (Kleidung, Sonne) to be warm ▷ vr: **sich ~** to warm up; (gegenseitig) to keep each other warm; **Wärmflasche** f hot-water bottle; **Warmstart** m (Inform) warm start

Warnblinkanlage f (Auto) warning flasher; **Warndreieck** nt (Auto) warning triangle; **warnen** vt to warn (vor +dat about, of); **Warnung** f warning

Warteliste f waiting list; **warten** vi to wait (auf +akk for); **warte mal!** wait (o hang on) a minute ▷ vt (Tech) to service

Wärter(in) m(f) attendant

Wartesaal m, **Wartezimmer** nt waiting room

Wartung f service; (das Warten) servicing

warum adv why

Warze (-, -n) f wart

was pron what; (fam: etwas) something; **~ kostet das?** what does it cost? how much is it?; **~ für ein Auto ist das?** what kind of car is that?; **~ für eine Farbe/Größe?** what colour/size?; **~?** (fam: wie bitte?) what?; **~ ist/gibt's?** what is it? what's up? **du weißt, ~ ich meine** you know what I mean; **~ (auch) immer** whatever; **soll ich dir ~ mitbringen?** do you want me to bring you anything?; **alles, ~ er hat** everything he's got

Waschanlage f (Auto) car wash;
waschbar adj washable;
Waschbär m raccoon;
Waschbecken nt washbasin

Wäsche (-, -n) f washing;
(schmutzig) laundry; (Bettwäsche)
linen; (Unterwäsche) underwear; **in
der ~** in the wash;
Wäscheklammer f clothes peg
(Brit) (o pin (US)); **Wäscheleine** f
clothesline

waschen (wusch, gewaschen) vt, vi
to wash; **Waschen und Legen**
shampoo and set ▷ vr: **sich ~** to
(have a) wash; **sich** (dat) **die Haare
~** to wash one's hair

Wäscherei f laundry;
Wäscheständer m clothes horse;
Wäschetrockner m tumble-drier

Waschgelegenheit f washing
facilities pl; **Waschlappen** m
flannel (Brit), washcloth (US); (fam:
Mensch) wet blanket;
Waschmaschine f washing
machine; **Waschmittel** nt,
Waschpulver nt washing
powder; **Waschraum** m
washroom; **Waschsalon** (-s, -s) m
launderette (Brit), laundromat
(US); **Waschstraße** f car wash

Wasser (-s, -) nt water;
fließendes ~ running water;
Wasserball m (Sport) water polo;
Wasserbob m jet ski;
wasserdicht adj watertight; (Uhr
etc) waterproof; **Wasserfall** m
waterfall; **Wasserfarbe** f
watercolour; **wasserfest** adj
watertight, waterproof;
Wasserhahn m tap (Brit), faucet
(US); **wässerig** adj watery;
Wasserkessel (-s, -) m kettle;
Wasserkocher (-s, -) m electric
kettle; **Wasserleitung** f water
pipe; **wasserlöslich** adj
water-soluble; **Wassermann** m
(Astr) Aquarius; **Wassermelone** f

water melon; **Wasserrutschbahn**
f water chute; **Wasserschaden**
m water damage; **wasserscheu**
adj scared of water; **Wasserski** m
nt water-skiing; **Wasserspiegel**
m surface of the water;
(Wasserstand) water level;
Wassersport m water sports pl;
wasserundurchlässig adj
watertight, waterproof;
Wasserverbrauch m water
consumption;
Wasserversorgung f water
supply; **Wasserwaage** f spirit
level; **Wasserwerk** nt
waterworks pl

waten vi to wade

Watt (-(e)s, -en) nt (Geo) mud flats
pl ▷ (-s, -) nt (Elek) watt

Watte (-, -n) f cotton wool;
Wattepad (-s, -s) m cotton pad;
Wattestäbchen nt cotton bud,
Q-tip® (US)

WC (-s, -s) nt toilet, restroom
(US); **WC-Reiniger** m toilet
cleaner

Web (-s) nt (Inform) Web;
Webseite f (Inform) web page

Wechsel (-s, -) m change;
(Spieler~: Sport) substitution;
Wechselgeld nt change;
wechselhaft adj (Wetter)
changeable; **Wechseljahre** pl
menopause sing; **Wechselkurs** m
exchange rate; **wechseln** vt to
change; (Blicke) to exchange; **Geld
~** to change some money; (in
Kleingeld) to get some change;
Euro in Pfund ~ to change euros
into pounds ▷ vi to change;
kannst du ~? can you change
this?; **Wechselstrom** m
alternating current, AC;
Wechselstube f bureau de
change

Weckdienst m wake-up call
service; **wecken** vt to wake (up);

Wecker (-s, -) m alarm clock; **Weckruf** m wake-up call

wedeln vi (Ski) to wedel; **mit etw ~** to wave sth; **mit dem Schwanz ~** to wag its tail; **der Hund wedelte mit dem Schwanz** the dog wagged its tail

weder conj: **~ ... noch ~** neither ... nor ...

weg adv (entfernt, verreist) away; (los, ab) off; **er war schon ~** he had already left (o gone); **Hände ~!** hands off; **weit ~** a long way away (o off)

Weg (-(e)s, -e) m way; (Pfad) path; (Route) route; **jdn nach dem ~ fragen** to ask sb the way; **auf dem ~ sein** to be on the way

weg|bleiben irr vi to stay away; **weg|bringen** irr vt to take away

wegen prep +gen o dat because of

weg|fahren irr vi to drive away; (abfahren) to leave; (in Urlaub) to go away; **Wegfahrsperre** f (Auto) (engine) immobilizer; **weg|gehen** irr vi to go away; **weg|kommen** irr vi to get away; (fig) **gut/schlecht ~** to come off well/badly; **weg|lassen** irr vt to leave out; **weg|laufen** irr vi to run away; **weg|legen** vt to put aside; **weg|machen** vt (fam) to get rid of; **weg|müssen** irr vi: **ich muss weg** I've got to go; **weg|nehmen** irr vt to take away; **weg|räumen** vt to clear away; **weg|rennen** irr vi to run away; **weg|schicken** vt to send away; **weg|schmeißen** irr vt to throw away; **weg|sehen** irr vi to look away; **weg|tun** irr vt to put away **Wegweiser** (-s, -) m signpost **weg|werfen** irr vt to throw away; **weg|wischen** vt to wipe off; **weg|ziehen** irr vi to move (away)

weh adj sore; siehe auch **wehtun**

wehen vt, vi to blow; (Fahne) to flutter

Wehen pl labour pains pl

Wehrdienst m military service

wehren vr: **sich ~** to defend oneself

weh|tun irr vi to hurt; **jdm/sich ~** to hurt sb/oneself

Weibchen nt: **es ist ein ~** (Tier) it's a she; **weiblich** adj feminine; (Bio) female

weich adj soft; **~ gekocht** (Ei) soft-boiled

Weichkäse m soft cheese; (Streichkäse) cheese spread; **weichlich** adj soft; (körperlich) weak; **Weichspüler** (-s, -) m (für Wäsche) (fabric) softener

Weide (-, -n) f (Baum) willow; (Grasfläche) meadow

weigern vr: **sich ~** to refuse; **Weigerung** f refusal

Weiher (-s, -) m pond

Weihnachten (-, -) nt Christmas; **Weihnachtsabend** m Christmas Eve; **Weihnachtsbaum** m Christmas tree; **Weihnachtsfeier** f Christmas party; **Weihnachtsferien** pl Christmas holidays pl (Brit), Christmas vacation sing (US); **Weihnachtsgeld** nt Christmas bonus; **Weihnachtsgeschenk** nt Christmas present; **Weihnachtskarte** f Christmas card; **Weihnachtslied** nt Christmas carol; **Weihnachtsmann** m Father Christmas, Santa (Claus)

● **WEIHNACHTSMARKT**
●
● The **Weihnachtsmarkt** is a
● market held in most large
● towns in Germany in the weeks
● prior to Christmas. People visit
● it to buy presents, toys and

- Christmas decorations, and to
- enjoy the festive atmosphere.
- Food and drink associated with
- the Christmas festivities can
- also be eaten and drunk there,
- for example, gingerbread and
- mulled wine.

Weihnachtsstern m (Bot)
poinsettia; **Weihnachtstag** m:
erster ~ Christmas Day; **zweiter
~** Boxing Day; **Weihnachtszeit** f
Christmas season

weil conj because

Weile (-) f while, short time; **es
kann noch eine ~ dauern** it could
take some time

Wein (-(e)s, -e) m wine; (Pflanze)
vine; **Weinbeere** f grape;
Weinberg m vineyard;
Weinbergschnecke f snail;
Weinbrand m brandy

weinen vt, vi to cry

Weinglas nt wine glass;
Weinkarte f wine list;
Weinkeller m wine cellar;
Weinlese (-, -n) f vintage;
Weinprobe f wine tasting;
Weintraube f grape

weise adj wise

Weise (-, -n) f manner, way; **auf
diese (Art und) ~** this way

weisen (wies, gewiesen) vt to
show

Weisheit f wisdom;
Weisheitszahn m wisdom
tooth

weiß adj white; **Weißbier** nt ~
wheat beer; **Weißbrot** nt white
bread; **weißhaarig** adj
white-haired; **Weißkohl** m,
Weißkraut nt (white) cabbage;
Weißwein m white wine

weit adj wide; (Begriff) broad;
(Reise, Wurf) long; (Kleid) loose; **wie
~ ist es …?** how far is it …?; **so
~ sein** to be ready ▷ adv far;

~ verbreitet widespread;
~ gereist widely travelled; **~ offen**
wide open; **das geht zu ~** that's
going too far, that's pushing it

weiter adj wider; (~ weg) farther
(away); (zusätzlich) further; **~e
Informationen** sing ▷ adv further; **~!**
go on; (weitergehen!) keep moving;
~ nichts/niemand
nothing/nobody else; **und so
~** and so on; **weiter|arbeiten** vi
to carry on working;
Weiterbildung f further training
(o education); **weiter|empfehlen**
irr vt to recommend;
weiter|erzählen vt: **nicht ~!**
don't tell anyone; **weiter|fahren**
irr vi to go on (nach to, bis as far
as); **weiter|geben** irr vt to pass
on; **weiter|gehen** irr vi to go on;
weiter|helfen irr vi: **jdm ~** to
help sb; **weiterhin** adv: **etw
~ tun** to go on doing sth;
weiter|machen vt, vi to
continue; **weiter|reisen** vi to
continue one's journey

weitgehend adj considerable
▷ adv largely; **weitsichtig** adj
long-sighted; (fig) far-sighted;
Weitsprung m long jump;
Weitwinkelobjektiv nt (Foto)
wide-angle lens

Weizen (-s, -) m wheat;
Weizenbier nt ~ wheat beer

○ **SCHLÜSSELWORT**

welche(r, s) interrogativ pron
which; **welcher von beiden?**
which (one) of the two?; **welchen
hast du genommen?** which (one)
did you take?; **welche eine …!**
what a …!; **welche Freude!** what
joy! ▷ indef pron some; (in Fragen)
any; **ich habe welche** I have some;
haben Sie welche? do you have

any? ▷ *relativ pron* (*bei Menschen*) who; (*bei Sachen*) which, that; **welche(r, s) auch immer** whoever/whichever/whatever

welk *adj* withered; **welken** *vi* to wither

Welle (-, -n) *f* wave; **Wellengang** *m* waves *pl*; **starker ~** heavy seas *pl*; **Wellenlänge** *f* (*a. fig*) wavelength; **Wellenreiten** *nt* surfing; **Wellensittich** (-s, -e) *m* budgerigar, budgie; **wellig** *adj* wavy

Wellness *f* health and beauty (*Brit*), wellness (*US*)

Welpe (-n, -n) *m* puppy

Welt (-, -en) *f* world; **auf der ~** in the world; **auf die ~ kommen** to be born; **Weltall** *nt* universe; **weltbekannt, weltberühmt** *adj* world-famous; **Weltkrieg** *m* world war; **Weltmacht** *f* world power; **Weltmeister(in)** *m(f)* world champion; **Weltmeisterschaft** *f* world championship; (*im Fußball*) World Cup; **Weltraum** *m* space; **Weltreise** *f* trip round the world; **Weltrekord** *m* world record; **Weltstadt** *f* metropolis; **weltweit** *adj* worldwide, global

wem *pron dat von* **wer** who ... to, (to) whom; **~ hast du's gegeben?** who did you give it to?; **~ gehört es?** who does it belong to?, whose is it?; **~ auch immer es gehört** whoever it belongs to

wen *pron akk von* **wer** who, whom; **~ hast du besucht?** who did you visit?; **~ möchten Sie sprechen?** who would you like to speak to?

Wende (-, -n) *f* turning point; (*Veränderung*) change; **die ~** (*Hist*) the fall of the Berlin Wall; **Wendekreis** *m* (*Auto*) turning circle

Wendeltreppe *f* spiral staircase

wenden (*wendete o wandte, gewendet o gewandt*) *vt, vi* to turn (round); (*um 180°*) to make a U-turn; **sich an jdn ~** to turn to sb; **bitte ~!** please turn over, PTO ▷ *vr:* **sich ~** to turn; **sich an jdn ~** to turn to sb

wenig *pron, adv* little; **~(e)** *pl* few; (*nur*) **ein ~ (klein)** ~ (just) a little (bit); **ein ~ Zucker** a little bit of sugar, a little sugar; **wir haben ~ Zeit** we haven't got much time; **zu ~** too little; *pl* too few; **nur ~ wissen** only a few know ▷ *adv:* **er spricht ~** he doesn't talk much; **~ bekannt** little known; **wenige** *pron pl* few *pl*; **wenigste(r, s)** *adj* least; **wenigstens** *adv* at least

⬤ SCHLÜSSELWORT

wenn *konj* **1** (*falls, bei Wünschen*) if; **wenn auch ..., selbst wenn ...** even if ...; **wenn ich doch ...** if only I ...
2 (*zeitlich*) when; **immer wenn** whenever

wennschon *adv:* **na ~** so what?

wer *pron* who; **~ war das?** who was that?; **~ von euch?** which (one) of you? ▷ *pron* anybody who, anyone who; **~ das glaubt, ist dumm** anyone who believes that is stupid; **~ auch immer** whoever ▷ *pron* somebody, someone; (*in Fragen*) anybody, anyone; **ist da ~?** is (there) anybody there?

Werbefernsehen *nt* TV commercials *pl*; **Werbegeschenk** *nt* promotional gift; **werben** (*warb, geworben*) *vt* to win; (*Mitglied*) to recruit ▷ *vi* to advertise; **Werbespot** (-s, -s) *m* commercial; **Werbung** *f* advertising

W

○ SCHLÜSSELWORT

werden (pt **wurde**, pp **geworden**
o (bei Passiv) **worden**) vi to
become; **was ist aus ihm/aus der
Sache geworden?** what became
of him/it?; **es ist nichts/gut
geworden** it came to
nothing/turned out well; **es wird
Nacht/Tag** it's getting dark/light;
mir wird kalt I'm getting cold; **mir
wird schlecht** I feel ill; **Erster
werden** to come o be first; **das
muss anders werden** that'll have
to change; **rot/zu Eis werden** to
turn red/to ice; **was willst du
(mal) werden?** what do you want
to be?; **die Fotos sind gut
geworden** the photos have come
out nicely
▷ als Hilfsverb 1 (bei Futur) **er wird
es tun** he will o he'll do it; **er wird
das nicht tun** he will not o he
won't do it; **es wird gleich regnen**
it's going to rain
2 (bei Konjunktiv) **ich würde ...** I
would ...; **er würde gern ...** he
would o he'd like to ...; **ich würde
lieber ...** I would o I'd rather ...
3 (bei Vermutung) **sie wird in der
Küche sein** she will be in the
kitchen
4 (bei Passiv) **gebraucht werden** to
be used; **er ist erschossen
worden** he has o he's been shot;
mir wurde gesagt, dass ... I was
told that ...

werfen (warf, geworfen) vt to
throw
Werft (-, -en) f shipyard,
dockyard
Werk (-(e)s, -e) nt (Kunstwerk, Buch
etc) work; (Fabrik) factory;
(Mechanismus) works pl; **Werkstatt**
(-, -stätten) f workshop; (Auto)

garage; **Werktag** m working
day; **werktags** adv on weekdays,
during the week; **Werkzeug** nt
tool; **Werkzeugkasten** m
toolbox
wert adj worth; **es ist etwa 50
Euro ~** it's worth about 50 euros;
das ist nichts ~ it's worthless;
Wert (-(e)s, -e) m worth; (Zahlen~)
(Fin) value; **~ legen auf** (+akk) to
attach importance to; **es hat
doch keinen ~** (Sinn) it's pointless;
Wertangabe f declaration of
value; **Wertbrief** m insured
letter; **Wertgegenstand** m
valuable object; **wertlos** adj
worthless; **Wertmarke** f token;
Wertpapiere pl securities pl;
Wertsachen pl valuables pl;
Wertstoff m recyclable waste;
wertvoll adj valuable
Wesen (-s, -) nt being; (Natur,
Charakter) nature
wesentlich adj significant;
(beträchtlich) considerable ▷ adv
considerably
weshalb adv why
Wespe (-, -n) f wasp;
Wespenstich m wasp sting
wessen pron gen von **wer**; whose

○ **WESSI**
○
○ A **Wessi** is a colloquial and often
○ derogatory word used to
○ describe a German from the
○ former West Germany. The
○ expression 'Besserwessi' is used
○ by East Germans to describe a
○ West German who is considered
○ to be a know-all.

West west; **Westdeutschland**
nt (als Landesteil) Western
Germany; (Hist) West Germany
Weste (-, -n) f waistcoat (Brit),
vest (US); (Wollweste) cardigan

Westen (-s) *m* west; **im ~ Englands** in the west of England; **der Wilde ~** the Wild West; **Westeuropa** *nt* Western Europe; **Westküste** *f* west coast; **westlich** *adj* western; *(Kurs, Richtung)* westerly; **Westwind** *m* west(erly) wind

weswegen *adv* why

Wettbewerb *m* competition; **Wettbüro** *nt* betting office; **Wette** (-, -*n*) *f* bet; **eine ~ abschließen** to make a bet; **die ~ gilt!** you're on; **wetten** *vt, vi* to bet *(auf +akk* on); **ich habe mit ihm gewettet, dass ...** I bet him that ...; **ich wette mit dir um 50 Euro** I'll bet you 50 euros; **~, dass?** wanna bet?

Wetter (-s, -) *nt* weather; **Wetterbericht** *m*, **Wettervorhersage** *f* weather forecast; **Wetterkarte** *f* weather map; **Wetterlage** *f* weather situation; **Wettervorhersage** *f* weather forecast

Wettkampf *m* contest; **Wettlauf** *m* race; **Wettrennen** *nt* race

WG (-, -s) *f abk* = **Wohngemeinschaft**

Whirlpool® (-s, -s) *m* jacuzzi®

Whisky (-s, -s) *m* *(schottisch)* whisky; *(irisch, amerikanisch)* whiskey

wichtig *adj* important

wickeln *vt* *(Schnur)* to wind *(um* round); *(Schal, Decke)* to wrap *(um* round); *(Baby)* to change a baby's nappy *(Brit)* o diaper *(US)*; **Wickelraum** *m* baby-changing room; **Wickeltisch** *m* baby-changing table

Widder (-s, -) *m* *(Zool)* ram; *(Astr)* Aries *sing*

wider *prep +akk* against

widerlich *adj* disgusting

widerrufen *irr vt* to withdraw; *(Auftrag, Befehl etc)* to cancel

widersprechen *irr vi* to contradict *(jdm* sb); **Widerspruch** *m* contradiction

Widerstand *m* resistance; **widerstandsfähig** *adj* resistant *(gegen* to)

widerwärtig *adj* disgusting

widerwillig *adj* unwilling

widmen *vt* to dedicate ▷ *vr*: **sich jdm/etw ~** to devote oneself to sb/sth; **Widmung** *f* dedication

○ SCHLÜSSELWORT

wie *adv* how; **wie groß/schnell?** how big/fast?; **wie wär's?** how about it?; **wie ist er?** what's he like?; **wie gut du das kannst!** you're very good at it; **wie bitte?** pardon?; *(entrüstet)* I beg your pardon!; **und wie!** and how!; **wie viel** how much; **wie viele Menschen** how many people; **wie weit** to what extent

▷ *konj* **1** *(bei Vergleichen)* **so schön wie ...** as beautiful as ...; **wie ich schon sagte** as I said; **wie du** like you; **singen wie ein ...** to sing like a ...; **wie (zum Beispiel)** such as (for example)

2 *(zeitlich)* **wie er das hörte, ging er** when he heard that he left; **er hörte, wie der Regen fiel** he heard the rain falling

wieder *adv* again; **~ ein(e) ...** another ...; **~ erkennen** to recognize; **etw ~ gutmachen** to make up for sth; **~ verwerten** to recycle

wieder|bekommen *irr vt* to get back

wiederbeschreibbar *adj* (CD, DVD) rewritable

wiederholen vt to repeat;
Wiederholung f repetition
Wiederhören nt (Tel) **auf**
~ goodbye
wieder|kommen irr vi to come
back
wieder|sehen irr vt to see
again; (wieder treffen) to meet
again; **Wiedersehen** (-s) nt
reunion; **auf ~!** goodbye
Wiedervereinigung f
reunification
Wiege (-, -n) f cradle; **wiegen**
(wog, gewogen) vt, vi to weigh
Wien (-s) nt Vienna
wies imperf von **weisen**
Wiese (-, -n) f meadow
Wiesel (-s, -) nt weasel
wieso adv why
wievielmal adv how often;
wievielte(r, s) adj: **zum ~n Mal?**
how many times?; **den**
Wievielten haben wir heute?
what's the date today?; **am**
Wievielten hast du Geburtstag?
which day is your birthday?
wieweit conj to what extent
Wi-Fi nt Wi-Fi
wild adj wild
Wild (-(e)s) nt game
wildfremd adj (fam) **ein ~er**
Mensch a complete (o total)
stranger; **Wildleder** nt suede;
Wildpark m game park;
Wildschwein nt (wild) boar;
Wildwasserfahren (-s) nt
whitewater rafting
Wille (-ns, -n) m will
willen prep +gen **um ... ~** for the
sake of ...; **um Himmels ~!**
(vorwurfsvoll) for heaven's sake;
(betroffen) goodness me
willkommen adj welcome; **jdn**
~ heißen to welcome sb
Wimper (-, -n) f eyelash;
Wimperntusche f mascara
Wind (-(e)s, -e) m wind

Windel (-, -n) f nappy (Brit),
diaper (US)
windgeschützt adj sheltered
from the wind; **windig** adj windy;
(fig) dubious; **Windjacke** f
windcheater; **Windmühle** f
windmill; **Windpark** m wind
farm; **Windpocken** pl chickenpox
sing; **Windschutzscheibe** f (Auto)
windscreen (Brit), windshield (US);
Windstärke f wind force;
Windsurfen (-s) nt windsurfing;
Windsurfer(in) m(f) windsurfer
Winkel (-s, -) m (Math) angle;
(Gerät) set square; (in Raum)
corner; **im rechten ~ zu** at right
angles to
winken vt, vi to wave
Winter (-s, -) m winter;
Winterausrüstung f (Auto)
winter equipment;
Winterfahrplan m winter
timetable; **winterlich** adj
wintry; **Wintermantel** m winter
coat; **Winterreifen** m winter
tyre; **Winterschlussverkauf** m
winter sales pl; **Wintersport** m
winter sports pl
Winterzeit f (Uhrzeit) winter
time (Brit), standard time (US)
winzig adj tiny
wir pron we; ~ **selbst** we
ourselves; ~ **alle** all of us; ~ **drei**
the three of us; ~ **sind's** it's us;
~ **nicht** not us
Wirbel (-s, -) m whirl; (Trubel)
hurly-burly; (Aufsehen) fuss; (Anat)
vertebra; **Wirbelsäule** f spine
wirken vi to be effective;
(erfolgreich sein) to work; (scheinen)
to seem
wirklich adj real; **Wirklichkeit** f
reality
wirksam adj effective; **Wirkung**
f effect
wirr adj confused; **Wirrwarr** (-s)
m confusion

Wirsing (-s) m savoy cabbage
Wirt (-(e)s, -e) m landlord; **Wirtin** f landlady
Wirtschaft f (Comm) economy; (Gaststätte) pub; **wirtschaftlich** adj (Pol, Comm) economic; (sparsam) economical
Wirtshaus nt pub
wischen vt, vi to wipe; **Wischer** (-s, -) m wiper
wissen (wusste, gewusst) vt to know; **weißt du schon, ...?** did you know ...?; **woher weißt du das?** how do you know?; **das musst du selbst ~** that's up to you; **Wissen** (-s) nt knowledge
Wissenschaft f science; **Wissenschaftler(in)** (-s, -) m(f) scientist; (Geisteswissenschaftler) academic; **wissenschaftlich** adj scientific; (geisteswissenschaftlich) academic
Witwe (-, -n) f widow; **Witwer** (-s, -) m widower
Witz (-(e)s, -e) m joke; **mach keine ~e!** you're kidding!; **das soll wohl ein ~ sein** you've got to be joking; **witzig** adj funny
wo adv where; **zu einer Zeit, ~ ...** at a time when ...; **überall, ~ ich hingehe** wherever I go ▷ conj: **jetzt, ~ du da bist** now that you're here; **~ ich gerade spreche** while I'm talking to you; **woanders** adv somewhere else
wobei adv: **~ mir einfällt ...** which reminds me ...
Woche (-, -n) f week; **während** (o **unter**) **der ~** during the week; **einmal die ~** once a week; **Wochenende** nt weekend; **am ~ at** (Brit) (o **on** (US)) the weekend; **wir fahren übers ~ weg** we're going away for the weekend; **Wochenendhaus** nt weekend cottage; **Wochenendtrip** m weekend trip; **Wochenendurlaub**

m weekend break; **Wochenkarte** f weekly (season) ticket; **wochenlang** adv for weeks (on end); **Wochenmarkt** m weekly market; **Wochentag** m weekday; **wöchentlich** adj, adv weekly
Wodka (-s, -s) m vodka
wodurch adv: **~ unterscheiden sie sich?** what's the difference between them?; **~ hast du es gemerkt?** how did you notice?; **wofür** adv (relativ) for which; (Frage) what ... for; **~ brauchst du das?** what do you need that for?
wog imperf von **wiegen**
woher adv where ... from; **wohin** adv where ... to

SCHLÜSSELWORT

wohl adv **1 wohl oder übel** whether one likes it or not
2 (wahrscheinlich) probably; (gewiss) certainly; (vielleicht) perhaps; **sie ist wohl zu Hause** she's probably at home; **das ist doch wohl nicht dein Ernst!** surely you're not serious; **das mag wohl sein** that may well be; **ob das wohl stimmt?** I wonder if that's true; **er weiß das sehr wohl** he knows that perfectly well

Wohl (-(e)s) nt: **zum ~!** cheers; **wohlbehalten** adv safe and sound; **wohl|fühlen** vr: **sich ~** (zufrieden) to feel happy; (gesundheitlich) to feel well; **Wohlstand** m prosperity, affluence; **wohl|tun** irr vi: **jdm ~** to do sb good; **Wohlwollen** nt goodwill
Wohnblock m block of flats (Brit), apartment house (US); **wohnen** vi to live; **Wohngemeinschaft** f shared flat

(Brit) (o apartment (US)); **ich wohne in einer ~** I share a flat (o apartment); **wohnhaft** adj resident; **Wohnküche** f kitchen-cum-living-room; **Wohnmobil** (-s, -e) nt camper, RV (US); **Wohnort** m place of residence; **Wohnsitz** m place of residence; **Wohnung** f flat (Brit), apartment (US); **Wohnungstür** f front door; **Wohnwagen** m caravan; **Wohnzimmer** nt living room

Wolf (-(e)s, **Wölfe**) m wolf

Wolke (-, -n) f cloud; **Wolkenkratzer** m skyscraper; **wolkenlos** adj cloudless; **wolkig** adj cloudy

Wolldecke f (woollen) blanket; **Wolle** (-, -n) f wool

⬤ SCHLÜSSELWORT

wollen (pt **wollte**, pp **gewollt** o (als Hilfsverb) **wollen**) vt, vi to want; **ich will nach Hause** I want to go home; **er will nicht** he doesn't want to; **er wollte das nicht** he didn't want it; **wenn du willst** if you like; **ich will, dass du mir zuhörst** I want you to listen to me
▷ Hilfsverb: **er will ein Haus kaufen** he wants to buy a house; **ich wollte, ich wäre ...** I wish I were ...; **etw gerade tun wollen** to be going to do sth

Wolljacke f cardigan
womit adv what ... with; **~ habe ich das verdient?** what have I done to deserve that?
womöglich adv possibly
woran adv **~ denkst du?** what are you thinking of?; **~ ist er gestorben?** what did he die of?; **~ sieht man das?** how can you tell?

worauf adv: **~ wartest du?** what are you waiting for?
woraus adv: **~ ist das gemacht?** what is it made of?
Workshop (-s, -s) m workshop
World Wide Web nt World Wide Web
Wort (-(e)s, **Wörter**) nt (Vokabel) word ▷ (-(e)s, -e) nt (Äußerung) word; **mit anderen ~en** in other words; **jdn beim ~ nehmen** to take sb at his/her word; **Wörterbuch** nt dictionary; **wörtlich** adj literal
worüber adv: **~ redet sie?** what is she talking about?
worum adv: **~ gehts?** what is it about?
worunter adv: **~ leidet er?** what is he suffering from?
wovon adv (relativ) from which; **~ redest du?** what are you talking about?; **wozu** adv (relativ) to/for which; (interrogativ) what ... for/to; (warum) why; **~?** what for?; **~ brauchst du das?** what do you need it for?; **~ soll das gut sein?** what's it for?; **~ hast du Lust?** what do you feel like doing?
Wrack (-(e)s, -s) nt wreck
Wucher (-s) m profiteering; **das ist ~!** that's daylight robbery!
wuchs imperf von **wachsen**
wühlen vi to rummage; (Tier) to root; (Maulwurf) to burrow
Wühltisch m bargain counter
wund adj sore; **Wunde** (-, -n) f wound
Wunder (-s, -) nt miracle; **es ist kein ~** it's no wonder; **wunderbar** adj wonderful, marvellous; **Wunderkerze** f sparkler; **Wundermittel** nt wonder cure; **wundern** vr: **sich ~** to be surprised (über +akk at) ▷ vt to surprise; **wunderschön** adj

beautiful; **wundervoll** *adj*
wonderful

Wundsalbe *f* antiseptic
ointment; **Wundstarrkrampf** *m*
tetanus

Wunsch (-(e)s, Wünsche) *m* wish
(nach for); **wünschen** *vt* to wish;
sich (dat) **etw ~** to want sth; **ich
wünsche dir alles Gute** I wish you
all the best; **wünschenswert** *adj*
desirable

wurde *imperf von* **werden**

Wurf (-s, Würfe) *m* throw; (Zool)
litter

Würfel (-s, -) *m* dice; (Math)
cube; **würfeln** *vi* to throw (the
dice); (Würfel spielen) to play dice
▷ *vt* (Zahl) to throw; (Gastr) to
dice; **Würfelzucker** *m* lump
sugar

Wurm (-(e)s, Würmer) *m* worm

Wurst (-, Würste) *f* sausage; **das
ist mir ~** (fam) I couldn't care less

Würstchen *nt* frankfurter

Würze (-, -n) *f* seasoning, spice

Wurzel (-, -n) *f* root;
Wurzelbehandlung *f* root canal
treatment

würzen *vt* to season, to spice;
würzig *adj* spicy

wusch *imperf von* **waschen**

wusste *imperf von* **wissen**

wüst *adj* (unordentlich) chaotic;
(ausschweifend) wild; (öde)
desolate; (fam: heftig) terrible

Wüste (-, -n) *f* desert

Wut (-) *f* rage, fury; **ich habe eine
~ auf ihn** I'm really mad at him;
wütend *adj* furious

WWW (-) *nt* abk = World Wide
Web WWW

X-Beine *pl* knock-knees *pl*;
x-beinig *adj* knock-kneed

x-beliebig *adj*: **ein ~es Buch** any
book (you like)

x-mal *adv* umpteen times

Xylophon (-s, -e) *nt* xylophone

Y Z

Yoga (-(s)) *m* o *nt* yoga
Yuppie (-s, -s) *m* (-, -s) *f* yuppie

zackig *adj* (*Linie etc*) jagged; (*fam: Tempo*) brisk
zaghaft *adj* timid
zäh *adj* tough; (*Flüssigkeit*) thick
Zahl (-, -en) *f* number; **zahlbar** *adj* payable; **zahlen** *vt, vi* to pay; ~ **bitte!** could I have the bill (*Brit*) (o check (*US*)) please?; **bar** ~ to pay cash; **zählen** *vt, vi* to count (*auf +akk* on); ~ **zu** to be one of; **Zahlenschloss** *nt* combination lock; **Zähler** (-s, -) *m* (*Gerät*) counter; (*für Strom, Wasser*) meter; **zahlreich** *adj* numerous; **Zahlung** *f* payment; **Zahlungsanweisung** *f* money order; **Zahlungsbedingungen** *pl* terms *pl* of payment
zahm *adj* tame; **zähmen** *vt* to tame
Zahn (-(e)s, *Zähne*) *m* tooth; **Zahnarzt** *m*, **Zahnärztin** *f* dentist; **Zahnbürste** *f*

toothbrush; **Zahncreme** f toothpaste; **Zahnersatz** m dentures pl; **Zahnfleisch** nt gums pl; **Zahnfleischbluten** nt bleeding gums pl; **Zahnfüllung** f filling; **Zahnklammer** f brace; **Zahnpasta** f, **Zahnpaste** f toothpaste; **Zahnradbahn** f rack railway (Brit) o railroad (US)); **Zahnschmerzen** pl toothache sing; **Zahnseide** f dental floss; **Zahnspange** f brace; **Zahnstocher** (-s, -) m toothpick

Zange (-, -n) f pliers pl; (Zuckerzange) tongs pl; (Beißzange, Zool) pincers pl; (Med) forceps pl

zanken vi to quarrel

Zäpfchen nt (Anat) uvula; (Med) suppository

zapfen vt (Bier) to pull; **Zapfsäule** f petrol (Brit) o gas (US)) pump

zappeln vi to wriggle; (unruhig sein) to fidget

zappen vi to zap, to channel-hop

zart adj (weich, leise) soft; (Braten etc) tender; (fein, schwächlich) delicate; **zartbitter** adj (Schokolade) plain, dark

zärtlich adj tender, affectionate; **Zärtlichkeit** f tenderness; **~en** pl hugs and kisses pl

Zauber (-s, -) m magic; (Bann) spell; **Zauberei** f magic; **Zauberer** (-s, -) m magician; (Künstler) conjuror; **Zauberformel** f (magic) spell; **zauberhaft** adj enchanting; **Zauberin** f sorceress; **Zauberkünstler(in)** m(f) magician, conjuror; **Zaubermittel** nt magic cure; **zaubern** vi to do magic; (Künstler) to do conjuring tricks; **Zauberspruch** m (magic) spell

Zaun (-(e)s, Zäune) m fence

z. B. abk = **zum Beispiel** e.g., eg

ZDF nt = **Zweites Deutsches Fernsehen** second German television channel

Zebra (-s, -s) nt zebra; **Zebrastreifen** m zebra crossing (Brit), crosswalk (US)

Zecke (-, -n) f tick

Zehe (-, -n) f toe; (Knoblauch) clove; **Zehennagel** m toenail; **Zehenspitze** f tip of the toes

zehn num ten; **Zehnerkarte** f ticket valid for ten trips; **Zehnkampf** m decathlon; **Zehnkämpfer(in)** m(f) decathlete; **zehnmal** adv ten times; **zehntausend** num ten thousand; **zehnte(r, s)** adj tenth; siehe auch **dritte**; **Zehntel** (-s, -) nt tenth; **Zehntelsekunde** f tenth of a second

Zeichen (-s, -) nt sign; (Schriftzeichen) character; **Zeichenblock** m sketch pad; **Zeichenerklärung** f key; **Zeichensetzung** f punctuation; **Zeichensprache** f sign language; **Zeichentrickfilm** m cartoon

zeichnen vt, vi to draw; **Zeichnung** f drawing

Zeigefinger m index finger; **zeigen** vt to show; **sie zeigte uns die Stadt** she showed us around the town; **zeig mal!** let me see ▷ vi to point (auf +akk to, at) ▷ vr: **sich ~** to show oneself; **es wird sich ~** time will tell; **Zeiger** (-s, -) m pointer; (Uhr) hand

Zeile (-, -n) f line

Zeit (-, -en) f time; **ich habe keine ~** I haven't got time; **lass dir ~** take your time; **das hat ~** there's no rush; **von ~ zu ~** from time to time; **Zeitansage** f (Tel) speaking clock (Brit), correct time (US); **Zeitarbeit** f temporary work; **zeitgenössisch** adj contemporary, modern; **zeitgleich** adj simultaneous ▷ adv at exactly the same time; **zeitig** adj early; **Zeitkarte** f season ticket; **zeitlich** adj (Reihenfolge) chronological; **es passt ~ nicht** it isn't a convenient time; **ich schaff es ~ nicht** I'm not going to make it; **Zeitlupe** f slow motion; **Zeitplan** m schedule; **Zeitpunkt** m point in time; **Zeitraum** m period (of time); **Zeitschrift** f magazine; **(wissenschaftliche) periodical**

Zeitung f newspaper; **es steht in der ~** it's in the paper(s); **Zeitungsanzeige** f newspaper advertisement; **Zeitungsartikel** m newspaper article; **Zeitungskiosk** m, **Zeitungsstand** m newsstand

Zeitunterschied m time difference; **(Menge)** time lag; **Zeitvertreib** (-(e)s, -e) m: **zum ~** to pass the time; **zeitweise** adv occasionally;
Zeitzone f time zone

Zelle (-, -n) f cell

Zellophan® (-s) nt cellophane®

Zelt (-(e)s, -e) nt tent; **zelten** vi to camp, to go camping; **Zeltplatz** m campsite, camping site

Zement (-(e)s, -e) m cement

Zentimeter m o nt centimetre

Zentner (-s, -) m (metric) hundredweight; (in Deutschland) fifty kilos; (in Österreich und der Schweiz) one hundred kilos

zentral adj central; **Zentrale** (-, -n) f central office; (Tel) exchange; **Zentralheizung** f central heating;
Zentralverriegelung f (Auto) central locking; **Zentrum** (-s, Zentren) nt centre

zerbrechen irr vt, vi to break; **zerbrechlich** adj fragile

Zeremonie (-, -n) f ceremony

zergehen irr vi to dissolve; (schmelzen) to melt

zerkleinern vt to cut up; (zerhacken) to chop (up);

zerkratzen vt to scratch;

zerlegen vt to take to pieces; (Fleisch) to carve; (Gerät, Maschine) to dismantle; **zerquetschen** vt to squash; **zerreißen** irr vt to tear to pieces ▷ vi to tear

zerren vt to drag; **sich** (dat) **einen Muskel ~** to pull a muscle ▷ vi to tug (an +dat at); **Zerrung** f (Med) pulled muscle

zerschlagen irr vt to smash ▷ vr: **sich ~** to come to nothing

zerschneiden irr vt to cut up

zerstören vt to destroy; **Zerstörung** f destruction

zerstreuen vt to scatter; (Menge) to disperse; (Zweifel etc) to dispel ▷ vr: **sich ~** (Menge) to disperse; **zerstreut** adj scattered; (Mensch) absent-minded; (kurzfristig) distracted

zerteilen vt to split up

Zertifikat (-(e)s, -e) nt certificate

Zettel (-s, -) m piece of paper; (Notizzettel) note

Zeug (-(e)s, -e) nt (fam) stuff; (Ausrüstung) gear; **dummes ~** nonsense

Zeuge (-n, -n) m, **Zeugin** f witness

Zeugnis nt certificate; (Schule) report; (Referenz) reference

z. H(d). abk = **zu Händen von** attn

zickig adj (fam) touchy, bitchy

Zickzack (-(e)s, -e) m: **im ~ fahren** to zigzag (across the road)

Ziege (-, -n) f goat

Ziegel (-s, -) m brick; (Dach) tile

Ziegenkäse m goat's cheese; **Ziegenpeter** m mumps

ziehen (zog, gezogen) vt to draw; (zerren) to pull; (Spielfigur) to move; (züchten) to rear ▷ vi (zerren) to pull; (sich bewegen) to move; (Rauch, Wolke etc) to drift; **den Tee**

Zufall m chance; (Ereignis) coincidence; **durch ~** by accident; **so ein ~!** what a coincidence; **zufällig** adj chance ▷ adv by chance; **weißt du ~, ob ...?** do you happen to know whether ...?

zufrieden adj content(ed); (befriedigt) satisfied; **lass sie ~** leave her alone; **zufrieden|geben** irr vr: **sich mit etw ~** to settle for sth; **Zufriedenheit** f contentment; (Befriedigtsein) satisfaction; **zufrieden|stellen** vt: **sie ist schwer zufriedenzustellen** she is hard to please

zu|fügen vt to add (dat to); **jdm Schaden/Schmerzen ~** to cause sb harm/pain

Zug (-(e)s, Züge) m (Eisenb) train; (Luft) draught; (Ziehen) pull; (Gesichtszug) feature; (Schach) move; (Charakterzug) trait; (an Zigarette) puff, drag; (Schluck) gulp

Zugabe f extra; (in Konzert etc) encore

Zugabteil nt train compartment

Zugang m access; **„kein ~!"** "no entry!"

Zugauskunft f (Stelle) train information office/desk; **Zugbegleiter(in)** m(f) guard (Brit), conductor (US)

zu|geben irr vt to admit; **zugegeben** adv admittedly

zu|gehen irr vi (schließen) to shut; **auf jdn/etw ~** to walk towards sb/sth; **dem Ende ~** to be coming to a close ▷ vi impers (sich ereignen) to happen; **es ging lustig zu** we/they had a lot of fun; **dort geht es streng zu** it's strict there

Zügel (-s, -) m rein

Zugführer(in) m(f) guard (Brit), conductor (US)

zugig adj draughty

zügig adj speedy

zugleich adv (zur gleichen Zeit) at the same time; (ebenso) both

Zugluft f draught

Zugpersonal nt train staff

zu|greifen irr vi (fig) to seize the opportunity; (beim Essen) to help oneself; **~ auf** (+akk) (Inform) to access

Zugrestaurant nt dining car, diner (US)

Zugriffsberechtigung f (Inform) access right

zugrunde adv: **~ gehen** to perish; **~ gehen an** (+dat) (sterben) to die of

Zugschaffner(in) m(f) ticket inspector; **Zugunglück** nt train crash

zugunsten prep +gen o dat in favour of

Zugverbindung f train connection

zu|haben irr vi to be closed

zu|halten irr vt: **sich** (dat) **die Nase ~** to hold one's nose; **sich** (dat) **die Ohren ~** to hold one's hands over one's ears; **die Tür ~** to hold the door shut

Zuhause (-s) nt home

zu|hören vi to listen (dat to); **Zuhörer(in)** m(f) listener

zu|kleben vt to seal

zu|kommen irr vi to come up (auf +akk to); **jdm etw ~ lassen** to give/send sb sth; **etw auf sich** (akk) **~ lassen** to take sth as it comes

zu|kriegen vt: **ich krieg den Koffer nicht zu** I can't shut the case

Zukunft (-, Zukünfte) f future; **zukünftig** adj future ▷ adv in future

zu|lassen irr vt (hereinlassen) to admit; (erlauben) to permit; (Auto) to license; (fam: nicht öffnen) to keep shut; **zulässig** adj permissible, permitted

zuletzt *adv* finally, at last

zuliebe *adv*: **jdm** ~ for sb's sake

zum *kontr von* **zu dem**; ~ **dritten Mal** for the third time; ~ **Scherz** as a joke; ~ **Trinken** for drinking

zu|machen *vt* to shut; (*Kleidung*) to do up ▷ *vi* to shut

zumindest *adv* at least

zu|muten *vt*: **jdm etw** ~ to expect sth of sb ▷ *vr*: **sich** (*dat*) **zu viel** ~ to overdo things

zunächst *adv* first of all; ~ **einmal** to start with

Zunahme (-, -n) *f* increase

Zuname *m* surname, last name

zünden *vt*, *vi* (*Auto*) to ignite, to fire; **Zündkabel** *nt* (*Auto*) ignition cable; **Zündkerze** *f* (*Auto*) spark plug; **Zündschloss** *nt* ignition lock; **Zündschlüssel** *m* ignition key; **Zündung** *f* ignition

zu|nehmen *irr vi* to increase; (*Mensch*) to put on weight ▷ *vt*: **5 Kilo** ~ to put on 5 kilos

Zunge (-, -n) *f* tongue

Zungenkuss *m* French kiss

zunichte|machen *vt* (*zerstören*) to ruin

zunutze *vr*: **sich** (*dat*) **etw** ~ **machen** to make use of sth

zu|parken *vt* to block

zur *kontr von* **zu der**

zurecht|finden *irr vr*: **sich** ~ to find one's way around; **zurecht|kommen** *irr vi* to cope (*mit etw* with sth); **zurecht|machen** *vt* to prepare ▷ *vr*: **sich** ~ to get ready

Zürich (-s) *nt* Zurich

zurück *adv* back

zurück|bekommen *irr vt* to get back; **zurück|blicken** *vi* to look back (*auf +akk* at); **zurück|bringen** *irr vt* (*hierhin*) to bring back; (*woandershin*) to take back; **zurück|erstatten** *vt* to refund; **zurück|fahren** *irr vi* to go back;

zurück|geben *irr vt* to give back; (*antworten*) to answer; **zurück|gehen** *irr vi* to go back; (*zeitlich*) to date back (*auf +akk* to)

zurück|halten *irr vt* to hold back; (*hindern*) to prevent ▷ *vr*: **sich** ~ to hold back; **zurückhaltend** *adj* reserved

zurück|holen *irr vt* to fetch back; **zurück|kommen** *irr vi* to come back; **auf etw** (*akk*) ~ to return (o get back) to sth; **zurück|lassen** *irr vt* to leave behind; **zurück|legen** *vt* to put back; (*Geld*) to put by; (*reservieren*) to keep back; (*Strecke*) to cover; **zurück|nehmen** *irr vt* to take back; **zurück|rufen** *irr vt* to call back; **zurück|schicken** *vt* to send back; **zurück|stellen** *vt* to put back; **zurück|treten** *irr vi* to step back; (*von Amt*) to retire; **zurück|verlangen** *vt*: **etw** ~ to ask for sth back; **zurück|zahlen** *vt* to pay back

zurzeit *adv* at present

Zusage *f* promise; (*Annahme*) acceptance; **zu|sagen** *vt* to promise ▷ *vi* to accept; **jdm** ~ (*gefallen*) to appeal to sb

zusammen *adv* together

Zusammenarbeit *f* collaboration; **zusammen|arbeiten** *vi* to work together

zusammen|brechen *irr vi* to collapse; (*psychisch*) to break down; **Zusammenbruch** *m* collapse; (*psychischer*) breakdown

zusammen|fassen *vt* to summarize; (*vereinigen*) to unite; **zusammenfassend** *adj* summarizing ▷ *adv* to summarize; **Zusammenfassung** *f* summary

zusammen|gehören *vi* to belong together; **zusammen|halten** *irr vi* to stick together

Zusammenhang m connection; **im/aus dem ~** in/out of context; **zusammen|hängen** irr vi to be connected; **zusammenhängend** adj coherent; **zusammenhang(s)los** adj incoherent

zusammen|klappen vi, vt to fold up

zusammen|knüllen vt to screw up

zusammen|kommen irr vi to meet; (sich ereignen) to happen together; **zusammen|legen** vt to fold up ▷ vi (Geld sammeln) to club together; **zusammen|nehmen** irr vt to summon up; **alles zusammengenommen** all in all ▷ vr: **sich ~** to pull oneself together; (fam) to get a grip, to get one's act together; **zusammen|passen** vi to go together; (Personen) to be suited; **zusammen|rechnen** vt to add up

Zusammensein (-s) nt get-together

zusammen|setzen vt to put together ▷ vr: **sich ~ aus** to be composed of; **Zusammensetzung** f composition

Zusammenstoß m crash, collision; **zusammen|stoßen** irr vi to crash (mit into)

zusammen|zählen vt to add up

zusammen|ziehen irr vi (in Wohnung etc) to move in together

Zusatz m addition; **zusätzlich** adj additional ▷ adv in addition

zu|schauen vi to watch; **Zuschauer(in)** (-s, -) m(f) spectator; **die ~** (pl) (Theat) the audience sing; **Zuschauertribüne** f stand

zu|schicken vt to send

Zuschlag m extra charge; (Fahrkarte) supplement

zuschlagpflichtig adj subject to an extra charge; (Eisenb) subject to a supplement

zu|schließen irr vt to lock up

zu|sehen irr vi to watch (jdm sb); **~, dass** (dafür sorgen) to make sure that

zu|sichern vt: **jdm etw ~** to assure sb of sth

Zustand m state, condition; **sie bekommt Zustände, wenn sie das sieht** (fam) she'll have a fit if she sees that

zustande adv: **~ bringen** to bring about; **~ kommen** to come about

zuständig adj (Behörde) relevant; **~ für** responsible for

Zustellung f delivery

zu|stimmen vi to agree (einer Sache dat to sth, jdm with sb); **Zustimmung** f approval

zu|stoßen irr vi (fig) to happen (jdm to sb)

Zutaten pl ingredients pl

zu|trauen vt: **jdm etw ~** to think sb is capable of sth; **das hätte ich ihm nie zugetraut** I'd never have thought he was capable of it; **ich würde es ihr ~** (etw Negatives) I wouldn't put it past her; **Zutrauen** (-s) nt confidence (zu in); **zutraulich** adj trusting; (Tier) friendly

zu|treffen irr vi to be correct; **~ auf** (+akk) to apply to; **Zutreffendes bitte streichen** please delete as applicable

Zutritt m entry; (Zugang) access; **~ verboten!** no entry

zuverlässig adj reliable; **Zuverlässigkeit** f reliability

Zuversicht f confidence; **zuversichtlich** adj confident

zuvor adv before; (zunächst) first; **zuvor|kommen** irr vi: **jdm ~** to beat sb to it; **zuvorkommend** adj obliging

Zuwachs (-es, Zuwächse) m increase, growth; (fam: Baby) addition to the family

zuwider adv: **es ist mir ~** I hate (o detest) it

zu|winken vi: **jdm ~** to wave to sb

zuzüglich prep +gen plus

zwang imperf von **zwingen**

Zwang (-(e)s, Zwänge) m (innerer) compulsion; (Gewalt) force

zwängen vt to squeeze (in +akk into) ▷ vr: **sich ~** to squeeze (in +akk into)

zwanglos adj informal

zwanzig num twenty; **zwanzigste(r, s)** adj twentieth; siehe auch **dritte**

zwar adv: **und ~ ...** (genauer) ..., to be precise; **das ist ~ schön, aber ...** it is nice, but ...; **ich kenne ihn ~, aber ...** I know him all right, but ...

Zweck (-(e)s, -e) m purpose; **zwecklos** adj pointless

zwei num two; **Zwei** (-, -en) f two; (Schulnote) = B; **Zweibettzimmer** nt twin room; **zweideutig** adj ambiguous; (unanständig) suggestive; **zweifach** adj, adv double

Zweifel (-s, -) m doubt; **zweifellos** adv undoubtedly; **zweifeln** vi to doubt (an etw dat sth); **Zweifelsfall** m: **im ~** in case of doubt

Zweig (-(e)s, -e) m branch

Zweigstelle f branch

zweihundert num two hundred; **zweimal** adv twice; **zweisprachig** adj bilingual; **zweispurig** adj (Auto) two-lane; **zweit** adv: **wir sind zu ~** there are two of us; **zweite(r, s)** adj second; siehe auch **dritte eine ~ Portion** a

second helping; **zweitens** adv secondly; (bei Aufzählungen) second; **zweitgrößte(r, s)** adj second largest; **Zweitschlüssel** m spare key

Zwerchfell nt diaphragm

Zwerg(in) (-(e)s, -e) m(f) dwarf

Zwetschge (-, -n) f plum

zwicken vt to pinch

Zwieback (-(e)s, -e) m rusk

Zwiebel (-, -n) f onion; (von Blume) bulb; **Zwiebelsuppe** f onion soup

Zwilling (-s, -e) m twin; **~e** (pl) (Astr) Gemini sing

zwingen (zwang, gezwungen) vt to force

zwinkern vi to blink; (absichtlich) to wink

zwischen prep +akk o dat between

Zwischenablage f (Inform) clipboard

zwischendurch adv in between

Zwischenfall m incident

Zwischenlandung f stopover

zwischenmenschlich adj interpersonal

Zwischenraum m space

Zwischenstopp (-s, -s) m stopover

Zwischensumme f subtotal

Zwischenzeit f: **in der ~** in the meantime

zwitschern vt, vi to twitter, to chirp

zwölf num twelve; **zwölfte(r, s)** adj twelfth; siehe auch **dritte**

Zylinder (-s, -) m cylinder; (Hut) top hat

zynisch adj cynical

Zypern (-s) nt Cyprus

Zyste (-, -n) f cyst

Mini-Sprachführer

Mini Phrasefinder

TOPICS		THEMEN

TOPICS | THEMEN

Hello!	Guten Tag!
Good evening!	Guten Abend!
Good night!	Gute Nacht!
Goodbye!	Auf Wiedersehen!
What's your name?	Wie heißen Sie?
My name is ...	Mein Name ist ...
This is ...	Das ist ...
my wife.	*meine Frau.*
my husband.	*mein Mann.*
my partner.	*mein Partner/*
	meine Partnerin.
Where are you from?	Wo kommen Sie her?
I come from ...	Ich komme aus ...
How are you?	Wie geht es Ihnen?
Fine, thanks.	Danke, gut.
And you?	Und Ihnen?
Do you speak English?	Sprechen Sie Englisch?
I don't understand German.	Ich verstehe kein Deutsch.
Thanks very much!	Vielen Dank!

Asking the Way | Erkundigungen

Where is the nearest ...?	Wo ist der/die/das nächste ...?
How do I get to ...?	Wie komme ich zum/zur/ nach ...?
Is it far?	Ist es weit?
How far is it?	Wie weit ist es?
Is this the right way to ...?	Bin ich hier richtig zum/zur/ nach ...?
I'm lost.	Ich habe mich verlaufen/ verfahren.
Can you show me on the map?	Können Sie mir das auf der Karte zeigen?
You have to turn round.	Kehren Sie um.
Go straight on.	Fahren Sie geradeaus.
Turn left/right.	Biegen Sie nach links/rechts ab.
Take the second street on the left/right.	Nehmen Sie die zweite Straße links/rechts.

Car Hire | Autovermietung

I want to hire ...	Ich möchte ... mieten.
a car.	*ein Auto*
a moped.	*ein Moped*
How much is it for ...?	Was kostet das für ...?
one day	*einen Tag*
a week	*eine Woche*
Is there a kilometre charge?	Verlangen Sie eine Kilometer- gebühr?
What is included in the price?	Was ist alles im Preis inbegriffen?
I'd like a child seat for a ... -year-old child.	Ich möchte einen Kindersitz für ein ... Jahre altes Kind.
What do I do if I have an accident/if I break down?	Was tue ich bei einem Unfall/ einer Panne?

Breakdowns | Pannen

My car has broken down.	Ich habe eine Panne.
Where is the next garage?	Wo ist die nächste Werkstatt?
The exhaust	*Der Auspuff*
The gearbox	*Das Getriebe*
The windscreen	*Die Windschutzscheibe*
... is broken.	... ist kaputt.
The brakes	*Die Bremsen*
The headlights	*Die Scheinwerfer*
The windscreen wipers	*Die Scheibenwischer*
... are not working.	... funktionieren nicht.
The battery is flat.	Die Batterie ist leer.
The car won't start.	Der Motor springt nicht an.
The engine is overheating.	Der Motor wird zu heiß.
I have a flat tyre.	Ich habe einen Platten.
Can you repair it?	Können Sie das reparieren?
When will the car be ready?	Wann ist das Auto fertig?

Parking | Parken

Can I park here?	Kann ich hier parken?
Do I need to buy a (car-parking) ticket?	Muss ich einen Parkschein lösen?
Where is the ticket machine?	Wo ist der Parkscheinautomat?
The ticket machine isn't working.	Der Parkscheinautomat funktioniert nicht.

Petrol Station | Tankstelle

Where is the nearest petrol station?	Wo ist die nächste Tankstelle?
Fill it up, please.	Volltanken bitte.

40 euros' worth of ..., please.	Für 40 Euro ... bitte.
diesel	*Diesel*
unleaded (economy) petrol	*Normalbenzin*
premium unleaded	*Super*
Pump number ... please.	Säule Nummer ... bitte.
Please check ...	Bitte überprüfen Sie ...
the tyre pressure.	*den Reifendruck.*
the oil.	*das Öl.*
the water.	*das Wasser.*

Accident — Unfall

Please call ...	Bitte rufen Sie ...
the police.	*die Polizei.*
the emergency doctor.	*den Notarzt.*
Here are my insurance details.	Hier sind meine Versicherungsangaben.
Give me your insurance details, please.	Bitte geben Sie mir Ihre Versicherungsangaben.
Can you be a witness for me?	Würden Sie das bezeugen?
You were driving too fast.	Sie sind zu schnell gefahren.
It wasn't your right of way.	Sie haben die Vorfahrt nicht beachtet.

Car Travel — Unterwegs mit dem Auto

What's the best route to ...?	Wie kommt man am besten nach/zu ...?
Where can I pay the toll?	Wo kann ich die Maut bezahlen?
I'd like a motorway tax sticker ...	Ich möchte einen Aufkleber für die Autobahngebühr/ eine Vignette ...
for a week.	*für eine Woche.*
for a month.	*für einen Monat.*

Do you have a road map of this area?	Haben Sie eine Straßenkarte von dieser Gegend?

Cycling | Fahrrad

Where is the cycle path to ...?	Wo ist der Radwanderweg nach ...?
Can I keep my bike here?	Kann ich hier mein Fahrrad unterstellen?
My bike has been stolen.	Mein Fahrrad ist gestohlen worden.
Where is the nearest bike repair shop?	Wo gibt es hier eine Fahrradwerkstatt?
The brake isn't working.	Die Bremse funktioniert nicht.
The gears aren't working.	Die Gangschaltung funktioniert nicht.
The chain is broken.	Die Kette ist gerissen.
I've got a flat tyre.	Ich habe einen Platten.
I need a puncture repair kit.	Ich brauche Reifenflickzeug.

Train | Eisenbahn

A single to ..., please.	Eine einfache Fahrt nach ... bitte.
Two returns to ..., please.	Zweimal hin und zurück nach ... bitte.
Is there a reduction ...?	Gibt es eine Ermäßigung ...?
for students	*für Studenten*
for pensioners	*für Rentner*
with this pass	*mit diesem Pass*
I'd like to reserve a seat on the train to ..., please.	Eine Platzkarte für den Zug nach ... bitte.
I want to book a couchette/a berth to ...	Ich möchte einen Liegewagenplatz/Schlafwagenplatz nach ... buchen.

When is the next train to ...?	Wann geht der nächste Zug nach ...?
Is there a supplement to pay?	Muss ich einen Zuschlag kaufen?
Do I need to change?	Muss ich umsteigen?
Where do I change?	Wo muss ich umsteigen?
Is this the train for ...?	Ist das der Zug nach ...?
I have a reservation.	Ich habe eine Platzkarte/ Reservierung.
Is this seat free?	Ist dieser Platz noch frei?
Where is the buffet car?	Wo ist der Speisewagen?
Where is coach number ...?	Wo ist Wagen Nummer ...?

Ferry | Fähre

Is there a ferry to ...?	Gibt es eine Fähre nach ...?
When is the next ferry to ...?	Wann geht die nächste Fähre nach ...?
When is the first/last ferry to ...?	Wann geht die erste/letzte Fähre nach ...?
How much is ...?	Was kostet ...?
a single	*die einfache Fahrt*
a return	*die Hin- und Rückfahrt*
How much is it for a car/ camper with ... people?	Was kostet es für eine Auto/ Wohnmobil mit ... Personen?
How long does the crossing take?	Wie lange dauert die Überfahrt?
Where is ...?	Wo ist ...?
the restaurant	*das Restaurant*
the duty-free shop	*der Duty-free-Shop*
Where is cabin number ...?	Wo ist Kabine Nummer ...?

Plane	Flugzeug
Where is ...?	Wo ist ...?
the taxi rank	*der Taxistand*
the bus stop	*die Bushaltestelle*
the information office	*die Information*
My luggage hasn't arrived.	Mein Gepäck ist nicht angekommen.
Where do I check in for the flight to ...?	Wo ist das Check-in für den Flug nach ...?
Which gate for the flight to ...?	Von welchem Ausgang geht der Flug nach ...?
When does boarding begin?	Wann beginnt das Einsteigen?
Window/aisle, please.	Fenster/Gang bitte.
I've lost my boarding pass/ my ticket.	Ich habe meine Einsteige-karte/meinen Flugschein verloren.

Local Public Transport	Öffentlicher Nahverkehr
How do I get to ...?	Wie komme ich zum/zur/ nach ...?
Where is the nearest ...?	Wo ist die nächste ...?
bus stop	*Bushaltestelle*
tram stop	*Straßenbahnhaltestelle*
underground station	*U-Bahn-Station*
Where is the bus station?	Wo ist der Busbahnhof?
Is there a reduction ...?	Gibt es eine Ermäßigung ...?
for students	*für Studenten*
for pensioners	*für Rentner*
with this card	*mit diesem Ausweis*
Do you have a map of the rail network?	Haben Sie eine Karte mit dem Streckennetz?
What is the next stop?	Was ist die nächste Halte-stelle?

Taxi	Taxi
Where can I get a taxi?	Wo bekomme ich hier ein Taxi?
Call me a taxi, please.	Bitte rufen Sie mir ein Taxi.
Please order me a taxi for ... o'clock.	Bitte bestellen Sie mir ein Taxi für ... Uhr.
To the airport/station, please.	Zum Flughafen/Bahnhof, bitte.
I'm in a hurry.	Ich habe es sehr eilig.
How much is it?	Was kostet die Fahrt?
I need a receipt.	Ich brauche eine Quittung.
Keep the change.	Stimmt so.
Stop here, please.	Bitte halten Sie hier.

Camping | Camping

Is there a campsite here?	Gibt es hier einen Campingplatz?
We'd like a site for ...	Wir möchten einen Platz für ...
a tent.	*ein Zelt.*
a camper van.	*ein Wohnmobil.*
a caravan.	*einen Wohnwagen.*
We'd like to stay one night/ ... nights.	Wir möchten eine Nacht/ ... Nächte bleiben.
How much is it per night?	Was kostet die Nacht?
Where are ...?	Wo sind ...?
the toilets	*die Toiletten*
the showers	*die Duschen*
Where is ...?	Wo ist ...?
the shop	*der Laden*
the site office	*die Verwaltung*
Can we camp here overnight?	Können wir über Nacht hier zelten?

Self-Catering | Ferienwohnung/-haus

English	German
Where do we get the key for the apartment/house?	Wo bekommen wir den Schlüssel für die Wohnung/ das Haus?
Do we have to pay extra for electricity/gas?	Müssen wir Strom/Gas extra bezahlen?
How does ... work?	Wie funktioniert ...?
the washing machine	*die Waschmaschine*
the cooker	*der Herd*
the heating	*die Heizung*
Who do I contact if there are any problems?	An wen kann ich mich bei Problemen wenden?
We need ...	Wir brauchen ...
a second key.	*einen zweiten Schlüssel.*
more sheets.	*mehr Bettwäsche.*

The gas has run out.	Das Gas ist alle.
There is no electricity.	Es gibt keinen Strom.
Where do we hand in the keys when we're leaving?	Wo geben wir die Schlüssel bei der Abreise ab?
Do we have to clean the apartment/the house before we leave?	Müssen wir die Wohnung/ das Haus vor der Abreise sauber machen?

Hotel | Hotel

Do you have a ... for tonight?	Haben Sie ein ... für heute Nacht?
single room	*Einzelzimmer*
double room	*Doppelzimmer*
with bath/shower	mit Bad/Dusche
I want to stay for one night/ ... nights.	Ich möchte eine Nacht/ ... Nächte bleiben.
I booked a room in the name of ...	Ich habe ein Zimmer auf den Namen ... reserviert.
I'd like another room.	Ich möchte ein anderes Zimmer.
What time is breakfast?	Wann gibt es Frühstück?
Where is breakfast served?	Wo gibt es Frühstück?
Can I have breakfast in my room?	Können Sie mir das Frühstück aufs Zimmer bringen?
Where is ...?	Wo ist ...?
the restaurant	*das Restaurant*
the bar	*die Bar*
the gym	*der Fitnessraum*
the swimming pool	*der Swimmingpool*
I'd like an alarm call for tomorrow morning at ...	Bitte wecken Sie mich morgen früh um ...
The key, please.	Den Schlüssel bitte.
Are there any messages for me?	Sind Nachrichten für mich da?

I'm looking for ...	Ich suche ...
I'd like ...	Ich möchte ...
Do you have ...?	Haben Sie ...?
Do you have this ...?	Haben Sie das ...?
in *another size*	*in einer anderen Größe*
in *another colour*	*in einer anderen Farbe*
in *another design*	*mit einem anderen Muster*
I take size ...	Ich trage Größe ...
I'll take it.	Ich nehme das.
Do you have anything else?	Haben Sie noch etwas anderes?
That's too expensive.	Das ist zu teuer.
I'm just looking.	Ich sehe mich nur um.
Do you take credit cards?	Nehmen Sie Kreditkarten?

Food Shopping | Lebensmittel

Where is the nearest ...?	Wo ist hier ...?
supermarket	*ein Supermarkt*
baker's	*eine Bäckerei*
butcher's	*eine Metzgerei*
greengrocer's	*ein Obst- und Gemüseladen*
Where is the market?	Wo ist der Markt?
When is the market on?	Wann ist Markt?
a kilo of ...	ein Kilo ...
a pound of ...	ein Pfund ...
200 grams of ...	200 Gramm ...
... slices ...	... Scheiben ...
a litre of ...	ein Liter ...
a bottle of ...	eine Flasche ...
a packet of ...	ein Päckchen ...

Photos and Videos | Foto und Video

A colour film, please.	Einen Farbfilm bitte.
With twenty-four/ thirty-six exposures.	Mit vierundzwanzig/ sechsunddreißig Bildern.
Can I have batteries for this camera, please?	Batterien für diesen Apparat bitte.
The camera is sticking.	Der Apparat klemmt.
Can you develop this film, please?	Bitte entwickeln Sie diesen Film.
I'd like the photos ...	Ich hätte die Bilder gern ...
matt.	*matt.*
glossy.	*Hochglanz.*
10 by 15 centimetres.	*im Format 10 mal 15.*
When will the photos be ready?	Wann sind die Fotos fertig?
How much do the photos cost?	Wie viel kosten die Bilder?
Are you allowed to take photos here?	Darf man hier fotografieren?
Could you take a photo of us, please?	Könnten Sie bitte ein Foto von uns machen?

Post Office | Post

Where is the nearest post office?	Wo ist die nächste Post?
When does the post office open?	Wann hat die Post geöffnet?
I'd like ... stamps for postcards/letters to Germany/Switzerland.	Ich möchte ... Briefmarken für Postkarten/Briefe nach Deutschland/in die Schweiz.
Where is the nearest postbox?	Wo ist hier ein Briefkasten?

Sightseeing | Besichtigungen

Where is the tourist office?	Wo ist die Touristen-information?
Do you have any leaflets about ...?	Haben Sie Broschüren über ...?
What sights can you visit here?	Welche Sehenswürdigkeiten gibt es hier?
Is there a guided tour in English?	Gibt es eine Stadtrundfahrt/ einen Stadtrundgang auf Englisch?
When is ... open?	Wann ist ... geöffnet?
the museum	*das Museum*
the church	*die Kirche*
the castle	*das Schloss*
How much does it cost to get in?	Was kostet der Eintritt?
Are there any reductions ...?	Gibt es eine Ermäßigung ...?
for students	*für Studenten*
for children	*für Kinder*
for pensioners	*für Rentner*
for the unemployed	*für Arbeitslose*
I'd like a catalogue.	Ich möchte einen Katalog.
Can I take photos here?	Kann ich hier fotografieren?
Can I film here?	Kann ich hier filmen?

Entertainment | Unterhaltung

What is there to do here?	Was kann man hier unter-nehmen?
Do you have a list of events?	Haben Sie einen Veranstal-tungskalender?
Where can we ...?	Wo kann man hier ...?
go dancing	*tanzen gehen*
hear live music	*Livemusik hören*

Where is there ...?	Wo gibt es hier ... ?
a nice pub	*eine nette Kneipe*
a good disco	*eine gute Disko*
What's on tonight ...?	Was gibt es heute Abend ...?
at the cinema	*im Kino*
at the theatre	*im Theater*
at the opera	*in der Oper*
at the concert hall	*in der Konzerthalle*
Where can I buy tickets	Wo kann ich Karten für ...
for ...?	kaufen?
the theatre	*das Theater*
the concert	*das Konzert*
the opera	*die Oper*
the ballet	*das Ballett*
How much is it to get in?	Was kostet der Eintritt?
I'd like a ticket/... tickets	Ich möchte eine Karte/
for ...	... Karten für ...
Are there any reductions	Gibt es eine Ermäßigung
for ...?	für ...?
children	*Kinder*
pensioners	*Rentner*
students	*Studenten*
the unemployed	*Arbeitslose*

At the Beach | Am Strand

Can you swim here/	Kann man hier/in diesem
in this lake?	See baden?
Where is the nearest quiet	Wo gibt es hier einen
beach?	ruhigen Strand?
Is there a beach with	Gibt es einen bewachten
lifeguards?	Strand?
How deep is the water?	Wie tief ist das Wasser?

What is the water temperature?	Wie viel Grad hat das Wasser?
Are there currents?	Gibt es hier Strömungen?
Is there a lifeguard?	Gibt es hier einen Rettungsschwimmer?
Where can you ...?	Wo kann man hier ...?
go surfing	*surfen*
go waterskiing	*Wasserski fahren*
go diving	*tauchen*
go paragliding	*Gleitschirm fliegen*
I'd like to hire ...	Ich möchte ... mieten.
a beach chair.	*einen Strandkorb*
a deckchair.	*einen Liegestuhl*
a sunshade.	*einen Sonnenschirm*
I'd like to hire ...	Ich möchte ... ausleihen.
a surfboard.	*ein Surfbrett*
a jet-ski.	*einen Jetski*
a rowing boat.	*ein Ruderboot*
a pedal boat.	*ein Tretboot*

Skiing | Ski

Where can I hire skiing equipment?	Wo kann ich eine Skiausrüstung ausleihen?
I'd like to hire ...	Ich möchte ... ausleihen.
downhill skis.	*Abfahrtski*
cross-country skis.	*Langlaufski*
ski boots.	*Skischuhe*
Where can I buy a ski pass?	Wo kann ich einen Skipass kaufen?
I'd like a ski pass ...	Ich möchte einen Skipass ...
for a day.	*für einen Tag.*
for five days.	*für fünf Tage.*
for a week.	*für sieben Tage.*

How much is a ski pass?	Wie viel kostet der Skipass?
Do you have a map of the ski runs?	Haben Sie eine Pistenkarte?
Where are the beginners' slopes?	Wo sind die Abfahrten für Anfänger?
How difficult is this slope?	Welchen Schwierigkeitsgrad hat diese Abfahrt?
Is there a ski school?	Gibt es eine Skischule?
What's the weather forecast?	Wie ist der Wetterbericht?
What is the snow like?	Wie ist der Schnee?
Is there a danger of avalanches?	Besteht Lawinengefahr?

Sport | Sport

Where can we ...?	Wo kann man hier ...?
play tennis/golf	*Tennis/Golf spielen*
go swimming	*schwimmen*
go riding	*reiten*
How much is it per hour?	Wie viel kostet es pro Stunde?
Where can I book a court?	Wo kann ich einen Platz buchen?
Where can I hire rackets?	Wo kann ich Schläger ausleihen?
Where can I hire a rowing boat/a pedal boat?	Wo kann ich ein Ruderboot/ein Tretboot mieten?
Do you need a fishing permit?	Braucht man einen Angelschein?
I'd like to see ...	Ich möchte ... ansehen.
a football match.	*ein Fußballspiel*
a horse race.	*ein Pferderennen*

RESTAURANT	RESTAURANT
A table for ... people, please.	Einen Tisch für ... Personen bitte.
The menu, please.	Die Speisekarte bitte.
The wine list, please.	Die Weinkarte bitte.
What do you recommend?	Was empfehlen Sie?
Do you have ...?	Haben Sie ...?
any vegetarian dishes	*vegetarische Gerichte*
children's portions	*Kinderportionen*
Does that contain ...?	Enthält das ...?
peanuts	*Erdnüsse*
alcohol	*Alkohol*
Can you bring (more) ..., please?	Bitte bringen Sie (noch) ...
I'll have ...	Ich nehme ...
The bill, please.	Zahlen bitte.
All together, please.	Bitte alles zusammen.
Separate bills, please.	Getrennte Rechnungen bitte.
Keep the change.	Stimmt so.
I didn't order this.	Das habe ich nicht bestellt.
The bill is wrong.	Die Rechnung stimmt nicht.
The food is cold/too salty.	Das Essen ist kalt/versalzen.

see also MENU READER   *siehe auch* SPEISEKARTE

Where can I make a phone call?	Wo kann ich hier telefonieren?
Where is the nearest card phone?	Wo ist das nächste Kartentelefon?
Where is the nearest coin box?	Wo ist der nächste Münzfernsprecher?
I'd like a ten euro phone card.	Ich möchte eine Telefonkarte für zehn Euro.
I'd like some coins for the phone, please.	Ich möchte Münzen für das Telefon bitte.
I'd like to make a reverse charge call.	Ich möchte ein R-Gespräch anmelden.
Hello.	Hallo.
This is ...	Hier ist ...
Who's speaking, please?	Wer spricht dort bitte?
Can I speak to Mr/Ms ..., please?	Kann ich bitte mit Herrn/Frau ... sprechen?
Extension ..., please.	Apparat ... bitte.
I'll phone back later.	Ich rufe später wieder an.
Where can I charge my mobile phone?	Wo kann ich mein Handy aufladen?
I need a new battery.	Ich brauche einen neuen Akku.
I can't get a network.	Hier ist kein Netz.
You're breaking up.	Die Verbindung ist sehr schlecht.

Passport/Customs | Pass/Zoll

Here is ...	Hier ist ...
my passport.	*mein Pass.*
my identity card.	*mein Personalausweis.*
my driving licence.	*mein Führerschein.*
Here are my vehicle documents.	Hier sind meine Fahrzeugpapiere.
The children are on this passport.	Die Kinder stehen in diesem Pass.
Do I have to pay duty on this?	Muss ich das verzollen?
This is ...	Das ist ...
a present.	*ein Geschenk.*
a sample.	*ein Warenmuster.*
This is for my own personal use.	Das ist für meinen persönlichen Gebrauch.
I'm on my way to ...	Ich bin auf der Durchreise nach ...

Changing Money | Bank

Where can I change money?	Wo kann ich hier Geld wechseln?
Is there a bank/bureau de change here?	Gibt es hier eine Bank/eine Wechselstube?
When is the bank/bureau de change open?	Wann ist die Bank/Wechselstube geöffnet?
I'd like to change ... euros into pounds/dollars.	Ich möchte ... Euro in Pfund/Dollar umtauschen.
I'd like to cash these traveller's cheques.	Ich möchte diese Reiseschecks einlösen.
What's the commission?	Wie hoch ist die Gebühr?
Can I use my credit card to get cash?	Kann ich hier mit meiner Kreditkarte Bargeld bekommen?

Where is the nearest cash machine?	Wo gibt es hier einen Geldautomaten?
The cash machine swallowed my card.	Der Geldautomat hat meine Karte geschluckt.
Can you give me some change, please.	Bitte geben Sie mir etwas Kleingeld.

Emergency Services | Notfalldienste

Help!	Hilfe!
Fire!	Feuer!
Please call ...	Bitte rufen Sie ...
the emergency doctor.	*den Notarzt.*
the fire brigade.	*die Feuerwehr.*
the police.	*die Polizei.*
I need to make an urgent phone call.	Ich muss dringend telefonieren.
I need an interpreter.	Ich brauche einen Dolmetscher.
Where is the police station?	Wo ist die Polizeiwache?
Where is the nearest hospital?	Wo ist das nächste Krankenhaus?
I want to report a theft.	Ich möchte einen Diebstahl melden.
... has been stolen.	... ist gestohlen worden.
There's been an accident.	Es ist ein Unfall passiert.
There are ... people injured.	Es gibt ... Verletzte.
My location is ...	Mein Standort ist ...
I've been ...	Ich bin ... worden.
robbed	*beraubt*
attacked	*überfallen*
raped	*vergewaltigt*
I'd like to phone my embassy.	Ich möchte mit meiner Botschaft sprechen.

Pharmacy	Apotheke
Where is the nearest pharmacy?	Wo gibt es hier eine Apotheke?
Which pharmacy provides emergency service?	Welche Apotheke hat Bereitschaft?
I'd like something for ...	Ich möchte etwas gegen ...
diarrhoea.	*Durchfall.*
a temperature.	*Fieber.*
travel sickness.	*Reisekrankheit.*
a headache.	*Kopfschmerzen.*
a cold.	*Erkältung.*
I'd like ...	Ich möchte ...
plasters.	*Pflaster.*
a bandage.	*einen Verband.*
I can't take ...	Ich vertrage kein ...
aspirin.	*Aspirin.*
penicillin.	*Penizillin.*
Is it safe to give to children?	Kann man das Kindern geben?
How should I take it?	Wie soll ich das einnehmen?

At the Doctor's	Beim Arzt
I need a doctor.	Ich brauche einen Arzt.
Where is casualty?	Wo ist die Notaufnahme?
I have a pain here.	Ich habe hier Schmerzen.
I feel ...	Mir ist ...
hot.	*heiß.*
cold.	*kalt.*
sick.	*übel.*
dizzy.	*schwindlig.*

I'm allergic to ...	Ich bin allergisch gegen ...
I am ...	Ich bin ...
pregnant.	*schwanger.*
diabetic.	*Diabetiker.*
HIV-positive.	*HIV-positiv.*
I'm on this medication.	Ich nehme dieses Medikament.
My blood group is ...	Meine Blutgruppe ist ...

At the Hospital · Krankenhaus

Which ward is ... in?	Auf welcher Station liegt ...?
When are visiting hours?	Wann ist die Besuchszeit?
I'd like to speak to ...	Ich möchte mit ... sprechen.
a doctor.	*einem Arzt*
a nurse.	*einer Krankenschwester*
I'd like to hire a phone.	Ich möchte ein Telefon mieten.
I'd like headphones for the TV, please.	Ich möchte Kopfhörer für das Fernsehen, bitte.
When will I be discharged?	Wann werde ich entlassen?

At the Dentist's · Beim Zahnarzt

I need a dentist.	Ich brauche einen Zahnarzt.
This tooth hurts.	Dieser Zahn tut weh.
One of my fillings has fallen out.	Mir ist eine Füllung herausgefallen.
I have an abscess.	Ich habe einen Abszess.
I want/don't want an injection for the pain.	Ich möchte eine/keine Spritze gegen die Schmerzen.
Can you repair my dentures?	Können Sie mein Gebiss reparieren?
I need a receipt for the insurance.	Ich brauche eine Quittung für die Versicherung.

Business Travel | Dienstreisen

I'd like to arrange a meeting with ...	Ich möchte eine Besprechung mit ... ausmachen.
I have an appointment with Mr/Ms ...	Ich haben einen Termin mit Herrn/Frau ...
Here is my card.	Hier ist meine Karte.
I work for ...	Ich arbeite für ...
How do I get to ...?	Wie komme ich ...?
your office	*zu Ihrem Büro*
Mr/Ms ...'s office	*zum Büro von Herrn/Frau ...*
the canteen	*zur Kantine*
I need an interpreter.	Ich brauche einen Dolmetscher.
Can you copy that for me, please?	Bitte kopieren Sie das für mich.
May I use ...?	Darf ich ... benutzen?
your phone	*Ihr Telefon*
your computer	*Ihren Computer*
your desk	*Ihren Schreibtisch*

Disabled Travellers | Behinderte

Where is the wheelchair-accessible entrance?	Wo ist der Eingang für Rollstuhlfahrer?
Is your hotel accessible to wheelchairs?	Ist Ihr Hotel rollstuhlgerecht?
I need a room ...	Ich brauche ein Zimmer ...
on the ground floor.	*im Erdgeschoss.*
with wheelchair access.	*für Rollstuhlfahrer.*
Do you have a lift for wheelchairs?	Haben Sie einen Aufzug für Rollstühle?
Where is the disabled toilet?	Wo ist die Behindertentoilette?
Is the train wheelchair accessible?	Kann ich als Rollstuhlfahrer in diesem Zug mitfahren?

Can you help me get on/off please?	Bitte helfen Sie mir beim Einsteigen/Aussteigen.
Where is the nearest repair shop for wheelchairs?	Wo gibt es hier eine Werkstatt für Rollstühle?
The wheels lock.	Die Räder blockieren.

Travelling with Children | Reisen mit Kindern

Is it OK to bring children here?	Können wir die Kinder mitbringen?
Are children allowed in, too?	Ist der Eintritt auch Kindern gestattet?
Is there a reduction for children?	Gibt es eine Ermäßigung für Kinder?
Do you have children's portions?	Haben Sie Kinderportionen?
Do you have ...?	Haben Sie ...?
a high chair	*einen Kinderstuhl*
a cot	*ein Kinderbett*
a child's seat	*einen Kindersitz*
a baby's changing table	*einen Wickeltisch*
Where can I change the baby?	Wo kann ich das Baby wickeln?
Where can I breast-feed the baby?	Wo kann ich das Baby stillen?
Can you warm this up, please?	Können Sie das bitte aufwärmen?
What is there for children to do?	Was können Kinder hier unternehmen?
Where is the nearest playground?	Wo gibt es hier einen Spielplatz?
Is there a child-minding service?	Gibt es hier eine Kinderbetreuung?
My son/daughter is ill.	Mein Sohn/meine Tochter ist krank.

I'd like to make a complaint.	Ich möchte mich beschweren.
To whom can I complain?	Bei wem kann ich mich beschweren?
I'd like to speak to the manager, please.	Ich möchte mit dem Geschäftsführer sprechen.
The light	Das Licht
The heating	Die Heizung
The shower	Die Dusche
... doesn't work.	... funktioniert nicht.
The room is ...	Das Zimmer ist ...
dirty.	schmutzig.
too small.	zu klein.
too cold.	zu kalt.
Can you clean the room, please?	Bitte machen Sie das Zimmer sauber.
Can you turn down the TV/the radio, please?	Bitte stellen Sie den Fernseher/ das Radio leiser.
The food is ...	Das Essen ist ...
cold.	kalt.
too salty.	versalzen.
This isn't what I ordered.	Das habe ich nicht bestellt.
We've been waiting for a very long time.	Wir warten schon sehr lange.
The bill is wrong.	Die Rechnung stimmt nicht.
I want my money back.	Ich möchte mein Geld zurück.
I'd like to exchange this.	Ich möchte das umtauschen.
I'm not satisfied with this.	Ich bin damit nicht zufrieden.

Alsterwasser lager shandy
Apfelkorn apple brandy
arme Ritter French toast
Backpflaumen prunes
Bauernfrühstück cooked breakfast of scrambled eggs, bacon, diced potatoes, onions, tomatoes
Berliner doughnut filled with jam
Bierschinken ham sausage
Bierwurst Bavarian boiled sausage
Bockwurst boiled sausage; a popular snack served with a bread roll
Dunkles dark beer
Eierkuchen pancakes
Eisbein boiled pork knuckle, often served with sauerkraut
Eiswein a rich, naturally sweet white wine made from grapes harvested after a period of frost
Fledermaus boiled beef in a horseradish cream
Fünfkornbrot wholemeal bread made with five different cereals
geschmort braised
Gewürzgurken gherkins
Hackbraten meatloaf

Helles light beer
Heuriger new wine
Jägerschnitzel escalope served with mushrooms and a wine sauce
Kasseler smoked pork
Knackwurst hot spicy sausage; a popular snack served with bread
Kraftsuppe consommé
Kroketten croquettes
Leberkäse pork liver meatloaf
Leinsamenbrot wholemeal bread with linseed
Linzer Torte latticed tart with jam topping
Malzbier dark malt beer
Maß a litre of beer
Mischbrot grey bread made with rye and wheat flour
Nockerln small dumplings
Pils, **Pilsner** a strong, slightly bitter lager
Pumpernickel very dark bread made with coarse wholemeal rye flour
Raclette melted cheese and potatoes
Räucherkäse smoked cheese
Reibekuchen potato cakes
Rösti fried diced potatoes, onions and bacon

Roulade beef olive
Sachertorte rich chocolate gâteau
Sauerbraten braised pickled beef served with dumplings and vegetables
Schwertfisch swordfish
Spanferkel suckling pig
Steinbutt turbot
Steinpilze porcini mushrooms

Stollen spiced loaf with candied peel traditionally eaten at Christmas
Wiener Schnitzel escalope fried in breadcrumbs
Wildbraten roast venison
Zervelatwurst fine beef and pork salami
Zigeunerschnitzel escalope in paprika sauce

apple turnover Apfeltasche

bangers and mash Kartoffelpüree mit Bratwurst, Zwiebeln und Soße

banoffee pie Törtchen mit einer Füllung aus Bananen, Toffee und Sahne

BLT (sandwich) Sandwich mit Schinkenspeck, Salat und Tomaten

bubble and squeak zusammen gebratene Fleischreste und Gemüse

butternut squash Moschuskürbis

Caesar salad Salatgericht aus Kopfsalat, Eiern, Parmesankäse und Vinaigrette

chocolate brownie kleiner Schokoladenkuchen

chicken Kiev Hähnchenbrust, mit Knoblauchbutter gefüllt

chicken nuggets Hähnchen-Nuggets

club sandwich dreilagiges, mit Toastbrot zubereitetes Sandwich

Cornish pasty Gebäckstück aus Blätterteig mit Fleischfüllung

English breakfast englisches Frühstück

filo pastry Blätterteig

haggis mit gehackten Schafsinnereien und Haferschrot gefüllter Schafsmagen

hash browns Rösti-Ecken

hotpot Fleischeintopf mit Kartoffeln

Irish stew Eintopf mit Hammelfleisch, Kartoffeln und Zwiebeln

monkfish Seeteufel

pavlova Baisertorte, mit Sahne und Früchten gefüllt

purée Püree

Quorn® proteinreicher Fleischersatz aus Gemüsesubstanz

savoy cabbage Wirsing

Scotch broth Gemüsesuppe mit Graupen und Hammelfleisch

Scotch egg hart gekochtes Ei in Wurstbrät, paniert und ausgebacken

scrumpy starker Cider aus Südwestengland

sea bass Wolfsbarsch

shortcrust pastry Mürbeteig

spare ribs Schälrippchen

MENU READER | SPEISEKARTE

Stilton englischer
Blauschimmelkäse
stout Starkbier
sundae Eisbecher mit Nüssen
und Sirup
Thousand Island dressing
Salatsoße aus Mayonnaise,
Ketchup, Paprika und Pickles
toad in the hole in Teig

gebackene Bratwürste
turbot Steinbutt
Waldorf salad Waldorfsalat
Welsh rarebit überbackene
Käseschnitte
Yorkshire pudding im
Backofen ausgebackener
Teig als Beilage zu
Fleischgerichten

a

abandon [ə'bændən] vt (desert) verlassen; (give up) aufgeben

abbey ['æbɪ] n Abtei f

abbreviate [əbriː'vɪeɪt] vt abkürzen; **abbreviation** [əbriːvɪ'eɪʃən] n Abkürzung f

ABC ['eɪbiː'siː] n (a. fig) Abc nt

abdicate ['æbdɪkeɪt] vi (king) abdanken; **abdication** [æbdɪ'keɪʃən] n Abdankung f

abdomen ['æbdəmən] n Unterleib m

ability [ə'bɪlɪtɪ] n Fähigkeit f; **able** ['eɪbl] adj fähig; **to be ~ to do sth** etw tun können

abnormal [æb'nɔːml] adj anormal

aboard [ə'bɔːd] adv, prep an Bord +gen

abolish [ə'bɒlɪʃ] vt abschaffen

aborigine [æbə'rɪdʒɪniː] n Ureinwohner(in) m(f) (Australiens)

abort [ə'bɔːt] vt (Med: foetus) abtreiben; (Space: mission) abbrechen; **abortion** [ə'bɔːʃən] n Abtreibung f

KEYWORD

a [eɪ, ə; æn, ən] (before vowel or silent h: **an**) indef art **1** ein, eine; **a woman** eine Frau; **a book** ein Buch; **an eagle** ein Adler; **she's a doctor** sie ist Ärztin

2 (instead of the number "one") ein, eine; **a year ago** vor einem Jahr; **a hundred/thousand** etc **pounds** (ein) hundert/(ein) tausend etc Pfund

3 (in expressing ratios, prices etc) pro; **3 a day/week** 3 pro Tag/Woche, 3 am Tag/in der Woche; **10 km an hour** 10 km pro Stunde/in der Stunde

AA abbr = **Automobile Association** britischer Automobilklub, ≈ ADAC m

aback adv: **taken ~** erstaunt

KEYWORD

about [ə'baʊt] adv **1** (approximately) etwa, ungefähr; **about a hundred/thousand** etc etwa hundert/tausend etc; **at about 2 o'clock** etwa um 2 Uhr; **I've just about finished** ich bin gerade fertig

2 (referring to place) herum, umher; **to leave things lying about** Sachen herumliegen lassen; **to run/walk** etc **about** herumrennen/gehen etc

3 to be about to do sth im Begriff sein, etw zu tun; **he was about to go to bed** er wollte gerade ins Bett gehen

▷ *prep* **1** *(relating to)* über +*akk*; **a book about London** ein Buch über London; **what is it about?** worum geht es?; *(book etc)* wovon handelt es?; **we talked about it** wir haben darüber geredet; **what o How about doing this?** wollen wir das machen?
2 *(referring to place)* um (... herum); **to walk about the town** in der Stadt herumgehen; **her clothes were scattered about the room** ihre Kleider waren über das ganze Zimmer verstreut

above [ə'bʌv] *adv* oben; **children aged 8 and ~** Kinder ab 8 Jahren; **on the floor ~** im Stockwerk höher ▷ *prep* über; **~ 40 degrees** über 40 Grad; **~ all** vor allem ▷ *adj* obig

abroad [ə'brɔːd] *adv* im Ausland; **to go ~** ins Ausland gehen

abrupt [ə'brʌpt] *adj (sudden)* plötzlich, abrupt

abscess ['æbsis] *n* Geschwür nt

absence ['æbsəns] *n* Abwesenheit *f*; **absent** ['æbsənt] *adj* abwesend; **to be ~** fehlen; **absent-minded** *adj* zerstreut

absolute ['æbsəluːt] *adj* absolut; *(power)* unumschränkt; *(rubbish)* vollkommen, total; **absolutely** *adv* absolut; *(true, stupid)* vollkommen; **~!** genau!; **you're ~ right** du hast/Sie haben völlig recht

absorb [əb'zɔːb] *vt* absorbieren; *(fig: information)* in sich aufnehmen; **absorbed** *adj*: **~ in sth** in etw vertieft; **absorbent** *adj* absorbierend; **~ cotton** *(US)* Watte *f*; **absorbing** *adj (fig)* faszinierend, fesselnd

abstain [əb'stein] *vi*: **to ~ (from voting)** sich (der Stimme) enthalten

abstract ['æbstrækt] *adj* abstrakt

absurd [əb'sɜːd] *adj* absurd

abundance [ə'bʌndəns] *n* Reichtum m *(of an +dat)*

abuse [ə'bjuːs] *n (rude language)* Beschimpfungen *pl*; *(mistreatment)* Missbrauch m ▷ [ə'bjuːz] *vt* *(misuse)* missbrauchen; **abusive** [ə'bjuːsiv] *adj* beleidigend

AC *abbr* = **alternating current** Wechselstrom m ▷ *abbr* = **air conditioning** Klimaanlage

a/c *abbr* = **account** Kto.

academic [ækə'demik] *n* Wissenschaftler(in) *m(f)* ▷ *adj* akademisch, wissenschaftlich

accelerate [æk'seləreit] *vi (car etc)* beschleunigen; *(driver)* Gas geben; **acceleration** [ækselə'reiʃən] *n* Beschleunigung *f*; **accelerator** [æk'seləreitə] *n* Gas(pedal) nt

accent ['æksənt] *n* Akzent m

accept [ək'sept] *vt* annehmen; *(agree to)* akzeptieren; *(responsibility)* übernehmen; **acceptable** [ək'septəbl] *adj* annehmbar

access ['ækses] *n* Zugang m; *(Inform)* Zugriff m; **accessible** [æk'sesəbl] *adj (easily)* zugänglich/erreichbar; *(place)* (leicht) erreichbar

accessory [æk'sesəri] *n* Zubehörteil nt

access road *n* Zufahrtsstraße *f*

accident ['æksidənt] *n* Unfall m; **by ~** zufällig; **accidental** [æksi'dentl] *adj* unbeabsichtigt; *(meeting)* zufällig; *(death)* durch Unfall; **~ damage** Unfallschaden m; **accident-prone** *adj* vom Pech verfolgt

acclimatize [ə'klaimətaiz] *vt*: **to ~ oneself** sich gewöhnen *(to* an +*akk)*

accommodate [əˈkɒmədeɪt] vt
unterbringen;
accommodation(s)
[əkɒməˈdeɪʃən(z)] n Unterkunft f

accompany [əˈkʌmpənɪ] vt
begleiten

accomplish [əˈkʌmplɪʃ] vt
erreichen

accord [əˈkɔːd] n: **of one's own**
~ freiwillig; **according to** prep
nach, laut +dat

account [əˈkaʊnt] n (in bank etc)
Konto nt; (narrative) Bericht m; **on**
~ of wegen; **on no ~** auf keinen
Fall; **to take into ~**
berücksichtigen, in Betracht
ziehen; **accountant** [əˈkaʊntənt]
n Buchhalter(in) m(f); **account for**
vt (explain) erklären; (expenditure)
Rechenschaft ablegen für;
account number n
Kontonummer f

accumulate [əˈkjuːmjʊleɪt] vt
ansammeln ▷ vi sich ansammeln

accuracy [ˈækjʊrəsɪ] n
Genauigkeit f; **accurate** [ˈækjʊrɪt]
adj genau

accusation [ækjʊˈzeɪʃən] n
Anklage f, Beschuldigung f

accusative [əˈkjuːzətɪv] n
Akkusativ m

accuse [əˈkjuːz] vt beschuldigen;
(Jur) anklagen (of wegen +gen); **~ sb**
of doing sth jdn beschuldigen,
etw getan zu haben; **accused** n
(Jur) Angeklagte(r) mf

accustom [əˈkʌstəm] vt
gewöhnen (to an +akk);
accustomed adj gewöhnt; **to get**
~ to sth sich an etw akk gewöhnen

ace [eɪs] n Ass nt ▷ adj Star-

ache [eɪk] n Schmerz m ▷ vi
wehtun

achieve [əˈtʃiːv] vt erreichen;
achievement n Leistung f

acid [ˈæsɪd] n Säure f ▷ adj sauer;
~ rain saurer Regen

acknowledge [əkˈnɒlɪdʒ] vt
(recognize) anerkennen; (admit)
zugeben; (receipt of letter etc)
bestätigen; **acknowledgement** n
Anerkennung f; (of letter)
Empfangsbestätigung f

acne [ˈæknɪ] n Akne f

acorn [ˈeɪkɔːn] n Eichel f

acoustic [əˈkuːstɪk] adj akustisch; **acoustics** [əˈkuːstɪks] npl
Akustik f

acquaintance [əˈkweɪntəns] n
(person) Bekannte(r) mf

acquire [əˈkwaɪə*] vt erwerben,
sich aneignen; **acquisition**
[ækwɪˈzɪʃn] n (of skills etc) Erwerb
m; (object) Anschaffung f

acrobat [ˈækrəbæt] n Akrobat(in)
m(f)

across [əˈkrɒs] prep über +akk; **he**
lives ~ the street er wohnt auf der
anderen Seite der Straße ▷ adv
hinüber, herüber; **100m ~** 100m
breit

act [ækt] n (deed) Tat f; (Jur: law)
Gesetz nt; (Theat) Akt m; (fig:
pretence) Schau f; **it's all an ~** es ist
alles nur Theater; **to be in the ~ of**
doing sth gerade dabei sein, etw
zu tun ▷ vi (take action) handeln;
(behave) sich verhalten; (Theat) spielen;
to ~ as (person) fungieren als; (thing)
dienen als ▷ vt (a part) spielen

action [ˈækʃən] n (of play, novel
etc) Handlung f; (in film Action
etc) Handlung f; (in film etc) Action
f; (Mil) Kampf m; **to take ~** etwas
unternehmen; **out of ~** (machine)
außer Betrieb; **to put a plan into**
~ einen Plan in die Tat umsetzen;
action replay n (Sport, TV)
Wiederholung f

activate [ˈæktɪveɪt] vt aktivieren;
active [ˈæktɪv] adj aktiv; (child)
lebhaft; **activity** [ækˈtɪvɪtɪ] n
Aktivität f; (occupation)
Beschäftigung f; (organized event)
Veranstaltung f

actor ['æktə°] n Schauspieler(in) m(f); **actress** ['æktrɪs] n Schauspielerin f

actual ['æktjʋəl] adj wirklich; **actually** adv eigentlich; (said in surprise) tatsächlich

acupuncture ['ækjʋpʌŋktʃə°] n Akupunktur f

acute [əˈkjuːt] adj (pain) akut; (sense of smell) fein; (Math: angle) spitz

ad [æd] abbr = **advertisement**

AD abbr = **Anno Domini** nach Christi, n. Chr.

adapt [əˈdæpt] vi sich anpassen (to +dat) ▷ vt anpassen (to +dat); (rewrite) bearbeiten (for für); **adaptable** adj anpassungsfähig; **adaptation** n (of book etc) Bearbeitung f; **adapter** n (Elec) Zwischenstecker m, Adapter m ▷ vt

add [æd] vt (ingredient) hinzufügen; (numbers) addieren; **add up** vi (make sense) stimmen ▷ vt (numbers) addieren

addict ['ædɪkt] n Süchtige(r) mf; **addicted** [əˈdɪktɪd] adj: **~ to alcohol/drugs** alkohol-/drogensüchtig

addition [əˈdɪʃən] n Zusatz m; (to bill) Hinzufügung f; (Math) Addition f; **in ~** außerdem, zusätzlich (to zu); **additional** adj zusätzlich, weiter; **additive** ['ædɪtɪv] n Zusatz m; **add-on** ['ædɒn] n Zusatzgerät nt

address [əˈdres] n Adresse f ▷ vt (letter) adressieren; (person) anreden

adequate ['ædɪkwɪt] adj (appropriate) angemessen; (sufficient) ausreichend; (time) genügend

adhesive [ədˈhiːsɪv] n Klebstoff m; **adhesive tape** n Klebstreifen m

adjacent [əˈdʒeɪsənt] adj benachbart

adjective ['ædʒəktɪv] n Adjektiv nt

adjoining [əˈdʒɔɪnɪŋ] adj benachbart, Neben-

adjust [əˈdʒʌst] vt einstellen; (put right also) richtig stellen; (speed, flow) regulieren; (in position) verstellen ▷ vi sich anpassen (to +dat); **adjustable** adj verstellbar

admin [ædˈmɪn] n (fam) Verwaltung f; **administration** [ədmɪnɪsˈtreɪʃən] n Verwaltung f; (Pol) Regierung f

admirable ['ædmɪrəbl] adj bewundernswert; **admiration** [ædmɪˈreɪʃən] n Bewunderung f; **admire** [ədˈmaɪə°] vt bewundern

admission [ədˈmɪʃən] n (entrance) Zutritt m; (to university etc) Zulassung f; (fee) Eintritt m; (confession) Eingeständnis nt; **admission charge**, **admission fee** n Eintrittspreis m; **admit** [ədˈmɪt] vt (let in) hereinlassen (to in +Akk); (to university etc) zulassen; (confess) zugeben, gestehen; **to be ~ted to hospital** ins Krankenhaus eingeliefert werden

adolescent [ædəˈlesnt] n Jugendliche(r) mf

adopt [əˈdɒpt] vt (child) adoptieren; (idea) übernehmen; **adoption** [əˈdɒpʃn] n (of child) Adoption f; (of idea) Übernahme f

adorable [əˈdɔːrəbl] adj entzückend; **adore** [əˈdɔː°] vt anbeten; (person) über alles lieben, vergöttern

ADSL abbr = **asymmetric digital subscriber line** ADSL f

adult ['ædʌlt] adj erwachsen; (film etc) für Erwachsene ▷ n Erwachsene(r) mf

adultery [əˈdʌltərɪ] n Ehebruch m

advance [ədˈvɑːns] n (money) Vorschuss m; (progress) Fortschritt

m; **in ~** im Voraus; **to book in ~**
vorbestellen ▷ *vi* (*move forward*)
vorrücken ▷ *vt* (*money*)
vorschießen; **advance booking** *n*
Reservierung *f*; (*Theat*) Vorverkauf
m; **advanced** *adj* (*modern*)
fortschrittlich; (*course, study*) für
Fortgeschrittene; **advance
payment** *n* Vorauszahlung *f*

advantage [əd'vɑːntɪdʒ] *n*
Vorteil *m*; **to take ~ of** (*exploit*)
ausnutzen; (*profit from*) Nutzen
ziehen aus; **it's to your ~** es ist in
deinem/Ihrem Interesse

adventure [əd'ventʃə°] *n*
Abenteuer *nt*; **adventure holiday**
n Abenteuerurlaub *m*; **adventure
playground** *n* Abenteuerspiel-
platz *m*; **adventurous**
[əd'ventʃərəs] *adj* (*person*)
abenteuerlustig

adverb ['ædvɜːb] *n* Adverb *nt*

adverse ['ædvɜːs] *adj* (*conditions
etc*) ungünstig; (*effect, comment etc*)
negativ

advert ['ædvɜːt] *n* Anzeige *f*;
advertise ['ædvətaɪz] *vt* werben
für; (*in newspaper*) inserieren; (*job*)
ausschreiben ▷ *vi* Reklame
machen; (*in newspaper*)
annoncieren (*for* für);
advertisement [əd'vɜːtɪsmənt]
n Werbung *f*; (*announcement*)
Anzeige *f*; **advertising** *n*
Werbung *f*

advice [əd'vaɪs] *n* Rat(schlag) *m*;
word o piece of ~ Ratschlag *m*;
take my ~ hör auf mich;
advisable [əd'vaɪzəbl] *adj* ratsam; **advise** [əd'vaɪz] *vt* raten
(*sb* jdm); **to ~ sb to do sth/not to
do sth** jdm zuraten/abraten, etw
zu tun

Aegean [iː'dʒiːən] *n*: **the ~ (Sea)**
die Ägäis

aerial ['eərɪəl] *n* Antenne *f* ▷ *adj*
Luft-

aerobatics [ɛərəʊ'bætɪks] *npl*
Kunstfliegen *nt*

aerobics [ɛə'rəʊbɪks] *nsing*
Aerobic *nt*

aeroplane ['eərəpleɪn] *n*
Flugzeug *nt*

afaik *abbr* = **as far as I know**;
(*SMS*) = soweit ich weiß

affair [ə'fɛə°] *n* (*matter, business*)
Sache *f*, Angelegenheit *f*; (*scandal*)
Affäre *f*; (*love affair*) Verhältnis *nt*

affect [ə'fɛkt] *vt* (*influence*)
(ein)wirken auf +*akk*; (*health,
organ*) angreifen; (*move deeply*)
berühren; (*concern*) betreffen;
affection [ə'fɛkʃən] *n* Zuneigung
f; **affectionate** [ə'fɛkʃənɪt] *adj*
liebevoll

affluent ['æfluənt] *adj*
wohlhabend

afford [ə'fɔːd] *vt* sich leisten; **I
can't ~ it** ich kann es mir nicht
leisten; **affordable** [ə'fɔːdəbl]
adj erschwinglich

Afghanistan [æf'gænɪstæn] *n*
Afghanistan *nt*

aforementioned
[əfɔː'menʃənd] *adj* oben genannt

afraid [ə'freɪd] *adj*: **to be ~** Angst
haben (*of* vor +*dat*); **to be ~ that ...**
fürchten, dass ...; **I'm ~ I don't
know** das weiß ich leider nicht

Africa ['æfrɪkə] *n* Afrika *nt*;
African *adj* afrikanisch ▷ *n*
Afrikaner(in) *m(f)*; **African
American, Afro-American** *n*
Afroamerikaner(in) *m(f)*

after ['ɑːftə°] *prep* nach; **ten
~ five** (US) zehn nach fünf; **to be
~ sb/sth** (*following, seeking*) hinter
jdm/etw her sein; **~ all**
schließlich; (*in spite of everything*)
(schließlich) doch ▷ *conj*
nachdem ▷ *adv*: **soon ~** bald
danach; **aftercare** *n*
Nachbehandlung *f*; **after-effect** *n*
Nachwirkung *f*

afternoon n Nachmittag m; **~, good ~** guten Tag!; **in the ~** nachmittags

afters npl Nachtisch m; **after-sales service** n Kundendienst m; **after-shave (lotion)** n Rasierwasser nt; **aftersun** n After-Sun-Lotion f; **afterwards** adv nachher; (after that) danach

again [əˈgen] adv wieder; (one more time) noch einmal; **not ~!** (nicht) schon wieder!; **~ and ~** immer wieder; **the same ~ please** das Gleiche noch mal bitte

against [əˈgenst] prep gegen; **~ my will** wider Willen; **~ the law** unrechtmäßig, illegal

age [eɪdʒ] n Alter nt; (period of history) Zeitalter nt; **at the ~ of four** im Alter von vier (Jahren); **what ~ is she?, what is her ~?** wie alt ist sie?; **to come of ~** volljährig werden; **under ~** minderjährig ▷ vi altern, alt werden; **aged** adj: **~ thirty** dreißig Jahre alt; **a son ~ twenty** ein zwanzigjähriger Sohn ▷ adj [ˈeɪdʒɪd] (elderly) betagt; **age group** n Altersgruppe f; **ageism** n Diskriminierung f aufgrund des Alters; **age limit** n Altersgrenze f

agency [ˈeɪdʒənsɪ] n Agentur f

agenda [əˈdʒendə] n Tagesordnung f

agent [ˈeɪdʒənt] n (Comm) Vertreter(in) m(f); (for writer, actor etc) Agent(in) m(f)

aggression [əˈgreʃn] n Aggression f; **aggressive** [əˈgresɪv] adj aggressiv

agitated adj aufgeregt; **to get ~** sich aufregen

AGM abbr = **Annual General Meeting** JHV f

ago [əˈgəʊ] adv: **two days ~** heute vor zwei Tagen; **not long ~** (erst) vor Kurzem

agonize [ˈægənaɪz] vi sich den Kopf zerbrechen (over über dat); **agonizing** adj qualvoll; **agony** [ˈægənɪ] n Qual f

agree [əˈgriː] vt (date, price etc) vereinbaren; **to ~ to do sth** sich bereit erklären, etw zu tun; **to ~ that ...** sich dat einig sein, dass ...; (decide) beschließen, dass ...; (admit) zugeben, dass ... ▷ vi (have same opinion, correspond) übereinstimmen (with mit); (consent) zustimmen; (come to an agreement) sich einigen (about, on auf +akk); (food) **not to ~ with sb** jdm nicht bekommen; **agreement** n (agreeing) Übereinstimmung f; (contract) Abkommen nt, Vereinbarung f

agricultural [ægrɪˈkʌltʃərəl] adj landwirtschaftlich, Landwirtschafts-; **agriculture** [ˈægrɪkʌltʃəʳ] n Landwirtschaft f

ahead [əˈhed] adv: **to be ~** führen, vorne liegen; **~ of** vor +dat; **to be ~ of sb** (person) jdm voraus sein; (thing) vor jdm liegen; **to be 3 metres ~** 3 Meter Vorsprung haben

aid [eɪd] n Hilfe f; **in ~ of** zugunsten +gen; **with the ~ of** mithilfe +gen ▷ vt helfen +dat; (support) unterstützen

Aids [eɪdz] n acr = **acquired immune deficiency syndrome** Aids nt

aim [eɪm] vt (gun, camera) richten (at auf +akk) ▷ vi: **to ~ at** (with gun etc) zielen auf +akk; (fig) abzielen auf +akk; **to ~ to do sth** beabsichtigen, etw zu tun ▷ n Ziel nt

air [eəʳ] n Luft f; **in the open ~** im Freien; (Radio, TV) **to be on the ~** (programme) auf Sendung sein;

(*station*) senden ▷ *vt* lüften;
airbag *n* (*Auto*) Airbag *m*;
air-conditioned *adj* mit
Klimaanlage; **air-conditioning** *n*
Klimaanlage *f*; **aircraft** *n*
Flugzeug *nt*; **airfield** *n* Flugplatz
m; **air force** *n* Luftwaffe *f*;
airgun *n* Luftgewehr *nt*;
airline *n* Fluggesellschaft *f*;
airmail *n* Luftpost *f*; **by ~** mit
Luftpost; **airplane** *n* (*US*)
Flugzeug *nt*; **air pollution** *n*
Luftverschmutzung *f*; **airport** *n*
Flughafen *m*; **airsick** *adj*
luftkrank; **airtight** *adj* luftdicht;
air-traffic controller *n* Fluglotse
m, Fluglotsin *f*; **airy** *adj* luftig;
(*manner*) lässig

aisle [aɪl] *n* Gang *m*; (*in church*)
Seitenschiff *nt*; **~ seat** Sitz *m* am
Gang

ajar [ə'dʒɑ:ʳ] *adj* (*door*) angelehnt

alarm [ə'lɑ:m] *n* (*warning*) Alarm
m; (*bell etc*) Alarmanlage *f* ▷ *vt*
beunruhigen; **alarm clock** *n*
Wecker *m*; **alarmed** *adj* (*protected*)
alarmgesichert; **alarming** *adj*
beunruhigend

Albania [æl'beɪnɪə] *n* Albanien
nt; **Albanian** *adj* albanisch ▷ *n*
(*person*) Albaner(in) *m(f)*; (*language*)
Albanisch *nt*

album ['ælbəm] *n* Album *nt*

alcohol ['ælkəhɒl] *n* Alkohol *m*;
alcohol-free *adj* alkoholfrei;
alcoholic [ælkə'hɒlɪk] *adj* (*drink*)
alkoholisch ▷ *n* Alkoholiker(in)
m(f); **alcoholism** *n* Alkoholismus
m

ale [eɪl] *n* Ale *nt* (*helles englisches
Bier*)

alert [ə'lɜ:t] *adj* wachsam ▷ *n*
Alarm *m* ▷ *vt* warnen (*to* vor +*dat*)

algebra ['ældʒɪbrə] *n* Algebra *f*

Algeria [æl'dʒɪərɪə] *n* Algerien *nt*

alibi ['ælɪbaɪ] *n* Alibi *nt*

alien ['eɪlɪən] *n* (*foreigner*)

Ausländer(in) *m(f)*; (*from space*)
Außerirdische(r) *mf*

align [ə'laɪn] *vt* ausrichten (*with*
auf +*akk*)

alike [ə'laɪk] *adj, adv* gleich;
(*similar*) ähnlich

alive [ə'laɪv] *adj* lebendig; **to
keep sth ~** etw am Leben
erhalten; **he's still ~** er lebt noch

O **KEYWORD**

all [ɔ:l] *adj* alle(r, s); **all day/night**
den ganzen Tag die ganze Nacht;
all men are equal alle Menschen
sind gleich; **all five came** alle fünf
kamen; **all the books/food** die
ganzen Bücher/das ganze Essen;
all the time die ganze Zeit (*über*);
all his life sein ganzes Leben
(lang)
▷ *pron* 1 alles; **I ate it all, I ate all of
it** ich habe alles gegessen; **all of
us/the boys went** wir gingen
alle/alle Jungen gingen; **we all sat
down** wir setzten uns alle
2 (*in phrases*): **above all** vor allem;
after all schließlich; **at all: not at
all** (*in answer to question*)
überhaupt nicht; (*in answer to
thanks*) gern geschehen; **I'm not at
all tired** ich bin überhaupt nicht
müde; **anything at all will do** es
ist egal, welche(r, s); **all in all** alles
in allem
▷ *adv* ganz; **all alone** ganz allein;
it's not as hard as all that so
schwer ist es nun auch wieder
nicht; **all the more/the better**
umso mehr/besser; **all but** fast;
the score is 2 all es steht 2 zu 2

allegation [ælɪ'ɡeɪʃən] *n*
Behauptung *f*; **alleged** *adj*
angeblich

allergic [ə'lɜ:dʒɪk] *adj* allergisch

(to gegen); **allergy** ['ælədʒɪ] *n*
Allergie *f*
alleviate [ə'liːvɪeɪt] *vt (pain)*
lindern
alley ['ælɪ] *n (enge)* Gasse;
(passage) Durchgang *m; (bowling)*
Bahn *f*
alliance [ə'laɪəns] *n* Bündnis *nt*
alligator ['ælɪgeɪtə°] *n* Alligator
m
all-night *adj (café, cinema)* die
ganze Nacht geöffnet
allocate ['æləkeɪt] *vt* zuweisen,
zuteilen *(to dat)*
allotment *n (plot)*
Schrebergarten *m*
allow [ə'laʊ] *vt (permit)* erlauben
(sb jdm); (grant) bewilligen; *(time)*
einplanen; **allow for** *vt*
berücksichtigen; *(cost etc)*
einkalkulieren; **allowance** *n (from
state)* Beihilfe *f; (from parent)*
Unterhaltsgeld *nt*
all right ['ɔːl'raɪt] *adj* okay, in
Ordnung; **I'm ~** mir geht's gut
▷ *adv (satisfactorily)* ganz gut
▷ *interj* okay
all-time *adj (record, high)* aller
Zeiten
allusion [ə'luːʒn] *n* Anspielung *f*
(to auf +akk)
ally ['ælaɪ] *n* Verbündete(r) *mf;*
(Hist) Alliierte(r) *mf*
almond ['ɑːmənd] *n* Mandel *f*
almost ['ɔːlməʊst] *adv* fast
alone [ə'ləʊn] *adj, adv* allein
along [ə'lɒŋ] *prep* entlang
+akk; **~ the river** den Fluss
entlang; *(position)* am Fluss
entlang ▷ *adv (onward)* weiter;
~ with zusammen mit; **all ~** die
ganze Zeit, von Anfang an;
alongside *prep* neben *+dat* ▷ *adv*
(walk) nebenher
aloud [ə'laʊd] *adv* laut
alphabet ['ælfəbet] *n* Alphabet
nt

alpine ['ælpaɪn] *adj* alpin; **Alps**
[ælps] *npl:* **the ~** die Alpen
already [ɔːl'redɪ] *adv* schon,
bereits
Alsace ['ælsæs] *n* Elsass *nt;*
Alsatian [æl'seɪʃən] *adj*
elsässisch ▷ *n* Elsässer(in) *m(f);*
(Brit: dog) Schäferhund *m*
also ['ɔːlsəʊ] *adv* auch
altar ['ɔːltə°] *n* Altar *m*
alter ['ɔːltə°] *vt* ändern;
alteration [ɔːltə'reɪʃən] *n*
Änderung *f;* **~s** *(to building)* Umbau
m
alternate [ɔːl'tɜːnət] *adj*
abwechselnd ▷ ['ɔːltəneɪt] *vi*
abwechseln *(with mit);*
alternating current *n*
Wechselstrom *m*
alternative [ɔːl'tɜːnətɪv] *adj*
Alternativ- ▷ *n* Alternative *f*
although [ɔːl'ðəʊ] *conj* obwohl
altitude ['æltɪtjuːd] *n* Höhe *f*
altogether [ɔːltə'geðə°] *adv (in
total)* insgesamt; *(entirely)* ganz
und gar
aluminium [ælju'mɪnɪəm], **aluminum** (US)
[ə'luːmɪnəm] *n*
Aluminium *nt*
always ['ɔːlweɪz] *adv* immer
am [æm] *present of* **be;** see **be**
am, a.m. *abbr* = **ante meridiem**
vormittags, vorm.
amateur ['æmətə°] *n* Ama-
teur(in) *m(f)* ▷ *adj* Amateur-;
(theatre, choir) Laien-
amaze [ə'meɪz] *vt* erstaunen;
amazed *adj* erstaunt *(at über
+akk);* **amazing** *adj* erstaunlich
Amazon ['æməzən] *n:* **~ (river)**
Amazonas *m*
ambassador [æm'bæsədə°] *n*
Botschafter *m*
amber ['æmbə°] *n* Bernstein *m*
ambiguity [æmbɪ'gjuːɪtɪ] *n*
Zweideutigkeit *f;* **ambiguous**
[æm'bɪgjʊəs] *adj* zweideutig

ambition [æm'bɪʃən] n Ambition f; *(ambitious nature)* Ehrgeiz m; **ambitious** [æm'bɪʃəs] adj ehrgeizig

ambulance ['æmbjʊləns] n Krankenwagen m

amend [ə'mend] vt *(law etc)* ändern

America [ə'merɪkə] n Amerika nt; **American** adj amerikanisch ▷ n Amerikaner(in) m(f); **native ~** Indianer(in) m(f)

amiable ['eɪmɪəbl] adj liebenswürdig

amicable ['æmɪkəbl] adj freundlich; *(relations)* freundschaftlich; *(Jur: settlement)* gütlich

amnesia [æm'niːzɪə] n Gedächtnisverlust m

among(st) [ə'mʌŋ(st)] prep unter +dat

amount [ə'maʊnt] n *(quantity)* Menge f; *(of money)* Betrag m; **a large/small ~ of ...** ziemlich viel/wenig ... ▷ vi: **to ~ to** *(total)* sich belaufen auf +akk

amp, ampere [æmp, 'æmpeə°] n Ampere nt

amplifier ['æmplɪfaɪə°] n Verstärker m

amputate ['æmpjʊteɪt] vt amputieren

Amtrak® ['æmtræk] n amerikanische Eisenbahngesellschaft

amuse [ə'mjuːz] vt amüsieren; *(entertain)* unterhalten; **amused** adj: **I'm not ~** das finde ich gar nicht lustig; **amusement** n *(enjoyment)* Vergnügen nt; *(recreation)* Unterhaltung f; **amusement arcade** n Spielhalle f; **amusement park** n Vergnügungspark m; **amusing** adj amüsant

an [æn, ən] art ein(e)

anaemic [ə'niːmɪk] adj blutarm

anaesthetic [ænɪs'θetɪk] n

Narkose f; *(substance)* Narkosemittel nt

analyse, analyze ['ænəlaɪz] vt analysieren; **analysis** [ə'næləsɪs] n Analyse f

anatomy [ə'nætəmɪ] n Anatomie f; *(structure)* Körperbau m

ancestor ['ænsestə°] n Vorfahr m

anchor ['æŋkə°] n Anker m ▷ vt verankern; **anchorage** n Ankerplatz m

anchovy ['æntʃəvɪ] n Sardelle f

ancient ['eɪnʃənt] adj alt; *(fam: person, clothes etc)* uralt

and [ænd, ənd] conj und

Andorra [æn'dɔːrə] n Andorra nt

anemic (US) see **anaemic**

anesthetic n (US) see **anaesthetic**

angel ['eɪndʒəl] n Engel m

anger ['æŋgə°] n Zorn m ▷ vt ärgern

angina, angina pectoris [æn'dʒaɪnə('pektərɪs)] n Angina Pectoris f

angle ['æŋgl] n Winkel m; *(fig)* Standpunkt m

angler ['æŋglə°] n Angler(in) m(f); **angling** ['æŋglɪŋ] n Angeln nt

angry ['æŋgrɪ] adj verärgert; *(stronger)* zornig; **to be ~ with sb** auf jdn böse sein

angular ['æŋgjʊlə°] adj eckig; *(face)* kantig

animal ['ænɪməl] n Tier nt; **animal rights** npl Tierrechte pl

animated ['ænɪmeɪtɪd] adj lebhaft; **~ film** Zeichentrickfilm m

aniseed ['ænɪsiːd] n Anis m

ankle ['æŋkl] n (Fuß)knöchel m

annex ['æneks] n Anbau m

anniversary [ænɪ'vɜːsərɪ] n Jahrestag m

announce [ə'naʊns] vt bekannt geben; *(officially)* bekannt machen; *(on radio, TV etc)* (Radio,

TV) ansagen; **announcement** n
Bekanntgabe f; (official)
Bekanntmachung f; (Radio, TV)
Ansage f; **announcer** n (Radio, TV)
Ansager(in) m(f)
annoy [ə'nɔɪ] vt ärgern;
annoyance n Ärger m; **annoyed**
adj ärgerlich; **to be ~ with sb**
(about sth) sich über jdn (über
etw) ärgern; **annoying** adj
ärgerlich; (person) lästig, nervig
annual [ˈænjʊəl] adj jährlich
▷ n Jahrbuch nt
anonymous [əˈnɒnɪməs] adj
anonym
anorak [ˈænəræk] n Anorak m
anorexia [ænəˈreksɪə] n Magersucht f; **anorexic** adj
magersüchtig
another [əˈnʌðəʳ] adj, pron
(different) ein(e) andere(r, s);
(additional) noch eine(r, s); **let me**
put it ~ way lass es mich anders
sagen
answer [ˈɑːnsəʳ] n Antwort f (to
auf +akk); (solution) Lösung f +gen
▷ vi antworten; (on phone) sich
melden ▷ vt (person) antworten
+dat; (letter, question) beantworten;
(telephone) gehen an +akk,
abnehmen; (door) öffnen; **answer**
back vi widersprechen; **answering**
machine, answerphone n Anrufbeant-
worter m
ant [ænt] n Ameise f
Antarctic [æntˈɑːktɪk] n
Antarktis f; **Antarctic Circle** n
südlicher Polarkreis
antelope [ˈæntɪləʊp] n Antilope f
antenna [ænˈtenə] (pl antennae)
n (Zool) Fühler m; (Radio) Antenne f
anti- [ˈæntɪ] pref Anti-, anti-;
antibiotic [ˈæntɪbaɪˈɒtɪk] n
Antibiotikum nt
anticipate [ænˈtɪsɪpeɪt] vt (expect:
trouble, question) erwarten,

rechnen mit; **anticipation**
[æntɪsɪˈpeɪʃən] n Erwartung f
anticlimax [ˈæntɪˈklaɪmæks] n
Enttäuschung f; **anticlockwise**
[ˈæntɪˈklɒkwaɪz] adv entgegen
dem Uhrzeigersinn
antidote [ˈæntɪdəʊt] n Gegenmittel nt; **antifreeze** n
Frostschutzmittel nt
Antipodes [ænˈtɪpədiːz] npl
Australien und Neuseeland
antiquarian [æntɪˈkwɛərɪən]
adj: **~ bookshop** Antiquariat nt
antique [ænˈtiːk] n Antiquität f
▷ adj antik; **antique shop** n
Antiquitätengeschäft nt
anti-Semitism [ˈæntɪˈsemɪtɪzm]
n Antisemitismus m; **antiseptic**
[æntɪˈseptɪk] n Antiseptikum nt
▷ adj antiseptisch; **antisocial** adj
(person) ungesellig; (behaviour)
unsozial, asozial; **antivirus** n
(Inform) Antiviren–; **antivirus**
software n Antivirensoftware f
antlers [ˈæntləz] npl Geweih nt
anxiety [æŋˈzaɪətɪ] n Sorge f
(about um); **anxious** [ˈæŋkʃəs] adj
besorgt (about um); (apprehensive)
ängstlich

O **KEYWORD**

any [ˈenɪ] adj 1 (in questions etc)
have you any butter? haben Sie
(etwas) Butter?; **have you any**
children? haben Sie Kinder?; **if**
there are any tickets left falls
noch Karten da sind
2 (with negative) **I haven't any**
money ich habe kein Geld
3 (no matter which) jede(r, s)
(beliebige); **any colour (at all)**
jede beliebige Farbe; **choose any**
book you like nehmen Sie ein
beliebiges Buch
4 (in phrases) **in any case** in jedem

Fall; **any day now** jeden Tag; **at any moment** jeden Moment; **at any rate** auf jeden Fall
▷ *pron* 1 *(in questions etc)* **have you got any?** haben Sie welche?; **can any of you sing?** kann (irgend)einer von euch singen? **2** *(with negative)* **I haven't any (of them)** ich habe keinen/keines (davon) **3** *(no matter which one(s))* **take any of those books (you like)** nehmen Sie irgendeines dieser Bücher
▷ *adv* 1 *(in questions etc)* **do you want any more soup/ sandwiches?** möchten Sie noch Suppe/Brote?; **are you feeling any better?** fühlen Sie sich etwas besser? **2** *(with negative)* **I can't hear him any more** ich kann ihn nicht mehr hören

anybody *pron (whoever one likes)* irgendjemand; *(everyone)* jeder; *(in question)* jemand; **anyhow** *adv*: **I don't want to talk about it, not now** ~ ich möchte nicht darüber sprechen, jedenfalls nicht jetzt; **they asked me not to go, but I went** ~ sie baten mich, nicht hinzugehen, aber ich bin trotzdem hingegangen; **anyone** *pron (whoever one likes)* irgendjemand; *(everyone)* jeder; *(in question)* jemand; **isn't there** ~ **you can ask?** gibt es denn niemanden, den du fragen kannst/den Sie fragen können?; **anyplace** *adv (US)* irgendwo; *(direction)* irgendwohin; *(everywhere)* überall

⭕ **KEYWORD**

anything ['ɛnɪθɪŋ] *pron* 1 *(in questions etc)* (irgend)etwas; **can you see anything?** können Sie etwas sehen? **2** *(with negative)* **I can't see anything** ich kann nichts sehen **3** *(no matter what)* **you can say anything you like** Sie können sagen, was Sie wollen; **anything will do** irgendetwas (wird genügen), irgendeine(r, s) (wird genügen); **he'll eat anything** er isst alles

anytime *adv* jederzeit; **anyway** *adv*: **I didn't want to go there** ~ ich wollte da sowieso nicht hingehen; **thanks** ~ trotzdem danke; ~ **as I was saying, ...** jedenfalls, wie ich schon sagte, ...; **anywhere** *adv* irgendwo; *(direction)* irgendwohin; *(everywhere)* überall

apart [ə'pɑːt] *adv* auseinander; ~ **from** außer; **live** ~ getrennt leben
apartment [ə'pɑːtmənt] *n (esp US)* Wohnung *f*; **apartment block** *n (esp US)* Wohnblock *m*
ape [eɪp] *n* (Menschen)affe *m*
aperitif [ə'perɪtɪf] *n* Aperitif *m*
aperture ['æpətjʊə] *n* Öffnung *f*; *(Foto)* Blende *f*
apologize [ə'pɒlədʒaɪz] *vi* sich entschuldigen; **apology** *n* Entschuldigung *f*
apostrophe [ə'pɒstrəfɪ] *n* Apostroph *m*
appalled [ə'pɔːld] *adj* entsetzt *(at über +akk)*; **appalling** *adj* entsetzlich
apparatus [æpə'reɪtəs] *n* Apparat *m*; *(piece of apparatus)* Gerät *nt*
apparent [ə'pærənt] *adj (obvious)* offensichtlich *(to für)*; *(seeming)* scheinbar; **apparently** *adv* anscheinend
appeal [ə'piːl] *vi* (dringend)

bitten (for um, to +akk); (Jur)
Berufung einlegen; **to ~ to sb** (be
attractive) jdm zusagen ▷ n Aufruf
m (to an +akk); (Jur) Berufung f;
(attraction) Reiz m; **appealing** adj
ansprechend, attraktiv

appear [əˈpɪə] vi erscheinen;
(Theat) auftreten; (seem) scheinen;
appearance n Erscheinen nt;
(Theat) Auftritt m; (look) Aussehen
nt

appendicitis [əpendɪˈsaɪtɪs] n
Blinddarmentzündung f;
appendix [əˈpendɪks] n Blinddarm m; (to book) Anhang m

appetite [ˈæpɪtaɪt] n Appetit m;
(fig: desire) Verlangen nt; (sexual)
Lust f; **appetizing** [ˈæpɪtaɪzɪŋ]
adj appetitlich, appetitanregend

applause [əˈplɔːz] n Beifall m,
Applaus m

apple [ˈæpl] n Apfel m; **apple
crumble** n mit Streuseln bestreutes
Apfeldessert; **apple juice** n
Apfelsaft m; **apple pie** n
gedeckter Apfelkuchen m; **apple
puree, apple sauce** n Apfelmus
nt; **apple tart** n Apfelkuchen m;
apple tree n Apfelbaum m

appliance [əˈplaɪəns] n Gerät nt;
applicable [əˈplɪkəbl] adj
anwendbar; (on forms) zutreffend;
applicant [ˈæplɪkənt] n Bewer-
ber(in)(m(f)); **application**
[æplɪˈkeɪʃən] n (request) Antrag m
(for auf +akk); (for job) Bewerbung f
(for um); **application form** n
Anmeldeformular nt; **apply**
[əˈplaɪ] vi (be relevant) zutreffen (to
auf +akk); (for job etc) sich
bewerben (for um) ▷ vt (cream,
paint etc) auftragen; (put into
practice) anwenden; (brakes)
betätigen

appoint [əˈpɔɪnt] vt (to post)
ernennen; **appointment** n
Verabredung f; (at doctor, hairdresser

etc, in business) Termin m; **by
~** nach Vereinbarung

appreciate [əˈpriːʃɪeɪt] vt (value)
zu schätzen wissen; (understand)
einsehen; **to be much ~d** richtig
gewürdigt werden ▷ vi (increase in
value) im Wert steigen;
appreciation [əpriːʃɪˈeɪʃən] n
(esteem) Anerkennung f,
Würdigung f; (of person also)
Wertschätzung f

apprehensive [æprɪˈhensɪv] adj
ängstlich

apprentice [əˈprentɪs] n Lehrling m

approach [əˈprəʊtʃ] vi sich
nähern ▷ vt (place) sich nähern
+dat; (person) herantreten an +akk;
(problem) angehen

appropriate [əˈprəʊprɪət] adj
passend; (to occasion) angemessen;
(remark) treffend; **appropriately**
adv passend; (expressed) treffend

approval [əˈpruːvəl] n (show of
satisfaction) Anerkennung f;
(permission) Zustimmung f (of zu);
approve [əˈpruːv] vt billigen
▷ vi: **to ~ of sth/sb** etw
billigen/von jdm etwas halten; **I
don't ~** ich missbillige das

approx [əˈprɒks] abbr =
approximately ca.; **approximate**
[əˈprɒksɪmɪt] adj ungefähr;
approximately adv ungefähr,
circa

apricot [ˈeɪprɪkɒt] n Aprikose f

April [ˈeɪprəl] n April m; see also
September

apron [ˈeɪprən] n Schürze f

aptitude [ˈæptɪtjuːd] n Begabung
f

aquaplaning [ˈækwəpleɪnɪŋ] n
(Auto) Aquaplaning nt

aquarium [əˈkweərɪəm] n
Aquarium nt

Aquarius [əˈkweərɪəs] n (Astr)
Wassermann m

Arab ['ærəb] n Araber(in) m(f); (horse) Araber m; **Arabian** [ə'reɪbɪən] adj arabisch; **Arabic** ['ærəbɪk] n (language) Arabisch nt ▷ adj arabisch

arbitrary ['ɑːbɪtrərɪ] adj willkürlich

arcade [ɑː'keɪd] n Arkade f; (shopping arcade) Einkaufspassage f

arch [ɑːtʃ] n Bogen m

archaeologist, **archeologist** (US) [ɑːkɪ'ɒlədʒɪst] n Archäologe m, Archäologin f; **archaeology**, **archeology** (US) [ɑːkɪ'ɒlədʒɪ] n Archäologie f

archaic [ɑː'keɪɪk] adj veraltet

archbishop [ɑːtʃ'bɪʃəp] n Erzbischof m

archery ['ɑːtʃərɪ] n Bogenschießen nt

architect ['ɑːkɪtekt] n Architekt(in) m(f); **architecture** [ɑːkɪ'tektʃə] n Architektur f

archive(s) ['ɑːkaɪv(z)] n(pl) Archiv nt

archway ['ɑːtʃweɪ] n Torbogen m

Arctic ['ɑːktɪk] n Arktis f; **Arctic Circle** n nördlicher Polarkreis

are [ə, unstressed ɑː°] present of **be**

area ['eərɪə] n (region, district) Gebiet nt, Gegend f; (amount of space) Fläche f; (part of building etc) Bereich m, Zone f; (fig: field) Bereich m; **the London ~** der Londoner Raum; **area code** n (Tel) Vorwahl f

aren't [ɑːnt] contr of **are not**

Argentina [ɑːdʒən'tiːnə] n Argentinien nt

argue ['ɑːgjuː] vi streiten (about, over über +akk); **to ~ that ...** behaupten, dass ...; **to ~ for/against ...** sprechen für/gegen ...; **argument** n (reasons) Argument nt; (quarrel)

Streit m; **to have an ~** sich streiten

Aries ['eəriːz] nsing (Astr) Widder m

arise [ə'raɪz] (**arose, arisen**) vi sich ergeben, entstehen; (problem, question, wind) aufkommen

aristocracy [ærɪs'tɒkrəsɪ] n (class) Adel m; **aristocrat** ['ærɪstəkræt] n Adlige(r) mf; **aristocratic** [ærɪstə'krætɪk] adj aristokratisch, adlig

arm [ɑːm] n Arm m; (sleeve) Ärmel m; (of armchair) Armlehne f ▷ vt bewaffnen; **armchair** ['ɑːmtʃeə°] n Lehnstuhl m

armed [ɑːmd] adj bewaffnet

armpit ['ɑːmpɪt] n Achselhöhle f

arms [ɑːmz] npl Waffen pl

army ['ɑːmɪ] n Armee f, Heer nt

A road ['eɪrəʊd] n (Brit) = Bundesstraße f

aroma [ə'rəʊmə] n Duft m, Aroma nt; **aromatherapy** [ərəʊmə'θerəpɪ] n Aromatherapie f

arose [ə'rəʊz] pt of **arise**

around [ə'raʊnd] adv herum, umher; (present) hier (irgendwo); (approximately) ungefähr; (with time) gegen; **he's ~ somewhere** er ist hier irgendwo in der Nähe ▷ prep (surrounding) um ... (herum); (about in) um ... herum

arr. abbr = **arrival**; **arrives** Ank.

arrange [ə'reɪndʒ] vt (put in order) (an)ordnen; (alphabetically) ordnen; (artistically) arrangieren; (agree to: meeting etc) vereinbaren, festsetzen; (holidays) festlegen; (organize) planen; **to ~ that ...** es so einrichten, dass ...; **we ~d to meet at eight o'clock** wir haben uns für acht Uhr verabredet; **it's all ~d** es ist alles arrangiert; **arrangement** n (layout) Anordnung f; (agreement)

Vereinbarung f, Plan m; **make ~s** Vorbereitungen treffen

arrest [ə'rest] vt (person) verhaften ▷ n Verhaftung f; **under ~** verhaftet

arrival [ə'raɪvl] n Ankunft f; **new ~** (person) Neuankömmling m; **arrivals** n (airport) Ankunftshalle f; **arrive** [ə'raɪv] vi ankommen (at bei, in +dat); **to ~ at a solution** eine Lösung finden

arrogant ['ærəgənt] adj arrogant

arrow ['ærəʊ] n Pfeil m

arse [ɑːs] n (vulg) Arsch m

art [ɑːt] n Kunst f, **the ~s** (pl) Geisteswissenschaften pl

artery ['ɑːtərɪ] n Schlagader f, Arterie f

art gallery n Kunstgalerie f, Kunstmuseum nt

arthritis [ɑː'θraɪtɪs] n Arthritis f

artichoke ['ɑːtɪtʃəʊk] n Artischocke f

article ['ɑːtɪkl] n Artikel m; (object) Gegenstand m

artificial [ɑːtɪ'fɪʃəl] adj künstlich, Kunst-; (smile etc) gekünstelt

artist ['ɑːtɪst] n Künstler(in) m(f); **artistic** [ɑː'tɪstɪk] adj künstlerisch

⊙ **KEYWORD**

as [æz, əz] conj 1 (referring to time) als; **as the years went by** mit den Jahren; **he came in as I was leaving** als er hereinkam, ging ich gerade; **as from tomorrow** ab morgen

2 (in comparisons) **as big as** so groß wie; **twice as big as** zweimal so groß wie; **as much/many as** so viel/so viele wie; **as soon as** sobald

3 (since, because) da; **he left early as he had to be home by 10** er

ging früher, da er um 10 zu Hause sein musste

4 (referring to manner, way) wie; **do as you wish** mach was du willst; **as she said** wie sie sagte

5 (concerning) **as for o to that** was das betrifft o angeht

6 **as if o though** als ob ▷ prep als; see also **long**; **he works as a driver** er arbeitet als Fahrer; see also **such**; **he gave it to me as a present** er hat es mir als Geschenk gegeben; see also **well**

asap [eɪeseɪ'piː, 'eɪsæp] acr = **as soon as possible** möglichst bald

ascertain [æsə'teɪn] vt feststellen

ash [æʃ] n (dust) Asche f; (tree) Esche f

ashamed [ə'ʃeɪmd] adj beschämt; **to be ~ (of sb/sth)** sich (für jdn/etw) schämen

ashore [ə'ʃɔː*] adv an Land

ashtray ['æʃtreɪ] n Aschenbecher m

Asia ['eɪʃə] n Asien nt; **Asian** adj asiatisch ▷ n Asiat(in) m(f)

aside [ə'saɪd] adv beiseite, zur Seite; **~ from** (esp US) außer

ask [ɑːsk] vt, vi fragen; (question) stellen; (request) bitten um; (invite) einladen; **to ~ sb the way** jdn nach dem Weg fragen; **to ~ sb to do sth** jdn darum bitten, etw zu tun; **ask for** vt bitten um

asleep [ə'sliːp] adj, adv: **to be ~ schlafen; **to fall ~** einschlafen

asparagus [əs'pærəgəs] n Spargel m

aspect ['æspekt] n Aspekt m

aspirin ['æsprɪn] n Aspirin® nt

ass [æs] n (a. fig) Esel m; (US vulg) Arsch m

assassinate [ə'sæsɪneɪt] vt ermorden; **assassination**

[əˈsæsıneıʃn] n Ermordung f;
~ attempt Attentat nt

assault [əˈsɔːlt] n Angriff m; (Jur)
Körperverletzung f ⊳ vt
überfallen, herfallen über +akk

assemble [əˈsembl] vt (parts)
zusammensetzen; (people)
zusammenrufen ⊳ vi sich
versammeln; **assembly**
[əˈsemblı] n (of people)
Versammlung f; (putting together)
Zusammensetzen nt; **assembly
hall** n Aula f

assert [əˈsɜːt] vt behaupten;
assertion [əˈsɜːʃən] n Behauptung f

assess [əˈses] vt einschätzen;
assessment n Einschätzung f

asset [ˈæset] n Vermögenswert
m; (fig) Vorteil m; **~s** pl Vermögen
nt

assign [əˈsaın] vt zuweisen;
assignment n Aufgabe f;
(mission) Auftrag m

assist [əˈsıst] vt helfen +dat;
assistance n Hilfe f; **assistant** n
Assistent(in) m(f), Mitarbeiter(in)
m(f); (in shop) Verkäufer(in) m(f);
assistant referee n (Sport)
Schiedsrichterassistent(in) m(f)

associate [əˈsəuʃıeıt] vt
verbinden (with mit); **association**
[əsəusıˈeıʃən] n (organization)
Verband m, Vereinigung f; **in
~ with ...** in Zusammenarbeit
mit ...

assorted [əˈsɔːtıd] adj gemischt;
assortment n Auswahl f (of an
+dat); (of sweets) Mischung f

assume [əˈsjuːm] vt annehmen
(that ... dass ...); (role, responsibility)
übernehmen; **assumption**
[əˈsʌmpʃən] n Annahme f

assurance f; (confidence) Zuversicht
f; **assure** [əˈʃuəˈ] vt (say
confidently) versichern +dat; **to**

~ sb of sth jdm etw zusichern; **to
be ~d of sth** einer Sache sicher
sein

asterisk [ˈæstərısk] n Sternchen
nt

asthma [ˈæsmə] n Asthma nt

astonish [əsˈtɒnıʃ] vt erstaunen;
astonished adj erstaunt (at
über); **astonishing** adj
erstaunlich; **astonishment** n
Erstaunen nt

astound [əˈstaund] vt sehr
erstaunen; **astounding** adj
erstaunlich

astray [əˈstreı] adv: **to go ~**
(letter etc) verloren gehen;
(person) vom Weg abkommen; **to
lead ~** irreführen, verführen

astrology [əsˈtrɒlədʒı] n
Astrologie f

astronaut [ˈæstrənɔːt] n Astro-
naut(in) m(f)

astronomy [əsˈtrɒnəmı] n
Astronomie f

asylum [əˈsaıləm] n (home)
Anstalt f; (political asylum) Asyl nt;
asylum seeker n
Asylbewerber(in) m(f)

○ **KEYWORD**

at [æt] prep 1 (referring to position,
direction) an +dat; bei +dat; (with
place) in +dat; **at the top** an der
Spitze; **at home/school** zu Hause,
zuhause (österreichisch,
schweizerisch)/in der Schule; **at the
baker's** beim Bäcker; **to look at
sth** auf etw akk blicken; **to throw
sth at sb** etw nach jdm werfen
2 (referring to time) **at 4 o'clock** um
4 Uhr; **at night** bei Nacht; **at
Christmas** zu Weihnachten; **at
times** manchmal
3 (referring to rates, speed etc) **at £1 a
kilo** zu £1 pro Kilo; **two at a time**

zwei auf einmal; **at 50 km/h** mit 50 km/h

4 (*referring to manner*) **at a stroke** mit einem Schlag; **at peace** in Frieden

5 (*referring to activity*) **to be at work** bei der Arbeit sein; **to play at cowboys** Cowboy spielen; **to be good at sth** gut in etw *dat* sein

6 (*referring to cause*) **surprised/annoyed at sth** überrascht/verärgert über etw *akk*; **I went at his suggestion** ich ging auf seinen Vorschlag hin

7 (*@ symbol*) At-Zeichen *nt*

ate [et, eɪt] *pt of* **eat**

athlete ['æθliːt] *n* Athlet(in) *m(f)*; (*track and field*) Leichtathlet(in) *m(f)*; (*sportsman*) Sportler(in) *m(f)*; **~'s foot** Fußpilz *m*; **athletic** [æθˈletɪk] *adj* sportlich; (*build*) athletisch; **athletics** *npl* Leichtathletik *f*

Atlantic [ətˈlæntɪk] *n*: **the ~ (Ocean)** der Atlantik

atlas ['ætləs] *n* Atlas *m*

ATM *abbr* = **automated teller machine** Geldautomat *m*

atmosphere ['ætməsfɪə] *n* Atmosphäre *f*; (*fig*) Stimmung *f*

atom ['ætəm] *n* Atom *nt*; **atomic** [əˈtɒmɪk] *adj* Atom-; **~ energy** Atomenergie *f*; **~ power** Atomkraft *f*

A to Z® ['eɪtəˈzed] *n* Stadtplan *m* (*in Buchform*)

atrocious [əˈtrəʊʃəs] *adj* grauenhaft; **atrocity** [əˈtrɒsɪtɪ] *n* Grausamkeit *f*; (*deed*) Gräueltat *f*

attach [əˈtætʃ] *vt* befestigen, anheften (*to an* +*dat*); **to ~ importance to sth** Wert auf etw *akk* legen; **to be ~ed to sb/sth** an jdm/etw hängen; **to ~ a file to an email** eine Datei an eine E-Mail anhängen; **attachment** *n*

(*affection*) Zuneigung *f*; (*Inform*) Attachment *nt*, Anhang *m*, Anlage *f*

attack [əˈtæk] *vt, vi* angreifen ▷ *n* Angriff *m* (*on auf* +*akk*); (*Med*) Anfall *m*

attempt [əˈtempt] *n* Versuch *m*; **to make an ~ to do sth** versuchen, etw zu tun ▷ *vt* versuchen

attend [əˈtend] *vt* (*go to*) teilnehmen an +*dat*; (*lectures, school*) besuchen ▷ *vi* (*be present*) anwesend sein; **attend to** *vt* sich kümmern um; (*customer*) bedienen; **attendance** *n* (*presence*) Anwesenheit *f*; (*people present*) Teilnehmerzahl *f*; **attendant** *n* (*in car park etc*) Wächter(in) *m(f)*; (*in museum*) Aufseher(in) *m(f)*

attention [əˈtenʃən] *n* Aufmerksamkeit *f*; **(your) ~ please** Achtung!; **to pay ~ to sth** etw beachten; **to pay ~ to sb** jdm aufmerksam zuhören; (*listen*) jdm/etw aufmerksam zuhören; **for the ~ of ...** zu Händen von ...; **attentive** [əˈtentɪv] *adj* aufmerksam

attic ['ætɪk] *n* Dachboden *m*; (*lived in*) Mansarde *f*

attitude ['ætɪtjuːd] *n* (*mental*) Einstellung *f* (*to, towards zu*); (*more general, physical*) Haltung *f*

attorney [əˈtɜːnɪ] *n* (*US: lawyer*) Rechtsanwalt *m*, Rechtsanwältin *f*

attract [əˈtrækt] *vt* anziehen; (*attention*) erregen; **to be ~ed to** *o* **by sb** sich zu jdm hingezogen fühlen; **attraction** [əˈtrækʃən] *n* Anziehungskraft *f*; (*thing*) Attraktion *f*; **attractive** *adj* attraktiv; (*thing, idea*) reizvoll

aubergine ['əʊbəʒiːn] *n* Aubergine *f*

auction ['ɔːkʃən] *n* Versteigerung *f*, Auktion *f* ▷ *vt* versteigern

audible ['ɔːdɪbl] adj hörbar

audience ['ɔːdɪəns] n Publikum nt; (Radio) Zuhörer pl; (TV) Zuschauer pl

audio ['ɔːdɪəʊ] adj Ton-

audition [ɔː'dɪʃən] n Probe f ⊳ vi (Theat) vorspielen, vorsingen

auditorium [ɔːdɪ'tɔːrɪəm] n Zuschauerraum m

Aug abbr = **August**

August ['ɔːɡəst] n August m; see also **September**

aunt [ɑːnt] n Tante f

au pair [əʊ'peə°] n Aupairmädchen nt, Aupairjunge m

Australia [ɒs'treɪlɪə] n Australien nt; **Australian** adj australisch ⊳ n Australier(in) m(f)

Austria ['ɒstrɪə] n Österreich nt; **Austrian** adj österreichisch ⊳ n Österreicher(in) m(f)

authentic [ɔː'θentɪk] adj echt; (signature) authentisch; **authenticity** [ɔː'θen'tɪsɪtɪ] n Echtheit f

author ['ɔːθə°] n Autor(in) m(f); (of report etc) Verfasser(in) m(f)

authority [ɔː'θɒrɪtɪ] n (power, expert) Autorität f; **an ~ on sth** eine Autorität auf dem Gebiet einer Sache; **the authorities** (pl) die Behörden pl; **authorize** ['ɔːθəraɪz] vt (permit) genehmigen; **to be ~d to do sth** offiziell berechtigt sein, etw zu tun

auto ['ɔːtəʊ] (pl **-s**) n (US) Auto nt

autobiography [ɔːtəʊbaɪ'ɒɡrəfɪ] n Autobiographie f; **autograph** ['ɔːtəɡrɑːf] n Autogramm nt

automatic [ɔːtə'mætɪk] adj automatisch; **~ gear change** (Brit), **~ gear shift** (US) Automatikschaltung f ⊳ n (car) Automatikwagen m

automobile ['ɔːtəməbiːl] n (US) Auto(mobil) nt; **autotrain**

['ɔːtəʊtreɪn] n (US) Autoreisezug m

autumn ['ɔːtəm] n (Brit) Herbst m

auxiliary [ɔːɡ'zɪlɪərɪ] adj Hilfs-; **~ verb** Hilfsverb nt ⊳ n Hilfskraft f

availability [əveɪlə'bɪlɪtɪ] n (of product) Lieferbarkeit f; (of resources) Verfügbarkeit f; **available** adj erhältlich; (existing) vorhanden; (product) lieferbar; (person) erreichbar; **to be/make ~ to sb** jdm zur Verfügung stehen/stellen; **they're only ~ in black** es gibt sie nur in Schwarz, sie sind nur in Schwarz erhältlich

avalanche ['ævəlɑːnʃ] n Lawine f

Ave abbr = **avenue**

avenue ['ævənjuː] n Allee f

average ['ævrɪdʒ] n Durchschnitt m; **on ~** im Durchschnitt ⊳ adj durchschnittlich; **~ speed** Durchschnittsgeschwindigkeit f; **of ~ height** von mittlerer Größe

avian flu ['eɪvɪən'fluː] n Vogelgrippe f

aviation [eɪvɪ'eɪʃən] n Luftfahrt f

avocado [ævə'kɑːdəʊ] (pl **-s**) n Avocado f

avoid [ə'vɔɪd] vt vermeiden; **to ~ sb** jdm aus dem Weg gehen; **avoidable** adj vermeidbar

awake [ə'weɪk] (awoke, awoken) vi aufwachen ⊳ adj wach

award [ə'wɔːd] n (prize) Preis m; (for bravery etc) Auszeichnung f ⊳ vt zuerkennen (to sb jdm); (present) verleihen (to sb jdm)

aware [ə'weə°] adj bewusst; **to be ~ of sth** sich dat einer Sache gen bewusst sein; **I was not ~ that ...** es war mir nicht klar, dass ...

away [ə'weɪ] adv weg; **to be ~** wegsehen; **he's ~** er ist nicht da; (on a trip) er ist verreist; (from school, work) er fehlt; (Sport) **they**

are (playing) ~ sie spielen
auswärts; *(with distance)* **three
miles** ~ drei Meilen (von hier)
entfernt; **to work** ~ drauflos
arbeiten

awful [ˈɔːfʊl] *adj* schrecklich,
furchtbar; **awfully** *adv* furchtbar

awkward [ˈɔːkwəd] *adj (clumsy)*
ungeschickt; *(embarrassing)*
peinlich; *(difficult)* schwierig

awning [ˈɔːnɪŋ] *n* Markise *f*

awoke [əˈwəʊk] *pt of* **awake**;
awoken [əˈwəʊkən] *pp of* **awoke**

ax *(US)*, **axe** [æks] *n* Axt *f*

axle [ˈæksl] *n (Tech)* Achse *f*

BA *abbr* = **Bachelor of Arts**

BSc *abbr* = **Bachelor of Science**

babe [beɪb] *n (fam)* Baby *nt*;
(fam: affectionate) Schatz *m*,
Kleine(r) *mf*

baby [ˈbeɪbɪ] *n* Baby *nt*; *(of animal)*
Junge(s) *nt*; *(fam: affectionate)*
Schatz *m*, Kleine(r) *mf*; **to have a**
~ ein Kind bekommen; **it's your**
~ *(fam: responsibility)* das ist dein
Bier; **baby carriage** *n (US)*
Kinderwagen *m*; **baby food** *n*
Babynahrung *f*; **babyish** *adj*
kindisch; **baby shower** *n (US)*
Party für die werdende Mutter;
baby-sit *irr vi* babysitten;
baby-sitter *n* Babysitter(in) *m(f)*

bachelor [ˈbætʃələ] *n* Junggeselle *m*; **Bachelor of
Arts/Science** *erster akademischer
Grad,* ≈ Magister/Diplom;
bachelorette *n* Junggesellin *f*;
bachelorette party *n (US)*

Junggesellinnenabschied; **bachelor party** n (US) *Junggesellenabschied*

back [bæk] n (of person, animal) Rücken m; (of house, coin etc) Rückseite f; (of chair) Rückenlehne f; (of car) Rücksitz m; (of train) Ende nt; (Sport: defender) Verteidiger(in) m(f); **at the ~ of ...**, (US) **in ~ of** (inside) hinten in ...; (outside) hinter ...; **~ to front** verkehrt herum ▷ vt (support) unterstützen; (car) rückwärtsfahren ▷ vi (go backwards) rückwärtsgehen o rückwärtsfahren ▷ adj Hinter-; **~ wheel** Hinterrad nt ▷ adv zurück; **they're ~** sie sind wieder da; **back away** vi sich zurückziehen; **back down** vi nachgeben; **back up** vi (car etc) zurücksetzen ▷ vt (support) unterstützen; (Inform) sichern; (car) zurückfahren

backache n Rückenschmerzen pl; **backbone** n Rückgrat nt; **backdate** vt zurückdatieren; **backdoor** n Hintertür f; **backfire** vi (plan) fehlschlagen; (Auto) fehlzünden; **background** n Hintergrund m; **backhand** n (Sport) Rückhand f; **backlog** n (of work) Rückstand m; **backpack** n (US) Rucksack m; **backpacker** n Rucksacktourist(in) m(f); **backpacking** n Rucksacktourismus m; **back seat** n Rücksitz m; **backside** n (fam) Po m; **back street** n Seitenstraßchen m; **backstroke** n Rückenschwimmen nt; **back-up** n (support) Unterstützung f; ~ (copy) (Inform) Sicherungskopie f; **backward** adj (child) zurückgeblieben; (region) rückständig; **~ movement** Rückwärtsbewegung f; **backwards** adv rückwärts; **backyard** n Hinterhof m

bacon ['beɪkən] n Frühstücksspeck m

bacteria [bæk'tɪərɪə] npl Bakterien pl

bad [bæd] (**worse, worst**) adj schlecht, schlimm; (smell) übel; **I have a ~ back** mir tut der Rücken weh; **I'm ~ at maths/sport** ich bin schlecht in Mathe/Sport; **to go ~** schlecht werden, verderben

badge [bædʒ] n Abzeichen nt

badger ['bædʒə] n Dachs m

badly ['bædlɪ] adv schlecht; **~ wounded** schwer verwundet; **to need sth ~** etw dringend brauchen; **bad-tempered** ['bæd'tempəd] adj schlecht gelaunt

bag [bæg] n (small) Tüte f; (larger) Beutel m; (handbag) Tasche f; **my ~s** (luggage) mein Gepäck

baggage ['bægɪdʒ] n Gepäck nt; **baggage allowance** n Freigepäck nt; **baggage (re)claim** n Gepäckrückgabe f

baggy ['bægɪ] adj (zu) weit; (trousers, suit) ausgebeult

bag lady ['bæg'leɪdɪ] n Stadtstreicherin f

bagpipes ['bægpaɪps] npl Dudelsack m

Bahamas [bə'hɑːməz] npl: **the ~** die Bahamas pl

bail [beɪl] n (money) Kaution f

bait [beɪt] n Köder m

bake [beɪk] vt, vi backen; **baked beans** npl weiße Bohnen in Tomatensoße; **baked potato** (pl **-es**) n in der Schale gebackene Kartoffel, Ofenkartoffel f; **baker** n Bäcker(in) m(f); **bakery** ['beɪkərɪ] n Bäckerei f; **baking powder** n Backpulver nt

balance ['bæləns] n (equilibrium) Gleichgewicht nt ▷ vt (make up for) ausgleichen; **balanced** adj

ausgeglichen; **balance sheet** n
Bilanz f

balcony ['bælkənɪ] n Balkon m

bald [bɔːld] adj kahl; **to be ~** eine
Glatze haben

Balkans ['bɔːlkənz] npl: **the ~**
der Balkan, die Balkanländer pl

ball [bɔːl] n Ball m; **to have a ~**
(fam) sich prima amüsieren

ballet ['bæleɪ] n Ballett nt; **ballet
dancer** n Balletttänzer(in) m(f)

balloon [bə'luːn] n (Luft)ballon
m

ballot ['bælət] n (geheime)
Abstimmung; **ballot box** n
Wahlurne f; **ballot paper** n
Stimmzettel m

ballpoint (pen) ['bɔːlpɔɪnt] n
Kugelschreiber m

ballroom ['bɔːlruːm] n Tanzsaal
m

Baltic ['bɔːltɪk] adj: **~ Sea** Ostsee
f; **the ~ States** die baltischen
Staaten

Baltics ['bɔːltɪks] n: **the ~** das
Baltikum nt

bamboo [bæm'buː] n Bambus m;
bamboo shoots npl
Bambussprossen pl

ban [bæn] n Verbot nt ▷ vt
verbieten

banana [bə'nɑːnə] n Banane f;
he's ~s er ist völlig durchgeknallt;
banana split n Bananensplit nt

band [bænd] n (group) Gruppe f;
(of criminals) Bande f; (Mus) Kapelle
f; (pop, rock etc) Band f; (strip) Band
nt

bandage ['bændɪdʒ] n Verband
m; (elastic) Bandage f ▷ vt
verbinden

B & B abbr = **bed and breakfast**

bang [bæŋ] n (noise) Knall m;
(blow) Schlag m ▷ vt, vi knallen;
(door) zuschlagen, zuknallen;
banger [bæŋə°] n (Brit fam:
firework) Knallkörper m; (sausage)

Würstchen nt; (fam: old car)
Klapperkiste f

bangs [bæŋz] npl (US: of hair)
Pony m

banish ['bænɪʃ] vt verbannen

banister(s) ['bænɪstə°] n (Treppen)geländer nt

bank [bæŋk] n (Fin) Bank f; (of
river etc) Ufer nt; **bank account** n
Bankkonto nt; **bank balance** n
Kontostand m; **bank card** n
Bankkarte f; **bank code** n
Bankleitzahl f; **bank holiday** n
gesetzlicher Feiertag

▶ **BANK HOLIDAY**

Als **bank holiday** wird in
Großbritannien ein gesetzlicher
Feiertag bezeichnet, an dem die
Banken geschlossen sind. Die
meisten dieser Feiertage,
abgesehen von Weihnachten
und Ostern, fallen auf Montage
im Mai und August. An diesen
langen Wochenenden (bank
holiday weekends) fahren viele
Briten in Urlaub, sodass dann
auf den Straßen, Flughäfen und
bei der Bahn sehr viel Betrieb
ist.

bank manager n Filialleiter(in)
m(f); **banknote** n Banknote f

bankrupt vt ruinieren; **to go
~** Pleite gehen

bank statement n
Kontoauszug m

baptism ['bæptɪzəm] n Taufe f;
baptize ['bæptaɪz] vt taufen

bar [bɑː°] n (for drinks) Bar f; (less
smart) Lokal nt; (rod) Stange f; (of
chocolate etc) Riegel m, Tafel f; (of
soap) Stück nt; (counter) Theke f
▷ prep außer; **~ none** ohne
Ausnahme

barbecue ['bɑːbɪkjuː] n (device)

Grill m; (party) Barbecue nt, Grillfete f; **to have a ~** grillen

barbed wire ['bɑːbd'waɪə°] n Stacheldraht m

barber ['bɑːbə°] n (Herren)friseur m

bar code ['bɑːkəʊd] n Strichkode m

bare [beə°] adj nackt; **~ patch** kahle Stelle; **barefoot** adj, adv barfuß; **bareheaded** adj, adv ohne Kopfbedeckung; **barely** adv kaum; (with age) knapp

bargain ['bɑːgɪn] n (cheap offer) günstiges Angebot, Schnäppchen nt; (transaction) Geschäft nt; **what a ~** das ist aber günstig! ▷ vi (ver)handeln

barge [bɑːdʒ] n (for freight) Lastkahn m; (unpowered) Schleppkahn m

bark [bɑːk] n (of tree) Rinde f; (of dog) Bellen nt ▷ vi (dog) bellen

barley ['bɑːlɪ] n Gerste f

barmaid ['bɑːmeɪd] n Barkeeperin f; **barman** ['bɑːmən] (pl **-men**) n Barkeeper m

barn [bɑːn] n Scheune f

barometer [bə'rɒmɪtə°] n Barometer nt

baroque [bə'rɒk] adj barock, Barock-

barracks ['bærəks] npl Kaserne f

barrel ['bærəl] n Fass nt; **barrel organ** n Drehorgel f

barricade [bærɪ'keɪd] n Barrikade f

barrier ['bærɪə°] n (obstruction) Absperrung f, Barriere f; (across road etc) Schranke f

barrow ['bærəʊ] n (cart) Schubkarren m

bartender ['bɑːtendə°] n (US) Barkeeper(in) m(f)

base [beɪs] n Basis f; (of lamp, pillar etc) Fuß m; (Mil) Stützpunkt m ▷ vt gründen (on auf +akk); **to be ~d on sth** auf etw dat basieren; **baseball** n Baseball m; **baseball cap** n Baseballmütze f; **basement** n Kellergeschoss nt

bash [bæʃ] (fam) n Schlag m; (fam) Party f ▷ vt hauen

basic ['beɪsɪk] adj einfach; (fundamental) Grund-; (importance, difference) grundlegend; (in principle) grundsätzlich; **the accomodation is very ~** die Unterkunft ist sehr bescheiden; **basically** adv im Grunde; **basics** npl: **the ~** das Wesentliche

basil ['bæzl] n Basilikum nt

basin ['beɪsn] n (for washing, valley) (Wasch)becken nt

basis ['beɪsɪs] n Basis f; **on the ~ of** aufgrund +gen; **on a monthly ~** monatlich

basket ['bɑːskɪt] n Korb m; **basketball** n Basketball m

Basque [bæsk] n (person) Baske m, Baskin f; (language) Baskisch nt ▷ adj baskisch

bass [beɪs] n (Mus) Bass m; (Zool) Barsch m ▷ adj (Mus) Bass-

bastard ['bɑːstəd] n (vulg: awful person) Arschloch nt

bat [bæt] n (Zool) Fledermaus f; (Sport: cricket, baseball) Schlagholz nt; (table tennis) Schläger m

batch [bætʃ] n Schwung m; (fam: of letters, books etc) Stoß m

bath [bɑːθ] n Bad nt; (tub) Badewanne f; **to have a ~** baden ▷ vt (child etc) baden

bathe [beɪð] vt, vi (wound etc) baden; **bath foam** ['bɑːθfəʊm] n Badeschaum m; **bathing cap** n Badekappe f; **bathing costume, bathing suit** (US) n Badeanzug m

bathmat ['bɑːθmæt] n Badevorleger m; **bathrobe** n Bademantel m; **bathroom** n Bad(ezimmer) nt; **baths** [bɑːðz] npl (Schwimm)bad

nt; **bath towel** *n* Badetuch *nt*;
bathtub *n* Badewanne *f*

baton ['bætən] *n* (Mus) Taktstock
m; (police) Schlagstock *m*

batter ['bætə'] *n* Teig *m* ▷ *vt*
heftig schlagen; **battered** *adj*
übel zugerichtet; (hat, car)
verbeult; (wife, baby) misshandelt

battery ['bætɹɪ] *n* (Elec) Batterie
f; **battery charger** *n* Ladegerät *nt*

battle ['bætl] *n* Schlacht *f*; (fig)
Kampf *m* (for um +akk); **battlefield**
n Schlachtfeld *nt*; **battlements**
npl Zinnen *pl*

Bavaria [bə'veərɪə] *n* Bayern *nt*;
Bavarian *adj* bay(e)risch ▷ *n*
Bayer(in) *m(f)*

bay [beɪ] *n* (of sea) Bucht *f*; (on
house) Erker *m*; (tree) Lorbeerbaum
m; **bay leaf** *n* Lorbeerblatt *nt*; **bay
window** *n* Erkerfenster *nt*

BBC *abbr* = **British Broadcasting
Corporation** BBC *f*

BC *abbr* = **before Christ** vor Christi
Geburt, v. Chr.

⭕ **KEYWORD**

be [bi:] (*pt* **was**, **were**, *pp* **been**) *vb
aux* 1 (with present participle: forming
continuous tenses): **what are you
doing?** was machst du (gerade)?;
it is raining es regnet; **I've been
waiting for you for hours** ich
warte schon seit Stunden auf dich
2 (with *pp*: forming passives): **to be
killed** getötet werden; **the thief
was nowhere to be seen** der Dieb
war nirgendwo zu sehen
3 (in tag questions) **it was fun,
wasn't it?** es hat Spaß gemacht,
nicht wahr?
4 (+to +infin) **the house is to be
sold** das Haus soll verkauft
werden; **he's not to open it** er darf
es nicht öffnen
▷ *vb* +complement 1 (usu) sein; **I'm

tired** ich bin müde; **I'm hot/cold**
mir ist heiß/kalt; **he's a doctor** er
ist Arzt; **2 and 2 are 4** 2 und 2 ist o
sind 4; **she's tall/pretty** sie ist
groß/hübsch; **be careful/quiet**
sei vorsichtig/ruhig
2 (of health) **how are you?** wie geht
es dir?; **he's very ill** er ist sehr
krank; **I'm fine now** jetzt geht es
mir gut
3 (of age) **how old are you?** wie alt
bist du?; **I'm sixteen (years old)**
ich bin sechzehn (Jahre alt)
4 (cost) **how much was the meal?**
was o wie viel hat das Essen
gekostet?; **that'll be £5.75, please**
das macht £5.75, bitte
▷ *vi* 1 (exist, occur etc) sein; **is there
a God?** gibt es einen Gott?; **be
that as it may** wie dem auch sei;
so be it also gut
2 (referring to place) sein; **I won't be
here tomorrow** ich werde morgen
nicht hier sein
3 (referring to movement) **where
have you been?** wo bist du
gewesen?; **I've been in the
garden** ich war im Garten
▷ *impers vb* 1 (referring to time,
distance, weather) sein; **it's 5
o'clock** es ist 5 Uhr; **it's 10 km to
the village** es sind 10 km bis zum
Dorf; **it's too hot/cold** es ist zu
heiß/kalt
2 (emphatic) **it's me** ich bin's; **it's
the postman** es ist der Briefträger

beach [bi:tʃ] *n* Strand *m*;
beachwear *n* Strandkleidung *f*

bead [bi:d] *n* (of glass, wood etc)
Perle *f*; (drop) Tropfen *m*

beak [bi:k] *n* Schnabel *m*

beam [bi:m] *n* (of wood etc) Balken
m; (of light) Strahl *m* ▷ *vi* (smile etc)
strahlen

bean [bi:n] *n* Bohne *f*; **bean curd**
n Tofu *m*

bear [beəʳ] (*pt* **bore**, **borne**) *vt* (carry) tragen; (tolerate) ertragen ▷ *n* Bär *m*; **bearable** *adj* erträglich

beard [bɪəd] *n* Bart *m*

beast [biːst] *n* Tier *nt*; (brutal person) Bestie *f*; (disliked person) Biest *nt*

beat [biːt] (**beat**, **beaten**) *vt* schlagen; (*as punishment*) prügeln; **to ~ sb at tennis** jdn im Tennis schlagen ▷ *n* (of heart, drum etc) Schlag *m*; (Mus) Takt *m*; (type of music) Beat *m*; **beat up** *vt* zusammenschlagen

beaten ['biːtn] *pp* of **beat**; **off the ~ track** abgelegen

beautiful ['bjuːtɪful] *adj* schön; (splendid) herrlich; **beauty** ['bjuːtɪ] *n* Schönheit *f*; **beauty spot** *n* (place) lohnendes Ausflugsziel

beaver ['biːvəʳ] *n* Biber *m*

became [bɪ'keɪm] *pt* of **become**

because [bɪ'kɒz] *adv, conj* weil ▷ *prep*: **~ of** wegen +gen o dat

become [bɪ'kʌm] (**became**, **become**) *vt* werden; **what's ~ of him?** was ist aus ihm geworden?

bed [bed] *n* Bett *nt*; (in garden) Beet *nt*; **bed and breakfast** *n* Übernachtung *f* mit Frühstück; **bedclothes** *npl* Bettwäsche *f*; **bedding** *n* Bettzeug *nt*; **bed linen** *n* Bettwäsche *f*; **bedroom** *n* Schlafzimmer *nt*; **bed-sit(ter)** *n* (fam) möblierte Einzimmerwohnung; **bedspread** *n* Tagesdecke *f*; **bedtime** *n* Schlafenszeit *f*

bee [biː] *n* Biene *f*

beech [biːtʃ] *n* Buche *f*

beef [biːf] *n* Rindfleisch *nt*; **beefburger** *n* Hamburger *m*; **beef tomato** (*pl* **-es**) *n* Fleischtomate *f*

beehive ['biːhaɪv] *n* Bienenstock *m*

been [biːn] *pp* of **be**

beer [bɪəʳ] *n* Bier *nt*; **beer garden** *n* Biergarten *m*

beetle ['biːtl] *n* Käfer *m*

beetroot ['biːtruːt] *n* Rote Bete

before [bɪ'fɔːʳ] *prep* vor; **the year ~ last** vorletztes Jahr; **the day ~ yesterday** vorgestern ▷ *conj* bevor o ehe ▷ *adv* vorher; **have you been there ~?** waren Sie/warst du schon einmal dort?; **beforehand** *adv* vorher

beg [beg] *vt*: **to ~ sb to do sth** jdn inständig bitten, etw zu tun ▷ *vi* (beggar) betteln (for um +akk)

began [bɪ'ɡæn] *pt* of **begin**

beggar ['begəʳ] *n* Bettler(in) *m(f)*

begin [bɪ'ɡɪn] (**began**, **begun**) *vt, vi* anfangen, beginnen; **to ~ to do sth** anfangen, etw zu tun; **beginner** *n* Anfänger(in) *m(f)*; **beginning** *n* Anfang *m*

begun [bɪ'ɡʌn] *pp* of **begin**

behalf [bɪ'hɑːf] *n*: **on ~ of**, in **~ of** (US) im Namen/Auftrag von; **on my ~** für mich

behave [bɪ'heɪv] *vi* sich benehmen; **~ yourself!** benimm dich!; **behavior** (US), **behaviour** [bɪ'heɪvjəʳ] *n* Benehmen *nt*

behind [bɪ'haɪnd] *prep* hinter; **to be ~ time** Verspätung haben ▷ *adv* hinten; **to be ~ with one's work** mit seiner Arbeit im Rückstand sein ▷ *n* (fam) Hinterteil *nt*

beige [beɪʒ] *adj* beige

being ['biːɪn] *n* (existence) Dasein *nt*; (person) Wesen *nt*

Belarus [belə'rʊs] *n* Weißrussland *nt*

belch [beltʃ] *n* Rülpser *m* ▷ *vi* rülpsen

belfry ['belfrɪ] *n* Glockenturm *m*

Belgian ['beldʒən] *adj* belgisch ▷ *n* Belgier(in) *m(f)*; **Belgium** ['beldʒəm] *n* Belgien *nt*

belief [bɪˈliːf] n Glaube m (in an +akk); (conviction) Überzeugung f; **it's my ~ that ...** ich bin der Überzeugung, dass ...; **believe** [bɪˈliːv] vt glauben; **believe in** vi glauben an +akk; **believer** n (Rel) Gläubige(r) mf

bell [bel] n (church) Glocke f; (bicycle, door) Klingel f; **bellboy** [ˈbelbɔɪ] n (esp US) Page m

bellows [ˈbeləʊz] npl (for fire) Blasebalg m

belly [ˈbelɪ] n Bauch m; **bellyache** n Bauchweh nt ⊳ vi (fam) meckern; **belly button** n (fam) Bauchnabel m; **bellyflop** n (fam) Bauchklatscher m

belong [bɪˈlɒŋ] vi gehören (to sb jdm); (to club) angehören +dat; **belongings** npl Habe f

below [bɪˈləʊ] prep unter ⊳ adv unten

belt [belt] n (round waist) Gürtel m; (safety belt) Gurt m; **below the ~** unter der Gürtellinie ⊳ vi (fam: go fast) rasen, düsen; **beltway** n (US) Umgehungsstraße f

bench [bentʃ] n Bank f

bend [bend] n Biegung f; (in road) Kurve f ⊳ vt (bend, bent) (curve) biegen; (head, arm) beugen ⊳ vi sich biegen; (person) sich beugen; **bend down** vi sich bücken

beneath [bɪˈniːθ] prep unter ⊳ adv darunter

beneficial [benɪˈfɪʃl] adj gut, nützlich (to für); **benefit** [ˈbenɪfɪt] n (advantage) Vorteil m; (profit) Nutzen m; **for your/his ~** deinetwegen/seinetwegen; **unemployment ~** Arbeitslosengeld nt ⊳ vt guttun +dat ⊳ vi Nutzen ziehen (from aus)

benign [bɪˈnaɪn] adj (person) gütig; (climate) mild; (Med) gutartig

bent [bent] pt, pp of **bend** ⊳ adj krumm; (fam) korrupt

beret [ˈbereɪ] n Baskenmütze f

Bermuda [bəˈmjuːdə] n **the ~s** pl die Bermudas (pl) ⊳ adj **~ shorts** pl Bermudashorts pl; **the ~ triangle** das Bermudadreieck

berry [ˈberɪ] n Beere f

berth [bɜːθ] n (for ship) Ankerplatz m; (in ship) Koje f; (in train) Bett nt ⊳ vt am Kai festmachen ⊳ vi anlegen

beside [bɪˈsaɪd] prep neben; **~ the sea/lake** am Meer/See; **besides** [bɪˈsaɪdz] prep außer ⊳ adv außerdem

besiege [bɪˈsiːdʒ] vt belagern

best [best] adj beste(r, s); **my ~ friend** mein bester o engster Freund; **the ~ thing (to do) would be to ...** das Beste wäre zu ...; (on food packaging) **~ before ...** mindestens haltbar bis ... ⊳ n der/die/das Beste; **all the ~** alles Gute; **to make the ~ of it** das Beste daraus machen ⊳ adv am besten; **I like this ~** das mag ich am liebsten; **best-before date** n Mindesthaltbarkeitsdatum nt; **best man** n [ˈbestˈmæn] (pl **men**) n Trauzeuge m; **bestseller** [ˈbestselə°] n Bestseller m

bet [bet] (bet, bet) vt, vi wetten (on auf +akk); **I ~ him £5 that ...** ich habe mit ihm um 5 Pfund gewettet, dass ...; **you ~** (fam) und ob!; **I ~ he'll be late** er kommt mit Sicherheit zu spät ⊳ n Wette f

betray [bɪˈtreɪ] vt verraten; **betrayal** n Verrat m

better [ˈbetə°] adj, adv besser; **to get ~** (healthwise) sich erholen, wieder gesund werden; (improve) sich verbessern; **I'm much ~ today** es geht mir heute viel besser; **you'd ~ go** du solltest/Sie

sollten lieber gehen; **a change for
the ~** eine Wendung zum Guten
betting ['betɪŋ] n Wetten nt;
betting shop n Wettbüro nt
between [bɪ'twiːn] prep
zwischen; (among) unter; **~ you
and me, ...** unter uns gesagt, ...
▷ adv: (in) ~ dazwischen
beverage ['bevərɪdʒ] n (formal)
Getränk nt
beware [bɪ'weə°] vt: **to ~ of sth**
sich vor etw +dat hüten; **"~ of the
dog"** „Vorsicht, bissiger Hund!"
bewildered [bɪ'wɪldəd] adj
verwirrt
beyond [bɪ'jɒnd] prep (place)
jenseits +gen; (time) über ...
hinaus; (out of reach) außerhalb
+gen; **it's ~ me** da habe ich keine
Ahnung, da bin ich überfragt
▷ adv darüber hinaus
bias ['baɪəs] n (prejudice) Vorurteil
nt, Voreingenommenheit f
bias(s)ed adj voreingenommen
bib [bɪb] n Latz m
Bible ['baɪbl] n Bibel f
bicycle ['baɪsɪkl] n Fahrrad nt
bid [bɪd] (bid, bid) vt (offer) bieten
▷ n (attempt) Versuch m; (offer)
Gebot nt
big [bɪg] adj groß; **it's no ~ deal**
(fam) es ist nichts Besonderes; **big
dipper** n (Brit) Achterbahn f;
big-headed [bɪg'hedɪd] adj
eingebildet
bike [baɪk] n (fam) Rad nt
bikini [bɪ'kiːnɪ] n Bikini m
bilberry ['bɪlbərɪ] n Heidelbeere f
bilingual [baɪ'lɪŋgwəl] adj
zweisprachig
bill [bɪl] n (account) Rechnung f;
(US: banknote) Banknote f; (Pol)
Gesetzentwurf m; (Zool) Schnabel
m; **billfold** ['bɪlfəʊld] n (US)
Brieftasche f
billiards ['bɪlɪədz] nsing Billard
nt; **billiard table** Billardtisch m

billion ['bɪlɪən] n Milliarde f
bin [bɪn] n Behälter m; (rubbish
bin) (Müll)eimer m; (for paper)
Papierkorb m
bind [baɪnd] (bound, bound) vt
binden; (bind together)
zusammenbinden; (wound)
verbinden; **binding** n (ski)
Bindung f; (book) Einband m
binge [bɪndʒ] n (fam: drinking)
Sauferei f; **to go on a ~** auf
Sauftour gehen
bingo ['bɪŋgəʊ] n Bingo nt
binoculars [bɪ'nɒkjʊləz] npl
Fernglas nt
biodegradable
['baɪəʊdɪ'greɪdəbl] adj biologisch
abbaubar
biography [baɪ'ɒgrəfɪ] n Bio-
grafie f
biological [baɪə'lɒdʒɪkəl] adj
biologisch; **biology** [baɪ'ɒlədʒɪ]
n Biologie f
birch [bɜːtʃ] n Birke f
bird [bɜːd] n Vogel m; (Brit fam:
girl, girlfriend) Tussi f; **bird flu** n
Vogelgrippe f; **bird watcher** n
Vogelbeobachter(in) m(f)
birth [bɜːθ] n Geburt f; **birth
certificate** n Geburtsurkunde f;
birth control n
Geburtenkontrolle f; **birthday** n
Geburtstag m; **happy ~** herzlichen
Glückwunsch zum Geburtstag;
birthday card n
Geburtstagskarte f; **birthday
party** n Geburtstagsfeier f;
birthplace n Geburtsort m
biscuit ['bɪskɪt] n (Brit) Keks m
bisexual [baɪ'seksjʊəl] adj
bisexuell
bishop ['bɪʃəp] n Bischof m; (in
chess) Läufer m
bit [bɪt] pt of **bite** n (piece)
Stück(chen) nt; (Inform) Bit nt; **a
~ (of ...)** (small amount) ein
bisschen ...; **a ~ tired** etwas müde;

~ by – allmählich; *(time)* **for a ~** ein Weilchen; **quite a ~** *(a lot)* ganz schön viel

bitch [bɪtʃ] *n (dog)* Hündin *f*; *(pej: woman)* Miststück *nt*, Schlampe *f*; **son of a ~** *(US: vulg)* Hurensohn *m*, Scheißkerl *m*; **bitchy** *adj* gemein, zickig

bite [baɪt] *(bit, bitten)* *vt, vi* beißen ▷ *n* Biss *m*; *(mouthful)* Bissen *m*; *(insect)* Stich *m*; **to have a ~** eine Kleinigkeit essen; **bitten** *pp of* **bite**

bitter ['bɪtə°] *adj* bitter; *(memory etc)* schmerzlich ▷ *n* (Brit: beer) halbdunkles Bier; **bitter lemon** *nt* Bitter Lemon *nt*

bizarre [bɪ'zɑː°] *adj* bizarr

black [blæk] *adj* schwarz; **blackberry** *n* Brombeere *f*; **blackbird** *n* Amsel *f*; **blackboard** *n* (Wand)tafel *f*; **black box** *n* (Aviat) Flugschreiber *m*; **blackcurrant** *n* Schwarze Johannisbeere; **black eye** *n* blaues Auge; **Black Forest** *n* Schwarzwald *m*; **Black Forest gateau** *n* Schwarzwälder Kirschtorte *f*; **blackmail** *n* Erpressung *f* ▷ *vt* erpressen; **black market** *n* Schwarzmarkt *m*; **blackout** *n* (Med) Ohnmacht *f*; **to have a ~** ohnmächtig werden; **black pudding** *n* ≈ Blutwurst *f*; **Black Sea** *n*: **the ~** das Schwarze Meer; **blacksmith** *n* Schmied(in) *m(f)*; **black tie** *n* Abendanzug *m*, Smoking *m*; **is it ~?** ist/besteht da Smokingzwang?

bladder ['blædə°] *n* Blase *f*

blade [bleɪd] *n (of knife)* Klinge *f*; *(of propeller)* Blatt *nt*; *(of grass)* Halm *m*

blame [bleɪm] *n* Schuld *f* ▷ *vt*: **to ~ sth on sb** jdm die Schuld an etw *dat* geben; **he is to ~** er ist daran schuld

bland [blænd] *adj (taste)* fade; *(comment)* nichtssagend

blank [blæŋk] *adj (page, space)* leer, unbeschrieben; *(look)* ausdruckslos; **~ cheque** Blankoscheck *m*

blanket ['blæŋkɪt] *n* (Woll)decke *f*

blast [blɑːst] *n (of wind)* Windstoß *m*; *(of explosion)* Druckwelle *f* ▷ *vt (blow up)* sprengen; **~! (fam)** Mist!, verdammt!

blatant ['bleɪtənt] *adj (undisguised)* offen; *(obvious)* offensichtlich

blaze [bleɪz] *vi* lodern; *(sun)* brennen ▷ *n (building)* Brand *m*; *(other fire)* Feuer *nt*; **a ~ of colour** eine Farbenpracht

blazer ['bleɪzə°] *n* Blazer *m*

bleach [bliːtʃ] *n* Bleichmittel *nt* ▷ *vt* bleichen

bleak [bliːk] *adj* öde, düster; *(future)* trostlos

bleary ['blɪərɪ] *adj (eyes)* trübe, verschlafen

bleed [bliːd] *(bled, bled)* *vi* bluten

blend [blend] *n* Mischung *f* ▷ *vt* mischen ▷ *vi* sich mischen; **blender** *n* Mixer *m*

bless [bles] *vt* segnen; **~ you!** Gesundheit!; **blessing** *n* Segen *m*

blew [bluː] *pt of* **blow**

blind [blaɪnd] *adj* blind; *(corner)* unübersichtlich; **to turn a ~ eye to sth** bei etw ein Auge zudrücken ▷ *n (for window)* Rollo *nt* ▷ *vt* blenden; **blind alley** *n* Sackgasse *f*; **blind spot** *n* (Auto) toter Winkel; *(fig)* schwacher Punkt

blink [blɪŋk] *vi* blinzeln; *(light)* blinken

bliss [blɪs] *n* (Glück)seligkeit *f*

blister ['blɪstə°] *n* Blase *f*

blizzard ['blɪzəd] n Schneesturm m

bloated ['bləʊtɪd] adj aufgedunsen

block [blɒk] n (of wood, stone, ice) Block m, Klotz m; (of buildings) Häuserblock m; **~ of flats** (Brit) Wohnblock m ▷ vt (road etc) blockieren; (pipe, nose) verstopfen; **blockage** ['blɒkɪdʒ] n Verstopfung f; **blockbuster** ['blɒkbʌstə°] n Knüller m; **block letters** npl Blockschrift f

blog [blɒg] n (Inform) Blog m, Weblog m ▷ vi bloggen

bloke [bləʊk] n (Brit fam) Kerl m, Typ m

blond(e) [blɒnd] adj blond ▷ n (person) Blondine f, blonder Typ

blood [blʌd] n Blut nt; **blood count** n Blutbild nt; **blood donor** n Blutspender(in) m(f); **blood group** n Blutgruppe f; **blood orange** n Blutorange f; **blood poisoning** n Blutvergiftung f; **blood pressure** n Blutdruck m; **blood sample** n Blutprobe f; **bloodsports** npl Sportarten, bei denen Tiere getötet werden; **bloodthirsty** adj blutrünstig; **bloody** adj (fam) verdammt, Scheiß-; (literal sense) blutig

bloom [bluːm] n Blüte f ▷ vi blühen

blossom ['blɒsəm] n Blüte f ▷ vi blühen

blot ['blɒt] n (of ink) Klecks m; (fig) Fleck m

blouse [blaʊz] n Bluse f; **big girl's ~** (fam) Schwächling m

blow [bləʊ] n Schlag m ▷ vi, vt (blew, blown) (wind) wehen, blasen; (person: trumpet etc) blasen; **to ~ one's nose** sich dat die Nase putzen; **blow out** vt (candle etc) ausblasen; **blow up** vi explodieren ▷ vt sprengen;

(balloon, tyre) aufblasen; (Foto: enlarge) vergrößern; **blow-dry** vt föhnen; **blowjob** n (fam) to give sb a ~ jdm einen blasen; **blown** [bləʊn] pp of **blow**; **blow-out** n (Auto) geplatzter Reifen

BLT n abbr = **bacon, lettuce and tomato sandwich** mit Frühstücksspeck, Kopfsalat und Tomaten belegtes Sandwich

blue [bluː] adj blau; (fam: unhappy) trübsinnig, niedergeschlagen; (film) pornografisch; (joke) anzüglich; (language) derb; **bluebell** n Glockenblume f; **blueberry** n Blaubeere f; **blue cheese** n Blauschimmelkäse m; **blues** npl: **the ~** (Mus) der Blues; **to have the ~** (fam) niedergeschlagen sein

blunder ['blʌndə°] n Schnitzer m

blunt [blʌnt] adj (knife) stumpf; (fig) unverblümt; **bluntly** adv geradeheraus

blurred [blɜːd] adj verschwommen, unklar

blush [blʌʃ] vi erröten

board [bɔːd] n (of wood) Brett nt; (committee) Ausschuss m; (of firm) Vorstand m; **~ and lodging** Unterkunft und Verpflegung; **on ~** an Bord ▷ vt (train, bus) einsteigen in +akk; (ship) an Bord +gen gehen; **boarder** n Pensionsgast m; (school) Internatsschüler(in) m(f); **board game** n Brettspiel n; **boarding card, boarding pass** n Bordkarte f, Einsteigekarte f; **boarding school** n Internat nt; **board meeting** n Vorstandssitzung f; **boardroom** n Sitzungssaal m (des Vorstands)

boast [bəʊst] vi prahlen (about mit) ▷ n Prahlerei f

boat [bəʊt] n Boot nt; (ship) Schiff nt; **boatman** n (hirer)

Bootsverleiher *m*; **boat race** *n*
Regatta *f*; **boat train** *n* Zug *m* mit
Schiffsanschluss
bob(sleigh) ['bɒbsleɪ] *n* Bob *m*
bodily ['bɒdɪlɪ] *adj* körperlich
▷ *adv* (*forcibly*) gewaltsam; **body**
['bɒdɪ] *n* Körper *m*; (*dead*) Leiche *f*;
(*of car*) Karosserie *f*; **bodybuilding**
n Bodybuilding *nt*; **bodyguard** *n*
Leibwächter *m*; (*group*) Leibwache
f; **body jewellery** *n*
Intimschmuck *m*; **body odour** *n*
Körpergeruch *m*; **body piercing** *n*
Piercing *nt*; **bodywork** *n*
Karosserie *f*
boil [bɔɪl] *vt, vi* kochen ▷ *n* (*Med*)
Geschwür *nt*; **boiler** *n* Boiler *m*;
boiling *adj* (*water etc*) kochend
(heiß); **I was ~** (*hot*) mir war
fürchterlich heiß; (*with rage*) ich
kochte vor Wut; **boiling point** *n*
Siedepunkt *m*
bold [bəʊld] *adj* kühn, mutig;
(*colours*) kräftig; (*type*) fett
Bolivia [bə'lɪvɪə] *n* Bolivien *nt*
bolt [bəʊlt] *n* (*lock*) Riegel *m*;
(*screw*) Bolzen *m* ▷ *vt* verriegeln
bomb [bɒm] *n* Bombe *f* ▷ *vt*
bombardieren
bond [bɒnd] *n* (*link*) Bindung *f*;
(*Fin*) Obligation *f*
bone [bəʊn] *n* Knochen *m*; (*of
fish*) Gräte *f*; **boner** *n* (*US fam*)
Schnitzer *m*; (*vulg: erection*) Ständer
m
bonfire ['bɒnfaɪə⁰] *n* Feuer *nt*
(im Freien)
bonnet ['bɒnɪt] *n* (*Brit Auto*)
Haube *f*; (*for baby*) Häubchen *nt*
bonny ['bɒnɪ] *adj* (*esp Scottish*)
hübsch
bonus ['bəʊnəs] *n* Bonus *m*,
Prämie *f*
boo [buː] *vt* auspfeifen,
ausbuhen ▷ *vi* buhen ▷ *n* Buhruf *m*
book [bʊk] *n* Buch *nt*; (*of tickets,*

stamps) Heft *nt* ▷ *vt* (*ticket etc*)
bestellen; (*hotel, flight etc*) buchen;
(*Sport*) verwarnen; **fully ~ed** (*up*)
ausgebucht; (*performance*)
ausverkauft; **book in** *vi*
eintragen; **to be ~ed in at a hotel**
ein Zimmer in einem Hotel
bestellt haben; **bookcase** *n*
Bücherregal *nt*; **booking** *n*
Buchung *f*; **booking office** *n*
(*Rail*) Fahrkartenschalter *m*; (*Theat*)
Vorverkaufsstelle *f*; **book-keeping**
n Buchhaltung *f*; **booklet** *n* (*a.
Inform*) Lesezeichen *nt*; **bookshelf**
n Bücherbord *nt*; **bookshelves**
Bücherregal *nt*; **bookshop**,
bookstore *n* (*esp US*)
Buchhandlung *f*
boom [buːm] *n* (*of business*)
Boom *m*; (*noise*) Dröhnen *nt* ▷ *vi*
(*business*) boomen; (*fam*) florieren;
(*voice etc*) dröhnen
boomerang ['buːməræŋ] *n*
Bumerang *m*
boost [buːst] *n* Auftrieb *m* ▷ *vt*
(*production, sales*) ankurbeln;
(*power, profits etc*) steigern;
booster (injection) *n*
Wiederholungsimpfung *f*
boot [buːt] *n* Stiefel *m*; (*Brit Auto*)
Kofferraum *m* ▷ *vt* (*Inform*) laden,
booten
booth [buːð] *n* (*at fair etc*) Bude *f*;
(*at trade fair etc*) Stand *m*
booze [buːz] *n* (*fam*) Alkohol *m*
▷ *vi* (*fam*) saufen
border ['bɔːdə⁰] *n* Grenze *f*; (*edge*)
Rand *m*; **north/south of the
Border** in Schottland/England;
borderline *n* Grenze *f*
bore [bɔː⁰] *pt of* **bear** ▷ *vt* (*hole
etc*) bohren; (*person*) langweilen
▷ *n* (*person*) Langweiler(in) *m(f)*,
langweiliger Mensch; (*thing*)
langweilige Sache; **bored** *adj*: **to
be ~** sich langweilen; **boredom** *n*

Langeweile f; **boring** adj
langweilig

born [bɔːn] adj: **he was ~ in London** er ist in London geboren

borne [bɔːn] pp of **bear**

borough ['bʌrə] n Stadtbezirk m

borrow ['bɒrəʊ] vt borgen

Bosnia-Herzegovina ['bɒzniəhɜːtsəgəʊˈviːnə] n Bosnien-Herzegowina nt; **Bosnian** ['bɒzniən] adj bosnisch ▷ n Bosnier(in) m(f)

boss [bɒs] n Chef(in) m(f), Boss m; **boss around** vt herumkommandieren; **bossy** adj herrisch

botanical [bəˈtænɪkəl] adj botanisch; **~ garden(s)** botanischer Garten

both [bəʊθ] adj beide; **~ the books** beide Bücher ▷ pron (people) beide; (things) beides; **~ (of) the boys** die beiden Jungs; **I like ~ of them** ich mag sie (alle) beide ▷ adv: **~ X and Y** sowohl X als auch Y

bother ['bɒðə*] vt (=irgern, belästigen; **it doesn't ~ me** das stört mich nicht; **he can't be ~ed with details** mit Details gibt er sich nicht ab; **I'm not ~ed** das ist mir egal ▷ vi sich kümmern (about um); **don't ~** (das ist) nicht nötig, lass es! ▷ n (trouble) Mühe f; (annoyance) Ärger m

bottle ['bɒtl] n Flasche f ▷ vt (in Flaschen) abfüllen; **bottle out** vi (fam) den Mut verlieren, aufgeben; **bottle bank** n Altglascontainer m; **bottled** adj in Flaschen; **~ beer** Flaschenbier nt; **bottleneck** n (fig) Engpass m; **bottle opener** n Flaschenöffner m

bottom ['bɒtəm] n (of container) Boden m; (underside) Unterseite f; (fam: of person) Po m; **at the ~ of the sea/table/page** auf dem

Meeresgrund/am Tabellenende/unten auf der Seite ▷ adj unterste(r, s); **to be ~ of the class/league** Klassenletzte(r)/Tabellenletzte(r) sein; **~ gear** (Auto) erster Gang

bought [bɔːt] pt, pp of **buy**

bounce [baʊns] vi (ball) springen, aufprallen; (cheque) platzen; **~ up and down** (person) herumhüpfen; **bouncy** adj (ball) gut springend; (person) munter; **bouncy castle®** n Hüpfburg f

bound [baʊnd] pt, pp of **bind** ▷ adj (tied up) gebunden; (obliged) verpflichtet; **to be ~ to do sth** (sure to) etw bestimmt tun (werden); (have to) etw tun müssen; **it's ~ to happen** es muss so kommen; **to be ~ for ...** auf dem Weg nach ... sein; **boundary** ['baʊndərɪ] n Grenze f

bouquet [bʊˈkeɪ] n (flowers) Strauß m; (of wine) Blume f

boutique [buːˈtiːk] n Boutique f

bow [bəʊ] n (ribbon) Schleife f; (instrument, weapon) Bogen m ▷ [baʊ] vi sich verbeugen ▷ [baʊ] n (with head) Verbeugung f; (of ship) Bug m

bowels ['baʊəlz] npl Darm m

bowl [bəʊl] n (basin) Schüssel f; (shallow) Schale f; (for animal) Napf m ▷ vt, vi (in cricket) werfen

bowler ['bəʊlə*] n (in cricket) Werfer(in) m(f); (hat) Melone f

bowling ['bəʊlɪŋ] n Kegeln nt; **bowling alley** n Kegelbahn f; **bowling green** n Rasen m zum Bowling-Spiel; **bowls** [bəʊlz] nsing (game) Bowling-Spiel nt

bow tie [bəʊˈtaɪ] n Fliege f

box [bɒks] n Schachtel f; (cardboard) Karton m; (bigger) Kasten m; (space on form) Kästchen nt; (Theat) Loge f; **boxer** n Boxer(in) m(f); **boxers, boxer**

shorts npl Boxershorts pl; **boxing** n (Sport) Boxen nt; **Boxing Day** n zweiter Weihnachtsfeiertag

boxing gloves npl Boxhandschuhe pl; **boxing ring** n Boxring m
box number n Chiffre f
box office n (cinema, theatre) Kasse f
boy [bɔɪ] n Junge m
boycott ['bɔɪkɒt] n Boykott m ▷ vt boykottieren
boyfriend ['bɔɪfrɛnd] n (fester) Freund m; **boy scout** n Pfadfinder m
bra [brɑː] n BH m
brace [breɪs] n (on teeth) Spange f
bracelet ['breɪslɪt] n Armband nt
braces ['breɪsɪz] npl (Brit) Hosenträger pl
bracket ['brækɪt] n (in text) Klammer f; (Tech) Träger m ▷ vt einklammern
brag [bræg] vi angeben
Braille [breɪl] n Blindenschrift f
brain [breɪn] n (Anat) Gehirn nt; (mind) Verstand m; **~s** (pl) (intelligence) Grips m; **brainwave** n Geistesblitz m; **brainy** adj schlau, clever
braise [breɪz] vt schmoren
brake [breɪk] n Bremse f ▷ vi

bremsen; **brake fluid** n Bremsflüssigkeit f; **brake light** n Bremslicht nt; **brake pedal** n Bremspedal nt
branch [brɑːntʃ] n (of tree) Ast m; (of family, subject) Zweig m; (of firm) Filiale f, Zweigstelle f; **branch off** vi (road) abzweigen
brand [brænd] n (Comm) Marke f
brand-new ['brænd'njuː] adj (funkel)nagelneu
brandy ['brændɪ] n Weinbrand m
brass [brɑːs] n Messing nt; (Brit fam: money) Knete f; **brass band** n Blaskapelle f
brat [bræt] n (pej, fam) Gör nt
brave [breɪv] adj tapfer, mutig; **bravery** ['breɪvərɪ] n Mut m
brawl [brɔːl] n Schlägerei f
brawn [brɔːn] n (strength) Muskelkraft f; (Gastr) Sülze f; **brawny** adj muskulös
Brazil [brə'zɪl] n Brasilien nt; **Brazilian** adj brasilianisch ▷ n Brasilianer(in) m(f); **brazil nut** n Paranuss f
bread [brɛd] n Brot m; **breadbin** (Brit), **breadbox** (US) n Brotkasten m; **breadcrumbs** npl Brotkrumen pl; (Gastr) Paniermehl nt; **breaded** adj paniert; **breadknife** n Brotmesser nt
breadth [brɛdθ] n Breite f
break [breɪk] n (fracture) Bruch m; (rest) Pause f; (short holiday) Kurzurlaub m; **give me a ~** gib mir eine Chance, hör auf damit! ▷ vt (**broke, broken**) (fracture) brechen; (in pieces) zerbrechen; (toy, device) kaputt machen; (promise) nicht halten; (silence) brechen; (law) verletzen; (journey) unterbrechen; (news) mitteilen (to sb jdm); **I broke my leg** ich habe mir das Bein gebrochen; **he broke it to her gently** er hat es ihr schonend beigebracht ▷ vi (come apart)

b

(auseinander)brechen; (in pieces) zerbrechen; (toy, device) kaputtgehen; (person) zusammenbrechen; (day, dawn) anbrechen; (news) bekannt werden; **break down** vi (car) eine Panne haben; (machine) versagen; (person) zusammenbrechen; **break in** vi (burglar) einbrechen; **break into** vt einbrechen in +akk; **break off** vi, vt abbrechen; **break out** vi ausbrechen; **to ~ in a rash** einen Ausschlag bekommen; **break up** vi aufbrechen; (meeting, organisation) sich auflösen; (marriage) in die Brüche gehen; (couple) sich trennen; **school breaks up on Friday** am Freitag beginnen die Ferien ▷ vt aufbrechen; (marriage) zerstören; (meeting) auflösen; **breakable** adj zerbrechlich; **breakage** n Bruch m; **breakdown** n (of car) Panne f; (of machine) Störung f; (of person, relations, system) Zusammenbruch m; **breakdown service** n Pannendienst m; **breakdown truck** n Abschleppwagen m

breakfast ['brɛkfəst] n Frühstück nt; **to have ~** frühstücken; **breakfast cereal** n Cornflakes, Muesli etc; **breakfast television** n Frühstücksfernsehen nt

break-in ['breɪkɪn] n Einbruch m; **breakup** ['breɪkʌp] n (of meeting, organisation) Auflösung f; (of marriage) Zerrüttung f

breast [brɛst] n Brust f; **breastfeed** vt stillen; **breaststroke** n Brustschwimmen nt

breath [brɛθ] n Atem m; **out of ~** außer Atem; **breathalyse, breathalyze** ['brɛθəlaɪz] vt (ins Röhrchen) blasen lassen; **breathalyser, breathalyzer** n Promillemesser m; **breathe** [briːð]

vt, vi atmen; **breathe in** vt, vi einatmen; **breathe out** vt, vi ausatmen; **breathless** ['brɛθlɪs] adj atemlos; **breathtaking** ['brɛθteɪkɪŋ] adj atemberaubend

bred [brɛd] pt, pp of **breed**

breed [briːd] n (race) Rasse f ▷ vi (bred, bred) sich vermehren ▷ vt züchten; **breeder** n Züchter(in) m(f); (fam) Hetero m; **breeding** n (of animals) Züchtung f; (of person) (gute) Erziehung f

breeze [briːz] n Brise f

brevity ['brɛvɪtɪ] n Kürze f

brew [bruː] vt (beer) brauen; (tea) kochen; **brewery** n Brauerei f

bribe ['braɪb] n Bestechungsgeld nt ▷ vt bestechen; **bribery** ['braɪbərɪ] n Bestechung f

brick [brɪk] n Backstein m; **bricklayer** n Maurer(in) m(f)

bride [braɪd] n Braut f; **bridegroom** n Bräutigam m; **bridesmaid** n Brautjungfer f

bridge [brɪdʒ] n Brücke f; (cards) Bridge nt

brief [briːf] adj kurz ▷ vt instruieren (on über +akk); **briefcase** n Aktentasche f; **briefs** npl Slip m

bright [braɪt] adj hell; (colour) leuchtend; (cheerful) heiter; (intelligent) intelligent; (idea) glänzend; **brighten up** vt aufhellen; (person) aufheitern ▷ vi sich aufheitern; (person) fröhlicher werden

brilliant ['brɪljənt] adj (sunshine, colour) strahlend; (person) brilliant; (idea) glänzend; (Brit fam) **it was ~** es war fantastisch

brim [brɪm] n Rand m

bring [brɪŋ] (brought, brought) vt bringen; (with one) mitbringen; **bring about** vt herbeiführen, bewirken; **bring back** vt zurückbringen; (memories) wecken; **bring down** vt (reduce)

senken; (*government etc*) zu Fall
bringen; **bring in** *vt*
hereinbringen; (*introduce*)
einführen; **bring out** *vt*
herausbringen; **bring round**,
bring to *vt* wieder zu sich
bringen; **bring up** *vt* (*child*)
aufziehen; (*question*) zur Sprache
bringen
brisk [brɪsk] *adj* (*trade*) lebhaft;
(*wind*) frisch
bristle ['brɪsl] *n* Borste *f*
Brit [brɪt] *n* (*fam*) Brite *m*, Britin *f*;
Britain ['brɪtn] *n* Großbritannien
nt; **British** ['brɪtɪʃ] *adj* britisch;
the ~ Isles (*pl*) die Britischen
Inseln *pl* ▷ *n* **the ~** (*pl*) die Briten *pl*
brittle ['brɪtl] *adj* spröde
broad [brɔːd] *adj* breit; (*accent*)
stark; **in ~ daylight** am helllichten
Tag ▷ (*US fam*) Frau *f*
B road ['biːrəʊd] *n* (*Brit*) =
Landstraße *f*
broadcast ['brɔːdkɑːst] *n*
Sendung *f* ▷ *irr vt, vi* (*radio*)
(*event*) übertragen
broaden ['brɔːdn] *vt*: **to ~ the
mind** den Horizont erweitern;
broad-minded *adj* tolerant
broccoli ['brɒkəlɪ] *n* Brokkoli *pl*
brochure ['brəʊʃjʊə°] *n* Prospekt
m, Broschüre *f*
broke [brəʊk] *pt of* **break** ▷ *adj*
(*Brit fam*) pleite; **broken**
['brəʊkən] *pp of* **break**;
broken-hearted *adj* untröstlich
broker ['brəʊkə°] *n* Makler(in)
m(f)
brolly ['brɒlɪ] *n* (*Brit*) Schirm *m*
bronchitis [brɒŋ'kaɪtɪs] *n*
Bronchitis *f*
bronze [brɒnz] *n* Bronze *f*
brooch [brəʊtʃ] *n* Brosche *f*
broom [bruːm] *n* Besen *m*
Bros [brɒs] *abbr* = **brothers** Gebr.
broth [brɒθ] *n* Fleischbrühe *f*
brothel ['brɒθl] *n* Bordell *nt*

brother ['brʌðə°] *n* Bruder *m*; **~s**
(*pl*) (*Comm*) Gebrüder *pl*; **brother-
in-law** (*pl* **brothers-in-law**) *n*
Schwager *m*
brought [brɔːt] *pt, pp of* **bring**
brow [braʊ] *n* (*eyebrow*)
(Augen)braue *f*; (*forehead*) Stirn *f*
brown [braʊn] *adj* braun; **brown
bread** *n* Mischbrot *nt*; (*wholemeal*)
Vollkornbrot *nt*; **brownie**
['braʊnɪ] *n* (*Gastr*) Brownie *m*;
(*Brit*) junge Pfadfinderin; **brown
paper** *n* Packpapier *nt*; **brown
rice** *n* Naturreis *m*; **brown sugar**
n brauner Zucker
browse [braʊz] *vi* (*in book*)
blättern; (*in shop*) schmökern,
herumschauen; **browser** *n*
(*Inform*) Browser *m*
bruise [bruːz] *n* blauer Fleck
▷ *vt*: **to ~ one's arm** sich *dat* einen
blauen Fleck am (Arm) holen
brunette [bruː'net] *n* Brünette
f
brush [brʌʃ] *n* Bürste *f*; (*for
sweeping*) Handbesen *m*; (*for
painting*) Pinsel *m* ▷ *vt* bürsten;
(*sweep*) fegen; **to ~ one's teeth**
sich *dat* die Zähne putzen; **brush
up** *vt* (*French etc*) auffrischen
Brussels sprouts
[brʌsl'spraʊts] *npl* Rosenkohl *m*,
Kohlsprossen *pl*
brutal ['bruːtl] *adj* brutal;
brutality [bruː'tælɪtɪ] *n* Bru-
talität *f*
BSE *abbr* = **bovine spongiform
encephalopathy** BSE *f*
bubble ['bʌbl] *n* Blase *f*; **bubble
bath** *n* Schaumbad *nt*,
Badeschaum *m*; **bubbly** ['bʌblɪ]
adj sprudelnd; (*person*)
temperamentvoll ▷ *n* (*fam*)
Schampus *m*
buck [bʌk] *n* (*animal*) Bock *m*; (*US
fam*) Dollar *m*
bucket ['bʌkɪt] *n* Eimer *m*

BUCKINGHAM PALACE

Der **Buckingham Palace** ist die offizielle Londoner Residenz der britischen Monarchen und liegt am St James's Park. Der Palast wurde 1703 für den Herzog von Buckingham erbaut, 1762 von George III gekauft, zwischen 1821 und 1836 von John Nash umgebaut und Anfang des 20. Jahrhunderts teilweise neu gestaltet. Teile des Buckingham Palace sind heute der Öffentlichkeit zugänglich.

buckle ['bʌkl] n Schnalle f ▷ vi (Tech) sich verbiegen ▷ vt zuschnallen

bud [bʌd] n Knospe f

Buddhism ['budɪzəm] n Buddhismus m; **Buddhist** adj buddhistisch ▷ n Buddhist(in) m(f)

buddy ['bʌdɪ] n (fam) Kumpel m

budget ['bʌdʒɪt] n Budget nt ▷ adj preisgünstig; **budget airline** n Billigflieger m

budgie ['bʌdʒɪ] n Wellensittich m

buff [bʌf] adj (US) muskulös; **in the ~** nackt ▷ n (enthusiast) Fan m

buffalo ['bʌfələʊ] (pl -es) n Büffel m

buffer ['bʌfəˀ] n (a. Inform) Puffer m

buffet ['bʊfeɪ] n (food) (kaltes) Büfett nt

bug [bʌg] n (Inform) Bug m, Programmfehler m; (listening device) Wanze f; (US: insect) Insekt nt; (fam: illness) Infektion f ▷ vt (fam) nerven

bugger ['bʌgəˀ] n (vulg) Scheißkerl m ▷ interj (vulg) Scheiße f; **bugger off** vi (vulg) abhauen, Leine ziehen

buggy® ['bʌgɪ] n (for baby) Buggy® m

build [bɪld] (**built, built**) vt bauen; **build up** vt aufbauen; **builder** n Bauunternehmer(in) m(f); **building** n Gebäude nt; **building site** n Baustelle f; **building society** n Bausparkasse f

built pt, pp of **build**; **built-in** adj (cupboard) Einbau-, eingebaut

bulb n (Bot) (Blumen)zwiebel f; (Elec) Glühbirne f

Bulgaria [bʌlˈgeərɪə] n Bulgarien nt; **Bulgarian** adj bulgarisch ▷ n (person) Bulgare m, Bulgarin f; (language) Bulgarisch nt

bulimia [bəˈlɪmɪə] n Bulimie f

bulk [bʌlk] n (size) Größe f; (greater part) Großteil m (of +gen); **in ~** en gros; **bulky** adj (goods) sperrig; (person) stämmig

bull [bʊl] n Stier m; **bulldog** n Bulldogge f; **bulldoze** ['bʊldəʊz] vt planieren; **bulldozer** n Planierraupe f

bullet ['bʊlɪt] n Kugel f

bulletin ['bʊlɪtɪn] n Bulletin nt; (announcement) Bekanntmachung f; (Med) Krankenbericht m; **bulletin board** n (US: Inform) schwarzes Brett

bullfight ['bʊlfaɪt] n Stierkampf m; **bullshit** n (fam) Scheiß m

bully ['bʊlɪ] n Tyrann m

bum [bʌm] n (Brit fam: backside) Po m; (US: vagrant) Penner m; (worthless person) Rumtreiber m; **bum around** vi herumgammeln

bumblebee ['bʌmblbiː] n Hummel f

bumf [bʌmf] (fam) n Infomaterial nt, Papierkram m

bump [bʌmp] n (Med: swelling) Beule f; (road) Unebenheit f; (blow) Stoß m ▷ vt stoßen; **to ~ one's head** sich dat den Kopf anschlagen (on an +dat); **bump into** vt stoßen gegen; (fam: meet)

(zufällig) begegnen +dat; **bumper**
n (Auto) Stoßstange f ▷ adj
(edition etc) Riesen-; (crop etc)
Rekord-; **bumpy** ['bʌmpɪ] adj
holp(e)rig

bun [bʌn] n süßes Brötchen nt

bunch [bʌntʃ] n (of flowers)
Strauß m; (fam: of people) Haufen m;
~ of keys Schlüsselbund m; **~ of
grapes** Weintraube f

bundle ['bʌndl] n Bündel nt

bungalow ['bʌŋɡələʊ] n Bungalow m

bungee jumping ['bʌndʒɪ-
dʒʌmpɪŋ] n Bungeejumping nt

bunk [bʌŋk] n Koje f; **bunk
bed(s)** n(pl) Etagenbett nt

bunker ['bʌŋkə°] n (Mil) Bunker
m

bunny ['bʌnɪ] n Häschen nt

buoy [bɔɪ] n Boje f; **buoyant**
['bɔɪənt] adj (floating)
schwimmend

BUPA ['buːpə] abbr (Brit) private
Krankenkasse

burden ['bɜːdn] n Last f

bureau ['bjuːrəʊ] n Büro nt;
(government department) Amt nt;
bureaucracy [bjʊˈrɒkrəsɪ] n
Bürokratie f; **bureaucratic**
[bjuːrəˈkrætɪk] adj bürokratisch;
bureau de change ['bjuːrəʊ də
ˈʃɑːnʒ] n Wechselstube f

burger ['bɜːɡə°] n Hamburger m

burglar ['bɜːɡlə°] n Einbre-
cher(in) m(f); **burglar alarm** n
Alarmanlage f; **burglarize** vt (US)
einbrechen in +akk; **burglary** n
Einbruch m; **burgle** ['bɜːɡl] vt
einbrechen in +akk

burial ['berɪəl] n Beerdigung f

burn [bɜːn] (burnt o **burned,
burnt** o **burned**) vt verbrennen;
(food, slightly) anbrennen; **to
~ one's hand** sich auf die Hand
verbrennen ▷ vi brennen ▷ n
(injury) Brandwunde f; (on material)

verbrannte Stelle; **burn down** vt,
vi abbrennen

burp [bɜːp] vi rülpsen ▷ vt (baby)
aufstoßen lassen

bursary ['bɜːsərɪ] n Stipendium nt

burst [bɜːst] (burst, burst) vt
platzen lassen ▷ vi platzen;
to ~ into tears in Tränen
ausbrechen

bury ['berɪ] vt begraben; (in grave)
beerdigen; (hide) vergraben

bus [bʌs] n Bus m; **bus driver** n
Busfahrer(in) m(f)

bush [bʊʃ] n Busch m

business ['bɪznɪs] n Geschäft nt;
(enterprise) Unternehmen nt;
(concern, affair) Sache f; **I'm here on
~** ich bin geschäftlich hier; **it's
none of your ~** das geht dich
nichts an; **business card** n
Visitenkarte f; **business class** n
(Aviat) Businessclass f;
businessman (pl **-men**) n
Geschäftsmann m; **business
studies** npl Betriebswirtschafts-
lehre f; **businesswoman** (pl
-women) n Geschäftsfrau f

bus service n Busverbindung f;
bus shelter n Wartehäuschen nt;
bus station n Busbahnhof m; **bus
stop** n Bushaltestelle f

bust [bʌst] n Büste f ▷ adj
(broken) kaputt; **to go ~** Pleite
gehen; **bust-up** n (fam) Krach m

busy ['bɪzɪ] adj beschäftigt;
(street, place) belebt; (esp US:
telephone) besetzt; **~ signal** (US)
Besetztzeichen nt

⭕ **KEYWORD**

but [bʌt, bət] conj 1 (yet) aber; **not
X but Y** nicht X sondern Y

2 (however) **I'd love to come, but
I'm busy** ich würde gern kommen,
bin aber beschäftigt

3 (showing disagreement, surprise etc)

but that's fantastic! (aber) das ist
ja fantastisch!
▷ prep (apart from, except): **nothing
but trouble** nichts als Ärger;
no-one but him can do it
niemand außer ihm kann es
machen; **but for you/your help**
ohne dich/deine Hilfe; **anything
but that** alles, nur das nicht
▷ adv (just, only) **she's but a child**
sie ist noch ein Kind; **had I but
known** wenn ich es nur gewusst
hätte; **I can but try** ich kann es
immerhin versuchen; **all but
finished** so gut wie fertig

butcher ['bʊtʃəʳ] n Fleischer(in)
m(f), Metzger(in) m(f)
butler ['bʌtləʳ] n Butler m
butt [bʌt] (US fam) n Hintern m
butter ['bʌtəʳ] n Butter f ▷ vt
buttern; **buttercup** n
Butterblume f; **butterfly** n
Schmetterling m
buttocks ['bʌtəks] npl Gesäß nt
button ['bʌtn] n Knopf m; (badge)
Button m ▷ vt zuknöpfen;
buttonhole n Knopfloch nt
buy [baɪ] n Kauf m ▷ vt (bought,
bought) kaufen (from von); **he
bought me a ring** er hat mir einen
Ring gekauft; **buyer** n Käufer(in)
m(f)
buzz [bʌz] n Summen nt; **to give
sb a ~** (fam) jdn anrufen ▷ vi
summen; **buzzer** ['bʌzəʳ] n
Summer m; **buzz word** n (fam)
Modewort nt

○ **KEYWORD**

by [baɪ] prep 1 (referring to cause,
agent) von, durch; **killed by
lightning** vom Blitz getötet; **a
painting by Picasso** ein Gemälde
von Picasso
2 (referring to method, manner) **by**

bus/car/train mit dem
Bus/Auto/Zug; **to pay by cheque**
per Scheck bezahlen; **by
moonlight** bei Mondschein; **by
saving hard, he ...** indem er
eisern sparte, ... er ...
3 (via, through) über +akk; **he came
in by the back door** er kam durch
die Hintertür herein
4 (close to, past) bei, an +dat; **a
holiday by the sea** im Urlaub am
Meer; **she rushed by me** sie eilte
an mir vorbei
5 (not later than) **by 4 o'clock** bis 4
Uhr; **by this time tomorrow**
morgen um diese Zeit; **by the
time I got here it was too late** als
ich hier ankam, war es zu spät
6 (during) **by day** bei Tag
7 (amount) **by the kilo/metre**
kiloweise/meterweise; **paid by
the hour** stundenweise bezahlt
8 (math, measure) **to divide by 3**
durch 3 teilen; **to multiply by 3**
mit 3 malnehmen; **a room 3
metres by 4** ein Zimmer 3 mal 4
Meter; **it's broader by a metre** es
ist (um) einen Meter breiter
9 (according to) nach; **it's all right
by me** von mir aus gern
10 (all) **by oneself** etc ganz allein
11 by the way übrigens
▷ adv 1 see go; pass etc
2 by and by irgendwann; (with
past tenses) nach einiger Zeit; **by
and large** (on the whole) im Großen
und Ganzen

bye-bye ['baɪ'baɪ] interj (fam)
Wiedersehen, tschüss
by-election n Nachwahl f;
bypass n Umgehungsstraße f;
(Med) Bypass m; **byproduct** n
Nebenprodukt nt; **byroad** n
Nebenstraße f; **bystander** n
Zuschauer(in) m(f)
byte [baɪt] n Byte nt

C

C [siː] n Celsius C

c abbr = circa ca

cab [kæb] n Taxi nt

cabbage ['kæbɪdʒ] n Kohl m

cabin ['kæbɪn] n (Naut) Kajüte f;
(Aviat) Passagierraum m; (wooden
house) Hütte f; **cabin crew** n
Flugbegleitpersonal nt; **cabin
cruiser** n Kajütboot nt

cabinet ['kæbɪnɪt] n Schrank m;
(for display) Vitrine f; (Pol) Kabinett
nt

cable ['keɪbl] n (Elec) Kabel nt;
cable-car n Seilbahn f; **cable
railway** n Drahtseilbahn f; **cable
television, cablevision** (US) n
Kabelfernsehen nt

cactus ['kæktəs] n Kaktus m

CAD abbr = **computer-aided
design** CAD nt

Caesarean [siː'zəərɪən] adj:
~ (section) Kaiserschnitt m

café ['kæfeɪ] n Café nt; **cafeteria**

[kæfɪ'tɪərɪə] n Cafeteria f;
cafetiere [kæfə'tjɛə°] n Kaf-
feebereiter m

cage [keɪdʒ] n Käfig m

Cairo ['kaɪərəʊ] n Kairo nt

cake [keɪk] n Kuchen m; **cake
shop** n Konditorei f

calamity [kə'læmɪtɪ] n Katastrophe f

calculate ['kælkjʊleɪt] vt
berechnen; (estimate) kalkulieren;
calculating adj berechnend;
calculation [kælkjʊ'leɪʃən] n
Berechnung f; (estimate)
Kalkulation f; **calculator**
['kælkjʊleɪtə°] n Taschenrechner
m

calendar ['kælɪndə°] n Kalender
m

calf [kɑːf] (pl **calves**) n Kalb nt;
(Anat) Wade f

California [kælɪ'fɔːnɪə] n Kali-
fornien nt

call [kɔːl] vt rufen; (name,
describe as) nennen; (Tel) anrufen;
(Inform, Aviat) aufrufen; **what's
this ~ed?** wie heißt das?; **that's
what I ~ service** das nenne ich
guten Service ▷ vi (shout) rufen
(for help um Hilfe); (visit)
vorbeikommen; **to ~ at the
doctor's** beim Arzt vorbeigehen;
(of train) halten ▷ n (shout) Ruf m; (Tel) Anruf; (Inform,
Aviat) Aufruf m; **to make a
~** telefonieren; **to give sb a ~** jdn
anrufen; **to be on
~** Bereitschaftsdienst haben; **call
back** vt, vi zurückrufen; **call for**
vt (come to pick up) abholen;
(demand, require) verlangen; **call off**
vt absagen

call centre n Callcenter nt; **caller**
n Besucher(in) m(f); (Tel)
Anrufer(in) m(f)

calm [kɑːm] n Stille f; (also of
person) Ruhe f; (of sea) Flaute f ▷ vt

beruhigen ▷ *adj* ruhig; **calm down** *vi* sich beruhigen
calorie ['kælərɪ] *n* Kalorie *f*
calves [kɑːvz] *pl of* **calf**
Cambodia [kæm'bəʊdɪə] *n* Kambodscha *nt*
camcorder ['kæmkɔːdə°] *n* Camcorder *m*
came [keɪm] *pt of* **come**
camel ['kæməl] *n* Kamel *nt*
camera ['kæmərə] *n* Fotoapparat *m*, Kamera *f*; **camera phone** ['kæmərəfəʊn] *n* Fotohandy *nt*
camomile ['kæməmaɪl] *n* Kamille *f*
camouflage ['kæməflɑːʒ] *n* Tarnung *f*
camp [kæmp] *n* Lager *nt*; (*camping place*) Zeltplatz *m* ▷ *vi* zelten, campen ▷ *adj* (*fam*) theatralisch, tuntig
campaign [kæm'peɪn] *n* Kampagne *f*; (*Pol*) Wahlkampf *m* ▷ *vi* sich einsetzen (*for/against* für/gegen)
campbed ['kæmpbed] *n* Campingliege *f*; **camper** ['kæmpə°] *n* (*person*) Camper(in) *m(f)*; (*van*) Wohnmobil *nt*; **camping** ['kæmpɪŋ] *n* Zelten *nt*, Camping *nt*; **campsite** ['kæmpsaɪt] *n* Zeltplatz *m*, Campingplatz *m*
campus ['kæmpəs] *n* (*of university*) Universitätsgelände *nt*, Campus *m*

○ **KEYWORD**

can [kæn] (*negative* **cannot, can't**, *conditional* **could**) *vb aux* 1 (*be able to, know how to*) können; **I can see you tomorrow, if you like** ich könnte Sie morgen sehen, wenn Sie wollen; **I can swim** ich kann schwimmen; **can you speak German?** sprechen Sie Deutsch?

2 (*may*) können, dürfen; **could I have a word with you?** könnte ich Sie kurz sprechen?

Canada ['kænədə] *n* Kanada *nt*; **Canadian** [kə'neɪdjən] *adj* kanadisch ▷ *n* Kanadier(in) *m(f)*
canal [kə'næl] *n* Kanal *m*
canary [kə'neərɪ] *n* Kanarienvogel *m*
cancel ['kænsəl] *vt* (*plans*) aufgeben; (*meeting, event*) absagen; (*Comm: order etc*) stornieren; (*contract*) kündigen; (*Inform*) löschen; (*Aviat: flight*) streichen; **to be ~led** (*event, train, bus*) ausfallen; **cancellation** [kænsə'leɪʃən] *n* Absage *f*; (*Comm*) Stornierung *f*; (*Aviat*) gestrichener Flug
cancer ['kænsə°] *n* (*Med*) Krebs *m*; **Cancer** *n* (*Astr*) Krebs *m*
candid ['kændɪd] *adj* (*person, conversation*) offen
candidate ['kændɪdət] *n* (*for post*) Bewerber(in) *m(f)*; (*Pol*) Kandidat(in) *m(f)*
candle ['kændl] *n* Kerze *f*; **candlelight** ['kændllaɪt] *n* Kerzenlicht *nt*; **candlestick** ['kændlstɪk] *n* Kerzenhalter *m*
candy ['kændɪ] *n* (*US*) Bonbon *nt*; (*quantity*) Süßigkeiten *pl*; **candy-floss** (*Brit*) Zuckerwatte *f*
cane [keɪn] *n* Rohr *nt*; (*stick*) Stock *m*
cannabis ['kænəbɪs] *n* Cannabis *m*
canned [kænd] *adj* Dosen-
cannot ['kænɒt] *contr of* **can not**
canny ['kænɪ] *adj* (*shrewd*) schlau
canoe [kə'nuː] *n* Kanu *nt*, **canoeing** *n* Kanufahren *nt*
can opener ['kænəʊpnə°] *n* Dosenöffner *m*
canopy ['kænəpɪ] *n* Baldachin *m*; (*awning*) Markise *f*; (*over entrance*) Vordach *nt*

can't [kɑːnt] *contr of* **can not**

canteen [kænˈtiːn] *n* (*in factory*) Kantine *f*; (*in university*) Mensa *f*

canvas [ˈkænvəs] *n* (*for sails, shoes*) Segeltuch *nt*; (*for tent*) Zeltstoff *m*; (*for painting*) Leinwand *f*

canvass [ˈkænvəs] *vi um* Stimmen werben (*for für*)

canyon [ˈkænjən] *n* Felsenschlucht *f*; **canyoning** [ˈkænjənɪŋ] *n* Canyoning *nt*

cap [kæp] *n* Mütze *f*; (*lid*) Verschluss *m*, Deckel *m*

capability [keɪpəˈbɪlɪtɪ] *n* Fähigkeit *f*; **capable** [ˈkeɪpəbl] *adj* fähig; **to be ~ of sth** zu etw fähig (o imstande) sein; **to be ~ of doing sth** etw tun können

capacity [kəˈpæsɪtɪ] *n* (*of building, container*) Fassungsvermögen *nt*; (*ability*) Fähigkeit *f*; (*function*) **in his ~ as ...** in seiner Eigenschaft als ...

cape [keɪp] *n* (*garment*) Cape *nt*, Umhang *m*; (*Geo*) Kap *nt*

caper [ˈkeɪpə³] *n* (*for cooking*) Kaper *f*

capital [ˈkæpɪtl] *n* (*Fin*) Kapital *nt*; (*letter*) Großbuchstabe *m*; **~ (city)** Hauptstadt *f*; **capitalism** *n* Kapitalismus *m*; **capital punishment** *n* die Todesstrafe

Capricorn [ˈkæprɪkɔːn] *n* (*Astr*) Steinbock *m*

capsize [kæpˈsaɪz] *vi* kentern

capsule [ˈkæpsjuːl] *n* Kapsel *f*

captain [ˈkæptɪn] *n* Kapitän *m*; (*army*) Hauptmann *m*

caption [ˈkæpʃən] *n* Bildunterschrift *f*

captive [ˈkæptɪv] *n* Gefangene(r) *mf*; **capture** [ˈkæptʃə³] *vt* (*person*) fassen, gefangen nehmen; (*town etc*) einnehmen; (*Inform: data*) erfassen ▷ *n* Gefangennahme *f*; (*Inform*) Erfassung *f*

car [kɑː³] *n* Auto *nt*; (*US Rail*)

Wagen *m*

carafe [kəˈræf] *n* Karaffe *f*

caramel [ˈkærəmel] *n* Karamelle *f*

caravan [ˈkærəvæn] *n* Wohnwagen *m*; **caravan site** *n* Campingplatz *m* für Wohnwagen

caraway (seed) [ˈkærəweɪ] *n* Kümmel *m*

carbohydrate [kɑːbəʊˈhaɪdreɪt] *n* Kohle(n)hydrat *nt*

car bomb *n* Autobombe *f*

carbon [ˈkɑːbən] *n* Kohlenstoff *m*; **carbon footprint** *n* ökologischer Fußabdruck

car boot sale *n* auf einem Parkplatz stattfindender Flohmarkt

carburettor, carburetor (US) [ˈkɑːbjʊretə³] *n* Vergaser *m*

card [kɑːd] *n* Karte *f*; (*material*) Pappe *f*; **cardboard** *n* Pappe *f*; **~ (box)** Karton *m* (*smaller*) Pappschachtel *f*; **card game** *n* Kartenspiel *nt*

cardigan [ˈkɑːdɪgən] *n* Strickjacke *f*

card index *n* Kartei *f*; **cardphone** [ˈkɑːdfəʊn] *n* Kartentelefon *nt*

care [keə³] *n* (*worry*) Sorge *f*; (*carefulness*) Sorgfalt *f*; (*looking after things, people*) Pflege *f*; **with ~** sorgfältig; (*cautiously*) vorsichtig; **to take ~** (*watch out*) vorsichtig sein; (*in address*) **~ of** bei; **to take ~ of** sorgen für, sich kümmern um ▷ *vi*: **I don't ~** es ist mir egal; **to ~ about sth** Wert auf etw akk legen; **he ~s about her** sie liegt ihm am Herzen; **care for** *vt* (*look after*) sorgen für, sich kümmern um; (*like*) mögen

career [kəˈrɪə³] *n* Karriere *f*, Laufbahn *f*; **career woman** (*pl* **women**) *n* Karrierefrau *f*; **careers adviser** *n* Berufsberater(in) *m(f)*

carefree [ˈkeəfriː] *adj* sorgenfrei; **careful, carefully** *adj*, *adv* sorgfältig; (*cautious, cautiously*)

vorsichtig; **careless, carelessly**
adj, adv nachlässig; *(driving etc)*
leichtsinnig; *(remark)*
unvorsichtig; **carer** ['kɛərə°] *n*
Betreuer(in) *m(f)*, Pfleger(in) *m(f)*;
caretaker ['kɛəteɪkə°] *n* Haus-
meister(in) *m(f)*; **careworker** *n*
Pfleger(in) *m(f)*
car-ferry ['ka:fɛri] *n* Autofähre *f*
cargo ['ka:gəʊ] *(pl* -(**e**)**s**) *n*
Ladung *f*
car hire, car hire company *n*
Autovermietung *f*
Caribbean [kærɪ'bi:ən] *n* Karibik
f ▷ adj karibisch
caring ['kɛərɪŋ] *adj* mitfühlend;
(parent, partner) liebevoll; *(looking
after sb)* fürsorglich
car insurance *n*
Kraftfahrzeugversicherung *f*
carnation [ka:'neɪʃən] *n* Nelke *f*
carnival ['ka:nɪvəl] *n* Volksfest
nt; (before Lent) Karneval *m*
carol ['kærəl] *n* Weihnachtslied *nt*
carp [ka:p] *n (fish)* Karpfen *m*
car park *n* Parkplatz *m*;
(multi-storey car park) Parkhaus *nt*
carpenter ['ka:pəntə°] *n* Zim-
mermann *m*
carpet ['ka:pɪt] *n* Teppich *m*
car phone *n* Autotelefon *nt*;
carpool *n* Fahrgemeinschaft *f*;
(vehicles) Fuhrpark *m ▷ vi* eine
Fahrgemeinschaft bilden; **car
rental** *n* Autovermietung *f*
carriage ['kærɪdʒ] *n (Brit Rail:
coach)* Wagen *m; (compartment)*
Abteil *nt; (horse-drawn)* Kutsche *f;
(transport)* Beförderung *f*;
carriageway *n (Brit: on road)*
Fahrbahn *f*
carrier ['kærɪə°] *n (Comm)*
Spediteur(in) *m(f)*; **carrier bag** *n*
Tragetasche *f*
carrot ['kærət] *n* Karotte *f*
carry ['kæri] *vt* tragen; *(in vehicle)*
befördern; *(have on one)* bei sich

haben; **carry on** *vi (continue)*
weitermachen; *(fam: make a scene)*
ein Theater machen *▷ vt
(continue)* fortführen; **to ~ on
working** weiter arbeiten; **carry
out** *vt (orders, plan)* ausführen,
durchführen
carrycot *n* Babytragetasche *f*
carsick ['ka:sɪk] *adj:* **he gets
~** ihm wird beim Autofahren übel
cart [ka:t] *n* Wagen *m*, Karren *m;
(US: shopping trolley)*
Einkaufswagen *m*
carton ['ka:tən] *n (Papp)*karton
m; (of cigarettes) Stange *f*
cartoon [ka:'tu:n] *n* Cartoon *m o
nt; (one drawing)* Karikatur *f; (film)*
(Zeichen)trickfilm *m*
cartridge ['ka:trɪdʒ] *n (for film)*
Kassette *f; (for gun, pen, printer)*
Patrone *f; (for copier)* Kartusche *f*
carve [ka:v] *vt, vi (wood)*
schnitzen; *(stone)* meißeln; *(meat)*
schneiden, tranchieren; **carving** *n
(in wood)* Schnitzerei *f; (in stone)*
Skulptur *f;* (Ski) Carving *nt*
car wash *n* Autowaschanlage *f*
case [keɪs] *n (crate)* Kiste *f; (box)*
Schachtel *f; (for jewels)* Schatulle *f;
(for spectacles)* Etui *nt; (Jur, matter)*
Fall *m;* **in ~** falls; **in that ~** in dem
Fall; **in ~ of fire** bei Brand; **it's a
~ of ...** es handelt sich hier um ...
cash [kæʃ] *n* Bargeld *nt;* **in ~** bar;
~ on delivery per Nachnahme
▷ vt (cheque) einlösen; **cash desk**
n Kasse *f;* **cash dispenser** *n*
Geldautomat *m;* **cashier** [kæ'ʃɪə°]
n Kassierer(in) *m(f)*; **cash
machine** *n (Brit)* Geldautomat *m*
cashmere ['kæʃmɪə°] *n* Kasch-
mirwolle *f*
cash payment *n* Barzahlung *f;*
cashpoint *n (Brit)* Geldautomat *m*
casing ['keɪsɪŋ] *n* Gehäuse *nt*
casino [kə'si:nəʊ] *(pl* -**s**) *n*
Kasino *nt*

cask [kɑːsk] n Fass nt

casserole ['kæsərəʊl] n Kasserole f; (food) Schmortopf m

cassette [kæ'set] n Kassette f; **cassette recorder** n Kassettenrekorder m

cast [kɑːst] (vb: **cast, cast**) vt (throw) werfen; (Theat, Cine) besetzen; (roles) verteilen ▷ n (Theat, Cine) Besetzung f; (Med) Gipsverband m; **cast off** vi (Naut) losmachen

caster ['kɑːstə°] n: ~ **sugar** Streuzucker m

castle ['kɑːsl] n Burg f

castrate [kæs'treɪt] vt kastrieren

casual ['kæʒjʊəl] adj (arrangement, remark) beiläufig; (attitude, manner) (nach)lässig, zwanglos; (dress) leger; (work, earnings) Gelegenheits-; (look, glance) flüchtig; ~ **wear** Freizeitkleidung f; ~ **sex** Gelegenheitssex m; **casually** adv (remark, say) beiläufig; (meet) zwanglos; (dressed) leger

casualty ['kæʒjʊəltɪ] n Verletzte(r) mf; (dead) Tote(r) mf; (department in hospital) Notaufnahme f

cat [kæt] n Katze f; (male) Kater m

catalog (US), **catalogue** ['kætəlɒg] n Katalog m ▷ vt katalogisieren

cataract ['kætərækt] n Wasserfall m; (Med) grauer Star

catarrh [kə'tɑː] n Katarr(h) m

catastrophe [kə'tæstrəfi] n Katastrophe f

catch [kætʃ] n (fish etc) Fang m ▷ vt (caught, caught) fangen; (thief) fassen; (train, bus etc) nehmen; (not miss) erreichen; to ~ **a cold** sich erkälten; to ~ **fire** Feuer fangen; **I didn't ~ that** das habe ich nicht verstanden; **catch on** vi (become popular) Anklang finden; **catch up** vt, vi: to ~ **with**

sb jdn einholen; to ~ **on sth** etw nachholen; **catching** adj ansteckend

category ['kætɪgərɪ] n Kategorie f

cater ['keɪtə°] vi die Speisen und Getränke liefern (for für); **cater for** vt (have facilities for) eingestellt sein auf +akk; **catering** n Versorgung f mit Speisen und Getränken, Gastronomie f; **catering service** n Partyservice m

caterpillar ['kætəpɪlə°] n Raupe f

cathedral [kə'θiːdrəl] n Kathedrale f, Dom m

Catholic ['kæθəlɪk] adj katholisch ▷ Katholik(in) m(f)

cat nap n (Brit) kurzer Schlaf; **cat's eyes** ['kætsaɪz] npl (in road) Katzenaugen pl, Reflektoren pl

catsup ['kætsəp] n (US) Ketschup nt o m

cattle ['kætl] npl Vieh nt

caught [kɔːt] pt, pp of **catch**

cauliflower ['kɒlɪflaʊə°] n Blumenkohl m; **cauliflower cheese** n Blumenkohl m in Käsesoße

cause [kɔːz] n (origin) Ursache f (of für); (reason) Grund m (for zu); (purpose) Sache f; **for a good** ~ für wohltätige Zwecke; **no ~ for alarm/complaint** kein Grund zur Aufregung/Klage ▷ vt verursachen

causeway ['kɔːzweɪ] n Damm m

caution ['kɔːʃən] n Vorsicht f; (Jur, Sport) Verwarnung f ▷ vt (ver)warnen; **cautious** ['kɔːʃəs] adj vorsichtig

cave [keɪv] n Höhle f; **cave in** vi einstürzen

cavity ['kævɪtɪ] n Hohlraum m; (in tooth) Loch nt

cayenne (pepper) [keɪ'en] n Cayennepfeffer m

CCTV *abbr* = **closed circuit television** Video-überwachungsanlage *f*

CD *abbr* = **Compact Disc** CD *f*; **CD player** *n* CD-Spieler *m*; **CD-ROM** *abbr* = **Compact Disc Read Only Memory** CD-ROM *f*; **CD-RW** *abbr* = **Compact Disc Rewritable** CD-RW *f*

cease [siːs] *vi* aufhören ▷ *vt* beenden; **to ~ doing sth** aufhören, etw zu tun; **cease fire** *n* Waffenstillstand *m*

ceiling ['siːlɪŋ] *n* Decke *f*

celebrate ['selɪbreɪt] *vt, vi* feiern; **celebrated** *adj* gefeiert; **celebration** [selɪ'breɪʃən] *n* Feier *f*; **celebrity** [sɪ'lebrɪtɪ] *n* Berühmtheit *f*, Star *m*

celeriac [sə'lerɪæk] *n* (Knollen)sellerie *m* of *f*; **celery** ['selərɪ] *n* (Stangen)sellerie *m* of *f*

cell [sel] *n* Zelle *f*; (US) see **cellphone**

cellar ['selə°] *n* Keller *m*

cello ['tʃeləʊ] (*pl* -**s**) *n* Cello *nt*

cellphone ['selfəʊn], **cellular phone** ['seljʊlə°fəʊn] *n* Mobiltelefon *nt*, Handy *nt*

Celt [kelt] *n* Kelte *m*, Keltin *f*; **Celtic** ['keltɪk] *adj* keltisch ▷ *n* (*language*) Keltisch *nt*

cement [sɪ'ment] *n* Zement *m*

cemetery ['semɪtrɪ] *n* Friedhof *m*

censorship ['sensəʃɪp] *n* Zensur *f*

cent [sent] *n* (*of dollar, euro etc*) Cent *m*

center *n* (US) see **centre**

centiliter (US), **centilitre** ['sentɪliːtə°] *n* Zentiliter *m*; **centimeter** (US), **centimetre** ['sentɪmiːtə°] *n* Zentimeter *m*

central ['sentrəl] *adj* zentral; **Central America** *n* Mittelamerika *nt*; **Central Europe** *n*

Mitteleuropa *nt*; **central heating** *n* Zentralheizung *f*; **centralize** *vt* zentralisieren; **central locking** *n* (Auto) Zentralverriegelung *f*; **central reservation** *n* (Brit) Mittelstreifen *m*; **central station** *n* Hauptbahnhof *m*

centre ['sentə°] *n* Mitte *f*; (*building, of city*) Zentrum *nt* ▷ *vt* zentrieren; **centre forward** *n* (Sport) Mittelstürmer *m*

century ['sentjʊrɪ] *n* Jahrhundert *nt*

ceramic [sɪ'ræmɪk] *adj* keramisch

cereal ['sɪərɪəl] *n* (*any grain*) Getreide *nt*; (*breakfast cereal*) Frühstücksflocken *pl*

ceremony ['serɪmənɪ] *n* Feier *f*, Zeremonie *f*

certain ['sɜːtən] *adj* sicher (*of +gen*); (*particular*) bestimmt; **for ~** mit Sicherheit; **certainly** *adv* sicher; (*without doubt*) bestimmt; **~!** aber sicher!; **~ not** ganz bestimmt nicht!

certificate [sə'tɪfɪkɪt] *n* Bescheinigung *f*; (*in school, of qualification*) Zeugnis *nt*; **certify** ['sɜːtɪfaɪ] *vt, vi* bescheinigen

cervical smear ['sɜːvɪkəl smɪə°] *n* Abstrich *m*

CFC *abbr* = **chlorofluorocarbon** FCKW *nt*

chain [tʃeɪn] *n* Kette *f* ▷ *vt*: **to ~ (up)** anketten; **chain reaction** *n* Kettenreaktion *f*; **chain store** *n* Kettenladen *m*

chair [tʃeə°] *n* Stuhl *m*; (*university*) Lehrstuhl *m*; (*armchair*) Sessel *m*; (*chairperson*) Vorsitzende(r) *mf*; **chairlift** *n* Sessellift *m*; **chairman** (*pl* -**men**) *n* Vorsitzende(r) *m*; (*of firm*) Präsident *m*; **chairperson** *n* Vorsitzende(r) *mf*; (*of firm*) Präsident(in) *m(f)*; **chairwoman**

(*pl* **-women**) *n* Vorsitzende *f*; (*of firm*) Präsidentin *f*

chalet ['ʃæleɪ] *n* (*in mountains*) Berghütte *f*; (*holiday dwelling*) Ferienhäuschen *nt*

chalk [tʃɔːk] *n* Kreide *f*

challenge ['tʃælɪndʒ] *n* Herausforderung *f* ▷ *vt* (*person*) herausfordern; (*statement*) bestreiten

chambermaid ['tʃeɪmbəˈmeɪd] *n* Zimmermädchen *nt*

chamois leather ['ʃæmwɑːˈleðə°] *n* (*for windows*) Fensterleder *nt*

champagne [ʃæm'peɪn] *n* Champagner *m*

champion ['tʃæmpɪən] *n* (*Sport*) Meister(in) *m(f)*; **championship** *n* Meisterschaft *f*

chance [tʃɑːns] *n* (*fate*) Zufall *m*; (*possibility*) Möglichkeit *f*; (*opportunity*) Gelegenheit *f*; (*risk*) Risiko *nt*; **by ~** zufällig; **he doesn't stand a ~** (*of winning*) er hat keinerlei Chance(, zu gewinnen)

chancellor ['tʃɑːnsələ°] *n* Kanzler(in) *m(f)*

chandelier [ʃændɪ'lɪə°] *n* Kronleuchter *m*

change [tʃeɪndʒ] *vt* verändern; (*alter*) ändern; (*money, wheel, nappy*) wechseln; (*exchange*) (um)tauschen; **to ~ one's clothes** sich umziehen; **to ~ trains** umsteigen; **to ~ gear** (*Auto*) schalten ▷ *vi* sich ändern; (*esp outwardly*) sich verändern; (*get changed*) sich umziehen ▷ *n* Veränderung *f*; (*alteration*) Änderung *f*; (*money*) Wechselgeld *nt*; (*coins*) Kleingeld *nt*; **for a ~** zur Abwechslung; **can you give me ~ for £10?** können Sie mir auf 10 Pfund herausgeben?; **change down** *vi* (*Brit Auto*) herunterschalten; **change over** *vi*

sich umstellen (*to auf +akk*); **change up** *vi* (*Brit Auto*) hochschalten

changeable *adj* (*weather*) veränderlich, wechselhaft; **change machine** *n* Geldwechsler *m*; **changing room** *n* Umkleideraum *m*

channel ['tʃænl] *n* Kanal *m*; (*Radio, TV*) Kanal *m*, Sender *m*; **the (English) Channel** der Ärmelkanal; **the Channel Islands** die Kanalinseln; **the Channel Tunnel** der Kanaltunnel; **channel-hopping** *n* Zappen *nt*

chaos ['keɪɒs] *n* Chaos *nt*; **chaotic** [keɪ'ɒtɪk] *adj* chaotisch

chap [tʃæp] *n* (*Brit fam*) Bursche *m*, Kerl *m*

chapel ['tʃæpəl] *n* Kapelle *f*

chapped ['tʃæpt] *adj* (*lips*) aufgesprungen

chapter ['tʃæptə°] *n* Kapitel *nt*

character ['kærəktə] *n* Charakter *m*, Wesen *nt*; (*in a play, novel etc*) Figur *f*; (*Typo*) Zeichen *nt*; **he's a real ~** er ist ein echtes Original; **characteristic** [kærəktə'rɪstɪk] *n* typisches Merkmal

charcoal ['tʃɑːkəʊl] *n* Holzkohle *f*

charge [tʃɑːdʒ] *n* (*cost*) Gebühr *f*; (*Jur*) Anklage *f*; **free of ~** gratis, kostenlos; **to be in ~ of** *vt* verantwortlich sein für *f* (*money*) verlangen; (*Jur*) anklagen; (*battery*) laden; **charge card** *n* Kundenkreditkarte *f*

charity ['tʃærɪtɪ] *n* (*institution*) wohltätige Organisation *f*; **a collection v** eine Sammlung für wohltätige Zwecke; **charity shop** *n* Geschäft einer 'charity', in dem freiwillige Helfer gebrauchte Kleidung, Bücher etc verkaufen

charm [tʃɑːm] *n* Charme *m* ▷ *vt* bezaubern; **charming** *adj* reizend, charmant

chart [tʃɑːt] n Diagramm nt; (map) Karte f; **the ~s** pl die Charts, die Hitliste

charter ['tʃɑːtə°] n Urkunde f
▷ vt (Naut, Aviat) chartern;
charter flight n Charterflug m

chase [tʃeɪs] vt jagen, verfolgen
▷ n Verfolgungsjagd f; (hunt) Jagd f

chassis ['ʃæsɪ] n (Auto) Fahrgestell nt

chat [tʃæt] vi plaudern; (Inform) chatten ▷ n Plauderei f; (Inform) Chat m; **chat up** vt anmachen, anbaggern; **chatroom** n (Inform) Chatroom m; **chat show** n Talkshow f; **chatty** adj geschwätzig

chauffeur ['ʃəʊfə°] n Chauffeur(in) m(f), Fahrer(in) m(f)

cheap [tʃiːp] adj billig; (of poor quality) minderwertig

cheat [tʃiːt] vt, vi betrügen; (in school, game) mogeln

Chechen ['tʃetʃen] adj tschetschenisch ▷ n Tschetschene m, Tschetschenin f; **Chechnya** n ['tʃetʃnɪə] n Tschetschenien nt

check [tʃek] vt (examine) überprüfen (for auf +akk); (Tech: adjustment etc) kontrollieren; (US: tick) abhaken; (Aviat: luggage) einchecken; (US: coat) abgeben ▷ n (examination, restraint) Kontrolle f; (US: restaurant bill) Rechnung f; (pattern) Karo(muster) nt; (US) see **cheque**; **check in** vi, vt (Aviat) einchecken; (into hotel) sich anmelden; **check out** vi sich abmelden, auschecken; **check up** vi nachprüfen; **to ~ on sb** Nachforschungen über jdn anstellen

checkers ['tʃekəz] nsing (US) Damespiel nt

check-in ['tʃekɪn] n (airport) Check-in m; (hotel) Anmeldung f; **check-in desk** n

Abfertigungsschalter m; **checking account** n (US) Scheckkonto nt; **check list** n Kontrollliste f; **checkout** n (supermarket) Kasse f; **checkout time** n (hotel) Abreise(zeit) f; **checkpoint** n Kontrollpunkt m; **checkroom** n (US) Gepäckaufbewahrung f; **checkup** n (Med) (ärztliche) Untersuchung

cheddar ['tʃedə°] n Cheddarkäse m

cheek [tʃiːk] n Backe f, Wange f; (insolence) Frechheit f; **what a ~** so eine Frechheit!; **cheekbone** n Backenknochen m; **cheeky** adj frech

cheer [tʃɪə°] n Beifallsruf m; **~s** (when drinking) prost!; (Brit fam: thanks) danke; (Brit: goodbye) tschüs ▷ vt zujubeln +dat ▷ vi jubeln; **cheer up** vt aufmuntern ▷ vi fröhlicher werden; **~!** Kopf hoch!; **cheerful** ['tʃɪəfʊl] adj fröhlich

cheese [tʃiːz] n Käse m; **cheeseboard** n Käsebrett nt; (as course) (gemischte) Käseplatte; **cheesecake** n Käsekuchen m

chef [ʃef] n Koch m; (in charge of kitchen) Küchenchef(in) m(f)

chemical ['kemɪkəl] adj chemisch ▷ Chemikalie f; **chemist** ['kemɪst] n (pharmacist) Apotheker(in) m(f); (industrial chemist) Chemiker(in) m(f); **~'s** (**shop**) Apotheke f; **chemistry** n Chemie f

cheque [tʃek] n (Brit) Scheck m; **cheque account** n (Brit) Girokonto nt; **cheque book** n (Brit) Scheckheft nt; **cheque card** n (Brit) Scheckkarte f

chequered ['tʃekəd] adj kariert

cherish ['tʃerɪʃ] vt (look after) liebevoll sorgen für; (hope) hegen; (memory) bewahren

cherry ['tʃerɪ] n Kirsche f; **cherry tomato** (pl **-es**) n Kirschtomate f

chess [tʃes] n Schach nt; **chessboard** n Schachbrett nt

chest [tʃest] n Brust f; (box) Kiste f; **~ of drawers** Kommode f

chestnut ['tʃesnʌt] n Kastanie f

chew [tʃuː] vt, vi kauen; **chewing gum** n Kaugummi m

chick [tʃɪk] n Küken nt; **chicken** n Huhn nt; (food: roast) Hähnchen nt; (coward) Feigling m; **chicken breast** n Hühnerbrust f; **chicken Kiev** n paniertes Hähnchen, mit Knoblauchbutter gefüllt; **chickenpox** n Windpocken pl; **chickpea** n Kichererbse f

chicory ['tʃɪkərɪ] n Chicorée f

chief [tʃiːf] n (of department etc) Leiter(in) m(f); (boss) Chef(in) m(f); (of tribe) Häuptling m ▷ adj Haupt-; **chiefly** adv hauptsächlich

child [tʃaɪld] n (pl **children**) n Kind nt; **child abuse** n Kindesmisshandlung f; **child allowance** n Kindergeld nt; **child benefit** (Brit) n Kindergeld nt; **childbirth** n Geburt f, Entbindung f; **childhood** n Kindheit f; **childish** adj kindisch; **child lock** n Kindersicherung f; **childproof** adj kindersicher; **children** ['tʃɪldrən] pl of **child**; **child seat** n Kindersitz m

Chile ['tʃɪlɪ] n Chile nt

chill [tʃɪl] n Kühle f; (Med) Erkältung f ▷ vt (wine) kühlen; **chill out** vi (fam) chillen, relaxen; **chilled** adj gekühlt

chilli ['tʃɪlɪ] n Pepperoni pl; (spice) Chili m; **chilli con carne** ['tʃɪlɪkɒn'kɑːnɪ] n Chili con carne nt

chilly ['tʃɪlɪ] adj kühl, frostig

chimney ['tʃɪmnɪ] n Schornstein m; **chimneysweep** n Schornsteinfeger(in) m(f)

chimpanzee [tʃɪmpæn'ziː] n Schimpanse m

chin [tʃɪn] n Kinn nt

china ['tʃaɪnə] n Porzellan nt

China ['tʃaɪnə] n China nt; **Chinese** [tʃaɪ'niːz] adj chinesisch ▷ n (person) Chinese m, Chinesin f; (language) Chinesisch nt; **Chinese leaves** npl Chinakohl m

chip [tʃɪp] n (of wood etc) Splitter m; (damage) angeschlagene Stelle; (Inform) Chip m; **~s** (Brit: potatoes) Pommes (frites) pl; (US: crisps) Kartoffelchips pl ▷ vt anschlagen, beschädigen; **chippie** (fam), **chip shop** n Frittenbude f

chiropodist [kɪ'rɒpədɪst] n Fußpfleger(in) m(f)

chirp [tʃɜːp] vi zwitschern

chisel ['tʃɪzl] n Meißel m

chitchat ['tʃɪttʃæt] n Gerede nt

chives [tʃaɪvz] npl Schnittlauch m

chlorine ['klɔːriːn] n Chlor nt

chocaholic, **chocoholic** ['tʃɒkəhɒlɪk] n Schokoladenfreak m; **choc-ice** ['tʃɒkaɪs] n Eis nt mit Schokoladenüberzug; **chocolate** ['tʃɒklɪt] n Schokolade f; (chocolate-coated sweet) Praline f; **a bar of ~** eine Tafel Schokolade; **a box of ~s** eine Schachtel Pralinen; **chocolate cake** n Schokoladenkuchen m; **chocolate sauce** n Schokoladensoße f

choice [tʃɔɪs] n Wahl f; (selection) Auswahl f ▷ adj auserlesen; (product) Qualitäts-

choir ['kwaɪə°] n Chor m

choke [tʃəʊk] vi sich verschlucken; (Sport) die Nerven verlieren ▷ vt erdrosseln ▷ n (Auto) Choke m

cholera ['kɒlərə] n Cholera f
cholesterol [kə'lestərəl] n Cholesterin nt
choose [tʃuːz] (**chose, chosen**) vt wählen; (pick out) sich aussuchen; **there are three to ~ from** es stehen drei zur Auswahl
chop [tʃɒp] vt (zer)hacken; (meat etc) klein schneiden ▷ n (meat) Kotelett nt; **to get the ~** gefeuert werden; **chopper** n Hackbeil nt; (fam: helicopter) Hubschrauber m; **chopsticks** npl Essstäbchen pl
chorus ['kɔːrəs] n Chor m; (in song) Refrain m
chose, chosen [tʃəʊz, 'tʃəʊzn] pt, pp of **choose**
chowder ['tʃaʊdə°] n (US) dicke Suppe mit Meeresfrüchten
christen ['krɪsn] vt taufen; **christening** n Taufe f; **Christian** ['krɪstɪən] adj christlich ▷ n Christ(in) m(f); **Christian name** n (Brit) Vorname m
Christmas ['krɪsməs] n Weihnachten pl; **Christmas bonus** n Weihnachtsgeld nt; **Christmas card** n Weihnachtskarte f; **Christmas carol** n Weihnachtslied nt; **Christmas Day** n der erste Weihnachtstag; **Christmas Eve** n Heiligabend m; **Christmas pudding** n Plumpudding m; **Christmas tree** n Weihnachtsbaum m
chronic ['krɒnɪk] adj (Med, fig) chronisch; (fam: very bad) miserabel
chrysanthemum [krɪ'sænθɪməm] n Chrysantheme f
chubby ['tʃʌbɪ] adj (child) pummelig; (adult) rundlich
chuck [tʃʌk] vt (fam) schmeißen; **chuck in** vt (fam: job) hinschmeißen; **chuck out** vt

(fam) rausschmeißen; **chuck up** vi (fam) kotzen
chunk [tʃʌŋk] n Klumpen m; (of bread) Brocken m; (of meat) Batzen m; **chunky** adj (person) stämmig
Chunnel ['tʃʌnəl] n (fam) Kanaltunnel m
church [tʃɜːtʃ] n Kirche f; **churchyard** n Kirchhof m
chute [ʃuːt] n Rutsche f
chutney ['tʃʌtnɪ] n Chutney m
CIA abbr = **Central Intelligence Agency** (US) CIA f
CID abbr = **Criminal Investigation Department** (Brit) ≈ Kripo f
cider ['saɪdə°] n ≈ Apfelmost m
cigar [sɪ'gɑː°] n Zigarre f
cigarette [sɪgə'ret] n Zigarette f
cinema ['sɪnəmə] n Kino nt
cinnamon ['sɪnəmən] n Zimt m
circle ['sɜːkl] n Kreis m ▷ vi kreisen; **circuit** ['sɜːkɪt] n Rundfahrt f; (on foot) Rundgang m; (for racing) Rennstrecke f; (Elec) Stromkreis m; **circular** ['sɜːkjʊlə°] adj (kreis)rund, kreisförmig ▷ n Rundschreiben nt; **circulation** [sɜːkjʊ'leɪʃən] n (of blood) Kreislauf m; (of newspaper) Auflage f
circumstances ['sɜːkəmstənsəz] npl (facts) Umstände pl; (financial condition) Verhältnisse pl; **in/under the ~** unter den Umständen; **under no ~** auf keinen Fall
circus ['sɜːkəs] n Zirkus m
cissy ['sɪsɪ] n (fam) Weichling m
cistern ['sɪstən] n Zisterne f; (of WC) Spülkasten m
citizen ['sɪtɪzn] n Bürger(in) m(f); (of nation) Staatsangehörige(r) mf; **citizenship** n Staatsangehörigkeit f
city ['sɪtɪ] n Stadt f; (large) Großstadt f; **the ~** (London's financial centre) die (Londoner)

City; **city centre** n Innenstadt f, Zentrum nt
civil ['sɪvɪl] adj (of town) Bürger-; (of state) staatsbürgerlich; (not military) zivil; **civil ceremony** n standesamtliche Hochzeit; **civil engineering** n Hoch- und Tiefbau m, Bauingenieurwesen nt; **civilian** [sɪ'vɪljən] n Zivilist(in) m(f); **civilization** [sɪvɪlaɪ'zeɪʃn] n Zivilisation f, Kultur f; **civilized** ['sɪvɪlaɪzd] adj zivilisiert, kultiviert; **civil partnership** n eingetragene Partnerschaft; **civil rights** npl Bürgerrechte pl; **civil servant** n (Staats)beamte(r) m, (Staats)beamtin f; **civil service** n Staatsdienst m; **civil war** n Bürgerkrieg m
CJD abbr = **Creutzfeld-Jakob disease** Creutzfeld-Jakob-Krankheit f
cl abbr = **centilitre(s)** cl
claim [kleɪm] vt beanspruchen; (apply for) beantragen; (demand) fordern; (assert) behaupten (that dass) ▷ n (demand) Forderung f (for für); (right) Anspruch m (to auf +akk); **~ for damages** Schadenersatzforderung f; **to make** o **put in a ~** (insurance) Ansprüche geltend machen; **claimant** n Antragsteller(in) m(f)
clam [klæm] n Venusmuschel f; **clam chowder** n (US) dicke Muschelsuppe (mit Sellerie, Zwiebeln etc)
clap [klæp] vi (Beifall) klatschen
claret ['klærɪt] n roter Bordeaux(wein)
clarify ['klærɪfaɪ] vt klären
clarinet [klærɪ'net] n Klarinette f
clarity ['klærɪtɪ] n Klarheit f
clash [klæʃ] vi (physically) zusammenstoßen (with mit); (argue) sich auseinandersetzen (with mit); (fig: colours) sich beißen

▷ n Zusammenstoß m; (argument) Auseinandersetzung f
clasp [klɑːsp] n (on belt) Schnalle f
class [klɑːs] n Klasse f ▷ vt einordnen, einstufen
classic ['klæsɪk] adj (mistake, example etc) klassisch ▷ n Klassiker m; **classical** ['klæsɪkəl] adj (music, ballet etc) klassisch
classification [klæsɪfɪ'keɪʃn] n Klassifizierung f; **classify** ['klæsɪfaɪ] vt klassifizieren; **classified advertisement** n Kleinanzeige f
classroom ['klɑːsrʊm] n Klassenzimmer nt
classy ['klɑːsɪ] adj (fam) nobel, exklusiv
clatter ['klætə*] vi klappern
clause [klɔːz] n (Ling) Satz m; (Jur) Klausel f
claw [klɔː] n Kralle f
clay [kleɪ] n Lehm m; (for pottery) Ton m
clean [kliːn] adj sauber; **~ driving licence** Führerschein ohne Strafpunkte ▷ vt sauber machen; (carpet etc) reinigen; (window, shoes, vegetables) putzen; (wound) säubern; **clean up** vt sauber machen ▷ vi aufräumen; **cleaner** n (person) Putzmann m, Putzfrau f; (substance) Putzmittel nt; **~'s** (firm) Reinigung f
cleanse [klenz] vt reinigen; (wound) säubern; **cleanser** n Reinigungsmittel nt
clear [klɪə*] adj klar; (distinct) deutlich; (conscience) rein; (free, road etc) frei; **to be ~ about sth** sich über etw im Klaren sein ▷ adv: **to stand ~** zurücktreten ▷ vt (road, room etc) räumen; (table) abräumen; (Jur: find innocent) freisprechen (of von) ▷ vi (fog, mist) sich verziehen; (weather) aufklaren; **clear away** vt

wegräumen; (dishes) abräumen; **clear off** vi (fam) abhauen; **clear up** vi (tidy up) aufräumen; (weather) sich aufklären ▷ vt (room) aufräumen; (litter) wegräumen; (matter) klären

clearance sale n Räumungsverkauf m; **clearing** n Lichtung f; **clearly** adv klar; (speak, remember) deutlich; (obviously) eindeutig; **clearout** n Entrümpelungsaktion f; **clearway** n (Brit) Straße f mit Halteverbot nt

clench [klentʃ] vt (fist) ballen; (teeth) zusammenbeißen

clergyman [ˈklɜːdʒɪmæn] (pl **-men**) n Geistliche(r) m; **clergywoman** [ˈklɜːdʒɪwʊmən] (pl **-women**) n Geistliche f

clerk [klɑːk, (US) klɜːk] n (in office) Büroangestellte(r) m/f; (US: salesperson) Verkäufer(in) m(f)

clever [ˈklevə°] adj schlau, klug; (idea) clever

cliché [ˈkliːʃeɪ] n Klischee nt

click [klɪk] n Klicken nt; (Inform) Mausklick m ▷ vi klicken; **to ~ on sth** (Inform) etw anklicken; **it ~ed** (fam) ich hab's/er hat's etc geschnallt, es hat gefunkt, es hat Klick gemacht; **they ~ed** sie haben sich gleich verstanden; **click on** vt (Inform) anklicken

client [ˈklaɪənt] n Kunde m, Kundin f; (Jur) Mandant(in) m(f)

cliff [klɪf] n Klippe f

climate [ˈklaɪmɪt] n Klima nt

climax [ˈklaɪmæks] n Höhepunkt m

climb [klaɪm] vi (person) klettern; (aircraft, sun) steigen; (road) ansteigen ▷ vt (mountain) besteigen; (tree etc) klettern auf +akk n Aufstieg m; **climber** n (mountaineer) Bergsteiger(in) m(f); **climbing** n Klettern nt,

Bergsteigen nt; **climbing frame** n Klettergerüst nt

cling [klɪŋ] (**clung, clung**) vi sich klammern (to an +akk); **cling film®** n Frischhaltefolie f

clinic [ˈklɪnɪk] n Klinik f; **clinical** adj klinisch

clip [klɪp] n Klammer f ▷ vt (fix) anklemmen (to an +akk); (fingernails) schneiden; **clipboard** n Klemmbrett nt; **clippers** npl Schere f; (for nails) Zwicker m

cloak [kləʊk] n Umhang m; **cloakroom** n (for coats) Garderobe f

clock [klɒk] n Uhr f; (Auto: fam) Tacho m; **round the ~** rund um die Uhr; **clockwise** adv im Uhrzeigersinn

clog [klɒg] n Holzschuh m ▷ vt verstopfen

cloister [ˈklɔɪstə°] n Kreuzgang m

clone [kləʊn] n Klon m ▷ vt klonen

close [kləʊs] adj nahe (to +dat); (friend, contact) eng; (resemblance) groß; **~ to the beach** in der Nähe des Strandes; **~ win** knapper Sieg; **on ~r examination** bei näherer o genauer Untersuchung ▷ adv [kləʊs] dicht; **he lives ~ by** er wohnt ganz in der Nähe ▷ vt [kləʊz] schließen; (road) sperren; (discussion, matter) abschließen ▷ vi [kləʊz] schließen ▷ n [kləʊz] Ende nt; **close down** vi schließen ▷ vt (factory) stillgelegt werden ▷ vt (shop) schließen; (factory) stilllegen; **closed** adj (road) gesperrt; (shop etc) geschlossen; **closed circuit television** n Videoüberwachungsanlage f; **closely** adv (related) eng, nah; (packed, follow) dicht; (attentively) genau

closet ['klɒzɪt] n (esp US) Schrank m

close-up ['kləʊsʌp] n Nahaufnahme f

closing ['kləʊzɪŋ] adj: ~ **date** letzter Termin; (for competition) Einsendeschluss m; ~ **time** (of shop) Ladenschluss m; (Brit: of pub) Polizeistunde f

closure ['kləʊʒə°] n Schließung f; Abschluss m; **to look for** ~ mit etw abschließen wollen

clot [klɒt] (**blood**) ~ Blutgerinnsel nt; (fam: idiot) Trottel m ▷ vi (blood) gerinnen

cloth [klɒθ] n (material) Tuch nt; (for cleaning) Lappen m

clothe [kləʊð] vt kleiden; **clothes** [kləʊðz] npl Kleider pl, Kleidung f; **clothes line** n Wäscheleine f; **clothes peg**, **clothespin** (US) n Wäscheklammer f; **clothing** ['kləʊðɪŋ] n Kleidung f

clotted ['klɒtɪd] adj: ~ **cream** dicke Sahne (aus erhitzter Milch)

cloud [klaʊd] n Wolke f; **cloudy** adj (sky) bewölkt; (liquid) trüb

clove [kləʊv] n Gewürznelke f; ~ **of garlic** Knoblauchzehe f

clover ['kləʊvə°] n Klee m; **cloverleaf** (pl **-leaves**) n Kleeblatt nt

clown [klaʊn] n Clown m

club [klʌb] n (weapon) Knüppel m; (society) Klub m, Verein m; (nightclub) Disko f; (golf club) Golfschläger m; ~**s** (Cards) Kreuz nt; **clubbing** n: **to go** ~ in die Disko gehen; **club class** n (Aviat) Businessclass f

clue [kluː] n Anhaltspunkt m, Hinweis m; **he hasn't a** ~ er hat keine Ahnung

clumsy ['klʌmzɪ] adj unbeholfen, ungeschickt

clung [klʌŋ] pt, pp of **cling**

clutch [klʌtʃ] n (Auto) Kupplung f ▷ vt umklammern; (book etc) an sich akk klammern

cm abbr = **centimetre(s)** cm

c/o abbr = **care of** bei

Co abbr = **company** Co

coach [kəʊtʃ] n (Brit: bus) Reisebus m; (Rail) (Personen)wagen m; (Sport: trainer) Trainer(in) m(f) ▷ vt Nachhilfeunterricht geben +dat; (Sport) trainieren; **coach (class)** n (Aviat) Economyclass f; **coach driver** n Busfahrer(in) m(f); **coach party** n Reisegruppe f (Bus); **coach station** n Busbahnhof m; **coach trip** n Busfahrt f; (tour) Busreise f

coal [kəʊl] n Kohle f

coalition [kəʊə'lɪʃən] n (Pol) Koalition f

coalmine ['kəʊlmaɪn] n Kohlenbergwerk nt; **coalminer** n Bergarbeiter m

coast [kəʊst] n Küste f; **coastguard** n Küstenwache f; **coastline** n Küste f

coat [kəʊt] n Mantel m; (jacket) Jacke f; (on animals) Fell nt, Pelz m; (of paint) Schicht f; ~ **of arms** Wappen nt; **coathanger** n Kleiderbügel m; **coating** n Überzug m; (layer) Schicht f

cobble(stone)s ['kɒbl(stəʊn)z] npl Kopfsteine pl; (surface) Kopfsteinpflaster nt

cobweb ['kɒbweb] n Spinnennetz nt

cocaine [kə'keɪn] n Kokain m

cock [kɒk] n Hahn m; (vulg: penis) Schwanz m; **cock up** vt (Brit fam) vermasseln, versauen; **cockerel** ['kɒkərəl] n junger Hahn

cockle ['kɒkl] n Herzmuschel f

cockpit ['kɒkpɪt] n (in plane, racing car) Cockpit nt; **cockroach** ['kɒkrəʊtʃ] n Kakerlake f; **cocktail**

['kɒkteɪl] n Cocktail m; **cock-up** n (Brit fam) **to make a ~ of sth** bei etw Mist bauen; **cocky** ['kɒkɪ] adj großspurig, von sich selbst überzeugt

cocoa ['kəʊkəʊ] n Kakao m

coconut ['kəʊkənʌt] n Kokosnuss f

cod [kɒd] n Kabeljau m

COD abbr = **cash on delivery** per Nachnahme

code [kəʊd] n Kode m

coeducational [kəʊedjʊ'keɪʃənl] adj (school) gemischt

coffee ['kɒfɪ] n Kaffee m; **coffee bar** n Café nt; **coffee break** n Kaffeepause f; **coffee maker** n Kaffeemaschine f; **coffee pot** n Kaffeekanne f; **coffee shop** n Café nt; **coffee table** n Couchtisch m

coffin ['kɒfɪn] n Sarg m

coil [kɔɪl] n Rolle f; (Elec) Spule f; (Med) Spirale f

coin [kɔɪn] n Münze f

coincide [kəʊɪn'saɪd] vi (happen together) zusammenfallen (with mit); **coincidence** [kəʊ'ɪnsɪdəns] n Zufall m

coke [kəʊk] n Koks m; **Coke®** Cola f

cola ['kəʊlə] n Cola f

cold [kəʊld] adj kalt; **I'm ~** mir ist kalt, ich friere ⊳ n Kälte f; (illness) Erkältung f, Schnupfen m; **to catch a ~** sich erkälten; **cold box** n Kühlbox f; **cold sore** n Herpes m; **cold turkey** n (fam) Totalentzug m; (symptoms) Entzugserscheinungen pl

coleslaw ['kəʊlslɔː] n Krautsalat m

collaborate [kə'læbəreɪt] vi zusammenarbeiten (with mit); **collaboration** [kəlæbə'reɪʃən] n Zusammenarbeit f; (of one party) Mitarbeit f

collapse [kə'læps] vi zusammenbrechen; (building etc) einstürzen ⊳ n Zusammenbruch m; (of building) Einsturz m; **collapsible** [kə'læpsəbl] adj zusammenklappbar, Klapp-

collar ['kɒlə°] n Kragen m; (for dog, cat) Halsband nt; **collarbone** n Schlüsselbein nt

colleague ['kɒliːg] n Kollege m, Kollegin f

collect [kə'lekt] vt sammeln; (fetch) abholen ⊳ vi sich sammeln; **collect call** n (US) R-Gespräch nt; **collected** adj (works) gesammelt; (person) gefasst; **collector** n Sammler(in) m(f); **collection** [kə'lekʃən] n Sammlung f; (Rel) Kollekte f; (from postbox) Leerung f

college ['kɒlɪdʒ] n (residential) College nt; (specialist) Fachhochschule f; (vocational) Berufsschule f; (US: university) Universität f; **to go to ~** (US) studieren

collide [kə'laɪd] vi zusammenstoßen; **collision** [kə'lɪʒən] n Zusammenstoß m

colloquial [kə'ləʊkwɪəl] adj umgangssprachlich

Cologne [kə'ləʊn] n Köln nt

colon ['kəʊlən] n (punctuation mark) Doppelpunkt m

colonial [kə'ləʊnɪəl] adj Kolonial-; **colonize** ['kɒlənaɪz] vt kolonisieren; **colony** ['kɒlənɪ] n Kolonie f

color n (US), **colour** ['kʌlə°] n Farbe f; (of skin) Hautfarbe f ⊳ vt anmalen; (dye) s färben; **colour-blind** adj farbenblind; **coloured** adj farbig; (biased) gefärbt; **colour film** n Farbfilm m; **colourful** adj (lit, fig) bunt; (life, past) bewegt; **colouring** n (in food etc) Farbstoff m; (complexion) Gesichtsfarbe f; **colourless** adj *(lit, fig)* farblos; **colour photo(graph)** *n* Farbfoto *nt*; **colour television** *n* Farbfernsehen *nt*

column ['kɒləm] *n* Säule *f*; *(of print)* Spalte *f*

comb [kəʊm] *n* Kamm *m* ▷ *vt* kämmen; **to ~ one's hair** sich kämmen

combination [kɒmbɪ'neɪʃən] *n* Kombination *f*; *(mixture)* Mischung *f (of aus)*; **combine** [kəm'baɪn] *vt* verbinden *(with mit)*; *(two things)* kombinieren

come [kʌm] **(came, come)** *vi* kommen; *(arrive)* ankommen; *(on list, in order)* stehen; *(with adjective: become)* werden; **~ and see us** besuchen Sie uns mal; **coming** ich komm ja schon!; **to ~ first/second** erster/zweiter werden; **to ~ true** wahr werden; **to ~ loose** sich lockern; **the years to ~** die kommenden Jahre; **there's one more to ~** es kommt noch eins/noch einer; **how ~ ...?** *(fam)* wie kommt es, dass ...?; **~ to think of it** *(fam)* wo es mir gerade einfällt; **come across** *vt (find)* stoßen auf +*akk*; **come back** *vi* zurückkommen; **I'll ~ to that** ich komme darauf zurück; **come down** *vi* herunterkommen; *(rain, snow, price)* fallen; **come from** *vt (result)* kommen von; **where do you ~?** wo kommen Sie her?; **~ London** ich komme aus London; **come in** *vi* hereinkommen; *(arrive)* ankommen; *(in race)* **to ~ fourth** Vierter werden; **come off** *vi (button, handle etc)* abgehen; *(succeed)* gelingen; **to ~ well/badly** gut/schlecht wegkommen; **come on** *vi (progress)* vorankommen; **~!** komm!; *(hurry)* beeil dich!; *(encouraging)* los!; **come out** *vi*

herauskommen; *(photo)* was werden; *(homosexual)* sich outen; **come round** *vi (visit)* vorbeikommen; *(regain consciousness)* wieder zu sich kommen; **come to** *vi (regain consciousness)* wieder zu sich kommen ▷ *vt (sum)* sich belaufen auf +*akk*; **when it comes to ...** wenn es um ... geht; **come up** *vi* hochkommen; *(sun, moon)* aufgehen; **to ~ (for discussion)** zur Sprache kommen; **come up to** *vt (approach)* zukommen auf +*akk*; *(water)* reichen bis zu; *(expectations)* entsprechen +*dat*; **come up with** *vt (idea)* haben; *(solution, answer)* kommen auf +*akk*; **to ~ a suggestion** einen Vorschlag machen

comedian [kə'miːdɪən] *n* Komiker(in *f) m(f)*

comedown ['kʌmdaʊn] *n* Abstieg *m*

comedy ['kɒmədɪ] *n* Komödie *f*, Comedy *f*

comfort ['kʌmfət] *n* Komfort *m*; *(consolation)* Trost *m* ▷ *vt* trösten; **comfortable** *adj* bequem; *(income)* ausreichend; *(temperature, life)* angenehm; **comforting** *adj* tröstlich

comic ['kɒmɪk] *n (magazine)* Comic(heft) *nt*; *(comedian)* Komiker(in *f) m(f)* ▷ *adj* komisch

coming ['kʌmɪŋ] *adj* kommend; *(event)* bevorstehend

comma ['kɒmə] *n* Komma *nt*

command [kə'mɑːnd] *n* Befehl *m*; *(control)* Führung *f*; *(Mil)* Kommando *nt* ▷ *vt* befehlen +*dat*

commemorate [kə'memәreɪt] *vt* gedenken +*gen*; **commemoration** [kəmemə'reɪʃən] *n*: **in ~ of** in Gedenken an +*akk*

comment ['kɒment] *n (remark)*

Bemerkung f; (note) Anmerkung f;
(official) Kommentar m (on zu); **no
~** kein Kommentar ▷ vi sich
äußern (on zu); **commentary**
['kɒmǝntrɪ] n Kommentar m (on
zu); (TV, Sport) Livereportage f;
commentator ['kɒmǝnteɪtǝ⁎] n
Kommentator(in) m(f); (TV, Sport)
Reporter(in) m(f)
commerce ['kɒmɜːs] n Handel
m; **commercial** [kǝ'mɜːʃǝl] adj
kommerziell; (training)
kaufmännisch; **~ break**
Werbepause f; **~ vehicle**
Lieferwagen m ▷ n (TV)
Werbespot m
commission [kǝ'mɪʃǝn] n
Auftrag m; (fee) Provision f;
(reporting body) Kommission f ▷ vt
beauftragen
commit [kǝ'mɪt] vt (crime)
begehen ▷ vr: **to ~ oneself** (to
undertake) sich verpflichten (to
zu); **commitment** n
Verpflichtung f; (Pol) Engagement
nt
committee [kǝ'mɪtɪ] n Ausschuss m, Komitee nt
commodity [kǝ'mɒdɪtɪ] n Ware
f
common ['kɒmǝn] adj (experience) allgemein, alltäglich;
(shared) gemeinsam; (widespread,
frequent) häufig; (pej)
gewöhnlich, ordinär; **to have
sth in ~** etw gemein haben ▷ n
(Brit: land) Gemeindewiese f;
commonly adv häufig,
allgemein; **commonplace** adj
alltäglich; (pej) banal;
commonroom n Gemeinschafts-
raum m; **Commons** n (Brit Pol)
the (House of) ~ das Unterhaus;
common sense n gesunder
Menschenverstand;
Commonwealth n Commonwealth nt; **~ of Independent

States Gemeinschaft f
Unabhängiger Staaten
communal ['kɒmjuːnl] adj
gemeinsam; (of a community)
Gemeinschafts-, Gemeinde-
communicate [kǝ'mjuːnɪkeɪt]
vi kommunizieren (with mit);
communication
[kǝmjuːnɪ'keɪʃǝn] n Kom-
munikation f, Verständigung f;
communications satellite n
Nachrichtensatellit m;
communications technology n
Nachrichtentechnik f;
communicative adj gesprächig
communion [kǝ'mjuːnɪǝn] n:
(Holy) Communion Heiliges
Abendmahl; (Catholic)
Kommunion f
communism ['kɒmjunɪzǝm] n
Kommunismus m; **communist**
['kɒmjunɪst] adj kommunistisch
▷ n Kommunist(in) m(f)
community [kǝ'mjuːnɪtɪ] n
Gemeinschaft f; **community
centre** n Gemeindezentrum nt;
community service n (Jur)
Sozialdienst m
commutation ticket n
[kɒmjuː'teɪʃǝntɪkɪt] n (US)
Zeitkarte f; **commute** [kǝ'mjuːt]
vi pendeln; **commuter** n
Pendler(in) m(f)
compact [kǝm'pækt] adj kompakt ▷ ['kɒmpækt] n (for
make-up) Puderdose f; (US: car) =
Mittelklassewagen m; **compact
camera** n Kompaktkamera f;
compact disc n Compact Disc f,
CD f
companion [kǝm'pænɪǝn] n
Begleiter(in) m(f)
company ['kʌmpǝnɪ] n
Gesellschaft f; (Comm) Firma f;
to keep sb ~ jdm Gesellschaft
leisten; **company car** n
Firmenauto nt

comparable ['kɒmpərəbl] adj
vergleichbar (with, to mit)

comparative [kəm'pærətɪv] adj
relativ ▷ n (Ling) Komparativ m;
comparatively adv
verhältnismäßig

compare [kəm'pɛə°] vt vergleichen (with, to mit); **~d with** o
to im Vergleich zu; **beyond
~** unvergleichlich; **comparison**
[kəm'pærɪsn] n Vergleich m; **in
~ with** im Vergleich mit (o zu)

compartment [kəm'pɑːtmənt]
n (Rail) Abteil nt; (in desk etc) Fach
nt

compass ['kʌmpəs] n Kompass
m; **~es** pl Zirkel m

compassion [kəm'pæʃən] n
Mitgefühl nt

compatible [kəm'pætɪbl] adj
vereinbar (with mit); (Inform)
kompatibel; **we're not ~** wir
passen nicht zueinander

compensate ['kɒmpenseɪt] vt
(person) entschädigen (for für) ▷ vi:
to ~ for sth Ersatz für etw leisten;
(make up for) etw ausgleichen;
compensation [kɒmpen'seɪʃən]
n Entschädigung f; (money)
Schadenersatz m; (Jur) Abfindung f

compete [kəm'piːt] vi konkur-
rieren (for um); (Sport) kämpfen (for
um); (take part) teilnehmen (in an
+dat)

competence ['kɒmpɪtəns] n
Fähigkeit f; (Jur) Zuständigkeit f;
competent adj fähig; (Jur)
zuständig

competition [kɒmpɪ'tɪʃən] n
(contest) Wettbewerb m; (Comm)
Konkurrenz f (for um);
competitive [kəm'petɪtɪv] adj
(firm, price, product)
konkurrenzfähig; **competitor**
[kəm'petɪtə°] n (Comm)
Konkurrent(in) m(f); (Sport)
Teilnehmer(in) m(f)

complain [kəm'pleɪn] vi klagen;
(formally) sich beschweren (about
über +akk); **complaint** n Klage f;
Beanstandung f; (formal)
Beschwerde f; (Med) Leiden nt

complement vt ergänzen

complete [kəm'pliːt] adj vollständig; (finished) fertig; (failure,
disaster) total; (happiness)
vollkommen; **are we ~?** sind wir
vollzählig? ▷ vt vervollständigen;
(finish) beenden; (form) ausfüllen;
completely adv völlig; **not ~ ...**
nicht ganz ...

complex ['kɒmpleks] adj komplex; (task, theory etc) kompliziert
▷ n Komplex m

complexion [kəm'plekʃən] n
Gesichtsfarbe f, Teint m

complicated ['kɒmplɪkeɪtɪd] adj
kompliziert; **complication**
['kɒmplɪkeɪʃən] n Komplikation
f

compliment ['kɒmplɪmənt] n
Kompliment nt; **complimentary**
[kɒmplɪ'mentərɪ] adj lobend;
(free of charge) Gratis-; **~ ticket**
Freikarte f

comply [kəm'plaɪ] vi: **to ~ with
the regulations** den Vorschriften
entsprechen

component [kəm'pəʊnənt] n
Bestandteil m

compose [kəm'pəʊz] vt (music)
komponieren; **to ~ oneself** sich
zusammennehmen; **composed**
adj gefasst; **to be ~ of** bestehen
aus; **composer** n Komponist(in)
m(f); **composition** [kɒmpə'zɪʃən]
n (of a group) Zusammensetzung f;
(Mus) Komposition f

comprehend [kɒmprɪ'hend] vt
verstehen; **comprehension**
[kɒmprɪ'henʃən] n Verständnis nt

comprehensive
[kɒmprɪ'hensɪv] adj umfassend;
~ school Gesamtschule f

compress [kəm'pres] vt
komprimieren

comprise [kəm'praɪz] vt
umfassen, bestehen aus

compromise ['kɒmprəmaɪz] n
Kompromiss m ▷ vi einen
Kompromiss schließen

compulsory [kəm'pʌlsərɪ] adj
obligatorisch; ~ **subject**
Pflichtfach nt

computer [kəm'pju:tə°] n
Computer m; **computer-aided** adj
computergestützt;
computer-controlled adj rèch-
nergesteuert; **computer game** n
Computerspiel nt;
computer-literate adj: **to be**
~ **with** dem Computer umgehen
können; **computer scientist** n
Informatiker(in) m(f); **computing**
n (subject) Informatik f

con [kɒn] (fam) n Schwindel m
▷ vt betrügen (out of um)

conceal [kən'si:l] vt verbergen
(from vor +dat)

conceivable [kən'si:vəbl] adj
denkbar, vorstellbar; **conceive**
[kən'si:v] vt (imagine) sich
vorstellen; (child) empfangen

concentrate ['kɒnsəntreɪt] vi
sich konzentrieren (on auf +akk);
concentration [kɒnsən'treɪʃən]
n Konzentration f

concept ['kɒnsept] n Begriff m

concern [kən'sɜ:n] n (affair)
Angelegenheit f; (worry) Sorge f;
(Comm: firm) Unternehmen nt; **it's
not my** ~ das geht mich nichts an;
there's no cause for ~ kein Grund
zur Beunruhigung ▷ vt (affect)
angehen; (have connection with)
betreffen; (be about) handeln von;
those ~ed die Betroffenen; **as far
as I'm** ~ed was mich betrifft;
concerned adj (anxious) besorgt;
concerning prep bezüglich,
hinsichtlich +gen

concert ['kɒnsət] n Konzert nt;
~ **hall** Konzertsaal m

concession [kən'seʃən] n Zu-
geständnis nt; (reduction)
Ermäßigung f

concise [kən'saɪs] adj knapp
gefasst, prägnant

conclude [kən'klu:d] vt (end)
beenden, (ab)schließen; (infer)
folgern (from aus); **to** ~ **that ...** zu
dem Schluss kommen, dass ...;
conclusion [kən'klu:ʒən] n
Schluss m, Schlussfolgerung f

concrete ['kɒŋkri:t] n Beton m
▷ adj konkret

concussion [kən'kʌʃən] n
Gehirnerschütterung f

condemn [kən'dem] vt
verdammen; (esp Jur)
verurteilen

condensed milk [kən'denst-] n
Kondensmilch f, Dosenmilch f

condition [kən'dɪʃən] n (state)
Zustand m; (requirement)
Bedingung f; **on** ~ **that ...** unter
der Bedingung, dass ...; ~**s** pl
(circumstances, weather)
Verhältnisse pl; **conditional** adj
bedingt; (Ling) Konditional-;
conditioner n Weichspüler m; (for
hair) Pflegespülung f

condo ['kɒndəʊ] (pl -**s**) n see
condominium

condolences [kən'dəʊlənsɪz]
npl Beileid nt

condom ['kɒndəm] n Kondom nt

condominium [kɒndə'mɪnɪəm]
n (US: apartment)
Eigentumswohnung f

conduct ['kɒndʌkt] n (behaviour)
Verhalten nt ▷ [kən'dʌkt] vt
führen, leiten; (orchestra)
dirigieren; **conductor**
[kən'dʌktə°] n (of orchestra)
Dirigent(in) m(f); (Brit: in bus)
Schaffner(in) m(f); (US: on train)
Zugführer(in) m(f)

cone [kəʊn] n Kegel m; (for ice cream) Waffeltüte f; (fir cone) (Tannen)zapfen m

conference ['kɒnfərəns] n Konferenz f

confess [kən'fes] vt, vi: **to ~ that ...** gestehen, dass ...; [kən'feʃən] n Geständnis nt; (Rel) Beichte f

confetti [kən'feti] n Konfetti nt

confidence ['kɒnfidəns] n Vertrauen nt (in zu); (assurance) Selbstvertrauen nt; **confident** adj (sure) zuversichtlich (that ... dass ...), überzeugt (of von); (self-assured) selbstsicher; **confidential** [kɒnfi'denʃəl] adj vertraulich

confine [kən'faɪn] vt beschränken (to auf +akk)

confirm [kən'fɜ:m] vt bestätigen; **confirmation** [kɒnfə'meɪʃən] n Bestätigung f; (Rel) Konfirmation f; **confirmed** adj überzeugt; (bachelor) eingefleischt

confiscate ['kɒnfiskeɪt] vt beschlagnahmen, konfiszieren

conflict ['kɒnflɪkt] n Konflikt m

confuse [kən'fju:z] vt verwirren; (sth with sth) verwechseln (with mit); (several things) durcheinanderbringen; **confused** adj (person) konfus, verwirrt; (account) verworren; **confusing** adj verwirrend; **confusion** [kən'fju:ʒən] n Verwirrung f; (of two things) Verwechslung f; (muddle) Chaos nt

congested [kən'dʒestɪd] adj verstopft; (overcrowded) überfüllt; **congestion** [kən'dʒestʃən] n Stau m

congratulate [kən'grætjʊleɪt] vt gratulieren (on zu); **congratulations** [kəngrætjʊ'leɪʃənz] npl Glück-

wünsche pl; **~!** gratuliere!, herzlichen Glückwunsch!

congregation [kɒngrɪ'geɪʃən] n (Rel) Gemeinde f

congress ['kɒŋgres] n Kongress m; (US) **Congress** der Kongress; **congressman** (pl **-men**), **congresswoman** (pl **-women**) n (US) Mitglied nt des Repräsentantenhauses

conifer ['kɒnɪfə°] n Nadelbaum m

conjunction [kən'dʒʌŋkʃən] n (Ling) Konjunktion f; **in ~ with** in Verbindung mit

conk out [kɒŋk 'aʊt] vi (fam: appliance, car) den Geist aufgeben, streiken; (person: die) ins Gras beißen

connect [kə'nekt] vt verbinden (with, to mit); (Elec, Tech: appliance etc) anschließen (to an +akk) ▷ vi (train, plane) Anschluss haben (with an +akk); **~ing flight** Anschlussflug m; **~ing train** Anschlusszug m; **connection** [kə'nekʃən] n Verbindung f; (link) Zusammenhang m; (for train, plane, electrical appliance) Anschluss m (with, to an +akk); (business etc) Beziehung f; **in ~ with** in Zusammenhang mit; **bad ~** (Tel) schlechte Verbindung; (Elec) Wackelkontakt m; **connector** n (Inform: computer) Stecker m

conscience ['kɒnʃəns] n Gewissen nt; **conscientious** [kɒnʃɪ'enʃəs] adj gewissenhaft

conscious ['kɒnʃəs] adj (act) bewusst; (Med) bei Bewusstsein; **to be ~** bei Bewusstsein sein; **consciousness** n Bewusstsein nt

consecutive [kən'sekjʊtɪv] adj aufeinanderfolgend

consent [kən'sent] n Zustimmung f ▷ vi zustimmen (to dat)

consequence ['kɒnsɪkwəns] n
Folge f, Konsequenz f;
consequently ['kɒnsɪkwəntlɪ]
adv folglich, deshalb

conservation [kɒnsə'veɪʃən] n
Erhaltung f; (nature conservation)
Naturschutz m; conservation
area n Naturschutzgebiet nt

conservative (Pol) Conservative
[kən'sɜːvətɪv] adj konservativ

conservatory [kən'sɜːvətrɪ] n
(greenhouse) Gewächshaus nt;
(room) Wintergarten m

consider [kən'sɪdə*] vt (reflect
on) nachdenken über, sich
überlegen; (take into account)
in Betracht ziehen; (regard) halten
für; he is ~ed (to be) ... er gilt als
...; considerable [kən'sɪdərəbl]
adj beträchtlich; considerate
[kən'sɪdərɪt] adj aufmerksam,
rücksichtsvoll; consideration
[kənsɪdə'reɪʃən] n (thoughtfulness)
Rücksicht f; (thought) Überlegung
f; to take sth into ~ etw in
Betracht ziehen; considering
[kən'sɪdərɪŋ] prep in Anbetracht
+gen ▷ conj da

consist [kən'sɪst] vi: to ~ of ...
bestehen aus ...

consistent [kən'sɪstənt] adj
(behaviour, process etc)
konsequent; (statements)
übereinstimmend; (argument)
folgerichtig; (performance, results)
beständig

consolation [kɒnsə'leɪʃən] n
Trost m; console [kən'səul] vt
trösten

consolidate [kən'sɒlɪdeɪt] vt
festigen

consonant ['kɒnsənənt] n
Konsonant m

conspicuous [kən'spɪkjuəs] adj
auffällig, auffallend

conspiracy [kən'spɪrəsɪ] n
Komplott nt; conspire

[kən'spaɪə*] vi sich verschwören
(against gegen)

constable ['kʌnstəbl] n (Brit)
Polizist(in) m(f)

Constance ['kɒnstəns] n Kon-
stanz nt; Lake ~ der Bodensee

constant ['kɒnstənt] adj (continual) ständig, dauernd;
(unchanging: temperature etc)
gleichbleibend; constantly adv
dauernd

consternation [kɒnstə'neɪʃən]
n (dismay) Bestürzung f

constituency [kən'stɪtjuənsɪ]
n Wahlkreis m

constitution [kɒnstɪ'tjuːʃən] n
Verfassung f; (of person)
Konstitution f

construct [kən'strʌkt] vt bauen;
construction [kən'strʌkʃən] n
(process, result) Bau m; (method)
Bauweise f; under ~ im Bau
befindlich; construction site
n Baustelle f; construction worker
n Bauarbeiter(in) m(f)

consulate ['kɒnsjulət] n Konsulat nt

consult [kən'sʌlt] vt um Rat
fragen; (doctor) konsultieren;
(book) nachschlagen in +dat;
consultant n (Med) Facharzt m,
Fachärztin f; consultation
[kɒnsəl'teɪʃən] n Beratung f;
(Med) Konsultation f; ~ room
Besprechungsraum m,
Sprechzimmer

consume [kən'sjuːm] vt verbrauchen; (food) konsumieren;
consumer n Verbraucher(in)
m(f); consumer-friendly adj
verbraucherfreundlich

contact ['kɒntækt] n (touch)
Berührung f; (communication)
Kontakt m; (person) Kontaktperson
f; to be/keep in ~ (with sb) (mit
jdm) in Kontakt sein/bleiben ▷ vt
sich in Verbindung setzen mit;

contact lenses npl Kontaktlinsen pl

contagious [kən'teɪdʒəs] adj ansteckend

contain [kən'teɪn] vt enthalten; **container** n Behälter m; (for transport) Container m

contaminate [kən'tæmɪneɪt] vt verunreinigen; (chemically) verseuchen; **~d by radiation** strahlenverseucht, verstrahlt; **contamination** [kəntæmɪ'neɪʃən] n Verunreinigung f; (by radiation) Verseuchung f

contemporary [kən'tempərərɪ] adj zeitgenössisch

contempt [kən'tempt] n Verachtung f; **contemptuous** adj verächtlich; **to be ~** voller Verachtung sein (of für)

content [kən'tent] adj zufrieden

content(s) ['kɒntent(s)] n pl Inhalt m

contest ['kɒntest] n (Wett)kampf m (for um); (competition) Wettbewerb m ▷ [kən'test] vt kämpfen um +akk; (dispute) bestreiten; **contestant** [kən'testənt] n Teilnehmer(in) m(f)

context ['kɒntekst] n Zusammenhang m; **out of ~** aus dem Zusammenhang gerissen

continent ['kɒntɪnənt] n Kontinent m, Festland nt; **the Continent** (Brit) das europäische Festland, der Kontinent; **continental** [kɒntɪ'nentl] adj kontinental; **~ breakfast** kleines Frühstück mit Brötchen und Marmelade, Kaffee oder Tee

continual [kən'tɪnjʊəl] adj (endless) ununterbrochen; (constant) dauernd, ständig; **continually** adv dauernd; (again and again) immer wieder; **continuation** [kəntɪnjʊ'eɪʃən] n

Fortsetzung f; **continue** [kən'tɪnjuː] vi weitermachen (with mit); (esp talking) fortfahren (with mit); (travelling) weiterfahren; (state, conditions) fortdauern, anhalten ▷ vt fortsetzen; **to be ~d** Fortsetzung folgt; **continuous** [kən'tɪnjʊəs] adj (endless) ununterbrochen; (constant) ständig

contraceptive [kɒntrə'septɪv] n Verhütungsmittel nt

contract ['kɒntrækt] n Vertrag m

contradict [kɒntrə'dɪkt] vt widersprechen +dat; **contradiction** [kɒntrə'dɪkʃən] n Widerspruch m

contrary ['kɒntrərɪ] n Gegenteil nt; **on the ~** im Gegenteil ▷ adj: **~ to** entgegen +dat

contrast ['kɒntrɑːst] n Kontrast m, Gegensatz m; **in ~ to** im Gegensatz zu ▷ [kən'trɑːst] vt entgegensetzen

contribute [kən'trɪbjuːt] vt, vi beitragen (to zu); (money) spenden (to für); **contribution** [kɒntrɪ'bjuːʃən] n Beitrag m

control [kən'trəʊl] vt (master) beherrschen; (temper etc) im Griff haben; (esp Tech) steuern; **to ~ oneself** sich beherrschen ▷ n Kontrolle f; (mastery) Beherrschung f; (esp Tech) Steuerung f; **~s** pl (knobs, switches etc) Bedienungselemente pl; (collectively) Steuerung f; **to be out of ~** außer Kontrolle sein; **control knob** n Bedienungsknopf m; **control panel** n Schalttafel f

controversial [kɒntrə'vɜːʃəl] adj umstritten

convalesce [kɒnvə'les] vi gesund werden; **convalescence** n Genesung f

convenience [kən'viːnɪəns] n (quality, thing) Annehmlichkeit f; **at**

your ~ wann es Ihnen passt; **with all modern ~s** mit allem Komfort; **convenience food** n Fertiggericht nt; **convenient** adj günstig, passend

convent ['kɒnvənt] n Kloster nt

convention [kən'venʃən] n (custom) Konvention f; (meeting) Konferenz f; **the Geneva Convention** die Genfer Konvention; **conventional** adj herkömmlich, konventionell

conversation [kɒnvə'seɪʃən] n Gespräch nt, Unterhaltung f

conversion [kən'vɜːʃən] n Umwandlung f (into in +akk); (of building) Umbau m (into zu); (calculation) Umrechnung f; **conversion table** n Umrechnungstabelle f; **convert** [kən'vɜːt] vt umwandeln; (person) bekehren; (Inform) konvertieren; **to ~ into euros** in Euro umrechnen; **convertible** n (Auto) Kabrio ▷ adj umwandelbar

convey [kən'veɪ] vt (carry) befördern; (feelings) vermitteln; **conveyor belt** n Förderband nt, Fließband nt

convict [kən'vɪkt] vt verurteilen (of wegen) ▷ ['kɒnvɪkt] n Strafgefangene(r) mf; **conviction** n (Jur) Verurteilung f; (strong belief) Überzeugung f

convince [kən'vɪns] vt überzeugen (of von); **convincing** adj überzeugend

cook [kʊk] vt, vi kochen ▷ n Koch m, Köchin f; **cookbook** n Kochbuch nt; **cooker** n Herd m; **cookery** n Kochkunst f; **~ book** Kochbuch nt; **cookie** n (US) Keks m; **cooking** n Kochen nt; (style of cooking) Küche f

cool [kuːl] adj kühl, gelassen; (fam: brilliant) cool, stark ▷ vt, vi (ab)kühlen; **~ it** reg dich ab! ▷ n:

to keep/lose one's ~ (fam) ruhig bleiben/durchdrehen; **cool down** vi abkühlen; (calm down) sich beruhigen

cooperate [kəʊ'ɒpəreɪt] vi zusammenarbeiten, kooperieren; **cooperation** [kəʊpərə'reɪʃən] n Zusammenarbeit f, Kooperation f; **cooperative** [kəʊ'ɒpərətɪv] adj hilfsbereit ▷ n Genossenschaft f

coordinate [kəʊ'ɔːdɪneɪt] vt koordinieren

cop [kɒp] n (fam: policeman) Bulle m

cope [kəʊp] vi zurechtkommen, fertig werden (with mit)

Copenhagen [kəʊpən'heɪgən] n Kopenhagen nt

copier ['kɒpɪə] n Kopierer m

copper ['kɒpə] n Kupfer nt; (Brit fam: policeman) Bulle m; (fam: coin) Kupfermünze f; **~s** Kleingeld nt

copy ['kɒpɪ] n Kopie f; (of book) Exemplar nt ▷ vt kopieren; (imitate) nachahmen; **copyright** n Urheberrecht nt

coral ['kɒrəl] n Koralle f

cord [kɔːd] n Schnur f; (material) Kordsamt m; **cordless** ['kɔːdlɪs] adj (phone) schnurlos

core [kɔːʳ] n (a. fig) Kern m; (of apple, pear) Kerngehäuse nt; **core business** n Kerngeschäft nt

cork [kɔːk] n (material) Kork m; (stopper) Korken m; **corkscrew** ['kɔːkskruː] n Korkenzieher m

corn [kɔːn] n Getreide nt, Korn nt; (US: maize) Mais m; (on foot) Hühnerauge nt; **~ on the cob** (gekochter) Maiskolben; **corned beef** n Cornedbeef nt

corner ['kɔːnəʳ] n Ecke f; (on road) Kurve f; (Sport) Eckstoß m ▷ vt in die Enge treiben; **corner shop** n Laden m an der Ecke

cornflakes ['kɔːfleɪks] npl Cornflakes pl

Cornish [ˈkɔːnɪʃ] adj kornisch; ~ **pasty** mit Fleisch und Kartoffeln gefüllte Pastete; **Cornwall** [ˈkɔːnwəl] n Cornwall nt

coronation [kɒrəˈneɪʃən] n Krönung f

corporation [kɔːpəˈreɪʃən] n (US Comm) Aktiengesellschaft f

corpse [kɔːps] n Leiche f

correct [kəˈrekt] adj (accurate) richtig; (proper) korrekt ▷ vt korrigieren, verbessern; **correction** n (esp written) Korrektur f

correspond [kɒrɪˈspɒnd] vi entsprechen (to dat); (two things) übereinstimmen; (exchange letters) korrespondieren; **corresponding** adj entsprechend

corridor [ˈkɒrɪdɔː] n (in building) Flur m; (in train) Gang m

corrupt [kəˈrʌpt] adj korrupt

cosmetic [kɒzˈmetɪk] adj kosmetisch; **cosmetics** npl Kosmetika pl; **cosmetic surgeon** n Schönheitschirurg(in) m(f); **cosmetic surgery** n Schönheitschirurgie f

cosmopolitan [kɒzməˈpɒlɪtən] adj international; (attitude) weltoffen

cost [kɒst] (cost, cost) vt kosten ▷ n Kosten pl; **at all ~s, at any ~** um jeden Preis; **~ of living** Lebenshaltungskosten pl; **costly** adj kostspielig

costume [ˈkɒstjuːm] n (Theat) Kostüm n

cosy [ˈkəʊzɪ] adj gemütlich

cot [kɒt] n (Brit) Kinderbett nt; (US) Campingliege f

cottage [ˈkɒtɪdʒ] n kleines Haus; (country cottage) Landhäuschen nt; **cottage cheese** n Hüttenkäse m; **cottage pie** n Hackfleisch mit Kartoffelbrei überbacken

cotton [ˈkɒtn] n Baumwolle f;

cotton candy n (US) Zuckerwatte f; **cotton wool** n (Brit) Watte f

couch [kaʊtʃ] n Couch f; (sofa) Sofa nt; **couchette** [kuːˈʃet] n Liegewagen(platz) m

cough [kɒf] vi husten ▷ n Husten m; **cough mixture** n Hustensaft m; **cough sweet** n Hustenbonbon nt

could [kʊd] pt of **can** konnte; conditional könnte; **~ you come earlier?** könntest du/könnten Sie früher kommen?

couldn't contr of **could not**

council [ˈkaʊnsl] n (Pol) Rat m; (local ~) Gemeinderat m; (town ~) Stadtrat m; **council estate** n Siedlung f des sozialen Wohnungsbaus; **council house** n Sozialwohnung f; **councillor** [ˈkaʊnsɪlə] n Gemeinderat m, Gemeinderätin f; **council tax** n Gemeindesteuer f

count [kaʊnt] vt, vi zählen; (include) mitrechnen ▷ n Zählung f; (noble) Graf m; **count on** vt (rely on) sich verlassen auf +akk; (expect) rechnen mit

counter [ˈkaʊntə] n (in shop) Ladentisch m; (in café) Theke f; (in bank, post office) Schalter m; **counter attack** n Gegenangriff m ▷ vi zurückschlagen; **counter-clockwise** adv (US) entgegen dem Uhrzeigersinn

counterpart [ˈkaʊntəpɑːt] n Gegenstück nt (of zu)

countess n Gräfin f

countless [ˈkaʊntlɪs] adj zahllos, unzählig

country [ˈkʌntrɪ] n Land nt; **in the ~** auf dem Land(e); **in this ~** hierzulande; **country cousin** n (fam) Landei nt; **country dancing** n Volkstanz m; **country house** n Landhaus nt; **countryman** n (compatriot) Landsmann m;

country music n Countrymusic f;
country road n Landstraße f;
countryside n Landschaft f; (rural area) Land nt

county ['kaʊntɪ] n (Brit) Grafschaft f; (US) Verwaltungsbezirk m; **county town** n (Brit) ≈ Kreisstadt f

couple ['kʌpl] n Paar nt; **a ~ of** ein paar

coupon ['ku:pɒn] n (voucher) Gutschein m

courage ['kʌrɪdʒ] n Mut m; **courageous** [kə'reɪdʒəs] adj mutig

courgette [kʊə'ʒet] n (Brit) Zucchini f

courier ['kʊrɪə°] n (for tourists) Reiseleiter(in) m(f); (messenger) Kurier m

course [kɔ:s] n (of study) Kurs m; (for race) Strecke f; (Naut, Aviat) Kurs m; (at university) Studiengang m; (in meal) Gang m; **of ~** natürlich; **in the ~ of** während

court [kɔ:t] n (Sport) Platz m; (Jur) Gericht nt

courteous ['kɜ:tɪəs] adj höflich; **courtesy** ['kɜ:təsɪ] n Höflichkeit f; **~ bus/coach** (gebührenfreier) Zubringerbus

courthouse ['kɔ:thaʊs] n (US) Gerichtsgebäude nt; **court order** n Gerichtsbeschluss m; **courtroom** n Gerichtssaal m; **courtyard** ['kɔ:tjɑːd] n Hof m

cousin ['kʌzn] n (male) Cousin m; (female) Cousine f

cover ['kʌvə°] vt bedecken (in, with mit); (distance) zurücklegen; (loan, costs) decken ▷ n (for bed etc) Decke f; (of cushion) Bezug m; (lid) Deckel m; (of book) Umschlag m; (**insurance**) ~ Versicherungsschutz m; **cover up** vt zudecken; (error etc) vertuschen; **coverage** n Berichterstattung f (of über +akk);

cover charge n Kosten pl für ein Gedeck; **covering; covering** n Decke f; **covering letter** n Begleitbrief m; **cover story** n (newspaper) Titelgeschichte f

cow [kaʊ] n Kuh f

coward ['kaʊəd] n Feigling m; **cowardly** adj feig(e)

cowboy ['kaʊbɔɪ] n Cowboy m

coy [kɔɪ] adj gespielt schüchtern, kokett

cozy ['kəʊzɪ] adj (US) gemütlich

CPU abbr = **central processing unit** Zentraleinheit f

crab [kræb] n Krabbe f

crabby ['kræbɪ] adj mürrisch, reizbar

crack [kræk] n Riss m; (in pottery, glass) Sprung m; (drug) Crack nt; **to have a ~ at sth** etw ausprobieren ▷ vi (pottery, glass) einen Sprung bekommen; (wood, ice etc) einen Riss bekommen; **to get ~ing** (fam) loslegen ▷ vt (bone) anbrechen; (nut, code) knacken

cracker ['krækə°] n (biscuit) Kräcker m; (Christmas ~) Knallbonbon nt; **crackers** adj (fam) verrückt, bekloppt; **he's ~** er hat nicht alle Tassen im Schrank

crackle ['krækl] vi knistern; (telephone, radio) knacken; **crackling** n (Gastr) Kruste f (des Schweinebratens)

cradle ['kreɪdl] n Wiege f

craft [krɑ:ft] n Handwerk nt; (art) Kunsthandwerk nt; (Naut) Boot nt; **craftsman** (pl **-men**) n Handwerker m; **craftsmanship** n Handwerkskunst f; (ability) handwerkliches Können

crafty ['krɑ:ftɪ] adj schlau

cram [kræm] vt stopfen (into in +akk); **to be ~med with ...** mit ... vollgestopft sein ▷ vi (revise for exam) pauken (for für)

cramp [kræmp] n Krampf m

cranberry ['krænbərɪ] n Preiselbeere f
crane [kreɪn] n (machine) Kran m; (bird) Kranich m
crap [kræp] n (vulg) Scheiße f; (rubbish) Mist m ▷ adj beschissen, Scheiß-
crash [kræʃ] vi einen Unfall haben; (two vehicles) zusammenstoßen; (plane, computer) abstürzen; (economy) zusammenbrechen; **to ~ into sth** gegen etw knallen ▷ vt einen Unfall haben mit ▷ n (car) Unfall m; (train) Unglück nt; (collision) Zusammenstoß m; (Aviat, Inform) Absturz m; (noise) Krachen nt; **crash barrier** n Leitplanke f; **crash course** n Intensivkurs m; **crash helmet** n Sturzhelm m; **crash landing** n Bruchlandung f
crate [kreɪt] n Kiste f; (of beer) Kasten m
crater ['kreɪtə°] n Krater m
craving ['kreɪvɪŋ] n starkes Verlangen, Bedürfnis nt
crawl [krɔːl] vi kriechen; (baby) krabbeln ▷ n (swimming) Kraul m; **crawler lane** n Kriechspur f
crayfish ['kreɪfɪʃ] n Languste f
crayon ['kreɪən] n Buntstift m
crazy ['kreɪzɪ] adj verrückt (about nach)
cream [kriːm] n (from milk) Sahne f, Rahm m; (polish, cosmetic) Creme f ▷ adj cremefarben; **cream cake** n (small) Sahnetörtchen nt; (big) Sahnetorte f; **cream cheese** n Frischkäse m; **creamer** n Kaffeeweißer m; **cream tea** n (Brit) Nachmittagstee mit Törtchen, Marmelade und Schlagsahne; **creamy** adj sahnig
crease [kriːs] n Falte f ▷ vt falten; (untidy) zerknittern
create [kriːˈeɪt] vt schaffen; (cause) verursachen; **creative**

['kriːˈeɪtɪv] adj schöpferisch; (person) kreativ; **creature** ['kriːtʃə°] n Geschöpf nt
crèche [kreʃ] n Kinderkrippe f
credible ['kredɪbl] adj (person) glaubwürdig; **credibility** n Glaubwürdigkeit f
credit ['kredɪt] n (Fin: amount allowed) Kredit m; (amount possessed) Guthaben nt; (recognition) Anerkennung f; **~s** (of film) Abspann m; **credit card** n Kreditkarte f; **credit crunch** n Kreditklemme f
creep [kriːp] (**crept, crept**) vi kriechen; **creeps** n: **he gives me the ~** er ist mir nicht ganz geheuer; **creepy** ['kriːpɪ] adj (frightening) gruselig, unheimlich
crept [krept] pt, pp of **creep**
cress [kres] n Kresse f
crest [krest] n Kamm m; (coat of arms) Wappen nt
crew [kruː] n Besatzung f, Mannschaft f
crib [krɪb] n (US) Kinderbett nt
cricket ['krɪkɪt] n (insect) Grille f; (game) Kricket nt
crime [kraɪm] n Verbrechen nt; **criminal** ['krɪmɪnl] n Verbrecher(in) m(f) ▷ adj kriminell, strafbar
cripple ['krɪpl] n Krüppel m ▷ vt verkrüppeln, lähmen
crisis ['kraɪsɪs] (pl **crises**) n Krise f
crisp [krɪsp] adj knusprig; **crisps** npl (Brit) Chips pl; **crispbread** n Knäckebrot m
criterion [kraɪˈtɪərɪən] n Kriterium nt
critic ['krɪtɪk] n Kritiker(in) m(f); **critical** adj kritisch; **critically** adv kritisch; **~ ill/injured** schwer krank/verletzt; **criticism** ['krɪtɪsɪzəm] n Kritik f; **criticize** ['krɪtɪsaɪz] vt kritisieren
Croat ['krəʊæt] n Kroate m,

Kroatin f; **Croatia** [krəʊˈeɪʃə] n Kroatien nt; **Croatian** [krəʊˈeɪʃən] adj kroatisch

crockery [ˈkrɒkərɪ] n Geschirr nt

crocodile [ˈkrɒkədaɪl] n Krokodil nt

crocus [ˈkrəʊkəs] n Krokus m

crop [krɒp] n (harvest) Ernte f; **crops** npl Getreide nt; **crop up** vi auftauchen

croquette [krəˈket] n Krokette f

cross [krɒs] n Kreuz nt; **to mark sth with a ~** etw ankreuzen ▷ vt (road, river etc) überqueren; (legs) übereinanderschlagen; **it -ed my mind** es fiel mir ein; **to ~ one's fingers** die Daumen drücken ▷ adj ärgerlich, böse; **cross out** vt durchstreichen

crossbar n (of bicycle) Stange f; (Sport) Querlatte f; **cross-country** adj: **~ running** Geländelauf m; **~ skiing** Langlauf m; **cross-examination** n Kreuzverhör nt; **cross-eyed** adj: **to be ~** schielen; **crossing** n (crossroads) (Straßen)kreuzung f; (for pedestrians) Fußgängerüberweg m; (on ship) Überfahrt f; **crossroads** nsing o pl Straßenkreuzung f; **cross section** n Querschnitt m; **crosswalk** n (US) Fußgängerüberweg m; **crossword (puzzle)** n Kreuzworträtsel nt

crouch [krautʃ] vi hocken

crouton [ˈkruːtɒn] n Croûton m

crow [krəʊ] n Krähe f

crowbar [ˈkrəʊbɑː°] n Brecheisen nt

crowd [kraud] n Menge f ▷ vi sich drängen (into in +akk; round um); **crowded** adj überfüllt

crown [kraun] n Krone f ▷ vt krönen; (fam) **and to ~ it all ...** und als Krönung ...

crucial [ˈkruːʃəl] adj entscheidend

crude [kruːd] adj primitiv; (humour, behaviour) derb, ordinär ▷ n: **~ (oil)** Rohöl nt

cruel [ˈkruəl] adj grausam (to zu, gegen); (unfeeling) gefühllos; **cruelty** n Grausamkeit f; **~ to animals** Tierquälerei f

cruise [kruːz] n Kreuzfahrt f ▷ vi (ship) kreuzen; (car) mit Reisegeschwindigkeit fahren; **cruise liner** n Kreuzfahrtschiff nt; **cruise missile** n Marschflugkörper m; **cruising speed** n Reisegeschwindigkeit f

crumb [krʌm] n Krume f

crumble [ˈkrʌmbl] vt, vi zerbröckeln ▷ n mit Streuseln überbackenes Kompott

crumpet [ˈkrʌmpɪt] n weiches Hefegebäck zum Toasten; (fam: attractive woman) Schnecke f

crumple [ˈkrʌmpl] vt zerknittern

crunchy [ˈkrʌntʃɪ] adj (Brit) knusprig

crusade [kruːˈseɪd] n Kreuzzug m

crush [krʌʃ] vt zerdrücken; (finger etc) quetschen; (spices, stone) zerstoßen ▷ n: **to have a ~ on sb** in jdn verknallt sein; **crushing** adj (defeat, remark) vernichtend

crust [krʌst] n Kruste f; **crusty** adj knusprig

crutch [krʌtʃ] n Krücke f

cry [kraɪ] vi (call) rufen; (scream) schreien; (weep) weinen ▷ n (call) Ruf m; (louder) Schrei m

crypt [krɪpt] n Krypta f

crystal [ˈkrɪstl] n Kristall m

cu abbr = **see you** (SMS, e-mail) bis bald

Cuba [ˈkjuːbə] n Kuba nt

cube [kjuːb] n Würfel m

cubic [ˈkjuːbɪk] adj Kubik-

cubicle [ˈkjuːbɪkl] n Kabine f

cuckoo ['kʊkuː] n Kuckuck m

cucumber ['kjuːkʌmbə°] n Salatgurke f

cuddle ['kʌdl] vt in den Arm nehmen; (amorously) schmusen mit ▷ n Liebkosung f, Umarmung f; **to have a ~** schmusen; **cuddly** adj verschmust; **cuddly toy** n Plüschtier nt

cuff [kʌf] n Manschette f; (US: trouser ~) Aufschlag m; **off the ~** aus dem Stegreif; **cufflink** n Manschettenknopf m

cuisine [kwɪˈziːn] n Kochkunst f, Küche f

cul-de-sac ['kʌldəsæk] n (Brit) Sackgasse f

culprit ['kʌlprɪt] n Schuldige(r) mf; (fig) Übeltäter(in) m(f)

cult [kʌlt] n Kult m

cultivate ['kʌltɪveɪt] vt (Agr: land) bebauen; (crop) anbauen; **cultivated** adj (person) kultiviert, gebildet

cultural ['kʌltʃərəl] adj kulturell, Kultur-; **culture** ['kʌltʃə°] n Kultur f; **cultured** adj gebildet, kultiviert; **culture vulture** (Brit fam) n Kulturfanatiker(in) m(f)

cumbersome ['kʌmbəsəm] adj (object) unhandlich

cumin ['kʌmɪn] n Kreuzkümmel m

cunning ['kʌnɪŋ] adj schlau; (person a.) gerissen

cup [kʌp] n Tasse f; (prize) Pokal m; **it's not his ~ of tea** das ist nicht sein Fall; **cupboard** ['kʌbəd] n Schrank m; **cup final** n Pokalendspiel nt; **cup tie** n Pokalspiel nt

cupola ['kjuːpələ] n Kuppel f

curable ['kjʊərəbl] adj heilbar

curb [kɜːb] n (US) see **kerb**

curd [kɜːd] n: **~ cheese**, **~s** ≈ Quark m

cure [kjʊə°] n Heilmittel nt (for

gegen); (process) Heilung f ▷ vt heilen; (Gastr) pökeln; (smoke) räuchern

curious ['kjʊərɪəs] adj neugierig; (strange) seltsam

curl [kɜːl] n Locke f ▷ vi sich kräuseln; **curly** adj lockig

currant ['kʌrənt] n (dried) Korinthe f; (red, black) Johannisbeere f

currency ['kʌrənsɪ] n Währung f; **foreign ~** Devisen pl

current ['kʌrənt] n (in water) Strömung f; (electric ~) Strom m ▷ adj (issue, affairs) aktuell, gegenwärtig; (expression) gängig; **current account** n Girokonto nt; **currently** adv zur Zeit

curriculum [kəˈrɪkjʊləm] n Lehrplan m; **curriculum vitae** [kəˈrɪkjʊləmˈviːtaɪ] n (Brit) Lebenslauf m

curry ['kʌrɪ] n Currygericht nt; **curry powder** n Curry(pulver) nt

curse [kɜːs] vi (swear) fluchen (at auf +akk) ▷ n Fluch m

cursor ['kɜːsə°] n (Inform) Cursor m

curt [kɜːt] adj schroff, kurz angebunden

curtain ['kɜːtn] n Vorhang m; **it was ~s for Benny** für Benny war alles vorbei

curve [kɜːv] n Kurve f ▷ vi einen Bogen machen; **curved** adj gebogen

cushion ['kʊʃən] n Kissen nt

custard ['kʌstəd] n dicke Vanillesoße, die warm oder kalt zu vielen englischen Nachspeisen gegessen wird

custom ['kʌstəm] n Brauch m; (habit) Gewohnheit f; **customary** ['kʌstəmrɪ] adj üblich; **custom-built** adj nach Kundenangaben gefertigt; **customer** ['kʌstəmə°] n Kunde

m, Kundin *f*; **customer loyalty
card** *n* Kundenkarte *f*; **customer
service** *n* Kundendienst *m*

customs [ˈkʌstəmz] *npl* (*organization, location*) Zoll *m*; **to pass
through ~** durch den Zoll gehen;
customs officer *n* Zollbeamte(r)
m, Zollbeamtin *f*

cut [kʌt] (**cut, cut**) *vt* schneiden;
(*cake*) anschneiden; (*wages,
benefits*) kürzen; (*prices*)
heruntersetzen; **I ~ my finger** ich
habe mir in den Finger
geschnitten ▷ *n* Schnitt *m*;
(*wound*) Schnittwunde *f*; (*reduction*)
Kürzung *f* (*in gen*); **price/tax ~**
Preissenkung/Steuersenkung *f*;
to be a ~ above the rest eine
Klasse besser als die anderen sein;
cut back *vt* (*workforce etc*)
reduzieren; **cut down** *vt* (*tree*)
fällen; **to ~ on sth** etwas
einschränken; **cut in** *vi* (*Auto*)
scharf einscheren; **to ~ on sb** jdn
schneiden; **cut off** *vt*
abschneiden; (*gas, electricity*)
abdrehen, abstellen; (*Tel*) **I was
~** ich wurde unterbrochen

cutback *n* Kürzung *f*

cute [kjuːt] *adj* putzig, niedlich;
(*US: shrewd*) clever

cutlery [ˈkʌtləri] *n* Besteck *nt*

cutlet [ˈkʌtlɪt] *n* (*pork*) Kotelett
nt; (*veal*) Schnitzel *nt*

cut-price *adj* verbilligt

cutting [ˈkʌtɪŋ] *n* (*from paper*)
Ausschnitt *m*; (*of plant*) Ableger *m*
▷ *adj* (*comment*) verletzend

CV *abbr* = **curriculum vitae**

cwt *abbr* = **hundredweight** =
Zentner, Ztr.

cybercafé [saɪbəˈkæfeɪ] *n*
Internetcafé *nt*; **cyberspace** *n*
Cyberspace *m*

cycle [ˈsaɪkl] *n* Fahrrad *nt* ▷ *vi*
Rad fahren; **cycle lane, cycle path**
n Radweg *m*; **cycling** *n*

Radfahren *nt*; **cyclist** [ˈsaɪklɪst]
n Radfahrer(in) *m(f)*

cylinder [ˈsɪlɪndə°] *n* Zylinder *m*

cynical [ˈsɪnɪkəl] *adj* zynisch

cypress [ˈsaɪprɪs] *n* Zypresse *f*

Cypriot [ˈsɪprɪət] *adj* zypriotisch
▷ *n* Zypriote *m*, Zypriotin *f*;
Cyprus [ˈsaɪprəs] *n* Zypern *nt*

czar [zɑː°] *n* Zar *m*; **czarina**
[zɑːˈriːnə] *n* Zarin *f*

Czech [tʃek] *adj* tschechisch ▷ *n*
(*person*) Tscheche *m*, Tschechin *f*;
(*language*) Tschechisch *nt*; **Czech
Republic** *n* Tschechische
Republik, Tschechien *nt*

d

dab [dæb] vt *(wound, nose etc)* betupfen *(with* mit)

dachshund ['dækshʊnd] n Dackel m

dad(dy) ['dæd(ɪ)] n Papa m, Vati m; **daddy-longlegs** nsing *(Brit)* Schnake; *(US)* Weberknecht m

daffodil ['dæfədɪl] n Osterglocke f

daft [dɑːft] adj *(fam)* blöd, doof

dahlia ['deɪlɪə] n Dahlie f

daily ['deɪlɪ] adj, adv täglich ▷ n *(paper)* Tageszeitung f

dairy ['dɛərɪ] n *(on farm)* Molkerei f; *(shop)* Milchgeschäft nt; **dairy products** npl Milchprodukte pl

daisy ['deɪzɪ] n Gänseblümchen nt

dam [dæm] n Staudamm m ▷ vt stauen

damage ['dæmɪdʒ] n Schaden m; **~s** pl *(Jur)* Schadenersatz m ▷ vt beschädigen; *(reputation, health)* schädigen, schaden +dat

damn [dæm] adj *(fam)* verdammt ▷ vt *(condemn)* verurteilen; **~ (it)!** verflucht! ▷ n: **he doesn't give a ~** es ist ihm völlig egal

damp [dæmp] adj feucht ▷ n Feuchtigkeit f; **dampen** ['dæmpən] vt befeuchten

dance [dɑːns] n Tanz m; *(event)* Tanzveranstaltung f ▷ vi tanzen; **dance floor** n Tanzfläche f; **dancer** n Tänzer(in) m(f); **dancing** n Tanzen nt

dandelion ['dændɪlaɪən] n Löwenzahn m

dandruff ['dændrəf] n Schuppen pl

Dane [deɪn] n Däne m, Dänin f

danger ['deɪndʒə*] n Gefahr f; **~ (sign)** Achtung!; **to be in ~** in Gefahr sein; **dangerous** adj gefährlich

Danish ['deɪnɪʃ] adj dänisch ▷ n *(language)* Dänisch nt; **the ~** pl die Dänen; **Danish pastry** n Plundergebäck nt

Danube ['dænjuːb] n Donau f

dare [dɛə*] vi: **to ~ (to) do sth** es wagen, etw zu tun; **I didn't ~ ask** ich traute mich nicht, zu fragen; **how ~ you** was fällt dir ein!; **daring** adj *(person)* mutig; *(film, clothes etc)* gewagt

dark [dɑːk] adj dunkel; *(gloomy)* düster, trübe; *(sinister)* finster; **~ chocolate** Bitterschokolade f; **~ green/blue** dunkelgrün/dunkelblau ▷ n Dunkelheit f; **in the ~** im Dunkeln; **dark glasses** npl Sonnenbrille f; **darkness** n Dunkelheit nt

darling ['dɑːlɪŋ] n Schatz m; *(also favourite)* Liebling m

darts [dɑːts] nsing *(game)* Darts nt

dash [dæʃ] vi stürzen, rennen

▷ vt: **to ~ hopes** Hoffnungen zerstören ▷ n (in text) Gedankenstrich m; (of liquid) Schuss m; **dashboard** n Armaturenbrett nt

data ['deɪtə] npl Daten pl; **data bank, data base** n Datenbank f; **data capture** n Datenerfassung f; **data processing** f; **data protection** n Datenschutz m

date [deɪt] n Datum nt; (for meeting, delivery etc) Termin m; (with person) Verabredung f; (with girlfriend/boyfriend etc) Date nt; (fruit) Dattel f; **what's the ~ (today)?** der Wievielte ist heute?; **out of ~** adj (news) aktuell; (fashion) zeitgemäß ▷ vt (letter etc) datieren; (person) gehen mit; **dated** adj altmodisch; **date of birth** n Geburtsdatum nt; **dating agency** n Partnervermittlung f

dative ['deɪtɪv] n Dativ m

daughter ['dɔːtə⁰] n Tochter f; **daughter-in-law** (pl **daughters-in-law**) n Schwiegertochter f

dawn [dɔːn] n Morgendämmerung f ▷ vi dämmern; **it ~ed on me** mir ging ein Licht auf

day [deɪ] n Tag m; **one ~** eines Tages; **by ~** bei Tage; **~ after ~, ~ by ~** Tag für Tag; **the ~ after/before** am Tag danach/zuvor; **the ~ after tomorrow** übermorgen; **these ~s** heutzutage; **in those ~s** damals; **let's call it a ~** Schluss für heute!; **daybreak** n Tagesanbruch m; **day-care center** (US), **day-care centre** n (Brit) Kita f (Kindertagesstätte); **daydream** n Tagtraum m ▷ vi (mit offenen Augen) träumen; **daylight**

Tageslicht nt; **in ~** bei Tage; **day nursery** n Kita f (Kindertagesstätte); **day return** n (Brit Rail) Tagesrückfahrkarte f; **daytime** n: **in the ~** bei Tage, tagsüber; **daytrip** n Tagesausflug m

dazed [deɪzd] adj benommen

dazzle ['dæzl] vt blenden; **dazzling** adj blendend, glänzend

dead [ded] adj tot; (limb) abgestorben ▷ adv genau; (fam) total, völlig; **~ tired** adj todmüde; **~ slow** (sign) Schritt fahren; **dead end** n Sackgasse f; **deadline** n Termin m; (period) Frist f; **~ for applications** Anmeldeschluss m; **deadly** adj tödlich ▷ adv: **~ dull** todlangweilig

deaf [def] adj taub; **deafen** vt taub machen; **deafening** adj ohrenbetäubend

deal [diːl] n (dealt, dealt) vt, vi (cards) geben, austeilen ▷ n (business ~) Abmachung f, (agreement) Abmachung f; **it's a ~** abgemacht!; **a good/great ~ of** ziemlich/sehr viel; **deal in** vt handeln mit; **deal with** vt (matter) sich beschäftigen mit; (book, film) behandeln mit; (successfully: person, problem) fertig werden mit; (matter) erledigen; **dealer** n (Comm) Händler(in) m(f); (drugs) Dealer(in) m(f); **dealings** npl (Comm) Geschäfte pl

dealt [delt] pt, pp of **deal**

dear [dɪə⁰] adj lieb, teuer; **Dear Sir or Madam** Sehr geehrte Damen und Herren; **Dear David** Lieber David ▷ n ▷ Schatz m; (as address) mein Schatz, Liebling; **dearly** adv (love) (heiß und) innig; (pay) teuer

death [deθ] n Tod m; (of project, hopes) Ende nt; (in accident etc) Todesfall m, Todesopfer nt; **death certificate** n Totenschein m;

death penalty n Todesstrafe f;
death toll n Zahl f der Todesopfer; **death trap** n Todesfalle f
debatable [dɪˈbeɪtəbl] adj
fraglich; (question) strittig; **debate**
[dɪˈbeɪt] n Debatte f ▷ vt
debattieren
debauched [dɪˈbɔːtʃt] adj
ausschweifend
debit [ˈdebɪt] n Soll nt ▷ vt
(account) belasten; **debit card** n
Geldkarte f
debris [ˈdebriː] n Trümmer pl
debt [det] n Schuld f; **to be in
~** verschuldet sein
debug [diːˈbʌg] vt (Inform) Fehler
beseitigen in +dat
decade [ˈdekeɪd] n Jahrzehnt nt
decadent [ˈdekədənt] adj
dekadent
decaff [ˈdiːkæf] n (fam) koffein-
freier Kaffee; **decaffeinated**
[diːˈkæfɪneɪtɪd] adj koffeinfrei
decanter [dɪˈkæntə*] n Dekanter
m, Karaffe f
decay [dɪˈkeɪ] n Verfall m;
(rotting) Verwesung f; (of tooth)
Karies f ▷ vi verfallen; (rot)
verwesen; (wood) vermodern;
(teeth) faulen; (leaves) verrotten
deceased [dɪˈsiːst] n: **the ~**
der/die Verstorbene
deceit [dɪˈsiːt] n Betrug m;
deceive [dɪˈsiːv] vt täuschen
December [dɪˈsembə*] n
Dezember m; see also **September**
decent [ˈdiːsənt] adj anständig
deception [dɪˈsepʃən] n Betrug
m; **deceptive** [dɪˈseptɪv] adj
täuschend, irreführend
decide [dɪˈsaɪd] vt (question)
entscheiden; (body of people)
beschließen; **I can't ~ what to do**
ich kann mich nicht entscheiden,
was ich tun soll ▷ vi sich
entscheiden; **to ~ on sth** (in favour
of sth) sich für etw entscheiden,

sich zu etw entschließen; **decided**
adj entschieden; (clear) deutlich;
decidedly adv entschieden
decimal [ˈdesɪml] adj Dezimal-;
decimal system n
Dezimalsystem nt
decipher [dɪˈsaɪfə*] vt entziffern
decision [dɪˈsɪʒən] n Entscheidung f (on über +akk); (of committee,
jury etc) Beschluss m; **to make a
~** eine Entscheidung treffen;
decisive [dɪˈsaɪsɪv] adj entscheidend; (person)
entscheidungsfreudig
deck [dek] n (Naut) Deck nt; (of
cards) Blatt nt; **deckchair** n
Liegestuhl m
declaration [dekləˈreɪʃən] n
Erklärung f; **declare** [dɪˈkleə*] vt
erklären; (state) behaupten (that
dass); (at customs) **have you
anything to ~?** haben Sie etwas
zu verzollen?
decline [dɪˈklaɪn] n Rückgang m
▷ vt (invitation, offer) ablehnen ▷ vi
(become less) sinken, abnehmen;
(health) sich verschlechtern
decode [diːˈkəʊd] vt
entschlüsseln
decompose [diːkəmˈpəʊz] vi sich
zersetzen
decontaminate
[diːkənˈtæmɪneɪt] vt entgiften;
(from radioactivity) entseuchen
decorate [ˈdekəreɪt] vt
(aus)schmücken; (wallpaper)
tapezieren; (paint) anstreichen;
decoration [dekəˈreɪʃən] n
Schmuck m; (process) Schmücken
nt; (wallpapering) Tapezieren nt;
(painting) Anstreichen nt;
Christmas ~s Weihnachts-
schmuck m; **decorator** n
Maler(in) m(f)
decrease [dɪˈkriːs] n Abnahme f
▷ [diːˈkriːs] vi abnehmen
dedicate [ˈdedɪkeɪt] vt widmen

(to sb jdm); **dedicated** adj (person)
engagiert; **dedication**
[dedɪˈkeɪʃən] n Widmung f;
(commitment) Hingabe f,
Engagement n

deduce [dɪˈdjuːs] vt folgern,
schließen (from aus, that dass)

deduct [dɪˈdʌkt] vt abziehen
(from von); **deduction**
[dɪˈdʌkʃən] n (of money) Abzug m; (conclusion)
(Schluss)folgerung f

deed [diːd] n Tat f

deep [diːp] adj tief; **deepen** vt
vertiefen; **deep-freeze** n
Tiefkühltruhe f; (upright)
Gefrierschrank m; **deep-fry** vt
frittieren

deer [dɪə°] n Reh nt; (with stag)
Hirsch m

defeat [dɪˈfiːt] n Niederlage f; **to
admit ~** sich geschlagen geben
▷ vt besiegen

defect [ˈdiːfekt] n Defekt m,
Fehler m; **defective** [dɪˈfektɪv]
adj fehlerhaft

defence [dɪˈfens] n Verteidigung
f; **defend** [dɪˈfend] vt
verteidigen; **defendant**
[dɪˈfendənt] n (Jur) Angeklagte(r)
mf; **defender** n (Sport)
Verteidiger(in) m(f); **defensive**
[dɪˈfensɪv] adj defensiv

deficiency [dɪˈfɪʃənsi] n Mangel
m; **deficient** adj mangelhaft;
deficit [ˈdefɪsɪt] n Defizit nt

define [dɪˈfaɪn] vt (word)
definieren; (duties, powers)
bestimmen; **definite** [ˈdefɪnɪt]
adj (clear) klar, eindeutig; (certain)
sicher; **it's ~** es steht fest;
definitely adv bestimmt;
definition [defɪˈnɪʃən] n Definition f; (Foto) Schärfe f

defrost [diːˈfrɒst] vt (fridge)
abtauen; (food) auftauen

degrading [dɪˈgreɪdɪŋ] adj
erniedrigend

degree [dɪˈgriː] n Grad m; (at
university) akademischer Grad; **a
certain/high ~ of** ein
gewisses/hohes Maß an +dat; **to a
certain ~** einigermaßen; **I have a
~ in chemistry** ≈ ich habe einen
Abschluss in Chemie

dehydrated [diːhaɪˈdreɪtɪd] adj
(food) getrocknet, Trocken-;
(person) ausgetrocknet

de-ice [diːˈaɪs] vt enteisen

delay [dɪˈleɪ] vt (postpone)
verschieben, aufschieben; **to be
~ed** (event) sich verzögern; **the
train/flight was ~ed** der Zug/die
Maschine hatte Verspätung ▷ vi
warten; (hesitate) zögern ▷ n
Verzögerung f; (of train etc)
Verspätung f; **without ~**
unverzüglich; **delayed** adj (train
etc) verspätet

delegate n [ˈdelɪgət] Dele-
gierte(r) mf ▷ [ˈdelɪgeɪt] vt
delegieren; **delegation**
[delɪˈgeɪʃən] n Abordnung f;
(foreign) Delegation f

delete [dɪˈliːt] vt (aus)streichen;
(Inform) löschen; **deletion** n
Streichung f; (Inform) Löschung f

deli [ˈdelɪ] n (fam)
Feinkostgeschäft nt

deliberate adj [dɪˈlɪbərət] adj
(intentional) absichtlich;
deliberately adv mit Absicht,
extra

delicate [ˈdelɪkɪt] adj (fine) fein;
(fragile) zart; (a. Med) empfindlich;
(situation) heikel

delicatessen [delɪkəˈtesn] nsing
Feinkostgeschäft nt

delicious [dɪˈlɪʃəs] adj köstlich,
lecker

delight [dɪˈlaɪt] n Freude f ▷ vt
entzücken; **delighted** adj sehr
erfreut (with über +akk); **delightful**
adj entzückend; (weather, meal etc)
herrlich

deliver | 322

deliver [dɪ'lɪvə*] vt (goods) liefern (to sb jdm); (letter, parcel) zustellen; (speech) halten; (baby) entbinden; **delivery** n Lieferung f; (of letter, parcel) Zustellung f; (of baby) Entbindung f; **delivery van** n Lieferwagen m

delude [dɪ'luːd] vt täuschen; **don't ~ yourself** mach dir nichts vor; **delusion** n Irrglaube m

de luxe [dɪ'lʌks] adj Luxus-

demand [dɪ'maːnd] vt verlangen (from von); (time, patience etc) erfordern ▷ n (request) Forderung f, Verlangen nt (for nach); (Comm: for goods) Nachfrage f; **on ~** auf Wunsch; **very much in ~** sehr gefragt; **demanding** adj anspruchsvoll

demented [dɪ'mentɪd] adj wahnsinnig

demerara [demə'reərə] n: **~ (sugar)** brauner Zucker

demister n Defroster m

demo ['deməʊ] (pl -s) n (fam) Demo f

democracy [dɪ'mɒkrəsɪ] n Demokratie f; **democrat**, **Democrat** (US Pol) ['deməkræt] Demokrat(in) m(f); **democratic** adj demokratisch; **the Democratic Party** (US Pol) die Demokratische Partei

demolish [dɪ'mɒlɪʃ] vt abreißen; (fig) zerstören; **demolition** [demə'lɪʃən] n Abbruch m

demonstrate ['demənstreɪt] vt, vi demonstrieren, beweisen; **demonstration** n Demonstration f

demoralize [dɪ'mɒrəlaɪz] vt demoralisieren

denial [dɪ'naɪəl] n Leugnung f; (official ~) Dementi nt

denim ['denɪm] n Jeansstoff m; **denim jacket** n Jeansjacke f; **denims** npl Bluejeans pl

Denmark ['denmaːk] n Dänemark nt

denomination [dɪnɒmɪ'neɪʃən] n (Rel) Konfession f; (Comm) Nennwert m

dense [dens] adj dicht; (fam: stupid) schwer von Begriff; **density** ['densɪtɪ] n Dichte f

dent [dent] n Beule f, Delle f ▷ vt einbeulen

dental ['dentl] adj Zahn-; **~ care** Zahnpflege f; **~ floss** Zahnseide f; **dentist** ['dentɪst] n Zahnarzt m, Zahnärztin; **dentures** ['dentʃəz] npl Zahnprothese f; (full) Gebiss nt

deny [dɪ'naɪ] vt leugnen, bestreiten; (refuse) ablehnen

deodorant [diː'əʊdərənt] n Deo(dorant) nt

depart [dɪ'paːt] vi abreisen; (bus, train) abfahren (for nach, from von); (plane) abfliegen (for nach, from von)

department [dɪ'paːtmənt] n Abteilung f; (at university) Institut nt; (Pol: ministry) Ministerium nt; **department store** n Kaufhaus nt

departure [dɪ'paːtʃə*] n (of person) Weggang m; (on journey) Abreise f (for nach); (of train etc) Abfahrt f (for nach); (of plane) Abflug m (for nach); **departure lounge** n (Aviat) Abflughalle f; **departure time** n Abfahrtzeit f; (Aviat) Abflugzeit f

depend [dɪ'pend] vi: **it ~s** es kommt darauf an (whether, if ob); **depend on** vt (thing) abhängen von; (person: rely on) sich verlassen auf +akk; (person, area etc) angewiesen sein auf +akk; **it ~s on the weather** es kommt auf das Wetter an; **dependable** adj zuverlässig; **dependence** n Abhängigkeit f (on von); **dependent** adj abhängig (on von)

deport [dɪ'pɔːt] vt ausweisen,

abschieben; **deportation**
[di:pɔ:ˈteɪʃən] n Abschiebung f

deposit [dɪˈpɒzɪt] n (down
payment) Anzahlung f; (security)
Kaution f; (for bottle) Pfand nt; (to
bank account) Einzahlung f; (in river
etc) Ablagerung f ▷ vt (put down)
abstellen, absetzen; (to bank
account) einzahlen; (sth valuable)
deponieren; **deposit account** n
Sparkonto nt

depot [ˈdepəʊ] n Depot nt

depreciate [dɪˈpriːʃɪeɪt] vi an
Wert verlieren

depress [dɪˈpres] vt (in mood)
deprimieren; **depressed** adj
(person) niedergeschlagen,
deprimiert; **~ area**
Notstandsgebiet nt; **depressing**
adj deprimierend; **depression**
[dɪˈpreʃən] n (in mood) Depression f;
(Meteo) Tief nt

deprive [dɪˈpraɪv] vt: **to ~ sb of
sth** jdn einer Sache berauben;
deprived adj (child) (sozial)
benachteiligt

dept abbr = **department** Abt.

depth [depθ] n Tiefe f

deputy [ˈdepjʊtɪ] adj stell-
vertretend, Vize- ▷ n
Stellvertreter(in) m(f); (US Pol)
Abgeordnete(r) mf

derail [dɪˈreɪl] vt entgleisen
lassen; **to be ~ed** entgleisen

deranged [dɪˈreɪndʒd] adj
geistesgestört

derivation [derɪˈveɪʃən] n
Ableitung f; **derive** [dɪˈraɪv] vt
ableiten (from von) ▷ abstammen
(from von)

dermatitis [dɜːməˈtaɪtɪs] n
Hautentzündung f

derogatory [dɪˈrɒgətərɪ] adj
abfällig

descend [dɪˈsend] vt, vi
hinabsteigen, hinuntergehen;
(person) **to ~** o **be ~ed from**

abstammen von; **descendant** n
Nachkomme m; **descent** [dɪˈsent]
n (coming down) Abstieg m; (origin)
Abstammung f

describe [dɪsˈkraɪb] vt beschreiben; **description**
[dɪsˈkrɪpʃən] n Beschreibung f

desert [ˈdezət] n Wüste f
▷ [dɪˈzɜːt] vt verlassen; (abandon)
im Stich lassen; **deserted** adj
verlassen; (empty) menschenleer

deserve [dɪˈzɜːv] vt verdienen

design [dɪˈzaɪn] n (plan) Entwurf
m; (of vehicle, machine)
Konstruktion f; (of object) Design
nt; (planning) Gestaltung f ▷ vt
entwerfen; (machine etc)
konstruieren; **~ed for sb/sth**
(intended) für jdn/etw konzipiert

designate [ˈdezɪgneɪt] vt
bestimmen

designer [dɪˈzaɪnəʳ] n
Designer(in) m(f); (Tech)
Konstrukteur(in) m(f); **designer
drug** n Designerdroge f

desirable [dɪˈzaɪərəbl] n
wünschenswert; (person)
begehrenswert; **desire** [dɪˈzaɪəʳ]
n Wunsch m (for nach); (esp sexual)
Begierde f (for nach) ▷ vt
wünschen; (ask for) verlangen; **if
~d** auf Wunsch

desk [desk] n Schreibtisch m;
(reception) Empfang m; (at airport
etc) Schalter m; **desktop
publishing** n Desktoppublishing
nt

desolate [ˈdesəlɪt] adj trostlos

despair [dɪsˈpeəʳ] n Verzweiflung f (at über +akk) ▷ vi
verzweifeln (of an +dat)

despatch [dɪsˈpætʃ] see **dispatch**

desperate [ˈdespərɪt] adj
verzweifelt; (situation)
hoffnungslos; **to be ~ for sth** etw
dringend brauchen, unbedingt
wollen; **desperation**

despicable | 324

[dɪspə'reɪʃən] n Verzweiflung f

despicable [dɪ'spɪkəbl] adj verachtenswert; **despise** [dɪ'spaɪz] vt verachten

despite [dɪ'spaɪt] prep trotz +gen

dessert [dɪ'zɜ:t] n Nachtisch m; **dessert spoon** n Dessertlöffel m

destination [destɪ'neɪʃən] n (of person) (Reise)ziel nt; (of goods) Bestimmungsort m

destiny ['destɪnɪ] n Schicksal nt

destroy [dɪ'strɔɪ] vt zerstören; (completely) vernichten; **destruction** [dɪ'strʌkʃən] n Zerstörung f; (complete) Vernichtung f; **destructive** [dɪ'strʌktɪv] adj zerstörerisch; (esp fig) destruktiv

detach [dɪ'tætʃ] vt abnehmen; (from form etc) abtrennen; (free) lösen (from von); **detachable** adj abnehmbar; (from form etc) abtrennbar; **detached** adj (attitude) distanziert, objektiv; **~ house** Einzelhaus nt

detail ['di:teɪl, (US) dɪ'teɪl] n Einzelheit f, Detail nt; (further) **~s from ...** Näheres erfahren Sie bei ...; **to go into ~** ins Detail gehen; **in ~** ausführlich; **detailed** adj detailliert, ausführlich

detain [dɪ'teɪn] vt aufhalten; (police) in Haft nehmen

detect [dɪ'tekt] vt entdecken; (notice) wahrnehmen; **detective** [dɪ'tektɪv] n Detektiv(in) m(f); **detective story** n Krimi m

detention [dɪ'tenʃən] n Haft f; (Sch) Nachsitzen nt

deter [dɪ'tɜ:°] vt abschrecken (from von)

detergent [dɪ'tɜ:dʒənt] n Reinigungsmittel nt; (soap powder) Waschmittel nt

deteriorate [dɪ'tɪərɪəreɪt] vi sich verschlechtern

determination [dɪtɜ:mɪ'neɪʃən] n Entschlossenheit f; **determine** [dɪ'tɜ:mɪn] vt bestimmen; **determined** adj (fest) entschlossen

deterrent [dɪ'terənt] n Abschreckungsmittel nt

detest [dɪ'test] vt verabscheuen; **detestable** adj abscheulich

detour ['di:tʊə°] n Umweg m; (of traffic) Umleitung f

deuce [dju:s] n (Tennis) Einstand m

devalue [di:'vælju:] vt abwerten

devastate ['devəsteɪt] vt verwüsten; **devastating** ['devəsteɪtɪŋ] adj verheerend

develop [dɪ'veləp] vt entwickeln; (illness) bekommen ▷ vi sich entwickeln; **developing country** n Entwicklungsland nt; **development** n Entwicklung f; (of land) Erschließung f

device [dɪ'vaɪs] n Vorrichtung f, Gerät nt

devil ['devl] n Teufel m; **devilish** adj teuflisch

devote [dɪ'vəʊt] vt widmen (to dat); **devoted** adj liebend; (servant etc) treu ergeben; **devotion** n Hingabe f

devour [dɪ'vaʊə°] vt verschlingen

dew [dju:] n Tau m

diabetes [daɪə'bi:ti:z] n Diabetes m, Zuckerkrankheit f; **diabetic** [daɪə'betɪk] adj zuckerkrank; für Diabetiker ▷ n Diabetiker(in) m(f)

diagnosis (diagnoses) [daɪəg'nəʊsɪs] (pl **diagnoses**) n Diagnose f

diagonal [daɪ'ægənl] adj diagonal

diagram ['daɪəgræm] n Diagramm nt

dial ['daɪəl] n Skala f; (of clock)

Zifferblatt nt ▷ vt (Tel) wählen; **dial code** n (US) Vorwahl f
dialect ['daɪəlɛkt] n Dialekt m
dialling code n (Brit) Vorwahl f; **dialling tone** n (Brit) Amtszeichen nt
dialogue, dialog (US) ['daɪəlɒg] n Dialog m
dial tone n (US) Amtszeichen nt
dialysis [daɪˈælɪsɪs] n (Med) Dialyse f
diameter [daɪˈæmɪtəʳ] n Durchmesser m
diamond ['daɪəmənd] n Diamant m; (Cards) Karo nt
diaper ['daɪpəʳ] n (US) Windel f
diarrhoea [daɪəˈriːə] n Durchfall m
diary ['daɪərɪ] n (Taschen)kalender m; (account) Tagebuch nt
dice [daɪs] npl Würfel pl; **diced** adj in Würfel geschnitten
dictate [dɪkˈteɪt] vt diktieren; **dictation** [dɪkˈteɪʃən] n Diktat nt
dictator [dɪkˈteɪtəʳ] n Diktator(in) m(f); **dictatorship** [dɪkˈteɪtəʃɪp] n Diktatur f
dictionary ['dɪkʃənrɪ] n Wörterbuch nt
did [dɪd] pt of **do**
didn't ['dɪdnt] contr of **did not**
die [daɪ] vi sterben (of an +dat); (plant, animal) eingehen; (engine) absterben; **to be dying to do sth** darauf brennen, etw zu tun; **I'm dying for a drink** ich brauche unbedingt was zu trinken; **die away** vi schwächer werden; (wind) sich legen; **die down** vi nachlassen; **die out** vi aussterben
diesel ['diːzəl] n (fuel, car) Diesel m; **~ engine** n Dieselmotor m
diet ['daɪət] n Kost f; (special food) Diät f ▷ vi eine Diät machen
differ ['dɪfəʳ] vi (be different) sich unterscheiden; (disagree) anderer Meinung sein; **difference**

['dɪfrəns] n Unterschied m; **it makes no ~ (to me)** es ist (mir) egal; **it makes a big ~** es macht viel aus; **different** adj andere(r, s); (with pl) verschieden; **to be quite ~** ganz anders sein (from als); (two people, things) völlig verschieden sein; **a ~ person** ein anderer Mensch; **differentiate** [dɪfəˈrɛnʃɪeɪt] vt, vi unterscheiden; **differently** ['dɪfrəntlɪ] adv anders (from als); (from one another) unterschiedlich
difficult ['dɪfɪkəlt] adj schwierig; **I find it ~** es fällt mir schwer; **difficulty** n Schwierigkeit f; **with ~** nur schwer; **to have ~ in doing sth** etw nur mit Mühe machen können
dig [dɪg] (dug, dug) vt, vi (hole) graben; **dig in** vi (fam: to food) reinhauen; **~!** greif(t) zu!; **dig up** vt ausgraben
digest [daɪˈdʒɛst] vt (a. fig) verdauen; **digestible** [dɪˈdʒɛstəbl] adj verdaulich; **digestion** [dɪˈdʒɛstʃən] n Verdauung f; **digestive** [dɪˈdʒɛstɪv] adj: **~ biscuit** (Brit) Vollkornkeks m
digit ['dɪdʒɪt] n Ziffer f; **digital** ['dɪdʒɪtəl] adj digital; **~ computer** Digitalrechner m; **~ watch/clock** Digitaluhr f; **digital camera** n Digitalkamera f; **digital television, digital TV** n Digitalfernsehen nt
dignified ['dɪgnɪfaɪd] adj würdevoll; **dignity** ['dɪgnɪtɪ] n Würde f
dilapidated [dɪˈlæpɪdeɪtɪd] adj baufällig
dilemma [daɪˈlɛmə] n Dilemma nt
dill [dɪl] n Dill m
dilute [daɪˈluːt] vt verdünnen
dim [dɪm] adj (light) schwach; (outline) undeutlich; (stupid)

schwer von Begriff ▷ vt
verdunkeln; (US Auto) abblenden;
~med headlights (US)
Abblendlicht nt

dime [daɪm] n (US)
Zehncentstück nt

dimension [daɪˈmenʃən] n
Dimension f; **~s** pl Maße pl

diminish [dɪˈmɪnɪʃ] vt
verringern ▷ vi sich verringern

dimple [ˈdɪmpl] n Grübchen nt

dine [daɪn] vi speisen; **dine out**
vi außer Haus essen; **diner** n Gast
m; (Rail) Speisewagen m; (US)
Speiselokal nt

dinghy [ˈdɪŋɪ] n Ding(h)i nt;
(inflatable) Schlauchboot nt

dingy [ˈdɪndʒɪ] adj düster; (dirty)
schmuddelig

dining car [ˈdaɪnɪŋkɑːʳ] n
Speisewagen m; **dining room** n
Esszimmer nt; (in hotel)
Speiseraum m; **dining table** n
Esstisch m

dinner [ˈdɪnəʳ] n Abendessen nt;
(lunch) Mittagessen nt; (public)
Diner nt; **to be at ~** beim Essen
sein; **to have ~** zu Abend/Mittag
essen; **dinner jacket** n Smoking
m; **dinner party** n
Abendgesellschaft f (mit Essen);
dinnertime n Essenszeit f

dinosaur [ˈdaɪnəsɔːʳ] n Dinosaurier m

dip [dɪp] vt tauchen (in in +akk);
to ~ (one's headlights) (Brit Auto)
abblenden; **~ped headlights**
Abblendlicht nt ▷ n (in ground)
Bodensenke f; (sauce) Dip m

diploma [dɪˈpləʊmə] n Diplom nt

diplomat [ˈdɪpləmæt] n Diplo-
mat(in) m(f); **diplomatic**
[dɪpləˈmætɪk] adj diplomatisch

dipstick [ˈdɪpstɪk] n Ölmessstab
m

(cause, consequence) unmittelbar;
~ debit (mandate)
Einzugsermächtigung f;
(transaction) Abbuchung f im
Lastschriftverfahren; **~ train**
durchgehender Zug ▷ vt (aim,
send) richten (at, to an +akk); (film)
die Regie führen bei; (traffic)
regeln; **direct current** n (Elec)
Gleichstrom m

direction [dɪˈrekʃən] n (course)
Richtung f; (Cine) Regie f; **in
the ~ of ...** in Richtung ...; **~s**
pl (to a place) Wegbeschreibung f

directly [dɪˈrektlɪ] adv direkt; (at
once) sofort

director [dɪˈrektəʳ] n Direk-
tor(in) m(f), Leiter(in) m(f); (of film)
Regisseur(in) m(f)

directory [dɪˈrektərɪ] n Adressbuch nt; (Tel) Telefonbuch nt;
~ enquiries o (US) **assistance** (Tel)
Auskunft f

dirt [dɜːt] n Schmutz m, Dreck m;
dirt cheap adj spottbillig; **dirt
road** n unbefestigte Straße; **dirty**
adj schmutzig

disability [dɪsəˈbɪlɪtɪ] n
Behinderung f; **disabled**
[dɪsˈeɪbld] adj behindert,
Behinderten- ▷ npl: **the ~** die
Behinderten

disadvantage [dɪsədˈvɑːntɪdʒ]
n Nachteil m; **at a ~** benachteiligt;
disadvantageous [dɪsædvɑːn-
ˈteɪdʒəs] adj unvorteilhaft,
ungünstig

disagree [dɪsəˈgriː] vi anderer
Meinung sein; (two people) sich
nicht einig sein; (two reports etc)
nicht übereinstimmen; **to ~ with
sb** mit jdm nicht übereinstimmen;
(food) jdm nicht bekommen;
disagreeable adj unangenehm;
(person) unsympathisch;
disagreement n Meinungsverschiedenheit f

direct [daɪˈrekt] adj direkt;

disappear [dɪsə'pɪə°] vi verschwinden; **disappearance** n Verschwinden nt

disappoint [dɪsə'pɔɪnt] vt enttäuschen; **disappointing** adj enttäuschend; **disappointment** n Enttäuschung f

disapproval [dɪsə'pruːvl] n Missbilligung f; **disapprove** [dɪsə'pruːv] vi missbilligen (of akk)

disarm [dɪs'ɑːm] vt entwaffnen ▷ vi (Pol) abrüsten; **disarmament** n Abrüstung f; **disarming** adj (smile, look) gewinnend

disaster [dɪ'zɑːstə°] n Katastrophe f; **disastrous** [dɪ'zɑːstrəs] adj katastrophal

disbelief [dɪsbə'liːf] n Ungläubigkeit f

disc [dɪsk] n Scheibe f, CD f; see also **disk**; (Anat) Bandscheibe f; **disc brake** n Scheibenbremse f

discharge ['dɪstʃɑːdʒ] n (Med) Ausfluss m ▷ [dɪs'tʃɑːdʒ] vt (person) entlassen; (emit) ausstoßen; (Med) ausscheiden

discipline ['dɪsɪplɪn] n Disziplin f

disc jockey ['dɪskdʒɒkɪ] n Diskjockey m

disclose [dɪs'kləʊz] vt bekannt geben; (secret) enthüllen

disco ['dɪskəʊ] (pl -s) n Disko f, Diskomusik f

discomfort [dɪs'kʌmfət] n (slight pain) leichte Schmerzen pl; (unease) Unbehagen nt

disconnect [dɪskə'nekt] vt (electricity, gas, phone) abstellen; (unplug) **to ~ the TV (from the mains)** den Stecker des Fernsehers herausziehen; (Tel) **I've been ~ed** das Gespräch ist unterbrochen worden

discontent [dɪskən'tent] n Unzufriedenheit f; **discontented** adj unzufrieden

discontinue [dɪskən'tɪnjuː] vt einstellen; (product) auslaufen lassen

discount ['dɪskaʊnt] n Rabatt m

discover [dɪs'kʌvə°] vt entdecken; **discovery** n Entdeckung f

discredit [dɪs'kredɪt] vt in Verruf bringen ▷ n Misskredit m

discreet [dɪs'kriːt] adj diskret

discrepancy [dɪs'krepənsɪ] n Unstimmigkeit f, Diskrepanz f

discriminate [dɪs'krɪmɪneɪt] vi unterscheiden; **to ~ against sb** jdn diskriminieren; **discrimination** [dɪskrɪmɪ'neɪʃən] n (different treatment) Diskriminierung f

discus ['dɪskəs] n Diskus m

discuss [dɪs'kʌs] vt diskutieren, besprechen; **discussion** [dɪs'kʌʃən] n Diskussion f

disease [dɪ'ziːz] n Krankheit f

disembark [dɪsɪm'bɑːk] vi von Bord gehen

disentangle ['dɪsɪn'tæŋgl] vt entwirren

disgrace [dɪs'greɪs] n Schande f ▷ vt Schande machen +dat; (family etc) Schande bringen über +akk; (less strong) blamieren; **disgraceful** adj skandalös

disguise [dɪs'gaɪz] vt verkleiden; (voice) verstellen ▷ n Verkleidung f, **in ~** verkleidet

disgust [dɪs'gʌst] n Abscheu m; (physical) Ekel m ▷ vt anekeln, anwidern; **disgusting** adj widerlich; (physically) ekelhaft

dish [dɪʃ] n (container) Schüssel f; (food) Gericht nt; **~es** pl (crockery) Geschirr nt; **to do/wash the ~es** abwaschen; **dishcloth** n (for washing) Spültuch nt; (for drying) Geschirrtuch nt

dishearten [dɪs'hɑ:tən] vt
entmutigen; **don't be -ed** lass den
Kopf nicht hängen!
dishonest [dɪs'ɒnɪst] adj
unehrlich
dishonour [dɪs'ɒnə°] n Schande
f
dish towel n (US) Geschirrtuch
nt; **dish washer** n
Geschirrspülmaschine f
dishy ['dɪʃi] adj (Brit fam) gut
aussehend
disillusioned [dɪsɪ'lu:ʒənd] adj
desillusioniert
disinfect [dɪsɪn'fekt] vt desinfizieren; **disinfectant** n
Desinfektionsmittel nt
disintegrate [dɪs'ɪntɪgreɪt]
vi zerfallen; (group) sich
auflösen
disjointed [dɪs'dʒɔɪntɪd] adj
unzusammenhängend
disk [dɪsk] n (Inform: floppy)
Diskette f; **disk drive** n
Diskettenlaufwerk nt; **diskette**
[dɪ'sket] n Diskette f
dislike [dɪs'laɪk] n Abneigung f
▷ vt nicht mögen; **to ~ doing sth**
etw ungern tun
dislocate ['dɪsləʊkeɪt] vt (Med)
verrenken, ausrenken
dismal ['dɪzməl] adj trostlos
dismantle [dɪs'mæntl] vt
auseinandernehmen; (machine)
demontieren
dismay [dɪs'meɪ] n Bestürzung f;
dismayed adj bestürzt
dismiss [dɪs'mɪs] vt (employee)
entlassen; **dismissal** n
Entlassung f
disobedience [dɪsə'bi:dɪəns] n
Ungehorsam m; **disobedient** adj
ungehorsam; **disobey** [dɪsə'beɪ]
vt nicht gehorchen +dat
disorder [dɪs'ɔːdə°] n (mess)
Unordnung f; (riot) Aufruhr m;
(Med) Störung f, Leiden nt

disorganized [dɪs'ɔːgənaɪzd] adj
chaotisch
disparaging adj geringschätzig
dispatch [dɪ'spætʃ] vt abschicken, abfertigen
dispensable [dɪ'spensəbl] adj
entbehrlich; **dispense** vt
verteilen; **dispense with** vt
verzichten auf +akk; **dispenser** n
Automat m
disperse [dɪ'spɜːs] vi sich
zerstreuen
display [dɪ'spleɪ] n (exhibition)
Ausstellung f, Show f; (of goods)
Auslage f; (Tech) Anzeige f, Display
nt ▷ vt zeigen; (goods) ausstellen
disposable [dɪ'spəʊzəbl] adj
(container, razor etc) Wegwerf-;
~ nappy Wegwerfwindel f;
disposal [dɪ'spəʊzəl] n Loswerden nt; (of waste) Beseitigung f; **to
be at sb's ~** jdm zur Verfügung
stehen; **to have at one's
~** verfügen über; **dispose of** vt
loswerden; (waste etc) beseitigen
dispute [dɪ'spjuːt] n Streit m;
(industrial) Auseinandersetzung f
▷ vt bestreiten
disqualification
[dɪskwɒlɪfɪ'keɪʃən] n Disquali-
fikation f; **disqualify**
[dɪs'kwɒlɪfaɪ] vt disqualifizieren
disregard [dɪsrɪ'gɑːd] vt nicht
beachten
disreputable [dɪs'repjʊtəbl] adj
verrufen
disrespect [dɪsrɪ'spekt] n
Respektlosigkeit f
disrupt [dɪs'rʌpt] vt stören;
(interrupt) unterbrechen;
disruption [dɪs'rʌpʃən] n
Störung f; (interruption)
Unterbrechung f
dissatisfied [dɪs'sætɪsfaɪd] adj
unzufrieden
dissent [dɪ'sent] n Widerspruch
m

dissolve [dɪ'zɒlv] vt auflösen
▷ vi sich auflösen

dissuade [dɪ'sweɪd] vt (davon abbringen) **to ~ sb from doing sth** jdn davon abbringen, etw zu tun

distance ['dɪstəns] n Entfernung f; **in the/from a ~** in/aus der Ferne; **distant** adj (a. in time) fern; (relative etc) entfernt; (person) distanziert

distaste [dɪs'teɪst] n Abneigung f (for gegen)

distil [dɪ'stɪl] vt destillieren; **distillery** n Brennerei f

distinct [dɪ'stɪŋkt] adj verschieden; (clear) klar, deutlich; **distinction** [dɪ'stɪŋkʃən] n (difference) Unterschied m; (in exam etc) Auszeichnung f; **distinctive** adj unverkennbar; **distinctly** adv deutlich

distinguish [dɪ'stɪŋgwɪʃ] vt unterscheiden (sth from sth etw von etw)

distort [dɪ'stɔ:t] vt verzerren; (truth) verdrehen

distract [dɪ'strækt] vt ablenken; **distraction** [dɪ'strækʃən] n Ablenkung f; (diversion) Zerstreuung f

distress [dɪ'stres] n (need, danger) Not f; (suffering) Leiden nt; (mental) Qual f; (worry) Kummer m ▷ vt mitnehmen, erschüttern; **distressed area** n Notstandsgebiet nt; **distress signal** n Notsignal nt

distribute [dɪ'strɪbju:t] vt verteilen; (Comm: goods) vertreiben; **distribution** [dɪstrɪ'bju:ʃən] n Verteilung f; (Comm: of goods) Vertrieb m; **distributor** [dɪ'strɪbjʊtə°] n (Auto) Verteiler m; (Comm) Händler(in) m(f)

district ['dɪstrɪkt] n Gegend f; (administrative) Bezirk m; **district attorney** n (US) Staatsanwalt m, Staatsanwältin f

distrust [dɪs'trʌst] vt misstrauen +dat ▷ n Misstrauen nt

disturb [dɪ'stɜ:b] vt stören; (worry) beunruhigen; **disturbance** n Störung f; **disturbing** adj beunruhigend

ditch [dɪtʃ] n Graben m ▷ vt (fam: person) den Laufpass geben +dat; (plan etc) verwerfen

ditto ['dɪtəʊ] n dito, ebenfalls

dive [daɪv] n (into water) Kopfsprung m; (Aviat) Sturzflug m; (fam) zwielichtiges Lokal ▷ vi (under water) tauchen; **diver** n Taucher(in) m(f)

diverse [daɪ'vɜ:s] adj verschieden; **diversion** [daɪ'vɜ:ʃən] n (of traffic) Umleitung f; (distraction) Ablenkung f; **divert** [daɪ'vɜ:t] vt ablenken; (traffic) umleiten

divide [dɪ'vaɪd] vt teilen; (in several parts, between people) aufteilen ▷ vi sich teilen; **dividend** ['dɪvɪdend] n Dividende f

divine [dɪ'vaɪn] adj göttlich

diving ['daɪvɪŋ] n (Sport)- tauchen nt; (jumping in) Springen nt; (Sport: from board) Kunstspringen nt; **diving board** n Sprungbrett nt; **diving goggles** npl Taucherbrille f; **diving mask** n Tauchmaske f

division [dɪ'vɪʒən] n Teilung f; (Math) Division f; (department) Abteilung f; (Sport) Liga f

divorce [dɪ'vɔ:s] n Scheidung f ▷ vt sich scheiden lassen von; **divorced** adj geschieden; **to get ~** sich scheiden lassen; **divorcee** [dɪvɔ:'si:] n Geschiedene(r) mf

DIY [di:aɪ'waɪ] abbr =

do-it-yourself; **DIY centre** n
Baumarkt m

dizzy ['dɪzɪ] adj schwindlig

DJ [di:'dʒeɪ] abbr = **dinner jacket**
Smoking m ▷ abbr = **disc jockey**
Diskjockey m, DJ m

DNA abbr = **desoxyribonucleic
acid** DNS f

KEYWORD

do [du:] (pt **did**, pp **done**) n (inf)
(party etc) Fete f
▷ vb aux **1** (in negative constructions
and questions) **I don't understand**
ich verstehe nicht; **didn't you
know?** wusstest du das nicht?;
what do you think? was meinen
Sie?
2 (for emphasis, in polite phrases) **she
does seem rather tired** sie
scheint wirklich sehr müde zu
sein; **do sit down/help yourself**
setzen Sie sich doch hin/greifen
Sie doch zu
3 (used to avoid repeating vb) **she
swims better than I do** sie
schwimmt besser als ich; **she
lives in Glasgow — so do I** sie
wohnt in Glasgow — ich auch
4 (in tag questions) **you like him,
don't you?** du magst/Sie mögen
ihn doch, oder?
▷ vt **1** (carry out, perform etc) tun,
machen; **what are you doing
tonight?** was machst du/machen
Sie heute Abend?; **I've got
nothing to do** ich habe nichts zu
tun; **to do one's hair/nails** sich
die Haare/Nägel machen
2 (car etc) fahren
▷ vi **1** (act, behave) **do as I do** mach
es wie ich
2 (get on, fare) **he's doing
well/badly at school** er ist
gut/schlecht in der Schule; **how
do you do?** guten Tag

3 (be suitable) gehen; (be sufficient)
reichen; **to make do (with)**
auskommen mit
do away with vt (kill)
umbringen; (abolish: law etc)
abschaffen
do up vt (laces, dress, buttons)
zumachen; (renovate: room, house)
renovieren
do with vt (need) brauchen; (be
connected) zu tun haben mit
do without vt, vi auskommen
ohne
do up vt (fasten) zumachen;
(parcel) verschnüren; (renovate)
wiederherrichten
do with vt (need) brauchen; **I
could ~ a drink** ich könnte einen
Drink gebrauchen
do without vt auskommen
ohne; **I can ~ your comments**
auf deine Kommentare kann ich
verzichten

dock [dɒk] n Dock nt; (Jur)
Anklagebank f; **docker** n
Hafenarbeiter m; **dockyard** n
Werft f

doctor ['dɒktə°] n Arzt m, Ärztin;
(in title, also academic) Doktor m

document ['dɒkjʊmənt] n
Dokument nt; **documentary**
[dɒkjʊ'mentərɪ] n Dokumentarfilm m; **documentation**
[dɒkjʊmen'teɪʃən] n Dokumen-
tation f

docusoap ['dɒkjʊsəʊp] n
Reality-Serie f, Dokusoap f

doddery ['dɒdərɪ] adj tatterig

dodgem ['dɒdʒəm] n Auto-
skooter m

dodgy ['dɒdʒɪ] adj nicht ganz in
Ordnung; (dishonest, unreliable)
zwielichtig; **he has a ~ stomach**
er hat sich den Magen verdorben

dog [dɒg] n Hund m; **dog food** n
Hundefutter nt; **doggie bag**

['dɒgɪbæg] n Tüte oder Box, in der Essensreste aus dem Restaurant mit nach Hause genommen werden können

do-it-yourself ['duːɪtjəˈself] n Heimwerken nt, Do-it-yourself nt ▷ adj Verderben-;

do-it-yourselfer n Bastler(in) m(f), Heimwerker(in) m(f)

doll [dɒl] n Puppe f

dollar ['dɒlə'] n Dollar m

dolphin ['dɒlfɪn] n Delphin m

domain n Domäne f; (Inform) Domain f

dome [dəʊm] n Kuppel f

domestic [dəˈmestɪk] adj häuslich; (within country) Innen-, Binnen-; **domestic animal** n Haustier nt; **domesticated** [dəˈmestɪkeɪtɪd] adj (person) häuslich; (animal) zahm; **domestic flight** n Inlandsflug m

domicile ['dɒmɪsaɪl] n (ständiger) Wohnsitz

dominant ['dɒmɪnənt] adj dominierend, vorherrschend; **dominate** ['dɒmɪneɪt] vt beherrschen

dominoes ['dɒmɪnəʊz] npl Domino(spiel) nt

donate [dəʊˈneɪt] vt spenden; **donation** n Spende f

done [dʌn] pp of **do** ▷ adj (cooked) gar; **well ~** durchgebraten

doner (kebab) ['dɒnəkəˈbæb] n Döner (Kebab) m

donkey ['dɒŋkɪ] n Esel m

donor ['dəʊnə] n Spender(in) m(f)

don't [dəʊnt] contr of **do not**

doom [duːm] n Schicksal nt; (downfall) Verderben nt

door [dɔː'] n Tür f; **doorbell** n Türklingel f; **door handle** n Türklinke f; **doorknob** n Türknauf m; **doormat** n Fußabtreter m; **doorstep** n Türstufe f; **right**

on our ~ direkt vor unserer Haustür

dope [dəʊp] (Sport) n (for athlete) Aufputschmittel nt ▷ vt dopen

dormitory ['dɔːmɪtrɪ] n Schlafsaal m; (US) Studentenwohnheim nt

dosage ['dəʊsɪdʒ] n Dosierung f; **dose** [dəʊs] n Dosis f ▷ vt dosieren

dot [dɒt] n Punkt m; **on the ~** auf die Minute genau, pünktlich

dotcom ['dɒtkɒm] n: ~ **(company)** Internetfirma f, Dotcom-Unternehmen nt

dote on [dəʊt ɒn] vt abgöttisch lieben

dotted line n punktierte Linie

double ['dʌbl] adj, adv doppelt; **~ the quantity** die zweifache Menge, doppelt so viel ▷ vt verdoppeln ▷ n (person) Doppelgänger(in) m(f); (Cine) Double nt; **double bass** n Kontrabass m; **double bed** n Doppelbett nt; **double-click** vt (Inform) doppelklicken; **double cream** n Sahne mit hohem Fettgehalt; **doubledecker** n Doppeldecker m; **double glazing** n Doppelverglasung f; **double-park** vi in zweiter Reihe parken; **double room** n Doppelzimmer nt; **doubles** npl (Sport: also match) Doppel nt

doubt [daʊt] n Zweifel m; **no ~** ohne Zweifel, zweifellos, wahrscheinlich; **to have one's ~s** Bedenken haben ▷ vt bezweifeln; (statement, word) anzweifeln; **I ~ it** das bezweifle ich; **doubtful** adj zweifelhaft, zweifelnd; **it is ~ whether ...** es ist fraglich, ob ...; **doubtless** adv ohne Zweifel, sicherlich

dough [dəʊ] n Teig m; **doughnut** n Donut m (rundes Hefegebäck)

dove [dʌv] n Taube f

down [daʊn] n Daunen pl; (fluff) Flaum m ▷ adv unten; (motion) nach unten; (towards speaker) herunter; (away from speaker) hinunter; **~ here/there** hier/dort unten; (downstairs) **they came ~ for breakfast** sie kamen zum Frühstück herunter; (southwards) **he came ~ from Scotland** er kam von Schottland herunter ▷ prep (towards speaker) herunter; (away from speaker) hinunter; **to drive ~ the hill/road** den Berg/die Straße hinunter fahren; (along) **to walk ~ the street** die Straße entlang gehen; **he's ~ the pub** (fam) er ist in der Kneipe ▷ vt (fam: drink) runterkippen ▷ adj niedergeschlagen, deprimiert

down-and-out adj heruntergekommen ▷ n Obdachlose(r) mf, Penner(in) m(f);
downcast adj niedergeschlagen;
downfall n Sturz m;
down-hearted adj entmutigt;
downhill adv bergab; **he's going ~** (fig) mit ihm geht es bergab

○ **DOWNING STREET**
○
○ **Downing Street** ist die Straße
○ in London, die von Whitehall
○ zum St James's Park führt, und
○ in der sich der offizielle
○ Wohnsitz des Premierministers
○ (Nr. 10) und des Finanzministers
○ (Nr. 11) befindet. Im weiteren
○ Sinne bezieht sich der Begriff
○ „Downing Street" auf die
○ britische Regierung.

download ['daʊnləʊd] vt herunterladen; **downloadable** adj (Inform) herunterladbar;
downmarket adj für den Massenmarkt; **down payment** n

Anzahlung f; **downpour** n Platzregen m; **downs** npl Hügelland nt; **downsize** vt verkleinern ▷ vi sich verkleinern

Down's syndrome ['daʊnz'sɪndrəʊm] n (Med) Downsyndrom nt

downstairs [daʊn'stɛəz] adv unten; (motion) nach unten; **downstream** adv flussabwärts; **downtime** n Ausfallzeit f; **downtown** adv (be, work etc) in der Innenstadt; (go) in die Innenstadt ▷ adj (US) in die Innenstadt; **~ Chicago** die Innenstadt von Chicago; **down under** adv (fam: in/to Australia) in/nach Australien; (in/to New Zealand) in/nach Neuseeland;
downwards adv, adj nach unten; (movement, trend) Abwärts-

doze [dəʊz] vi dösen ▷ n Nickerchen nt

dozen ['dʌzn] n Dutzend nt; **two ~ eggs** zwei Dutzend Eier; **~s of times** x-mal

DP abbr = **data processing** DV f

drab [dræb] adj trist; (colour) düster

draft [drɑːft] n (outline) Entwurf m; (US Mil) Einberufung f

drag [dræg] vt schleppen ▷ n (fam) **to be a ~** (boring) stinklangweilig sein; (laborious) ein ziemlicher Schlauch sein; **drag on** vi sich in die Länge ziehen

dragon ['drægən] n Drache m; **dragonfly** n Libelle f

drain [dreɪn] n Abfluss m ▷ vt (water, oil) ablassen; (vegetables etc) abgießen; (land) entwässern, trockenlegen ▷ vi (of water) abfließen; **drainpipe** n Abflussrohr nt

drama ['drɑːmə] n (a. fig) Drama nt; **dramatic** [drə'mætɪk] adj dramatisch

drank [dræŋk] *pt of* **drink**
drapes [dreɪps] *npl* (*US*)
Vorhänge *pl*
drastic ['dræstɪk] *adj* drastisch
draught [drɑːft] *n* (Luft)zug *m*;
there's a ~ es zieht; **on ~** (*beer*)
vom Fass; **draughts** *nsing*
Damespiel *nt*; **draughty** *adj*
zugig
draw [drɔː] (**drew, drawn**) *vt*
(*pull*) ziehen; (*crowd*) anlocken,
anziehen; (*picture*) zeichnen ▷ *vi*
(*Sport*) unentschieden spielen ▷ *n*
(*Sport*) Unentschieden *nt*;
(*attraction*) Attraktion *f*; (*for lottery*)
Ziehung *f*; **draw out** *vt*
herausziehen; (*money*) abheben;
draw up *vt* (*formulate*) entwerfen;
(*list*) erstellen ▷ *vi* (*car*) anhalten;
drawback *n* Nachteil *m*;
drawbridge *n* Zugbrücke *f*
drawer ['drɔːʳ] *n* Schublade *f*
drawing ['drɔːɪŋ] *n* Zeichnung *f*;
drawing pin *n* Reißzwecke *f*
drawn [drɔːn] *pp of* **draw**
dread [dred] *n* Furcht *f* (*of* vor
+*dat*) ▷ *vt* sich fürchten vor +*dat*;
dreadful *adj* furchtbar;
dreadlocks *npl* Rastalocken *pl*
dream [driːm] (**dreamed** *o*
dreamt, dreamed *o* **dreamt**) *vt, vi*
träumen (*about* von) ▷ *n* Traum *m*;
dreamt [dremt] *pt, pp of* **dream**
dreary ['drɪərɪ] *adj* (*weather,
place*) trostlos; (*book etc*) langweilig
drench [drentʃ] *vt* durchnässen
dress [dres] *n* Kleidung *f*;
(*garment*) Kleid *nt* ▷ *vt* anziehen;
(*Med: wound*) verbinden; **to get
~ed** sich anziehen; **dress up** *vi*
sich fein machen; (*in costume*) sich
verkleiden (*as* als); **dress circle** *n*
(*Theat*) erster Rang; **dresser** *n*
Anrichte *f*; (*US: dressing table*)
(Frisier)kommode *f*; **dressing** *n*
(*Gastr*) Dressing *nt*, Soße *f*; (*Med*)
Verband *m*; **dressing gown** *n*

Bademantel *m*; **dressing room** *n*
(*Theat*) Künstlergarderobe *f*;
dressing table *n*
Frisierkommode *f*; **dress
rehearsal** *n* (*Theat*) Generalprobe
f
drew [druː] *pt of* **draw**
dried [draɪd] *adj* getrocknet;
(*milk, flowers*) Trocken-; **~ fruit**
Dörrobst *nt*; **drier** ['draɪəʳ] *n see*
dryer
drift [drɪft] *vi* treiben ▷ *n* (*of
snow*) Verwehung *f*; (*fig*) Tendenz *f*;
if you get my ~ wenn du mich
richtig verstehst/wenn Sie mich
richtig verstehen
drill [drɪl] *n* Bohrer *m* ▷ *vt, vi*
bohren
drink [drɪŋk] (**drank, drunk**) *vt,
vi* trinken ▷ *n* Getränk *nt*;
(*alcoholic*) Drink *m*; **drink-driving**
n (*Brit*) Trunkenheit *f* am Steuer;
drinking water *n* Trinkwasser
nt
drip [drɪp] *n* Tropfen *m* ▷ *vi*
tropfen; **drip-dry** *adj* bügelfrei;
dripping *n* Bratenfett *nt* ▷ *adj*:
~ (wet) tropfnass
drive [draɪv] (**drove, driven**) *vt*
(*car, person in car*) fahren; (*force:
person, animal*) treiben; (*Tech*)
antreiben; **to ~ sb mad** jdn
verrückt machen ▷ *vi* fahren ▷ *n*
Fahrt *f*; (*entrance*) Einfahrt *f*,
Auffahrt *f*; (*Inform*) Laufwerk *nt*; **to
go for a ~** spazieren fahren; **drive
away, drive off** *vi* wegfahren
▷ *vt* vertreiben
drive-in *adj* Drive-in-; **~ cinema** *n*
(*US*) Autokino *nt*
driven ['drɪvn] *pp of* **drive**
driver ['draɪvəʳ] *n* Fahrer(in)
m(f); (*Inform*) Treiber *m*; **~'s license**
n (*US*) Führerschein *m*; **~'s seat**
n Fahrersitz *m*; **driving** ['draɪvɪŋ]
n (*Auto*)fahren *nt*; **he likes ~** er
fährt gern Auto; **driving lesson** *n*

Fahrstunde *f*; **driving licence** *n* (Brit) Führerschein *m*; **driving school** *n* Fahrschule *f*; **driving seat** *n* (Brit) Fahrersitz *m*; **to be on the ~** alles im Griff haben; **driving test** *n* Fahrprüfung *f*

drizzle ['drɪzl] *n* Nieselregen *m* ▷ *vi* nieseln

drop [drɒp] *n* (of liquid) Tropfen *m*; (fall in price etc) Rückgang *m* ▷ *vt* (a. fig: give up) fallen lassen ▷ *vi* (fall) herunterfallen; (figures, temperature) sinken, zurückgehen; **drop by**, **drop in** *vi* vorbeikommen; **drop off** *vi* (to sleep) einnicken; **drop out** *vi* (withdraw) aussteigen; (university) das Studium abbrechen; **dropout** *n* Aussteiger(in) *m(f)*

drought [draʊt] *n* Dürre *f*

drove [drəʊv] *pt of* **drive**

drown [draʊn] *vi* ertrinken ▷ *vt* ertränken

drowsy ['draʊzɪ] *adj* schläfrig

drug [drʌg] *n* (Med) Medikament *nt*, Arznei *f*; (addictive) Droge *f*; (narcotic) Rauschgift *nt*; **to be on ~s** drogensüchtig sein ▷ *vt* (mit Medikamenten) betäuben; **drug addict** *n* Rauschgiftsüchtige(r) *mf*; **drug dealer** *n* Drogenhändler(in) *m(f)*; **druggist** *n* (US) Drogist(in) *m(f)*; **drugstore** *n* (US) Drogerie *f*

drum [drʌm] *n* Trommel *f*; **~s** *pl* Schlagzeug *nt*; **drummer** *n* Schlagzeuger(in) *m(f)*

drunk [drʌŋk] *pp of* **drink** ▷ *adj* betrunken; **to get ~** sich betrinken ▷ *n* Betrunkene(r) *mf*; (alcoholic) Trinker(in) *m(f)*; **drunk-driving** *n* (US) Trunkenheit *f* am Steuer; **drunken** *adj* betrunken, besoffen

dry [draɪ] *adj* trocken ▷ *vt* trocknen; (dishes, oneself, one's hands etc) abtrocknen ▷ *vi* trocknen, trocken werden; **dry out**

vi trocknen; **dry up** *vi* austrocknen; **dry-clean** *vt* chemisch reinigen; **dry-cleaning** *n* chemische Reinigung; **dryer** *n* Trockner *m*; (for hair) Föhn *m*; (over head) Trockenhaube *f*

DTP *abbr* = **desktop publishing** DTP *nt*

dual ['djʊəl] *adj* doppelt; **~ carriageway** (Brit) zweispurige Schnellstraße *f*; **~ nationality** doppelte Staatsangehörigkeit

dubbed [dʌbd] *adj* (film) synchronisiert

dubious ['dju:bɪəs] *adj* zweifelhaft

duchess ['dʌtʃəs] *n* Herzogin *f*

duck [dʌk] *n* Ente *f*

dude [du:d] *n* (US fam) Typ *m*; **a cool ~** ein cooler Typ

due [dju:] *adj* (time) fällig; (fitting) angemessen; **in ~ course** zu gegebener Zeit; **~ to** infolge +*gen*, wegen +*gen* ▷ *adv*: **~ south/north** *etc* direkt nach Norden/Süden *etc*

dug [dʌg] *pt*, *pp of* **dig**

duke [dju:k] *n* Herzog *m*

dull [dʌl] *adj* (colour, light, weather) trübe; (boring) langweilig

duly ['dju:lɪ] *adv* ordnungsgemäß; (as expected) wie erwartet

dumb [dʌm] *adj* stumm; (fam: stupid) doof, blöde

dumb-bell ['dʌmbel] *n* Hantel *f*

dummy ['dʌmɪ] *n* (sham) Attrappe *f*; (in shop) Schaufensterpuppe *f*; (Brit: teat) Schnuller *m*; (fam: person) Dummkopf *m* ▷ *adj* unecht, Schein-; **~ run** Testlauf *m*

dump [dʌmp] *n* Abfallhaufen *m*; (fam: place) Kaff *nt* ▷ *vt* (lit, fig) abladen; (fam) **he ~ed her** er hat mir ihr Schluss gemacht

dumpling ['dʌmplɪŋ] *n* Kloß *m*, Knödel *m*

dune [dju:n] *n* Düne *f*

dung [dʌŋ] n (manure) Mist m
dungarees [dʌŋɡə'riːz] npl
Latzhose f
dungeon ['dʌndʒən] n Kerker m
duplex ['djuːpleks] n
zweistöckige Wohnung; (US)
Doppelhaushälfte f
duplicate ['djuːplɪkɪt] n Dup-
likat nt ▷ ['djuːplɪkeɪt] vt (make
copies of) kopieren; (repeat)
wiederholen
durable ['djʊərəbl] adj haltbar;
duration [djʊə'reɪʃən] n Dauer f
during ['djʊərɪŋ] prep (time)
während +gen
dusk [dʌsk] n Abenddämmerung f
dust [dʌst] n Staub m ▷ vt
abstauben; **dustbin** n (Brit)
Mülleimer m; **dustcart** n (Brit)
Müllwagen m; **duster** n
Staubtuch nt; **dust jacket** n
Schutzumschlag m; **dustman** n
(Brit) Müllmann m; **dustpan** n
Kehrschaufel f; **dusty** adj staubig
Dutch [dʌtʃ] adj holländisch ▷ n
(language) Holländisch nt; **to
speak/talk double ~** (fam)
Quatsch reden; **the ~** pl die
Holländer; **Dutchman** (pl **-men**)
n Holländer m; **Dutchwoman** (pl
-women) n Holländerin f
duty ['djuːtɪ] n Pflicht f; (task)
Aufgabe f; (tax) Zoll m; **on/off ~** im
Dienst/nicht im Dienst; **to be on
~** Dienst haben; **duty-free** adj
zollfrei; **~ shop** Dutyfreeshop m
duvet ['duːveɪ] n Federbett nt
DVD n abbr = **digital versatile
disk** DVD f; **DVD player** n
DVD-Player m; **DVD recorder** n
DVD-Rekorder m
dwelling ['dwelɪŋ] n Wohnung f
dwindle ['dwɪndl] vi schwinden
dye [daɪ] n Farbstoff m ▷ vt
färben
dynamic [daɪ'næmɪk] adj
dynamisch

dynamo ['daɪnəməʊ] n Dynamo m
dyslexia [dɪs'leksɪə] n Legasthenie
f; **dyslexic** adj legasthenisch; **to
be ~** Legastheniker(in) sein

e

E [i:] abbr = **east** (geo) O; abbr = **ecstasy** (drug) Ecstasy nt

E111 form n ≈ Auslandskrankenschein m

each [i:tʃ] adj jeder/jede/jedes ▷ pron jeder/jede/jedes; **I'll have one of ~** ich nehme von jedem eins; **they ~ have a car** jeder von ihnen hat ein Auto; **~ other** einander, sich; **for/against ~ other** füreinander/gegeneinander ▷ adv je; **they cost 10 euros ~** sie kosten je 10 Euro, sie kosten 10 Euro das Stück

eager ['i:gǝ°] adj eifrig; **to be ~ to do sth** darauf brennen, etw zu tun

eagle ['i:gl] n Adler m

ear [ɪǝ°] n Ohr nt; **earache** n Ohrenschmerzen pl; **eardrum** n Trommelfell nt

earl [ɜːl] n Graf m

early ['ɜːlɪ] adj, adv früh; **to be 10 minutes ~** 10 Minuten zu früh kommen; **at the earliest** frühestens; **in ~ June/2008** Anfang Juni/2008; **~ retirement** vorzeitiger Ruhestand; **~ warning system** Frühwarnsystem nt

earn [ɜːn] vt verdienen

earnest ['ɜːnɪst] adj ernst; **in ~** im Ernst

earnings ['ɜːnɪŋz] npl Verdienst m, Einkommen nt

earplug n Ohrenstöpsel m, Ohropax® nt; **earring** n Ohrring m

earth [ɜːθ] n Erde f; **what on ~ ...?** was in aller Welt ...? ▷ vt erden; **earthenware** n Tonwaren pl; **earthquake** n Erdbeben nt

earwig ['ɪǝwɪg] n Ohrwurm m

ease [i:z] vt (pain) lindern; (burden) erleichtern ▷ n (easiness) Leichtigkeit f; **to feel at ~** sich wohlfühlen; **to feel ill at ~** sich nicht wohlfühlen; **easily** ['i:zɪlɪ] adv leicht; **he is ~ the best** er ist mit Abstand der Beste

east [i:st] n Osten m; **to the ~ of** östlich von ▷ adv (go, face) nach Osten ▷ adj Ost-; **~ wind** Ostwind m; **eastbound** adj (in) Richtung Osten

Easter ['i:stǝ°] n Ostern nt; **at ~** zu Ostern; **Easter egg** n Osterei nt; **Easter Sunday** n Ostersonntag m

eastern ['i:stǝn] adj Ost-, östlich; **Eastern Europe** Osteuropa nt; **East Germany** n Ostdeutschland nt; **former ~** die ehemalige DDR, die neuen Bundesländer pl; **eastwards** ['i:stwǝdz] adv nach Osten

easy ['i:zɪ] adj leicht; (task, solution) einfach; (life) bequem; (manner) ungezwungen; **easy-going** adj gelassen

eat [i:t] (**ate, eaten**) vt essen; (animal) fressen; **eat out** vi zum

Essen ausgehen; **eat up** vt
aufessen; (animal) auffressen
eaten ['iːtn] pp of **eat**
eavesdrop ['iːvzdrɒp] vi (heimlich) lauschen; **to ~ on sb** jdn
belauschen
eccentric [ɪk'sentrɪk] adj
exzentrisch
echo ['ekəʊ] (pl **-es**) n Echo nt
▷ vi widerhallen
ecological [iːkə'lɒdʒɪkl] adj
ökologisch; **~ disaster**
Umweltkatastrophe f; **ecology**
[ɪ'kɒlədʒɪ] n Ökologie f
economic [iːkə'nɒmɪk] adj
wirtschaftlich, Wirtschafts-; **~ aid**
Wirtschaftshilfe f; **economical**
adj wirtschaftlich; (person) sparsam;
economics nsing o pl
Wirtschaftswissenschaft f;
economist [ɪ'kɒnəmɪst] n
Wirtschaftswissenschaftler(in)
m(f); **economize** [ɪ'kɒnəmaɪz] vi
sparen (on an +dat); **economy**
[ɪ'kɒnəmɪ] n (of state) Wirtschaft
f; (thrift) Sparsamkeit f; **economy
class** n (Aviat) Economyclass f
ecstasy ['ekstəsɪ] n Ekstase f;
(drug) Ecstasy f
eczema ['eksɪmə] n Ekzem nt
edge [edʒ] n Rand m; (of knife)
Schneide f; **on ~** nervös; **edgy**
['edʒɪ] adj nervös
edible ['edɪbl] adj essbar
Edinburgh ['edɪnbərə] n Edin-
burg nt
edit ['edɪt] vt (series, newspaper
etc) herausgeben; (text) redigieren;
(film) schneiden; (Inform)
editieren; **edition** [ɪ'dɪʃən] n
Ausgabe f; **editor** n Redakteur(in)
m(f); (of series etc) Herausgeber(in)
m(f); **editorial** [edɪ'tɔːrɪəl] adj
Redaktions- ▷ n Leitartikel m
educate ['edjʊkeɪt] vt (child)
erziehen; (at school, university)
ausbilden; (public) aufklären;

educated adj gebildet;
education [edjʊ'keɪʃən] n
Erziehung f; (studies, training)
Ausbildung f; (subject of study)
Pädagogik f; (system) Schulwesen
nt; (knowledge) Bildung f;
educational adj pädagogisch;
(instructive) lehrreich; **~ television**
Schulfernsehen nt
eel [iːl] n Aal m
eerie ['ɪərɪ] adj unheimlich
effect [ɪ'fekt] n Wirkung f (on auf
+akk); **to come into ~** in Kraft
treten; **effective** adj wirksam,
effektiv
effeminate [ɪ'femɪnət] adj (of
man) tuntig
efficiency [ɪ'fɪʃənsɪ] n Leistungsfähigkeit f; (of method)
Wirksamkeit f; **efficient** adj
(Tech) leistungsfähig; (method)
wirksam, effizient
effort ['efət] n Anstrengung f;
(attempt) Versuch m; **to make an
~** sich anstrengen; **effortless** adj
mühelos
e.g. abbr = **exempli gratia (for
example)** z. B.
egg [eg] n Ei nt; **eggcup** n
Eierbecher m; **eggplant** n (US)
Aubergine f; **eggshell** n
Eierschale f
ego ['iːgəʊ] (pl **-s**) n Ich nt;
(self-esteem) Selbstbewusstsein nt;
ego(t)ist ['egəʊ(t)ɪst] n Ego-
zentriker(in) m(f)
Egypt ['iːdʒɪpt] n Ägypten nt;
Egyptian [ɪ'dʒɪpʃən] adj
ägyptisch ▷ n Ägypter(in) m(f)
eiderdown ['aɪdədaʊn] n
Daunendecke f
eight [eɪt] num acht; **at the age
of ~** im Alter von acht Jahren; **it's
~ (o'clock)** es ist acht Uhr ▷ n (a.
bus etc) Acht f; (boat) Achter m;
eighteen [eɪ'tiːn] num achtzehn
▷ n Achtzehn f; see also **eight**;

eighteenth adj achtzehnte(r, s);
see also **eighth**; **eighth** [eɪtθ] adj
achte(r, s); see also **eighth**; **the ~ of**
Juni ▷ n (fraction) Achtel nt; **an
~ of a litre** ein Achtelliter;
eightieth ['eɪtɪə] adj achtzig-
ste(r, s); see also **eighth**; **eighty**
['eɪtɪ] num achtzig ▷ n Achtzig f;
see also **eighth**

Eire ['eərə] n die Republik Irland
either ['aɪðəʳ] conj: **~ ... or**
entweder ... oder ▷ pron: **~ of the
two** eine(r, s) von beiden ▷ adj:
on ~ side auf beiden Seiten ▷ adv:
I won't go ~ ich gehe auch nicht
eject [ɪ'dʒekt] vt ausstoßen;
(person) vertreiben
elaborate [ɪ'læbərət] adj (complex) kompliziert; (plan)
ausgeklügelt; (decoration)
kunstvoll ▷ vi [ɪ'læbəreɪt] **could
you ~ on that?** könntest
du/könnten Sie mehr darüber
sagen?
elastic [ɪ'læstɪk] adj elastisch;
~ band Gummiband nt
elbow ['elbəʊ] n Ellbogen m; **to
give sb the ~** (fam) jdm den
Laufpass geben
elder ['eldəʳ] adj (of two) älter ▷ n
Ältere(r) mf; (Bot) Holunder m;
elderly adj ältere(r, s) ▷ n: **the
~** die älteren Leute; **eldest**
['eldɪst] adj älteste(r, s)
elect [ɪ'lekt] vt wählen; **he was
~ed chairman** er wurde zum
Vorsitzenden gewählt; **election**
[ɪ'lekʃən] n Wahl f; **election
campaign** n Wahlkampf m;
electioneering [ɪlekʃə'nɪərɪŋ] n
Wahlpropaganda f; **electorate**
[ɪ'lektərɪt] n Wähler pl
electric [ɪ'lektrɪk] adj elektrisch;
(car, motor, razor etc) Elektro-;
~ blanket Heizdecke f; **~ cooker**
Elektroherd m; **~ current**
elektrischer Strom; **~ shock**

Stromschlag m; **electrical** adj
elektrisch; **~ goods/appliances**
Elektrogeräte; **electrician**
[ɪlek'trɪʃən] n Elektriker(in) m(f);
electricity [ɪlek'trɪsɪtɪ] n Elektrizität f; **electrocute**
[ɪ'lektrəʊkjuːt] vt durch einen
Stromschlag töten; **electronic**
[ɪlek'trɒnɪk] adj elektronisch

elegance ['elɪgəns] n Eleganz f;
elegant adj elegant
element ['elɪmənt] n Element
nt; **an ~ of truth** ein Körnchen
Wahrheit; **elementary**
[elɪ'mentərɪ] adj einfach; (basic)
grundlegend; **~ stage**
Anfangsstadium nt; **~ school** (US)
Grundschule f; **~ maths/French**
Grundkenntnisse in
Mathematik/Französisch
elephant ['elɪfənt] n Elefant m
elevator ['elɪveɪtəʳ] n (US)
Fahrstuhl m
eleven [ɪ'levn] num elf
▷ n (team, bus etc) Elf f see
eight; **eleventh** [ɪ'levnθ] adj
elfte(r, s) ▷ n (fraction) Elftel nt
see **eighth**
eligible ['elɪdʒəbl] adj infrage
kommend; (for grant etc)
berechtigt; **~ for a
pension/competition**
pensions-/teilnahmeberechtigt;
~ bachelor begehrter Junggeselle
eliminate [ɪ'lɪmɪneɪt] vt
ausschließen (from aus),
ausschalten; (problem etc)
beseitigen; **elimination** n
Ausschluss m (from aus); (of problem
etc) Beseitigung f
elm [elm] n Ulme f
elope [ɪ'ləʊp] vi durchbrennen
(with sb mit jdm)
eloquent ['eləkwənt] adj
redegewandt
else [els] adv: **anybody/any-
thing ~** (in addition) sonst (noch)

jemand/etwas; (other) ein anderer/etwas anderes; **somebody ~** jemand anders; **everyone ~** alle anderen; **or ~** sonst; **elsewhere** adv anderswo, woanders; (direction) woandershin

ELT abbr = **English Language Teaching**

email ['i:meɪl] vi, vt mailen (sth to sb jdm etw) ▷ n E-Mail f; **email address** n E-Mail-Adresse f

emancipated [ɪ'mænsɪpeɪtɪd] adj emanzipiert

embankment [ɪm'bæŋkmənt] n Böschung f; (for railway) Bahndamm m

embargo [ɪm'bɑ:gəʊ] (pl -es) n Embargo nt

embark [ɪm'bɑ:k] vi an Bord gehen

embarrass [ɪm'bærəs] vt in Verlegenheit bringen; **embarrassed** adj verlegen; **embarrassing** adj peinlich

embassy ['embəsɪ] n Botschaft f

embrace [ɪm'breɪs] vt umarmen ▷ n Umarmung f

embroider [ɪm'brɔɪdə°] vt besticken; **embroidery** n Stickerei f

embryo ['embrɪəʊ] (pl -s) n Embryo m

emerald ['emərəld] n Smaragd m

emerge [ɪ'mɜ:dʒ] vi auftauchen; **it ~d that ...** es stellte sich heraus, dass ...

emergency [ɪ'mɜ:dʒənsɪ] n Notfall m ▷ adj Not-; **~ exit** Notausgang m; **~ landing** Notlandung f; **~ room** (US) Unfallstation f; **~ service** Notdienst m; **~ stop** Vollbremsung f

emigrate ['emɪgreɪt] vi auswandern

emit [ɪ'mɪt] vt ausstoßen; (heat) abgeben

emoticon [ɪ'məʊtɪkən] n (Inform) Emoticon nt

emotion [ɪ'məʊʃən] n Emotion f, Gefühl nt; **emotional** adj (person) emotional; (experience, moment, scene) ergreifend

emperor ['empərə°] n Kaiser m

emphasis ['emfəsɪs] n Betonung f; **emphasize** ['emfəsaɪz] vt betonen; **emphatic**, **emphatically** [ɪm'fætɪk, -lɪ] adj, adv nachdrücklich

empire ['empaɪə°] n Reich nt

employ [ɪm'plɔɪ] vt beschäftigen; (hire) anstellen; (use) anwenden; **employee** [emplɔɪ'i:] n Angestellte(r) mf; **employer** n Arbeitgeber(in) m(f); **employment** n Beschäftigung f; (position) Stellung f; **employment agency** n Stellenvermittlung f

empress ['emprɪs] n Kaiserin f

empty ['emptɪ] adj leer ▷ vt (contents) leeren; (container) ausleeren

enable [ɪ'neɪbl] vt: **to ~ sb to do sth** es jdm ermöglichen, etw zu tun

enamel [ɪ'næməl] n Email nt; (of teeth) Zahnschmelz m

enchanting [ɪn'tʃɑ:ntɪŋ] adj bezaubernd

enclose [ɪn'kləʊz] vt einschließen; (in letter) beilegen (in, with dat); **enclosure** [ɪn'kləʊʒə°] n (for animals) Gehege nt; (in letter) Anlage f

encore ['ɒŋkɔ:°] n Zugabe f

encounter [ɪn'kaʊntə°] n . Begegnung f ▷ vt (person) begegnen +dat; (difficulties) stoßen auf +akk

encourage [ɪn'kʌrɪdʒ] vt ermutigen; **encouragement** n Ermutigung f

encyclopaedia
[ensaɪkləʊ'pi:dɪə] n Lexikon nt, Enzyklopädie f

end [end] n Ende nt; (of film, play etc) Schluss m; (purpose) Zweck m; **at the ~ of** May Ende Mai; **in the ~** schließlich; **to come to an ~** zu Ende gehen ▷ vt beenden ▷ vi enden; **end up** vi enden

endanger [ɪn'deɪndʒə*] vt gefährden; **~ed species** vom Aussterben bedrohte Art

endeavour [ɪn'devə*] n Bemühung f ▷ vi sich bemühen (to do sth etw zu tun)

ending ['endɪŋ] n (of book) Ausgang m; (last part) Schluss m; (of word) Endung f; **endless** ['endlɪs] adj endlos; (possibilities) unendlich

endurance [ɪn'djʊərəns] n Ausdauer f; **endure** [ɪn'djʊə*] vt ertragen

enemy ['enɪmɪ] n Feind(in) m(f) ▷ adj feindlich

energetic [enə'dʒetɪk] adj energiegeladen; (active) aktiv; **energy** ['enədʒɪ] n Energie f

enforce [ɪn'fɔ:s] vt durchsetzen; (obedience) erzwingen

engage [ɪn'geɪdʒ] vt (employ) einstellen; (singer, performer) engagieren; **engaged** adj verlobt; (toilet, telephone line) besetzt; **to get** ~ sich verloben (to mit); **engaged tone** n (Brit Tel) Belegtzeichen nt; **engagement** n (to marry) Verlobung f; ~ **ring** Verlobungsring m; **engaging** adj gewinnend

engine ['endʒɪn] n (Auto) Motor m; (Rail) Lokomotive f; ~ **failure** (Auto) Motorschaden m; ~ **trouble** (Auto) Defekt m am Motor; **engineer** [endʒɪ'nɪə*] n Ingenieur(in) m(f); (US Rail) Lokomotivführer(in) m(f);

engineering [endʒɪ'nɪərɪŋ] n Technik f; (mechanical ~) Maschinenbau m; (subject) Ingenieurwesen nt; **engine immobilizer** n (Auto) Wegfahrsperre f

England ['ɪŋglənd] n England nt; **English** adj englisch; **he's** ~ er ist Engländer; **the** ~ **Channel** der Ärmelkanal ▷ n (language) Englisch nt; **in** ~ auf Englisch; **to translate into** ~ ins Englische übersetzen; (people) **the** ~ pl die Engländer; **Englishman** (pl -**men**) n Engländer m; **Englishwoman** (pl -**women**) n Engländerin f

engrave [ɪn'greɪv] vt eingravieren; **engraving** n Stich m

engrossed [ɪn'grəʊst] adj vertieft (in sth in etw akk)

enigma [ɪ'nɪgmə] n Rätsel nt

enjoy [ɪn'dʒɔɪ] vt genießen; **I** ~ **reading** ich lese gern; **he ~s teasing her** es macht ihm Spaß, sie aufzuziehen; **did you ~ the film?** hat dir der Film gefallen?; **enjoyable** adj angenehm; (entertaining) unterhaltsam; **enjoyment** n Vergnügen nt; (stronger) Freude f (of an +dat)

enlarge [ɪn'lɑ:dʒ] vt vergrößern; (expand) erweitern; **enlargement** n Vergrößerung f

enormous, enormously [ɪ'nɔ:məs, -lɪ] adj, adv riesig, ungeheuer

enough [ɪ'nʌf] adj genug; **that's** ~ das reicht!; (stop it) Schluss damit!; **I've had** ~ das hat mir gereicht; (to eat) ich bin satt ▷ adv genug, genügend

enquire [ɪn'kwaɪə*] vi sich erkundigen (about nach); **enquiry** [ɪn'kwaɪərɪ] n (question) Anfrage f; (for information) Erkundigung f (about über +akk); (investigation)

Untersuchung f; **"Enquiries"** „Auskunft"

enrol [ɪnˈrəʊl] vi sich einschreiben; (for course, school) sich anmelden; **enrolment** n Einschreibung f, Anmeldung f

en suite [ɒnˈswiːt] adj, n: **room with ~ (bathroom)** Zimmer nt mit eigenem Bad

ensure [ɪnˈʃʊə°] vt sicherstellen

enter [ˈentə°] vt eintreten in +akk, betreten; (drive into) einfahren in +akk; (country) einreisen in +akk; (in list) eintragen; (Inform) eingeben; (race, contest) teilnehmen an +dat ▷ vi (towards speaker) hereinkommen; (away from speaker) hineingehen

enterprise [ˈentəpraɪz] n (Comm) Unternehmen nt

entertain [entəˈteɪn] vt (guest) bewirten; (amuse) unterhalten; **entertaining** adj unterhaltsam; **entertainment** n (amusement) Unterhaltung f

enthusiasm [ɪnˈθjuːzɪæzəm] n Begeisterung f; **enthusiastic** [ɪnθjuːzɪˈæstɪk] adj begeistert (about von)

entice [ɪnˈtaɪs] vt locken; (lead astray) verleiten

entire, entirely [ɪnˈtaɪə°, -lɪ] adj, adv ganz

entitle [ɪnˈtaɪtl] vt (qualify) berechtigen (to zu); (name) betiteln

entrance [ˈentrəns] n Eingang m; (for vehicles) Einfahrt f; (entering) Eintritt m; (Theat) Auftritt m; **entrance exam** n Aufnahmeprüfung f; **entrance fee** n Eintrittsgeld nt

entrust [ɪnˈtrʌst] vt: **to ~ sb with sth** jdm etw anvertrauen

entry [ˈentrɪ] n (way in) Eingang m; (entering) Eintritt m; (in vehicle) Einfahrt f; (into country) Einreise f;

(admission) Zutritt m; (in diary, accounts) Eintrag m; **"no ~"** „Eintritt verboten"; (for vehicles) „Einfahrt verboten"; **entry phone** n Türsprechanlage f

E-number n (food additive) E-Nummer f

envelope [ˈenvələʊp] n (Brief)umschlag m

enviable [ˈenvɪəbl] adj beneidenswert; **envious** [ˈenvɪəs] adj neidisch

environment [ɪnˈvaɪərənmənt] n Umgebung f; (ecology) Umwelt f; **environmental** [ɪnvaɪərənˈmentəl] adj Umwelt-; **~ pollution** Umweltverschmutzung f; **environmentalist** n Umweltschützer(in) m(f)

envy [ˈenvɪ] n Neid m (of auf +akk) ▷ vt beneiden (sb sth jdn um etw)

epic [ˈepɪk] n Epos nt; (film) Monumentalfilm m

epidemic [epɪˈdemɪk] n Epidemie f

epilepsy [ˈepɪlepsɪ] n Epilepsie f; **epileptic** [epɪˈleptɪk] adj epileptisch

episode [ˈepɪsəʊd] n Episode f; (TV) Folge f

epoch [ˈiːpɒk] n Zeitalter nt, Epoche f

equal [ˈiːkwl] adj gleich (to +dat) ▷ n Gleichgestellte(r) mf ▷ vt gleichen; (match) gleichkommen +dat; **two times two ~s four** zwei mal zwei ist gleich vier; **equality** [ɪˈkwɒlɪtɪ] n Gleichheit f; (equal rights) Gleichberechtigung f; **equalize** vi (Sport) ausgleichen; **equalizer** n (Sport) Ausgleichstreffer m; **equally** adv gleich; (on the other hand) andererseits; **equation** [ɪˈkweɪʒən] n (Math) Gleichung f

equator [ɪˈkweɪtə°] n Äquator m

equilibrium | 342

equilibrium [iːkwɪˈlɪbrɪəm] n Gleichgewicht nt

equip [ɪˈkwɪp] vt ausrüsten; (kitchen) ausstatten; **equipment** n Ausrüstung f; (for kitchen) Ausstattung f; **electrical ~** Elektrogeräte pl

equivalent [ɪˈkwɪvələnt] adj gleichwertig (to dat); (corresponding) entsprechend (to dat) ▷ n Äquivalent nt; (amount) gleiche Menge; (in money) Gegenwert m

era [ˈɪərə] n Ära f, Zeitalter nt

erase [ɪˈreɪz] vt ausradieren; (tape, disk) löschen; **eraser** n Radiergummi m

erect [ɪˈrekt] adj aufrecht ▷ vt (building, monument) errichten; (tent) aufstellen; **erection** n Errichtung f; (Anat) Erektion f

erode [ɪˈrəʊd] vt zerfressen; (land) auswaschen; (rights, power) aushöhlen; **erosion** [ɪˈrəʊʒən] n Erosion f

erotic [ɪˈrɒtɪk] adj erotisch

err [ɜː] vi sich irren

errand [ˈerənd] n Besorgung f

erratic [ɪˈrætɪk] adj (behaviour) unberechenbar; (bus link etc) unregelmäßig; (performance) unbeständig

error [ˈerə] n Fehler m; **in ~** irrtümlicherweise; **error message** n (Inform) Fehlermeldung f

erupt [ɪˈrʌpt] vi ausbrechen

escalator [ˈeskəleɪtə] n Rolltreppe f

escalope [ˈeskələp] n Schnitzel nt

escape [ɪˈskeɪp] n Flucht f; (from prison etc) Ausbruch m; **to have a narrow ~** gerade noch davonkommen; **there's no ~** (fig) es gibt keinen Ausweg ▷ vt (pursuers) entkommen +dat; (punishment etc) entgehen +dat ▷ vi (from pursuers) entkommen (from dat); (from prison etc) ausbrechen (from dat); (leak: gas) ausströmen; (water) auslaufen

escort [ˈeskɔːt] n (companion) Begleiter(in) m(f); (guard) Eskorte f ▷ vt [ɪˈskɔːt] (lady) begleiten

especially [ɪˈspeʃəlɪ] adv besonders

espionage [ˈespɪənɑːʒ] n Spionage f

Esquire [ɪˈskwaɪə] n (Brit: in address): **J. Brown, Esq** Herrn J. Brown

essay [ˈeseɪ] n Aufsatz m; (literary) Essay m

essential [ɪˈsenʃəl] adj (necessary) unentbehrlich, unverzichtbar; (basic) wesentlich ▷ n **the ~s** pl das Wesentliche; **essentially** adv im Wesentlichen

establish [ɪˈstæblɪʃ] vt (set up) gründen; (introduce) einführen; (relations) aufnehmen; (prove) nachweisen; **to ~ that ...** feststellen, dass ...; **establishment** n Institution f; (business) Unternehmen nt

estate [ɪˈsteɪt] n Gut nt; (of deceased) Nachlass m; (housing ~) Siedlung f; (country house) Landsitz m; **estate agent** n (Brit) Grundstücksmakler(in) m(f), Immobilienmakler(in) m(f); **estate car** n (Brit) Kombiwagen m

estimate [ˈestɪmət] n Schätzung f; (Comm: of price) Kostenvoranschlag m ▷ [ˈestɪmeɪt] vt schätzen

Estonia [eˈstəʊnɪə] n Estland nt; **Estonian** [eˈstəʊnɪən] ▷ adj estnisch; ▷ n (person) Este m; Estin f; (language) Estnisch nt

estuary [ˈestjʊərɪ] n Mündung f

etching [ˈetʃɪŋ] n Radierung f

eternal, eternally [ɪˈtɜːnl, -nəlɪ]

adj, adv ewig; **eternity** *n*
Ewigkeit *f*

ethical ['eθɪkəl] *adj* ethisch;
ethics ['eθɪks] *npl* Ethik *f*

Ethiopia [iːθɪˈəʊpɪə] *n* Äthiopien
nt

ethnic ['eθnɪk] *adj* ethnisch;
(clothes etc) landesüblich;
~ minority ethnische Minderheit

e-ticket ['iːtɪkɪt] *n* E-Ticket *nt*

EU *abbr* = **European Union** EU *f*

euphemism ['juːfɪmɪzəm] *n*
Euphemismus *m*

euro ['jʊərəʊ] *(pl* **-s)** *n* (Fin) Euro
m; **Eurocheque** ['jʊərəʊtʃek] *n*
Euroscheck *m;* **Europe** ['jʊərəp] *n*
Europa *nt;* **European** [jʊərəˈpiːən]
adj europäisch; **~ Parliament**
Europäisches Parlament; **~ Union**
Europäische Union *nt;*
Europäer(in) *m(f);* **Eurosceptic**
['jʊərəʊskeptɪk] *n*
Euroskeptiker(in) *m(f);*
Eurotunnel *n* Eurotunnel *m*

evacuate [ɪˈvækjʊeɪt] *vt (place)*
räumen; *(people)* evakuieren

evade [ɪˈveɪd] *vt* ausweichen
+dat; *(pursuers)* sich entziehen *+dat*

evaluate [ɪˈvæljʊeɪt] *vt*
auswerten

evaporate [ɪˈvæpəreɪt] *vi* ver-
dampfen; *(fig)* verschwinden; **~d
milk** Kondensmilch *f*

even ['iːvən] *adj (flat)* eben;
(regular) gleichmäßig; *(equal)*
gleich; *(number)* gerade; **the score
is ~** es steht unentschieden ⊳ *adv*
sogar; **~ you** selbst du (o sogar
du/Sie; **~ if** selbst wenn, wenn
auch; **~ though** obwohl; **not
~** nicht einmal; **~ better** noch
besser; **even out** *vi (prices)* sich
einpendeln

evening ['iːvnɪŋ] *n* Abend *m;* **in
the ~** abends, am Abend; **this
~** heute Abend; **evening class** *n*
Abendkurs *m;* **evening dress** *n*

(generally) Abendkleidung *f;*
(woman's) Abendkleid *nt*

evenly ['iːvənlɪ] *adv* gleichmäßig

event [ɪˈvent] *n* Ereignis *nt;*
(organized) Veranstaltung *f; (Sport:
discipline)* Disziplin *f;* **in the ~ of** im
Falle +gen; **eventful** *adj*
ereignisreich

eventual [ɪˈventʃʊəl] *adj (final)*
letztendlich; **eventually**
[ɪˈventʃʊəlɪ] *adv (at last)* am Ende;
(given time) schließlich

ever ['evəʳ] *adv (at any time)*
je(mals); **don't ~ do that again** tu
das ja nie wieder; **he's the best
~** er ist der Beste, den es je
gegeben hat; **have you ~ been to
the States?** bist du schon einmal
in den Staaten gewesen?; **for
~** (für) immer; **for ~ and ~** auf
immer und ewig; **so ...?** *(fam)*
äußerst ...; **~ so drunk** ganz schön
betrunken

every ['evrɪ] *adj* jeder/jede/
jedes; **~ day** jeden Tag; **~ other
day** jeden zweiten Tag; **~ five
days** alle fünf Tage; **I have ~
reason to believe that ...** ich
habe allen Grund anzunehmen,
dass ...; **everybody** *pron* jeder,
alle *pl;* **everyday** *adj*
(commonplace) alltäglich; *(clothes,
language etc)* Alltags-; **everyone**
pron jeder, alle *pl;* **everything**
pron alles; **everywhere** *adv*
überall; *(with direction)* überallhin

evidence ['evɪdəns] *n* Beweise
pl; (single piece) Beweis *m;*
(testimony) Aussage *f; (signs)*
Spuren *pl;* **evident**, **evidently** *adj,
adv* offensichtlich

evil ['iːvl] *adj* böse ⊳ *n* Böse(s) *nt;*
an ~ ein Übel

evolution [iːvəˈluːʃən] *n* Entwicklung *f; (of life)* Evolution *f;*
evolve [ɪˈvɒlv] *vi* sich entwickeln

ex- [eks] *pref* Ex-, ehemalig;

~boyfriend Exfreund *m*; **~wife** frühere Frau, Exfrau *f*; **ex** *n* (*fam*) Verflossene(r) *mf*

exact [ɪɡˈzækt] *adj* genau; **exactly** *adv* genau; **not - fast** nicht gerade schnell

exaggerate [ɪɡˈzædʒəreɪt] *vt, vi* übertreiben; **exaggerated** *adj* übertrieben; **exaggeration** *n* Übertreibung *f*

exam [ɪɡˈzæm] *n* Prüfung *f*; **examination** [ɪɡzæmɪˈneɪʃən] *n* (*Med etc*) Untersuchung *f*, Prüfung *f*; (*at university*) Examen *nt*; (*at customs etc*) Kontrolle *f*; **examine** [ɪɡˈzæmɪn] *vt* untersuchen (*for auf +akk*); (*check*) kontrollieren, prüfen; **examiner** *n* Prüfer(in) *m(f)*

example [ɪɡˈzɑːmpl] *n* Beispiel *nt* (*of für +akk*); **for -** zum Beispiel

excavation [ekskəˈveɪʃən] *n* Ausgrabung *f*

exceed [ɪkˈsiːd] *vt* überschreiten, übertreffen; **exceedingly** *adv* äußerst

excel [ɪkˈsel] *vt* übertreffen; **he ~led himself** er hat sich selbst übertroffen ▷ *vi* sich auszeichnen (*in* in +*dat*, *at* bei); **excellent, excellently** [ˈeksələnt, -lɪ] *adj, adv* ausgezeichnet

except [ɪkˈsept] *prep*: **~ außer** +*dat*; **~ for** abgesehen von ▷ *vt* ausnehmen; **exception** [ɪkˈsepʃən] *n* Ausnahme *f*; **exceptional, exceptionally** [ɪkˈsepʃənl, -nəlɪ] *adj, adv* außergewöhnlich

excess [ek'ses] *n* Übermaß *nt* (*of an* +*dat*); **excess baggage** *n* Übergepäck *nt*; **excesses** *npl* Exzesse *pl*; (*drink, sex*) Ausschweifungen *pl*; **excessive, excessively** *adj, adv* übermäßig; **excess weight** *n* Übergewicht *nt*

exchange [ɪksˈtʃeɪndʒ] *n* Austausch *m* (*for gegen*); (*of bought items*) Umtausch *m* (*for gegen*); (*Fin*) Wechsel *m* (*for gegen*); (*Tel*) Vermittlung *f*, Zentrale *f* ▷ *vt* austauschen; (*goods*) tauschen; (*bought items*) umtauschen (*for gegen*); (*money, blows*) wechseln; **exchange rate** *n* Wechselkurs *m*

excite [ɪkˈsaɪt] *vt* erregen; **excited** *adj* aufgeregt; **to get ~** sich aufregen; **exciting** *adj* aufregend; (*book, film*) spannend

exclamation [eksklə'meɪʃən] *n* Ausruf *m*; **exclamation mark, exclamation point** (*US*) *n* Ausrufezeichen *nt*

exclude [ɪksˈkluːd] *vt* ausschließen; **exclusion** [ɪksˈkluːʒən] *n* Ausschluss *m*; **exclusive** [ɪksˈkluːsɪv] *adj* (*select*) exklusiv; (*sole*) ausschließlich; **exclusively** *adv* ausschließlich

excrement [ˈekskrɪmənt] *n* Kot *m*, Exkremente *pl*

excruciating [ɪksˈkruːʃɪeɪtɪŋ] *adj* fürchterlich, entsetzlich

excursion [ɪksˈkɜːʃən] *n* Ausflug *m*

excusable [ɪksˈkjuːzəbl] *adj* entschuldbar; **excuse** [ɪksˈkjuːz] *vt* entschuldigen; **~ me** Entschuldigung!; **to ~ sb for sth** jdm etw verzeihen; **to ~ sb from sth** jdn von etw befreien ▷ [ɪksˈkjuːs] *n* Entschuldigung *f*, Ausrede *f*

ex-directory [eksdərˈrektərɪ] *adj*: **to be ~** (*Brit Tel*) nicht im Telefonbuch stehen

execute [ˈeksɪkjuːt] *vt* (*carry out*) ausführen; (*kill*) hinrichten; **execution** *n* (*killing*) Hinrichtung *f*; (*carrying out*) Ausführung *f*; **executive** [ɪɡˈzekjʊtɪv] *n* (*Comm*) leitender Angestellter, leitende Angestellte

exemplary [ɪgˈzemplərɪ] adj beispielhaft

exempt [ɪgˈzempt] adj befreit (from von) ▷ vt befreien

exercise [ˈeksəsaɪz] n (in school, sports) Übung f; (movement) Bewegung f; **to get more ~** mehr Sport treiben; **exercise bike** n Heimtrainer m; **exercise book** n Heft nt

exert [ɪgˈzɜːt] vt (influence) ausüben

exhaust [ɪgˈzɔːst] n (fumes) Abgase pl; (Auto) **~ (pipe)** Auspuff m; **exhausted** adj erschöpft; **exhausting** adj anstrengend

exhibit [ɪgˈzɪbɪt] n (in exhibition) Ausstellungsstück nt; **exhibition** [eksɪˈbɪʃən] n Ausstellung f; **exhibitionist** [eksɪˈbɪʃənɪst] n Selbstdarsteller(in) m(f); **exhibitor** n Aussteller(in) m(f)

exhilarating [ɪgˈzɪləreɪtɪŋ] adj belebend, erregend

exile [ˈeksaɪl] n Exil nt; (person) Verbannte(r) mf ▷ vt verbannen

exist [ɪgˈzɪst] vi existieren; (live) leben (on von); **existence** n Existenz f; **to come into ~** entstehen; **existing** adj bestehend

exit [ˈeksɪt] n Ausgang m; (for vehicles) Ausfahrt f; **exit poll** n Umfrage direkt nach dem Wahlgang

exorbitant [ɪgˈzɔːbɪtənt] adj astronomisch

exotic [ɪgˈzɒtɪk] adj exotisch

expand [ɪksˈpænd] vt ausdehnen, erweitern ▷ vi sich ausdehnen; **expansion** [ɪksˈpænʃən] n Expansion f, Erweiterung f

expect [ɪksˈpekt] vt erwarten; (suppose) annehmen; **he ~s me to do it** er erwartet, dass ich es mache; **I ~ it'll rain** es wird wohl regnen; **I ~ so** ich denke schon

▷ vi: **she's ~ing** sie bekommt ein Kind

expedition [ekspɪˈdɪʃən] n Expedition f

expenditure [ɪksˈpendɪtʃə°] n Ausgaben pl

expense [ɪksˈpens] n Kosten pl; (single cost) Ausgabe f; **(business) ~s** pl Spesen pl; **at sb's ~** auf jds Kosten; **expensive** [ɪksˈpensɪv] adj teuer

experience [ɪksˈpɪərɪəns] n Erfahrung f; (particular incident) Erlebnis nt; **by/from ~** aus Erfahrung ▷ vt erfahren, erleben; (hardship) durchmachen; **experienced** adj erfahren

experiment [ɪksˈperɪmənt] n Versuch m, Experiment nt ▷ vi experimentieren

expert [ˈekspɜːt] n Experte m, Expertin f; (professional) Fachmann m, Fachfrau f; (Jur) Sachverständige(r) mf ▷ adj fachmännisch, Fach-; **expertise** [ekspəˈtiːz] n Sachkenntnis f

expire [ɪksˈpaɪə°] vi (end) ablaufen; **expiry date** [ɪksˈpaɪərədeɪt] n Verfallsdatum nt

explain [ɪksˈpleɪn] vt erklären (sth to sb jdm etw); **explanation** [ekspləˈneɪʃən] n Erklärung f

explicit [ɪksˈplɪsɪt] adj ausdrücklich, eindeutig

explode [ɪksˈpləʊd] vi explodieren

exploit [ɪksˈplɔɪt] vt ausbeuten

explore [ɪksˈplɔː°] vt erforschen

explosion [ɪksˈpləʊʒən] n Explosion f; **explosive** [ɪksˈpləʊsɪv] adj explosiv ▷ n Sprengstoff m

export [ekˈspɔːt] vt, vi exportieren ▷ n [ˈekspɔːt] Export m ▷ adj (trade) Export-

expose [ɪksˈpəʊz] vt (to danger

express | 346

etc) aussetzen (*to dat*); (*uncover*)
freilegen; (*imposter*) entlarven;
exposed *adj* (*position*)
ungeschützt; **exposure**
[ɪk'spəʊʒə°] *n* (*Med*)
Unterkühlung *f*; (*Foto: time*)
Belichtung(szeit) *f*; **24 ~s** 24
Aufnahmen

express [ɪk'spres] *adj* (*speedy*)
Express-, Schnell-; **~ delivery**
Eilzustellung *f* ▷ *n* (*Rail*)
Schnellzug *m* ▷ *vt* ausdrücken
▷ *vr*: **to ~ oneself** sich
ausdrücken; **expression**
[ɪk'spreʃən] *n* (*phrase*) Ausdruck
m; (*look*) Gesichtsausdruck *m*;
expressive *adj* ausdrucksvoll;
expressway *n* (*US*) Schnellstraße
f

extend [ɪk'stend] *vt* (*arms*)
ausstrecken; (*lengthen*) verlängern;
(*building*) vergrößern, ausbauen;
(*business, limits*) erweitern;
extension [ɪk'stenʃən] *n*
(*lengthening*) Verlängerung *f*; (*of
building*) Anbau *m*; (*Tel*) Anschluss
m; (*of business, limits*) Erweiterung
f; **extensive** [ɪk'stensɪv] *adj*
(*knowledge*) umfangreich; (*use*)
häufig; **extent** [ɪk'stent] *n*
(*length*) Länge *f*; (*size*) Ausdehnung
f; (*scope*) Umfang *m*, Ausmaß *nt*; **to
a certain/large ~** in
gewissem/hohem Maße

exterior [ek'stɪərɪə°] *n* Äußere(s)
nt

external [ek'stɜːnl] *adj* äußere(r, s), Außen-; **externally** *adv*
äußerlich

extinct [ɪk'stɪŋkt] *adj* (*species*)
ausgestorben

extinguish [ɪk'stɪŋgwɪʃ] *vt*
löschen; **extinguisher** *n*
Löschgerät *nt*

extra ['ekstrə] *adj* zusätzlich;
~ charge Zuschlag *m*; **~ time**
(*Sport*) Verlängerung *f* ▷ *adv*

besonders; **~ large** (*clothing*)
übergroß ▷ *npl*: **~s** zusätzliche
Kosten *pl*; (*food*) Beilagen *pl*;
(*accessories*) Zubehör *nt*; (*for car etc*)
Extras *pl*

extract [ɪk'strækt] *vt* herausziehen (*from aus*); (*tooth*)
ziehen ▷ ['ekstrækt] *n* (*from book
etc*) Auszug *m*

extraordinary [ɪk'strɔːdɪnrɪ] *adj*
außerordentlich; (*unusual*)
ungewöhnlich; (*amazing*)
erstaunlich

extreme [ɪk'striːm] *adj* äußer-
ste(r, s); (*drastic*) extrem ▷ *n*
Extrem *nt*; **extremely** *adv*
äußerst, höchst; **extreme sports**
npl Extremsportarten *pl*;
extremist [ɪk'striːmɪst] *adj*
extremistisch ▷ *n* Extremist *m*

extricate ['ekstrɪkeɪt] *vt* befreien
(*from aus*)

extrovert ['ekstrəʊvɜːt] *adj*
extrovertiert

exuberance [ɪg'zuːbərəns] *n*
Überschwang *m*; **exuberant** *adj*
überschwänglich

exultation [egzʌl'teɪʃən] *n* Jubel
m

eye [aɪ] *n* Auge *nt*; **to keep an
~ on sb/sth** auf jdn/etw
aufpassen ▷ *vt* mustern;
eyebrow *n* Augenbraue *f*;
eyelash *n* Wimper *f*; **eyelid** *n*
Augenlid *nt*; **eyeliner** *n* Eyeliner
m; **eyeopener** *n*: **that was an
~** das hat mir die Augen geöffnet;
eyeshadow *n* Lidschatten *m*;
eyesight *n* Sehkraft *f*; **eyesore** *n*
Schandfleck *m*; **eye witness** *n*
Augenzeuge *m*, Augenzeugin *f*

f

fabric ['fæbrɪk] n Stoff m
fabulous ['fæbjʊlǝs] adj
  sagenhaft
façade [fǝ'sɑːd] n (a. fig) Fassade
  f
face [feɪs] n Gesicht nt; (of clock)
  Zifferblatt nt; (of mountain) Wand f;
  in the ~ of trotz +gen; **to be ~ to
  ~ (people)** einander
  gegenüberstehen ▷ vt, vi (person)
  gegenüberstehen +dat; (at table)
  gegenübersitzen +dat; **to ~ north
  (room)** nach Norden gehen; **to
  ~ (up to) the facts** den Tatsachen
  ins Auge sehen; **to be ~d with sth**
  mit etw konfrontiert sein; **face lift**
  n Gesichtsstraffung f; (fig)
  Verschönerung f; **face powder** n
  Gesichtspuder m
facet ['fæsɪt] n (fig) Aspekt m
face value n Nennwert m
facial ['feɪʃǝl] adj Gesichts- ▷ n
  (fam) (kosmetische)
  Gesichtsbehandlung f

facilitate [fǝ'sɪlɪteɪt] vt
  erleichtern
facility [fǝ'sɪlɪtɪ] n (building etc to
  be used) Einrichtung f, Möglichkeit
  f; (installation) Anlage f; (skill)
  Gewandtheit f
fact [fækt] n Tatsache f; **as a
  matter of ~, in ~** eigentlich,
  tatsächlich
factor ['fæktǝ³] n Faktor m
factory ['fæktǝrɪ] n Fabrik f;
  factory outlet n Fabrikverkauf m
factual ['fæktjʊǝl] adj sachlich
faculty ['fækǝltɪ] n Fähigkeit f;
  (at university) Fakultät f; (US:
  teaching staff) Lehrkörper m
fade [feɪd] vi (a. fig) verblassen;
  faded adj verblasst, verblichen
faff about ['fæfǝbaʊt] vi (Brit
  fam) herumwursteln
fag [fæg] n (Brit fam: cigarette)
  Kippe f; (US fam pej) Schwule(r) m
Fahrenheit ['færǝnhaɪt] n
  Fahrenheit
fail [feɪl] vt (exam) nicht bestehen
  ▷ vi versagen; (plan, marriage)
  scheitern; (student) durchfallen;
  (eyesight) nachlassen; **words ~ me**
  ich bin sprachlos; **failing** n
  Schwäche f; **failure** ['feɪljǝ³] n
  (person) Versager(in) m(f); (act, a.
  Tech) Versagen nt; (of engine etc)
  Ausfall m; (of plan, marriage)
  Scheitern nt
faint [feɪnt] adj schwach; (sound)
  leise; (fam) **I haven't the ~est
  (idea)** ich habe keinen blassen
  Schimmer ▷ vi ohnmächtig
  werden (with vor +dat); **faintness**
  n (Med) Schwächegefühl nt
fair [feǝ³] adj (hair) (dunkel)blond;
  (skin) hell; (just) gerecht, fair;
  (reasonable) ganz ordentlich; (in
  school) befriedigend; (weather)
  schön; (wind) günstig; **a
  ~ number/amount of** ziemlich
  viele/viel ▷ adv: **to play ~** fair

spielen; *(fig)* fair sein; **~ enough** in
Ordnung; ▷ *n (fun~)* Jahrmarkt *m*;
(Comm) Messe *f*; **fair-haired** *adj*
(dunkel)blond; **fairly** *adv*
(honestly) fair; *(rather)* ziemlich

fairy ['feərɪ] *n* Fee *f*; **fairy tale** *n*
Märchen *nt*

faith [feɪθ] *n (trust)* Vertrauen *nt*
(in sb zu jdm); *(Rel)* Glaube *m*;
faithful, faithfully *adj, adv* treu;
Yours ~ly Hochachtungsvoll

fake [feɪk] *n (thing)* Fälschung *f*
▷ *adj* vorgetäuscht ▷ *vt* fälschen

falcon ['fɔːlkən] *n* Falke *m*

fall [fɔːl] *(fell, fallen)* *vi* fallen;
(from a height, badly) stürzen; **to
~ ill** krank werden; **to ~ asleep**
einschlafen; **to ~ in love** sich
verlieben ▷ *n* Fall *m*; *(accident, fig:
of regime)* Sturz *m*; *(decrease)* Sinken
nt (in +gen); *(US: autumn)* Herbst *m*;
fall apart *vi* auseinanderfallen;
fall behind *vi* zurückbleiben;
(with work, rent) in Rückstand
geraten; **fall down** *vi (person)*
hinfallen; **fall off** *vi*
herunterfallen; *(decrease)*
zurückgehen; **fall out** *vi (quarrel)* sich
herausfallen; *(quarrel)* sich
streiten; **fall over** *vi* hinfallen;
fall through *vi (plan etc)* ins
Wasser fallen

fallen ['fɔːlən] *pp of* **fall**

fallout ['fɔːlaʊt] *n* radioaktiver
Niederschlag, Fall-out *m*

false [fɔːls] *adj* falsch; *(artificial)*
künstlich; **false alarm** *n* blinder
Alarm; **false start** *n (Sport)*
Fehlstart *m*; **false teeth** *npl*
(künstliches) Gebiss

fame [feɪm] *n* Ruhm *m*

familiar [fə'mɪlɪə°] *adj* vertraut,
bekannt; **to be ~ with** vertraut
sein mit, gut kennen; **familiarity**
[fəmɪlɪˈærɪtɪ] *n* Vertrautheit *f*

family ['fæmɪlɪ] *n* Familie *f*;
(including relations) Verwandtschaft

f; **family man** *n* Familienvater *m*;
family name *n* Familienname *m*,
Nachname *m*; **family practitioner**
n (US) Allgemeinarzt *m*,
Allgemeinärztin *f*

famine ['fæmɪn] *n* Hungersnot *f*;
famished ['fæmɪʃt] *adj*
ausgehungert

famous ['feɪməs] *adj* berühmt

fan [fæn] *n (hand-held)* Fächer *m*;
(Elec) Ventilator *m*; *(admirer)* Fan *m*

fanatic [fə'nætɪk] *n* Fanatiker(in)
m(f)

fancy ['fænsɪ] *adj (elaborate)*
kunstvoll; *(unusual)* ausgefallen
▷ *vt (like)* gernhaben; **he fancies
her** er steht auf sie; **~ that!** stell dir
vor!, so was!; **fancy dress** *n*
Kostüm *nt*, Verkleidung *f*

fan heater ['fænhiːtə°] *n*
Heizlüfter *m*; **fanlight** *n*
Oberlicht *nt*

fan mail *n* Fanpost *f*

fantasise ['fæntəsaɪz] *vi* träumen *(about von)*; **fantastic**
[fæn'tæstɪk] *adj (a. fam)*
fantastisch; **that's ~** *(fam)* das ist
ja toll!; **fantasy** ['fæntəzɪ] *n*
Fantasie *f*

far [fɑː°] *(further o farther,
furthest o farthest)* *adj* weit; **the
~ end of the room** das andere
Ende des Zimmers; **the Far East**
der Ferne Osten ▷ *adv* weit;
~ better viel besser; **by ~ the best**
bei weitem der/die/das Beste; **as
~ as ...** bis zum o zur ...; *(with place
name)* bis nach ...; **as ~ as I'm
concerned** was mich betrifft, von
mir aus; **so ~** soweit, bisher;
faraway *adj* weit entfernt; *(look)*
verträumt

fare [feə°] *n* Fahrpreis *m*; *(money)*
Fahrgeld *m*

farm [fɑːm] *n* Bauernhof *m*, Farm
f; **farmer** *n* Bauer *m*, Bäuerin *f*,
Landwirt(in) *m(f)*; **farmhouse**

Bauernhaus nt; **farming** n
Landwirtschaft f; **farmland** n
Ackerland nt; **farmyard** n Hof m

far-reaching ['fɑːriːtʃɪŋ] adj
weit reichend; **far-sighted** adj
weitsichtig; (fig) weitblickend

fart [fɑːt] n (fam) Furz m; **old
~** (fam: person) alter Sack ▷ vi (fam)
furzen

farther ['fɑːðə⁰] adj, adv
comparative of **far**; see **further**

farthest ['fɑːðɪst] adj, adv
superlative of **far**; see **furthest**

fascinating ['fæsɪneɪtɪŋ] adj
faszinierend; **fascination** n
Faszination f

fascism ['fæʃɪzəm] n Faschismus
m; **fascist** ['fæʃɪst] adj
faschistisch ▷ Faschist(in) m(f)

fashion ['fæʃən] n (clothes) Mode
f; (manner) Art (und Weise) f; **to be
in ~** (in) Mode sein; **out of
~** unmodisch; **fashionable,
fashionably** adj, adv (clothes,
person) modisch; (author, pub etc) in
Mode

fast [fɑːst] adj schnell; **to be
~** (clock) vorgehen ▷ adv schnell;
(firmly) fest; **to be ~ asleep** fest
schlafen ▷ n Fasten nt ▷ vi
fasten; **fastback** n (Auto)
Fließheck nt

fasten ['fɑːsn] vt (attach)
befestigen (to an +dat); (do up)
zumachen; **~ your seatbelts** bitte
anschnallen; **fastener, fastening**
n Verschluss m

fast food n Fast Food nt; **fast
forward** n (for tape)
Schnellvorlauf m; **fast lane** n
Überholspur f

fat [fæt] adj dick; (meat) fett ▷ n
Fett nt

fatal ['feɪtl] adj tödlich

fate [feɪt] n Schicksal nt

fat-free adj (food) fettfrei

father ['fɑːðə⁰] n Vater m; (priest)

Pfarrer m ▷ vt (child) zeugen;
Father Christmas n der
Weihnachtsmann; **father-in-law**
(pl **fathers-in-law**) n
Schwiegervater m

fatigue [fə'tiːg] n Ermüdung
f

fattening ['fætnɪŋ] adj: **to be
~** dick machen; **fatty** ['fætɪ] adj
(food) fettig

faucet ['fɔːsɪt] n (US)
Wasserhahn m

fault [fɔːlt] n (in machine) Fehler m;
Defekt m; (Elec) Störung f; (blame)
Schuld f; **it's your ~** du bist daran
schuld; **faulty** adj fehlerhaft;
(Tech) defekt

favor (US), **favour** ['feɪvə⁰] n
(approval) Gunst f; (kindness)
Gefallen m; **in ~ of:** **I'm in ~ (of
going)** ich bin dafür(, dass wir
gehen); **to do sb a ~** jdm einen
Gefallen tun ▷ vt (prefer)
vorziehen; **favourable** adj
günstig (to, for für); **favourite**
['feɪvrɪt] n Liebling m,
Favorit(in) m(f) ▷ adj Lieblings-

fax [fæks] vt faxen ▷ n Fax nt;
fax number n Faxnummer f

faze [feɪz] vt (fam) aus der
Fassung bringen

FBI abbr = **Federal Bureau of
Investigation** FBI nt

fear [fɪə⁰] n Angst f (of vor +dat)
▷ vt befürchten; **fearful** adj
(timid) ängstlich, furchtsam;
(terrible) fürchterlich; **fearless** adj
furchtlos

feasible ['fiːzəbl] adj machbar

feast [fiːst] n Festessen nt

feather ['feðə⁰] n Feder f

feature ['fiːtʃə⁰] n (facial)
(Gesichts)zug m; (characteristic)
Merkmal nt; (of car etc)
Ausstattungsmerkmal nt; (in the
press) (Cine) Feature nt ▷ vt
bringen, (als Besonderheit)

zeigen; **feature film** n Spielfilm
m

February ['februəri] n Februar
m; see also **September**

fed [fed] pt, pp of **feed**

federal ['fedərəl] adj Bundes-;
**the Federal Republic of
Germany** die Bundesrepublik
Deutschland

fed-up [fed'ʌp] adj: **to be ~ with
sth** etw satthaben; **I'm ~** ich habe
die Nase voll

fee [fiː] n Gebühr f; (of doctor,
lawyer) Honorar nt

feeble ['fiːbl] adj schwach

feed [fiːd] (**fed, fed**) vt (baby,
animal) füttern; (support) ernähren
▷ n (for baby) Mahlzeit f; (for
animals) Futter nt; (Inform: paper ~)
Zufuhr f; **feed in** vt (information)
eingeben; **feedback** n
(information) Feed-back nt

feel [fiːl] (**felt, felt**) vt (sense)
fühlen; (pain) empfinden; (touch)
anfassen; (think) meinen ▷ vi
(person) sich fühlen; **I ~ cold** mir ist
kalt; **do you ~ like a walk?** hast du
Lust, spazieren zu gehen?; **feeling**
n Gefühl nt

feet [fiːt] pl of **foot**

fell [fel] pt of **fall** ▷ vt (tree) fällen

fellow ['feləʊ] n Kerl m, Typ m;
~ **citizen** Mitbürger(in) m(f);
~ **countryman** Landsmann m;
~ **worker** Mitarbeiter(in) m(f)

felt [felt] pt, pp of **feel** ▷ n Filz m;
felt tip, felt-tip pen n Filzstift m

female ['fiːmeɪl] n (of animals)
Weibchen nt ▷ adj weiblich;
~ **doctor** Ärztin f; **feminine**
['feminin] adj weiblich; **feminist**
['feminist] n Feminist(in) m(f)
▷ adj feministisch

fence [fens] n Zaun m

fencing n (Sport) Fechten nt

fender ['fendə²] n (US Auto)
Kotflügel m

fennel ['fenl] n Fenchel m

fern [fɜːn] n Farn m

ferocious [fə'rəʊʃəs] adj wild

ferry ['feri] n Fähre f ▷ vt
übersetzen

fertile ['fɜːtaɪl] adj fruchtbar;
fertility [fə'tɪlɪti] n Fruchtbarkeit
f; **fertilize** ['fɜːtɪlaɪz] vt (Bio)
befruchten; (Agr: land) düngen;
fertilizer n Dünger m

festival ['festivəl] n (Rel) Fest nt;
(Art, Mus) Festspiele pl; (pop music)
Festival nt; **festive** ['festiv] adj
festlich; **festivities** [fe'stivitiz] n
Feierlichkeiten pl

fetch [fetʃ] vt holen; (collect)
abholen; (in sale, money)
einbringen; **fetching** adj reizend

fetish ['fetiʃ] n Fetisch m

fetus ['fiːtəs] n (US) Fötus m

fever ['fiːvə²] n Fieber nt;
feverish adj (Med) fiebrig; (fig)
fieberhaft

few [fjuː] adj, pron pl wenige pl; **a
~** pl ein paar; **fewer** adj weniger;
fewest adj wenigste(r, s)

fiancé [fi'ãnsei] n Verlobte(r) m;
fiancée n Verlobte f

fiasco [fi'æskəʊ] (pl -s o US -es) n
Fiasko nt

fiber (US), **fibre** ['faɪbə²] n
Faser f; (material) Faserstoff m

fickle ['fikl] adj unbeständig

fiction ['fikʃən] n (novels)
Prosaliteratur f; **fictional** adj;
fictitious [fik'tiʃəs] adj erfunden

fiddle ['fidl] n Geige f; (trick)
Betrug m ▷ vt (accounts, results)
frisieren; **fiddle with** vt
herumfummeln an +dat; **fiddly**
adj knifflig

fidelity [fi'deliti] n Treue f

fidget ['fidʒit] vi zappeln;
fidgety adj zappelig

field [fiːld] n Feld nt;
(grass-covered) Wiese f; (fig: of work)
(Arbeits)gebiet nt

fierce [fɪəs] adj heftig; (animal, appearance) wild; (criticism, competition) scharf

fifteen [fɪf'tiːn] num fünfzehn ▷ n Fünfzehn f; see also **eight**; **fifteenth** adj fünfzehnte(r, s); see also **eighth**; **fifth** [fɪfθ] adj fünfte(r, s) ▷ n (fraction) Fünftel nt; see also **eighth**; **fifty** ['fɪftɪ] num fünfzig ▷ n Fünfzig f; see also **eight**; **fiftieth** adj fünfzigste(r, s); see also **eighth**

fig [fɪg] n Feige f

fight [faɪt] (fought, fought) vi kämpfen (with, against gegen, for, over um) ▷ vt (person) kämpfen mit; (fig: disease, fear etc) bekämpfen ▷ n Kampf m; (brawl) Schlägerei f; (argument) Streit m; **fight back** vi zurückschlagen; **fight off** vt abwehren; **fighter** n Kämpfer(in) m(f)

figurative ['fɪgərətɪv] adj übertragen

figure ['fɪgəʳ] n (person) Gestalt f; (of person) Figur f; (number) Zahl f, Ziffer f; (amount) Betrag m; **a four-figure sum** eine vierstellige Summe ▷ vt (US: think) glauben ▷ vi (appear) erscheinen; **figure out** vt (work out) herausbekommen; **I can't figure him out** ich werde aus ihm nicht schlau; **figure skating** n Eiskunstlauf m

file [faɪl] n (tool) Feile f; (dossier) Akte f; (Inform) Datei f; (folder) Aktenordner m; **on ~** in den Akten ▷ vt (metal, nails) feilen; (papers) ablegen (under unter) ▷ vi: **to ~ in/out** hintereinander hereinkommen/hinausgehen; **filing cabinet** n Aktenschrank m

fill [fɪl] vt füllen; (tooth) plombieren; (post) besetzen; **fill in** vt (hole) auffüllen; (form) ausfüllen; (tell) informieren (on über); **fill out**

vt (form) ausfüllen; **fill up** vi (Auto) volltanken

fillet ['fɪlɪt] n Filet nt

filling ['fɪlɪŋ] n (Gastr) Füllung f; (for tooth) Plombe f; **filling station** n Tankstelle f

film [fɪlm] n Film ▷ vt (scene) filmen; **film star** n Filmstar m; **film studio** n Filmstudio nt

filter ['fɪltəʳ] n Filter m; (traffic lane) Abbiegespur f ▷ vt filtern

filth [fɪlθ] n Dreck m; **filthy** adj dreckig

fin [fɪn] n Flosse f

final ['faɪnl] adj letzte(r, s); (stage, round) End-; (decision, version) endgültig; **~ score** Schlussstand m ▷ n (Sport) Endspiel nt; (competition) Finale nt; **~s pl** Abschlussexamen nt; **finalize** vt die endgültige Form geben +dat; **finally** adv (lastly) zuletzt; (eventually) schließlich, endlich

finance [faɪ'næns] n Finanzwesen nt; **~s pl** Finanzen pl ▷ vt finanzieren; **financial** [faɪ'nænʃəl] adj finanziell; (adviser, crisis, policy etc) Finanz-

find [faɪnd] (found, found) vt finden; **he was found dead** er wurde tot aufgefunden; **I ~ myself in difficulties** ich befinde mich in Schwierigkeiten; **she ~s it difficult/easy** es fällt ihr schwer/leicht; **find out** vt herausfinden; **findings** npl (Jur) Ermittlungsergebnis nt; (of report, Med) Befund m

fine [faɪn] adj (thin) dünn, fein; (good) gut; (splendid) herrlich; (clothes) elegant; (weather) schön; **I'm ~** es geht mir gut; **that's ~** das ist OK ▷ adv (well) gut ▷ n (Jur) Geldstrafe f ▷ vt (Jur) mit einer Geldstrafe belegen; **fine arts** npl: **the ~** die schönen Künste pl;

finely adv (cut) dünn; (ground) fein

finger ['fɪŋgə*] n Finger m ▷ vt herumfingern an +dat; **fingernail** n Fingernagel m; **fingerprint** n Fingerabdruck m; **fingertip** n Fingerspitze f

finicky ['fɪnɪkɪ] adj (person) pingelig; (work) knifflig

finish ['fɪnɪʃ] n Ende nt; (Sport) Finish nt; (line) Ziel nt; (of product) Verarbeitung f ▷ vt beenden; (book etc) zu Ende lesen; (food aufessen; (drink) austrinken ▷ vi zu Ende gehen; (song, story) enden; (person) fertig sein; (stop) aufhören; **have you ~ed?** bist du fertig?; **to ~ first/second** (Sport) als erster/zweiter durchs Ziel gehen; **finishing line** n Ziellinie f

Finland ['fɪnlənd] n Finnland nt; **Finn** n Finne m, Finnin f; **Finnish** adj finnisch ▷ n (language) Finnisch nt

fir [fɜː*] n Tanne f

fire [faɪə*] n Feuer nt; (house etc) Brand m; **to set ~ to sth** etw in Brand stecken; **to be on ~** brennen ▷ vt (bullets, rockets) abfeuern; (fam: dismiss) feuern ▷ vi (Auto: engine) zünden; **to ~ at sb** auf jdn schießen; **fire alarm** n Feuermelder m; **fire brigade** n Feuerwehr f; **fire engine** n Feuerwehrauto nt; **fire escape** n Feuerleiter f; **fire extinguisher** n Feuerlöscher m; **firefighter** n Feuerwehrmann m, Feuerwehrfrau f; **fireman** n Feuerwehrmann m; **fireplace** n (offener) Kamin; **fireproof** adj feuerfest; **fire station** n Feuerwache f; **firewood** n Brennholz nt; **fireworks** npl Feuerwerk nt

firm [fɜːm] adj fest; (person) **to be ~** entschlossen auftreten ▷ n Firma f

first [fɜːst] adj erste(r, s) ▷ adv (at first) zuerst; (firstly) erstens; (arrive, finish) als erste(r); (happen) zum ersten Mal; **~ of all** zuallererst ▷ n (person) Erste(r) m|f; (Auto: gear) erster Gang; **at ~** zuerst, anfangs; **first aid** n erste Hilfe; **first-class** adj erstklassig; (compartment, ticket) erster Klasse; **~ mail** (Brit) bevorzugt beförderte Post ▷ adv (travel) erster Klasse; **first floor** n (Brit) erster Stock; (US) Erdgeschoss nt; **first lady** n (US) Frau f des Präsidenten; **firstly** adv erstens; **first name** n Vorname m; **first night** n (Theat) Premiere f; **first-rate** adj erstklassig

fir tree n Tannenbaum m

fish [fɪʃ] n Fisch m; **~ and chips** (Brit) frittierter Fisch mit Pommes frites ▷ vi fischen; (with rod) angeln; **to go ~ing** fischen/angeln gehen; (with rod) angeln; **fishbone** n Gräte f; **fishcake** n Fischfrikadelle f; **fish farm** n Fischzucht f; **fish finger** n (Brit) Fischstäbchen nt; **fishing** ['fɪʃɪŋ] n Fischen nt; (with rod) Angeln nt; (as industry) Fischerei f; **fishing boat** n Fischerboot nt; **fishing line** n Angelschnur f; **fishing rod** n Angelrute f; **fishing village** n Fischerdorf nt; **fishmonger** ['fɪʃmʌŋgə*] n Fischhändler(in) m(f); **fish stick** n (US) Fischstäbchen nt; **fish tank** n Aquarium nt

fishy ['fɪʃɪ] adj (fam: suspicious) faul

fist [fɪst] n Faust f

fit [fɪt] adj (Med) gesund; (Sport) in Form, fit; (suitable) geeignet; **to keep ~** sich in Form halten ▷ vi passen +dat; (attach) anbringen (to an +dat); (install) einbauen (in in +akk) ▷ vi passen; (in space, gap) hineinpassen ▷ n (of clothes) Sitz m; (Med) Anfall m; **it's a good ~ es**

passt gut; **fit in** vt (accommodate) unterbringen; (find time for) einschieben ▷ vi (in space) hineinpassen; (plans, ideas) passen; **he doesn't ~ (here)** er passt nicht hierher; **to ~ with sb's plans** sich mit jds Plänen vereinbaren lassen; **fitness** n (Med) Gesundheit f; (Sport) Fitness f; **fitness trainer** n (Sport) Fitnesstrainer(in) m(f); **fitted carpet** n Teppichboden m; **fitted kitchen** n Einbauküche f; **fitting** adj passend ▷ n (of dress) Anprobe f; **~s** pl Ausstattung f

five [faɪv] num fünf ▷ n Fünf f; see also **eight**; **fiver** n (Brit fam) Fünfpfundschein m

fix [fɪks] vt befestigen (to an +dat); (settle) festsetzen; (place, time) ausmachen; (repair) reparieren; **fixer** n (drug addict) Fixer(in) m(f); **fixture** ['fɪkstʃə⁰] n (Sport) Veranstaltung f; (match) Spiel nt; (in building) Installationsteil m; **~s (and fittings)** pl Ausstattung f

fizzy ['fɪzɪ] adj sprudelnd; **~ drink** Limo f

flabbergasted ['flæbəgɑːstɪd] adj (fam) platt

flabby ['flæbɪ] adj (fat) wabbelig

flag [flæg] n Fahne f; **flagstone** n Steinplatte f

flake [fleɪk] n Flocke f ▷ vi: **to ~ (off)** abblättern

flamboyant [flæm'bɔɪənt] adj extravagant

flame [fleɪm] n Flamme f; (person) **an old ~** eine alte Liebe

flan [flæn] n (fruit ~) Obstkuchen m

flannel ['flænl] n Flanell m; (Brit: face ~) Waschlappen m; (fam: waffle) Geschwafel nt ▷ vi herumlabern

flap [flæp] n Klappe f; (fam) **to be in a ~** rotieren ▷ vt (wings) schlagen mit ▷ vi flattern

flared [flɛəd] adj (trousers) mit Schlag; **flares** npl Schlaghose f

flash [flæʃ] n Blitz m; (news ~) Kurzmeldung f; (Foto) Blitzlicht nt; **in a ~** im Nu ▷ vt: **to ~ one's (head)lights** die Lichthupe betätigen ▷ vi aufblinken; (brightly) aufblitzen; **flashback** n Rückblende f, Flashback m; **flashlight** ['flæʃlaɪt] n (Photo) Blitzlicht nt; (US: torch) Taschenlampe f; **flashy** adj grell, schrill; (pej) protzig

flat [flæt] adj flach; (surface) eben; (drink) abgestanden; (tyre) platt; (battery) leer; (refusal) glatt ▷ n (Brit: rooms) Wohnung f; (Auto) Reifenpanne f; **flat screen** n (Inform) Flachbildschirm m; **flatten** vt platt machen, einebnen

flatter ['flætə⁰] vt schmeicheln +dat; **flattering** adj schmeichelhaft

flatware ['flætwɛə⁰] n (US) Besteck nt

flavor (US), **flavour** ['fleɪvə⁰] n Geschmack m ▷ vt Geschmack geben +dat; (with spices) würzen; **flavouring** n Aroma nt

flaw [flɔː] n Fehler m; **flawless** adj fehlerlos; (complexion) makellos

flea [fliː] n Floh m

fled [fled] pt, pp of **flee**

flee [fliː] vi (fled, fled) vi fliehen

fleece [fliːs] n (of sheep) Vlies nt; (soft material) Fleece m; (jacket) Fleecejacke f

fleet [fliːt] n Flotte f

Flemish ['flemɪʃ] adj flämisch ▷ n (language) Flämisch nt

flesh [fleʃ] n Fleisch nt

flew [fluː] pt of **fly**

flex [fleks] n (Brit Elec) Schnur f

flexibility [fleksɪ'bɪlɪtɪ] n Biegsamkeit f; (fig) Flexibilität f; **flexible** ['fleksɪbl] adj biegsam;

(plans, person) flexibel; **flexitime** n gleitende Arbeitszeit, Gleitzeit f
flicker ['flɪkə'] vi flackern; *(TV)* flimmern
flies [flaɪz] pl of **fly** ▷ n
flight [flaɪt] n Flug m; *(escape)* Flucht f; **~ of stairs** Treppe f; **flight attendant** n Flugbegleiter(in) m(f); **flight recorder** n Flugschreiber m
flimsy ['flɪmzɪ] adj leicht gebaut, nicht stabil; *(thin)* hauchdünn; *(excuse)* fadenscheinig
fling [flɪŋ] **(flung, flung)** vt schleudern ▷ n: **to have a ~** eine (kurze) Affäre haben
flip [flɪp] vt schnippen; **to ~ a coin** eine Münze werfen; **flip through** vt *(book)* durchblättern; **flipchart** n Flipchart m
flipper ['flɪpə'] n Flosse f
flirt [flɜːt] vi flirten
float [fləʊt] n *(for fishing)* Schwimmer m; *(in procession)* Festwagen m; *(money)* Wechselgeld nt ▷ vi schwimmen; *(in air)* schweben
flock [flɒk] n *(of sheep)* *(Rel)* Herde f; *(of birds)* Schwarm m; *(of people)* Schar f
flog [flɒg] vt auspeitschen; *(Brit fam)* verscheuern
flood [flʌd] n Hochwasser nt, Überschwemmung f; *(fig)* Flut f ▷ vt überschwemmen; **floodlight** n Flutlicht nt; **floodlit** adj *(building)* angestrahlt
floor [flɔː'] n Fußboden m; *(storey)* Stock m; **ground ~** *(Brit)*, **first ~** *(US)* Erdgeschoss nt; **first ~** *(Brit)*, **second ~** *(US)* erster Stock; **floorboard** n Diele f
flop [flɒp] n *(fam: failure)* Reinfall m, Flop m ▷ vi losschwimmen, floppen
floppy disk ['flɒpɪ'dɪsk] n Diskette f
Florence ['flɒrəns] n Florenz f

florist ['flɒrɪst] n Blumenhändler(in) m(f); **florist's (shop)** ['flɒrɪsts] n Blumengeschäft m(f)
flounder ['flaʊndə'] n *(fish)* Flunder f
flour ['flaʊə'] n Mehl nt
flourish ['flʌrɪʃ] vi gedeihen; *(business)* gut laufen; *(boom)* florieren ▷ vt *(wave about)* schwenken; **flourishing** adj blühend
flow [fləʊ] n Fluss m; **to go with the ~** mit dem Strom schwimmen ▷ vi fließen
flower ['flaʊə'] n Blume f ▷ vi blühen; **flower bed** n Blumenbeet nt; **flowerpot** n Blumentopf m
flown [fləʊn] pp of **fly**
flu [fluː] n *(fam)* Grippe f
fluent ['fluːənt] adj *(Italian etc)* fließend; **to be ~ in German** fließend Deutsch sprechen
fluid ['fluːɪd] n Flüssigkeit f ▷ adj flüssig
flung [flʌŋ] pt, pp of **fling**
fluorescent [fluə'resnt] adj fluoreszierend, Leucht-
flush [flʌʃ] n *(lavatory)* Wasserspülung f; *(blush)* Röte f ▷ vi *(lavatory)* spülen
flute [fluːt] n Flöte f
fly [flaɪ] **(flew, flown)** vt, vi fliegen; **how time flies** wie die Zeit vergeht! ▷ n *(insect)* Fliege f; **~/flies** (pl) *(on trousers)* Hosenschlitz m; **fly-drive** n Urlaub m mit Flug und Mietwagen; **flyover** n *(Brit)* Straßenüberführung f, Eisenbahnüberführung f; **flysheet** n Überzelt nt
FM abbr = **frequency modulation** = UKW
FO abbr = **Foreign Office** ≈ AA nt
foal [fəʊl] n Fohlen nt

foam [fəʊm] n Schaum m ▷ vi schäumen

fob off [fɒb ɒf] vt: **to fob sb off with sth** jdm etw andrehen

focus ['fəʊkəs] n Brennpunkt m; **in/out of ~** (photo) scharf/unscharf ▷ vt (camera) scharf/unscharf eingestellt ▷ vt (camera) scharf stellen ▷ vi sich konzentrieren (on auf +akk)

foetus ['fiːtəs] n Fötus m

fog [fɒg] n Nebel m; **foggy** adj neblig; **fog light** n (Auto: at rear) Nebelschlussleuchte f

foil [fɔɪl] vt vereiteln ▷ n Folie f

fold [fəʊld] vt falten ▷ vi (fam: business) eingehen ▷ n Falte f; **fold up** vt (map etc) zusammenfalten; (chair etc) zusammenklappen ▷ vi (fam: business) eingehen; **folder** n (portfolio) Aktenmappe f; (pamphlet) Broschüre f; (Inform) Ordner m; **folding** adj zusammenklappbar; (bicycle, chair) Klapp-

folk [fəʊk] n Leute pl; (Mus) Folk m; **my ~s** pl (fam) meine Leute ▷ adj Volks-

follow ['fɒləʊ] vt folgen +dat; (pursue) verfolgen; (understand) folgen können +dat; (career, news etc) verfolgen; **as ~s** wie folgt ▷ vi folgen; (result) sich ergeben (from aus); **follow up** vt (request, rumour) nachgehen +dat, weiter verfolgen; **follower** n Anhänger(in) m(f); **following** adj folgend; **the ~ day** am (darauf)folgenden Tag ▷ prep nach; **follow up** n (event, book etc) Fortsetzung f

fond [fɒnd] adj: **to be ~ of** gernhaben; **fondly** adv (with love) liebevoll; **fondness** n Vorliebe f; (for people) Zuneigung f

fondue ['fɒnduː] n Fondue nt

font [fɒnt] n Taufbecken nt; (Typo) Schriftart f

food [fuːd] n Essen nt, Lebensmittel pl; (for animals) Futter nt; (groceries) Lebensmittel pl; **food poisoning** n Lebensmittelvergiftung f; **food processor** n Küchenmaschine f; **foodstuff** n Lebensmittel nt

fool [fuːl] n Idiot m, Narr m; **to make a ~ of oneself** sich blamieren ▷ vt (deceive) hereinlegen ▷ vi: **to ~ around** herumalbern; (waste time) herumtrödeln; **foolish** adj dumm; **foolproof** adj idiotensicher

foot [fʊt] n (pl **feet** [fiːt]) n Fuß m; (measure) Fuß m (30,48 cm); **on ~** zu Fuß ▷ vt (bill) bezahlen; **foot-and-mouth disease** n Maul- und Klauenseuche f; **football** n Fußball m; (US: American ~) Football m; **footballer** n Fußballspieler(in) m(f); **footbridge** n Fußgängerbrücke f; **footing** n (hold) Halt m; **footlights** npl Rampenlicht nt; **footnote** n Fußnote f; **footpath** n Fußweg m; **footprint** n Fußabdruck m; **footwear** n Schuhwerk nt

O KEYWORD

for [fɔː*] prep 1 für; **is this for me?** ist das für mich?; **the train for London** der Zug nach London; **he went for the paper** er ging die Zeitung holen; **give it to me — what for?** gib es mir — warum?
2 (because of) wegen; **for this reason** aus diesem Grunde
3 (referring to distance) **there are roadworks for 5 km** die Baustelle ist 5 km lang; **we walked for miles** wir sind meilenweit gegangen

4 (referring to time) seit; (with future sense) für; **he was away for 2 years** er war zwei Jahre lang weg **5** (+infin clauses) **it is not for me to decide** das kann ich nicht entscheiden; **for this to be possible ...** damit dies möglich wird/wurde ...
6 (in spite of) trotz +gen o (inf) dat; **for all his complaints** obwohl er sich ständig beschwert ▷ conj denn

forbade [fə'bæd] pt of **forbid**
forbid [fə'bɪd] (**forbade, forbidden**) vt verbieten
force [fɔːs] n Kraft f; (compulsion) Zwang m, Gewalt; **to come into ~** in Kraft treten; **the Forces** pl die Streitkräfte ▷ vt zwingen; **forced** adj (smile) gezwungen; **~ landing** Notlandung f; **forceful** adj kraftvoll
forceps ['fɔːseps] npl Zange f
forearm ['fɔːrɑːm] n Unterarm m
forecast ['fɔːkɑːst] vt voraussagen; (weather) vorhersagen ▷ n Vorhersage f
forefinger ['fɔːfɪŋɡə°] n Zeigefinger m
foreground ['fɔːɡraʊnd] n Vordergrund m
forehand ['fɔːhænd] n (Sport) Vorhand f
forehead ['fɔːhed, 'fɒrɪd] n Stirn f
foreign ['fɒrən] adj ausländisch; **foreigner** n Ausländer(in) m(f); **foreign exchange** n Devisen pl; **foreign language** n Fremdsprache f; **foreign minister** n Außenminister(in) m(f); **Foreign Office** n (Brit) Außenministerium nt; **Foreign Secretary** n (Brit) Außenminister(in) m(f); **foreign policy** n Außenpolitik f

foremost ['fɔːməʊst] adj erste(r, s); (leading) führend
forerunner ['fɔːrʌnə°] n Vorläufer(in) m(f)
foresee [fɔː'siː] irr vt vorhersehen; **foreseeable** adj absehbar
forest ['fɒrɪst] n Wald m; **forestry** ['fɒrɪstrɪ] n Forstwirtschaft f
forever [fə'revə°] adv für immer
forgave [fə'ɡeɪv] pt of **forgive**
forge [fɔːdʒ] n Schmiede f ▷ vt schmieden; (fake) fälschen; **forger** n Fälscher(in) m(f); **forgery** n Fälschung f
forget [fə'ɡet] (**forgot, forgotten**) vt, vi vergessen; **to ~ about sth** etw vergessen; **forgetful** adj vergesslich; **forgetfulness** n Vergesslichkeit f; **forget-me-not** n Vergissmeinnicht nt
forgive [fə'ɡɪv] (**forgave, forgiven**) irr vt verzeihen; **to ~ sb for sth** jdm etw verzeihen
forgot [fə'ɡɒt] pt of **forget**
forgotten [fə'ɡɒtn] pp of **forget**
fork [fɔːk] n Gabel f; (in road) Gabelung f ▷ vi (road) sich gabeln
form [fɔːm] n (shape) Form f; (class) Klasse f; (document) Formular nt; (person) **to be in (good) ~** in Form sein ▷ vt bilden
formal ['fɔːml] adj förmlich, formell; **formality** [fɔː'mælɪtɪ] n Formalität f
format ['fɔːmæt] n Format nt ▷ vt (Inform) formatieren
former ['fɔːmə°] adj frühere(r, s); (opposite of latter) erstere(r, s); **formerly** adv früher
formidable ['fɔːmɪdəbl] adj gewaltig; (opponent) stark
formula ['fɔːmjʊlə] n Formel f
formulate ['fɔːmjʊleɪt] vt formulieren

forth [fɔːθ] adv: **and so ~** und so weiter; **forthcoming** [fɔːθ'kʌmɪŋ] adj kommend, bevorstehend

fortify ['fɔːtɪfaɪ] vt verstärken; (for protection) befestigen

fortieth ['fɔːtɪɪθ] adj vierzigste(r, s); see also **eighth**

fortnight ['fɔːtnaɪt] n vierzehn Tage pl

fortress ['fɔːtrɪs] n Festung f

fortunate ['fɔːtʃənɪt] adj glücklich; **I was ~** ich hatte Glück; **fortunately** adv zum Glück; **fortune** ['fɔːtʃən] n (money) Vermögen nt; **good ~** Glück nt; **fortune-teller** n Wahrsager(in) m(f)

forty ['fɔːtɪ] num vierzig ▷ n Vierzig f; see also **eight**

forward ['fɔːwəd] adv vorwärts ▷ n (Sport) Stürmer(in) m(f) ▷ vt (send on) nachsenden; (Inform) weiterleiten; **forwards** adv vorwärts

foster child ['fɒstətʃaɪld] n Pflegekind nt; **foster parents** npl Pflegeeltern pl

fought [fɔːt] pt, pp of **fight**

foul [faʊl] adj (weather) schlecht; (smell) übel ▷ n (Sport) Foul nt

found [faʊnd] pt, pp of **find** ▷ vt (establish) gründen; **foundations** [faʊn'deɪʃənz] npl Fundament nt

fountain ['faʊntɪn] n Springbrunnen m; **fountain pen** n Füller m

four [fɔː°] num vier ▷ n Vier f; see also **eight**; **fourteen** ['fɔː'tiːn] num vierzehn ▷ n Vierzehn f; see also **eight**; **fourteenth** adj vierzehnte(r, s); see also **eighth**; **fourth** [fɔːθ] adj vierte(r, s); see also **eighth**

four-wheel drive n Allradantrieb m; (car) Geländewagen m

fowl [faʊl] n Geflügel nt

fox [fɒks] n (a. fig) Fuchs m

fraction ['frækʃən] n (Math) Bruch m; (part) Bruchteil m; **fracture** ['fræktʃə°] n (Med) Bruch m ▷ vt brechen

fragile ['frædʒaɪl] adj zerbrechlich

fragment ['frægmənt] n Bruchstück nt

fragrance ['freɪgrəns] n Duft m; **fragrant** adj duftend

frail [freɪl] adj gebrechlich

frame [freɪm] n Rahmen m; (of spectacles) Gestell nt; **~ of mind** Verfassung f ▷ vt einrahmen; **to ~ sb** (fam: incriminate) jdm etwas anhängen; **framework** n Rahmen m, Struktur f

France [frɑːns] n Frankreich nt

frank [fræŋk] adj offen

frankfurter ['fræŋkfɜːtə°] n (Frankfurter) Würstchen nt

frankly ['fræŋklɪ] adv offen gesagt; **quite ~** ganz ehrlich; **frankness** n Offenheit f

frantic ['fræntɪk] adj (activity) hektisch; (effort) verzweifelt; **~ with worry** außer sich vor Sorge

fraud [frɔːd] n (trickery) Betrug m; (person) Schwindler(in) m(f)

freak [friːk] n Anomalie f; (animal, person) Missgeburt f; (fam: fan) Fan m, Freak m ▷ adj (conditions) außergewöhnlich, seltsam; **freak out** vi (fam) ausflippen

freckle ['frekl] n Sommersprosse f

free [friː] adj, adv frei; (without payment) gratis, kostenlos; **for ~** umsonst ▷ vt befreien; **freebie** ['friːbɪ] n (fam) Werbegeschenk nt; **it was a ~** es war gratis; **freedom** ['friːdəm] n Freiheit f; **freefone** ['friːfəʊn] adj: **a ~ number** eine gebührenfreie

Nummer; **free kick** n (Sport)
Freistoß m

freelance ['fri:lɑ:ns] adj
freiberuflich tätig; (artist)
freischaffend ▷ n Freiberufler(in)
m(f)

free-range ['fri:reɪndʒ] adj (hen)
frei laufend; **~ eggs** pl Freilandeier
pl

freeway ['fri:weɪ] n (US)
(gebührenfreie) Autobahn

freeze [fri:z] (froze, frozen) vi
(feel cold) frieren; (of lake etc)
zufrieren; (water etc) gefrieren ▷ vt
einfrieren; **freezer** n
Tiefkühltruhe f; (in fridge)
Gefrierfach nt; **freezing** adj
eiskalt; **I'm ~** mir ist eiskalt;
freezing point n Gefrierpunkt m

freight [freɪt] n (goods) Fracht f;
(money charged) Frachtgebühr f;
freight car n (US) Güterwagen m;
freight train n (US) Güterzug m

French [frentʃ] adj französisch
▷ n (language) Französisch nt; **the
~** pl die Franzosen; **French bean** n
grüne Bohne; **French bread** n
Baguette f; **French dressing** n
Vinaigrette f; **French fries** (US)
npl Pommes frites pl; **French kiss**
n Zungenkuss m; **Frenchman** (pl
-men) n Franzose m; **French
toast** n (US) in Ei und Milch
getunktes gebratenes Brot; **French
window(s)** n(pl) Balkontür f,
Terrassentür f; **Frenchwoman** (pl
-women) n Französin f

frequency ['fri:kwənsɪ] n
Häufigkeit f; (Phys) Frequenz f;
frequent ['fri:kwənt] adj häufig;
frequently adv häufig

fresco ['freskəʊ] (pl -es) n Fresko
nt

fresh [freʃ] adj frisch; (new) neu;
freshen vi: **to ~ up** (person) sich
frisch machen; **fresher, freshman**
(pl -men) n Erstsemester nt;

freshwater fish n
Süßwasserfisch m

Fri abbr = **Friday** Fr

friction ['frɪkʃən] n (a. fig)
Reibung f

Friday ['fraɪdeɪ] n Freitag m; see
also **Tuesday**

fridge [frɪdʒ] n Kühlschrank m

fried [fraɪd] adj gebraten;
~ potatoes Bratkartoffeln pl;
~ egg Spiegelei nt; **~ rice**
gebratener Reis

friend [frend] n Freund(in) m(f);
(less close) Bekannte(r) m f; **to make
~s with sb** sich mit jdm
anfreunden; **we're good ~** wir
sind gut befreundet; **friendly** adj
freundlich; **to be ~ with sb** mit
jdm befreundet sein ▷ n (Sport)
Freundschaftsspiel nt; **friendship**
['frendʃɪp] n Freundschaft f

fright [fraɪt] n Schrecken m;
frighten vt erschrecken; **to be
~ed** Angst haben; **frightening** adj
beängstigend

frill [frɪl] n Rüsche f; **~s** (fam)
Schnickschnack

fringe [frɪndʒ] n (edge) Rand m;
(on shawl etc) Fransen pl; (hair)
Pony m

frivolous ['frɪvələs] adj leichtsinnig; (remark) frivol

frizzy ['frɪzɪ] adj kraus

frog [frɒg] n Frosch m

O   KEYWORD

from [frɒm] prep 1 (indicating
starting place) von; (indicating origin
etc) aus +dat; **a letter/telephone
call from my sister** ein
Brief/Anruf von meiner
Schwester; **where do you come
from?** woher kommen Sie?; **to
drink from the bottle** aus der
Flasche trinken

2 (indicating time) von ... an; (past) seit; **from one o'clock to o until o till two** von ein Uhr bis zwei; **from January (on)** ab Januar **3** (indicating distance) von ... (entfernt) **4** (indicating price, number etc) ab +dat; **from £10** ab £10; **there were from 20 to 30 people there** es waren zwischen 20 und 30 Leute da **5** (indicating difference) **he can't tell red from green** er kann nicht zwischen Rot und Grün unterscheiden; **to be different from sb/sth** anders sein als jd/etw **6** (because of, based on) **from what he says** aus dem, was er sagt; **weak from hunger** schwach vor Hunger

front [frʌnt] n Vorderseite f; (of house) Fassade f; (in war, of weather) Front f; (at seaside) Promenade f; **in ~, at the ~** vorne; **in ~ of** vor; **up ~** (in advance) vorher, im Voraus ▷ adj vordere(r, s), Vorder-; (first) vorderste(r, s) ▷ **~ door** Haustür f; **~ page** Titelseite f; **~ seat** Vordersitz m; **~ wheel** Vorderrad nt

frontier [frʌntɪə°] n Grenze f

front-wheel drive n (Auto) Frontantrieb m

frost [frɒst] n Frost m; (white ~) Reif m; **frosting** n (US) Zuckerguss m; **frosty** adj frostig

froth [frɒθ] n Schaum m; **frothy** adj schaumig

frown [fraʊn] vi die Stirn runzeln

froze [frəʊz] pt of **freeze**

frozen [frəʊzn] pp of **freeze** ▷ adj (food) tiefgekühlt, Tiefkühl-

fruit [fruːt] n (as collective, a. type) Obst nt; (single ~, a. fig) Frucht f;

fruit machine n Spielautomat m; **fruit salad** n Obstsalat m

frustrated [frʌˈstreɪtɪd] adj frustriert; **frustratration** n Frustration f, Frust m

fry [fraɪ] vt braten; **frying pan** n Bratpfanne f

fuchsia [ˈfjuːʃə] n Fuchsie f

fuck [fʌk] vt (vulg) ficken; **~ off** verpiss dich!; **fucking** adj (vulg) Scheiß-

fudge [fʌdʒ] n weiche Karamellsüßigkeit

fuel [fjʊəl] n Kraftstoff m; (for heating) Brennstoff m; **fuel consumption** n Kraftstoffverbrauch m; **fuel gauge** n Benzinuhr f; fuel oil n Gasöl nt; **fuel rod** n Brennstab m; **fuel tank** n Tank m; (for oil) Öltank m

fugitive [ˈfjuːdʒɪtɪv] n Flüchtling m

fulfil [fʊlˈfɪl] vt erfüllen

full [fʊl] adj voll; (person: satisfied) satt; (member, employment) Voll(zeit)-; (complete) vollständig; **~ of ...** voller ... gen; **full beam** n (Auto) Fernlicht nt; **full moon** n Vollmond m; **full stop** n Punkt m; **full-time** adj; **~ job** Ganztagsarbeit f; **fully** adv völlig; (recover) voll und ganz; (discuss) ausführlich

fumble [ˈfʌmbl] vi herumfummeln (with, at an +dat)

fumes [fjuːmz] npl Dämpfe pl; (of car) Abgase pl

fun [fʌn] n Spaß m; **for ~** zum Spaß; **it's ~** es macht Spaß; **to make ~ of** sich lustig machen über +akk

function [ˈfʌŋkʃən] n Funktion f; (event) Feier f; (reception) Empfang m ▷ vi funktionieren; **function key** n (Inform) Funktionstaste f

fund [fʌnd] n Fonds m; **~s** pl Geldmittel pl

fundamental [fʌndəˈmentl]
adj grundlegend; **fundamentally**
adv im Grunde

funding [ˈfʌndɪŋ] n finanzielle
Unterstützung

funeral [ˈfjuːnərəl] n Beerdigung f

funfair [ˈfʌnfɛəˀ] n Jahrmarkt m

fungus [ˈfʌŋgəs] (pl **fungi** o
funguses) n Pilz m

funicular [fjuːˈnɪkjʊləˀ] n Seilbahn f

funnel [ˈfʌnl] n Trichter m; (of
steamer) Schornstein m

funny [ˈfʌnɪ] adj (amusing)
komisch, lustig; (strange) seltsam

fur [fɜːˀ] n Pelz m; (of animal) Fell
nt

furious [ˈfjʊərɪəs] adj wütend
(with sb auf jdn)

furnished [ˈfɜːnɪʃd] adj möb-
liert; **furniture** [ˈfɜːnɪtʃəˀ] n
Möbel pl; **piece of ~** Möbelstück nt

further [ˈfɜːðəˀ] comparative of **far**
▷ adj weitere(r, s); **~ education**
Weiterbildung f; **until ~ notice** bis
auf weiteres ▷ adv weiter;
furthest [ˈfɜːðɪst] superlative of
far ▷ adj am weitesten entfernt
▷ adv am weitesten

fury [ˈfjʊərɪ] n Wut f

fuse [fjuːz] n (Elec) Sicherung f
▷ vi (Elec) durchbrennen; **fuse box**
n Sicherungskasten m

fuss [fʌs] n Theater nt; **to make a
~** (ein) Theater machen; **fussy** adj
(difficult) schwierig, kompliziert;
(attentive to detail) pingelig

future [ˈfjuːtʃəˀ] adj künftig ▷ n
Zukunft f

fuze (US) see **fuse**

fuzzy [ˈfʌzɪ] adj (indistinct)
verschwommen; (hair) kraus

g

gable [ˈgeɪbl] n Giebel m

gadget [ˈgædʒɪt] n Vorrichtung f,
Gerät nt

Gaelic [ˈgeɪlɪk] adj gälisch ▷ n
(language) Gälisch nt

gain [geɪn] vt (obtain, win)
gewinnen; (advantage, respect) sich
verschaffen; (wealth) erwerben;
(weight) zunehmen ▷ vi (improve)
gewinnen (in an +dat); (clock)
vorgehen ▷ n Gewinn m (in an
+dat)

gale [geɪl] n Sturm m

gall bladder [ˈgɔːlblædəˀ] n
Gallenblase f

gallery [ˈgælərɪ] n Galerie f,
Museum nt

gallon [ˈgælən] n Gallone f; ((Brit)
4,546 l, (US) 3,79 l)

gallop [ˈgæləp] n Galopp m ▷ vi
galoppieren

gallstone [ˈgɔːlstəʊn] n Gallenstein m

Gambia ['gæmbɪə] n Gambia nt

gamble ['gæmbl] vi um Geld spielen, wetten ▷ n: **it's a ~** es ist riskant; **gambling** n Glücksspiel nt

game [geɪm] n Spiel nt; (animals) Wild nt; **a ~ of chess** eine Partie Schach; **~s** (in school) Sport m; **game show** n (TV) Gameshow f

gammon ['gæmən] n geräucherter Schinken

gang [gæŋ] n (of criminals, youths) Bande f, Gang f, Clique f ▷ vt: **to ~ up on** sich verschwören gegen

gangster ['gæŋstə*] n Gangster m

gangway ['gæŋweɪ] n (for ship) Gangway f; (Brit: aisle) Gang m, Gangway f

gap [gæp] n (hole) Lücke f; (in time) Pause f; (in age) Unterschied m

gape [geɪp] vi (mit offenem Mund) starren

gap year n Jahr zwischen Schulabschluss und Studium, das oft zu Auslandsaufenthalten genutzt wird

garage ['gærɑːʒ] n Garage f; (for repair) (Auto)werkstatt f; (for fuel) Tankstelle f

garbage ['gɑːbɪdʒ] n (US) Müll m; (fam: nonsense) Quatsch m; **garbage can** n (US) Mülleimer m; (outside) Mülltonne f; **garbage truck** n (US) Müllwagen m

garden ['gɑːdn] n Garten m; (public) **~s** pl Park m; **garden centre** n Gartencenter nt; **gardener** n Gärtner(in) m(f); **gardening** n Gartenarbeit f

gargle ['gɑːgl] vi gurgeln

gargoyle ['gɑːgɔɪl] n Wasserspeier m

garlic ['gɑːlɪk] n Knoblauch m; **garlic bread** n Knoblauchbrot nt; **garlic butter** n Knoblauchbutter f

gas [gæs] n Gas nt; (US: petrol)

Benzin nt; **to step on the ~** Gas geben; **gas cooker** n (US) Gasherd m; **gas cylinder** n Gasflasche f; **gas fire** n Gasofen m

gasket ['gæskɪt] n Dichtung f

gas lighter n (for cigarettes) Gasfeuerzeug nt; **gas mask** n Gasmaske f; **gas meter** n Gaszähler m

gasoline ['gæsəliːn] n (US) Benzin nt

gasp [gɑːsp] vi keuchen; (in surprise) nach Luft schnappen

gas pedal n (US) Gaspedal nt; **gas pump** n (US) Zapfsäule f; **gas station** n (US) Tankstelle f; **gas tank** n (US) Benzintank m

gastric ['gæstrɪk] adj Magen-; **~ flu** Magen-Darm-Grippe f; **~ ulcer** Magengeschwür nt

gasworks ['gæswɜːks] n Gaswerk nt

gate [geɪt] n Tor nt; (barrier) Schranke f; (Aviat) Gate nt, Flugsteig m

gateau ['gætəʊ] n (pl **gateaux**) n Torte f

gateway n Tor nt

gather ['gæðə*] vt (collect) sammeln; **to ~ speed** beschleunigen ▷ vi (assemble) sich versammeln; (understand) schließen (from aus); **gathering** n Versammlung f

gauge [geɪdʒ] n Meßgerät nt

gauze [gɔːz] n Gaze f; (for bandages) Mull m

gave [geɪv] pt of **give**

gay [geɪ] adj (homosexual) schwul; **~ marriage** (fam) Homoehe f

gaze [geɪz] n Blick m ▷ vi starren

GCSE abbr = **general certificate of secondary education** (school) Abschlussprüfung f der Sekundarstufe, = mittlere Reife

gear [gɪə*] n (Auto) Gang m; (equipment) Ausrüstung f; (clothes)

geese | 362

Klamotten *pl*; **to change ~** schalten; **gearbox** *n* Getriebe *nt*; **gear change**, **gear shift** (US) *n* Gangschaltung *f*; **gear lever**, **gear stick** (US) *n* Schalthebel *m*

geese [giːs] *pl of* **goose**

gel [dʒel] *n* Gel *nt* ▷ *vi* gelieren; **they really ~led** sie verstanden sich auf Anhieb

gem [dʒem] *n* Edelstein *m*; (*fig*) Juwel *nt*

Gemini ['dʒemɪniː] *nsing* (*Astr*) Zwillinge *pl*

gender ['dʒendə°] *n* Geschlecht *nt*

gene [dʒiːn] *n* Gen *nt*

general ['dʒenərəl] *adj* allgemein; **~ knowledge** Allgemeinbildung *f*; **~ election** Parlamentswahlen *pl*; **generalize** ['dʒenrəlaɪz] *vi* verallgemeinern; **generally** ['dʒenrəlɪ] *adv* im Allgemeinen

generation [dʒenə'reɪʃən] *n* Generation *f*; **generation gap** *n* Generationsunterschied *m*

generator ['dʒenəreɪtə°] *n* Generator *m*

generosity [dʒenə'rɒsɪtɪ] *n* Großzügigkeit *f*; **generous** ['dʒenərəs] *adj* großzügig; (*portion*) reichlich

genetic [dʒɪ'netɪk] *adj* genetisch; **~ research** Genforschung *f*; **~ technology** Gentechnik *f*; **genetically modified** *adj* gentechnisch verändert, genmanipuliert; *see also* **GM**

Geneva [dʒɪ'niːvə] *n* Genf *nt*; **Lake ~** der Genfer See

genitals ['dʒenɪtlz] *npl* Geschlechtsteile *pl*

genitive ['dʒenɪtɪv] *n* Genitiv *m*

genius ['dʒiːnɪəs] *n* Genie *nt*

gentle ['dʒentl] *adj* sanft; (*touch*) zart; **gentleman** (*pl* **-men**) *n*

Herr *m*; (*polite man*) Gentleman *m*

gents [dʒents] *n*: "**~**" (*lavatory*) „Herren", **the ~** *pl* die Herrentoilette

genuine ['dʒenjuɪn] *adj* echt

geographical [dʒɪə'græfɪkəl] *adj* geografisch; **geography** [dʒɪ'ɒgrəfɪ] *n* Geografie *f*; (*at school*) Erdkunde *f*

geological [dʒɪə'lɒdʒɪkəl] *adj* geologisch; **geology** [dʒɪ'ɒlədʒɪ] *n* Geologie *f*

geometry [dʒɪ'ɒmɪtrɪ] *n* Geometrie *f*

geranium [dʒɪ'reɪnɪəm] *n* Geranie *f*

gerbil ['dʒɜːbəl] *n* (*Zool*) Wüstenrennmaus *f*

germ [dʒɜːm] *n* Keim *m*; (*Med*) Bazillus *m*

German ['dʒɜːmən] *adj* deutsch; **she's ~** sie ist Deutsche; **~ shepherd** Deutscher Schäferhund ▷ *n* (*person*) Deutsche(r) *mf*; (*language*) Deutsch *nt*; **in ~** auf Deutsch; **German measles** *nsing* Röteln *pl*; **Germany** ['dʒɜːmənɪ] *n* Deutschland *nt*

gesture ['dʒestʃə°] *n* Geste *f*

🔵 **KEYWORD**

get [get] (*pt*, *pp* **got**, *pp* **gotten** (US)) *vi* **1** (*become*, *be*) werden; **to get old/tired** alt/müde werden; **to get married** heiraten

2 (*go*) (an)kommen, gehen

3 (*begin*) **to get to know sb** jdn kennenlernen; **let's get going** *o* **started!** fangen wir an!

4 (*modal vb aux*) **you've got to do it** du musst/Sie müssen es tun

▷ *vt* **1 to get sth done** (*do*) etw machen; (*have done*) etw machen lassen; **to get sth going** *o* **to go** etw in Gang bringen *o* bekommen

to get sb to do sth jdn dazu bringen, etw zu tun

2 (*obtain: money, permission, results*) erhalten; (*find: job, flat*) finden; (*fetch: person, object*) holen; **to get sth for sb** jdm etw besorgen; **get me Mr Jones, please** (*Tel*) verbinde/verbinden Sie mich bitte mit Mr Jones; **get a life!** (*annoyed*) mach dich mal locker!, reg dich bloß ab!

3 (*receive: present, letter*) bekommen, kriegen; (*acquire: reputation etc*) erwerben

4 (*catch*) bekommen, kriegen; (*hit: target etc*) treffen, erwischen; **get him!** (*to dog*) fass!

5 (*take, move*) bringen; **to get sth to sb** jdm etw bringen

6 (*understand*) verstehen; (*hear*) mitbekommen; **I've got it!** ich hab's!

7 (*have, possess*) **to have got sth** etw haben

get about *vi* herumkommen, (*news*) sich verbreiten

get across *vi* **to s.th** über etw *akk* kommen; *vt:* **to get sth across** (*communicate*) etw klarmachen

get along *vi* (*people*) (gut) zurecht-/auskommen (*with*) mit; (*depart*) sich *akk* auf den Weg machen

get at *vt* (*reach*) herankommen an +*akk*; (*facts*) herausbekommen; **what are you getting at?** worauf wollen Sie hinaus?, was meinst du damit?; **to get at sb** (*nag*) an jdm herumnörgeln

get away *vi* (*leave*) sich *akk* davonmachen, weggkommen; (*escape*) **to get away from sth** von etw *dat* entkommen; **to get away with sth** mit etw davonkommen

get back *vi* (*return*) zurückkommen; (*Tel*) **to get back**

to s.o. jdn zurückrufen
▷ *vt* zurückbekommen

get by *vi* (*pass*) vorbeikommen; (*manage*) zurecht-/auskommen (*on*) mit

get down *vi* (*her*)untergehen; **to get down to** in Angriff nehmen, (*find time to do*) kommen zu; ▷ *vt* (*depress*) fertigmachen; **it gets me down** (*fam*) es macht mich fertig; **to get sth down** (*write*) etw aufschreiben

get in *vi* (*train*) ankommen; (*arrive home*) heimkommen

get into *vt* (*enter*) hinein-/hereinkommen in +*akk*; (*car, train etc*) einsteigen in +*akk*; (*clothes*) anziehen; (*rage, panic etc*) geraten in +*akk*; **to get into trouble** in Schwierigkeiten kommen

get off *vi* (*from train etc*) aussteigen; (*from horse*) absteigen; (*fam: be enthusiastic*) **to get off on sth** auf etw abfahren; ▷ *vt* (*nail, sticker*) los-/abbekommen; (*clothes*) ausziehen

get on *vi* (*progress*) vorankommen; (*be friends*) auskommen; (*age*) alt werden; (*onto train etc*) einsteigen; (*onto horse etc*) aufsteigen
▷ *vt* etw *akk* vorantreiben, mit etw *akk* loslegen

get out *vi* (*of house*) herauskommen; (*of vehicle*) aussteigen; **get out!** raus!
▷ *vt* (*take out*) herausholen; (*stain, nail*) herausbekommen

get out of *vi* (*duty etc*) herumkommen

get over *vi* (*illness*) sich *akk* erholen von; (*surprise*) verkraften; (*news*) fassen; (*loss*) sich abfinden mit

get round *vi* herumkommen um; *vt* (*fig*) (*person*) herumkriegen

get through vi (Tel) durchkommen; (to) zu

get together vi zusammenkommen

get up vi aufstehen
▷ vt hinaufbringen; (go up) hinaufgehen; (organize) auf die Beine stellen

get up to vi (reach) erreichen; (prank etc) anstellen

getaway n Flucht f;

get-together n Treffen nt

Ghana ['gɑːnə] n Ghana nt

gherkin ['gɜːkɪn] n Gewürzgurke f

ghetto ['gɛtəʊ] n (pl -es) n Ghetto nt

ghost [gəʊst] n Gespenst nt; (of sb) Geist m

giant ['dʒaɪənt] n Riese m ▷ adj riesig

giblets ['dʒɪblɪts] npl Geflügelinnereien pl

Gibraltar [dʒɪ'brɔːltə] n Gibraltar nt

giddy ['gɪdɪ] adj schwindlig

gift [gɪft] n Geschenk nt; (talent) Begabung f; **gifted** adj begabt; **giftwrap** vt als Geschenk verpacken

gigantic [dʒaɪ'gæntɪk] adj riesig

giggle ['gɪgl] vi kichern ▷ n Gekicher nt

gill [gɪl] n (of fish) Kieme f

gimmick ['gɪmɪk] n (for sales, publicity) Gag m

gin [dʒɪn] n Gin m

ginger ['dʒɪndʒə] n Ingwer m ▷ adj (colour) kupferrot; (cat) rötlichgelb; **ginger ale** n Gingerale m; **ginger beer** n Ingwerlimonade f; **gingerbread** n Lebkuchen m (mit Ingwergeschmack); **ginger(-haired)** adj rotblond; **gingerly** adv (move) vorsichtig

gipsy ['dʒɪpsɪ] n Zigeuner(in) m(f)

giraffe [dʒɪ'rɑːf] n Giraffe f

girl [gɜːl] n Mädchen nt; **girlfriend** n (feste) Freundin f; **girl guide** n (Brit), **girl scout** (US) Pfadfinderin f

gist [dʒɪst] n: **to get the ~ (of it)** das Wesentliche verstehen

give [gɪv] (gave, given) vt geben; (as present) schenken (to sb jdm); (state: name etc) angeben; (speech) halten; (blood) spenden; **to ~ sb sth** jdm etw geben/schenken ▷ vi (yield) nachgeben; **give away** vt (give free) verschenken; (secret) verraten; **give back** vt zurückgeben; **give in** vi aufgeben; **give up** vt, vi aufgeben; **give way** vi (collapse, yield) nachgeben; (traffic) die Vorfahrt beachten

given ['gɪvn] pp of **give** ▷ adj (fixed) festgesetzt; (certain) bestimmt; **~ name** (US) Vorname m ▷ conj: **~ that ...** angesichts der Tatsache, dass ...

glacier ['glæsɪə] n Gletscher m

glad [glæd] adj froh (about über); **I was ~ (to hear) that ...** es hat mich gefreut, dass ...; **gladly** ['glædlɪ] adv gerne

glance [glɑːns] n Blick m ▷ vi einen Blick werfen (at auf +akk)

gland [glænd] n Drüse f; **glandular fever** n Drüsenfieber nt

glare [glɛə] n grelles Licht; (stare) stechender Blick ▷ vi (angrily) **to ~ at sb** jdn böse anstarren; **glaring** adj (mistake) krass

glass [glɑːs] n Glas nt; **~es** pl Brille f

glen [glɛn] n (Scot) (enges) Bergtal nt

glide [glaid] vi gleiten; (hover) schweben; **glider** n Segelflugzeug nt; **gliding** n Segelfliegen nt

glimmer ['glɪmə°] n (of hope) Schimmer m

glimpse [glɪmps] n flüchtiger Blick

glitter ['glɪtə°] vi glitzern; (eyes) funkeln

glitzy [glɪtsɪ] adj (fam) glanzvoll, Schickimicki-

global ['gləʊbəl] adj global, Welt-; **~ warming** die Erwärmung der Erdatmosphäre; **globe** [gləʊb] sp2; n (sphere) Kugel f; (world) Erdball m; (map) Globus m

gloomily ['gluːmɪlɪ], **gloomy** adv, adj düster

glorious ['glɔːrɪəs] adj (victory, past) ruhmreich; (weather, day) herrlich; **glory** ['glɔːrɪ] n Herrlichkeit f

gloss [glɒs] n (shine) Glanz m

glossary ['glɒsərɪ] n Glossar nt

glossy ['glɒsɪ] adj (surface) glänzend ▷ n (magazine) Hochglanzmagazin nt

glove [glʌv] n Handschuh m; **glove compartment** n Handschuhfach nt

glow [gləʊ] vi glühen

glucose ['gluːkəʊs] n Traubenzucker m

glue [gluː] n Klebstoff m ▷ vt kleben

glutton ['glʌtn] n Vielfraß m; **~ for punishment** (fam) Masochist m

GM abbr = **genetically modified** Gen-; **~ foods** gentechnisch veränderte Lebensmittel

GMT abbr = **Greenwich Mean Time** WEZ f

go [gəʊ] (went, gone) vi gehen; (in vehicle, travel) fahren; (plane) fliegen; (road) führen (to nach); (depart: train, bus) (ab)fahren;

(person) (fort)gehen; (disappear) verschwinden; (time) vergehen; (function) gehen, funktionieren; (machine, engine) laufen; (fit, suit) passen (with zu); (fail) nachlassen; **I have to ~** ich muss zum Arzt/nach London ich muss zum Arzt/nach London; **to ~ shopping** einkaufen gehen; **to ~ for a walk/swim** spazieren/schwimmen gehen; **has he gone yet?** ist er schon weg?; **the wine ~es in the cupboard** der Wein kommt in den Schrank; **to get sth ~ing** etw in Gang setzen; **to keep ~ing** weitermachen; (machine etc) weiterlaufen; **how's the job ~ing?** was macht der Job?; **his memory/eyesight is going** sein Gedächtnis lässt nach/seine Augen werden schwach; **to ~ deaf/mad/grey** taub/verrückt/grau werden ▷ vb aux: **to be ~ing to do sth** etw tun werden; **I was ~ing to do it** ich wollte es tun ▷ n (pl **-es**) (attempt) Versuch m; **can I have another ~?** darf ich noch mal (probieren)?; **it's my ~** ich bin dran; **in one ~** auf einen Schlag; (drink) in einem Zug; **go after** vt insep nachfahren +dat; (vehicle) nachfahren +dat; **go ahead** vi (in front) vorausgehen; (start) anfangen; **go away** vi weggehen; (on holiday, business) verreisen; **go back** vi (return) zurückgehen; **we ~ a long way** wir kennen uns schon ewig; **go by** vi vorbeigehen; (vehicle) vorbeifahren; (years, time) vergehen ▷ vt (judge by) gehen nach; **go down** vi (sun, ship) untergehen; (flood, temperature) zurückgehen; (price) sinken; **to ~ well/badly** gut/schlecht ankommen; **go in** vi hineingehen; **go into** vt (enter) hineingehen in +akk; (crash) fahren gegen, hineinfahren in +akk; **to ~ teaching/politics/the army** Lehrer werden/in die Politik gehen/zum Militär gehen; **go off** vi (depart) weggehen; (in vehicle) wegfahren; (lights) ausgehen; (milk etc) sauer werden; (gun, bomb, alarm) losgehen ▷ vt (dislike) nicht mehr mögen; **go on** vi (continue) weitergehen; (lights) angehen; **to ~ with** o doing sth etw weitermachen; **go out** vi (leave house) hinausgehen; (fire, light, person socially) ausgehen; **to ~ for a meal** essen gehen; **go up** vi (temperature, price) steigen; (lift) hochfahren; **go without** vt verzichten auf +akk; (food, sleep) auskommen ohne

go-ahead ['gəʊəhed] adj (progressive) fortschrittlich ▷ n grünes Licht

goal [gəʊl] n (aim) Ziel nt; (Sport) Tor nt; **goalie, goalkeeper** n Torwart m, Torfrau f; **goalpost** n Torpfosten m

goat [gəʊt] n Ziege f

gob [gɒb] n (Brit fam) Maul nt; **shut your ~** halt's Maul! ▷ vi spucken; **gobsmacked** (fam: surprised) platt

god [gɒd] n Gott m; **thank God** Gott sei Dank; **godchild** (pl -children) n Patenkind nt; **goddaughter** n Patentochter f; **goddess** ['gɒdes] n Göttin f; **godfather** n Pate m; **godmother** n Patin f; **godson** n Patensohn m

goggles npl Schutzbrille f; (for skiing) Skibrille f; (for diving) Taucherbrille f

going ['gəʊɪŋ] adj (rate) üblich; **goings-on** npl Vorgänge pl

go-kart ['gəʊkɑːt] n Gokart m

gold [gəʊld] n Gold nt; **golden** adj golden; **goldfish** n Goldfisch m; **gold-plated** adj vergoldet

golf [gɒlf] n Golf nt; **golf ball** n Golfball m; **golf club** n Golfschläger m; (association) Golfklub m; **golf course** n Golfplatz m; **golfer** n Golfspieler(in) m(f)

gone [gɒn] pp of **go**; **he's ~** er ist weg ▷ prep: **just ~ three** kurz nach drei

good [gʊd] n (benefit) Wohl nt; (morally good things) Gute(s) nt; **for the ~ of** zum Wohle +gen; **it's for your own ~** es ist zu deinem/Ihrem Besten o Vorteil; **it's no ~** (doing sth) es hat keinen Sinn o Zweck; (thing) es taugt nichts; **for ~** für immer ▷ adj (better, best) gut; (suitable) passend; (thorough) gründlich; (well-behaved) brav; (kind) nett, lieb; **to be ~ at sport/maths** gut in Sport/Mathe sein; **to be no ~ at sport/maths** schlecht in Sport/Mathe sein; **it's ~ for you** es tut dir gut; **this is ~ for colds** das ist gut gegen Erkältungen; **too ~ to be true** zu schön, um wahr zu sein; **this is just not ~ enough** so geht das nicht; **a ~ three hours** gute drei Stunden; **~ morning/evening** guten Morgen/Abend; **~ night** gute Nacht; **to have a ~ time** sich gut amüsieren

goodbye [gʊd'baɪ] interj auf Wiedersehen

Good Friday n Karfreitag m

good-looking adj gut aussehend

goods [gʊdz] npl Waren pl, Güter pl; **goods train** n (Brit) Güterzug m

goodwill [gʊd'wɪl] n Wohlwollen nt

goose [guːs] n (pl **geese**) n Gans f

▷ vt (fam) **to ~ s.o.** jdn in den
Arsch kneifen; **gooseberry**
['guzbərɪ] n Stachelbeere f; **goose
bumps** n, **goose pimples** npl
Gänsehaut f

gorge [gɔːdʒ] n Schlucht f

gorgeous ['gɔːdʒəs] adj
wunderschön; **he's ~** er sieht toll
aus

gorilla [gə'rɪlə] n Gorilla m

gossip ['gosɪp] n (talk) Klatsch m;
(person) Klatschtante f ▷ vi
klatschen, tratschen

got [gɒt] pt, pp of **get**

gotten ['gɒtn] (US) pp of **get**

govern ['gʌvən] vt regieren;
(province etc) verwalten;
government n Regierung f;
governor n Gouverneur(in) m(f);
govt abbr = **government**
Regierung f

gown [gaʊn] n Abendkleid nt;
(academic) Robe f

GP abbr = **General Practitioner**
Allgemeinarzt, Allgemeinärztin

GPS n abbr = **global positioning
system** GPS nt

grab [græb] vt packen; (person)
schnappen

grace [greɪs] n Anmut f; (prayer)
Tischgebet nt; **5 days' ~** 5 Tage
Aufschub; **graceful** adj anmutig

grade [greɪd] n Niveau nt; (of
goods) Güteklasse f; (mark) Note f;
(US: year) Klasse f; **to make the
~** es schaffen; **grade crossing** n
(US) Bahnübergang m; **grade
school** n (US) Grundschule f

gradient ['greɪdɪənt] n (upward)
Steigung f; (downward) Gefälle nt

gradual, gradually ['grædjʊəl,
-lɪ] adj, adv allmählich

graduate ['grædjʊt] n Uniab-
solvent(in) m(f),
Hochschulabsolvent(in) m(f)
▷ ['grædjʊeɪt] vi einen
akademischen Grad erwerben

grain [greɪn] n (cereals) Getreide
nt; (of corn, sand) Korn nt; (in wood)
Maserung f

gram [græm] n Gramm nt

grammar ['græmə] n Grammatik f; **grammar school** n (Brit)
≈ Gymnasium nt

gran [græn] n (fam) Oma f

grand [grænd] adj (pej)
hochnäsig; (posh) vornehm ▷ n
(fam) 1000 Pfund bzw. 1000 Dollar

grand(d)ad n (fam) Opa m;
granddaughter n Enkelin f;
grandfather n Großvater m;
grandma n (fam) Oma f;
grandmother n Großmutter f;
grandpa n (fam) Opa m;
grandparents npl Großeltern pl;
grandson n Enkel m

grandstand n (Sport) Tribüne f

granny ['grænɪ] n (fam) Oma f

grant [grɑːnt] vt gewähren (sb
sth jdm etw); **to take sb/sth for
~ed** jdn/etw als selbstverständlich
hinnehmen ▷ n Subvention f,
finanzielle Unterstützung f; (for
university) Stipendium nt

grape [greɪp] n Weintraube f;
grapefruit n Grapefruit f; **grape
juice** n Traubensaft m

graph [grɑːf] n Diagramm nt;
graphic ['græfɪk] adj grafisch;
(description) anschaulich

grasp [grɑːsp] vt ergreifen;
(understand) begreifen

grass [grɑːs] n Gras nt; (lawn)
Rasen m; **grasshopper** n
Heuschrecke f

grate [greɪt] n Feuerrost m ▷ vi
kratzen ▷ vt (cheese) reiben

grateful, gratefully ['greɪtfʊl,
-fəlɪ] adj, adv dankbar

grater ['greɪtə*] n Reibe f

gratifying ['grætɪfaɪɪŋ] adj
erfreulich

gratitude ['grætɪtjuːd] n Dank-
barkeit f

grave [greɪv] n Grab nt ▷ adj
ernst; (mistake) schwer
gravel ['grævəl] n Kies m
graveyard ['greɪvjɑːd] n Friedhof m
gravity ['grævɪtɪ] n Schwerkraft
f; (seriousness) Ernst m
gravy ['greɪvɪ] n Bratensoße
f

gray [greɪ] adj (US) grau
graze [greɪz] vi (of animals)
grasen ▷ vt (touch) streifen; (Med)
abschürfen ▷ n (Med)
Abschürfung f
grease [griːs] n (fat) Fett nt;
(lubricant) Schmiere f ▷ vt
einfetten; (Tech) schmieren;
greasy [griːsɪ] adj fettig; (hands,
tools) schmierig; (fam: person)
schleimig
great [greɪt] adj groß; (fam: good)
großartig, super; **a ~ deal of** viel;
Great Britain ['greɪt'brɪtn] n
Großbritannien nt;
great-grandfather n Urgroßvater m; **great-grandmother** n
Urgroßmutter f; **greatly** adv sehr;
~ disappointed zutiefst
enttäuscht
Greece [griːs] n Griechenland nt
greed [griːd] n Gier f (for nach);
(for food) Gefräßigkeit f; **greedy**
adj gierig; (for food) gefräßig
Greek [griːk] adj griechisch ▷ n
(person) Grieche m, Griechin f;
(language) Griechisch nt; **it's all
~ to me** ich verstehe nur
Bahnhof
green [griːn] adj grün; **~ with
envy** grün/gelb vor Neid ▷ n
(colour; for golf) Grün nt; (village ~)
Dorfwiese f; **~s** (vegetables) grünes
Gemüse; **the Greens, the Green
Party** (Pol) die Grünen; **green card**
n (US: work permit)
Arbeitserlaubnis f; (Brit: for car)
grüne Versicherungskarte f;

greengage n Reneklode f;
greengrocer n Obst- und
Gemüsehändler(in) m(f);
greenhouse n Gewächshaus nt;
~ effect Treibhauseffekt m;
Greenland n Grönland nt; **green
pepper** n grüner Paprika; **green
salad** n grüner Salat
Greenwich Mean Time
['grenɪdʒ'miːntaɪm] n west-
europäische Zeit
greet [griːt] vt grüßen; **greeting**
n Gruß m
grew [gruː] pt of **grow**
grey [greɪ] adj grau; **grey-haired**
adj grauhaarig; **greyhound** n
Windhund m
grid [grɪd] n Gitter nt; **gridlock** n
Verkehrsinfarkt m; **gridlocked** adj
(roads) völlig verstopft; (talks)
festgefahren
grief [griːf] n Kummer m; (over
loss) Trauer f
grievance ['griːvəns] n
Beschwerde f
grieve [griːv] vi trauern (for um)
grill [grɪl] n (on cooker) Grill m ▷ vt
grillen
grim [grɪm] adj (face, humour)
grimmig; (situation, prospects)
trostlos
grin [grɪn] n Grinsen nt ▷ vi
grinsen
grind [graɪnd] (**ground, ground**)
vt mahlen; (sharpen) schleifen; (US:
meat) durchdrehen, hacken
grip [grɪp] n Griff m; **get a
~** nimm dich zusammen!; **to get
to ~s with sth** etw in den Griff
bekommen ▷ vt packen; **gripping**
adj (exciting) spannend
groan [grəʊn] vi stöhnen (with
vor +dat)
grocer ['grəʊsə°] n Lebensmit-
telhändler(in) m(f); **groceries** npl
Lebensmittel pl
groin [grɔɪn] n (Anat) Leiste f;

groin strain n (Med) Leistenbruch m
groom [gru:m] n Bräutigam m
▷ vt: **well ~ed** gepflegt
grope [grəʊp] vi tasten ▷ vt
(sexually harrass) befummeln
gross [grəʊs] adj (coarse) derb;
(extreme: negligence, error) grob;
(disgusting) ekelhaft; (Comm)
brutto; **~ national product**
Bruttosozialprodukt nt; **~ salary**
Bruttogehalt nt
grotty ['grɒtɪ] adj (fam) mies,
vergammelt
ground [graʊnd] pt, pp of **grind**
▷ n Boden m, Erde f; (Sport) Platz
m; **~s** pl (around house)
(Garten)anlagen pl; (reasons)
Gründe pl; (of coffee) Satz m; **on
(the) ~s of** aufgrund von; **ground
floor** n (Brit) Erdgeschoss nt;
ground meat n (US) Hackfleisch
nt
group [gru:p] n Gruppe f ▷ vt
gruppieren
grouse [graʊs] (pl -) n (bird)
Schottisches Moorhuhn;
(complaint) Nörgelei f
grow [grəʊ] (grew, grown) vi
wachsen; (increase) zunehmen (in
an); (become) werden; **to ~ old** alt
werden; **to ~ into ...** sich
entwickeln zu ... ▷ vt (crop, plant)
ziehen; (commercially) anbauen;
I'm ~ing a beard ich lasse mir
einen Bart wachsen; **grow up** vi
aufwachsen; (mature) erwachsen
werden; **growing** adj wachsend;
a ~ number of people immer
mehr Leute
growl [graʊl] vi knurren
grown [grəʊn] pp of **grow**
grown-up [grəʊnʌp] adj
erwachsen ▷ n Erwachsene(r) mf;
growth [grəʊθ] n Wachstum nt;
(increase) Zunahme f; (Med)
Wucherung f

grubby ['grʌbɪ] adj schmuddelig
grudge [grʌdʒ] n Abneigung f
(against gegen) ▷ vt: **to ~ sb sth**
jdm etw nicht gönnen
gruelling ['grʊəlɪŋ] adj
aufreibend; (pace) mörderisch
gruesome ['gru:səm] adj
grausig
grumble ['grʌmbl] vi murren
(about über +akk)
grumpy ['grʌmpɪ] adj (fam)
mürrisch, grantig
grunt [grʌnt] vi grunzen
G-string ['dʒi:strɪŋ] n String m,
Stringtanga m
guarantee [gærən'ti:] n Garantie f (of für); **it's still under ~** es ist
noch Garantie darauf ▷ vt
garantieren
guard [ga:d] n (sentry) Wache f;
(in prison) Wärter(in) m(f); (Brit
Rail) Schaffner(in) m(f) ▷ vt
bewachen; **a closely ~ed
secret** ein streng gehütetes
Geheimnis
guardian ['ga:dɪən] n Vormund
m; **~ angel** Schutzengel m
guess [ges] n Vermutung f;
(estimate) Schätzung f; **have a
~ rate mal!** ▷ vt, vi raten;
(estimate) schätzen; **I ~ you're
right** du hast wohl recht; **I ~ so** ich
glaube schon
guest [gest] n Gast m; **be my
~** nur zu!; **guest-house** n Pension
f; **guest room** n Gästezimmer
nt
guidance ['gaɪdəns] n (direction)
Leitung f; (advice) Rat m;
(counselling) Beratung f; **for your
~** zu Ihrer Orientierung; **guide**
[gaɪd] n (person) Führer(in) m(f);
(tour) Reiseleiter(in) m(f); (book)
Führer m; (girl ~) Pfadfinderin f
▷ vt führen; **guidebook** n
Reiseführer m; **guide dog** n
Blindenhund m; **guided tour** n

Führung f (of durch); **guidelines**
npl Richtlinien pl
guilt [gɪlt] n Schuld f; **guilty** adj
schuldig (of gen); (look)
schuldbewusst; **to have a
~ conscience** ein schlechtes
Gewissen haben
guinea pig ['gɪnɪ pɪg] n
Meerschweinchen nt; (person)
Versuchskaninchen nt
guitar [gɪ'tɑː°] n Gitarre f
gulf [gʌlf] n Golf m; (gap) Kluft f;
Gulf States npl Golfstaaten pl
gull [gʌl] n Möwe f
gullible ['gʌlɪbl] adj
leichtgläubig
gulp [gʌlp] n (kräftiger) Schluck
▷ vi schlucken
gum [gʌm] n (around teeth, usu pl)
Zahnfleisch nt; (chewing ~)
Kaugummi m
gun [gʌn] n Schusswaffe f; (rifle)
Gewehr nt; (pistol) Pistole f;
gunfire n Schüsse pl,
Geschützfeuer nt; **gunpowder** n
Schießpulver nt; **gunshot** n
Schuss m
gush [gʌʃ] vi (heraus)strömen
(from aus)
gut [gʌt] n Darm m; **~s** pl
(intestines) Eingeweide; (courage)
Mumm m
gutter ['gʌtə°] n (for roof)
Dachrinne f; (in street) Rinnstein m,
Gosse f; **gutter press** n
Skandalpresse f
guy [gaɪ] n (man) Typ m, Kerl m; **~s**
pl (US) Leute pl
gym [dʒɪm] n Turnhalle f; (for
working out) Fitnesscenter nt;
gymnasium [dʒɪm'neɪzɪəm] n
Turnhalle f; **gymnastics**
[dʒɪm'næstɪks] nsing Turnen nt;
gym-toned adj durchtrainiert
gynaecologist [gaɪnɪ'kɒlədʒɪst]
n Frauenarzt m, Frauenärztin f,
Gynäkologe m, Gynäkologin f;

gynaecology n Gynäkologie f,
Frauenheilkunde f
gypsy ['dʒɪpsɪ] n Zigeuner(in)
m(f)

h

habit ['hæbɪt] n Gewohnheit f;
habitual [hə'bɪtjuəl] adj
gewohnt; (drinker, liar)
gewohnheitsmäßig

hack [hæk] vt hacken; **hacker** n
(Inform) Hacker(in) m(f)

had [hæd] pt, pp of **have**

haddock ['hædək] n Schellfisch
m

hadn't ['hædnt] contr of **had not**

haemophiliac, hemophiliac (US)
[hiːməʊ'fɪliæk] n Bluter(in) m(f);
haemorrhage, hemorrhage (US)
['hemərɪdʒ] n Blutung f ▷ vi
bluten; **haemorrhoids,
hemorrhoids** (US) ['hemərɔɪdz]
npl Hämorrhoiden pl

haggis ['hægɪs] n (Scot) mit
gehackten Schafsinnereien und
Haferschrot gefüllter Schafsmagen

Hague [heɪg] n: **the ~** Den Haag

hail [heɪl] n Hagel m ▷ vi hageln
▷ vt: **to ~ sb as sth** jdn als etw

feiern; **hailstone** n Hagelkorn nt;
hailstorm n Hagelschauer m

hair [heə°] n Haar nt, Haare pl; **to
do one's ~** sich frisieren; **to get
one's ~ cut** sich dat die Haare
schneiden lassen; **hairbrush** n
Haarbürste f; **hair conditioner** n
Haarspülung f; **haircut** n
Haarschnitt m; **to have a ~** sich
dat die Haare schneiden lassen;
hairdo (pl **-s**) n Frisur f;
hairdresser n Friseur m, Friseuse
f; **hairdryer** n Haartrockner m;
(hand-held) Fön® m; (over head)
Trockenhaube f; **hair gel** n
Haargel nt; **hairpin** n Haarnadel f;
hair remover n
Enthaarungsmittel nt; **hair spray**
n Haarspray nt; **hair style** n
Frisur f; **hairy** adj haarig,
behaart; (fam: dangerous) brenzlig

hake [heɪk] n Seehecht m

half [hɑːf] (pl **halves**) n Hälfte f;
(Sport: of game) Halbzeit f; **to cut in
~** halbieren ▷ adj halb; **three and
a ~ pounds** dreieinhalb Pfund;
~ an hour, a ~ hour eine halbe
Stunde; **one and a ~** eineinhalb,
anderthalb ▷ adv halb, zur Hälfte;
~ past three, ~ three halb vier; **at
~ past** um halb; **~ asleep** fast
eingeschlafen; **she's ~ German** sie
ist zur Hälfte Deutsche; **~ as big
(as)** halb so groß (wie); **half board**
n Halbpension f; **half fare** n
halber Fahrpreis; **half-hearted**
adj halbherzig; **half-hour** n halbe
Stunde; **half moon** n Halbmond
m; **half pint** n = Viertelliter m o nt;
half price n: **at ~** zum halben
Preis; **half-term** n (at school)
Ferien pl in der Mitte des
Trimesters; **half-time** n Halbzeit
f; **halfway** adv auf halbem Wege;
halfwit n (fam) Trottel m

halibut ['hælɪbət] n Heilbutt m

hall [hɔːl] n (building) Halle f; (for

audience) Saal *m; (entrance ~)* Flur *m;
(large)* Diele *f;* **~ of residence** (Brit)
Studentenwohnheim *nt*

hallmark ['hɔːlmaːk] *n* Stempel
m; (fig) Kennzeichen *nt*

hallo [hʌ'ləʊ] *interj* hallo

Hallowe'en [hæləʊ'iːn] *n* Halloween *nt (Tag vor Allerheiligen, an
dem sich Kinder verkleiden und von Tür
zu Tür gehen)*

● HALLOWE'EN
●
● **Hallowe'en** ist der 31. Oktober,
● der Vorabend von Allerheiligen,
● und nach altem Glauben an dem
● Abend, an dem man Geister und
● Hexen sehen kann. In
● Großbritannien und vor allem in
● den USA feiern die Kinder
● Hallowe'en, indem sie sich
● verkleiden und mit selbst
● gemachten Laternen aus
● Kürbissen von Tür zu Tür
● ziehen.

halo ['heɪləʊ] *(pl* **-es)** *n (of saint)*
Heiligenschein *m*

halt [hɔːlt] *n* Pause *f,* Halt *m;* **to
come to a ~** zum Stillstand
kommen ▷ *vt, vi* anhalten

halve [haːv] *vt* halbieren

ham [hæm] *n* Schinken *m;* **~ and
eggs** Schinken mit Spiegelei

hamburger ['hæmbɜːgə°] *n (Gastr)*
Hamburger *m*

hammer ['hæmə°] *n* Hammer *m
▷ vt, vi* hämmern

hammock ['hæmək] *n* Hängematte *f*

hamper ['hæmpə°] *vt* behindern
▷ *n (as gift)* Geschenkkorb *m; (for
picnic)* Picknickkkorb *m*

hamster ['hæmstə°] *n* Hamster *m*

hand [hænd] *n* Hand *f; (of clock,
instrument)* Zeiger *m; (in card game)*
Blatt *nt;* **to be made by**

~ Handarbeit sein; **~s up!** Hände
hoch!; *(at school)* meldet euch!; **~s
off!** Finger weg!; **on the one ~ ...,
on the other ~...** einerseits ...,
andererseits ...; **to give sb a ~** jdm
helfen *(with bei);* **it's in his ~s** er
hat es in der Hand; **to be in good
~s** gut aufgehoben sein; **to get
out of ~** außer Kontrolle geraten
▷ *vt (pass)* reichen *(to sb jdm);*
hand down *vt (tradition)*
überliefern; *(heirloom)* vererben;
hand in *vt* einreichen; *(at school,
university etc)* abgeben; **hand out**
vt verteilen; **hand over** *vt*
übergeben

handbag *n* Handtasche *f;*
handbook *n* Handbuch *nt;*
handbrake *n* (Brit) Handbremse
f; **handcuffs** *npl* Handschellen *pl;*
handful *n* Handvoll *f;* **handheld
PC** *n* Handheld *m*

handicap ['hændɪkæp] *n*
Behinderung *f,* Handikap *m* ▷ *vt*
benachteiligen; **handicapped** *adj*
behindert; **the ~** die Behinderten

handicraft ['hændɪkraːft] *n*
Kunsthandwerk *nt*

handkerchief ['hæŋkətʃɪf] *n*
Taschentuch *nt*

handle ['hændl] *n* Griff *m; (of
door)* Klinke *f; (of cup etc)* Henkel *m;
(for winding)* Kurbel *f* ▷ *vt (touch)*
anfassen; *(deal with: matter)* sich
befassen mit; *(people, machine etc)*
umgehen mit; *(situation, problem)*
fertig werden mit; **handlebars** *npl*
Lenkstange *f*

hand luggage ['hændlʌgɪdʒ] *n*
Handgepäck *nt;* **handmade** *adj*
handgefertigt; **to be ~** Handarbeit
sein; **handout** *n (sheet)* Handout
nt, Thesenpapier *nt;* **handset** *n*
Hörer *m;* **please replace the
~** bitte legen Sie auf; **hands-free
phone** *n* Freisprechanlage *f;*
handshake *n* Händedruck *m*

handsome ['hænsəm] *adj* (man) gut aussehend

hands-on ['hændz'ɒn] *adj* praxisorientiert; **~ experience** praktische Erfahrung

handwriting ['hændraɪtɪŋ] *n* Handschrift f

handy ['hændɪ] *adj* (useful) praktisch

hang [hæŋ] (**hung, hung**) *vt* (auf)hängen; (execute: hanged, hanged) hängen; **to ~ sth on sth** etw an etw akk hängen ▷ *vi* hängen ▷ *n*: **he's got the ~ of it** er hat den Dreh raus; **hang about** *vi* sich herumtreiben, rumhängen; **hang on** *vi* sich festhalten (to an +dat); (fam: wait) warten; **to ~ on to sth** etw behalten; **hang up** *vt* (Tel) auflegen ▷ *vt* aufhängen

hangar ['hæŋə°] *n* Flugzeughalle f

hanger ['hæŋə°] *n* Kleiderbügel m

hang glider ['hæŋglaɪdə°] *n* (Flug)drachen m; (person) Drachenflieger(in) m(f); **hang-gliding** *n* Drachenfliegen nt

hangover ['hæŋəʊvə°] *n* (bad head) Kater m; (relic) Überbleibsel nt

hankie ['hæŋkɪ] *n* (fam) Taschentuch nt

happen ['hæpən] *vi* geschehen; (sth strange, unpleasant) passieren; **if anything should ~ to me** wenn mir etwas passieren sollte; **it won't ~ again** es wird nicht wieder vorkommen; **I ~ed to be passing** ich kam zufällig vorbei; **happening** *n* Ereignis nt, Happening nt

happily ['hæpɪlɪ] *adv* fröhlich, glücklich; (luckily) glücklicherweise; **happiness** ['hæpɪnəs] *n* Glück nt; **happy** ['hæpɪ] *adj* glücklich; (satisfied)

~ with sth mit etw zufrieden; (willing) **to be ~ to do sth** etw gerne tun; **Happy Christmas** fröhliche Weihnachten!; **Happy New Year** ein glückliches Neues Jahr!; **Happy Birthday** herzlichen Glückwunsch zum Geburtstag!; **happy hour** *n* Happy Hour f (Zeit, in der man in Bars Getränke zu günstigeren Preisen bekommt)

harass ['hærəs] *vt* (ständig) belästigen; **harassment** *n* Belästigung f; (at work) Mobbing nt; **sexual ~** sexuelle Belästigung

harbor (US), **harbour** ['hɑːbə°] *n* Hafen m

hard [hɑːd] *adj* hart; (difficult) schwer, schwierig; (harsh) hart(herzig); **don't be ~ on him** sei nicht zu streng zu ihm; **it's ~ to believe** es ist kaum zu glauben ▷ *adv* (work) schwer; (run) schnell; (rain, snow) stark; **to try ~/~er sth** dat große/mehr Mühe geben; **hardback** *n* gebundene Ausgabe; **hard-boiled** *adj* (egg) hart gekocht; **hard copy** *n* (Inform) Ausdruck m; **hard disk** *n* (Inform) Festplatte f; **hard up** *adj* knapp bei Kasse; **harden** *vt* härten ▷ *vi* hart werden; **hardened** *adj* (person) abgehärtet (to gegen); **hard-hearted** *adj* hartherzig; **hardliner** *n* Hardliner(in) m(f); **hardly** ['hɑːdlɪ] *adv* kaum; **~ ever** fast nie; **hardship** ['hɑːdʃɪp] *n* Not f; **hard shoulder** *n* (Brit) Standspur f; **hardware** *n* (Inform) Hardware f, Haushalts- und Eisenwaren pl; **hard-working** *adj* fleißig, tüchtig

hare [heə°] *n* Hase m

harm [hɑːm] *n* Schaden m; (bodily) Verletzung f; **it wouldn't do any ~** es würde nicht schaden ▷ *vt* schaden +dat; (person) verletzen; **harmful** *adj* schädlich; **harmless** *adj* harmlos

harp [hɑːp] n Harfe f
harsh [hɑːʃ] adj (climate, voice)
rau; (light, sound) grell; (severe)
hart, streng
harvest ['hɑːvɪst] n Ernte f;
(time) Erntezeit f ▷ vt ernten
has [hæz] pres of **have**
hash [hæʃ] n (Gastr) Haschee nt;
(fam: hashish) Haschisch nt; **to
make a ~ of sth** etw vermasseln;
hash browns npl (US) =
Kartoffelpuffer/Rösti mit
Zwiebeln pl
hassle ['hæsl] n Ärger m; (fuss)
Theater nt; **no ~** kein Problem ▷ vt
bedrängen
hasn't ['hæznt] contr of **has not**
haste [heɪst] n Eile f; **hastily,
hasty** adv, adj hastig; (rash)
vorschnell
hat [hæt] n Hut m
hatch [hætʃ] n (Naut) Luke f; (in
house) Durchreiche f; **hatchback**
['hætʃbæk] n (car) Wagen m mit
Hecktür
hate [heɪt] vt hassen; **I ~ doing
this** ich mache das sehr ungern
▷ n Hass m (of auf +akk)
haul [hɔːl] vt ziehen, schleppen
▷ n (booty) Beute f; **haulage**
['hɔːlɪdʒ] n Transport m; (trade)
Spedition f; **haunted** adj: **a
~ house** ein Haus, in dem es spukt

○ **KEYWORD**

have [hæv] (pt, pp had) vb aux **1**
haben; (esp with vbs of motion) sein;
to have arrived/slept
angekommen sein/geschlafen
haben; **to have been** gewesen
sein; **having eaten** o **when he
had eaten, he left** nachdem er
gegessen hatte, ging er
2 (in tag questions) **you've done it,
haven't you?** du hast/Sie haben
es doch gemacht, oder nicht?

3 (in short answers and questions)
**you've made a mistake — so I
have/no I haven't** du hast/Sie
haben einen Fehler gemacht — ja,
stimmt/nein; **we haven't paid —
yes we have!** wir haben nicht
bezahlt — doch!; **I've been there
before, have you?** ich war schon
einmal da, du/Sie auch?
▷ modal vb aux (be obliged): **to
have (got) to do sth** etw tun
müssen; **you haven't to tell her**
du darfst es ihr nicht erzählen
▷ vt **1** (possess) haben; **he has (got)
blue eyes** er hat blaue Augen; **I
have (got) an idea** ich habe eine
Idee
2 (referring to meals etc) **to have
breakfast/a cigarette**
frühstücken/eine Zigarette
rauchen
3 (receive, obtain etc) haben; **may I
have your address?** kann ich
deine/Ihre Adresse haben?; **to
have a baby** ein Kind bekommen
4 (maintain, allow) **he will have it
that he is right** er besteht darauf,
dass er recht hat; **I won't have it**
das lasse ich mir nicht bieten
5 to have sth done etw machen
lassen; **to have sb do sth** jdn etw
machen lassen; **he soon had
them all laughing** er brachte sie
alle zum Lachen
6 (experience, suffer) **she had her
bag stolen** man hat ihr die Tasche
gestohlen; **he had his arm broken**
er hat sich den Arm gebrochen
7 (+noun: take, hold etc) **to have a
walk/rest** spazieren gehen/sich
ausruhen; **to have a
meeting/party** eine
Besprechung/Party haben;
have on vt (be wearing) anhaben;
(have arranged) vorhaben; (Brit)
you're having me on du
verarschst mich doch;

have out vt: **to have it out with sb** (settle problem) etw mit jdm bereden

Hawaii [hə'waiːi] n Hawaii nt
hawk [hɔːk] n Habicht m
hay [heɪ] n Heu nt; **hay fever** n Heuschnupfen m
hazard ['hæzəd] n Gefahr f; (risk) Risiko nt; **hazardous** adj gefährlich; **~ waste** Sondermüll m; **hazard warning lights** npl Warnblinkanlage f
haze [heɪz] n Dunst m
hazelnut ['heɪzlnʌt] n Haselnuss f
hazy ['heɪzɪ] adj (misty) dunstig; (vague) verschwommen
he [hiː] pron er
head [hed] n Kopf m; (leader) Leiter(in) m(f); (at school) Schulleiter(in) m(f); (at state) Staatsoberhaupt nt; **at the ~ of** an der Spitze von; (tossing coin) **~s or tails?** Kopf oder Zahl? ▷ adj (leading) Ober-; **~ boy** Schulsprecher m; **~ girl** Schulsprecherin f ▷ vt anführen; (organization) leiten; **head for** vt zusteuern auf +akk; **he's heading for trouble** er wird Ärger bekommen
headache n Kopfschmerzen pl, Kopfweh nt; **header** n (football) Kopfball m; (dive) Kopfsprung m; **headfirst** adj kopfüber; **headhunt** vt (Comm) abwerben; **heading** n Überschrift f; **headlamp**, **headlight** n Scheinwerfer m; **headline** n Schlagzeile f; **headmaster** n Schulleiter m; **headmistress** n Schulleiterin f; **head-on collision** adj Frontalzusammenstoß m; **headphones** npl Kopfhörer m; **headquarters** npl (of firm) Zentrale f; **headrest**, **head**

restraint n Kopfstütze f;
headscarf (pl **-scarves**) n Kopftuch nt; **head teacher** n Schulleiter(in) m(f)
heal [hiːl] vt, vi heilen
health [helθ] n Gesundheit f; **good/bad for one's ~** gesund/ungesund; **your ~!** zum Wohl!; **~ and beauty** Wellness; **health centre** n Ärztezentrum nt; **health club** n Fitnesscenter nt; **health food** n Reformkost f; **~ shop**, **~ store** Bioladen m; **health insurance** n Krankenversicherung f; **health service** n Gesundheitswesen nt; **healthy** adj gesund
heap [hiːp] n Haufen m; **~s of** (fam) jede Menge ▷ vt, vi häufen
hear [hɪə°] (heard, heard) vt, vi hören; **to ~ about sth** von etw erfahren; **I've ~ of it/him** ich habe schon davon/von ihm gehört; **hearing** n Gehör nt; (Jur) Verhandlung f; **hearing aid** n Hörgerät nt; **hearsay** n: **from ~** vom Hörensagen
heart [hɑːt] n Herz nt; **to lose/take ~** den Mut verlieren/Mut fassen; **to learn by ~** auswendig lernen; (cards) **~s** Herz nt; **queen of ~s** Herzdame f; **heart attack** n Herzanfall m; **heartbeat** n Herzschlag m; **heartbreaking** adj herzzerreißend; **heartbroken** adj todunglücklich, untröstlich; **heartburn** n Sodbrennen nt; **heart failure** n Herzversagen nt; **heartfelt** adj tief empfunden; **heartless** adj herzlos; **heart-throb** n (fam) Schwarm m; **heart-to-heart** n offene Aussprache; **hearty** [hɑːtɪ] adj (meal, appetite) herzhaft; (welcome) herzlich
heat [hiːt] n Hitze f; (pleasant) Wärme f; (temperature) Temperatur

f; (Sport) Vorlauf m ▷ vt (house, room) heizen; **heat up** vi warm werden ▷ vt aufwärmen; **heated** adj beheizt; (fig) hitzig; **heater** n Heizofen m; (Auto) Heizung f

heath [hi:θ] n (Brit) Heide f; **heather** ['heðə°] n Heidekraut nt

heating ['hi:tɪŋ] n Heizung f; **heat resistant** adj hitzebeständig; **heatwave** n Hitzewelle f

heaven ['hevn] n Himmel m; **heavenly** adj himmlisch

heavily ['hevɪlɪ] adv (rain, drink etc) stark; **heavy** ['hevɪ] adj schwer; (rain, traffic, smoker etc) stark; **heavy goods vehicle** n Lastkraftwagen m

Hebrew ['hi:bru:] adj hebräisch ▷ n (language) Hebräisch nt

hectic ['hektɪk] adj hektisch

he'd [hi:d] contr of **he had; he would**

hedge [hedʒ] n Hecke f

hedgehog ['hedʒhɒg] n Igel m

heel [hi:l] n (Anat) Ferse f; (of shoe) Absatz m

hefty ['heftɪ] adj schwer; (person) stämmig; (fine, amount) saftig

height [haɪt] n Höhe f; (of person) Größe f

heir [ɛə°] n Erbe m; **heiress** ['ɛərɪs] n Erbin f

held [held] pt, pp of **hold**

helicopter ['helɪkɒptə°] n Hubschrauber m; **helipad** ['helɪpɔːt] n Hubschrauber-landeplatz m

hell [hel] n Hölle f; **go to ~** scher dich zum Teufel ▷ interj verdammt!; **that's a ~ of a lot of money** das ist verdammt viel Geld

he'll [hi:l] contr of **he will; he shall**

hello [hʌ'ləʊ] interj hallo

helmet ['helmɪt] n Helm m

help [help] n Hilfe f ▷ vt, vi helfen +dat (with bei); **to ~ sb (to) do sth** jdm helfen, etw zu tun; **can I ~?** kann ich (Ihnen) behilflich sein?; **I couldn't ~ laughing** ich musste einfach lachen; **I can't ~ it** ich kann nichts dafür; **~ yourself** bedienen Sie sich; **helpful** adj (person) hilfsbereit; (useful) nützlich; **helping** n Portion f; **helpless** adj hilflos

hem [hem] n Saum m

hemophiliac [hi:məʊ'fɪlɪæk] n (US) Bluter m; **hemorrhage** ['hemərɪdʒ] n (US) Blutung f; **hemorrhoids** ['hemərɔɪdz] npl (US) Hämorrhoiden pl

hen [hen] n Henne f

hen night n (Brit) Junggesellinnenabschied m

hence [hens] adv (reason) daher

henpecked ['henpekt] adj: **to be ~** unter dem Pantoffel stehen

hepatitis [hepə'taɪtɪs] n Hepatitis f

her [hɜː°] adj ihr; **she's hurt ~ leg** sie hat sich dat das Bein verletzt ▷ pron (direct object) sie; (indirect object) ihr; **do you know ~?** kennst du sie?; **can you help ~?** kannst du ihr helfen?; **it's ~** sie ist's

herb [hɜːb] n Kraut nt

herbal medicine ['hɜːbəl-] n Pflanzenheilkunde f; **herbal tea** n Kräutertee m

herd [hɜːd] n Herde f; **herd instinct** n Herdentrieb m

here [hɪə°] adv hier; (to this place) hierher; **come ~** komm her; **I won't be ~ for lunch** ich bin zum Mittagessen nicht da; **~ and there** hier und da, da und dort

hereditary [hɪ'redɪtərɪ] adj erblich; **hereditary disease** n Erbkrankheit f; **heritage** ['herɪtɪdʒ] n Erbe nt

hernia ['hɜːnɪə] n Leistenbruch m, Eingeweidebruch m

hero ['hɪərəʊ] (pl **-es**) n Held m

heroin ['herəʊɪn] n Heroin nt

heroine ['herəʊɪn] n Heldin f; **heroism** ['herəʊɪzəm] n Heldentum nt

herring ['herɪŋ] n Hering m

hers [hɜːz] pron ihre(r, s); **this is ~** das gehört ihr; **a friend of ~** ein Freund von ihr

herself [hɜːˈself] pron (reflexive) sich; **she's bought ~ a flat** sie hat sich eine Wohnung gekauft; **she needs it for ~** sie braucht es für sich (selbst); (emphatic) **she did it ~** sie hat es selbst gemacht; (all) **by ~** allein

he's [hiːz] contr of **he is**; **he has**

hesitant ['hezɪtənt] adj zögernd; **hesitate** ['hezɪteɪt] vi zögern; **don't ~ to ask** fragen Sie ruhig; **hesitation** n Zögern nt; **without ~** ohne zu zögern

heterosexual [hetərəʊˈsekʃʊəl] adj heterosexuell ⊳ n Heterosexuelle(r) mf

HGV abbr = **heavy goods vehicle** LKW m

hi [haɪ] interj hi, hallo

hiccup ['hɪkʌp] n Schluckauf m; (minor problem) Problemchen nt; **to have (the) ~s** Schluckauf haben

hid [hɪd] pt of **hide**

hidden ['hɪdn] pp of **hide**

hide [haɪd] (pt **hid**, pp **hidden**) vt verstecken (from vor +dat); (feelings, truth) verbergen; (cover) verdecken ⊳ vi sich verstecken (from vor +dat)

hideous ['hɪdɪəs] adj scheußlich

hiding ['haɪdɪŋ] n (beating) Tracht f Prügel; (concealment) **to be in ~** sich versteckt halten; **hiding place** n Versteck nt

hi-fi ['haɪfaɪ] n Hi-Fi nt; (system) Hi-Fi-Anlage f

high [haɪ] adj hoch; (wind) stark; (living) im großen Stil; (on drugs) high ⊳ adv hoch ⊳ n (Meteo) Hoch nt; **highchair** n Hochstuhl m; **high** adj höher; **higher education** n Hochschulbildung f; **high flier** n Hochbegabte(r) (m)f; **high heels** npl Stöckelschuhe pl; **high jump** n Hochsprung m; **Highlands** npl (schottisches) Hochland nt; **highlight** n (in hair) Strähnchen nt; (fig) Höhepunkt m ⊳ vt (with pen) hervorheben; **highlighter** n Textmarker m; **highly** adv hoch, sehr; **~ paid** hoch bezahlt; **I think ~ of him** ich habe eine hohe Meinung von ihm; **high-performance** adj Hochleistungs-; **high school** n (US) Highschool f, ≈ Gymnasium nt; **high-speed** adj Hochgeschwindigkeits-; **~ train** Hochgeschwindigkeitszug m; **high street** n Hauptstraße f; **high tech** adj Hightech- ⊳ n Hightech nt; **high tide** n Flut f; **highway** n (US) ≈ Autobahn f; (Brit) Landstraße f

hijack ['haɪdʒæk] vt entführen, hijacken; **hijacker** n Entführer(in) m(f), Hijacker m

hike [haɪk] vi wandern ⊳ n Wanderung f; **hiker** n Wanderer m, Wanderin f; **hiking** n Wandern nt

hilarious [hɪˈleərɪəs] adj zum Schreien komisch

hill [hɪl] n Hügel m; (higher) Berg m; **hilly** adj hügelig

him [hɪm] pron (direct object) ihn; (indirect object) ihm; **do you know ~?** kennst du ihn?; **can you help ~?** kannst du ihm helfen?; **it's ~** er ist's; **~ too** er auch

himself [hɪmˈself] pron (reflexive) sich; **he's bought ~ a flat** er hat sich eine Wohnung gekauft; **he needs it for ~** er braucht es für sich (selbst); (emphatic) **he did it ~**

~ er hat es selbst gemacht; (**all**) by ~ allein

hinder ['hɪndə°] vt behindern; **hindrance** ['hɪndrəns] n Behinderung f

Hindu ['hɪnduː] adj hinduistisch ▷ n Hindu m; **Hinduism** ['hɪnduːɪzəm] n Hinduismus m

hinge [hɪndʒ] n Scharnier nt; (on door) Angel f

hint [hɪnt] n Wink m, Andeutung f; (trace) Spur f ▷ vi andeuten (at akk)

hip [hɪp] n Hüfte f

hippopotamus [hɪpə'pɒtəməs] n Nilpferd nt

hire ['haɪə°] vt (worker) anstellen; (car, bike etc) mieten ▷ n Miete f; **for ~** (taxi) frei; **hire car** n Mietwagen m; **hire charge** n Benutzungsgebühr f; **hire purchase** n Ratenkauf m

his [hɪz] adj sein; **he's hurt ~ leg** er hat sich dat das Bein verletzt ▷ pron seine(r, s); **it's ~** es gehört ihm; **a friend of ~** ein Freund von ihm

historic [hɪ'stɒrɪk] adj (significant) historisch; **historical** adj (monument etc) historisch; (studies etc) geschichtlich; **history** ['hɪstərɪ] n Geschichte f

hit [hɪt] n (blow) Schlag m; (on target) Treffer m; (successful film, CD etc) Hit m ▷ vt (**hit, hit**) schlagen; (bullet, stone etc) treffen; **the car ~ the tree** das Auto fuhr gegen einen Baum; **to ~ one's head on sth** sich dat den Kopf an etw dat stoßen; **hit (up)on** vt stoßen auf +akk; **hit-and-run** adj: **~ accident** Unfall m mit Fahrerflucht

hitch [hɪtʃ] vt (pull up) hochziehen ▷ n Schwierigkeit f; **without a ~** reibungslos

hitch-hike ['hɪtʃhaɪk] vi trampen; **hitch-hiker** n Tramper(in)

m(f); **hitchhiking** n Trampen nt

HIV abbr = **human immunodeficiency virus** HIV nt; **~ positive/negative** HIV-positiv/negativ

hive [haɪv] n Bienenstock m

HM abbr = **His/Her Majesty**

HMS abbr = **His/Her Majesty's Ship**

hoarse [hɔːs] adj heiser

hoax [həʊks] n Streich m, Jux m; (false alarm) blinder Alarm

hob [hɒb] n (of cooker) Kochfeld nt

hobble ['hɒbl] vi humpeln

hobby ['hɒbɪ] n Hobby nt

hobo ['həʊbəʊ] (pl **-es**) n (US) Penner(in) m(f)

hockey ['hɒkɪ] n Hockey nt

hold [həʊld] vt (**held, held**) halten; (contain) enthalten; (be able to contain) fassen; (post, office) innehaben; (value) behalten; (meeting) abhalten; (person as prisoner) gefangen halten; **to ~ one's breath** den Atem anhalten; **to ~ hands** Händchen halten; **~ the line** (Tel) bleiben Sie am Apparat ▷ vi halten; (weather) sich halten ▷ n (grasp) Halt m; (of ship, aircraft) Laderaum m; **hold back** vt zurückhalten; (keep secret) verheimlichen; **hold on** vi sich festhalten; (wait) warten; (Tel) dranbleiben; **to ~ to sth** etw festhalten; **hold out** vt ausstrecken; (offer) hinhalten; (offer) bieten ▷ vi durchhalten; **hold up** vt hochhalten; (support) stützen; (delay) aufhalten; **holdall** n Reisetasche f; **holder** n (person) Inhaber(in) m(f); **holdup** n (in traffic) Stau m; (robbery) Überfall m

hole [həʊl] n Loch nt; (of fox, rabbit) Bau m; **~ in the wall** (cash dispenser) Geldautomat m

holiday ['hɒlɪdeɪ] n (day off)
freier Tag; (public ~) Feiertag m;
(vacation) Urlaub m; (at school)
Ferien pl; on ~ im Urlaub; to go on
~ Urlaub machen; holiday camp
n Ferienlager nt; holiday home n
Ferienhaus nt; (flat)
Ferienwohnung f; holidaymaker
n Urlauber(in) m(f); holiday
resort n Ferienort m

Holland ['hɒlənd] n Holland nt

hollow ['hɒləʊ] adj hohl; (words)
leer ▷ n Vertiefung f

holly ['hɒlɪ] n Stechpalme f

holy ['həʊlɪ] adj heilig; Holy
Week n Karwoche f

home [həʊm] n Zuhause nt;
(area, country) Heimat f; (institution)
Heim nt; at ~ zu Hause; to make
oneself at ~ es sich dat bequem
machen; away from ~ verreist
▷ adv: to go ~ nach Hause
gehen/fahren; home address n
Heimatadresse f; home country
n Heimatland nt; home game n
(Sport) Heimspiel nt; homeless adj
obdachlos; homely adj häuslich;
(US: ugly) unscheinbar;
home-made adj selbst gemacht;
home movie n Amateurfilm m;
Home Office n (Brit)
Innenministerium nt

homeopathic adj (US) see
homoeopathic

home page ['həʊmpeɪdʒ] n
(Inform) Homepage f; Home
Secretary n (Brit)
Innenminister(in) m(f); homesick
adj: to be ~ Heimweh haben;
home town n Heimatstadt f;
homework n Hausaufgaben pl

homicide ['hɒmɪsaɪd] n (US)
Totschlag m

homoeopathic
[həʊmɪəʊˈpæθɪk] adj
homöopathisch

homosexual [hɒməʊˈsɛksjʊəl]

adj homosexuell ▷ n Homosex-
uelle(r) mf

Honduras [hɒnˈdjʊərəs] n
Honduras nt

honest ['ɒnɪst] adj ehrlich;
honesty n Ehrlichkeit f

honey ['hʌnɪ] n Honig m;
honeycomb n Honigwabe f;
honeydew melon n
Honigmelone f; honeymoon n
Flitterwochen pl

Hong Kong [hɒŋ ˈkɒŋ] n
Hongkong nt

honor (US) see honour; honorary
['ɒnərərɪ] adj (member, title etc)
Ehren-, ehrenamtlich; honour
['ɒnə] vt ehren; (cheque) einlösen;
(contract) einhalten ▷ n Ehre f; in
~ of zu Ehren von; honourable adj
ehrenhaft; honours degree n
akademischer Grad mit Prüfung im
Spezialfach

hood [hʊd] n Kapuze f; (Auto)
Verdeck nt; (US Auto) Kühlerhaube
f

hoof [huːf] (pl hooves) n Huf
m

hook [hʊk] n Haken m; hooked
adj (keen) besessen (on von);
(drugs) abhängig sein (on von)

hooligan ['huːlɪɡən] n Hooligan
m

hoot [huːt] vi (Auto) hupen

Hoover® ['huːvə] n Staubsauger
m; hoover vi, vt staubsaugen

hop [hɒp] vi hüpfen ▷ n (Bot)
Hopfen m

hope [həʊp] vi, vt hoffen (for auf
+akk); I ~ so/~ not
hoffentlich/hoffentlich nicht; I
~ (that) we'll meet ich hoffe, dass
wir uns sehen werden ▷ n
Hoffnung f; there's no ~ es ist
aussichtslos; hopeful adj
hoffnungsvoll; hopefully adv (full
of hope) hoffnungsvoll; (I hope so)
hoffentlich; hopeless adj

hoffnungslos; (incompetent) miserabel

horizon [hə'raɪzn] n Horizont m; **horizontal** [hɒrɪ'zɒntl] adj horizontal

hormone ['hɔːməʊn] n Hormon nt

horn [hɔːn] n Horn nt; (Auto) Hupe f

hornet ['hɔːnɪt] n Hornisse f

horny ['hɔːnɪ] adj (fam) geil

horoscope ['hɒrəskəʊp] n Horoskop nt

horrible, horribly ['hɒrɪbl, -blɪ] adj, adv schrecklich; **horrid, horridly** ['hɒrɪd, -lɪ] adj, adv abscheulich; **horrify** ['hɒrɪfaɪ] vt entsetzen; **horror** ['hɒrə⁺] n Entsetzen nt; **~s** (things) Schrecken pl

hors d'oeuvre [ɔː'dɜːvr] n Vorspeise f

horse [hɔːs] n Pferd nt; **horse chestnut** n Rosskastanie f; **horsepower** n Pferdestärke f, PS nt; **horse racing** n Pferderennen nt; **horseradish** n Meerrettich m; **horse riding** n Reiten nt; **horseshoe** n Hufeisen nt

horticulture ['hɔːtɪkʌltʃə⁺] n Gartenbau m

hose, hosepipe [həʊz, 'həʊzpaɪp] n Schlauch m

hospitable [hɒ'spɪtəbl] adj gastfreundlich

hospital ['hɒspɪtl] n Krankenhaus nt

hospitality [hɒspɪ'tælɪtɪ] n Gastfreundschaft f

host [həʊst] n Gastgeber m; (TV: of show) Moderator(in) m(f), Talkmaster(in) m(f) ▷ vt (party) geben; (TV: TV show) moderieren

hostage ['hɒstɪdʒ] n Geisel f

hostel ['hɒstəl] n Wohnheim nt; (youth ~) Jugendherberge f

hostess ['həʊstɪs] n (of a party) Gastgeberin f

hostile ['hɒstaɪl] adj feindlich; **hostility** [hɒs'tɪlɪtɪ] n Feindseligkeit f

hot [hɒt] adj heiß; (drink, food, water) warm; (spiced) scharf; **I'm (feeling) ~** mir ist heiß; **hot cross bun** n Rosinenbrötchen mit einem Kreuz darauf, hauptsächlich zu Ostern gegessen; **hot dog** n Hotdog m

hotel [həʊ'tel] n Hotel nt; **hotel room** n Hotelzimmer nt

hothouse n Treibhaus nt; **hotline** n Hotline f; **hotplate** n Kochplatte f; **hotspot** n (Inform) Hotspot m; **hot-water bottle** n Wärmflasche f

hour ['aʊə⁺] n Stunde f; **to wait for ~s** stundenlang warten; **~s** pl (of shops etc) Geschäftszeiten pl; **hourly** adj stündlich

house [haʊs] (pl **houses**) n Haus nt; **at my ~** bei mir (zu Hause); **to my ~** zu mir (nach Hause); **on the ~** auf Kosten des Hauses; **the House of Commons/Lords** das britische Unterhaus/Oberhaus; **the Houses of Parliament** das britische Parlamentsgebäude ▷ [haʊz] vt unterbringen; **houseboat** n Hausboot nt; **household** n Haushalt m; **~ appliance** Haushaltsgerät nt; **house-husband** n Hausmann m; **housekeeping** n Haushaltung f; (money) Haushaltsgeld nt; **house-trained** adj stubenrein; **house-warming (party)** n Einzugsparty f; **housewife** (pl **-wives**) n Hausfrau f; **house wine** n Hauswein m; **housework** n Hausarbeit f

housing ['haʊzɪŋ] n (houses) Wohnungen pl; (house building) Wohnungsbau m; **housing**

benefit n Wohngeld nt; **housing development**, **housing estate** (Brit) n Wohnsiedlung f
hover ['hɒvə°] vi schweben; **hovercraft** n Luftkissenboot nt
how [hau] adv wie; ~ **many** wie viele; ~ **much** wie viel; ~ **are you?** wie geht es Ihnen?; ~ **are things?** wie geht's?; ~'**s work?** was macht die Arbeit?; ~ **about ...?** wie wäre es mit ...?; **however** [hau'evə°] conj (but) jedoch, aber ▷ adv (no matter how) wie, ... auch; ~ **much it costs** wie viel es auch kostet; ~ **you do it** wie man es auch macht
howl [haul] vi heulen; **howler** ['haulə°] n (fam) grober Schnitzer
HP, **hp** (Brit) abbr = **hire purchase** Ratenkauf m ▷ abbr = **horsepower** PS
HQ abbr = **headquarters**
hubcap ['hʌbkæp] n Radkappe f
hug [hʌg] vt umarmen ▷ n Umarmung f
huge [hjuːdʒ] adj riesig
hum [hʌm] vi, vt summen
human ['hjuːmən] adj menschlich; ~ **rights** Menschenrechte pl ▷ n: ~ (**being**) Mensch m; **humanitarian** [hjuːmænɪ'teəriən] adj humanitär; **humanity** [hjuː'mænɪtɪ] n Menschheit f; (kindliness) Menschlichkeit f; **humanities** Geisteswissenschaften pl
humble ['hʌmbl] adj demütig; (modest) bescheiden
humid ['hjuːmɪd] adj feucht; **humidity** [hjuː'mɪdɪtɪ] n (Luft)feuchtigkeit f
humiliate [hjuː'mɪlɪeɪt] vt demütigen; **humiliation** [hjuːmɪlɪ'eɪʃn] n Erniedrigung f, Demütigung f
humor (US) see **humour**;

humorous ['hjuːmərəs] adj humorvoll; (story) lustig, witzig; **humour** ['hjuːmə°] n Humor m; **sense of** ~ Sinn m für Humor
hump [hʌmp] n Buckel m
hunch [hʌntʃ] n Gefühl nt, Ahnung f ▷ vt (back) krümmen; **hunchback** n Bucklige(r) mf
hundred ['hʌndrəd] num: **one** ~, **a** ~ (ein)hundert; **a** ~ **and one** hundert(und)eins; **two** ~ zweihundert; **hundredth** adj hundertste(r, s) ▷ n (fraction) Hundertstel nt; **hundredweight** n Zentner m (50,8 kg)
hung [hʌŋ] pt, pp of **hang**
Hungarian [hʌŋ'gɛərɪən] adj ungarisch ▷ n (person) Ungar(in) m(f); (language) Ungarisch nt; **Hungary** ['hʌŋgərɪ] n Ungarn nt
hunger ['hʌŋgə°] n Hunger m; **hungry** ['hʌŋgrɪ] adj hungrig; **to be** ~ Hunger haben
hunk [hʌŋk] n (fam) gut gebauter Mann; **hunky** ['hʌŋkɪ] adj (fam) gut gebaut
hunt [hʌnt] n Jagd f; (search) Suche f (for nach) ▷ vt, vi jagen; (search) suchen (for nach); **hunting** n Jagen nt, Jagd f
hurdle ['hɜːdl] n (a. fig) Hürde f; **the 400m ~s** der 400m-Hürdenlauf
hurl [hɜːl] vt schleudern
hurricane ['hʌrɪkən] n Orkan m
hurried ['hʌrɪd] adj eilig; **hurry** ['hʌrɪ] n Eile f; **to be in a** ~ es eilig haben; **there's no** ~ es eilt nicht ▷ vi sich beeilen; ~ (**up**) mach schnell! ▷ vt antreiben
hurt [hɜːt] vt wehtun +dat; (wound: person, feelings) verletzen; **I've** ~ **my arm** ich habe mir am Arm wehgetan ▷ vi wehtun; **my arm** ~**s** mir tut der Arm weh

h

husband ['hʌzbənd] n Ehemann m

husky ['hʌskɪ] adj rau ▷ n Schlittenhund m

hut [hʌt] n Hütte f

hyacinth ['haɪəsɪnθ] n Hyazinthe f

hybrid ['haɪbrɪd] n Kreuzung f

hydroelectric ['haɪdrəʊ'lektrɪk] adj: ~ power station Wasserkraftwerk nt

hydrofoil ['haɪdrəʊfɔɪl] n Tragflächenboot nt

hydrogen ['haɪdrədʒən] n Wasserstoff m

hygiene ['haɪdʒiːn] n Hygiene f; **hygienic** [haɪ'dʒiːnɪk] adj hygienisch

hymn [hɪm] n Kirchenlied nt

hyperlink ['haɪpəlɪŋk] n Hyperlink m; **hypermarket** n Großmarkt m; **hypersensitive** adj überempfindlich

hyphen ['haɪfən] n Bindestrich m

hypnosis [hɪp'nəʊsɪs] n Hypnose f; **hypnotize** ['hɪpnətaɪz] vt hypnotisieren

hypochondriac [haɪpəʊ'kɒndrɪæk] n eingebildete(r) Kranke(r), eingebildete Kranke

hypocrisy ['hɪ'pɒkrəsɪ] n Heuchelei f; **hypocrite** ['hɪpəkrɪt] n Heuchler(in) m(f)

hypodermic [haɪpə'dɜːmɪk] adj, n: ~ (**needle**) Spritze f

hypothetical [haɪpəʊ'θetɪkəl] adj hypothetisch

hysteria [hɪ'stɪərɪə] n Hysterie f; **hysterical** [hɪ'sterɪkəl] adj hysterisch; (amusing) zum Totlachen

---

I [aɪ] pron ich

ice [aɪs] n Eis nt ▷ vt (cake) glasieren; **iceberg** n Eisberg m; **iceberg lettuce** n Eisbergsalat m; **icebox** n (US) Kühlschrank m; **icecold** adj eiskalt; **ice cream** n Eis nt; **ice cube** n Eiswürfel m; **iced** adj eisgekühlt; (coffee, tea) Eis-; (cake) glasiert; **ice hockey** n Eishockey nt

Iceland ['aɪslənd] n Island nt; **Icelander** n Isländer(in) m(f); **Icelandic** [aɪs'lændɪk] adj isländisch ▷ n (language) Isländisch nt

ice lolly ['aɪslɒlɪ] n (Brit) Eis nt am Stiel; **ice rink** n Kunsteisbahn f; **ice skating** n Schlittschuhlaufen nt

icing ['aɪsɪŋ] n (on cake) Zuckerguss m

icon ['aɪkɒn] n Ikone f; (Inform) Icon nt, Programmsymbol nt

icy ['aɪsɪ] adj (slippery) vereist; (cold) eisig

I'd [aɪd] contr of **I would**; **I had**

ID abbr = **identification** Ausweis m

idea [aɪ'dɪə] n Idee f; **(I've) no ~** (ich habe) keine Ahnung; **that's my ~ of ...** so stelle ich mir ... vor

ideal [aɪ'dɪəl] n Ideal nt ▷ adj ideal; **ideally** adv ideal; (before statement) idealerweise

identical [aɪ'dentɪkəl] adj identisch; **~ twins** eineiige Zwillinge

identify [aɪ'dentɪfaɪ] vt identifizieren; **identity** [aɪ'dentɪtɪ] n Identität f; **identity card** n Personalausweis m

idiom ['ɪdɪəm] n Redewendung f; **idiomatic** adj idiomatisch

idiot ['ɪdɪət] n Idiot(in) m(f)

idle ['aɪdl] adj (doing nothing) untätig; (worker) unbeschäftigt; (machines) außer Betrieb; (lazy) faul; (promise, threat) leer

idol ['aɪdl] n Idol nt; **idolize** ['aɪdəlaɪz] vt vergöttern

idyllic [ɪ'dɪlɪk] adj idyllisch

i.e. abbr = **id est** d.h.

O KEYWORD

if [ɪf] conj 1 wenn; (in case also) falls; **if I were you** wenn ich Sie wäre
2 (although) **(even) if** (selbst o auch) wenn
3 (whether) ob
4 **if so/not** wenn ja/nicht; **if only ...** wenn ... doch nur ...; **if only I could** wenn ich doch nur könnte; see also **as**

ignition [ɪg'nɪʃən] n Zündung f; **ignition key** n (Auto) Zündschlüssel m

ignorance ['ɪgnərəns] n Unwissenheit f; **ignorant** adj

unwissend; **ignore** [ɪg'nɔː°] vt ignorieren, nicht beachten

I'll [aɪl] contr of **I will**; **I shall**

ill [ɪl] adj krank; **~ at ease** unbehaglich

illegal [ɪ'liːgəl] adj illegal

illegitimate [ɪlɪ'dʒɪtɪmət] adj unzulässig; (child) unehelich

illiterate [ɪ'lɪtərət] adj: **to be ~** Analphabet(in) sein

illness ['ɪlnəs] n Krankheit f

illuminate [ɪ'luːmɪneɪt] vt beleuchten; **illuminating** adj (remark) aufschlussreich

illusion [ɪ'luːʒən] n Illusion f; **to be under the ~ that ...** sich einbilden, dass ...

illustrate ['ɪləstreɪt] vt illustrieren; **illustration** n Abbildung f, Bild nt

I'm [aɪm] contr of **I am**

image ['ɪmɪdʒ] n Bild nt; (public ~) Image nt; **imaginable** [ɪ'mædʒɪnəbl] adj denkbar; **imaginary** [ɪ'mædʒɪnərɪ] adj eingebildet; **~ world** Fantasiewelt f; **imagination** [ɪmædʒɪ'neɪʃən] n Fantasie f; (mistaken) Einbildung f; **imaginative** [ɪ'mædʒɪnətɪv] adj fantasievoll; **imagine** [ɪ'mædʒɪn] vt sich vorstellen; (wrongly) sich einbilden; **~! stell dir vor!**

imbecile ['ɪmbəsiːl] n Trottel m

imitate ['ɪmɪteɪt] vt nachahmen, nachmachen; **imitation** n Nachahmung f ▷ adj imitiert, Kunst-

immaculate [ɪ'mækjulɪt] adj tadellos; (spotless) makellos

immature [ɪmə'tjuə°] adj unreif

immediate [ɪ'miːdɪət] adj unmittelbar; (instant) sofortig; (reply) umgehend; **immediately** adv sofort

immense, immensely [ɪ'mens, -lɪ] adj, adv riesig, enorm

immersion heater [ɪˈmɜːʃn
hiːtə] n Boiler m
immigrant [ˈɪmɪɡrənt] n Ein-
wanderer m, Einwanderin f;
immigration [ɪmɪˈɡreɪʃən] n
Einwanderung f; (facility)
Einwanderungskontrolle f
immobilize [ɪˈməʊbɪlaɪz] vt
lähmen; **immobilizer** n (Auto)
Wegfahrsperre f
immoral [ɪˈmɒrəl] adj
unmoralisch
immortal [ɪˈmɔːtl] adj
unsterblich
immune [ɪˈmjuːn] adj (Med)
immun (from, to gegen); **immune
system** n Immunsystem nt
impact [ˈɪmpækt] n Aufprall m;
(effect) Auswirkung f (on auf +akk)
impatience [ɪmˈpeɪʃəns] n
Ungeduld f; **impatient**,
impatiently adj, adv ungeduldig
impeccable [ɪmˈpekəbl] adj
tadellos
impede [ɪmˈpiːd] vt behindern
imperative [ɪmˈperətɪv] adj
unbedingt erforderlich ▷ n (Ling)
Imperativ m
imperfect [ɪmˈpɜːfɪkt] adj
unvollkommen; (goods) fehlerhaft
▷ n (Ling) Imperfekt nt;
imperfection [ɪmpəˈfekʃən] n
Unvollkommenheit f; (fault) Fehler
m
imperial [ɪmˈpɪərɪəl] adj kaiser-
lich, Reichs-; **imperialism** n
Imperialismus m
impertinence [ɪmˈpɜːtɪnəns] n
Unverschämtheit f, Zumutung f;
impertinent adj unverschämt
implant [ˈɪmplɑːnt] n (Med)
Implantat nt
implausible [ɪmˈplɔːzəbl] adj
unglaubwürdig
implement [ˈɪmplɪmənt] n
Werkzeug nt, Gerät nt
▷ [ˈɪmplɪment] vt durchführen

implication [ɪmplɪˈkeɪʃən] n
Folge f, Auswirkung f; (logical)
Schlussfolgerung f; **implicit**
[ɪmˈplɪsɪt] adj implizit,
unausgesprochen; **imply**
[ɪmˈplaɪ] vt (indicate) andeuten;
(mean) bedeuten; **are you ~ing
that ...** wollen Sie damit sagen,
dass ...
impolite [ɪmpəˈlaɪt] adj
unhöflich
import [ɪmˈpɔːt] vt einführen,
importieren ▷ n [ˈɪmpɔːt] Einfuhr f, Import m
importance [ɪmˈpɔːtəns] n
Bedeutung f; **of no ~** unwichtig;
important adj wichtig (to sb für
jdn); (significant) bedeutend;
(influential) einflussreich
import duty [ˈɪmpɔːt djuːtɪ] n
Einfuhrzoll m; **import licence** n
Einfuhrgenehmigung f
impose [ɪmˈpəʊz] vt (conditions)
auferlegen (on dat); (penalty,
sanctions) verhängen (on gegen);
imposing [ɪmˈpəʊzɪŋ] adj eindrucksvoll, imposant
impossible [ɪmˈpɒsəbl] adj
unmöglich
impotence [ˈɪmpətəns] n
Machtlosigkeit f; (sexual)
Impotenz f; **impotent** adj
machtlos; (sexually) impotent
impractical [ɪmˈpræktɪkəl] adj
unpraktisch; (plan)
undurchführbar
impress [ɪmˈpres] vt beeindrucken; **impression** [ɪmˈpreʃən]
n Eindruck m; **impressive** adj
eindrucksvoll
imprison [ɪmˈprɪzn] vt inhaf-
tieren; **imprisonment** n
Inhaftierung f
improbability [ɪmprɒbəˈbɪlɪtɪ]
n Unwahrscheinlichkeit f;
improbable [ɪmˈprɒbəbl] adj
unwahrscheinlich

improper [ɪmˈprɔpə°] *adj*
(*indecent*) unanständig; (*use*)
unsachgemäß

improve [ɪmˈpruːv] *vt*
verbessern ▷ *vi* sich verbessern,
besser werden; (*patient*)
Fortschritte machen;
improvement *n* Verbesserung *f*
(*in* +gen; *on* gegenüber); (*in*
appearance) Verschönerung *f*

improvise [ˈɪmprəvaɪz] *vt, vi*
improvisieren

impulse [ˈɪmpʌls] *n* Impuls *m*;
impulsive [ɪmˈpʌlsɪv] *adj*
impulsiv

O **KEYWORD**

in [ɪn] *prep* **1** (*indicating place,
position*) in +*dat*; (*with motion*) in
+*akk*: **in here/there** hier/dort; **in
London** in London; **in the United
States** in den Vereinigten Staaten
2 (*indicating time: during*) in +*dat*:
in summer im Sommer; **in 1988** (im
Jahre) 1988; **in the afternoon**
nachmittags, am Nachmittag
3 (*indicating time: in the space of*)
innerhalb von; **I'll see you in 2
weeks** *o* **in 2 weeks' time** ich sehe
dich/Sie in zwei Wochen
4 (*indicating manner, circumstances,
state etc*) in +*dat*: **in the sun/rain**
in der Sonne/im Regen; **in
English/French** auf
Englisch/Französisch; **in a
loud/soft voice** mit lauter/leiser
Stimme
5 (*with ratios, numbers*) **1 in 10** jeder
Zehnte; **20 pence in the pound** 20
Pence pro Pfund; **they lined up in
twos** sie stellten sich in
Zweierreihe auf
6 (*referring to people, works*) **the
disease is common in children**
die Krankheit ist bei Kindern
häufig; **in Dickens** bei Dickens;

we have a loyal friend in him er
ist uns ein treuer Freund
7 (*indicating profession etc*) **to be in
teaching/the army** Lehrer,
Lehrerin/beim Militär sein; **to be
in publishing** im Verlagswesen
arbeiten
8 (*with present participle*) **in saying
this, I ...** wenn ich das sage, ... ich;
in accepting this view, he ... weil
er diese Meinung akzeptierte, ...
er
▷ *adv*: **to be in** (*person: at home,
work*) da sein; (*train, ship, plane*)
angekommen sein; (*in fashion*) in
sein; **to ask sb in** jdn hereinbitten;
to run/limp *etc* **in**
hereingerannt/gehumpelt *etc*
kommen
▷ *n*: **the ins and outs** (*of proposal,
situation etc*) die Feinheiten

inability [ɪnəˈbɪlɪtɪ] *n* Unfähig-
keit *f*

inaccessible [ɪnækˈsesəbl] *adj*
(*a. fig*) unzugänglich

inaccurate [ɪnˈækjʊrɪt] *adj*
ungenau

inadequate [ɪnˈædɪkwət] *adj*
unzulänglich

inapplicable [ɪnəˈplɪkəbl] *adj*
unzutreffend

inappropriate [ɪnəˈprəʊprɪət]
adj unpassend; (*clothing*)
ungeeignet; (*remark*)
unangebracht

inborn [ˈɪnˈbɔːn] *adj* angeboren

incapable [ɪnˈkeɪpəbl] *adj*
unfähig (*of zu*); **to be ~ of doing
sth** nicht imstande sein, etw zu
tun

incense [ˈɪnsens] *n* Weihrauch
m

incentive [ɪnˈsentɪv] *n* Anreiz *m*

incessant, incessantly [ɪnˈsesnt,
-lɪ] *adj, adv* unaufhörlich

incest [ˈɪnsest] *n* Inzest *m*

inch [ɪntʃ] n Zoll m (2,54 cm)

incident ['ɪnsɪdənt] n Vorfall m; (disturbance) Zwischenfall m; **incidentally** [ɪnsɪ'dentlɪ] adv nebenbei bemerkt, übrigens

inclination [ɪnklɪ'neɪʃən] n Neigung f; **inclined** ['ɪnklaɪnd] adj: **to be ~ to do sth** dazu neigen, etw zu tun

include [ɪn'kluːd] vt einschließen; (on list, in group) aufnehmen; **including** prep einschließlich (+gen); **not ~ service** Bedienung nicht inbegriffen; **inclusive** [ɪn'kluːsɪv] adj einschließlich (of +gen); (price) Pauschal-

incoherent [ɪnkəʊ'hɪərənt] adj zusammenhanglos

income ['ɪnkʌm] n Einkommen nt; (from business) Einkünfte pl; **income tax** n Einkommensteuer f; (on wages, salary) Lohnsteuer f; **incoming** ['ɪnkʌmɪŋ] adj ankommend; (mail) eingehend

incompatible [ɪnkəm'pætəbl] adj unvereinbar; (people) unverträglich; (Inform) nicht kompatibel

incompetent [ɪn'kɒmpɪtənt] adj unfähig

incomplete [ɪnkəm'pliːt] adj unvollständig

incomprehensible [ɪnkɒmprɪ'hensəbl] adj unverständlich

inconceivable [ɪnkən'siːvəbl] adj unvorstellbar

inconsiderate [ɪnkən'sɪdərət] adj rücksichtslos

inconsistency [ɪnkən'sɪstənsɪ] n Inkonsequenz f; (contradictory) Widersprüchlichkeit f; **inconsistent** adj inkonsequent; (contradictory) widersprüchlich; (work) unbeständig

inconvenience [ɪnkən'viːnɪəns] n Unannehmlichkeit f; (trouble) Umstände pl; **inconvenient** adj ungünstig, unbequem; (time) **it's ~ for me** es kommt mir ungelegen; **if it's not too ~ for you** wenn es dir/Ihnen passt

incorporate [ɪn'kɔːpəreɪt] vt aufnehmen (into in +akk); (include) enthalten

incorrect [ɪnkə'rekt] adj falsch; (improper) inkorrekt

increase ['ɪnkriːs] n Zunahme f (in an +dat); (in amount, speed) Erhöhung f (in +gen) ▷ [ɪn'kriːs] vt (price, taxes, salary, speed etc) erhöhen; (wealth) vermehren; (number) vergrößern; (business) erweitern ▷ vi zunehmen (in an +dat); (prices) steigen; (in size) größer werden; (in number) sich vermehren; **increasingly** [ɪn'kriːsɪŋlɪ] adv zunehmend

incredible, incredibly [ɪn'kredəbl, -blɪ] adj, adv unglaublich; (very good) fantastisch

incredulous [ɪn'kredjʊləs] adj ungläubig, skeptisch

incriminate [ɪn'krɪmɪneɪt] vt belasten

incubator ['ɪnkjʊbeɪtə*] n Brutkasten m

incurable [ɪn'kjʊərəbl] adj unheilbar

indecent [ɪn'diːsnt] adj unanständig

indecisive [ɪndɪ'saɪsɪv] adj (person) unentschlossen; (result) nicht entscheidend

indeed [ɪn'diːd] adv tatsächlich; (as answer) allerdings; **very hot ~** wirklich sehr heiß

indefinite [ɪn'defɪnɪt] adj unbestimmt; (postpone) auf unbestimmte Zeit

independence [ɪndɪ'pendəns]
n Unabhängigkeit f

- INDEPENDENCE DAY

- Der **Independence Day**, der 4.
  Juli, ist in den USA ein
  gesetzlicher Feiertag zum
  Gedenken an die
  Unabhängigkeitserklärung am
  4. Juli 1776, mit der die 13
  amerikanischen Kolonien ihre
  Freiheit und Unabhängigkeit
  von Großbritannien erklärten.

independent [ɪndɪ'pendənt]
adj unabhängig (of von); (person)
selbstständig
indescribable [ɪndɪ'skraɪbəbl]
adj unbeschreiblich
index ['ɪndeks] n Index m,
Verzeichnis nt; **index finger** n
Zeigefinger m
India ['ɪndɪə] n Indien nt; **Indian**
['ɪndɪən] adj indisch; (Native
American) indianisch ▷ n Inder(in)
m(f); (Native American) Indianer(in)
m(f); **Indian Ocean** n Indischer
Ozean; **Indian summer** n Spät-
sommer m, Altweibersommer m
indicate ['ɪndɪkeɪt] vt (show)
zeigen; (instrument) anzeigen;
(suggest) hinweisen auf +akk ▷ vi
(Auto) blinken; **indication**
[ɪndɪ'keɪʃn] n (sign) Anzeichen nt
(of für); **indicator** [ˈɪndɪkeɪtəʳ] n
(Auto) Blinker m
indifferent [ɪn'dɪfrənt] adj (not
caring) gleichgültig (to, towards
gegenüber); (mediocre)
mittelmäßig
indigestible [ɪndɪ'dʒestəbl] adj
unverdaulich; **indigestion**
[ɪndɪ'dʒestʃən] n Verdau-
ungsstörung f
indignity [ɪn'dɪgnɪtɪ] n Demütigung f

indirect, indirectly [ɪndɪ'rekt, -lɪ]
adj, adv indirekt
indiscreet [ɪndɪ'skriːt] adj
indiskret
indispensable [ɪndɪ'spensəbl]
adj unentbehrlich
indisposed [ɪndɪ'spəʊzd] adj
unwohl
indisputable [ɪndɪ'spjuːtəbl]
adj unbestreitbar; (evidence)
unanfechtbar
individual [ɪndɪ'vɪdjʊəl] n
Einzelne(r) mf ▷ adj einzeln;
(distinctive) eigen, individuell;
~ **case** Einzelfall m; **individually**
adv (separately) einzeln
Indonesia [ɪndəʊ'niːzjə] n
Indonesien nt
indoor ['ɪndɔː'] adj (shoes)
Haus-; (plant, games) Zimmer-;
(Sport: football, championship, record
etc) Hallen-; **indoors** adv drinnen,
im Haus
indulge [ɪn'dʌldʒ] vi: **to ~ in sth**
sich dat etw gönnen; **indulgence**
n Nachsicht f; (enjoyment)
(übermäßig) Genuss; (luxury)
Luxus m; **indulgent** adj
nachsichtig (with gegenüber)
industrial [ɪn'dʌstrɪəl] adj
Industrie-, industriell; ~ **estate**
Industriegebiet nt; **industry**
['ɪndəstrɪ] n Industrie f
inedible [ɪn'edɪbl] adj nicht
essbar, ungenießbar
ineffective [ɪnɪ'fektɪv] adj
unwirksam, wirkungslos;
inefficient [ɪnɪ'fɪʃnt] adj unwirksam; (use,
machine) unwirtschaftlich; (method
etc) unrationell
ineligible [ɪn'elɪdʒəbl] adj nicht
berechtigt (for zu)
inequality [ɪnɪ'kwɒlɪtɪ] n
Ungleichheit f
inevitable [ɪn'evɪtəbl] adj
unvermeidlich; **inevitably** adv
zwangsläufig

inexcusable [ɪnɪks'kjuːzəbl]
adj unverzeihlich; **that's ~** das
kann man nicht verzeihen

inexpensive [ɪnɪks'pɛnsɪv] *adj*
preisgünstig

inexperience [ɪnɪks'pɪərɪəns]
n Unerfahrenheit *f*;
inexperienced *adj* unerfahren

inexplicable [ɪnɪks'plɪkəbl] *adj*
unerklärlich

infallible [ɪn'fælɪbl] *adj*
unfehlbar

infamous ['ɪnfəməs] *adj* (person)
berüchtigt (*for* wegen); (deed)
niederträchtig

infancy ['ɪnfənsɪ] *n* frühe
Kindheit; **infant** ['ɪnfənt] *n*
Säugling *m*; (small child)
Kleinkind *nt*; **infant school** *n*
Vorschule *f*

infatuated [ɪn'fætjʊeɪtɪd] *adj*
vernarrt (*with* in +*akk*), verknallt
(*with* in +*akk*)

infect [ɪn'fɛkt] *vt* (person)
anstecken; (wound) infizieren;
infection [ɪn'fɛkʃən] *n* Infektion
f; **infectious** [ɪn'fɛkʃəs] *adj*
ansteckend

inferior [ɪn'fɪərɪə] *adj* (in quality)
minderwertig; (in rank)
untergeordnet; **inferiority**
[ɪnfɪərɪ'ɒrɪtɪ] *n* Minderwertigkeit
f; **~ complex** Minderwertigkeitskomplex *m*

infertile [ɪn'fɜːtaɪl] *adj*
unfruchtbar

infidelity [ɪnfɪ'dɛlɪtɪ] *n* Untreue
f

infinite ['ɪnfɪnɪt] *adj* unendlich

infinitive [ɪn'fɪnɪtɪv] *n* (Ling)
Infinitiv *m*

infinity [ɪn'fɪnɪtɪ] *n* Unend-
lichkeit *f*

infirmary [ɪn'fɜːmərɪ] *n*
Krankenhaus *nt*

inflame [ɪn'fleɪm] *vt* (Med)
entzünden; **inflammation**

[ɪnflə'meɪʃən] *n* (Med)
Entzündung *f*

inflatable [ɪn'fleɪtəbl] *adj* auf-
blasbar; **~ dinghy** Schlauchboot
nt; **inflate** [ɪn'fleɪt] *vt*
aufpumpen; (by blowing)
aufblasen; (prices) hochtreiben

inflation [ɪn'fleɪʃən] *n* Inflation
f

inflexible [ɪn'flɛksəbl] *adj*
unflexibel

inflict [ɪn'flɪkt] *vt*: **to ~ sth on sb**
jdm etw zufügen; (punishment)
jdm etw auferlegen; (wound) jdm
etw beibringen

in-flight [ɪn'flaɪt] *adj* (catering,
magazine) Bord-; **~ entertainment**
Bordprogramm *nt*

influence ['ɪnflʊəns] *n* Einfluss
m (*on auf* +*akk*) ▷ *vt* beeinflussen;
influential [ɪnflʊ'ɛnʃəl] *adj*
einflussreich

influenza [ɪnflʊ'ɛnzə] *n* Grippe
f

inform [ɪn'fɔːm] *vt* informieren
(*of, about* über +*akk*); **to keep sb
~ed** jdn auf dem Laufenden halten

informal [ɪn'fɔːməl] *adj* zwanglos, ungezwungen

information [ɪnfə'meɪʃən] *n*
Auskunft *f*, Informationen *pl*; **for
your ~** zu deiner/Ihrer
Information; **further ~** weitere
Informationen, Weiteres;
information desk *n*
Auskunftsschalter *m*; **information
technology** *n* Informations-
technik *f*; **informative**
[ɪn'fɔːmətɪv] *adj* aufschlussreich

infra-red [ɪnfrə'rɛd] *adj* infrarot

infrastructure ['ɪnfrəstrʌktʃə] *n* Infrastruktur
f

infuriate [ɪn'fjʊərɪeɪt] *vt* wütend
machen; **infuriating** *adj* äußerst
ärgerlich

infusion [ɪn'fjuːʒən] *n* (herbal
tea) Aufguss *m*; (Med) Infusion *f*

ingenious [ɪnˈdʒiːnɪəs] *adj (person)* erfinderisch; *(device)* raffiniert; *(idea)* genial

ingredient [ɪnˈɡriːdɪənt] *n (Gastr)* Zutat *f*

inhabit [ɪnˈhæbɪt] *vt* bewohnen; **inhabitant** *n* Einwohner(in) *m(f)*

inhale [ɪnˈheɪl] *vt* einatmen; *(cigarettes, Med)* inhalieren; **inhaler** *n* Inhalationsgerät *nt*

inherit [ɪnˈherɪt] *vt* erben; **inheritance** *n* Erbe *nt*

inhibited [ɪnˈhɪbɪtɪd] *adj* gehemmt; **inhibition** [ɪnhɪˈbɪʃən] *n* Hemmung *f*

in-house [ˈɪnhaʊs] *adj* intern

inhuman [ɪnˈhjuːmən] *adj* unmenschlich

initial [ɪˈnɪʃəl] *adj* anfänglich; **~ stage** Anfangsstadium *nt* ▷ *vt* mit Initialen unterschreiben; **initially** *adv* anfangs; **initials** *npl* Initialen *pl*

initiative [ɪˈnɪʃətɪv] *n* Initiative *f*

inject [ɪnˈdʒekt] *vt (drug etc)* einspritzen; **to ~ sb with sth** jdm etw (ein)spritzen; **injection** *n* Spritze *f*, Injektion *f*

in-joke [ˈɪndʒəʊk] *n* Insiderwitz *m*

injure [ˈɪndʒəʳ] *vt* verletzen; **to ~ one's leg** sich *dat* das Bein verletzen; **injury** [ˈɪndʒərɪ] *n* Verletzung *f*

injustice [ɪnˈdʒʌstɪs] *n* Ungerechtigkeit *f*

ink [ɪŋk] *n* Tinte *f*; **ink-jet printer** *n* Tintenstrahldrucker *m*

inland [ˈɪnlənd] *adj* Binnen- ▷ *adv* landeinwärts; **inland revenue** *f (Brit)* Finanzamt *nt*

in-laws [ˈɪnlɔːz] *npl (fam)* Schwiegereltern *pl*

inline skates [ˈɪnlaɪnskeɪts] *npl* Inlineskates *pl*, Inliner *pl*

inmate [ˈɪnmeɪt] *n* Insasse *m*

inn [ɪn] *n* Gasthaus *nt*

innate [ɪˈneɪt] *adj* angeboren

inner [ˈɪnəʳ] *adj* innere(r, s); **~ city** Innenstadt *f*

innocence [ˈɪnəsns] *n* Unschuld *f*; **innocent** *adj* unschuldig

innovation [ɪnəʊˈveɪʃən] *n* Neuerung *f*

innumerable [ɪˈnjuːmərəbl] *adj* unzählig

inoculate [ɪˈnɒkjʊleɪt] *vt* impfen *(against* gegen); **inoculation** [ɪnɒkjʊˈleɪʃən] *n* Impfung *f*

in-patient [ˈɪnpeɪʃənt] *n* stationärer Patient, stationäre Patientin

input [ˈɪnpʊt] *n (contribution)* Beitrag *m*; *(Inform)* Eingabe *f*

inquest [ˈɪnkwest] *n* gerichtliche Untersuchung (einer Todesursache)

inquire [ɪnˈkwaɪəʳ] *see* enquire; **inquiry** [ɪnˈkwaɪərɪ] *see* enquiry

insane [ɪnˈseɪn] *adj* wahnsinnig; *(Med)* geisteskrank; **insanity** [ɪnˈsænɪtɪ] *n* Wahnsinn *m*

insatiable [ɪnˈseɪʃəbl] *adj* unersättlich

inscription [ɪnˈskrɪpʃən] *n (on stone etc)* Inschrift *f*

insect [ˈɪnsekt] *n* Insekt *nt*; **insecticide** [ɪnˈsektɪsaɪd] *n* Insektenbekämpfungsmittel *nt*; **insect repellent** *n* Insektenschutzmittel *nt*

insecure [ɪnsɪˈkjʊəʳ] *adj (person)* unsicher; *(shelves)* instabil

insensitive [ɪnˈsensɪtɪv] *adj* unempfindlich *(to* gegen); *(unfeeling)* gefühllos; **insensitivity** [ɪnsensɪˈtɪvɪtɪ] *n* Unempfindlichkeit *f (to* gegen); *(unfeeling nature)* Gefühllosigkeit *f*

inseparable [ɪnˈsepərəbl] *adj* unzertrennlich

insert [ɪnˈsɜːt] *vt* einfügen; *(coin)* einwerfen; *(key etc)* hineinstecken

▷ *n* (in magazine) Beilage *f*;
insertion *n* (in text) Einfügen *nt*
inside ['ın'saıd] *n*: **the ~** das
Innere; (surface) die Innenseite;
from the ~ von innen ▷ *adj*
innere(r, s), Innen-; **~ lane** (Auto)
Innenspur *f*; (Sport) Innenbahn *f*
▷ *adv* (place) innen; (direction)
hinein; **to go ~** hineingehen
▷ *prep* (place) innen in +dat; (into) in +akk
... hinein; (time, within) innerhalb
+gen; **inside out** *adv* verkehrt
herum; (know) in- und auswendig;
insider *n* Eingeweihte(r) *mf*,
Insider(in) *m(f)*
insight ['ınsaɪt] *n* Einblick *m*
(into in +akk)
insignificant [ınsıg'nıfıkənt]
adj unbedeutend
insincere [ınsın'sıə°] *adj* un-
aufrichtig, falsch
insinuate [ın'sınjʊeɪt] *vt*
andeuten; **insinuation**
[ınsınjʊ'eɪʃən] *n* Andeutung *f*
insist [ın'sıst] *vi* darauf bestehen;
to ~ on sth auf etw *dat* bestehen;
insistent *adj* hartnäckig
insoluble [ın'sɒljʊbl] *adj*
unlösbar
insomnia [ın'sɒmnıə] *n* Schlaf-
losigkeit *f*
inspect [ın'spekt] *vt* prüfen,
kontrollieren; **inspection** *n*
Prüfung *f*; (check) Kontrolle *f*;
inspector *n* (police ~)
Inspektor(in) *m(f)*; (senior)
Kommissar(in) *m(f)*; (on bus etc)
Kontrolleur(in) *m(f)*
inspiration [ınspı'reıʃən] *n*
Inspiration *f*; **inspire** [ın'spaɪə°]
vt (respect) einflößen (in *dat*);
(person) inspirieren
install [ın'stɔːl] *vt* (software)
installieren; (furnishings) einbauen
installment, **instalment**
[ın'stɔːlmənt] *n* Rate *f*; (of story)
Folge *f*; **to pay in ~s** auf Raten

zahlen; **installment plan** *n* (US)
Ratenkauf *m*
instance ['ınstəns] *n* (of
discrimination) Fall *m*; (example)
Beispiel *nt* (of/für +akk); **for ~** zum
Beispiel
instant ['ınstənt] *n* Augenblick
m ▷ *adj* sofortig; **instant coffee**
n löslicher Kaffee *m*; **instantly** *adv*
sofort
instead [ın'sted] *adv* stattdes-
sen; **instead of** *prep* (an)statt
+gen; **~ of me** an meiner Stelle;
~ of going (an)statt zu gehen
instinct ['ınstıŋkt] *n* Instinkt *m*;
instinctive, instinctively
[ın'stıŋktıv, -lı] *adj, adv*
instinktiv
institute ['ınstıtjuːt] *n* Institut
nt; **institution** [ınstı'tjuːʃən] *n*
(organisation) Institution *f*,
Einrichtung *f*; (home) Anstalt *f*
instruct [ın'strʌkt] *vt* anweisen;
instruction [ın'strʌkʃən] *n*
(teaching) Unterricht *m*; (command)
Anweisung *f*; **~s for use**
Gebrauchsanweisung *f*;
instructor *n* Lehrer(in) *m(f)*; (US)
Dozent(in) *m(f)*
instrument ['ınstrəmənt] *n*
Instrument *nt*; **instrument panel**
n Armaturenbrett *nt*
insufficient [ınsə'fıʃənt] *adj*
ungenügend
insulate ['ınsjʊleıt] *vt* (Elec)
isolieren; **insulating tape** *n*
Isolierband *nt*; **insulation**
[ınsjʊ'leıʃən] *n* Isolierung *f*
insulin ['ınsjʊlın] *n* Insulin *nt*
insult ['ınsʌlt] *n* Beleidigung *f*
▷ [ın'sʌlt] *vt* beleidigen;
insulting [ın'sʌltıŋ] *adj*
beleidigend
insurance [ın'ʃʊərəns] *n* Versicherung *f*; **~ company** *n*
Versicherungsgesellschaft *f*;
~ policy Versicherungspolice *f*;

insure [ɪnˈʃʊəʳ] vt versichern (against gegen)

intact [ɪnˈtækt] adj intakt

intake [ˈɪnteɪk] n Aufnahme f

integrate [ˈɪntɪˈɡreɪt] vt integrieren (into in +akk); **integration** n Integration f

integrity [ɪnˈteɡrɪtɪ] n Integrität f, Ehrlichkeit f

intellect [ˈɪntɪlekt] n Intellekt m; **intellectual** [ˈɪntɪˈlektjʊəl] adj intellektuell; (interests etc) geistig

intelligence [ɪnˈtelɪdʒəns] n (understanding) Intelligenz f; **intelligent** adj intelligent

intend [ɪnˈtend] vt beabsichtigen; **to ~ to do sth** vorhaben, etw zu tun

intense [ɪnˈtens] adj intensiv; (pressure) enorm; (competition) heftig; **intensity** n Intensität f; **intensive** adj intensiv; **intensive care unit** n Intensivstation f; **intensive course** n Intensivkurs m

intent [ɪnˈtent] adj: **to be ~ on doing sth** fest entschlossen sein, etw zu tun; **intention** [ɪnˈtenʃən] n Absicht f; **intentional**, **intentionally** adj, adv absichtlich

interact [ɪntərˈækt] vi aufeinander einwirken; **interaction** f, Wechselwirkung f; **interactive** adj interaktiv

interchange [ˈɪntətʃeɪndʒ] n (of motorways) Autobahnkreuz nt; **interchangeable** [ɪntəˈtʃeɪndʒəbl] adj austauschbar

intercity [ɪntəˈsɪtɪ] n Intercityzug m, IC m

intercom [ˈɪntəkɒm] n (Gegen)sprechanlage f

intercourse [ˈɪntəkɔːs] n (sexual) Geschlechtsverkehr m

interest [ˈɪntrɪst] n Interesse nt; (Fin: on money) Zinsen pl; (Comm: share) Anteil m; **to be of ~** von Interesse sein (to für) ▷ vt interessieren; **interested** adj interessiert (in an +dat); **to be ~ed in** sich interessieren für; **are you ~ in coming?** hast du Lust, mitzukommen?; **interest-free** adj zinsfrei; **interesting** adj interessant; **interest rate** n ' Zinssatz m

interface [ˈɪntəfeɪs] n (Inform) Schnittstelle f

interfere [ɪntəˈfɪəʳ] vi (meddle) sich einmischen (with, in in +akk); **interference** n Einmischung f; (TV, Radio) Störung f

interior [ɪnˈtɪərɪəʳ] adj Innen-; n Innere(s) nt; (of car) Innenraum m; (of house) Innenausstattung f

intermediate [ɪntəˈmiːdɪət] adj Zwischen-; **~ stage** n Zwischenstadium nt

intermission [ɪntəˈmɪʃən] n Pause f

intern [ɪnˈtɜːn] n Assistent(in) m(f)

internal [ɪnˈtɜːnl] adj innere(r, s); (flight) Inlands-; **~ revenue** n (US) Finanzamt nt; **internally** adv innen; (in body) innerlich

international [ɪntəˈnæʃnəl] adj international; **~ match** n Länderspiel nt; **~ flight** n Auslandsflug m ▷ n (Sport: player) Nationalspieler(in) m(f)

Internet [ˈɪntənet] n (Inform) Internet nt; **Internet access** n Internetzugang m; **Internet auction** n Internetauktion f; **Internet banking** n Onlinebanking nt; **Internet café** n Internetcafé nt; **Internet connection** n Internetanschluss m; **Internet provider** n Internetprovider m

interpret [ɪnˈtɜːprɪt] vi, vt

(translate) dolmetschen; *(explain)* interpretieren; **interpretation** [ɪntɜːprɪˈteɪʃən] n Interpretation f; **interpreter** [ɪnˈtɜːprɪtə°] n Dolmetscher(in) m(f)

interrogate [ɪnˈterəgeɪt] vt verhören; **interrogation** n Verhör nt

interrupt [ɪntəˈrʌpt] vt unterbrechen; **interruption** [ɪntəˈrʌpʃən] n Unterbrechung f

intersection [ɪntəˈsekʃən] n (of roads) Kreuzung f

interstate [ɪntəˈsteɪt] n (US) zwischenstaatlich; **~ highway** = Bundesautobahn f

interval [ˈɪntəvəl] n (space, time) Abstand m; (theatre etc) Pause f

intervene [ɪntəˈviːn] vi eingreifen (in in); **intervention** [ɪntəˈvenʃən] n Eingreifen nt; (Pol) Intervention f

interview [ˈɪntəvjuː] n Interview nt; (for job) Vorstellungsgespräch nt ▷ vt interviewen; (job applicant) ein Vorstellungsgespräch führen mit; **interviewer** n Interviewer(in) m(f)

intestine [ɪnˈtestɪn] n Darm m; **~s** pl Eingeweide pl

intimate [ˈɪntɪmət] adj (friends) vertraut, eng; (atmosphere) gemütlich; (sexually) intim

intimidate [ɪnˈtɪmɪdeɪt] vt einschüchtern; **intimidation** n Einschüchterung f

into [ˈɪntʊ] prep in +akk; (crash) gegen; **to change ~ sth** (turn ~) zu etw werden; (put on) sich dat etw anziehen; **to translate ~ French** ins Französische übersetzen; **to be ~ sth** (fam) auf etw akk stehen

intolerable [ɪnˈtɒlərəbl] adj unerträglich

intolerant [ɪnˈtɒlərənt] adj intolerant

intoxicated [ɪnˈtɒksɪkeɪtɪd] adj betrunken; (fig) berauscht

intricate [ˈɪntrɪkət] adj kompliziert

intrigue [ɪnˈtriːg] vt faszinieren; **intriguing** adj faszinierend, fesselnd

introduce [ɪntrəˈdjuːs] vt (person) vorstellen (to sb jdm); (sth new) einführen (to in +akk); **introduction** [ɪntrəˈdʌkʃən] n Einführung f (to in +akk); (to book) Einleitung f (to zu); (to person) Vorstellung f

introvert [ˈɪntrəʊvɜːt] n Introvertierte(r) mf

intuition [ɪntjuːˈɪʃn] n Intuition f

invade [ɪnˈveɪd] vt einfallen in +akk

invalid [ˈɪnvəlɪd] n Kranke(r) mf; (disabled) Invalide m ▷ adj [ɪnˈvælɪd] (not valid) ungültig

invaluable [ɪnˈvæljʊəbl] adj äußerst wertvoll, unschätzbar

invariably [ɪnˈveərɪəblɪ] adv ständig; (every time) jedes Mal, ohne Ausnahme

invasion [ɪnˈveɪʒən] n Invasion f (of in +akk), Einfall m (of in +akk)

invent [ɪnˈvent] vt erfinden; **invention** [ɪnˈvenʃən] n Erfindung f; **inventor** n Erfinder(in) m(f)

inverted commas [ɪnˈvɜːtɪd ˈkɒmaz] npl Anführungszeichen pl

invest [ɪnˈvest] vt, vi investieren (in +akk)

investigate [ɪnˈvestɪgeɪt] vt untersuchen; **investigation** [ɪnvestɪˈgeɪʃən] n Untersuchung f (into +gen)

investment [ɪnˈvestmənt] n Investition f; **it's a good ~** es ist eine gute Anlage; (it'll be useful) es macht sich bezahlt

invigorating [ɪnˈvɪɡəreɪtɪŋ] *adj*
erfrischend, belebend; *(tonic)*
stärkend

invisible [ɪnˈvɪzəbl] *adj*
unsichtbar

invitation [ɪnvɪˈteɪʃən] *n* Einladung *f*; **invite** [ɪnˈvaɪt] *vt*
einladen

invoice [ˈɪnvɔɪs] *n (bill)*
Rechnung *f*

involuntary [ɪnˈvɒləntərɪ] *adj*
unbeabsichtigt

involve [ɪnˈvɒlv] *vt* verwickeln
(in sth in etw akk); *(entail)* zur Folge
haben; **to be ~d in sth** *(participate
in)* an etw *dat* beteiligt sein; **I'm
not ~d** *(affected)* ich bin nicht
betroffen

inward [ˈɪnwəd] *adj* innere(r, s);
inwardly *adv* innerlich; **inwards**
adv nach innen

iodine [ˈaɪədiːn] *n* Jod *nt*

IOU [aɪəʊˈjuː] *abbr* = **I owe you**
Schuldschein *m*

iPod® [ˈaɪpɒd] *n* iPod® *m*

IQ *abbr* = **intelligence quotient** IQ
m

Iran [ɪˈrɑːn] *n* der Iran

Iraq [ɪˈrɑːk] *n* der Irak

Ireland [ˈaɪələnd] *n* Irland *nt*

iris [ˈaɪrɪs] *n (flower)* Schwertlilie
f; *(of eye)* Iris *f*

Irish [ˈaɪrɪʃ] *adj* irisch; **~ coffee**
Irish Coffee *m*; **~ Sea** die Irische
See ▷ *n (language)* Irisch *nt*; **the
~ pl** die Iren *pl*; **Irishman** *(pl* **-men)**
n Ire *m*; **Irishwoman** *(pl* **-women)**
n Irin *f*

iron [ˈaɪən] *n* Eisen *nt*; *(for ironing)*
Bügeleisen *nt* ▷ *adj* eisern ▷ *vt*
bügeln

ironic(al) [aɪˈrɒnɪk(əl)] *adj*
ironisch

ironing board *n* Bügelbrett *nt*

irony [ˈaɪrənɪ] *n* Ironie *f*

irrational [ɪˈræʃənl] *adj*
irrational

irregular [ɪˈreɡjʊlə°] *adj*
unregelmäßig; *(shape)*
ungleichmäßig

irrelevant [ɪˈreləvənt] *adj*
belanglos, irrelevant

irreplaceable [ɪrɪˈpleɪsəbl] *adj*
unersetzlich

irresistible [ɪrɪˈzɪstəbl] *adj*
unwiderstehlich

irrespective of [ɪrɪˈspektɪv ɒv]
prep ungeachtet +gen

irresponsible [ɪrɪˈspɒnsəbl] *adj*
verantwortungslos

irretrievable [ɪrɪˈtriːvəbl] *adv*
unwiederbringlich; *(loss)*
unersetzlich

irritable [ˈɪrɪtəbl] *adj* reizbar;
irritate [ˈɪrɪteɪt] *vt (annoy)*
ärgern; *(deliberately)* reizen;
irritation [ɪrɪˈteɪʃən] *n (anger)*
Ärger *m*; *(Med)* Reizung *f*

IRS *abbr* = **Internal Revenue
Service** *(US)* Finanzamt *nt*

is [ɪz] *present of* **be** ist

Islam [ˈɪzlɑːm] *n* Islam *m*; **Islamic**
[ɪzˈlæmɪk] *adj* islamisch

island [ˈaɪlənd] *n* Insel *f*; **Isle**
[aɪl] *n (in names)* **the ~ of Man** die
Insel Man; **the ~ of Wight** die Insel
Wight; **the British ~s** die
Britischen Inseln

isn't [ˈɪznt] *contr of* **is not**

isolate [ˈaɪsəleɪt] *vt* isolieren;
isolated *adj (remote)* abgelegen;
(cut off) abgeschnitten *(from von)*;
an ~ case ein Einzelfall; **isolation**
[aɪsəˈleɪʃən] *n* Isolierung *f*

Israel [ˈɪzreɪl] *n* Israel *nt*; **Israeli**
[ɪzˈreɪlɪ] *adj* israelisch ▷ *n* Israeli
m of

issue [ˈɪʃuː] *n (matter)* Frage *f*;
(problem) Problem *nt*; *(subject)*
Thema *nt*; *(of newspaper etc)*
Ausgabe *f*; **that's not the ~** darum
geht es nicht ▷ *vt* ausgeben; *(document)* ausstellen; *(orders)*
erteilen; *(book)* herausgeben

it [ɪt] *pron* **1** (*specific: subject*) er/sie/es; (*direct object*) ihn/sie/es; (*indirect object*) ihm/ihr/ihm; **about/from/in/of it** darüber/davon/darin/davon **2** (*impers*) es; **it's raining** es regnet; **it's Friday tomorrow** morgen ist Freitag; **who is it? — it's me** wer ist da? — ich (bin's)

IT *abbr* = **information technology** IT *f*

Italian [ɪˈtæljən] *adj* italienisch ▷ *n* Italiener(in) *m(f)*; (*language*) Italienisch *nt*

italic [ɪˈtælɪk] *adj* kursiv ▷ *npl*: **in ~s** kursiv

Italy [ˈɪtəlɪ] *n* Italien *nt*

itch [ɪtʃ] *n* Juckreiz *m*; **I have an ~** mich juckt es ▷ *vi* jucken; **he is ~ing to ...** es juckt ihn, zu ...; **itchy** *adj* juckend

it'd [ˈɪtd] *contr* of **it would**; **it had**

item [ˈaɪtəm] *n* (*article*) Gegenstand *m*; (*in catalogue*) Artikel *m*; (*on list, in accounts*) Posten *m*; (*on agenda*) Punkt *m*; (*in show programme*) Nummer *f*; (*in news*) Bericht *m*; (*TV, radio*) Meldung *f*

itinerary [aɪˈtɪnərərɪ] *n* Reiseroute *f*

it'll [ˈɪtl] *contr* of **it will**; **it shall**

its [ɪts] *pron* sein; (*feminine form*) ihr

it's [ɪts] *contr* of **it is**; **it has**

itself [ɪtˈsɛlf] *pron* (*reflexive*) sich; (*emphatic*) **the house ~** das Haus selbst *o* an sich; **by ~** allein; **the door closes (by) ~** die Tür schließt sich von selbst

I've [aɪv] *contr* of **I have**

ivory [ˈaɪvərɪ] *n* Elfenbein *nt*

ivy [ˈaɪvɪ] *n* Efeu *m*

j

jab [dʒæb] *vt* (*needle, knife*) stechen (*into* in +*akk*) ▷ *n* (*fam*) Spritze *f*

jack [dʒæk] *n* (*Auto*) Wagenheber *m*; (*Cards*) Bube *m*; **jack in** *vt* (*fam*) aufgeben, hinschmeißen; **jack up** *vt* (*car etc*) aufbocken

jacket [ˈdʒækɪt] *n* Jacke *f*; (*of man's suit*) Jackett *nt*; (*of book*) Schutzumschlag *m*; **jacket potato** (*pl* **-es**) *n* (*in der Schale*) gebackene Kartoffel

jack-knife [ˈdʒæknaɪf] (*pl* **jack-knives**) *n* Klappmesser *nt* ▷ *vi* (*truck*) sich quer stellen

jackpot [ˈdʒækpɒt] *n* Jackpot *m*

jacuzzi® [dʒəˈkuːzɪ] *n* (*bath*) Whirlpool® *m*

jail [dʒeɪl] *n* Gefängnis *nt* ▷ *vt* einsperren

jam [dʒæm] *n* Konfitüre *f*, Marmelade *f*; (*traffic* ~) Stau *m* ▷ *vt* (*street*) verstopfen; (*machine*) blockieren; **to be ~med** (stuck) klemmen; **to ~ on the brakes** eine Vollbremsung machen

Jamaica [dʒəˈmeɪkə] n Jamaika nt

jam-packed adj proppenvoll

janitor [ˈdʒænɪtər] n (US) Hausmeister(in) m(f)

Jan abbr = **January** Jan

January [ˈdʒænjʊəri] n Januar m

Japan [dʒəˈpæn] n Japan nt; **Japanese** [dʒæpəˈniːz] adj japanisch ▷ n (person) Japaner(in) m(f); (language) Japanisch nt

jar [dʒɑːʳ] n Glas nt

jaundice [ˈdʒɔːndɪs] n Gelbsucht f

javelin [ˈdʒævlɪn] n Speer m; (Sport) Speerwerfen nt

jaw [dʒɔː] n Kiefer m

jazz [dʒæz] n Jazz m

jealous [ˈdʒeləs] adj eifersüchtig (of auf +akk); **don't make me ~** mach mich nicht neidisch; **jealousy** n Eifersucht f

jeans [dʒiːnz] npl Jeans pl

jeep® [dʒiːp] n Jeep® m

jelly [ˈdʒelɪ] n Gelee nt; (on meat) Gallert nt; (dessert) Götterspeise f; (US: jam) Marmelade f; **jelly baby** n (sweet) Gummibärchen m; **jellyfish** n Qualle f

jeopardize [ˈdʒepədaɪz] vt gefährden

jerk [dʒɜːk] n Ruck m; (fam: idiot) Trottel m ▷ vt ruckartig bewegen ▷ vi (rope) rucken; (muscles) zucken

Jerusalem [dʒəˈruːsələm] n Jerusalem nt

jet [dʒet] n (of water etc) Strahl m; (nozzle) Düse f; (aircraft) Düsenflugzeug nt; **jet foil** n Tragflächenboot nt; **jetlag** n Jetlag m (Müdigkeit nach langem Flug)

Jew [dʒuː] n Jude m, Jüdin f

jewel [ˈdʒuːəl] n Edelstein m; (esp fig) Juwel m; **jeweller, jeweler** (US) n Juwelier(in) m(f); **jewellery, jewelry** (US) n Schmuck m

Jewish [ˈdʒuːɪʃ] adj jüdisch; **she's ~** sie ist Jüdin

jigsaw (puzzle) [ˈdʒɪgsɔː(pʌzl)] n Puzzle nt

jilt [dʒɪlt] vt den Laufpass geben +dat

jingle [ˈdʒɪŋgl] n (advert) Jingle m; (verse) Reim m

jitters [ˈdʒɪtərz] npl (fam) **to have the ~** Bammel haben; **jittery** adj (fam) ganz nervös

job [dʒɒb] n (piece of work) Arbeit f; (task) Aufgabe f; (occupation) Stellung f, Job m; **what's your ~?** was machen Sie beruflich?; **it's a good ~ you did that** gut, dass du das gemacht hast; **jobcentre** n Arbeitsvermittlungsstelle f, Arbeitsamt nt; **job-hunting** n: **to go ~** auf Arbeitssuche gehen; **jobless** adj arbeitslos; **job seeker** n Arbeitssuchende(r) mf; **jobseeker's allowance** n Arbeitslosengeld nt; **job-sharing** n Arbeitsplatzteilung f

jockey [ˈdʒɒkɪ] n Jockey m

jog [dʒɒg] vt (person) anstoßen ▷ vi (run) joggen; **jogging** n Jogging nt; **to go ~** joggen gehen

john [dʒɒn] n (US fam) Klo nt

join [dʒɔɪn] vt (put together) verbinden (to mit); (club etc) beitreten +dat; **to ~ sb** sich jdm anschließen; (sit with) sich zu jdm setzen ▷ vi (unite) sich vereinigen; (rivers) zusammenfließen ▷ n Verbindungsstelle f; (seam) Naht f; **join in** vi, vt mitmachen (sth bei etw)

joint [dʒɔɪnt] n (of bones) Gelenk nt; (in pipe etc) Verbindungsstelle f; (of meat) Braten m; (of marijuana)

Joint *m* ▷ *adj* gemeinsam; **joint account** *n* Gemeinschaftskonto *nt*; **jointly** *adv* gemeinsam

joke [dʒəʊk] *n* Witz *m*; (*prank*) Streich *m*; **for a ~** zum Spaß; **it's no ~** das ist nicht zum Lachen ▷ *vi* Witze machen; **you must be joking** das ist ja wohl nicht dein Ernst!

jolly [ˈdʒɒlɪ] *adj* lustig, vergnügt

Jordan [ˈdʒɔːdən] *n* (*country*) Jordanien *nt*; (*river*) Jordan *m*

jot down [dʒɒt daʊn] *vt* sich notieren; **jotter** *n* Notizbuch *nt*

journal [ˈdʒɜːnl] *n* (*diary*) Tagebuch *nt*; (*magazine*) Zeitschrift *f*; **journalism** *n* Journalismus *m*; **journalist** *n* Journalist(in) *m(f)*

journey [ˈdʒɜːnɪ] *n* Reise *f*; (*esp on stage, by car, train*) Fahrt *f*

joy [dʒɔɪ] *n* Freude *f* (*at* über +*akk*); **joystick** *n* (*Inform*) Joystick *m*; (*Aviat*) Steuerknüppel *m*

judge [dʒʌdʒ] *n* Richter(in) *m(f)*; (*Sport*) Punktrichter(in) *m(f)* ▷ *vt* beurteilen (*by* nach); **as far as I can ~** meinem Urteil nach ▷ *vi* urteilen (*by* nach); **judg(e)ment** (*Jur*) Urteil *nt*; (*opinion*) Ansicht *f*; **an error of ~** Fehleinschätzung *f*

judo [ˈdʒuːdəʊ] *n* Judo *nt*

jug [dʒʌg] *n* Krug *m*

juggle [ˈdʒʌgl] *vi* (*lit, fig*) jonglieren (*with* mit)

juice [dʒuːs] *n* Saft *m*; **juicy** *adj* saftig; (*story, scandal*) pikant

July [dʒuːˈlaɪ] *n* Juli *m*; *see also* **September**

jumble [ˈdʒʌmbl] *n* Durcheinander *nt* ▷ *vt*: **to ~ (up)** durcheinanderwerfen; (*facts*) durcheinanderbringen; **jumble sale** *n* (*for charity*) Flohmarkt *m*, Wohltätigkeitsbasar *m*

jumbo [ˈdʒʌmbəʊ] *adj* (*sausage etc*) Riesen-; **jumbo jet** *n* Jumbojet *m*

jump [dʒʌmp] *vi* springen; (*nervously*) zusammenzucken; **to ~ to conclusions** voreilige Schlüsse ziehen; **to ~ from one thing to another** dauernd das Thema wechseln ▷ *vt* (*a. fig: omit*) überspringen; **to ~ the lights** bei Rot über die Kreuzung fahren; **to ~ the queue** sich vordrängen ▷ *n* Sprung *m*; (*for horses*) Hindernis *nt*; **jumper** *n* Pullover *m*; (*US: dress*) Trägerkleid *nt*; (*person, horse*) Springer(in) *m(f)*; **jumper cable** (*US*), **jump lead** *n* (*Brit Auto*) Starthilfekabel *nt*

junction [ˈdʒʌŋkʃən] *n* (*of roads*) Kreuzung *f*; (*Rail*) Knotenpunkt *m*

June [dʒuːn] *n* Juni *m*; *see also* **September**

jungle [ˈdʒʌŋgl] *n* Dschungel *m*

junior [ˈdʒuːnɪə*] *adj* (*younger*) jünger; (*lower position*) untergeordnet (*to sb* jdm) ▷ *n*: **she's two years my ~** sie ist zwei Jahre jünger als ich; **junior high (school)** *n* (*US*) ≈ Mittelschule *f*; **junior school** *n* (*Brit*) Grundschule *f*

junk [dʒʌŋk] *n* (*trash*) Plunder *m*; **junk food** *n* Nahrungsmittel *pl* mit geringem Nährwert, Junkfood *nt*; **junkie** *n* (*fam*) Junkie *m*, Fixer(in) *m(f)*; (*fig: fan*) Freak *m*; **junk mail** *n* Reklame *f*; (*Inform*) Junkmail *f*; **junk shop** *n* Trödelladen *m*

jury [ˈdʒʊərɪ] *n* Geschworene *pl*; (*in competition*) Jury *f*

just [dʒʌst] *adj* gerecht ▷ *adv* (*recently*) gerade; (*exactly*) genau; **~ as expected** genau wie erwartet; **~ as nice** genauso nett; (*barely*) **~ in time** gerade noch rechtzeitig; (*immediately*) **~ before/after ...** gleich vor/nach ...; (*small distance*) **~ round the corner** gleich um die Ecke; (*a little*)

~ over an hour etwas mehr als eine Stunde; (only) **~ the two of us** nur wir beide; **~ a moment** Moment mal; (absolutely, simply) **it was ~ fantastic** es war einfach klasse; **~ about** so etwa; (more or less) mehr oder weniger; **~ about ready** fast fertig

justice ['dʒʌstɪs] n Gerechtigkeit f; **justifiable** [dʒʌstɪ'faɪəbl] adj berechtigt; **justifiably** adv zu Recht; **justify** ['dʒʌstɪfaɪ] vt rechtfertigen

jut [dʒʌt] vi: **to ~ (out)** herausragen

juvenile ['dʒuːvənaɪl] n adj Jugend-, jugendlich ⊳ n Jugendliche(r) mf

k

k abbr = **thousand**; **15k** 15 000
K abbr = **kilobyte** KB
kangaroo [kæŋgə'ruː] n Känguru nt
karaoke [kærɪ'əʊki] n Karaoke nt
karate [kə'rɑːtɪ] n Karate nt
kart [kɑːt] n Gokart m
kayak ['kaɪæk] n Kajak m o nt; **kayaking** ['kaɪækɪŋ] n Kajakfahren nt
Kazakhstan [kæzæk'stɑːn] n Kasachstan nt
kebab [kə'bæb] n (shish ~) Schaschlik nt o m; (doner ~) Kebab m
keel [kiːl] n (Naut) Kiel m; **keel over** vi (boat) kentern; (person) umkippen
keen [kiːn] adj begeistert (on von); (hardworking) eifrig; (mind, wind) scharf; (interest, feeling) stark; **to be ~ on sb** von jdm angetan sein; **she's ~ on riding** sie reitet

gern; **to be ~ to do sth** darauf erpicht sein, etw zu tun

keep [ki:p] *(kept, kept)* vt *(retain)* behalten; *(secret)* für sich behalten; *(observe)* einhalten; *(promise)* halten; *(run: shop, diary, accounts)* führen; *(animals)* halten; *(support, family etc)* unterhalten, versorgen; *(store)* aufbewahren; **to ~ sb waiting** jdn warten lassen; **to ~ sb from doing sth** jdn davon abhalten, etw zu tun; **to ~ sth clean/secret** etw sauber/geheim halten; **"~ clear"** "(bitte) frei halten"; **~ this to yourself** behalten Sie das für sich ▷ vi *(food)* sich halten; *(remain, with adj)* bleiben; **~ quiet** sei ruhig!; **~ left** links fahren; **to ~ doing sth** *(repeatedly)* etw immer wieder tun; **~ at it** mach weiter so!; **it ~s happening** es passiert immer wieder ▷ n *(livelihood)* Unterhalt m; **keep back** vi zurückbleiben ▷ vt zurückhalten; *(information)* verschweigen *(from sb jdm)*; **keep off** vt *(person, animal)* fernhalten; **"~ off the grass"** "Betreten des Rasens verboten"; **keep on** vi weitermachen; *(walking)* weitergehen; *(in car)* weiterfahren; **to ~ doing sth** *(persistently)* etw immer wieder tun ▷ vt *(coat etc)* anbehalten; **keep out** vt nicht hereinlassen ▷ vi draußen bleiben; **"~ out"** *(on sign)* Eintritt verboten; **keep to** vt *(road, path)* bleiben auf +dat; *(plan etc)* sich halten an +akk; **to ~ the point** bei der Sache bleiben; **keep up** vi Schritt halten *(with mit)* ▷ vt *(maintain)* aufrechterhalten; *(speed)* halten; **to ~ appearances** den Schein wahren; **keep it up!** *(fam)* weiter so!

keeper n *(museum etc)* Aufseher(in) m(f); *(goal-)* Torwart

m; *(zoo ~)* Tierpfleger(in) m(f);
keep-fit n Fitnesstraining nt;
~ exercises Gymnastik f

kennel ['kenl] n Hundehütte f;
kennels n Hundepension f

Kenya ['kenjə] n Kenia nt

kept [kept] pt, pp of **keep**

kerb [kɜ:b] n Randstein m

kerosene ['kerəsi:n] n *(US)* Petroleum nt

ketchup ['ketʃʌp] n Ketchup nt o m

kettle ['ketl] n Kessel m

key [ki:] n Schlüssel m; *(of piano, computer)* Taste f; *(Mus)* Tonart f; *(for map etc)* Zeichenerklärung f ▷ vt: **to ~ in** *(Inform)* eingeben ▷ adj entscheidend; **keyboard** n *(piano, computer)* Tastatur f; **keyhole** n Schlüsselloch nt; **keypad** n *(Inform)* Nummernblock m; **keyring** n Schlüsselring m

kick [kik] n Tritt m; *(Sport)* Stoß m; **I get a ~ out of it** *(fam)* es turnt mich an ▷ vt, vi treten; **kick out** vt *(fam)* rausschmeißen *(of aus)*; **kick-off** n *(Sport)* Anstoß m

kid [kid] n *(child)* Kind nt ▷ vt *(tease)* auf den Arm nehmen ▷ vi Witze machen; **you're ~ding** das ist doch nicht dein Ernst!; **no ~ding** aber echt!

kidnap ['kidnæp] vt entführen; **kidnapper** n Entführer(in) m(f); **kidnapping** n Entführung f

kidney ['kidni] n Niere f; **kidney machine** n künstliche Niere

kill [kil] vt töten; *(esp intentionally)* umbringen; *(weeds)* vernichten; **killer** n Mörder(in) m(f)

kilo ['ki:ləʊ] *(pl -s)* n Kilo nt; **kilobyte** n Kilobyte nt; **kilogramme** n Kilogramm nt; **kilometer** *(US)*, **kilometre** n Kilometer m; **~s per hour**

Stundenkilometer pl; **kilowatt** n Kilowatt nt

kilt [kɪlt] n Schottenrock m

kind [kaɪnd] adj nett, freundlich (to zu) ▷ n Art f; (of coffee, cheese etc) Sorte f; **what ~ of …?** was für ein(e) …?; **this ~ of …** so ein(e) …; **~ of** (+ adj) irgendwie

kindergarten ['kɪndəgɑːtn] n Kindergarten m

kindly ['kaɪndlɪ] adj nett, freundlich ▷ adv liebenswürdigerweise; **kindness** ['kaɪndnəs] n Freundlichkeit f

king [kɪŋ] n König m; **kingdom** n Königreich nt; **kingfisher** n Eisvogel m; **king-size** adj im Großformat; (bed) extra groß

kipper ['kɪpə'] n Räucherhering m

kiss [kɪs] n Kuss m; **~ of life** Mund-zu-Mund-Beatmung f ▷ vt küssen

kit [kɪt] n (equipment) Ausrüstung f; (fam) Sachen pl; (sports ~) Sportsachen pl; (belongings, clothes) Sachen pl; (for building sth) Bausatz m

kitchen ['kɪtʃɪn] n Küche f; **kitchen foil** n Alufolie f; **kitchen scales** n (object) Küchenwaage f; **kitchen unit** n Küchenschrank m; **kitchenware** n Küchengeschirr nt

kite [kaɪt] n Drachen m

kitten ['kɪtn] n Kätzchen nt

kiwi ['kiːwiː] n (fruit) Kiwi f

km abbr = **kilometres** km

knack [næk] n Dreh m, Trick m; **to get/have got the ~** den Dreh herauskriegen/heraushaben; **knackered** ['nækəd] adj (Brit fam) fix und fertig, kaputt

knee [niː] n Knie nt; **kneecap** n Kniescheibe f; **knee-jerk** adj (reaction) reflexartig; **kneel** [niːl] vi (knelt o kneeled, knelt o kneeled)

vi knien; (action, ~ down) sich hinknien

knelt [nelt] pt, pp of **kneel**

knew [njuː] pt of **know**

knickers ['nɪkəz] npl (Brit fam) Schlüpfer m

knife [naɪf] n (pl **knives**) n Messer nt

knight [naɪt] n Ritter m; (in chess) Pferd nt, Springer m

knit [nɪt] vt, vi stricken; **knitting** n (piece of work) Strickarbeit f; (activity) Stricken nt; **knitting needle** n Stricknadel f; **knitwear** n Strickwaren pl

knob [nɒb] n (on door) Knauf m; (on radio etc) Knopf m

knock [nɒk] vt (with hammer etc) schlagen; (accidentally) stoßen; **to ~ one's head** sich dat den Kopf anschlagen ▷ vi klopfen (on, at an +akk) ▷ n (blow) Schlag m; (on door) Klopfen nt; **there was a ~ (at the door)** es hat geklopft; **knock down** vt (object) umstoßen; (person) niederstoßen; (with car) anfahren; (building) abreißen; **knock out** vt (stun) bewusstlos schlagen; (boxer) k.o. schlagen; **knock over** vt umstoßen; (with car) anfahren; **knocker** n Türklopfer m; **knockout** n Knockout m, K.o. nt

knot [nɒt] n Knoten m

know [nəʊ] (**knew**, **known**) vt, vi wissen; (be acquainted with: people, places) kennen; (recognize) erkennen; (language) können; **I'll let you ~** ich sage dir Bescheid; **I ~ some French** ich kann etwas Französisch; **to get to ~ sb** jdn kennenlernen; **to be ~n as** bekannt sein als; **know about** vt Bescheid wissen über +akk; **(subject)** sich auskennen in +dat; **(cars, horses etc)** sich auskennen mit; **know of** vt kennen; **not that**

I ~ nicht dass ich wüsste;
know-all n (fam) Klugscheißer m;
know-how n Kenntnis f,
Know-how nt; **knowing** adj
wissend; (look, smile) vielsagend;
knowledge ['nɒlɪdʒ] n Wissen
nt; (of a subject) Kenntnisse pl; **to
(the best of) my** ~ meines
Wissens
known [nəʊn] pp of **know**
knuckle ['nʌkl] n (Finger)knöchel m; (Gastr) Hachse f;
knuckle down vi sich an die
Arbeit machen
Koran [kɔ'rɑːn] n Koran m
Korea [kə'rɪə] n Korea nt
Kosovo ['kɒsɒvəʊ] n der Kosovo
kph abbr = **kilometres per hour**
km/h
Kremlin ['kremlɪn] n: **the** ~ der
Kreml
Kurd [kɜːd] n Kurde m, Kurdin f;
Kurdish adj kurdisch
Kuwait [kʊ'weɪt] n Kuwait nt

L abbr (Brit Auto) = **learner**
LA abbr = **Los Angeles**
lab [læb] n (fam) Labor nt
label ['leɪbl] n Etikett nt; (tied)
Anhänger m; (adhesive) Aufkleber
m; (record ~) Label nt ▷ vt
etikettieren; (pej) abstempeln
laboratory [lə'bɒrətərɪ] n Labor
nt

- **LABOR DAY**
-
- Der **Labor Day** ist in den USA
- und Kanada der Name für den
- Tag der Arbeit. Er wird dort als
- gesetzlicher Feiertag am ersten
- Montag im September
- begangen.

laborious [lə'bɔːrɪəs] adj
mühsam; **labor** (US), **labour**
['leɪbəʳ] n Arbeit f; (Med) Wehen
pl; **to be in** ~ Wehen haben ▷ adj

(Pol) Labour-; ~ **Party** Labour Party f; **labor union** n (US) Gewerkschaft f; **labourer** n Arbeiter(in) m(f)

lace [leɪs] n (fabric) Spitze f; (of shoe) Schnürsenkel m ▷ vt: **to ~ (up)** zuschnüren; **lace-up** n Schnürschuh m

lack [læk] vt, vi: **to be ~ing** fehlen; **sb ~s o is ~ing in sth** es fehlt jdm an etw dat; **we ~ the time** uns fehlt die Zeit ▷ n Mangel m (of an +dat)

lacquer ['lækə°] n Lack m; (Brit: hair ~) Haarspray nt

lad [læd] n Junge m

ladder ['lædə°] n Leiter f; (in tight) Laufmasche f

laddish ['lædɪʃ] adj (Brit) machohaft

laden ['leɪdn] adj beladen (with mit)

ladies [-] ladies' room = Damentoilette f

lad mag n Männerzeitschrift f

lady ['leɪdɪ] n Dame f; (as title) Lady f; **ladybird, ladybug** (US) n Marienkäfer m; **Ladyshave®** n Epiliergerät nt

lag [læg] vi: **to ~ (behind)** zurückliegen ▷ vt (pipes) isolieren

lager ['lɑːgə°] n helles Bier; **~ lout** betrunkener Rowdy

lagging ['lægɪn] n Isolierung f

laid [leɪd] pt, pp of **lay; laid-back** adj (fam) cool, gelassen

lain [leɪn] pp of **lie**

lake [leɪk] n See m; **the Lake District** Seengebiet im Nordwesten Englands

lamb [læm] n Lamm nt; (meat) Lammfleisch nt; **lamb chop** n Lammkotelett nt

lame [leɪm] adj lahm; (excuse) faul; (argument) schwach

lament [lə'ment] n Klage f ▷ vt beklagen

laminated ['læmɪneɪtɪd] adj beschichtet

lamp [læmp] n Lampe f; (in street) Laterne f; (in car) Licht nt, Scheinwerfer m; **lamppost** n Laternenpfahl m; **lampshade** n Lampenschirm m

land [lænd] n Land nt ▷ vi (from ship) an Land gehen; (Aviat) landen ▷ vt (passengers) absetzen; (goods) abladen; (plane) landen; **landing** n Landung f; (on stairs) Treppenabsatz m; **landing stage** n Landesteg m; **landing strip** n Landebahn f

landlady n Hauswirtin f, Vermieterin f; **landlord** n (of house) Hauswirt m, Vermieter m; (of pub) Gastwirt m; **landmark** n Wahrzeichen nt; (event) Meilenstein m; **landowner** n Grundbesitzer(in) m(f); **landscape** n Landschaft f; (format) Querformat nt; **landslide** n (Geo) Erdrutsch m

lane [leɪn] n (in country) enge Landstraße, Weg m; (in town) Gasse f; (of motorway) Spur f; (Sport) Bahn f; **to get in ~** (in car) sich einordnen

language ['læŋgwɪdʒ] n Sprache f; (style) Ausdrucksweise f

lantern ['læntən] n Laterne f

lap [læp] n Schoß m; (in race) Runde f ▷ vt (in race) überholen

lapse [læps] n (mistake) Irrtum m; (moral) Fehltritt m ▷ vi ablaufen

laptop ['læptɒp] n Laptop m

large [lɑːdʒ] adj groß; **by and ~** im Großen und Ganzen; **largely** adv zum größten Teil; **large-scale** adj groß angelegt, Groß-

lark [lɑːk] n (bird) Lerche f

laryngitis [lærɪn'dʒaɪtɪs] n Kehlkopfentzündung f; **larynx** ['lærɪŋks] n Kehlkopf m

laser ['leɪzə°] n Laser m; **laser printer** n Laserdrucker m

lash [læʃ] vt peitschen; **lash out**
vi (with fists) um sich schlagen;
(spend money) sich in Unkosten
stürzen (on mit)

lass [læs] n Mädchen nt

last [lɑːst] adj letzte(r, s); **the
~ but one** der/die/das vorletzte;
~ night gestern Abend; **~ but not
least** nicht zuletzt ▷ adv zuletzt;
(last time) das letzte Mal; **at
~** endlich ▷ n (person) Letzte(r) mf;
(thing) Letzte(s) nt; **he was the
~ to leave** er ging als Letzter ▷ vi
(continue) dauern; (remain in good
condition) durchhalten; (remain
good) sich halten; (money)
ausreichen; **lasting** adj
dauerhaft; (impression) nachhaltig;
lastly adv schließlich;
last-minute adj in letzter
Minute; **last name** n Nachname
m

late [leɪt] adj spät; (after proper
time) zu spät; (train etc) verspätet;
(dead) verstorben; **to be ~** zu spät
kommen; (train etc) Verspätung
haben ▷ adv spät; (after proper
time) zu spät; **late availibility
flight** n Last-Minute-Flug m;
lately adv in letzter Zeit; **late
opening** n verlängerte
Öffnungszeiten pl; **later** ['leɪtə°]
adj, adv später; **see you ~** bis
später; **latest** ['leɪtɪst] adj
späteste(r, s) (most recent)
neueste(r, s) ▷ n: **the ~** (news) das
Neueste; **at the ~** spätestens

Latin ['lætɪn] n Latein nt ▷ adj
lateinisch; **Latin America** n
Lateinamerika nt;
Latin-American adj
lateinamerikanisch ▷ n Latein-
amerikaner(in) m(f)

latter ['lætə°] adj (second of two)
letztere(r, s); (last: part, years)
letzte(r, s), später

Latvia ['lætvɪə] n Lettland nt;

Latvian ['lætvɪən] ▷ adj lettisch;
▷ n (person) Lette m; Lettin f;
(language) Lettisch nt

laugh [lɑːf] n Lachen nt; **for a
~** aus Spaß ▷ vi lachen (at, about
über +akk); **to ~ at sb** sich über jdn
lustig machen; **it's no ~ing
matter** es ist nichts zum Lachen;
laughter ['lɑːftə°] n Gelächter nt

launch [lɔːntʃ] n (launching, of
ship) Stapellauf m; (of rocket)
Abschuss m; (of product)
Markteinführung f; (with hype)
Lancierung f; (event)
Eröffnungsfeier f ▷ vt (ship) vom
Stapel lassen; (rocket) abschießen;
(product) einführen; (with hype)
lancieren; (project) in Gang setzen

launder ['lɔːndə°] vt waschen
und bügeln; (fig: money) waschen;
launderette [lɔːn'dret] n (Brit),
laundromat ['lɔːndrəmæt] n (US)
Waschsalon m; **laundry** ['lɔːndrɪ]
n (place) Wäscherei f; (clothes)
Wäsche f

lavatory ['lævətrɪ] n Toilette f

lavender ['lævɪndə°] n Lavendel
m

lavish ['lævɪʃ] adj verschwende-
risch; (furnishings etc) üppig; (gift)
großzügig

law [lɔː] n Gesetz nt; (system)
Recht nt; (for study) Jura; (of sport)
Regel f; **against the
~** gesetzwidrig; **law-abiding** adj
gesetzestreu; **law court** n
Gerichtshof m; **lawful** adj
rechtmäßig

lawn [lɔːn] n Rasen m;
lawnmower n Rasenmäher m

lawsuit ['lɔːsuːt] n Prozess m;

lawyer ['lɔːjə°] n Rechtsanwalt
m, Rechtsanwältin f

laxative ['læksətɪv] n Abführmittel nt

lay [leɪ] pt of **lie** ▷ vt (laid, laid)
legen; (table) decken; (vulg)

poppen, bumsen; (egg) legen ▷ adj Laien-; **lay down** vt hinlegen; **lay off** vt (workers) (vorübergehend) entlassen; (stop attacking) in Ruhe lassen; **lay on** vt (provide) anbieten; (organize) veranstalten, bereitstellen; **layout** n Faulenzer(in) m(f); **lay-by** n Parkbucht f; (bigger) Parkplatz m

layer ['leɪə°] n Schicht f

layman ['leɪmən] n Laie m

layout ['leɪaʊt] n Gestaltung f; (of book etc) Lay-out nt

laze [leɪz] vi faulenzen; **laziness** ['leɪzɪnɪs] n Faulheit f; **lazy** ['leɪzɪ] adj faul; (day, time) gemütlich

lb abbr = **pound** Pfd.

lead [led] n Blei nt ▷ vt, vi [li:d] (**led, led**) führen; (group etc) leiten; **to ~ the way** vorangehen; **this is ~ing nowhere** das bringt uns nicht weiter ▷ n [li:d] n (race) Führung f; (distance, time ahead) Vorsprung m (over vor +dat); (of police) Spur f; (Theat) Hauptrolle f; (dog's) Leine f; (Elec: flex) Leitung f; **lead astray** vt irreführen; **lead away** vt wegführen; **lead back** vi zurückführen; **lead on** vi anführen; **lead to** vt (street) hinführen nach; (result in) führen zu; **lead up to** vt (drive) führen zu

leaded ['ledɪd] adj (petrol) verbleit

leader ['li:də°] n Führer(in) m(f); (of party) Vorsitzende(r) mf; (of project, expedition) Leiter(in) m(f); (Sport: in race) der/die Erste; (in league) Tabellenführer m; **leadership** ['li:dəʃɪp] n Führung f

lead-free ['led'fri:] adj (petrol) bleifrei

leading ['li:dɪŋ] adj führend, wichtig

leaf [li:f] n (pl **leaves**) n Blatt nt;

leaflet ['li:flɪt] n Prospekt m; (pamphlet) Flugblatt nt; (with instructions) Merkblatt nt

league [li:g] n Bund m; (Sport) Liga f

leak [li:k] n (gap) undichte Stelle; (escape) Leck nt; **to take a ~** (fam) pinkeln gehen ▷ vi (pipe etc) undicht sein; (liquid etc) auslaufen; **leaky** adj undicht

lean [li:n] adj (meat) mager; (face) schmal; (person) drahtig ▷ vi (**leant** o **leaned, leant** o **leaned**) (not vertical) sich neigen; (rest) **to ~ against sth** sich an etw akk lehnen; (support oneself) **to ~ on sth** sich auf etw akk stützen ▷ vt lehnen (on, against an +akk); **lean back** vi sich zurücklehnen; **lean forward** vi sich vorbeugen; **lean over** vi sich hinüberbeugen; **lean towards** vt tendieren zu

leant [lent] pt, pp of **lean**

leap [li:p] n Sprung m ▷ vi (**leapt** o **leaped, leapt** o **leaped**) springen; **leapt** [lept] pt, pp of **leap**; **leap year** n Schaltjahr nt

learn [lɜ:n] (**learnt** o **learned, learnt** o **learned**) vt, vi lernen; (find out) erfahren; **to ~ (how) to swim** schwimmen lernen; **learned** ['lɜ:nɪd] adj gelehrt; **learner** n Anfänger(in) m(f); (Brit: driver) Fahrschüler(in) m(f)

learnt [lɜ:nt] pt, pp of **learn**

lease [li:s] n (of land, premises etc) Pacht f; (contract) Pachtvertrag m; (of house, car etc) Miete f; (contract) Mietvertrag m ▷ vt pachten; (house, car etc) mieten; **lease out** vt vermieten, verpachten; **leasing** n Leasing nt

least [li:st] adj wenigste(r, s); (slightest) geringste(r, s) ▷ adv am wenigsten; **~ expensive** billigste(r, s) ▷ n: **the ~** das Mindeste; **not in the ~** nicht im geringsten; **at ~** wenigstens; *(with number)* mindestens

leather ['leðə°] *n* Leder *nt* ⊳ *adj* ledern, Leder-

leave [li:v] *n (time off)* Urlaub *m*; **on ~** auf Urlaub; **to take one's ~** Abschied nehmen *(of* von) ⊳ *vt* **(left, left)** *(place, person)* verlassen; *(not remove, not change)* lassen; *(~ behind: message, scar etc)* hinterlassen; *(forget)* hinter sich lassen; *(after death)* hinterlassen *(to sb* jdm); *(entrust)* überlassen *(to sb* jdm); **to be left** *(remain)* übrig bleiben; **~ me alone** lass mich in Ruhe!; **don't ~ it to the last minute** warte nicht bis zur letzten Minute ⊳ *vi* (weg)gehen, (weg)fahren; *(on journey)* abreisen; *(bus, train)* abfahren *(for* nach); **leave behind** *vt* zurücklassen; *(scar etc)* hinterlassen; *(forget)* hinter sich lassen; **leave out** *vt* auslassen; *(person)* ausschließen *(of* von)

leaves [li:vz] *pl of* **leaf**

leaving do [li:vɪŋ du:] *n* Abschiedsfeier *f*

Lebanon ['lebənən] *n*: **the ~** der Libanon

lecture ['lektʃə°] *n* Vortrag *m*; *(at university)* Vorlesung *f*; **to give a ~** einen Vortrag/eine Vorlesung halten; **lecturer** *n* Dozent/-in *m(f)*; **lecture theatre** *n* Hörsaal *m*

led [led] *pt, pp of* **lead**

LED *abbr* = **light-emitting diode** Leuchtdiode *f*

ledge [ledʒ] *n* Leiste *f*; *(window ~)* Sims *m* *o* *nt*

leek [li:k] *n* Lauch *m*

left [left] *pt, pp of* **leave** ⊳ *adj* linke(r, s) ⊳ *adv (position)* links; *(movement)* nach links ⊳ *n (side)* linke Seite; **the Left** *(Pol)* die Linke; **on/to the ~** links *(of* von); **move/fall to the ~** nach links

rücken/fallen; **left-hand** *adj* linke(r, s); **~ bend** Linkskurve *f*; **~ drive** Linkssteuerung *f*; **left-handed** *adj* linkshändig; **left-hand side** *n* linke Seite

left-luggage locker *n* Gepäckschließfach *nt*; **left-luggage office** *n* Gepäckaufbewahrung *f*

leftovers *npl* Reste *pl*

left wing *n* linker Flügel; **left-wing** *adj* *(Pol)* linksgerichtet

leg [leg] *n* Bein *nt*; *(of meat)* Keule *f*

legacy ['legəsɪ] *n* Erbe *nt*, Erbschaft *f*

legal ['li:gəl] *adj* Rechts-, rechtlich; *(allowed)* legal; *(limit, age)* gesetzlich; **~ aid** Rechtshilfe *f*; **legalize** *vt* legalisieren; **legally** *adv* legal

legend ['ledʒənd] *n* Legende *f*

legible, legibly ['ledʒəbl, -blɪ] *adj, adv* leserlich

legislation [ledʒɪs'leɪʃn] *n* Gesetze *pl*

legitimate [lɪ'dʒɪtɪmət] *adj* rechtmäßig, legitim

legroom ['legrʊm] *n* Beinfreiheit *f*

leisure ['leʒə°] *n (time)* Freizeit *f* ⊳ *adj* Freizeit-; **~ centre** Freizeitzentrum *nt*; **leisurely** ['leʒəlɪ] *adj* gemächlich

lemon ['lemən] *n* Zitrone *f*; **lemonade** [lemə'neɪd] *n* Limonade *f*; **lemon curd** *n* Brotaufstrich aus Zitronen, Butter, Eiern und Zucker; **lemon juice** *n* Zitronensaft *m*; **lemon sole** *n* Seezunge *f*

lend [lend] *(lent, lent)* *vt* leihen; **to ~ sb sth** jdm etw leihen; **to (sb) ~ a hand** (jdm) behilflich sein; **lending library** *n* Leihbücherei *f*

length [leŋθ] *n* Länge *f*; **4 metres in ~** 4 Meter lang; **what**

~ is it? wie lange ist es?; **for any ~ of time** für längere Zeit; **at ~** (lengthily) ausführlich; **lengthen** ['lɛŋθən] vt verlängern; **lengthy** adj sehr lange; (dragging) langwierig

lenient ['liːnɪənt] adj nachsichtig

lens [lɛnz] n Linse f; (Foto) Objektiv nt

lent [lɛnt] pt, pp of **lend**

Lent [lɛnt] n Fastenzeit f

lentil ['lɛntl] n (Bot) Linse f

Leo ['liːəʊ] (pl **-s**) n (Astr) Löwe m

leopard ['lɛpəd] n Leopard m

lesbian ['lɛzbɪən] adj lesbisch ▷ n Lesbe f

less [lɛs] adj, adv, n weniger; **~ and ~** immer weniger; (~ often) immer seltener; **lessen** ['lɛsn] vi abnehmen, nachlassen ▷ vt verringern; (pain) lindern; **lesser** ['lɛsə°] adj geringer; (amount) kleiner

lesson ['lɛsn] n (at school) Stunde f; (unit of study) Lektion f; (fig) Lehre f; (Rel) Lesung f; **~s start at 9** der Unterricht beginnt um 9

let [lɛt] (**let, let**) vt lassen; (lease) vermieten; **to ~ sb have sth** jdm etw geben; **~'s go** gehen wir; **to ~ go** (of sth) (etw) loslassen; **let down** vt herunterlassen; (fail to help) im Stich lassen; (disappoint) enttäuschen; **let in** vt hereinlassen; **let off** vt (bomb) hochgehen lassen; (person) laufen lassen; **let out** vt hinauslassen; (secret) verraten; (scream etc) ausstoßen; **let up** vi nachlassen; (stop) aufhören

lethal ['liːθəl] adj tödlich

let's contr = **let us**

letter ['lɛtə°] n (of alphabet) Buchstabe m; (message) Brief m; (official ~) Schreiben nt; **letter**

bomb n Briefbombe f; **letterbox** n Briefkasten m

lettuce ['lɛtɪs] n Kopfsalat m

leukaemia, leukemia (US) [luːˈkiːmɪə] n Leukämie f

level ['lɛvl] adj (horizontal) waagerecht; (ground) eben; (two things, two runners) auf selber Höhe; **to be with sb/sth** mit jdm/etw auf gleicher Höhe sein; **~ on points** punktgleich ▷ adv (run etc) auf gleicher Höhe, gleich auf; **to draw ~** (in race) gleichziehen (with mit); (in game) ausgleichen ▷ n (altitude) Höhe f; (standard) Niveau nt; (amount, degree) Grad m; **to be on a ~ with** auf gleicher Höhe sein mit ▷ vt (ground) einebnen; **level crossing** n (Brit) (schienengleicher) Bahnübergang m; **level-headed** adj vernünftig

lever ['liːvə°, (US) 'lɛvə°] n Hebel m; (fig) Druckmittel nt; **lever up** vt hochstemmen

liability [laɪəˈbɪlɪtɪ] n Haftung f; (burden) Belastung f; (obligation) Verpflichtung f; **liable** ['laɪəbl] adj: **to be ~ for sth** (responsible) für etw haften; **~ for tax** steuerpflichtig

liar ['laɪə°] n Lügner(in) m(f)

Lib Dem [lɪbˈdɛm] abbr = **Liberal Democrat**

liberal ['lɪbərəl] adj (generous) großzügig; (broad-minded) offen; **Liberal Democrat** n (Brit Pol) Liberaldemokrat(in) m(f) ▷ adj liberaldemokratisch

liberate ['lɪbəreɪt] vt befreien; **liberation** [lɪbəˈreɪʃn] n Befreiung f

Liberia [laɪˈbɪərɪə] n Liberia nt

liberty ['lɪbətɪ] n Freiheit f

Libra ['liːbrə] n (Astr) Waage f

library ['laɪbrərɪ] n Bibliothek f; (lending ~) Bücherei f

Libya | 406

Libya ['lɪbɪə] *n* Libyen *nt*
lice [laɪs] *pl of* **louse**
licence ['laɪsəns] *n* (permit)
  Genehmigung *f*; (Comm) Lizenz *f*;
  (driving ~) Führerschein *m*; **license**
  ['laɪsəns] *n* (US) *see* **licence** ▷ *vt*
  genehmigen; **licensed** *adj*
  (restaurant etc) mit
  Schankerlaubnis; **license plate** *n*
  (US Auto) Nummernschild *nt*;
  licensing hours *npl*
  Ausschankzeiten *pl*
lick [lɪk] *vt* lecken ▷ *n* Lecken
  nt
licorice ['lɪkərɪs] *n* Lakritze *f*
lid [lɪd] *n* Deckel *m*; (eye-) Lid *nt*
lie [laɪ] *n* Lüge *f*; **~ detector**
  Lügendetektor *m* ▷ *vi* lügen; **to**
  ~ to sb jdn belügen ▷ *vi* (**lay, lain**)
  (rest, be situated) liegen; (~ down)
  sich legen; (snow) liegen bleiben;
  to be lying third an dritter Stelle
  liegen; **lie about** *vi* herumliegen;
  lie down *vi* sich hinlegen
Liechtenstein ['lɪktənstaɪn] *n*
  Liechtenstein *nt*
lie in [laɪ'ɪn] *n*: **to have a**
  ~ ausschlafen
life [laɪf] (*pl* **lives**) *n* Leben *nt*; **to**
  get ~ lebenslänglich bekommen;
  there isn't much ~ here hier ist
  nicht viel los; **how many lives**
  were lost? wie viele sind ums
  Leben gekommen?; **life assurance**
  n Lebensversicherung *f*; **lifebelt** *n*
  Rettungsring *m*; **lifeboat** *n*
  Rettungsboot *nt*; **lifeguard** *n*
  Bademeister(in) *m(f)*,
  Rettungsschwimmer(in) *m(f)*; **life**
  insurance *n* Lebensversicherung
  f; **life jacket** *n* Schwimmweste *f*;
  lifeless *adj* (dead) leblos; **lifelong**
  adj lebenslang; **life preserver** *n*
  (US) Rettungsring *m*; **life-saving**
  adj lebensrettend; **life-size(d)** *adj*
  in Lebensgröße; **life span** *n*
  Lebensspanne *f*; **life style** *n*

Lebensstil *m*; **lifetime** *n*
  Lebenszeit *f*
lift [lɪft] *vt* (hoch)heben; (ban)
  aufheben ▷ *n* (Brit: elevator)
  Aufzug *m*, Lift *m*; **to give sb a ~** jdn
  im Auto mitnehmen; **lift up** *vt*
  hochheben; **lift-off** *n* Start *m*
ligament ['lɪgəmənt] *n* Band *nt*
light [laɪt] (*lit o* **lighted**, *lit o*
  lighted) *vt* beleuchten; (fire,
  cigarette) anzünden ▷ *n* Licht *nt*;
  (lamp) Lampe *f*; **~s** *pl* (Aut)
  Beleuchtung *f*; (traffic ~s) Ampel *f*;
  in the ~ of angesichts +gen ▷ *adj*
  (bright) hell; (not heavy, easy) leicht;
  (punishment) milde; (taxes) niedrig;
  ~ blue/green hellblau/hellgrün;
  light up *vt* (illuminate) beleuchten
  ▷ *vi* (a. eyes) aufleuchten
light bulb *n* Glühbirne *f*
lighten ['laɪtn] *vi* hell werden
  ▷ *vt* (give light to) erhellen; (make
  less heavy) leichter machen; (fig)
  erleichtern
lighter ['laɪtə*] *n* (cigarette ~)
  Feuerzeug *nt*
light-hearted *adj* unbeschwert;
lighthouse *n* Leuchtturm *m*;
lighting *n* Beleuchtung *f*; **lightly**
  adv leicht; **light meter** *n* (Foto)
  Belichtungsmesser *m*
lightning ['laɪtnɪŋ] *n* Blitz *m*
lightweight *adj* leicht
like [laɪk] *vt* mögen, gernhaben;
  he ~s swimming er schwimmt
  gern; **would you ~ ...?** hättest
  du/hätten Sie gern ...?; **I'd ~ to go**
  home ich möchte nach Hause
  (gehen); **I don't ~ the film** der
  Film gefällt mir nicht ▷ prep vor;
  what's it/he ~? wie ist es/er?; **he**
  looks ~ you er sieht dir/Ihnen
  ähnlich; **that/this** so; **likeable**
  ['laɪkəbl] *adj* sympathisch
likelihood ['laɪklɪhʊd] *n* Wahrscheinlichkeit *f*; **likely** ['laɪklɪ]
  adj wahrscheinlich; **the bus is**

~ to be late der Bus wird wahrscheinlich Verspätung haben; **he's not (at all) ~ to come** (höchst)wahrscheinlich kommt er nicht

like-minded ['laɪk'maɪndɪd] *adj* gleich gesinnt

likewise ['laɪkwaɪz] *adv* ebenfalls; **to do ~** das Gleiche tun

liking ['laɪkɪŋ] *n* (for person) Zuneigung *f*; (for type, things) Vorliebe *f* (for für)

lilac ['laɪlək] *n* Flieder *m* ▷ *adj* fliederfarben

lily ['lɪlɪ] *n* Lilie *f*; **~ of the valley** Maiglöckchen *nt*

limb [lɪm] *n* Glied *nt*

limbo ['lɪmbəʊ] *n*: **in ~** (plans) auf Eis gelegt

lime [laɪm] *n* (tree) Linde *f*; (fruit) Limone *f*; (substance) Kalk *m*; **lime juice** *n* Limonensaft *m*; **limelight** *n* (fig) Rampenlicht *nt*

limerick ['lɪmərɪk] *n* Limerick *m* (fünfzeiliges komisches Gedicht)

limestone ['laɪmstəʊn] *n* Kalkstein *m*

limit ['lɪmɪt] *n* Grenze *f*; (for pollution etc) Grenzwert *m*; **there's a ~ to that** dem sind Grenzen gesetzt; **to be over the ~** (speed) das Tempolimit überschreiten; (alcohol consumption) fahruntüchtig sein; **that's the ~** jetzt reicht's!, das ist die Höhe! ▷ *vt* beschränken (to auf +akk); (freedom, spending) einschränken; **limitation** [lɪmɪ'teɪʃən] *n* Beschränkung *f*; (of freedom, spending) Einschränkung *f*; **limited** *adj* begrenzt; **~ liability company** Gesellschaft *f* mit beschränkter Haftung, GmbH *f*; **public ~ company** Aktiengesellschaft *f*

limousine ['lɪməziːn] *n* Limousine *f*

limp [lɪmp] *vi* hinken ▷ *adj* schlaff

line [laɪn] *n* Linie *f*; (written) Zeile *f*; (rope) Leine *f*; (on face) Falte *f*; (row) Reihe *f*; (US: queue) Schlange *f*; (Rail) Bahnlinie *f*; (between A and B) Strecke *f*; (Tel) Leitung *f*; (range of items) Kollektion *f*; **hold the ~** bleiben Sie am Apparat; **to stand in ~** Schlange stehen; **in ~ with** in Übereinstimmung mit; **something along those ~s** etwas in dieser Art; **drop me a ~** schreib mir ein paar Zeilen; **~s** (Theat) Text *m* ▷ *vt* (clothes) füttern; (streets) säumen; **lined** *adj* (paper) liniert; (face) faltig; **line up** vi sich aufstellen; (US: form queue) sich anstellen

linen ['lɪnɪn] *n* Leinen *nt*; (sheets etc) Wäsche *f*

liner ['laɪnə°] *n* Überseedampfer *m*, Passagierschiff *nt*

linger ['lɪŋgə°] *vi* verweilen; (smell) nicht weggehen

lingerie ['lænʒəriː] *n* Damenunterwäsche *f*

lining ['laɪnɪŋ] *n* (of clothes) Futter *nt*; (brake ~) Bremsbelag *m*

link [lɪŋk] *n* (connection) Verbindung *f*; (of chain) Glied *nt*; (relationship) Beziehung *f* (with zu); (between events) Zusammenhang *m*; (Internet) Link *m* ▷ *vt* verbinden

lion ['laɪən] *n* Löwe *m*; **lioness** *n* Löwin *f*

lip [lɪp] *n* Lippe *f*; **lipstick** *n* Lippenstift *m*

liqueur [lɪ'kjʊə°] *n* Likör *m*

liquid ['lɪkwɪd] *n* Flüssigkeit *f* ▷ *adj* flüssig

liquidate ['lɪkwɪdeɪt] *vt* liquidieren

liquidizer ['lɪkwɪdaɪzə°] *n* Mixer *m*

liquor ['lɪkə°] *n* Spirituosen *pl*

liquorice ['lɪkərɪs] n Lakritze f
Lisbon ['lɪzbən] n Lissabon nt
lisp [lɪsp] vt, vi lispeln
list [lɪst] n Liste f ⊳ vi (ship)
Schlagseite haben ⊳ vt auflisten,
aufzählen; **~ed building** unter
Denkmalschutz stehendes
Gebäude
listen ['lɪsn] vi zuhören, horchen
(for sth auf etw akk); **listen to** vt
(person) zuhören +dat; (radio)
hören; (advice) hören auf; **listener**
n Zuhörer(in) m(f); (to radio)
Hörer(in) m(f)
lit [lɪt] pt, pp of **light**
liter ['liːtə'] n (US) Liter m
literacy ['lɪtərəsɪ] n Fähigkeit f
zu lesen und zu schreiben; **literal**
['lɪtərəl] adj (translation, meaning)
wörtlich; (actual) buchstäblich;
literally adv (translate, take sth)
wörtlich; (really) buchstäblich,
wirklich; **literary** ['lɪtərərɪ] adj
literarisch; (critic, journal etc)
Literatur-; (language) gehoben;
literature ['lɪtrɪtʃə'] n Literatur
f; (brochures etc)
Informationsmaterial nt
Lithuania [lɪθju:ˈeɪnjə] n Litauen
nt; **Lithuanian** [lɪθju:ˈeɪnjən]
⊳ adj litauisch; ⊳ n (person)
Litauer(in) m(f); (language)
Litauisch nt
litre ['liːtə'] n Liter m
litter ['lɪtə'] n Abfälle pl; (of
animals) Wurf m ⊳ vt: **to be ~ed
with** übersät sein mit; **litter bin** n
Abfalleimer m
little ['lɪtl] adj (**smaller,
smallest**) klein; (in quantity)
wenig; **a ~ while ago** vor kurzer
Zeit ⊳ adv, n (**fewer, fewest**)
wenig; **a ~** ein bisschen, ein
wenig; **as ~ as possible** so wenig
wie möglich; **for as ~ as £5** ab nur
5 Pfund; **I see very ~ of them** ich
sehe sie sehr selten; **~ by ~** nach

und nach; **little finger** n kleiner
Finger
live [laɪv] adj lebendig; (Elec)
geladen, unter Strom; (TV, Radio:
event) live; **~ broadcast**
Direktübertragung f ⊳ [lɪv] vi
leben; (not die) überleben; (dwell)
wohnen; **you ~ and learn** man
lernt nie aus ⊳ vt (life) führen; **to
~ a life of luxury** im Luxus leben; **to
live on** vi weiterleben ⊳ vt: **to
~ sth** von etw leben; (feed) sich von
etw ernähren; **to earn enough to
~** genug verdienen, um davon zu
leben; **live together** vi
zusammenleben; **live up to** vt
(reputation) gerecht werden +dat;
(expectations) entsprechen +dat;
live with vt (parents etc) wohnen
bei; (partner) zusammenleben mit;
(difficulty) **you'll just have to ~ it**
du musst dich/Sie müssen sich
eben damit abfinden
liveliness ['laɪvlɪnɪs] n Lebhaf-
tigkeit f; **lively** ['laɪvlɪ] adj
lebhaft
liver ['lɪvə'] n Leber f
lives [laɪvz] pl of **life**
livestock ['laɪvstɒk] n Vieh nt
living ['lɪvɪŋ] n Lebensunterhalt
m; **what do you do for a ~?** was
machen Sie beruflich? ⊳ adj
lebend; **living room** n
Wohnzimmer nt
lizard ['lɪzəd] n Eidechse f
llama ['lɑːmə] n (Zool) Lama nt
load [ləʊd] n Last f; (cargo)
Ladung f; (Tech, fig) Belastung f; **~s
of** (fam) massenhaft; **it was a ~ of
rubbish** (fam) es war
grottenschlecht ⊳ vt (vehicle)
beladen; (Inform) laden; (film)
einlegen
loaf [ləʊf] (pl **loaves**) n: **a ~ of
bread** ein (Laib) Brot (m)nt
loan [ləʊn] n (item leant)
Leihgabe f; (Fin) Darlehen nt; **on**

~ geliehen ▷ vt leihen (*to sb* jdm)

loathe [ləʊð] vt verabscheuen

loaves [ləʊvz] pl of **loaf**

lobby ['lɒbɪ] n Vorhalle f; (*Pol*) Lobby f

lobster ['lɒbstə*] n Hummer m

local ['ləʊkəl] adj (*traffic, time etc*) Orts-; (*radio, news, paper*) Lokal-; (*government, authority*) Kommunal-; (*anaesthetic*) örtlich; **~ call** (*Tel*) Ortsgespräch nt; **~ elections** Kommunalwahlen pl; **~ time** Ortszeit f; **~ train** Nahverkehrszug m; **the ~ shops** die Geschäfte am Ort ▷ n (*pub*) Stammlokal nt; **the ~s** pl die Ortsansässigen pl; **locally** adv örtlich, am Ort

locate [ləʊ'keɪt] vt (*find*) ausfindig machen; (*position*) legen; (*establish*) errichten; **to be ~d** sich befinden (*in, at* in +dat); **location** [ləʊ'keɪʃən] n (*position*) Lage f; (*Cine*) Drehort m

loch [lɒx] n (*Scot*) See m

lock [lɒk] n Schloss nt; (*Naut*) Schleuse f; (*of hair*) Locke f ▷ vt (*door etc*) abschließen ▷ vi (*door etc*) sich abschließen lassen; (*wheels*) blockieren; **lock in** vt einschließen, einsperren; **lock out** vt aussperren; **lock up** vt (*house*) abschließen; (*person*) einsperren

locker ['lɒkə*] n Schließfach nt; **locker room** n (*US*) Umkleideraum m

locksmith ['lɒksmɪθ] n Schlosser(in) m(f)

locust ['ləʊkəst] n Heuschrecke f

lodge [lɒdʒ] n (*small house*) Pförtnerhaus nt; (*porter's ~*) Pförtnerloge f ▷ vi in Untermiete wohnen (*with* bei); (*get stuck*) stecken bleiben; **lodger** n Untermieter(in) m(f); **lodging** n Unterkunft f

loft [lɒft] n Dachboden m

log [lɒg] n Klotz m; (*Naut*) Log nt; **to keep a ~ of sth** über etw Buch führen; **log in, log on** vi (*Inform*) sich einloggen; **log off, log out** vi (*Inform*) sich ausloggen

logic ['lɒdʒɪk] n Logik f; **logical** adj logisch

login ['lɒgɪn] n (*Inform*) Log-in nt, Anmeldung f

logo ['lɒgəʊ] (pl **-s**) n Logo nt

loin [lɔɪn] n Lende f

loiter ['lɔɪtə*] vi sich herumtreiben

lollipop ['lɒlɪpɒp] n Lutscher m; **~ man/lady** (*Brit*) Schülerlotse m, Schülerlotsin f

lolly ['lɒlɪ] n Lutscher m

London ['lʌndən] n London nt; **Londoner** n Londoner(in) m(f)

loneliness ['ləʊnlɪnɪs] n Einsamkeit f; **lonely** ['ləʊnlɪ], (*esp US*) **lonesome** ['ləʊnsəm] adj einsam

long [lɒŋ] adj lang; (*distance*) weit; **it's a ~ way** es ist weit (*to* nach); **for a ~ time** lange; **how ~ is the film?** wie lange dauert der Film?; **in the ~ run** auf die Dauer ▷ adv lange; **not for ~** nicht lange; **~ ago** vor langer Zeit; **before ~** bald; **all day ~** den ganzen Tag; **no ~er** nicht mehr; **as ~ as** solange ▷ vi sich sehnen (*for* nach); (*be waiting*) sehnsüchtig warten (*for* auf); **long-distance call** n Ferngespräch nt; **long drink** n Longdrink m; **long-haul flight** n Langstreckenflug m; **longing** n Sehnsucht f (*for* nach); **longingly** adv sehnsüchtig; **longitude** ['lɒŋgɪtjuːd] n Länge f; **long jump** n Weitsprung m; **long-life milk** n H-Milch f; **long-range** adj Langstrecken-, Fern-; **~ missile** Langstreckenrakete f; **long-sighted** adj weitsichtig; **long-standing** adj alt, langjährig; **long-term** adj

langfristig; (car park, effect etc)
Langzeit-; **~ unemployment**
Langzeitarbeitslosigkeit f; **long
wave** n Langwelle f

loo [luː] n (Brit fam) Klo nt

look [lʊk] n Blick m; (appearance)
~(s) pl Aussehen nt; **I'll have a
~** ich schau mal nach; **to have a
~ at sth** sich dat etw ansehen; **can
I have a ~?** darf ich mal sehen?
▷ vi schauen, gucken; (with prep)
sehen; (search) nachsehen; (appear)
aussehen; (**I'm) just ~ing** ich
schaue nur; **it ~s like rain** es sieht
nach Regen aus ▷ vt: **~ what
you've done** sieh dir mal an, was
du da angestellt hast; (appear) **he
~s his age** man sieht ihm sein Alter
an; **to ~ one's best** sehr vorteilhaft
aussehen; **look after** vt (care for)
sorgen für; (keep an eye on) aufpassen auf +akk; **look at** vt
ansehen, anschauen; **look back** vi
sich umsehen; (fig) zurückblicken;
look down on vt (fig) herabsehen
auf +akk; **look for** vt suchen; **look
forward to** vt sich freuen auf +akk;
look into vt (investigate) untersuchen; **look out** vi hinaussehen
(of the window zum Fenster); (watch
out) Ausschau halten (for nach); (be
careful) aufpassen, Acht geben (for
auf +akk); **~!** Vorsicht!; **look up** vi
aufsehen ▷ vt (word etc)
nachschlagen; **look up to** vt
aufsehen zu

loony ['luːnɪ] adj (fam) bekloppt

loop [luːp] n Schleife f

loose [luːs] adj locker; (knot,
button) lose; **loosen** vt lockern;
(knot) lösen

loot [luːt] n Beute f

lop-sided ['lɒp'saɪdɪd] adj schief

lord [lɔːd] n (ruler) Herr m; (Brit:
title) Lord m; **the Lord (God)** Gott
der Herr; **the (House of) Lords**
(Brit) das Oberhaus

lorry ['lɒrɪ] n (Brit) Lastwagen m

lose [luːz] n (lost, lost) vt
verlieren; (chance) verpassen; **to
~ weight** abnehmen; **to ~ one's
life** umkommen ▷ vi verlieren;
(clock, watch) nachgehen; **loser** n
Verlierer(in) m(f); **loss** [lɒs] n
Verlust m; **lost** [lɒst] pt, pp of **lose**;
we're ~ wir haben uns verlaufen
▷ adj verloren; **lost-and-found**
(US), **lost property (office)** n
Fundbüro nt

lot [lɒt] n (fam: batch) Menge f,
Haufen m, Stoß m; **this is the first
~** das ist die erste Ladung; **a
~** viel(e); **a ~ of money** viel Geld;
~s of people viele Leute; **the
(whole) ~** alles; (people) alle

lotion ['ləʊʃən] n Lotion f

lottery ['lɒtərɪ] n Lotterie f

loud [laʊd] adj laut; (colour)
schreiend; **loudspeaker** n
Lautsprecher m; (of stereo) Box f

lounge [laʊndʒ] n Wohnzimmer
nt; (in hotel) Aufenthaltsraum m;
(at airport) Warteraum m ▷ vi sich
herumlümmeln

louse [laʊs] n (pl **lice**) n Laus f;
lousy ['laʊzɪ] adj (fam) lausig

lout [laʊt] n Rüpel m

lovable ['lʌvəbl] adj liebenswert

love [lʌv] n Liebe f (of zu); (person,
address) Liebling m, Schatz m;
(Sport) null; **to be in ~** verliebt sein
(with sb in jdn); **to fall in ~** sich
verlieben (with sb in jdn); **to make
~ to** (o **with) sb** mit jdm schlafen;
(in letter) **he sends his ~** er lässt
grüßen; **give her my ~** grüße sie
von mir; **~, Tom** liebe Grüße, Tom
▷ vt (person) lieben; (activity) sehr
gerne mögen; **to ~ to do sth** etw
für sein Leben gerne tun; **I'd ~ a
cup of tea** ich hätte liebend gern
eine Tasse Tee; **love affair** n
(Liebes)verhältnis nt; **love letter** n

Liebesbrief m; **love life** n
Liebesleben nt; **lovely** ['lʌvlɪ] adj
schön, wunderschön; (charming)
reizend; **we had a ~ time** es war
sehr schön; **lover** ['lʌvə] n Liebhaber(in) m(f); **loving** adj liebevoll
low [ləʊ] adj niedrig; (rank)
niedere(r, s); (level, note, neckline)
tief; (intelligence, density) gering;
(quality, standard) schlecht; (not
loud) leise; (depressed)
niedergeschlagen; **we're ~ on
petrol** wir haben kaum noch
Benzin ▷ n (Meteo) Tief nt;
low-calorie adj kalorienarm;
lowcut adj (dress) tief
ausgeschnitten; **low-emission**
adj schadstoffarm; **lower** ['ləʊə*]
adj niedriger; (storey, class etc)
untere(r, s) ▷ vt herunterlassen;
(eyes, price) senken; (pressure)
verringern; **low-fat** adj fettarm;
low tide [ləʊ'taɪd] n Ebbe f
loyal ['lɔɪəl] adj treu; **loyalty** n
Treue f
lozenge ['lɒzɪndʒ] n Pastille f

L-PLATES

Als **L-Plates** werden in
Großbritannien die weißen
Schilder mit einem roten „L"
bezeichnet, die vorn und hinten
an jedem von einem
Fahrschüler gesteuerten
Fahrzeug befestigt werden
müssen. Fahrschüler müssen
einen vorläufigen Führerschein
beantragen und dürfen damit
unter der Aufsicht eines
erfahrenen Autofahrers auf
allen Straßen außer
Autobahnen fahren.

Ltd abbr = **limited** ≈ GmbH f
lubricant ['luːbrɪkənt] n
Schmiermittel nt, Gleitmittel nt
luck [lʌk] n Glück nt; **bad ~** Pech

nt; **luckily** adv glücklicherweise,
zum Glück; **lucky** adj (number, day
etc) Glücks-; **to be ~** Glück haben
ludicrous ['luːdɪkrəs] adj
grotesk
luggage ['lʌgɪdʒ] n Gepäck nt;
luggage compartment n
Gepäckraum m; **luggage rack** n
Gepäcknetz nt
lukewarm ['luːkwɔːm] adj
lauwarm
lullaby ['lʌləbaɪ] n Schlaflied nt
lumbago [lʌm'beɪgəʊ] n Hexenschuss m
luminous ['luːmɪnəs] adj
leuchtend
lump [lʌmp] n Klumpen m; (Med)
Schwellung f; (in breast) Knoten m;
(of sugar) Stück nt; **lump sum** n
Pauschalsumme f; **lumpy** adj
klumpig
lunacy ['luːnəsɪ] n Wahnsinn m;
lunatic ['luːnətɪk] adj wahnsinnig ▷ n Wahnsinnige(r) mf
lunch, luncheon [lʌntʃ, -ən] n
Mittagessen nt; **to have ~** zu
Mittag essen; **lunch break, lunch
hour** n Mittagspause f;
lunchtime n Mittagszeit f
lung [lʌŋ] n Lunge f
lurch [lɜːtʃ] n: **to leave sb in the
~** jdn im Stich lassen
lurid ['ljʊərɪd] adj (colour) grell;
(details) widerlich
lurk [lɜːk] vi lauern
lust [lʌst] n (sinnliche) Begierde
(for nach)
Luxembourg ['lʌksəmbɜːg] n
Luxemburg nt; **Luxembourger**
[lʌksəm'bɜːgə*] n Luxemburger(in)
m(f)
luxurious [lʌg'zʊərɪəs] adj luxuriös, Luxus-; **luxury** ['lʌkʃərɪ] n
(a. luxuries pl) Luxus m; **~ goods**
Luxusgüter pl
lynx [lɪŋks] n Luchs m
lyrics ['lɪrɪks] npl Liedtext m

m

m *abbr* = **metre** m
M *abbr (street)* = **Motorway** A; *(size)* = **medium** M
MA *abbr* = **Master of Arts** Magister Artium *m*
ma [maː] *n (fam)* Mutti *f*
mac [mæk] *n (Brit fam)* Regenmantel *m*
macaroon [mækəˈruːn] *n* Makrone *f*
Macedonia [masɪˈdəʊnɪə] *n* Mazedonien *nt*
machine [məˈʃiːn] *n* Maschine *f*; **machine gun** *n* Maschinengewehr *nt*; **machinery** [məˈʃiːnərɪ] *n* Maschinen *pl*; *(fig)* Apparat *m*; **machine washable** *adj* waschmaschinenfest
mackerel [ˈmækrəl] *n* Makrele *f*
macro [ˈmækrəʊ] *(pl -s)* *n (Inform)* Makro *nt*
mad [mæd] *adj* wahnsinnig, verrückt; *(dog)* tollwütig; *(angry)*

wütend, sauer *(at auf +akk)*; *(fam)* **~ about** *(fond of)* verrückt nach; **to work like ~** wie verrückt arbeiten; **are you ~?** spinnst du/spinnen Sie?
madam [ˈmædəm] *n* gnädige Frau
mad cow disease [mædˈkaʊdɪˈziːz] *n* Rinderwahnsinn *m*; **maddening** *adj* zum Verrücktwerden
made [meɪd] *pt, pp of* **make**
made-to-measure [ˈmeɪdtəˈmeʒəʳ] *adj* nach Maß; **~ suit** Maßanzug *m*
madly [ˈmædlɪ] *adv* wie verrückt; *(with adj)* wahnsinnig; **madman** [ˈmædmən] *(pl -men)* *n* Verrückte(r) *m*; **madwoman** [ˈmædwʊmən] *(pl -women)* *n* Verrückte *f*; **madness** [ˈmædnɪs] *n* Wahnsinn *m*
magazine [mægəˈziːn] *n* Zeitschrift *f*
maggot [ˈmægət] *n* Made *f*
magic [ˈmædʒɪk] *n* Magie *f*; *(activity)* Zauberei *f*; *(fig: effect)* Zauber *m*; **as if by ~** wie durch Zauberei ▷ *adj* Zauber-; *(powers)* magisch; **magician** [məˈdʒɪʃən] *n* Zauberer *m*, Zaub(r)erin *f*
magnet [ˈmægnɪt] *n* Magnet *m*; **magnetic** [mægˈnetɪk] *adj* magnetisch; **magnetism** [ˈmægnɪtɪzəm] *n (fig)* Anziehungskraft *f*
magnificent, magnificently [mægˈnɪfɪsənt, -lɪ] *adj, adv* herrlich, großartig
magnify [ˈmægnɪfaɪ] *vt* vergrößern; **magnifying glass** *n* Vergrößerungsglas *nt*, Lupe *f*
magpie [ˈmægpaɪ] *n* Elster *f*
maid [meɪd] *n* Dienstmädchen *nt*; **maiden name** *n* Mädchenname *m*; **maiden voyage** *n* Jungfernfahrt *f*

mail [meɪl] n Post f; (e-mail) Mail f ▷ vt (post) aufgeben; (send) mit der Post schicken (to an +akk); **mailbox** n (US) Briefkasten m; (Inform) Mailbox f; **mailing list** n Adressenliste f; **mailman** n (pl **-men**) (US) Briefträger m; **mail order** n Bestellung f per Post; **mail order firm** n Versandhaus nt; **mailshot** n Mailing nt

main [meɪn] adj Haupt-; ~ **course** Hauptgericht nt; **the** ~ **thing** die Hauptsache ▷ n (pipe) Hauptleitung f; **mainframe** n Großrechner m; **mainland** n Festland nt; **mainly** adv hauptsächlich; **main road** n Hauptverkehrsstraße f; **main street** n (US) Hauptstraße f

maintain [meɪnˈteɪn] vt (keep up) aufrechterhalten; (machine, roads) instand halten; (service) warten; (claim) behaupten; **maintenance** [ˈmeɪntənəns] n Instandhaltung f; (Tech) Wartung f

maize [meɪz] n Mais m

majestic [məˈdʒestɪk] adj majestätisch; **majesty** [ˈmædʒɪstɪ] n Majestät f; **Your/His/Her Majesty** Eure/Seine/Ihre Majestät

major [ˈmeɪdʒəʳ] adj (bigger) größer; (important) bedeutend; ~ **part** Großteil m; (role) wichtige Rolle; ~ **road** Hauptverkehrsstraße f; (Mus) **A** ~ A-Dur nt ▷ vi (US) **to** ~ **in sth** etw als Hauptfach studieren

Majorca [məˈjɔːkə] n Mallorca nt

majority [məˈdʒɒrɪtɪ] n Mehrheit f; **to be in the** ~ in der Mehrzahl sein

make [meɪk] n Marke f ▷ vt (**made, made**) machen; (manufacture) herstellen; (clothes) anfertigen; (dress) nähen; (soup)

zubereiten; (bread, cake) backen; (tea, coffee) kochen; (speech) halten; (earn) verdienen; (decision) treffen; **it's made of gold** es ist aus Gold; **to** ~ **sb do sth** jdn dazu bringen, etw zu tun; (force) jdn zwingen, etw zu tun; **she made us wait** sie ließ uns warten; **what ~s you think that?** wie kommen Sie darauf; **it ~s the room look smaller** es lässt den Raum kleiner wirken; **to** ~ **(it to) the airport** (reach) den Flughafen erreichen; (in time) es zum Flughafen schaffen; **he never really made it** er hat es nie zu etwas gebracht; **she didn't** ~ **it through the night** sie hat die Nacht nicht überlebt; (calculate) **I** ~ **it £5/a quarter to six** nach meiner Rechnung kommt es auf 5 Pfund/nach meiner Uhr ist es dreiviertel sechs; **he's just made for this job** er ist für diese Arbeit wie geschaffen; **make for** vt zusteuern auf +akk; **make of** vt (think of) halten von; **I couldn't** ~ **anything of it** ich wurde daraus nicht schlau; **make off** vi sich davonmachen (with mit); **make out** vi zurechtkommen ▷ vt (cheque) ausstellen; (list) aufstellen; (understand) verstehen; (discern) ausmachen; **to** ~ **(that) ...** es so hinstellen, als ob ...; **make up** vt (team etc) bilden; (face) schminken; (invent: story etc) erfinden; **to** ~ **one's mind** sich entscheiden; **to make (it) up with sb** sich mit jdm aussöhnen ▷ vi sich versöhnen; **make up for** vt ausgleichen; (time) aufholen

make-believe adj Fantasie-; **makeover** n gründliche Veränderung, Verschönerung f; **maker** n (Comm) Hersteller(in) m(f); **makeshift** adj behelfsmäßig; **make-up** n

maladjusted | 414

Make-up nt, Schminke f; **making**
['meɪkɪŋ] n Herstellung f
maladjusted [mælə'dʒʌstɪd] adj
verhaltensgestört
malaria [mə'leərɪə] n Malaria f
Malaysia [mə'leɪzɪə] n Malaysia
nt
male [meɪl] n Mann m; (animal)
Männchen nt ▷ adj männlich;
~ chauvinist Chauvi m, Macho m;
~ nurse Krankenpfleger m
malfunction [mæl'fʌŋkʃən] vi
nicht richtig funktionieren ▷ n
Defekt m
malice ['mælɪs] n Bosheit f;
malicious [mə'lɪʃəs] adj boshaft;
(behaviour, action) böswillig;
(damage) mutwillig
malignant [mə'lɪgnənt] adj
bösartig
mall [mɔːl] n (US)
Einkaufszentrum nt
malnutrition [mælnjʊ'trɪʃən] n
Unterernährung f
malt [mɔːlt] n Malz nt
Malta ['mɔːltə] n Malta nt;
Maltese [mɔːl'tiːz] adj
maltesisch ▷ n (person)
Malteser(in) m(f); (language)
Maltesisch nt
maltreat [mæl'triːt] vt schlecht
behandeln; (violently) misshandeln
mammal ['mæməl] n Säugetier
nt
mammoth ['mæməθ] adj
Mammut-, Riesen-
man [mæn] (pl **men**) n (male)
Mann m; (human race) der Mensch,
die Menschen pl (in chess) Figur f
▷ vt besetzen
manage ['mænɪdʒ] vi zurechtkommen; **can you ~?** schaffst du
es?; **to ~ without sth** ohne etw
auskommen, auf etw verzichten
können ▷ vt (control) leiten;
(musician, sportsman) managen;
(cope with) fertig werden mit; (task,

portion, climb etc) schaffen; **to ~ to
do sth** es schaffen, etw zu tun;
manageable adj (object)
handlich; (task) zu bewältigen;
management n Leitung f;
(directors) Direktion f; (subject)
Management nt,
Betriebswirtschaft f;
management consultant n
Unternehmensberater(in) m(f);
manager n Geschäftsführer(in)
m(f); (departmental ~)
Abteilungsleiter(in) m(f); (of
branch, bank) Filialleiter(in) m(f); (of
musician, sportsman) Manager(in)
m(f); **managing director** n
Geschäftsführer(in) m(f)
mane [meɪn] n Mähne f
maneuver (US) see **manoeuvre**
mango ['mæŋgəʊ] (pl **-es**) n
Mango f
man-hour n Arbeitsstunde f
manhunt n Fahndung f
mania ['meɪnɪə] n Manie f;
maniac ['meɪnɪæk] n Wahnsin-
nige(r) mf; (fan) Fanatiker(in)
m(f)
manicure ['mænɪkjʊə°] n
Maniküre f
manipulate [mə'nɪpjʊleɪt] vt
manipulieren
mankind [mæn'kaɪnd] n
Menschheit f
manly ['mænlɪ] adj männlich
man-made ['mænmeɪd] adj
(product) künstlich
manner ['mænə°] n Art f; **in this
~** auf diese Art und Weise; **~s** pl
Manieren pl
manoeuvre [mə'nuːvə°] n
Manöver nt ▷ vt, vi manövrieren
manor ['mænə°] n: **~ (house)**
Herrenhaus nt
manpower ['mænpaʊə°] n
Arbeitskräfte pl
mansion ['mænʃən] n Villa f; (of
old family) Herrenhaus nt

manslaughter ['mænslɔːtə°] n Totschlag m

mantelpiece ['mæntlpiːs] n Kaminsims m

manual ['mænjʊəl] adj manuell, Hand- ▷ n Handbuch nt

manufacture [mænjʊˈfæktʃə°] vt herstellen ▷ n Herstellung f; **manufacturer** n Hersteller m

manure [məˈnjʊə°] n Dung m; (esp artificial) Dünger m

many ['menɪ] (**more**, **most**) adj, pron viele; **~ times** oft; **not ~ people** nicht viele Leute; **too ~ problems** zu viele Probleme

map [mæp] n Landkarte f; (of town) Stadtplan m

maple ['meɪpl] n Ahorn m

marathon ['mærəθən] n Marathon m

marble ['mɑːbl] n Marmor m; (for playing) Murmel f

march [mɑːtʃ] vi marschieren ▷ n Marsch m; (protest) Demonstration f

March [mɑːtʃ] n März m; see also **September**

mare [meə] n Stute f

margarine [mɑːdʒəˈriːn] n Margarine f

margin ['mɑːdʒɪn] n Rand m; (extra amount) Spielraum m; (Comm) Gewinnspanne f; **marginal** adj (difference etc) geringfügig

marijuana [mærɪjuˈɑːnə] n Marihuana nt

marine [məˈriːn] adj Meeres-

marital ['mærɪtl] adj ehelich; **~ status** Familienstand m

maritime ['mærɪtaɪm] adj See-

marjoram ['mɑːdʒərəm] n Majoran m

mark [mɑːk] n (spot) Fleck m; (at school) Note f; (sign) Zeichen n; ▷ vt (make ~) Flecken machen auf +akk; (indicate) markieren;

(schoolwork) benoten, korrigieren; Flecken machen auf +akk;

markedly ['mɑːkɪdlɪ] adv merklich; (with comp adj) wesentlich;

marker n (in book) Lesezeichen nt; (pen) Marker m

market ['mɑːkɪt] n Markt m; (stock ~) Börse f ▷ vt (Comm: new product) auf den Markt bringen; (goods) vertreiben; **marketing** n Marketing nt; **market leader** n Marktführer m; **market place** n Marktplatz m; **market research** n Marktforschung f

marmalade ['mɑːməleɪd] n Orangenmarmelade f

maroon [məˈruːn] adj rötlich braun

marquee [mɑːˈkiː] n großes Zelt

marriage ['mærɪdʒ] n Ehe f; (wedding) Heirat f (to mit);

married ['mærɪd] adj (person) verheiratet

marrow ['mærəʊ] n (bone ~) Knochenmark nt; (vegetable) Kürbis m

marry ['mærɪ] vt heiraten; (join) trauen; (take as husband, wife) heiraten ▷ vi: **to ~ / to get married** heiraten

marsh [mɑːʃ] n Marsch f, Sumpf m

marshal ['mɑːʃəl] n (at rally etc) Ordner m; (US: police) Bezirkspolizeichef m

martial arts ['mɑːʃəlˈɑːts] npl Kampfsportarten pl

martyr ['mɑːtə°] n Märtyrer(in) m(f)

marvel ['mɑːvəl] n Wunder nt ▷ vi staunen (at über +akk); **marvellous, marvelous** (US) adj wunderbar

marzipan ['mɑːzɪˈpæn] n Marzipan nt o m

mascara [mæˈskɑːrə] n Wimperntusche f

mascot ['mæskɒt] n Maskottchen nt

masculine ['mæskjʊlɪn] adj männlich

mashed [mæʃt] adj ~ **potatoes** pl Kartoffelbrei m, Kartoffelpüree nt

mask [mɑːsk] n (a. Inform) Maske f ▷ vt (feelings) verbergen

masochist ['mæsəʊkɪst] n Masochist(in) m(f)

mason ['meɪsn] n (stone~) Steinmetz(in) m(f); **masonry** n Mauerwerk nt

mass [mæs] n Masse f; (of people) Menge f; (Rel) Messe f; ~**es of** massenhaft

massacre ['mæsəkə°] n Blutbad nt

massage ['mæsɑːʒ] n Massage f ▷ vt massieren

massive ['mæsɪv] adj (powerful) gewaltig; (very large) riesig

mass media ['mæs'miːdɪə] npl Massenmedien pl; **mass-produce** vt in Massenproduktion herstellen; **mass production** n Massenproduktion f

master ['mɑːstə°] n Herr m; (of dog) Besitzer m, Herrchen nt; (teacher) Lehrer m; (artist) Meister m ▷ vt meistern; (language etc) beherrschen; **masterly** adj meisterhaft; **masterpiece** n Meisterwerk nt

masturbate ['mæstəbeɪt] vi masturbieren

mat [mæt] n Matte f; (for table) Untersetzer m

match [mætʃ] n Streichholz nt; (Sport) Wettkampf m; (ball games) Spiel nt; (tennis) Match nt ▷ vt (be like, suit) passen zu; (equal) gleichkommen +dat ▷ vi zusammenpassen; **matchbox** n Streichholzschachtel f; **matching** adj (one item)

passend; (two items) zusammenpassend

mate [meɪt] n (companion) Kumpel m; (of animal) Weibchen nt/Männchen nt ▷ vi sich paaren

material [mə'tɪərɪəl] n Material nt; (for book etc, cloth) Stoff m; **materialistic** [mətɪərɪə'lɪstɪk] adj materialistisch; **materialize** [mə'tɪərɪəlaɪz] vi zustande kommen; (hope) wahr werden

maternal [mə'tɜːnl] adj mütterlich; **maternity** [mə'tɜːnɪtɪ] adj: ~ **dress** Umstandskleid nt; ~ **leave** Elternzeit f (der Mutter); ~ **ward** Entbindungsstation f

math [mæθ] n (US fam) Mathe f; **mathematical** [mæθə'mætɪkəl] adj mathematisch; **mathematics** [mæθə'mætɪks] nsing Mathematik f; **maths** [mæθs] nsing (Brit fam) Mathe f

matinée ['mætɪneɪ] n Nachmittagsvorstellung f

matter ['mætə°] n (substance) Materie f; (affair) Sache f; **a personal** ~ eine persönliche Angelegenheit; **a** ~ **of taste** eine Frage des Geschmacks; **no** ~ **how/what** egal wie/was; **what's the** ~? was ist los?; **as a** ~ **of fact** eigentlich; **a** ~ **of time** eine Frage der Zeit ▷ vi darauf ankommen, wichtig sein; **it doesn't** ~ es macht nichts; **matter-of-fact** adj sachlich, nüchtern

mattress ['mætrəs] n Matratze f

mature [mə'tjʊə°] adj reif ▷ vi reif werden; **maturity** [mə'tjʊərɪtɪ] n Reife f

maximum ['mæksɪməm] adj Höchst-, höchste(r, s); ~ **speed** Höchstgeschwindigkeit f ▷ n Maximum nt

may [meɪ] (**might**) vb aux (be

possible) können; (have permission) dürfen; **it ~ rain** es könnte regnen; **~ I smoke?** darf ich rauchen?; **it ~ not happen** es passiert vielleicht gar nicht; **we ~ as well go** wir können ruhig gehen

May [meɪ] n Mai m; see also **September**

maybe ['meɪbiː] adv vielleicht

May Day ['meɪdeɪ] n der erste Mai

mayo ['meɪəʊ] (US fam), **mayonnaise** [meɪə'neɪz] n Mayo f, Mayonnaise f, Majonäse f

mayor [mɛə°] n Bürgermeister m

maze [meɪz] n Irrgarten m; (fig) Wirrwarr nt

MB abbr = **megabyte** MB nt

⭕ **KEYWORD**

me [miː] pron **1** (direct) mich; **it's me** ich bin's
2 (indirect) mir; **give them to me** gib sie mir
3 (after prep) (+akk) mich; (+dat) mir; **with/without me** mit mir/ohne mich

meadow ['medəʊ] n Wiese f

meal [miːl] n Essen nt, Mahlzeit f; **to go out for a ~** essen gehen; **meal pack** n (US) tiefgekühltes Fertiggericht; **meal time** n Essenszeit f

mean [miːn] (meant, meant) vt (signify) bedeuten; (have in mind) meinen; (intend) vorhaben; **I ~ it** ich meine das ernst; **what do you ~ (by that)?** was willst du damit sagen?; **to ~ to do sth** etw tun wollen; **it was ~t for you** es war für dich bestimmt (o gedacht); **it was ~t to be a joke** es sollte ein Witz sein ▷ vi: **he ~s well** er

meint es gut ▷ adj (stingy) geizig; (spiteful) gemein (to zu); **meaning** ['miːnɪŋ] n Bedeutung f; (of life, poem) Sinn m; **meaningful** adj sinnvoll; **meaningless** adj (text) ohne Sinn

means [miːnz] (pl **means**) n Mittel nt; (pl: funds) Mittel pl; **by ~ of** durch, mittels; **by all ~** selbstverständlich; **by no ~** keineswegs; **~ of transport** Beförderungsmittel

meant [ment] pt, pp of **mean**

meantime ['miːntaɪm] adv: **in the ~** inzwischen; **meanwhile** ['miːnwaɪl] adv inzwischen

measles ['miːzlz] nsing Masern pl; **German ~** Röteln pl

measure ['meʒə°] vt, vi messen ▷ n (unit, device for measuring) Maß f; (step) Maßnahme f; **to take ~s** Maßnahmen ergreifen; **measurement** n (amount measured) Maß nt

meat [miːt] n Fleisch nt; **meatball** n Fleischbällchen nt

mechanic [mɪ'kænɪk] n Mechaniker(in) m(f); **mechanical** adj mechanisch; **mechanics** nsing Mechanik f; **mechanism** ['mekənɪzəm] n Mechanismus m

medal ['medl] n Medaille f; (decoration) Orden m; **medalist** (US), **medallist** ['medəlɪst] n Medaillengewinner(in) m(f)

media ['miːdɪə] npl Medien pl

median strip ['miːdɪən strɪp] n (US) Mittelstreifen m

mediate ['miːdɪeɪt] vi vermitteln

medical ['medɪkəl] adj medizinisch; (treatment etc) ärztlich; **~ student** Medizinstudent(in) m(f) ▷ n Untersuchung f; **Medicare** ['medɪkeə°] n (US) Krankenkasse f für ältere Leute; **medication**

[medɪˈkeɪʃən] n Medikamente pl;
to be on ~ Medikamente nehmen;
medicinal [meˈdɪsɪnl] adj Heil-;
~ **herbs** Heilkräuter pl; **medicine**
[ˈmedsɪn] n Arznei f; (science)
Medizin f

medieval [medɪˈiːvəl] adj
mittelalterlich

mediocre [miːdɪˈəʊkə*] adj
mittelmäßig

meditate [ˈmedɪteɪt] vi meditieren; (fig) nachdenken (on über
+akk)

Mediterranean
[medɪtəˈreɪnɪən] n (sea)
Mittelmeer nt; (region)
Mittelmeerraum m

medium [ˈmiːdɪəm] adj (quality,
size) mittlere(r, s); (steak)
halbdurch; ~ **(dry)** (wine)
halbtrocken; ~ **sized** mittelgroß;
~ **wave** Mittelwelle f ▷ n (pl
media) Medium nt; (means) Mittel
nt

meet [miːt] (**met, met**) vt
treffen; (by arrangement) sich
treffen mit; (difficulties) stoßen auf
+akk; (get to know) kennenlernen;
(requirement, demand) gerecht
werden +dat; (deadline) einhalten;
pleased to ~ you sehr angenehm!;
to ~ sb at the station jdn vom
Bahnhof abholen ▷ vi sich
treffen; (become acquainted) sich
kennenlernen; **we've met**
(before) wir kennen uns schon;
meet up vt sich treffen (with
mit); **meet with** vt (group)
zusammenkommen mit;
(difficulties, resistance etc) stoßen
auf +akk; **meeting** n Treffen nt;
(business ~) Besprechung f; (of
committee) Sitzung f; (assembly)
Versammlung f; **meeting place**,
meeting point n Treffpunkt m

megabyte [ˈmegəbaɪt] n
Megabyte nt

melody [ˈmelədɪ] n Melodie f

melon [ˈmelən] n Melone f

melt [melt] vt, vi schmelzen

member [ˈmembə*] n Mitglied
nt; (of tribe, species) Angehörige(r)
mf; **Member of Parliament**
Parlamentsabgeordnete(r) mf;
membership n Mitgliedschaft f;
membership card n
Mitgliedskarte f

memento [məˈmentəʊ] (pl **-es**)
n Andenken nt (of an +akk)

memo [ˈmeməʊ] (pl **-s**) n
Mitteilung f, Memo nt; **memo pad**
n Notizblock m

memorable [ˈmemərəbl] adj
unvergesslich; **memorial**
[mɪˈmɔːrɪəl] n Denkmal nt (to
für); **memorize** [ˈmeməraɪz] vt
sich einprägen, auswendig lernen;
memory [ˈmemərɪ] n Gedächtnis nt; (Inform: of computer)
Speicher m; (sth recalled)
Erinnerung f; **in ~ of** zur
Erinnerung an +akk; **memory
stick** n (Inform) Memorystick® m

men [men] pl of **man**

menace [ˈmenɪs] n Bedrohung f;
(danger) Gefahr f

mend [mend] vt reparieren;
(clothes) flicken ▷ n: **on the ~** auf
dem Wege der Besserung

meningitis [menɪnˈdʒaɪtɪs] n
Hirnhautentzündung f

menopause [ˈmenəʊpɔːz] n
Wechseljahre pl

mental [ˈmentl] adj geistig;
mentality [menˈtælɪtɪ] n Mentalität f; **mentally** [ˈmentəlɪ] adv
geistig; ~ **handicapped** geistig
behindert; ~ **ill** geisteskrank

mention [ˈmenʃən] n Erwäh-
nung f ▷ vt erwähnen (to sb jdm
gegenüber); **don't ~ it** bitte sehr,
gern geschehen

menu [ˈmenjuː] n Speisekarte f;
(Inform) Menü nt

merchandise ['mɜːtʃəndaɪz] n Handelsware f; **merchant** ['mɜːtʃənt] adj Handels-

merciful ['mɜːsɪful] adj gnädig; **mercifully** adv glücklicherweise

mercury ['mɜːkjʊrɪ] n Quecksilber nt

mercy ['mɜːsɪ] n Gnade f

mere [mɪə] adj bloß; **merely** ['mɪəlɪ] adv bloß, lediglich

merge [mɜːdʒ] vi verschmelzen; (Auto) sich einfädeln; (Comm) fusionieren; **merger** n (Comm) Fusion f

meringue [mə'ræŋ] n Baiser nt

merit ['merɪt] n Verdienst nt; (advantage) Vorzug m

merry ['merɪ] adj fröhlich; (fam: tipsy) angeheitert; **Merry Christmas** Fröhliche Weihnachten!; **merry-go-round** n Karussell nt

mess [mes] n Unordnung f; (muddle) Durcheinander nt; (dirty) Schweinerei f; (trouble) Schwierigkeiten pl; **in a ~** (muddled) durcheinander; (untidy) unordentlich; (fig: person) in der Klemme; **to make a ~ of sth** etw verpfuschen; **to look a ~** unmöglich aussehen; **mess about** vi (tinker with) herummurksen (with an +dat); (play the fool) herumalbern; (do nothing in particular) herumgammeln; **mess up** vt verpfuschen; (make untidy) in Unordnung bringen; (dirty) schmutzig machen

message ['mesɪdʒ] n Mitteilung f, Nachricht f; (meaning) Botschaft f; **can I give him a ~?** kann ich ihm etwas ausrichten?; **please leave a ~** (on answerphones) bitte hinterlassen Sie eine Nachricht; **I get the ~** ich hab's verstanden

messenger ['mesɪndʒə°] n Bote m

messy ['mesɪ] adj (untidy) unordentlich; (situation etc) verfahren

met [met] pt, pp of **meet**

metal ['metl] n Metall nt; **metallic** [mɪ'tælɪk] adj metallisch

meteorology [miːtɪə'rɒlədʒɪ] n Meteorologie f

meter ['miːtə°] n Zähler m; (parking meter) Parkuhr f; (US) see **metre**

method ['meθəd] n Methode f; **methodical** [mɪ'θɒdɪkəl] adj methodisch

meticulous [mɪ'tɪkjʊləs] adj (peinlich) genau

metre ['miːtə°] n Meter m o nt; **metric** ['metrɪk] adj metrisch; **~ system** Dezimalsystem nt

Mexico ['meksɪkəʊ] n Mexiko nt

mice [maɪs] pl of **mouse**

mickey ['mɪkɪ] n: **to take the ~ (out of sb)** (fam) (jdn) auf den Arm nehmen

microchip ['maɪkrəʊtʃɪp] n (Inform) Mikrochip m; **microphone** n Mikrofon nt; **microscope** n Mikroskop nt; **microwave (oven)** n Mikrowelle(nherd) f(m)

mid [mɪd] adj: **in ~ January** Mitte Januar; **he's in his ~ forties** er ist Mitte vierzig

midday ['mɪd'deɪ] n Mittag m; **at ~** mittags

middle ['mɪdl] n Mitte f; (waist) Taille f; **in the ~ of** mitten in +dat; **to be in the ~ of doing sth** gerade dabei sein, etw zu tun ▷ adj mittlere(r, s), Mittel-; **the ~ one** der/die/das Mittlere; **middle-aged** adj mittleren Alters; **Middle Ages** npl: **the ~** das Mittelalter; **middle-class** adj mittelständisch; (bourgeois)

bürgerlich; **middle classes** npl:
the ~ der Mittelstand; **Middle
East** n: **the ~** der Nahe Osten;
middle name n zweiter
Vorname

Midlands ['mɪdləndz] npl: **the
~** Mittelengland nt

midnight ['mɪdnaɪt] n Mitternacht f

midst [mɪdst] n: **in the ~ of**
mitten in +dat

midsummer ['mɪdsʌmə°] n
Hochsommer m; **Midsummer's
Day** Sommersonnenwende f

midway [mɪd'weɪ] adv auf
halbem Wege; **~ through the film**
nach der Hälfte des Films;

midweek [mɪd'wiːk] adj, adv in
der Mitte der Woche

midwife ['mɪdwaɪf] (pl **-wives**) n
Hebamme f

midwinter [mɪd'wɪntə°] n
tiefster Winter

might [maɪt] pt of **may**;
(possibility) könnte; (permission)
dürfte; (would) würde; **they ~ still
come** sie könnten noch nicht kommen;
he ~ have let me know er hätte
mir doch Bescheid sagen können;
I thought she ~ change her mind
ich dachte schon, sie würde sich
anders entscheiden ▷ n Macht f,
Kraft f

mighty ['maɪtɪ] adj gewaltig;
(powerful) mächtig

migraine ['miːgreɪn] n Migräne
f

migrant ['maɪgrənt] n (bird)
Zugvogel m; **~ worker**
Gastarbeiter(in) m(f); Migrant(in)
m(f); **migrate** [maɪ'greɪt] vi
abwandern; (birds) nach Süden
ziehen

mike [maɪk] n (fam) Mikro nt

Milan [mɪ'læn] n Mailand nt

mild [maɪld] adj mild; (person)
sanft; **mildly** adv: **to put it**

~ gelinde gesagt; **mildness** n
Milde f

mile [maɪl] n Meile f (=1,609 km);
for ~s (and ~s) = kilometerweit; **~s
per hour** Meilen pro Stunde; **~s
better than** hundertmal besser
als; **mileage** n Meilen pl,
Meilenzahl f; **mileometer**
[maɪ'lɒmɪtə°] n =
Kilometerzähler m; **milestone** n
(a. fig) Meilenstein m

militant ['mɪlɪtənt] adj militant;
military ['mɪlɪtərɪ] adj Militär-,
militärisch

milk [mɪlk] n Milch f ▷ vt
melken; **milk chocolate** n
Vollmilchschokolade f; **milkman**
(pl **-men**) n Milchmann m; **milk
shake** n Milchshake m,
Milchmixgetränk nt

mill [mɪl] n Mühle f; (factory)
Fabrik f

millennium [mɪ'lenɪəm] n
Jahrtausend nt

milligramme ['mɪlɪɡræm] n
Milligramm nt; **milliliter** (US),
millilitre n Milliliter m;
millimeter (US), **millimetre** n
Millimeter m

million ['mɪljən] n Million f; **five
~** fünf Millionen; **~s of people**
Millionen von Menschen;
millionaire [mɪljə'neə°] n Millionär(in) m(f)

mime [maɪm] n Pantomime f
▷ vt, vi mimen; **mimic** ['mɪmɪk]
n Imitator(in) m(f) ▷ vt, vi
nachahmen; **mimicry** ['mɪmɪkrɪ]
n Nachahmung f

mince [mɪns] vt (zer)hacken
▷ n (meat) Hackfleisch nt;
mincemeat n süße Gebäckfüllung
aus Rosinen, Äpfeln, Zucker, Gewürzen
und Talg; **mince pie** n mit
'mincemeat' gefülltes süßes
Weihnachtsgebäck

mind [maɪnd] n (intellect)

Verstand m; (also person) Geist m;
out of sight, he is out of ~ aus den
Augen, aus dem Sinn; **he is out of
his ~** er ist nicht bei Verstand; **to
keep sth in ~** etw im Auge
behalten; **do you have sth in ~?**
denken Sie an etwas Besonderes?;
I've a lot on my ~ mich
beschäftigt so vieles im Moment;
to change one's ~ es sich dat
anders überlegen ▷ vt (look after)
aufpassen auf +akk; (object to)
etwas haben gegen; **~ you, ...**
allerdings ...; **I wouldn't ~ ...** ich
hätte nichts gegen ...; **"~ the
step"** „Vorsicht Stufe" ▷ vi etwas
dagegen haben; **do you ~ if I ...**
macht es Ihnen etwas aus, wenn
ich ...; **I don't ~** es ist mir egal,
meinetwegen; **never ~** macht
nichts

mine [maɪn] pron meine(r, s);
this is ~ das gehört mir; **a friend
of ~** ein Freund von mir ▷ n
(coalmine) Bergwerk nt; (Mil) Mine
f; **miner** n Bergarbeiter(in) m(f)

mineral ['mɪnərəl] n Mineral nt;
mineral water n Mineralwasser
nt

mingle ['mɪŋgl] vi sich mischen
(with unter +akk)

miniature ['mɪnɪtʃə°] adj
Miniatur-

minibar ['mɪnɪbɑː] n Minibar f;
minibus n Kleinbus m; **minicab** n
Kleintaxi nt

minimal ['mɪnɪml] adj minimal;
minimize ['mɪnɪmaɪz] vt auf ein
Minimum reduzieren; **minimum**
['mɪnɪməm] n Minimum nt ▷ adj
Mindest-

mining ['maɪnɪŋ] n Bergbau m

miniskirt n Minirock m

minister ['mɪnɪstə°] n (Pol)
Minister(in) m(f); (Rel) Pastor(in)
m(f), Pfarrer(in) m(f); **ministry**
['mɪnɪstrɪ] n (Pol) Ministerium nt

minor ['maɪnə°] adj kleiner;
(insignificant) unbedeutend;
(operation, offence) harmlos; **~ road**
Nebenstraße f; (Mus) **A ~** a-Moll nt
▷ n (Brit: under 18)
Minderjährige(r) mf; **minority**
[maɪ'nɒrɪtɪ] n Minderheit f

mint [mɪnt] n Minze f; (sweet)
Pfefferminz(bonbon) nt; **mint
sauce** n Minzsoße f

minus ['maɪnəs] prep minus;
(without) ohne

minute [maɪ'njuːt] adj winzig;
in ~ detail genauestens ▷ ['mɪnɪt]
n Minute f; **just a ~** Moment mal;
any ~ jeden Augenblick; **~s pl** (of
meeting) Protokoll nt

miracle ['mɪrəkl] n Wunder nt;
miraculous [mɪ'rækjʊləs] adj
unglaublich

mirage ['mɪrɑːʒ] n Fata Morgana
f, Luftspiegelung f

mirror ['mɪrə°] n Spiegel m

misbehave [mɪsbɪ'heɪv] vi sich
schlecht benehmen

miscalculation
['mɪskælkjʊ'leɪʃən] n Fehlkalku-
lation f; (misjudgement)
Fehleinschätzung f

miscarriage [mɪs'kærɪdʒ] n
(Med) Fehlgeburt f

miscellaneous [mɪsɪ'leɪnɪəs]
adj verschieden

mischief ['mɪstʃɪf] n Unfug m;
mischievous ['mɪstʃɪvəs] adj
(person) durchtrieben; (glance)
verschmitzt

misconception [mɪskən'sepʃən]
n falsche Vorstellung

misconduct [mɪs'kɒndʌkt] n
Vergehen nt

miser ['maɪzə°] n Geizhals m

miserable ['mɪzərəbl] adj (person) todunglücklich; (conditions,
life) elend; (pay, weather)
miserabel

miserly ['maɪzəlɪ] adj geizig

misery ['mɪzərɪ] n Elend nt; (suffering) Qualen pl

misfit ['mɪsfɪt] n Außenseiter(in) m(f)

misfortune [mɪsˈfɔːtʃən] n Pech nt

misguided [mɪsˈgaɪdɪd] adj irrig; (optimism) unangebracht

misinform [mɪsɪnˈfɔːm] vt falsch informieren

misinterpret [mɪsɪnˈtɜːprɪt] vt falsch auslegen

misjudge [mɪsˈdʒʌdʒ] vt falsch beurteilen

mislay [mɪsˈleɪ] irr vt verlegen

mislead [mɪsˈliːd] irr vt irreführen; **misleading** adj irreführend

misprint ['mɪsprɪnt] n Druckfehler m

mispronounce [mɪsprəˈnaʊns] vt falsch aussprechen

miss [mɪs] vt (fail to hit, catch) verfehlen; (not notice, hear) nicht mitbekommen; (be too late for) verpassen; (chance) versäumen; (regret the absence of) vermissen; **I ~ you** du fehlst mir ▷ vi nicht treffen; (shooting) danebenschießen; (ball, shot etc) danebengehen; **miss out** vt auslassen ▷ vi: **to ~ on sth** etw verpassen

Miss [mɪs] n (unmarried woman) Fräulein nt

missile ['mɪsaɪl] n Geschoss nt; (rocket) Rakete f

missing ['mɪsɪŋ] adj (person) vermisst; (thing) fehlend; **to be/go ~** vermisst werden, fehlen

mission ['mɪʃən] n (Pol, Mil, Rel) Auftrag m, Mission f; **missionary** ['mɪʃənrɪ] n Missionar(in) m(f)

mist [mɪst] n (feiner) Nebel m; (haze) Dunst m; **mist over, mist up** vi sich beschlagen

mistake [mɪˈsteɪk] n Fehler m; **by ~** aus Versehen ▷ irr vt

(**mistook, mistaken**)
(misunderstand) falsch verstehen; (mix up) verwechseln (for mit); **there's no mistaking ...** ... ist unverkennbar; (meaning) ... ist unmissverständlich;

mistaken adj (idea, identity) falsch; **to be ~** sich irren, falschliegen

mistletoe ['mɪsltəʊ] n Mistel f

mistreat [mɪsˈtriːt] vt schlecht behandeln

mistress ['mɪstrɪs] n (lover) Geliebte f

mistrust [mɪsˈtrʌst] n Misstrauen nt (of gegen) ▷ vt misstrauen +dat

misty ['mɪstɪ] adj neblig; (hazy) dunstig

misunderstand [mɪsʌndəˈstænd] irr vt, vi falsch verstehen; **misunderstanding** n Missverständnis nt; (disagreement) Differenz f

mitten ['mɪtn] n Fausthandschuh m

mix [mɪks] n (mixture) Mischung f ▷ vt mischen; (blend) vermischen (with mit); (drinks, music) mixen; **to ~ business with pleasure** das Angenehme mit dem Nützlichen verbinden ▷ vi (liquids) sich vermischen lassen; **mix up** vt (mix) zusammenmischen; (confuse) verwechseln (with mit); **mixed** adj gemischt; **a ~ bunch** eine bunt gemischte Truppe; **~ grill** Mixed Grill m; **~ vegetables** Mischgemüse nt; **mixer** n (for food) Mixer m; **mixture** ['mɪkstʃəˈ] n Mischung f; (Med) Saft m; **mix-up** n Durcheinander nt, Missverständnis nt

ml abbr = **millilitre** ml

mm abbr = **millimetre** mm

moan [məʊn] n Stöhnen nt; (complaint) Gejammer nt ▷ vi

stöhnen; (complain) jammern, meckern (about über +akk)

mobile ['məʊbaɪl] adj beweglich; (on wheels) fahrbar ▷ n (phone) Handy nt; **mobile phone** n Mobiltelefon nt, Handy nt

mobility [məʊ'bɪlɪtɪ] n Beweglichkeit f

mock [mɒk] vt verspotten ▷ adj Schein-; **mockery** n Spott m

mod cons ['mɒd'kɒnz] abbr = **modern conveniences** (moderner) Komfort

mode [məʊd] n Art f; (Inform) Modus m

model ['mɒdl] n Modell nt; (example) Vorbild nt; (fashion ~) Model nt ▷ adj (miniature) Modell-; (perfect) Muster- ▷ vt (make) formen ▷ vi: **she ~s for Versace** sie arbeitet als Model bei Versace

modem ['məʊdem] n Modem nt

moderate ['mɒdərət] adj mäßig; (views, politics) gemäßigt; (income, success) mittelmäßig ▷ n (Pol) Gemäßigte(r) mf ▷ ['mɒdəreɪt] vt mäßigen; **moderation** [mɒdə'reɪʃən] n Mäßigung f; **in ~** mit Maßen

modern ['mɒdən] adj modern; ~ **history** neuere Geschichte; ~ **Greek** Neugriechisch nt; **modernize** ['mɒdənaɪz] vt modernisieren

modest ['mɒdɪst] adj bescheiden; **modesty** n Bescheidenheit f

modification [mɒdɪfɪ'keɪʃən] n Abänderung f; **modify** ['mɒdɪfaɪ] vt abändern

moist [mɔɪst] adj feucht; **moisten** ['mɔɪsn] vt befeuchten; **moisture** ['mɔɪstʃə°] n Feuchtigkeit f; **moisturizer** n Feuchtigkeitscreme f

molar ['məʊlə°] n Backenzahn m

mold (US) see **mould**

mole [məʊl] n (spot) Leberfleck m; (animal) Maulwurf m

molecule ['mɒlɪkjuːl] n Molekül nt

molest [məʊ'lest] vt belästigen

molt (US) see **moult**

molten ['məʊltən] adj geschmolzen

mom [mɒm] n (US) Mutti f

moment ['məʊmənt] n Moment m, Augenblick m; **just a ~** Moment mal!; **at** (o for) **the ~** im Augenblick; **in a ~** gleich

momentous [məʊ'mentəs] adj bedeutsam

Monaco ['mɒnəkəʊ] n Monaco nt

monarchy ['mɒnəkɪ] n Monarchie f

monastery ['mɒnəstrɪ] n (for monks) Kloster nt

Monday ['mʌndeɪ] n Montag m; see also **Tuesday**

monetary ['mʌnɪtərɪ] adj (reform, policy, union) Währungs-; ~ **unit** Geldeinheit f

money ['mʌnɪ] n Geld nt; **to get one's ~'s worth** auf seine Kosten kommen; **money order** n Postanweisung f

mongrel ['mʌŋɡrəl] n Promenadenmischung f

monitor ['mɒnɪtə°] n (screen) Monitor m ▷ vt (progress etc) überwachen; (broadcasts) abhören

monk [mʌŋk] n Mönch m

monkey ['mʌŋkɪ] n Affe m; ~ **business** Unfug m

monopolize [mə'nɒpəlaɪz] vt monopolisieren; (fig: person, thing) in Beschlag nehmen; **monopoly** [mə'nɒpəlɪ] n Monopol nt

monotonous [mə'nɒtənəs] adj eintönig, monoton

monsoon [mɒn'suːn] n Monsun m

monster ['mɒnstə°] n (animal,

thing) Monstrum nt ▷ adj Riesen-;
monstrosity [mɒnˈstrɒsɪtɪ] n
Monstrosität f; *(thing)* Ungetüm
nt

Montenegro [mɒntɪˈniːɡrəʊ] n
Montenegro nt

month [mʌnθ] n Monat m;
monthly adj monatlich; *(ticket,
salary)* Monats- ▷ adv monatlich
▷ n *(magazine)* Monatsschrift f

monty [ˈmɒntɪ] n: **to go the full
~** *(fam: strip)* alle Hüllen fallen
lassen; *(go the whole hog)* aufs
Ganze gehen

monument [ˈmɒnjʊmənt] n
Denkmal nt *(to für)*; **monumental**
[mɒnjʊˈmentl] adj *(huge)*
gewaltig

mood [muːd] n *(of person)*
Laune f; *(a. general)* Stimmung f;
**to be in a good/bad
~** gute/schlechte Laune haben;
to be in the ~ for sth zu etw
aufgelegt sein; **I'm not in the
~** ich fühle mich nicht danach;
moody adj launisch

moon [muːn] n Mond m; **to be
over the ~** *(fam)* überglücklich
sein; **moonlight** n Mondlicht nt
▷ vi schwarzarbeiten; **moonlit**
adj *(night, landscape)* mondhell

moor [mɔː] n Moor nt ▷ vt, vi
festmachen; **moorings** npl
Liegeplatz m; **moorland** n
Moorland nt, Heideland nt

moose [muːs] n *(pl ~)* n Elch m

mop [mɒp] n Mopp m; **mop up**
vt aufwischen

mope [məʊp] vi Trübsal blasen

moped [ˈməʊped] n *(Brit)* Moped
nt

moral [ˈmɒrəl] adj moralisch;
(values) sittlich ▷ n Moral f; **~s** pl
Moral f; **morale** [mɒˈrɑːl] n
Stimmung f, Moral f; **morality**
[məˈrælɪtɪ] n Moral f, Ethik f

morbid [ˈmɔːbɪd] adj krankhaft

KEYWORD

more [mɔː] adj *(greater in number
etc)* mehr; *(additional)* noch mehr;
do you want (some) more tea?
möchtest du/möchten Sie noch
etwas Tee?; **I have no** o **I don't
have any more money** ich habe
kein Geld mehr
▷ *pron (greater amount)* mehr;
(further o additional amount) noch
mehr; **is there any more?** gibt es
noch mehr?; *(left over)* ist noch
etwas da?; **there's no more** es ist
nichts mehr da
▷ *adv* mehr; **more
dangerous/easily** *etc (than)*
gefährlicher/einfacher *etc* (als);
more and more immer mehr;
more and more excited immer
aufgeregter; **more or less** mehr
oder weniger; **more than ever**
mehr denn je; **more beautiful
than ever** schöner denn je

moreish adj *(food)* **these
crisps are really ~** ich kann mit
diesen Chips einfach nicht
aufhören; **moreover** adv
außerdem

morgue [mɔːɡ] n Leichen-
schauhaus nt

morning [ˈmɔːnɪŋ] n Morgen m;
in the ~ am Morgen, morgens;
(tomorrow) morgen früh; **this
~** heute morgen ▷ adj Morgen-;
(early) Früh-; *(walk etc)*
morgendlich; **morning after pill**
n die Pille danach; **morning
sickness** n Schwangerschafts-
übelkeit f

Morocco [məˈrɒkəʊ] n Marokko
nt

moron [ˈmɔːrɒn] n Idiot(in) m(f)

morphine [ˈmɔːfiːn] n Morphium nt

morsel ['mɔ:sl] *n* Bissen *m*

mortal ['mɔ:tl] *adj* sterblich; (*wound*) tödlich ▷ *n* Sterbliche(r) *mf;* **mortality** (*death rate*) Sterblichkeitsziffer *f;* **mortally** *adv* tödlich

mortgage ['mɔ:ɡɪdʒ] *n* Hypothek *f* ▷ *vt* mit einer Hypothek belasten

mortified ['mɔ:tɪfaɪd] *adj:* **I was ~** es war mir schrecklich peinlich

mortuary ['mɔ:tjʊərɪ] *n* Leichenhalle *f*

mosaic [məʊˈzeɪɪk] *n* Mosaik *nt*

Moscow ['mɒskəʊ] *n* Moskau *nt*

Moslem ['mɒzləm] *adj, n* see **Muslim**

mosque [mɒsk] *n* Moschee *f*

mosquito [mɒˈski:təʊ] (*pl* **-es**) *n* (*Stech*)mücke *f;* (*tropical*) Moskito *m;* **~ net** Moskitonetz *nt*

moss [mɒs] *n* Moos *nt*

most [məʊst] *adj* meiste *pl,* die meisten; **in ~ cases** in den meisten Fällen ▷ *adv* (*with verbs*) am meisten; (*with adj*) ...ste; (*with adv*) am ...sten; (*very*) äußerst, höchst; **he ate (the) ~** er hat am meisten gegessen; **the ~ beautiful/interesting** der/die/das schönste/interessanteste; **~ interesting** hochinteressant! ▷ *n* das meiste, der größte Teil; (*people*) die meisten; **~ of the money/players** das meiste Geld/die meisten Spieler; **for the ~ part** zum größten Teil; **five at the ~** höchstens fünf; **to make the ~ of sth** etw voll ausnützen; **mostly** *adv* (*most of the time*) meistens; (*mainly*) hauptsächlich; (*for the most part*) größtenteils

MOT *abbr* = **Ministry of Transport; ~ (test)** = TÜV *m*

motel [məʊˈtel] *n* Motel *nt*

moth [mɒθ] *n* Nachtfalter *m;*

(*wool-eating*) Motte *f;* **mothball** *n* Mottenkugel *f*

mother ['mʌðə*] *n* Mutter *f* ▷ *vt* bemuttern; **mother-in-law** (*pl* **mothers-in-law**) *n* Schwiegermutter *f;* **mother-to-be** (*pl* **mothers-to-be**) *n* werdende Mutter

motif [məʊˈti:f] *n* Motiv *m*

motion ['məʊʃən] *n* Bewegung *f;* (*in meeting*) Antrag *m;* **motionless** *adj* bewegungslos

motivate ['məʊtɪveɪt] *vt* motivieren; **motive** ['məʊtɪv] *n* Motiv *m*

motor ['məʊtə*] *n* Motor *m;* (*fam: car*) Auto *nt* ▷ *adj* Motor-; **Motorail train®** *n* (*Brit*) Autoreisezug *m;* **motorbike** *n* Motorrad *nt;* **motorboat** *n* Motorboot *nt;* **motorcycle** *n* Motorrad *nt;* **motor industry** *n* Automobilindustrie *f;* **motoring** ['məʊtərɪŋ] *n* Autofahren *nt;* **~ organization** Automobilklub *m;* **motorist** ['məʊtərɪst] *n* Autofahrer(in) *m(f);* **motor oil** *n* Motorenöl *nt;* **motor racing** *n* Autorennsport *m;* **motor scooter** *n* Motorroller *m;* **motor show** *n* Automobilausstellung *f;* **motor vehicle** *n* Kraftfahrzeug *nt;* **motorway** *n* (*Brit*) Autobahn *f*

motto ['mɒtəʊ] (*pl* **-es**) *n* Motto *nt*

mould [məʊld] *n* Form *f;* (*mildew*) Schimmel *m* ▷ *vt* (*a. fig*) formen; **mouldy** ['məʊldɪ] *adj* schimmelig

moult [məʊlt] *vi* sich mausern, haaren

mount [maʊnt] *vt* (*horse*) steigen auf +*akk;* (*exhibition etc*) organisieren; (*painting*) mit einem Passepartout versehen ▷ *vi:* **to ~ (up)** (an)steigen ▷ *n* Passepartout *nt*

mountain ['maʊntɪn] n Berg m;
mountain bike n Mountainbike
nt; **mountaineer** [maʊntɪ'nɪə°]
n Bergsteiger(in) m(f);
mountaineering [maʊntɪ'nɪərɪŋ]
n Bergsteigen nt; **mountainous**
adj bergig; **mountainside** n
Berghang m

mourn [mɔːn] vt betrauern ▷ vi
trauern (for um); **mourner** n
Trauernde(r) mf; **mournful** adj
trauervoll; **mourning** n Trauer f;
to be in ~ trauern (for um)

mouse [maʊs] (pl **mice**) n (a.
Inform) Maus f; **mouse mat,
mouse pad** (US) n Mauspad m;
mouse trap n Mausefalle f

mousse [muːs] n (Gastr) Creme f;
(styling ~) Schaumfestiger m

moustache [mə'stæʃ] n
Schnurrbart m

mouth [maʊθ] n Mund m; (of
animal) Maul nt; (of cave) Eingang
m; (of bottle etc) Öffnung f; (of river)
Mündung f; **to keep one's ~ shut**
(fam) den Mund halten; **mouthful**
n (of drink) Schluck m; (of food)
Bissen m; **mouth organ** n
Mundharmonika f; **mouthwash** n
Mundwasser nt; **mouthwatering**
adj appetitlich, lecker

move [muːv] n (movement)
Bewegung f; (in game) Zug m; (step)
Schritt m; (moving house) Umzug m;
to make a ~ (in game) ziehen;
(leave) sich auf den Weg machen;
to get a ~ on (with sth) sich (mit
etw) beeilen ▷ vt bewegen;
(object) rücken; (car) wegfahren;
(transport: goods) befördern;
(people) transportieren; (in job)
versetzen; (emotionally) bewegen,
rühren; **I can't ~ it** (stuck, too heavy)
ich bringe es nicht von der Stelle;
to ~ (house) umziehen ▷ vi sich
bewegen; (change place) gehen;
(vehicle, ship) fahren; (move house,

town etc) umziehen; (in game)
ziehen; **move about** vi sich
bewegen; (travel) unterwegs sein;
move away vi weggehen; (move
town) wegziehen; **move in** vi (to
house) einziehen; **move off** vi
losfahren; **move on** vi
weitergehen; (vehicle)
weiterfahren; **move out** vi
ausziehen; **move up** vi (in queue
etc) aufrücken; **movement** n
Bewegung f

movie ['muːvɪ] n Film m; **the ~s**
(the cinema) das Kino; **movie
theatre** n (US) Kino nt

moving ['muːvɪŋ] adj (emotionally) ergreifend, berührend

mow [məʊ] (mowed, mown o
mowed) vt mähen; **mower** n
(lawn~) Rasenmäher m

mown [məʊn] pp of **mow**

Mozambique [məʊzæm'biːk] n
Mosambik nt

MP abbr = **Member of Parliament**
Parlamentsabgeordnete(r) mf

mph abbr = **miles per hour** Meilen
pro Stunde

MPV n abbr = **multi-purpose
vehicle** Mehrzweckfahrzeug nt

MP3 player [empiːˈθriː'pleɪə°]
n MP3-Player m

Mr ['mɪstə°] n (written form of
address) Herr

Mrs ['mɪsɪz] n (written form of
address) Frau

Ms [məz] n (written form of address
for any woman, married or unmarried)
Frau

MS n abbr = **multiple sclerosis** MS
f

Mt abbr = **Mount** Berg m

much [mʌtʃ] (more, most) adj
viel; **we haven't got ~ time** wir
haben nicht viel Zeit; **how
~ money?** wie viel Geld? ▷ adv
viel; (with verb) sehr; **~ better**
besser; **I like it very ~** es gefällt

mir sehr gut; **I don't like it ~** ich mag es nicht besonders; **thank you very ~** danke sehr; **I thought as ~** das habe ich mir gedacht; **~ as I like him** so sehr ich ihn mag; **we don't see them ~** wir sehen sie nicht sehr oft; **~ the same** first gleich ▷ n viel; **as ~ as you want** so viel du willst; **he's not ~ of a cook** er ist kein großer Koch

muck [mʌk] n (fam) Dreck m; **muck about** vi (fam) herumalbern; **muck up** vt (fam) dreckig machen; (spoil) vermasseln; **mucky** adj dreckig

mucus ['mjuːkəs] n Schleim m

mud [mʌd] n Schlamm m

muddle ['mʌdl] n Durcheinander nt; **to be in a ~** ganz durcheinander sein ▷ vt: **to ~ (up)** durcheinanderbringen; **muddled** adj konfus

muddy ['mʌdɪ] adj schlammig; (shoes) schmutzig; **mudguard** ['mʌdgɑːd] n Schutzblech nt

muesli ['mjuːzlɪ] n Müsli nt

muffin ['mʌfɪn] n Muffin m; (Brit) weiches, flaches Milchbrötchen aus Hefeteig, das meist getoastet und mit Butter gegessen wird

muffle ['mʌfl] vt (sound) dämpfen; **muffler** n (US) Schalldämpfer m

mug [mʌg] n (cup) Becher m; (fam: fool) Trottel m ▷ vt (attack and rob) überfallen; **mugging** n Raubüberfall m

muggy ['mʌgɪ] adj (weather) schwül

mule [mjuːl] n Maulesel m

mull over [mʌl 'əʊvə*] vt nachdenken über +akk

mulled [mʌld] adj: **~ wine** Glühwein m

multicolored (US), **multicoloured** ['mʌltɪkʌləd] adj bunt; **multicultural** adj

multikulturell; **multi-grade** adj: **~ oil** Mehrbereichsöl nt; **multilingual** adj mehrsprachig; **multinational** n (company) Multi m

multiple ['mʌltɪpl] n Vielfache(s) nt ▷ adj mehrfach; (several) mehrere; **multiple-choice (method)** n Multiple-Choice-Verfahren nt; **multiple sclerosis** [skləˈrəʊsɪs] n Multiple Sklerose f

multiplex ['mʌltɪpleks] adj, n: **~ (cinema)** Multiplexkino nt

multiplication [mʌltɪplɪˈkeɪʃən] n Multiplikation f; **multiply** ['mʌltɪplaɪ] vt multiplizieren (by mit) ▷ vi sich vermehren

multi-purpose ['mʌltɪˈpɜːpəs]-adj Mehrzweck-; **multistorey (car park)** n Parkhaus nt; **multitasking** n (Inform) Multitasking nt

mum [mʌm] n (fam: mother) Mutti f, Mami f

mumble ['mʌmbl] vt, vi murmeln

mummy ['mʌmɪ] n (dead body) Mumie f; (fam: mother) Mutti f, Mami f

mumps [mʌmps] nsing Mumps m

munch [mʌntʃ] vt, vi mampfen

Munich ['mjuːnɪk] n München nt

municipal [mjuːˈnɪsɪpəl] adj städtisch

mural ['mjʊərəl] n Wandgemälde nt

murder ['mɜːdə*] n Mord m; **the traffic was ~** der Verkehr war die Hölle ▷ vt ermorden; **murderer** n Mörder(in) m(f)

murky ['mɜːkɪ] adj düster; (water) trüb

murmur ['mɜːmə*] vt, vi murmeln

muscle ['mʌsl] n Muskel m;
muscular ['mʌskjʊlə°] adj (strong)
muskulös; (cramp, pain etc) Muskel-
nt
museum [mjuː'zɪəm] n Museum
nt
mushroom ['mʌʃruːm] n (ess-
barer) Pilz; (button ~) Champignon
m ▷ vi (fig) emporschießen
mushy ['mʌʃɪ] adj breiig; **~ peas**
Erbsenmus m
music ['mjuːzɪk] n Musik f;
(printed) Noten pl; **musical** adj
(sound) melodisch; (person)
musikalisch; **~ instrument**
Musikinstrument nt ▷ n (show)
Musical nt; **musically** adv
musikalisch; **musician**
[mjuː'zɪʃən] n Musiker(in) m(f)
Muslim ['mʊzlɪm] adj
moslemisch ▷ n Moslem m,
Muslime f
mussel ['mʌsl] n Miesmuschel f
must [mʌst] vb (had to, had to) vb
aux (need to) müssen; (in negation)
dürfen; **I ~n't forget that** ich darf
das nicht vergessen; (certainty) **he
~ be there by now** er ist
inzwischen bestimmt schon da;
(assumption) **I ~ have lost it** ich
habe es wohl verloren; **~ you?**
muss das sein? ▷ n Muss nt
mustache ['mʌstæʃ] n (US)
Schnurrbart m
mustard ['mʌstəd] n Senf m; **to
cut the ~** es bringen
mustn't ['mʌsnt] contr of **must
not**
mute [mjuːt] adj stumm
mutter ['mʌtə°] vt, vi murmeln
mutton ['mʌtn] n Ham-
melfleisch nt
mutual ['mjuːtjʊəl] adj gegenseitig; **by ~ consent** in
gegenseitigem Einvernehmen
my [maɪ] adj mein; **I've hurt
~ leg** ich habe mir das Bein
verletzt

Myanmar ['maɪænmɑː] n
Myanmar nt
myself [maɪ'self] pron (reflexive)
mich akk, mir dat; **I've hurt ~** ich
habe mich verletzt; **I've bought
~ a flat** ich habe mir eine
Wohnung gekauft; **I need it for
~** ich brauche es für mich (selbst);
(emphatic) **I did it ~** ich habe es
selbst gemacht; **(all) by ~** allein
mysterious [mɪ'stɪərɪəs] adj
geheimnisvoll, mysteriös;
(inexplicable) rätselhaft; **mystery**
['mɪstərɪ] n Geheimnis nt; (puzzle)
Rätsel nt; **it's a ~ to me** es ist mir
schleierhaft; **mystify** ['mɪstɪfaɪ]
vt verblüffen
myth [mɪθ] n Mythos m; (fig:
untrue story) Märchen nt; **mythical**
adj mythisch; (fig: untrue)
erfunden; **mythology**
[mɪ'θɒlədʒɪ] n Mythologie f

n

N *abbr* = **north** N

nag [næg] *vt, vi* herumnörgeln (*sb* an jdm); **nagging** *n* Nörgelei *f*

nail [neɪl] *n* Nagel *m* ▷ *vt* nageln (*to* an); **nail down** *vt* festnageln; **nailbrush** *n* Nagelbürste *f*; **nail clippers** *npl* Nagelknipser *m*; **nailfile** *n* Nagelfeile *f*; **nail polish** *n* Nagellack *m*; **nail polish remover** *n* Nagellackentferner *m*; **nail scissors** *npl* Nagelschere *f*; **nail varnish** *n* Nagellack *m*

naive [naɪˈiːv] *adj* naiv

naked [ˈneɪkɪd] *adj* nackt

name [neɪm] *n* Name *m*; **his ~ is ...** er heißt ...; **what's your ~?** wie heißen Sie?; (*reputation*) **to have a good/bad ~** einen guten/schlechten Ruf haben ▷ *vt* nennen (*after* nach); (*sth new*) benennen; (*nominate*) ernennen (*as* als/zu); **a boy ~d ...** ein Junge

namens ...; **namely** *adv* nämlich; **name plate** *n* Namensschild *nt*

nan bread [ˈnɑːnˈbred] *n* (*warm serviertes*) *indisches Fladenbrot*

nanny [ˈnænɪ] *n* Kindermädchen *nt*

nap [næp] *n*: **to have/take a ~** ein Nickerchen machen

napkin [ˈnæpkɪn] *n* (*at table*) Serviette *f*

Naples [ˈneɪplz] *n* Neapel *nt*

nappy [ˈnæpɪ] *n* (*Brit*) Windel *f*

narcotic [nɑːˈkɒtɪk] *n* Rauschgift *nt*

narrate [nəˈreɪt] *vt* erzählen; **narration** [nəˈreɪʃən] , **narrative** [ˈnærətɪv] *n* Erzählung *f*; **narrator** [nəˈreɪtə°] *n* Erzähler(in) *m(f)*

narrow [ˈnærəʊ] *adj* eng, schmal; (*victory, majority*) knapp; **to have a ~ escape** mit knapper Not davonkommen ▷ *vi* sich verengen; **narrow down** *vt* einschränken (*to sth auf etw akk*); **narrow-minded** *adj* engstirnig

nasty [ˈnɑːstɪ] *adj* ekelhaft; (*person*) fies; (*remark*) gehässig; (*accident, wound etc*) schlimm

nation [ˈneɪʃən] *n* Nation *f*; **national** [ˈnæʃənl] *adj* national; **~ anthem** Nationalhymne *f*; **National Health Service** (*Brit*) staatlicher Gesundheitsdienst; **~ insurance** (*Brit*) Sozialversicherung *f*; **~ park** Nationalpark *m*; **~ service** Wehrdienst *m*; **~ socialism** (*Hist*) Nationalsozialismus *m* ▷ *n* Staatsbürger(in) *m(f)*

● **NATIONAL TRUST**

● Der **National Trust** ist ein 1895
● gegründeter Natur- und
● Denkmalschutzverband in
● Großbritannien, der Gebäude
● und Gelände von besonderem

● historischen oder ästhetischen
● Interesse erhält und der
● Öffentlichkeit zugänglich
● macht.

nationality [næʃˈnælɪtɪ] n
Staatsangehörigkeit f;
Nationalität f; **nationalize**
[ˈnæʃnəlaɪz] vt verstaatlichen;
nationwide adj, adv landesweit
native [ˈneɪtɪv] adj einheimisch;
(inborn) angeboren, natürlich;
Native American Indianer(in)
m(f); **~ country** Heimatland nt; **a
~ German** ein gebürtiger
Deutscher, eine gebürtige
Deutsche; **~ language**
Muttersprache f; **~ speaker**
Muttersprachler(in) m(f) ▷ n
Einheimische(r) mf; (in colonial
context) Eingeborene(r) mf
nativity play [nəˈtɪvɪtɪpleɪ] n
Krippenspiel nt
NATO [ˈneɪtəʊ] acr = **North
Atlantic Treaty Organization**
Nato f
natural [ˈnætʃrəl] adj natürlich;
(law, science, forces etc) Natur-;
(inborn) angeboren; **~ gas** Erdgas
nt; **~ resources** Bodenschätze pl;
naturally adv natürlich; (by
nature) von Natur aus; **it comes
~ to her** es fällt ihr leicht
nature [ˈneɪtʃə*] n Natur f;
(type) Art f; **it is not in my ~** es
entspricht nicht meiner Art;
by ~ von Natur aus; **nature
reserve** n Naturschutzgebiet nt
naughty [ˈnɔːtɪ] adj (child)
ungezogen; (cheeky) frech
nausea [ˈnɔːsɪə] n Übelkeit f
nautical [ˈnɔːtɪkəl] adj nautisch;
~ mile Seemeile f
nave [neɪv] n Hauptschiff nt
navel [ˈneɪvəl] n Nabel m
navigate [ˈnævɪɡeɪt] vi navi-
gieren; (in car) lotsen, dirigieren;

navigation [nævɪˈɡeɪʃən] n
Navigation f; (in car) Lotsen nt
navy [ˈneɪvɪ] n Marine f; **~ blue**
Marineblau nt
Nazi [ˈnɑːtsɪ] n Nazi m
NB abbr = **nota bene** NB
NE abbr = **northeast** NO
near [nɪə*] adj nahe; **in the
~ future** in nächster Zukunft; **that
was a ~ miss** (◇ thing) das war
knapp; (with price) ... **or ~est offer**
Verhandlungsbasis ... ▷ adv in der
Nähe; **so ~ so nahe; come ~er**
näher kommen; (event) näher
rücken ▷ prep: **~ (to)** (space) nahe
an +dat; (vicinity) in der Nähe +gen;
~ the sea nahe am Meer; **~ the
station** in der Nähe des Bahnhofs,
in Bahnhofsnähe; **nearby** adj
nahe gelegen ▷ adv in der Nähe;
nearly adv fast; **nearside** n
(Auto) Beifahrerseite f;
near-sighted adj kurzsichtig
neat [niːt] adj ordentlich; (work,
writing) sauber; (undiluted) pur
necessarily [nesəˈserɪlɪ] adv
notwendigerweise; **not ~** nicht
unbedingt; **necessary** [ˈnesəsərɪ]
adj notwendig, nötig; **it's ~ to ...**
man muss ...; **it's not ~ for him to
come** er braucht nicht
mitzukommen; **necessity**
[nɪˈsesɪtɪ] n Notwendigkeit f; **the
bare necessities** das absolut
Notwendigste; **there is no ~ to ...**
man braucht nicht (zu) ..., man
muss nicht ...
neck [nek] n Hals m; (size)
Halsweite f; **back of the ~** Nacken
m; **necklace** [ˈneklɪs] n
Halskette f; **necktie** n (US)
Krawatte f
nectarine [ˈnektərɪn] n Nektarine f
née [neɪ] adj geborene
need [niːd] n (requirement)
Bedürfnis nt (for für); (necessity)

Notwendigkeit f; (poverty) Not f; **to be in ~ of sth** etw brauchen; **if ~(s) be** wenn nötig; **there is no ~ to ...** man braucht nicht (zu) ..., man muss nicht ... ▷ vt brauchen; **I ~ to speak to you** ich muss mit dir reden; **you ~n't go** du brauchst nicht (zu) gehen, du musst nicht gehen

needle ['niːdl] n Nadel f
needless, needlessly ['niːdlɪs, -lɪ] adj, adv unnötig; **~ to say** selbstverständlich
needy ['niːdɪ] adj bedürftig
negative ['negətɪv] n (Ling) Verneinung f; (Foto) Negativ nt ▷ adj negativ; (answer) verneinend
neglect [nɪ'glekt] n Vernachlässigung f ▷ vt vernachlässigen; **to ~ to do sth** es versäumen, etw zu tun; **negligence** ['neglɪdʒəns] n Nachlässigkeit f; **negligent** adj nachlässig
negligible ['neglɪdʒəbl] adj unbedeutend; (amount) geringfügig
negotiate [nɪ'gəʊʃɪeɪt] vi verhandeln; **negotiation** [nɪgəʊʃɪ'eɪʃən] n Verhandlung f
neigh [neɪ] vi (horse) wiehern
neighbor (US), **neighbour** ['neɪbə°] n Nachbar(in) m(f); **neighbo(u)rhood** n Nachbarschaft f; **neighbo(u)ring** adj benachbart
neither ['naɪðə°] adj, pron keine(r, s) von beiden; **~ of you/us** keiner von euch/uns beiden ▷ adv: **~ ... nor ...** weder ... noch ... ▷ conj: **I'm not going - ~ am I** ich gehe nicht - ich auch nicht
neon ['niːɒn] n Neon nt; **~ sign** n (advertisement) Leuchtreklame f
nephew ['nefjuː] n Neffe m
nerd [nɜːv] n (fam) Schwachkopf m; **he's a real computer ~** er ist ein totaler Computerfreak

nerve [nɜːv] n Nerv m; **he gets on my ~s** er geht mir auf die Nerven; (courage) **to keep/lose one's ~** die Nerven behalten/verlieren; (cheek) **to have the ~ to do sth** die Frechheit besitzen, etw zu tun; **nerve-racking** adj nervenaufreibend; **nervous** ['nɜːvəs] adj (apprehensive) ängstlich; (on edge) nervös; **nervous breakdown** n Nervenzusammenbruch m
nest [nest] n Nest nt ▷ vi nisten
net [net] n Netz nt; **the Net** (Internet) das Internet; **on the ~** im Netz ▷ adj (price, weight) Netto-; **~ profit** Reingewinn m; **netball** n Netzball m
Netherlands ['neðələndz] npl: **the ~** die Niederlande pl
nettle ['netl] n Nessel f
network ['netwɜːk] n Netz nt; (TV, Radio) Sendenetz nt; (Inform) Netzwerk nt; **networking** n Networking nt (das Knüpfen und Pflegen von Kontakten, die dem beruflichen Fortkommen dienen)
neurosis [njʊə'rəʊsɪs] n Neurose f; **neurotic** [njʊə'rɒtɪk] adj neurotisch
neuter ['njuːtə°] adj (Bio) geschlechtslos; (Ling) sächlich
neutral ['njuːtrəl] adj neutral ▷ n (gear in car) Leerlauf m
never ['nevə°] adv nie(mals); **~ before** noch nie; **~ mind** macht nichts!; **never-ending** adj endlos; **nevertheless** [nevəðə'les] adv trotzdem
new [njuː] adj neu; **this is all ~ to me** das ist für mich noch ungewohnt; **newcomer** n Neuankömmling m; (in job, subject) Neuling m
New England [njuː'ɪŋglənd] n Neuengland nt

Newfoundland ['nju:fəndlənd]
n Neufundland *nt*

newly ['nju:lɪ] *adv* neu; ~ **made**
(*cake*) frisch gebacken;
newly-weds *npl* Frischvermählte
pl; **new moon** Neumond *m*

news [nju:z] *nsing* (*piece of* ~)
Nachricht *f*; (*Radio, TV*)
Nachrichten *pl*; **good** ~ ein
erfreuliche Nachricht; **what's the**
~? was gibt's Neues?; **have you**
heard the ~? hast du das Neueste
gehört?; **that's ~ to me** das ist mir
neu; **newsagent**, **news dealer**
(*US*) *n* Zeitungshändler(in) *m(f)*;
news bulletin *n*
Nachrichtensendung *f*; **news flash**
n Kurzmeldung *f*; **newsgroup** *n*
(*Inform*) Diskussionsforum *nt*,
Newsgroup *f*; **newsletter** *n*
Mitteilungsblatt *nt*; **newspaper**
['nju:speɪpə'] *n* Zeitung *f*

New Year ['nju:'jɪə'] *n* das
neue Jahr; **Happy** ~ (ein) frohes
Neues Jahr!; (*toast*) Prosit
Neujahr!; **~'s Day** Neujahr *nt*,
Neujahrstag *m*; **~'s Eve**
Silvesterabend *m*; **~'s resolution**
guter Vorsatz fürs neue Jahr

New York [nju:'jɔ:k] *n* New
York *nt*

New Zealand [nju:'zi:lənd] *n*
Neuseeland *nt* ▷ *adj*
neuseeländisch; **New Zealander**
n Neuseeländer(in) *m(f)*

next [nekst] *adj* nächste(r, s);
the week after ~ übernächste
Woche; **~ time I see him** wenn ich
ihn das nächste Mal sehe; **you're**
~ du bist jetzt dran ▷ *adv* als
Nächstes; (*then*) dann, darauf; **~ to**
neben +*dat*; **~ to last** vorletzte(r,
s); **~ to impossible** nahezu
unmöglich; **the ~ best thing** das
Nächstbeste; **~ door** nebenan

NHS *abbr* = **National Health**
Service

Niagara Falls [naɪ'ægrə'fɔ:lz]
npl Niagarafälle *pl*

nibble ['nɪbl] *vt* knabbern an
+*dat*; **nibbles** *npl* Knabberzeug *nt*

Nicaragua [nɪkə'rægjuə] *n*
Nicaragua *nt*

nice [naɪs] *adj* nett, sympathisch;
(*taste, food, drink*) gut; (*weather*)
schön; **~ and ...** schön ...; **be ~ to**
him sei nett zu ihm; **have a ~ day**
(*US*) schönen Tag noch!; **nicely** *adv*
nett; (*well*) gut; **that'll do ~** das
genügt vollauf

nick [nɪk] *vt* (*fam: steal*) klauen;
(*capture*) schnappen

nickel ['nɪkl] *n* (*Chem*) Nickel *nt*;
(*US: coin*) Nickel *m*

nickname ['nɪkneɪm] *n*
Spitzname *m*

nicotine ['nɪkəti:n] *n* Nikotin *nt*;
nicotine patch *n* Nikotinpflaster
nt

niece [ni:s] *n* Nichte *f*

Nigeria [naɪ'dʒɪərɪə] *n* Nigeria
nt

night [naɪt] *n* Nacht *f*; (*before bed*)
Abend *m*; **good** ~ gute Nacht!; **at**
(*o by*) ~ nachts; **to have an early**
~ früh schlafen gehen; **nightcap** *n*
Schlummertrunk *m*; **nightclub** *n*
Nachtklub *m*; **nightdress** *n*
Nachthemd *nt*; **nightie** ['naɪtɪ] *n*
(*fam*) Nachthemd *nt*

nightingale ['naɪtɪŋgeɪl] *n*
Nachtigall *f*

night life ['naɪtlaɪf] *n*
Nachtleben *nt*; **nightly** *adv* (*every*
evening) jeden Abend; (*every night*)
jede Nacht; **nightmare**
['naɪtmɛə'] *n* Albtraum *m*;
nighttime *n* Nacht *f*; **at** ~ nachts

nil [nɪl] *n* (*Sport*) null

Nile [naɪl] *n* Nil *m*

nine [naɪn] *num* neun; ~ **times**
out of ten so gut wie immer ▷ *n*
(*a. bus etc*) Neun *f*; *see also* **eight**;
nineteen [naɪn'ti:n] *num*

neunzehn ▷ n (a. bus etc) Neunzehn f; see also **eight**; **nineteenth** adj neunzehnte(r, s); see also **eighth**; **ninetieth** ['naɪntɪəθ] adj neunzigste(r, s); see also **eighth**; **ninety** ['naɪntɪ] num neunzig f; ▷ n Neunzig f; see also **eight**; **ninth** [naɪnθ] adj neunte(r, s) ▷ n (fraction) Neuntel nt; see also **eighth**

nipple ['nɪpl] n Brustwarze f

nitrogen ['naɪtrədʒən] n Stickstoff m

⊙ **KEYWORD**

no [nəʊ] (pl **noes**) adv (opposite of yes) nein; **to answer to** (to question) mit Nein antworten; (to request) Nein o nein sagen; **no thank you** nein, danke ▷ adj (not any) kein(e); **I have no money/time** ich habe kein Geld/keine Zeit; **"no smoking"** „Rauchen verboten" ▷ n Nein nt; (no vote) Neinstimme f

nobility [nəʊ'bɪlɪtɪ] n Adel m; **noble** ['nəʊbl] adj (rank) adlig; (quality) edel ▷ n Adlige(r) mf

nobody ['nəʊbədɪ] pron niemand; (emphatic) keiner; **~ knows** keiner weiß es; **~ else** sonst niemand, kein anderer ▷ n Niemand m

no-claims bonus [nəʊ'kleɪmzbəʊnəs] n Schadenfreiheitsrabatt m

nod [nɒd] vi, vt nicken; **nod off** vi einnicken

noise [nɔɪz] n (loud) Lärm m; (sound) Geräusch nt; **noisy** adj laut; (crowd) lärmend

nominate ['nɒmɪneɪt] vt (in election) aufstellen; (appoint) ernennen

nominative ['nɒmɪnətɪv] n (Ling) Nominativ m

nominee [nɒmɪ'niː] n Kandidat(in) m(f)

non- [nɒn] pref Nicht-; (with adj) nicht-, un-; **non-alcoholic** adj alkoholfrei

none [nʌn] pron keine(r, s); **~ of them** keiner von ihnen; **~ of it is any use** nichts davon ist brauchbar; **there are ~ left** es sind keine mehr da; (with comparative) **to be ~ the wiser** auch nicht schlauer sein; **I was ~ the worse for it** es hat mir nichts geschadet

nonentity [nɒ'nentɪtɪ] n Null f

nonetheless [nʌnðə'les] adv nichtsdestoweniger, dennoch

non-event n Reinfall m; **non-existent** adj nicht vorhanden; **non-fiction** n Sachbücher pl; **non-iron** adj bügelfrei; **non-polluting** adj schadstofffrei; **non-resident** n: **"open to ~s"** „auch für Nichthotelgäste"; **non-returnable** adj: **~ bottle** Einwegflasche f

nonsense ['nɒnsəns] n Unsinn m; **don't talk ~** red keinen Unsinn

non-smoker [nɒn'sməʊkə*] n Nichtraucher(in) m(f); **non-smoking** adj Nichtraucher-; **~ area** Nichtraucherbereich m; **nonstop** adj (train) durchgehend; (flight) Nonstop- ▷ adv (talk) ununterbrochen; (travel) ohne Unterbrechung; (fly) ohne Zwischenlandung; **non-violent** adj gewaltfrei

noodles ['nuːdlz] npl Nudeln pl

noon [nuːn] n Mittag m; **at ~** um 12 Uhr mittags

no one ['nəʊwʌn] pron niemand; (emphatic) keiner; **~ else** sonst niemand, kein anderer

nor [nɔː] conj: **neither ... ~ ...**

weder ... noch ...; **I don't smoke, ~ does he** ich rauche nicht, er auch nicht

norm [nɔːm] n Norm f

normal ['nɔːməl] adj normal; **to get back to ~** sich wieder normalisieren; **normally** adv (usually) normalerweise

north [nɔːθ] n Norden m; **to the ~ of** nördlich von ▷ adv (go, face) nach Norden ▷ adj Nord-; **~ wind** Nordwind m; **North America** n Nordamerika nt; **northbound** adj (in) Richtung Norden; **northeast** n Nordosten m; **to the ~ of** nordöstlich von ▷ adv (go, face) nach Nordosten ▷ adj Nordost-; **northern** ['nɔːðən] adj nördlich; **~ France** Nordfrankreich nt; **Northern Ireland** n Nordirland nt; **North Pole** n Nordpol m; **North Sea** n Nordsee f; **northwards** adv nach Norden; **northwest** n Nordwesten m; **to the ~ of** nordwestlich von ▷ adv (go, face) nach Nordwesten ▷ adj Nordwest-

Norway ['nɔːweɪ] n Norwegen nt; **Norwegian** [nɔːˈwiːdʒən] adj norwegisch ▷ n (person) Norweger(in) m(f); (language) Norwegisch nt

nos. abbr = **numbers** Nr.

nose [nəʊz] n Nase f; **nose around** vi herumschnüffeln; **nosebleed** n Nasenbluten nt; **nose-dive** n Sturzflug m; **to take a ~** abstürzen

nosey ['nəʊzɪ] see **nosy**

nostalgia [nɒsˈtældʒɪə] n Nostalgie f (for nach); **nostalgic** adj nostalgisch

nostril ['nɒstrɪl] n Nasenloch nt

nosy ['nəʊzɪ] adj neugierig

not [nɒt] adv nicht; **~ a** kein; **~ one of them** kein einziger von ihnen; **he is ~ an expert** er ist kein

Experte; **I told him ~ to (do it)** ich sagte ihm, er solle es nicht tun; **~ at all** überhaupt nicht, keineswegs; (don't mention it) gern geschehen; **~ yet** noch nicht

notable ['nəʊtəbl] adj bemerkenswert; **note** [nəʊt] n (written) Notiz f; (short letter) paar Zeilen pl; (on scrap of paper) Zettel m; (comment in book etc) Anmerkung f; (bank~) Schein m; (Mus: sign) Note f; (sound) Ton m; **to make a ~ of sth** sich dat etw notieren; **~s** (of lecture etc) Aufzeichnungen pl; **to take ~s** sich dat Notizen machen (of über +akk) ▷ vt (notice) bemerken (that dass); (write down) notieren; **notebook** n Notizbuch nt; (Inform) Notebook nt; **notepad** n Notizblock m; **notepaper** n Briefpapier nt

nothing ['nʌθɪŋ] n nichts; **~ but ...** lauter ...; **for ~** umsonst; **he thinks ~ of it** er macht sich nichts daraus

notice ['nəʊtɪs] n (announcement) Bekanntmachung f; (on ~ board) Anschlag m; (attention) Beachtung f; (advance warning) Ankündigung f; (to leave job, flat etc) Kündigung f; **at short ~** kurzfristig; **until further ~** bis auf weiteres; **to give sb ~** jdm kündigen; **to hand in one's ~** kündigen; **to take (no) ~ of (sth)** etw (nicht) beachten; **take no ~** kümmere dich nicht darum! ▷ vt bemerken; **noticeable** adj erkennbar; (visible) sichtbar; **to be ~** auffallen; **notice board** n Anschlagtafel f

notification [nəʊtɪfɪˈkeɪʃən] n Benachrichtigung f (of von); **notify** ['nəʊtɪfaɪ] vt benachrichtigen (of von)

notion ['nəʊʃən] n Idee f

notorious [nəʊˈtɔːrɪəs] adj berüchtigt

nought [nɔːt] n Null f

noun [naʊn] n Substantiv nt

nourish [ˈnʌrɪʃ] vt nähren;
nourishing adj nahrhaft;
nourishment n Nahrung f

novel [ˈnɒvəl] n Roman m ▷ adj
neuartig; **novelist** n
Schriftsteller(in) m(f); **novelty** n
Neuheit f

November [nəʊˈvembə°] n
November m; see also **September**

novice [ˈnɒvɪs] n Neuling m

now [naʊ] adv (at the moment)
jetzt; (introductory phrase) also;
right ~ jetzt gleich; **just ~** gerade;
by ~ inzwischen; **from ~ on** ab
jetzt; **~ and again** (o then) ab und
zu; **nowadays** adv heutzutage

nowhere [ˈnəʊwɛə°] adv nirgends; **we're getting ~** wir
kommen nicht weiter; **~ near**
noch lange nicht

nozzle [ˈnɒzl] n Düse f

nuclear [ˈnjuːklɪə°] adj (energy
etc) Kern-; **~ power station**
Kernkraftwerk nt; **nuclear waste**
n Atommüll m

nude [njuːd] adj nackt ▷ n (person) Nackte(r) mf; (painting etc) Akt
m

nudge [nʌdʒ] vt stupsen; **nudist**
[ˈnjuːdɪst] n Nudist(in) m(f),
FKK-Anhänger(in) m(f); **nudist
beach** n FKK-Strand m

nuisance [ˈnjuːsns] n Ärgernis
nt; (person) Plage f; **what a ~** wie
ärgerlich!

nuke [njuːk] (US fam) n (bomb)
Atombombe f ▷ vt eine
Atombombe werfen auf +akk

numb [nʌm] adj taub, gefühllos
▷ vt betäuben

number [ˈnʌmbə°] n Nummer f;
(Math) Zahl f; (quantity) (An)zahl f;
in small/large ~s in
kleinen/großen Mengen; **a ~ of
times** mehrmals ▷ vt (give a

number to) nummerieren; (count)
zählen (among sb); **his days are
~ed** seine Tage sind gezählt;
number plate n (Brit Auto)
Nummernschild nt

numeral [ˈnjuːmərəl] n Ziffer f;
numerical [njuːˈmerɪkəl] adj
numerisch; (superiority)
zahlenmäßig; **numerous**
[ˈnjuːmərəs] adj zahlreich

nun [nʌn] n Nonne f

Nuremberg [ˈnjʊərəmbɜːg] n
Nürnberg nt

nurse [nɜːs] n Krankenschwester
f; (male ~) Krankenpfleger m ▷ vt
(patient) pflegen; (baby) stillen;
nursery n Kinderzimmer nt; (for
plants) Gärtnerei f; (tree)
Baumschule f; **nursery rhyme** n
Kinderreim m; **nursery school** n
Kindergarten m; **~ teacher**
Kindergärtner(in) m(f),
Erzieher(in) m(f); **nursing** n
(profession) Krankenpflege f;
~ home Privatklinik f

nut [nʌt] n Nuss f; (Tech: for bolt)
Mutter f; **nutcase** n (fam)
Spinner(in) m(f); **nutcracker** n,
nutcrackers npl Nussknacker m

nutmeg [ˈnʌtmeg] n Muskat m,
Muskatnuss f

nutrient [ˈnjuːtrɪənt] n Nährstoff
m

nutrition [njuːˈtrɪʃən] n Ernährung f; **nutritious** [njuːˈtrɪʃəs]
adj nahrhaft

nuts [nʌts] (fam) adj verrückt; **to
be ~ about sth** nach etw verrückt
sein ▷ npl (testicles) Eier pl

nutshell [ˈnʌtʃel] n Nussschale f;
in a ~ kurz gesagt

nutter [ˈnʌtə°] n (fam)
Spinner(in) m(f); **nutty** [ˈnʌtɪ]
adj (fam) verrückt

NW abbr = **northwest** NW

nylon® [ˈnaɪlɒn] n Nylon® nt
▷ adj Nylon-

O

O [əʊ] n (Tel) Null f
oak [əʊk] n Eiche f ▷ adj Eichen-
OAP abbr = **old-age pensioner** Rentner(in) m(f)
oar [ɔːʳ] n Ruder nt
oasis [əʊˈeɪsɪs] n (pl **oases**) n Oase f
oatcake [ˈəʊtkeɪk] n Haferkeks m
oath [əʊθ] n (statement) Eid m
oats [əʊts] npl Hafer m; (Gastr) Haferflocken pl
obedience [əˈbiːdɪəns] n Gehorsam m; **obedient** adj gehorsam; **obey** [əˈbeɪ] vt, vi gehorchen +dat
object [ˈɒbdʒɪkt] n Gegenstand m; (abstract) Objekt nt; (purpose) Ziel nt ▷ [əbˈdʒekt] vi dagegen sein; (raise objection) Einwände erheben (to gegen); (morally) Anstoß nehmen (to an +dat); **do you ~ to my smoking?** haben Sie

etwas dagegen, wenn ich rauche?; **objection** [əbˈdʒekʃən] n Einwand m
objective [əbˈdʒektɪv] n Ziel nt ▷ adj objektiv; **objectivity** [ɒbdʒekˈtɪvɪtɪ] n Objektivität f
obligation [ɒblɪˈgeɪʃən] n (duty) Pflicht f; (commitment) Verpflichtung f; **no ~** unverbindlich; **obligatory** [əˈblɪgətərɪ] adj obligatorisch; **oblige** [əˈblaɪdʒ] vt: **to ~ sb to do sth** jdn (dazu) zwingen, etw zu tun; **he felt ~d to accept the offer** er fühlte sich verpflichtet, das Angebot anzunehmen
oblique [əˈbliːk] adj schräg; (angle) schief
oboe [ˈəʊbəʊ] n Oboe f
obscene [əbˈsiːn] adj obszön
obscure [əbˈskjʊəʳ] adj unklar; (unknown) unbekannt
observant [əbˈzɜːvənt] adj aufmerksam; **observation** [ɒbzəˈveɪʃən] n (watching) Beobachtung f; (remark) Bemerkung f; **observe** [əbˈzɜːv] vt (notice) bemerken; (watch) beobachten; (customs) einhalten
obsessed [əbˈsest] adj besessen (with an idea etc von einem Gedanken etc); **obsession** [əbˈseʃən] n Manie f
obsolete [ˈɒbsəliːt] adj veraltet
obstacle [ˈɒbstəkl] n Hindernis nt (to für); **to be an ~ to sth** einer Sache im Weg stehen
obstinate [ˈɒbstɪnət] adj hartnäckig
obstruct [əbˈstrʌkt] vt versperren; (pipe) verstopfen; (hinder) behindern, aufhalten; **obstruction** [əbˈstrʌkʃən] n Blockierung f; (of pipe) Verstopfung f; (obstacle) Hindernis nt
obtain [əbˈteɪn] vt erhalten; **obtainable** adj erhältlich

obvious ['ɒbvɪəs] adj
offensichtlich; **it was ~ to me
that ...** es war mir klar, dass ...;
obviously adv offensichtlich

occasion [ə'keɪʒən] n Gelegenheit f; (special event) (großes)
Ereignis nt; **on the ~ of** anlässlich
+gen; **special** besonderer Anlass;
occasional, occasionally adj, adv
gelegentlich

occupant ['ɒkjʊpənt] n (of
house) Bewohner(in) m(f); (of
vehicle) Insasse m, Insassin f;
occupation [ɒkjʊ'peɪʃən] n
Beruf m; (pastime) Beschäftigung f;
(of country etc) Besetzung f;
occupied adj (country, seat, toilet)
besetzt; (person) beschäftigt; **to
keep sb/oneself ~** jdn/sich
beschäftigen; **occupy** ['ɒkjʊpaɪ]
vt (country) besetzen; (time)
beanspruchen; (mind, person)
beschäftigen

occur [ə'kɜ:ʳ] vi vorkommen;
~ to sb jdm einfallen; **occurrence**
[ə'kʌrəns] n (event) Ereignis nt;
(presence) Vorkommen nt

ocean ['əʊʃən] n Ozean m; (US:
sea) das Meer nt

o'clock [ə'klɒk] adv: **5 ~** 5 Uhr; **at
10 ~** um 10 Uhr

octagon ['ɒktəgən] n Achteck
nt

October [ɒk'təʊbəʳ] n Oktober
m; see also **September**

octopus ['ɒktəpəs] n Tintenfisch m

odd [ɒd] adj (strange) sonderbar;
(not even) ungerade; (one missing)
einzeln; **to be the ~ one out** nicht
dazugehören; **~ jobs**
Gelegenheitsarbeiten pl; **odds** npl
Chancen pl; **against all
~** entgegen allen Erwartungen;
~ and ends (fam) Kleinkram pl

odometer [əʊ'dɒmɪtəʳ] n (US
Auto) Meilenzähler m

odor (US), **odour** ['əʊdəʳ] n
Geruch m

⚪ **KEYWORD**

of [ɒv, əv] prep 1 von +dat ≈ use of
gen; **the history of Germany** die
Geschichte Deutschlands; **a friend
of ours** ein Freund von uns; **a boy
of 10** ein 10-jähriger Junge;
that was kind of you das war
sehr freundlich von Ihnen
2 (expressing quantity, amount,
dates etc) **a kilo of flour** ein Kilo
Mehl; **how much of this do you
need?** wie viel brauchen Sie
(davon)?; **there were 3 of them
(people)** es waren 3 (davon); (objects)
es gab 3 (davon); **a cup of
tea/vase of flowers** eine
Tasse Tee/Vase mit Blumen;
the 5th of July der 5. Juli
3 (from, out of) aus; **a bridge made
of wood** eine Holzbrücke, eine
Brücke aus Holz

off [ɒf] adv (away) weg, fort; (free)
frei; (switch) ausgeschaltet; (milk)
sauer; **a mile ~** eine Meile
entfernt; **I'll be ~ now** ich gehe
jetzt; **to have the day/Monday
~** heute/Montag freihaben; **the
lights are ~** die Lichter sind aus;
the concert is ~ das Konzert fällt
aus; **I got 10 % ~** ich habe 10 %
Nachlass bekommen ▷ prep (away
from) von; **to jump/fall ~ the roof**
vom Dach springen/fallen; **to get
~ the bus** aus dem Bus
aussteigen; **he's ~ work/school**
hat frei/schulfrei; **to take £20
~ the price** den Preis um 20 Pfund
herabsetzen

offence [ə'fens] n (crime)
Straftat f; (minor) Vergehen nt; (to
feelings) Kränkung f; **to
cause/take ~** Anstoß

erregen/nehmen; **offend** [ə'fend]
vt kränken; (eye, ear) beleidigen;
offender n Straffällige(r) mf;
offense (US) see **offence**;
offensive [ə'fensɪv] adj anstößig;
(insulting) beleidigend; (smell) übel,
abstoßend ▷ n (Mil) Offensive f

offer ['ɒfə°] n Angebot nt; **on**
~ (Comm) im Angebot ▷ vt
anbieten (to sb jdm); (money, a
chance etc) bieten

offhand [ɒf'hænd] adj lässig
▷ adv (say) auf Anhieb

office ['ɒfɪs] n Büro nt; (position)
Amt nt; **doctor's** ~ (US) Arztpraxis
f; **office block** n Bürogebäude nt;
office hours npl Dienstzeit f;
(notice) Geschäftszeiten pl; **officer**
['ɒfɪsə°] n (Mil) Offizier(in) m(f);
(official) Polizeibeamte(r) m,
Polizeibeamtin f; **office worker**
['ɒfɪswɜːkə°] n Büroangestellte(r)
mf; **official** [ə'fɪʃəl] adj offiziell;
(report etc) amtlich; ~ **language**
Amtssprache f ▷ n Beamte(r) m,
Beamtin f, Repräsentant(in)
m(f)

off-licence ['ɒflaɪsəns] n (Brit)
Wein- und Spirituosenhandlung f;
off-line adj (Inform) offline;
off-peak adj außerhalb der
Stoßzeiten; (rate, ticket) verbilligt;
off-putting adj abstoßend,
entmutigend, irritierend;
off-season adj außerhalb der
Saison

offshore ['ɒfʃɔ:°] adj küstennah,
Küsten-; (oil rig) im Meer; **offside**
['ɒf'saɪd] n (Auto) Fahrerseite f;
(Sport) Abseits nt

often ['ɒfən] adv oft; **every so**
~ von Zeit zu Zeit

oil [ɔɪl] n Öl nt ▷ vt ölen; **oil level**
n Ölstand m; **oil painting** n
Ölgemälde nt; **oil-rig** n
(Öl)bohrinsel f; **oil slick** n
Ölteppich m; **oil tanker** n

Öltanker m; (truck) Tankwagen m;
oily adj ölig; (skin, hair) fettig

ointment ['ɔɪntmənt] n Salbe f

OK, okay [əʊ'keɪ] adj (fam) okay,
in Ordnung; **that's** ~ **by** (o **with**)
me das ist mir recht

old [əʊld] adj alt; **old age** n Alter
nt; ~ **pension** Rente f; ~ **pensioner**
Rentner(in) m(f); **old-fashioned**
adj altmodisch; **old people's
home** n Altersheim nt

olive ['ɒlɪv] n Olive f; **olive oil** n
Olivenöl nt

Olympic [əʊ'lɪmpɪk] adj olym-
pisch; **the** ~ **Games, the** ~**s** pl die
Olympischen Spiele pl, die
Olympiade

omelette ['ɒmlət] n Omelett nt

omission [əʊ'mɪʃən] n Auslas-
sung f; **omit** [əʊ'mɪt] vt
auslassen

O **KEYWORD**

on [ɒn] prep **1** (indicating position)
auf +dat; (with vb of motion) auf
+akk; (on vertical surface, part of
body) an +dat/akk; **it's on the table**
es ist auf dem Tisch; **she put the
book on the table** sie legte das
Buch auf den Tisch; **on the left**
links

2 (indicating means, method,
condition etc) **on foot** (go, be) zu
Fuß; **on the train/plane** (go) mit
dem Zug/Flugzeug; (be) im
Zug/Flugzeug; **on the
telephone/television** am
Telefon/im Fernsehen; **to be on
drugs** Drogen nehmen; **to be on
holiday/business** im Urlaub/auf
Geschäftsreise sein

3 (referring to time) **on Friday** (am)
Freitag; **on Fridays** freitags; **on
June 20th** am 20. Juni; **a week on
Friday** Freitag in einer Woche; **on
arrival he …** als er ankam, … er …

4 (about, concerning) über +akk
▷ adv **1** (referring to dress) an; **she put her boots/hat on** sie zog ihre Stiefel an/setzte ihren Hut auf **2** (further, continuously) weiter; **to walk on** weitergehen
▷ adj **1** (functioning, in operation: machine, TV, light) an; (tap) aufgedreht; (brakes) angezogen; **is the meeting still on?** findet die Versammlung noch statt?; **there's a good film on** es läuft ein guter Film **2** **that's not on!** (inf) (of behaviour) das ist nicht drin!

once [wʌns] adv (one time, in the past) einmal; (at the same time) gleichzeitig; **~ more** noch einmal; **for ~** ausnahmsweise (einmal); **~ in a while** ab und zu mal ▷ conj wenn ... einmal; **~ you've got used to it** sobald Sie sich daran gewöhnt haben

oncoming ['ɒnkʌmɪŋ] adj entgegenkommend; **~ traffic** Gegenverkehr m

O KEYWORD

one [wʌn] num eins; (with noun, referring back to noun) ein(e/r); **it is one (o'clock)** es ist eins, es ist ein Uhr; **one hundred and fifty** einhundertfünfzig
▷ adj **1** (sole) einzige(r, s); **the one book which** das einzige Buch, welches **2** (same) derselbe/dieselbe/dasselbe; **they came in the one car** sie kamen alle in dem einen Auto **3** (indef) **one day I discovered ...** eines Tages bemerkte ich ...
▷ pron **1** eine(r, s); **do you have a red one?** haben Sie einen

roten/eine rote/ein rotes?; **this one** diese(r, s); **that one** der/die/das; **which one?** welche(r, s)?; **one by one** einzeln **2 one another** einander; **do you two ever see one another?** seht ihr beide euch manchmal? **3** (impers) man; **one never knows** man kann nie wissen; **to cut one's finger** sich in den Finger schneiden

one-off adj einmalig ▷ n: **a ~** etwas Einmaliges; **one-parent family** n Einelternfamilie f; **one-piece** adj einteilig; **oneself** pron (reflexive) sich; **one-way** adj: **~ street** Einbahnstraße f; **~ ticket** (US) einfache Fahrkarte

onion ['ʌnjən] n Zwiebel f

on-line ['ɒnlaɪn] adj (Inform) online; **~ banking** Homebanking nt

only ['əʊnlɪ] adv nur; (with time) erst; **~ yesterday** erst gestern; **he's ~ four** er ist erst vier; **~ just arrived** gerade erst angekommen ▷ adj einzige(r, s); **~ child** Einzelkind nt

o.n.o. abbr = **or nearest offer** VB

onside [ɒn'saɪd] adv (Sport) nicht im Abseits

onto ['ɒntʊ] prep auf +akk; (vertical surface) an +akk; **to be ~ sb** jdm auf die Schliche gekommen sein

onwards ['ɒnwədz] adv voran, vorwärts; **from today ~** von heute an, ab heute

open ['əʊpən] adj offen; **in the ~ air** im Freien; **~ to the public** für die Öffentlichkeit zugänglich; **the shop is ~ all day** das Geschäft hat den ganzen Tag offen ▷ vt öffnen, aufmachen; (meeting, account, new building)

eröffnen; (road) dem Verkehr
übergeben ▷ vi (door, window etc)
aufgehen, sich öffnen; (shop, bank)
öffnen, aufmachen; (begin)
anfangen (with mit); **open-air** adj
Freiluft-; **open day** n Tag m der
offenen Tür; **opening** n Öffnung
f; (beginning) Anfang m; (official, of
exhibition etc) Eröffnung f;
(opportunity) Möglichkeit f;
~ hours (= times) Öffnungszeiten
pl; **openly** adv offen;
open-minded adj aufgeschlossen; **open-plan** adj: **~ office**
Großraumbüro nt

opera ['ɒpərə] n Oper f; **opera
glasses** npl Opernglas nt; **opera
house** n Oper f, Opernhaus nt;
opera singer n Opernsänger(in)
m(f)

operate ['ɒpəreɪt] vt (machine)
bedienen; (brakes, lights) betätigen
▷ vi (machine) laufen; (bus etc)
verkehren (between zwischen); **to
~ (on sb)** (Med) (jdn) operieren;
operating theatre n
Operationssaal m; **operation**
[ɒpə'reɪʃən] n (of machine)
Bedienung f; (functioning)
Funktionieren nt; (Med) Operation
f (on an +dat); (undertaking)
Unternehmen nt; **in ~** (machine) in
Betrieb; **to have an ~** operiert
werden (for wegen); **operator**
['ɒpəreɪtə⁰] n: **to phone the ~** die
Vermittlung anrufen

opinion [ə'pɪnjən] n Meinung f
(on zu); **in my ~** meiner Meinung
nach

opponent [ə'pəʊnənt] n Geg-
ner(in) m(f)

opportunity [ɒpə'tjuːnɪtɪ] n
Gelegenheit f

oppose [ə'pəʊz] vt sich
widersetzen +dat; (idea) ablehnen;
opposed adj: **to be ~ to sth**
gegen etw sein; **as ~ to** im

Gegensatz zu; **opposing** adj
(team) gegnerisch; (points of view)
entgegengesetzt

opposite ['ɒpəzɪt] adj (house)
gegenüberliegend; (direction)
entgegengesetzt; **the ~ sex** das
andere Geschlecht ▷ adv
gegenüber ▷ prep gegenüber
+dat; **~ me** mir gegenüber ▷ n
Gegenteil nt

opposition [ɒpə'zɪʃən] n
Widerstand m (to gegen); (Pol)
Opposition f

oppress [ə'pres] vt unterdrücken; **oppressive** adj (heat)
drückend

opt [ɒpt] vi: **to ~ for sth** sich für
etw entscheiden; **to ~ to do sth**
sich entscheiden, etw zu tun

optician [ɒp'tɪʃən] n Optiker(in)
m(f)

optimist ['ɒptɪmɪst] n Opti-
mist(in) m(f); **optimistic**
[ɒptɪ'mɪstɪk] adj optimistisch

option ['ɒpʃən] n Möglichkeit f;
(Comm) Option f; **to have no
~** keine Wahl haben; **optional** adj
freiwillig; **~ extras** (Auto) Extras
pl

or [ɔː⁰] conj oder; (otherwise)
sonst; (after neg) noch; **hurry up,
~ (else) we'll be late** beeil dich,
sonst kommen wir zu spät

oral ['ɔːrəl] adj mündlich; **~ sex**
Oralverkehr m ▷ n (exam)
Mündliche(s) nt; **oral surgeon** n
Kieferchirurg(in) m(f)

orange ['ɒrɪndʒ] n Orange f
▷ adj orangefarben; **orange juice**
n Orangensaft m

orbit ['ɔːbɪt] n Umlaufbahn f; **to
be out of ~** (fam) nicht zu
erreichen sein ▷ vt umkreisen

orchard ['ɔːtʃəd] n Obstgarten m

orchestra ['ɔːkɪstrə] n Orchester nt; (US Theat) Parkett nt

orchid ['ɔːkɪd] n Orchidee f

ordeal [ɔː'diːl] *n* Tortur *f*; (*emotional*) Qual *f*

order ['ɔːdə*] *n* (*sequence*) Reihenfolge *f*; (*good arrangement*) Ordnung *f*; (*command*) Befehl *m*; (*Jur*) Anordnung *f*; (*condition*) Zustand *m*; (*Comm*) Bestellung *f*; **out of ~** (*not functioning*) außer Betrieb; (*unsuitable*) nicht angebracht; **in ~** (*items*) richtig geordnet; (*all right*) in Ordnung; **in ~ to do sth** um etw zu tun ▷ *vt* (*arrange*) ordnen; (*command*) befehlen; **to ~ sb to do sth** jdm befehlen, etw zu tun; (*food, product*) bestellen; **order form** *n* Bestellschein *m*

ordinary ['ɔːdnrɪ] *adj* gewöhnlich, normal; (*average*) durchschnittlich

ore [ɔː*] *n* Erz *nt*

organ ['ɔːgən] *n* (*Mus*) Orgel *f*; (*Anat*) Organ *nt*

organic [ɔː'gænɪk] *adj* organisch; (*farming, vegetables*) Bio-, Öko-; **~ farmer** Biobauer *m*, Biobäuerin *f*; **~ food** Biokost *f*

organization [ɔːgənaɪ'zeɪʃən] *n* Organisation *f*; (*arrangement*) Ordnung *f*; **organize** ['ɔːgənaɪz] *vt* organisieren; **organizer** *n* (*elektronisches*) Notizbuch

orgasm ['ɔːgæzəm] *n* Orgasmus *m*

orgy ['ɔːdʒɪ] *n* Orgie *f*

oriental [ɔːrɪ'entəl] *adj* orientalisch

orientation [ɔːrɪenteɪʃən] *n* Orientierung *f*

origin ['ɒrɪdʒɪn] *n* Ursprung *m*; (*of person*) Herkunft *f*; **original** [ə'rɪdʒɪnl] *adj* (*first*) ursprünglich; (*painting*) original; (*idea*) originell ▷ *n* Original *nt*; **originality** [ərɪdʒɪ'nælɪtɪ] *n* Originalität *f*; **originally** *adv* ursprünglich

Orkneys ['ɔːknɪz] *npl*, **Orkney Islands** *npl* Orkneyinseln *pl*

ornament ['ɔːnəmənt] *n* Schmuckgegenstand *m*; **ornamental** [ɔːnə'mentl] *adj* dekorativ

orphan ['ɔːfən] *n* Waise *f*, Waisenkind *nt*; **orphanage** ['ɔːfənɪdʒ] *n* Waisenhaus *nt*

orthodox ['ɔːθədɒks] *adj* orthodox

orthopaedic, **orthopedic** (*US*) [ɔːθəʊ'piːdɪk] *adj* orthopädisch

ostentatious [ɒstenteɪʃəs] *adj* protzig

ostrich ['ɒstrɪtʃ] *n* (*Zool*) Strauß *m*

other ['ʌðə*] *adj, pron* andere(r, s); **any ~ questions?** sonst noch Fragen?; **the ~ day** neulich; **every ~ day** jeden zweiten Tag; **any person ~ than him** alle außer ihm; **someone/something or ~** irgendjemand/irgendetwas; **otherwise** *adv*; (*differently*) anders

OTT *adj abbr* = **over the top** übertrieben

otter ['ɒtə*] *n* Otter *m*

ought [ɔːt] *vb aux* (*obligation*) sollte; (*probability*) dürfte; (*stronger*) müsste; **you ~ to do that** du solltest/Sie sollten das tun; **he ~ to win** er müsste gewinnen; **that ~ to do** das müsste reichen

ounce [aʊns] *n* Unze *f* (*28,35 g*)

our [aʊə*] *adj* unser; **ours** *pron* unsere(r, s); **this is ~** das gehört uns; **a friend of ~** ein Freund von uns; **ourselves** *pron* (*reflexive*) uns; **we enjoyed ~** wir haben uns amüsiert; **we've got the house to ~** wir haben das Haus für uns; (*emphatic*) **we did it ~** wir haben es selbst gemacht; (**all**) **by ~** allein

out [aʊt] *adv* hinaus/heraus; (*not*

indoors) draußen; (*not at home*) nicht zu Hause; (*not alight*) aus; (*unconscious*) bewusstlos; (*published*) herausgekommen; (*results*) bekannt gegeben; **have you been ~ yet?** warst du/waren Sie schon draußen?; **I was ~ when they called** ich war nicht da, als sie vorbeikamen; **to be ~ and about** unterwegs sein; **the sun is ~** die Sonne scheint; **the fire is ~** das Feuer ist ausgegangen; (*wrong*) **the calculation is (way) ~** die Kalkulation stimmt (ganz und gar) nicht; **they're ~ to get him** sie sind hinter ihm her ▷ *vt* (*fam*) outen

outback ['autbæk] *n* (*in Australia*) **the ~** das Hinterland

outboard ['autbɔːd] *adj*: **~ motor** Außenbordmotor *m*

outbreak ['autbreik] *n* Ausbruch *m*

outburst ['autbɜːst] *n* Ausbruch *m*

outcast ['autkɑːm] *n* Ergebnis *nt*

outcry ['autkrai] *n* (*public protest*) Protestwelle *f* (*against* gegen)

outdo [aut'duː] *irr vt* übertreffen

outdoor ['autdɔː°] *adj* Außen-; (*Sport*) im Freien; **~ swimming pool** Freibad *nt*; **outdoors** [aut'dɔːz] *adv* draußen, im Freien

outer ['autə°] *adj* äußere(r, s); **outer space** *n* Weltraum *m*

outfit ['autfit] *n* Ausrüstung *f*; (*clothes*) Kleidung *f*

outgoing ['autgəuiŋ] *adj* kontaktfreudig

outgrow [aut'grəu] *irr vt* (*clothes*) herauswachsen aus

outing ['autiŋ] *n* Ausflug *m*

outlet ['autlet] *n* Auslass *m*, Abfluss *m*; (US) Steckdose *f*; (*shop*) Verkaufsstelle *f*

outline ['autlain] *n* Umriss *m*; (*summary*) Abriss *m*

outlive [aut'liv] *vt* überleben

outlook ['autluk] *n* Aussicht(en) *f(pl)*; (*prospects*) Aussichten *pl*; (*attitude*) Einstellung *f* (*on* zu)

outnumber [aut'nʌmbə°] *vt* zahlenmäßig überlegen sein +*dat*; **~ed** zahlenmäßig unterlegen

out of ['autəv] *prep* (*motion, motive, origin*) aus; (*position, away from*) außerhalb +*gen*; **~ danger/sight/breath** außer Gefahr/Sicht/Atem; **made ~ wood** aus Holz gemacht; **we are ~ bread** wir haben kein Brot mehr; **out-of-date** *adj* veraltet; **out-of-the-way** *adj* abgelegen

outpatient ['autpeiʃənt] *n* ambulanter Patient, ambulante Patientin

output ['autput] *n* Produktion *f*; (*of engine*) Leistung *f*; (*Inform*) Ausgabe *f*

outrage ['autreidʒ] *n* (*great anger*) Empörung *f* (*at* über); (*wicked deed*) Schandtat *f*; (*crime*) Verbrechen *nt*; (*indecency*) Skandal *m*; **outrageous** [aut'reidʒəs] *adj* unerhört; (*clothes, behaviour etc*) unmöglich, schrill

outright ['autrait] *adv* (*killed*) sofort ▷ *adj* total; (*denial*) völlig; (*winner*) unbestritten

outside [aut'said] *n* Außenseite *f*; **on the ~** außen ▷ *adj* äußere(r, s), Außen-; (*chance*) sehr gering ▷ *adv* außen; **to go ~** nach draußen gehen ▷ *prep* außerhalb +*gen*; **outsider** *n* Außenseiter(in) *m(f)*

outskirts ['autskɜːts] *npl* (*of town*) Stadtrand *m*

outstanding [aut'stændiŋ] *adj* hervorragend; (*debts etc*) ausstehend

outward ['autwəd] *adj* äußere(r, s); **~ journey** Hinfahrt *f*;

outwardly adv nach außen hin;
outwards adv nach außen

oval ['əʊvəl] adj oval

ovary ['əʊvərɪ] n Eierstock m

ovation [əʊ'veɪʃən] n Ovation f,
Applaus m

oven ['ʌvn] n Backofen m; **oven
glove** n Topfhandschuh m;
ovenproof adj feuerfest;
oven-ready adj bratfertig

over ['əʊvə°] prep (position) über
+dat; (motion) über +akk; **they
spent a long time ~** it sie haben
lange dazu gebraucht; **from all
~ England** aus ganz England;
~ £20 mehr als 20 Pfund; **~ the
phone/radio** am Telefon/im
Radio; **to talk ~ a glass of wine**
sich bei einem Glas Wein
unterhalten; **~ and above** this
darüber hinaus; **~ the summer**
während des Sommers ▷ adv
(across) hinüber/herüber; (finished)
vorbei; (match, play etc) zu Ende;
(left) übrig; (more) mehr;
~ there/in America da
drüben/drüben in Amerika; **~ to
you** du bist/Sie sind dran; **it's (all)
~** between us es ist aus zwischen
uns; **~ and ~ again** immer wieder;
to start (all) ~ again noch einmal
von vorn anfangen; **children of 8
and ~** Kinder ab 8 Jahren

over- ['əʊvə°] pref über-

overall ['əʊvərɔːl] n (Brit) Kittel
m ▷ adj (situation) allgemein;
(length) Gesamt-; **~ majority**
absolute Mehrheit ▷ adv
insgesamt; **overalls** npl Overall
m

overboard ['əʊvəbɔːd] adv über
Bord

overbooked [əʊvə'bʊkt] adj
überbucht; **overbooking** n
Überbuchung f

overcharge [əʊvə'tʃɑːdʒ] vt zu
viel verlangen von

overcoat ['əʊvəkəʊt] n Wintermantel m

overcome [əʊvə'kʌm] irr vt
überwinden; **~ by sleep/emotion**
von Schlaf/Rührung übermannt;
we shall ~ wir werden siegen

overcooked [əʊvə'kʊkt] adj
verkocht; (meat) zu lange gebraten

overcrowded [əʊvə'kraʊdɪd]
adj überfüllt

overdo [əʊvə'duː] irr vt übertreiben; **overdone** adj
übertrieben; (food) zu lange
gekocht; (meat) zu lange gebraten

overdose ['əʊvədəʊs] n Über-
dosis f

overdraft ['əʊvədrɑːft] n Kon-
toüberziehung f; **overdrawn**
[əʊvə'drɔːn] adj überzogen

overdue [əʊvə'djuː] adj
überfällig

overestimate [əʊvər'estɪmeɪt]
vt überschätzen

overexpose [əʊvəriks'pəʊz] vt (Foto)
überbelichten

overflow [əʊvə'fləʊ] vi
überlaufen

overhead ['əʊvəhed] adj (Aviat)
~ locker Gepäckfach nt;
~ projector Overheadprojektor m;
~ railway Hochbahn f
▷ [əʊvə'hed] adv oben;
overhead, (Brit) **overheads** n
(Comm) allgemeine
Geschäftskosten pl

overhear [əʊvə'hɪə°] irr vt zufällig
mit anhören

overheat [əʊvə'hiːt] vi (engine)
heiß laufen

overjoyed [əʊvə'dʒɔɪd] adj
überglücklich (at über)

overland ['əʊvəlænd] adj Über-
land- ▷ [əʊvə'lænd] adv (travel)
über Land

overlap [əʊvə'læp] vi (dates etc)
sich überschneiden; (objects) sich
teilweise decken

overload | 444

overload [əʊvə'ləʊd] vt überladen

overlook [əʊvə'lʊk] vt (view from above) überblicken; (not notice) übersehen; (pardon) hinwegsehen über +akk

overnight [əʊvə'naɪt] adj (journey, train) Nacht-; **~ bag** Reisetasche f; **~ stay** Übernachtung f ▷ adv über Nacht

overpass ['əʊvəpɑːs] n Überführung f

overpay [əʊvə'peɪ] vt überbezahlen

overrule [əʊvə'ruːl] vt verwerfen; (decision) aufheben

overseas [əʊvə'siːz] adj Übersee-; ausländisch; (fam) Auslands- ▷ adv (go) nach Übersee; (live, work) in Übersee

oversee [əʊvə'siː] irr vt beaufsichtigen

overshadow [əʊvə'ʃædəʊ] vt überschatten

overshoot [əʊvə'ʃuːt] irr vt (runway) hinausschießen über +akk; (turning) vorbeifahren +dat

oversight ['əʊvəsaɪt] n Versehen nt

oversimplify [əʊvə'sɪmplɪfaɪ] vt zu sehr vereinfachen

oversleep [əʊvə'sliːp] irr vi verschlafen

overtake [əʊvə'teɪk] irr vt, vi überholen

overtime ['əʊvətaɪm] n Überstunden pl

overturn [əʊvə'tɜːn] vt, vi umkippen

overweight [əʊvə'weɪt] adj: **to be ~** Übergewicht haben

overwhelm [əʊvə'welm] vt überwältigen; **overwhelming** adj überwältigend

overwork [əʊvə'wɜːk] n Überarbeitung f ▷ vi sich

überarbeiten; **overworked** adj überarbeitet

owe [əʊ] vt schulden; **to ~ sth to sb** (money) jdm etw schulden; (favour etc) jdm etw verdanken; **how much do I ~ you?** was bin ich dir/Ihnen schuldig?; **owing to** prep wegen +gen

owl [aʊl] n Eule f

own [əʊn] vt besitzen ▷ adj eigen; **on one's ~** allein; **he has a flat of his ~** er hat eine eigene Wohung; **own up** vi: **to ~ to sth** etw zugeben; **owner** n Besitzer(in) m(f); (of business) Inhaber(in) m(f); **ownership** n Besitz m; **under new ~** unter neuer Leitung

ox [ɒks] (pl **oxen**) n Ochse m; **oxtail** ['ɒksteɪl] n Ochsenschwanz m; **~ soup** Ochsenschwanzsuppe f; **oxygen** ['ɒksɪdʒən] n Sauerstoff m

oyster ['ɔɪstə*] n Auster f

oz abbr = **ounces** Unzen pl

Oz ['ɒz] n (fam) Australien nt

ozone ['əʊzəʊn] n Ozon nt; **~ layer** Ozonschicht f

P

p abbr = **page** S.; abbr = **penny,
pence**

p.a. abbr = **per annum**

pace [peɪs] n (speed) Tempo nt;
(step) Schritt m; **pacemaker** n
(Med) Schrittmacher m

Pacific [pəˈsɪfɪk] n: **the
~ (Ocean)** der Pazifik; **Pacific
Standard Time** n pazifische Zeit

pacifier [ˈpæsɪfaɪə] n (US: for
baby) Schnuller m

pack [pæk] n (of cards) Spiel nt;
(esp US: of cigarettes) Schachtel f;
(gang) Bande f; (US: backpack)
Rucksack m ▷ vt (case) packen;
(clothes) einpacken ▷ vi (for
holiday) packen; **pack in** vt (Brit
fam: job) hinschmeißen; **package**
[ˈpækɪdʒ] n (a. Inform, fig) Paket
nt; **package deal** n
Pauschalangebot nt; **package
holiday** n; **package tour** n
Pauschalreise f; **packaging** n

(material) Verpackung f; **packed
lunch** n (Brit) Lunchpaket nt;
packet n Päckchen nt; (of
cigarettes) Schachtel f

pad [pæd] n (of paper)
Schreibblock m; (padding) Polster
nt; **padded envelope** n
wattierter Umschlag; **padding** n
(material) Polsterung f

paddle [ˈpædl] n (for boat) Paddel
nt ▷ vi (in boat) paddeln;
paddling pool n (Brit)
Planschbecken nt

padlock [ˈpædlɒk] n Vorhänge-
schloss nt

page [peɪdʒ] n (of book etc) Seite f

pager [ˈpeɪdʒə] n Piepser m

paid [peɪd] pt, pp of **pay** ▷ adj
bezahlt

pain [peɪn] n Schmerz m; **to be in
~** Schmerzen haben; **she's a (real)
~** sie nervt; **painful** adj (physically)
schmerzhaft; (embarrassing)
peinlich; **painkiller** n
schmerzstillendes Mittel

painstaking adj sorgfältig

paint [peɪnt] n Farbe f ▷ vt
anstreichen; (picture) malen;
paintbrush n Pinsel m; **painter** n
Maler(in) m(f); **painting** n
(picture) Bild nt, Gemälde nt

pair [peə] n Paar nt; **a ~ of shoes**
ein Paar Schuhe; **a ~ of scissors**
eine Schere; **a ~ of trousers** eine
Hose

pajamas [pəˈdʒɑːməz] npl (US)
Schlafanzug m

Pakistan [pɑːkɪˈstɑːn] n Pakistan nt

pal [pæl] n (fam) Kumpel m

palace [ˈpæləs] n Palast m

pale [peɪl] adj (face) blass, bleich;
(colour) hell

palm [pɑːm] n (of hand) Handfläche
f; **~ (tree)** Palme f; **palmtop
(computer)** n Palmtop(computer) m

pamper ['pæmpə°] vt
verhätscheln
pan [pæn] n (saucepan) Topf m;
(frying pan) Pfanne f; **pancake**
['pænkeɪk] n Pfannkuchen m;
Pancake Day n (Brit)
Fastnachtsdienstag m
pandemic [pæn'demɪk] n Pandemie f
panel ['pænl] n (of wood) Tafel f;
(in discussion) Diskussionsteil-
nehmer pl; (in jury) Jurymitglieder
pl
panic ['pænɪk] n Panik f ▷ vi in
Panik geraten; **panicky** ['pænɪkɪ]
adj panisch
pansy ['pænzɪ] n (flower)
Stiefmütterchen nt
panties ['pæntɪz] npl (Damen)
slip m
pantomime ['pæntəmaɪm] n
(Brit) um die Weihnachtszeit
aufgeführte Märchenkomödie
pants [pænts] npl Unterhose f;
(esp US: trousers) Hose f
pantyhose ['pæntɪhəʊz] npl
(US) Strumpfhose f; **panty-liner** n
Slipeinlage f
paper ['peɪpə°] n Papier nt;
(newspaper) Zeitung f; (exam)
Klausur f; (for reading at conference)
Referat nt; **~s** pl (identity papers)
Papiere pl; **~ bag** Papiertüte f;
~ cup Pappbecher m ▷ vt (wall)
tapezieren; **paperback** n
Taschenbuch nt; **paper clip** n
Büroklammer f; **paper feed** n (of
printer) Papiereinzug m; **paper
round** n: **to do a ~** Zeitungen
austragen; **paperwork** n
Schreibarbeit f
parachute ['pærəʃuːt] n Fallschirm m ▷ vi abspringen
paracetamol [pærə'siːtəmɒl] n
(tablet) Paracetamoltablette
f
parade [pə'reɪd] n (procession)

Umzug m; (Mil) Parade f ▷ vi
vorbeimarschieren
paradise ['pærədaɪs] n Paradies
nt
paragliding ['pærəglaɪdɪŋ] n
Gleitschirmfliegen nt
paragraph ['pærəgrɑːf] n Absatz
m
parallel ['pærəlel] adj parallel
▷ n (Math, fig) Parallele f
paralyze ['pærəlaɪz] vt lähmen;
(fig) lahmlegen
paranoid ['pærənɔɪd] adj
paranoid
paraphrase ['pærəfreɪz] vt
umschreiben; (sth spoken) anders
ausdrücken
parasailing ['pærəseɪlɪŋ] n
Parasailing nt
parasol ['pærəsɒl] n Sonnenschirm m
parcel ['pɑːsl] n Paket nt
pardon ['pɑːdn] n (Jur)
Begnadigung f; **~ me/I beg your
~** verzeih/verzeihen Sie bitte;
(objection) aber ich bitte dich/Sie; **I
beg your ~?/~ me?** wie bitte?
parent ['pɛərənt] n Elternteil m;
~s pl Eltern pl; **~s-in-law** pl
Schwiegereltern pl; **parental**
[pə'rentl] adj elterlich, Eltern-
parish ['pærɪʃ] n Gemeinde f
park [pɑːk] n Park m ▷ vt, vi
parken; **parking** n Parken nt; **"no
~"** "Parken verboten"; **parking
brake** n (US) Handbremse f;
parking disc n Parkscheibe f;
parking fine n Geldbuße f für
falsches Parken; **parking lights**
npl (US) Standlicht nt; **parking lot**
n (US) Parkplatz m; **parking meter**
n Parkuhr f; **parking place**,
parking space n Parkplatz m;
parking ticket n Strafzettel m
parliament ['pɑːləmənt] n Parlament nt
parrot ['pærət] n Papagei m

parsley ['pɑːslɪ] n Petersilie f

parsnip ['pɑːsnɪp] n Pastinake f (längliches, weißes Wurzelgemüse)

part [pɑːt] n Teil m; (of machine) Teil nt; (Theat) Rolle f; (US: in hair) Scheitel m; **to take ~** teilnehmen (in an +dat); **for the most ~** zum größten Teil ▷ adj Teil- ▷ vt (separate) trennen; (hair) scheiteln ▷ vi (people) sich trennen

partial ['pɑːʃəl] adj (incomplete) teilweise, Teil-

participant [pɑːˈtɪsɪpənt] n Teilnehmer(in) m(f); **participate** [pɑːˈtɪsɪpeɪt] vi teilnehmen (in an +dat)

particular [pəˈtɪkjʊləʳ] adj (specific) bestimmt; (exact) genau; (fussy) eigen; **in ~** insbesondere ▷ n **~s** pl (details) Einzelheiten pl; (about person) Personalien pl; **particularly** adv besonders

parting ['pɑːtɪŋ] n (farewell) Abschied m; (Brit: in hair) Scheitel m

partly ['pɑːtlɪ] adv teilweise

partner ['pɑːtnəʳ] n Partner(in) m(f); **partnership** n Partnerschaft f

partridge ['pɑːtrɪdʒ] n Rebhuhn nt

part-time ['pɑːt'taɪm] adj Teilzeit- ▷ adv: **to work ~** Teilzeit arbeiten

party ['pɑːtɪ] n (celebration) Party f; (Pol, Jur) Partei f; (group) Gruppe f ▷ vi feiern

pass [pɑːs] vt (on foot) vorbeigehen an +dat; (in car etc) vorbeifahren an +dat; (time) verbringen; (exam) bestehen; (law) verabschieden; **to ~ sth to sb, to ~ sb sth** jdm etw reichen; **to ~ the ball to sb** jdm den Ball zuspielen ▷ vi (on foot) vorbeigehen; (in car etc) vorbeifahren; (years) vergehen; (in exam) bestehen ▷ n (document) Ausweis m; (Sport) Pass m; **pass**

away vi (die) verscheiden; **pass by** vi (on foot) vorbeigehen; (in car etc) vorbeifahren ▷ vt (on foot) vorbeigehen an +dat; (in car etc) vorbeifahren an +dat; **pass on** vt weitergeben (to an +akk); (disease) übertragen (to auf +akk); **pass out** vi (faint) ohnmächtig werden; **pass round** vt herumreichen

passage ['pæsɪdʒ] n (corridor) Gang m; (in book, music) Passage f; **passageway** n Durchgang m

passenger ['pæsɪndʒəʳ] n Passagier(in) m(f); (on bus) Fahrgast m; (on train) Reisende(r) mf; (in car) Mitfahrer(in) m(f)

passer-by ['pɑːsəˈbaɪ] (pl **passers-by**) n Passant(in) m(f)

passion ['pæʃən] n Leidenschaft f; **passionate** ['pæʃənɪt] adj leidenschaftlich; **passion fruit** n Passionsfrucht f

passive ['pæsɪv] adj passiv; **~ smoking** Passivrauchen nt ▷ n: **~ (voice)** (Ling) Passiv nt

passport ['pɑːspɔːt] n (Reise)pass m; **passport control** n Passkontrolle f

password ['pɑːswɜːd] n (Inform) Passwort nt

past [pɑːst] n Vergangenheit f ▷ adv (by) vorbei; **it's five ~** es ist fünf nach ▷ adj (years) vergangen; (president etc) ehemalig; **in the ~ two months** in den letzten zwei Monaten ▷ prep (telling time) nach; **half ~ 10** halb 11; **to go ~ sth** an etw dat vorbeigehen/-fahren

pasta ['pæstə] n Nudeln pl

paste [peɪst] vt (stick) kleben; (Inform) einfügen ▷ n (glue) Kleister m

pastime ['pɑːstaɪm] n Zeitvertreib m

pastry ['peɪstrɪ] n Teig m; (cake) Stückchen

pasty ['pæstɪ] n (Brit) Pastete f

patch [pætʃ] n (area) Fleck m; (for mending) Flicken ▷ vt flicken; **patchy** adj (uneven) ungleichmäßig

pâté ['pæteɪ] n Pastete f

paternal [pə'tɜ:nl] adj väterlich; **~ grandmother** Großmutter f väterlicherseits; **paternity leave** [pə'tɜ:nɪtɪli:v] n Elternzeit f (des Vaters)

path [pɑ:θ] n (a. Inform) Pfad m; (a. fig) Weg m

pathetic [pə'θetɪk] adj (bad) kläglich, erbärmlich; **it's ~** es ist zum Heulen

patience ['peɪʃəns] n Geduld f; (Brit Cards) Patience f; **patient** adj geduldig ▷ n Patient(in) m(f)

patio ['pætɪəʊ] n Terrasse f

patriotic [pætrɪ'ɒtɪk] adj patriotisch

patrol car [pə'trəʊlkɑ:ᵊ] n Streifenwagen m; **patrolman** (pl **-men**) n (US) Streifenpolizist m

patron ['peɪtrən] n (sponsor) Förderer m, Förderin f; (in shop) Kunde m, Kundin f

patronize ['pætrənaɪz] vt (treat condescendingly) von oben herab behandeln; **patronizing** adj (attitude) herablassend

pattern ['pætən] n Muster nt

pause [pɔ:z] n Pause f ▷ vi (speaker) innehalten

pavement ['peɪvmənt] n (Brit) Bürgersteig m; (US) Pflaster nt

pay [peɪ] (paid, paid) vt bezahlen; **he paid (me) £20 for it** er hat (mir) 20 Pfund dafür gezahlt; **to ~ attention** Acht geben (to auf +akk); **to ~ sb a visit** jdn besuchen ▷ vi zahlen; (be profitable) sich bezahlt machen; **to ~ for sth** etw bezahlen ▷ n Bezahlung f, Lohn m; **pay back** vt (money) zurückzahlen; **pay in** vt (into account) einzahlen; **payable**

adj zahlbar; (due) fällig; **payday** n Zahltag m; **payee** [peɪ'i:] n Zahlungsempfänger(in) m(f); **payment** n Bezahlung f; (money) Zahlung f; **pay-per-view** adj Pay-per-View-; **pay phone** n Münzfernsprecher m; **pay TV** n Pay-TV nt

PC abbr = **personal computer** PC m; abbr = **politically correct** politisch korrekt

PDA abbr = **personal digital assistant** PDA m

PE abbr = **physical education** (school) Sport m

pea [pi:] n Erbse f

peace [pi:s] n Frieden m; **peaceful** adj friedlich

peach [pi:tʃ] n Pfirsich m

peacock ['pi:kɒk] n Pfau m

peak [pi:k] n (of mountain) Gipfel m; (fig) Höhepunkt m; **peak period** n Stoßzeit f; (season) Hochsaison

peanut ['pi:nʌt] n Erdnuss f; **peanut butter** n Erdnussbutter f

pear [peəᵊ] n Birne f

pearl [pɜ:l] n Perle f

pebble ['pebl] n Kiesel m

pecan [pɪ'kæn] n Pekannuss f

peck [pek] vt, vi picken; **peckish** adj (Brit fam) ein bisschen hungrig

peculiar [pɪ'kju:lɪəᵊ] adj (odd) seltsam; **~ to** charakteristisch für; **peculiarity** [pɪkjʊlɪ'ærɪtɪ] n (singular quality) Besonderheit f; (strangeness) Eigenartigkeit f

pedal ['pedl] n Pedal nt

pedestrian [pɪ'destrɪən] n Fußgänger(in) m(f); **pedestrian crossing** n Fußgängerüberweg m

pee [pi:] vi (fam) pinkeln

peel [pi:l] n Schale f ▷ vt schälen ▷ vi (paint etc) abblättern; (skin etc) sich schälen

peer [pɪəᵊ] n Gleichaltrige(r) mf ▷ vi starren

peg [peg] n (for coat etc) Haken m; (for tent) Hering m; (**clothes**) ~ (Wäsche)klammer f

pelvis ['pelvɪs] n Becken nt

pen [pen] n (ball-point) Kuli m, Kugelschreiber m; (fountain ~) Füller m

penalize ['piːnəlaɪz] vt (punish) bestrafen; **penalty** ['penltɪ] n (punishment) Strafe f; (in football) Elfmeter m

pence [pens] pl of **penny**

pencil ['pensl] n Bleistift m; **pencil sharpener** n (Bleistift)spitzer m

penetrate ['penɪtreɪt] vt durchdringen; (enter into) eindringen in +akk

penfriend ['penfrend] n Brieffreund(in) m(f)

penguin ['peŋgwɪn] n Pinguin m

penicillin [penɪ'sɪlɪn] n Penizillin nt

peninsula [pɪ'nɪnsjʊlə] n Halbinsel f

penis ['piːnɪs] n Penis m

penknife ['pennaɪf] (pl **penknives**) n Taschenmesser nt

penny ['penɪ] (pl **pence** o **pennies**) n (Brit) Penny m; (US) Centstück nt

pension ['penʃən] n Rente f; (for civil servants, executives etc) Pension f; **pensioner** n Rentner(in) m(f); **pension plan, pension scheme** n Rentenversicherung f

penultimate [pɪ'nʌltɪmət] adj vorletzte(r, s)

people ['piːpl] npl (persons) Leute pl; (von Staat) Volk nt; (inhabitants) Bevölkerung f; **people carrier** n Minivan m

pepper ['pepə°] n Pfeffer m; (vegetable) Paprika m; **peppermint** n (sweet) Pfefferminz nt

per [pɜː°] prep pro; ~ **annum** pro Jahr; ~ **cent** Prozent nt

percentage [pə'sentɪdʒ] n Prozentsatz m

perceptible [pə'septəbl] adj wahrnehmbar

percolator ['pɜːkəleɪtə°] n Kaffeemaschine f

percussion [pə'kʌʃən] n (Mus) Schlagzeug nt

perfect ['pɜːfɪkt] adj perfekt; (utter) völlig ▷ [pə'fekt] vt vervollkommnen; **perfectly** adv perfekt; (utterly) völlig

perform [pə'fɔːm] vt (task) ausführen; (play) aufführen; (Med: operation) durchführen ▷ vi (Theat) auftreten; **performance** n (show) Vorstellung f; (efficiency) Leistung f

perfume ['pɜːfjuːm] n Duft m; (substance) Parfüm nt

perhaps [pə'hæps] adv vielleicht

period ['pɪərɪəd] n (length of time) Zeit f; (in history) Zeitalter nt; (school) Stunde f; (Med) Periode f; (US: full stop) Punkt m; **for a ~ of three years** für einen Zeitraum von drei Jahren; **periodical** [pɪərɪ'ɒdɪkəl] n Zeitschrift f

peripheral [pə'rɪfərəl] n (Inform) Peripheriegerät nt

perjury ['pɜːdʒərɪ] n Meineid m

perm [pɜːm] n Dauerwelle f

permanent, permanently ['pɜːmənənt, -lɪ] adj, adv ständig

permission [pə'mɪʃən] n Erlaubnis f; **permit** ['pɜːmɪt] n Genehmigung f ▷ [pə'mɪt] vt erlauben, zulassen; **to ~ sb to do sth** jdm erlauben, etw zu tun

persecute ['pɜːsɪkjuːt] vt verfolgen

perseverance [pɜːsɪ'vɪərəns] n Ausdauer f

persist [pə'sɪst] vi (in belief etc) bleiben (in bei); (rain, smell) andauern; **persistent** adj beharrlich

person ['pɜːsn] n Mensch m; (in official context) Person f; **in ~** persönlich; **personal** adj persönlich; (private) privat; **personality** [pɜːsə'nælətɪ] n Persönlichkeit f; **personal organizer** n Organizer m; **personal stereo** (pl **-s**) n Walkman® m; **personnel** [pɜːsə'nel] n Personal nt

perspective [pə'spektɪv] n Perspektive f

persuade [pə'sweɪd] vt überreden; (convince) überzeugen; **persuasive** [pə'sweɪsɪv] adj überzeugend

perverse [pə'vɜːs] adj eigensinnig; abwegig; **pervert** ['pɜːvɜːt] n Perverse(r) mf ⊳ [pə'vɜːt] vt (morally) verderben; **perverted** [pə'vɜːtɪd] adj pervers

pessimist ['pesɪmɪst] n Pessimist(in) m(f); **pessimistic** [pesɪ'mɪstɪk] adj pessimistisch

pest [pest] n (insect) Schädling m; (fig: person) Nervensäge f; (thing) Plage f; **pester** ['pestə°] vt plagen; **pesticide** ['pestɪsaɪd] n Schädlingsbekämpfungsmittel nt

pet [pet] n (animal) Haustier nt; (person) Liebling m

petal ['petl] n Blütenblatt nt

petition [pə'tɪʃən] n Petition f

petrol ['petrəl] n (Brit) Benzin nt; **petrol pump** n (at garage) Zapfsäule f; **petrol station** n Tankstelle f; **petrol tank** n Benzintank m

pharmacy ['fɑːməsɪ] n (shop) Apotheke f; (science) Pharmazie f

phase [feɪz] n Phase f

PhD abbr = **Doctor of Philosophy** Dr. phil; (dissertation) Doktorarbeit f; **to do one's ~** promovieren

pheasant ['feznt] n Fasan m

phenomenon [fɪ'nɒmɪnən] (pl **phenomena**) n Phänomen nt

Philippines ['fɪlɪpiːnz] npl Philippinen pl

philosophical [fɪlə'sɒfɪkəl] adj philosophisch; (fig) gelassen; **philosophy** [fɪ'lɒsəfɪ] n Philosophie f

phone [fəʊn] n Telefon nt ⊳ vt, vi anrufen; **phone book** n Telefonbuch nt; **phone bill** n Telefonrechnung f; **phone booth**, **phone box** (Brit) n Telefonzelle f; **phonecall** n Telefonanruf m; **phonecard** n Telefonkarte f; **phone-in** n Rundfunkprogramm, bei dem Hörer anrufen können; **phone number** n Telefonnummer f

photo ['fəʊtəʊ] (pl **-s**) n Foto nt; **photo booth** n Fotoautomat m; **photocopier** ['fəʊtəʊkɒpiə°] n Kopiergerät nt; **photocopy** ['fəʊtəʊkɒpɪ] n Fotokopie f ⊳ vt fotokopieren; **photograph** ['fəʊtəgrɑːf] n Fotografie f, Aufnahme f ⊳ vt fotografieren; **photographer** [fə'tɒgrəfə°] n Fotograf(in) m(f); **photography** [fə'tɒgrəfɪ] n Fotografie f

phrase [freɪz] n (expression) Redewendung f, Ausdruck m; **phrase book** n Sprachführer m

physical ['fɪzɪkəl] adj (bodily) körperlich, physisch ⊳ n ärztliche Untersuchung; **physically** adv (bodily) körperlich, physisch; **~ handicapped** körperbehindert

physics ['fɪzɪks] nsing Physik f

physiotherapy [fɪzɪə'θerəpɪ] n Physiotherapie f

physique [fɪ'ziːk] n Körperbau m

piano ['pjɑːnəʊ] (pl **-s**) n Klavier nt

pick [pɪk] n (flowers, fruit) pflücken; (choose) auswählen; (team) aufstellen; **pick out** vt auswählen; **pick up** vi (lift up) aufheben; (collect) abholen; (learn) lernen

pickle ['pɪkl] n (food) (Mixed) Pickles pl ▷ vt einlegen

pickpocket ['pɪkpɒkɪt] n Taschendieb(in) m(f)

picnic ['pɪknɪk] n Picknick nt

picture ['pɪktʃə°] n Bild nt; **to go to the ~s** (Brit) ins Kino gehen ▷ vt (visualize) sich vorstellen; **picture book** n Bilderbuch nt; **picturesque** [pɪktʃə'resk] adj malerisch

pie [paɪ] n (meat) Pastete f; (fruit) Kuchen m

piece [piːs] n Stück nt; (part) Teil nt; (in chess) Figur f; (in draughts) Stein m; **a ~ of cake** ein Stück Kuchen; **to fall to ~s** auseinanderfallen

pier [pɪə°] n Pier m

pierce [pɪəs] vt durchstechen, durchbohren; (cold, sound) durchdringen; **pierced** adj (part of body) gepierct; **piercing** adj durchdringend

pig [pɪg] n Schwein nt

pigeon ['pɪdʒən] n Taube f; **pigeonhole** n (compartment) Ablegefach nt

piggy ['pɪgɪ] adj (fam) verfressen; **pigheaded** ['pɪg'hedɪd] adj dickköpfig; **piglet** ['pɪglət] n Ferkel nt; **pigsty** ['pɪgstaɪ] n Schweinestall m; **pigtail** ['pɪgteɪl] n Zopf m

pile [paɪl] n (heap) Haufen m; (one on top of another) Stapel m; **pile up** vi (accumulate) sich anhäufen

piles [paɪlz] npl Hämorr(ho)iden pl

pile-up ['paɪlʌp] n (Auto) Massenkarambolage f

pilgrim ['pɪlgrɪm] n Pilger(in) m(f)

pill [pɪl] n Tablette f; **the ~** (Antibaby)pille; **to be on the ~** die Pille nehmen

pillar ['pɪlə°] n Pfeiler m

pillow ['pɪləʊ] n (Kopf)kissen nt; **pillowcase** n (Kopf)kissenbezug m

pilot ['paɪlət] n (Aviat) Pilot(in) m(f)

pimple ['pɪmpl] n Pickel m

pin [pɪn] n (for fixing) Nadel f; (in sewing) Stecknadel f; (Tech) Stift m; **I've got ~s and needles in my leg** mein Bein ist mir eingeschlafen ▷ vt (fix with ~) heften (to an +akk)

PIN [pɪn] acr = **personal identification number** ~ **(number)** PIN f, Geheimzahl f

pinch [pɪntʃ] n (of salt) Prise f ▷ vt zwicken; (fam: steal) klauen ▷ vi (shoe) drücken

pine [paɪn] n Kiefer f

pineapple ['paɪnæpl] n Ananas f

pink [pɪŋk] adj rosa

pinstripe(d) ['pɪnstraɪp(t)] adj Nadelstreifen-

pint [paɪnt] n Pint nt (Brit: 0,57 l, US: 0,473l); (Brit: glass of beer) Bier nt

pious ['paɪəs] adj fromm

pip [pɪp] n (of fruit) Kern m

pipe [paɪp] n (for smoking) Pfeife f; (for water, gas) Rohrleitung f

pirate ['paɪərɪt] n Pirat(in) m(f); **pirated copy** n Raubkopie f

Pisces ['paɪsiːz] nsing (Astr) Fische pl; **she's a ~** sie ist Fisch

piss [pɪs] vi (vulg) pissen n (vulg) Pisse f; **to take the ~ out of sb** jdn verarschen; **piss off** vi (vulg) sich verpissen; **~! verpiss dich!; pissed** adj (Brit fam: drunk) sturzbesoffen; (US fam: annoyed) stocksauer

pistachio [pɪ'stɑːʃɪəʊ] (pl -s) n Pistazie f

piste [piːst] n (Ski) Piste f

pistol ['pɪstl] n Pistole f

pit [pɪt] n (hole) Grube f; (coalmine) Zeche f; **the ~s** (motor racing) die Box; **to be the ~s** (fam) grottenschlecht sein

pitch [pɪtʃ] n (Sport) Spielfeld nt; (Mus: of instrument) Tonlage f; (of voice) Stimmlage f ▷ vt (tent)

p

aufschlagen; (*throw*) werfen; **pitch-black** *adj* pechschwarz

pitcher ['pɪtʃə*] *n* (US: *jug*) Krug *m*

pitiful ['pɪtɪful] *adj* (*contemptible*) jämmerlich

pitta bread ['pɪtə] *n* Pittabrot *nt*

pity ['pɪtɪ] *n* Mitleid *nt*; **what a ~** wie schade; **it's a ~** es ist schade ▷ *vt* Mitleid haben mit

pizza ['piːtsə] *n* Pizza *f*

place [pleɪs] *n* (*spot, in text*) Stelle *f*; (*town etc*) Ort; (*house*) Haus *nt*; (*position, seat, on course*) Platz *m*; **~ of birth** Geburtsort *m*; **at my ~** bei mir; **in third ~** auf dem dritten Platz; **to three decimal ~s** bis auf drei Stellen nach dem Komma; **out of ~** nicht an der richtigen Stelle; (*fig: remark*) unangebracht; **in ~ of** anstelle von; **in the first ~** (*firstly*) erstens; (*immediately*) gleich; (*in any case*) überhaupt ▷ *vt* (*put*) stellen, setzen; (*lay flat*) legen; (*advertisement*) setzen (in *in +akk*); (*Comm: order*) aufgeben; **place mat** *n* Set *nt*

plague [pleɪg] *n* Pest *f*

plaice [pleɪs] *n* Scholle *f*

plain [pleɪn] *adj* (*clear*) klar, deutlich; (*simple*) einfach; (*not beautiful*) unattraktiv; (*yoghurt*) Natur-; (*Brit: chocolate*) (Zart)bitter- ▷ *n* Ebene *f*; **plainly** *adv* (*frankly*) offen; (*simply*) einfach; (*obviously*) eindeutig

plait [plæt] *n* Zopf *m* ▷ *vt* flechten

plan [plæn] *n* Plan *m*; (*for essay etc*) Konzept *nt* ▷ *vt* planen; **to ~ to do sth, to ~ on doing sth** vorhaben, etw zu tun ▷ *vi* planen

plane [pleɪn] *n* (*aircraft*) Flugzeug *nt*; (*tool*) Hobel *m*

planet ['plænɪt] *n* Planet *m*

plank [plæŋk] *n* Brett *nt*

plant [plɑːnt] *n* Pflanze *f*; (*equipment*) Maschinen *pl*; (*factory*) Werk *nt* ▷ *vt* (*tree etc*) pflanzen

plantation [plæn'teɪʃən] *n* Plantage *f*

plaque [plæk] *n* Gedenktafel *f*; (*on teeth*) Zahnbelag *m*

plaster ['plɑːstə*] *n* (*Brit Med: sticking ~*) Pflaster *nt*; (*on wall*) Verputz *m*; **to have one's arm in ~** den Arm in Gips haben

plastered ['plɑːstəd] *adj* (*fam*) besoffen; **to get (absolutely) ~** sich besaufen

plastic ['plæstɪk] *n* Kunststoff *m*; **to pay with ~** mit Kreditkarte bezahlen ▷ *adj* Plastik-; **plastic bag** *n* Plastiktüte *f*; **plastic surgery** *n* plastische Chirurgie *f*

plate [pleɪt] *n* (*for food*) Teller *m*; (*flat sheet*) Platte *f*; (*plaque*) Schild *nt*

platform ['plætfɔːm] *n* (*Rail*) Bahnsteig *m*; (*at meeting*) Podium *nt*

platinum ['plætɪnəm] *n* Platin *nt*

play [pleɪ] *n* Spiel *nt*; (*Theat*) (Theater)stück *nt* ▷ *vt* spielen; (*another player or team*) spielen gegen; **to ~ the piano** Klavier spielen; **to ~ a part in** (*fig*) eine Rolle spielen bei ▷ *vi* spielen; **play at** *vt*: **what are you ~ing at?** was soll das?; **play back** *vt* abspielen; **play down** *vt* herunterspielen

playacting *n* Schauspielerei *f*; **playback** *n* Wiedergabe *f*; **player** *n* Spieler(in) *m(f)*; **playful** *adj* (*person*) verspielt; (*remark*) scherzhaft; **playground** *n* Spielplatz *m*; (*in school*) Schulhof *m*; **playgroup** *n* Spielgruppe *f*; **playing card** *n* Spielkarte *f*; **playing field** *n* Sportplatz *m*; **playmate** *n* Spielkamerad(in) *m(f)*; **playwright** *n* Dramatiker(in) *m(f)*

plc *abbr* = **public limited company** AG *f*

plea [pliː] *n* Bitte *f* (for um)

plead [pliːd] *vi* dringend bitten (with sb jdn); (Jur) **to ~ guilty** sich schuldig bekennen

pleasant, pleasantly ['plɛznt, -lɪ] *adj, adv* angenehm

please [pliːz] *interj* bitte; **more tea? - yes,** ~ noch Tee? - ja, bitte ▷ *vt* (be agreeable to) gefallen +*dat*; ~ **yourself** wie du willst/Sie wollen; **pleased** *adj* zufrieden; (glad) erfreut; ~ **to meet you** freut mich, angenehm; **pleasing** *adj* erfreulich; **pleasure** ['plɛʒə°] *n* Vergnügen *nt*, Freude *f*; **it's a** ~ gern geschehen

pledge [plɛdʒ] *n* Versprechen *nt* ▷ *vt* versprechen

plenty ['plɛntɪ] *n*: ~ **of** eine Menge, viel(e); **to be** ~ genug sein, reichen; **I've got** ~ ich habe mehr als genug ▷ *adv* (US fam) ganz schön

pliable ['plaɪəbl] *adj* biegsam

pliers ['plaɪəz] *npl* (Kombi)zange *f*

plimsoll ['plɪmsəl] *n* (Brit) Turnschuh *m*

plonk [plɒŋk] *n* (Brit fam: wine) billiger Wein ▷ *vt*: **to ~ sth (down)** etw hinknallen

plot [plɒt] *n* (of story) Handlung *f*; (conspiracy) Komplott *nt*; (of land) Stück *nt* Land, Grundstück *nt* ▷ *vi* ein Komplott schmieden

plough, plow (US) [plaʊ] *n* Pflug *m* ▷ *vt, vi* (Agr) pflügen; **ploughman's lunch** *n* (Brit) in einer Kneipe serviertes Gericht aus Käse, Brot, Mixed Pickles etc

pluck [plʌk] *vt* (eyebrows, guitar) zupfen; (chicken) rupfen; **pluck up** *vt*: **to ~ (one's) courage** Mut aufbringen

plug [plʌg] *n* (for sink, bath) Stöpsel *m*; (Elec) Stecker *m*; (Auto) (Zünd)kerze *f*; (fam: publicity)

Schleichwerbung *f* ▷ *vt* (fam: advertise) Reklame machen für; **plug in** *vt* anschließen

plum [plʌm] *n* Pflaume *f* ▷ *adj* (fam: job etc) Super-

plumber ['plʌmə°] *n* Klempner(in) *m(f)*; **plumbing** ['plʌmɪŋ] *n* (fittings) Leitungen *pl*; (craft) Installieren *nt*

plump [plʌmp] *adj* rundlich

plunge [plʌndʒ] *n* (knife) stoßen; (into water) tauchen ▷ *vi* stürzen; (into water) tauchen

plural ['plʊərəl] *n* Plural *m*

plus [plʌs] *prep* plus; (as well as) und ▷ *adj* Plus-; **20 ~** mehr als 20 ▷ *n* (fig) Plus *nt*

plywood ['plaɪwʊd] *n* Sperrholz *nt*

pm *abbr* = **post meridiem; at 3** ~ um 3 Uhr nachmittags; **at 8** ~ um 8 Uhr abends

pneumonia [njuːˈməʊnɪə] *n* Lungenentzündung *f*

poached [pəʊtʃt] *adj* (egg) pochiert, verloren

PO Box *abbr* = **post office box** Postfach *n*

pocket ['pɒkɪt] *n* Tasche *f* ▷ *vt* (put in ~) einstecken; **pocketbook** *n* (US: wallet) Brieftasche *f*; **pocket calculator** *n* Taschenrechner *m*; **pocket money** *n* Taschengeld *nt*

podcast ['pɒdkɑːst] *n* Podcast *m*

poem ['pəʊɪm] *n* Gedicht *nt*; **poet** ['pəʊɪt] *n* Dichter(in) *m(f)*; **poetic** [pəʊˈɛtɪk] *adj* poetisch; **poetry** ['pəʊɪtrɪ] *n* (art) Dichtung *f*; (poems) Gedichte *pl*

point [pɔɪnt] *n* (spot) Stelle *f*; (sharp tip) Spitze *f*; (moment) Zeitpunkt *m*; (purpose) Zweck *m*; (idea) Argument *nt*; (decimal) Dezimalstelle *f*; **~s** *pl* (Rail) Weiche *f*; **~ of view** Standpunkt *m*; **three ~ two** drei Komma zwei; **at some ~** irgendwann (mal); **to get**

to the ~ zur Sache kommen;
there's no ~ es hat keinen Sinn; **I
was on the ~ of leaving** ich wollte
gerade gehen ▷ vt (gun etc)
richten (at auf +akk); **to ~ one's
finger at** mit dem Finger zeigen
auf +akk ▷ vi (with finger etc)
zeigen (at, to auf +akk); **point out**
vt (indicate) aufzeigen; (mention)
hinweisen auf +akk; **pointed** adj
spitz; (question) gezielt; **pointer** n
(on dial) Zeiger m; (tip) Hinweis m;
pointless adj sinnlos
poison ['pɔɪzn] n Gift nt ▷ vt
vergiften; **poisonous** adj giftig
poke [pəʊk] vt (with stick, finger)
stoßen, stupsen; (put) stecken
Poland ['pəʊlənd] n Polen nt
polar ['pəʊlə⁰] adj Polar-, polar;
~ bear Eisbär m
pole [pəʊl] n Stange f; (Geo, Elec)
Pol m
Pole [pəʊl] n Pole m, Polin f
pole vault n Stabhochsprung m
police [pə'liːs] n Polizei f; **police
car** n Polizeiwagen m; **policeman**
(pl **-men**) n Polizist m; **police
station** n (Polizei)wache f;
policewoman (pl **-women**) n
Polizistin f
policy ['pɒlɪsɪ] n (plan) Politik f;
(principle) Grundsatz m; (insurance
~) (Versicherungs)police f
polio ['pəʊlɪəʊ] n Kinderlähmung f
polish ['pɒlɪʃ] n (for furniture)
Politur f; (for floor) Wachs nt; (for
shoes) Creme f; (shine) Glanz m;
(fig) Schliff m ▷ vt polieren;
(shoes) putzen; (fig) den letzten
Schliff geben +dat
Polish ['pəʊlɪʃ] adj polnisch ▷ n
Polnisch nt
polite [pə'laɪt] adj höflich;
politeness n Höflichkeit f
political, **politically** [pə'lɪtɪkəl, -ɪ]
adj, adv politisch; **~ly correct**
politisch korrekt; **politician**

[pɒlɪ'tɪʃən] n Politiker(in) m(f);
politics ['pɒlɪtɪks] nsing o pl
Politik f
poll [pəʊl] n (election) Wahl f;
(opinion ~) Umfrage f
pollen ['pɒlən] n Pollen m,
Blütenstaub m; **pollen count** n
Pollenflug m
polling station ['pəʊlɪŋsteɪʃən]
n Wahllokal nt
pollute [pə'luːt] vt verschmutzen; **pollution** [pə'luːʃən] n
Verschmutzung f
pompous ['pɒmpəs] adj aufge-
blasen; (language) geschwollen
pond [pɒnd] n Teich m
pony ['pəʊnɪ] n Pony nt;
ponytail n Pferdeschwanz m
poodle ['puːdl] n Pudel m
pool [puːl] n (swimming ~)
Schwimmbad nt; (private)
Swimmingpool m; (of spilt liquid,
blood) Lache f; (game) Poolbillard
nt ▷ vt (money etc)
zusammenlegen
poor [pɔː⁰] adj arm; (not good)
schlecht ▷ npl: **the ~** die Armen
pl; **poorly** adv (badly) schlecht
▷ adj (Brit) krank
pop [pɒp] n (music) Pop m; (noise)
Knall m ▷ vt (put) stecken;
(balloon) platzen lassen ▷ vi
(balloon) platzen; (cork) knallen; **to
~ in** (person) vorbeischauen; **pop
concert** n Popkonzert nt;
popcorn n Popcorn nt
Pope [pəʊp] n Papst m
pop group n Popgruppe f; **pop music** n
Popmusik f
poppy ['pɒpɪ] n Mohn m
Popsicle® ['pɒpsɪkl] n (US) Eis
nt am Stiel
pop star ['pɒpstaː⁰] n Popstar m
popular ['pɒpjʊlə⁰] adj (well-
-liked) beliebt (with bei);
(widespread) weit verbreitet

population [pɒpjʊ'leɪʃən] n
Bevölkerung f; (of town) Einwohner
pl

porcelain ['pɔːslɪn] n Porzellan
nt

porch [pɔːtʃ] n Vorbau m; (US:
verandah) Veranda f

porcupine ['pɔːkjupaɪn] n
Stachelschwein nt

pork [pɔːk] n Schweinefleisch nt;
pork chop n Schweinekotelett;
pork pie n Schweinefleischpastete
f

porn [pɔːn] n Porno m;
pornographic [pɔːnə'græfɪk] adj
pornografisch; **pornography**
[pɔː'nɒɡrəfɪ] n Pornografie f

porridge ['pɒrɪdʒ] n Haferbrei m

port [pɔːt] n (harbour) Hafen m;
(town) Hafenstadt f; (Naut: left side)
Backbord nt; (wine) Portwein m;
(Inform) Anschluss m

portable ['pɔːtəbl] adj tragbar;
(radio) Koffer-

portal ['pɔːtl] n (Inform) Portal nt

porter ['pɔːtə°] n Pförtner(in)
m(f); (for luggage) Gepäckträger m

porthole ['pɔːthəʊl] n Bullauge
nt

portion ['pɔːʃən] n Teil m; (of
food) Portion f

portrait ['pɔːtrɪt] n Porträt nt

portray [pɔː'treɪ] vt darstellen

Portugal ['pɔːtjʊɡl] n Portugal
nt; **Portuguese** [pɔːtʃʊ'ɡiːz] adj
portugiesisch ▷ n Portugiese m,
Portugiesin f; (language)
Portugiesisch nt

pose [pəʊz] n Haltung f ▷ vi
posieren ▷ vt (threat, problem)
darstellen

posh [pɒʃ] adj (fam) piekfein

position [pə'zɪʃən] n Stellung f;
(place) Position f, Lage f; (job) Stelle
f; (opinion) Standpunkt m; **to be in
a ~ to do sth** in der Lage sein, etw
zu tun; **in third ~** auf dem dritten

Platz ▷ vt aufstellen; (Inform:
cursor) positionieren

positive ['pɒzɪtɪv] adj positiv;
(convinced) sicher

possess [pə'zes] vt besitzen;
possession [pə'zeʃən] n ~(s pl)
Besitz m; **possessive** adj (person)
besitzergreifend

possibility [pɒsə'bɪlɪtɪ] n
Möglichkeit f; **possible** ['pɒsəbl]
adj möglich; **if ~** wenn möglich; **as
big/soon as ~** so groß/bald wie
möglich; **possibly** adv (perhaps)
vielleicht; **I've done all I ~ can** ich
habe mein Möglichstes getan

post [pəʊst] n (mail) Post f; (pole)
Pfosten m; (job) Stelle f ▷ vt
(letters) aufgeben; **to keep sb ~ed**
jdn auf dem Laufenden halten;
postage ['pəʊstɪdʒ] n Porto nt;
~ and packing Porto und
Verpackung; **postal** adj Post-;
(Brit) **~ order** Postanweisung f;
postbox n Briefkasten m;
postcard n Postkarte f; **postcode**
n (Brit) Postleitzahl f

poster ['pəʊstə°] n Plakat nt,
Poster nt

postgraduate [pəʊst'grædjuɪt]
n jmd, der seine Studien nach dem
ersten akademischen Grad weiterführt

postman ['pəʊstmən] (pl **-men**)
n Briefträger m; **postmark** n
Poststempel m

postmortem [pəʊst'mɔːtəm] n
Autopsie f

post office ['pəʊstɒfɪs] n Post f

postpone [pə'spəʊn] vt verschieben (till auf +akk)

posture ['pɒstʃə°] n Haltung f

pot [pɒt] n Topf m; (tea-, coffee ~)
Kanne f; (fam: marijuana) Pot nt
▷ vt (plant) eintopfen

potato [pə'teɪtəʊ] (pl **-es**) n
Kartoffel f; **potato chips** (US) npl
Kartoffelchips pl; **potato peeler** n
Kartoffelschäler m

potent ['pəʊtənt] adj stark
potential [pəʊ'tenʃəl] adj
potenziell ▷ n Potenzial nt;
potentially adv potenziell
pothole ['pɒthəʊl] n Höhle f; (in
road) Schlagloch nt
potter about ['pɒtərəbaʊt] vi
herumhantieren
pottery ['pɒtərɪ] n (objects)
Töpferwaren pl
potty ['pɒtɪ] adj (Brit fam)
verrückt ▷ n Töpfchen nt
poultry ['pəʊltrɪ] n Geflügel
nt
pounce [paʊns] vi: **to ~ on** sich
stürzen auf +akk
pound [paʊnd] n (money) Pfund
nt; (weight) Pfund nt (0,454 kg); **a
~ of cherries** ein Pfund Kirschen;
ten-~ note Zehnpfundschein
m
pour [pɔː] vt (liquid) gießen; (rice,
sugar etc) schütten; **to ~ sb sth**
(drink) jdm etw eingießen;
pouring adj (rain) strömend
poverty ['pɒvətɪ] n Armut f
powder ['paʊdə] n Pulver nt;
(cosmetic) Puder m; **powdered
milk** n Milchpulver nt; **powder
room** n Damentoilette f
power [paʊə] n Macht f;
(ability) Fähigkeit f; (strength)
Stärke f; (Elec) Strom m; **to be in
~** an der Macht sein ▷ vt
betreiben, antreiben;
power-assisted steering n
Servolenkung f; **power cut** n
Stromausfall m; **powerful** adj
(politician person) mächtig; (engine,
government) stark; (argument)
durchschlagend; **powerless** adj
machtlos; **power station** n
Kraftwerk nt

p&p abbr = **postage and packing**
PR abbr = **public relations** ▷ abbr =
proportional representation
practical, practically ['præktɪkəl,

-l] adj, adv praktisch; **practice**
['præktɪs] n (training) Übung f;
(custom) Gewohnheit f; (doctor's,
lawyer's) Praxis f; **in ~** (in reality) in
der Praxis; **out of ~** außer Übung;
to put sth into ~ etw in die Praxis
umsetzen ▷ vt, vi (US) see
practise; practise ['præktɪs] vt
(instrument, movement) üben;
(profession) ausüben ▷ vi üben;
(doctor, lawyer) praktizieren
Prague [prɑːɡ] n Prag nt
praise [preɪz] n Lob nt ▷ vt
loben
pram [præm] n (Brit)
Kinderwagen m
prawn [prɔːn] n Garnele f,
Krabbe f; **prawn crackers** npl
Krabbenchips pl
pray [preɪ] vi beten; **to ~ for sth**
(fig) stark auf etw akk hoffen;
prayer ['preə] n Gebet nt
pre- [priː] pref vor-, prä-
preach [priːtʃ] vi predigen
prearrange [priːə'reɪndʒ] vt im
Voraus vereinbaren
precaution [prɪ'kɔːʃən] n Vor-
sichtsmaßnahme f
precede [prɪ'siːd] vt vorausgehen +dat; **preceding** adj
vorhergehend
precinct ['priːsɪŋkt] n (Brit:
pedestrian ~) Fußgängerzone f;
(Brit: shopping ~) Einkaufsviertel nt;
(US: district) Bezirk m
precious ['preʃəs] adj kostbar;
~ stone Edelstein m
précis ['preɪsiː] n Zusammenfassung f
precise, precisely [prɪ'saɪs, -lɪ]
adj, adv genau
precondition [priːkən'dɪʃən] n
Vorbedingung f
predecessor ['priːdɪsesə] n
Vorgänger(in) m(f)
predicament [prɪ'dɪkəmənt] n
missliche Lage

predict [prɪ'dɪkt] vt voraussagen; **predictable** adj vorhersehbar; (person) berechenbar

predominant [prɪ'dɒmɪnənt] adj vorherrschend; **predominantly** adv überwiegend

preface ['prefɪs] n Vorwort nt

prefer [prɪ'fɜː] vt vorziehen (to dat), lieber mögen (to als); **to ~ to do sth** etw lieber tun; **preferably** ['prefrəblɪ] adv vorzugsweise, am liebsten; **preference** ['prefərəns] n (liking) Vorliebe f; **preferential** [prefə'renʃəl] adj: **to get ~ treatment** bevorzugt behandelt werden

prefix ['priːfɪks] n (US Tel) Vorwahl f

pregnancy ['pregnənsɪ] n Schwangerschaft f; **pregnant** ['pregnənt] adj schwanger; **two months ~** im zweiten Monat schwanger

prejudice ['predʒʊdɪs] n Vorurteil nt; **prejudiced** adj (person) voreingenommen

preliminary [prɪ'lɪmɪnərɪ] adj (measures) vorbereitend; (results) vorläufig; (remarks) einleitend

premature ['premətʃʊə] adj vorzeitig; (hasty) voreilig

premiere ['premɪeə] n Premiere f

premises ['premɪsɪz] npl (offices) Räumlichkeiten pl; (of factory, school) Gelände nt

premium-rate [priː'mɪəmreɪt] adj (Tel) zum Höchsttarif

preoccupied [priː'ɒkjʊpaɪd] adj: **to be ~ with sth** mit etw sehr beschäftigt sein

prepaid [priː'peɪd] adj vorausbezahlt; (envelope) frankiert

preparation [prepə'reɪʃən] n Vorbereitung f; **prepare** [prɪ'peə] vt vorbereiten (for auf +akk); (food)

zubereiten; **to be ~d to do sth** bereit sein, etw zu tun ▷ vi sich vorbereiten (for auf +akk)

prerequisite [priː'rekwɪzɪt] n Voraussetzung f

prescribe [prɪ'skraɪb] vt vorschreiben; (Med) verschreiben; **prescription** [prɪ'skrɪpʃən] n Rezept nt

presence ['prezns] n Gegenwart f; **present** [preznt] adj (in attendance) anwesend (at bei); (current) gegenwärtig; **~ tense** Gegenwart f, Präsens nt ▷ n (gift) Geschenk nt; **at ~** zurzeit ▷ ['prezent] vt (TV, Radio) präsentieren; (problem) darstellen; (report etc) vorlegen; **to ~ sb with sth** jdm etw überreichen; **present-day** adj heutig; **presently** adv bald; (at present) zurzeit

preservative [prɪ'zɜːvətɪv] n Konservierungsmittel nt

preserve [prɪ'zɜːv] vt erhalten; (food) einmachen, konservieren

president ['prezɪdənt] n Präsident(in) m(f); **presidential** [prezɪ'denʃəl] adj Präsidenten-; (election) Präsidentschafts-

press [pres] n (newspapers, machine) Presse f ▷ vt (push) drücken; **to ~ a button** auf einen Knopf drücken ▷ vi (push) drücken; **pressing** adj dringend; **press-stud** n Druckknopf m; **press-up** n (Brit) Liegestütz m; **pressure** ['preʃə] n Druck m; **to be under ~** unter Druck stehen; **to put ~ on sb** jdn unter Druck setzen; **pressure cooker** n Schnellkochtopf m; **pressurize** ['preʃəraɪz] vt (person) unter Druck setzen

presumably [prɪ'zjuːməblɪ] adv vermutlich; **presume** [prɪ'zjuːm] vt, vi annehmen

presumptuous [prɪˈzʌmptʃʊəs] *adj* anmaßend

presuppose [priːsəˈpəʊz] *vt* voraussetzen

pretend [prɪˈtend] *vt*: **to ~ that** so tun als ob; **to ~ to do sth** vorgeben, etw zu tun ▷ *vi*: **she's ~ing** sie tut nur so

pretentious [prɪˈtenʃəs] *adj* anmaßend; (*person*) wichtigtuerisch

pretty [ˈprɪtɪ] *adj* hübsch ▷ *adv* ziemlich

prevent [prɪˈvent] *vt* verhindern; **to ~ sb from doing sth** jdn daran hindern, etw zu tun

preview [ˈpriːvjuː] *n* (*Cine*) Voraufführung *f*; (*trailer*) Vorschau *f*

previous, previously [ˈpriːvɪəs, -lɪ] *adj, adv* früher

prey [preɪ] *n* Beute *f*

price [praɪs] *n* Preis *m* ▷ *vt*: **it's ~d at £10** es ist mit 10 Pfund ausgezeichnet; **priceless** *adj* unbezahlbar; **price list** *n* Preisliste *f*; **price tag** *n* Preisschild *nt*

prick [prɪk] *n* Stich *m*; (*vulg: penis*) Schwanz *m*; (*vulg: person*) Arsch *m* ▷ *vt* stechen in +*akk*; **to ~ one's finger** sich *dat* in den Finger stechen; **prickly** [ˈprɪklɪ] *adj* stachelig

pride [praɪd] *n* Stolz *m*; (*arrogance*) Hochmut *m* ▷ *vt*: **to ~ oneself on sth** auf etw *akk* stolz sein

priest [priːst] *n* Priester *m*

primarily [ˈpraɪmərɪlɪ] *adv* vorwiegend; **primary** [ˈpraɪmərɪ] *adj* Haupt-; **~ education** Grundschulausbildung *f*; **~ school** Grundschule *f*

prime [praɪm] *adj* Haupt-; (*excellent*) erstklassig ▷ *n*: **in one's ~** in den besten Jahren; **prime minister** *n* Premierminister(in) *m(f)*; **prime time** *n* (*TV*) Hauptsendezeit *f*

primitive [ˈprɪmɪtɪv] *adj* primitiv

primrose [ˈprɪmrəʊz] *n* Schlüsselblume *f*

prince [prɪns] *n* Prinz *m*; (*ruler*) Fürst *m*; **princess** [prɪnˈses] *n* Prinzessin *f*; Fürstin *f*

principal [ˈprɪnsɪpəl] *adj* Haupt-, wichtigste(r, s) ▷ *n* (*school*) Rektor(in) *m(f)*

principle [ˈprɪnsəpl] *n* Prinzip *nt*; **in ~** im Prinzip; **on ~** aus Prinzip

print [prɪnt] *n* (*picture*) Druck *m*; (*Foto*) Abzug *m*; (*made by feet, fingers*) Abdruck *m*; **out of ~** vergriffen ▷ *vt* drucken; (*photo*) abziehen; (*write in block letters*) in Druckschrift schreiben; **print out** *vt* (*Inform*) ausdrucken; **printed matter** *n* Drucksache *f*; **printer** *n* Drucker *m*; **printout** *n* (*Inform*) Ausdruck *m*

prior [ˈpraɪəʳ] *adj* früher; **a ~ engagement** eine vorher getroffene Verabredung; **~ to sth** vor etw *dat*; **~ to going abroad, she had ...** bevor sie ins Ausland ging, hatte sie ...

priority [praɪˈɒrɪtɪ] *n* (*thing having precedence*) Priorität *f*

prison [ˈprɪzn] *n* Gefängnis *nt*; **prisoner** *n* Gefangene(r) *mf*; **~ of war** Kriegsgefangene(r) *mf*

privacy [ˈprɪvəsɪ] *n* Privatleben *nt*; **private** [ˈpraɪvɪt] *adj* privat; (*confidential*) vertraulich ▷ *n* einfacher Soldat; **in ~** privat; **privately** *adv* privat; (*confidentially*) vertraulich; **privatize** [ˈpraɪvətaɪz] *vt* privatisieren

privilege [ˈprɪvɪlɪdʒ] *n* Privileg *nt*; **privileged** *adj* privilegiert

prize [praɪz] *n* Preis *m*; **prize money** *n* Preisgeld *nt*; **prizewinner** *n* Gewinner(in) *m(f)*; **prizewinning** *adj* preisgekrönt

pro [prəʊ] (pl **-s**) n (professional) Profi m; **the ~s and cons** pl das Für und Wider

pro- [prəʊ] pref pro-

probability [prɒbəˈbɪlɪtɪ] n Wahrscheinlichkeit f; **probable** [ˈprɒbəbl] adj; **probably** [ˈprɒbəblɪ, -blɪ] adj, adv wahrscheinlich

probation [prəˈbeɪʃən] n Probezeit f; (Jur) Bewährung f

probe [prəʊb] n (investigation) Untersuchung f ▷ vt untersuchen

problem [ˈprɒbləm] n Problem nt; **no ~** kein Problem!

procedure [prəˈsiːdʒəˀ] n Verfahren nt

proceed [prəˈsiːd] vi (continue) fortfahren; (set about sth) vorgehen ▷ vt: **to ~ to do sth** anfangen, etw zu tun; **proceedings** npl (Jur) Verfahren nt; **proceeds** [ˈprəʊsiːdz] npl Erlös m

process [ˈprəʊses] n Prozess m, Vorgang m; (method) Verfahren nt ▷ vt (application etc) bearbeiten; (food, data) verarbeiten; (film) entwickeln

procession [prəˈseʃən] n Umzug m

processor [ˈprəʊsesəˀ] n (Inform) Prozessor m; (Gastr) Küchenmaschine f

produce [ˈprɒdjuːs] n (Agr) Produkte pl, Erzeugnisse pl ▷ [prəˈdjuːs] vt (manufacture) herstellen, produzieren; (on farm) erzeugen; (film, play, record) produzieren; (cause) hervorrufen; (evidence, results) liefern; **producer** n (manufacturer) Hersteller(in) m(f); (of film, play, record) Produzent(in) m(f); **product** [ˈprɒdʌkt] n Produkt nt, Erzeugnis nt; **production** [prəˈdʌkʃən] n Produktion f; (Theat) Inszenierung f; **productive** [prəˈdʌktɪv] adj produktiv; (land) ertragreich

prof [prɒf] n (fam) Prof m

profession [prəˈfeʃən] n Beruf m; **professional** [prəˈfeʃənl] n Profi m ▷ adj beruflich; (expert) fachlich; (sportsman, actor etc) Berufs-

professor [prəˈfesəˀ] n Professor(in) m(f); (US: lecturer) Dozent(in) m(f)

proficient [prəˈfɪʃənt] adj kompetent (in in +dat)

profile [ˈprəʊfaɪl] n Profil nt; **to keep a low ~** sich vornehm

profit [ˈprɒfɪt] n Gewinn m ▷ vi profitieren (by, from von); **profitable** adj rentabel

profound [prəˈfaʊnd] adj tief; (idea, thinker) tiefgründig; (knowledge) profund

program [ˈprəʊgræm] n (Inform) Programm nt; (US) see **programme** ▷ vt (Inform) programmieren; (US) see **programme**

programme [ˈprəʊgræm] n Programm nt; (TV, Radio) Sendung f ▷ vt programmieren; **programmer** n Programmierer(in) m(f); **programming** n (Inform) Programmieren nt; **~ language** Programmiersprache f

progress [ˈprəʊgres] n Fortschritt m; **to make ~** Fortschritte machen ▷ [prəˈgres] vi (work, illness etc) fortschreiten; (improve) Fortschritte machen; **progressive** [prəˈgresɪv] adj (person, policy) fortschrittlich; **progressively** [prəˈgresɪvlɪ] adv zunehmend

prohibit [prəˈhɪbɪt] vt verbieten

project [ˈprɒdʒekt] n Projekt nt

projector [prəˈdʒektəˀ] n Projektor m

prolong [prəˈlɒŋ] vt verlängern

prom [prɒm] n (at seaside) Promenade f; (Brit: concert) Konzert nt (bei dem ein Großteil des Publikums im Parkett Stehplätze hat); (US:

dance) Ball für die Schüler und
Studenten von Highschools oder
Colleges

prominent ['prɒmɪnənt] *adj*
(politician, actor etc) prominent;
(easily seen) auffallend

promiscuous [prə'mɪskjʊəs]
adj promisk

promise ['prɒmɪs] *n* Versprechen *n* ▷ *vt* versprechen; **to**
~ sb jdm etw versprechen; **to**
~ to do sth versprechen, etw zu
tun ▷ *vi* versprechen; **promising**
adj vielversprechend

promote [prə'məʊt] *vt (in rank)*
befördern; *(help on)* fördern;
(Comm) werben für; **promotion**
[prə'məʊʃən] *n (in rank)*
Beförderung *f*; *(Comm)* Werbung *f*
(of für)

prompt [prɒmpt] *adj* prompt;
(punctual) pünktlich ▷ *adv*: **at two**
o'clock ~ Punkt zwei Uhr ▷ *vt*
(Theat: actor) soufflieren *+dat*

prone [prəʊn] *adj*: **to be ~ to sth**
zu etw neigen

pronounce [prə'naʊns] *vt*
(word) aussprechen; **pronounced**
adj ausgeprägt; **pronunciation**
[prənʌnsɪ'eɪʃən] *n* Aussprache *f*

proof [pruːf] *n* Beweis *m*; *(of*
alcohol) Alkoholgehalt *m*

prop [prɒp] *n* Stütze *f*; *(Theat)*
Requisit *n* ▷ *vt*: **to ~ sth**
against sth etw gegen etw
lehnen; **prop up** *vt* stützen; *(fig)*
unterstützen

proper ['prɒpə*] *adj* richtig;
(morally correct) anständig

property ['prɒpətɪ] *n*
Eigentum *nt*; *(house)* Haus *nt*; *(land)*
Grundbesitz *m*; *(characteristic)*
Eigenschaft *f*

proportion [prə'pɔːʃən] *n*
Verhältnis *nt*; *(share)* Teil *m*; **~s** *pl*
(size) Proportionen *pl*; **in ~ to** im
Verhältnis zu; **proportional** *adj*

proportional; **~ representation**
Verhältniswahlrecht *nt*

proposal [prə'pəʊzl] *n* Vorschlag
m; **~ (of marriage)** (Heirats)antrag
m; **propose** [prə'pəʊz] *vt*
vorschlagen ▷ *vi (offer marriage)*
einen Heiratsantrag machen *(to sb*
jdm)

proprietor [prə'praɪətə*] *n*
Besitzer(in) *m(f)*; *(of pub, hotel)*
Inhaber(in) *m(f)*

prose [prəʊz] *n* Prosa *f*

prosecute ['prɒsɪkjuːt] *vt* verfolgen *(for* wegen)

prospect ['prɒspekt] *n* Aussicht
f

prosperity [prɒ'sperɪtɪ] *n*
Wohlstand *m*; **prosperous** *adj*
wohlhabend; *(business)* gut
gehend

prostitute ['prɒstɪtjuːt] *n* Pros-
tituierte(r) *mf*

protect [prə'tekt] *vt* schützen
(from, against vor *+dat*, gegen);
protection [prə'tekʃən] *n* Schutz
m (from, against vor *+dat*, gegen);
protective *adj* beschützend;
(clothing etc) Schutz-

protein ['prəʊtiːn] *n* Protein *nt*

protest [prə'təʊtest] *n* Protest *m*;
(demonstration)
Protestkundgebung *f* ▷ [prə'test]
vi protestieren *(against* gegen);
(demonstrate) demonstrieren

Protestant ['prɒtɪstənt] *adj*
protestantisch ▷ *n* Protestant(in)
m(f)

proud, **proudly** [praʊd, -lɪ] *adj*,
adv stolz *(of* auf *+akk*)

prove [pruːv] *vt* beweisen; *(turn*
out to be) sich erweisen als

proverb ['prɒvɜːb] *n* Sprichwort
nt

provide [prə'vaɪd] *vt* zur
Verfügung stellen; *(drinks, music*
etc) sorgen für; *(person)* versorgen
(with mit); **provide for** *vt (family*

etc) sorgen für; **provided** *conj*: ~ **(that)** vorausgesetzt, dass; **provider** *n* (*Inform*) Provider *m*

provision [prəˈvɪʒən] *n* (*condition*) Bestimmung *f*; ~**s** *pl* (*food*) Proviant *m*

provisional, provisionally [prəˈvɪʒənl, -l] *adj, adv* provisorisch

provoke [prəˈvəʊk] *vt* provozieren; (*cause*) hervorrufen

proximity [prɒkˈsɪmɪtɪ] *n* Nähe *f*

prudent [ˈpruːdənt] *adj* klug; (*person*) umsichtig

prudish [ˈpruːdɪʃ] *adj* prüde

prune [pruːn] *n* Backpflaume *f* ▷ *vt* (*tree etc*) zurechtstutzen

PS *abbr* = **postscript** PS *nt*

psalm [sɑːm] *n* Psalm *m*

pseudo [ˈsjuːdəʊ] *adj* pseudo-, Pseudo-; **pseudonym** [ˈsjuːdənɪm] *n* Pseudonym *nt*

PST *abbr* = **Pacific Standard Time**

psychiatric [saɪkɪˈætrɪk] *adj* psychiatrisch; (*illness*) psychisch; **psychiatrist** [saɪˈkaɪətrɪst] *n* Psychiater(in) *m(f)*; **psychiatry** [saɪˈkaɪətrɪ] *n* Psychiatrie *f*; **psychic** [ˈsaɪkɪk] *adj* übersinnlich; **I'm not** ~ ich kann keine Gedanken lesen; **psychoanalysis** [saɪkəʊəˈnæləsɪs] *n* Psychoanalyse *f*; **psychoanalyst** [saɪkəʊˈænəlɪst] *n* Psychoanalytiker(in) *m(f)*; **psychological** [saɪkəˈlɒdʒɪkəl] *adj* psychologisch; **psychology** [saɪˈkɒlədʒɪ] *n* Psychologie *f*; **psychopath** [ˈsaɪkəʊpæθ] *n* Psychopath(in) *m(f)*

pt *abbr* = **pint**

pto *abbr* = **please turn over** b.w.

pub [pʌb] *n* (*Brit*) Kneipe *f*

● **PUB**
●
● Ein **pub** ist ein Gasthaus mit
● einer Lizenz zum Ausschank von

● alkoholischen Getränken. Ein
● "Pub" besteht meist aus
● verschiedenen gemütlichen
● (**lounge, snug**) oder
● einfacheren (**public bar**)
● Räumen, in denen oft auch
● Spiele wie Darts, Domino und
● Poolbillard zur Verfügung
● stehen. In "Pubs" werden vor
● allem mittags auch Mahlzeiten
● angeboten (**pub lunch**). Die
● Sperrstunde wurde 2005
● aufgehoben. Dennoch sind
● "Pubs" oft nur von 11 bis 23 Uhr
● geöffnet. Nachmittags bleiben
● sie häufig geschlossen.

puberty [ˈpjuːbətɪ] *n* Pubertät *f*

public [ˈpʌblɪk] *n*: **the (general)** ~ die (breite) Öffentlichkeit; **in** ~ in der Öffentlichkeit ▷ *adj* öffentlich; (*relating to the State*) Staats-; ~ **convenience** (*Brit*) öffentliche Toilette; ~ **holiday** gesetzlicher Feiertag; ~ **opinion** die öffentliche Meinung; ~ **relations** *pl* Öffentlichkeitsarbeit *f*, Public Relations *pl*; ~ **school** (*Brit*) Privatschule *f*; **publication** [pʌblɪˈkeɪʃən] *n* Veröffentlichung *f*; **publicity** [pʌbˈlɪsɪtɪ] *n* Publicity *f*; (*advertisements*) Werbung *f*; **publish** [ˈpʌblɪʃ] *vt* veröffentlichen; **publisher** *n* Verleger(in) *m(f)*; (*company*) Verlag *m*; **publishing** *n* Verlagswesen *nt*

pub lunch [ˈpʌbˈlʌntʃ] *n* (*oft einfacheres*) Mittagessen in einer Kneipe

pudding [ˈpʊdɪŋ] *n* (*course*) Nachtisch *m*

puddle [ˈpʌdl] *n* Pfütze *f*

puff [pʌf] *vi* (*pant*) schnaufen

puffin [ˈpʌfɪn] *n* Papageientaucher *m*

puff paste (US), **puff pastry** ['pʌf peɪstrɪ] n Blätterteig m
pull [pʊl] n Ziehen nt; **to give sth a ~** an etw dat ziehen ▷ vt (cart, tooth) ziehen; (rope, handle) ziehen an +dat; (fam: date) abschleppen; **to ~ a muscle** sich einen Muskel zerren; **to ~ sb's leg** jdn auf den Arm nehmen ▷ vi ziehen; **pull apart** vt (separate) auseinanderziehen; **pull down** vt (blind) herunterziehen; (house) abreißen; **pull in** vi hineinfahren; (stop) anhalten; **pull off** vt (deal etc) zuwege bringen; (clothes) ausziehen; **pull on** vt (clothes) anziehen; **pull out** vi (car from lane) ausscheren; (train) abfahren; (withdraw) aussteigen (of aus) ▷ vt herausziehen; (tooth) ziehen; (troops) abziehen; **pull round, pull through** vi durchkommen; **pull up** vt (raise) hochziehen; (chair) heranziehen ▷ vi anhalten
pullover ['pʊləʊvə°] n Pullover m
pulp [pʌlp] n Brei m; (of fruit) Fruchtfleisch nt
pulpit ['pʊlpɪt] n Kanzel f
pulse [pʌls] n Puls m
pump [pʌmp] n Pumpe f; (in petrol station) Zapfsäule f; **pump up** vt (tyre etc) aufpumpen
pumpkin ['pʌmpkɪn] n Kürbis m
pun [pʌn] n Wortspiel nt
punch [pʌntʃ] n (blow) (Faust)schlag m; (tool) Locher m; (hot drink) Punsch m; (cold drink) Bowle f ▷ vt (strike) schlagen; (ticket, paper) lochen
punctual, punctually ['pʌŋktjʊəl, -ɪ] adj, adv pünktlich
punctuation [pʌŋktjʊˈeɪʃən] n Interpunktion f; **punctuation mark** n Satzzeichen nt
puncture ['pʌŋktʃə°] n (flat tyre) Reifenpanne f

punish ['pʌnɪʃ] vt bestrafen; **punishment** n Strafe f; (action) Bestrafung f
pupil ['pjuːpl] n (school) Schüler(in) m(f)
puppet ['pʌpɪt] n Marionette f
puppy ['pʌpɪ] n junger Hund
purchase ['pɜːtʃɪs] n Kauf m ▷ vt kaufen
pure [pjʊə°] adj rein; (clean) sauber; (utter) pur; **purely** ['pjuːəlɪ] adv rein; **purify** ['pjʊərɪfaɪ] vt reinigen; **purity** ['pjʊərɪtɪ] n Reinheit f
purple ['pɜːpl] adj violett
purpose ['pɜːpəs] n Zweck m; (of person) Absicht f; **on ~** absichtlich
purr [pɜː°] vi (cat) schnurren
purse [pɜːs] n Geldbeutel m; (US: handbag) Handtasche f
pursue [pəˈsjuː] vt (person, car) verfolgen; (hobby, studies) nachgehen +dat; **pursuit** [pəˈsjuːt] n (chase) Verfolgung f; (occupation) Beschäftigung f; (hobby) Hobby nt
pus [pʌs] n Eiter m
push [pʊʃ] n Stoß m ▷ vt (person) stoßen; (car, chair etc) schieben; (button) drücken; (drugs) dealen ▷ vi (in crowd) drängeln; **push in** vi (in queue) sich vordrängeln; **push off** vi (fam: leave) abhauen; **push on** vi (with job) weitermachen; **push up** vt (prices) hochtreiben; **pushchair** n (Brit) Sport(kinder)wagen m; **pusher** n (of drugs) Dealer(in) m(f); **push-up** n (US) Liegestütz m; **pushy** adj (fam) aufdringlich, penetrant
put [pʊt] vt (put, put) vt tun; (upright) stellen; (flat) legen; (express) ausdrücken; (write) schreiben; **he ~ his hand in his pocket** er steckte die Hand in die Tasche; **he ~ his hand on her shoulder** er legte ihr die Hand auf

die Schulter; **to ~ money into one's account** Geld auf sein Konto einzahlen; **put aside** vt *(money)* zurücklegen; **put away** vt *(tidy away)* wegräumen; **put back** vt zurücklegen; *(clock)* zurückstellen; **put down** vt *(in writing)* aufschreiben; *(Brit: animal)* einschläfern; *(rebellion)* niederschlagen; **to put the phone down** (den Hörer) auflegen; **to put one's name down for sth** sich für etw eintragen; **put forward** vt *(idea)* vorbringen; *(name)* vorschlagen; *(clock)* vorstellen; **put in** vt *(install)* einbauen; *(submit)* einreichen; **put off** vt *(switch off)* ausschalten; *(postpone)* verschieben; **to put sb off doing sth** jdn davon abbringen, etw zu tun; **put on** vt *(switch on)* anmachen; *(clothes)* anziehen; *(hat, glasses)* aufsetzen; *(make-up, CD)* auflegen; *(play)* aufführen; **to put the kettle on** Wasser aufsetzen; **to put weight on** zunehmen; **put out** vt *(hand, foot)* ausstrecken; *(light, cigarette)* ausmachen; **put up** vt *(hand)* hochheben; *(picture)* aufhängen; *(tent)* aufstellen; *(building)* errichten; *(price)* erhöhen; *(person)* unterbringen; **to ~ with** sich abfinden mit; **I won't ~ with it** das lasse ich mir nicht gefallen

putt [pʌt] vt, vi *(Sport)* putten

puzzle [ˈpʌzl] n Rätsel nt; *(toy)* Geduldsspiel nt; **(jigsaw)** ~ Puzzle nt ▷ vt vor ein Rätsel stellen; **it ~s me** es ist mir ein Rätsel; **puzzling** adj rätselhaft

pyjamas [prˈdʒɑːməz] npl Schlafanzug m

pylon [ˈpaɪlən] n Mast m

pyramid [ˈpɪrəmɪd] n Pyramide f

---

quartet ...

(of year) Vie... Vierteldoll... eine Viert... *(Brit)* *(o ~ v...* Viertel n... Vierteln... Viertel ... *(Mil)* Qu...

quarte ...

quay [...

queas ...
ist üb...

queer ...
card... ...

quee ...
sel... ho...
Sc...

qu ...
lo... ...

q ...

quack [kwæk] vi qu...

quaint [kweɪnt] adj (...
tradition) kurios; *(picture...* malerisch

qualification [kwɒlɪfɪˈk... n *(for job)* Qualifikation f; (... school, university)* Abschluss n...

qualified [ˈkwɒlɪfaɪd] adj *(f... job)* qualifiziert; **qualify** vt *(li...* einschränken; **to be qualified t... do sth** berechtigt sein, etw zu t... ▷ vi *(finish training)* seine Ausbildung abschließen; *(contest etc)* sich qualifizieren

quality [ˈkwɒlɪtɪ] n Qualität f; *(characteristic)* Eigenschaft f

quantity [ˈkwɒntɪtɪ] n Menge f, Quantität f

quarantine [ˈkwɒrəntiːn] n Quarantäne f

quarrel [ˈkwɒrəl] n Streit m ▷ vi sich streiten

quarter [ˈkwɔːtə°] n Viertel nt;

...erteljahr nt; (US: coin)
...ar m; **a ~ of an hour**
...elstunde; **~ to/past**
...of/after (US) **three**
...r/nach drei ▷ vt
quarter final n
...nale nt; **quarters** npl
...artier nt

... [kwɔː'tet] n Quartett m
...kiː] n Kai m
...y ['kwiːzi] adj: **I feel ~** mir
...el

... [kwiːn] n Königin f; (in
..., chess) Dame f
...r [kwɪə°] adj (strange)
...sam, sonderbar; (pej:
...nosexual) schwul ▷ n (pej)
...hwule(r) m

...ench [kwɛntʃ] vt (thirst)
...schen

...ery ['kwɪərɪ] n Frage f ▷ vt
...nfrage stellen; (bill) reklamieren
question [kwɛstʃən] n Frage f;
that's out of the ~ das kommt
nicht infrage ▷ vt (person)
befragen; (suspect) verhören;
(express doubt about) bezweifeln;
questionable adj zweifelhaft;
(improper) fragwürdig; **question**
mark n Fragezeichen nt;
questionnaire [kwɛstʃə'nɛə°] n
Fragebogen m

queue [kjuː] n (Brit) Schlange f;
to jump the ~ sich vordrängeln
▷ vi: **to ~ (up)** Schlange stehen
quibble ['kwɪbl] vi kleinlich sein;
(argue) streiten
quiche [kiːʃ] n Quiche
quick [kwɪk] adj schnell; (short)
kurz; **be ~** mach schnell!; **quickly**
adv schnell
quid [kwɪd] (pl **quid**) n (Brit fam)
Pfund nt; **20 ~** 20 Pfund
quiet ['kwaɪət] adj (not noisy)
leise; (peaceful, calm) still, ruhig; **be**
~ sei still!; **to keep ~ about sth**
über etw akk nichts sagen ▷ n

Stille f, Ruhe f; **quiet down** (US),
quieten down ['kwaɪətən'daʊn]
vi sich beruhigen ▷ vt beruhigen;
quietly adv leise; (calmly) ruhig
quilt [kwɪlt] n (Stepp)decke f
quit [kwɪt] (**quit** o **quitted, quit** o
quitted) vt (leave) verlassen; (job)
aufgeben; **to ~ doing sth**
aufhören, etw zu tun ▷ vi
aufhören; (resign) kündigen
quite [kwaɪt] adv (fairly)
ziemlich; (completely) ganz, völlig; **I**
don't ~ understand ich verstehe
das nicht ganz; **~ a few** ziemlich
viele; **~ so** richtig!
quits [kwɪts] adj: **to be ~ with sb**
mit jdm quitt sein
quiver ['kwɪvə°] vi zittern
quiz [kwɪz] n (competition) Quiz
nt
quota ['kwəʊtə] n Anteil m;
(Comm, Pol) Quote f
quotation [kwəʊ'teɪʃən] n Zitat
nt; (price) Kostenvoranschlag m;
quotation marks npl
Anführungszeichen pl; **quote**
[kwəʊt] vt (text, author) zitieren;
(price) nennen ▷ n Zitat nt; (price)
Kostenvoranschlag m; **in ~s** in
Anführungszeichen

r

rabbi ['ræbaɪ] n Rabbiner m
rabbit ['ræbɪt] n Kaninchen nt
rabies ['reɪbiːz] nsing Tollwut f
raccoon [rə'kuːn] n Waschbär m
race [reɪs] n (competition) Rennen nt; (people) Rasse f ▷ vt um die Wette laufen/fahren ▷ vi (rush) rennen; **racecourse** n Rennbahn f; **racehorse** n Rennpferd nt; **racetrack** n Rennbahn f
racial ['reɪʃəl] adj Rassen-; **~ discrimination** Rassendiskriminierung f
racing ['reɪsɪŋ] n (horse) ~ Pferderennen nt; (motor) ~ Autorennen nt; **racing car** n Rennwagen m
racism ['reɪsɪzəm] n Rassismus m; **racist** ['reɪsɪst] n Rassist(in) m(f) ▷ adj rassistisch
rack [ræk] n Ständer m, Gestell nt ▷ vt: **to ~ one's brains** sich dat den Kopf zerbrechen

racket ['rækɪt] n (Sport) Schläger m; (noise) Krach m
radar ['reɪdɑː°] n Radar nt o m; **radar trap** n Radarfalle f
radiation [reɪdɪ'eɪʃən] n (radio-active) Strahlung f
radiator ['reɪdɪeɪtə°] n Heiz-körper m; (Auto) Kühler m
radical ['rædɪkəl] adj radikal
radio ['reɪdɪəʊ] (pl -s) n Rundfunk m, Radio m
radioactivity [reɪdɪəʊæk'tɪvɪtɪ] n Radioaktivität f
radio alarm ['reɪdɪəʊə'lɑːm] n Radiowecker m; **radio station** n Rundfunksstation f
radiotherapy [reɪdɪəʊ'θerəpɪ] n Strahlenbehandlung f
radish ['rædɪʃ] n Radieschen nt
radius ['reɪdɪəs] n Radius m; **within a five-mile** ~ im Umkreis von fünf Meilen (of um)
raffle ['ræfl] n Tombola f; **raffle ticket** n Los nt
raft [rɑːft] n Floß nt
rag [ræg] n Lumpen m; (for cleaning) Lappen m
rage [reɪdʒ] n Wut f; **to be all the** ~ der letzte Schrei sein ▷ vi toben; (disease) wüten
raid [reɪd] n Überfall m (on auf +akk); (by police) Razzia f (on gegen) ▷ vt (bank etc) überfallen; (by police) eine Razzia machen in +dat
rail [reɪl] n (on stairs, balcony etc) Geländer nt; (of ship) Reling f; (Rail) Schiene f; **railcard** n (Brit) ≈ Bahncard® f; **railing** n Geländer nt; **~s** pl (fence) Zaun m; **railroad** n (US) Eisenbahn f; **railroad station** n (US) Bahnhof m; **railway** n (Brit) Eisenbahn f; **railway line** n Bahnlinie f; (track) Gleis m; **railway station** n Bahnhof m
rain [reɪn] n Regen m ▷ vi regnen; **it's ~ing** es regnet; **rainbow** n Regenbogen m;

raincoat n Regenmantel m;
rainfall n Niederschlag m;
rainforest n Regenwald m; **rainy**
adj regnerisch
raise [reɪz] n (US: of wages/salary)
Gehalts-/Lohnerhöhung f ▷ vt
(lift) hochheben; (increase)
erhöhen; (family) großziehen;
(livestock) züchten; (money)
aufbringen; (objection) erheben; **to
~ one's voice** laut werden
raisin ['reɪzn] n Rosine f
rally ['rælɪ] n (Pol) Kundgebung f;
(Auto) Rallye f; (Tennis) Ballwechsel
m
RAM [ræm] acr = **random access
memory** RAM m
ramble ['ræmbl] n Wanderung f
▷ vi (walk) wandern; (talk)
schwafeln
ramp [ræmp] n Rampe f
ran [ræn] pt of **run**
ranch [rɑːntʃ] n Ranch f
rancid ['rænsɪd] adj ranzig
random ['rændəm] adj
willkürlich ▷ n: **at ~** (choose)
willkürlich; (fire) ziellos
rang [ræŋ] pt of **ring**
range [reɪndʒ] n (selection)
Auswahl f (of an +dat); (Comm)
Sortiment nt (of an +dat); (of
missile, telescope) Reichweite f; (of
mountains) Kette f; **in this price
~** in dieser Preisklasse ▷ vi: **to
~ from ... to ...** gehen von ... bis ...;
(temperature, sizes, prices) liegen
zwischen ... und ...
rank [ræŋk] n (Mil) Rang m; (social
position) Stand m ▷ vt einstufen
ransom ['rænsəm] n Lösegeld nt
rap [ræp] n (Mus) Rap m
rape [reɪp] n Vergewaltigung f
▷ vt vergewaltigen
rapid, rapidly ['ræpɪd, -lɪ] adj, adv
schnell
rapist ['reɪpɪst] n Vergewaltiger
m

rare [reə°] adj selten, rar;
(especially good) vortrefflich; (steak)
blutig; **rarely** adv selten; **rarity**
['reərɪtɪ] n Seltenheit f
rash [ræʃ] adj unbesonnen ▷ n
(Med) (Haut)ausschlag m
rasher ['ræʃə°] n: **~ (of bacon)**
(Speck)scheibe f
raspberry ['rɑːzbərɪ] n Himbeere f
rat [ræt] n Ratte f; (pej: person)
Schwein nt
rate [reɪt] n (proportion, frequency)
Rate f; (speed) Tempo nt; **~ (of
exchange)** (Wechsel)kurs m; **~ of
inflation** Inflationsrate f; **~ of
interest** Zinssatz m; **at any ~** auf
jeden Fall ▷ vt (evaluate)
einschätzen (as als)
rather ['rɑːðə°] adv (in preference)
lieber; (fairly) ziemlich; **I'd ~ stay
here** ich würde lieber hierbleiben;
I'd ~ not lieber nicht; **or ~** (more
accurately) vielmehr
ratio ['reɪʃɪəʊ] (pl **-s**) n Verhältnis
nt
rational ['ræʃənl] adj rational;
rationalize ['ræʃnəlaɪz] vt
rationalisieren
rattle ['rætl] n (toy) Rassel f ▷ vt
(keys, coins) klimpern mit; (person)
durcheinanderbringen ▷ vi (window) klappern; (bottles) klirren;
rattle off vt herunterrasseln;
rattlesnake n Klapperschlange
f
rave [reɪv] vi (talk wildly)
fantasieren; (rage) toben; (enthuse)
schwärmen (about von) ▷ n (Brit:
event) Raveparty f
raven ['reɪvn] n Rabe m
raving ['reɪvɪŋ] adv: **~ mad** total
verrückt
ravishing ['rævɪʃɪŋ] adj
hinreißend
raw [rɔː] adj (food) roh; (skin)
wund; (climate) rau

ray [reɪ] n (of light) Strahl m; ~ **of hope** Hoffnungsschimmer m

razor ['reɪzə°] n Rasierapparat m; **razor blade** n Rasierklinge f

Rd n abbr = **road** Str.

re [riː] prep (Comm) betreffs +gen

RE abbr = **religious education**

reach [riːtʃ] n: **within/out of (sb's)** ~ in/außer (jds) Reichweite; **within easy ~ of the shops** nicht weit von den Geschäften ▷ vt (arrive at, contact) erreichen; (come down/up as far as) reichen bis zu; (contact) **can you ~ it?** kommst du/kommen Sie dran?; **reach for** vt greifen nach; **reach out** vi die Hand ausstrecken; **to ~ for** greifen nach

react [riːˈækt] vi reagieren (to auf +akk); **reaction** [riːˈækʃən] n Reaktion f (to auf +akk); **reactor** [riːˈæktə°] n Reaktor m

read [riːd] (**read, read**) vt lesen; (meter) ablesen; **to ~ sth to sb** jdm etw vorlesen ▷ vi: **to ~ to sb** jdm vorlesen; **it ~s well** es liest sich gut; **it ~s as follows** es lautet folgendermaßen; **read out** vt vorlesen; **read through** vt durchlesen; **read up on** vi nachlesen (über +akk); **readable** adj (book) lesenswert; (handwriting) lesbar; **reader** n Leser(in) m(f); **readership** n Leserschaft f

readily ['redɪlɪ] adv (willingly) bereitwillig; ~ **available** leicht erhältlich

reading ['riːdɪŋ] n (action) Lesen nt; (from meter) Zählerstand m; **reading glasses** npl Lesebrille f; **reading lamp** n Leselampe f; **reading list** n Leseliste f; **reading matter** n Lektüre f

readjust [riːəˈdʒʌst] vt (mechanism etc) neu einstellen ▷ vi sich wieder anpassen (to an +akk)

ready ['redɪ] adj fertig, bereit; **to**

be ~ to do sth (willing) bereit sein, etw zu tun; **are you ~ to go?** bist du so weit?; **to get sth ~** etw fertig machen; **to get (oneself)** ~ sich fertig machen; **ready cash** n Bargeld nt; **ready-made** adj (product) Fertig-; (clothes) Konfektions-; ~ **meal** n Fertiggericht nt

real [rɪəl] adj wirklich; (actual) eigentlich; (genuine) echt; (idiot etc) richtig ▷ adv (fam, esp US) echt; **for** ~ echt; **this time it's for** ~ diesmal ist es ernst; **get** ~ sei realistisch!; **real ale** n Ale nt; **real estate** n Immobilien pl

realistic, realistically [rɪəˈlɪstɪk, -əlɪ] adj, adv realistisch; **reality** [riːˈælɪtɪ] n Wirklichkeit f; **in** ~ in Wirklichkeit; **reality TV** n Reality-TV nt; **realization** [rɪəlaɪˈzeɪʃən] n (awareness) Erkenntnis f; **realize** ['rɪəlaɪz] vt (understand) begreifen; (plan, idea) realisieren; **I ~d (that)** ... mir wurde klar, dass ...

really ['rɪəlɪ] adv wirklich

real time [rɪəlˈtaɪm] n (Inform) **in** ~ in Echtzeit

realtor ['rɪəltə°] n (US) Grundstücksmakler(in) m(f)

reappear [riːəˈpɪə°] vi wieder erscheinen

rear [rɪə°] adj hintere(r, s), Hinter- ▷ n (of building, vehicle) hinterer Teil m; **at the ~ of** hinter +dat; (inside) hinten in +dat; **rear light** n (Auto) Rücklicht nt

rearm [riːˈɑːm] vi wieder aufrüsten

rearrange [riːəˈreɪndʒ] vt (furniture, system) umstellen; (meeting) verlegen (for auf +akk)

rear-view mirror
['rɪəvjuːˈmɪrə°] n Rückspiegel m; **rear window** n (Auto) Heckscheibe f

reason ['ri:zn] n (cause) Grund m (for für); (ability to think) Verstand m; (common sense) Vernunft f; **for some ~** aus irgendeinem Grund ▷ vi: **to ~ with sb** mit jdm vernünftig reden; **reasonable** adj (person, price) vernünftig; (offer) akzeptabel; (chance) reell; (food, weather) ganz gut; **reasonably** adv vernünftig; (fairly) ziemlich

reassure [ri:ə'ʃʊəˠ] vt beruhigen; **she ~d me that ...** sie versicherte mir, dass ...

rebel ['rebl] n Rebell(in) m(f) ▷ [rɪ'bel] vi rebellieren; **rebellion** [rɪ'belɪən] n Aufstand m

reboot [ri:'bu:t] vt, vi (Inform) rebooten

rebound [rɪ'baʊnd] vi (ball etc) zurückprallen

rebuild [ri:'bɪld] irr vt wieder aufbauen

recall [rɪ'kɔ:l] vt (remember) sich erinnern an +akk; (call back) zurückrufen

recap ['ri:kæp] vt, vi rekapitulieren

receipt [rɪ'si:t] n (document) Quittung f; (receiving) Empfang m; **~s** pl (money) Einnahmen pl

receive [rɪ'si:v] vt (news etc) erhalten, bekommen; (visitor) empfangen; **receiver** n (Tel) Hörer m; (Radio) Empfänger m

recent ['ri:snt] adj (event) vor Kurzem stattgefunden; (photo) neueste(r,s); (invention) neu; **in ~ years** in den letzten Jahren; **recently** adv vor Kurzem; (in the last few days or weeks) in letzter Zeit

reception [rɪ'sepʃən] n Empfang m; **receptionist** n (in hotel) Empfangschef m, Empfangsdame f; (woman in firm) Empfangsdame f; (Med) Sprechstundenhilfe f

recess [rɪ'ses] n (in wall) Nische f; (US: in school) Pause f

recession [rɪ'seʃən] n Rezession f

recharge [ri:'tʃɑ:dʒ] vt (battery) aufladen; **rechargeable** [ri:'tʃɑ:dʒəbl] adj wiederaufladbar

recipe ['resɪpɪ] n Rezept nt (for für)

recipient [rɪ'sɪpɪənt] n Empfänger(in) m(f)

reciprocal [rɪ'sɪprəkəl] adj gegenseitig

recite [rɪ'saɪt] vt vortragen; (details) aufzählen

reckless ['rekləs] adj leichtsinnig; (driving) gefährlich

reckon ['rekən] vt (calculate) schätzen; (think) glauben ▷ vi: **to ~ with/on** rechnen mit

reclaim [rɪ'kleɪm] vt (baggage) abholen; (expenses, tax) zurückverlangen

recline [rɪ'klaɪn] vi (person) sich zurücklehnen; **reclining seat** n Liegesitz m

recognition ['rekəg'nɪʃən] n (acknowledgement) Anerkennung f; **in ~ of** in Anerkennung +gen; **recognize** ['rekəgnaɪz] vt erkennen; (approve officially) anerkennen

recommend [rekə'mend] vt empfehlen; **recommendation** [rekəmən'deɪʃən] n Empfehlung f

reconfirm [ri:kən'fɜ:m] vt (flight etc) rückbestätigen

reconsider [ri:kən'sɪdəˠ] vt noch einmal überdenken ▷ vi es sich dat noch einmal überlegen

reconstruct [ri:kən'strʌkt] vt wieder aufbauen; (crime) rekonstruieren

record [rɪ'kɔ:d] n (Mus) (Schall)platte f; (best performance) Rekord m; **~s** pl (files) Akten pl; **to keep a ~ of** Buch führen über +akk ▷ adj (time etc) Rekord- ▷ [rɪ'kɔ:d] vt (write down) aufzeichnen; (on

tape etc) aufnehmen; **~ed message**
Ansage f; **recorded delivery** n
(Brit) **by ~** per Einschreiben

recorder [rɪˈkɔːdə⁰] n (Mus)
Blockflöte f; **(cassette)**
~ (Kassetten)rekorder m;

recording [rɪˈkɔːdɪŋ] n (on tape
etc) Aufnahme f; **record player**
[ˈrekɔːdpleɪə⁰] n Plattenspieler m

recover [rɪˈkʌvə⁰] vt (money, item)
zurückbekommen; (appetite,
strength) wiedergewinnen ▷ vi
sich erholen

recreation [rekrɪˈeɪʃən] n
Erholung f; **recreational** adj
Freizeit-; **~ vehicle** (US)
Wohnmobil nt

recruit [rɪˈkruːt] n (Mil)
Rekrut(in) m(f); (in firm,
organization) neues Mitglied ▷ vt
(Mil) rekrutieren; (members)
anwerben; (staff) einstellen;
recruitment agency n
Personalagentur f

rectangle [ˈrektæŋgl] n
Rechteck nt; **rectangular**
[rekˈtæŋgə⁰] adj rechteckig

rectify [ˈrektɪfaɪ] vt berichtigen

recuperate [rɪˈkuːpəreɪt] vi sich
erholen

recyclable [riːˈsaɪkləbl] adj
recycelbar, wiederverwertbar;
recycle [riːˈsaɪkl] vt recyceln,
wiederverwerten; **~d paper**
Recyclingpapier nt; **recycling** n
Recycling nt, Wiederverwertung f

red [red] adj cpr ▷ n: **in the ~** in
den roten Zahlen; **Red Cross** n
Rotes Kreuz; **red cabbage** n
Rotkohl m; **redcurrant** n (rote)
Johannisbeere

redeem [rɪˈdiːm] vt (Comm)
einlösen

red-handed [redˈhændɪd] adj:
to catch sb ~ jdn auf frischer Tat
ertappen; **redhead** n
Rothaarige(r) mf

redial [riːˈdaɪəl] vt, vi nochmals
wählen

redirect [riːdaɪˈrekt] vt (traffic)
umleiten; (forward) nachsenden

red light [redˈlaɪt] n (traffic
signal) rotes Licht; **to go through
the ~** bei Rot über die Ampel
fahren; **red meat** n
Rind-, Lamm-, Rehfleisch

redo [riːˈduː] irr vt nochmals
machen

reduce [rɪˈdjuːs] vt reduzieren
(to auf +akk, by um); **reduction**
[rɪˈdʌkʃən] n Reduzierung f; (in
price) Ermäßigung f

redundant [rɪˈdʌndənt] adj
überflüssig; **to be made
~** entlassen werden

red wine [redˈwaɪn] n Rotwein
m

reef [riːf] n Riff nt

reel [riːl] n Spule f; (on fishing rod)
Rolle f; **reel off** vt herunterrasseln

ref [ref] n (fam: referee) Schiri m

refectory [rɪˈfektərɪ] n (at
college) Mensa f

refer [rɪˈfɜː⁰] vt: **to ~ sb to sb/sth**
jdn an jdn/etw verweisen; **to
~ sth to** (query, problem) etw an
jdn weiterleiten ▷ vi: **to ~ to**
(mention, allude to) sich beziehen
auf +akk; (book) nachschlagen in
+dat

referee [refəˈriː] n Schiedsrich-
ter(in) m(f); (in boxing) Ringrichter
m; (Brit: for job) Referenz f

reference [ˈrefrəns] n (allusion)
Anspielung f (to auf +akk); (for job)
Referenz f; (in book) Verweis m;
~ (number) (in document)
Aktenzeichen nt; **with ~ to** mit
Bezug auf +akk; **reference book** n
Nachschlagewerk nt

referendum [refəˈrendəm] (pl
referenda) n Referendum nt

refill [ˈriːfɪl] vt [riːˈfɪl] nachfüllen
▷ n (for ballpoint pen) Ersatzmine f

refine [rɪˈfaɪn] vt (purify)
raffinieren; (improve) verfeinern;
refined adj (genteel) fein
reflect [rɪˈflɛkt] vt reflektieren;
(fig) widerspiegeln ▷ vi
nachdenken (on über +akk);
reflection [rɪˈflɛkʃən] n (image)
Spiegelbild nt; (thought)
Überlegung f; **on** ~ nach reiflicher
Überlegung
reflex [ˈriːflɛks] n Reflex m
reform [rɪˈfɔːm] n Reform f ▷ vt
reformieren; (person) bessern
refrain [rɪˈfreɪn] vi: **to ~ from
doing sth** es unterlassen, etw zu
tun
refresh [rɪˈfrɛʃ] vt erfrischen;
refresher course n
Auffrischungskurs m; **refreshing**
adj erfrischend; **refreshments** npl
Erfrischungen pl
refrigerator [rɪˈfrɪdʒəreɪtə°] n
Kühlschrank m
refuel [riːˈfjʊəl] vt, vi auftanken
refugee [rɛfjʊˈdʒiː] n Flüchtling
m
refund [ˈriːfʌnd] n (of money)
Rückerstattung f; **to get a ~ (on
sth)** sein Geld (für etw)
zurückbekommen ▷ [rɪˈfʌnd] vt
zurückerstatten
refusal [rɪˈfjuːzəl] n (to do sth)
Weigerung f; **refuse** [ˈrɛfjuːs] n
Müll m, Abfall m ▷ [rɪˈfjuːz] vt
ablehnen; **to ~ sb sth** jdm etw
verweigern; **to ~ to do sth** sich
weigern, etw zu tun ▷ vi sich
weigern
regain [rɪˈgeɪn] vt wiedergewinnen, wiedererlangen; **to
~ consciousness** wieder zu
Bewusstsein kommen
regard [rɪˈgɑːd] n: **with ~ to** in
Bezug auf +akk; **in this ~** in dieser
Hinsicht; **~s** (at end of letter) mit
freundlichen Grüßen; **give my ~s
to ...** viele Grüße an ... +akk ▷ vt:

to ~ sb/sth as sth jdn/etw als etw
betrachten; **as ~s ...** was ...
betrifft; **regarding** prep bezüglich
+gen; **regardless** adj: **~ of** ohne
Rücksicht auf +akk ▷ adv
trotzdem; **to carry on ~** einfach
weitermachen
regime [reɪˈʒiːm] n (Pol) Regime
nt
region [ˈriːdʒən] n (of country)
Region f, Gebiet nt; **in the ~ of**
(about) ungefähr; **regional** adj
regional
register [ˈrɛdʒɪstə°] n Register
nt; (school) Namensliste f ▷ vt
(with an authority) registrieren
lassen; (birth, death, vehicle)
anmelden ▷ vi (at hotel, for course)
sich anmelden; (at university) sich
einschreiben; **registered** adj
eingetragen; (letter)
eingeschrieben; **by ~ post** per
Einschreiben; **registration**
[rɛdʒɪˈstreɪʃən] n (for course)
Anmeldung f; (at university)
Einschreibung f; (Auto: number)
(polizeiliches) Kennzeichen;
registration form n
Anmeldeformular nt; **registration
number** n (Auto) (polizeiliches)
Kennzeichen; **registry office**
[ˈrɛdʒɪstrɪɒfɪs] n Standesamt nt
regret [rɪˈgrɛt] n Bedauern nt
▷ vt bedauern; **regrettable** adj
bedauerlich
regular [ˈrɛgjələ°] adj regelmäßig; (size) normal ▷ n (client)
Stammkunde m, Stammkundin f;
(in bar) Stammgast m; (petrol)
Normalbenzin nt; **regularly** adv
regelmäßig
regulate [ˈrɛgjʊleɪt] vt
regulieren; (using rules) regeln;
regulation [rɛgjʊˈleɪʃən] n (rule)
Vorschrift f
rehabilitation [riːəbɪlɪˈteɪʃən]
n Rehabilitation f

rehearsal [rɪ'hɜːsəl] n Probe f; **rehearse** vt, vi proben

reign [reɪn] n Herrschaft f ▷ vi herrschen (over über +akk)

reimburse [riːɪm'bɜːs] vt (person) entschädigen; (expenses) zurückerstatten

reindeer ['reɪndɪə°] n Rentier nt

reinforce [riːɪn'fɔːs] vt verstärken

reinstate [riːɪn'steɪt] vt (employee) wieder einstellen; (passage in text) wieder aufnehmen

reject ['riːdʒekt] n (Comm) Ausschussartikel m ▷ [rɪ'dʒekt] vt ablehnen; **rejection** [rɪ'dʒekʃən] n Ablehnung f

relapse [rɪ'læps] n Rückfall m

relate [rɪ'leɪt] vt (story) erzählen; (connect) in Verbindung bringen (to mit) ▷ vi: **to ~ to** (refer) sich beziehen auf +akk; **related** adj verwandt (to mit); **relation** [rɪ'leɪʃən] n (relative) Verwandte(r) mf; (connection) Beziehung f; **~s** pl (dealings) Beziehungen pl; **relationship** n (connection) Beziehung f; (between people) Verhältnis nt

relative ['relətɪv] n Verwandte(r) mf ▷ adj relativ; **relatively** adv relativ, verhältnismäßig

relax [rɪ'læks] vi sich entspannen; **~!** reg dich nicht auf! ▷ vt (grip, conditions) lockern; **relaxation** [riːlæk'seɪʃən] n (rest) Entspannung f; **relaxed** adj entspannt; **relaxing** adj entspannend

release [rɪ'liːs] n (from prison) Entlassung f; **new/recent ~** (film, CD) Neuerscheinung f ▷ vt (animal, hostage) freilassen; (prisoner) entlassen; (handbrake) lösen; (news) veröffentlichen; (film, CD) herausbringen

relent [rɪ'lent] vi nachgeben;

relentless, relentlessly adj, adv (merciless) erbarmungslos; (neverending) unaufhörlich

relevance ['reləvəns] n Relevanz f (to für); **relevant** adj relevant (to für)

reliable, reliably [rɪ'laɪəbl, -blɪ] adj, adv zuverlässig; **reliant** [rɪ'laɪənt] adj: **~ on** abhängig von

relic ['relɪk] n (from past) Relikt nt

relief [rɪ'liːf] n (from anxiety, pain) Erleichterung f; (assistance) Hilfe f; **relieve** [rɪ'liːv] vt (pain) lindern; (boredom) überwinden; (take over from) ablösen; **I'm ~d** ich bin erleichtert

religion [rɪ'lɪdʒən] n Religion f; **religious** [rɪ'lɪdʒəs] adj religiös

relish ['relɪʃ] n (for food) würzige Soße f ▷ vt (enjoy) genießen; **I don't ~ the thought of it** der Gedanke behagt mir gar nicht

reluctant [rɪ'lʌktənt] adj widerwillig; **to be ~ to do sth** etw nur ungern tun; **reluctantly** adv widerwillig

rely on [rɪ'laɪ ɒn] vt sich verlassen auf +akk; (depend on) abhängig sein von

remain [rɪ'meɪn] vi bleiben; (be left over) übrig bleiben; **remainder** n (a. Math) Rest m; **remaining** adj übrig; **remains** npl Überreste pl

remark [rɪ'mɑːk] n Bemerkung f ▷ vt: **to ~ that** bemerken, dass ▷ vi: **to ~ on sth** über etw akk eine Bemerkung machen; **remarkable, remarkably** adj, adv bemerkenswert

remarry [riː'mærɪ] vi wieder heiraten

remedy ['remədɪ] n Mittel nt (for gegen) ▷ vt abhelfen +dat

remember [rɪ'membə°] vt sich erinnern an +akk; **to ~ to do sth** daran denken, etw zu tun; **I ~ seeing her** ich erinnere mich daran, sie gesehen zu haben; **I must ~ that** das muss ich mir merken ▷ *vi* sich erinnern

Remembrance Day [rɪˈmembrənsˌdeɪ] *n* (*Brit*) = Volkstrauertag *m*

● **REMEMBRANCE DAY**
●
● **Remembrance Sunday/Day** ist
● der britische Gedenktag für die
● Gefallenen der beiden
● Weltkriege und anderer Kriege.
● Er fällt auf einen Sonntag vor
● oder nach dem 11. November
● (am 11.11.1918 endete der Erste
● Weltkrieg) und wird mit einer
● Schweigeminute,
● Kranzniederlegungen an
● Kriegerdenkmälern und dem
● Tragen von Anstecknadeln in
● Form einer Mohnblume
● begangen.

remind [rɪˈmaɪnd] *vt*: **to ~ sb of/about sb/sth** jdn an jdn/etw erinnern; **to ~ sb to do sth** jdn daran erinnern, etw zu tun; **that ~s me** dabei fällt mir ein ...; **reminder** *n* (*to pay*) Mahnung *f*

reminisce [remɪˈnɪs] *vi* in Erinnerungen schwelgen (*about an* +akk); **reminiscent** [remɪˈnɪsənt] *adj*: **to be ~ of** erinnern an +akk

remittance *n* Überweisung *f* (*to an* +akk)

remnant [ˈremnənt] *n* Rest *m*

remote [rɪˈməʊt] *adj* (*place*) abgelegen; (*slight*) gering ▷ *n* (*TV*) Fernbedienung *f*; **remote control** *n* Fernsteuerung *f*; (*device*) Fernbedienung *f*

removal [rɪˈmuːvəl] *n* Entfernung *f*; (*Brit*: *move from house*) Umzug *m*; **removal firm** *n* (*Brit*) Spedition *f*; **remove** [rɪˈmuːv] *vt* entfernen; (*lid*) abnehmen;

(*clothes*) ausziehen; (*doubt, suspicion*) zerstreuen

rename [riːˈneɪm] *vt* umbenennen

renew [rɪˈnjuː] *vt* erneuern; (*licence, passport, library book*) verlängern lassen; **renewable** *adj* (*energy*) erneuerbar

renounce [rɪˈnaʊns] *vt* verzichten auf +akk; (*faith, opinion*) abschwören +dat

renovate [ˈrenəveɪt] *vt* renovieren

renowned [rɪˈnaʊnd] *adj* berühmt (*for* für)

rent [rent] *n* Miete *f*; **for ~** (*US*) zu vermieten ▷ *vt* (*as hirer, tenant*) mieten; (*as owner*) vermieten; **~ed car** Mietwagen *m*; **rent out** *vt* vermieten; **rental** *n* Miete *f*; (*for car, TV etc*) Leihgebühr *f* ▷ *adj* Miet-

reorganize [riːˈɔːɡənaɪz] *vt* umorganisieren

rep [rep] *n* Vertreter(in) *m(f)*

repair [rɪˈpeəʳ] *n* Reparatur *f* ▷ *vt* reparieren; (*damage*) wiedergutmachen; **repair kit** *n* Flickzeug *nt*

repay [riːˈpeɪ] *irr vt* (*money*) zurückzahlen; **to ~ sb for sth** (*fig*) sich bei jdm für etw revanchieren

repeat [rɪˈpiːt] *n* (*Radio, TV*) Wiederholung *f* ▷ *vt* wiederholen; **repetition** [repəˈtɪʃən] *n* Wiederholung *f*; **repetitive** [rɪˈpetɪtɪv] *adj* sich wiederholend

rephrase [riːˈfreɪz] *vt* anders formulieren

replace [rɪˈpleɪs] *vt* ersetzen (*with* durch); (*put back*) zurückstellen, zurücklegen; **replacement** *n* (*thing, person*) Ersatz *m*; (*temporarily in job*) Vertretung *f*; **replacement part** *n* Ersatzteil *nt*

replay [ˈriːpleɪ] *n*: (*action*)

~ Wiederholung f ▷ [rɪ:'pleɪ] vt
(game) wiederholen
replica ['replɪkə] n Kopie f
reply [rɪ'plaɪ] n Antwort f ▷ vi
antworten; **to ~ to sb/sth**
jdm/auf etw *akk* antworten ▷ vt:
to ~ that antworten, dass
report [rɪ'pɔ:t] n Bericht m;
(school) Zeugnis nt ▷ vt (tell)
berichten; (give information against)
melden; (to police) anzeigen ▷ vi
(present oneself) sich melden; **to ~
sick** sich krankmelden; **report
card** n (US: school) Zeugnis nt;
reporter n Reporter(in) m(f)
represent [reprɪ'zent] vt darstellen; (speak for) vertreten;
representation [reprɪzen'teɪʃən]
n (picture etc) Darstellung f;
representative [reprɪ'zentətɪv]
n Vertreter(in) m(f); (US Pol)
Abgeordnete(r) mf ▷ adj
repräsentativ (of für)
reprimand ['reprɪmɑ:nd] n Tadel
m ▷ vt tadeln
reprint ['ri:prɪnt] n Nachdruck m
reproduce [ri:prə'dju:s] vt (copy)
reproduzieren ▷ vi (Bio) sich
fortpflanzen; **reproduction**
[ri:prə'dʌkʃən] n (copy)
Reproduktion f; (Bio)
Fortpflanzung f
reptile ['reptaɪl] n Reptil nt
republic [rɪ'pʌblɪk] n Republik f;
republican adj republikanisch
▷ n Republikaner(in) m(f)
repulsive [rɪ'pʌlsɪv] adj
abstoßend
reputable ['repjʊtəbl] adj seriös
reputation [repjʊ'teɪʃən] n Ruf
m; **he has a ~ for being difficult**
er hat den Ruf, schwierig zu sein
request [rɪ'kwest] n Bitte f (for
um); **on ~** auf Wunsch ▷ vt bitten
um; **to ~ sb to do sth** jdn bitten,
etw zu tun
require [rɪ'kwaɪə°] vt (need)

brauchen; (desire) verlangen; **what
qualifications are ~d?** welche
Qualifikationen sind
erforderlich?; **required** adj
erforderlich; **requirement** n
(condition) Anforderung f; (need)
Bedingung f
rerun ['ri:rʌn] n Wiederholung f
rescue ['reskju:] n Rettung f; **to
come to sb's ~** jdm zu Hilfe
kommen ▷ vt retten; **rescue
party** n Rettungsmannschaft f
research [rɪ'sɜ:tʃ] n Forschung f
▷ vi forschen (into über +akk) ▷ vt
erforschen; **researcher** n
Forscher(in) m(f)
resemblance [rɪ'zembləns] n
Ähnlichkeit f (to mit); **resemble**
[rɪ'zembl] vt ähneln +dat
resent [rɪ'zent] vt übel nehmen
reservation [rezə'veɪʃən] n
(booking) Reservierung f; (doubt)
Vorbehalt m; **I have a ~** (in hotel,
restaurant) ich habe reserviert;
reserve [rɪ'zɜ:v] n (store) Vorrat m
(of an +dat); (manner)
Zurückhaltung f; (Sport)
Reservespieler(in) m(f); (game ~)
Naturschutzgebiet nt ▷ vt (book in
advance) reservieren; **reserved** adj
reserviert
reservoir ['rezəvwɑ:°] n (for
water) Reservoir nt
reside [rɪ'zaɪd] vi wohnen;
residence ['rezɪdəns] n Wohnsitz m; (living) Aufenthalt m;
~ permit Aufenthaltsgenehmigung f; **~ hall** Studentenwohnheim nt; **resident**
['rezɪdənt] n (in house)
Bewohner(in) m(f); (in town, area)
Einwohner(in) m(f)
resign [rɪ'zaɪn] vt (post)
zurücktreten von; (job) kündigen
▷ vi (from post) zurücktreten; (from
job) kündigen; **resignation**
[rezɪg'neɪʃən] n (from post)

Rücktritt m; (from job) Kündigung f; **resigned** adj resigniert; **he is ~ to it** er hat sich damit abgefunden

resist [rɪˈzɪst] vt widerstehen +dat; **resistance** n Widerstand m (to gegen)

resit [riːˈsɪt] (Brit) irr vt wiederholen ▷ [ˈriːsɪt] n Wiederholungsprüfung f

resolution [rezəˈluːʃən] n (intention) Vorsatz m; (decision) Beschluss m

resolve [rɪˈzɒlv] vt (problem) lösen

resort [rɪˈzɔːt] n (holiday ~) Urlaubsort m; (health ~) Kurort m; **as a last ~** als letzter Ausweg ▷ vi: **to ~ to** greifen zu; (violence) anwenden

resources [rɪˈsɔːsɪz] npl (money) (Geld)mittel pl; (mineral ~) Bodenschätze pl

respect [rɪˈspekt] n Respekt m (for vor +dat); (consideration) Rücksicht f (for auf +akk); **with ~ to** in Bezug auf +akk; **in this ~** in dieser Hinsicht; **with all due ~** bei allem Respekt ▷ vt respektieren; **respectable** [rɪˈspektəbl] adj (person, family) angesehen; (district) anständig; (achievement, result) beachtlich; **respected** [rɪˈspektɪd] adj angesehen

respective [rɪˈspektɪv] adj jeweilig; **respectively** adv: **5 % and 10 %** = 5 % beziehungsweise 10 %

respiratory [rɪˈspɪrətərɪ] adj: **~ problems** (o **trouble**) Atembeschwerden pl

respond [rɪˈspɒnd] vi antworten (to auf +akk); (react) reagieren (to auf +akk); (to treatment) ansprechen (to auf +akk); **response** [rɪˈspɒns] n Antwort f; (reaction) Reaktion f; **in ~ to** als Antwort auf +akk

responsibility [rɪspɒnsəˈbɪlɪtɪ] n Verantwortung f; **that's her ~** dafür ist sie verantwortlich; **responsible** [rɪˈspɒnsəbl] adj verantwortlich (for für); (trustworthy) verantwortungsbewusst; (job) verantwortungsvoll

rest [rest] n (relaxation) Ruhe f; (break) Pause f; (remainder) Rest m; **to have** (o **take**) **a ~** sich ausruhen; (break) Pause machen; **the ~ of the wine/the people** der Rest des Weins/der Leute ▷ vi (relax) sich ausruhen; (lean) lehnen (on, against an +dat, gegen)

restaurant [ˈrestərɒnt] n Restaurant nt; **restaurant car** n (Brit) Speisewagen m

restful [ˈrestfʊl] adj (holiday etc) erholsam, ruhig; **restless** [ˈrestləs] adj unruhig

restore [rɪˈstɔː] vt (painting, building) restaurieren; (order) wiederherstellen; (give back) zurückgeben

restrain [rɪˈstreɪn] vt (person, feelings) zurückhalten; **to ~ oneself** sich beherrschen

restrict [rɪˈstrɪkt] vt beschränken (to auf +akk); **restricted** adj beschränkt; **restriction** [rɪˈstrɪkʃən] n Einschränkung f (on +gen)

rest room [ˈrestruːm] n (US) Toilette f

result [rɪˈzʌlt] n Ergebnis nt; (consequence) Folge f; **as a ~ of** infolge +gen ▷ vi: **to ~ in** führen zu; **to ~ from** sich ergeben aus

resume [rɪˈzjuːm] vt (work, negotiations) wieder aufnehmen; (journey) fortsetzen

résumé [ˈrezjʊmeɪ] n Zusammenfassung f; (US: curriculum vitae) Lebenslauf m

resuscitate [rɪˈsʌsɪteɪt] *vt* wiederbeleben

retail [ˈriːteɪl] *adv* im Einzelhandel; **retailer** *n* Einzelhändler(in) *m(f)*

retain [rɪˈteɪn] *vt* behalten; *(heat)* halten

rethink [riːˈθɪŋk] *irr vt* noch einmal überdenken

retire [rɪˈtaɪə*] *vi (from work)* in den Ruhestand treten; *(withdraw)* sich zurückziehen; **retired** *adj (person)* pensioniert; **retirement** *n (time of life)* Ruhestand *m*; **retirement age** *n* Rentenalter *nt*

retrace [rɪˈtreɪs] *vt* zurückverfolgen

retrain [riːˈtreɪn] *vi* sich umschulen lassen

retreat [rɪˈtriːt] *n (Mil)* Rückzug *m (from aus)*; *(refuge)* Zufluchtsort *m* ▷ *vi (Mil)* sich zurückziehen; *(step back)* zurückweichen

retrieve [rɪˈtriːv] *vt (recover)* wiederbekommen; *(rescue)* retten; *(data)* abrufen

retrospect [ˈretrəʊspekt] *n*: **in ~** rückblickend; **retrospective** [retrəʊˈspektɪv] *adj* rückblickend; *(pay rise)* rückwirkend

return [rɪˈtɜːn] *n (going back)* Rückkehr *f*; *(giving back)* Rückgabe *f*; *(profit)* Gewinn *m*; *(Brit: ~ ticket)* Rückfahrkarte *f*; *(plane ticket)* Rückflugticket *nt*; *(Tennis)* Return *m*; **in ~** als Gegenleistung *(for für)*; **many happy ~s (of the day)** herzlichen Glückwunsch zum Geburtstag! ▷ *vi (person)* zurückkehren; *(doubts, symptoms)* wieder auftreten; **to ~ to school/work** wieder in die Schule/die Arbeit gehen ▷ *vt (give back)* zurückgeben; **I ~ed his call** ich habe ihn zurückgerufen; **returnable** *adj (bottle)* Pfand-;

return flight *n (Brit)* Rückflug *m*; *(both ways)* Hin- und Rückflug *m*; **return key** *n (Inform)* Eingabetaste *f*; **return ticket** *n (Brit)* Rückfahrkarte *f*; *(for plane)* Rückflugticket *nt*

reunification [riːjuːnɪfɪˈkeɪʃən] *n* Wiedervereinigung *f*

reunion [riːˈjuːnjən] *n (party)* Treffen *nt*; **reunite** [riːjuːˈnaɪt] *vt* wieder vereinigen

reusable [riːˈjuːzəbl] *adj* wiederverwendbar

reveal [rɪˈviːl] *vt (make known)* enthüllen; *(secret)* verraten; *(show)* zeigen; **revealing** *adj* aufschlussreich; *(dress)* freizügig

revenge [rɪˈvendʒ] *n* Rache *f*; *(in game)* Revanche *f*; **to take ~ on sb (for sth)** sich an jdm (für etw) rächen

revenue [ˈrevənjuː] *n* Einnahmen *pl*

reverse [rɪˈvɜːs] *n (back)* Rückseite *f*; *(opposite)* Gegenteil *nt*; *(Auto: ~ gear)* Rückwärtsgang *m* ▷ *adj*: **in ~ order** in umgekehrter Reihenfolge ▷ *vt (order)* umkehren; *(decision)* umstoßen; *(car)* zurücksetzen; **to ~ the charges** *(Brit)* ein R-Gespräch führen ▷ *vi (Auto)* rückwärtsfahren

review [rɪˈvjuː] *n (of book, film etc)* Rezension *f*; Kritik *f*; **to be under ~** überprüft werden ▷ *vt (book, film etc)* rezensieren; *(re-examine)* überprüfen

revise [rɪˈvaɪz] *vt* revidieren; *(text)* überarbeiten; *(Brit: in school)* wiederholen ▷ *vi (Brit, in school)* (für eine Prüfung) lernen; **revision** [rɪˈvɪʒən] *n (of text)* Überarbeitung *f*; *(Brit, in school)* Wiederholung *f*

revitalize [riːˈvaɪtəlaɪz] *vt* neu beleben

revive [rɪ'vaɪv] vt (person) wiederbeleben; (tradition, interest) wieder aufleben lassen ▷ vi (regain consciousness) wieder zu sich kommen

revolt [rɪ'vəʊlt] n Aufstand m; **revolting** adj widerlich

revolution [revə'lu:ʃən] n (Pol, fig) Revolution f; (turn) Umdrehung f; **revolutionary** adj revolutionär ▷ n Revolutionär(in) m(f)

revolve [rɪ'vɒlv] vi. sich drehen (around um); **revolver** n Revolver m; **revolving door** n Drehtür f

reward [rɪ'wɔːd] n Belohnung f ▷ vt belohnen; **rewarding** adj lohnend

rewind [riː'waɪnd] irr vt (tape) zurückspulen

rewritable [riː'raɪtəbl] adj (CD, DVD) wiederbeschreibbar; **rewrite** irr vt (write again; recast) umschreiben

rheumatism ['ruːmətɪzəm] n Rheuma nt

Rhine [raɪn] n Rhein m

rhinoceros [raɪ'nɒsərəs] n Nashorn nt

Rhodes [rəʊdz] n Rhodos nt

rhubarb ['ruːbɑːb] n Rhabarber m

rhyme [raɪm] n Reim m ▷ vi sich reimen (with auf +akk)

rhythm ['rɪðəm] n Rhythmus m

rib [rɪb] n Rippe f

ribbon ['rɪbən] n Band nt

rice [raɪs] n Reis m; **rice pudding** n Milchreis m

rich [rɪtʃ] adj reich; (food) schwer ▷ npl: **the ~** die Reichen pl

rickety ['rɪkɪtɪ] adj wackelig

rid [rɪd] (rid, rid) vt: **to get ~ of sb/sth** jdn/etw loswerden

ridden ['rɪdn] pp of **ride**

riddle ['rɪdl] n Rätsel nt

ride [raɪd] (rode, ridden) vt (horse) reiten; (bicycle) fahren ▷ vi

(on horse) reiten; (on bike) fahren ▷ n (in vehicle, on bike) Fahrt f; (on horse) (Aus)ritt m; **to go for a ~** (in car, on bike) spazieren fahren; (on horse) reiten gehen; **to take sb for a ~** (fam) jdn verarschen; **rider** n (on horse) Reiter(in) m(f); (on bike) Fahrer(in) m(f)

ridiculous [rɪ'dɪkjʊləs] adj lächerlich; **don't be ~** red keinen Unsinn!

riding ['raɪdɪŋ] n Reiten nt; **to go ~** reiten gehen ▷ adj Reit-

rifle ['raɪfl] n Gewehr nt

rig [rɪg] n: **oil ~** Bohrinsel f ▷ vt (election etc) manipulieren

right [raɪt] adj (correct, just) richtig; (opposite of left) rechte(r, s); (clothes, job etc) passend; **to be ~** (person) recht haben; (clock) richtig gehen; **that's ~** das stimmt! ▷ n Recht nt (to auf +akk); (side) rechte Seite; **the Right** (Pol) die Rechte; **to take a ~** (Auto) rechts abbiegen; **on the ~** rechts (of von); **to the ~** nach rechts; (on the ~) rechts (of von) ▷ adv (towards the ~) nach rechts; (directly) direkt; (exactly) genau: **to turn ~** (Auto) rechts abbiegen; **~ away** sofort; **~ now** im Moment; (immediately) sofort; **right angle** n rechter Winkel; **right-hand drive** n Rechtssteuerung f ▷ adj rechtsgesteuert; **right-handed** adj: **he is ~** er ist Rechtshänder; **right-hand side** n rechte Seite; **on the ~** auf der rechten Seite; **rightly** adv zu Recht; **right of way** n: **to have ~** (Auto) Vorfahrt haben; **right wing** n (Pol, Sport) rechter Flügel; **right-wing** adj Rechts-; **~ extremist** Rechtsradikale(r) mf

rigid ['rɪdʒɪd] adj (stiff) starr; (strict) streng

rigorous, rigorously ['rɪgərəs, -lɪ] adj, adv streng

rim [rɪm] n (of cup etc) Rand m; (of wheel) Felge f

rind [raɪnd] n (of cheese) Rinde f; (of bacon) Schwarte f; (of fruit) Schale f

ring [rɪŋ] **(rang, rung)** vt, vi (bell) läuten; (Tel) anrufen ▷ n (on finger, in boxing) Ring m; (circle) Kreis m; (at circus) Manege f; **to give sb a ~** (Tel) jdn anrufen; **ring back** vt, vi zurückrufen; **ring up** vt, vi anrufen

ring binder n Ringbuch nt

ringleader n Anführer(in) m(f)

ring road n (Brit) Umgehungsstraße f

ringtone n Klingelton m

rink [rɪŋk] n (ice ~) Eisbahn f; (for roller-skating) Rollschuhbahn f

rinse [rɪns] vt spülen

riot ['raɪət] n Aufruhr m

rip [rɪp] n Riss m ▷ vt zerreißen; **to ~ sth open** etw aufreißen ▷ vi reißen; **rip off** vt (fam: person) übers Ohr hauen; **rip up** vt zerreißen

ripe [raɪp] adj (fruit) reif; **ripen** vi reifen

rip-off ['rɪpɒf] n: **that's a ~** (fam: too expensive) das ist Wucher

rise [raɪz] **(rose, risen)** vi (from sitting, lying) aufstehen; (sun) aufgehen; (prices, temperature) steigen; (ground) ansteigen; (in revolt) sich erheben ▷ n (increase) Anstieg m (in +gen); (pay ~) Gehaltserhöhung f; (to power, fame) Aufstieg m (to zu); (slope) Steigung f; **risen** ['rɪzn] pp of **rise**

risk [rɪsk] n Risiko nt ▷ vt riskieren; **to ~ doing sth** es riskieren, etw zu tun; **risky** adj riskant

risotto [rɪ'zɒtəʊ] (pl **-s**) n Risotto nt

ritual ['rɪtjʊəl] n Ritual nt ▷ adj rituell

rival ['raɪvəl] n Rivale m, Rivalin f (for um); (Comm) Konkurrent(in) m(f); rivalry n Rivalität f; (Comm, Sport) Konkurrenz f

river ['rɪvə°] n Fluss m; **the River Thames** (Brit), **the Thames River** (US) die Themse; **riverside** n Flussufer nt ▷ adj am Flussufer

road [rəʊd] n Straße f; (fig) Weg m; **on the ~** (travelling) unterwegs, mit dem Auto/Bus etc fahren; **roadblock** n Straßensperre f; **roadmap** n Straßenkarte f; **road rage** n aggressives Verhalten im Straßenverkehr; **roadside** n: **at (o by) the ~** am Straßenrand; **roadsign** n Verkehrsschild nt; **road tax** n Kraftfahrzeugsteuer f; **roadworks** npl Bauarbeiten pl; **roadworthy** adj fahrtüchtig

roar [rɔː°] n (of person, lion) Brüllen nt; (von Verkehr) Donnern nt ▷ vi (person, lion) brüllen (with vor +dat)

roast [rəʊst] n Braten m ▷ adj: **~ beef** Rinderbraten m; **~ chicken** Brathähnchen nt; **~ pork** Schweinebraten m; **~ potatoes** pl im Backofen gebratene Kartoffeln ▷ vt (meat) braten

rob [rɒb] vt bestehlen; (bank, shop) ausrauben; **robber** n Räuber(in) m(f); **robbery** n Raub m

robe [rəʊb] n (US: dressing gown) Morgenrock m; (of judge, priest etc) Robe f, Talar m

robin ['rɒbɪn] n Rotkehlchen nt

robot ['rəʊbɒt] n Roboter m

robust [rəʊ'bʌst] adj robust; (defence) stark

rock [rɒk] n (substance) Stein m; (boulder) Felsbrocken m; (Mus) Rock m; **stick of ~** (Brit) Zuckerstange f; **on the ~s** (drink) mit Eis; *(marriage)* gescheitert ▷ *vt, vi (swing)* schaukeln; *(dance)* rocken; **rock climbing** *n* Klettern *nt;* **to go ~** klettern gehen

rocket ['rɒkɪt] *n* Rakete *f; (in salad)* Rucola *m*

rocking chair ['rɒkɪntʃeə⁽ʳ⁾] *n* Schaukelstuhl *m*

rocky ['rɒkɪ] *adj (landscape)* felsig; *(path)* steinig

rod [rɒd] *n (bar)* Stange *f; (fishing ~)* Rute *f*

rode [rəʊd] *pt of* **ride**

rogue [rəʊg] *n* Schurke *m,* Gauner *m*

role [rəʊl] *n* Rolle *f;* **role model** *n* Vorbild *nt*

roll [rəʊl] *n (of film, paper etc)* Rolle *f; (bread ~)* Brötchen *nt* ▷ *vt (move by ~ing)* rollen; *(cigarette)* drehen ▷ *vi (move by ~ing)* rollen; *(ship)* schlingern; *(camera)* laufen; **roll out** *vt (pastry)* ausrollen; **roll over** *vi (person)* sich umdrehen; **roll up** *vi (fam: arrive)* antanzen ▷ *vt (carpet)* aufrollen; **to roll one's sleeves up** die Ärmel hochkrempeln

roller [n *(hair ~)*] (Locken)wickler *m;* **Rollerblades®** *npl* Inlineskates *pl;* **rollerblading** *n* Inlineskaten *nt;* **roller coaster** *n* Achterbahn *f;* **roller skates** *npl* Rollschuhe *pl;* **roller-skating** *n* Rollschuhlaufen *nt;* **rolling pin** *n* Nudelholz *nt;* **roll-on** *(deodorant) n* Deoroller *m*

ROM [rɒm] *acr =* **read only memory** ROM *m*

Roman ['rəʊmən] *adj* römisch ▷ *n* Römer(in) *m(f);* **Roman Catholic** *adj* römisch-katholisch ▷ *n* Katholik(in) *m(f)*

romance [rəʊ'mæns] *n* Romantik *f; (love affair)* Romanze *f*

Romania [rəʊ'meɪnɪə] *n* Rumänien *nt;* **Romanian** *adj*

rumänisch ▷ *n* Rumäne *m,* Rumänin *f; (language)* Rumänisch *nt*

romantic [rəʊ'mæntɪk] *adj* romantisch

roof [ruːf] *n* Dach *nt;* **roof rack** *n* Dachgepäckträger *m*

rook [rʊk] *n (in chess)* Turm *m*

room [ruːm] *n* Zimmer *nt,* Raum *m; (large, for gatherings etc)* Saal *m; (space)* Platz *m; (fig)* Spielraum *m;* **to make ~ for** Platz machen für; **roommate** *n* Zimmergenosse *m,* Zimmergenossin *f;* Mitbewohner(in) *m(f);* **room service** *n* Zimmerservice *m;* **roomy** *adj* geräumig; *(garment)* weit

root [ruːt] *n* Wurzel *f;* **root out** *vt (eradicate)* ausrotten; **root vegetable** *n* Wurzelgemüse *nt*

rope [rəʊp] *n* Seil *nt;* **to know the ~s** *(fam)* sich auskennen

rose [rəʊz] *pt of* **rise** ▷ *n* Rose *f*

rosé ['rəʊzeɪ] *n* Rosé(wein) *m*

rot [rɒt] *vi* verfaulen

rota ['rəʊtə] *n (Brit)* Dienstplan *m*

rotate [rəʊ'teɪt] *vt (turn)* rotieren lassen ▷ *vi* rotieren; **rotation** [rəʊ'teɪʃən] *n (turning)* Rotation *f;* **in ~** abwechselnd

rotten ['rɒtn] *adj (decayed)* faul; *(mean)* gemein; *(unpleasant)* scheußlich; *(ill)* elend

rough [rʌf] *adj (not smooth)* rau; *(path)* uneben; *(coarse, violent)* grob; *(crossing)* stürmisch; *(without comforts)* hart; *(unfinished, makeshift)* grob; *(approximate)* ungefähr; **~ draft** Rohentwurf *m;* **I have a ~ idea** ich habe eine ungefähre Vorstellung ▷ *adv:* **to sleep ~** im Freien schlafen ▷ *vt:* **to ~ it** primitiv leben ▷ *n:* **to write sth in ~** etw ins Unreine schreiben; **roughly** *adv* grob; *(approximately)* ungefähr

round [raʊnd] *adj* rund ▷ *adv:* **all ~** (on all sides) rundherum; **the long way ~** der längere Weg; **I'll be ~ at 8** ich werde um acht Uhr da sein; **the other way ~** umgekehrt ▷ *prep* (surrounding) um (... herum); **~** (**about**) (approximately) ungefähr; **~ the corner** um die Ecke; **to go ~ the world** um die Welt reisen; **she lives ~ here** sie wohnt hier in der Gegend ▷ *n* Runde *f*; (of bread, toast) Scheibe *f*; **it's my ~** (of drinks) die Runde geht auf mich ▷ *vt* (corner) biegen um; **round off** *vt* abrunden; **round up** *vt* (number, price) aufrunden

roundabout *n* (Brit Auto) Kreisverkehr *m*; (Brit: merry-go-round) Karussell *nt* ▷ *adj* umständlich; **round-the-clock** *adj* rund um die Uhr; **round trip** *n* Rundreise *f*; **round-trip ticket** *n* (US) Rückfahrkarte *f*; (for plane) Rückflugticket *nt*

rouse [raʊz] *vt* (from sleep) wecken

route [ruːt] *n* Route *f*; (bus, plane etc service) Linie *f*; (fig) Weg *m*

routine [ruːˈtiːn] *n* Routine *f* ▷ *adj* Routine-

row[1] [raʊ] *n* (line) Reihe *f*; **three times in a ~** dreimal hintereinander ▷ *vt, vi* (boat) rudern ▷ [raʊ] *n* (noise) Krach *m*; (dispute) Streit *m*

rowboat [ˈraʊbəʊt] *n* (US) Ruderboot *nt*

row house [ˈraʊhaʊs] *n* (US) Reihenhaus *nt*

rowing [ˈraʊɪŋ] *n* Rudern *nt*; **rowing boat** *n* (Brit) Ruderboot *nt*; **rowing machine** *n* Rudergerät *nt*

royal [ˈrɔɪəl] *adj* königlich; **royalty** *n* (family) Mitglieder *pl* der königlichen Familie; **royalties** *pl* (from book, music) Tantiemen *pl*

RSPCA *abbr* = **Royal Society for the Prevention of Cruelty to Animals** britischer Tierschutzverein

RSPCC *abbr* = **Royal Society for the Prevention of Cruelty to Children** britischer Kinderschutzverein

RSVP *abbr* = **répondez s'il vous plaît** u. A. w. g.

rub [rʌb] *vt* reiben; **rub in** *vt* einmassieren; **rub out** *vt* (with eraser) ausradieren

rubber [ˈrʌbə*] *n* Gummi *m*; (Brit: eraser) Radiergummi *m*; (US fam: contraceptive) Gummi *m*; **rubber band** *n* Gummiband *nt*; **rubber stamp** *n* Stempel *m*

rubbish [ˈrʌbɪʃ] *n* Abfall *m*; (nonsense) Quatsch *m*; (poor-quality thing) Mist *m*; **don't talk ~** red keinen Unsinn!; **rubbish bin** *n* Mülleimer *m*; **rubbish dump** *n* Müllabladeplatz *m*

rubble [ˈrʌbl] *n* Schutt *m*

ruby [ˈruːbɪ] *n* (stone) Rubin *m*

rucksack [ˈrʌksæk] *n* Rucksack *m*

rude [ruːd] *adj* (impolite) unhöflich; (indecent) unanständig

rug [rʌg] *n* Teppich *m*; (next to bed) Bettvorleger *m*; (for knees) Wolldecke *f*

rugby [ˈrʌgbɪ] *n* Rugby *nt*

rugged [ˈrʌgɪd] *adj* (coastline) zerklüftet; (features) markant

ruin [ˈruːɪn] *n* Ruine *f*; (financial, social) Ruin *m* ▷ *vt* ruinieren

rule [ruːl] *n* Regel *f*; (governing) Herrschaft *f*; **as a ~** in der Regel ▷ *vt, vi* (govern) regieren; (decide) entscheiden; **ruler** *n* Lineal *nt*; (person) Herrscher(in) *m(f)*

rum [rʌm] *n* Rum *m*

rumble [ˈrʌmbl] *vi* (stomach) knurren; (train, truck) rumpeln

rummage [ˈrʌmɪdʒ] *vi:* **~** (**around**) herumstöbern

rumor (US), **rumour** ['ruːmə°] n Gerücht nt

run [rʌn] vt (race, distance) laufen; (machine, engine, computer program, water) laufen lassen; (manage) leiten, führen; (car) unterhalten; **I ran her home** ich habe sie nach Hause gefahren ▷ vi laufen; (move quickly) rennen; (bus, train) fahren; (path etc) verlaufen; (machine, engine, computer program) laufen; (flow) fließen; (colours, make-up) verlaufen; **to ~ for President** für die Präsidentschaft kandidieren; **to be ~ning low** knapp werden; **my nose is ~ning** mir läuft die Nase; **it ~s in the family** es liegt in der Familie ▷ n (on foot) Lauf m; (in car) Spazierfahrt f; (series) Reihe f; (sudden demand) Ansturm m (on auf +akk); (in tights) Laufmasche f; (in cricket, baseball) Lauf m; **to go for a ~** laufen gehen; (in car) eine Spazierfahrt machen; **in the long ~** auf die Dauer; **on the ~** auf der Flucht (from vor +dat); **run about** vi herumlaufen; **run away** vi weglaufen; **run down** vt (with car) umfahren; (criticize) heruntermachen; **to be ~** (tired) abgespannt sein; **run into** vt (meet) zufällig treffen; (problem) stoßen auf +akk; **run off** vi weglaufen; **run out** vi (person) hinausrennen; (liquid) auslaufen; (lease, time) ablaufen; (money, supplies) ausgehen; **he ran ~ of money** ihm ging das Geld aus; **run over** vt (with car) überfahren; **run up** vt (debt, bill) machen

rung [rʌŋ] pp of **ring**

runner ['rʌnə°] n (athlete) Läufer(in) m(f); **to do a ~** (fam) wegrennen; **runner bean** n (Brit) Stangenbohne f

running ['rʌnɪŋ] n (Sport) Laufen nt; (management) Leitung f, Führung f ▷ adj (water) fließend; **~ costs** Betriebskosten pl; (for car) Unterhaltskosten pl; **3 days** ~ 3 Tage hintereinander

runny ['rʌnɪ] adj (food) flüssig; (nose) laufend

runway ['rʌnweɪ] n Start- und Landebahn f

rural ['rʊərəl] adj ländlich

rush [rʌʃ] n Eile f; (for tickets etc) Ansturm m (for auf +akk); **to be in a ~** es eilig haben; **there's no ~** es eilt nicht ▷ vt (do too quickly) hastig machen; (meal) hastig essen; **to ~ sb to hospital** jdn auf dem schnellsten Weg ins Krankenhaus bringen; **don't ~ me** dräng mich nicht ▷ vi (hurry) eilen; **don't ~** lass dir Zeit; **rush hour** n Hauptverkehrszeit f

rusk [rʌsk] n Zwieback m

Russia ['rʌʃə] n Russland nt; **Russian** adj russisch ▷ n Russe m, Russin f; (language) Russisch nt

rust [rʌst] n Rost m ▷ vi rosten; **rustproof** adj rostfrei; **rusty** ['rʌstɪ] adj rostig

ruthless ['ruːθləs] adj rücksichtslos; (treatment, criticism) schonungslos

rye [raɪ] n Roggen m; **rye bread** n Roggenbrot nt

S

S *abbr* = **south** S

sabotage ['sæbətɑːʒ] *vt* sabotieren

sachet ['sæʃeɪ] *n* Päckchen *nt*

sack [sæk] *n* (*bag*) Sack *m*; **to get the ~** (*fam*) rausgeschmissen werden ▷ *vt* (*fam*) rausschmeißen

sacred ['seɪkrɪd] *adj* heilig

sacrifice ['sækrɪfaɪs] *n* Opfer *nt* ▷ *vt* opfern

sad [sæd] *adj* traurig

saddle ['sædl] *n* Sattel *m*

sadistic [sə'dɪstɪk] *adj* sadistisch

sadly ['sædlɪ] *adv* (*unfortunately*) leider

safari [sə'fɑːrɪ] *n* Safari *f*

safe [seɪf] *adj* (*free from danger*) sicher; (*out of danger*) in Sicherheit; (*careful*) vorsichtig; **have a ~ journey!** gute Fahrt! ▷ *n* Safe *m*; **safeguard** *n* Schutz *m* ▷ *vt* schützen (*against* vor +*dat*); **safely** *adv* sicher; (*arrive*) wohlbehalten;

(*drive*) vorsichtig; **safety** *n* Sicherheit *f*; **safety belt** *n* Sicherheitsgurt *m*; **safety pin** *n* Sicherheitsnadel *f*

Sagittarius [sædʒɪ'teərɪəs] *n* (*Astr*) Schütze *m*

Sahara [sə'hɑːrə] *n*: **the ~** (**Desert**) die (Wüste) Sahara

said [sed] *pt*, *pp of* **say**

sail [seɪl] *n* Segel *nt*; **to set ~** losfahren (*for* nach) ▷ *vi* (*in yacht*) segeln; (*on ship*) mit dem Schiff fahren; (*ship*) auslaufen (*for* nach) ▷ *vt* (*yacht*) segeln mit; (*ship*) steuern; **sailboat** *n* (*US*) Segelboot *nt*; **sailing** *n*: **to go ~** segeln gehen; **sailing boat** (*Brit*) Segelboot *nt*; **sailor** *n* Seemann *m*; (*in navy*) Matrose *m*

saint [seɪnt] *n* Heilige(r) *mf*

sake [seɪk] *n*: **for the ~ of** um +*gen* ... willen; **for your ~** deinetwegen, dir zuliebe

salad ['sæləd] *n* Salat *m*; **salad cream** *n* (*Brit*) majonäseartige Salatsoße; **salad dressing** *n* Salatsoße *f*

salary ['sælərɪ] *n* Gehalt *nt*

sale [seɪl] *n* Verkauf *m*; (*at reduced prices*) Ausverkauf *m*; **the ~s** *pl* (*in summer, winter*) der Schlussverkauf; **for ~** zu verkaufen; **sales clerk** *n* (*US*) Verkäufer(in) *m(f)*; **salesman** (*pl* **-men**) *n* Verkäufer *m*; (*rep*) Vertreter *m*; **sales rep** *n* Vertreter(in) *m(f)*; **sales tax** *n* (*US*) Verkaufssteuer *f*; **saleswoman** (*pl* **-women**) *n* Verkäuferin *f*; (*rep*) Vertreterin *f*

salmon ['sæmən] *n* Lachs *m*

saloon [sə'luːn] *n* (*ship's lounge*) Salon *m*; (*US: bar*) Kneipe *f*

salt [sɔːlt] *n* Salz *nt* ▷ *vt* (*flavour*) salzen; (*roads*) mit Salz streuen; **salt cellar**, **salt shaker** (*US*) *n* Salzstreuer *m*; **salty** *adj* salzig

salvage ['sælvidʒ] vt bergen (from aus); (fig) retten

same [seim] adj: **the ~** (similar) der/die/das gleiche, die gleichen pl; (identical) der-/die-/dasselbe, dieselben pl; **they live in the ~ house** sie wohnen im selben Haus ▷ pron: **the ~** (similar) der/die/das Gleiche, die Gleichen pl; (identical) der-/die-/dasselbe, dieselben pl; **all the ~** trotzdem; **the ~ to you** gleichfalls; **it's all the ~ to me** es ist mir egal ▷ adv: **the ~** gleich; **they look the ~** sie sehen gleich aus

sample ['sɑːmpl] n Probe f; (of fabric) Muster nt ▷ vt probieren

sanctions ['sæŋkʃənz] npl (Pol) Sanktionen pl

sanctuary ['sæŋktjʋəri] n (refuge) Zuflucht f; (for animals) Schutzgebiet nt

sand [sænd] n Sand m

sandal ['sændl] n Sandale f

sandpaper n Sandpapier nt ▷ vt schmirgeln

sandwich ['sænwidʒ] n Sandwich nt

sandy ['sændi] adj (full of sand) sandig; **~ beach** Sandstrand m

sane [sein] adj geistig gesund, normal; (sensible) vernünftig

sang [sæŋ] pt of **sing**

sanitary ['sænitəri] adj hygienisch; **sanitary napkin** (US), **sanitary towel** n Damenbinde f

sank [sæŋk] pt of **sink**

Santa (Claus) ['sæntə('klɔːz)] n der Weihnachtsmann

sarcastic [sɑːˈkæstik] adj sarkastisch

sardine [sɑːˈdiːn] n Sardine f

Sardinia [sɑːˈdiniə] n Sardinien nt

sari [ˈsɑːri] n Sari m (von indischen Frauen getragenes Gewand)

sat [sæt] pt, pp of **sit**

Sat abbr = **Saturday** Sa.

satellite ['sætəlait] n Satellit m; **satellite dish** n Satellitenschüssel f; **satellite TV** n Satellitenfernsehen nt

satin ['sætin] n Satin m

satisfaction [sætisˈfækʃən] n (contentment) Zufriedenheit f; **is that to your ~?** bist du/sind Sie damit zufrieden?; **satisfactory** [sætisˈfæktəri] adj zufriedenstellend; **satisfied** ['sætisfaid] adj zufrieden (with mit); **satisfy** ['sætisfai] vt zufriedenstellen; (convince) überzeugen; (conditions) erfüllen; (need, demand) befriedigen; **satisfying** adj befriedigend

Saturday ['sætədei] n Samstag m, Sonnabend m; see also **Tuesday**

sauce [sɔːs] n Soße f; **saucepan** n Kochtopf m; **saucer** n Untertasse f

saucy ['sɔːsi] adj frech

Saudi Arabia ['saʊdiəˈreibiə] n Saudi-Arabien nt

sauna ['sɔːnə] n Sauna f

sausage ['sɔsidʒ] n Wurst f; **sausage roll** n mit Wurst gefülltes Blätterteigröllchen

savage ['sævidʒ] adj (person, attack) brutal; (animal) wild

save [seiv] vt (rescue) retten (from vor +dat); (money, time, electricity etc) sparen; (strength) schonen; (Inform) speichern; **to ~ sb's life** jdm das Leben retten ▷ vi sparen ▷ n (in football) Parade f; **save up** vi sparen (for auf +akk); **saving** n (of money) Sparen nt; **~s** pl Ersparnisse pl; **~s account** Sparkonto nt

savory (US), **savoury** ['seivəri] adj (not sweet) pikant

saw [sɔː] (**sawed, sawn**) vt, vi sägen ▷ n (tool) Säge f ▷ pt of **see**; **sawdust** n Sägemehl nt

saxophone ['sæksəfəʊn] n Saxophon nt

say [seɪ] (**said, said**) vt sagen (to sb jdm); (prayer) sprechen; **what does the letter ~?** was steht im Brief?; **the rules - that ...** in den Regeln heißt es, dass ...; **he's said to be rich** er soll reich sein ▷ n: **to have a ~ in sth** ein wenig Mitspracherecht haben ▷ adv zum Beispiel; **saying** n Sprichwort nt

scab [skæb] n (on cut) Schorf m

scaffolding ['skæfəʊldɪŋ] n (Bau)gerüst nt

scale [skeɪl] n (of music) Maßstab m; (on thermometer etc) Skala f; (of pay) Tarifsystem nt; (Mus) Tonleiter f; (of fish, snake) Schuppe f; **to -** maßstabsgerecht; **on a large/small ~** in großem/kleinem Umfang; **scales** npl (for weighing) Waage f

scalp [skælp] n Kopfhaut f

scan [skæn] vt (examine) genau prüfen; (read quickly) überfliegen; (Inform) scannen ▷ n (Med) Ultraschall m; **scan in** vt (Inform) einscannen

scandal ['skændl] n Skandal m; **scandalous** adj skandalös

Scandinavia [skændɪ'neɪvɪə] n Skandinavien nt; **Scandinavian** adj skandinavisch ▷ n Skandinavier(in) m(f)

scanner ['skænə°] n Scanner m

scapegoat ['skeɪpgəʊt] n Sündenbock m

scar [skɑː°] n Narbe f

scarce ['skeəs] adj selten; (in short supply) knapp; **scarcely** adv kaum

scare ['skeə°] n (general alarm) Panik f ▷ vt erschrecken; **to be ~d** Angst haben (of vor +dat)

scarf [skɑːf] (pl **-scarves**) n Schal m; (on head) Kopftuch nt

scarlet ['skɑːlət] adj scharlachrot; **scarlet fever** n Scharlach m

scary ['skeərɪ] adj (film, story) gruselig

scatter ['skætə°] vt verstreuen; (seed, gravel) streuen; (disperse) auseinandertreiben

scene [siːn] n (location) Ort m; (division of play) (Theat) Szene f; (view) Anblick m; **to make a ~** eine Szene machen; **scenery** ['siːnərɪ] n (landscape) Landschaft f; (Theat) Kulissen pl; **scenic** ['siːnɪk] adj (landscape) malerisch; **~ route** landschaftlich schöne Strecke

scent [sent] n (perfume) Parfüm nt; (smell) Duft m

sceptical ['skeptɪkəl] adj (Brit) skeptisch

schedule ['ʃedjuːl, 'skedʒʊəl] n (plan) Programm nt; (of work) Zeitplan m; (list) Liste f; (US: of trains, buses, air traffic) Fahr-, Flugplan m; **on ~** planmäßig; **to be behind ~ with sth** mit etw in Verzug sein ▷ vt: **the meeting is ~d for next Monday** die Besprechung ist für nächsten Montag angesetzt; **scheduled** adj (departure, arrival) planmäßig; **~ flight** Linienflug m

scheme [skiːm] n (plan) Plan m; (project) Projekt nt; (dishonest) Intrige f ▷ vi intrigieren

schizophrenic [skɪtsə'frenɪk] adj schizophren

scholar ['skɒlə°] n Gelehrte(r) mf; **scholarship** n (grant) Stipendium nt

school [skuːl] n Schule f; (university department) Fachbereich m; (US: university) Universität f; **school bag** n Schultasche f; **schoolbook** n Schulbuch nt; **schoolboy** n Schüler m; **school bus** n Schulbus m; **schoolgirl**

sciatica | 484

Schülerin f; **schoolteacher** n
Lehrer(in) m(f); **schoolwork** n
Schularbeiten pl

sciatica [saɪˈætɪkə] n Ischias m

science [ˈsaɪəns] n Wissenschaft
f; (natural ~) Naturwissenschaft f;
science fiction n Sciencefiction
f; **scientific** [saɪənˈtɪfɪk] adj
wissenschaftlich; **scientist**
[ˈsaɪəntɪst] n Wissenschaftler(in)
m(f); (in natural sciences)
Naturwissenschaftler(in) m(f)

scissors [ˈsɪzəz] npl Schere f

scone [skɒn] n kleines süßes
Hefebrötchen mit oder ohne Rosinen,
das mit Butter oder Dickrahm und
Marmelade gegessen wird

scoop [skuːp] n (exclusive story)
Exklusivbericht m; **~ of
ice-cream** eine Kugel Eis ▷ vt: **to
~ (up)** schaufeln

scooter [ˈskuːtə°] n (Motor)-
roller m; (toy) (Tret)roller m

scope [skəʊp] n Umfang m;
(opportunity) Möglichkeit f

score [skɔː°] n (Sport) Spielstand
m; (final result) Spielergebnis nt; (in
quiz etc) Punktestand m; (Mus)
Partitur f; **to keep (the
~** mitzählen ▷ vt (goal) schießen;
(points) punkten ▷ vi (keep ~)
mitzählen; **scoreboard** n
Anzeigetafel f

scorn [skɔːn] n Verachtung f;
scornful adj verächtlich

Scorpio [ˈskɔːpɪəʊ] (pl **-s**) n (Astr)
Skorpion m

scorpion [ˈskɔːpɪən] n Skorpion m

Scot [skɒt] n Schotte m, Schottin
f; **Scotch** [skɒtʃ] n (whisky)
schottischer Whisky, Scotch m

Scotch tape® n (US) Tesafilm®
m

Scotland [ˈskɒtlənd] n Schottland nt; **Scotsman** (pl **-men**) n
Schotte m; **Scotswoman** (pl

-women) n Schottin f; **Scottish**
adj schottisch

scout [skaʊt] n (boy ~) Pfadfinder
m

scowl [skaʊl] vi finster blicken

scrambled eggs npl Rührei nt

scrap [skræp] n (bit) Stückchen
nt, Fetzen m; (metal) Schrott m ▷ vt
(car) verschrotten; (plan)
verwerfen; **scrapbook** n
Sammelalbum nt

scrape [skreɪp] n (scratch)
Kratzer m ▷ vt (car) schrammen;
(wall) streifen; **to ~ one's knee**
sich das Knie schürfen; **scrape
through** vi (exam) mit knapper
Not bestehen

scrap heap [ˈskræphiːp] n
Schrotthaufen m; **scrap metal** n
Schrott m; **scrap paper** n
Schmierpapier nt

scratch [skrætʃ] n (mark) Kratzer
m; **to start from ~** von vorne
anfangen ▷ vt kratzen; (car)
zerkratzen; **to ~ one's arm** sich
am Arm kratzen ▷ vi kratzen;
(~ oneself) sich kratzen

scream [skriːm] n Schrei m ▷ vi
schreien (with vor +dat); **to ~ at sb**
jdn anschreien

screen [skriːn] n (TV, Inform)
Bildschirm m; (Cine) Leinwand f
▷ vt (protect) abschirmen; (hide)
verdecken; (film) zeigen;
(applicants, luggage) überprüfen;
screenplay n Drehbuch nt;
screensaver n (Inform)
Bildschirmschoner m

screw [skruː] n Schraube f ▷ vt
(vulg: have sex with) ficken; **to ~ sth
to sth** etw akk an etw akk schrauben;
to ~ off/on (lid)
ab-/aufschrauben; **screw up** vt
(paper) zusammenknüllen; (make a
mess of) vermasseln; **screwdriver**
n Schraubenzieher m; **screw top**
n Schraubverschluss m

scribble ['skrɪbl] vt, vi kritzeln

script [skrɪpt] n (of play) Text m; (of film) Drehbuch nt; (style of writing) Schrift f

scroll down ['skrəʊl'daʊn] vi (Inform) runterscrollen; **scroll up** vi (Inform) raufscrollen; **scroll bar** n (Inform) Scrollbar f

scrub [skrʌb] vt schrubben; **scrubbing brush, scrub brush** (US) n Scheuerbürste f

scruffy ['skrʌfɪ] adj vergammelt

scrupulous, scrupulously ['skruːpjʊləs, -lɪ] adj, adv gewissenhaft; (painstaking) peinlich genau

scuba-diving n ['skuːbədaɪvɪŋ] n Sporttauchen nt

sculptor(in) ['skʌlptə°] m(f); **sculpture** ['skʌlptʃə°] n (Art) Bildhauerei f; (statue) Skulptur f

sea [siː] n Meer nt, See f; **seafood** n Meeresfrüchte pl; **sea front** n Strandpromenade f; **seagull** n Möwe f

seal [siːl] n (animal) Robbe f; (stamp, impression) Siegel nt; (Tech) Verschluss m; (ring etc) Dichtung f ▷ vt versiegeln; (envelope) zukleben

seam [siːm] n Naht f

search [sɜːtʃ] n Suche f(for nach); **to do a ~ for** (Inform) suchen nach; **in ~ of** auf der Suche nach ▷ vi suchen (for nach) ▷ vt durchsuchen; **search engine** n (Inform) Suchmaschine f

seashell ['siːʃel] n Muschel f; **seashore** n Strand m; **seasick** adj seekrank; **seaside** n: **at the ~** am Meer; **to go to the ~** ans Meer fahren; **seaside resort** n Seebad nt

season ['siːzn] n Jahreszeit f; (Comm) Saison f; **high/low**

~ Hoch-/Nebensaison f ▷ vt (flavour) würzen

seasoning n Gewürz nt

season ticket n (Rail) Zeitkarte f; (Theat) Abonnement nt; (Sport) Dauerkarte f

seat [siːt] n (place) Platz m; (chair) Sitz m; **take a ~** setzen Sie sich ▷ vt: **the hall ~s 300** der Saal hat 300 Sitzplätze; **please be ~ed** bitte setzen Sie sich; **to remain ~ed** sitzen bleiben; **seat belt** n Sicherheitsgurt m

sea view ['siːvjuː] n Seeblick m; **seaweed** n Seetang m

secluded [sɪˈkluːdɪd] adj abgelegen

second ['sekənd] adj zweite(r, s); **the ~ of June** der zweite Juni ▷ adv (in ~ position) an zweiter Stelle; (secondly) zweitens; **he came ~** er ist Zweiter geworden ▷ n (of time) Sekunde f; (moment) Augenblick m; **~ (gear)** der zweite Gang; (~ helping) zweite Portion; **just a ~!** (einen) Augenblick!; **secondary** adj (less important) zweitrangig; **~ education** höhere Schulbildung f; **~ school** weiterführende Schule; **second-class** adj (ticket) zweiter Klasse; **~ stamp** Briefmarke für nicht bevorzugt beförderte Sendungen ▷ adv (travel) zweiter Klasse; **second-hand** adj, adv gebraucht; (information) aus zweiter Hand; **secondly** adv zweitens; **second-rate** adj (pej) zweitklassig

secret ['siːkrət] n Geheimnis nt ▷ adj geheim; (admirer) heimlich

secretary ['sekrətrɪ] n Sekretär(in) m(f); (minister) Minister(in) m(f); **Secretary of State** n (US) Außenminister(in) m(f); **secretary's office** n Sekretariat nt

secretive ['si:krətɪv] adj (person) geheimnisstuerisch; **secretly** ['si:krətlɪ] adv heimlich

sect [sekt] n Sekte f

section ['sekʃən] n (part) Teil m; (of document) Abschnitt m; (department) Abteilung f

secure [sɪ'kjʊə'] adj (safe) sicher (from vor +dat); (firmly fixed) fest ▷ vt (make firm) befestigen; (window, door) fest verschließen; **securely** adv fest; (safely) sicher; **security** [sɪ'kjʊərɪtɪ] n Sicherheit f

sedative ['sedətɪv] n Beruhigungsmittel nt

seduce [sɪ'dju:s] vt verführen; **seductive** [sɪ'dʌktɪv] adj verführerisch; (offer) verlockend

see [si:] (saw, seen) vt sehen; (understand) verstehen; (check) nachsehen; (accompany) bringen; (visit) besuchen; (talk to) sprechen; **to ~ the doctor** zum Arzt gehen; **to ~ sb home** jdn nach Hause begleiten; **I saw him swimming** ich habe ihn schwimmen sehen; **~ you** tschüs!; **~ you on Friday** bis Freitag! ▷ vi sehen; (understand) verstehen; (check) nachsehen; **(you) ~** siehst du; **we'll ~** mal sehen; **see about** vt (attend to) sich kümmern um; **see off** vt (say goodbye to) verabschieden; **see out** vt (show out) zur Tür bringen; **see through** vt: **to see sth through** etw zu Ende bringen; **to ~ sb/sth through** jdn/etw durchschauen; **see to** vt sich kümmern um; **~ it that ...** sieh zu, dass ...

seed [si:d] n (of plant) Samen m; (in fruit) Kern m; **seedless** adj kernlos

seedy ['si:dɪ] adj zwielichtig

seek [si:k] (sought, sought) vt suchen; (fame) streben nach; **to ~ sb's advice** jdn um Rat fragen

seem [si:m] vi scheinen; **he ~s (to be) honest** er scheint ehrlich zu sein; **it ~s to me that ...** es scheint mir, dass ...

seen [si:n] pp of **see**

seesaw ['si:sɔ:] n Wippe f

see-through adj durchsichtig

segment ['segmənt] n Teil m

seize [si:z] vt packen; (confiscate) beschlagnahmen; (opportunity, power) ergreifen

seldom ['seldəm] adv selten

select [sɪ'lekt] adj (exclusive) exklusiv ▷ vt auswählen; **selection** [sɪ'lekʃən] n Auswahl f (of an +dat); **selective** adj (choosy) wählerisch

self [self] (pl **selves**) n Selbst nt, Ich nt; **he's his old ~ again** er ist wieder ganz der Alte; **self-adhesive** adj selbstklebend; **self-assured** n selbstsicher; **self-catering** adj für Selbstversorger; **self-centred** adj egozentrisch; **self-confidence** n Selbstbewusstsein nt; **self-confident** adj selbstbewusst; **self-conscious** adj befangen, verklemmt; **self-contained** adj (flat) separat; **self-control** n Selbstbeherrschung f; **self-defence** n Selbstverteidigung f; **self-employed** adj selbstständig; **self-evident** adj offensichtlich

selfish adj, **selfishly** ['selfɪʃ, -lɪ] adj, adv egoistisch, selbstsüchtig; **selfless, selflessly** adj, adv selbstlos

self-pity ['self'pɪtɪ] n Selbstmitleid nt; **self-portrait** n Selbstporträt nt; **self-respect** n Selbstachtung f; **self-service** n Selbstbedienung f ▷ adj Selbstbedienungs-

sell [sel] (sold, sold) vt verkaufen; **to ~ sb sth, to ~ sth to**

sb jdm etw verkaufen; **do you ~ postcards?** haben Sie Postkarten? ▷ vi (product) sich verkaufen; **sell out** vt: **to be sold ~** ausverkauft sein; **sell-by date** n Haltbarkeitsdatum nt

Sellotape® ['seləʊteɪp] n (Brit) Tesafilm® m

semester [sɪ'mestə*] n Semester nt

semi ['semɪ] n (Brit: house) Doppelhaushälfte f; **semicircle** n Halbkreis m; **semicolon** n Semikolon nt; **semidetached (house)** n (Brit) Doppelhaushälfte f; **semifinal** n Halbfinale nt

seminar ['semɪnɑ:*] n Seminar nt

semiskimmed milk ['semɪskɪmd'mɪlk] n Halbfettmilch f

senate ['senət] n Senat m; **senator** n Senator(in) m(f)

send [send] (**sent, sent**) vt schicken; **to ~ sb sth, to ~ sth to sb** jdm etw schicken; **~ her my best wishes** grüße sie von mir; **send away** vt wegschicken ▷ vi: **to ~ for** anfordern; **send back** vt zurückschicken; **send for** vt (person) holen lassen; (by post) anfordern; **send off** vt (by post) abschicken; **send out** vt (invitations etc) verschicken ▷ vi: **to ~ for sth** etw holen lassen

sender ['sendə*] n Absender(in) m(f)

senior ['si:nɪə*] adj (older) älter; (high-ranking) höher; (pupils) älter; **he is ~ to me** er ist mir übergeordnet ▷ n: **he's eight years my ~** er ist acht Jahre älter als ich; **senior citizen** n Senior(in) m(f)

sensation [sen'seɪʃən] n Gefühl nt; (excitement, person, thing)

Sensation f; **sensational** adj sensationell

sense [sens] n (faculty, meaning) Sinn m; (feeling) Gefühl nt; (understanding) Verstand m; **~ of smell/taste** Geruchs-/ Geschmackssinn m; **to have a ~ of humour** Humor haben; **to make ~** (sentence etc) einen Sinn ergeben; (be sensible) Sinn machen; **in a ~** gewissermaßen ▷ vt spüren; **senseless** adj (stupid) sinnlos

sensible, sensibly ['sensəbl, -blɪ] adj, adv vernünftig

sensitive ['sensɪtɪv] adj empfindlich (to gegen); (easily hurt) sensibel; (subject) heikel

sensual ['sensjʊəl] adj sinnlich

sensuous ['sensjʊəs] adj sinnlich

sent [sent] pt, pp of **send**

sentence ['sentəns] n (Ling) Satz m; (Jur) Strafe f ▷ vt verurteilen (to zu)

sentiment ['sentɪmənt] n (sentimentality) Sentimentalität f; (opinion) Ansicht f; **sentimental** [sentɪ'mentl] adj sentimental

separate ['seprət] adj getrennt, separat; (individual) einzeln ▷ ['sepəreɪt] vt trennen (from von); **they are ~d** (couple) sie leben getrennt ▷ vi sich trennen; **separately** adv getrennt; (singly) einzeln

September [sep'tembə*] n September m; **in ~** im September; **on the 2nd of ~** am 2. September; **at the beginning/in the middle/at the end of ~** Anfang/Mitte/Ende September; **last/next ~** letzten/nächsten September

septic ['septɪk] adj vereitert

sequel ['si:kwəl] n (to film, book) Fortsetzung f (to von)

sequence ['si:kwəns] n (order) Reihenfolge f

Serbia ['sɜ:bjə] n Serbien nt

sergeant ['sɑ:dʒənt] n Polizeimeister(in) m(f); (Mil) Feldwebel(in) m(f)

serial ['sɪərɪəl] n (TV) Serie f; (in newspaper etc) Fortsetzungsroman m ▷ adj (Inform) seriell; **~ number** Seriennummer f

series ['sɪərɪz] nsing Reihe f; (TV, Radio) Serie f

serious ['sɪərɪəs] adj ernst; (injury, illness, mistake) schwer; (discussion) ernsthaft; **are you ~?** ist das dein Ernst?; **seriously** adv ernsthaft; (hurt) schwer; **~?** im Ernst?; **to take sb ~** jdn ernst nehmen

sermon ['sɜ:mən] n (Rel) Predigt f

servant ['sɜ:vənt] n Diener(in) m(f); **serve** [sɜ:v] vt (customer) bedienen; (food) servieren; (one's country etc) dienen +dat; (sentence) verbüßen; **I'm being ~d** ich werde schon bedient; **it ~s him right** es geschieht ihm recht ▷ vi dienen (as als), aufschlagen ▷ n Aufschlag m

server [Inform] Server m

service ['sɜ:vɪs] n (in shop, hotel) Bedienung f; (activity, amenity) Dienstleistung f; (set of dishes) Service n; (Auto) Inspektion f; (Tech) Wartung f; (Rel) Gottesdienst m, Aufschlag m; **train/bus ~** Zug-/Busverbindung f; **"~ not included"** „Bedienung nicht inbegriffen" ▷ vt (Auto, Tech) warten; **service area** n (on motorway) Raststätte f (mit Tankstelle); **service charge** n Bedienung f; **service provider** n (Inform) Provider m; **service station** n Tankstelle f

session ['seʃən] n (of court, assembly) Sitzung f

set [set] (**set, set**) vt (place) stellen; (lay flat) legen; (arrange) anordnen; (table) decken; (trap, record) aufstellen; (time, price) festsetzen; (watch, alarm) stellen (for auf +akk); **to ~ sb a task** jdm eine Aufgabe stellen; **to ~ free** freilassen; **to ~ a good example** ein gutes Beispiel geben; **the novel is ~ in London** der Roman spielt in London ▷ vi (sun) untergehen; (become hard) fest werden; (bone) zusammenwachsen ▷ n (collection of things) Satz m; (of cutlery, furniture) Garnitur f; (group of people) Kreis m; (Radio, TV) Apparat m, Satz m; (Theat) Bühnenbild nt; (Cine) (Film)kulisse f ▷ adj (agreed, prescribed) festgelegt; (ready) bereit; **~ meal** Menü nt; **set aside** vt (money) beiseitelegen; (time) einplanen; **set off** vi aufbrechen (for nach) ▷ vt (alarm) auslösen; (enhance) hervorheben; **set out** vi aufbrechen (for nach) ▷ vt (chairs, chesspieces etc) aufstellen; (state) darlegen; **to ~ to do sth** (intend) beabsichtigen, etw zu tun; **set up** vt (firm, organization) gründen; (stall, tent, camera) aufbauen; (meeting) vereinbaren ▷ vi: **to ~ as a doctor** sich als Arzt niederlassen

setback n Rückschlag m

settee [se'ti:] n Sofa nt, Couch f

setting ['setɪŋ] n (of novel, film) Schauplatz m; (surroundings) Umgebung f

settle ['setl] vt (bill, debt) begleichen; (dispute) beilegen; (question) klären; (stomach) beruhigen ▷ vi: **to ~ (down)** (feel at home) sich einleben; (calm down) sich beruhigen; **settle in** vi (in place) sich einleben; (in job) sich eingewöhnen; **settle up** vi (be)zahlen; **to ~ with sb** mit jdm

abrechnen; **settlement** n (of bill,
debt) Begleichung f; (colony)
Siedlung f; **to reach a ~** sich
einigen

setup ['sɛtʌp] n (organization)
Organisation f; (situation)
Situation f

seven ['sɛvn] num sieben ▷ n
Sieben f; see also **eight; seventeen**
['sɛvn'tiːn] num siebzehn ▷ n
Siebzehn f; see also **eight;
seventeenth** adj siebzehnte(r, s);
see also **eighth; seventh** ['sɛvnθ]
adj siebte(r, s) ▷ n (fraction)
Siebtel nt; see also **eighth;
seventieth** ['sɛvntɪθ] adj sieb-
zigste(r, s); see also **eighth;
seventy** ['sɛvntɪ] num siebzig;
~-one einundsiebzig ▷ n Siebzig
f; **to be in one's seventies** in den
Siebzigern sein; see also **eight**

several ['sɛvrəl] adj, pron
mehrere

severe [sɪ'vɪə*] adj (strict) streng;
(serious) schwer; (pain) stark;
(winter) hart; **severely** adv
(harshly) hart; (seriously) schwer

sew [səʊ] (**sewed, sewn**) vt, vi
nähen

sewage ['suːɪdʒ] n Abwasser nt;
sewer ['suːə*] n Abwasserkanal m

sewing ['səʊɪŋ] n Nähen nt;
sewing machine n Nähmaschine
f

sewn [səʊn] pp of **sew**

sex [sɛks] n Sex m; (gender)
Geschlecht nt; **to have ~** Sex
haben (with mit); **sexism**
['sɛksɪzəm] n Sexismus m; **sexist**
['sɛksɪst] adj sexistisch ▷ n Sex-
ist(in) m(f); **sex life** n
Sex(ual)leben nt

sexual ['sɛksjʊəl] adj sexuell;
~ discrimination/harassment
sexuelle Diskriminierung/
Belästigung; **~ intercourse**
Geschlechtsverkehr m; **sexuality**

[sɛksjʊ'ælɪtɪ] n Sexualität f;
sexually adv sexuell

sexy ['sɛksɪ] adj sexy, geil

Seychelles ['seɪʃelz] npl Seychellen pl

shabby ['ʃæbɪ] adj schäbig

shack [ʃæk] n Hütte f

shade [ʃeɪd] n (shadow) Schatten
m; (for lamp) (Lampen)schirm m;
(colour) Farbton m; **~s** (US:
sunglasses) Sonnenbrille f ▷ vt
(from sun) abschirmen; (in drawing)
schattieren

shadow ['ʃædəʊ] n Schatten m

shady ['ʃeɪdɪ] adj schattig; (fig)
zwielichtig

shake [ʃeɪk] (**shook, shaken**) vt
schütteln; (shock) erschüttern; **to
~ hands with sb** jdm die Hand
geben; **to ~ one's head** den Kopf
schütteln ▷ vi (tremble) zittern;
(building, ground) schwanken;
shake off vt abschütteln; **shaken**
['ʃeɪkn] pp of **shake**; **shaky** ['ʃeɪkɪ]
adj (trembling) zittrig; (table, chair,
position) wackelig; (weak) unsicher

shall [ʃæl] (**should**) vb aux
werden; (in questions) sollen; **I ~ do
my best** ich werde mein Bestes
tun; **~ I come too?** soll ich
mitkommen?; **where ~ we go?** wo
gehen wir hin?

shallow ['ʃæləʊ] adj (a. fig)
seicht; (person) oberflächlich

shame [ʃeɪm] n (feeling of ~)
Scham f; (disgrace) Schande f; **what
a ~!** wie schade!; **~ on you!** schäm
dich/schämen Sie sich!; **it's a
~ that ...** schade, dass ...

shampoo [ʃæm'puː] n Shampoo
nt; **to have a ~ and set** sich die
Haare waschen und legen lassen
▷ vt (hair) waschen; (carpet)
schamponieren

shandy ['ʃændɪ] n Radler m,
Alsterwasser nt

shan't [ʃɑːnt] contr of **shall not**

shape [ʃeɪp] n Form f;
(unidentified figure) Gestalt f; **in
the ~ of** in Form +gen; **to be in
good ~** (healthwise) in guter
Verfassung sein; **to take ~** (plan,
idea) Gestalt annehmen ▷ vt (clay,
person) formen; **-shaped** [ʃeɪpt]
suf -förmig; **shapeless** adj
formlos

share [ʃeə°] n Anteil +dat (in, of an
m); (Fin) Aktie f ▷ vt, vi teilen;
shareholder n Aktionär(in) m(f)

shark [ʃɑːk] n (Zool) Haifisch m

sharp [ʃɑːp] adj scharf; (pin) spitz;
(person) scharfsinnig; (pain) heftig;
(increase, fall) abrupt; **C/F ~** (Mus)
Cis/Dis nt ▷ adv: **at 2 o'clock
~** Punkt 2 Uhr; **sharpen** vt (knife)
schärfen; (pencil) spitzen;
sharpener n (pencil ~) Spitzer m

shatter [ˈʃætə°] vt zerschmet-
tern; (fig) zerstören ▷ vi
zerspringen; **shattered** adj
(exhausted) kaputt

shave [ʃeɪv] (shaved, shaved o
shaven) vt rasieren ▷ vi sich
rasieren ▷ n Rasur f; **that was a
close ~** (fig) das war knapp; **shave
off** vt: **to shave one's beard off**
sich den Bart abrasieren; **shaven**
[ˈʃeɪvn] pp of **shave** ▷ adj (head)
kahl geschoren; **shaver** n (Elec)
Rasierapparat m; **shaving brush**
n Rasierpinsel m; **shaving foam** n
Rasierschaum m; **shaving tackle**
n Rasierzeug nt

shawl [ʃɔːl] n Tuch nt

she [ʃiː] pron sie

shed [ʃed] (shed, shed) n
Schuppen m ▷ vt (tears, blood)
vergießen; (hair, leaves) verlieren

she'd [ʃiːd] contr of **she had; she
would**

sheep [ʃiːp] (pl -) n Schaf nt;
sheepdog n Schäferhund m;
sheepskin n Schaffell nt

sheer [ʃɪə°] adj (madness) rein;

(steep) steil; **by ~ chance** rein
zufällig

sheet [ʃiːt] n (on bed) Betttuch nt;
(of paper) Blatt nt; (of metal) Platte f;
(of glass) Scheibe f; **a ~ of paper**
ein Blatt Papier

shelf [ʃelf] (pl **shelves**) n
Bücherbord nt, Regal nt; **shelves** pl
(item of furniture) Regal nt

she'll [ʃiːl] contr of **she will; she
shall**

shell [ʃel] n (of egg, nut) Schale f;
(sea~) Muschel f ▷ vt (peas, nuts)
schälen; **shellfish** n (as food)
Meeresfrüchte pl

shelter [ˈʃeltə°] n (protection)
Schutz m; (accommodation)
Unterkunft f; (bus ~)
Wartehäuschen nt ▷ vt schützen
(from vor +dat) ▷ vi sich
unterstellen; **sheltered** adj (spot)
geschützt; (life) behütet

shelve [ʃelv] vt (fig) aufschieben;
shelves pl of **shelf**

shepherd [ˈʃepəd] n Schäfer m;
shepherd's pie n
Hackfleischauflauf mit Decke aus
Kartoffelpüree

sherry [ˈʃerɪ] n Sherry m

she's [ʃiːz] contr of **she is; she has**

shield [ʃiːld] n Schild m; (fig)
Schutz m ▷ vt schützen (from vor
+dat)

shift [ʃɪft] n (change)
Veränderung f; (period at work,
workers) Schicht f; (on keyboard)
Umschalttaste f ▷ vt (furniture etc)
verrücken; (stain) entfernen; **to
~ gear(s)** (US Auto) schalten ▷ vi
(move) sich bewegen; (move up)
rutschen; **shift key** n
Umschalttaste f

shin [ʃɪn] n Schienbein nt

shine [ʃaɪn] (shone, shone) vi
(be shiny) glänzen; (sun) scheinen;
(lamp) leuchten ▷ vt (polish)
polieren ▷ n Glanz m

shingles ['ʃɪŋglz] nsing (Med) Gürtelrose f

shiny ['ʃaɪnɪ] adj glänzend

ship [ʃɪp] n Schiff nt ▷ vt (send) versenden; (by ship) verschiffen; **shipment** n (goods) Sendung f; (sent by ship) Ladung f; **shipwreck** n Schiffbruch m; **shipyard** n Werft f

shirt [ʃɜːt] n Hemd nt

shit [ʃɪt] n (vulg) Scheiße f; (person) Arschloch nt; ~! Scheiße!; **shitty** ['ʃɪtɪ] adj (fam) beschissen

shiver ['ʃɪvə°] vi zittern (with vor +dat)

shock [ʃɒk] n (mental, emotional) Schock m; **to be in** ~ unter Schock stehen ▷ ~ (Elec) einen Schlag bekommen ▷ vt schockieren; **shock absorber** n Stoßdämpfer m; **shocked** adj schockiert (by über +akk); **shocking** adj schockierend; (awful) furchtbar

shoe [ʃuː] n Schuh m; **shoehorn** n Schuhlöffel m; **shoelace** n Schnürsenkel m; **shoe polish** n Schuhcreme f

shone [ʃɒn] pt, pp of **shine**

shook [ʃʊk] pt of **shake**

shoot [ʃuːt] (**shot, shot**) vt (wound) anschießen; (kill) erschießen; (Cine) drehen; (fam: heroin) drücken ▷ vi (with gun, move quickly) schießen; **to ~ at sb** auf jdn schießen ▷ n (of plant) Trieb m; **shooting** n (exchange of gunfire) Schießerei f; (killing) Erschießung f

shop [ʃɒp] n Geschäft nt, Laden m ▷ vi einkaufen; **shop assistant** n Verkäufer(in) m(f); **shopkeeper** n Geschäftsinhaber(in) m(f); **shoplifting** n Ladendiebstahl m; **shopper** n Käufer(in) m(f); **shopping** n (activity) Einkaufen nt; (goods) Einkäufe pl; **to do the**

~ einkaufen; **to go** ~ einkaufen gehen; **shopping bag** n Einkaufstasche f; **shopping cart** n (US) Einkaufswagen m; **shopping center** (US), **shopping centre** n Einkaufszentrum nt; **shopping list** n Einkaufszettel m; **shopping trolley** n (Brit) Einkaufswagen m; **shop window** n Schaufenster nt

shore [ʃɔː°] n Ufer nt; **on** ~ an Land

short [ʃɔːt] adj kurz; (person) klein; **to be** ~ **of money** knapp bei Kasse sein; **to be** ~ **of time** wenig Zeit haben; ~ **of breath** kurzatmig; **to cut** ~ (holiday) abbrechen; **we are two** ~ wir haben zwei zu wenig; **it's** ~ **for ...** das ist die Kurzform von ... ▷ n (drink, Elec) Kurze(r) m; **shortage** n Knappheit f (of an +dat); **shortbread** n Buttergebäck nt; **short circuit** n Kurzschluss m; **shortcoming** n Unzulänglichkeit f; (of person) Fehler m; **shortcut** n (quicker route) Abkürzung f; (Inform) Shortcut m; **shorten** vt kürzen; (in time) verkürzen; **shorthand** n Stenografie f; **shortlist** n: **to be on the** ~ in der engeren Wahl sein; **short-lived** adj kurzlebig; **shortly** adv bald; **shorts** npl Shorts pl; **short-sighted** adj (a. fig) kurzsichtig; **short-sleeved** adj kurzärmelig; **short-stay car park** n Kurzzeitparkplatz m; **short story** n Kurzgeschichte f; **short-term** adj kurzfristig; **short wave** n Kurzwelle f

shot [ʃɒt] pt, pp of **shoot** n (from gun, in football) Schuss m; (Foto, Cine) Aufnahme f; (injection) Spritze f; (of alcohol) Schuss m

should [ʃʊd] pt of **shall** ▷ vb aux: **I** ~ **go now** ich sollte jetzt gehen; **what** ~ **I do?** was soll ich tun?; **you** ~**n't have said that** das hättest du/hätten Sie nicht sagen sollen; **that ~ be enough** das müsste reichen

shoulder ['ʃəʊldə°] n Schulter f

shouldn't ['ʃʊdnt] contr of **should not**

should've ['ʃʊdəv] contr of **should have**

shout [ʃaʊt] n Schrei m; (call) Ruf m ▷ vt rufen; (order) brüllen ▷ vi schreien; **to ~ at** anschreien; **to ~ for help** um Hilfe rufen

shove [ʃʌv] vt (person) schubsen; (car, table etc) schieben ▷ vi (in crowd) drängeln

shovel ['ʃʌvl] n Schaufel f ▷ vt schaufeln

show [ʃəʊ] (showed, shown) vt zeigen; **to ~ sb sth, to ~ sth to sb** jdm etw zeigen; **to ~ sb in** jdn hereinführen; **to ~ sb out** jdn zur Tür bringen ▷ n (Cine, Theat) Vorstellung f; (TV) Show f; (exhibition) Ausstellung f; **show off** vi (pej) angeben; **show round** vt herumführen; **to show sb round the house/the town** jdm das Haus/die Stadt zeigen; **show up** vi (arrive) auftauchen

shower ['ʃaʊə°] n Dusche f; (rain) Schauer m; **to have** (o **take) a ~** duschen ▷ vi (wash) duschen; **~ gel** n Duschgel nt

showing ['ʃəʊɪŋ] n (Cine) Vorstellung f

shown [ʃəʊn] pp of **show**

showroom ['ʃəʊruːm] n Ausstellungsraum m

shrank [ʃræŋk] pt of **shrink**

shred [ʃred] n (of paper, fabric) Fetzen m ▷ vt (in shredder) (im Reißwolf) zerkleinern; **shredder** n (for paper) Reißwolf m

shrimp [ʃrɪmp] n Garnele f

shrink [ʃrɪŋk] (shrank, shrunk) vi schrumpfen; (clothes) eingehen

shrivel ['ʃrɪvl] vi: **to ~ (up)**

schrumpfen; (skin) runzlig werden; (plant) welken

Shrove Tuesday ['ʃrəʊv'tjuːzdeɪ] n Fastnachtsdienstag m

shrub [ʃrʌb] n Busch m, Strauch m

shrug [ʃrʌg] vt, vi: **to ~ (one's shoulders)** die Achseln zucken

shrunk [ʃrʌŋk] pp of **shrink**

shudder ['ʃʌdə°] vi schaudern; (ground, building) beben

shuffle ['ʃʌfl] vt, vi mischen

shut [ʃʌt] (shut, shut) vt zumachen, schließen; **~ your face!** (fam) halt den Mund! ▷ vi schließen ▷ adj geschlossen; **we're ~** wir haben geschlossen; **shut down** vt schließen ▷ vi schließen; (computer) sich ausschalten; **shut in** vt einschließen; **shut out** vt (lock out) aussperren; **to shut oneself out** sich aussperren; **shut up** vt (lock up) abschließen; (silence) zum Schweigen bringen ▷ vi (keep quiet) den Mund halten; **~!** halt den Mund!; **shutter** n (on window) (Fenster)laden m; **shutter release** n Auslöser m; **shutter speed** n Belichtungszeit f

shuttle bus ['ʃʌtlbʌs] n Shuttlebus m

shuttlecock ['ʃʌtlkɒk] n Federball m

shuttle service ['ʃʌtlsɜːvɪs] n Pendelverkehr m

shy [ʃaɪ] adj schüchtern; (animal) scheu

Siberia [saɪ'bɪərɪə] n Sibirien nt

Sicily ['sɪsɪlɪ] n Sizilien nt

sick [sɪk] adj krank; (joke) makaber; **to be ~** (Brit: vomit) sich übergeben; **to be off ~** wegen Krankheit fehlen; **I feel ~** mir ist schlecht; **to be ~ of sb/sth** jdn/etw satthaben; **it makes me**

~ (fig) es ekelt mich an; **sickbag** n
Spucktüte f; **sick leave** n: **to be
on ~** krankgeschrieben sein;
sickness n Krankheit f; (Brit:
nausea) Übelkeit f; **sickness
benefit** n (Brit) Krankengeld nt

side [saɪd] n Seite f; (of road) Rand
m; (of mountain) Hang m; (Sport)
Mannschaft f; **by my ~** neben mir;
~ by ~ nebeneinander ▷ adj (door)
Seiten-; **sideboard** n Anrichte f;
sideburns npl Koteletten pl; **side
dish** n Beilage f; **side effect** n
Nebenwirkung f; **sidelight** n (Brit
Auto) Parklicht nt; **side order** n
Beilage f; **side road** n Nebenstraße f; **side street** n Seitenstraße
f; **sidewalk** n (US) Bürgersteig m;
sideways adv seitwärts

sieve [sɪv] n Sieb nt

sift [sɪft] vt (flour etc) sieben

sigh [saɪ] n Seufzer m ▷ vi seufzen

sight [saɪt] n (power of seeing)
Sehvermögen nt; (view, thing seen)
Anblick m; **~s** pl (of city etc)
Sehenswürdigkeiten pl; **to have
bad ~** schlecht sehen; **to lose ~ of**
aus den Augen verlieren; **out of
~** außer Sicht; **sightseeing** n: **to
go ~** Sehenswürdigkeiten
besichtigen; **~ tour** Rundfahrt f

sign [saɪn] n Zeichen nt; (notice,
road ~) Schild nt ▷ vt
unterschreiben ▷ vi unterschreiben; **to ~ for sth** den
Empfang einer Sache gen
bestätigen; **to ~ in/out** sich
ein-/austragen; **sign on** vi (Brit:
register as unemployed) sich
arbeitslos melden; **sign up** vi (for
course) sich einschreiben; (Mil) sich
verpflichten

signal ['sɪɡnl] n Signal nt ▷ vi
(car driver) blinken

signature ['sɪɡnətʃə°] n Unterschrift f

significant [sɪɡ'nɪfɪkənt] adj
(important) bedeutend, wichtig;
(meaning sth) bedeutsam;
significantly adv (considerably)
bedeutend

sign language ['saɪnlæŋɡwɪdʒ]
n Zeichensprache f; **signpost** n
Wegweiser m

silence ['saɪləns] n Stille f; (of
person) Schweigen nt; **~!** Ruhe! ▷ vt
zum Schweigen bringen; **silent**
adj still; (taciturn) schweigsam;
she remained ~ sie schwieg

silk [sɪlk] n Seide f ▷ adj Seiden-

silly ['sɪlɪ] adj dumm, albern;
don't do anything ~ mach keine
Dummheiten; **the ~ season** n
Sommerloch

silver ['sɪlvə°] n Silber nt; (coins)
Silbermünzen pl ▷ adj
Silber-, silbern; **silver-plated** adj
versilbert; **silver wedding** n
silberne Hochzeit

SIM card ['sɪm-] n (Tel) SIM-Karte f

similar ['sɪmɪlə°] adj ähnlich (to
dat); **similarity** [sɪmɪ'lærɪtɪ] n
Ähnlichkeit f (to mit); **similarly**
adv (equally) ebenso

simple ['sɪmpl] adj einfach;
(unsophisticated) schlicht; **simplify**
['sɪmplɪfaɪ] vt vereinfachen;
simply adv einfach; (merely) bloß;
(dress) schlicht

simulate ['sɪmjʊleɪt] vt
simulieren

simultaneous, simultaneously
[sɪməl'teɪnɪəs, -lɪ] adj, adv
gleichzeitig

sin [sɪn] n Sünde f ▷ vi sündigen

since [sɪns] adv seitdem; (in the
meantime) inzwischen ▷ prep seit
+dat; **ever ~ 1995** schon seit 1995
▷ conj (time) seit, seitdem;
(because) da, weil; **ever ~ I've
known her** seit ich sie kenne; **it's
ages ~ I've seen him** ich habe
ihn seit Langem nicht mehr
gesehen

sincere [sɪn'sɪə°] *adj* aufrichtig;
sincerely *adv* aufrichtig;
Yours ~ mit freundlichen
Grüßen

sing [sɪŋ] **(sang, sung)** *vt, vi*
singen

Singapore [sɪŋgə'pɔ:°] *n* Singapur *nt*

singer ['sɪŋə°] *n* Sänger(in) *m(f)*

single ['sɪŋgl] *adj (one only)*
einzig; *(not double)* einfach; *(bed,
room)* Einzel–; *(unmarried)* ledig;
(Brit: ticket) einfach ▷ *n (Brit:
ticket)* einfache Fahrkarte; *(Mus)*
Single *f*; **a ~ to London, please**
(Brit Rail) einfach nach London,
bitte; **single out** *vt (choose)*
auswählen; **single-handed**,
single-handedly *adv* im
Alleingang; **single parent** *n*
Alleinerziehende(r) *mf*; **single
supplement** *n (for hotel room)*
Einzelzimmerzuschlag *m*

singular ['sɪŋgjʊlə°] *n* Singular
m

sinister ['sɪnɪstə°] *adj*
unheimlich

sink [sɪŋk] **(sank, sunk)** *vt (ship)*
versenken ▷ *vi* sinken ▷ *n*
Spülbecken *nt*; *(in bathroom)*
Waschbecken *nt*

sip [sɪp] *vt* nippen an +*dat*

sir [sɜ:°] *n*: **yes, ~** ja(, mein Herr);
can I help you, ~? kann ich Ihnen
helfen?; **Sir James** *(title)* Sir James

sister ['sɪstə°] *n* Schwester *f*;
(Brit: nurse) Oberschwester *f*;
sister-in-law *(pl* **sisters-in-law)** *n*
Schwägerin *f*

sit [sɪt] **(sat, sat)** *vi (be sitting)*
sitzen; *(~ down)* sich setzen;
(committee, court) tagen ▷ *vt (Brit:
exam)* machen; **sit down** *vi* sich
hinsetzen; **sit up** *vi (from lying
position)* sich aufsetzen

sitcom ['sɪtkɒm] *n* Situ-
ationskomödie *f*

site [saɪt] *n* Platz *m*; *(building ~)*
Baustelle *f*; *(web~)* Site *f*

sitting ['sɪtɪŋ] *n (meeting, for
portrait)* Sitzung *f*; **sitting room** *n*
Wohnzimmer *nt*

situated ['sɪtjʊeɪtɪd] *adj*: **to be
~** liegen

situation [sɪtjʊ'eɪʃən] *n (circum-
stances)* Situation *f*, Lage *f*; *(job)*
Stelle *f*; **"~s vacant/wanted"** *(Brit)*
„Stellenangebote/Stellengesuche"

six [sɪks] *num* sechs ▷ *n* Sechs *f*;
see also **eight**; **sixpack** *n (of beer
etc)* Sechserpack *m*; **sixteen**
['sɪks'ti:n] *num* sechzehn ▷ *n*
Sechzehn *f*; *see also* **eight**;
sixteenth *adj* sechzehnte(r, s); *see
also* **eighth**; **sixth** [sɪksθ] *adj*
sechste(r, s); **~ form** *(Brit)* =
Oberstufe *f* ▷ *n (fraction)* Sechstel
nt; *see also* **eighth**; **sixtieth**
['sɪkstɪɪθ] *adj* sechzigste(r, s); *see
also* **eighth**; **sixty** ['sɪkstɪ] *num*
sechzig; **~-one** einundsechzig ▷ *n*
Sechzig *f*; **to be in one's sixties** in
den Sechzigern sein; *see also* **eight**

size [saɪz] *n* Größe *f*; **what ~ are
you?** welche Größe hast du/haben
Sie?; **a ~ too big** eine Nummer zu
groß

sizzle ['sɪzl] *vi (Gastr)* brutzeln

skate [skeɪt] *n* Schlittschuh *m*;
(roller ~) Rollschuh *m* ▷ *vi*
Schlittschuh laufen; *(roller~)*
Rollschuh laufen; **skateboard** *n*
Skateboard *nt*; **skating** *n* Eislauf
m; *(roller~)* Rollschuhlauf *m*;
skating rink *n* Eisbahn *f*; *(for
roller-skating)* Rollschuhbahn *f*

skeleton ['skelɪtn] *n (a. fig)*
Skelett *n*

skeptical *n (US) see* **sceptical**

sketch [sketʃ] *n* Skizze *f*; *(Theat)*
Sketch *m* ▷ *vt* skizzieren;
sketchbook *n* Skizzenbuch *n*

ski [ski:] *n* Ski *m* ▷ *vi* Ski laufen;
ski boot *n* Skistiefel *m*

skid [skɪd] vi (Auto) schleudern

skier ['skiːəʳ] n Skiläufer(in) m(f);
skiing n Skilaufen nt; **to go ~** Ski
laufen gehen; **~ holiday** Skiurlaub
m; **skiing instructor** n
Skilehrer(in) m(f)

skilful, skilfully ['skɪlfʊl, -fəlɪ]
adj, adv geschickt

ski-lift ['skiːlɪft] n Skilift m

skill [skɪl] n Geschick nt; (acquired
technique) Fertigkeit f; **skilled** adj
geschickt (at, in in +dat); (worker)
Fach-; (work) fachmännisch

skim [skɪm] vt: **to ~ (off)** (fat etc)
abschöpfen; **to ~ (through)** (read)
überfliegen; (meal) ausfallen
lassen; (school, lesson) schwänzen

ski pants ['skiːpænts] npl
Skihose f; **ski pass** n Skipass m;
ski pole n Skistock m; **ski resort**
n Skiort m

skirt [skɜːt] n Rock m

ski run ['skiːrʌn] n (Ski)abfahrt
f; **ski stick** n Skistock m; **ski tow**
n Schlepplift m

skittle ['skɪtl] n Kegel m; **~s**
(game) Kegeln nt

skive [skaɪv] vi: **to ~ (off)** (Brit)
(from school) schwänzen; (from
work) blaumachen

skull [skʌl] n Schädel m

sky [skaɪ] n Himmel m;
skydiving n Fallschirmspringen
nt; **skylight** n Dachfenster nt;
skyscraper n Wolkenkratzer m

slam [slæm] vt (door) zuschlagen;
slam on vt: **to slam the brakes
on** voll auf die Bremse treten

slander ['slɑːndəʳ] n Verleumdung f ▷ vt verleumden

slang [slæŋ] n Slang m

slap [slæp] n Klaps m; (across face)
Ohrfeige f ▷ vt schlagen; **to ~ sb's
face** jdn ohrfeigen

slash [slæʃ] n (punctuation mark)
Schrägstrich m ▷ vt (face, tyre)
aufschlitzen; (prices) stark
herabsetzen

slate [sleɪt] n (rock) Schiefer m;
(roof~) Schieferplatte f

slaughter ['slɔːtəʳ] vt (animals)
schlachten; (people) abschlachten

Slav [slɑːv] adj slawisch ▷ n
Slawe m, Slawin f

slave [sleɪv] n Sklave m, Sklavin f;
slave away vi schuften;
slave-driver n (fam)
Sklaventreiber(in) m(f); **slavery**
['sleɪvərɪ] n Sklaverei f

sleaze [sliːz] n (corruption)
Korruption f; **sleazy** adj (bar,
district) zwielichtig

sledge [sledʒ] n Schlitten m

sleep [sliːp] (**slept, slept**) n
schlafen; **to ~ with sb** mit jdm
schlafen ▷ n Schlaf m; **to put to
~** (animal) einschläfern; **sleep in** vi
(lie in) ausschlafen; **sleeper** n
(Rail: train) Schlafwagenzug m;
(carriage) Schlafwagen m; **sleeping
bag** n Schlafsack m; **sleeping car**
n Schlafwagen m; **sleeping pill** n
Schlaftablette f; **sleepless** adj
schlaflos; **sleepover** n Übernachtung f (bei Freunden etc); **sleepy** adj
schläfrig; (place) verschlafen

sleet [sliːt] n Schneeregen m

sleeve [sliːv] n Ärmel m;
sleeveless adj ärmellos

sleigh [sleɪ] n (Pferde)schlitten m

slender ['slendəʳ] adj schlank;
(fig) gering

slept [slept] pt, pp of **sleep**

slice [slaɪs] n Scheibe f; (of cake,
tart, pizza) Stück nt ▷ vt: **to ~ (up)**
in Scheiben schneiden; **sliced
bread** n geschnittenes Brot

slid [slɪd] pt, pp of **slide**

slide [slaɪd] (**slid, slid**) vt gleiten lassen; (push) schieben ▷ vi gleiten; (slip) rutschen ▷ n (Foto) Dia nt; (in playground) Rutschbahn f; (Brit: for hair) Spange f

slight [slaɪt] adj leicht; (problem, difference) klein; **not in the ~est** nicht im Geringsten; **slightly** adv etwas; (injured) leicht

slim [slɪm] adj (person) schlank; (book) dünn; (chance, hope) gering ▷ vi abnehmen

slime [slaɪm] n Schleim m; **slimy** adj schleimig

sling [slɪŋ] (**slung, slung**) vt werfen ▷ n (for arm) Schlinge f

slip [slɪp] n (mistake) Flüchtigkeitsfehler m; **~ of paper** Zettel m ▷ vt (put) stecken; to **~ on/off** (garment) an-/ausziehen; **it ~ped my mind** ich habe es vergessen ▷ vi (lose balance) (aus)rutschen; **slip away** vi (leave) sich wegstehlen; **slipper** n Hausschuh m; **slippery** adj (path, road) glatt; (soap, fish) glitschig; **slip-road** n (Brit: onto motorway) Auffahrt f; (off motorway) Ausfahrt f

slit [slɪt] (**slit, slit**) vt aufschlitzen ▷ n Schlitz m

slope [sləʊp] n Neigung f; (side of hill) Hang m ▷ vi (be sloping) schräg sein; **sloping** adj (floor, roof) schräg

sloppy [ˈslɒpɪ] adj (careless) schlampig; (sentimental) rührselig

slot [slɒt] n (opening) Schlitz m; (Inform) Steckplatz m; **we have a ~ free at 2** (free time) um 2 ist noch ein Termin frei; **slot machine** n Automat m; (for gambling) Spielautomat m

Slovak [ˈsləʊvæk] adj slowakisch ▷ n (person) Slowake m, Slowakin f; (language) Slowakisch nt; **Slovakia** [sləʊˈvækɪə] n Slowakei f

Slovene [ˈsləʊviːn], **Slovenian** [sləʊˈviːnɪən] adj slowenisch ▷ n (person) Slowene m, Slowenin f; (language) Slowenisch nt; **Slovenia** [sləʊˈviːnɪə] n Slowenien nt

slow [sləʊ] adj langsam; (business) flau; **to be ~** (clock) nachgehen; (stupid) begriffsstutzig sein; **slow down** vi langsamer werden; (when driving/walking) langsamer fahren/gehen; **slowly** adv langsam; **slow motion**: **in ~** in Zeitlupe

slug [slʌg] n (Zool) Nacktschnecke f

slum [slʌm] n Slum m

slump [slʌmp] n Rückgang m (in an +dat) ▷ vi (onto chair etc) sich fallen lassen; (prices) stürzen

slung [slʌŋ] pt, pp of **sling**

slur [slɜː] n (insult) Verleumdung f; **slurred** [slɜːd] adj undeutlich

slush [slʌʃ] n (snow) Schneematsch m

slut [slʌt] n (pej) Schlampe f

smack [smæk] n Klaps m ▷ vt: **to ~ sb** jdm einen Klaps geben ▷ vi: **to ~ of** riechen nach

small [smɔːl] adj klein; **small ads** npl (Brit) Kleinanzeigen pl; **small change** n Kleingeld nt; **small letters** npl: **in ~** in Kleinbuchstaben; **smallpox** n Pocken pl; **small print**: **the ~** das Kleingedruckte; **small-scale** adj (map) in kleinem Maßstab; **small talk** n Konversation f, Smalltalk m

smart [smɑːt] adj (elegant) schick; (clever) clever; **smartarse**, **smartass** (US) n (fam) Klugscheißer m/f(m); **smart card** n Chipkarte f; **smartly** adv (dressed) schick; **smartphone** n (Tel) Smartphone nt

smash [smæʃ] n (car crash) Zusammenstoß m, Schmetterball *m* ⊳ *vt* (*break*) zerschlagen; (*fig: record*) brechen, deutlich übertreffen ⊳ *vi* (*break*) zerbrechen; **to ~ into** (*car*) krachen gegen

smear [smɪəʳ] *n* (*mark*) Fleck *m*; (*Med*) Abstrich *m*; (*fig*) Verleumdung *f* ⊳ *vt* (*spread*) schmieren; (*make dirty*) beschmieren; (*fig*) verleumden

smell [smɛl] (**smelt** *o* **smelled, smelt** *o* **smelled**) *vt* riechen ⊳ *vi* riechen (*of* nach); (*unpleasantly*) stinken ⊳ *n* Geruch *m*; (*unpleasant*) Gestank *m*; **smelly** *adj* übel riechend; **smelt** [smɛlt] *pt, pp* of **smell**

smile [smaɪl] *n* Lächeln *nt* ⊳ *vi* lächeln; **to ~ at sb** jdn anlächeln

smock [smɒk] *n* Kittel *m*

smog [smɒg] *n* Smog *m*

smoke [sməʊk] *n* Rauch *m* ⊳ *vi* rauchen; (*food*) räuchern ⊳ *vi* rauchen; **smoke alarm** *n* Rauchmelder *m*; **smoked** *adj* (*food*) geräuchert; **smoke-free** *adj* (*zone, building*) rauchfrei; **smoker** *n* Raucher(in) *m(f)*; **smoking** *n* Rauchen *nt*; **"no ~"** „Rauchen verboten"

smooth [smuːð] *adj* glatt; (*flight, crossing*) ruhig; (*movement*) geschmeidig; (*without problems*) reibungslos; (*pej: person*) aalglatt ⊳ *vt* (*hair, dress*) glatt streichen; (*surface*) glätten; **smoothly** *adv* reibungslos; **to run ~** (*engine*) ruhig laufen

smudge [smʌdʒ] *vt* (*writing, lipstick*) verschmieren

smug [smʌg] *adj* selbstgefällig

smuggle [ˈsmʌgl] *vt* schmuggeln; **to ~ in/out** herein-/herausschmuggeln

smutty [ˈsmʌtɪ] *adj* (*obscene*) schmutzig

snack [snæk] *n* Imbiss *m*; **to have**

a ~ eine Kleinigkeit essen; **snack bar** *n* Imbissstube *f*

snail [sneɪl] *n* Schnecke *f*; **snail mail** *n* (*fam*) Schneckenpost *f*

snake [sneɪk] *n* Schlange *f*

snap [snæp] *n* (*photo*) Schnappschuss *m* ⊳ *adj* (*decision*) spontan ⊳ *vt* (*break*) zerbrechen; (*rope*) zerreißen ⊳ *vi* (*break*) brechen; (*rope*) reißen; (*bite*) schnappen (*at* nach); **snap off** *vt* (*break*) abbrechen; **snap fastener** *n* (US) Druckknopf *m*; **snapshot** *n* Schnappschuss *m*

snatch [snætʃ] *vt* (*grab*) schnappen

sneak [sniːk] *vi* (*move*) schleichen; **sneakers** *npl* (US) Turnschuhe *pl*

sneeze [sniːz] *vi* niesen

sniff [snɪf] *vi* schniefen; (*smell*) schnüffeln (*at* an +*dat*) ⊳ *vt* schnuppern an +*dat*; (*glue*) schnüffeln

snob [snɒb] *n* Snob *m*; **snobbish** *adj* versnobt

snog [snɒg] *vi, vt* knutschen

snooker [ˈsnuːkəʳ] *n* Snooker *nt*

snoop [snuːp] *vi*: **to ~ (around)** (herum)schnüffeln

snooze [snuːz] *n, vi*: **to (have a) ~** ein Nickerchen machen

snore [snɔːʳ] *vi* schnarchen

snorkel [ˈsnɔːkl] *n* Schnorchel *m*; **snorkelling** *n* Schnorcheln *nt*; **to go ~** schnorcheln gehen

snout [snaʊt] *n* Schnauze *f*

snow [snəʊ] *n* Schnee *m* ⊳ *vi* schneien; **snowball** *n* Schneeball *m*; **snowboard** *n* Snowboard *nt*; **snowboarding** *n* Snowboarding *nt*; **snowdrift** *n* Schneewehe *f*; **snowdrop** *n* Schneeglöckchen *nt*; **snowflake** *n* Schneeflocke *f*; **snowman** (*pl* **-men**) *n* Schneemann *m*; **snowplough,**

s

snowplow (US) n Schneepflug m;
snowstorm n Schneesturm m;
snowy adj (region) schneereich;
(landscape) verschneit

snug [snʌg] adj (person, place)
gemütlich

snuggle up ['snʌglʌp] vi: **to
~ to sb** sich an jdn ankuscheln

O **KEYWORD**

so [səʊ] adv 1 (thus) so; (likewise)
auch; **so saying he walked away**
indem er das sagte, ging er; **if so**
wenn ja; **I didn't do it — you did
so!** ich hab das nicht gemacht —
hast du wohl!; **so do I, so am I** etc
ich auch; **so it is!** tatsächlich!; **I
hope/think so** hoffentlich/ich
glaube schon; **so far** bis jetzt
2 (in comparisons etc: to such a
degree) so; **so quickly/big (that)**
so schnell/groß, dass; **I'm so glad
to see you** ich freue mich so,
dich/Sie zu sehen
3 **so many** so viele; **so much work**
so viel Arbeit; **I love you so much**
ich liebe dich so sehr
4 (phrases): **or so** etwa 10; **so
long!** (inf) (goodbye) tschüss!
▷ conj 1 (expressing reason) **so as to**
um ... zu; **so (that)** damit
2 (expressing result) also; **so I was
right after all** ich hatte also doch
recht; **so you see ...** wie du
siehst/Sie sehen ...

soak [səʊk] vt durchnässen;
(leave in liquid) einweichen; **I'm ~ed**
ich bin klatschnass; **soaking** adj:
~ (**wet**) klatschnass

soap [səʊp] n Seife f; **soap**
(opera) n Seifenoper f; **soap
powder** n Waschpulver nt

sob [sɒb] vi schluchzen

sober ['səʊbə'] adj nüchtern;
sober up vi nüchtern werden

so-called ['səʊ'kɔːld] adj
sogenannt

soccer ['sɒkə'] n Fußball m

sociable ['səʊʃəbl] adj gesellig

social ['səʊʃəl] adj sozial;
(sociable) gesellig; **socialist** adj
sozialistisch ▷ n Sozialist(in)
m(f); **socialize** vi unter die Leute
gehen; **social networking** n
Netzwerken nt; **social security** n
(Brit) Sozialhilfe f; (US)
Sozialversicherung f

society [sə'saɪətɪ] n Gesellschaft
f; (club) Verein m

sock [sɒk] n Socke f

socket ['sɒkɪt] n (Elec) Steckdose
f

soda ['səʊdə] n (~ water) Soda f;
(US: pop) Limo f; **soda water** n
Sodawasser nt

sofa ['səʊfə] n Sofa nt; **sofa bed**
n Schlafcouch f

soft [sɒft] adj weich; (quiet) leise;
(lighting) gedämpft; (kind)
gutmütig; (weak) nachgiebig;
~ **drink** alkoholfreies Getränk;
softly adv sanft; (quietly) leise;
software n (Inform) Software f

soil [sɔɪl] n Erde f; (ground) Boden
m

solar ['səʊlə'] adj Sonnen-, Solar-
solarium [sə'lɛərɪəm] n
Solarium nt

sold [səʊld] pt, pp of **sell**

soldier ['səʊldʒə'] n Soldat(in)
m(f)

sole [səʊl] n Sohle f; (fish)
Seezunge f ▷ vt besohlen ▷ adj
einzig; (owner, responsibility)
alleinig; **solely** adv nur

solemn ['sɒləm] adj feierlich;
(person) ernst

solicitor [sə'lɪsɪtə'] n (Brit)
Rechtsanwalt m, Rechtsanwältin f

solid ['sɒlɪd] adj (hard) fest; (gold,
oak etc) massiv; (-ly built) solide;
(meal) kräftig

solitary ['sɒlɪtərɪ] adj einsam; (single) einzeln; **solitude** ['sɒlɪtjuːd] n Einsamkeit f

solo ['səʊləʊ] n (Mus) Solo nt

soluble ['sɒljʊbl] adj löslich; **solution** [sə'luːʃən] n Lösung f (to +gen); **solve** [sɒlv] vt lösen

somber (US), **sombre** ['sɒmbə°] adj düster

○ **KEYWORD**

some [sʌm] adj 1 (a certain amount o number of) einige; (a few) ein paar; (with singular nouns) etwas; **some tea/biscuits** etwas Tee/ein paar Kekse; **I've got some money, but not much** ich habe ein bisschen Geld, aber nicht viel
2 (certain: in contrasts) manche(r, s); **some people say that ...** manche Leute sagen, dass ...
3 (unspecified) irgendein(e); **some woman was asking for you** da hat eine Frau nach dir/Ihnen gefragt; **some day** eines Tages; **some day next week** irgendwann nächste Woche
▷ pron 1 (a certain number) einige; **have you got some?** hast du/haben Sie welche?
2 (a certain amount) etwas; **I've read some of the book** ich habe das Buch teilweise gelesen
▷ adv: **some 10 people** etwa 10 Leute

somebody pron jemand; **~ (or other)** irgendjemand; **~ else** jemand anders; **someday** adv irgendwann; **somehow** adv irgendwie; **someone** pron see **somebody**; **someplace** adv (US) see **somewhere**; **something** ['sʌmθɪŋ] pron etwas; **~ (or other)** irgendetwas; **~ else** etwas anderes; **~ nice** etwas Nettes;

would you like ~ to drink? möchtest du/möchten Sie etwas trinken? ▷ adv: **~ like 20** ungefähr 20; **sometime** adv irgendwann; **sometimes** adv manchmal; **somewhat** adv ein wenig; **somewhere** adv irgendwo; (to a place) irgendwohin; **~ else** irgendwo anders; (to another place) irgendwo anders hin

son [sʌn] n Sohn m

song [sɒŋ] n Lied nt; Song m

son-in-law ['sʌnɪnlɔː] n (pl **sons-in-law**) n Schwiegersohn m

soon [suːn] adv bald; (early) früh; **too ~** zu früh; **as ~ as I ...** sobald ich ...; **as ~ as possible** so bald wie möglich; **sooner** adv (time) früher; (for preference) lieber

soot [sʊt] n Ruß m

soothe [suːð] vt beruhigen; (pain) lindern

sophisticated [sə'fɪstɪkeɪtɪd] adj (person) kultiviert; (machine) hoch entwickelt; (plan) ausgeklügelt

sophomore ['sɒfəmɔː°] n (US) College-Student(in) m(f) im zweiten Jahr

soppy ['sɒpɪ] adj (fam) rührselig

soprano [sə'prɑːnəʊ] n Sopran m

sore [sɔː°] adj: **to be ~** wehtun; **to have a ~ throat** Halsschmerzen haben ▷ n wunde Stelle

sorrow ['sɒrəʊ] n Kummer m

sorry ['sɒrɪ] adj (sight, figure) traurig; (I'm) ~ (excusing) Entschuldigung!; **I'm ~** (regretful) es tut mir leid; **~? wie bitte?; I feel ~ for him** er tut mir leid

sort [sɔːt] n Art f; **what ~ of film is it?** was für ein Film ist das?; **a ~ of** eine Art +gen; **all ~s of things** alles Mögliche ▷ adv: **~ of** (fam) irgendwie ▷ vt sortieren; **everything's ~ed** (dealt with) alles ist geregelt; **sort out** vt (classify etc) sortieren; (problems) lösen

sought [sɔːt] pt, pp of **seek**

soul [səʊl] n Seele f; (music) Soul m

sound [saʊnd] adj (healthy) gesund; (safe) sicher; (sensible) vernünftig; (theory) stichhaltig; (thrashing) tüchtig ▷ n (noise) Geräusch nt; (Mus) Klang m; (TV) Ton m ▷ vt: **to ~ the alarm** Alarm schlagen; **to ~ one's horn** hupen ▷ vi (alarm) klingen (like wie); **soundcard** n (Inform) Soundkarte f; **sound effects** npl Klangeffekte pl; **soundproof** adj schalldicht; **soundtrack** n (of film) Filmmusik f, Soundtrack m

soup [suːp] n Suppe f

sour ['saʊə] adj sauer; (fig) mürrisch

source [sɔːs] n Quelle f; (fig) Ursprung m

sour cream [saʊə'kriːm] n saure Sahne

south [saʊθ] n Süden m; **to the ~ of** südlich von ▷ adv (go, face) nach Süden ▷ adj Süd-; **South Africa** n Südafrika nt; **South African** adj südafrikanisch ▷ n Südafrikaner(in) m(f); **South America** n Südamerika nt; **South American** adj südamerikanisch ▷ n Südamerikaner(in) m(f); **southbound** adj (in) Richtung Süden; **southern** ['sʌðən] adj Süd-, südlich; **~ Europe** Südeuropa nt; **southwards** ['saʊθwədz] adv nach Süden

souvenir [suːvə'nɪə] n Andenken nt (of an +akk)

sow [səʊ] (**sowed, sown** o **sowed**) vt (a. fig) säen; (field) besäen ▷ [saʊ] n (pig) Sau f

soya bean ['sɔɪə'biːn] n Sojabohne f

soy sauce ['sɔɪ'sɔːs] n Sojasoße f

spa [spaː] n (place) Kurort m

space [speɪs] n (room) Platz m, Raum m; (outer ~) Weltraum m; (gap) Zwischenraum m; (for parking) Lücke f; **space bar** n Leertaste f; **spacecraft** (pl ~) n Raumschiff nt; **space ship** n Raumschiff nt; **space shuttle** n Raumfähre f

spacing ['speɪsɪŋ] n (in text) Zeilenabstand m; **double ~** zweizeiliger Abstand

spacious ['speɪʃəs] adj geräumig

spade [speɪd] n Spaten m; **~s** Pik nt

spaghetti [spə'getɪ] nsing Spaghetti pl

Spain [speɪn] n Spanien nt

spam [spæm] n (Inform) Spam m

Spaniard ['spænɪəd] n Spanier(in) m(f); **Spanish** ['spænɪʃ] adj spanisch ▷ n (language) Spanisch nt

spanner ['spænə] n (Brit) Schraubenschlüssel m

spare [speə] adj (as replacement) Ersatz-; **~ part** Ersatzteil nt; **~ room** Gästezimmer nt; **~ time** Freizeit f; **~ tyre** Ersatzreifen m ▷ n (~ part) Ersatzteil nt ▷ vt (lives, feelings) verschonen; **can you ~ (me) a moment?** hättest du/hätten Sie einen Moment Zeit?

spark [spaːk] n Funke m; **sparkle** ['spaːkl] vi funkeln; **sparkling wine** n Schaumwein m, Sekt m; **spark plug** n ['spaːkplʌg] n Zündkerze f

sparrow ['spærəʊ] n Spatz m

sparse [spaːs] adj spärlich; **sparsely** adv: **~ populated** dünn besiedelt

spasm ['spæzəm] n Krampf m

spat [spæt] pt, pp of **spit**

speak [spiːk] (**spoke, spoken**) vt sprechen; **can you ~ French?** sprechen Sie Französisch?; **to**

~ one's mind seine Meinung sagen ▷ vi sprechen (to mit, zu); (make speech) reden; **~ing** (Tel) am Apparat; **so to ~** sozusagen; **~ for yourself** das meinst auch nur du!; **speak up** vi (louder) lauter sprechen; **speaker** n Sprecher(in) m(f); (public ~) Redner(in) m(f); (loud~) Lautsprecher m, Box f

special ['speʃəl] adj besondere(r, s), speziell ▷ n (on menu) Tagesgericht nt; (TV, Radio) Sondersendung f; **special delivery** n Eilzustellung f; **special effects** npl Spezialeffekte pl; **specialist** n Spezialist(in) m(f); (Tech) Fachmann m, Fachfrau f; (Med) Facharzt m, Fachärztin f; **speciality** [speʃi'ælɪtɪ] n Spezialität f; **specialize** vi sich spezialisieren (in auf +akk); **specially** adv besonders; (specifically) extra; **special offer** n Sonderangebot nt; **specialty** n (US) see **speciality**

species ['spi:ʃiːz] nsing Art f

specific [spə'sɪfɪk] adj spezifisch; (precise) genau; **specify** ['spesɪfaɪ] vt genau angeben

specimen ['spesɪmən] n (sample) Probe f; (example) Exemplar n

specs [speks] npl (fam) Brille f

spectacle ['spektəkl] n Schauspiel nt

spectacles npl Brille f

spectacular [spek'tækjʊlə°] adj spektakulär

spectator [spek'teɪtə°] n Zuschauer(in) m(f)

sped [sped] pt, pp of **speed**

speech [spi:tʃ] n (address) Rede f; (faculty) Sprache f; **to make a ~** eine Rede halten; **speechless** adj sprachlos (with vor +dat)

speed [spi:d] n (SMS) (sped o speeded, sped o speeded) vi rasen; (exceed

~ limit) zu schnell fahren ▷ n Geschwindigkeit f; (of film) Lichtempfindlichkeit f; **speed up** vt beschleunigen ▷ vi schneller werden/fahren; (drive faster) schneller fahren; **speedboat** n Rennboot nt; **speed bump** n Bodenschwelle f; **speed camera** n Blitzgerät nt; **speed limit** n Geschwindigkeitsbegrenzung f; **speedometer** [spɪ'dɒmɪtə°] n Tachometer m; **speed trap** n Radarfalle f; **speedy** adj schnell

spell [spel] (spelt o spelled, spelt o spelled) vt buchstabieren; **how do you ~ ...?** wie schreibt man ...? ▷ n (period) Weile f; (enchantment) Zauber m; **a cold/hot ~** (weather) ein Kälteeinbruch/eine Hitzewelle; **spellchecker** n (Inform) Rechtschreibprüfung f; **spelling** n Rechtschreibung f; (of a word) Schreibweise f; **~ mistake** Schreibfehler m

spelt [spelt] pt, pp of **spell**

spend [spend] (spent, spent) vt (money) ausgeben (on für); (time) verbringen; **spending money** n Taschengeld nt

spent [spent] pt, pp of **spend**

sperm [spɜːm] n Sperma nt

sphere [sfɪə°] n (globe) Kugel f; (fig) Sphäre f

spice [spaɪs] n Gewürz nt; (fig) Würze f ▷ vt würzen; **spicy** ['spaɪsɪ] adj würzig; (fig) pikant

spider ['spaɪdə°] n Spinne f

spike [spaɪk] n (on railing etc) Spitze f; (on shoe, tyre) Spike m

spill [spɪl] (spilt o spilled, spilt o spilled) vt verschütten

spin [spɪn] (spun, spun) vi (turn) sich drehen; (washing) schleudern; **my head is ~ing** mir dreht sich alles ▷ vt (turn) drehen; (coin) hochwerfen ▷ n (turn) Drehung f

spinach ['spɪnɪtʃ] n Spinat m

spin doctor n Spindoktor m (Verantwortlicher für die schönrednerische Öffentlichkeitsarbeit besonders von Politikern)

spin-drier ['spɪndraɪə°] n Wäscheschleuder f; **spin-dry** vt schleudern

spine [spaɪn] n Rückgrat nt; (of animal, plant) Stachel m; (of book) Rücken m

spiral ['spaɪərəl] n Spirale f ▷ adj spiralförmig; **spiral staircase** n Wendeltreppe f

spire ['spaɪə°] n Turmspitze f

spirit ['spɪrɪt] n (essence, soul) Geist m; (humour, mood) Stimmung f; (courage) Mut m; (verve) Elan m; **~s** pl (drinks) Spirituosen pl

spiritual ['spɪrɪtjʊəl] adj geistig; (Rel) geistlich

spit [spɪt] (**spat, spat**) vi spucken ▷ n (for roasting) (Brat)spieß m; (saliva) Spucke f; **spit out** vt ausspucken

spite [spaɪt] n Boshaftigkeit f; **in ~ of** trotz +gen; **spiteful** adj boshaft

spitting image ['spɪtɪŋ'ɪmɪdʒ] n: **he's the ~ of you** er ist dir/Ihnen wie aus dem Gesicht geschnitten

splash [splæʃ] vt (person, object) bespritzen ▷ vi (liquid) spritzen; (play in water) planschen

splendid ['splendɪd] adj herrlich

splinter ['splɪntə°] n Splitter m

split [splɪt] (**split, split**) vt (stone, wood) spalten; (share) teilen ▷ vi (stone, wood) sich spalten; (seam) platzen ▷ n (in stone, wood) Spalt m; (in clothing) Riss m; (fig) Spaltung f; **split up** vi (couple) sich trennen ▷ vt (divide up) aufteilen; **split ends** npl (Haar)spliss m; **splitting** adj (headache) rasend

spoil [spɔɪl] (**spoiled** o **spoilt,**

spoiled o **spoilt**) vt verderben; (child) verwöhnen ▷ vi (food) verderben

spoilt [spɔɪlt] pt, pp of **spoil**

spoke [spəʊk] pt of **speak** ▷ n Speiche f

spoken ['spəʊkən] pp of **speak**

spokesperson ['spəʊkspɜːsən] (pl **-people**) n Sprecher(in) m(f)

sponge [spʌndʒ] n (for washing) Schwamm m; **sponge bag** n Kulturbeutel m; **sponge cake** n Biskuitkuchen m

sponsor ['spɒnsə°] n (of event, programme) Sponsor(in) m(f) ▷ vt unterstützen; (event, programme) sponsern

spontaneous, spontaneously [spɒn'teɪnɪəs, -lɪ] adj, adv spontan

spool [spuːl] n Spule f

spoon [spuːn] n Löffel m

sport [spɔːt] n Sport m; **sports car** n Sportwagen m; **sports centre** n Sportzentrum nt; **sports club** n Sportverein m; **sportsman** (pl **-men**) n Sportler m; **sportswear** n Sportkleidung f; **sportswoman** (pl **-women**) n Sportlerin f; **sporty** adj sportlich

spot [spɒt] n (dot) Punkt m; (of paint, blood etc) Fleck m; (place) Stelle f; (pimple) Pickel m; **on the ~** vor Ort; (at once) auf der Stelle ▷ vt (notice) entdecken; (difference) erkennen; **spotless** adj (clean) blitzsauber; **spotlight** n (lamp) Scheinwerfer m; **spotty** adj (pimply) pickelig

spouse [spaʊs] n Gatte m, Gattin f

spout [spaʊt] n Schnabel m

sprain [spreɪn] n Verstauchung f ▷ vt: **to ~ one's ankle** sich den Knöchel verstauchen

sprang [spræŋ] pt of **spring**

spray [spreɪ] n (liquid in can)

Spray nt o m; (~ (can)) Spraydose f
▷ vt (plant, insects) besprühen;
(car) spritzen

spread [spred] (**spread, spread**)
vt (open out) ausbreiten; (news,
disease) verbreiten; (butter, jam)
streichen; (bread, surface)
bestreichen ▷ vi (news, disease,
fire) sich verbreiten ▷ n (of disease,
religion etc) Verbreitung f; (for bread)
Aufstrich m; **spreadsheet** n
(Inform) Tabellenkalkulation f

spring [sprɪŋ] (**sprang, sprung**)
vi (leap) springen ▷ n (season)
Frühling m; (coil) Feder f; (water)
Quelle f; **springboard** n
Sprungbrett nt; **spring onion** n
(Brit) Frühlingszwiebel f; **spring
roll** n (Brit) Frühlingsrolle f;
springy adj (mattress) federnd

sprinkle ['sprɪŋkl] vt streuen;
(liquid) (be)träufeln; **to ~ sth with
sth** etw mit etw bestreuen; (with
liquid) etw mit etw besprengen;
sprinkler n (for lawn)
Rasensprenger m; (for fire)
Sprinkler m

sprint [sprɪnt] vi rennen; (Sport)
sprinten

sprout [spraʊt] n (of plant) Trieb
m; (from seed) Keim m; (**Brussels**)
~s pl Rosenkohl m; sich sprießen

sprung [sprʌŋ] pp of **spring**

spun [spʌn] pt, pp of **spin**

spy [spaɪ] n Spion(in) m(f) ▷ vi
spionieren; **to ~ on sb** jdm
nachspionieren ▷ vt erspähen

squad [skwɒd] n (Sport) Kader m;
(police ~) Kommando nt

square [skweə°] n (shape)
Quadrat nt; (open space) Platz m;
(on chessboard etc) Feld nt ▷ adj (in
shape) quadratisch; **2 ~ metres** 2
Quadratmeter; **2 metres ~** 2 Meter
im Quadrat ▷ vt: **3 ~d** 3 hoch 2;
square root n Quadratwurzel f

squash [skwɒʃ] n (drink)

Fruchtsaftgetränk nt; (Sport)
Squash nt; (US: vegetable) Kürbis m
▷ vt zerquetschen

squat [skwɒt] vi (be crouching)
hocken; **to ~ (down)**
(hin)hocken

squeak [skwi:k] vi (door, shoes
etc) quietschen; (animal) quieken

squeal [skwi:l] vi (person)
kreischen (with vor +dat)

squeeze [skwi:z] vt drücken;
(orange) auspressen ▷ vi: **to ~ into
the car** sich in den Wagen
hineinzwängen; **squeeze up** vi
(on bench etc) zusammenrücken

squid [skwɪd] n Tintenfisch m

squint [skwɪnt] vi schielen; (in
bright light) blinzeln

squirrel ['skwɪrəl] n Eichhörnchen nt

squirt [skwɜ:t] vt, vi (liquid)
spritzen

Sri Lanka [sri:'læŋkə] n Sri
Lanka nt

st abbr = **stone** Gewichtseinheit (6,35
kg)

St abbr = **saint** St.; abbr = **street** Str.

stab [stæb] vt (person) einstechen
auf +akk; (to death) erstechen;
stabbing adj (pain) stechend

stabilize ['steɪbəlaɪz] vt
stabilisieren ▷ vi sich
stabilisieren

stable ['steɪbl] n Stall m ▷ adj
stabil

stack [stæk] n (pile) Stapel m
▷ vt: **to ~ (up)** (auf)stapeln

stadium ['steɪdɪəm] n Stadion
nt

staff [stɑ:f] n (personnel) Personal
nt, Lehrkräfte pl

stag [stæg] n Hirsch m

stag night n (Brit)
Junggesellenabschied m

stage [steɪdʒ] n (Theat) Bühne f;
(of project, life etc) Stadium nt; (of
journey) Etappe f; **at this ~** zu

stagger | 504

diesem Zeitpunkt ▷ vt (Theat) aufführen, inszenieren; (demonstration) veranstalten

stagger ['stægə'] vi wanken ▷ vt (amaze) verblüffen; **staggering** adj (amazing) umwerfend; (amount, price) schwindelerregend

stagnate [stæg'neɪt] vi (fig) stagnieren

stain [steɪn] n Fleck m; **stained-glass window** n Buntglasfenster nt; **stainless steel** n rostfreier Stahl; **stain remover** n Fleck(en)entferner m

stair [steə'] n (Treppen)stufe f; **~s** pl Treppe f; **staircase** n Treppe f

stake [steɪk] n (post) Pfahl m; (in betting) Einsatz m; (Fin) Anteil m (in an +dat); **to be at ~** auf dem Spiel stehen

stale [steɪl] adj (bread) alt; (engine) abwürgen ▷ vi (driver) den schal

stalk [stɔːk] n Stiel m ▷ vt (wild animal) sich anpirschen an +akk; (person) nachstellen +dat

stall [stɔːl] n (in market) (Verkaufs)stand m; (in stable) Box f; **~s** pl (Theat) Parkett nt ▷ vt (engine) abwürgen ▷ vi (driver) den Motor abwürgen; (car) stehen bleiben; (delay) Zeit schinden

stamina ['stæmɪnə] n Durchhaltevermögen nt

stammer ['stæmə'] vi, vt stottern

stamp [stæmp] n (postage ~) Briefmarke f; (for document) Stempel m ▷ vt (passport etc) stempeln; (mail) frankieren; **stamped addressed envelope** n frankierter Rückumschlag

stand [stænd] vi (stood, stood) stehen; (as candidate) kandidieren ▷ vt (place) stellen; (endure) aushalten; **I can't ~ her** ich kann sie nicht ausstehen ▷ n (stall)

Stand m; (seats in stadium) Tribüne f; (for coats, bicycles) Ständer m; (for small objects) Gestell nt; **stand around** vi herumstehen; **stand by** vi (be ready) sich bereithalten; (be inactive) danebenstehen ▷ vt (fig: person) halten zu; (decision, promise) stehen zu; **stand for** vt (represent) stehen für; (tolerate) hinnehmen; **stand in for** vt einspringen für; **stand out** vi (be noticeable) auffallen; **stand up** vi (get up) aufstehen ▷ vt (inf: boyfriend) versetzen; **stand up for** vt sich einsetzen für; **stand up to** vt: **to ~ sb** jdm die Stirn bieten

standard ['stændəd] n (norm) Norm f; **~ of living** Lebensstandard m ▷ adj Standard-

standardize ['stændədaɪz] vt vereinheitlichen

stand-by ['stændbaɪ] n (thing in reserve) Reserve f; **on ~** in Bereitschaft ▷ adj (flight, ticket) Stand-by-; **standing order** n (at bank) Dauerauftrag m; **standpoint** ['stændpɔɪnt] n Standpunkt m; **standstill** ['stændstɪl] n Stillstand m; **to come to a ~** stehen bleiben; (fig) zum Erliegen kommen

stank [stæŋk] pt of **stink**

staple ['steɪpl] n (for paper) Heftklammer f ▷ vt heften (to an +akk); **stapler** n Hefter m

star [stɑː'] n Stern m; (person) Star m ▷ vt: **the film ~s Hugh Grant** der Film zeigt Hugh Grant in der Hauptrolle ▷ vi die Hauptrolle spielen

starch [stɑːtʃ] n Stärke f

stare [steə'] vi starren; **to ~ at** anstarren

starfish ['stɑːfɪʃ] n Seestern m

star sign ['stɑːsaɪn] n Sternzeichen nt

start [stɑːt] n (beginning) Anfang m, Beginn m; (Sport) Start m; (lead) Vorsprung m; **from the ~** von Anfang an ▷ vt anfangen; (car, engine) starten; (business, family) gründen; **to ~ to do sth, to ~ doing sth** anfangen, etw zu tun ▷ vi (begin) anfangen; (car) anspringen; (on journey) aufbrechen; (Sport) starten; (jump) zusammenfahren; **~ing from Monday** ab Montag; **start off** vt (discussion, process etc) anfangen, beginnen ▷ vi (begin) anfangen, beginnen; (on journey) aufbrechen; **start over** vi (US) wieder anfangen; **start up** vi (in business) anfangen ▷ vt (car, engine) starten; (business) gründen; **starter** n (Brit: first course) Vorspeise f; (Auto) Anlasser m; **starting point** n (a. fig) Ausgangspunkt m

startle ['stɑːtl] vt erschrecken; **startling** adj überraschend

starve [stɑːv] vi hungern; (to death) verhungern; **I'm starving** ich habe einen Riesenhunger

state [steɪt] n (condition) Zustand m; (Pol) Staat m; **the (United) States** die (Vereinigten) Staaten ▷ adj Staats-; (control, education) staatlich ▷ vt erklären; (facts, name etc) angeben; **stated** adj (fixed) festgesetzt

statement ['steɪtmənt] n (official declaration) Erklärung f; (to police) Aussage f; (from bank) Kontoauszug m

state-of-the-art [steɪtəvðiːˈɑːt] adj hochmodern, auf dem neuesten Stand der Technik

static ['stætɪk] adj (unchanging) konstant

station ['steɪʃən] n (for trains, buses) Bahnhof m; (underground ~) Station f; (police ~, fire ~) Wache f; (TV, Radio) Sender m ▷ vt (Mil) stationieren

stationer's ['steɪʃənəz] n: **~ (shop)** Schreibwarengeschäft nt; **stationery** n Schreibwaren pl

station wagon ['steɪʃənwægən] n (US) Kombiwagen m

statistics [stəˈtɪstɪks] nsing (science) Statistik f; (figures) Statistiken pl

statue ['stætjuː] n Statue f

status ['steɪtəs] n Status m; (prestige) Ansehen nt; **status bar** n (Inform) Statuszeile f

stay [steɪ] n Aufenthalt m ▷ vi bleiben; (with friends, in hotel) wohnen (with bei); **to ~ the night** übernachten; **stay away** vi wegbleiben; **to ~ from sb** sich von jdm fernhalten; **stay behind** vi zurückbleiben; (at work) länger bleiben; **stay in** vi (at home) zu Hause bleiben; **stay out** vi (not come home) wegbleiben; **stay up** vi (at night) aufbleiben

steady ['stedɪ] adj (speed) gleichmäßig; (progress, increase) stetig; (job, income, girlfriend) fest; (worker) zuverlässig; (hand) ruhig; **they've been going ~ for two years** sie sind seit zwei Jahren fest zusammen ▷ vt (nerves) beruhigen; **to ~ oneself** Halt finden

steak [steɪk] n Steak nt; (of fish) Filet nt

steal [stiːl] (stole, stolen) vt stehlen; **to ~ sth from sb** jdm etw stehlen

steam [stiːm] n Dampf m ▷ vt (Gastr) dämpfen; **steam up** vi (window) beschlagen; **steamer** n (Gastr) Dampfkochtopf m; (ship) Dampfer m; **steam iron** n Dampfbügeleisen nt

steel [stiːl] n Stahl m ▷ adj Stahl-

steep [stiːp] adj steil
steeple ['stiːpl] n Kirchturm m
steer [stɪə°] vt, vi steuern; (car, bike etc) lenken; **steering** n (Auto) Lenkung f; **steering wheel** n Steuer nt, Lenkrad nt
stem [stem] n (of plant, glass) Stiel m
step [step] n Schritt m; (stair) Stufe f; (measure) Maßnahme f; **~ by ~** Schritt für Schritt ▷ vi treten; **~ this way, please** hier entlang, bitte; **step down** vi (resign) zurücktreten
stepbrother n Stiefbruder m; **stepchild** (pl **-children**) n Stiefkind nt; **stepfather** n Stiefvater m
stepladder n Trittleiter f
stepmother n Stiefmutter f; **stepsister** n Stiefschwester f
stereo ['sterɪəʊ] (pl **-s**) n; **~ (system)** Stereoanlage f
sterile ['sterail] adj steril; **sterilize** ['sterilaiz] vt sterilisieren
sterling ['stɜːlɪŋ] n (Fin) das Pfund Sterling
stew [stjuː] n Eintopf m
steward ['stjuːəd] n (on plane, ship) Steward m; **stewardess** n Stewardess f
stick [stɪk] (stuck, stuck) vt (with glue etc) kleben; (pin etc) stecken; (fam: put) tun ▷ vi (get jammed) klemmen; (hold fast) haften ▷ n Stock m; (hockey ~) Schläger m; (of chalk) Stück m; (of celery, rhubarb) Stange f; **stick out** vt: **to stick one's tongue out (at sb)** (jdm) die Zunge herausstrecken ▷ vi (protrude) vorstehen; (ears) abstehen; (be noticeable) auffallen; **stick to** vt (rules, plan etc) sich halten an +akk; **sticker** ['stɪkə°] n Aufkleber m; **sticky** ['stɪkɪ] adj klebrig;

(weather) schwül; **~ label** Aufkleber m; **~ tape** Klebeband nt
stiff [stɪf] adj steif
stifle ['staifl] vt (yawn etc, opposition) unterdrücken; **stifling** adj drückend
still [stɪl] adj still; (drink) ohne Kohlensäure ▷ adv (yet, even now) (immer) noch; (all the same) immerhin; (sit, stand) still; **he ~ doesn't believe me** er glaubt mir immer noch nicht; **keep ~** halt still!; **bigger/better ~** noch größer/besser
still life (pl **still lives**) n Stillleben nt
stimulate ['stɪmjʊleɪt] vt anregen, stimulieren; **stimulating** adj anregend
sting [stɪŋ] (stung, stung) vt (wound with ~) stechen ▷ vi (eyes, ointment etc) brennen ▷ n (insect wound) Stich m
stingy ['stɪndʒɪ] adj (fam) geizig
stink [stɪŋk] (stank, stunk) vi stinken (of nach) ▷ n Gestank m
stir [stɜː°] vt (mix) (um)rühren; **stir up** vt (mob) aufhetzen; (memories) wachrufen; **to ~ trouble** Unruhe stiften; **stir-fry** vt (unter Rühren) kurz anbraten
stitch [stɪtʃ] n (in sewing) Stich m; (in knitting) Masche f; **to have a ~ (pain)** Seitenstechen haben; **he had to have ~es** er musste genäht werden; **she had her ~es out** ihr wurden die Fäden gezogen; **to be in ~es** (fam) sich kaputtlachen ▷ vt nähen; **stitch up** vt (hole, wound) nähen
stock [stɒk] n (supply) Vorrat m (of an +dat); (of shop) Bestand m; (for soup etc) Brühe f; **~s and shares** npl Aktien und Wertpapiere pl; **to be in/out of ~** vorrätig/nicht vorrätig sein; **to**

take ~ Inventur machen; (fig) Bilanz ziehen ▷ vt (keep in shop) führen; **stock up** vi sich eindecken (on, with mit)

stockbroker n Börsenmakler(in) m(f)

stock cube n Brühwürfel m

stock exchange n Börse f

stocking ['stɒkɪŋ] n Strumpf m

stock market n ['stɒkɑːkɪt] n Börse f

stole [stəʊl] pt of **steal**; **stolen** ['stəʊlən] pp of **steal**

stomach ['stʌmək] n Magen m; (belly) Bauch m; **on an empty ~** auf leeren Magen; **stomach-ache** n Magenschmerzen pl; **stomach upset** n Magenverstimmung f

stone [stəʊn] n Stein m; (seed) Kern m, Stein m; (weight) britische Gewichtseinheit (6,35 kg) ▷ adj Stein-, aus Stein; **stony** adj (ground) steinig

stood [stʊd] pt, pp of **stand**

stool [stuːl] n Hocker m

stop [stɒp] n Halt m; (for bus, tram, train) Haltestelle f; **to come to a ~** anhalten ▷ vt (vehicle, passer-by) anhalten; (put an end to) ein Ende machen +dat; (cease) aufhören mit; (prevent from happening) verhindern; (bleeding) stillen; (engine, machine) abstellen; (payments) einstellen; (cheque) sperren; **to ~ doing sth** aufhören, etw zu tun; **to ~ sb (from) doing sth** jdn daran hindern, etw zu tun; **~ it** hör auf (damit)! ▷ vi (vehicle) anhalten; (during journey) Halt machen; (pedestrian, clock, heart) stehen bleiben; (rain, noise) aufhören; (stay) bleiben; **stop by** vi vorbeischauen; **stop over** vi Halt machen; (overnight) übernachten; **stopgap** n Provisorium nt, Zwischenlösung f; **stopover** n (on journey)

Zwischenstation f; **stopper** n Stöpsel m; **stop sign** n Stoppschild nt; **stopwatch** n Stoppuhr f

storage ['stɔːrɪdʒ] n Lagerung f; **store** [stɔː°] n (supply) Vorrat m (of an +dat); (place for storage) Lager nt; (large shop) Kaufhaus nt; (US: shop) Geschäft nt ▷ vt lagern; (Inform) speichern; **storecard** n Kundenkreditkarte f; **storeroom** n Lagerraum m

storey ['stɔːrɪ] n (Brit) Stock m, Stockwerk nt

storm [stɔːm] n Sturm m; (thunder~) Gewitter nt ▷ vt, vi (with movement) stürmen; **stormy** adj stürmisch

story ['stɔːrɪ] n Geschichte f; (plot) Handlung f; (US: of building) Stock m, Stockwerk nt

stout [staʊt] adj (fat) korpulent

stove [stəʊv] n Herd m; (for heating) Ofen m

stow [stəʊ] vt verstauen; **stowaway** n blinder Passagier

straight [streɪt] adj (not curved) gerade; (hair) glatt; (honest) ehrlich ▷ adv (directly) direkt; (immediately) sofort; (drink) pur; (think) klar; **~ ahead** geradeaus; **to go ~ on** geradeaus weitergehen/ weiterfahren; **straightaway** adv sofort; **straightforward** adj einfach; (person) aufrichtig, unkompliziert

strain [streɪn] n Belastung f ▷ vt (eyes) überanstrengen; (rope, relationship) belasten; (vegetables) abgießen; **to ~ a muscle** sich einen Muskel zerren; **strained** adj (laugh, smile) gezwungen; (relations) gespannt; **~ muscle** Muskelzerrung f; **strainer** n Sieb nt

strand [strænd] n (of wool) Faden

m; (of hair) Strähne *f* ▷ *vt:* **to be (left) ~ed** *(person)* festsitzen

strange [streɪndʒ] *adj* seltsam; *(unfamiliar)* fremd; **strangely** *adv* seltsam; **~ enough** seltsamerweise; **stranger** *n* Fremde(r) *mf;* **I'm a ~ here** ich bin hier fremd

strangle ['stræŋgl] *vt (kill)* erdrosseln

strap [stræp] *n* Riemen *m; (on dress etc)* Träger *m; (on watch)* Band *nt* ▷ *vt (fasten)* festschnallen *(to an +dat);* **strapless** *adj* trägerlos

strategy ['strætɪdʒɪ] *n* Strategie *f*

straw [strɔː] *n* Stroh *nt; (drinking ~)* Strohhalm *m*

strawberry *n* Erdbeere *f*

stray [streɪ] *n* streunendes Tier ▷ *adj (cat, dog)* streunend ▷ *vi* streunen

streak ['striːk] *n (of colour, dirt)* Streifen *m; (in hair)* Strähne *f; (in character)* Zug *m*

stream [striːm] *n (flow of liquid)* Strom *m; (brook)* Bach *m* ▷ *vi* strömen; **streamer** *n (of paper)* Luftschlange *f*

street [striːt] *n* Straße *f;* **streetcar** *n (US)* Straßenbahn *f;* **street lamp, street light** *n* Straßenlaterne *f;* **street map** *n* Stadtplan *m*

strength [streŋθ] *n* Kraft *f,* Stärke *f;* **strengthen** *vt* verstärken; *(fig)* stärken

strenuous ['strenjʊəs] *adj* anstrengend

stress [stres] *n* Stress *m; (on word)* Betonung *f;* **to be under ~** im Stress sein ▷ *vt* betonen; *(put under ~)* stressen; **stressed** *adj:* **~ (out)** gestresst

stretch [stretʃ] *n (of land)* Stück *nt; (of road)* Strecke *f* ▷ *vt (material, shoes)* dehnen; *(rope, canvas)*

spannen; *(person in job etc)* fordern; **to ~ one's legs** *(walk)* sich die Beine vertreten ▷ *vi (person)* sich strecken; *(area)* sich erstrecken *(to* bis zu); **stretch out** *vt:* **to stretch one's hand/legs out** die Hand/die Beine ausstrecken, ausstrecken ▷ *vi (reach)* sich strecken; *(lie down)* sich ausstrecken; **stretcher** *n* Tragbahre *f*

strict, strictly [strɪkt, -lɪ] *adj, adv (severe(ly))* streng; *(exact(ly))* genau; **~ speaking** genauer gesagt

strike [straɪk] *(struck, struck) vt (match)* anzünden; *(hit)* schlagen; *(find)* finden; **it struck me as strange** es kam mir seltsam vor ▷ *vi (stop work)* streiken; *(attack)* zuschlagen; *(clock)* schlagen ▷ *n (by workers)* Streik *m;* **to be on ~** streiken; **strike up** *vt (conversation)* anfangen; *(friendship)* schließen; **striking** *adj* auffallend

string [strɪŋ] *n (for tying)* Schnur *f; (Mus, Tennis)* Saite *f;* **the ~s** *pl (section of orchestra)* die Streicher *pl*

strip [strɪp] *n* Streifen *m; (Brit: of footballer etc)* Trikot *nt* ▷ *vi (undress)* sich ausziehen, strippen

stripe [straɪp] *n* Streifen *m;* **striped** *adj* gestreift

stripper ['strɪpə] *n* Stripper(in) *m(f); (paint ~)* Farbentferner *m*

strip-search ['strɪpsɜːtʃ] *n* Leibesvisitation *f (bei der man sich ausziehen muss)*

striptease ['strɪptiːz] *n* Striptease *m*

stroke [strəʊk] *n (Med, Tennis etc)* Schlag *m; (of pen, brush)* Strich *m* ▷ *vt* streicheln

stroll [strəʊl] *n* Spaziergang *m* ▷ *vi* spazieren; **stroller** *n (US: for baby)* Buggy *m*

strong [strɒŋ] *adj* stark; *(healthy)*

robust; (wall, table) stabil; (shoes) fest; (influence, chance) groß; **strongly** adv stark; (believe) fest; (constructed) stabil

struck [strʌk] pt, pp of **strike**

structural, structurally ['strʌktʃərəl, -lɪ] adj strukturell; **structure** ['strʌktʃə] n Struktur f; (building, bridge) Konstruktion f, Bau m

struggle ['strʌgl] n Kampf m (for um) ▷ vi (fight) kämpfen (for um); (do sth with difficulty) sich abmühen; **to ~ to do sth** sich abmühen, etw zu tun

stub [stʌb] n (of cigarette) Kippe f; (of ticket, cheque) Abschnitt m ▷ vt: **to ~ one's toe** sich den Zeh stoßen (on an +dat)

stubble ['stʌbl] n Stoppelbart m; (field) Stoppeln pl

stubborn ['stʌbən] adj (person) stur

stuck [stʌk] pt, pp of **stick** ▷ adj: **to be ~** (jammed) klemmen; (at a loss) nicht mehr weiterwissen; **to get ~** (car in snow etc) stecken bleiben

student ['stju:dənt] n Student(in) m(f), Schüler(in) m(f)

studio ['stju:dɪəʊ] n (pl **-s**) Studio nt

studious ['stju:dɪəs] adj fleißig

study ['stʌdɪ] n (investigation) Untersuchung f; (room) Arbeitszimmer nt ▷ vt, vi studieren

stuff [stʌf] n Zeug nt, Sachen pl ▷ vt (push) stopfen; (Gastr) füllen; **to ~ oneself** (fam) sich vollstopfen; **stuffing** n (Gastr) Füllung f

stuffy ['stʌfɪ] adj (room) stickig; (person) spießig

stumble ['stʌmbl] vi stolpern; (when speaking) stocken

stun [stʌn] vt (shock) fassungslos

machen; **I was ~ned** ich war fassungslos (o völlig überrascht)

stung [stʌŋ] pt, pp of **sting**

stunk [stʌŋk] pp of **stink**

stunning ['stʌnɪŋ] adj (marvellous) fantastisch; (beautiful) atemberaubend; (very surprising, shocking) überwältigend; unfassbar

stunt [stʌnt] n (Cine) Stunt m

stupid ['stju:pɪd] adj dumm; **stupidity** [stju:'pɪdɪtɪ] n Dummheit f

sturdy ['stɜːdɪ] adj robust; (building, car) stabil

stutter ['stʌtə*] vi, vt stottern

stye [staɪ] n (Med) Gerstenkorn nt

style [staɪl] n Stil m ▷ vt (hair) stylen; **styling mousse** n Schaumfestiger m; **stylish** ['staɪlɪʃ] adj elegant, schick

subconscious [sʌb'kɒnʃəs] adj unterbewusst ▷ n: **the ~** das Unterbewusstsein

subdivide [sʌbdɪ'vaɪd] vt unterteilen

subject ['sʌbdʒɪkt] n (topic) Thema nt; (in school) Fach nt; (citizen) Staatsangehörige(r) mf; (of kingdom) Untertan(in) m(f); (Ling) Subjekt nt; **to change the ~** das Thema wechseln ▷ adj [səb'dʒekt]: **to be ~ to** (dependent on) abhängen von; (under control of) unterworfen sein +dat

subjective [səb'dʒektɪv] adj subjektiv

sublet [sʌb'let] irr vt untervermieten (to an +akk)

submarine [sʌbmə'riːn] n U-Boot m

submerge [səb'mɜːdʒ] vt (put in water) eintauchen ▷ vi tauchen

submit [səb'mɪt] vt (application, claim) einreichen ▷ vi (surrender) sich ergeben

subordinate [sə'bɔːdɪnət] adj

untergeordnet (to +dat) ▷ n
Untergebene(r) mf
subscribe [səb'skraɪb] vi: **to
~ to** (magazine etc) abonnieren;
subscription [səb'skrɪpʃən] n (to
magazine etc) Abonnement nt; (to
club etc) (Mitglieds)beitrag m
subsequent ['sʌbsɪkwənt] adj
nach(folgend); **subsequently** adv
später, anschließend
subside [səb'saɪd] vi (floods)
zurückgehen; (storm) sich legen;
(building) sich senken
substance ['sʌbstəns] n Substanz f
substantial [səb'stænʃəl] adj
beträchtlich; (improvement)
wesentlich; (meal) reichhaltig;
(furniture) solide
substitute ['sʌbstɪtjuːt] n Ersatz
m; (Sport) Ersatzspieler(in) m(f)
▷ vt: **to ~ A for B** B durch A
ersetzen
subtitle ['sʌbtaɪtl] n Untertitel
m
subtle ['sʌtl] adj (difference, taste)
fein; (plan) raffiniert
subtotal ['sʌbtəʊtl] n
Zwischensumme f
subtract [səb'trækt] vt abziehen
(from von)
suburb ['sʌbɜːb] n Vorort m; **in
the ~s** am Stadtrand; **suburban**
[sə'bɜːbən] adj vorstädtisch,
Vorstadt-
subway ['sʌbweɪ] n (Brit)
Unterführung f; (US Rail) U-Bahn f
succeed [sək'siːd] vi erfolgreich
sein; **he ~ed (in doing it)** es gelang
ihm(, es zu tun) ▷ vt nachfolgen
+dat; **succeeding** adj
nach(folgend; **success** [sək'ses] n
Erfolg m; **successful, successfully**
adj, adv erfolgreich
successive [sək'sesɪv] adj
aufeinanderfolgend; **successor** n
Nachfolger(in) m(f)

succulent ['sʌkjulənt] adj saftig
succumb [sə'kʌm] vi erliegen (to
+dat)
such [sʌtʃ] adj solche(r, s); **~ a
book** so ein Buch, ein solches
Buch; **it was ~ a success that ...**
es war solch ein Erfolg, dass ...;
~ as wie ▷ adv so; **~ a hot day** so
ein heißer Tag ~ s ▷ pron: **as ~** als
solche(r, s)
suck [sʌk] vt (toffee etc) lutschen;
(liquid) saugen; **it ~s** (fam) das ist
beschissen
Sudan [su'dɑːn] n: (**the**) **~** der
Sudan
sudden ['sʌdn] adj plötzlich; **all
of a ~** ganz plötzlich; **suddenly**
adv plötzlich
sudoku [su'dəʊkuː] n Sudoku nt
sue [suː] vt verklagen
suede [sweɪd] n Wildleder nt
suffer ['sʌfə°] vt erleiden ▷ vi
leiden; **to ~ from** (Med) leiden an
+dat
sufficient, sufficiently
[sə'fɪʃənt, -lɪ] adj, adv
ausreichend
suffocate ['sʌfəkeɪt] vt, vi
ersticken
sugar ['ʃʊgə°] n Zucker m ▷ vt
zuckern; **sugar bowl** n
Zuckerdose f; **sugary** adj (sweet)
süß
suggest [sə'dʒest] vt vorschlagen; (imply) andeuten; **I ~ saying
nothing** ich schlage vor, nichts zu
sagen; **suggestion** n (proposal)
Vorschlag m; **suggestive** adj
vielsagend; (sexually) anzüglich
suicide ['sʊɪsaɪd] n (act)
Selbstmord m; **suicide bomber** n
Selbstmordattentäter(in) m(f);
suicide bombing n
Selbstmordattentat nt
suit [suːt] n (man's clothes) Anzug
m; (lady's clothes) Kostüm nt; (Cards)
Farbe f ▷ vt (be convenient for)

passen +dat; (clothes, colour) stehen +dat; (climate, food) bekommen +dat; **suitable** adj geeignet (for für); **suitcase** n Koffer m

suite [swiːt] n (of rooms) Suite f; (sofa and chairs) Sitzgarnitur f

sulk [sʌlk] vi schmollen; **sulky** adj eingeschnappt

sultana [sʌlˈtɑːnə] n (raisin) Sultanine f

sum [sʌm] n Summe f; (money a.) Betrag m; (calculation) Rechenaufgabe f; **sum up** vt, vi (summarize) zusammenfassen

summarize [ˈsʌməraɪz] vt, vi zusammenfassen; **summary** n Zusammenfassung f

summer [ˈsʌməʳ] n Sommer m; **summer camp** n (US) Ferienlager nt; **summer holidays** n Sommerferien pl; **summertime** n: **in (the) ~** im Sommer

summit [ˈsʌmɪt] n (a. Pol) Gipfel m

summon [ˈsʌmən] vt (doctor, fire brigade etc) rufen; (to one's office) zitieren; **summon up** vt (courage, strength) zusammennehmen

summons [ˈsʌmənz] nsing (Jur) Vorladung f

sumptuous [ˈsʌmptjʊəs] adj luxuriös; (meal) üppig

sun [sʌn] n Sonne f ▷ vt: **to ~ oneself** sich sonnen

Sun abbr = **Sunday** So.

sunbathe vi sich sonnen; **sunbathing** n Sonnenbaden nt; **sunbed** n Sonnenbank f; **sunblock** n Sonnenblocker m; **sunburn** n Sonnenbrand m; **sunburnt** adj: **to be/get ~** einen Sonnenbrand haben/bekommen

sundae [ˈsʌndeɪ] n Eisbecher m

Sunday [ˈsʌndɪ] n Sonntag m; see also **Tuesday**

sung [sʌŋ] pp of **sing**

sunglasses [ˈsʌŋglɑːsɪz] npl

Sonnenbrille f; **sunhat** n Sonnenhut m

sunk [sʌŋk] pp of **sink**

sunlamp [ˈsʌnlæmp] n Höhensonne f; **sunlight** n Sonnenlicht nt; **sunny** [ˈsʌnɪ] adj sonnig; **sun protection factor** n Lichtschutzfaktor m; **sunrise** n Sonnenaufgang m; **sunroof** n (Auto) Schiebedach nt; **sunscreen** n Sonnenschutzmittel nt; **sunset** n Sonnenuntergang m; **sunshade** n Sonnenschirm m; **sunshine** n Sonnenschein m; **sunstroke** n Sonnenstich m; **suntan** n (Sonnen)bräune f; **to get/have a ~** braun werden/sein; **~ lotion** (o **oil**) Sonnenöl nt

super [ˈsuːpəʳ] adj (fam) toll

superb [suːˈpɜːb, -ˈlɪ] adj, adv ausgezeichnet

superficial, superficially [suːpəˈfɪʃəl, -lɪ] adj, adv oberflächlich

superfluous [suˈpɜːfluəs] adj überflüssig

superglue [ˈsuːpəgluː] n Sekundenkleber m

superior [suˈpɪərɪəʳ] adj (better) besser (to als); (higher in rank) höhergestellt (to als), höher ▷ n (in rank) Vorgesetzte(r) mf

supermarket [ˈsuːpəmɑːkɪt] n Supermarkt m

supersede [suːpəˈsiːd] vt ablösen

supersonic [suːpəˈsɒnɪk] adj Überschall-

superstition [suːpəˈstɪʃən] n Aberglaube m; **superstitious** [suːpəˈstɪʃəs] adj abergläubisch

superstore [ˈsuːpəstɔːʳ] n Verbrauchermarkt m

supervise [ˈsuːpəvaɪz] vt beaufsichtigen; **supervisor** [ˈsuːpəvaɪzə] n Aufsicht f; (at university) Doktorvater m

supper ['sʌpə°] n Abendessen nt; (late-night snack) Imbiss

supplement ['sʌplɪmənt] n (extra payment) Zuschlag m; (of newspaper) Beilage f ▷ vt ergänzen; **supplementary** [sʌplɪ'mentəri] adj zusätzlich

supplier [sə'plaɪə°] n Lieferant(in) m(f); **supply** [sə'plaɪ] vt (deliver) liefern; (drinks, music etc) sorgen für; **to ~ sb with sth** (provide) jdn mit etw versorgen ▷ n (stock) Vorrat m (of an +dat)

support [sə'pɔːt] n Unterstützung f; (Tech) Stütze f ▷ vt (hold up) tragen, stützen; (provide for) ernähren, unterhalten; (speak in favour of) unterstützen; **he ~s Manchester United** er ist Manchester-United-Fan

suppose [sə'pəʊz] vt (assume) annehmen; **I ~ so** ich denke schon; **I ~ not** wahrscheinlich nicht; **you're not ~d to smoke here** du darfst/Sie dürfen hier nicht rauchen; **supposedly** [sə'pəʊzɪdlɪ] adv angeblich; **supposing** conj angenommen

suppress [sə'pres] vt unterdrücken

surcharge ['sɜːtʃɑːdʒ] n Zuschlag m

sure [ʃʊə°] adj sicher; **I'm (not) ~** ich bin mir (nicht) sicher; **make ~ you lock up** vergiss/vergessen Sie nicht abzuschließen ▷ adv: **~!** klar!; **~ enough** tatsächlich; **surely** adv: **~ you don't mean it?** das ist nicht dein/Ihr Ernst, oder?

surf [sɜːf] n Brandung f ▷ vi (Sport) surfen ▷ vt: **to ~ the net** im Internet surfen

surface ['sɜːfɪs] n Oberfläche f ▷ vi auftauchen; **surface mail** n: **by ~** auf dem Land-/Seeweg

surfboard ['sɜːfbɔːd] n Surfbrett nt; **surfer** n Surfer(in) m(f);

surfing n Surfen nt; **to go ~** surfen gehen

surgeon ['sɜːdʒən] n Chirurg(in) m(f); **surgery** ['sɜːdʒərɪ] n (operation) Operation f; (room) Praxis f, Sprechzimmer nt; (consulting time) Sprechstunde f; **to have ~** operiert werden

surname ['sɜːneɪm] n Nachname m

surpass [sɜːˈpɑːs] vt übertreffen

surplus ['sɜːpləs] n Überschuss m (of an +dat)

surprise [sə'praɪz] n Überraschung f ▷ vt überraschen; **surprising** adj überraschend; **surprisingly** adv überraschenderweise, erstaunlicherweise

surrender [sə'rendə°] vi sich ergeben (to +dat) ▷ vt (weapon, passport) abgeben

surround [sə'raʊnd] vt umgeben; (stand all round) umringen; **surrounding** adj (countryside) umliegend ▷ n **~s** pl Umgebung f

survey ['sɜːveɪ] n (opinion poll) Umfrage f; (of literature etc) Überblick m (of über +akk); (of land) Vermessung f ▷ [sɜːˈveɪ] vt (look out over) überblicken; (land) vermessen

survive [sə'vaɪv] vt, vi überleben

susceptible [sə'septəbl] adj empfänglich (to für); (Med) anfällig (to für)

sushi ['suːʃɪ] n Sushi nt

suspect ['sʌspekt] n Verdächtige(r) mf ▷ adj verdächtig ▷ [sə'spekt] vt verdächtigen (of +gen); (think likely) vermuten

suspend [sə'spend] vt (from work) suspendieren; (payment) vorübergehend einstellen; (player) sperren; (hang up) aufhängen; **suspender** n (Brit) Strumpfhalter

m; **~s** pl (US: for trousers)
Hosenträger pl

suspense [sə'spens] n Spannung f

suspicious [sə'spɪʃəs] adj
misstrauisch (of sb/sth jdm/etw
gegenüber); (causing suspicion)
verdächtig

SUV abbr = **sport utility vehicle**
SUV m, Geländewagen m

swallow ['swɒləʊ] n (bird)
Schwalbe f ▷ vt, vi schlucken

swam [swæm] pt of **swim**

swamp [swɒmp] n Sumpf m

swan [swɒn] n Schwan m

swap [swɒp] vt, vi tauschen; **to
~ sth for sth** etw gegen etw
eintauschen

sway [sweɪ] vi schwanken

swear [sweəʳ] (**swore**,
sworn) vi (promise) schwören;
(curse) fluchen; **to ~ at sb** jdn
beschimpfen; **swear by** vt (have
faith in) schwören auf +akk;
swearword n Fluch m

sweat [swet] n Schweiß m ▷ vi
schwitzen; **sweatband** n
Schweißband nt; **sweater** n
Pullover m; **sweatshirt** n
Sweatshirt nt; **sweaty** adj
verschwitzt

swede [swiːd] n Steckrübe f

Swede [swiːd] n Schwede m,
Schwedin f; **Sweden** n Schweden
nt; **Swedish** adj schwedisch ▷ n
(language) Schwedisch nt

sweep [swiːp] (**swept**, **swept**)
vt, vi (with brush) kehren, fegen;
sweep up vt (dirt etc) zusammenkehren, zusammenfegen

sweet [swiːt] n (Brit: candy)
Bonbon nt; (dessert) Nachtisch m
▷ adj süß; (kind) lieb;
sweet-and-sour adj süßsauer;
sweetcorn n Mais m; **sweeten** vt
(tea etc) süßen; **sweetener** n
(substance) Süßstoff m; **sweet**

potato n Süßkartoffel f

swell [swel] (**swelled, swollen** o
swelled) vi: **to ~ (up)**
(an)schwellen ▷ adj (US fam) toll;
swelling n (Med) Schwellung f

sweltering ['sweltərɪŋ] adj (heat)
drückend

swept [swept] pt, pp of **sweep**

swift [swɪft] adj schnell

swig [swɪg] n (fam) Schluck m

swim [swɪm] (**swam, swum**) vi
schwimmen ▷ n: **to go for a
~** schwimmen gehen; **swimmer** n
Schwimmer(in) m(f); **swimming** n
Schwimmen nt; **to go
~** schwimmen gehen; **swimming
cap** n (Brit) Badekappe f;
swimming costume n (Brit)
Badeanzug m; **swimming pool** n
Schwimmbad nt; (private, in hotel)
Swimmingpool m; **swimming
trunks** npl (Brit) Badehose f;
swimsuit n Badeanzug m

swindle ['swɪndl] vt betrügen
(out of um)

swine [swaɪn] n (person)
Schwein nt

swing [swɪŋ] (**swung, swung**)
vt, vi (object) schwingen ▷ n (for
child) Schaukel f

swipe [swaɪp] vt (credit card etc)
durchziehen; (fam: steal) klauen;
swipe card n Magnetkarte f

Swiss [swɪs] adj schweizerisch
▷ n Schweizer(in) m(f)

switch [swɪtʃ] n (Elec) Schalter m
▷ vi (change) wechseln (to zu);
switch off vt abschalten,
ausschalten; **switch on** vt
anschalten, einschalten;
switchboard n (Tel) Vermittlung f

Switzerland ['swɪtsələnd] n die
Schweiz

swivel ['swɪvl] vi sich drehen
▷ vt drehen; **swivel chair** n
Drehstuhl m

swollen ['swəʊlən] pp of **swell**

▷ *adj* (*Med*) geschwollen; (*stomach*) aufgebläht

swop [swɒp] *see* **swap**

sword [sɔ:d] *n* Schwert *nt*

swore [swɔ:[r]] *pt of* **swear**

sworn [swɔ:n] *pp of* **swear**

swot [swɒt] *vi* (*Brit fam*) büffeln (for für)

swum [swʌm] *pp of* **swim**

swung [swʌŋ] *pt, pp of* **swing**

syllable ['sɪləbl] *n* Silbe *f*

syllabus ['sɪləbəs] *n* Lehrplan *m*

symbol ['sɪmbəl] *n* Symbol *nt*; **symbolic** [sɪm'bɒlɪk] *adj* symbolisch; **symbolize** *vt* symbolisieren

symmetrical [sɪ'metrɪkəl] *adj* symmetrisch

sympathetic [sɪmpə'θetɪk] *adj* mitfühlend; (*understanding*) verständnisvoll; **sympathize** ['sɪmpəθaɪz] *vi* mitfühlen (with sb mit jdm); **sympathy** ['sɪmpəθɪ] *n* Mitleid *nt*; (after death) Beileid *nt*; (understanding) Verständnis *nt*

symphony ['sɪmfənɪ] *n* Sinfonie *f*

symptom ['sɪmptəm] *n* (a. fig) Symptom *nt*

synagogue ['sɪnəgɒg] *n* Synagoge *f*

synonym ['sɪnənɪm] *n* Synonym *nt*; **synonymous** [sɪ'nɒnɪməs] *adj* synonym (with mit)

synthetic [sɪn'θetɪk] *adj* (material) synthetisch

syphilis ['sɪfɪlɪs] *n* Syphilis *f*

Syria ['sɪrɪə] *n* Syrien *nt*

syringe [sɪ'rɪndʒ] *n* Spritze *f*

system ['sɪstəm] *n* System *nt*; **systematic** [sɪstə'mætɪk] *adj* systematisch; **system disk** *n* (*Inform*) Systemdiskette *f*; **system(s) software** *n* (*Inform*) Systemsoftware *f*

t

tab [tæb] *n* (for hanging up coat etc) Aufhänger *m*; (*Inform*) Tabulator *m*; **to pick up the ~** (fam) die Rechnung übernehmen

table ['teɪbl] *n* Tisch *m*; (list) Tabelle *f*; **~ of contents** Inhaltsverzeichnis *nt*; **tablecloth** *n* Tischdecke *f*; **tablelamp** *n* Tischlampe *f*; **tablemat** *n* Set *nt*; **tablespoon** *n* Servierlöffel *m*; (in recipes) Esslöffel *m*

tablet ['tæblət] *n* (*Med*) Tablette *f*

table tennis ['teɪbltenɪs] *n* Tischtennis *nt*; **table wine** *n* Tafelwein *m*

tabloid ['tæblɔɪd] *n* Boulevardzeitung *f*

taboo [tə'bu:] *n* Tabu *nt* ▷ *adj* tabu

tacit, tacitly ['tæsɪt, -lɪ] *adj, adv* stillschweigend

tack [tæk] *n* (small nail) Stift *m*; (US: thumb~) Reißzwecke *f*

tackle ['tækl] n (Sport) Angriff m; (equipment) Ausrüstung f ▷ vt (deal with) in Angriff nehmen; (Sport) angreifen; (verbally) zur Rede stellen (about wegen)

tacky ['tækı] adj trashig, heruntergekommen

tact [tækt] n Takt m; **tactful, tactfully** adj, adv taktvoll; **tactic(s)** ['tæktɪk(s)] n(pl) Taktik f; **tactless, tactlessly** ['tæktləs, -lı] adj, adv taktlos

tag [tæg] n (label) Schild nt; (with maker's name) Etikett nt

Tahiti [tɑː'hiːtı] n Tahiti nt

tail [teɪl] n Schwanz m; **heads or ~s?** Kopf oder Zahl?; **tailback** n (Brit) Rückstau m; **taillight** n (Auto) Rücklicht nt

tailor ['teɪləʳ] n Schneider(in) m(f)

tailpipe ['teɪlpaɪp] n (US Auto) Auspuffrohr nt

tainted ['teɪntɪd] adj (US: food) verdorben

Taiwan [taɪ'wæn] n Taiwan nt

take [teɪk] (**took, taken**) vt nehmen; (~ along with one) mitnehmen; (~ to a place) bringen; (subtract) abziehen (from von); (capture: person) fassen; (gain, obtain) bekommen; (Fin, Comm) einnehmen; (train, taxi) nehmen, fahren mit; (trip, walk, holiday, exam, course, photo) machen; (bath) nehmen; (phone call) entgegennehmen; (decision, precautions) treffen; (risk) eingehen; (advice, job) annehmen; (consume) zu sich nehmen; (tablets) nehmen; (heat, pain) ertragen; (react to) aufnehmen; (have room for) Platz haben für; **I'll ~ it** (item in shop) ich nehme es; **how long does it ~?** wie lange dauert es?; **it ~s 4 hours** man braucht 4 Stunden; **do you ~ sugar?** nimmst

du/nehmen Sie Zucker?; **I ~ it that ...** ich nehme an, dass ...; **to ~ part** in teilnehmen an; **to ~ place** stattfinden; **take after** vt nachschlagen +dat; **take along** vt mitnehmen; **take apart** vt auseinandernehmen; **take away** vt (remove) wegnehmen (from sb jdm); (subtract) abziehen (from von); **take back** vt (return) zurückbringen; (retract) zurücknehmen; (remind) zurückversetzen (to in +akk); **take down** vt (picture, curtains) abnehmen; (write down) aufschreiben; **take in** vt (understand) begreifen; (give accommodation to) aufnehmen; (deceive) hereinlegen; (include) einschließen; (show, film etc) mitnehmen; **take off** vi (plane) starten ▷ vt (clothing) ausziehen; (hat, lid) abnehmen; (deduct) abziehen; (Brit: imitate) nachmachen; **to take a day off** sich einen Tag freinehmen; **take on** vt (undertake) übernehmen; (employ) einstellen; (Sport) antreten gegen; **take out** vt (wallet etc) herausnehmen; (person, dog) ausführen; (insurance) abschließen; (money from bank) abheben; (book from library) ausleihen; **take over** vt übernehmen ▷ vi: **he took over (from me)** er hat mich abgelöst; **take to** vt: **I've taken to her/it** ich mag sie/es; **to ~ doing sth** (begin) anfangen, etw zu tun; **take up** vt (carpet) hochnehmen; (space) einnehmen; (time) in Anspruch nehmen; (hobby) anfangen mit; (new job) antreten; (offer) annehmen

takeaway n (Brit: meal) Essen nt zum Mitnehmen

taken ['teɪkn] pp of **take** ▷ adj

(seat) besetzt; **to be ~ with** angetan sein von
takeoff ['teɪkɒf] *n* (*Aviat*) Start *m*; (*imitation*) Nachahmung *f*; **takeout** (*US*) *see* **takeaway**; **takeover** *n* (*Comm*) Übernahme *f*
takings ['teɪkɪŋz] *npl* Einnahmen *pl*
tale [teɪl] *n* Geschichte *f*
talent ['tælənt] *n* Talent *nt*; **talented** *adj* begabt
talk [tɔːk] *n* (*conversation*) Gespräch *nt*; (*rumour*) Gerede *nt*; (*to audience*) Vortrag *m* ▷ *vi* sprechen, reden; (*have conversation*) sich unterhalten; **to ~ to** (**o with**) **sb** (**about sth**) mit jdm (über etw *akk*) sprechen; (*nonsense*) reden; (*politics, business*) reden über +*akk*; **to ~ sb into doing/out of doing sth** jdn überreden/jdm ausreden, etw zu tun; **talk over** *vt* besprechen
talkative *adj* gesprächig; **talk show** *n* Talkshow *f*
tall [tɔːl] *adj* groß; (*building, tree*) hoch; **he is 6ft ~** er ist 1,80m groß
tame [teɪm] *adj* zahm; (*joke, story*) fade ▷ *vt* (*animal*) zähmen
tampon ['tæmpɒn] *n* Tampon *m*
tan [tæn] *n* (*on skin*) (Sonnen)bräune *f*; **to get/have a ~** braun werden/sein ▷ *vi* braun werden
tangerine [tændʒə'riːn] *n* Mandarine *f*
tango ['tæŋɡəʊ] *n* Tango *m*
tank [tæŋk] *n* Tank *m*; (*for fish*) Aquarium *nt*; (*Mil*) Panzer *m*
tanker ['tæŋkə*] *n* (*ship*) Tanker *m*; (*vehicle*) Tankwagen *m*
tanned [tænd] *adj* (*by sun*) braun
tantalizing ['tæntəlaɪzɪŋ] *adj* verlockend
Tanzania [tænzə'nɪə] *n* Tansania *nt*

tap [tæp] *n* (*for water*) Hahn *m* ▷ *vt, vi* klopfen; **to ~ sb on the shoulder** jdm auf die Schulter klopfen; **tap-dance** *vi* steppen
tape [teɪp] *n* (*adhesive ~*) Klebeband *nt*; (*for tape recorder*) Tonband *nt*; (*cassette*) Kassette *f*; (*video*) Video *nt* ▷ *vt* (*record*) aufnehmen; **tape up** *vt* (*parcel*) zukleben; **tape measure** *n* Maßband *nt*; **tape recorder** *n* Tonbandgerät *nt*
tapestry ['tæpɪstrɪ] *n* Wandteppich *m*
tap water ['tæpwɔːtə*] *n* Leitungswasser *nt*
target ['tɑːɡɪt] *n* Ziel *nt*; (*board*) Zielscheibe *f*; **target group** *n* Zielgruppe *f*
tariff ['tærɪf] *n* (*price list*) Preisliste *f*; (*tax*) Zoll *m*
tarmac ['tɑːmæk] *n* (*Aviat*) Rollfeld *nt*
tart [tɑːt] *n* (*fruit ~*) (Obst)kuchen *m*; (*small*) (Obst)törtchen *nt*; (*fam, pej: prostitute*) Nutte *f*; (*fam: promiscuous person*) Schlampe *f*
tartan ['tɑːtən] *n* Schottenkaro *nt*; (*material*) Schottenstoff *m*
tartar(e) sauce ['tɑːtə'sɔːs] *n* Remouladensoße *f*
task [tɑːsk] *n* Aufgabe *f*; (*duty*) Pflicht *f*; **taskbar** *n* (*Inform*) Taskbar *f*
Tasmania [tæz'meɪnɪə] *n* Tasmanien *nt*
taste [teɪst] *n* Geschmack *m*; (*sense of ~*) Geschmackssinn *m*; (*small quantity*) Kostprobe *f*; **it has a strange ~** es schmeckt komisch ▷ *vt* schmecken; (*try*) probieren ▷ *vi* (*food*) schmecken (nach); **to ~ good/strange** gut/komisch schmecken; **tasteful, tastefully** *adj, adv* geschmackvoll; **tasteless** *adj, adv* geschmacklos; **tasty** *adj* lecker

tattered ['tætəd] adj (clothes) zerlumpt; (fam: person) angespannt; **I'm absolutely ~** ich bin mit den Nerven am Ende

tattoo [tə'tu:] n (on skin) Tätowierung f

taught [tɔ:t] pt, pp of **teach**

Taurus ['tɔ:rəs] n (Astr) Stier m

tax [tæks] n Steuer f (on auf +akk) ▷ vt besteuern; **taxable** adj steuerpflichtig; **taxation** [tæk'seɪʃən] n Besteuerung f; **tax bracket** n Steuerklasse f; **tax disc** n (Brit Auto) Steuermarke f; **tax-free** adj steuerfrei

taxi ['tæksɪ] n Taxi nt ▷ vi (plane) rollen; **taxi driver** n Taxifahrer(in) m(f); **taxi rank** (Brit), **taxi stand** n Taxistand m

tax return n Steuererklärung f

tea [ti:] n Tee m; (afternoon ~) ≈ Kaffee und Kuchen; (meal) frühes Abendessen; **teabag** n Teebeutel m; **tea break** n (Tee)pause f

teach [ti:tʃ] (**taught, taught**) vt (person, subject) unterrichten; **to ~ sb (how) to dance** jdm das Tanzen beibringen ▷ vi unterrichten; **teacher** n Lehrer(in) m(f); **teaching** n (activity) Unterrichten nt; (profession) Lehrberuf m

teacup ['ti:kʌp] n Teetasse f

team [ti:m] n (Sport) Mannschaft f, Team nt; **teamwork** n Teamarbeit f

teapot ['ti:pɒt] n Teekanne f

tear [tɪə°] n (in eye) Träne f

tear [tɛə°] (**tore, torn**) vt zerreißen; **to ~ a muscle** sich einen Muskel zerren ▷ n (in material etc) Riss m; **tear down** vt (building) abreißen; **tear up** vt (paper) zerreißen

tearoom ['ti:rʊm] n Teestube f,

Café, in dem in erster Linie Tee serviert wird

tease [ti:z] vt (person) necken (about wegen)

tea set n Teeservice nt; **teashop** n Teestube f; **teaspoon** n Teelöffel m; **tea towel** n Geschirrtuch nt

technical ['teknɪkəl] adj technisch; (knowledge, term, dictionary) Fach-; **technically** adv technisch gesehen

technique [tek'ni:k] n Technik f

techno ['teknəʊ] n Techno f

technological [teknə'lɒdʒɪkəl] adj technologisch; **technology** [tek'nɒlədʒɪ] n Technologie f, Technik f

tedious ['ti:dɪəs] adj langweilig

teen(age) ['ti:n(eɪdʒ)] adj (fashions etc) Teenager-; **teenager** n Teenager m; **teens** [ti:nz] npl: **in one's ~** im Teenageralter

teeth [ti:θ] pl of **tooth**

teetotal ['ti:'təʊtl] adj abstinent

telegraph pole ['telɪgrɑ:fpəʊl] n (Brit) Telegrafenmast m

telephone ['telɪfəʊn] n Telefon nt ▷ vi telefonieren ▷ vt anrufen; **telephone banking** n Telefonbanking nt; **telephone book** n Telefonbuch nt; **telephone booth, telephone box** (Brit) n Telefonzelle f; **telephone call** n Telefonanruf m; **telephone directory** n Telefonbuch nt; **telephone number** n Telefonnummer f

telephoto lens ['telɪfəʊtəʊ'lenz] n Teleobjektiv nt

telescope ['telɪskəʊp] n Teleskop nt

televise ['telɪvaɪz] vt im Fernsehen übertragen; **television** ['telɪvɪʒən] n Fernsehen nt; **television programme** n Fernsehsendung f; **television (set)** n Fernseher m

teleworking ['telɪwɜːkɪŋ] n
Telearbeit f

tell [tel] (**told, told**) vt (say,
inform) sagen (sb sth jdm etw);
(story) erzählen; (truth) sagen;
(difference) erkennen; (reveal secret)
verraten; **to ~ sb about sth** jdm
von etw erzählen; **to ~ sth from
sth** etw von etw unterscheiden
▷ vi (be sure) wissen; **tell apart** vt
unterscheiden; **tell off** vt
schimpfen

telling adj aufschlussreich

telly ['telɪ] n (Brit fam) Glotze f; **on
(the) ~** in der Glotze

temp [temp] n Aushilfskraft f
▷ vi als Aushilfskraft arbeiten

temper ['tempə°] n (anger) Wut f;
(mood) Laune f; **to lose one's ~** die
Beherrschung verlieren; **to have a
bad ~** jähzornig sein;
temperamental
[tempərə'mentl] adj (moody)
launisch

temperature ['temprɪtʃə°] n
Temperatur f; (Med: high ~) Fieber
nt; **to have a ~** Fieber haben

temple ['templ] n Tempel m;
(Anat) Schläfe f

temporarily ['tempərərɪlɪ] adv
vorübergehend; **temporary**
['tempərərɪ] adj vorübergehend;
(road, building) provisorisch

tempt [tempt] vt in Versuchung
führen; **I'm ~ed to accept** ich bin
versucht anzunehmen;
temptation [temp'teɪʃən] n
Versuchung f; **tempting** adj
verlockend

ten [ten] num zehn ▷ n Zehn f;
see also **eight**

tenant ['tenənt] n Mieter(in)
m(f); (of land) Pächter(in) m(f)

tend [tend] vi: **to ~ to do sth**
(person) dazu neigen, etw zu tun;
to ~ towards neigen zu;
tendency ['tendənsɪ] n Tendenz

f; **to have a ~ to do sth** (person)
dazu neigen, etw zu tun

tender ['tendə°] adj (loving)
zärtlich; (sore) empfindlich; (meat)
zart

tendon ['tendən] n Sehne f

Tenerife [tenə'riːf] n Teneriffa nt

tenner ['tenə°] n (Brit fam: note)
Zehnpfundschein m; (amount) zehn
Pfund

tennis ['tenɪs] n Tennis nt;
tennis ball n Tennisball m; **tennis
court** n Tennisplatz m; **tennis
racket** n Tennisschläger m

tenor ['tenə°] n Tenor m

tenpin bowling, tenpins (US)
['tenpɪn'bəʊlɪŋ, 'tenpɪnz] n
Bowling nt

tense [tens] adj angespannt;
(stretched tight) gespannt; **tension**
['tenʃən] n Spannung f; (strain)
Anspannung f

tent [tent] n Zelt nt

tenth [tenθ] adj zehnte(r, s) ▷ n
(fraction) Zehntel nt; see also **eighth**

tent peg n ['tentpeg] n Hering m;
tent pole n Zeltstange f

term [tɜːm] n (in school, at
university) Trimester nt; (expression)
Ausdruck m; **~s** pl (conditions)
Bedingungen pl; **to be on good ~s
with sb** mit jdm gut auskommen;
to come to ~s with sth sich mit
etw abfinden; **in the long/short
~** langfristig/kurzfristig; **in ~s
of ...** was ... betrifft

terminal ['tɜːmɪnl] n (bus ~ etc)
Endstation f; (Aviat) Terminal m;
(Inform) Terminal nt; (Elec) Pol m
▷ adj (Med) unheilbar; **terminally**
adv (ill) unheilbar

terminate ['tɜːmɪneɪt] vt (contract) lösen; (pregnancy) abbrechen
▷ vi (train, bus) enden

terminology [tɜːmɪ'nɒlədʒɪ] n
Terminologie f

terrace ['terəs] n (of houses)

Häuserreihe f; (in garden etc)
Terrasse f; **terraced** adj (garden)
terrassenförmig angelegt;
terraced house n (Brit)
Reihenhaus nt
terrible ['terəbl] adj schrecklich
terrific [tə'rɪfɪk] adj (very good)
fantastisch
terrify ['terɪfaɪ] vt erschrecken;
to be terrified schreckliche Angst
haben (of vor +dat)
territory ['terɪtərɪ] n Gebiet nt
terror ['terə] n Schrecken m;
(Pol) Terror m; **terrorism** n
Terrorismus m; **terrorist** n
Terrorist(in) m(f)
test [test] n Test m, Klassenarbeit
f; (driving ~) Prüfung f; **to put to
the ~** auf die Probe stellen ▷ vt
testen, prüfen; (patience, courage
etc) auf die Probe stellen
Testament ['testəmənt] n: **the
Old/New ~** das Alte/Neue
Testament
test-drive ['testdraɪv] vt Probe
fahren
testicle ['testɪkl] n Hoden m
testify ['testɪfaɪ] vi (Jur)
aussagen
test tube ['testtju:b] n
Reagenzglas nt
tetanus ['tetənəs] n Tetanus m
text [tekst] n Text m; (of
document) Wortlaut m; (sent by
mobile phone) SMS f ▷ vt (message)
simsen, SMSen; **to ~ sb** jdm
simsen, jdm eine SMS schicken;
I'll ~ it to you ich schicke es dir per
SMS
textbook n Lehrbuch nt
texting ['tekstɪŋ] n SMS-
Messaging nt; **text message** n
SMS f; **text messaging** n
SMS-Messaging nt
texture ['tekstʃə] n
Beschaffenheit f
Thailand ['taɪlənd] n Thailand nt

Thames [temz] n Themse f
than [ðæn] prep, conj als;
bigger/faster ~ me
größer/schneller als ich; **I'd rather
walk ~ drive** ich gehe lieber zu
Fuß als mit dem Auto
thank [θæŋk] vt danken +dat;
~ you danke; **~ you very much**
vielen Dank; **thankful** adj
dankbar; **thankfully** adv (luckily)
zum Glück; **thankless** adj
undankbar; **thanks** npl Dank m;
~ dankel; ~ to dank +gen

● **THANKSGIVING DAY**
●
● **Thanksgiving (Day)** ist ein
● Feiertag in den USA, der auf den
● vierten Donnerstag im
● November fällt. Er soll daran
● erinnern, wie die Pilgerväter die
● gute Ernte im Jahre 1621
● feierten. In Kanada gibt es einen
● ähnlichen Erntedanktag (der
● aber nichts mit den Pilgervätern
● zu tun hat) am zweiten Montag
● im Oktober.

○ **KEYWORD**

that [ðæt, ðət] adj (demonstrative)
(pl those) der/die/das, jene(r, s);
that one das da
▷ pron 1 (demonstrative) (pl those)
das; **who's/what's that?** wer ist
da/was ist das?; **is that you?** bist
du/sind Sie das?; **that's what he
said** genau das hat er gesagt;
what happened after that? was
passierte danach?; **that is** das
heißt
2 (relative) (subj) der/die/das, die;
(direct obj) den/die/das, die;
(indirect obj) dem/der/dem, denen;
all (that) I have alles, was ich
habe
3 (relative) (of time); **the day (that)**

an dem Tag, als; **the winter (that) he came** in dem Winter, in dem er kam

▷ *conj* dass; **he thought that I was ill** er dachte, dass ich krank sei, er dachte, ich sei krank

▷ *adv* (*demonstrative*) so; **I can't work that much** ich kann nicht so viel arbeiten

that's [ðæts] *contr of* **that is; that has**

thaw [θɔ:] *vi* tauen; (*frozen food*) auftauen ▷ *vt* auftauen lassen

⊙ **KEYWORD**

the [ðə, ði:] *def art* 1 der/die/das; **to play the piano/violin** Klavier/Geige spielen; **I'm going to the butcher's/the cinema** ich gehe zum Fleischer/ins Kino; **Elizabeth the First** Elisabeth die Erste

2 (*+adj to form noun*) das, die; **the rich and the poor** die Reichen und die Armen

3 (*in comparisons*) **the more he works the more he earns** je mehr er arbeitet, desto mehr verdient er

theater (*US*), **theatre** ['θɪətə°] *n* Theater nt; (*for lectures etc*) Saal m

theft [θeft] *n* Diebstahl m

their [ðeə°] *adj* ihr; (*unidentified person*) sein; **they cleaned ~ teeth** sie putzten sich die Zähne; **someone has left ~ umbrella here** jemand hat seinen Schirm hier vergessen; **theirs** *pron* ihre(r, s); (*unidentified person*) seine(r, s); **it's ~** es gehört ihnen; **a friend of ~** ein Freund von ihnen; **someone has left ~ here** jemand hat seins hier liegen lassen

them [ðem, ðəm] *pron* (*direct object*) sie; (*indirect object*) ihnen;

(*unidentified person*) ihn/ihm, sie/ihr; **do you know ~?** kennst du/kennen Sie sie?; **can you help ~?** kannst du/können Sie ihnen helfen?; **it's ~** sie sind's; **if anyone has a problem you should help ~** wenn jemand ein Problem hat, solltest du/sollten Sie ihm helfen

theme [θi:m] *n* (*Mus*) Motiv nt; **~ park** Themenpark m; **~ song** Titelmusik f

themselves [ðəm'selvz] *pron* sich; **they hurt ~** sie haben sich verletzt; **they ~ were not there** sie selbst waren nicht da; **they did it ~** sie haben es selbst gemacht; **they are not dangerous in ~** an sich sind sie nicht gefährlich; (**all**) **by ~** allein

then [ðen] *adv* (*at that time*) damals; (*next*) dann; (*therefore*) also; (*furthermore*) ferner; **from ~ on** von da an; **by ~** bis dahin

▷ *adj* damalig

theoretical, theoretically [θɪə'retɪkəl, -ɪ] *adj, adv* theoretisch

theory ['θɪərɪ] *n* Theorie f; **in ~** theoretisch

therapy ['θerəpɪ] *n* Therapie f

⊙ **KEYWORD**

there [ðeə°] *adv* 1 **there is/there are** es o da ist/sind; (*there exists/exist also*) es gibt; **there are 3 of them** (*people, things*) es gibt 3 davon; **there has been an accident** da war ein Unfall

2 (*place*) da, dort; (*direction*) dahin, dorthin; **put it in/on there** leg es dahinein/dorthinauf

3 **there, there** (*esp to child*) na, na

thereabouts *adv* (*approximately*) so ungefähr; **therefore** *adv* daher, deshalb

thermometer [θə'mɒmɪtə°] n
Thermometer nt

Thermos® ['θɜːməs] n: ~ **(flask)**
Thermosflasche® f

these [ðiːz] pron, adj diese; **I
don't like ~ apples** ich mag diese
Äpfel nicht; **~ are not my books**
das sind nicht meine Bücher

thesis ['θiːsɪs] (pl **theses**) n (for
PhD) Doktorarbeit f

they [ðeɪ] pron pl sie; (people in
general) man; (unidentified person)
er/sie; **~ are rich** sie sind reich;
~ say that ... man sagt, dass ...; **if
anyone looks at this, ~ will see
that ...** wenn sich jemand dies
ansieht, wird er erkennen, dass ...

they'd [ðeɪd] contr of **they had;
they would**

they'll [ðeɪl] contr of **they will;
they shall**

they've [ðeɪv] contr of **they have**

thick [θɪk] adj dick; (fog) dicht;
(liquid) dickflüssig; (fam: stupid)
dumm; **thicken** vi (fog) dichter
werden; (sauce) dick werden ▷ vt
(sauce) eindicken

thief [θiːf] (pl **thieves**) n
Dieb(in) m(f)

thigh [θaɪ] n Oberschenkel m

thimble ['θɪmbl] n Fingerhut m

thin [θɪn] adj dünn

thing [θɪŋ] n Ding nt; (affair)
Sache f; **my ~s** pl meine Sachen pl;
how are ~s? wie geht's?; **I can't
see a ~** ich kann nichts sehen; **he
knows a ~ or two about cars** er
kennt sich mit Autos aus

think [θɪŋk] (**thought, thought**)
vt, vi denken; (believe) meinen; **I
~ so** ich denke schon; **I don't ~ so**
ich glaube nicht; **think about** vt
denken an +akk; (reflect on)
nachdenken über +akk; (have
opinion of) halten von; **think of** vt
denken an +akk; (devise) sich
ausdenken; (have opinion of) halten

von; (remember) sich erinnern an
+akk; **think over** vt überdenken;
think up vt sich ausdenken

third [θɜːd] adj dritte(r, s); **the
Third World** die Dritte Welt ▷ n
(fraction) Drittel nt; **in ~ (gear)** im
dritten Gang; see also **eighth;
thirdly** adv drittens; **third-party
insurance** n Haftpflichtversicherung f

thirst [θɜːst] n Durst m (for nach);
thirsty adj: **to be ~** Durst haben

thirteen ['θɜː'tiːn] num dreizehn
▷ n Dreizehn f; see also **eight;
thirteenth** adj dreizehnte(r, s);
see also **eighth; thirtieth** ['θɜːtɪɪθ]
adj dreißigste(r, s); see also **eighth;
thirty** ['θɜːtɪ] num dreißig;
~-one einunddreißig ▷ n Dreißig
f; **to be in one's thirties** in den
Dreißigern sein; see also **eight**

○ **KEYWORD**

this [ðɪs] adj (demonstrative) (pl
these) diese(r, s); **this evening**
heute Abend; **this one** diese(r, s)
(da)
▷ pron (demonstrative) (pl these)
dies, das; **who/what is this?**
wer/was ist das?; **this is where I
live** hier wohne ich; **this is what
he said** das hat er gesagt; **this is
Mr Brown** dies ist Mr Brown; (on
telephone) hier ist Mr Brown
▷ adv (demonstrative) **this
high/long etc** so groß/lang etc

thistle [θɪsl] n Distel f

thong [θɒŋ] n String m

thorn [θɔːn] n Dorn m, Stachel m

thorough ['θʌrə] adj gründlich;
thoroughly adv gründlich; (agree
etc) völlig

those [ðəʊz] pron die da, jene;
~ who diejenigen, die ▷ adj die,
jene

though [ðəʊ] conj obwohl; **as ~ s** ob ▷ adv aber

thought [θɔːt] pt, pp of **think** ▷ n Gedanke m; (thinking) Überlegung f; **thoughtful** adj (kind) rücksichtsvoll; (attentive) aufmerksam; (in Gedanken versunken) nachdenklich; **thoughtless** adj (unkind) rücksichtslos, gedankenlos

thousand ['θaʊzənd] num: (one) **~, a ~** tausend; **five ~** fünftausend; **~s of** Tausende pl

thrash [θræʃ] vt (hit) verprügeln; (defeat) vernichtend schlagen

thread [θred] n Faden m ▷ vt (needle) einfädeln; (beads) auffädeln

threat [θret] n Drohung f; (danger) Bedrohung f (to für); **threaten** vt bedrohen; **threatening** adj bedrohlich

three [θriː] num drei ▷ n Drei f; see also **eight**; **three-dimensional** adj dreidimensional; **three-piece suit** n Anzug m mit Weste; **three-quarters** npl drei Viertel pl

threshold ['θreʃhəʊld] n Schwelle f

threw [θruː] pt of **throw**

thrifty ['θrɪftɪ] adj sparsam

thrilled [θrɪld] adj: **to be ~ (with sth)** sich (über etw akk) riesig freuen; **thriller** n Thriller m; **thrilling** adj aufregend

thrive [θraɪv] vi gedeihen (on bei); (fig, business) florieren

throat [θrəʊt] n Hals m, Kehle f

throbbing ['θrɒbɪŋ] adj (pain, headache) pochend

thrombosis [θrɒm'bəʊsɪs] n Thrombose f; **deep vein ~** tiefe Venenthrombose f

throne [θrəʊn] n Thron m

through [θruː] prep durch; (time) während +gen; (because of) aus, durch; (US: up to and including) bis;

arranged ~ him durch ihn arrangiert ▷ adv durch; **to put sb ~** (Tel) jdn verbinden (to mit) ▷ adj (ticket, train) durchgehend; **~ flight** Direktflug m; **to be ~ with sb/sth** mit jdm/etw fertig sein;

throughout [θruː'aʊt] prep (place) überall in +dat; (time) während +gen; **~ the night** die ganze Nacht hindurch ▷ adv überall; (time) die ganze Zeit

throw [θrəʊ] (**threw**, **thrown**) vt werfen; (rider) abwerfen; (party) geben; **to ~ sth to sb, to ~ sb sth** jdm etw zuwerfen; **I was ~n by his question** seine Frage hat mich aus dem Konzept gebracht ▷ n Wurf m; **throw away** vt wegwerfen; **throw in** vt (include) dazugeben; **throw out** vt (unwanted object) wegwerfen; (person) hinauswerfen (of aus); **throw up** vt, vi (fam: vomit) sich übergeben; **throw-in** n Einwurf m

thrown [θrəʊn] pp of **throw**

thru (US) see **through**

thrush [θrʌʃ] n Drossel f

thrust [θrʌst] (**thrust**, **thrust**) vt, vi (push) stoßen

thruway ['θruːweɪ] n (US) Schnellstraße f

thumb [θʌm] n Daumen m ▷ vt: **to ~ a lift** per Anhalter fahren; **thumbtack** n (US) Reißzwecke f

thunder ['θʌndə°] n Donner m ▷ vi donnern; **thunderstorm** n Gewitter nt

Thur(s) abbr = **Thursday** Do.

Thursday ['θɜːzdɪ] n Donnerstag m; see also **Tuesday**

thus [ðʌs] adv (in this way) so; (therefore) somit, also

thyme [taɪm] n Thymian m

Tibet [tɪ'bet] n Tibet nt

tick [tɪk] n (Brit: mark) Häkchen nt ▷ vt (name) abhaken; (box, answer) ankreuzen ▷ vi (clock) ticken

ticket ['tɪkɪt] n (for train, bus) (Fahr)karte f; (plane ~) Flugschein m, Ticket nt; (for theatre, match, museum etc) (Eintritts)karte f; (price ~) (Preis)schild nt; (raffle ~) Los nt; (for car park) Parkschein m; (for traffic offence) Strafzettel m; **ticket collector**, **ticket inspector** (Brit) n Fahrkartenkontrolleur(in) m(f); **ticket machine** n (for public transport) Fahrscheinautomat m; (in car park) Parkscheinautomat m; **ticket office** n (Rail) Fahrkartenschalter m; (Theat) Kasse f

tickle ['tɪkl] vt kitzeln; **ticklish** ['tɪklɪʃ] adj kitzlig

tide [taɪd] n Gezeiten pl; **the ~ is in/out** es ist Flut/Ebbe

tidy ['taɪdɪ] adj ordentlich ▷ vt aufräumen; **tidy up** vt, vi aufräumen

tie [taɪ] n (neck~) Krawatte f; (Sport) Unentschieden nt; (bond) Bindung f ▷ vt (attach, do up) binden (to an +akk); (~ together) zusammenbinden; (knot) machen ▷ vi (Sport) unentschieden spielen; **tie down** vt festbinden (to an +dat); (fig) binden; **tie up** vt (dog) anbinden; (parcel) verschnüren; (shoelace) binden; (boat) festmachen; **I'm tied up** (fig) ich bin beschäftigt

tiger ['taɪgə*] n Tiger m

tight [taɪt] adj (clothes) eng; (knot) fest; (screw, lid) fest sitzend; (control, security measures) streng; (timewise) knapp; (schedule) eng ▷ adv (shut) fest; (pull) stramm; **hold ~** festhalten!; **sleep ~** schlaf gut!; **tighten** vt (knot, rope, screw) anziehen; (belt) enger machen; (restrictions, control) verschärfen; **tights** npl (Brit) Strumpfhose f

tile [taɪl] n (on roof) Dachziegel m; (on wall, floor) Fliese f; **tiled** adj (roof) Ziegel-; (floor, wall) gefliest

till [tɪl] n Kasse f ▷ prep, conj see **until**

tilt [tɪlt] vt kippen; (head) neigen ▷ vi sich neigen

time [taɪm] n Zeit f; (occasion) Mal nt; (Mus) Takt m; **local ~** Ortszeit; **what ~ is it?**, **what's the ~?** wie spät ist es?, wie viel Uhr ist es?; **to take one's ~** (over sth) sich (bei etw) Zeit lassen; **to have a good ~** Spaß haben; **in two weeks' ~** in zwei Wochen; **at ~s** manchmal; **at the same ~** gleichzeitig; **all the ~** die ganze Zeit; **by the ~ he ...** bis er ...; (in past) als er ...; **for the ~ being** vorläufig; **in ~** (not late) rechtzeitig; **on ~** pünktlich; **the first ~** das erste Mal; **this ~** diesmal; **five ~s five** fünfmal fünf; **six ~s** fünf mal sechs; **four ~s a year** viermal im Jahr; **three at a ~** drei auf einmal ▷ vt (with stopwatch) stoppen; **you ~d that well** das hast du/haben Sie gut getimt; **time difference** n Zeitunterschied m; **time limit** n Frist f; **timer** n Timer m; (switch) Schaltuhr f; **time-saving** adj zeitsparend; **time switch** n Schaltuhr f; **timetable** n (for public transport) Fahrplan m; (school) Stundenplan m; **time zone** n Zeitzone f

timid ['tɪmɪd] adj ängstlich

timing ['taɪmɪŋ] n (coordination) Timing nt, zeitliche Abstimmung f

tin [tɪn] n (metal) Blech nt; (Brit: can) Dose f; **tinfoil** n Alufolie f; **tinned** [tɪnd] adj (Brit) aus der Dose; **tin opener** n (Brit) Dosenöffner m

tinsel ['tɪnsl] n ~ Lametta nt

tint [tɪnt] n (Farb)ton m; (in hair) Tönung f; **tinted** adj getönt

tiny ['taɪnɪ] *adj* winzig

tip [tɪp] *n* (money) Trinkgeld *nt*; (hint) Tipp *m*; (end) Spitze *f*; (of cigarette) Filter *m*; (Brit: rubbish ~) Müllkippe *f* ▷ *vt* (waiter) Trinkgeld geben +*dat*; **tip over** *vt, vi* (overturn) umkippen

tipsy ['tɪpsɪ] *adj* beschwipst

tiptoe ['tɪptəʊ] *n*: **on ~** auf Zehenspitzen

tire ['taɪə*] *n* (US) see **tyre** ▷ *vt* müde machen ▷ *vi* müde werden; **tired** *adj* müde; **to be ~ of** jdn/etw satthaben; **to be ~ of doing sth** es satthaben, etw zu tun; **tireless** *adj*, **tirelessly** *adv* unermüdlich; **tiresome** *adj* lästig; **tiring** *adj* ermüdend

Tirol [tɪ'rəʊl] see **Tyrol**

tissue ['tɪʃuː] *n* (Anat) Gewebe *nt*; (paper handkerchief) Tempotaschentuch® *nt*, Papier(taschen)tuch *nt*; **tissue paper** *n* Seidenpapier *nt*

tit [tɪt] *n* (bird) Meise *f*; (fam: breast) Titte *f*

title ['taɪtl] *n* Titel *m*

titter ['tɪtə] *vi* kichern

KEYWORD

to [tuː, tə] *prep* **1** (direction) zu, nach; **I go to France/school** ich gehe nach Frankreich/zur Schule; **to the left** nach links

2 (as far as) bis

3 (with expressions of time) vor; **a quarter to 5** Viertel vor 5

4 (for, of) für; **secretary to the director** Sekretärin des Direktors

5 (expressing indirect object) **to give sth to sb** jdm etw geben; **to talk to sb** mit jdm sprechen; **I sold it to a friend** ich habe es einem Freund verkauft

6 (in relation to) zu; **30 miles to the gallon** 30 Meilen pro Gallone

7 (purpose, result) zu; **to my surprise** zu meiner Überraschung ▷ *with vb* **1** (infin) **to go/eat** gehen/essen; **to want to do sth** etw tun wollen; **to try/start to do sth** versuchen/anfangen, etw zu tun; **he has a lot to lose** er hat viel zu verlieren

2 (with vb omitted) **I don't want to** ich will (es) nicht

3 (purpose, result) um; **I did it to help you** ich tat es, um dir/Ihnen zu helfen

4 (after adj etc) ready to use gebrauchsfertig; **too old/young to ...** zu alt/jung, um ... zu ...

▷ *adv*: **push/pull the door to** die Tür zuschieben/zuziehen

toad [təʊd] *n* Kröte *f*; **toadstool** *n* Giftpilz *m*

toast [təʊst] *n* (bread, drink) Toast *m*; **a piece o slice) of ~** eine Scheibe Toast; **to propose a ~ to sb** einen Toast auf jdn ausbringen ▷ *vt* (bread) toasten; (person) trinken auf +*akk*; **toaster** *n* Toaster *m*

tobacco [tə'bækəʊ] *n* (pl **-s**) *n* Tabak *m*; **tobacconist's** [tə'bækənɪsts] *n*: **~ (shop)** Tabakladen *m*

toboggan [tə'bɒgən] *n* Schlitten *m*

today [tə'deɪ] *adv* heute; **a week ~** heute in einer Woche; **~'s newspaper** die Zeitung von heute

toddler ['tɒdlə*] *n* Kleinkind *nt*

toe [təʊ] *n* Zehe *f*, Zeh *m*; **toenail** *n* Zehennagel *m*

toffee ['tɒfɪ] *n* (sweet) Karamellbonbon *nt*; **toffee apple** *n* kandierter Apfel; **toffee-nosed** *adj* hochnäsig

tofu ['təʊfuː] *n* Tofu *m*

together [tə'geðə*] *adv*

zusammen; **I tied them ~** ich habe sie zusammengebunden

toilet ['tɔɪlət] n Toilette f; **to go to the ~** auf die Toilette gehen; **toilet bag** n Kulturbeutel m; **toilet paper** n Toilettenpapier nt; **toiletries** ['tɔɪlətrɪz] npl Toilettenartikel pl; **toilet roll** n Rolle f Toilettenpapier

token ['təʊkən] n Marke f; (in casino) Spielmarke f; (voucher, gift ~) Gutschein m; (sign) Zeichen nt

Tokyo ['təʊkɪəʊ] n Tokio nt

told [təʊld] pt, pp of **tell**

tolerant ['tɒlərənt] adj tolerant (of gegenüber); **tolerate** ['tɒləreɪt] vt tolerieren (noise, pain, heat) ertragen

toll [təʊl] n (charge) Gebühr f; **the death ~** die Zahl der Toten; **toll-free** adj, adv (US Tel) gebührenfrei; **toll road** n gebührenpflichtige Straße

tomato [tə'mɑːtəʊ] (pl **-es**) n Tomate f; **tomato juice** n Tomatensaft m; **tomato ketchup** n Tomatenketchup m o nt; **tomato sauce** n Tomatensoße f; (Brit: ketchup) Tomatenketchup m o nt

tomb [tuːm] n Grabmal nt; **tombstone** n Grabstein m

tomorrow [tə'mɒrəʊ] adv morgen; **~ morning** morgen früh; **~ evening** morgen Abend; **the day after ~** übermorgen; **a week (from) ~/~ week** morgen in einer Woche

ton [tʌn] n (Brit) Tonne f (1016 kg); (US) Tonne f (907 kg); **~s of books** (fam) eine Menge Bücher

tone [təʊn] n Ton m; **tone down** vt mäßigen; **toner** ['təʊnə] n (for printer) Toner m; **toner cartridge** n Tonerpatrone f

tongs [tɒŋz] npl Zange f; (curling ~) Lockenstab m

tongue [tʌŋ] n Zunge f

tonic ['tɒnɪk] n (Med) Stärkungsmittel nt; **~ (water)** Tonic nt; **gin and ~** Gin m Tonic

tonight [tə'naɪt] adv heute Abend; (during night) heute Nacht

tonsils ['tɒnslz] npl Mandeln pl; **tonsillitis** [tɒnsɪ'laɪtɪs] n Mandelentzündung f

too [tuː] adv zu; (also) auch; **~ fast** zu schnell; **~ much/many** zu viel/viele; **me ~** ich auch; **she liked it ~** ihr gefiel es auch

took [tʊk] pt of **take**

tool [tuːl] n Werkzeug nt; **toolbar** n (Inform) Symbolleiste f; **toolbox** n Werkzeugkasten m

tooth [tuːθ] (pl **teeth**) n Zahn m; **toothache** n Zahnschmerzen pl; **toothbrush** n Zahnbürste f; **toothpaste** n Zahnpasta f; **toothpick** n Zahnstocher m

top [tɒp] n (of tower, class, company etc) Spitze f; (of mountain) Gipfel m; (of tree) Krone f; (of street) oberes Ende; (of tube, pen) Kappe f; (of box) Deckel m; (of bikini) Oberteil nt; (sleeveless) Top nt; **at the ~ of the page** oben auf der Seite; **at the ~ of the league** an der Spitze der Liga; **on ~** oben; **on ~ of** auf +dat; (in addition to) zusätzlich zu; **in ~ (gear)** im höchsten Gang; **over the ~** übertrieben ▷ adj (floor, shelf) oberste(r, s); (price, note) höchste(r, s); (best) Spitzen-; (pupil, school) beste(r, s) ▷ vt (exceed) übersteigen; (be better than) übertreffen; (league) an erster Stelle liegen in +dat; **~ped with cream** mit Sahne obendrauf; **top up** vt auffüllen; **can I top you up?** darf ich dir nachschenken?

topic ['tɒpɪk] n Thema nt; **topical** adj aktuell

topless ['tɒpləs] adj, adv oben ohne

topping ['tɒpɪŋ] n (on top of pizza, ice-cream etc) Belag m, Garnierung f

top-secret ['tɒp'si:krət] adj streng geheim

torch [tɔ:tʃ] n (Brit) Taschenlampe f

tore [tɔ:ʳ] pt of **tear**

torment ['tɔ:ment] vt quälen

torn [tɔ:n] pp of **tear**

tornado [tɔ:'neɪdəʊ] (pl **-es**) n Tornado m

torrential [tə'renʃəl] adj (rain) sintflutartig

tortoise ['tɔ:təs] n Schildkröte f

torture ['tɔ:tʃəʳ] n Folter f; (fig) Qual f ▷ vt foltern

Tory ['tɔ:rɪ] (Brit) n Tory m, Konservative(r) mf ▷ adj Tory-

toss [tɒs] vt (throw) werfen; (salad) anmachen; **to ~ a coin** eine Münze werfen ▷ n: **I don't give a ~** (fam) es ist mir scheißegal

total ['təʊtl] n (of figures, money) Gesamtsumme f; **a ~ of 30** insgesamt 30; **in ~** insgesamt ▷ adj total; (sum etc) Gesamt- ▷ vt (amount to) sich belaufen auf +akk; **totally** adv total

touch [tʌtʃ] n (act of ~ing) Berührung f; (sense of ~) Tastsinn m; (trace) Spur f; **to be/keep in ~ with sb** mit jdm in Verbindung stehen/bleiben; **to get in ~ with sb** sich mit jdm in Verbindung setzen; **to lose ~ with sb** den Kontakt zu jdm verlieren ▷ vt (feel) berühren; (emotionally) bewegen; **touch on** vt (topic) berühren; **touchdown** n (Aviat) Landung f; (Sport) Touchdown m; **touching** adj (moving) rührend; **touch screen** n Touchscreen m, Berührungsbildschirm m; **touchy** adj empfindlich, zickig

tough [tʌf] adj hart; (meat) zäh; (material) robust; (meat) zäh

tour ['tʊəʳ] n Tour f (of durch); (of town, building) Rundgang m (of durch); (pop group etc) Tournee f ▷ vt eine Tour/einen Rundgang/eine Tournee machen durch ▷ vi (on holiday) umherreisen; **tour guide** n Reiseleiter(in) m(f)

tourism ['tʊərɪzəm] n Tourismus m, Fremdenverkehr m; **tourist** n Tourist(in) m(f); **tourist class** n Touristenklasse f; **tourist guide** n (book) Reiseführer m; (person) Fremdenführer(in) m(f); **tourist office** n Fremdenverkehrsamt nt

tournament ['tʊənəmənt] n Turnier nt

tour operator ['tʊərɒpəreɪtəʳ] n Reiseveranstalter m

tow [təʊ] vt abschleppen; (caravan, trailer) ziehen; **tow away** vt abschleppen

towards [tə'wɔ:dz] prep: **~ me** mir entgegen, auf mich zu; **we walked ~ the station** wir gingen in Richtung Bahnhof; **my feelings ~ him** meine Gefühle ihm gegenüber; **she was kind ~ me** sie war nett zu mir

towel ['taʊəl] n Handtuch nt

tower ['taʊəʳ] n Turm m; **tower block** n (Brit) Hochhaus nt

town [taʊn] n Stadt f; **town center** (US), **town centre** n Stadtmitte f, Stadtzentrum nt; **town hall** n Rathaus nt

towrope ['təʊrəʊp] n Abschleppseil nt; **tow truck** n (US) Abschleppwagen m

toxic ['tɒksɪk] adj giftig, Gift-

toy [tɔɪ] n Spielzeug nt; **toy with** vt spielen mit; **toyshop** n Spielwarengeschäft nt

trace [treɪs] n Spur f; **without**

~ spurlos ▷ vt (find) ausfindig machen; **tracing paper** n Pauspapier nt

track [træk] n (mark) Spur f; (path) Weg m; (Rail) Gleis nt; (on CD, record) Stück nt; **to keep/lose ~ of sb/sth** jdn/etw im Auge behalten/aus den Augen verlieren; **track down** vt ausfindig machen; **trackball** n (Inform) Trackball m; **tracksuit** n Trainingsanzug m

tractor ['træktə°] n Traktor m

trade [treɪd] n (commerce) Handel m; (business) Geschäft nt; (skilled job) Handwerk nt ▷ vi handeln (in mit) ▷ vt (exchange) tauschen (for gegen); **trademark** n Warenzeichen nt; **tradesman** (pl **-men**) n (shopkeeper) Geschäftsmann m; (workman) Handwerker m; **trade(s) union** n (Brit) Gewerkschaft f

tradition [trə'dɪʃən] n Tradition f; **traditional, traditionally** adj, adv traditionell

traffic ['træfɪk] n Verkehr m; (pej: trading) Handel m (in mit); **traffic circle** n (US) Kreisverkehr m; **traffic island** n Verkehrsinsel f; **traffic jam** n Stau m; **traffic lights** npl Verkehrsampel f; **traffic warden** n (Brit) ≈ Politesse f

tragedy ['trædʒədɪ] n Tragödie f; **tragic** ['trædʒɪk] adj tragisch

trail [treɪl] n Spur f; (path) Weg m ▷ vt (follow) verfolgen; (drag) schleppen; (drag behind) hinter sich herziehen; (Sport) zurückliegen hinter +dat ▷ vi (hang loosely) schleifen; (Sport) weit zurückliegen; **trailer** n Anhänger m; (US: caravan) Wohnwagen m; (Cine) Trailer m

train [treɪn] n (Rail) Zug m ▷ vt (teach) ausbilden; (Sport) trainieren ▷ vi (Sport) trainieren; **to ~ as** (o **to be**) **a teacher** eine Ausbildung als Lehrer machen; **trained** adj (person, voice) ausgebildet; **trainee** n Auszubildende(r) mf; (academic, practical) Praktikant(in) m(f); **traineeship** n Praktikum nt; **trainer** n (Sport) Trainer(in) m(f); **-s** (Brit: shoes) Turnschuhe pl; **training** n Ausbildung f; (Sport) Training nt; **train station** n Bahnhof m

tram ['træm] n (Brit) Straßenbahn f

tramp [træmp] n Landstreicher(in) m(f) ▷ vi trotten

tranquillizer ['træŋkwɪlaɪzə°] n Beruhigungsmittel nt

transaction n (piece of business) Geschäft nt

transatlantic ['trænzæt'læntɪk] adj transatlantisch; **~ flight** Transatlantikflug m

transfer ['trænsfə°] n (of money) Überweisung f; (US: ticket) Umsteigekarte f ▷ [træns'fɜː°] vt (money) überweisen (to sb an jdn); (patient) verlegen; (employee) versetzen; (Sport) transferieren ▷ vi (on journey) umsteigen; **transferable** [træns'fɜːrəbl] adj übertragbar

transform [træns'fɔːm] vt umwandeln; **transformation** [trænsfə'meɪʃən] n Umwandlung f

transfusion [træns'fjuːʒən] n Transfusion f

transistor [træn'zɪstə°] n Transistor m; **~ (radio)** n Transistorradio nt

transition [træn'zɪʃən] n Übergang m (from ... to von ... zu)

transit lounge ['trænzɪtlaʊndʒ] n Transitraum m; **transit passenger** n Transitreisende(r) mf

translate [trænz'leɪt] vt, vi
übersetzen; **translation**
[trænz'leɪʃən] n Übersetzung f;
translator [trænz'leɪtə°] n
Übersetzer(in) m(f)
transmission [trænz'mɪʃən] n
(Auto) Getriebe nt
transparent [træns'pærənt] adj
durchsichtig; (fig) offenkundig
transplant [træns'plɑːnt] (Med)
vt transplantieren ▷ ['trænsplɑːnt]
n (operation) Transplantation f
transport ['trænspɔːt] n (of
goods, people) Beförderung f; **public
~** öffentliche Verkehrsmittel pl
▷ [træns'pɔːt] vt befördern,
transportieren; **transportation**
[trænspɔː'teɪʃən] n see **transport**
trap [træp] n Falle f ▷ vt: **to be
~ped** (in snow, job etc) festsitzen
trash [træʃ] n (book, film etc)
Schund m; (US: refuse) Abfall m;
trash can n (US) Abfalleimer m;
trashy adj niveaulos; (novel)
Schund-
traumatic [trɔː'mætɪk] adj
traumatisch
travel ['trævl] n Reisen pl ▷ vi
(journey) reisen ▷ vt (distance)
zurücklegen; (country) bereisen;
travel agency, **travel agent** n
(company) Reisebüro nt; **traveler**
(US) see **traveller**; **traveler's
check** (US) see **traveller's cheque**;
travel insurance n
Reiseversicherung f; **traveller** n
Reisende(r) mf; **traveller's cheque**
n (Brit) Reisescheck m; **travelsick**
n reisekrank
tray [treɪ] n Tablett nt; (for mail
etc) Ablage f; (of printer, photocopier)
Fach nt
tread [tred] n (on tyre) Profil nt;
tread on [tred] (trod, trodden)
vt treten auf +akk
treasure ['treʒə°] n Schatz m
▷ vt schätzen

treat [triːt] n besondere Freude;
it's my ~ das geht auf meine
Kosten ▷ vt behandeln; **to ~ sb
(to sth)** jdn (zu etw) einladen; **to
~ oneself to sth** sich etw leisten;
treatment ['triːtmənt] n
Behandlung f
treaty ['triːtɪ] n Vertrag m
tree [triː] n Baum m
tremble ['trembl] vi zittern
tremendous [trə'mendəs] adj
gewaltig; (fam: very good) toll
trench [trentʃ] n Graben m
trend [trend] n Tendenz f;
(fashion) Mode f, Trend m; **trendy**
adj trendy
trespass ['trespəs] vi: **"no ~ing"**
"Betreten verboten"
trial ['traɪəl] n (Jur) Prozess m;
(test) Versuch m; **by ~ and error**
durch Ausprobieren; **trial period**
n (for employee) Probezeit f
triangle ['traɪæŋgl] n Dreieck nt;
(Mus) Triangel m; **triangular**
[traɪ'æŋgjʊlə°] adj dreieckig
tribe [traɪb] n Stamm m
trick [trɪk] n Trick m; (mischief)
Streich m ▷ vt hereinlegen
tricky ['trɪkɪ] adj (difficult)
schwierig, heikel; (situation)
verzwickt
trifle ['traɪfl] n Kleinigkeit f; (Brit
Gastr) Trifle nt (Nachspeise aus
Biskuit, Wackelpudding, Obst,
Vanillesoße und Sahne)
trigger ['trɪgə°] n (of gun) Abzug
m ▷ vt: **to ~ (off)** auslösen
trim [trɪm] vt (hair, beard)
nachschneiden; (nails) schneiden;
(hedge) stutzen ▷ n: **just a ~,
please** nur etwas nachschneiden,
bitte; **trimmings** npl (decorations)
Verzierungen pl; (extras) Zubehör
nt; (Gastr) Beilagen pl
trip [trɪp] n Reise f; (outing)
Ausflug m ▷ vi stolpern (over über
+akk)

triple ['trɪpl] *adj* dreifach ▷ *adv*: **~ the price** dreimal so teuer ▷ *vi* sich verdreifachen; **triplet** ['trɪplɪt] *n* Drilling *m*

tripod ['traɪpɒd] *n* (Foto) Stativ *nt*

trite [traɪt] *adj* banal

triumph ['traɪʌmf] *n* Triumph *m*

trivial ['trɪvɪəl] *adj* trivial

trod [trɒd] *pt of* **tread**

trodden *pp of* **tread**

trolley ['trɒlɪ] *n* (Brit: in shop) Einkaufswagen *m*; (for luggage) Kofferkuli *m*; (serving ~) Teewagen *m*

trombone [trɒm'bəʊn] *n* Posaune *f*

troops [tru:ps] *npl* (Mil) Truppen *pl*

trophy ['trəʊfɪ] *n* Trophäe *f*

tropical ['trɒpɪkl] *adj* tropisch

trouble ['trʌbl] *n* (problems) Schwierigkeiten *pl*; (worry) Sorgen *pl*; (effort) Mühe *f*; (unrest) Unruhen *pl*; (Med) Beschwerden *pl*; **to be in ~** in Schwierigkeiten sein; **to get into ~** (with authority) Ärger bekommen; **to make ~** Schwierigkeiten machen ▷ *vt* (worry) beunruhigen; (disturb) stören; **my back's troubling me** mein Rücken macht mir zu schaffen; **sorry to ~ you** ich muss dich/Sie leider kurz stören; **troubled** *adj* (worried) beunruhigt; **trouble-free** *adj* problemlos; **troublemaker** *n* Unruhestifter(in) *m(f)*; **troublesome** *adj* lästig

trousers ['traʊzəz] *npl* Hose *f*; **trouser suit** *n* (Brit) Hosenanzug *m*

trout [traʊt] *n* Forelle *f*

truck [trʌk] *n* Lastwagen *m*; (Brit Rail) Güterwagen *m*; **trucker** *n* (US: driver) Lastwagenfahrer(in) *m(f)*

true [tru:] *adj* (factually correct) wahr; (genuine) echt; **to come ~** wahr werden

truly ['tru:lɪ] *adv* wirklich; **Yours ~** (in letter) mit freundlichen Grüßen

trumpet ['trʌmpɪt] *n* Trompete *f*

trunk [trʌŋk] *n* (of tree) Stamm *m*; (Anat) Rumpf *m*; (of elephant) Rüssel *m*; (piece of luggage) Überseekoffer *m*; (US Auto) Kofferraum *m*; **trunks** *npl*: **(swimming) ~** Badehose *f*

trust [trʌst] *n* (confidence) Vertrauen *nt* (in zu) ▷ *vt* vertrauen +*dat*; **trusting** *adj* vertrauensvoll; **trustworthy** *adj* vertrauenswürdig

truth [tru:θ] *n* Wahrheit *f*; **truthful** *adj* ehrlich; (statement) wahrheitsgemäß

try [traɪ] *n* Versuch *m* ▷ *vt* (attempt) versuchen; (~ out) ausprobieren; (sample) probieren; (Jur: person) vor Gericht stellen; (courage, patience) auf die Probe stellen ▷ *vi* versuchen; (make effort) sich bemühen; **~ and come** versuch zu kommen; **try on** *vt* (clothes) anprobieren; **try out** *vt* ausprobieren

T-shirt ['ti:ʃɜ:t] *n* T-Shirt *nt*

tub [tʌb] *n* (for ice-cream, margarine) Becher *m*

tube [tju:b] *n* (pipe) Rohr *nt*; (of rubber, plastic) Schlauch *m*; (for toothpaste, glue etc) Tube *f*; **the Tube** (in London) die U-Bahn

tube station *n* ['tju:bsteɪʃən] *n* U-Bahn-Station *f*

tuck [tʌk] *vt* (put) stecken; **tuck in** *vt* (shirt) in die Hose stecken; (blanket) feststecken; (person) zudecken ▷ *vi* (eat) zulangen

Tue(s) *abbr* = **Tuesday** Di.

Tuesday ['tju:zdɪ] *n* Dienstag *m*;

on ~ (am) Dienstag; **on ~s** dienstags; **this/last/next ~** diesen/letzten/nächsten Dienstag; **(on) ~ morning/ afternoon/evening** (am) Dienstagmorgen/-nachmittag/ -abend; **every ~** jeden Dienstag; **a week on ~/~ week** Dienstag in einer Woche

tug [tʌɡ] vt ziehen; **she ~ged his sleeve** sie zog an seinem Ärmel ▷ vi ziehen (at an +dat)

tuition [tjuˈɪʃən] n Unterricht m; (US: fees) Studiengebühren pl; **~ fees** pl Studiengebühren pl

tulip [ˈtjuːlɪp] n Tulpe f

tumble [ˈtʌmbl] vi (person, prices) fallen; **tumble dryer** n Wäschetrockner m; **tumbler** n (glass) (Becher)glas nt

tummy [ˈtʌmɪ] n (fam) Bauch m; **tummyache** n (fam) Bauchweh nt

tumor (US), **tumour** [ˈtjuːməʳ] n Tumor m

tuna [ˈtjuːnə] n Thunfisch m

tune [tjuːn] n Melodie f; **to be in/out of ~** (instrument) gestimmt/verstimmt sein; (singer) richtig/falsch singen ▷ vt (instrument) stimmen; (radio) einstellen (to auf +akk); **tuner** n (in stereo system) Tuner m

Tunisia [tjuːˈnɪzɪə] n Tunesien nt

tunnel [ˈtʌnl] n Tunnel m; (under road, railway) Unterführung f

turban [ˈtɜːbən] n Turban m

turbulence [ˈtɜːbjʊləns] n (Aviat) Turbulenzen pl; **turbulent** adj stürmisch

Turk [tɜːk] n Türke m, Türkin f

turkey [ˈtɜːkɪ] n Truthahn m

Turkey [ˈtɜːkɪ] n die Türkei; **Turkish** adj türkisch ▷ n (language) Türkisch nt

turmoil [ˈtɜːmɔɪl] n Aufruhr m

turn [tɜːn] n (rotation) Drehung f; (performance) Nummer f; **to make a left ~** nach links abbiegen; **at the ~ of the century** um die Jahrhundertwende; **it's your ~** du bist/Sie sind dran; **in ~, by ~s** abwechselnd; **to take ~s** sich abwechseln ▷ vt (wheel, key, screw) drehen; (to face other way) umdrehen; (corner) biegen um; (page) umblättern; (transform) verwandeln (into in +akk) ▷ vi (rotate) sich drehen; (to face other way) sich umdrehen; (change direction: driver, car) abbiegen; (become) werden; (weather) umschlagen; **to ~ into sth** (become) sich in etw akk verwandeln; **to ~ cold/green** kalt/grün werden; **to ~ left/right** links/rechts abbiegen; **turn away** vt (person) abweisen; (person) zurückweisen ▷ vi (go back) umkehren; **turn down** vt (refuse) ablehnen; (radio, TV) leiser stellen; (heating) kleiner stellen; **turn off** vi abbiegen ▷ vt (switch off) ausschalten; (tap) zudrehen; (engine, electricity) abstellen; **turn on** vt (switch on) einschalten; (tap) aufdrehen; (engine, electricity) anstellen; (fam: person) anmachen, antörnen; **turn out** vt (light) ausmachen; (pockets) leeren ▷ vi (develop) sich entwickeln; **as it turned out** wie sich herausstellte; **turn over** vi umdrehen; (page) umblättern ▷ vi (person) sich umdrehen; (car) sich überschlagen; (TV) umschalten (to auf +akk); **turn round** vt (to face other way) umdrehen ▷ vi (person) sich umdrehen; (go back) umkehren; **turn to** vt sich zuwenden +dat; **turn up** vi (person, lost object) auftauchen ▷ vt (radio, TV) lauter stellen; (heating) höher stellen; **turning** n (in road) Abzweigung f; **turning point** n Wendepunkt m

turnip ['tɜːnɪp] n Rübe f

turnover ['tɜːnəʊvə°] n (Fin) Umsatz m

turnpike ['tɜːnpaɪk] n (US) gebührenpflichtige Autobahn

turntable ['tɜːnteɪbl] n (on record player) Plattenteller m

turn-up ['tɜːnʌp] n (Brit: on trousers) Aufschlag m

turquoise ['tɜːkwɔɪz] adj türkis

turtle ['tɜːtl] n (Brit) Wasserschildkröte f; (US) Schildkröte f

tutor ['tjuːtə°] n (private) Privatlehrer(in) m(f); (Brit: at university) Tutor(in) m(f)

tux [tʌks], **tuxedo** [tʌk'siːdəʊ] (pl -s) n (US) Smoking m

TV ['tiː'viː] n Fernsehen nt; (~ set) Fernseher m; **to watch ~** fernsehen; **on ~** im Fernsehen ▷ adj Fernseh-; **~ programme** Fernsehsendung f

tweed [twiːd] n Tweed m

tweezers ['twiːzəz] npl Pinzette f

twelfth [twelfθ] adj zwölfte(r, s); see also **eighth**; **twelve** [twelv] num zwölf ▷ n Zwölf f; see also **eight**

twentieth ['twentɪɪθ] adj zwanzigste(r, s); see also **eighth**; **twenty** ['twentɪ] num zwanzig; **~-one** einundzwanzig ▷ n Zwanzig f; **to be in one's twenties** in den Zwanzigern sein; see also **eight**

twice [twaɪs] adv zweimal; **~ as much/many** doppelt so viel/viele

twig [twɪg] n Zweig

twilight ['twaɪlaɪt] n (in evening) Dämmerung f

twin [twɪn] n Zwilling m ▷ adj (brother etc) Zwillings-; **~ beds** zwei

Einzelbetten ▷ vt: **York is ~ned with Münster** York ist eine Partnerstadt von Münster

twinge [twɪndʒ] n (pain) stechender Schmerz

twinkle ['twɪŋkl] vi funkeln

twin room n Zweibettzimmer nt; **twin town** n Partnerstadt f

twist [twɪst] vt (turn) drehen, winden; (distort) verdrehen; **I've ~ed my ankle** ich bin mir dem Fuß umgeknickt

two [tuː] num zwei; **to break sth in ~** etw in zwei Teile brechen ▷ n Zwei f; **the ~ of them** die beiden; see also **eight**; **two-dimensional** adj zweidimensional; (fig) oberflächlich; **two-faced** adj falsch, heuchlerisch; **two-piece** adj zweiteilig; **two-way** adj: **~ traffic** Gegenverkehr

type [taɪp] n (sort) Art f; (typeface) Schrift(art) f; **what ~ of car is it?** was für ein Auto ist das?; **he's not my ~** er ist nicht mein Typ; **typeface** n Schrift(art) f; **typewriter** n Schreibmaschine f

typhoid ['taɪfɔɪd] n Typhus m

typhoon [taɪ'fuːn] n Taifun m

typical ['tɪpɪkəl] adj typisch (of für)

typing error ['taɪpɪnərə°] n Tippfehler m

tyre [taɪə°] n (Brit) Reifen m; **tyre pressure** n Reifendruck m

Tyrol [tɪ'rəʊl] n: **the ~** Tirol nt

U

UFO ['juːfəʊ] *acr* = **unidentified flying object** Ufo *nt*

Uganda [juːˈɡændə] *n* Uganda *nt*

ugly ['ʌɡlɪ] *adj* hässlich

UHT *adj abbr* = **ultra-heat treated** ~ **milk** H-Milch *f*

UK *abbr* = **United Kingdom**

Ukraine [juːˈkreɪn] *n*: **the** ~ die Ukraine

ulcer ['ʌlsə°] *n* Geschwür *nt*

ulterior [ʌlˈtɪərɪə°] *adj*: ~ **motive** Hintergedanke *m*

ultimate ['ʌltɪmət] *adj* (*final*) letzte(r, s); (*authority*) höchste(r, s); **ultimately** *adv* letzten Endes; (*eventually*) schließlich; **ultimatum** [ʌltɪˈmeɪtəm] *n* Ultimatum *nt*

ultra- ['ʌltrə] *pref* ultra-

ultrasound ['ʌltrəsaʊnd] *n* (*Med*) Ultraschall *m*

umbrella [ʌmˈbrelə] *n* Schirm *m*

umpire ['ʌmpaɪə°] *n* Schieds-richter(in) *m(f)*

umpteen ['ʌmptiːn] *num* (*fam*) zig; ~ **times** zigmal

un- [ʌn] *pref* un-

UN *n sing abbr* = **United Nations** VN, Vereinte Nationen *pl*

unable [ʌnˈeɪbl] *adj*: **to be** ~ **to do sth** etw nicht tun können

unacceptable [ʌnəˈkseptəbl] *adj* unannehmbar

unaccountably [ʌnəˈkaʊntəblɪ] *adv* unerklärlicherweise

unaccustomed [ʌnəˈkʌstəmd] *adj*: **to be** ~ **to sth** etw nicht gewohnt sein

unanimous, unanimously [juːˈnænɪməs, -lɪ] *adj, adv* einmütig

unattached [ʌnəˈtætʃt] (*without partner*) ungebunden

unattended [ʌnəˈtendɪd] *adj* (*luggage, car*) unbeaufsichtigt

unauthorized [ʌnˈɔːθəraɪzd] *adj* unbefugt

unavailable [ʌnəˈveɪləbl] *adj* nicht erhältlich; (*person*) nicht erreichbar

unavoidable [ʌnəˈvɔɪdəbl] *adj* unvermeidlich

unaware [ʌnəˈwɛə°] *adj*: **to be** ~ **of sth** sich einer Sache *dat* nicht bewusst sein; **I was** ~ **that ...** ich wusste nicht, dass ...

unbalanced [ʌnˈbælənst] *adj* unausgewogen; (*mentally*) gestört

unbearable [ʌnˈbɛərəbl] *adj* unerträglich

unbeatable [ʌnˈbiːtəbl] *adj* unschlagbar

unbelievable [ʌnbɪˈliːvəbl] *adj* unglaublich

unblock [ʌnˈblɒk] *vt* (*pipe*) frei machen

unbutton [ʌnˈbʌtn] *vt* aufknöpfen

uncertain [ʌnˈsɜːtən] adj
unsicher

uncle [ˈʌŋkl] n Onkel m

uncomfortable [ʌnˈkʌmfətəbl]
adj unbequem

unconditional [ʌnkənˈdɪʃənl]
adj bedingungslos

unconscious [ʌnˈkɒnʃəs] adj
(Med) bewusstlos; **to be ~ of sth**
sich einer Sache dat nicht bewusst
sein; **unconsciously** adv
unbewusst

uncork [ʌnˈkɔːk] vt entkorken

uncover [ʌnˈkʌvə°] vt
aufdecken

undecided [ʌndɪˈsaɪdɪd] adj
unschlüssig

undeniable [ʌndɪˈnaɪəbl] adj
unbestreitbar

under [ˈʌndə°] prep (beneath)
unter +dat; (with motion) unter
+akk; **children ~ eight** Kinder
unter acht; **~ an hour** weniger als
eine Stunde ▷ adv (beneath)
unten; (with motion) darunter;
children aged eight and ~ Kinder
bis zu acht Jahren; **under-age** adj
minderjährig

undercarriage [ˈʌndəkærɪdʒ] n
Fahrgestell nt

underdog [ˈʌndədɒɡ] n (outsider)
Außenseiter(in) m(f)

underdone [ʌndəˈdʌn] adj
(Gastr) nicht gar, durch;
(deliberately) nicht durchgebraten

underestimate [ʌndərˈestɪmeɪt] vt unterschätzen

underexposed [ʌndərɪksˈpəʊzd]
adj (Foto) unterbelichtet

undergo [ʌndəˈɡəʊ] irr vt
(experience) durchmachen;
(operation, test) sich unterziehen
+dat

undergraduate [ʌndəˈɡrædjuət]
n Student(in) m(f)

underground [ˈʌndəɡraʊnd] adj
unterirdisch ▷ n (Brit Rail) U-Bahn

f; **underground station** n
U-Bahn-Station f

underlie [ʌndəˈlaɪ] irr vt
zugrunde liegen +dat

underline [ʌndəˈlaɪn] vt
unterstreichen

underlying [ʌndəˈlaɪɪŋ] adj
zugrunde liegend

underneath [ʌndəˈniːθ] prep
unter; (with motion) unter +akk
▷ adv darunter

underpants [ˈʌndəpænts] npl
Unterhose f; **undershirt**
[ˈʌndəʃɜːt] n (US) Unterhemd nt;
undershorts [ˈʌndəʃɔːts] npl (US)
Unterhose f

understand [ʌndəˈstænd] irr vt,
vi verstehen; **I ~ that ...** (been told)
ich habe gehört, dass ...;
(sympathize) ich habe Verständnis
dafür, dass ...; **to make oneself
understood** sich verständlich
machen; **understandable** adj
verständlich; **understanding** adj
verständnisvoll

undertake [ʌndəˈteɪk] irr vt
(task) übernehmen; **to ~ to do sth**
sich verpflichten, etw zu tun;
undertaker n Leichenbestat-
ter(in) m(f); **~'s** (firm)
Bestattungsinstitut nt

underwater [ʌndəˈwɔːtə°] adv
unter Wasser ▷ adj Unterwasser-

underwear [ˈʌndəweə°] n
Unterwäsche f

undesirable [ʌndɪˈzaɪərəbl] adj
unerwünscht

undo [ʌnˈduː] irr vt (unfasten)
aufmachen; (work)
zunichtemachen; (Inform)
rückgängig machen

undoubtedly [ʌnˈdaʊtɪdlɪ] adv
zweifellos

undress [ʌnˈdres] vt ausziehen;
to get ~ed sich ausziehen ▷ vi
sich ausziehen

undue [ʌnˈdjuː] adj übermäßig

unduly [ʌnˈdjuːlɪ] *adv*
übermäßig

unearth [ʌnˈɜːθ] *vt (dig up)*
ausgraben; *(find)* aufstöbern

unease [ʌnˈiːz] *n* Unbehagen *nt*;
uneasy *adj (person)* unbehaglich;
I'm ~ about it mir ist nicht wohl
dabei

unemployed [ʌnɪmˈplɔɪd] *adj*
arbeitslos ▷ *b npl*: **the ~** die
Arbeitslosen *pl*; **unemployment**
[ʌnɪmˈplɔɪmənt] *n* Arbeitslosigkeit *f*; **unemployment
benefit** *n* Arbeitslosengeld *nt*

unequal [ʌnˈiːkwəl] *adj*
ungleich

uneven [ʌnˈiːvən] *adj (surface,
road)* uneben; *(contest)* ungleich

unexpected [ʌnɪkˈspektɪd] *adj*
unerwartet

unfair [ʌnˈfɛə*] *adj* unfair

unfamiliar [ʌnfəˈmɪljə*] *adj*: **to
be ~ with sb/sth** jdn/etw nicht
kennen

unfasten [ʌnˈfɑːsn] *vt*
aufmachen

unfit [ʌnˈfɪt] *adj* ungeeignet (for
für); *(in bad health)* nicht fit

unforeseen [ʌnfɔːˈsiːn] *adj*
unvorhergesehen

unforgettable [ʌnfəˈgɪvəbl] *adj*
unvergesslich

unforgivable [ʌnfəˈgɪvəbl] *adj*
unverzeihlich

unfortunate [ʌnˈfɔːtʃnət] *adj
(unlucky)* unglücklich; **it is ~
that ...** es ist bedauerlich, dass ...;
unfortunately *adv* leider

unfounded [ʌnˈfaʊndɪd] *adj*
unbegründet

unhappy [ʌnˈhæpɪ] *adj (sad)*
unglücklich, unzufrieden; **to be
~ with sth** mit etw unzufrieden
sein

unhealthy [ʌnˈhelθɪ] *adj*
ungesund

unheard-of [ʌnˈhɜːdɒv] *adj*
(unknown) gänzlich unbekannt;
(outrageous) unerhört

unhelpful [ʌnˈhelpfʊl] *adj* nicht
hilfreich

unhitch [ʌnˈhɪtʃ] *vt (caravan,
trailer)* abkoppeln

unhurt [ʌnˈhɜːt] *adj* unverletzt

uniform [ˈjuːnɪfɔːm] *n* Uniform
f ▷ *adj* einheitlich

unify [ˈjuːnɪfaɪ] *vt* vereinigen

unimportant [ʌnɪmˈpɔːtənt]-
adj unwichtig

uninhabited [ʌnɪnˈhæbɪtɪd] *adj*
unbewohnt

uninstall [ʌnɪnˈstɔːl] *vt (Inform)*
deinstallieren

unintentional [ʌnɪnˈtenʃənl]
adj unabsichtlich

union [ˈjuːnjən] *n (uniting)*
Vereinigung *f*; *(alliance)* Union *f*;
Union Jack *n* Union Jack *m*
(britische Nationalflagge)

unique [juːˈniːk] *adj* einzigartig

unit [ˈjuːnɪt] *n* Einheit *f*; *(of
system, machine)* Teil *nt*; *(in school)*
Lektion *f*

unite [juːˈnaɪt] *vt* vereinigen;
the United Kingdom das
Vereinigte Königreich; **the United
Nations** *pl* die Vereinten Nationen
pl; **the United States (of
America)** *pl* die Vereinigten
Staaten (von Amerika) *pl* ▷ *vi* sich
vereinigen

universe [ˈjuːnɪvɜːs] *n* Univer-
sum *nt*

university [juːnɪˈvɜːsɪtɪ] *n*
Universität *f*

unkind [ʌnˈkaɪnd] *adj* unfreundlich (to zu)

unknown [ʌnˈnəʊn] *adj*
unbekannt (to +dat)

unleaded [ʌnˈledɪd] *adj* bleifrei

unless [ənˈles] *conj* es sei denn,
wenn ... nicht; **don't do it ~ I tell
you to** mach das nicht, es sei
denn, ich sage es dir; **~ I'm**

mistaken ... wenn ich mich nicht irre ...

unlicensed [ʌnˈlaɪsənst] adj (to sell alcohol) ohne Lizenz

unlike [ʌnˈlaɪk] prep (in contrast to) im Gegensatz zu; **it's ~ her to be late** es sieht ihr gar nicht ähnlich, zu spät zu kommen; **unlikely** [ʌnˈlaɪklɪ] adj unwahrscheinlich

unload [ʌnˈləʊd] vt ausladen

unlock [ʌnˈlɒk] vt aufschließen

unlucky [ʌnˈlʌkɪ] adj unglücklich; **to be ~** Pech haben

unmistakable [ʌnmɪˈsteɪkəbl] adj unverkennbar

unnecessary [ʌnˈnesəsərɪ] adj unnötig

unobtainable [ʌnəbˈteɪnəbl] adj nicht erhältlich

unoccupied [ʌnˈɒkjʊpaɪd] adj (seat) frei; (building, room) leer stehend

unpack [ʌnˈpæk] vt, vi auspacken

unpleasant [ʌnˈpleznt] adj unangenehm

unplug [ʌnˈplʌg] vt: **to ~ sth** den Stecker von etw herausziehen

unprecedented [ʌnˈpresɪdəntɪd] adj beispiellos

unpredictable [ʌnprɪˈdɪktəbl] adj (person, weather) unberechenbar

unreasonable [ʌnˈriːznəbl] adj unvernünftig; (demand) übertrieben

unreliable [ʌnrɪˈlaɪəbl] adj unzuverlässig

unsafe [ʌnˈseɪf] adj nicht sicher; (dangerous) gefährlich

unscrew [ʌnˈskruː] vt abschrauben

unsightly [ʌnˈsaɪtlɪ] adj unansehnlich

unskilled [ʌnˈskɪld] adj (worker) ungelernt

unsuccessful [ʌnsəkˈsesful] adj erfolglos

unsuitable [ʌnˈsuːtəbl] adj ungeeignet (for für)

until [ənˈtɪl] prep bis; **not ~** erst; **from Monday ~ Friday** von Montag bis Freitag; **he didn't come home ~ midnight** er kam erst um Mitternacht nach Hause; **~ then** bis dahin ▷ conj bis; **she won't come ~ you invite her** sie kommt erst, wenn du sie einlädst/wenn Sie sie einladen

unusual, unusually [ʌnˈjuːʒʊəl, -ɪ] adj, adv ungewöhnlich

unwanted [ʌnˈwɒntɪd] adj unerwünscht, ungewollt

unwell [ʌnˈwel] adj krank; **to feel ~** sich nicht wohlfühlen

unwilling [ʌnˈwɪlɪŋ] adj: **to be ~ to do sth** nicht bereit sein, etw zu tun

unwind [ʌnˈwaɪnd] irr vt abwickeln ▷ vi (relax) sich entspannen

unwrap [ʌnˈræp] vt auspacken

unzip [ʌnˈzɪp] vt den Reißverschluss aufmachen an +dat; (Inform) entzippen

○ **KEYWORD**

up [ʌp] prep: **to be up sth** oben auf etw dat sein; **to go up sth** (auf) etw akk hinaufgehen; **go up that road** gehen Sie die Straße hinauf
▷ adv **1** (upwards, higher) oben; **put it up a bit higher** stell es etwas weiter nach oben; **up there** da oben, dort oben; **up above** hoch oben
2 to be up (out of bed) auf sein; (prices, level) gestiegen sein; (building, tent) stehen
3 up to (as far as) bis; **up to now** bis jetzt

4 to be up to (*depending on*): **it's up to you** das hängt von dir ab; (*equal to*): **he's not up to it** (*job, task etc*) er ist dem nicht gewachsen; (*inf: be doing*) (*showing disapproval, suspicion*) **what is he up to?** was führt er im Schilde?; **his work is not up to the required standard** seine Arbeit entspricht nicht dem geforderten Niveau
▷ n: **ups and downs** (*in life, career*) Höhen und Tiefen *pl*

upbringing ['ʌpbrɪŋɪŋ] *n* Erziehung *f*

update [ʌp'deɪt] *n* (*list etc*) Aktualisierung *f*; (*software*) Update *nt* ▷ *vt* (*list etc, person*) auf den neuesten Stand bringen, aktualisieren

upgrade [ʌp'greɪd] *vt* (*computer*) aufrüsten; **we were ~d** das Hotel hat uns ein besseres Zimmer gegeben

upheaval [ʌp'hi:vəl] *n* Aufruhr *m*; (*Pol*) Umbruch *m*

uphill [ʌp'hɪl] *adv* bergauf

upon [ə'pɒn] *prep* see **on**

upper ['ʌpə°] *adj* obere(r, s); (*arm, deck*) Ober-

upright ['ʌpraɪt] *adj, adv* aufrecht

uprising [ʌp'raɪzɪŋ] *n* Aufstand *m*

uproar ['ʌprɔ:°] *n* Aufruhr *m*

upset [ʌp'set] *irr vt* (*overturn*) umkippen; (*disturb*) aufregen; (*sadden*) bestürzen; (*offend*) kränken; (*plans*) durcheinanderbringen ▷ *adj* (*disturbed*) aufgeregt; (*sad*) bestürzt; (*offended*) gekränkt; **~ stomach** ['ʌpset] Magenverstimmung *f*

upside down [ʌpsaɪd'daʊn] *adv* verkehrt herum; (*fig*) drunter und drüber; **to turn sth ~** (*box etc*)

etw umdrehen/durchwühlen

upstairs [ʌp'steəz] *adv* oben; (*go, take*) nach oben

up-to-date ['ʌptə'deɪt] *adj* modern; (*fashion, information*) aktuell; **to keep sb ~** jdn auf dem Laufenden halten

upwards ['ʌpwədz] *adv* nach oben

urban ['ɜ:bən] *adj* städtisch, Stadt-

urge [ɜ:dʒ] *n* Drang *m* ▷ *vt*: **to ~ sb to do sth** jdn drängen, etw zu tun; **urgent, urgently** ['ɜ:dʒənt, -lɪ] *adj, adv* dringend

urine ['jʊərɪn] *n* Urin *m*

URL *abbr* = **uniform resource locator** (*Comput*) URL-Adresse *f*

us [ʌs] *pron* uns; **do they know ~?** kennen sie uns?; **can he help ~?** kann er uns helfen?; **it's ~** wir sind's; **both of ~** wir beide

US, USA *nsing abbr* = **United States (of America)** USA *pl*

use [ju:s] *n* (*using*) Gebrauch *m*; (*for specific purpose*) Benutzung *f*; **to make ~ of** Gebrauch machen von; **in/out of ~** in/außer Gebrauch; **it's no ~ (doing that)** es hat keinen Zweck(, das zu tun); **it's (of) no ~ to me** das kann ich nicht brauchen ▷ [ju:z] *vt* benutzen, gebrauchen; (*for specific purpose*) verwenden; (*method*) anwenden; **use up** *vt* aufbrauchen

used [ju:zd] *adj* (*secondhand*) gebraucht ▷ *vb aux*: **to be ~d to sb/sth** an jdn/etw gewöhnt sein; **to get ~d to sb/sth** sich an jdn/etw gewöhnen; **she ~d to live here** sie hat früher mal hier gewohnt; **useful** *adj* nützlich; **useless** *adj* nutzlos; (*unusable*) unbrauchbar; (*pointless*) zwecklos; **user** ['ju:zə°] *n* Benutzer(in) *m(f)*;

user-friendly adj
benutzerfreundlich

usual ['juːʒʊəl] adj üblich,
gewöhnlich; **as ~** wie üblich;
usually adv normalerweise

utensil [juːˈtensl] n Gerät nt

uterus ['juːtərəs] n Gebärmutter
f

utilize ['juːtɪlaɪz] vt verwenden

utmost ['ʌtməʊst] adj äußerst;
to do one's ~ sein Möglichstes
tun

utter ['ʌtə*] adj völlig ▷ vt von
sich geben; **utterly** adv völlig

U-turn ['juːtɜːn] n (Auto) Wende
f; **to do a ~** wenden; (fig) eine
Kehrtwendung machen

vacancy ['veɪkənsɪ] n (job)
offene Stelle; (room) freies Zimmer;
vacant ['veɪkənt] adj (room,
toilet) frei; (post) offen; (building)
leer stehend; **vacate** [vəˈkeɪt] vt
(room, building) räumen; (seat) frei
machen

vacation [vəˈkeɪʃən] n (US)
Ferien pl, Urlaub m; (at university)
(Semester)ferien pl; **to go on ~** in
Urlaub fahren; **~ course**
Ferienkurs m

vaccinate ['væksɪneɪt] vt
impfen; **vaccination**
[væksɪˈneɪʃən] n Impfung f; **~ card**
Impfpass m

vacuum ['vækjʊm] n Vakuum nt
▷ vt, vi (staub)saugen; **vacuum
(cleaner)** n Staubsauger m

vagina [vəˈdʒaɪnə] n Scheide f

vague [veɪg] adj (imprecise) vage;
(resemblance) entfernt; **vaguely**
adv in etwa, irgendwie

V

vain [veɪn] adj (attempt)
vergeblich; (conceited) eitel; **in
~** vergeblich, umsonst; **vainly** adv
(in vain) vergeblich

valentine (card)
['væləntaɪn(kɑːd)] n Valentins-
karte f; **Valentine's Day** n
Valentinstag m

valid ['vælɪd] adj (ticket, passport
etc) gültig; (argument) stichhaltig;
(claim) berechtigt

valley ['vælɪ] n Tal nt

valuable ['væljʊəbl] adj wertvoll;
(time) kostbar; **valuables** npl
Wertsachen pl

value ['væljuː] n Wert m ▷ vt
(appreciate) schätzen; **value added
tax** n Mehrwertsteuer f

valve [vælv] n Ventil nt

van [væn] n (Auto) Lieferwagen m

vanilla [vəˈnɪlə] n Vanille f

vanish ['vænɪʃ] vi verschwinden

vanity ['vænɪtɪ] n Eitelkeit f;
vanity case n Schminkkoffer m

vapor (US), **vapour** ['veɪpə] n
(mist) Dunst m; (steam) Dampf
m

variable ['veərɪəbl] adj (weather,
mood) unbeständig; (quality)
unterschiedlich; (speed, height)
regulierbar; **varied** ['veərɪd] adj
(interests, selection) vielseitig;
(career) bewegt; (work, diet)
abwechslungsreich; **variety**
[vəˈraɪətɪ] n (diversity)
Abwechslung f; (assortment)
Vielfalt f (of an +dat); (type) Art f;
various ['veərɪəs] adj
verschieden

varnish ['vɑːnɪʃ] n Lack m ▷ vt
lackieren

vary ['veərɪ] vt (alter) verändern
▷ vi (be different) unterschiedlich
sein; (fluctuate) sich verändern;
(prices) schwanken

vase [vɑːz, ?? veɪz] (US) n Vase f

vast [vɑːst] adj riesig; (area) weit

VAT [væt] abbr = **value added tax**
Mehrwertsteuer f, MwSt.

Vatican ['vætɪkən] n: **the ~** der
Vatikan

VCR [viːsiːˈɑː°] abbr = **video
cassette recorder** Videorekorder
m

VD [viːˈdiː] abbr = **venereal
disease** Geschlechtskrankheit f

VDU [viːdiːˈjuː] abbr = **visual
display unit**

veal [viːl] n Kalbfleisch nt

vegan ['viːgən] n Veganer(in)
m(f)

vegetable ['vedʒtəbl] n Gemüse
nt

vegetarian [vedʒɪˈteərɪən] n
Vegetarier(in) m(f) ▷ adj
vegetarisch

veggie ['vedʒɪ] n (fam)
Vegetarier(in) m(f); Gemüse nt
▷ adj vegetarisch; **veggieburger**
n Veggieburger m, Gemüseburger
m

vehicle ['viːɪkl] n Fahrzeug nt

veil [veɪl] n Schleier m

vein [veɪn] n Ader f

Velcro® ['velkrəʊ] n Klettband
nt

velvet ['velvɪt] n Samt m

vending machine
['vendɪŋməʃiːn] n Automat m

venetian blind [vɪˈniːʃənˈblaɪnd]
n Jalousie f

Venezuela [veneˈzweɪlə] n
Venezuela nt

Venice ['venɪs] n Venedig nt

venison ['venɪsn] n Rehfleisch
nt

vent [vent] n Öffnung f

ventilate ['ventɪleɪt] vt lüften;
ventilation [ventɪˈleɪʃən] n
Belüftung f; **ventilator**
['ventɪleɪtə°] n (in room)
Ventilator m; **to be on a ~** (Med)
künstlich beatmet werden

venture ['ventʃə°] n (project)

Unternehmung f; (Comm) Unternehmen nt ▷ vi (go) (sich) wagen

venue ['venjuː] n (for concert etc) Veranstaltungsort m; (Sport) Austragungsort m

verb [vɜːb] n Verb nt; **verbal** adj (agreement) mündlich; (skills) sprachlich; **verbally** adv mündlich

verdict ['vɜːdɪkt] n Urteil nt

verge [vɜːdʒ] n (of road) (Straßen)rand m; **to be on the ~ of doing sth** im Begriff sein, etw zu tun ▷ vi: **to ~ on** grenzen an +akk

verification [ˌverɪfɪ'keɪʃən] n (confirmation) Bestätigung f; (check) Überprüfung f; **verify** ['verɪfaɪ] vt (confirm) bestätigen; (check) überprüfen

vermin ['vɜːmɪn] npl Schädlinge pl; (insects) Ungeziefer nt

verruca [vɛ'ruːkə] n Warze f

versatile ['vɜːsətaɪl] adj vielseitig

verse [vɜːs] n (poetry) Poesie f; (stanza) Strophe f

version ['vɜːʃən] n Version f

versus ['vɜːsəs] prep gegen

vertical ['vɜːtɪkəl] adj senkrecht, vertikal

very ['verɪ] adv sehr; **~ much** sehr ▷ adj: **the ~ book I need** genau das Buch, das ich brauche; **at that ~ moment** gerade in dem Augenblick; **at the ~ top** ganz oben; **the ~ best** der/die/das Allerbeste

vest [vest] n (Brit) Unterhemd nt; (US: waistcoat) Weste f

vet [vet] n Tierarzt m, Tierärztin f

veto ['viːtəʊ] (pl -es) n Veto nt ▷ vt sein Veto einlegen gegen

VHF abbr = **very high frequency** UKW

via ['vaɪə] prep über +akk

viable ['vaɪəbl] adj (plan)

realisierbar; (company) rentabel

vibrate [vaɪ'breɪt] vi vibrieren; **vibration** [vaɪ'breɪʃən] n Vibration f

vicar ['vɪkə] n Pfarrer(in) m(f)

vice [vaɪs] n (evil) Laster nt; (Tech) Schraubstock m ▷ pref Vize-; **~-chairman** stellvertretender Vorsitzender; **~-president** Vizepräsident(in) m(f)

vice versa [vaɪs'vɜːsə] adv umgekehrt

vicinity [vɪ'sɪnɪtɪ] n: **in the ~** in der Nähe (of +gen)

vicious ['vɪʃəs] adj (violent) brutal; (malicious) gemein; **vicious circle** n Teufelskreis m

victim ['vɪktɪm] n Opfer nt

Victorian [vɪk'tɔːrɪən] adj viktorianisch

victory ['vɪktərɪ] n Sieg m

video ['vɪdɪəʊ] (pl -s) adj Video- ▷ n Video nt; (recorder) Videorekorder m ▷ vt (auf Video) aufnehmen; **video camera** n Videokamera f; **video cassette** n Videokassette f; **video clip** n Videoclip m; **video game** n Videospiel nt; **videophone** n Bildtelefon nt; **video recorder** n Videorekorder m; **video shop** n Videothek f; **videotape** n Videoband nt ▷ vt (auf Video) aufnehmen

Vienna [vɪ'enə] n Wien nt

Vietnam [vjet'næm] n Vietnam nt

view [vjuː] n (sight) Blick m (of auf +akk); (vista) Aussicht f; (opinion) Ansicht f, Meinung f; **in ~ of** angesichts +gen ▷ vt (situation, event) betrachten; (house) besichtigen; **viewer** n (for slides) Diabetrachter m; (TV) Zuschauer(in) m(f); **viewpoint** n (fig) Standpunkt m

vigilant ['vɪdʒɪlənt] adj wachsam

vile [vaɪl] *adj* abscheulich; (*weather, food*) scheußlich

village ['vɪlɪdʒ] *n* Dorf *nt*; **villager** *n* Dorfbewohner(in) *m(f)*

villain ['vɪlən] *n* Schurke *m*; (*in film, story*) Bösewicht *m*

vine [vaɪn] *n* (Wein)rebe *f*

vinegar ['vɪnɪgə*] *n* Essig *m*

vineyard ['vɪnjəd] *n* Weinberg *m*

vintage ['vɪntɪdʒ] *n* (*of wine*) Jahrgang *m*; **vintage wine** *n* edler Wein

vinyl ['vaɪnɪl] *n* Vinyl *nt*

viola [vɪ'əʊlə] *n* Bratsche *f*

violate ['vaɪəleɪt] *vt* (*treaty*) brechen; (*rights, rule*) verletzen

violence ['vaɪələns] *n* (*brutality*) Gewalt *f*; (*of person*) Gewalttätigkeit *f*; **violent** *adj* (*brutal*) brutal; (*death*) gewaltsam

violet ['vaɪələt] *n* Veilchen *nt*

violin [vaɪə'lɪn] *n* Geige *f*, Violine *f*

VIP *abbr* = **very important person** VIP *mf*

virgin ['vɜːdʒɪn] *n* Jungfrau *f*

Virgo ['vɜːgəʊ] *n* (*Astr*) Jungfrau *f*

virile ['vɪraɪl] *adj* (*man*) männlich

virtual ['vɜːtjʊəl] *adj* (*Inform*) virtuell; **virtually** *adv* praktisch; **virtual reality** *n* virtuelle Realität

virtue ['vɜːtjuː] *n* Tugend *f*; **by ~ of** aufgrund +*gen*; **virtuous** ['vɜːtjʊəs] *adj* tugendhaft

virus ['vaɪrəs] *n* (*Med, Inform*) Virus *m*

visa ['viːzə] *n* Visum *nt*

visibility [vɪzɪ'bɪlɪtɪ] *n* (*Meteo*) Sichtweite *f*; **good/poor ~** gute/schlechte Sicht; **visible** ['vɪzəbl] *adj* sichtbar; (*evident*) sichtlich; **visibly** *adv* sichtlich

vision ['vɪʒən] *n* (*power of sight*) Sehvermögen *nt*; (*foresight*) Weitblick *m*; (*dream, image*) Vision *f*

visit ['vɪzɪt] *n* Besuch *m*; (*stay*) Aufenthalt *m* ▷ *vt* besuchen; **visiting hours** *npl* Besuchszeiten *pl*; **visitor** *n* Besucher(in) *m(f)*; **~'s book** Gästebuch *nt*; **visitor centre** *n* Informationszentrum *nt*

visor ['vaɪzə*] *n* (*on helmet*) Visier *nt*; (*Auto*) Blende *f*

visual ['vɪzjʊəl] *adj* Seh-; (*image, joke*) visuell; **~ aid** Anschauungsmaterial *nt*; **~ display unit** Monitor *m*; **visualize** *vt* sich vorstelle; **visually** *adv* visuell; **~ impaired** sehbehindert

vital ['vaɪtl] *adj* (*essential*) unerlässlich, wesentlich; (*argument, moment*) entscheidend; **vitality** [vaɪ'tælɪtɪ] *n* Vitalität *f*; **vitally** *adv* äußerst

vitamin ['vɪtəmɪn] *n* Vitamin *nt*

vivacious [vɪ'veɪʃəs] *adj* lebhaft

vivid ['vɪvɪd] *adj* (*description*) anschaulich; (*memory*) lebhaft; (*colour*) leuchtend

V-neck ['viːnek] *n* V-Ausschnitt *m*

vocabulary [vəʊ'kæbjʊlərɪ] *n* Wortschatz *m*, Vokabular *nt*

vocal ['vəʊkəl] *adj* (*of the voice*) Stimm-; (*group*) Gesangs-; (*protest, person*) lautstark

vocation [vəʊ'keɪʃən] *n* Berufung *f*; **vocational** *adj* Berufs-

vodka ['vɒdkə] *n* Wodka *m*

voice [vɔɪs] *n* Stimme *f* ▷ *vt* äußern; **voice mail** *n* Voicemail *f*

void [vɔɪd] *n* Leere *f* ▷ *adj* (*Jur*) ungültig; **~ of** (ganz) ohne

volcano [vɒl'keɪnəʊ] (*pl* **-es**) *n* Vulkan *m*

volley ['vɒlɪ] *n* (*Tennis*) Volley *m*; **volleyball** *n* Volleyball *m*

volt [vəʊlt] *n* Volt *nt*; **voltage** *n* Spannung *f*

volume ['vɒljuːm] *n* (*of sound*) Lautstärke *f*; (*space occupied by sth*)

Volumen nt; (size, amount) Umfang m; (book) Band m; **volume control** n Lautstärkeregler m

voluntary, voluntarily ['vɒləntəri, -li] adj, adv freiwillig; (unpaid) ehrenamtlich; **volunteer** [vɒlən'tɪə°] n Freiwillige(r) mf ▷ vi sich freiwillig melden ▷ vt: **to ~ to do sth** sich anbieten, etw zu tun

voluptuous [və'lʌptjuəs] adj sinnlich

vomit ['vɒmɪt] vi sich übergeben

vote [vəʊt] n Stimme f; (ballot) Wahl f; (result) Abstimmungsergebnis nt; (right to vote) Wahlrecht nt ▷ vt (elect) wählen; **they ~d him chairman** sie wählten ihn zum Vorsitzenden ▷ vi wählen; **to ~ for/against sth** für/gegen etw stimmen; **voter** n Wähler(in) m(f)

voucher ['vaʊtʃə°] n Gutschein m

vow [vaʊ] n Gelöbnis nt ▷ vt: **to ~ to do sth** geloben, etw zu tun

vowel ['vaʊəl] n Vokal m

voyage ['vɔɪdʒ] n Reise f

vulgar ['vʌlgə°] adj vulgär, ordinär

vulnerable ['vʌlnərəbl] adj verwundbar; (sensitive) verletzlich

vulture ['vʌltʃə°] n Geier m

W abbr = **west** W

wade [weɪd] vi (in water) waten

wafer ['weɪfə°] n (Rel) Hostie f; **wafer-thin** adj hauchdünn

waffle ['wɒfl] n Waffel f; (Brit fam: empty talk) Geschwafel nt ▷ vi (Brit fam) schwafeln

wag [wæg] vt (tail) wedeln mit

wage [weɪdʒ] n Lohn m

waggon (Brit), **wagon** ['wægən] n (horse-drawn) Fuhrwerk nt; (Brit Rail) Waggon m; (US Auto) Wagen m

waist [weɪst] n Taille f; **waistcoat** n (Brit) Weste f; **waistline** n Taille f

wait [weɪt] n Wartezeit f ▷ vi warten (for auf +akk); **to ~ and see** abwarten; **~ a minute** Moment mal; **wait up** vi aufbleiben

waiter n Kellner m; **~!** Herr Ober!

waiting n: **"no ~"** "Halteverbot";

waiting list n Warteliste f;
waiting room n (Med)
Wartezimmer nt; (Rail) Wartesaal
m
waitress n Kellnerin f
wake [weɪk] (woke o waked,
woken o waked) vt wecken ▷ vi
aufwachen; **wake up** vt
aufwecken ▷ vi aufwachen;
wake-up call n (Tel) Weckruf m
Wales [weɪlz] n Wales nt
walk [wɔːk] n Spaziergang m;
(ramble) Wanderung f; (route) Weg
m; **to go for a ~** es sind
it's only a five-minute ~ es sind
nur fünf Minuten zu Fuß ▷ vi
gehen; (stroll) spazieren gehen;
(ramble) wandern ▷ vt (dog)
ausführen; **walking** n: **to go
~** wandern; **walking shoes** npl
Wanderschuhe pl; **walking stick** n
Spazierstock m
Walkman® (pl -s) n Walkman®
m
wall [wɔːl] n (inside) Wand f;
(outside) Mauer f
wallet ['wɒlɪt] n Brieftasche
f
wallpaper ['wɔːlpeɪpə*] n
Tapete f; (Inform)
Bildschirmhintergrund m ▷ vt
tapezieren
walnut ['wɔːlnʌt] n (nut)
Walnuss f
waltz [wɔːlts] n Walzer m
wander ['wɒndə*] vi (person)
herumwandern
want [wɒnt] n (lack) Mangel m
(of an +dat); (need) Bedürfnis nt; **for
~ of** aus Mangel an +dat ▷ vt
(desire) wollen; (need) brauchen; **I
~ to stay here** ich will hier
bleiben; **he doesn't ~ to** er will
nicht
WAP phone ['wæpfəʊn] n
WAP-Handy nt
war [wɔː*] n Krieg m

ward [wɔːd] n (in hospital)
Station f; (child) Mündel nt
warden ['wɔːdən] n Aufseher(in)
m(f); (in youth hostel) Herbergsvater
m, Herbergsmutter f
wardrobe ['wɔːdrəʊb] n
Kleiderschrank m
warehouse ['weəhaʊs] n
Lagerhaus nt
warfare ['wɔːfeə*] n Krieg m;
(techniques) Kriegsführung f
warm [wɔːm] adj warm;
(welcome) herzlich; **I'm ~** mir ist
warm ▷ vt wärmen; (food)
aufwärmen; **warm over** vt (US:
food) aufwärmen; **warm up** vt
(food) aufwärmen; (room)
erwärmen ▷ vi (food, room) warm
werden; (Sport) sich aufwärmen;
warmly adv warm; (welcome)
herzlich; **warmth** n Wärme f; (of
welcome) Herzlichkeit f
warn [wɔːn] vt warnen (of,
against vor +dat); **to ~ sb not to do
sth** jdn davor warnen, etw zu tun;
warning n Warnung f; **warning
light** n Warnlicht nt; **warning
triangle** n (Auto) Warndreieck nt
warranty ['wɒrəntɪ] n Garantie
f
wart [wɔːt] n Warze f
wary ['weərɪ] adj vorsichtig;
(suspicious) misstrauisch
was [wɒz, wəz] pt of **be**
wash [wɒʃ] n: **to have a ~** sich
waschen; **it's in the ~** es ist in der
Wäsche ▷ vt waschen; (plates,
glasses etc) abwaschen; **to ~ one's
hands** sich dat die Hände
waschen; **to ~ the dishes** (das
Geschirr) abwaschen ▷ vi (clean
oneself) sich waschen; **wash off** vt
abwaschen; **wash up** vi (Brit:
wash dishes) abwaschen; (US: clean
oneself) sich waschen; **washable**
adj waschbar; **washbag** n (US)
Kulturbeutel m; **washbasin** n

Waschbecken nt; **washcloth** n (US) Waschlappen m; **washer** n (Tech) Dichtungsring m; (washing machine) Waschmaschine f; **washing** n (laundry) Wäsche f; **washing machine** n Waschmaschine f; **washing powder** n Waschpulver nt; **washing-up** n (Brit) Abwasch m; **to do the ~** abwaschen; **washing-up liquid** n (Brit) Spülmittel nt; **washroom** n (US) Toilette f

wasn't ['wɒznt] contr of **was not**

wasp [wɒsp] n Wespe f

waste [weɪst] n (materials) Abfall m; (wasting) Verschwendung f; **it's a ~ of time** das ist Zeitverschwendung ▷ adj (superfluous) überschüssig ▷ vt verschwenden (on an +akk); (opportunity) vertun; **waste bin** n Abfalleimer m; **wastepaper basket** n Papierkorb m

watch [wɒtʃ] n (timepiece) (Armband)uhr f ▷ vt (observe) beobachten; (guard) aufpassen auf +akk; (film, play, programme) sich dat ansehen; **to ~ TV** fernsehen ▷ vi zusehen; (guard) Wache halten; **to ~ for sb/sth** nach jdm/etw Ausschau halten; **~ out** pass auf!; **watchdog** n Wachhund m; (fig) Aufsichtsbehörde f; **watchful** adj wachsam

water ['wɔːtə°] n Wasser nt ▷ vt (plant) gießen ▷ vi (eye) tränen; **my mouth is ~ing** mir läuft das Wasser im Mund zusammen; **water down** vt verdünnen; **watercolor** (US), **watercolour** n (painting) Aquarell nt; (paint) Wasserfarbe f; **watercress** n (Brunnen)kresse f; **waterfall** n Wasserfall m; **watering can** n Gießkanne f; **water level** n

Wasserstand m; **watermelon** n Wassermelone f; **waterproof** adj wasserdicht; **water-skiing** n Wasserskilaufen nt; **water sports** npl Wassersport m; **watertight** adj wasserdicht; **water wings** npl Schwimmflügel pl; **watery** adj wässerig

wave [weɪv] n Welle f ▷ vt (move to and fro) schwenken; (hand, flag) winken mit ▷ vi (person) winken; (flag) wehen; **wavelength** n Wellenlänge f; **to be on the same ~** (fig) die gleiche Wellenlänge haben; **wavy** ['weɪvɪ] adj wellig

wax [wæks] n Wachs nt; (in ear) Ohrenschmalz nt

way [weɪ] n Weg m; (direction) Richtung f; (manner) Art f; **can you tell me the ~ to ... ?** wie komme ich (am besten) zu ... ?; **we went the wrong ~** wir sind in die falsche Richtung gefahren/gegangen; **to lose one's ~** sich verirren; **to make ~ for sb/sth** jdm/etw Platz machen; **to get one's own ~** seinen Willen durchsetzen; **"give ~"** (Auto) „Vorfahrt achten"; **the other ~ round** andersherum; **one ~ or another** irgendwie; **in a ~** in gewisser Weise; **in the ~** im Weg; **by the ~** übrigens; **"~ in"** „Eingang"; **"~ out"** „Ausgang"; **no ~** (fam) kommt nicht infrage!

we [wiː] pron wir

weak [wiːk] adj schwach; **weaken** vt schwächen ▷ vi schwächer werden

wealth [welθ] n Reichtum m; **wealthy** adj reich

weapon ['wepən] n Waffe f

wear [weə°] n (wore, worn) vt (have on) tragen; **what shall I ~?** was soll ich anziehen? ▷ vi (become worn) sich abnutzen ▷ n: **~ (and tear)** Abnutzung f; **wear**

off vi (diminish) nachlassen; **wear
out** vt abnutzen; (person)
erschöpfen ▷ vi sich
abnutzen

weather ['weðə'] n Wetter nt;
I'm feeling under the ~ ich fühle
mich nicht ganz wohl; **weather
forecast** n Wettervorhersage
f

weave [wi:v] (**wove** o **weaved**,
woven o **weaved**) vt (cloth)
weben; (basket etc) flechten

web [web] n (a. fig) Netz nt; **the
Web** das Web, das Internet;
webcam ['webkæm] n Webcam
f; **web page** n Webseite f;
website n Website f

we'd [wi:d] contr of **we had; we
would**

Wed abbr = **Wednesday** Mi.

wedding ['wedɪŋ] n Hochzeit f;
wedding anniversary n
Hochzeitstag m; **wedding dress** n
Hochzeitskleid nt; **wedding ring**
n Ehering m

wedding shower n (US) Party für
die zukünftige Braut

wedge [wedʒ] n (under door etc)
Keil m; (of cheese etc) Stück nt, Ecke
f

Wednesday ['wenzdeɪ] n
Mittwoch m; see also **Tuesday**

wee [wi:] adj klein ▷ vi (fam)
Pipi machen

weed [wi:d] n Unkraut nt ▷ vt
jäten

week [wi:k] n Woche f; **twice a
~** zweimal in der Woche; **a ~ on
Friday/Friday ~** Freitag in einer
Woche; **a ~ last Friday** letzten
Freitag vor einer Woche; **in two
~s' time, in two ~s** in zwei
Wochen; **for ~s** wochenlang;
weekday n Wochentag m;
weekend n Wochenende nt;
weekend break n
Wochenendurlaub m; **weekly** adj,

adv wöchentlich; (magazine)
Wochen-

weep [wi:p] (**wept, wept**) vi
weinen

weigh [weɪ] vt, vi wiegen; **it ~s
20 kilos** es wiegt 20 Kilo; **weigh
up** vt abwägen; (person)
einschätzen; **weight** [weɪt] n
Gewicht nt; **to lose/put on
~** abnehmen/zunehmen;
weightlifting n Gewichtheben
nt; **weight training** n
Krafttraining nt; **weighty** adj
(important) schwerwiegend

weird [wɪəd] adj seltsam; **weirdo**
['wɪədəʊ] n Spinner(in) m(f)

welcome ['welkəm] n Empfang
m ▷ adj willkommen; (news)
angenehm; **~ to London**
willkommen in London! ▷ vt
begrüßen; **welcoming** adj
freundlich

welfare ['welfeə'] n Wohl nt; (US:
social security) Sozialhilfe f; **welfare
state** n Wohlfahrtsstaat m

well [wel] n Brunnen m ▷ adj (in
good health) gesund; **are you ~?**
geht es dir/Ihnen gut?; **to feel
~** sich wohlfühlen; **get ~** soon
gute Besserung! ▷ interj nun; **~, I
don't know** nun, ich weiß nicht
▷ adv gut; **~ done** gut gemacht!; **it
may ~ be** das kann wohl sein; **as
~** (in addition) auch; **~ over 60** weit
über 60

we'll [wi:l] contr of **we will; we
shall**

well-behaved [welbɪ'heɪvd]
adj brav; **well-being** n Wohl nt;
well-built (person) gut gebaut;
well-done adj (steak)
durchgebraten; **well-earned** adj
wohlverdient

wellingtons ['welɪŋtənz] npl
Gummistiefel pl

well-known [wel'nəʊn] adj
bekannt; **well-off** adj (wealthy)

wohlhabend; **well-paid** adj gut
bezahlt

Welsh [welʃ] adj walisisch ▷ n
(language) Walisisch nt; **the ~ pl** die
Waliser pl; **Welshman** (pl **-men**) n
Waliser m; **Welshwoman** (pl
-women) n Waliserin f

went [went] pt of **go**

wept [wept] pt, pp of **weep**

were [wɜː] pt of **be**

we're [wɪə] contr of **we are**

weren't [wɜːnt] contr of **were not**

west [west] n Westen m; **the
West** (Pol) der Westen m ▷ adv (go,
face) nach Westen ▷ adj West-;
westbound adj (in) Richtung
Westen; **western** adj
West-, westlich; **Western Europe**
Westeuropa nt ▷ n (Cine) Western
m; **West Germany** n (the
former) ~ (das ehemalige)
Westdeutschland nt; **westwards**
['westwədz] adv nach Westen

wet [wet] **(wet, wet)** adj ▷ vt: **to
~ oneself** in die Hose machen
▷ adj nass, feucht; **"~ paint"**
"frisch gestrichen"; **wet suit** n
Taucheranzug m

we've [wiːv] contr of **we have**

whale [weɪl] n Wal m

wharf [wɔːf] (pl **-s** o **wharves**) n
Kai m

⭕ **KEYWORD**

what [wɒt] adj **1** (in questions)
welche(r, s) was für ein(e);
what size is it? welche Größe ist
das?
2 (in exclamations) was für ein(e);
what a mess! was für ein
Durcheinander!
▷ pron (interrogative/relative) was;
what are you doing? was machst
du/machen Sie gerade?; **what are
you talking about?** wovon redest

du/reden Sie?; **what's your
name?** wie heißt du/heißen Sie?;
what is it called? wie heißt das?;
what about …? wie wär's mit …?;
I saw what you did ich habe
gesehen, was du gemacht
hast/Sie gemacht haben
▷ excl (disbelieving) wie, was;
what, no coffee! wie, kein
Kaffee?; **I've crashed the car —
what!** ich hatte einen
Autounfall — was!

whatever pron: **I'll do ~ you
want** ich tue alles, was du
willst/Sie wollen; **~ he says** egal,
was er sagt

what's [wɒts] contr of **what is;
what has**

wheat [wiːt] n Weizen m

wheel [wiːl] n Rad nt; (steering
wheel) Lenkrad nt ▷ vt (bicycle,
trolley) schieben; **wheelbarrow** n
Schubkarren m; **wheelchair** n
Rollstuhl m; **wheel clamp** n
Parkkralle f

⭕ **KEYWORD**

when [wen] adv wann
▷ conj **1** (at, during, after the time
that) wenn; (in past) als; **she was
reading when I came in** sie las,
als ich hereinkam; **be careful
when you cross the road** sei
vorsichtig, wenn du über die
Straße gehst/seien Sie vorsichtig,
wenn Sie über die Straße gehen
2 (on, at which) als; **on the day
when I met him** an dem Tag, an
dem ich ihn traf
3 (whereas) wo … doch

whenever adv (every time) immer
wenn; **come ~ you like** komm,
wann immer du willst/kommen
Sie, wann immer sie wollen

w

where [wɛəˀ] *adv* wo; **~ are you going?** wohin gehst du/gehen Sie?; **~ are you from?** woher kommst du/kommen Sie? ▷ *conj* wo; **that's ~ I used to live** da habe ich früher gewohnt; **whereabouts** [ˈwɛərəˈbaʊts] *adv* wo ▷ *n* [ˈwɛərəbaʊts] Aufenthaltsort *m*; **whereas** [wɛərˈæz] *conj* während, wohingegen; **whereby** *adv* wodurch; **wherever** [wɛərˈevəˀ] *conj* wo immer; **~ that may be** wo immer das sein mag; **~ I go** überall, wohin ich gehe

whether [ˈwɛðəˀ] *conj* ob

○ KEYWORD

which [wɪtʃ] *adj* **1** *(interrogative) (direct, indirect)* welche(r, s); **which one?** welche(r, s)?
2 in which case in diesem Fall; **by which time** zu dieser Zeit
▷ *pron* **1** *(interrogative)* welche(r, s); *(of people also)* wer
2 *(relative)* der/die/das; *(referring to people)* was; **the apple which you ate/which is on the table** der Apfel, den du gegessen hast/der auf dem Tisch liegt; **he said he saw her, which is true** er sagte, er habe sie gesehen, was auch stimmt

whichever *adj, pron* welche(r, s) auch immer

while [waɪl] *n*: **a ~** eine Weile; **for a ~** eine Zeit lang; **a short ~ ago** vor Kurzem ▷ *conj* während; *(although)* obwohl

whine [waɪn] *vi (person)* jammern

whip [wɪp] *n* Peitsche *f* ▷ *vt (beat)* peitschen; **~ped cream** Schlagsahne *f*

whirl [wɜːl] *vt, vi* herumwirbeln;

whirlpool *n (in river, sea)* Strudel *m; (pool)* Whirlpool *m*

whisk [wɪsk] *n* Schneebesen *m* ▷ *vt (cream etc)* schlagen

whisker [ˈwɪskəˀ] *n (of animal)* Schnurrhaar *nt*; **~s** *pl (of man)* Backenbart *m*

whisk(e)y [ˈwɪskɪ] *n* Whisky *m*

whisper [ˈwɪspəˀ] *vi, vt* flüstern; **to ~ sth to sb** jdm etw zuflüstern

whistle [ˈwɪsl] *n* Pfiff *m*; *(instrument)* Pfeife *f* ▷ *vt, vi* pfeifen

white [waɪt] *n (of egg)* Eiweiß *nt*; *(of eye)* Weiße *nt* ▷ *adj* weiß; *(with fear)* blass; *(coffee)* mit Milch/Sahne; **White House** *n*: **the ~** das Weiße Haus; **white lie** *n* Notlüge *f*; **white meat** *n* helles Fleisch; **white sauce** *n* weiße Soße; **white water rafting** *n* Rafting *nt*; **white wine** *n* Weißwein *m*

Whitsun [ˈwɪtsn] *n* Pfingsten *nt*

○ KEYWORD

who [huː] *pron* **1** *(interrogative)* wer; *(akk)* wen; *(dat)* wem; **who is it?, who's there?** wer ist da?
2 *(relative)* der/die/das; **the woman/man who spoke to me** die Frau/der Mann, die/der mit mir sprach

whoever [huːˈevəˀ] *pron* wer auch immer; **~ you choose** wen auch immer du wählst/Sie wählen

whole [həʊl] *adj* ganz ▷ *n* Ganze(s) *nt*; **the ~ of my family** meine ganze Familie; **on the ~** im Großen und Ganzen; **wholefood** *n (Brit)* Vollwertkost *f*; **~ store** Bioladen *m*; **wholeheartedly** *adv* voll und ganz; **wholemeal** *adj (Brit)* Vollkorn-; **wholesale** *adv (buy, sell)* im Großhandel; **wholesome**

adj gesund; **whole wheat** adj
Vollkorn-; **wholly** ['həʊlɪ] adv
völlig

○ **KEYWORD**

whom [huːm] pron 1
(interrogative) (akk) wen; (dat) wem;
whom did you see? wen hast
du/haben Sie gesehen?; **to whom
did you give it?** wem hast
du/haben Sie es gegeben?
2 (relative) (akk) den/die/das; (dat)
dem/der/dem; **the man whom
I saw/to whom I spoke** der
Mann, den ich sah/mit dem ich
sprach

whooping cough ['huːpɪŋkɒf]
n Keuchhusten m

whose [huːz] adj (in questions)
wessen; (in relative clauses)
dessen/deren/dessen, deren pl;
~ bike is that? wessen Fahrrad ist
das? ▷ pron (in questions) wessen;
~ is this? wem gehört das?

○ **KEYWORD**

why [waɪ] adv warum, weshalb
▷ conj warum, weshalb; **that's
not why I'm here** ich bin nicht
deswegen hier; **that's the reason
why** deshalb
▷ excl (expressing surprise, shock) na
so was; (explaining) also dann;
why, it's you! na so was, du
bist/Sie sind es!

wicked ['wɪkɪd] adj böse; (fam:
great) geil
wide [waɪd] adj breit; (skirt,
trousers) weit; (selection) groß
▷ adv weit; **wide-angle lens** n
Weitwinkelobjektiv nt;
wide-awake adj hellwach;
widely adv weit; **~ known**

allgemein bekannt; **widen** vt
verbreitern; (fig) erweitern;
wide-open adj weit offen;
widescreen TV n
Breitbildfernseher m; **widespread**
adj weit verbreitet

widow ['wɪdəʊ] n Witwe f;
widowed adj verwitwet;
widower n Witwer m
width [wɪdθ] n Breite f
wife [waɪf] (pl **wives**) n
(Ehe)frau f
Wi-Fi ['waɪfaɪ] n Wi-Fi nt
wig [wɪg] n Perücke f
wiggle ['wɪgl] vt wackeln mit
wild [waɪld] adj. wild; (violent)
heftig; (plan, idea) verrückt ▷ n: **in
the ~** in freier Wildbahn; **wildlife**
n Tier- und Pflanzenwelt f; **wildly**
adv wild; (exaggerated) maßlos

○ **KEYWORD**

will [wɪl] vb aux 1 (forms future
tense) werden; **I will finish it
tomorrow** ich mache es morgen
zu Ende
2 (in conjectures, predictions) **he will**
o **he'll be there by now** er dürfte
jetzt da sein; **that will be the
postman** das wird der Postbote
sein
3 (in commands, requests, offers) **will
you be quiet!** sei/seien Sie
endlich still!; **will you help me?**
hilfst du/helfen Sie mir?; **will you
have a cup of tea?** trinkst
du/trinken Sie eine Tasse Tee?; **I
won't put up with it!** das lasse ich
mir nicht gefallen!
▷ vt wollen
▷ n Wille m; (jur) Testament nt

willing adj bereitwillig; **to be ~ to
do sth** bereit sein, etw zu tun;
willingly adv gern(e)
willow ['wɪləʊ] n Weide f

w

willpower ['wɪlpaʊə] n Willenskraft f

wimp [wɪmp] n Weichei nt

win [wɪn] (**won, won**) vt, vi gewonnen ▷ n Sieg m; **win over, win round** vt für sich gewinnen

wind [waɪnd] (**wound, wound**) vt (rope, bandage) wickeln; **wind down** vt (car window) herunterkurbeln; **wind up** vt (clock) aufziehen; (car window) hochkurbeln; (meeting, speech) abschließen; (person) aufziehen, ärgern

wind [wɪnd] n Wind m; (Med) Blähungen pl; **wind farm** n Windpark m; **wind instrument** n Blasinstrument nt; **windmill** n Windmühle f

window ['wɪndəʊ] n Fenster nt; (counter) Schalter m; **~ of opportunity** Chance f, Gelegenheit f; **window box** n Blumenkasten m; **windowpane** n Fensterscheibe f; **window-shopping** n: **to go ~** einen Schaufensterbummel machen; **windowsill** n Fensterbrett nt

windpipe ['wɪndpaɪp] n Luftröhre f; **windscreen** n (Brit) Windschutzscheibe f; **windscreen wiper** n (Brit) Scheibenwischer m; **windshield** n (US) Windschutzscheibe f; **windshield wiper** n (US) Scheibenwischer m; **windsurfer** n Windsurfer(in) m(f); (board) Surfbrett nt; **windsurfing** n Windsurfen nt

windy ['wɪndɪ] adj windig

wine [waɪn] n Wein m; **wine bar** n Weinlokal nt; **wineglass** n Weinglas nt; **wine list** n Weinkarte f; **wine tasting** n (event) Weinprobe f

wing [wɪŋ] n Flügel m; (Brit Auto)

Kotflügel m; **~s** pl (Theat) Kulissen pl

wink [wɪŋk] vi zwinkern; **to ~ at sb** jdm zuzwinkern

winner ['wɪnə*] n Gewinner(in) m(f); (Sport) Sieger(in) m(f); **winning** adj (team, horse etc) siegreich; **~ number** Gewinnzahl f ▷ n **~s** pl Gewinn m

winter ['wɪntə*] n Winter m; **winter sports** npl Wintersport m; **wint(e)ry** ['wɪntrɪ] adj winterlich

wipe [waɪp] vt abwischen; **to ~ one's nose** sich dat die Nase putzen; **to ~ one's feet** (on mat) sich dat die Schuhe abtreten; **wipe off** vt abwischen; **wipe out** vt (destroy) vernichten; (data, debt) löschen; (epidemic etc) ausrotten

wire ['waɪə*] n Draht m; (Elec) Leitung f; (US: telegram) Telegramm nt ▷ vt (plug in) anschließen; (US Tel) telegrafieren (sb sth jdm etw); **wireless** ['waɪələs] adj drahtlos

wisdom ['wɪzdəm] n Weisheit f; **wisdom tooth** n Weisheitszahn m

wise, wisely [waɪz, -lɪ] adj, adv weise

wish [wɪʃ] n Wunsch m (for nach); **with best ~es** (in letter) herzliche Grüße ▷ vt wünschen, wollen; **to ~ sb good luck/Merry Christmas** jdm viel Glück/frohe Weihnachten wünschen; **I ~ I'd never seen him** ich wünschte, ich hätte ihn nie gesehen

witch [wɪtʃ] n Hexe f

O KEYWORD

with [wɪð] prep 1 (accompanying, in the company of) mit; **we stayed with friends** wir übernachteten

bei Freunden; **I'll be with you in a minute** einen Augenblick, ich bin sofort da; **I'm not with you** (I don't understand) das verstehe ich nicht; **to be with it** (inf) (up-to-date) auf dem Laufenden sein; (alert) (voll) da sein inf
2 (descriptive, indicating manner etc) mit; **the man with the grey hat** der Mann mit dem grauen Hut; **red with anger** rot vor Wut

withdraw [wɪðˈdrɔː] irr vt zurückziehen; (money) abheben; (comment) zurücknehmen ▷ vi sich zurückziehen

wither [ˈwɪðə°] vi (plant) verwelken

withhold [wɪðˈhəʊld] irr vt vorenthalten (from sb jdm)

within [wɪðˈɪn] prep innerhalb +gen; **~ walking distance** zu Fuß erreichbar

without [wɪðˈaʊt] prep ohne; **~ asking** ohne zu fragen

withstand [wɪðˈstænd] irr vt standhalten +dat

witness [ˈwɪtnəs] n Zeuge m, Zeugin f ▷ vt. Zeuge sein; **witness box, witness stand** (US) n Zeugenstand m

witty [ˈwɪtɪ] adj geistreich

wives [waɪvz] pl of **wife**

WMD abbr = **weapon of mass destruction** Massenvernichtungswaffe

wobble [ˈwɒbl] vi wackeln; **wobbly** adj wackelig

wok [wɒk] n Wok m

woke [wəʊk] pt of **wake**

woken [ˈwəʊkn] pp of **wake**

wolf [wʊlf] (pl **wolves**) n Wolf m

woman [ˈwʊmən] (pl **women**) n Frau f

womb [wuːm] n Gebärmutter f

women [ˈwɪmɪn] pl of **woman**

won [wʌn] pt, pp of **win**

wonder [ˈwʌndə°] n (marvel) Wunder nt; (surprise) Staunen nt ▷ vt, vi (speculate) sich fragen; **I ~ what/if ...** ich frage mich, was/ob ...; **wonderful** adj, adv wunderbar

won't [wəʊnt] contr of **will not**

wood [wʊd] n Holz nt; **~s** Wald m; **wooden** adj Holz-; (fig) hölzern; **woodpecker** n Specht m; **woodwork** n (wooden parts) Holzteile pl; (in school) Werken nt

wool [wʊl] n Wolle f; **woollen, woolen** (US) adj Woll-

word [wɜːd] n Wort nt; (promise) Ehrenwort nt; **~s** pl (of song) Text m; **to have a ~ with sb** mit jdm sprechen; **in other ~s** mit anderen Worten ▷ vt formulieren; **wording** n Formulierung f; **word processing** n Textverarbeitung f; **word processor** n (program) Textverarbeitungsprogramm nt

wore [wɔː°] pt of **wear**

work [wɜːk] n Arbeit f; (of art, literature) Werk nt; **~ of art** Kunstwerk nt; **he's at ~** er ist in/auf der Arbeit; **out of ~** arbeitslos ▷ vi arbeiten (at, on an +dat); (machine, plan) funktionieren; (medicine) wirken; (succeed) klappen ▷ vt (machine) bedienen; **work out** vi (plan) klappen; (sum) aufgehen; (person) trainieren ▷ vt (price, speed etc) ausrechnen; (plan) ausarbeiten; **work up** vt: **to get worked up** sich aufregen; **workaholic** [wɜːkəˈhɒlɪk] n Arbeitstier nt; **worker** n Arbeiter(in) m(f); **working class** n Arbeiterklasse f; **workman** (pl **-men**) n Handwerker m; **workout** n (Sport) Fitnesstraining nt, Konditionstraining nt; **work permit** n Arbeitserlaubnis f;

workplace n Arbeitsplatz m; **workshop** n Werkstatt f; (meeting) Workshop m; **work station** n (Inform) Workstation f

world [wɜːld] n Welt f; **world championship** n Weltmeisterschaft f; **World War** n: **~ I/II, the First/Second** ~ der Erste/Zweite Weltkrieg; **world-wide** adj, adv weltweit; **World Wide Web** n World Wide Web nt

worm [wɜːm] n Wurm m

worn [wɔːn] pp of **wear** ▷ adj (clothes) abgetragen; (tyre) abgefahren; **worn-out** adj abgenutzt; (person) erschöpft

worried [ˈwʌrɪd] adj besorgt; **be ~ about** sich dat Sorgen machen um; **worry** [ˈwʌrɪ] n Sorge f ▷ vi sich Sorgen machen +dat ▷ vi sich Sorgen machen (about um); **don't ~!** keine Sorge!; **worrying** adj beunruhigend

worse [wɜːs] adj comparative of **bad**; schlechter; (pain, mistake etc) schlimmer ▷ adv comparative of **badly**; schlechter; **worsen** vt verschlechtern ▷ vi sich verschlechtern

worship [ˈwɜːʃɪp] vt anbeten, anhimmeln

worst [wɜːst] adj superlative of **bad**; schlechteste(r, s); (pain, mistake etc) schlimmste(r, s) ▷ adv superlative of **badly**; am schlechtesten ▷ n: **the ~ is over** das Schlimmste ist vorbei; **at (the) ~** schlimmstenfalls

worth [wɜːθ] n Wert m; **£10 ~ of food** Essen für 10 Pfund ▷ adj: **it is ~ £50** es ist 50 Pfund wert; **~ seeing** sehenswert; **it's ~ it** (rewarding) es lohnt sich; **worthless** adj wertlos; **worthwhile** adj lohnend, lohnenswert; **worthy** [ˈwɜːðɪ]

adj (deserving respect) würdig; **to be ~ of sth** etw verdienen

KEYWORD

would [wʊd] vb aux **1** (conditional tense) **if you asked him he would do it** wenn du ihn fragtest/Sie ihn fragten, würde er es tun; **if you had asked him he would have done it** wenn du ihn gefragt hättest/Sie ihn gefragt hätten, hätte er es getan

2 (in offers, invitations, requests) **would you like a biscuit?** möchtest du/möchten Sie einen Keks?; **would you ask him to come in?** würdest du/würden Sie ihn bitte hereinbitten?

3 (in indirect speech) **I said I would do it** ich sagte, ich würde es tun

4 (emphatic) **it WOULD have to snow today!** es musste ja ausgerechnet heute schneien!

5 (insistence) **she wouldn't behave** sie wollte sich partout nicht anständig benehmen

6 (conjecture) **it would have been midnight** es mag ungefähr Mitternacht gewesen sein; **it would seem so** es sieht wohl so aus

7 (indicating habit) **he would go there on Mondays** er ging jeden Montag dorthin

wouldn't [ˈwʊdnt] contr of **would not**

would've [ˈwʊdəv] contr of **would have**

wound [wuːnd] n Wunde f ▷ vt verwunden; (fig) verletzen ▷ [waʊnd] pt, pp of **wind**

wove [wəʊv] pt of **weave**

woven [ˈwəʊvn] pp of **weave**

wrap [ræp] vt (parcel, present) einwickeln; **to ~ sth round sth**

etw um etw wickeln; **wrap up** vt
(parcel, present) einwickeln ▷ vi
(dress warmly) sich warm anziehen;
wrapper n (of sweet) Papier nt;
wrapping paper n Packpapier nt;
(giftwrap) Geschenkpapier nt
wreath [riːθ] n Kranz m
wreck [rek] n (ship, plane, car)
Wrack nt; **a nervous ~** ein
Nervenbündel m ▷ vt (car) zu
Schrott fahren; (fig) zerstören;
wreckage ['rekɪdʒ] n Trümmer pl
wrench [rentʃ] n (tool)
Schraubenschlüssel m
wrestling ['reslɪŋ] n Ringen nt
wring out ['rɪŋ'aʊt] (**wrung,
wrung**) vt auswringen
wrinkle ['rɪŋkl] n Falte f
wrist [rɪst] n Handgelenk nt;
wristwatch n Armbanduhr f
write [raɪt] (**wrote, written**) vt
schreiben; (cheque) ausstellen ▷ vi
schreiben; **to ~ to sb** jdm
schreiben; **write down** vt
aufschreiben; **write off** vt (debt,
person) abschreiben; (car) zu
Schrott fahren ▷ vi **to ~ off for
sth** etw anfordern; **write out** vt
(name etc) ausschreiben; (cheque)
ausstellen; **write-protected** adj
(Inform) schreibgeschützt; **writer**
n Verfasser(in) m(f); (author)
Schriftsteller(in) m(f); **writing** n
Schrift f; (profession) Schreiben nt;
in ~ schriftlich; **writing paper** n
Schreibpapier nt
written ['rɪtən] pp of **write**
wrong [rɒŋ] adj (incorrect) falsch;
(morally) unrecht; **you're ~** du
hast/Sie haben unrecht; **what's
~ with your leg?** was ist mit
deinem/Ihrem Bein los?; **you've
got the ~ number** du bist/Sie sind
falsch verbunden; **I dialled the
~ number** ich habe mich
verwählt; **don't get me
~** versteh/verstehen Sie mich

nicht falsch; **to go ~** (plan)
schiefgehen; **wrongly** adv falsch;
(unjustly) zu Unrecht
wrote [rəʊt] pt of **write**
WWW abbr = **World Wide Web**
WWW

xenophobia [zenəˈfəʊbɪə] *n*
Ausländerfeindlichkeit *f*
XL *abbr* = **extra large** XL, übergroß
Xmas [ˈkrɪsməs] *n* Weihnachten
nt
X-ray [ˈeksreɪ] *n* (*picture*)
Röntgenaufnahme *f* ▷ *vt* röntgen
xylophone [ˈzaɪləfəʊn] *n* Xylo

yacht [jɒt] *n* Jacht *f*; **yachting** *n*
Segeln *nt*; **to go ~** segeln gehen
yam [jæm] *n* (US) Süßkartoffel
f
yard [jɑːd] *n* Hof *m*; (US: *garden*)
Garten *m*; (*measure*) Yard *nt* (0,91 m)
yd *abbr* = **yard(s)**
year [ˈjɪə*] *n* Jahr *nt*; **this/last/
next ~** dieses/letztes/nächstes
Jahr; **he is 28 ~s old** er ist 28 Jahre
alt; **~ ago** vor Jahren; **a
five-year-old** ein(e)
Fünfjährige(r); **yearly** *adj, adv*
jährlich
yearn [jɜːn] *vi* sich sehnen (*for*
nach +*dat*); **to ~ to do sth** sich
danach sehnen, etw zu tun
yeast [jiːst] *n* Hefe *f*
yell [jel] *vi, vt* schreien; **to ~ at sb**
jdn anschreien
yellow [ˈjeləʊ] *adj* gelb; **~ card**

(Sport) gelbe Karte; **~ fever**
Gelbfieber nt; **~ line** (Brit) =
Halteverbot nt; **double ~ line** (Brit)
= absolutes Halteverbot; **the**
Yellow Pages® pl die Gelben
Seiten pl

yes [jɛs] adv ja; (answering
negative question) doch; **to say ~ to**
sth ja zu etw sagen ▷ n Ja nt

yesterday [ˈjɛstədeɪ] adv
gestern; **~ morning/evening**
gestern Morgen/Abend; **the day**
before ~ vorgestern; **~'s**
newspaper die Zeitung von
gestern

yet [jɛt] adv (still) noch; (up to
now) bis jetzt; (in a question:
already) schon; **he hasn't arrived**
~ er ist noch nicht gekommen;
have you finished ~? bist du/sind
Sie schon fertig?; **~ again** schon
wieder; **as ~** bis jetzt ▷ conj doch

yield [jiːld] n Ertrag m ▷ vt
(result, crop) hervorbringen; (profit,
interest) bringen ▷ vi nachgeben
(to +dat); (Mil) sich ergeben (to
+dat); **"~"** (US Auto) Vorfahrt
beachten!

yoga [ˈjəʊɡə] n Yoga nt

yog(h)urt [ˈjɒɡət] n Jog(h)urt m

yolk [jəʊk] n Eigelb nt

Yorkshire pudding
[ˈjɔːkʃəˈpʊdɪŋ] n gebackener
Eierteig, der meist zum Roastbeef
gegessen wird

O **KEYWORD**

you [juː] pron 1 (subj, in
comparisons: familiar form) (sg) du;
(pl) ihr; (in letters) Du, Ihr; (polite
form) Sie; **you Germans** ihr
Deutschen; **she's younger than**
you sie ist jünger als du
2 (direct object, after prep +akk)
(familiar form) (sg) dich; (pl) euch;
(in letters) Dich, Euch; (polite form)

Sie; **I know you** ich kenne
dir/euch/Sie
3 (indirect object, after prep +dat)
(familiar form) (sg) dir; (pl) euch; (in
letters) Dir, Euch; (polite form)
Ihnen; **I gave it to you** ich gab es
dir/euch/Ihnen
4 (impers) (one) (subj) man; (direct
object) einen; (indirect object)
einem; **fresh air does you good**
frische Luft tut (einem) gut

you'd [juːd] controf you had; you
would; **~ better leave** du
solltest/Sie sollten gehen

you'll [juːl] controf you will; you
shall

young [jʌŋ] adj jung ▷ n **the**
~ pl (~ people) die jungen Leute pl;
(animals) die Jungen pl; **youngster**
[ˈjʌŋstə*] n Jugendliche(r)
mf

your [ˈjɔː*] adj sing dein; polite
form Ihr; pl euer; polite form Ihr;
have you hurt ~ leg? hast du
dir/haben Sie sich das Bein
verletzt?

you're [jʊə*] controf you are

yours [jɔːz] pron sing deine(r, s);
polite form Ihre(r, s); pl eure(r, s);
polite form Ihre(r, s); **is this ~?**
gehört das dir/Ihnen?; **a friend of**
~ ein Freund von dir/Ihnen

yourself [jɔːˈsɛlf] pron sing dich;
polite form sich; **have you hurt ~?**
hast du dich/haben Sie sich
verletzt?; **did you do it ~?** hast
du/haben Sie es selbst gemacht?;
(all) by ~ allein; **yourselves** pron
pl euch; polite form sich; **have you**
hurt ~? habt ihr euch/haben Sie
sich verletzt?; **did you do it ~?**
habt ihr/haben Sie es selbst
gemacht?; **(all) by ~** allein

youth [juːθ] n (period) Jugend f;
(young man) junger Mann; (young
people) Jugend f; **youth group**

Y

Jugendgruppe f: **youth hostel** n
Jugendherberge f
you've [ju:v] contr of **you have**
yucky ['jʌkɪ] adj (fam) eklig
yummy ['jʌmɪ] adj (fam) lecker
yuppie, yuppy ['jʌpɪ] n Yuppie
m

Z

zap [zæp] vt (Inform) löschen; (in
computer game) abknallen ▷ vi (TV)
zappen; **zapper** n (TV)
Fernbedienung f: **zapping** n (TV)
ständiges Umschalten, Zapping nt
zebra ['zebrə, ?? 'zi:brə] (US) n
Zebra nt; **zebra crossing** n (Brit)
Zebrastreifen m
zero [zɪərəʊ] (pl **-es**) n Null f; **10
degrees below ~** 10 Grad unter
null
zest [zest] n (enthusiasm)
Begeisterung f
zigzag ['zɪgzæg] n Zickzack m
▷ vi (person, vehicle) im Zickzack
gehen/fahren; (path) im Zickzack
verlaufen
zinc [zɪŋk] n Zink nt
zip [zɪp] n (Brit) Reißverschluss m
▷ vt: **to ~ (up)** den Reißverschluss
zumachen; (Inform) zippen; **zip
code** n (US) Postleitzahl f: **Zip
disk®** n (Inform) ZIP-Diskette f: